COMMERCIAL TRANSACTIONS

Commercial Transactions

Text, Cases, and Problems

JONATHAN A. EDDY
Visiting Professor of Law
Louisiana State University

PETER WINSHIP
Associate Professor of Law
Southern Methodist University

Little, Brown and Company
Boston   Toronto

HAL

Published simultaneously in Canada
by Little, Brown & Company (Canada) Limited

Printed in the United States of America

To Debbie, Amy, Hart, and Emily

and

To Marion, Verity, and Adam

Summary of Contents

Table of Contents

Preface

There has not been a truly revolutionary casebook in commercial law since Karl Llewellyn's Cases and Materials on the Law of Sales in 1930. Perhaps there is good reason for this when the law itself has undergone such rapid and constant change. And in truth, casebooks share more common features than those that distinguish them, and quite similar materials can be made to do quite different things in the hands of diverse and creative instructors.

Nonetheless, these materials do differ in some significant respects from most current casebooks. We choose to start our study of commercial law by considering promissory notes and principles of suretyship. This decision is in part functionally dictated: secured transactions usually involve a promissory note, and also frequently involve sureties. Second, we believe that the note represents the simplest type of negotiable instrument and is therefore a good vehicle for the introduction of basic principles of negotiability. We then treat secured transactions, following the once heretical view that it is preferable to teach secured transactions prior to the law of sales. The final section of the book examines the law and use of checks and drafts. This sequence is justified by the fact that checks and drafts serve as payment media, increasingly in competition wth such devices as credit cards and electronic fund transfers. It is also justified pedagogically by the fact that such instruments are only understandable in conjunction with the bank collection system.

We believe that the above organization is desirable in the context of an integrated commercial law course. But we do not expect all consumers of these materials to share our predilections, and we recognize that the format of the commercial law curriculum differs widely among schools. From the outset, therefore, we have striven to make these materials readily adaptable to use in the widest possible variety of curricular structures. As a result, they may be used as well for stand-alone courses in sales, commercial paper, or secured transactions, and in courses that combine two, but not all, of these areas. *A fortiori,* instructors who teach an integrated course but prefer a different sequence will face no major barriers.

Both authors taught their courses in this area as pure problem courses at one time but have come to believe that such an approach has certain unacceptable drawbacks. The Code is starting to enter middle age; it has acquired in some areas a case law encrustation that must be considered if an accurate sense of the current state of the law is to be presented. More important, cases provide a needed context that problems alone cannot, in giving a fuller sense of the business setting or illustrating techniques of statutory construction. In regard to the latter, we confess that we have included opinions that we consider bad examples, in addition to well reasoned expositions of majority positions. In recent years this use of cases has fallen into some disfavor; we adhere to the traditional view that the careful examination of mistakes can be quite helpful. Throughout, we have tried to tailor carefully our editing of the cases to conform with the underlying reasons for their inclusion. We remain devotees of the problem method nevertheless, and the reader will find sufficient problems present to cover each area. Although we assume that many instructors will wish to use their own problems as supplements or substitutes, this is an option rather than a necessity.

These materials incorporate a substantial bias towards coverage of commercial, rather than consumer, transactions. First, this bias follows the Code, which includes relatively few provisions specifically addressed to consumer settings (and has been roundly criticized by some for that reason). Second, we believe that the student has a serious need to gain familiarity with typical business patterns to appreciate how commercial equities may differ from the more familiar equities of consumer transactions. As a corollary to these two points, we think it desirable to evaluate the Code against the mercantile backdrop whose problems it was meant to address squarely; a critique of its adequacy for consumer settings may then proceed on a more informed basis.

Commercial law is an intricate subject, but its study can be a very pleasurable experience. We hope that students will find as they study these materials the same sense of discovery we find in our work.

> *Jonathan A. Eddy*
> Baton Rouge, Louisiana
>
> *Peter Winship*
> Dallas, Texas

February 1985

Acknowledgments

We wish to acknowledge the institutional support of Southern Methodist University Law School, Dallas, and Garvey, Schubert, Adams, & Barer, Seattle, as well as generations of secretaries and research assistants. Specifically we note the devotion and long hours of Linda Becker, Carolyn Magers, and Corie Roper. Our efforts have been enhanced by the critique afforded by law students at Berkeley, S.M.U., the University of Puget Sound, Virginia, and Washington (Seattle), all of whom studied from draft materials. Mr. Eddy also wishes to acknowledge the critique of Howard R. Eddy, of the Office of the Attorney General, Province of British Columbia, the research and editorial assistance of D. H. Eddy, of the Washington State Bar, and the consistent encouragement and material support of Michael D. Garvey and Paul R. Verkuil.

Gilmore, The Commercial Doctrine of Good Faith Purchase, 63 Yale L.J. 1057, 1068-1069 (1954). Reprinted by permission of the Yale Law Journal Company and Fred B. Rothman & Co.

G. Gilmore, Security Interests in Personal Property 293-294, 346-348, 359-360, 466-467, 876-879, 932 (1965). Reprinted with the permission of Little, Brown & Company.

Goetz & Scott, Liquidated Damages, Penalties and the Just Compensation Principle: Some Notes on an Enforcement Model and a Theory of Efficient Breach, 77 Colum. L. Rev. 554, 554-555, 558-562, 593-594 (1977). Copyright © 1977 by the Directors of the Columbia Law Review Association. All rights reserved. Reprinted by permission.

Goetz & Scott, Measuring Sellers' Damages: The Lost-Profits Puzzle, 31 Stan. L. Rev. 323, 330-331, 346-349 (1978). Copyright 1978 by the Board of Trustees of the Leland Stanford Junior University.

W. Hawkland, A Transactional Guide to the Uniform Commercial Code 995-999 (1964). Copyright © 1964 by The American Law Institute. Reprinted with the permission of the American Law Institute-American Bar Association Committee on Continuing Professional Education.

W. Hawkland, Commercial Paper 101 (2d ed. 1979). Copyright © 1979 by The American Law Institute. Reprinted with the permission of the American Law Institute-American Bar Association Committee on Continuing Professional Education.

P. Hunt, C. Williams, & G. Donaldson, Basic Business Finance: A Text 108, 286-287, 296-298, 306 (4th ed. 1971). Copyright © 1971 Richard D. Irwin, Inc. Reprinted with the permission of the publisher.

Incoterm, "Free on Board." Copyright © 1980 by ICC Publishing Corporation. Reprinted with permission of the ICC Publishing Corporation. All rights reserved.

Jackson & Peters, Quest for Uncertainty: A Proposal for Flexible Resolution of Inherent Conflicts Between Article 2 and Article 9 of the Uniform Commercial Code, 87 Yale L.J. 907, 985-986, 925-930 (1978). Reprinted by permission of The Yale Law Journal Company and Fred B. Rothman & Co., with the permission of the authors.

Leff, Unconscionability and the Code—The Emperor's New Clause, 115 U. Pa. Law Rev. 485, 523 (1967). Copyright 1967 by the University of Pennsylvania Law Review. Reprinted by permission of the copyright holder.

Mellinkoff, The Language of the Uniform Commercial Code, 77 Yale L.J. 185, 192-193 (1967). Reprinted by permission of The Yale Law Journal Company and Fred B. Rothman & Co., with the permission of the author.

Miller, Taking a Look at the Commercial Finance Contract, 65 American Bar Association Journal 628, 628-630 (1979). Copyright © 1979. Reprinted with the permission of the American Bar Association Journal.

Model Rules of Professional Conduct, Rules 1.6, 3.3 (1983), copyright by the American Bar Association. All rights reserved. Reprinted by permission.

Note, Cognovit Judgments: Some Constitutional Considerations, 70 Colum. L. Rev. 1118, 1130 (1970). Copyright © 1971 by the Directors of the

Priest, Breach and Remedy for the Tender of Nonconforming Goods under the Uniform Commercial Code: An Economic Approach, 91 Harv. L. Rev. 960, 963-968 (1978). Copyright © 1978 by the Harvard Law Review Association. Reprinted by permission.

Reisman, What the Commercial Lawyer Should Know About Commercial Finance and Factoring, 79 Com. L.J. 146, 148-151 (1974). Copyright © 1974 by the Commercial Law League of America. Reprinted by permission.

Report & Second Draft: The Revised Uniform Sales Act 38-39, 100-103, 185-186 (1941). Reprinted with the permission of the National Conference of Commissioners on Uniform State Laws.

Restatement of the Law Second, Contracts 2d §336 (1981). Copyright © 1981 by The American Law Institute. Reprinted with the permission of The American Law Institute.

Restatement of the Law, Security §§36, 122, 128, 129 and Comments (1941). Copyright © 1941 by The American Law Institute. Reprinted with the permission of The American Law Institute.

Rosenthal, Negotiability—Who Needs It?, 71 Colum. L. Rev. 375, 377-381, 384-385 (1971). Copyright © 1971 by the Directors of the Columbia Law Review Association, Inc. All rights reserved. Reprinted by permission.

Taylor, UCC Section 2-207: An Integration of Legal Abstractions and Transactional Reality, 46 U. Cinn. L. Rev. 419, 437 (1977). Reprinted with permission of the publisher and author.

Uniform Laws Annotated, Uniform Commercial Code Forms and Materials, Form 9:1600. Copyright © 1968 West Publishing Company. Reprinted by permission.

J. White & R. Summers, Handbook of the Law under the Uniform Commercial Code 904-905 (2d ed. 1980). Reprinted by permission of the authors and West Publishing Company.

Winship, The "True" Consignment under the Uniform Commercial Code, and Related Peccadilloes, 29 Sw. L.J. 825, 846-848 (1975). Copyright 1976, by Southern Methodist University. Reprinted with permission from Southwestern Law Journal and the author.

Special Notice

Throughout the text the Uniform Commercial Code is cited as the Code or by specific section numbers as follows: UCC 2-202. Cases have been edited so as to conform citations to state enactments of the Code to the foregoing citation form. Unless otherwise stated, all citations to the Code in the text and problems are to the 1972 Official Text.

The Uniform Commercial Code Reporting Service is cited throughout as — UCC Rep. —(e.g., 26 UCC Rep. 345).

The Bankruptcy Code, 11 U.S.C.§—, is cited throughout as BC—(e.g., BC 362).

We adhere to the Code's usage as to gender: unless the context otherwise requires, words of the masculine gender include the feminine and neuter. When the sense indicates, words of neuter gender may also refer to feminine and masculine gender.

COMMERCIAL TRANSACTIONS

General Introduction

Although the term *commercial law* is not a term of art in American law it has become synonymous in recent years with the legal rules contained in the Uniform Commercial Code. The Code's organizing principle is the *commercial transaction*. As the General Comment introducing the official text of the Code states, the draftsmen believed that the commercial transaction is a "single subject of the law, notwithstanding its many facets."

> A single transaction may very well involve a contract for sale, followed by a sale, the giving of a check or draft for a part of the purchase price, and the acceptance of some form of security for the balance. The check or draft may be negotiated and will ultimately pass through one or more banks for collection. If the goods are shipped or stored the subject matter of the sale may be covered by a bill of lading or warehouse receipt or both. Or it may be that the entire transaction was made pursuant to a letter of credit either domestic or foreign. Obviously, every phase of commerce involved is but a part of one transaction, namely, the sale of and payment for goods. . . . This Act purports to deal with all the phases which may ordinarily arise from start to finish. [General Comment, Uniform Commercial Code Official Text at xvi-xvii (1978).]

Note what the draftsmen's definition of commercial transaction does *not* include. First, the Code is comprised of private law rather than public law rules. The commercial law of the Code is contract law; the parties may exclude or vary the effect of virtually all the Code's rules. The UCC does not include, in other words, rules regulating anti-competitive acts or consumer transactions. Second, the Code separates substantive rules from procedural ones, such as rules on commercial arbitration and enforcement of judgments in commercial matters. Third, the Code omits systematic coverage of some topics, such as suretyship and personal property leases, that are as equally related to the distribution of goods as those topics that are covered by the Code. Tempting as it is to deal at length with these different perspectives and topics, we emphasize here the UCC concepts and rules. A glance at the 1978 Official Text of the Code, with its 11 articles and 778 pages of text and comment, suggests that to limit our study only to UCC topics may be more than enough.

Unfortunately at this point we cannot offer a key to unlock all of the Code's hidden treasures. Only after working through these course materials with constant reference to the Code will many of you begin to feel comfortable with it. For those of you unfamiliar with a long and complicated statutory text we offer the following working outline of steps to take when you confront a problem governed by the Code. Refer to the outline when analyzing the prob-

1

lems and cases set out in the following chapters: you should find it a convenient way to organize your approach to the material.[1]

1. Study carefully the factual context, particularly the agreement of the parties as determined from their communications, course of performance and dealing, and usage of trade. Remember that much of commercial law is contract law.

2. Read and reread the statutory text. Do so in the light of its "reason" or purpose and the general principles and concepts applicable throughout the Code.

3. When determining the "reason" of a text, consider the Official Comments, drafting history, and pre-Code law.

4. Examine the case-law gloss on the text, remembering the Code's general purpose to make the law uniform. UCC 1-102(2)(c).

NOTES & QUESTIONS

1. *The Uniform Commercial Code as a code.* Does the working outline adequately account for the fact that the UCC is a code? Commentators have disagreed about the significance of the codification. Compare Hawkland, Uniform Commercial "Code" Methodology, 1962 U. Ill. L.F. 291 (because UCC is a "true" code, gaps should be filled by analogy rather than by non-Code law, and court opinions should be given less precedential value) with Kripke, The Principles Underlying the Drafting of the Uniform Commercial Code, 1962 U. Ill. L.F. 321 (draftsmen had anticodification predilection and merely wanted to correct false starts in case-law development and to encourage trade usage as an institution for growth) and Gilmore, In Memoriam: Karl Llewellyn, 71 Yale L.J. 813 (1962) (Llewellyn wanted "case-law Code" that would accommodate future developments, but practitioners advising him wanted detailed and precise statute).

Further reading: Mentschikoff, Highlights of the Uniform Commercial Code, 27 Mod. L. Rev. 167 (1964); Nickles, Problems of Sources of Law Relationships under the Uniform Commercial Code (Parts 1-3), 31 Ark. L. Rev. 1, 171 (1977), 34 Ark. L. Rev. 1 (1980); Note, The Uniform Commercial Code as a Premise for Judicial Reasoning, 65 Colum. L. Rev. 880 (1965); Note, How Appellate Opinions Should Justify Decisions Made Under the Uniform Commercial Code, 29 Stan. L. Rev. 1245 (1977).

2. *Supereminent principles.* When reading a particular statutory text in the UCC you should keep in mind the general principles that apply to all Code rules. UCC 1-102(2) states:

---

1. For a similar set of guidelines, with an explanation of the jurisprudential assumptions of the Code draftsmen and numerous examples applying the guidelines, see McDonnell, Purposive Interpretation of the Uniform Commercial Code: Some Implications for Jurisprudence, 126 U. Pa. L. Rev. 795 (1978).

(2) Underlying purposes and policies of this Act are
   (a) to simplify, clarify and modernize the law governing commercial transactions;
   (b) to permit the continued expansion of commercial practices through custom, usage and agreement of the parties;
   (c) to make uniform the law among the various jurisdictions.

See also Comment 1 to this provision.

In addition, the UCC provides for general concepts or principles.

(a) The Code explicitly sets out some of these concepts: the *suppletory* nature of most Code rules (UCC 1-102(3)), *good faith* (UCC 1-201(19), 1-203, 2-103(1)(b)), *usage of trade* (UCC 1-205), and *unconscionability* (UCC 2-302).

(b) Other principles can be derived from separate but functionally similar Code provisions, such as the general principles on the security of property interests.

(c) Extra-Code general principles may be implicit in Code provisions or in the common law and equity principles that supplement the Code (UCC 1-103). Recent literature suggests, for example, that *efficiency* may be one such general principle.

3. *"Official" comments.* How much weight should one give the "official" comments? UCC 1-102(3)(f) of the 1952 text, which was the first complete official text published by the sponsors, contained the following provision: "The Comments of the National Conference of Commissioners on Uniform State Laws and the American Law Institute may be consulted in the construction and application of this Act but, if text and comment conflict, text controls." The 1956 Recommendations of the Editorial Board deleted this provision with the explanation that "paragraph (3)(f) was deleted because the old comments were clearly out of date and it was not known when new ones could be prepared." Even though NCCUSL and ALI reviewed and adopted the 1952 comments, it is not clear to what extent subsequent revisions were examined by the sponsors.

To what extent can one talk of "official" comments if state legislatures did not have the comments before them? Annotated copies of the UCC as adopted in a particular jurisdiction often are printed with special state law comments. Sometimes these comments are background notes prepared at the time a state legislature is considering adoption of the Code; sometimes they are prepared by prominent practitioners or academicians. William Hawkland (see Note 1 supra), for example, prepared New Jersey Study Comments as director of a commission established by the New Jersey legislature to study the Code. Homer Kripke (see Note 1) also wrote Practice Commentaries to Article 9 of the New York Uniform Commercial Code.

Karl Llewellyn, as the Chief Reporter of the Code project, had strong feelings about the need to prepare detailed comments to be published with the official text of the Code. In response to an attack on the comments he stated:

[W]e are troubled by a matter of what I can only refer to as a democratic feeling and democratic decency. Miss Mentschikoff did not call to your attention the fact that by her estimate there has been active participation on the work of this draft to date of more than a thousand lawyers in the United States—lawyers, and interested informed businessmen. She feels that to be—and I think rightly— as fine an example of the democratic process in producing legislation as one could well think of.

I refer here now to the possible sabotage of that kind of work by the work of individuals. Note, if these comments are not given effective status as permissive guides to the courts, something else is going to acquire unofficial status in a surreptitious and, to my mind, outrageous fashion. That "something else" is going to be the "Authoritative Text on the Code" written by some of the Reporters. We know what happens when that kind of text turns up. We had that kind of text on the old Uniform Sales Act prepared by its draftsman, [Samuel Williston] and the history of that has been that through the years, two times out of three, the court has not read or applied the statute. [Transcript of Discussion, Joint Meeting on the Uniform Commercial Code 9-10 (ALI & NCCUSL 1950).]

See also Mentschikoff, The Uniform Commercial Code: An Experiment in Democracy in Drafting, 36 A.B.A.J. 419 (1950).

The only draftsman who did not comply with Llewellyn's injunction against treatises by those who participated in the drafting of the Code was Grant Gilmore (see Note 1 supra), who wrote a study of Article 9 (secured transactions) with his characteristic appreciation for the fallibility of statutory draftsmen. Several draftsmen, however, have written less comprehensive commentaries on the product of their efforts. See, e.g., Coogan, The New UCC Article 9, 86 Harv. L. Rev. 477 (1973). In addition, draftsmen have participated in panel discussions subsequently published in law journals. See, e.g., 43 Ohio St. L.J. 535 (1982), 33 Bus. Law. 2491 (1978), 29 Bus. Law. 973 (1974), 25 Bus. Law. 307 (1970), 87 Banking L.J. 579 (1970). Should these comments be given greater weight than the analyses of nondraftsmen?

The Permanent Editorial Board, established in 1961 by the NCCUSL and ALI to monitor nonuniform amendments and to propose official amendments to the Code, uses several devices to make "official" comments. When submitting the 1972 revision of Article 9 the Board proposed that the amendments were to be presumed to be declaratory of the pre-1972 text unless a change was clearly intended (UCC 11-108), thereby providing an official gloss on the earlier provisions. In addition, by a letter of October 27, 1964, the Board invited courts to request the Board to file amicus curiae briefs on troublesome questions of interpretation. As a consequence the Board has submitted briefs in several important cases. See, e.g., DuBay v. Williams, 417 F.2d 1277 (9th Cir. 1969). One such brief is reproduced in Mentschikoff, Peaceful Repossession under the UCC, A Constitutional and Economic Analysis, 14 Wm. & Mary L. Rev. 767 (1973). What weight should be given to these Board interpretations?

Further reading: Skilton, Some Comments on the Comments to the Uniform Commercial Code, 1966 Wis. L. Rev. 597.

4. *Drafting history.* One must distinguish between official texts and pre-1952 draft texts. Official texts were promulgated in 1952, 1957, 1958, 1962, 1972, and 1978. Minor amendments to the 1962 text were also adopted in 1966. These texts are readily accessible in most law school libraries; the pre-1952 drafts may occasionally be found. The most widely circulated drafts are listed in M. Ezer, Uniform Commercial Code Bibliography 1-4 (1972). For the aficionado there are "confidential" drafts in some of the larger law school libraries.

UCC 1-102(3)(g) of the 1952 Official Text stated: "Prior drafts of text and comments may not be used to ascertain legislative intent." The 1956 Recommendations of the Editorial Board omitted the paragraph with the cryptic note that "paragraph (3)(g) was deleted because the changes from the text enacted in Pennsylvania in 1953 are clearly legitimate legislative history." Where does this leave prior drafts as aids to interpretation?

One should distinguish this general drafting history from the legislative history within each jurisdiction. With the exception of major studies in New York and California most state legislatures generated little history. Variations on the uniform text in some states may, however, be explained by unofficial commentaries, and the legislative policies may be inferred from the variations themselves.

Further reading: Braucher, The Legislative History of the Uniform Commercial Code, 58 Colum. L. Rev. 798 (1958); Schnader, A Short History of the Preparation and Enactment of the Uniform Commercial Code, 22 U. Miami L. Rev. 1 (1967).

5. *Pre-Code law.* UCC 1-103 provides that the principles of pre-Code law and equity supplement the UCC provisions "unless displaced by the particular provisions of this Act." Comment 1 uses the words *explicitly displaced,* suggesting that displacement of pre-Code principles should be exceptional.

UCC 1-103 refers to principles and not specific legal rules. Many of the Code provisions can be traced back to pre-Code uniform legislation. Note that each official comment includes a reference to any pertinent earlier uniform statutory provisions. How much weight should be given to court decisions construing these prior provisions?

6. *The interpretation of statutes and "situation sense."* Karl Llewellyn stressed the role of facts in determining the appropriate rule of decision in a particular case. Llewellyn incorporates this emphasis in his concept of "situation sense," which classifies cases according to common factual patterns and applies rules of law appropriate to each class. Llewellyn suggested that the following quotation from Levin Goldschmidt expresses this concept beautifully.

Every fact-pattern of common life, so far as the legal order can take it in, carries within itself its appropriate, natural rules, its right law. This is a natural law which is real, not imaginary; it is not a creature of mere reason, but rests on the solid foundation of what reason can recognize in the nature of man and of the life conditions of the time and place; it is thus not eternal nor changeless nor everywhere the same, but it is indwelling in the very circumstances of life. The highest task of law-giving consists in uncovering and implementing this immanent law. [K. Llewellyn, The Common Law Tradition, Deciding Appeals 122 (1960) (quoting from a translation of the Preface to Kritik des Entwurfs eines Handelsgesetzbuchs).]

While Llewellyn discussed situation sense primarily in connection with common law decision-making, he did suggest in passing that the concept also applies to statutory interpretation. Id. at 380. For an illustration of how the study of situation sense illuminates Code analysis, see Eddy, On the "Essential" Purposes of Limited Remedies: The Metaphysics of UCC Section 2-719(2), 65 Calif. L. Rev. 28 (1977).

Further reading: W. Twining, Karl Llewellyn and the Realist Movement 270-301 (1973).

7. *The Uniform Commercial Code in historical context.* You should not forget that the Code was not drafted and enacted in a historical vacuum. The late Grant Gilmore, a draftsman of Article 9, devoted much of his writing to showing the humble and limited role of the writers of the statutes and to placing the UCC in its historical context. See, e.g., G. Gilmore, The Ages of American Law 81-86, (1977); Gilmore, Commercial Law in the United States: Its Codification and Other Misadventures, in Aspects of Comparative Commercial Law 449 (J. Ziegel & W. Foster eds. 1969); Gilmore, On Statutory Obsolescence, 39 U. Colo. L. Rev. 461 (1967). Other authors not specializing in commercial law have also commented on commercial codification as a historical phenomenon. See Friedman, Law Reform in Historical Perspective, 13 St. Louis U.L.J. 351, 354-359 (1969) (UCC essentially "a scheme of law professors, hungry for quality and order in a tool of *their* trade. To the business community the code was and is mostly irrelevant"); Ferguson, Legal Ideology and Commercial Interests: The Social Origins of the Commercial Law Codes, 4 Br. J. of Law & Soc. 18 (1977) (analysis of the ideology of principal proponents of commercial codification in England, noting that proponents were not businessmen). To what extent should this historical perspective affect your analysis of the cases and problems set out in the following chapters?

8. *Other aids to statutory construction.* Many states have codified guidelines to aid in statutory construction. Although adopted in only three jurisdictions, the Uniform Statutory Construction Act is a useful codification of many generally accepted principles of construction. Unif. Stat. Constr. Act, 14 U.L.A. 513 (1965) (adopted in Colorado, Iowa, Wisconsin). For a typical statute see Code Construction Act, Tex. Rev. Civ. Stat. Ann. art. 5429b-2 (Vernon Supp. 1984). The Texas act provides not only rules on the construction of words and phrases, (e.g., §2.01 states that words and phrases "shall be read in context and construed according to the rules of grammar and common usage") but

also general guidelines on construction (e.g., §3.02 states a presumption that a statute will operate only prospectively). Compare the four steps in the working outline set out above with the following section of the Texas act:

> Sec. 3.03. In construing a statute, whether or not the statute is considered ambiguous on its face, a court may consider among other matters the
> (1) object sought to be obtained;
> (2) circumstances under which the statute was enacted;
> (3) legislative history;
> (4) common law or former statutory provisions, including laws upon the same or similar subjects;
> (5) consequences of a particular construction;
> (6) administrative construction of the statute; and
> (7) title, preamble, and emergency provision.

How helpful are these statutory guidelines?

For further general reading on statutory interpretation, see R. Dickerson, The Interpretation and Application of Statutes (1975) (expresses, inter alia, reservations about the utility of statutory construction acts, see ch. 14); Llewellyn, Remarks on the Theory of Appellate Decision and the Rules and Canons About How Statutes Are to be Construed, 3 Vand. L. Rev. 395 (1950) (demonstrates that every maxim of construction has a counter-maxim). See generally C. Sands, [Sutherland's] Statutes and Statutory Construction (4th ed. 1972).

PART I

Introduction to Commercial Paper

The following two chapters introduce the basic concepts underlying the law governing commercial paper or, in pre-UCC terminology, the law of negotiable instruments. Chapter 1 explores the obligations of the debtor who issues a promissory note. Chapter 2 focuses on the obligations of the surety who adds his promise to that of the principal debtor. Both chapters build on contract and property concepts you have already studied and provide a foundation for your study of personal property secured transactions (Part II) and payment systems (Part IV). As you read the following materials you should identify the extent to which contract and property rules are displaced to accommodate commercial needs.

CHAPTER 1

The Promissory Note

A. BASIC CONCEPTS

A promissory note is a promise by one party (the "maker" of the note) to pay another party (the "payee" of the note). As such, it may simply evidence a contractual promise to pay. Over the years, however, such notes have acquired certain stylized attributes. A note that has these attributes is a *negotiable instrument* and is governed by Article 3 of the Uniform Commercial Code (UCC). Since ours is a credit economy, promises to pay money have a very important role. And because negotiable instruments are governed by rules that are generally more favorable to the payee than ordinary rules of contract law, transactions are frequently structured so that any extension of credit will be embodied in a promissory note given by the borrower to the lender.

Since the need for credit arises in an almost infinite variety of situations, so too does the use of notes. The purchaser of a home, for example, will typically pay a required percentage of the purchase price as a down payment and sign a note for the balance payable to the mortgage lender. The same is true when purchasing costly items of personal property: automobiles, aircraft, boats, and furniture or household appliances. In most of the foregoing examples it is likely that the note will be *secured:* in the case of a house, by a mortgage; in the other instances, by a UCC Article 9 security interest. Depending on the credit-worthiness of the note's maker, the lender may also require another party to cosign the note as surety. Whether or not it is secured, and whether or not it is cosigned by another party, a negotiable promissory note provides advantages over a simple contractual promise. An explanation of these advantages is the subject matter of this chapter.

Law students often have had a degree of personal acquaintance with promissory notes in the contexts described above. It should be evident, however, that counterparts to the above transactions exist throughout the world of commerce and finance. For instance, the owner of a shopping center or large downtown office building is no more likely to pay cash for its purchase than is the typical homeowner. Just as in the case of residential real estate, if the seller receives the full purchase price in cash only a portion will come from the buyer: the balance will represent proceeds of a mortgage loan obtained by the buyer, who also will have signed a note. The same pattern may apply in the acquisition of expensive equipment, such as computerized welding equipment for an assembly line or a fleet of new aircraft for an airline.

Capital goods of such high value create another credit need in the economy. The manufacturer of large commercial aircraft, like the developer of a large office building, cannot bear its construction costs out-of-pocket—it must borrow to pay them. Again an extension of credit, again the presence of a note. A retailer with sizeable inventory and substantial accounts receivable representing rights to future payment for goods sold on credit likewise does not want to keep its capital tied up—so it borrows from a bank or finance company, signing a note and granting a security interest in its inventory and accounts.

As is evident from the foregoing, the functions of the promissory note are as varied as the functions of credit. And the form of the note will vary with the function being served.

For instance, since the 1930s the most common form of mortgage lending has been the 25- or 30-year amortized term loan. Much equipment lending has followed the same pattern, but with a term consonant with the shorter useful life of the equipment: the borrower makes equal installment payments over the life of the loan, and each payment is applied partially to interest and partially to principal. In the early years of the loan virtually the entire payment is applied to interest, but as the principal amount is gradually reduced, more and more of each installment is available to reduce principal until both interest and principal have been paid in full.

Traditionally such loans were set at fixed rates. In recent years, however, the volatility of interest rates has made lenders wary of long-term lending at fixed rates, and term loans with variable or floating rates have come into increased use. At the same time, very high rates have placed installment payments beyond the reach of many potential borrowers. One response has been to borrow money on an "interest only" basis (or even with "negative amortization"—that is, with current payments less than currently accruing interest), with a "balloon payment" after a specified time—perhaps 18 to 36 months. In such situations the borrower is often gambling on falling interest rates (allowing refinancing) or on the sale of the financed property before the balloon payment is due.

In certain contexts term loans are not the norm. For instance, in financing inventory and accounts receivable lenders do not really expect to be "paid off." Rather, they are extending a fluctuating line of credit. The amount available under the line of credit depends on a number of factors, one of which will be the value of the collateral securing the loan. The interest rate also usually "floats," being tied to an index rate (usually referred to as the bank's prime rate). Occasionally a lender will operate a line of credit with very loose documentation, but in the great majority of cases, one of several patterns is followed. The borrower is required to sign a "demand note" (that is, a note that is payable whenever the lender "calls" the note, by making demand for its

```
                                              San Francisco, CA
                                              August 15, 1984

  $ _____5000.00_____

  _____On demand_____ I (we) promise to pay

  to the order of _____Paula Payee_____

  _____Five Thousand_____ Dollars.

  For Value Received.                 John Jones
```

FORM 1-1
Short Form Demand Note

repayment). See Form 1-1. This may be in a face amount equal to the maximum credit available to the borrower, whether or not the borrower has drawn upon the full credit available. Or separate demand notes may be signed in the actual amount of each draw. Occasionally the notes, rather than being demand notes, may be term notes with short maturities (e.g., 30, 60, or 90 days). Even if the note is a demand note in the face amount of the credit, but especially when it has a short maturity, it is many lenders' practice to require the borrower to "renew" the note at frequent intervals by signing a new note and having the old notes cancelled. A bank or finance company may finance a customer for years on this basis while holding a succession of renewal notes, each of which by its terms has been payable on demand.

The note is not the only type of negotiable instrument governed by Article 3: the article also provides the legal principles applicable to checks and drafts.[1] While the basic concepts and principles that apply to notes are in most cases identical to those applicable to checks and drafts, notes serve a separate function in the business context. The note is principally a credit instrument; checks and drafts are principally means of providing current payment. Although short-term credit may be extended, the financing aspect is incidental to the payment aspect.[2]

notes
_v_
drafts

---

1. The check, familiar to all students, is actually a special kind of draft. Drafts other than checks are usually not encountered in consumer settings. Discussion of both drafts and checks is deferred until Chapter 15 for reasons given in the text. Article 3 also governs certificates of deposit, a specialized form of bank note not discussed in the text.

2. This statement is certainly true with respect to checks, but oversimplifies the use of drafts, which may serve a mixture of payment and financing functions. For clarity's sake, however, it is best to postpone treatment of the sophisticated use of drafts to finance transactions. As payment media, checks and drafts compete increasingly with credit cards and electronic funds transfer systems (EFTS), including debit cards. All these payment forms, which are related in function to one another but not to the note, are treated in Part IV of these course materials.

Notes may vary widely to meet the needs of the transactions in which they are utilized. A simple short-form demand note appears in Form 1-1. For purposes of contrast, examine the long-form promissory note reproduced infra in Form 3-2. Both are similar to preprinted forms in common use by banks, insurance companies, title insurance companies, furniture dealers, or anyone else extending credit or connected with lending transactions on a regular basis. In addition, multitudinous "standard" forms exist in form books or preprinted by legal form printing companies. To this array must be added "tailor-made" notes drafted by attorneys for particular transactions and the inevitable do-it-yourself notes drawn by individuals.

One of the basic issues of negotiable instruments law is whether a particular instrument has been drafted in such a way that it meets the requirements of negotiability. These requirements are referred to technically as the "formal requisites" of negotiability. While it is exceedingly simple to draft an instrument that meets these requirements (see Form 1-1, or examine a check from your checkbook), an elaborate body of law has grown up defining the exact contours of these formal requisites. This issue is considered in Part B infra. For the present, it is assumed that the note is question is negotiable. The materials that follow explore the procedural and substantive advantages of holding a negotiable instrument.

VIRGINIA NATIONAL BANK v. HOLT
216 Va. 500, 219 S.E.2d 881, 18 UCC Rep. 440 (1975)

COMPTON, Justice. In this appeal, which results from a suit on a negotiable instrument, we deal with proof of a signature. Pertinent to our consideration are the following italicized portions of UCC 3-307:

> *Burden of establishing signatures, defenses and due course.*—(1) Unless specifically denied in the pleadings each signature on an instrument is admitted. *When the effectiveness of a signature is put in issue*
>> (a) *the burden of establishing it is on the party claiming under the signature; but*
>> (b) *the signature is presumed to be genuine or authorized* except where the action is to enforce the obligation of a purported signer who has died or become incompetent before proof is required.
>
> (2) *When signatures are* admitted or *established, production of the instrument entitles a holder to recover on it unless the defendant establishes a defense.*
>
> (3) After it is shown that a defense exists a person claiming the right of a holder in due course has the burden of establishing that he or some person under whom he claims is in all respects a holder in due course.

In May 1974, the plaintiff, Virginia National Bank, filed a motion for judgment against the defendants, Edgar M. Holt and Gustava H. Holt, his wife, jointly and severally, seeking recovery of the face amount of a "Homestead Waiving Promissory Note," plus interest and attorney's fees. The instrument, payable to the order of the Bank and allegedly made by the Holts to evidence an indebtedness, was dated December 12, 1973, was due 90 days after date, and was in the amount of $6,000.

Edgar M. Holt was duly served with process, but failed to appear or file pleadings in response. A default judgment in the amount sued was entered against him in August 1974.

In her pleadings, Gustava H. Holt generally denied liability and specifically denied that the instrument was signed by her. On November 20, 1974, judgment was entered on a jury verdict in her favor and we granted the Bank a writ of error.

The dispositive issue is whether the evidence relating to the genuineness of Mrs. Holt's signature on the instrument presented a question of fact to be decided by the jury. We hold that it did not and reverse.

We will summarize only the evidence pertinent to the issue we decide. Testifying for the Bank was one of its commercial loan officers, who did not handle the Holt transaction but through whom the instrument in question was introduced into evidence, and two other witnesses, one of whom was an expert in handwriting analysis, whose statements supported the Bank's position that the signature on the note was in fact the defendant's.

Mrs. Holt did not appear at the trial, but her attorney endeavored to show that his client did not execute the instrument. During cross-examination, the loan officer, over the Bank's objection based on the hearsay rule, was required to answer whether he was present during the taking of Mrs. Holt's discovery deposition in July 1974 when she "denied that she signed the note?" The record shows that the witness responded: "Yes, I was. Somewhat surprised."[1] No other statement was elicited by defendant's counsel from any of the Bank's witnesses which would support the defendant's claim that she did not sign the writing.

The only evidence offered in the defendant's behalf was a set of answers previously filed by the Bank to six interrogatories propounded by her attorney. Those responses indicated that the Bank did not know of any witness who saw the defendant sign the note or who heard her admit that she signed it. They further indicated that the Bank had no information that she ever authorized her husband to sign her name to any promissory note or that she ever ratified any act of his in signing her name to such a writing.

By a motion to strike at the conclusion of the evidence, and again by a motion to set aside after the verdict, the Bank moved for judgment in its favor contending, as it does on appeal, that the foregoing hearsay testimony on cross-examination was erroneously admitted and, in the alternative, that even if such evidence was properly received, the defendant had failed, as a matter of law, to overcome the presumption established by UCC 3-307 that her signature was genuine and authorized. The trial court, in refusing to sustain the

---

1. This answer should probably read "Yes. I was somewhat surprised."

lower ct
— err

motion to strike and in overruling the motion to set aside, ruled that the question of whether the signature was genuine was for the jury. This was error.

UCC 3-307, inter alia, sets out the burden of proof in an action which seeks recovery upon an "instrument"[2] and deals with issues arising, in such a suit, from a challenge of the genuineness or authorization of signatures. 2 R. Anderson, Uniform Commercial Code §3-307:3 (2d ed. 1971). Under that section, each signature on an instrument is admitted unless, as in this case, the

(the way it work)

"effectiveness" of the signature is put in issue by a special denial. The burden of establishing[3] the genuineness of the signature is then upon the party claiming under the signature and relying on its "effectiveness," but such a party is aided by a presumption that it is genuine or authorized. In this context, "presumption" means that "the trier of fact must find the existence of the fact presumed unless and until evidence is introduced which would support a finding of its nonexistence." UCC 1-201(31).

The effect of the presumption is to eliminate any requirement that the plaintiff prove the signature is authentic until some evidence is introduced which would support a finding that the signature is forged or unauthorized. UCC 3-307, Official Comment 1. It is based upon the fact that in the normal course of events forged or unauthorized signatures are very uncommon, and that evidence of such is usually within the defendant's control or more accessible to him. Id. Therefore, under UCC 3-307, the party denying a signature must make some sufficient showing of the grounds for the denial before the plaintiff is put to his proof. The evidence need not be sufficient to require entry of summary judgment in the defendant's favor, "but it must be enough to support his denial by permitting a finding in his favor." Id. "Until the party denying the signature introduces such sufficient evidence, the presumption requires a finding for the party relying on the effectiveness of the signature." UCC 3-307, Virginia Comment. See 2 F. Hart & W. Willier, Commercial Paper Under the Uniform Commercial Code §2.07(2) (1975).

held

An application of the foregoing analysis of the statute to the facts of this case demonstrates that the Bank was entitled to entry of summary judgment in its favor at the conclusion of all the evidence, since no material issue of fact requiring resolution by a jury was presented. Rule 3:18.

The defendant's specific denial put the genuineness of the defendant's signature in issue. Because of the foregoing presumption, the signature, which appeared to be that of Gustava H. Holt, was presumed to be genuine and the defendant was thus required to present "sufficient evidence" in support of the denial of genuineness. This she failed to do. We will assume, but not decide, that the disputed answer during cross-examination was properly admitted in evidence. Nonetheless, we conclude that this bit of testimony is insufficient to

---

2. See UCC 3-102(1)(e) and 3-104(1).

3. " 'Burden of establishing' a fact means the burden of persuading the triers of fact that the existence of the fact is more probable than its nonexistence." UCC 1-201(8).

sustain a finding that the signature was forged or unauthorized. Furthermore, the answers to interrogatories furnish no support to the defendant's claimed defense. A forgery or an unauthorized signature may not be shown by merely demonstrating the plaintiff's apparent lack of evidence on that issue.

We hold, therefore, that the defendant has failed, as a matter of law, to make a sufficient showing to support a finding that she, or her authorized representative, did not in fact write her name on the instrument. The presumption then requires a finding that the signature on the instrument is genuine and effective. Accordingly, production of the instrument entitled the Bank to recover, because the defendant established no defense, UCC 3-307(2), and it was error to submit the case to the jury.

For these reasons, the judgment in favor of Gustava H. Holt will be reversed and final judgment will be entered in favor of the Bank.

NOTES & QUESTIONS

1. _Procedural advantages of a note over a contractual promise._ In *Virginia National Bank* the bank held Mrs. Holt's note. Suppose instead that the plaintiff is Dealer, who brings an action against Mrs. Holt to recover $6,000. Assume that in the action Dealer introduces a writing purporting to be a contract between Dealer and Mrs. Holt. The writing bears signatures alleged to be Dealer's and Mrs. Holt's and states that Dealer agrees to sell Mrs. Holt a certain Buick automobile, for which Mrs. Holt agrees to pay $6,000. What must Dealer plead and establish to make a prima facie case for recovery against Mrs. Holt? In the principal case, was the testimony of the handwriting experts necessary to the outcome? See UCC 3-307, 3-408 Comment 3; Fed. R. Civ. P. 9. See generally Kinyon, Actions on Commercial Paper: Holder's Procedural Advantage Under Article Three, 65 Mich. L. Rev. 1441 (1967).

2. _Substantive advantages of a note over a contractual promise._ Developer sold 20 building lots, with streets and utilities completed, to different individuals and took back contracts calling for a total payment of $1 million. Developer assigned these contracts to Warbucks in exchange for a $900,000 loan and directed the individuals to start paying directly to Warbucks. Warbucks received no payments, and when he contacted the first individual, he was informed that the purchasers had discovered during recent rains that all the lots were in a floodplain and, further, that Developer had misrepresented the zoning classifications of both the subject properties and the immediately adjacent parcels. What difficulties may Warbucks face in enforcing the contracts against the individual purchasers? Restatement (Second) of Contracts §336(1) summarizes the rights of an assignee of a contract right as follows:

> By an assignment the assignee acquires a right against the obligor only to the extent that the obligor is under a duty to the assignor; and if the right of the

assignor would be avoidable by the obligor or unenforceable against him if no
assignment had been made, the right of the assignee is subject to the infirmity.

See also UCC 9-318(1).

As you will see infra, Warbucks might be better off if Developer had
taken promissory notes from the purchasers of the building lots and then
"negotiated" (delivered each note with Developer's signature on the back) the
note to Warbucks. Why? Because if Warbucks qualifies as a "holder in due
course" he will take the purchasers' obligations free of most defenses they
might have against Developer. See UCC 3-305, 3-306.

B. NEGOTIABILITY, NEGOTIATION, AND HOLDING IN DUE COURSE

The preceding materials suggest some of the reasons why a party who is to
extend credit often bargains to obtain a promissory note embodying the borrower's promise to pay. Two issues are basic to any legal analysis of a transaction involving the rights of one who may hold a promissory note. The first is
simply whether the writing in question is a *negotiable instrument*: that is, does it
satisfy the formal requisites of negotiability so as to fall within the scope of
Article 3's rules? Second, assuming that the instrument is negotiable, has the
instrument been *negotiated*—transferred in such a way that the party now in
possession of it is a *holder?*

Assuming positive answers to these two inquiries, a third issue may arise:
has the holder acquired the instrument under circumstances that will confer
the special status of *holder in due course?* Only if a party to the note asserts a
defense, or if a third party claims the note, will holder-in-due-course status be
important; such a holder will take free of most defenses and claims; a mere
holder takes the note subject to them.

In the following cases and materials each of these issues is examined in
sequence.

1. *Formal Requisites of Negotiability*

VON FRANK v. HERSHEY NATIONAL BANK
269 Md. 138, 306 A.2d 207, 12 UCC Rep. 689 (1973)

DIGGES, Judge. . . .

This litigation concerns the liability of the appellants [James von Frank
and Joseph Barrett] on two notes, one dated May 1, 1969, the other, June 10
of that year. The note of May 1 reads:

The June 10 note is identical except for the date and the fact that the signature of Stanley Stoller (S. S. Stoller) appears only once, as president of the corporation, and does not appear below the attestation line and to the left of the other signatures.

The facts leading up to the execution of these notes can be narrated as follows: in November 1968 the appellants, together with Stanley S. Stoller, met in Hershey, Pennsylvania, with a representative of Hershey Estates Corporation to discuss the purchase by appellants and Stoller of two radio stations owned by a wholly owned subsidiary of that corporation. These negotiations apparently proceeded so well that, at the conclusion of the meeting, arrangements were made for the prospective purchasers to meet with John Baum, vice president and cashier of the Hershey National Bank [a Pennsylvania financial institution]. The purpose of this meeting was to discuss the prospects of obtaining a bank loan of $20,000 for the East Penn Broadcasting Corporation, a company to be newly organized, owned, directed and administered by appellants and Stoller. This money was necessary in order to fulfill a Federal Communications Commission requirement for a license transfer. At this initial bank meeting, Baum testified that he informed the purchasers that no funds could be loaned to their new corporation unless they were personally responsible for the indebtedness. Additionally, he informed them that their personal financial statements would be required before the Bank would further consider the loan. This request for financial statements was complied with and Barrett, a Washington stockbroker, and von Frank, then president of a Maryland bank, supplied detailed statements showing their net worth. Stoller supplied a statement which in Baum's words, "was such that the [Bank] couldn't have relied on his personal net worth." East Penn never filed a financial statement.

Apparently satisfied that the appellants' financial statements justified the loan, the Bank notified East Penn, through its president, Stoller, that it had an approved line of credit for $20,000. At this point we should mention that Barrett and von Frank are both residents of Bethesda, Maryland, while Stoller was the man on the scene in Pennsylvania. It is probably because of the inconvenience to appellants of having to travel to Pennsylvania that appellee was made aware of a corporate resolution that authorized Stoller, as president of East Penn, to sign a valid corporate obligation on his signature alone.

Finally, in April of 1969, East Penn was ready to draw on its line of credit. Stoller so informed the Bank and obtained the printed form that was to become the May 1, 1969 note in order to have it properly signed by the appellants. Stoller met appellants one night at a restaurant in Bethesda where the signing ceremony took place. Barrett and von Frank both claim that the printed note form they signed that night did not have on it the words "president," "seal," or "sec'y"; but that they instructed Stoller to add their respective corporate titles after their names. The appellants make the same contention about the July 10 note which they say they signed in blank when they received it in the mail and then returned it to Stoller. No explanation is offered by these signators as to why they did not place so important a detail, as they understood the addition of the corporate office to be, on the notes themselves while they had pen in hand. The trial judge found that each note, when presented to the Bank and as received in evidence, was complete and no additions were made except to date them and place the Bank number in the lower left hand corner.

The East Penn investment did not prove successful and by January 1970 the interest due on the notes was in default. The Bank made demand on the appellants that they honor their obligation as co-makers and when they still did not pay, this suit was instituted. Appellants resist the Bank's claim on the grounds that they are not personally liable on the notes. . . .

The parties have proceeded throughout this litigation on the assumption that these notes were negotiable and therefore governed by the provisions of the UCC. We find the notes to be non-negotiable and the UCC to be inapplicable. Therefore, the liability of the parties is determined as a matter of simple contract law. See UCC 1-103, 3-805 Official Comments. Cf. Vain v. Gordon, 249 Md. 134, 136, 238 A.2d 872 (1968); Roth v. Baltimore Trust Co., 161 Md. 340, 348, 158 A. 32 (1931). We also note that, although the UCC has been adopted in both Maryland and Pennsylvania, the parties here proceeded on the assumption that the law of Maryland and not that of Pennsylvania was applicable. However, from the record, it would seem that the law of Pennsylvania would govern this transaction. But, as no notice was given of an intention to rely on Pennsylvania law, and there was no waiver of the requirement, pursuant to Code (1957, 1971 Repl. Vol.), Art. 35, §50, we are not required to take judicial notice of the law of that state other than to presume it is like that of Maryland. . . .

Under the Maryland UCC, to be negotiable, an instrument must, among other requirements, "be payable to order or to bearer." (UCC 3-104(1)(d)). The absence of these magic words renders a note non-negotiable. Here, the notes in question contain just a "promise to pay to the Hershey National Bank" the amount due. However, UCC 3-805 entitled "instruments not payable to order or to bearer" specifies that:

This Article *applies* to any instrument whose terms do not include transfer and *which is otherwise negotiable within this Article* but which is not payable to order or to bearer, except that there can be no holder in due course of such an instrument. (Emphasis added.)

The official comments to this section indicate that: "This section covers the 'non-negotiable instrument.' As it has been used by most courts, this term has been a technical one of art. It does not refer to a writing, such as a note containing an express condition, which is not negotiable and is entirely outside of the scope of this Article and to be treated as a simple contract. It refers to a particular type of instrument which meets all requirements as to form of a negotiable instrument except that it is not payable to order or to bearer."

Thus, while these notes could still be governed by the Code even though they lack words of negotiability, they must meet all other "requirements as to form of a negotiable instrument" except for that. The notes here do not conform to this standard. UCC 3-112(1)(d) provides that the negotiability of an instrument is not affected by "a term authorizing confession of judgment on the instrument if it is not paid when due." We held in Stankovich v. Lehman, 230 Md. 426, 187 A.2d 309 (1963), a case decided under the Negotiable Instruments Act, that the authorization to confess judgment "as of any term" permitted entry of judgment at any time prior to the maturity of the note and therefore destroyed negotiability. [The note provided that it was payable six months after date.—Eds.] As was stated by Judge Hammond for this Court in *Stankovich,* supra at 430, 187 A.2d at 312: "It would seem logical that if the statute, as it does, preserves negotiability only if the confession of judgment is at or after maturity, the warrant to confess must expressly, or by necessary implication, restrict its exercise to that time if the note is to be negotiable, and that if the warrant is silent as to the time when it can be exercised, the reasonable implication must be that it can be done at any time. Most of the cases involving this general area of the law have arisen in Pennsylvania, and the Courts of that State have held that notes containing stipulations for confession of judgment without specification or limitation as to time are, like those expressly authorizing judgment prior to maturity, non-negotiable."

We held in *Vain v. Gordon,* supra, 249 Md. at 136, 238 A.2d 872, that the UCC has not changed the law on this point. [The note in *Vain* provided that it was payable one year after date.—Eds.] The notes here being silent on the time when confession of judgment can occur must be read to mean that it can be done at any time and therefore they are non-negotiable.

It is significant, and somewhat ironic, that the authorities relied on by this Court in *Stankovich* and *Vain* are Pennsylvania cases. They have likewise held that the UCC has not changed the law and continue to hold that a provision of a note authorizing confession of judgment before it is due, such as we have here, renders it non-negotiable. . . .

Since these non-negotiable notes are not governed by the UCC, their effect is, as already noted, determined under principles of simple contract law.

Under that law, appellants cannot escape personal liability. Although the corporation, as principal, was fully disclosed, its agents would not be insulated from liability if there was an agreement between the parties that the appellants would be so liable. . . .

At best from appellants' standpoint, the appearance of the name of the corporation before their signatures renders the capacity in which they signed ambiguous and this permits "extraneous proof, as between the original parties, to show the true character of the instrument, and what party—the principal, or agent, or both—is liable." Haile v. Peirce, [32 Md. 327 (1870)]. . . . Here, the evidence is clear, as found by the trial judge, that individual liability was intended. . . .

In sum, we think that the trial court correctly found the appellants personally liable on these notes and will affirm its judgment.

didn't have titles, etc.

NOTES & QUESTIONS

1. *Words of negotiability.* As *von Frank* indicates, one of the formal requisites of negotiability is that the instrument "be payable to order or to bearer." UCC 3-104(1)(d). Both "to order" and "to bearer" are terms of art, further defined in UCC 3-110 and 3-111. "Pay John Doe" is neither an order nor a bearer instrument; it is not a negotiable instrument, but falls within the rule of UCC 3-805. "Pay to the order of one barrel No. 1 Diesel Fuel" is a bearer instrument and is negotiable if it meets the other requisites of UCC 3-104. See UCC 3-111, Comment 2. The "order or bearer" requirement is often referred to as a requirement that the instrument contain "words of negotiability."

2. *Purposeful characterization.* UCC 3-805 states the effect of an instrument payable to a named party without words of negotiability ("Pay John Doe"). It is not uncommon, particularly in the context of transactions between family members or other closely-related parties, purposely to draw an instrument payable to a specific payee. Why might that be so? Would the same reasons be relevant in the principal case?

no more ???

3. *Characterization by other means.* Compare UCC 3-105(1)(c) with UCC 3-105(2)(a). When setting up transactions it is common for an attorney to insist upon a statement in the note utilizing either the "reference" language of subsection (1), or the "subject to" language of subsection (2). How does the outcome of bargaining over this issue compare with inclusion or omission of words of negotiability?

4. *Form and substance in the law of formal requisites.* As the foregoing case and notes indicate, the rules surrounding negotiability are both technical and highly formalistic. Professor Gilmore, however, states: "Few generalizations have been more often repeated, or by generations of lawyers more devoutly believed, than this: negotiability is a matter rather of form than substance. It is bred in the bone of every lawyer that an instrument to be negotiable must be 'a courier without luggage. '. . . Few generalizations, legal or otherwise, have ever been less true; the truth is, in this as in every other field of commercial

law, substance has always prevailed over form. 'The law' has always been in a constant state of flux as it struggles to adjust itself to changing methods of business practice; what purport to be formal rules of abstract logic are merely *ad hoc* responses to particular situations." Gilmore, The Commercial Doctrine of Good Faith Purchase, 63 Yale L.J. 1057, 1068-1069 (1954).

If Professor Gilmore is right, is the elaborate codification in UCC 3-104 through 3-112 not a misguided effort that may stultify desirable developments? At the same time, courts with less insight than Professor Gilmore may judge cases in the light of the "devout beliefs" that Gilmore debunks.

5. *Traps for the unwary: clarity in formalism.* To the extent that the technical requisites are formally adhered to, it is obvious that a premium is placed upon a firm grasp of their detail, and potential surprises await the unwary or poorly counseled due to minute variations in wording. Should not parties, including the lay person, be able to tell with ease whether a note is or is not negotiable? Would it be objectionable to allow a note to be negotiable or not simply by conspicuously labeling it as such? Cf. UCC 5-102 (letter of credit is letter of credit if it conspicuously so states).

6. *Negotiability by contract.* A contract may contain a waiver-of-defense clause, by which it is agreed that the obligor will not set up against assignees defenses that would be available against the assignor. In the absence of fraud such clauses are normally valid in commercial contexts (see UCC 9-206); although prohibitions exist in the consumer context, they are related to similar limitations upon cut off of defenses by use of a negotiable instrument, discussed at p. 59 infra. If such results can be achieved by contract, how significant is "true" negotiability under Article 3 (through compliance with formal requisites) as opposed to "negotiability by contract" through use of waiver-of-defense clauses?

Remember that Article 3 does not purport to be the exclusive statement of rules on negotiable instruments. UCC 3-103 does not cover money, documents of title, and investment securities; it also refers to other Code articles for rules on bank collection and secured transactions. Comment 1 to UCC 3-104 notes that special state statutes may make negotiable a written promise to deliver commodities rather than to pay money, and, as noted, UCC 3-805 makes Article 3 rules (except holder-in-due-course rules) applicable to instruments that comply with all the formal requisites except use of "order" or "bearer" language.

2. Transfer and Negotiation

BECKER v. NATIONAL BANK & TRUST CO.
222 Va. 716, 284 S.E.2d 793, 32 UCC Rep. 1083 (1981)

CARRICO, Chief Justice. In this case involving the Uniform Commercial Code, National Bank and Trust Company (the Bank) sought recovery below on six promissory notes executed respectively by each of six couples (collectively, the Makers). The Bank held the notes as collateral for a loan made to United Leasing Corporation (United) and instituted the present action against the Makers upon United's default. The parties agreed to submit the case to the trial court upon discovery depositions and pretrial briefs. Ruling that the Bank was a holder in due course entitled to recover on the notes, the court entered a separate judgment against each set of makers. We granted the Makers an appeal.

The record shows that, in 1972, Dr. Sven Ebbesson induced six of his colleagues in the medical field to join him in a cattle venture. The venture consisted of a corporation known as Solhem Farm, Inc., with Ebbesson as president and major shareholder, and a partnership known as Polled Exotics Limited Partnership (Polled), with Ebbesson as general partner and his six colleagues as limited partners.

To commence the business, Ebbesson negotiated with Edward Shield, president of United, to have United purchase cattle and lease them to Polled. As collateral to insure performance of the lease obligations, Polled transferred to United seven promissory notes, each executed by a different partner and his wife and made payable to the order of Polled. The transfer to United was evidenced by a separate assignment agreement and not by any writing entered upon, or attached to, the notes themselves.

Shield, on behalf of United, negotiated with the Bank for a loan to purchase the cattle to be leased to Polled. As collateral, United transferred to the Bank the cattle lease executed by Polled and the seven promissory notes United had received from Polled.

After the Bank's loan to United was closed, the cattle operation commenced and the Makers began paying United the annual installments due on their notes. Ultimately, the cattle venture suffered financial reverses, and the Makers undertook an investigation of the operation. Thereafter, the Makers ceased paying the notes and instituted a fraud action against Polled in the United States District Court for the Western District of Virginia. Finding that the notes had been procured from the Makers by fraud, the District Court declared the notes void *ab initio* as between the Makers and Polled. The Bank was not a party to this proceeding.[4]

Following cessation of the Makers' payments, United defaulted on its loan obligation to the Bank. The Bank obtained judgment against United for the balance due on the debt and, failing to secure satisfaction of that judgment, brought the present action against the Makers.

On appeal, the focal point of the controversy between the parties is a provision contained in each of the notes executed by the Makers. The provision reads:

4. The Makers state in their brief that the United States Bankruptcy Court for the Western District of Virginia found that United had procured the cattle lease from Polled by fraud. The Makers state also that the Bank was not a party to this proceeding.

issue: did U. have authorization to negotiate to let BK be a holder — due course

> The makers of this Note agree that Polled Exotics Limited Partnership, or its assignees, may freely assign or negotiate this Note in whole or in part from time to time without notice to the makers; however, if the makers of this Note are given notice of such an assignment or negotiation, the makers agree to acknowledge receipt thereof in writing.

UCC 1-102(3) provides that "[t]he effect of provisions of this act may be varied by agreement." The Official Comment to this section reads in part: "2. Subsection (3) states affirmatively at the outset that freedom of contract is a principle of the Code: 'the effect' of its provisions may be varied by 'agreement.' The meaning of the statute itself must be found in its text, including its definitions, and in appropriate extrinsic aids; it cannot be varied by agreement. . . . Thus private parties cannot make an instrument negotiable within the meaning of Article 3 except as provided in Section 3-104; nor can they change the meaning of such terms as 'bona fide purchaser,' 'holder in due course,' or 'due negotiation,' as used in this Act. But an agreement can change the legal consequences which would otherwise flow from the provisions of the Act."

In reaching the conclusion that the Bank was a holder in due course not subject to the fraud defenses of the Makers, the trial court held that the parties had "contract[ed] as to the effect of the Commercial Code's provisions" by providing for the assignment of the notes "without suffering the usual effect of loss of negotiability." Thus, the court found, United had the "capacity to negotiate the notes" to the extent that the Bank became a holder in due course.

The Makers contend that by allowing the disputed provision of the notes to stand, the trial court has permitted the parties to vary the meaning of such UCC terms as "due negotiation" and "holder in due course." This is the very sort of change that the UCC prohibits, the Makers insist, and, hence, the trial court's findings are erroneous.

On the other hand, the Bank contends that the disputed provision did not change "any concept or definition" of the UCC. The Bank argues that the "language of the Notes only varied the legal consequence of lost negotiability" which would otherwise have attended an assignment of the Notes to United Leasing." The Bank maintains that, since this type of variance is allowed by the UCC, the trial court properly held United was authorized to negotiate the notes so as to permit the Bank to become a holder in due course.

B's arg

We agree with the Bank that by allowing United, a mere assignee, to negotiate the notes, the disputed provision varied the legal consequences ordinarily attending an assignment. We do not agree, however, that only legal consequences were altered; we believe the provision also changed concepts or definitions of the UCC contrary to the previously quoted Official Comment. In pertinent part, UCC 3-202 provides:

> (1) Negotiation is the transfer of an instrument in such form that the transferee becomes a holder. If the instrument is payable to order it is negotiated by

assign → makes initial note non-negot

negotiate = indorsement & delivery

delivery with any necessary indorsement; if payable to bearer it is negotiated by delivery.

(2) An indorsement must be written by or on behalf of the holder and on the instrument or on a paper so firmly affixed thereto as to become a part thereof.

In UCC 1-201(20), a holder is defined as "a person who is in possession of . . . an instrument . . . issued or indorsed to him or to his order or to bearer or in blank." And, in UCC 3-302, a holder in due course is defined as a "holder who takes the instrument" under specified conditions.

These sections provide that, before a transferee of a promissory note can become a holder in due course, he must first qualify as a holder. A transferee may become a holder of order paper only by "negotiation," that is, by indorsement and delivery, and the indorsement must be by or on behalf of a person who is himself a holder.

held

Without the disputed provision, it is clear that, because United took the notes by mere assignment and not through the indorsement of Polled, United was not a holder. Thus, United could not "negotiate" the notes so as to permit its transferee, the Bank, to qualify as a holder. Therefore, to the extent that the disputed provision purported to authorize United, as a mere assignee, to negotiate the notes, the provision necessarily changed the meaning of the terms "holder" and "due negotiation" and, hence, of the term "holder in due course."

When the provision is given its obvious import relative to the order paper in question, it attempts to equate a "holder" with a mere possessor and to make "due negotiation" synonymous with delivery accompanied only by assignment. Correspondingly, the provision attempts to convert the meaning of "holder in due course" to one who possesses order paper by assignment. But the UCC does not permit this sort of alteration of the meaning of the inviolable terms "due negotiation" and "holder in due course." We hold, therefore, that the judgments entered against the Makers are erroneous. Accordingly, we will reverse the judgments and remand the case for further proceedings not inconsistent with the views expressed in this opinion.

clause invalid

NOTES & QUESTIONS

1. *Order paper and bearer paper.* An instrument may originally be drawn in either order form or bearer form. An example of order paper would be:

April 1, 1984

On demand, without grace, pay to the order of John Jones $1000.00.

/s/ *Maker*

See also UCC 3-110.

An example of bearer paper would be:

April 1, 1984

On demand, without grace, pay to the bearer of this note $1000.00.

/s/ *Maker*

See also UCC 3-111.

An order instrument may be negotiated only upon indorsement by the named payee (here, John Jones) and delivery. Bearer paper, in contrast, may be negotiated by delivery alone. The mechanics of negotiation are set forth in UCC 3-202.

2. *Necessary indorsements.* The notion of a *necessary indorsement* is a key concept of negotiable instruments law. Although this term of art appears in UCC 3-202, the Code assumes an understanding of the term; it does not define it. However, the concept is not difficult: an indorsement is a necessary indorsement if the instrument is currently in order form, so that negotiation requires the current holder's indorsement. Thus, in the first example above, the note is in order form. If Jones wishes to negotiate the note he must *both* indorse it and deliver it. His indorsement is a necessary indorsement. In the second example above, Jones may negotiate the bearer note by delivery alone. Although he may indorse it, his indorsement is not essential to the negotiation of the note: it is not a necessary indorsement.

3. *Special and blank indorsements.* Just as paper may be issued in either order or bearer form, it may be indorsed so as to give it either order or bearer character. Take the first example above: when John Jones negotiates the note, he may indorse it "pay to the order of Sally Smith /s/ John Jones" or simply "pay Sally Smith /s/ John Jones." Either indorsement is effective as a special indorsement. UCC 3-204. Upon delivery of the instrument to Sally Smith, she will become the holder of specially indorsed paper. Such paper is treated as order paper; she may further negotiate the paper only by delivery *and* indorsement: hers is a necessary indorsement. It is possible, however, that Jones will simply indorse the note in blank (/s/ John Jones) and deliver it to Smith. In that case, he will have converted the paper to bearer paper. Smith may now negotiate the paper simply by delivering it. If she does indorse the paper when she negotiates it, her indorsement is not a necessary one.

As it passes through commerce, an instrument may be converted back and forth from order to bearer form. As the student may have deduced, there are certain risks in holding paper in bearer form. The potential recipient of bearer paper may therefore request that it be issued in order form or specially indorsed to his order. Indeed, the holder of bearer paper may convert it to order paper himself: see UCC 3-204(3) and Comment.

4. *Difficulties with the Code's definitional scheme.* The Code's draftsmanship in this area is unsatisfying and circular, and has been criticized as a poor presentation of previously clear and well-established principles.

MELLINKOFF, THE LANGUAGE OF THE UNIFORM COM-
MERCIAL CODE, 77 Yale L.J. 185, 192-193 (1967): "The basic concept of
the law of negotiable instruments is defined as follows:

> *Negotiation* is the transfer of an instrument in such form that the transferee be-
> comes a *holder*. If the instrument is payable to order it is negotiated by delivery
> with any necessary *indorsement;* if payable to bearer it is negotiated by delivery.
> [UCC 3-202(1).]

With key words italicized, it becomes clearer that to discover what *negotiation* is
you first have to know what is meant by *holder* and *indorsement*.
  "The very next section tells you something about indorsement:

> An *indorsement* must be written by or on behalf of the *holder* and on the instrument
> or on a paper so firmly affixed thereto as to become a part thereof. [UCC 3-
> 202(2).]

  "The search for the sense of *negotiation* that hinges on *indorsement* thus
doubles back on the same *holder* that is a part of the definition of *negotiation.*
Holder must be the way out. Naturally, it is defined:

> *'Holder'* means a person who is in possession of a document of title or an instru-
> ment or an investment security drawn, issued or *indorsed* to him or to his order or
> to bearer or in blank. [UCC 1-201(20).]

  "At this point your cry of despair is mingled with the shriek of the
wounded draftsman who has just bitten himself squarely in the back. For the
negotiation which led to *holder* has led to *indorsement* which leads back to *holder.*
And the *negotiation* which led to *indorsement* has led to *holder* which leads back to
indorsement.
  "From the dizzying shuttle between *holder* and *indorsement* there is only one
escape. In order to understand the UCC definitions in the area of negotiable
instruments, you must first know the law of negotiable instruments. In other
words, the Code is not a code that tells a student or a banker or a lawyer what
the law is. It is rather a compilation of notes that may serve to remind you of
law you had better know before you read the UCC."
  See also Whaley, Forged Indorsements and the UCC's "Holder," 6 Ind.
L. Rev. 45 (1972); White, Some Petty Complaints about Article Three, 65
Mich. L. Rev. 1315, 1322-1323 (1967).
  5. *Title: "tracing the path of an instrument."*
  (a) Maker signs a note to the order of Jones. Jones indorses the note in
blank; it is stolen from his desk drawer by Fingers. Fingers gives the note to
Smith in payment of a long-standing debt to her. Smith demands payment
from Maker. Is she entitled to payment? Will payment discharge Maker on

the note? Is Smith a holder? Has the note been negotiated at each step on its path into Smith's hands?

(b) Assume exactly the same facts, except that rather than Jones indorsing the note, it is stolen by Fingers, who indorses Jones' signature upon it. How will the same questions be answered?

(c) Assume that the note is originally issued in bearer form; otherwise the facts are as in (b). How will the same questions be answered?

In answering the above problems, take two differing approaches. First try to analyze each "transfer" of the instrument by asking whether a "negotiation" of the instrument was effected by that transfer: apply UCC 3-202 and UCC 3-204 as starting points. See also UCC 3-404. As a second approach, simply ask whether Smith is a *holder* as defined by UCC 1-201(20). As to the liability of Maker and the issue of discharge, see UCC 3-413(1) and 3-603. Do the two approaches suggested above yield consistent answers in each case?

While the Code may lack elegance, or even clarity, the correct results in the above cases have not been in doubt for well over a century.

In (a) Smith is entitled to enforce the note; she is a holder of it notwithstanding the fact that she derives title through a thief. UCC 3-301. Good faith payment to her will discharge Maker. UCC 3-603. If Smith is also a holder in due course she is entitled to payments even if Maker has notice of the theft. UCC 3-603, 3-305, and Miller v. Race, 1 Burr. 452, 97 Eng. Rep. 398 (King's Bench 1758) (owner of bank note payable to bearer could not recover possession of note from bona fide purchaser for value who took through robber of note).

In (b) Smith is not a "true" holder (notwithstanding her apparent conformity with UCC 1-201(20)), and does not have good title to the instrument because the instrument *lacks a necessary indorsement in the chain of title.* (As to the procedural burdens of establishing or denying signatures, however, recall Virginia National Bank v. Holt, supra.)

Problem (c) receives the same answer as (a), because again the theft is of bearer paper. Finger's signature upon the instrument is a forgery, but it is not the forgery of a necessary indorsement.

Two indelible principles should be retained from the above problems: first, that a forged *necessary* indorsement usually creates a break in the chain of title that will not be "laundered" by any number of good faith, clean-hands dealings downstream; second, that it is never safe to analyze a negotiable instruments problem without first "running the chain of title" of the instrument by tracing its path from its first issuance to final transfer to the party now in possession of it.

6. *Transfer, assignment, and negotiation.* Only those transfers of a negotiable instrument made in formal compliance with the requisites of UCC 3-202 and 3-204 are negotiations of the instrument that confer the rights of a holder upon the transferee. But a negotiable instrument can be assigned, just like other property or ordinary contract rights. Transfer without negotiation confers the rights stated in UCC 3-201. Essentially, such a transferee is in the position of

an ordinary transferee of property or assignee of contract rights, and often has the additional right specifically to enforce indorsement and thereupon upgrade his or her status to that of a holder.

7. *Diagram of* Becker *facts.* Application of normal rules of *Becker*'s facts may be diagrammed as follows:

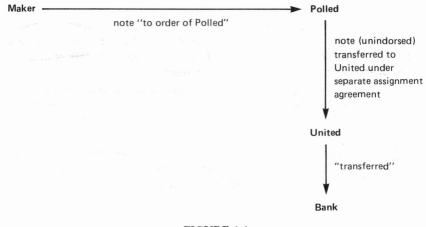

FIGURE 1-1
Path of *Becker* Note

Ignore for the moment the "special provision" contained in each of the notes, and focus on the path of these notes through commerce. Polled could have negotiated the notes to United by indorsing them "Pay to the order of United, /s/ Polled," or "Pay United /s/ Polled" (special indorsements) or simply "/s/ Polled" (a blank indorsement). Any of these actions, together with delivery of the notes to United, would have constituted negotiation under UCC 3-202. Accordingly, United would then be the holder of the instrument. However, Polled did none of these acts. It assigned the instruments, under a separate agreement, to United. UCC 3-201 determines United's rights in such a situation, as noted above.

The court then states that United "transferred" the notes to Bank as collateral. There is a frustrating lack of clarity in the opinion as to the mechanics of this transfer. The trial court held that United gave the "capacity to negotiate the notes." Let us assume that United did indorse the notes in its own name: the instrument would then run as follows: drawn to the order of Polled; transferred by separate assignment to United (still reading payable to the order of Polled and unindorsed by Polled); indorsed by United, either in blank or in favor of Bank. In technical terms, the note as originally issued was order paper; therefore the indorsement of the named payee (Polled) was a *necessary* indorsement if the paper was to be further negotiated (see UCC 3-

202(1), 3-202(2)). (Note, however, that a transferee who gives value has the *holder*
specifically enforceable right to have the transferor's unqualified indorsement — *due* ?
by virtue of UCC 3-201(3).) Since this did not occur, United did not become *course*?
a holder (see again UCC 1-201(20)). Since an indorsement "must be written
by or on behalf of the holder" (UCC 3-202(2)), United's signature was ineffective to confer on the bank status as a holder. If United signed "Polled" and
then signed "United," the result would be no different. United's "signature" of
Polled's name is unauthorized, and therefore wholly inoperative. UCC 3-404
(see also Comment 1). The instrument still lacks Polled's necessary indorsement, so United cannot become a holder of it; United therefore cannot effectively indorse it (UCC 3-202), and Bank cannot become a holder of it. Such
would be the ordinary analysis. A contrary result could be accounted for only
by some effect of the special provision contained in the notes in question.

8. *Construing the special provision.* It appears most probable that the instruments in *Becker* followed the path set forth in the preceding note. In the trial
court's analysis, the normal result should not obtain; as that court read the
special provision in the notes, the makers had specifically agreed that Polled *lower ct*
or its assignees (such as United) might freely assign or *negotiate* the notes. The *held*
trial court held this a valid contractual modification of the principle that
United could further negotiate the notes only if United was itself a holder and
not a mere assignee. The Virginia Supreme Court seems on sound ground in
attacking this analysis.

The provision in issue is somewhat inartful. Although the bank's analysis
of the purpose of the term is strained, it is not immediately clear what purpose
its draftsman *did* have in mind. Reread the provision carefully in its entirety.
Neither assignment nor negotiation requires notice to the maker of a note. In
saying that these actions can be taken without notice to the maker, the provision is mere surplusage, and at most appears to drive home to the makers
Polled's probable intention to assign or negotiate the note, quite possibly as
collateral. The provision's final clause may add something by providing a
mechanism for clarifying who was entitled to payment in the event of assignment.

Suppose the provision had been intended to allow the result reached by
the trial court. Could it have been drafted in such a manner to circumvent the
supreme court's objections? For instance, in some forms of security agreements
it is common to include a provision authorizing the lender to take possession of
instruments or documents the borrower holds, and granting the lender a
power of attorney to indorse them on borrower's behalf. Will the provision in
Becker bear the construction that it conferred authority upon United, as agent
or subagent, to take those actions necessary to effect negotiation? Does it
appear that United took such actions? If a clause was explicitly drawn to
confer such authority, would it be open to the supreme court's objections? To
other objections?

9. *Further terminology.* In addition to the terms *necessary* indorsement, *blank*
indorsement, and *special* indorsement, the student will encounter the terms

restrictive indorsement and *qualified* indorsement. The most common restrictive indorsement is "for deposit only," which is often utilized when a check is indorsed. Restrictive indorsements are defined in UCC 3-205, but their effects are governed by a number of provisions. We will examine restrictive indorsements again in Chapter 16, The Bank Collection System. A qualified indorsement is an indorsement in which the indorser places an indorsement on the instrument but prefaces his signature by such words as "without recourse." This form is commonly employed where the indorsement in question is a necessary indorsement (so that the instrument cannot be further negotiated without it), but the indorser wishes to limit his liability. Effects of qualified indorsements are discussed infra in conjunction with the liabilities of an indorser and again in Chapter 15.

3.   Holding in Due Course

ARCANUM NATIONAL BANK v. HESSLER
69 Ohio St. 2d 549, 433 N.E.2d 204, 33 UCC Rep. 604 (1982)

Syllabus by the Court

1. A transferee who takes a note with notice of a defense on the part of any person is not a holder in due course.

2. A transferee is not a holder in due course, when, in an action by the transferee of a note against the makers, the trier of fact finds an irregularity on the face of the note which calls into question the validity of the note, the terms of the note, the ownership of the note or creates an ambiguity as to the party to pay, and there is sufficient evidence to support such finding.

3. A transferee does not take an instrument in good faith and is therefore not a holder in due course when there are sufficient facts to indicate the transferee, by virtue of its unusually close relationship with the transferor, had reason to know or should have known of infirmities in the underlying transaction from which the instrument originated.

Appellant, Kenneth Hessler, was in the business of raising hogs for the John Smith Grain Company. John Smith Grain Company or J & J Farms, Inc., would deliver hogs to appellant and require appellant to sign a promissory note payable to John Smith Grain Company to cover the cost of the hogs and feed. Without the knowledge or consent of appellant, John Smith Grain Company would then sell the note to appellee, Arcanum National Bank. Appellee would credit the John Smith Grain Company with the face amount of the note and open a commercial loan account for appellant. The first such transaction, according to the bank's records, was August 28, 1974. The hogs were usually sold by J & J Farms, Inc. to Producer's Livestock Association, and a portion of the proceeds were applied to satisfy appellant's note and loan account. Appellant received a flat fee and a share of the net profits.

On January 4, 1977, appellant signed a promissory note payable to John Smith Grain Company for hogs delivered on that date. J & J Farms, Inc. had previously mortgaged the hogs to Producer's Livestock Association. Accordingly, in its separate findings of fact and conclusions of law, the trial court found appellant received no consideration for the note.

Appellant signed his name and was advised by C. North, Jr., an officer and director of both John Smith Grain Company and J & J Farms, Inc., to sign his wife's name, Carla Hessler, on the note; appellant then placed his initials, K.H., after her name. John Smith Grain Company as payee assigned this note to appellee, Arcanum National Bank.

In early 1977, Producer's Livestock Association took the hogs from appellant's farm because of the serious financial difficulties of John Smith Grain Company. John Smith Grain Company was later placed in receivership, and no funds were available to pay appellee bank for appellant's note.

Appellee bank sued appellant and Carla Hessler in the Common Pleas Court of Darke County to collect the face amount of the note, viz., $16,800. Appellee's motion to dismiss Carla Hessler was granted.

The trial court held appellee was a holder in due course of the note, and appellant's defense of want of consideration could not be asserted against appellee. The Court of Appeals affirmed. This cause is now before this court pursuant to the allowance of a motion to certify the record.

KRUPANSKY, Justice. The sole issue in this case is whether appellee is a holder in due course who takes the note free from appellant's defense of want of consideration.

In a suit by the holder of a note against the maker, the holder obtains a great advantage if granted the status of holder in due course. R.C. Chapter 1303 (UCC Article 3) provides that a holder in due course takes the instrument free from most defenses and claims. UCC 3-305. One such defense which is of no avail when raised against a holder in due course is want of consideration, the defense raised by appellant.

Whether one is a holder in due course is an issue which does not arise unless it is shown a defense exists. Once it is established a defense exists, the holder has the full burden of proving holder in due course status in all respects. UCC 3-307(3).

There are five requirements which under UCC 3-302 one must meet in order to establish holder in due course status: viz., (1) one must be a "holder" as defined in UCC 1-201; (2) one must be in possession of an "instrument," as explained in UCC 3-102(1)(e); (3) "value," as set forth in UCC 3-303, must have been given for the instrument; (4) the instrument must have been taken in "good faith," as defined at UCC 1-201; and (5) the purchaser must take the instrument without notice that it is overdue or has been dishonored or of any defense against or claim to it on the part of any person, as detailed at UCC 3-

304. All five of these requirements must be met to qualify as a holder in due course. A transferee who otherwise qualifies as a holder in due course, but who takes an instrument with notice of a defense to it on the part of any person is therefore not a holder in due course. Likewise, one who does not take an instrument in good faith is not a holder in due course.

not holder in due course b/c
① knowledge of defense

I

Appellant contends appellee has not established holder in due course status because appellee took the instrument with notice of a defense against it. We agree. The requirement that the purchaser take the instrument without notice of a claim or defense in order to qualify as a holder in due course is explained, under the heading of "Notice to Purchaser," at UCC 3-304, which provides in relevant part:

> (1) The purchaser has notice of a claim or defense if:
>   (a) The instrument is so incomplete, bears such visible evidence of forgery or alteration, or is otherwise so irregular as to call into question its validity, terms or ownership or to create an ambiguity as to the party to pay; . . .

Whether a transferee has taken an instrument with notice of a defense depends upon all the facts and circumstances of a particular situation and is generally a question of fact to be determined by the trier of fact. . . . One situation when a bank was denied holder in due course status was found in First National Bank v. Otto Huber & Sons, Inc., 394 F. Supp. 1284 (D.S.D. 1975). This case held the bank had notice of a defense because of an ambiguity involving the due date; the note was considered irregular on its face. Similarly, when a transferee receives a note which is blank except for the maker's signature, the note is irregular on its face. The transferee takes with notice of a defense and is therefore not a holder in due course of the note. Salter v. Mutual Finance Co., 106 Ohio App. 20, 153 N.E.2d 216 (1957).

In the case *sub judice,* the trial court, sitting as fact finder, weighed the evidence of the relationship between appellee and appellants and reasoned: "The defect on the promissory note is that the signature of Carla Hessler was added by Kenneth Hessler and, since the Arcanum National Bank handled the Hesslers' personal finances, it should have noticed that there was a defect on the face of the instrument. . . . The note also bears the initials 'K. H.' indicating that Kenneth Hessler had signed Carla Hessler's name." Accordingly, the trial court specifically found "this 'irregularity' does call into question the validity of the note, the terms of the note, the ownership of the note or create an ambiguity as to the party who is to pay the note." Thus, the trial court, while specifically finding appellee took the note with notice of a defense, nonetheless erroneously held appellee bank qualified as holder in due course.

We hold, therefore, when the trier of fact finds a transferee took a note with notice of a defense, the legal conclusion which follows from such finding is the transferee cannot benefit from holder in due course status and the maker may assert all valid defenses. Since the fact finder in this case specifically found appellee bank took the note with notice of a defense, appellee cannot qualify as a holder in due course.

② not - good faith II

Appellant also contends, in essence, appellee bank failed in its burden of proving holder in due course status because appellee failed to establish it took the note in good faith as required under UCC 3-302(1)(b).

"Good faith" is defined as "honesty in fact in the conduct or transaction concerned." UCC 1-201(19). Under the "close connectedness" doctrine, which was established by the Supreme Court of New Jersey in Unico v. Owen, 50 N.J. 101, 232 A.2d 405 (1967), a transferee does not take an instrument in good faith when the transferee is so closely connected with the transferor that the transferee may be charged with knowledge of an infirmity in the underlying transaction. The rationale for the close connectedness doctrine was enunciated in Unico, at pages 109-110, 232 A.2d 405, as follows: "In the field of negotiable instruments, good faith is a broad concept. The basic philosophy of the holder in due course status is to encourage free negotiability of commercial paper by removing certain anxieties of one who takes the paper as an innocent purchaser knowing no reason why the paper is not sound as its face would indicate. It would seem to follow, therefore, that the more the holder knows about the underlying transaction, and particularly the more he controls or participates or becomes involved in it, the less he fits the role of a good faith purchaser for value; the closer his relationship to the underlying agreement which is the source of the note, the less need there is for giving him the tension-free rights considered necessary in a fast-moving, credit-extending world."

Soon after the decision in *Unico* was reached, the close connectedness doctrine was adopted by Ohio courts. Headnote No. 2 in American Plan Corp. v. Woods, 16 Ohio App. 2d 1, 240 N.E.2d 886 (1968), announced the following: "A transferee of a negotiable note does not take in 'good faith' and is not a holder in due course of a note given in the sale of consumer goods where the transferee is a finance company involved with the seller of the goods, and which has a pervasive knowledge of factors relating to the terms of the sale."

Similarly, in Security Central Natl. Bank v. Williams, 52 Ohio App. 2d 175, 368 N.E.2d 1264 (1976), a finding that the transferee did not take the note in good faith was justified when the transferee bank was alerted to the possibility that the underlying transaction which generated the note was not a completely above-board transaction.

According to White and Summers, noted authorities on the Uniform

Commercial Code, the following five factors are indicative of a close connection between the transferee and transferor: (1) Drafting by the transferee of forms for the transferor; (2) approval or establishment or both of the transferor's procedures by the transferee (e.g., setting the interest rate, approval of a referral sales plan); (3) an independent check by the transferee on the credit of the debtor or some other direct contact between the transferee and the debtor; (4) heavy reliance by the transferor upon the transferee (e.g., transfer by the transferor of all or substantial part of his paper to the transferee); and (5) common or connected ownership or management of the transferor and transferee. White & Summers, Uniform Commercial Code 481 (1972).

An analysis of the above factors in relation to the facts of this case, as set forth in the trial court's findings, reveals an unusually close relationship between appellee bank (the transferee), the John Smith Grain Company (the transferor-payee) and J & J Farms, Inc.

Appellee provided John Smith Grain Company with the forms used in the transaction and supplied the interest rate to be charged. At the time of the purchase of the first note, appellee bank ran an independent credit check on appellant. There is evidence of a heavy reliance by John Smith Grain Company upon appellee bank insofar as it was customary for the grain company to transfer substantially all of its commercial paper to appellee bank. There was not only a common director of appellee and John Smith Grain Company, but also common directors or management between John Smith Grain Company and J & J Farms, Inc. H. K. Smith was a director of appellee bank and the president and director of John Smith Grain Company. C. North, Jr., was an officer and director of both John Smith Grain Company and J & J Farms, Inc. John Milton Smith was officer and director of John Smith Grain Company and officer of J & J Farms, Inc. In addition, the trial court found that B. Henninger, the executive vice-president of appellee who had previously been employed by John Smith Grain Company, frequented John Smith Grain Company several times a week between November 1976 and January 1977 to advise the officers of John Smith Grain Company on business practices. During that time, John Smith Grain Company was experiencing serious financial difficulties.

The facts of this case clearly indicate such close connectedness between appellee bank and John Smith Grain Company as to impute knowledge by appellee bank of infirmities in the underlying transaction. The trial court specifically found, in its separate findings of fact and conclusions of law, the relationship between appellee bank and J & J Farms was not an arm's length relationship. In spite of this finding, the trial court erroneously concluded "the facts do not permit the court to void the holder in due course protections under these circumstances."

The trial court reasoned as follows: "Even if the bank were aware, through its Director, Tim [H. K.] Smith, of the perilous financial condition of John Smith Grain Company, the bank had every right to anticipate that the note could be paid by J & J Farms when the pigs were sold." Given the circumstances of this case, i.e., the common directors or management between appellee bank, John Smith Grain Company and J & J Farms, Inc., the trial court as fact finder could quite reasonably conclude appellee was aware, at the time it bought the note, of the troubled financial situation of John Smith Grain Company.

The trial court, however, missed the point. Not only do the facts indicate appellee bank was aware of the impending bankruptcy of John Smith Grain Company, but they also show appellee had reason to know of a fatal infirmity in the underlying transaction, viz., there was no consideration given by John Smith Grain Company for the note. C. North, Jr., an officer and director of both John Smith Grain Company and J & J Farms, Inc., obtained appellant's signature and advised appellant to sign his wife's name on the note. As an officer and director of J & J Farms, Inc., C. North, Jr., undoubtedly was aware that at the time he obtained appellant's signature, the hogs had already been mortgaged by J & J Farms, Inc. It is well-established in Ohio a corporation can act only through its officer and agents, and the knowledge of the officers of a corporation is at once the knowledge of the corporation. . . . If North, as officer and director of both John Smith Grain Company and J & J Farms, Inc., knew there was no consideration for the note, then such knowledge is imputed to both corporations. Thus, H. K. Smith, as president and director of John Smith Grain Company, had ample reason to know of the failure of consideration; and since H. K. Smith was also a director of appellee bank, his knowledge is imputed to appellee bank.

The executive vice-president of appellee bank, B. Henninger, who had previously been employed by John Smith Grain Company, was also in close contact with John Smith Grain Company at the time appellant signed the note. According to the trial court's conclusions, at the time appellant's signature was obtained on the note, B. Henninger was meeting several times a week with the officers of John Smith Grain Company to advise them on business practices. At that time, the officers of John Smith Grain Company included H. K. Smith, who was also a director of appellee bank, and C. North, Jr., who was also an officer and director of J & J Farms, Inc.

Given these facts, one cannot conclude with absolute certainty that appellee bank had actual knowledge of the failure of consideration. As appellant correctly states in his brief, however, the doctrine of close connectedness was developed in part because of the difficulty of proving the transferee's actual knowledge of problems in the underlying transaction. The doctrine allows the court to imply knowledge by the transferee when the relationship between the transferee and transferor is sufficiently close to warrant such an implication.

Under the circumstances of this case, we find the relationship between appellee bank and John Smith Grain Company was so entwined that it was error for the trial court not to apply the doctrine of close connectedness to find appellee bank failed to carry its burden of proving good faith.

If we accept the trial court's findings of fact and apply the close connectedness doctrine, we can reach only one conclusion, viz., appellee bank did not take the note in good faith.

Upon either one or both of the above reasoned theories, i.e., (1) notice of a defense and (2) close connectedness doctrine, we find the Court of Appeals erred in affirming the trial court's finding that appellee bank was a holder in due course. The judgment of the Court of Appeals is, therefore reversed.

William B. BROWN, Justice, concurring. . . . This court's finding that appellee bank cannot qualify as a holder in due course since it took the note with notice of a defense is, in my opinion, dispositive of the case at bar. As such, it is unnecessary for this court to additionally determine whether appellee failed to qualify as a holder in due course under the close connectedness doctrine.

NOTES & QUESTIONS

1. *Holder in due course: holder, instrument.* The first two requisites of holder-in-due-course status are that the instrument be negotiable and that the party in possession be a holder. A student or lawyer who overlooks these requirements may confer holder-in-due course status on a person who is not even a holder and has no rights on the instrument. Conversely, if the instrument is negotiable and the party seeking enforcement is a holder, holder-in-due-course status is often irrelevant. As the notes following *Becker* indicate, production of an instrument entitles a holder to recover on it unless the defendant establishes a defense. UCC 3-307(2); see also UCC 3-301. Full discussion of the effect of holder-in-due-course status upon availability of defenses is deferred until Part C of this chapter.

2. *Good faith.* Compare the definition of good faith applicable within Article 3 (including 3-302) with the more expansive definition in UCC 2-103(1)(b), which is applicable to merchants in sales transactions governed by Article 2. In earlier drafts of the Code an attempt was made to incorporate some requirement of commercial reasonability into Article 3 as well, but the present wholly subjective standard eventually prevailed. What policy, if any, supports protecting professionals, such as merchants and bankers, who have not exercised the degree of care or precautionary practices usual for a prudent merchant or banker taking an instrument?

3. *Value.* Compare the definition of value in Article 3 (UCC 3-303) with the Code's general definition of value in UCC 1-201(44). How do they differ? Can these differences be accounted for on any rational basis?

4. *Notice of defenses.* UCC 3-304 provides a rather extensive elaboration of circumstances under which a purchaser is or is not deemed to have notice of a defense. See also UCC 1-201(25) through (27). What specific facts gave Arcanum National Bank notice of a defense? If a note is signed

/s/ *Jim Jones*
/s/ *The Jones Corporation, J. J.*

does it follow that there can never be a holder in due course of the note? Is that the alternative holding in the principal case?

It is noteworthy that the defense of which the purchaser has notice need not ultimately be upheld; the invalid defense may defeat holder-in-due-course status, leaving the holder subject to another defense the holder had no notice of whatever. Why should this be so?

Note: The "Close Connectedness" Doctrine

Arcanum cites four authorities in its discussion of the close-connectedness doctrine: *Unico,* which it regards as establishing the doctrine, two Ohio appellate court decisions it identifies as adopting the doctrine, and J. White & R. Summers, Uniform Commercial Code (1972).

The *Unico* opinion is lengthy and somewhat lacking in clarity. It seems highly pertinent, however, that the holder in *Unico* was a partnership formed expressly for the purpose of financing the seller, Universal Stereo Corporation. 50 N.J. 101, 114; 232 A.2d 405, 412, 4 UCC Rep. 542, 551. Two of the factors noted by White & Summers are heavy reliance by the seller upon the lender and common or connected ownership or management.

American Plan, which *Arcanum* states adopted *Unico*'s doctrine in Ohio, fits the *Unico* paradigm only in certain respects. Although not clearly articulated in the opinion, it might be inferred that seller sold a substantial portion of its notes to American Plan Corporation, a finance company. The finance company bought the notes for their "face value," that is, the principal amount of the note. Each note was subject to a $215 carrying charge, but the opinion fails to state the amount or other terms of the note, so that the effective interest rate cannot be deduced from the opinion. Perhaps the strongest resemblance between *Unico* and *American Plan* is the degree to which the consumer purchaser was "hung out to dry" on the underlying transaction. Aside from the apparent shoddy quality of the merchandise sold, it was uncontroverted that the nature of the papers she was signing was misrepresented to defendant, who neither realized she was making nor intended to make a note. As the court held that this provided a real defense (good even against a holder in due course), its alternative holding on close-connectedness was purely gratuitous. The court also remarked that the note in question was of doubtful negotiability but declined to decide that issue since it had not been raised on appeal.

In *American Plan,* the court particularly disapproved the fact that the finance company supplied the seller with notes and other forms, made a credit investigation of the makers of the notes, and reserved the right to refuse to purchase paper that it felt was "risky." Do not all of these actions indicate prudence by a lender? If you wished to buy a car and went to your bank to obtain a loan, which of the above steps would you expect the bank to take? If you obtained the loan and signed a note to the bank, would you have a defense to payment of the note if the car was a lemon? If, instead, the bank purchases your note from the dealer, should it have any less concern about your ability to pay or the form of the note? Following *American Plan,* would you advise the finance company simply to make a direct extension of credit to the purchaser? Is one form of financing preferable to the other? Note that "preferable" might refer to prudent business practices or to the least expensive or most efficient way of allocating costs.

The second Ohio case cited, *Security Central National Bank,* is quite different from both *American Plan* and *Arcanum.* The case also involves a highly dubious sales scheme. The seller's sales representative was a former bank employee; the vice-president of the bank who handled the account resigned "because of the Art Sales matter and several other matters." The note in question, for about $3,000, had been purchased by the bank for $500, half of which represented accrued interest. The trial court, in ruling on a motion for a new trial, stated: "Now, the Court listened to the evidence and I think the Court was legitimate in drawing whatever legitimate inferences it may from the facts that was testified to and the Court drew the inference from the facts that there was a knowledge between the seller of the goods, Mr. Skaggs, who was involved with Art Sales, [and] Mr. Grant Reed, who was vice-president of the bank. . . . The bank acts through its employees, its agents, its vice-president, and what have you, and I find from the evidence that they had pervasive knowledge of the factors involved in the sale of these items, that there was a connection there, in fact, and that they were not holders in due course with negotiable notes. They did not take them in good faith as required. . . ." 368 N.E.2d 1264, 1265 (1976). The exact issue on appeal was whether the trial court's finding that the bank did not take the instrument in good faith was against the manifest weight of the evidence. The court held it was not.

The court's syllabus and its opinion are cast in broad terms of "facts sufficient to alert a bank to a possibility that the deal was not above-board," and would thus appear to import an objective good-faith standard. The trial court finding seems to be that the vice-president was dishonest in fact and that the bank was bound by the act of its agent. The appellate court provides little insight into whether the evidence supported knowledge of infirmity of the particular sale, resting as it does on the "almost inherently suspect" type of business. Id. at 1266.

A principal effect of the close-connectedness doctrine is to avoid the difficulty (or impossibility) of showing the holder's knowledge of fraud in a *particular* transaction, when knowledge of a pattern of fraudulent dealing may be obvious. *Unico* fits this pattern; so does *Security Central National Bank,* although the doctrine was perhaps unnecessary to the result, as noted. How well does *American Plan* fit such a pattern? *Arcanum?*

A number of cases have rejected the suggestion that under the close-connectedness doctrine, bad faith or notice of a defense may be proved simply by showing knowledge of a pattern of questionable dealing. Universal C.I.T. Credit Corp. v. Ingel, 347 Mass. 19, 196 N.E.2d 847, 2 UCC Rep. 82, 3 UCC Rep. 303 (1964), although antedating *Unico,* is perhaps the most frequently cited (aluminum siding case; trial judge properly excluded evidence that holder was aware of complaints by previous customers of seller).

The importance of the close-connectedness doctrine in consumer settings has been vitiated due to subsequent legislative and regulatory actions that have effectively abolished the holder-in-due course doctrine in consumer transactions. See Part G infra. The continued vitality of the close-connected-ness doctrine in commercial contexts remains a question mark at present.

C. LIABILITY "ON THE INSTRUMENT"

Liability may exist in many forms in connection with negotiable instruments. The law in this field is made up of a complex web of contract, tort, warranty, and property theories. The term liability "on the instrument," however, is once again a term of art: it refers to the contractual liability of one who has signed an instrument in some capacity. UCC 3-401 states one of the most basic principles of the law of commercial paper:

> (1) No person is liable *on an instrument* unless his signature appears thereon. [Emphasis added]

A person whose signature does not appear on an instrument may have con-tractual or other liabilities arising from the underlying transaction giving rise to the instrument and may also be subject to liability due to the manner in which he or she has dealt with the instrument, such as for breach of warranty or for conversion. These are themes that will be pursued in later sections. In this section the immediate object is to explore such issues as the following: how does one become liable *on an instrument* within the meaning of UCC 3-401? What are the various capacities and how does one determine the capacity in which one can sign an instrument? What are the parameters of liability im-posed by the statutory contracts that Article 3 ascribes to signatories in par-ticular capacities?

1. Liability of the Maker

We begin with an examination of the simplest contract for which the Code provides, the contract of a maker of a promissory note. The statutory content of a maker's contract is set forth in UCC 3-413(1):

> The maker . . . engages that he will pay the instrument according to its tenor at the time of his engagement or as completed pursuant to Section 3-115 on in-complete instruments.

Problem 1-1. Son writes to his father, who is wintering in Trinidad, that he is short of cash for his next semester at school and for skiing. Father writes back enclosing the following instrument, which he instructs Son "to fill in at your pleasure for any amount up to $5,000, and take it to Mr. Diamond at the bank." Son dutifully fills in the instrument for $5,000. He then takes it to Mr. Diamond, who gives Son $5,000 in exchange for the note as completed.

Trinidad
January 10, 1984

The undersigned hereby promises to pay, on demand, without grace, the sum of _____ ($_____) to Aspen National Bank, together with interest thereon from the date hereof until the date of payment at the rate from time-to-time current for said Bank's Personal Credit Lines, and in the event of default at said Bank's Prime Lending Rate plus 5%, together with costs and expenses incurred in enforcing this obligation, including reasonable attorney's fees.

/s/ *Herbert Warbucks, Jr.*

What is Warbucks' obligation?

Problem 1-2. On the same facts, Son, who is enjoying an exceptionally fine ski season, decides that $7,500 would be a more appropriate figure, and completes the note accordingly. What is Warbucks' obligation?

ST. REGIS PAPER CO. v. WICKLUND
93 Wash. 2d 497, 610 P.2d 903, 28 UCC Rep. 1065 (1980)

DOLLIVER, Justice. Wicklund Builders, Inc., and its president, defendant Vernon Wicklund, had done business with plaintiff St. Regis Paper Company for several years on an open account basis. Wicklund agreed with Ralph Munger, credit manager of St. Regis, to sign a promissory note for certain past due amounts. Munger filled in the blank spaces of the standard form note and wrote "personal guaranty" in a blank space in a paragraph referring to security for the note. He later crossed out these words, initialed the change, and substituted the word "none." Wicklund signed the note without designating that he was signing it in a representative or corporate capacity.

St. Regis sued Wicklund individually on the note. Wicklund counterclaimed for reformation alleging a mutual mistake and that the parties intended only the corporation to be bound rather than Wicklund as an individual. Over the objection of St. Regis, Wicklund testified he had discussed the note with Munger and that both parties understood only the corporation would be liable on the promissory note. The trial court allowed the parol evidence: "I am going to overrule the objection. It would appear to me the authorities currently hold that in a reformation action, parol evidence is admissible on the question of reformation, so I will overrule the objection."

Wicklund further testified that he objected to the words "personal guar-

anty" and had Munger cross them out as he did not want to be personally
bound on the note.

On the other hand, Munger's testimony by deposition stated that he
understood the note was to be a personal obligation; that he wrote the words
"personal guaranty" in by mistake and that he crossed them out and initialed
them on his own initiative.

The trial court held in favor of Wicklund. In its findings of fact the court
said that, "the inclusion of the words 'personal guaranty' and the subsequent
striking of those words by Mr. Munger, is confusing and raises a question as to
the parties' intentions at the time." The court also found there was no reasonable explanation for the inclusion and subsequent striking of the words "personal guaranty" other than the fact that the question of Wicklund's personal
liability on the note arose, was discussed, and the parties agreed he was not to
be personally liable. The court further stated that clear, cogent and convincing evidence existed that the note did not embody the intent of the parties and
that a mutual mistake was made in failing to indicate Wicklund's representative capacity.

On the basis of its findings of fact, the court concluded that as a result of
the mutual mistake the note should be reformed to provide that Wicklund
signed the note for the corporation and not as an individual. The court entered
judgment reflecting this conclusion. Judgment was also entered against Wicklund Builders, Inc., in the amount of $21,492.98, plus interest and costs. . . .
[The Court of Appeals reversed, concluding that the plaintiff's objection to the
admission of the parol evidence should have been sustained.]

Two issues are presented: (1) Did the trial court err in allowing parol
evidence to establish that the parties intended only the corporation to be liable
on the promissory note? and (2) Did the trial court err in reforming the note to
indicate that Wicklund signed only as an agent of Wicklund Builders, Inc.?

As to the first issue, St. Regis contends the admission of parol evidence is
prohibited by UCC 3-403. This section provides:

(1) A signature may be made by an agent or other representative, and his
authority to make it may be established as in other cases of representation. No
particular form of appointment is necessary to establish such authority.
(2) An authorized representative who signs his own name to an instrument
    (a) is personally obligated if the instrument neither names the person rep-
        resented nor shows that the representative signed in a representative
        capacity;
    (b) except as otherwise established between the immediate parties, is per-
        sonally obligated if the instrument names the person represented but
        does not show that the representative signed in a representative capac-
        ity, or if the instrument does not name the person represented but does
        show that the representative signed in a representative capacity.
(3) Except as otherwise established the name of an organization preceded or
followed by the name and office of an authorized individual is a signature made
in a representative capacity.

St. Regis also cites the official comments to UCC 3-403(2)(a) which states "A signature [of the agent alone] . . . personally obligates the agent and parol evidence is inadmissible under subsection (2)(a) to disestablish his obligation." UCC 3-403, Comment 3.

Wicklund, however, contends reformation because of mutual mistake is available regardless of UCC 3-403. In Akers v. Sinclair, 37 Wash. 2d 693, 226 P.2d 225 (1950), we stated the rule on reformation for mutual mistake: "Where both parties have an identical intention as to the terms to be embodied in a proposed written conveyance, assignment, contract or discharge, and a writing executed by them is materially at variance with that intention, either party can get a decree that the writing shall be reformed so that it shall express the intention of the parties, if innocent third persons will not be unfairly affected thereby. 2 Restatement of Contracts, 968, §504." *Akers,* at 702, 226 P.2d at 230. In Leonard v. Washington Employers, Inc., 77 Wash. 2d 271, 278, 461 P.2d 538, 543 (1969), we said: "In the first place, the parol evidence rule is not applicable in actions for reformation. . . . The reason is clear. The remedy of reformation is granted when necessary to conform a writing to correctly reflect the agreement actually reached by the parties. . . . In order to determine whether there was a mutual understanding which preceded the writing, and if so, what the mutual understanding was, parol must be admitted before a court can pass upon the question of whether the writing should be reformed."

Does UCC 3-403 eliminate the equitable remedy of reformation because of mutual mistake and prohibit the admission of parol evidence to prove mutual mistake? We hold it does not. UCC 1-103 states:

> Unless displaced by the particular provisions of this Act, the principles of law and equity, including the law merchant and the law relative to capacity to contract, principal and agent, estoppel, fraud, misrepresentation, duress, coercion, *mistake,* bankruptcy, or other validating or invalidating cause shall supplement its provisions. (Italics ours).

The official comments to this section state: "Purposes of Changes: 1. . . . [T]his section indicates the continued applicability to commercial contracts of all supplemental bodies of law except insofar as they are *explicitly* displaced by this Act. . . ." (Italics ours) UCC 1-103, Comment 1.

There is nothing in UCC 3-403 which explicitly—or indeed even by reference—states the equitable remedy of reformation because of mutual mistake is no longer available. Neither by case law nor by the statutes of this state has reformation because of mutual mistake been eliminated. The defense was raised properly by defendant and parol evidence as to mutual mistake was properly admitted by the trial court. See J. White & R. Summers, Uniform Commercial Code §2-11, at 75-76 (1972).

The Court of Appeals was correct in its contention the signature on the note was unambiguous and thus not subject to explanation by parol evidence. However, it is not the contention of defendant that the signature is ambiguous but rather that it was a mutual mistake that the note itself was signed by Wicklund in his individual capacity. . . . [The Supreme Court then held that there was substantial evidence to support the trial court's findings that the parties did not intend for Wicklund to be personally bound on the note.—EDS.]

The Court of Appeals is reversed and the judgment of the trial court is reinstated.

NOTES & QUESTIONS

1. *Form of the note.* The Washington Supreme Court's opinion does not indicate as clearly as it might the form of the note, which is as follows:

PROMISSORY NOTE

28934.49 _____ JAN 18 _____, 19 73

FOR VALUE RECEIVED, without grace, I promise to pay to the
order of ____ST Regis Paper Co
the principal sum of Twenty Eight Thousand Nine hundred Thirty four and 49/00
(28934.49) with interest thereon from date hereof at the rate of _____ per cent, per annum until maturity.

Said principal, together with interest as aforesaid, shall be paid in monthly payments as follows (such payments including interest): ____ON DEMAND

($_____) or more

on the _____ day of _____, 19____, and a like sum on the _____ day of each and every month thereafter until the said principal sum, together with interest thereon, shall have been fully paid. Said principal and interest shall be paid in lawful money of the United States, and shall bear interest from maturity until paid at the rate of __8%__ per cent, per annum.

If default be made in the payment of this note, or any part thereof, or any interest thereon, then the principal sum with accrued interest shall at once become due and collectible without notice, time being of the essence of this contract, and said principal sum and interest shall bear interest from such default until paid at the rate of ____8%____ per cent, per annum.

In case suit is instituted to collect this note or any portion thereof, I promise to pay such additional sum as the court may adjudge reasonable as attorney fees in such suit.

This note with interest is secured by a __Personal Guaranty__ NONE mortgage of even date herewith executed and delivered by the makers hereof to the said payee conveying certain real estate described therein situate in _____ County, State of Washington.

This contract is to be construed in all respects and enforced according to the laws of the State of Washington.

X _____

PIONEER NATIONAL TITLE INSURANCE COMPANY   FORM 5195

is this negotiable?

Since the note nowhere indicated an obligation of any party other than Wicklund, the court of appeals held the note unambiguous, and not subject to explanation by parol. On this narrow point the supreme court agreed. The court of appeals was obviously influenced in its decision by Wicklund's testimony at trial that he knew the difference between a signature on behalf of the company and a signature as an individual, that he had signed many documents on behalf of the company, and that such documents "would normally already be prepared with the name *Wicklund Builders, Inc. and then a space for my signature and then, 'President' typed in."* (Court's emphasis.) 24 Wash. App. 552, 561, 597 P.2d 926, 932 (1979).

On the other hand, the supreme court gave great weight to the insertion and subsequent deletion of the words "personal guaranty." Is there any explanation for the insertion and deletion other than that offered by Wicklund?

2. *Fraud.* Given his version of what transpired, could Wicklund have argued that St. Regis had attempted to defraud him? How would that argument differ from the theory employed by Wicklund's attorney? What would be the difference in proof of fact required? How would Wicklund's theory, if established, affect his rights and liabilities and those of St. Regis? How would you sum up the comparative advantages and disadvantages of the two theories from Wicklund's perspective?

3. *Parol evidence in the law of negotiable instruments.* Students may recall the Code's parol evidence rule for sales transactions, UCC 2-202, from their first year Contracts course. Article 3, unlike Article 2, lacks a single provision dealing with problems of parol evidence. Rather, treatment of the issue is sprinkled throughout the article, UCC 3-403 being simply an example. The emphasis on formalities in the law of negotiable instruments may seem to make a strict formulation both appropriate and justified by concerns about commercial certainty and predictability; on the other hand, the highly stylized nature of such instruments increases the likelihood, as a practical matter, that agreements extrinsic to the instrument will exist. Insofar as written agreements are concerned, this problem is addressed by UCC 3-119; extrinsic parol agreements receive a far more equivocal treatment. Professor Ellen Jordan has provided a brief but thoughtful consideration of several aspects of the problem; see Jordan, "Just Sign Here—It's Only a Formality": Parol Evidence in the Law of Commercial Paper, 13 Ga. L. Rev. 43 (1978).

4. *Application of the rules of UCC 3-403.* Wicklund testified at trial that when he signed documents on behalf of the company the signature was usually made as follows:

Wicklund Builders, Inc. [typed]
/s/ *Vernon Wicklund* [handwritten]
President [typed]

Which subsection of UCC 3-403 applies to a signature in this form? Is Wicklund liable personally? May this result be altered by extrinsic evidence? Is the corporation liable? May this result be altered by extrinsic evidence? Does it make any difference whether the instrument is in the hands of a holder who dealt with Wicklund, a holder who did not deal with Wicklund, or a holder in due course? Consider UCC 3-404 and 1-201(39) in addition to UCC 3-403.

Suppose Wicklund signs a note as follows, the entire "signature" being handwritten:

Wicklund Builders, Inc.
Vernon Wicklund

Which subsection of UCC 3-403 applies? May either UCC 1-201(39) or 3-402 be applicable? If Wicklund is personally liable under UCC 3-403, in what capacity is he liable? In what capacity would he be liable under UCC 3-402?

Wicklund signs a note "Wicklund Builders, Inc." Under what circumstances, if any, would Wicklund be personally liable on this note?

Conversely, Wicklund signs a note "Vernon Wicklund" and then seeks to establish that the note is a corporate, not a personal obligation (the facts of the principal case, omitting the stricken "personal guaranty" aspect). Assuming that in normal circumstances this obligates Wicklund personally under UCC 3-403(2)(a), does it follow that Wicklund Builders, Inc., is not liable? See UCC 3-403, Comment 2, and UCC 3-401, Comment 1. Are the comments clearly supported by the language of UCC 1-201(39), 3-401 or 3-403?

The above examples all involve notes; it is not uncommon to seek the signature of an officer (who will frequently also be a shareholder) on a note to obtain personal liability. This is particularly so in the case of small, closely-held corporations. UCC 3-403 makes no distinction between notes and other forms of paper, such as checks. It is equally common even for large corporations to sign payroll checks with an authorized facsimile signature, which will be the personal name of the signatory and may or may not indicate a corporate office. The corporation's name will not appear on the check in the lower right-hand corner, where by custom a drawer's signature is placed, but in the printed heading on the check, together with an address and sundry other information. Do signatures in either form bind the signatory personally under UCC 3-403? Is it plausible that anyone giving or receiving such an instrument believes that an individual and not a corporate obligation is intended?

5. *Ambiguity as to the party who must pay.* In several of the above instances, it appears to be ambiguous whether the signature binds principal or agent. Are such signatures considered ambiguous within the meaning of UCC 3-402? Can there be a holder in due course of such instruments? See UCC 3-302, 3-304(1)(a).

2.   Liability of an Indorser

As we have seen, no person is liable *on an instrument* unless his signature appears thereon. UCC 3-401. By signing an instrument, however, one may take on quite differing types of liability, depending upon the capacity and manner in which one signs.

A broad distinction is sometimes made between *primary* and *secondary* parties to the instrument. The maker's contract, which we have just examined, is the contract of a primary party. An indorser who signs a note, however, is said to be only "secondarily" liable. The distinction is not merely a matter of commercial expectation: *secondary party* is a defined term (UCC 3-102(1)(d)), and the legal obligation of an indorser as a secondary party differs substantially from the liability of a maker.

Compare UCC 3-413(1) with UCC 3-414, and then consider the problems that follow.

Problem 1-3. Maker makes a $5,000 note payable July 1 to order of Payee, who indorses in favor of Holder. Holder, having made no demand for payment upon Maker, files suit July 2, naming Maker and Payee as defendants. What result?

Problem 1-4. Maker makes a $5,000 note payable July 1 to order of Bearer and delivers it to Smith in exchange for a loan. Smith delivers the note to Wells in satisfaction of a long-standing debt to her. On July 1, Wells asks payment from Maker, who says that he cannot make payment until the end of the week. Wells phones Smith and tells him she will file suit against him on the note July 2 unless paid by either Maker or Smith by 5 P.M. that day. Wells files suit the next day, naming only Smith as a defendant. Is Maker a necessary party to the action? May Smith seek dismissal of the action on other grounds? If Smith pays Wells on the morning of July 2, can he recover from Maker? If so, on what theories?

Problem 1-5. On the same facts as the preceding problem, Wells requires Smith to indorse the note. What result? Suppose alternatively that Wells does not require an indorsement. Smith indorses anyway, prefacing his signature with the words "Pay Kate Wells, without recourse." What result? Why might Smith voluntarily indorse the note?

Nominally, the secondary liability of an indorser is predicated on satisfaction of three conditions precedent: dishonor, any necessary notice of dishonor, and any necessary protest. In the context of notes, however, this statement is somewhat misleading. Most notes waive all these conditions except dishonor, and the Code gives effect to such waivers. UCC 3-511.

Dishonor. In the context of notes, dishonor occurs when due presentment for payment is made to the maker and payment is refused, or when presentment has been excused and the instrument is not duly paid. UCC 3-507. Since notes by their terms usually waive presentment, as a practical matter dishonor usually occurs when a note is not paid at maturity, without the necessity for any action by the holder against the maker.

Notice of dishonor. The manner of satisfying the second condition of an indorser's liability is detailed in UCC 3-508. Again, it is customary for notes to include a waiver of notice of dishonor, and the Code again gives effect to such waivers. UCC 3-501, 3-511.

Protest. Protest is a manner of formally certifying dishonor. UCC 3-509. Under the Code, protest is only *necessary* in order to charge indorsers of drafts or checks payable outside the United States. UCC 3-501(3). It is therefore only marginally applicable to the liability of indorsers of notes. In any event, standard note forms almost always contain an express waiver of protest.

It is important to bear in mind that indorsement contracts are placed not only on notes but also on checks and drafts, and that *secondary party* is defined to include drawers of checks and drafts as well as indorsers. Waiver provisions are rarely present in checks and are only occasionally encountered in drafts. The Code's sections relating to presentment, dishonor, and notice of dishonor require careful reading and a good deal of cross-referencing in order to ascertain the liability of any secondary party. We will further elaborate on secondary liability in Chapter 15 where, in the context of checks and drafts, the conditions will be most easily understood.

It also bears re-emphasizing that the above liability is the indorser's *contractual* liability *on the instrument*. An indorsement may be made incidental to the instrument's transfer. In such a case the indorser will assume not only the contractual liabilities of an indorser, but the warranty liabilities of a transferor.[3] See text at p. 53 *infra*.

An indorser's contract on an instrument usually will be obtained in connection with an underlying transaction.[4] The possibility of liabilities arising out of that transaction and the effect upon them of the indorser's giving of the instrument are also considered *infra*.

3. *Defenses; Holder-in-Due-Course Status*

The liability of a party on an instrument is contractual in nature, and like other promisors, the liable party may seek to raise a defense to his contract, such as fraud, duress, or failure of consideration. A person who is not a holder in due course takes an instrument subject to the same defenses available against a simple contract claim. UCC 3-306. But a party who is able to establish his status as a holder in due course by meeting the requirements of UCC 3-302 takes free of all claims to the instrument by other parties, and all but a very limited number of defenses. UCC 3-305. The limited class of defenses good against a holder in due course are frequently referred to as "real defenses," while those that are cut off against a holder in due course are denominated "personal defenses." Although the Code does not employ this terminology, it is firmly rooted in the usage of courts and lawyers. Unless a valid defense is shown to exist, it is irrelevant to contractual liability whether a holder is also a holder in due course, but once a defense is established, the burden is on the party seeking enforcement to establish holder-in-due-course status. UCC 3-307.

---

3. Not all transferors indorse, and not all indorsers transfer: a party may have the status of both and be subject to liability on both bases, or may have only one or the other. Additionally, a transferor may alter both his or her contractual liability (as seen supra) and warranty liability (discussed infra) by indorsing without recourse. In addition to assuming contractual liability, a transferor also assumes more extensive warranty liability when he is also indorser.

4. A party may indorse an instrument merely to lend his credit to it. Such an indorser is called an "accommodation party." The liabilities of such parties are treated more fully in Chapter 2.

Problems in this section focus on the distinction between real and personal defenses, but also review requirements of holder-in-due-course status, to which the student should remain alert.

Problem 1-6. Able borrows $5,000 from Baker and gives Baker his note to the order of Baker in that amount. Within a year Able repays Baker but neglects to obtain the cancellation or surrender of the note. Baker sells the note to Charles for $2,000. Charles has no knowledge that Able has repaid Baker. Does Able have a defense? See UCC 3-601, 3-603, 3-306. May Charles recover notwithstanding the defense? See UCC 3-302, 3-305, 3-602. *Effect of Disc. against the DC.*

Problem 1-7. Able contracts with Baker to pave Able's driveway. The contract price is $3,000, and Baker requests payment in advance. Able refuses. Instead, he gives Baker his promissory note for $3,000, payable to the order of Baker in 30 days. Baker gives the note to Charles, one of his trade creditors, in satisfaction of a long-outstanding debt. After completing about 80 percent of the driveway, Baker quits because the job is taking more time than he has estimated. May Charles successfully enforce Able's note? See UCC 3-306, 3-305, 3-302, 3-303.

Problem 1-8. Able borrows $5,000 from Baker and gives Baker a $5,000 demand note in bearer form. Baker loses the note and asks Able to give him a replacement note. Able refuses to do so unless and until Baker agrees to indemnify Able for any subsequent liability. While Baker is considering this, Donald appears and demands payment of the note. Does Able have a defense to payment? If Able pays Donald, what is Able's potential liability to Baker? See UCC 3-603, 3-601, 3-306, 3-305.

Problem 1-9. *T* is trustee of a trust. *B* is the sole beneficiary of the trust. *M* makes a note for $10,000 payable to the trust. *T,* as trustee, transfers the note to herself for $10,000 in cash. After default on the note *T* brings an action to enforce the note in her individual capacity. *M* defends the action on the ground that the transfer from *T,* as trustee, to *T,* as an individual, is a breach of her fiduciary duty of loyalty to the trust beneficiary. What result? See UCC 3-301, 3-304, 3-305, 3-302, 3-306.

Problem 1-10. Able borrows $5,000 from Baker and gives Baker his demand promissory note in bearer form in like amount. Baker skillfully raises the amount of the note to $50,000 and sells it to Charles in exchange for Charles' promise to lend Baker $40,000. Charles has no knowledge of Baker's chicanery. When Charles makes demand, does Able have a defense? See UCC 3-601, 3-602, 3-407, 3-306, 3-305, 3-302, 3-303.

Problem 1-11. Able contracts with Baker to pave his driveway for $3,000. Baker says he will need some money for materials. Able makes out a note stating "On demand pay Baker the sum of $_____," and tells Baker to fill it in for the amount he needs. Baker takes the instrument to Builder's Supply and orders materials. In the presence of the manager, he fills in the note for the purchase price of the materials and indorses it to Builder's Supply. Baker takes the materials he purchases and completes another job and never paves Able's driveway. Does Able have a defense to enforcement of the note by Builder's Supply? See UCC 3-306, 3-302, 3-304, 3-305. See also 3-104, 3-805.

Problem 1-12. Xanadu, a developer, plats some raw acreage. He sells building lots to Michael, Morris, and Maureen, and obtains from each an installment note for $25,000 as part of the transaction. Each makes a downpayment of $2,500 but discovers prior to the first installment payment date that Xanadu has made several material misrepresentations to induce them to enter into the land purchase contracts. Xanadu discounts all three notes to Mortgage Broker, who had paid a fair valuation for the notes and had no knowledge of Xanadu's misrepresentations when it purchased the notes. When all three makers fail to make the first installment payment, Mortgage Broker gives notice of acceleration under a provision in the notes and demands payment in full from all three makers. When the three refuse, Mortgage Broker sells the notes to Shark. Shark has full knowledge of the situation and buys the notes for a 50 percent discount. Morris, without Shark's knowledge, has meanwhile filed a petition in bankruptcy and has been granted a discharge on the debt. Shark seeks to enforce all three notes. Do any of the makers have defenses good against Shark? See UCC 3-306, 3-305, 3-302, 3-104, 3-106, 3-109, 3-304. See also UCC 3-201. If Xanadu now further purchases the notes from Shark, what will be Xanadu's rights?

Problem 1-13. *M* is induced by fraud to issue a note in the amount of $10,000 to *P*'s order. To satisfy an antecedent debt in the amount of $6,000, *P* indorses the note to *X*, who takes the note without actual knowledge of any defense to the instrument. *X* borrows money from Bank, under an agreement by which Bank is to provide additional discretionary advances to *X*. *X* requests an additional advance. Prior to making the advance, Bank requires that *X* surrender the note to Bank. *X* subsequently defaults on the loan. Bank requires *X* to indorse the note, which is then one month overdue, to the order of Bank, and sues *M* and *P*. What defenses are available to *M* and *P*? See UCC 3-305, 3-302, 3-303, 3-304, 3-306, 3-408, 3-201.

Problem 1-14. Hart holds a demand note made by Bluster, which Hart obtained when he loaned Bluster $125,000 in connection with a real estate development. Hart indorses the note to his 17-year-old nephew, Gullible, and tells him to "hold on to it for your college years." Gullible is persuaded to indorse the note to Circe, his girl friend, an MBA student. She tells him it is silly to let the money stand idle, and she will arrange to invest it in high-yield government bonds. Actually she uses it as collateral for a loan from Flash and speculates in the commodities markets with the proceeds. Flash knows nothing of Circe's agreement with Gullible. Her speculations are disastrous, and within a year she has lost nearly the entire amount. When Flash requests repayment, Circe says he will have to look to the note, and indorses it to him. Flash then approaches Hart and relates the entire story to him, Circe having finally confided in Flash. Hart asks Flash to indorse the note to the order of Hart, pays off Flash, and says he, Hart, will deal with the problem. Hart now retains you. He suggests that the original loan to Bluster may have been usurious. He states that he would prefer to sue Bluster but will sue anyone. He wants to know who is liable on the instrument to him, and whether any of those parties may have valid defenses against him. Advise. See, in addition to sections you have previously consulted, UCC 3-207, 3-208.

D. THE NOTE AS PROPERTY

A piece of paper with words that comply with the formal requirements for an Article 3 promissory note not only evidences a promise to pay money but also *is* the promise itself. The law has reified the promise: it is frequently said to be "merged" in the paper. The note therefore has value determined not by its worth as scrap paper but by the likelihood that the promise embodied in the paper will be carried out.

Reification of the promise has a number of legal consequences associated with ownership and possession of property. The obligation is transferred not by an assignment but by physical delivery of the paper with any necessary indorsement. UCC 3-202(1). The owner of a note may use it as collateral to secure a loan from a third party, as will be explained in Chapter 3. But a lender who is granted a security interest must take possession of the note in order to perfect its security interest. A creditor of the note's holder may not garnish the maker or the other parties obligated on the note, and a judgment creditor obtains an execution lien only when the sheriff, armed with a writ of execution, physically takes possession of the paper.

Two property characteristics of commercial paper play a special role in allocating losses from forgery and other wrongdoing: the paper may be converted by unauthorized exercise of dominion over it, and its transfer creates implied warranties. Chapter 17 will explore at greater length these aspects of commercial paper; here we merely introduce the statutory provisions.

1. Conversion

UCC 3-419(1) sets out specific examples of when the "owner" of an instrument has a cause of action for conversion. In addition, most courts have supplemented the statutory examples by recognizing common law conversion actions (see UCC 1-103). The least obvious but most frequently litigated commercial paper conversion case is conversion by payment on a forged indorsement (UCC 3-419(1)(c)). If Maker issues an order note to Payee and Employee forges Payee's signature and collects the note from Maker, the Maker has converted the instrument by payment on the forged indorsement, and the payee may ground an action on UCC 3-419. Employee has also converted the note, by exercising dominion over it without authorization, but the conversion action will be based on the common law rather than the UCC.

Problem 1-15. As part of a settlement agreement with Wholesaler, Re-tailer issues to Attorney, who represents Wholesaler in the settlement negotia-tions, a 90-day note made payable to the order of Attorney, who is to hold the note for the convenience of Wholesaler. When Attorney presents the note for payment, Retailer takes possession and promises to have its bank issue a check later in the day. When Attorney returns in the afternoon Retailer announces it will not pay and cannot return the note because an employee has misplaced it. On subsequent inquiries at Retailer's bank Attorney learns that Retailer is not paying its current obligations on a regular basis. What rights does Wholesaler have? What would you advise it to do? See UCC 3-419.

2. Warranties

UCC 3-417 provides that when a person transfers a negotiable instrument or presents it for payment he makes the warranties set out in that section. Con-ceptually these warranties are similar to the warranties that arise when goods are sold, although the content of the warranties obviously differs. *Transfer warranties* are made by a person who transfers an instrument for consideration to his transferee and to any subsequent holder who takes in good faith by indorsement (UCC 3-417(2)). *Presentment warranties* are made by a person who obtains payment or acceptance to the person who in good faith pays or accepts (UCC 3-417(1)). When the banking system is used for collection of commer-cial paper similar warranties are implied (UCC 4-207).

The Code's regulation of commercial paper warranties does not contem-plate agreements modifying or excluding the statutory warranties. The Code itself provides for only one form of modification, which affects only one of five transfer warranties: by a transfer "without recourse" the transferor warrants that he has *no knowledge* of a defense of any party good against him whereas the warranty implied in the absence of this restrictive language is that there *is no* such defense (UCC 3-417(3)). The Code says nothing about agreements to make other modifications, to exclude all warranties, or to make additional express warranties.[5] Most legal problems in this area, however, turn on statu-tory interpretation rather than on attempts to modify the statutory framework.

<hr>

5. The most common express warranty used in connection with commercial paper is the "P.E.G." stamped on the backs of items collected by banks. With respect to this Judge Goldberg has remarked: "The P.E.G. stamp employed by banks stands for 'Prior endorsements guaranteed.' While the Uniform Commercial Code, as will be seen, frequently fails to provide clear answers to

The warranty provisions both overlap with and supplement the rules on the contractual obligations of parties to an instrument. Remember that you undertake a contractual obligation only if your name appears on the instrument with your approval. Even if you sign an instrument, your contractual liability may be conditioned on presentment, dishonor, and notice of dishonor. Moreover, you may be discharged from your obligations by specified acts, such as payment or cancellation of a signature.

You may be liable for breach of warranty, however, whether or not you are liable in contract. Warranty liability may arise, for example, whether or not your signature appears on the instrument. If you transfer a bearer instrument you undertake no contractual obligations, but you make transfer warranties. Presentment and notice of dishonor are also irrelevant when a claim is made that you have breached a warranty. Indeed, because the breach of warranty claim accrues at the time of breach, a warranty claim may be brought even before the instrument is due. The warranty claim may also survive the discharge of your contractual obligations. Even the remedies differ. A party claiming that you have breached a warranty may be able to rescind the transaction or recover the reasonably forseeable damages caused by the breach (cf. UCC 4-207(3)), whereas the party claiming for breach of your contractual obligation usually may not rescind and may recover only the face amount of the instrument.

The similarity between the transfer and presentment warranties may cause confusion. Both warranties cover (1) title, (2) signatures, and (3) alterations. But the persons making the warranties, the persons to whom they are made, and the content of each warranty differs. A transferor for consideration makes these warranties to his or her immediate transferee together with warranties with respect to (4) defenses and (5) knowledge of insolvency proceedings (UCC 3-417(2)). If the transferor transfers by indorsement he also makes these warranties to "subsequent holders" (not "transferees") who take in good faith. The transferor does not make *transfer* warranties to the person who pays or accepts because the payor is not a subsequent "holder," but the transferor does make *presentment* warranties as a "prior transferor" when the instrument is presented for payment or acceptance (UCC 3-417(1)).

Problem 1-16. For services rendered, Maker issues a 90-day note payable to the order of Art for $1,000. Art changes the amount payable to $6,000 and transfers the note to Ben in satisfaction of a pre-existing debt. As security for a loan Ben transfers the note to Carl, who takes the instrument in good faith and without notice of the alteration.

---

questions in the area of negotiable instruments, it is unequivocal in its insistence that indorsement is to be spelled with the letter 'i.' Bankers, who claim to know much of such weighty matters, may insist on beginning with 'e,' but this practice could be attributed to the bankers' understandable reluctance to stamp 'Pay any Bank PIG' on the backs of the checks they handle." Perini Corp. v. First National Bank, 553 F.2d 398, 401 n.1 (5th Cir. 1977).

(a) On maturity Maker refuses to pay more than $1,000 (see UCC 3-407(3)). May Carl recover the difference from Art or Ben? See UCC 3-417(2).

(b) On maturity Maker does not notice the alteration and pays $6,000 to Carl. Can Maker recover from anyone? See UCC 3-417(1).

E.   EFFECT ON THE UNDERLYING OBLIGATION

An instrument usually embodies an obligation to pay money to a payee arising from some transaction such as the sale of goods or loan of money. By virtue of UCC 3-802(1)(b) this underlying obligation is suspended until maturity of the instrument. If the instrument is dishonored the underlying obligation is revived and the holder may bring an action either on the obligation or the instrument. If the instrument is paid at maturity the issuer's liability on both the underlying obligation and the instrument will be discharged. The Code goes further by providing that discharge on the instrument for whatever reason will also discharge the underlying obligation although, as we noted above, warranty actions may survive. These general rules are subject to contrary agreement of the parties, and there is a presumption that an underlying obligation is discharged when the obligor delivers commercial paper issued by a bank. UCC 3-802(1)(a).

O'NEILL v. STEPPAT
270 N.W.2d 375, 24 UCC Rep. 1214 (S.D. 1978)

PORTER, Justice (on reassignment). This appeal presents a question dealing with the interrelationship between various Articles of the Uniform Commercial Code. The trial court concluded that the UCC Article 2 four year statute of limitations applies to an action to collect on a promissory note given in part payment of a contract for sale. The court granted defendant buyers' motion for summary judgment. We reverse.   NO SJ for buyers

On August 31, 1970, sellers and buyers entered into a purchase agreement concerning the sale of a business in Gregory, along with certain personal property. The purchase price for the fixtures, equipment, and tools was $2,487.50 and for the parts inventory was $13,165.36. The schedule of payments was to be as follows: $1,000.00 on signing the contract; $9,000.00 on September 15, 1970; $5,000.00 on January 1, 1971; and the balance on September 1, 1971. The unpaid balance of the purchase price was to draw interest at eight percent.

Buyers executed and delivered to sellers their promissory note, financing statement and security agreement covering all equipment, tools and merchandise used or held by buyers in connection with the business that was transferred. The note was executed on October 15, 1970, for $6,516.82, to become due on September 1, 1971, with eight percent interest.

Sellers sued on December 29, 1975, to recover the amount of the note due on September 1, 1971, plus interest. The action was, therefore, brought over four years after the due date. The trial court granted buyers' motion for summary judgment, based on the four-year statute of limitations set out in UCC 2-725(1). Sellers contend that the applicable statute is SDCL 15-2-13, which sets a six-year limitation on actions to recover on obligations. The trial court, after noting the paucity of legal authority on the question, concluded that the action was one for the breach of a contract for sale and that UCC 2-725(1) bars the action.

Sellers have sought to recover on the note, not on the contract. That the note might have been given in payment for a contract for sale is not relevant in this action, except insofar as defenses to the underlying obligation may be asserted as defenses to an action on the note. See UCC 3-301 to 3-307. Buyers, by signing a negotiable note, made a separate promise:

> The maker or acceptor [of a negotiable instrument] engages that he will pay the instrument according to its tenor at the time of his engagement or as completed pursuant to Section 3-115 on incomplete instruments. (UCC 3-413(1).)

This separate promise gives rise to a separate remedy on the note, as indicated by UCC 3-802(1):

> Unless otherwise agreed where an instrument is taken for an underlying obligation
> (a) the obligation is pro tanto discharged if a bank is drawer, maker or acceptor of the instrument and there is no recourse on the instrument against the underlying obligor; and
> (b) in any other case the obligation is suspended pro tanto until the instrument is due or if it is payable on demand until its presentment. *If the instrument is dishonored action may be maintained on either the instrument or the obligation;* discharge of the underlying obligor on the instrument also discharges him on the obligation. (Emphasis added.)

Since a bank is not the drawer, maker or acceptor of the instrument, subsection (b) is applicable. The clear intent is that the holder of a note taken for an underlying contract has a choice of remedies. He can sue on the note or the underlying contract. . . . Sellers chose to sue on the note.

We must then determine what statute of limitations applies to actions on a note under UCC Article 3. Since Article 3 has no statute of limitations, we refer to SDCL 15-2-13(1), which provides a six-year limitation on actions "upon a contract, obligation, or liability, express or implied. . . ." The action was therefore timely.

Buyers argue that since the underlying contract was one for sale of goods under UCC Article 2, the four-year statute of limitations, UCC 2-725(1), should bar the action. This argument is without merit. UCC 2-701 provides that:

> Remedies for breach of any obligation or promise collateral or ancillary to a contract for sale are not impaired by the provisions of this Article.

The promissory note is an "obligation or promise collateral or ancillary to" any contract for sale. 2 Anderson, Uniform Commercial Code §2-701.3 at 319 (1971). The remedy on the note is thus not impaired by the Article 2 statute of limitations, UCC 2-725(1).[1]

We therefore reverse the judgment and remand the case for trial.

NOTES & QUESTIONS

1. *Accrual of cause of action on instrument.* When did the cause of action on the instrument in *O'Neill* accrue so that the statute of limitations began to run? See UCC 3-122. If buyers had given a demand note when would the action have accrued? What if buyers had given a certificate of deposit due on September 1, 1971?

Note that a cause of action accrues separately on each installment of an installment note as that installment falls due. As a practical matter, most notes have an acceleration clause that, if the holder properly exercises by giving any necessary notice, will make the accelerated amount due on the date of acceleration, and a cause of action for this amount will then accrue.

2. *Suspension of underlying obligation.* If sellers had brought an action on the underlying sales transaction on August 1, 1975, would UCC 2-725 have barred their action?

If one month after the buyers in *O'Neill* take delivery of the business they discover the equipment is not as warranted by the sellers, may the buyers revoke acceptance or recover damages (as permitted by UCC Art. 2) or is their claim suspended by UCC 3-802? See UCC 3-207.

Problem 1-17. In payment for the $8,000 purchase price of a tractor Buyer agrees to transfer to Seller, with Buyer's indorsement, a six-month note payable to the order of Buyer for $8,500 made by Cooperative. When the note matures Seller waits one month before demanding payment from Cooperative. On demand Cooperative dishonors because it is insolvent. Does Seller have recourse against Buyer either on the instrument or on the underlying sales contract? Would your answer be different if Buyer had transferred to Seller a certificate of deposit by a bank that subsequently became insolvent? See UCC 3-606, 3-802.

1. Since sellers in this case seek to recover on the note, and we have held that the action on the note is not barred by the UCC Article 2 statute of limitations, we do not find it necessary to determine whether the contract for sale is governed by Article 2. . . .

Problem 1-18. As part of a loan transaction, Debtor makes and issues to Bank a six-month note for $30,000 at 16 percent interest. At the end of six months Bank agrees to renew the note for a further three months at 17 percent interest. Debtor signs a "renewal note" incorporating the new terms. Bank stamps "Paid" on the first note but retains it in its files. Is Debtor discharged on the first note? If so, has Debtor's "underlying obligation" to repay the loan from Bank been discharged? Would your answer be different if Bank surrenders the first note to Debtor? See UCC 3-605, 3-802.

F.   LOST INSTRUMENTS

The owner of an Article 3 negotiable instrument may be unable to present it for payment at maturity because it has been lost, destroyed, or stolen. As we have already seen, however, to be a *holder* and thereby have the procedural advantages of enforcing a negotiable instrument the owner must have possession of the original instrument. Nevertheless, despite the merger of the underlying obligation into the physical piece of paper, the owner does not forfeit all rights when he or she is unable to produce the instrument. UCC 3-804 permits the owner to bring an action against any prior party to the instrument on proof of ownership, the terms of the instrument, and the facts that prevent the owner from producing it. If the owner does not show that the instrument has been destroyed, however, the court may order him or her to provide security to indemnify the defendant from potential claimants who may later present the instrument for payment.

Problem 1-19. Client makes a note payable to the order of Accountant for services rendered. Client tells his employee to mail the note to Accountant but instead the employee forges Accountant's signature and transfers the note to Bank for cash, which he keeps. Both Accountant and Bank demand payment from Client. What should Client do? Does Accountant have any claim against Bank? See UCC 3-419, 3-603, 3-804.

Problem 1-20. Patient has a claim against Driver for physical injuries suffered in a car accident. In settlement of the claim Patient takes Driver's note, payable in three months. Patient has second thoughts about the settlement, destroys the note, and brings an action on the tort claim. Driver's attorney advises that the settlement agreement is a valid defense to the court action and that the destruction of the note discharges Driver's liability on both the note and the underlying claim. Is Driver's attorney correct? See UCC 3-605, 3-802, 3-804.

G.   EXCURSUS: WHY NEGOTIABILITY?

The usual rationale in favor of negotiability is that it is a necessary condition for the creation of a market for commercial paper. The existence of the market reduces the cost of credit and of payment collection systems. Note how the doctrines we have studied in this chapter support the ready marketability of commercial paper. Rules governing the form of negotiable instruments permit a potential purchaser to determine the nature and value of an instrument by examining the instrument itself without extended investigation into its background. Statutory rules on transfer and negotiation allow the potential purchaser to determine the obligations of prior parties without reading the fine print of a lengthy contract document and to transfer these obligations at minimal cost. Procedural advantages of holding a negotiable instrument reduce potential costs of enforcement, while the substantive advantages of taking the instrument free from many of the potential defenses of prior parties increases the likelihood that these obligations ultimately will be performed.

Negotiability, however, has its costs. Parties to a note, for example, take the risk that they will have to pay a holder the face amount of the note at maturity notwithstanding some defense they may have arising out of the transaction in which the note was issued or transferred. Parties may not understand these risks or may be unable to calculate these risks because they are unsophisticated or lack sufficient information. To justify negotiability, therefore, requires at the very least the comparison of these costs to consumers with the gains from the lower cost of credit. Schwartz, Optimality and the Cutoff of Defenses against Financers and Consumer Sales, 15 B.C. Indus. & Com. L. Rev. 499, 509-513 (1974).

In the last few decades negotiability has been under attack. Commentators have questioned whether there is a need for negotiability, especially in consumer transactions where the consumer's promissory note is usually not negotiated more than once and where there is a great danger that the risks of signing negotiable paper are not appreciated. Courts have responded to such concerns by developing doctrines like the *close-connectedness* doctrine discussed in *Arcanum* (p. 32 supra), which make some holders take an instrument subject to defenses on the underlying transaction. Also, legislatures have adopted statutes restricting the use of negotiable instruments in consumer transactions and preserving consumer claims or defenses. In response to similar concerns the Federal Trade Commission has limited negotiability indirectly by requiring certain commercial paper to include a clause that preserves defenses and in effect makes the paper nonnegotiable. See generally Rohner, Holder in Due Course in Consumer Transactions: Requiem, Revival or Reformation?, 60 Cornell L. Rev. 1019 (1975).

Critics have suggested that legislation restricting negotiability would increase the cost of consumer credit, especially for low-income groups considered high credit risks. Studies of the effect of restrictive legislation, however, are inconclusive. Federal Trade Commission, Staff Report on the Proposed Amendment to the Trade Regulation Rule on Preservation of Consumer's Claims and Defenses 122-143 (1978).

ROSENTHAL, NEGOTIABILITY—WHO NEEDS IT?
71 Colum. L. Rev. 375, 377-381 (1971)

A Bank of England bearer note, while not yet legal in 1756, was, according to Lord Mansfield, "treated as money, as cash." In the leading case of Miller v. Race [97 Eng. Rep. 398 (K.B. 1758)] he concluded that when such a bearer note was stolen and subsequently sold to a bona fide purchaser, it had to belong to the purchaser rather than to the previous owner, because of "the consequences to trade and commerce . . . which would be most incommoded by a contrary determination."

While the negotiable character of certain kinds of instruments had earlier been given some measure of protection in specialized commercial courts in England, this decision seems to have been the first clear-cut holding of its kind by a common-law court. Several points should be noted. (1) A claim of ownership was cut off—no defense against payment of the instrument was involved. (2) The note in question was of a type customarily passed from hand to hand, serving many of the purposes of paper money, which did not exist in England at the time. (3) Without the free circulation of such "money," business would have been impeded.

The negotiable promissory note of today is quite a different instrument, serving different purposes, and the consequences of its negotiability are quite different in impact. By far the most commonly employed variety of the species today is the note given by the installment purchaser of goods to reflect the unpaid portion of the purchase price. Typically, such a note is transferred just once, from the dealer to the lender (usually either a finance company or a bank), and thereafter remains in the possession of the latter or its lawyers until it is either paid off or offered in evidence in Court. Its negotiable character is of no importance with respect to claims of ownership, as it is unlikely to be lost or stolen. Even if it is, the last indorsement will have been a special indorsement to the order of the lender; without the genuine further indorsement of the latter there can be no subsequent holder, much less a holder in due course.

The only significant consequence of the negotiability of such a note is that it cuts off the defenses of the maker. If, for example, the purchaser gives the note in payment for a refrigerator, the finance company is entitled to full payment regardless of whether the refrigerator fails to work or whether its sale was accomplished through fraudulent misrepresentations or, indeed, whether it was ever delivered at all. And it may be small comfort to the buyer, forced to pay the finance company in full, to know that he has a cause of action against the seller, which may at best be collectible with difficulty and may in many cases be worthless because the seller is insolvent or has left town.

A promissory note of this kind, and a consequence of negotiability that works in this fashion, are a far cry from the stolen Bank of England note, and the protection accorded its purchaser, in Miller v. Race. Whether the finance company should be allowed to prevail free of the maker's defenses raises questions that ought to be decided on their own merits, and not merely through the absent-minded application of a doctrine created to meet an entirely different situation. The social evils flowing from negotiability in this circumstance[18] have become manifest, and there has been a clear trend in both the courts and the legislatures toward amelioration of its consequences. In particular, the unfairness to the poorest members of the community of the law governing consumer installment purchases has generated a reaction that is giving rise to a major alteration in it. This departure is being accomplished, not by modification of the provisions of Article 3 of the Code, but by legislative action forbidding the use of negotiable instruments in consumer installment transactions and by judicial attempts to stretch the facts to deny holder in due course status to finance companies. Since the installment buyer can be similarly harmed even without a negotiable instrument if there is a clause in his purchase contract waiving, as against an assignee of his obligation, any defenses on the contract that he may have, legislatures and courts have also been moving in the direction of declaring such clauses invalid.

It is not clear whether the apparent weakness in the opposition to these changes springs from a lack of genuine need on the part of sellers or lenders for continuation of the power to cut off buyers' defenses. While there has been ground to believe that where this protection is denied, credit nevertheless will remain available, a recent study suggests that this may not be so.

If an exception is carved out, should it be limited to consumer paper, or should it be applied to promissory notes across the board? Thus far, the demand for reform has been confined largely to the former. While there may be small commercial purchasers also in need of similar protection, and while

---

18. The same problem can arise even without the use of a negotiable instrument, through employment of a clause in the contract between the buyer and the seller whereby the buyer waives as against an assignee any defenses he may have against the seller. . . . Such waiver clauses have in turn been invalidated by some courts and legislatures. . . .

Dealers and lenders have responded by suggesting to the buyer that he go out and borrow the money with which to pay for his purchase in cash. Since the loan is at least theoretically independent of the purchase, the obligation to repay it in accordance with its terms would then be immune from defenses based on the purchase transaction even in states barring waiver of defenses clauses. Routine referral by the dealer of his customers to the same lender would seem to be a subterfuge intended to avoid the policy behind a rule forbidding use of a negotiable promissory note or a waiver of defenses clause; on the other hand, many loans are made by completely independent lending institutions on an individual, ad hoc, basis, in order to enable the borrowers to make consumer purchases, and it may not be socially desirable to jeopardize this source of credit. It is not easy to draft legislation, or frame the basis of a judicial doctrine, that draws the line between these two situations.

there may be other situations in which unfair advantage seems to be taken of makers of promissory notes, there does not appear in such cases to be a resulting social problem of comparable dimension. On the other hand, we need to know more about the range of other uses to which promissory notes are put in today's economy, and about the circumstances in which the cutting off of claims and defenses in connection with such notes serves legitimate needs or works undue hardship.[27]

FEDERAL TRADE COMMISSION HOLDER-IN-DUE-COURSE REGULATIONS
16 C.F.R. §433 (1984)

§433.1   DEFINITIONS

(a) Person. An individual, corporation, or any other business organization.

(b) Consumer. A natural person who seeks or acquires goods or services for personal, family, or household use.

(c) Creditor. A person who, in the ordinary course of business, lends purchase money or finances the sale of goods or services to consumers on a deferred payment basis; Provided, such person is not acting, for the purposes of a particular transaction, in the capacity of a credit card issuer.

(d) Purchase money loan. A cash advance which is received by a consumer in return for a "Finance Charge" within the meaning of the Truth in Lending Act and Regulation Z, which is applied, in whole or substantial part, to a purchase of goods or services from a seller who (1) refers consumers to the creditor or (2) is affiliated with the creditor by common control, contract, or business arrangement.

(e) Financing a sale. Extending credit to a consumer in connection with a "Credit Sale" within the meaning of the Truth in Lending Act and Regulation Z.

(f) Contract. Any oral or written agreement, formal or informal, between a creditor and a seller, which contemplates or provides for cooperative or concerted activity in connection with the sale of goods or services to consumers or the financing thereof.

(g) Business arrangement. Any understanding, procedure, course of dealing, or arrangement, formal or informal, between a creditor and a seller, in connection with the sale of goods or services to consumers or the financing thereof.

27. The establishment in the Code of different rules for commercial and noncommercial situations would not be unique. Compare the wide range of differences in treatment of merchants and non-merchants in connection with the sale of goods under article 2 of the Code, as well as the effect of commercial status upon the rights of a holder of a document of title under article 7. . . .

(h) Credit card issuer. A person who extends to cardholders the right to use a credit card in connection with purchases of goods or services.

(i) Consumer credit contract. Any instrument which evidences or embodies a debt arising from a "Purchase Money Loan" transaction or a "financed sale" as defined in paragraphs (d) and (e).

(j) Seller. A person who, in the ordinary course of business, sells or leases goods or services to consumers.

---

§433.2   PRESERVATION OF CONSUMERS' CLAIMS AND DEFENSES, UNFAIR OR DECEPTIVE ACTS OR PRACTICES

In connection with any sale or lease of goods or services to consumers, in or affecting commerce as "commerce" is defined in the Federal Trade Commission Act, it is an unfair or deceptive act or practice within the meaning of Section 5 of that Act for a seller, directly or indirectly, to:

(a) Take or receive a consumer credit contract which fails to contain the following provision in at least ten point, bold face, type:

Notice

Any holder of this consumer credit contract is subject to all claims and defenses which the debtor could assert against the seller of goods or services obtained pursuant hereto or with the proceeds hereof. Recovery hereunder by the debtor shall not exceed amounts paid by the debtor hereunder.

or, (b) Accept, as full or partial payment for such sale or lease, the proceeds of any purchase money loan (as purchase money loan is defined herein), unless any consumer credit contract made in connection with such purchase money loan contains the following provision in at least ten point, bold face, type:

Notice

Any holder of this consumer credit contract is subject to all claims and defenses which the debtor could assert against the seller of goods or services obtained with the proceeds hereof. Recovery hereunder by the debtor shall not exceed amounts paid by the debtor hereunder.

FEDERAL TRADE COMMISSION, PRESERVATION OF CONSUMERS' CLAIMS AND DEFENSES: STATEMENT OF BASIS AND PURPOSE
40 Fed. Reg. 53506, 53509 (Nov. 18, 1975)

Criticism of application of the holder in due course doctrine to consumer transactions has concentrated on the fact that it places the risk of a seller's misconduct on the party least able to bear the burden—the individual consumer. It also enables a merchant who engages in disreputable and unethical sales practices to establish and maintain a source of payment which assures him a place in the market, notwithstanding continuing breaches of contract and warranty. The relatively equal bargaining power which characterizes dealings between merchants is absent in consumer transactions, which are consummated by the use of standard form contracts which the customer must sign as a condition of purchase. Consumers without sufficient resources or business sophistication are frequently unable to press their claims effectively against dishonest sellers; moreover, the seller may be beyond the reach of an effective remedy. Because he is prevented from asserting the seller's breach of warranty or failure to perform against the assignee of the consumer's instrument, the consumer loses his most effective weapon—nonpayment.

Between an innocent consumer, whose dealings with an unreliable seller are, at most, episodic, and a finance institution qualifying as "a holder in due course," the financer is in a better position both to protect itself and to assume the risk of a seller's reliability. The financer may have recourse against the seller based on the seller's endorsement of the instrument, or it may have a full recourse agreement with the seller and withhold part of the payments to the seller as a reserve. In addition, financial institutions usually protect themselves by warranties from the merchant as to freedom of the obligation from customer defenses. As the National Commission on Consumer Finance recognized, financial institutions which purchase consumer paper are in a better position to control the credit practices of retail merchants: "They can choose the retailers and suppliers with whom they will do business. If a financial institution is subject to consumers' defenses against payment, such as failure of consideration, nondelivery, etc., it will discontinue purchase of paper from those merchants who cause trouble thereby forcing the many merchants who desire to stay in business but need financial institutions to buy their consumer credit paper to "now react responsibly to consumer complaints in order to keep the avenue of credit open."

The foregoing discussion suggests that waivers of defenses and promissory notes which result in foreclosures of substantial pre-existing equities between parties to a transfer of money have little or no place in consumer transactions.

CHAPTER 2

The Surety

A. INTRODUCTION TO THE LAW OF SURETYSHIP

Suretyship is "the relation which exists where one person has undertaken an obligation and another person is also under an obligation or other duty to the obligee, who is entitled to but one performance, and as between the two who are bound, one rather than the other should perform." Restatement of Security §82 (1941). This abstract statement of the basic suretyship relations can be illustrated by Figure 2-1.

Assume that a college student (principal) wishes to buy a car but has no credit record and does not have enough cash to buy the car outright. The seller (creditor) may agree to grant credit if the student's father or mother

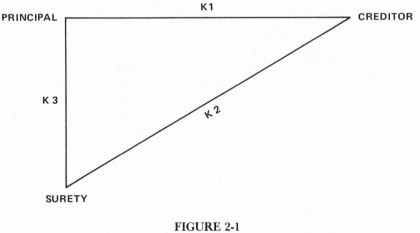

FIGURE 2-1
Surety Relationship

agrees to act as surety by promising to pay if the student should be unable or unwilling when payment is due. Both the student and the parent have an obligation to pay the seller; the seller, however, is not entitled to more than the agreed purchase price (one performance); and, as between the parent and the student, the student should make the payment.

The familiar example of the college student's purchase of a car embodies the same basic pattern that appears in many different commercial contexts. Perhaps the most institutionalized surety arrangement is the surety bond written by a corporation that specializes in evaluating risks and is compensated for acting as a surety. These surety bonds often have elaborate provisions, many of which have become boilerplate. They are common in the context of construction contracts where the surety guaranties to the owner that construction will be completed (*performance bond*) and that subcontractors and suppliers will be paid (*payment bond*). Professional sureties also write *fidelity bonds* to protect employers against unfaithful employees. Banks, for example, take out *Bankers Blanket Bonds* to insure themselves against losses from both unfaithful employees and forgery or alteration of items they handle. Less institutionalized examples of suretyship agreements are the separate agreements signed by individuals to guaranty performance of some act, usually the repayment of loans extended to the principal debtor. Major shareholders or officers of a close corporation, for example, frequently sign agreements providing a continuing guaranty of the corporation's obligations to its financer or principal trade creditors.

An important variation on the separate guaranty agreement is the surety who agrees to secure the principal debtor's obligation by signing a negotiable instrument such as a promissory note. The creditor thus obtains all the procedural and substantive advantages of holding commercial paper and may enforce the instrument against both the principal debtor and the surety, who signs the instrument to accommodate the debtor. We study this last form of suretyship in Part B of this chapter. Even the special rules governing such obligations, however, operate against the background of the principles and rules common to all suretyship arrangements.

The law of suretyship remains uncodified common law in most jurisdictions.[1] Furthermore, the case law is quite dated, with leading cases often stemming from the late nineteenth century. Both commercial and legal terminology vary considerably. The distinction between *suretyship* and *guaranty* is particularly confusing. Generally (but not universally) it has been accepted

---

1. Some recent consumer legislation protects consumers, like neighbors or family members, who agree to act as sureties without compensation in connection with consumer transactions. The Uniform Consumer Credit Code, for example, requires special notice to be given to sureties in consumer credit transactions. UCCC §3.208. The Federal Trade Commission has defined as an unfair or deceptive act the misrepresentation of the nature or extent of the potential liability of a cosigner in a consumer transaction. 16 C.F.R. §444.3 (1984). The Bankruptcy Code also protects nonprofessional sureties when the principal debtor has filed for adjustment of debts in a Chapter 13 proceeding by staying the creditor from enforcing the surety's obligation. 11 U.S.C. §1301 (Supp. 1984). These statutory provisions, however, are the exception.

that surety is the broader term. A surety has a primary duty to perform, usually jointly or jointly and severally with the principal debtor, while the guarantor has a separate undertaking with the creditor that is expressly conditioned on default by the principal debtor on his obligation to the creditor. L. Simpson, Handbook on the Law of Suretyship §14 (1950). Fortunately, for most purposes it is unnecessary to distinguish between suretyship and guaranty because the legal consequences are usually the same. Indeed, the Restatement of Security uses the two terms interchangeably. Restatement of Security, §82, Comment G. However, you must remain alert to the possibility that courts in some jurisdictions may give particular weight to the use of one or the other of these terms. When this occurs, the principal issues usually concern the availability of certain defenses to the surety, and whether prior resort to the principal debtor is a condition precedent to enforcement of the surety's obligation.

The Restatement of Security (1941) was the last of the initial restatements of the common law undertaken by the American Law Institute. It attempts to bring some order to the disarray and variant terminology prevalent in the case law. The black letter principles and rules of suretyship law are set out in its Division II (§§82-211). This backdrop was assumed by the drafters of the Uniform Commercial Code, whose major foray into suretyship law was the codification of the rules governing *accommodation parties* (UCC 3-415, 3-416, 3-606).[2] This term traditionally has been used to refer to a surety's undertaking when the surety signs a negotiable instrument to accommodate the principal obligor who is also a party to the instrument.

No matter what the source of suretyship law, the legal rules regulate three basic contractual relations: (1) the contract between the creditor and the principal debtor, (2) the contract between the creditor and the surety, and (3) the contract between the surety and the principal debtor. To these basic relations should be added another potential set, that between cosureties of the same principal debtor.

1.   The Contract Between the Creditor and the Principal Debtor

The contractual obligation secured by the surety's promise is of little interest to the law of suretyship. The debtor, for example, may be obligated to pay for goods, repay a loan, or perform an act such as building a house. Regular contract law normally applies to the transaction.

What is of interest to the law of suretyship, however, is whether the surety may take advantage of the principal debtor's defenses to the creditor's contract action. The debtor may have such defenses as lack of capacity, want or failure of consideration, fraud, mistake, or duress. The creditor may be unable to enforce the contract because the statute of limitations has run or because the

---

2. The UCC itself defines *surety* as "includ[ing] guarantor" (UCC 1-201(40)).

debt has been discharged in bankruptcy. The surety will want to know whether these defenses can be used if the creditor seeks to enforce the surety's contractual obligations.

Case law has evolved a number of specific rules on which defenses are available to the surety. See, for example, Restatement of Security §§117-118; L. Simpson, Handbook of the Law of Suretyship §§52-62. The principal debtor's incapacity or bankruptcy is not a defense because the creditor bargained for the surety's promise to protect against just such defenses. Want or failure of consideration does discharge the surety, however, because there is no principal obligation to secure. In most jurisdictions fraud and duress by the creditor on the principal debtor also discharge the surety because they are risks unknown to the surety at the time he agreed to act as surety, and the creditor's concealment of the risk is a fraud on the surety directly.[3]

2.   The Contract Between the Creditor and the Surety

The surety's contract with the creditor is also subject to general contract rules, but there are several recurring problems given special treatment.

Consideration for the surety's contractual obligation to the creditor must be present, but the consideration supporting the principal debtor's contractual obligation also supports the surety's obligation. As a consequence, if the surety agrees to secure the debtor before or at the same time as the debtor contracts with the creditor there is no problem, but if the surety agrees to act as surety after the debtor is already obligated, the creditor must provide new consideration. For example, the creditor might extend the time within which the debtor must perform.

Even if there is consideration a creditor seeking to enforce a surety's obligation may be met with a statute of frauds defense. Recognizing that the role of surety is particularly susceptible to false allegations, the English Statute of Frauds required that the surety's contract be in writing. 29 Car. 2, ch. 3, §4 (1677). The case law gloss on similar American statutes provides numerous refinements, which the Restatement (Second) of Contracts §§112-123 (1981) summarizes. See also Restatement of Security §89.

Assuming that a creditor may enforce the surety's promise under normal contract principles, he will be entitled in most jurisdictions to proceed directly against the surety when the principal obligation falls due without having to pursue the principal debtor or liquidate collateral securing the obligation. The parties may agree, of course, that the creditor will look first to the principal debtor or collateral: in some jurisdictions a statute or case law may discharge a surety if, after the surety requests the creditor to proceed against the principal debtor, the creditor fails to do so in a specified time. This rule is usually

---

3. To what extent can these rules be justified on the grounds of efficiency? For example, as between the creditor and the surety, who is more likely to be able to determine at least cost (a) the debtor's incapacity, (b) want of consideration?

traced to the case of Pain v. Packard, 13 Johns. 174 (N.Y. Sup. Ct. 1816) (creditor bound to use due diligence to protect known surety by proceeding against principal debtor after surety's request, and surety discharged absent such diligence). The Restatement of Security §130 rejects the rule of Pain v. Packard on the grounds that the creditor has no duty to protect the surety when the surety can protect himself by exoneration or reimbursement from the debtor, as will be discussed below.

Even in jurisdictions where the creditor may proceed directly against the surety, the creditor must still take into account the maxim that the surety is a favorite of the law. Courts regularly construe the surety's contract against the creditor and in favor of the surety, frequently justifying their attitude with a reference to the principle expressed in the cryptic Latin tag *strictissimi juris*. Some courts suggest that less protection is necessary for the professional surety than for the uncompensated nonprofessional.

The impact of this approach is felt most in cases holding that any modification of the principal obligation discharges the surety. If analyzed in terms of the risk initially undertaken by the surety, many of the results may be justified where the risk of having to perform is increased. Some courts, however, discharge the surety even if the modification does not increase the surety's risk. For example, if the creditor and debtor agree to change the interest calculation on the principal loan, the surety is discharged if the change increases the risk the debtor is unable to pay and the surety is asked to perform. Even if the creditor agrees to lower interest payments and thereby lightens the debtor's burden the surety may be discharged in some jurisdictions. The doctrinal justification for such decisions is simply that the surety's risk may not be altered without its consent.

Several rules have evolved to protect the creditor who modifies the principal debt but does not intend to release the surety. The surety may consent to the modification or release and thereby remain bound. Alternatively, a creditor may reserve his rights against the surety at the time he releases the principal debtor. The reason for permitting a reservation to have this effect is that the modification or release is merely the creditor's covenant not to sue the debtor on the obligation, which continues to exist, and the surety is unaffected because his rights of exoneration and reimbursement may still be enforced against the debtor. Courts have been unpersuaded by the surety's argument that a modification or release may make it more likely that the surety will have to perform.[4]

---

4. These rules on modification and release have been restated in the following sections of the Restatement of Security.

§122. Release of Principal.

Where the creditor releases a principal, the surety is discharged, unless
(a) the surety consents to remain liable notwithstanding the release, or
(b) the creditor in the release reserves his rights against the surety.

Comment: . . . b. Rationale. Where the surety and principal are bound jointly, the release of one is the release of both unless the rights of the obligee are reserved against the other. See Restatement of Contracts, §§121, 122. [Restatement (Second) of Contracts §§294, 295 (1981).] Where the surety and principal are not bound jointly, but the obligation of the surety is to answer for the

3.   The Contract Between the Surety and the Principal Debtor

If a surety is called upon to perform his contract with the creditor because the principal debtor has defaulted, the surety has three remedies against the debtor: exoneration, reimbursement, and subrogation.

a.   Exoneration

When a creditor calls upon a surety to perform, the surety before per-

---

duty of the principal, the termination of the principal's duty is also a termination of the surety's obligation. If the principal has no longer a duty as a result of the creditor's act, the surety should not be held to an obligation to answer for a default of that duty. Furthermore, if the surety could be compelled to pay after the principal's release, he would be entitled to reimbursement if he had become a surety at the principal's request or with his consent. Such an outcome would be unfair to the principal after a release because it would afford the creditor a means of attacking the principal indirectly through the surety. . . .

d.   Reservation of rights by creditor. Where the creditor releases the principal but reserves his rights against the surety, this is construed as a covenant not to sue the principal. Historically, the covenant not to sue did not prevent a suit in violation of the covenant, although a liability might be incurred by such a suit. The creditor, by a release with reservation of rights against the surety, was in effect notifying the principal that, in spite of the release, the surety might pay as the result of compulsion or voluntarily and that the principal would then be liable to reimburse the surety. Since the release was regarded as only a covenant not to sue, even the surety's right of subrogation was technically preserved. The reservation of rights showed that the creditor had no intention to release the surety. The principal had no cause for complaint since, having accepted his release with the reservation, he necessarily accepted the consequence that the liability might still be enforced against him through action by the surety.

There are probably instances where the rule stated in this Section has the advantage of encouraging compositions.

§128.   Modification of Principal's Duty.

Where, without the surety's consent, the principal and the creditor modify their contract otherwise than by extension of time of payment

(a)   the surety, other than a compensated surety, is discharged unless the modification is of a sort that can only be beneficial to the surety, and

(b)   the compensated surety is

(i)   discharged if the modification materially increases his risk, and

(ii)   not discharged if the risk is not materially increased, but his obligation is reduced to the extent of loss due to the modification.

§129.   Extension of Time to Principal.

(1) Subject to the rule stated in Subsection (2) and to the rules in respect of negotiable instruments, where the principal and creditor, without the surety's consent, make a binding agreement to extend the time of payment by the principal, the surety is discharged unless the creditor in the extension agreement reserves his rights against the surety.

(2) Where the surety is a compensated surety he is discharged only to the extent that he is harmed by the extension.

Comment: . . . a. Rationale. A binding extension of time by the creditor to the principal is a form of modification of the principal's duty; see §128. Its effect is stated separately because it is a form of modification under which the creditor can reserve his rights against the surety. The basic reason for the rule stated in Subsection (1) is that the surety should not be bound on a duty of the principal which he has not guaranteed. The rule can also be supported because of the possibility that the risk of the surety will be increased by the extension.

Furthermore, if the surety were not discharged, the creditor, notwithstanding the extension, might at once enforce his right against the surety, and if the surety satisfied his obligation, the latter could proceed immediately against the principal for reimbursement. Under such a rule too the surety's right to subrogation would be affected since he could not enforce the right of the creditor by subrogation until the period of the extension has expired.

forming may bring an equitable suit against the principal debtor requesting a decree ordering the debtor to exonerate ("to take the burden from") the surety by discharging the surety's contractual obligations to the debtor. Restatement of Security §112. This equitable suit is distinct from any legal action brought by the creditor against the surety, and the suit does not bar the creditor from proceeding to judgment against the surety. Absent any equitable defenses, courts grant the decree to protect sureties from the hardship of having to perform and then seek reimbursement from the principal debtor. In practice sureties do not often seek exoneration.

b.   Reimbursement

If instead of obtaining an equitable decree ordering exoneration the surety decides to perform, he may recover from the principal debtor in an action for reimbursement. Restatement of Security §104. The action may be on an express promise of the debtor to reimburse the surety or it may be implied from the debtor's consent to having the surety act as surety. The right to reimbursement arises as soon as the surety performs any part of the obligation for which the debtor is principally responsible. Even if the surety pays only part of the principal obligation, for example, he has the right to reimbursement for this amount. The principal debtor is not relieved of the obligation to reimburse the surety if the surety performs, despite a personal defense of the surety or a defense of the debtor available to the surety of which the surety has no knowledge. Indeed, Restatement of Security §108 states that the surety also has a right to reimbursement even if the surety knows of a defense of the principal when the surety performs "under business compulsion." Some defenses of the principal are not available to the surety. Lack of capacity provides the principal with a defense not only to an action by the creditor but also to an action by the surety seeking reimbursement.

c.   Subrogation

If the surety performs following the principal debtor's default, not only may an action be brought against the debtor for reimbursement but the surety is also subrogated to any rights of the creditor against the debtor. Restatement of Security §141. If, for example, the creditor holds collateral that also secured the principal obligation the surety is entitled to that collateral to secure the right to reimbursement: the surety thus "steps into the shoes" of the creditor. In other words, the law treats the transfer of right by subrogation as an equitable assignment, a right that exists even if the surety-debtor contract makes no mention of it. An important condition to this right to subrogation is that the principal debtor's obligation be performed in full, even if the surety is only responsible for part performance.

4. Rights Between Cosureties

When more than one surety agree to secure the principal debtor's obligation they are *cosureties*. Restatement of Security §§144-164. Normally cosureties are jointly and severally liable to the creditor. If the creditor pursues only one surety, that surety may seek exoneration from the other sureties or recover from them in an action for contribution. In the absence of an agreement to share the burden in some other proportion, it is assumed that as among themselves each cosurety will share equally in the cost of performance. This right to contribution is secured by the right to be subrogated to the creditor's rights against the cosureties. Sureties may also agree among themselves that one or more of them shall be entitled to full reimbursement from the others. Those entitled to full reimbursement from their cosureties are sometimes referred to as *subsureties*.

Problem 2-1. The Alliance for Rural Progress (ARP) is a nonprofit organization whose purposes include fostering development of business owned by minority groups and migrant workers in rural areas. It acts as both a lending and consulting agency. Its executive board members and officers do not themselves have substantial business or financial expertise so they have formed an informal advisory board. The advisory board is composed primarily of bank personnel, including loan officers and the branch manager of the local branch of Western National Bank (WNB).

Gomez approaches ARP with a proposal for a restaurant, and, after consulting with its advisory board, ARP decides to participate in the Gomez transaction. WNB extends a $90,000 loan to Gomez to finance improvements to the restaurant and to provide working capital. The note Gomez signed provides for a schedule of quarterly payments and for interest at WNB's prime rate plus 4 percent, an effective rate of 18 to 25 percent during the period in question. It also provides for costs and attorneys' fees. Gomez secures the loan by granting a first deed of trust in favor of WNB on nine acres of unimproved commercially-zoned property adjacent to a freeway interchange currently under construction. The bank's appraisal values the land at $180,000.

WNB also requires, as a condition of the loan, that ARP purchase and pledge with WNB certain "Growbonds" issued by WNB. This collateral is in the principal amount of $60,000 and has an interest yield of 6 percent. ARP does not sign the Gomez note but does sign a standard bank pledge agreement form pledging the collateral in question to secure the Gomez loan. The form also waives any right to notice, demand, presentment, notice of demand or presentment, consents to extension or modification of the terms of the loan, relieves WNB from any obligation to maintain collateral, and allows WNB to substitute or release collateral in its discretion. WNB's branch manager tells ARP that the document is a necessary form but that ARP is not personally liable on the Gomez note. The manager characterizes the pledge as a precaution and states that WNB will first pursue Gomez if any default arises.

The loan goes into default almost immediately, apparently due to poor management and to cost overruns on improvements to the restaurant. Both WNB and ARP are aware of Gomez's default on the WNB loan because they have been in regular contact with Gomez, who promises to continue payments as soon as business improves. On one occasion ARP brings the loan current by making a third cash advance to Gomez, who in turn pays the bank.

When the loan has been in default for about a year, accrued interest has raised the total amount of indebtedness to about $120,000. At this point, with no notice to ARP, WNB "cashes out" ARP's "Growbonds." After deducting early withdrawal penalties in the amount of about $4,000 WNB applies the net proceeds to reduce the balance on the Gomez loan, notifies both ARP and Gomez of these actions after the fact, and invites them to meet with bank officials to discuss payoff of the balance of the loan.

These negotiations continue over a period of several months. WNB repeatedly presses ARP to bring the loan current and guaranty payment of the balance, in return for which WNB will agree to assign WNB's deed of trust to the extent ARP has made or will in the future make payment. ARP declines and negotiations continue.

Late in the year, with a balance of about $70,000 on the loan, Gomez sells the property adjacent to the freeway for $100,000. WNB receives payment of the loan balance and releases the deed of trust it holds on the land. This action is also taken without notice to ARP.

Leon, executive director of ARP, comes to your office to complain of ARP's treatment at the hands of WNB. What advice can you provide?

In connection with this problem, note the following rule stated in the Restatement of Security:

§36.   *Owner of Pledged Chattel as Surety*

(1)   Where a pledge is made as security for the obligation of a third party, the pledgor is a surety to the extent of the pledged chattel.

(2)   Where a third person authorizes the pledge of his chattel to secure the obligation of a pledgor and this fact is known to the pledgee, the owner of the chattel is a surety to the extent of the pledged chattel.

Cf. UCC 9-112. This rule is also applicable to real estate mortgages.

B.   ACCOMMODATION PARTIES

First and foremost, to assume the role of surety is to assume a liability: under certain circumstances the surety must pay the obligation of another. However, as the preceding materials indicate, the surety has often been regarded as "a favorite of the law." It is a special status, often entitling a party to special rights and defenses. In contrast, much of the law of negotiable instruments is designed to facilitate the summary enforcement of rights against parties to the instrument and to preclude the assertion of defenses by such parties. When an instrument has been signed by a party with the intention of being liable only as a surety, reconciliation of the law of suretyship with the general law of negotiable instruments has proved troublesome.

Article 3 defines an accommodation party as "one who signs the instrument in any capacity for the purpose of lending his name to another party to it." UCC 3-415(1). The language "for the purpose of lending his name to another party to it" clearly connotes suretyship status, but the phrase "in any capacity" may be confusing to the uninitiated. Consider the following ways in which a party might "lend his name" on an instrument:

(1) Daughter applies to Bank for a car loan. Bank agrees to grant the loan if Mother will sign as comaker a note payable to the order of Bank. Mother has "lent her name" (i.e., credit) to Daughter by cosigning the note. The *capacity* in which Mother has signed is as a maker. She is also an *accommodation* maker; although Bank knows this from direct dealing, later holders of the note might not. Nothing in the form of the signature indicates accommodation status.

(2) Against the same background as in (1), Mother signs the note. Although her signature is placed directly beneath Daughter's, on a line marked *"Comaker,"* she follows her signature with the word *guarantor*. Mother has still signed in the capacity of maker. She is still an accommodation maker. She has now created a presumption, however, not only with respect to Bank but as to others who may deal with the instrument, that her signature is by way of accommodating her comaker.

(3) Creditor approaches a financially-troubled company about a delinquent account. Corporation's president asks Creditor to accept Corporation's note for the amount of the account payable. Creditor agrees, provided that President personally indorses the note. The note is made out to the order of Creditor and signed (in a clearly representative capacity) by President. President then signs his own name elsewhere on the note. This is a signature in an ambiguous capacity. Under the rule of UCC 3-402, President has signed in the capacity of an indorser. He is also an accommodation indorser. This fact is known to Creditor, who dealt with President. Additionally, under the rule of UCC 3-415(4), the fact that the indorsement is not in the chain of title gives notice of its accommodation character to later takers of the instrument.

(4) Against the same background as in (3), President makes a corporate note, signing as a maker in a clearly representative capacity. However, he names himself personally as payee, and then indorses the note on its reverse side to the order of Creditor. President has again made an indorser's contract. He has also accommodated Corporation, just as in (3). However, this fact is not apparent on the face of the instrument.

(5) Corporation is in need of working capital. Shareholder makes a substantial note payable to Corporation with the expectation that Corporation will use the note as collateral. Corporation, as payee, indorses the note and pledges it to Finance Company as collateral for a loan. Shareholder has accommodated Corporation by signing the note as maker: again this is not apparent from the face of the note.

The foregoing examples are intended to emphasize several propositions. First, a party may accommodate another party to an instrument by signing in many different ways. In each case, the obligation of the accommodation party is determined in the first instance by establishing what form of contract (i.e., in what contractual capacity) the accommodating party signs. Second, accommodation status may be either apparent on the face of the instrument, as in examples (2) and (3), or latent, as in examples (1), (4), and (5). Known accommodation status does not mean that the accommodation party is not liable: the very purpose of Bank in obtaining Mother's signature in (1) is to have Mother as well as Daughter liable on the note. However, an accommodation party is not liable to the party accommodated. UCC 3-415(5). Thus, if Daughter pays the note in (1), she is not entitled to contribution from Mother. This principle is perhaps most vividly illustrated by Example (5). On its face, this is Shareholder's note payable to Corporation and then indorsed to Bank. If Shareholder refuses payment Creditor can be expected to turn to Corporation, who is liable as indorser. If Corporation now sues Shareholder as a maker, Shareholder will assert that notwithstanding the fact that Corporation appears as payee, Corporation is the party accommodated. Thus, although an indorser who takes up the instrument is normally entitled to enforce Shareholder's contract, Corporation may not.

It bears reiteration that status as an accommodation party is in the first instance a contractual obligation in some capacity and not a defense. Nevertheless, establishing accommodation status may be crucial to establishing nonliability when the party seeking enforcement is the party accommodated, and it may also be important to establishing the availability of defenses dependent on status as an accommodation party.

1. Establishing Accommodation Status

A first and crucial question concerns the means by which one is able to establish accommodation status. As noted, certain types of signatures establish the accommodation character of the signature, so that any taker of the instrument will be held to have notice of the status. The most important of these is the "irregular indorsement," that is, the indorsement outside of the instrument's chain of title. UCC 3-415(4). This must be read in connection with UCC 3-402.

Problem 2-2. In which, if any, of the cases below has John Jones signed as an accommodation party? If so, in what capacity? **Note:** In all cases below only the part of the note text that is relevant to the problem is reproduced. For the full text of a short form note from which the forms below are abstracted, review Form 1-1, p. 13 supra.

Note A

San Francisco, CA	November 1, 1984

Pay to the order of _____*Sam Smith*_____

The John Jones Co.

by _____*John Jones*_____
President
John Jones

Note B

San Francisco, CA	November 1, 1984

Pay to the order of _____*Sam Smith*_____

The John Jones Co.

by _____*Ken Jones*_____
President

Attest: _____*John Jones*_____

Note C (front)

San Francisco, CA	November 1, 1984

Pay to the order of _____*Sam Smith*_____

The John Jones Co.

by _____*John Jones*_____
President

B. Accommodation Parties

Note C (back: alternatives 1-4)

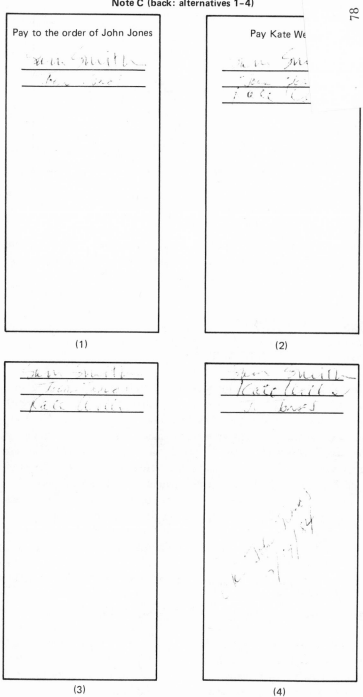

(1)

(2)

(3)

(4)

Pay to the order of John Jones

Pay Kate We

Note D

San Francisco, CA	November 1, 1984

Pay to the order of _____ *Sam Smith* _____

The John Jones Co.

by _____ *John Jones* _____
    President
John Jones

If a party signs in a manner that does not provide notice of accommodation status, under what circumstances will a party be allowed to prove accommodation by extrinsic evidence, and with what effect?

WILLIS v. WILLIS
30 UCC Rep. 1332, 1341-1345 (D.D.C. 1980), *aff'd on this point*, 655 F.2d 1333, 32 UCC Rep. 202 (D.C. Cir. 1981)

[Charles Willis led a group of investors who purchased a controlling interest in Alaska Airlines, Inc. (AA) in 1958. He was married at the time to Elizabeth Firestone Willis, daughter of Harvey Firestone of the Firestone Tire Company family. The original loan to finance the stock purchase was made to both Charles and Elizabeth. It was secured by a pledge of 25,000 shares of AA stock, registered to the Willises as joint tenants, and by 5001 shares of Firestone Co. stock of which 4700 were Elizabeth's separate property. Renewal notes in varying amounts and with varying specific collateral were made over the years. In 1969, the Willises were on the verge of divorce; Charles, in Seattle, signed another renewal note and sent it to Elizabeth's attorney in Washington, D.C. Although this note contains a signature blank for Elizabeth Firestone Willis, Elizabeth never signed it. On the day following the Willises' divorce, this note was sent by Elizabeth's attorney to Harvey Firestone at the latter's request. Without the knowledge or consent of Charles, Harvey co-signed the note, and it was given to the payee, The Firestone Bank. Following Harvey's death and a claim by the Firestone Bank against Harvey's estate, Harvey's executor paid the note in full. To resolve issues concerning the respective rights of Harvey and Elizabeth to reimbursement or contribution, it was first necessary for the court to determine whether Harvey or Elizabeth had signed the respective notes by way of accommodation. The court's determination of other issues (a number of which were reversed on appeal) have been

omitted; additional facts appear in the course of the excerpt that follows.—
EDS.]

UCC 3-415(1) states, "An accommodation party is one who signs the instrument in any capacity for the purpose of lending his name to another party to it." Official comment 1 to this section explains that "an accommodation party is always a surety . . . and it is his only distinguishing feature." Elizabeth Willis asserts that she was merely an accommodation maker when she signed the notes with her husband; Harvey Firestone contends that his status as an accommodation maker is derived from his daughter, whom he allegedly replaced as surety on the 1969 note. The court is unpersuaded by the contentions of Elizabeth and Mr. Firestone and it finds that she was a co-maker of the notes signed with her husband. Because Mr. Firestone can acquire no greater rights than the party to the note whom he replaced, he too was a co-maker.

At the outset, the court notes that the burden of proof rests upon the party who claims accommodation status. . . . The standard which must be applied in determining whether a party has satisfied this burden is well developed. One commentator explains: "The intent of the parties is the significant element in determining whether a given party is an accommodation party and the identity of the party accommodated. If the intent is not expressed, the purpose for which the commercial paper is executed or used is the significant element. . . . Another way of stating the purpose of the paper criterion is as a receiving of the benefit. Where a person receives no direct benefit from the execution of the paper, it is likely that he will be regarded as an accommodation party but not if he receives a benefit. Illustrative of this distinction, it has been held that where a co-signer of a note receives a benefit from the proceeds of the note such person is a co-maker and not an accommodation party." R. Anderson, 2 Uniform Commercial Code §3-415:9 (1971); . . . Courts confronted with the borrowing activities of spouses have regularly applied this standard and their findings have invariably turned upon the question of whether the spouse seeking accommodation status was directly benefited by the proceeds of the loan. Compare Riegler v. Riegler, 244 Ark. 483, 426 S.W.2d 789, 791 (1968) and Feltman v. National Bank of Georgia, 146 Ga. App. 434, 246 S.E.2d 434 (1978) (both finding benefit to spouse) with Seaboard Finance Co. v. Dorman, 4 Conn. Cir. 154, 227 A.2d 441 (1966); Fithian v. Jamar, 286 Md. 161, 410 A.2d 569 (1979); Kerney v. Kerney, 386 A.2d 1100 (R.I. 1978) (all finding no benefit to spouse).

Another additional rule of construction is helpful in this case. Where corporate shareholders co-sign notes which benefit their corporation, one court has ruled that the signers received a direct benefit by using the proceeds from the note to preserve their interests in the corporation. Common Wealth Insurance Systems, Inc. v. Kersten, 40 Cal. App. 3d 1014, 1029, 115 Cal. Rptr. 653, 663 (1974). Thus, Professors White and Summers explain that a corporate shareholder should clearly "indicate his status when he signs an instrument as an accommodation party." J. White & R. Summers, Uniform Commercial

Code §13-13, at 522 (2nd ed. 1980). With these rules in mind, the court shall examine Elizabeth Willis' claim.

Elizabeth Willis submits that she derived no benefits from any of the proceeds of the loans entered into by her husband. She evidently had no personal interest in either the aviation industry, the State of Alaska, or Alaska Airlines, Inc. Moreover, she played no role in the management of the airline and she had no enthusiasm for *any* of her investments. Indeed, she took no pleasure in visiting the AA headquarters in Seattle because she considered that city to be merely "Akron with a view." Elizabeth was a woman of independent means, who had no need for the AA stock purchased with the proceeds of the loan. Based on these considerations, Elizabeth would have the court conclude that she received no "benefit" from the notes which she signed with her husband. The court, however, is not persuaded that such a finding is appropriate.

First, Mrs. Willis' lack of personal benefit from or financial interest in, the affairs of her spouse is not controlling; rather, the prime considerations for the court are Elizabeth's *pecuniary* interests and pecuniary benefits. In this case, Elizabeth clearly derived a direct pecuniary benefit from the proceeds of the loan which was made to her and Charles. The original loans for $224,000 were used to purchase 32,000 shares of stock which were registered in Charles and Elizabeth's names. By virtue of the loan Elizabeth became a joint owner of a controlling interest in a large corporation; her investment appreciated and at one point, she was the joint owner of over $320,000 worth of AA stock, all derived from this $224,000 loan. See pl ex 51 (showing market listing of AA stock in excess of $10 per share). When her husband borrowed an additional $164,000 from the Irving Trust Company, the bulk of this loan provided financial assistance to a corporation in which Elizabeth had a significant interest. As a major shareholder, she again derived a direct benefit from the proceeds of the loan.[5] Finally, Elizabeth was unequivocally benefited by the additional $50,000 which she and her husband borrowed in July, 1967; although the money was *intended* to be used to purchase an Alaskan bank, it was *in fact* deposited in Elizabeth's personal account. By receiving exclusive control over the proceeds of this last loan, Elizabeth was clearly one who directly benefited from the transaction.

Because the intent of the parties is significant, the court must also examine the relevant evidence on this point. The only document presented to the court which discusses the liability of the parties to the notes is a memo prepared for Mr. Firestone by his accountants. Def ex 132; see Deposition of Howard W. Harrell at 35-37 (June 22, 1979). This memorandum discusses the extent of Elizabeth's assets and liabilities and offers suggestions on how to

---

5. The court does not find the omission of Elizabeth's name from the Irving loan significant. She assumed liability for the funds borrowed from Irving when she signed the first note with The Firestone Bank. Moreover, it is clear that the original Firestone loan was essentially a renewal of the original U.S. Trust note. In matters of renewal notes, the intent underlying the original note must control, absent evidence to the contrary. R. Anderson, 2 Uniform Commercial Code §3-415:7 (1971). No such evidence has been presented here.

improve her financial condition. The memorandum describes the note as "a joint liability loan of Elizabeth and Charlie Willis." Def ex 132. Nowhere does it suggest that Elizabeth was merely an accommodation maker. Certainly, if Elizabeth had intended to appear as a surety for her husband, this intent would have been expressed to those entrusted with providing advice on her financial problems.

Elizabeth has relied on Kerney v. Kerney, 386 A.2d 1100 (1978) as persuasive precedent for her position. The court, however, finds *Kerney* entirely distinguishable. In *Kerney,* a married couple borrowed money and used the proceeds to benefit an insurance business in which both were employed. The wife, however, was the *sole* owner of the business. Based on this fact, the court concluded that the husband, who served as general manager, did not receive any direct benefit from the proceeds of the loans and that he was therefore an accommodation party. 386 A.2d at 1102. In the present case, by contrast, *both* parties to the notes had an interest in the corporation which benefited from the loans and, more importantly, the loans were used to acquire property (AA stock) which was jointly held. The case most similar to the one before the court is Feltman v. National Bank of Georgia, 146 Ga. App. 434, 246 S.E.2d 434 (1978). In *Feltman,* the husband and wife co-signed a note in the amount of $100,000. The wife, who was "endowed with a substantial personal financial estate," also purchased a certificate of deposit in the same amount. Like Elizabeth Willis, she took no personal interest in the business ventures of her husband. The husband, however, employed the proceeds of the note to purchase real estate which was titled in both of their names. In view of this direct benefit, the court concluded that the wife was a co-maker with her husband. Although this court is not bound by the holding in *Feltman,* it finds that the analysis provided by that decision offers persuasive guidance.

In light of the foregoing, the court concludes that Elizabeth Willis received a direct benefit from the proceeds of the notes which she signed with her husband and thus, it was not the intent of the parties to those notes that Elizabeth sign in an accommodation status. Accordingly, the court concludes that Elizabeth Willis was not an accommodation party within the meaning of UCC 3-415(1).

Having found that Elizabeth Willis was not an accommodation maker, the court must reach a similar conclusion with respect to her father. Although Mr. Firestone played no direct role in the borrowing activities of his daughter between 1958 and 1968 it is undisputed that he may stand in no better position than the party to the note whom he replaces. Accordingly, the court finds that Harvey Firestone was not an accommodation maker on the notes dated September 30, 1969.

Problem 2-3. Andrews and Jenkins are interested in forming a partnership to conduct a printing business and approach Bank for a loan to purchase equipment. Bank refuses to lend the money unless both spouses sign the note as well. At a meeting at Bank, during which a loan officer of Bank and both couples are present, Andrews details his plan for the printing business, in which he is to play the major managerial role. Andrews, Jenkins, and both spouses then all sign the note as makers. No formal partnership agreement is ever drawn up. The business does not flourish. Andrew draws between 70 and 75 percent of the profits during the brief period when there are profits. After less than a year Bank calls its note, which has been paid in full by Mrs. Jenkins from her personal funds. What are her rights against the other makers?

Problem 2-4. Son approaches car dealer and asks for a loan to purchase a sports car. Dealer balks, but says that he will grant the loan if the note is signed as comaker by Son's girl friend, Goodbucks. Son and Goodbucks both sign the note as makers. Over coffee in the Town Cafe, Son's father, Old-school, tells Dealer he'd like to know where Son came up with the money for his new car. Dealer cheerfully explains that Son and Goodbucks cosigned a note. Flustered by this revelation, Oldschool stops by Dealer's showroom and asks to see the note. When Dealer displays the note, Oldschool states "he never should have done that," and writes across the face of the note "Guaranteed. Oldschool." Dealer subsequently discounts the paper by indorsing it to National Bank. Son, who has been making payments on the note to Bank, splits for California and the loan goes into default. What are Bank's rights against the parties? What are Dealer's rights if he takes up the note when pressed by Bank? What are the rights as between Oldschool, Goodbucks, and Son? See UCC 3-413, 3-415, 3-416.

Problem 2-5. UCC 3-415(5) states that the paying accommodation party has an action "on the instrument" against the party accommodated. This section reverses pre-Code law in some jurisdictions and may be of great practical importance in instances where the note is secured, provides for an advantageous interest rate, attorney's fees, or the like. Suppose in either of the two preceding problems a comaker tries unsuccessfully to show accommodation status. He is still entitled to contribution. Does his action have the attributes of an action "on the instrument"? See UCC 3-603(2).

2. Defenses

In Chapter 1 we analyzed the defenses normally asserted by a party liable on an instrument. Under Article 3 these issues are generally resolved by posing and answering two questions. First, does the party seeking enforcement have the status of holder in due course? If not, the party being held may interpose any defense that would be a defense on a simple contract. UCC 3-306. If, however, a holder in due course seeks enforcement of liability on the instrument, a second question must be answered: is the defense in issue one of the limited number of "real" defenses good even against a holder in due course? UCC 3-305.

An accommodation party may lend his name by signing an instrument in any capacity. An initially plausible analysis, therefore, might be that one simply identifies the capacity in which an accommodation party is bound and then applies Article 3's usual analytic structure. Unfortunately the issues presented are not so readily resolved; the above analysis is adequate to solve only a portion of the entire set of problems.

An accommodation party "is always a surety." UCC 3-415, Comment 1. Recall the diagram of a suretyship relation we considered in Part A. Superimpose upon that diagram the respective roles played when a party indorses another's note to accommodate the maker; the party's relationship will then be as indicated in Figure 2-2.

In the example below, the capacity in which the accommodation party has signed is as an indorser, and the K2 contract is his contract on the instrument.

The first set of defenses an indorser may wish to raise are directly related to the indorsement contract (K2). As a surety, however, the indorser may also wish to raise other matters: for instance, the principal fraudulently induced the indorser into serving as surety (a K3 matter), or the creditor fraudulently induced the K1 contract and valid defenses to the K1 contract are available to the surety. In addition, the accommodation party may wish to interpose defenses traditionally viewed as "suretyship defenses": discharge through modification of the principal obligation is an example. The Code appears to address some of these issues either obliquely or not at all. In the materials that follow, we introduce some of the Code's troublesome formulations but seek to provide reasonable guidance through the thicket.

We examine first the defenses that are clearly rooted in the K2 contract itself.

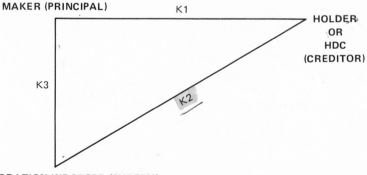

FIGURE 2-2
Accommodation Party Relationship

Problem 2-6. Son obtains a loan for use in his fledgling construction business. Lender requires that Father indorse the note. When Son defaults three years later, Bank attempts to hold Father liable. Father defends on the ground that his obligation was discharged in bankruptcy, Father himself having fallen on hard times in the intervening years. Does it matter whether Bank, who now holds the note, has the status of holder or holder in due course? When a debtor is discharged in bankruptcy his unsecured creditors are injoined from trying to collect on prepetition claims that were allowed in the bankruptcy proceedings except when a creditor can show that his claim falls within an exception to discharge, such as when the claim arose through the debtor's fraud. See Bankruptcy Code §§523, 524.

Problem 2-7. On the same basic facts, Father argues instead that he was fraudulently induced to indorse the note by Lender, who collaborated with Son to misrepresent the business purpose of the loan. Again, does it matter whether Bank, who now holds the note, has the status of holder or holder in due course?

In the above instances, a customary analysis focused upon holder-in-due-course doctrine, and the distinction between real and personal defenses appears to yield appropriate results. But the Code's provisions are sometimes unclear even in this area.

A persistent problem is that of the "gratuitous" surety. Leaving aside professionals, most sureties are uncompensated. Certainly this is true of most accommodation parties who lend their names out of either a close business or personal relationship. One might argue endlessly about whether, although uncompensated, such parties receive some benefit. Those with long memories will recall that the issue of benefit to the promisor (here the accommodation party) is simply not relevant to modern contract theory. To the extent that consideration doctrine retains vitality, general contract theory is easily satisfied as follows: creditor bargained for the accommodation party's indorsement in exchange for lending money to the principal. The same consideration that supports the principal's contract as maker supports the accommodation party's contract as indorser. Aside from a lawyer's occasional pragmatic desire to obfuscate, the contention that the accommodation party received no consideration should be a losing argument in this bald form.

The plot thickens, however, when the facts are changed slightly. Suppose that the accommodation party argues instead that the holder of the note first approached him seeking an indorsement a month after the note was issued, five months before it was due? Under general contract law and the general law of suretyship the accommodation party has a reasonable defense on the theory that past consideration is no consideration. The defense would be personal, not real, and the outcome would therefore be determined by whether the holder was also a holder in due course.

Article 3, however, does not as a general proposition adhere to the "past consideration" doctrine. UCC 3-408 provides:

> Want or failure of consideration is a defense as against any person not having the rights of a holder in due course (Section 3-305), except that no consideration is necessary for an instrument or obligation thereon given in payment of or as security for an antecedent obligation of any kind. Nothing in this section shall be taken to displace any statute outside this Act under which a promise is enforceable notwithstanding lack or failure of consideration. Partial failure of consideration is a defense pro tanto whether or not the failure is in an ascertained or liquidated amount.

In addition, the Code's principal section on accommodation parties states in part (UCC 3-415(2)):

> When the instrument has been taken for value before it is due the accommodation party is liable in the capacity in which he has signed even though the taker knows of the accommodation.

Both provisions are susceptible of more than one interpretation. To sharpen your understanding of UCC 3-415(2) consider the following problems. Then reread both UCC 3-408 and 3-415(2) and analyze the principal case following the problems.

Problem 2-8. *A* accommodates *B* as comaker on a $5,000 note payable to the order of *C.* In consideration for the note, *C* advances *B* $5,000, which *B* pockets; *B* then disappears. *C* negotiates the paper for value to *D,* who in turn negotiates to *E.* At maturity *E* discovers that *B* has skipped and forces *D* to take up the note. *D,* having satisfied *E,* sues *A.* What result?

Problem 2-9. Assume the same facts as in Problem 2-8, except that *D,* when he acquires the note from *C,* is a donee. He does not further negotiate the note, and sues *A* at maturity. What result?

Problem 2-10. Assume the same facts as in Problem 2-8, except that *C* never made the intended advance to *B. D* acquires the note from *C* as a holder in due course and sues *A* at maturity. What result?

Problem 2-11. Assume the same facts as in the immediately preceding problem, except that when signing the note, *A* had written "comaker and surety" following his name. What result?

FRANKLIN NATIONAL BANK v. EUREZ CONSTRUCTION CORP.
60 Misc. 2d 499, 301 N.Y.S.2d 845, 6 UCC Rep. 634 (Sup. Ct. 1969)

MEYER, J. [Plaintiff stated four causes of action. Discussion of all but the third cause has been omitted.—EDS.] In this action, tried without a jury, plaintiff bank seeks . . . to recover from Eurez, J. J. White Ready Mix Concrete Corporation and John J. White, as indorser, on the note, it having been dishonored when due. . . .

Its right to recover against defendants J. J. White Ready Mix Concrete Corp. and John J. White on the third cause of action is less clear, however. UCC 3-201(3) provides that "Negotiation takes effect only when the indorsement is made. . . ." As to any defense of which the transferee of an instrument payable to order has notice prior to the time "indorsement is made," the transferee is not a holder in due course, UCC 1-201(20); 3-202(1), 3-302(1)(c). Defendants J. J. White Ready Mix Concrete Corp. and John J. White urge as a complete defense to the third cause of action that the note was made by the corporate defendant and indorsed by the individual defendant as an accommodation to Eurez and without consideration. They urge that under UCC 3-306(c) and 3-408 want of consideration is a defense against one who is not a holder in due course. Plaintiff, relying on UCC 3-415(1) and (2) argues that absence of consideration is not available as a defense to an accommodation-maker or indorser when the instrument is taken for value before it is due. Though the court finds that defendant J. J. White Ready Mix Concrete Corporation made, and defendant John J. White indorsed, the note in suit as an accommodation to defendant Eurez and without consideration, it holds plaintiff's interpretation of the Uniform Commercial Code to be correct and, therefore, awards plaintiff judgment against them as well as defendant Eurez on the third cause of action.

As Professor Peters states "While Section 3-415(2) seems to opt for liability in this situation the outcome is by no means clear," (Peters, Suretyship Under Article 3 of the Uniform Commercial Code, 77 Yale L.J. 833, 848). The problem arises because UCC 3-408 states that "Want or failure of consideration is a defense as against any person not having the rights of a holder in due course (Section 3-305), except that no consideration is necessary for an instrument or obligation thereon given in payment of or as security for an antecedent obligation of any kind," but fails to except cases in which an accommodation party signs without consideration. Under well known rules of construction that omission would lead to the conclusion that want of consideration to the accommodation maker and indorser is a defense available to them, were it not for the provision of 3-415(1) and (2).

UCC 3-415(1) provides that "An accommodation party is one who signs the instrument in any capacity for the purpose of lending his name to another party to it" and subdivision (2) states that "When the instrument has been taken for value before it is due the accommodation party is liable in the capacity in which he has signed even though the taker knows of the accommodation." Nothing in subdivision (1) suggests that consideration running to an accommodation maker is a sine qua non of his liability; indeed Official Comment 2 to UCC 3-415 makes clear that its definition includes both gratuitous · and paid sureties. Furthermore, nothing in subdivision (2) requires that the accommodation party have received value. Ostensibly its purpose is to protect the taker when the instrument has been taken for value and before maturity. In light of the phrase "before it is due" it seems unreasonable to construe the Code to require that value has been given at the time of issuance in order to hold an accommodation maker, but see Peters (op. cit. supra, 77 Yale L.J. at 845). Nor can the concluding clause ("even though the taker knows of the accommodation") be seized upon as limiting the effect of the subdivision to the negation of knowledge of accommodation status as a defense, for that construction would either make UCC 3-304(4)(c) superfluous or in view of the provisions of that section and UCC 3-302 would make meaningless the reference in UCC 3-415(2) to taking for value and before maturity. If UCC 3-415(2) was not intended to give status to a taker for value before maturity different from the status he would have as a holder in due course, the section should have referred not to a "taker" but to a "holder who when he takes" (compare UCC 3-302(1) which uses the phrase "holder who takes"), especially since "holder" is expressly defined in UCC 1-201(20) whereas the Code nowhere defines "taker," and since the predecessor to UCC 3-415(2), section 55 of the Negotiable Instruments Law (U.N.I.L. §29), used the phrase "holder for value." Some significance must also be accorded the fact that though Professor Brannan pressed for amendment of the Negotiable Instruments Law provisions to substitute in place of "holder for value" the words "one who is in other respects a holder in due course," Brannan, Some Necessary Amendments of the Negotiable Instruments Law, 26 Harv. L. Rev. 493, the draftsmen of the Uniform Commercial Code (who, it may be presumed, were aware of the Brannan article), while modifying the Negotiable Instruments Law concept to include not only taking "for value" (which was the sole U.N.I.L. criterion) but also taking "before it [the instrument] is due," and to drop the former §52 (U.N.I.L. §26) definition of "holder for value" as "erroneous and misleading, since a holder who does not himself give value cannot qualify as a holder in due course in his own right merely because value has previously been given for the instrument," Official Comment 1 to UCC 3-303, nevertheless did not incorporate in UCC 3-415 all of the holder in due course criteria and substituted for the word "holder" previously used the word "taker." It seems fair to argue from this that the draftsmen did not intend to require that a taker for value before maturity have holder in due course status in order to hold an accommodation party liable. The difficulty with the argument is that it proves too much, for to paraphrase Professor Brannan (op. cit. supra at p.498), if the argument is sound, a taker of accommodation paper occupies a position superior to that of any other purchaser of negotiable paper, since there are no other requirements for his recovery except that he be a taker for value and before maturity, see also 1955 Report Law Rev. Comm. (Leg. Doc. [1955] No. 65), Vol. 2, pp. 918-919. It is not now necessary to determine to what extent defenses other than want of consideration are available against a taker for value before maturity who is not a holder in due course, cf. UCC 3-306(c) and 3-408. It is sufficient to note that Official Comment 3 to UCC 3-415 states that: "The obligation of the accommodation party is supported by any due consideration for which the instrument is taken before it is due" and to hold on the basis of that comment and the history and wording of the section, that there is no want of consideration within the meaning of UCC 3-408 when consideration moves before maturity to the party accommodated, even though the accommodation maker receives no consideration for executing the instrument.

The conclusion thus reached, while it reads into UCC 3-408 an exception which the draftsmen of the Code have not articulated, can be supported by a number of additional arguments. "Consideration" is distinguished from "value" throughout Article 3 of the Code, Official Comment 1 to UCC 3-408; Official Comment 2 to UCC 3-303. "Consideration" refers to what the obligor has received for his obligation and is important only on the question whether the obligation can be enforced against him, ibid. "Value" on the other hand refers to what the holder or taker has given up and is important only on the question whether the holder "qualifies as a particular kind of holder." (Official Comment 2 to UCC 3-303.) The fact that in §3-424 of the May 1949 Draft of the Uniform Commercial Code, the sentence which became UCC 3-415(2) of the Code in its final form began "When the instrument has been taken for consideration before it is due . . ." (italics supplied) and that the word "consideration" was changed to "value" in the spring 1950 draft, when read together with Official Comment 3 to UCC 3-415 ("The obligation of the accommodation party is supported by any consideration [sic] for which the instrument is taken before it is due," [emphasis supplied]), suggests that the draftsmen intended the taker's right to enforce an instrument against an accommodation party to turn on whether the taker had given value, rather than whether the accommodation party had received consideration.

Secondly, UCC 1-103 provides that: "Unless displaced by the particular provisions of this Act, the provisions of law and equity, including the law merchant . . . shall supplement its provisions." The rule of law prior to the Code was that one who receives before maturity a note signed by the maker for the accommodation of another is not affected by the mere fact that it was made without consideration. . . . The omission from UCC 3-408 of any exception covering the situation suggests an intention on the part of the draftsmen to change the rule; the fact that gratuitous accommodation is covered by UCC 3-415, the specific language of UCC 3-415(2) and the absence of any logical basis for change suggest an intention to preserve the prior rule. If the latter reasons be an insufficient basis for concluding that the prior rule continues, it is likewise impossible to view the omission from UCC 3-408 as a displacement "by the particular provisions of this Act" of the prior rule. Absent such displacement, the prior rule continues.

Thirdly, UCC 1-102(2)(c) of the Code directs that it be liberally construed to promote its purposes and policies, one of which is "to make uniform the law among the various jurisdictions." Though based on somewhat different reasoning, there are cases in other jurisdictions holding that one who is not a holder in due course but who takes accommodation paper for value before it is due may, under UCC 3-415(2), enforce it against the accommodation maker . . . and that want of consideration is no defense to an accommodation maker. . . . Brief mention must also be made of a few additional points.

While defendants J. J. White Ready Mix Concrete Corp. and John J. White were accommodation parties, plaintiff bank did not know that fact when it took the note. That it did not does not, however, change the result in light of the wording of UCC 3-415(2). Defendant White's testimony was that when he gave the note to Alfredo Rezendi he told him it was not to be used unless Eurez needed it to make its payroll. Defendants presented no proof that when the note was discounted by Eurez no part of its proceeds was required by Eurez to make its payroll, but in any event, the court finds that plaintiff took the note without notice of that restriction and may, therefore, enforce it even if the note was in fact used in violation of the restriction. . . .

[Judgment for plaintiff.]

Note

Chancellor Hawkland summarizes results in some typical situations as follows:

"While not entirely free from doubt, those in banking circles and in the commercial community generally believe in the existence, under Section 3-408, of rules regarding antecedent consideration that may be illustrated by the following three hypotheticals:

"(i) Accommodation party and principal debtor sign original note. The note is subsequently extended without any new consideration being supplied, and both sign the new note. Conclusion: There is consideration (antecedent) that binds the accommodation party.

"(ii) Principal debtor signs a note on account of either antecedent or present consideration and indicates to the payee that he will procure an accommodation party. He does so, and the accommodation party signs at a later time. Conclusion: The accommodation party is liable. The antecedent consideration of the principal debtor supports the contract of the accommodation party.

"(iii) Principal debtor signs a note on account of present or antecedent consideration. Subsequently, and not as part of the original transaction, the accommodation party is induced to sign the same note without being provided

any new consideration. Conclusion: The accommodation party is not liable."
W. Hawkland, Commercial Paper 101 (2d ed. 1979).

The second set of defenses we postulated above are those arising from the relationship between the accommodation party and the principal, or as defenses to the principal contract. One may take two rather different tacks in analyzing such cases. Under the first analysis, one turns to suretyship law to determine whether the asserted defense is considered a defense available to the surety against the creditor. If the answer is no, proceed no further. If the answer is yes, then apply Article 3's usual analysis. Under the second analysis, weight is placed upon UCC 3-415(3):

> As against a holder in due course and without notice of the accommodation oral proof of the accommodation is not admissible to give the accommodation party the benefit of discharges dependent on his character as such. In other cases the accommodation character may be shown by oral proof.

Problem 2-12. Father cosigns as maker a note for the purpose of accommodating Son on a loan obtained for use in Son's fledgling construction business. Three years later, Son defaults and Son's debt is discharged in bankruptcy. When Bank sues Father, Father interposes Son's discharge as a defense. Does it matter whether Father's signature also indicated accommodation status? Whether Bank otherwise had notice of the accommodation? Whether Bank is a holder in due course or only a holder?

Problem 2-13. On the same basic facts as in Problem 2-12, Father now argues that (a) Son fraudulently induced Father to enter into the contract or (b) Lender fraudulently induced Son to enter into the contract. Again, does it matter whether Father's signature also indicated accommodation status? Whether Bank is a holder in due course or only a holder?

Problem 2-14. Lee obtained a loan in the amount of $30,000 from Credit Union. Before granting the loan, Credit Union required Lee to provide co-makers, which Lee did. The loan was granted and became delinquent early in the following summer. No attempt was made at that time to collect the note. Late in the summer Lee appeared at a dinner meeting of Credit Union's board of directors and delivered a postdated check in an amount sufficient to bring the loan current through the date on the check. Although the check was postdated two months, Lee assured the directors it would be covered when payable. On that assurance Credit Union did nothing further until October. It then presented the check, which was dishonored due to insufficient funds. Up through this point, Credit Union made no attempt to collect from the comakers, nor did it notify them of the delinquencies or its acceptance of the postdated check. In August of the following year Credit Union learned that Lee had filed a petition in bankruptcy. At that time it first contacted one of the comakers and sued her on the note. Credit Union objected to admission of oral evidence to show the accommodation status of the comakers. It is conceded, however, that Credit Union is a holder in due course. Is the evidence admissible? What is the liability of the comakers?

Problem 2-15. In a jurisdiction that followed the doctrine of Pain v. Packard in pre-Code law (see text at p. 69 supra), what is the vitality of the doctrine under the Code?

The final class of defenses that must be considered are the "classic" suretyship defenses, such as modification of the principal obligation. These defenses seem clearly within the ambit of UCC 3-415(3). The accommodation party's liability may also be affected by UCC 3-606:

Section 3-606. Impairment of Recourse or of Collateral

(1) The holder discharges any party to the instrument to the extent that without such party's consent the holder
   (a) without express reservation of rights releases or agrees not to sue any person against whom the party has to the knowledge of the holder a right of recourse or agrees to suspend the right to enforce against such person the instrument or collateral or otherwise discharges such person, except that failure or delay in effecting any required presentment, protest or notice of dishonor with respect to any such person does not discharge any party as to whom presentment, protest or notice of dishonor is effective or unnecessary; or
   (b) unjustifiably impairs any collateral for the instrument given by or on behalf of the party or any person against whom he has a right of recourse.
(2) By express reservation of rights against a party with a right of recourse the holder preserves
   (a) all his rights against such party as of the time when the instrument was originally due; and
   (b) the right of the party to pay the instrument as of that time; and
   (c) all rights of such party to recourse against others.

ETELSON v. SUBURBAN TRUST CO.
263 Md. 376, 283 A.2d 408, 9 UCC Rep. 1371 (1971)

FINAN, Judge. The appellants, Jerome A. and Marilyn F. Etelson, contest a decision of the Circuit Court for Montgomery County (Levine, J.) awarding a judgment in the amount of $2,455.07 against them, as the endorsers of a promissory note, and in favor of the appellee, Suburban Trust Company (Bank).

On July 31, 1969, the Bank made a loan to the J. M. Kalista Company, Inc., a Maryland corporation. Mr. Etelson, as the President of the Kalista Company, executed on behalf of the corporation a promissory note payable to the order of the Bank in the amount of $2,400.00. As security for this transaction the Bank accepted a security interest in a 1969 truck owned by the corporation, and additionally demanded that Mr. and Mrs. Etelson guarantee the payment of the note. Although a financing statement covering the truck was signed by Mr. Etelson on July 31, 1969, the Bank did not attempt to perfect its interest by filing until January 28, 1970, fifteen days after the Kalista Company had been declared bankrupt in the United States District Court for the District of Maryland.

At some time prior to March 5, 1970, and after default by the Kalista Company on the note, the Bank repossessed the truck. On April 6, 1970, the Trustee in Bankruptcy notified the Bank that in view of the late filing date of the financing statement, the Bank had lost the priority of its security interest. The Bank then released the truck to the Trustee in Bankruptcy who subsequently sold it at public auction for 1,400.00.

The Bank then brought an action on the note against the Etelsons, as the endorsers. The Etelsons attempting to rely on UCC 3-606(1)(b), 9-207(1) and 9-302(1), defended on the grounds that the Bank, by its negligence in failing to make a timely recording of the financing statement, had impaired the security and therefore could not recover from the endorsers, or in the alternative, that the sum of $1,400.00 received from the sale of the truck by the Trustee in Bankruptcy, should be applied against the endorsers' indebtedness to the Bank.

The following significant language appears in the endorsement on the back of the note:

> I/We, the endorser(s), do hereby jointly and severally (1) guarantee the payment of this note; (2) consent to any modification of the terms of the note or the release or exchange of any collateral without notice; and (3) authorize judgment by confession against each of us under the terms on the face of the note.
>
> /s/ *Jerome A. Etelson*
> /s/ *Marilyn F. Etelson*

The trial court in rejecting the Etelsons' arguments, which were premised on the negligence of the Bank in its untimely filing of the financing statement, commented: ". . . the failure of the plaintiff [Bank] to record the instrument so as to make the collateral available for partial satisfaction is not available as a defense since the plaintiff [Bank] violated no duty which it owed to the defendants to record timely."

From a judgment in favor of the Bank in the amount of $2,454.07, the Etelsons appealed.

We have been referred to no Maryland cases, and have found none dispositive of the issue before us. However, there are cases from other jurisdictions upon which the appellants rely which generally hold that where a creditor releases or negligently fails to protect security put in his possession or under his control by the principal debtor, the obligation of the endorser will be extinguished to the extent of the value of the security so released or left unprotected. Shaffer v. Davidson, 445 P.2d 13 (Wyo. 1968); . . . It would further appear that Anderson's Uniform Commercial Code, Vol. 3, §3-606:8, pg. 129 (Second Edition), supports this view.[1]

In the instant case, however, the Etelsons by agreeing to the broad language of the endorsement limited the protection to which they might have otherwise been entitled under the UCC. It is clear from the express wording of the endorsement that the Bank could have released the collateral at any time without notice to the Etelsons and without the release affecting the Etelsons' obligation to pay. It would be illogical to rule that the Bank had a duty to file the financing statement and its failure to do so released the endorsers, when under the endorsement it could have released the collateral with impunity.

The UCC recognizes that there may be times where parties to an instrument may choose to alter the general provisions of the UCC to meet their particular purposes. UCC 1-102(3).[2] The appellants did not attack the propriety of the endorsement in the court below nor do they on appeal. Additionally, it appears from the record that the Bank was the party which sought the collateral as security for its own benefit and the taking of the chattel mortgage as security for the loan was not part of any inducement extended to the Etelsons to obtain their endorsement. In fact, as guarantors of "payment" of the loan their liability is indistinguishable from that of a co-maker. See Official Comment, UCC 3-416.

Under the facts of this case, the lower court was correct in holding that the Bank owed no duty to the Etelsons to record the financing statement and hence the failure to file did not affect their obligations as endorsers.

Judgment affirmed, appellants to pay costs.

Problem 2-16. Ivan L. Anderson and Stanley D. Lee are majority stockholders, directors, and officers of the St. Charles Lumber and Fuel Co. Ander-

---

1. "The failure to perfect a security interest under Article 9 is an 'impairing' of collateral within the discharge provision of Article 3. Consequently, where a creditor is given a chattel mortgage on an automobile to secure payment of a note, the chattel mortgage constitutes 'collateral' and if the creditor fails to file the mortgage with the result that it has no effect as against a subsequent purchaser of the automobile, there is a failure to preserve collateral within the meaning of Code, §9-207, and an accommodation maker on the note is discharged under Code, §3-606." Anderson, supra at 129-130.

2. UCC 1-102(3) states, "The effect of provisions of this Act may be varied by agreement, except as otherwise provided in this Act and except that the obligations of good faith, diligence, reasonableness and care prescribed by this Act may not be disclaimed by agreement but the parties may by agreement determine the standards by which the performance of such obligations is to be measured if such standards are not manifestly unreasonable."

son and Lee negotiate with Wohlhuter for a $50,000 loan. Wohlhuter makes
the loan and receives a promissory note signed as follows:

Ivan L. Anderson	St. Charles Lumber and Fuel Co.
Stanley D. Lee	By: Ivan L. Anderson (Seal)
	President
Ann P. Lee	Attest: Stanley D. Lee (Seal)
Annette Anderson	Secretary

A security agreement (chattel mortgage) under which the corporation
pledges its inventory as collateral secures the loan. The agreement provides
that the inventory is to be maintained in such an amount that the indebtedness owed by the debtor to the secured party at all times will not exceed 80
percent of the value of the security.

The note and security agreement are given to Wohlhuter on February 15,
1966, and he files the security agreement in the office of the county recorder of
deeds on February 17, 1966. He does not, however, file either a copy of the
security agreement or a financing statement with the secretary of state. Assume as a result that the security interest is not properly perfected. No principal payments are made by the St. Charles Lumber and Fuel Co. during the
time the Andersons and Lees own the corporation, but the interest is paid as
accrued.

In June of 1968, the Andersons and the Lees sell all of their stock in the
St. Charles Lumber and Fuel Co. to Barrett Paper Co. and resign as officers.
At the time of the sale there is sufficient inventory on hand to satisfy the
security agreement made with Wohlhuter. Wohlhuter is made aware of the
disposition and sale of the lumber company. The Barrett Paper Co. is informed of the outstanding mortgage on the inventory and makes a $15,000
payment on the principal of the note to Wohlhuter at this time.

Subsequently, in November of 1969, the St. Charles Lumber and Fuel
Co. finds itself in financial trouble and sells all its inventory of plywood and
lumber supplies to another company in a bulk transfer, apparently at a time
when the inventory on hand is sufficient to satisfy the original security agreement. The purchaser is unaware, however, of the Wohlhuter security interest
in the inventory. During the six months following the sale the lumber and
plywood are consumed. In mid-1970, Wohlhuter sues to recover from Ivan
Anderson, Stanley Lee, and their spouses. What result?

PART II

Personal Property Secured Transactions

We turn now to another legal institution designed to decrease the risk that an obligation will not be performed: the security interest in personal property. Assume Lender lends $10,000 to Borrower and Borrower promises to repay the loan in one year. Lender may decrease his risk of loss if Borrower does not repay by using the *Article 9 secured transaction*. Under this mechanism Borrower designates some of his property as available to Lender if Borrower should not repay as promised. Upon Borrower's default, Lender may dispose of this property without going to court and may apply the proceeds to Borrower's debt. Moreover, if Lender has properly publicized his interest, his claim will have priority over other potential claimants to the property. Although personal property secured transactions were known before the Code, Article 9 unifies and simplifies the several pre-Code mechanisms (pledge, chattel mortgage, conditional sale, etc.) that governed the use of personal property as security. The following chapters explore Article 9, its place within the framework of the Code, and its relation to other federal and state regulation.

Although the following chapters stand on their own they also build on the previous two chapters. A Code security interest "secures payment or performance of an obligation" (UCC 1-201(37)), and this *obligation* is very often represented by the promissory note studied in Chapter 1. Similarly, although the surety arrangement explored in Chapter 2 is conceptually and legally distinct from the collateral security arrangement, the two arrangements are functionally equivalent in that they both decrease the risk of loss if the principal obligor does not perform as promised.[1] Moreover, you will find in practice that

---

1. For a general comparison of personal property security arrangements and surety arrangements, see Peters, Suretyship Under Article 3 of the Uniform Commercial Code, 77 Yale L.J. 833, 833-835 (1968). The author notes the "irreducible costs of collateral security arrangements" that may be avoided by the use of a surety arrangement. "A borrower may well have misgivings both about the notoriety and about the controls which a secured transaction is likely to entail. The Code minimizes these drawbacks, but it cannot eliminate them: a secured creditor must still perfect, in order to prevail over competing third parties, and perfection will ordinarily take the form of a financing statement placed on a public record; a secured creditor must still police, for maximum protection in the event of his debtor's bankruptcy, and policing must, despite the

many creditors will request both collateral and a guaranty agreement. You should therefore keep the previous chapters in mind as you go through the following materials.

comforting repeal of Benedict v. Ratner, [268 U.S. 353 (1925)], encompass at least the proceeds from collateral and perhaps even the acquisition of collateral. No well-advised secured creditor will be likely to forego these protective maneuvers, and their execution involves real costs to the borrower. Not only must he bear the expenses of administration inherent in a secured transaction, but he must also run the risk that the filing of the financing statement may impede the flow of unsecured credit from independent suppliers and servicers." Id. at 833-834.

CHAPTER 3

Introduction: Equipment Financing

A. INTRODUCTION TO PERSONAL PROPERTY SECURITY LAW

The following overview is designed to give you an aerial photograph of Article 9 with the significant landmarks pointed out. Keep the landmarks in sight and you will not get lost. Remember that you are not entering Dante's forest: the paths through the trees may be obscure at first, but others have gone before you and have returned with enlightenment. Do not lose hope.

These landmarks in Article 9 cluster around five basic questions:

1. Is the transaction governed by Article 9?
2. Is the transaction enforceable by the parties?
3. Is proper notice of the enforceable transaction given to third parties?
4. Does the secured party have priority over specific classes of competing claimants?
5. What rights and duties do the parties to the transaction have when the debtor defaults on the underlying obligation?

1. Scope of an Article 9 Secured Transaction

When asking whether Article 9 governs a transaction there are three major clusters of questions to be considered:

(a) Is the transaction *functionally* one where personal property or a fixture is being used to secure payment or performance of an obligation? The test is function, *not* form. A businessman may wish to give the transaction a particular form. He might structure the acquisition of equipment as a lease in order to take advantage of income tax benefits. Article 9 does not prohibit the use of this form, but the article's provisions will apply to the transaction if functionally the lessor is financing the purchase price. Because scope questions of this kind require looking through form to substance, they can be quite troubling to the unwary lawyer who is unfamiliar with the true nature of the transaction. UCC 9-102 and 1-201(37) are the Code landmarks, but you must also look to the growing body of case law to learn to recognize the facts that show what the function of a transaction actually is.

(b) A transaction may meet the functional test outlined above but be excluded from the scope of Article 9 because of some extrinsic policy reason. UCC 9-104 sets out these exclusions. There is no unifying theme underlying the reasons for the exclusions; you must check UCC 9-104 until you are familiar with the transactions excluded. You will have to be careful because a transaction may not be omitted from Article 9 for all purposes. For example, the use of bank deposit accounts as collateral is not included because these accounts do not customarily serve as commercial collateral, but when the accounts include the proceeds of other collateral some of the rules of Article 9 apply (UCC 9-104(*l*)).

(c) A transaction that involves contacts with several states may meet the functional test and not be excluded, but there still may be a question of *which state's version* of Article 9 applies. UCC 1-105 and 9-103 try to answer these conflict-of-laws questions. (In jurisdictions where the 1962 Code is still in force you will also have to consult UCC 9-102.) Because all jurisdictions except Louisiana have adopted some version of Article 9 many potential conflicts have been eliminated. As a practical matter the question of which law applies arises primarily when you try to decide where to file a financing statement (a public notice to third parties).

To sum up, you will answer scope questions by consulting UCC 1-105, 1-201(37), 9-102, 9-103, and 9-104. As a matter of logical priority you will ask scope questions first. We suggest that your analysis should follow the steps outlined above. You should note, however, that although most secured transactions will not raise scope problems, those relatively few transactions that do are often complex.

Example 1. Dealer sells a washing machine to Buyer for use in Buyer's home. Buyer makes a down payment of $100 and agrees to pay the remaining $360 in equal monthly installments over 24 months. Buyer signs a document entitled "Conditional Sales Agreement," which sets out the payment terms and grants to Dealer a security interest in the washing machine to secure Buyer's payment obligation. This transaction is governed by Article 9 of the Uniform Commercial Code. Buyer has granted a security interest in personal property (UCC 1-201(37), 9-102(1)(a)) in a transaction not excluded from the coverage of Article 9 (UCC 9-104). That the document uses the pre-Code language of conditional sales makes no difference (UCC 9-102(2)). Nor would it make a difference that the washing machine became a *fixture* as defined by non-Code state law because Article 9 also covers security interests in fixtures (UCC 9-102(1)(a), 9-313).

To decide that Article 9 applies to the transaction does not mean, of course, that other law does not also apply. Article 9 as enacted in a particular jurisdiction may subject the transaction not only to its own provisions but also to the provisions of other state legislation. This is quite likely here because it is a consumer transaction (UCC 9-203(4); see UCC 1-104). The transaction is also a sales transaction, and Article 2 of the Code will govern the sales aspects of the agreement (for example, issues as to the quality of the washing machine; see UCC 2-102). In addition, federal law such as the truth-in-lending provisions of the Consumer Credit Protection Act (15 U.S.C. §§1601-1667e) may apply no matter what the Code or other state law provides.

2. Creation of an Enforceable Security Interest

Article 9 regulates *consensual* security interests in personal property and fixtures. The agreement that creates or provides for a security interest is called a *security agreement*. To determine whether the agreement is *enforceable* and when the security interest *attaches* you will consult UCC 9-203. (In jurisdictions where the 1962 Code is still in force you will consult both UCC 9-203 and 9-204.)

To be enforceable the security agreement either must be in a writing that describes the collateral and is signed by the debtor or the secured party must take possession of the collateral pursuant to agreement. This requirement is in the nature of a statute of frauds. In addition, the secured party must give value (for example, by making or promising to make a loan) and the debtor must have rights in the property used as collateral.

The Code distinguishes *enforceability* from *attachment*. A security interest attaches when it becomes enforceable against specific collateral but the parties may agree to delay the time when the security interest will attach.[1]

There are several refinements to this basic scheme. If the debtor disposes of any property to which the security interest has attached, the interest will attach automatically to the identifiable *proceeds* received on the disposition unless the security agreement otherwise provides. This new interest in proceeds may be *in addition to* the interest in the property disposed of because the original interest continues notwithstanding disposition unless the secured party has agreed to the disposition or, with some exceptions, the disposition was in the ordinary course of business. UCC 9-203(3), 9-306(2). A security interest will

---

1. Although the draftsmen made a conscious effort to avoid using terminology associated with pre-Code security devices (e.g., lien, pledge, mortgage), Article 9 continues to share terms with related areas of the law. *Attachment*, for example, is used in Article 9 to refer to when a security interest comes into existence. See 1962 UCC 9-204; 1972 UCC 9-203(1) (combining concept of attachment with that of enforceability). The term *attachment*, however, is also used in non-Code law to refer to the writ of attachment, which is a non-consensual judicial writ by which a party to litigation may obtain a lien on another party's property. You may have read U.S. Supreme Court decisions exploring due process limitations on state judicial process, such as prejudgment attachment. See, for example, Fuentes v. Shevin, 407 U.S. 67 (1972) (summary seizure under replevin statute unconstitutional where writ issued prejudgment on ex parte application to court clerk without notice to possessor of property and without opportunity for prompt judicial hearing).

also attach automatically to other property subsequently acquired by the debtor if the security agreement includes an *after-acquired property clause* that describes the property. UCC 9-204(1).

While "fringe" problems will arise as they do in any area of the law, you should note the simplicity of the Code's requirements for creation of a security interest and how easily these requirements will be met in most cases. Consider the credit purchase of a TV set by a consumer from a retailer who wishes to retain a security interest in the goods sold. The sale of the set itself will satisfy both the requirement that the secured party give value and that the debtor have rights in the collateral. Because the interest will be nonpossessory (that is, the consumer-debtor rather than the seller-secured party will be in possession of the set), a writing is required. However, the sales slip evidencing the sale may be drafted to serve this purpose by simply providing in it that the seller retains a security interest. If the retailer fills in a description of the set on the face of this sales slip and requires the debtor to sign it, all the requirements for the creation of an enforceable security interest are fulfilled and the security interest will attach to the set.

To sum up, if you wish to determine whether a security agreement is enforceable you should consult UCC 9-203 (and UCC 9-204 where applicable).

To understand the consequences of having an enforceable security agreement with a security interest attached you must consult UCC 9-201: the security agreement is effective "according to its terms between the parties, against purchasers of the collateral and against creditors"—except where the Code provides otherwise. As we shall see, the Code provides otherwise in many cases.

Example 2. Dealer sells a washing machine to Buyer for use in his home. Buyer makes a down payment of $100. Buyer agrees to pay the remaining $360 in equal monthly installments over the next 24 months and orally grants Dealer a security interest in the washing machine to secure payment of this obligation. The washing machine is delivered to Buyer. Dealer does not have an attached security interest in the washing machine. Buyer has not signed a security agreement and Dealer does not have possession of the washing machine. Dealer, therefore, may not enforce the security interest against the debtor or third parties. UCC 9-203(1). Note that the contract for sale of the washing machine *is* enforceable because the price is less than $500 and therefore not subject to the Article 2 statute of frauds. UCC 2-201(1); cf. UCC 1-206.

3.   Perfection of the Security Interest

In practice you will find many disputes turn on whether or not a security interest is *perfected*. Although there are several exceptions noted below, perfection of the security interest occurs when the interest has attached, as described above, and is publicized. Publicity of the secured party's interest is usually given by filing a short notice (called a financing statement) in a public file but publicity may also be given by having the secured party take possession of the collateral.

The consequence of perfecting a security interest is that the secured party will have priority over many, but not all, potential conflicting claims of third parties. The law may make exceptions to the secured party's priority to promote other policies. Once the secured party perfects its interest, however, it has taken all the steps possible to maximize the legal effectiveness of the interest.

To determine whether a security interest is perfected requires you to take the following steps:

(a) classify the collateral within the elaborate definitions of UCC 9-105, 9-106, and 9-109;

(b) determine whether the interest is a purchase money security interest under UCC 9-107;

(c) find out if the security interest has attached as outlined above (UCC 9-203, 9-204);

(d) determine if a filing is required by UCC 9-302 or whether the exceptions to filing set out in that section apply;

(e) check UCC 9-304 to see if that section requires the secured party to take possession in order to perfect the interest;

(f) if filing is required or permitted, examine UCC 9-401, 9-402, and 9-403 to determine if a validly-completed notice was filed in the proper office and has not lapsed by the passage of time.

Filing a notice will be the normal means of perfecting a security interest in most cases you encounter. Taking possession of collateral is in theory a substitute means of perfecting in many cases and is even required in the case of money and most instruments. In addition, you should note two other means of perfecting an interest. A purchase money security interest in consumer goods is "automatically perfected" on attachment without the need to file (UCC 9-302(1)(d)). Temporary perfection without the need to file is also provided in specialized commercial contexts where the debtor has possession of very specific types of collateral for a short period of time (UCC 9-304(4) and (5), and 9-306(3)).

All this detail may bewilder you at first. Remember, though, that the basic directions on how to perfect an interest are set out in UCC 9-302 through 9-306. If you read these sections and follow the steps outlined above you should be able to determine quickly and accurately whether a security interest is perfected.

One final note on a point that generation after generation of students stumbles over: the Code distinguishes between a *security agreement,* which creates or provides for a security interest, and a *financing statement,* which is the notice filed to perfect the security interest. The requirements of a security agreement under UCC 9-203 are only two: that the debtor sign the agreement, and that the agreement describe the collateral. The *statutory* function of this writing, as noted, is to serve as a writing for statute of frauds purposes. The *business* function, however, is also to serve as a statement of the agreement between the parties. Thus in certain types of secured transactions the security agreement may run to several pages, since it will include not merely the statutory minimum requirements but many clauses covering additional rights and duties of the parties, such as a clause requiring the debtor to maintain insurance covering the collateral.

The requirements of the financing statement are found in UCC 9-402; they are likewise minimal. As a matter of practice, virtually all states have adopted a simple form that meets UCC 9-402's requirements, and most UCC filings are made using this standard form. The function of the financing statement is simply to provide a public record that will serve to place other creditors, potential lenders, or purchasers on notice of the possible existence of a security interest in property of the debtor. We explore this distinction further in the material following this note.

Example 3. Dealer sells a washing machine to Buyer for use in Buyer's home. By written agreement Dealer retains a security interest in the washer to secure payment of the purchase price. Dealer does not file a financing statement. Notwithstanding his failure to file, Dealer has a perfected security interest. He is a seller who retained a security interest to secure the purchase price of goods (purchase money security interest), and the goods were bought for use primarily in the household (consumer goods). Dealer's security interest, therefore, is automatically perfected (UCC 9-302(1)(d)).

4. Priority of Competing Claims to the Same Collateral

The fourth major landmark in the law of secured transactions is the area of priorities. As we noted above, the perfection of a security interest increases the protection that a secured party enjoys against third parties but does not give absolute protection. Some third party claimants are given a special priority that enables them to take priority over even a perfected security interest. Furthermore, the priority that certain claimants will enjoy against a secured party will depend in some instances upon the mode of perfection the secured party has chosen where more than one mode is available. The Code's rules determining priorities appear in UCC 9-301, and 9-306 through 9-316. More specifically, the three most likely competing claimants will be the lien creditor (UCC 9-301),[2] the buyer in ordinary course (UCC 9-306, 9-307), and another secured party (UCC 9-312).

2. A lien is an interest in or charge against property to secure payment of a debt or performance of an obligation. The holder of a lien on property has a claim against the property that can be enforced by foreclosure and that will have priority over most of the claims of unsecured creditors and subsequent lienholders. Liens may arise by judicial process, by statute, or by agree-

An illustration of how a priority rule works will show the difference between priority and perfection. Assume that a retailer obtains a line of credit from a bank secured by a security interest in all the retailer's inventory. Assume further that the bank has properly perfected this security interest by filing an appropriate financing statement with the secretary of state. If at some later time the retailer files a petition in bankruptcy, the bank will receive protection against the trustee in bankruptcy as representative of the unsecured creditors of the retailer. Under both the Bankruptcy Code and the Uniform Commercial Code the trustee has the rights of a lien creditor. The strict UCC authority for the bank's protection is UCC 9-201. If the security interest is unperfected, the trustee will be able to invoke a very broad exception to UCC 9-201, to wit, UCC 9-301, which subordinates the interest of an unperfected security interest holder to a broad range of other claimants, including the lien creditor. Since the bank has perfected its interest, however, the trustee loses the benefit of his rights as a lien creditor under UCC 9-301.

You should not read the above example as saying that the bank will win against all potential claimants. Indeed, strictly speaking, the only assured result of perfecting a security interest is that the secured party will not lose to a third party who can cite only UCC 9-301 in support of his claim to priority. For example, in the above illustration, assume that an expensive item is sold out of the retailer's inventory to a consumer. Bank then attempts to assert its security interest. Good sense tells us that banks financing inventory should not, as a general rule, be able to assert that security interest against the collateral in the hands of a buyer in ordinary course; a contrary result would be disruptive of retail trade or inventory financing or both. The Code comes to the same conclusion as our common sense, in this instance in UCC 9-306(2), 9-307(1).

Note that, as a matter of logical structure, this priority for the buyer is simply another exception to the "general" rule of UCC 9-201. The *logical* structure of the Code is to provide for a "general" rule of protection against

---

ment. An Article 9 security interest might be described as a consensual lien. The lien creditor in UCC 9-301 is a creditor who has obtained a lien by judicial process (e.g., by attachment, levy, or the like) although the assignee for the benefit of creditors and the trustee in bankruptcy, whose liens might be said to arise by statute, are also deemed lien creditors. See UCC 9-301(3).

When you come across the word *lien* you should be careful to read it in context. A *judgment lien* usually arises when a judgment is rendered and adopted (recorded in a special book kept by the clerk of the court rendering the judgment) but, with the exception of three states, this lien only attaches to real property. A *judicial lien* includes liens that arise through legal process and may include judgment liens. See, for example, the definition of *judicial lien* in BC 101(30). Unfortunately, usage is not always consistent. The Internal Revenue Code, for example, uses the term *judgment lien creditor* in a sense that includes not only the judgment lien but also liens that may arise by levy of execution. See 26 U.S.C. §§6321-6323 (1982); 26 C.F.R. §301.623(h)-1(g) (1984).

For the purposes of UCC 9-301 it is important to know the date on which a lien is deemed effective. The Code does not provide an answer and unfortunately state law is not uniform. In some states the lien may arise only when a sheriff levies on property by taking it into his custody; in some states the lien may arise when the writ is delivered to the sheriff and continue in effect if the sheriff levies promptly; in yet other states the lien may arise when the sheriff levies but for priority purposes be deemed to relate back to the date on which the writ was delivered to the sheriff. If you look at UCC 9-301 closely you will see how these different rules might lead to different results.

third parties in UCC 9-201. This rule is applicable as soon as the secured party has created an enforceable security interest: it does not require that the interest be perfected. However, UCC 9-201, the general rule, is applicable "unless otherwise provided." A very broad provision to the contrary, effective whenever the security interest is unperfected, is found in UCC 9-301. A series of narrower provisions to the contrary, applicable even though the security interest in question is perfected, is found in the priority rules of UCC 9-306 to 9-316.

Example 4. Dealer sells a washing machine to Buyer, a consumer, and retains by written agreement a security interest in the washer to secure payment of the purchase price. Dealer does not file a financing statement but, as explained in Example 3, Dealer's interest is automatically perfected. To what extent is Dealer protected against potential claims to the property by third parties?

(a) Dealer's interest has priority over the claims of Buyer's general unsecured creditors regardless of whether Dealer's interest is perfected. UCC 9-201.

(b) As a perfected security interest Dealer's interest has priority over the claims of Buyer's lien creditors. UCC 9-201, 9-301.

(c) As a perfected purchase money security interest Dealer's interest will be prior to virtually all competing secured parties. UCC 9-312(4); cf. 9-312(5).

(d) Unless Dealer agrees to the disposition of the washer by Buyer, Dealer will have priority over most purchasers from Buyer. UCC 9-306; cf. 9-307(1). Dealer's interest is cut off, however, if Buyer sells to another consumer who does not know about the security interest. Only by filing is Dealer protected from this possibility. UCC 9-307(2).

5.   Remedies upon Default

The final landmark of Article 9 is Part 5, which sets out the remedies available to a secured party upon the default of the debtor and the protections afforded the debtor against creditor overreaching. The Code provisions governing these questions are all located in the 9-500s. In increasing instances these provisions must be read in conjunction with special debtor-protection legislation, particularly if a consumer credit transaction is involved. From an analytic perspective, the issues of remedy upon default are not complex. The key idea is that, subject to certain statutory safeguards to protect the debtor, a secured party may take possession of the collateral and dispose of it without going to court— although the secured party is not precluded from going to court. These flexible rules are designed to decrease expenses and increase the amount realized on the disposition. The most common legal problems are whether the secured party repossessed the collateral without breaching the peace, whether he disposed of the goods in a commercially reasonable manner, and, if not, what the consequences are. No matter what legal rights the secured party may have, however, he will often have to face the practical problem of deciding what to do when a debtor is recalcitrant: go to court or wait until the debtor finally surrenders the collateral.

You should bear in mind two points. First, *default* is not defined; it generally includes a failure to make payments when due. The secured party, however, will usually include much more extensive provisions in the security agreement listing events that shall or may constitute default. Second, a secured party has available all the Code's remedies upon default, regardless of whether the security interest is perfected.

Example 5. Dealer sells a washing machine to Buyer, who makes a down payment and agrees to pay the balance in 24 monthly installments. The security agreement provides that if Buyer does not pay an installment when due he will be in default and Dealer shall have the rights of a secured party under the Uniform Commercial Code. After five monthly payments Buyer fails to make a payment. Dealer repossesses the washing machine, accelerates payment of the remaining installments, gives notice to Buyer that he plans to sell it by private sale after two weeks, sells it, and claims a deficiency (i.e., the difference between what is owed to Dealer, including repossession and resale expenses, and what was received by Dealer from disposition of the washing machine). Buyer is responsible for the deficiency.

Note the protections the Code provides the Buyer. There are limits on permissible contract clauses limiting or waiving Dealer's responsibilities in the default proceedings (UCC 9-501(3)), and repossession must not breach the peace (UCC 9-503). After default Buyer has the right to redeem the washing machine by tendering the amount owed to the Dealer (UCC 9-506). If Dealer proposes to keep the washing machine in satisfaction of the amount owed ("strict foreclosure"), Buyer may force him to sell the machine in the hope of realizing a surplus to be turned over to Buyer (UCC 9-505). Disposition of the washing machine requires prior notice be given to Buyer and that all actions be taken in a commercially reasonable manner (UCC 9-504). Buyer may restrain Dealer or recover damages if Dealer does not comply with the Code provisions (UCC 9-507).

You should not be misled, however, by this overly simplified summary of the Code provisions. Most default proceedings do not involve redemption, strict foreclosure, or commercially unreasonable actions. Most creditors, it has been suggested, act in a commercially reasonable manner because they wish to minimize their losses. A deficiency judgment against a defaulting debtor is not likely to offer much solace to a creditor.

Note: Secured Financing in a Business Context

The proliferation of financial institutions is a twentieth-century phenomenon. At the end of the nineteenth century commercial banks and the securities markets were the primary external sources of business funds. Banks, however, were conservative in their lending policies, and the securities markets were a source of funds primarily for larger enterprises. Rapid industrial expansion and growing consumer demand for durable goods, especially the automobile, created a need for new credit institutions. Sales finance companies financed the installment sales of equipment and consumer durables by taking assignments of the contracts. Commercial finance companies financed riskier smaller ventures and looked to accounts receivable and inventory as collateral. Credit unions and personal finance companies supplied funds directly to con-

TABLE 3-1
Major Sources of Funds for American Business

Instruments or form in which funds are acquired	*Major suppliers of funds*
Normal trade credit	Vendors selling to the firm[1]
Accrued expenses	Miscellaneous creditors[1]
Accrued U.S. income taxes	U.S. government[1]
Special credits from suppliers	Major vendors[2]
Customer loans and advances	Major customers[2]
Short-term bank loans	Commercial banks[2]
Loans from specialized lending companies	Business finance companies, factors, sales finance companies[2]
Commercial paper (short-term notes payable)	Nonfinancial corporations, banks and other financial institutions[3]
Term bank loans	Commercial banks[3]
Term loans—directly placed with nonbank lenders	Insurance companies, pension funds, small-business investment companies[3]
Long-term debt instruments (bonds, notes, debentures, mortgages)	Primarily insurance companies, pension funds, savings banks and other institutional investors, (to lesser extent) individual investors[4]
Preferred stock	Institutional investors, individual investors[4]
Common stock	Individual investors, institutional investors[4]
Inflows from operations represented by retained earnings; noncash charges to earnings (depreciation, etc.)	Operations of the business[5]

Notes: The following notes indicate the broad classification of sources and the classification by length of term.
1. Spontaneous: Short term.
2. Negotiated: Short term.
3. Negotiated: Intermediate term.
4. Negotiated: Long term.
5. Operational: Long term.

(Source: P. Hunt, C. Williams & G. Donaldson, Basic Business Finance: A Text, p. 112 (1974))

sumers. The Depression, the war effort, and reconstruction after World War II also saw the introduction of government lending institutions that continue to be important in the financing of agriculture, transportation, and small business ventures.

The markets served by these financial institutions have changed significantly, especially in the last two decades. For many years banks were content to lend money to finance companies either directly or indirectly by the purchase of short-term commercial paper issued by the finance companies. In recent years, however, commercial banks have competed vigorously in markets formerly left to the finance companies, such as accounts-receivable financing and consumer lending. The present call for deregulation and the expansion of financial intermediaries into new markets suggests that the present trend toward greater competition in all credit markets will continue.

For the purposes of these materials, commercial banks and finance companies are the most important financial intermediaries. Among the more important restrictions in this context are the limitations on loans to any one customer (e.g., 12 U.S.C. §84), the reserve requirements that may restrict the availability of credit (e.g., 12 U.S.C. §461; 12 C.F.R. §204), and the prohibition on banks acting as guarantors or sureties. By contrast, finance companies are usually subject to less elaborate and stringent state law regulation, except for loans to consumers. The lending of all institutions, however, is usually subject to the same state or federal usury laws that prescribe the maximum interest rates that may be charged.

While secured lending is clearly important to these institutions, one should not overestimate the importance of Article 9 security interests for either the lender or the borrower. Lenders rely primarily on the three C's (Capital, Character, Capacity) and usually look to collateral and legal proceedings as a last resort. Indeed, much short-term lending by commercial banks to business customers is unsecured. From the perspective of the businessman borrower, loans secured by collateral are only one of a variety of sources of funding, as Table 3-1, supra, illustrates.

The authors of the business finance text from which Table 3-1 is adapted go on to state both the importance and limitations of secured financing.

P. HUNT, C. WILLIAMS & G. DONALDSON, BASIC BUSINESS FINANCE: A TEXT
286-287, 306 (1974)

Why do lenders so frequently prefer a *secured position* to the status of an unsecured creditor? As suggested earlier, lenders take collateral primarily as a means of reducing the risk of loss through nonrepayment of their loans. The risks of loss may be reduced by a secured position in several ways:

1. Under many security arrangements, close contact with the borrower is

required in order to maintain an effective secured position. As a byproduct of the security arrangement, the lender often gains a more complete and up-to-date acquaintance with the borrower's affairs than he would have obtained as an unsecured creditor.

2. Under many security arrangements the lender obtains a close and continuing control over assets vital to the borrower's business. This control helps to prevent the sale or diversion of assets that the lender is looking to as an ultimate source of repayment of his loan. Some lenders would be willing to accept an unsecured status provided no other creditor could obtain a prior claim. By taking key assets as security, the lender assures himself that these assets cannot be pledged to another creditor who would thereby gain priority over unsecured lenders. If the lender has full confidence in the borrower, he may seek to gain this same objective through an agreement that the borrower will not pledge assets to other lenders. Such compacts, known as *negative pledge agreements,* are used with some frequency.

3. Finally, and most basically, if the borrower encounters serious financial difficulties and cannot meet his obligations, the secured lender expects to enjoy a prior claim to the security and to the net proceeds from its disposition. . . .

Earlier in this chapter, advantages that borrowers might obtain from effective use of their assets as security for loans—greater credit, lower interest rates than on unsecured borrowing, etc.—were discussed. It is appropriate at this point to consider the serious disadvantages that can result from injudicious giving of security.

First, the increased availability of credit by giving security may encourage excessively heavy use of debt. Any borrowing involves risk to the borrower—financial risk added to the normal risks of doing business. The increased risks of debt should be appreciated and accepted only after careful and full consideration.

Second, for many firms, there is great advantage (not to say comfort) in retaining reserves of borrowing power for use in financial extremity or to finance particularly desirable investment opportunities that may develop. Obviously, security, once committed, no longer is available as the basis for further credit: and the firm that ties up all of its attractive security is in the same exposed position as the general who has committed all his reserves to battle. When secured borrowing is undertaken, the borrower should appreciate that if he concedes more security than really is required and further credit subsequently is needed, it may be hard indeed to get the old lender to release security or to dilute his own cushion by lending more against the same security.

Third, most firms depend heavily on continued trade credit from suppliers, extended on an unsecured basis. As the firm commits more and more of its best assets as security for loans, the trade creditors increasingly depend on the shrinking and poorer assets left unpledged. While it is difficult to determine in advance the exact extent to which pledging of assets can be carried without jeopardizing the continued availability of trade credit, excessive pledging of assets can result in impairment or loss of credit from alert suppliers and other unsecured creditors.

NOTES & QUESTIONS

1. *Monitoring.* Reread the above excerpt critically. It is much less true under the Code than under prior law that a lender is "required" to maintain close contact with the borrower in order to maintain an effective secured position. In any event, does anything prevent an unsecured creditor from maintaining close contact? Other commentators have suggested that secured credit is justified because it *lowers* the need and cost of monitoring the debtor. See Jackson & Kronman, Secured Financing and Priorities Among Creditors, 88 Yale L.J. 1143 (1979) (summarized at p. 215 infra).

2. *Leverage.* The authors gloss over a point of great practical importance to many lenders and their counsel: the added leverage that a secured lender enjoys if it becomes necessary to restructure the loan or if the lender would like to influence management practices. Under this view, security interests are valued as much for the potential threat they pose to the borrower as for the actual advantages enjoyed by the lender if it is necessary to resort to the security. But it is important to remember that a financer will only lend if he has determined *as a business matter* that the loan is likely to be repaid by this borrower. Collateral does not turn a bad loan into a good loan; it may, however, make a good loan slightly better.

3. *Interest rates.* The authors state that secured lending lowers interest rates. How do you square this observation with the fact that rates on so-called asset-based loans (secured lending) are usually higher than rates on unsecured loans?

4. *Further reading:* Students who do not have a business background may find it useful to consult Commercial Financing (M. Lazere ed. 1968). Texts prepared for business school students may also be useful. See, for example, E. Brigham, Financial Management Theory and Practice chs. 9-10 (2d ed. 1979); P. Hunt, C. Williams & G. Donaldson, Basic Business Finance: A Text (1974); J. Van Horne, Financial Management and Policy (5th ed. 1980); J. Weston & E. Brigham, Managerial Finance chs. 8, 15 (6th ed. 1978). For further reading on the institutional framework in which secured financing takes place, see R. Goldsmith, Financial Intermediaries (1968).

Problem 3-1. The president of the Small Tool Manufacturing Co., Inc., shows you, as outside counsel, the latest balance sheet set out below.[3] She asks

3. For guidance on how to read a balance sheet, see Merrill Lynch, Pierce, Fenner & Smith, How to Read a Financial Report (5th ed. 1981). Note that although students who have no business background frequently worry about competing with students who do, there are times when no background is an advantage. Ask a business person, for example, what *accounts receivable*

TABLE 3-2
Small Tool Manufacturing Co., Inc.
Balance Sheet—December 31, 198____

ASSETS   *(in thousands)*

Current Assets
  Cash   550
  Investment securities (at cost)   850
  Accounts receivable
    (Less allowance for bad debt: $200,000)   2,300
  Inventories   3,700

    Total current assets   7,400
Fixed Assets
  Land   750
  Building   4,800
  Machinery   1,450
  Office equipment   200

                                                                      7,200
  (Less accumulated depreciation)   2,200

    Net fixed assets   5,000

Prepayment of expenses; Deferred charges   150
Cash value of life insurance   150
Intangibles (good will, patent, trademarks)   100
   TOTAL ASSETS $12,800

LIABILITIES

Current Liabilities
  Accounts payable   1,450
  Notes payable   1,200
  Accrued expenses payable   380
  Income tax payable   320

    Total current liabilities   3,350
Long-term Liabilities
  First mortgage bonds
    (8% interest, due 1990)   2,500
  Debenture (10½% interest, due 1995)   2,000

    Total long-term liabilities   4,500

    Total Liabilities   7,850

---

include and then compare the response with the UCC definition of *account* (UCC 9-106). For the purposes of the Code, of course, the limited definition of *account* will control. For another example of a "special" Code definition, see the definition of *debtor*. See generally Mellinkoff, The Language of the Uniform Commercial Code, 77 Yale L.J. 185, 186-204 (1967) ("for all its substantive contributions, the UCC is a slipshod job of draftsmanship").

TABLE 3-2 (continued)

SHAREHOLDERS' EQUITY   *(in thousands)*

Capital Stock	
Preferred shares ($100 par value;	
6% cumulative; 100,000 authorized)	
20,000 issued & outstanding	2,000
Common shares ($1.00 par value;	
1,000,000 authorized)	
650,000 issued & outstanding	650
Retained earnings	2,300
Total Shareholders' Equity	4,950
TOTAL LIABILITIES AND SHAREHOLDERS' EQUITY	$12,800

whether you can tell if any of the corporation's assets could be used for collateral to secure a loan that she hopes to negotiate with the corporation's bank. Advise her. Does the balance sheet suggest any additional problems you may want to explore further? See UCC 9-102, 9-104, 9-105, 9-106, 9-109.

Note that this problem requires you to look closely at the Code's elaborate system of classifying collateral. Correct classification is important primarily when you are determining how to perfect a security interest in the collateral, but there are also other consequences. A useful collection of special rules for particular types of collateral is set out in Comment 5 to UCC 9-102. For a skeptical view of the utility of the Code's classification scheme, see 1 G. Gilmore, Security Interests in Personal Property 291-294 (1965) ("Anyone who approaches the Article for the first time will do well to bear in mind that the forbidding string of definitions in Part I of the Article can for most purposes be disregarded.").

Problem 3-2. Small Tool Manufacturing Co., Inc., borrows $100,000 from Chicago National Bank, and to secure repayment of the loan its president orally agrees to grant the bank a security interest in specific drills, molds, and other heavy equipment. The bank official in charge of the account asks you to review his first draft of the basic agreement.

> Small Tool Manufacturing Company of 113 East 60th Street, Chicago, Illinois, hereinafter called Owner, for value of $10 in hand paid, hereby contracts with and agrees to grant and convey to Chicago National Bank, The Loop, Chicago, Illinois, hereinafter called Financier, an Article 9 property right in certain specific equipment listed in Schedule A attached hereto and incorporated herein by reference, and any and all additions, accessions, and substitutions thereto or therefor, all of which shall be called the Security, to collateralize the repayment of $100,000, hereinafter called Debt, which is provided for in a note of even date signed by Melanie Smith, Pres.

Advise him. See UCC 9-203, 9-105, 9-109, 9-110.

B.   A PROTOTYPE TRANSACTION: EQUIPMENT FINANCING

In the remainder of this chapter we examine more closely the skeleton of Article 9 introduced in the preceding section. We present a simple transaction in which a buyer obtains financing from a bank for the purchase of equipment and grants to the bank a security interest in the equipment to secure repayment of the loan.[4] We explore the transaction by breaking it down into the four different elements of a secured transaction discussed in the previous section: attachment, perfection, priorities, and default. Do not hesitate to look back at that section. Learning to cope with the Code is a cumulative process.

Apex Publishing Co., Inc. (Apex) is a Texas corporation with its head office and plant in Austin, Texas. Its main business is the printing and publishing of The Austin Diplomat, a daily newspaper, and Texas Commerce, a monthly magazine with a growing national circulation. To modernize its existing printing equipment and to allow for diversification, Apex management decided in November 1980 to invest in additional printing equipment. As a first step, management decides to purchase a bookbinding machine and they contact the Houston plant of American Business Machines, Inc. (ABM), a Delaware corporation. Apex and ABM reach agreement in December on the appropriate model, price, and delivery date. ABM indicates that it has a model ready for delivery by truck on receipt of the purchase price.

To finance the purchase, Apex negotiates a loan with its bank, Austin State Bank (Bank). The attorney for Bank files a financing statement (Form 3-1) with the Texas Secretary of State on January 2, 1981. Samuel Clemens, president of Apex, signs the installment note (Form 3-2) and security agreement (Form 3-3) on January 9th. At this time Bank issues a cashier's check for the purchase price payable to the order of Apex and ABM. Apex forwards the check with its indorsement to ABM. On January 12 ABM acknowledges receipt of the check and indicates that the bookbinder will be forwarded by truck from Houston on January 19 to arrive in Austin that same day. The machine is delivered as planned. ABM representatives install the bookbinder during the next three days and it begins production on January 23.

---

4. The following prototype transaction has the buyer obtain financing. This prototype sets out only one of a number of possible ways the purchase of equipment can be financed; Chapter 5 will look at some of these variations. If you are interested, you will find useful the discussion in Leary, Leasing and Other Techniques of Financing Equipment Under the U.C.C., 42 Temple L.Q. 217 (1969). For the business background of equipment financing see Commercial Financing ch. 7 (M. Lazere ed. 1968).

Under the pre-Code law of most jurisdictions the buyer in the prototype would have granted the bank a chattel mortgage interest in the equipment. Although the bank is financing the purchase of the equipment, it is not the seller and usually would not qualify as a conditional seller under pre-Code conditional sales statutes. This is not to say that the prototype could not have been restructured under pre-Code law in patterns similar to those to be explored in Chapter 5. Nevertheless, the correct legal classification of a particular business pattern was crucial when determining the validity of a pre-Code security interest. For further discussion, see 1 G. Gilmore, Security Interests in Personal Property ch. 2 (1965).

Uniform Commercial Code—FINANCING STATEMENT—Form UCC-1 (Rev. 6-19-75)

Filing Fee $3.00   IMPORTANT—Read instructions on back before filling out form

This Financing Statement is presented to a Filing Officer for filing pursuant to the Uniform Commercial Code.

1. Debtor(s) Name and Mailing Address: (Do not abbreviate)	2. Secured Party(ies) Name and Address:	3. For Filing Officer (Date, Time, Number and Filing Office):
Apex Publishing Co., Inc. 2500 Red River Austin, TX 78705	Austin State Bank 4321 Guadelupe Austin, Texas 78751	

4. This Financing Statement covers the following types (or items) of property.
(WARNING: If collateral is crops, fixtures, timber or minerals, read instructions on back.)

Printing Equipment

5. Name and Address of Assignee of Secured Party: (Use this space to describe collateral, if needed)

Check only if applicable   Number of additional sheets presented ___0___
☐ This Financing Statement is to be filed for record in the real estate records.   ☐ Products of collateral are also covered.

6. This Statement is signed by the Secured Party instead of the Debtor to perfect a security interest in collateral
(Please check   ☐ already subject to a security interest in another jurisdiction when it was brought into this state, or when the debtor's location was
appropriate box)   ☐ changed to this state, or
                      ☐ already subject to a financing statement filed in another county.
                      ☐ which is proceeds of the original collateral described above in which a security interest was perfected, or
                      ☐ as to which the filing has lapsed, or
                      ☐ acquired after a change of name, identity or corporate structure of the debtor.

Apex Publishing Co., Inc.   Use whichever signature line is applicable.   The Austin State Bank

By _Samuel Clemens_   By _James A. Campbell_
(1) Filing Officer Copy - Numerical   Signature(s) of Debtor(s)   Signature(s) of Secured Party(ies)

STANDARD FORM—FORM UCC-1 (REV. 6-19-75) APPROVED BY THE SECRETARY OF STATE OF TEXAS—FORM 15-1548—

FORM 3-1
Financing Statement

113

FORM 3-2
Installment Note

$**54,489.00   No. 21,435   Due: January 9, 1986

Austin, Texas   Date: January 9, 1981

The undersigned, for value received, promises to pay to the order of The Austin State Bank, at its office at 4321 Guadalupe, Austin, Texas, Fifty-four thousand four hundred eighty-nine and xx/100 Dollars payable in 60 monthly installments of $**908.15 each beginning February 9, 1981 and the same date of each month thereafter, until paid in full, with interest at the rate of _____ percent per annum payable on the principal remaining from time to time unpaid.

It is agreed that if default be made in the payment of any of said installments of principal or interest, the entire balance of principal remaining unpaid shall at the option of the holder hereof without notice be and become forthwith due and payable. If the holder exercises this option to accelerate payment, principal and past-due interest shall bear interest at the highest rate permitted by applicable law or, if no such rate is established by applicable law, then at the rate of 18 percent per annum.

The makers, signers, sureties, and endorsers of this Note severally waive demand, presentment, notice of dishonor, notice of intent to demand or accelerate payment hereof, diligence in collecting, grace, notice, and protest, and agree to one or more extensions for any period or periods of time and partial payments, before or after maturity, without prejudice to the holder; and if this Note shall be collected by legal proceedings or through a probate or bankruptcy court, or shall be placed in the hands of an attorney for collection after default or maturity, the undersigned agrees to pay all costs of collection, including reasonable attorney's fees.

Should this Note be signed by more than one party, all of the obligations herein contained shall be the joint and several obligations of each signer hereof.

This installment Note is secured by a security interest granted by makers of this note in a security agreement of even date herewith.

All agreements between the undersigned and the holder hereof, whether now existing or hereafter arising and whether written or oral, are hereby limited so that in no contingency, whether by reason of demand for payment or acceleration of the maturity hereof or otherwise, shall the interest contracted for, charged or received by the holder hereof exceed the maximum amount permissible under applicable law.

This Note shall be construed in accordance with the laws of the State of Texas and the laws of the United States applicable to transactions in Texas.

Apex Publishing Co., Inc.

By: /s/ Samuel Clemens

President

FORM 3-3
Security Agreement

1   Apex Publishing Co., Inc., 2500 Red River, Austin, Travis
2   County, Texas (Debtor), hereby grants to The Austin State Bank
3   (Bank) a security interest in the following goods located in
4   Debtor's plant at 2500 Red River, Austin:
5   One ABM Model 3-B Bookbinder with optional work table
6   together with all parts, fittings, accessories, equipment, special
7   tools, renewals and replacements of all or any part thereof, and
8   other goods of the same class whether now owned or hereafter
9   acquired by Debtor (all hereinafter called Collateral), to secure
10   (i) the payment of a note dated January 9, 1981, executed and
11   delivered by Debtor to Bank in the sum of $54,489.00, payable
12   as to principal and interest as therein provided; (ii) further
13   advances, to be evidenced by additional notes if such advances
14   are made at Bank's option; (iii) all other liabilities (primary,
15   secondary, direct, contingent, sole, joint, or general) due or to
16   become due or which may be hereafter contracted or acquired,
17   of Debtor to Bank; and (iv) performance by Debtor of the
18   agreements hereinafter set forth.
19   Debtor Warrants: (a) Debtor is the owner of the Collateral
20   clear of all liens and security interests except the security interest
21   granted hereby; (b) Debtor has the right to make this
22   agreement; (c) the Collateral is used or bought for use primarily
23   for business purposes and will be left at the address specified
24   above; (d) the Collateral is being acquired by Debtor with the
25   proceeds of the note identified above, and the Bank is hereby
26   authorized to pay the proceeds of the loan directly to the seller
27   of the Collateral as shown on Bank's records; (e) the Collateral
28   will not be attached or affixed to real estate in such a manner
29   that it will become a fixture. [Delete (d) or (e) if inapplicable,
30   but if (e) is deleted describe real estate concerned and give name
31   of record owner here:]
32   _____.
33   Debtor Agrees that it:
34   1. Will pay the Bank all amounts payable on the note
35   mentioned above and all other notes held by Bank as and when
36   the same shall be due and payable, whether at maturity, by
37   acceleration or otherwise, and will perform all terms of said notes
38   and this or any other security or loan agreement between Debtor
39   and Bank, and will discharge all said liabilities.
40   2. Will defend the Collateral against the claims and
41   demands of all persons.
42   3. Will insure the Collateral against all hazards requested
43   by Bank in form and amount satisfactory to Bank. If Debtor fails

FORM 3-3 (continued)

44   to obtain insurance, Bank shall have the right to obtain it at
45   Debtor's expense. Debtor assigns to Bank all right to receive
46   proceeds of insurance not exceeding the unpaid balance under
47   the note, directs any insurer to pay all proceeds directly to Bank,
48   and authorizes Bank to endorse any draft for the proceeds.
49   4. Will keep the Collateral in good condition and repair,
50   reasonable wear and tear excepted, and will permit Bank and its
51   agents to inspect the Collateral at any time.
52   5. Will pay as part of the debt hereby secured all amounts,
53   including attorney's fees, with interest thereon paid by Bank
54   (a) for taxes, levies, insurance, repairs to or maintenance of the
55   Collateral, and (b) in taking possession of, disposing of or
56   preserving the Collateral after any default hereinafter described.
57   6. Will not permit any of the Collateral to be removed from
58   the above-mentioned location without the prior written consent
59   of the Bank.
60   7. Will immediately advise Bank in writing of any change
61   in any of Debtor's places of business, or the opening of any new
62   place of business.
63   8. Will not (a) permit any liens or security interests (other
64   than Bank's security interest) to attach to any of the Collateral;
65   (b) permit any of the Collateral to be levied upon under any
66   legal process; (c) dispose of any of the Collateral without the
67   prior written consent of Bank; (d) permit anything to be done
68   that may impair the value of any of the Collateral or the
69   security intended to be afforded by this agreement; or (e) permit
70   the Collateral to become an accession to other goods.
71   9. Bank is hereby appointed Debtor's attorney-in-fact to do
72   all acts and things that Bank may deem necessary to perfect and
73   continue perfected the security interest created by this security
74   agreement and to protect the Collateral.
75   Until default Debtor may retain possession of the Collateral
76   and use it in any lawful manner not inconsistent with the
77   agreements herein, or with the terms and conditions of any
78   policy of insurance thereon.
79   Upon default by Debtor in the performance of any covenant
80   or agreement herein or in the discharge of any liability to Bank,
81   or if any warranty should prove untrue, Bank shall have all of
82   the rights and remedies of a secured party under the Uniform
83   Commercial Code or other applicable law and all rights
84   provided herein, in the notes mentioned above or in any other
85   applicable security or loan agreement, all of which rights and
86   remedies shall, to the full extent permitted by law, be

FORM 3-3 (continued)

87   cumulative. Bank may require Debtor to assemble the Collateral
88   and make it available to Bank at a place to be designated by
89   Bank that is reasonably convenient to Bank and Debtor. Any
90   notice of sale, disposition or other intended action by Bank, sent
91   to Debtor at the address specified above or such other address of
92   Debtor as may from time to time be shown on Bank's records, at
93   least five days prior to such action, shall constitute reasonable   *pleas*
94   notice to Debtor. The waiver of any default hereunder shall not   *notice =*
95   be a waiver of any subsequent default.   *5 days*
96   All rights of Bank hereunder shall inure to the benefit of its
97   successors and assigns; and all obligations of Debtor shall bind
98   its heirs, executors, administrators, successors and assigns. If there
99   be more than one Debtor, their obligations hereunder shall be
100 joint and several.
101   This agreement is executed on *January 9, 1981*.

102   Apex Publishing Co., Inc.
103   (Debtor)

104   By: /s/   *Samuel Clemens*

105   Title: President

Note: Austin State Bank's loan file for Apex will undoubtedly contain many more documents. Among the more important might be a board of directors resolution authorizing corporate borrowing, separate guaranty agreements, and insurance documentation. For a summary of recommended bank loan review procedures, see Stimson, Loan Review at the Hands-on Level, J. Com. Bank Lending, Nov. 1979, at 20-23.

C.   ATTACHMENT: THE SECURITY AGREEMENT

When you review the Apex-Austin State Bank prototype transaction you will conclude no doubt that the bank has an attached and enforceable security interest in the ABM bookbinder. Recall that UCC 9-203(1) sets out the following prerequisites for attachment and enforceability:

> (a) the collateral is in the possession of the secured party pursuant to agreement, or the debtor has signed a security agreement, which contains a description of

the collateral and in addition, when the security interest covers crops growing or to be grown or timber to be cut, a description of the land concerned;

(b) value has been given; and

(c) the debtor has rights in the collateral.

In the prototype Apex has satisfied these prerequisites. It has signed, through an authorized agent, a written security agreement that describes the bookbinder (see UCC 9-110); the bank has given value by making the purchase money loan (see UCC 1-201(44)); and Apex is the owner of the bookbinder. Moreover, although the parties could have agreed to delay attachment (see UCC 9-203(2)), they did not choose to do so.

Problem 3-3. Review the prototype transaction and consider not *whether* the security interest attached but *when* it attached.   9-203(1)

(a) When did Austin State Bank give *value*? The Code's general definition of value includes "a binding commitment to extend credit," "the extension of immediately available credit whether or not drawn upon," and "any consideration sufficient to support a simple contract." UCC 1-201(44)(a),(d). Did the Bank give value when it signed the financing statement on January 2? When it issued the cashier's check on January 9? When ABM received the check? When ABM received the proceeds of the cashier's check?

(b) When did Apex obtain rights in the collateral? Consider two possibilities: when Apex received title and when Apex received a special property in the bookbinder by identification to the sales contract.

(i) The residual rule on passage of title in a sales transaction is that, unless the parties otherwise explicitly agree, title passes to the buyer when the seller "completes his performance with reference to the physical delivery of the goods." UCC 2-401(2). Title to the bookbinder, therefore, appears to have passed on January 19, although without knowing the delivery terms of the sales contract we cannot be sure where it passed or at what time on January 19. But must Apex have title to the goods before it has rights to the bookbinder under UCC 9-203(1)(c)? Cf. UCC 9-202 (title to collateral immaterial).

(ii) An alternative analysis recognizes rights when the debtor first is given even a limited property interest. Under Article 2, Apex will have a special property and an insurable interest when the bookbinder was *identified* to the sales contract. UCC 2-501, 2-502. On the facts set out in the prototype, when was the ABM bookbinder identified?

(c) As between Apex and the Bank does it matter when the security interest attaches? (We will see in a subsequent part of this chapter that the time of attachment may determine when a security interest is perfected. See UCC 9-303.)

Problem 3-4. Assume you are outside counsel for the Austin State Bank in the prototype set out above. You are asked to review Bank's security agreement to see if revisions must be made. With the following notes and questions in mind, prepare to comment on the forms and to suggest appropriate revisions.

NOTES & QUESTIONS

1. *Form books.* The intelligent use of forms and form books is an important component of a lawyer's drafting skill and requires that an attorney understand the legal or practical problem with which each clause attempts to deal. Obviously this requires careful reading. Only after the purpose of the provision is understood should the draftsman undertake to draft the clause.

Several national form books are frequently referred to: F. Hart & W. Willier, Forms and Procedures under the Uniform Commercial Code (1963); 4 & 5 U.L.A., Uniform Commercial Code Master Edition: Uniform Commercial Code Forms and Materials (R. Henson & W. Davenport eds. 1968). Specialized form books adapted to a state's version of the UCC are also frequently available.

2. *Role of lawyers; drafting forms.* A lawyer may be called on to prepare forms for a client, negotiate the terms of a specific secured transaction, advise the client on legal alternatives when a transaction goes sour, litigate issues concerning repossession and disposition of collateral following default, or sue for a deficiency. Depending on his role, the attorney must take into account different ethical considerations. See generally V. Countryman, Problems of Professional Responsibility under the Uniform Commercial Code (1969).

Consider the problem of drafting forms. Unless a transaction involves a great deal of money it is unlikely that a lawyer will be called on to draft a security agreement specifically tailored to a particular deal. A lawyer may, however, be asked to draft forms that will then be used by the client in a variety of transactions. When drafting a form what ethical limitations must the lawyer consider? Would the following rule be helpful?

> *4.3   Illegal, Fraudulent, or Unconscionable Transactions*
>
> A lawyer shall not conclude an agreement, or assist a client in concluding an agreement, that the lawyer knows or reasonably should know is illegal, contains legally prohibited terms, would work a fraud, or would be held to be unconscionable as a matter of law.

"Comment: Although a lawyer is generally not responsible for the substantive fairness of the result of a negotiation, the lawyer has a duty to see that the product is not offensive to the law. There are many legal proscriptions concerning contractual arrangements. Being a party to some types of agreement is a penal offense. Some types of contractual provisions are prohibited by law, such as provisions purporting to waive certain legally conferred rights. Modern commercial law provides that grossly unfair contracts are unconscionable and may therefore be invalid. Such proscriptions are intended to secure definite legal rights. As an officer of the legal system, a lawyer is required to observe them. On the other hand, there are legal rules that simply make certain contractual provisions unenforceable, allowing one or both parties to avoid the obligation. Inclusion of such provisions in a contract may be unwise but it is not ethically improper, nor is it improper to include a provision whose legality is subject to reasonable argument.

"A lawyer is not obliged to make an independent investigation of the circumstances of a transaction to assure that it is legally unimpeachable. . . . [A] lawyer is not absolved of responsibility for a legally offensive transaction simply because the client takes the final step in carrying it out. For example, a lawyer who prepared a form contract containing legally proscribed terms is involved in a transaction in which the form is used, even though the lawyer does not participate in a specific transaction." Commission on Evaluation of Professional Standards, Discussion Draft of ABA Model Rules of Professional Conduct (January 30, 1980). (This proposed rule was subsequently withdrawn by the commission without comment.) See also A.B.A. Code of Professional Responsibility, EC 7-8 and EC 7-9; V. Countryman, Problems of Professional Responsibility under the Uniform Commercial Code 86-87 (1969).

3. *Client use of form.* Frequently an attorney will not be present when a form security agreement is used in a transaction. What are the attorney's obligations to explain when and how to use the form? When blanks are to be filled in or boxes checked should there be directions printed on the form itself? Consider, for example, a blank for the description of collateral. What are the legal requirements with respect to the specificity of the description? See UCC 9-203(1)(a), 9-110. Can this be explained on the form? Should it? Will the advent of computer programs help to solve this problem? See Boyd & Saxon, The A-9: A Program for Drafting Security Agreements Under Article 9 of the Uniform Commercial Code, 1981 ABF Res. J. 637.

4. *Security agreement.* Should both the debtor and the secured party sign the security agreement? Does the writing memorialize an "agreement"? See UCC 1-201(3). Are there advantages to having the secured party sign a security agreement? See UCC 9-203(1)(a), 9-402(1).

5. *Sample clauses.* Compare the prototype security agreement with the following clauses from another form (2 W. Hawkland, A Transactional Guide to the Uniform Commercial Code 995-999 (1964)).

(a) DESCRIPTION OF COLLATERAL.

Whereas, Debtor desires to grant Bank a Security Interest pursuant to the Uniform Commercial Code (Pa.) in the following described property together with all equipment, parts, accessories and attachments and any and all replacements and additions herein collectively called Collateral:

Description of collateral (State whether new–used)	Make or manufacturer	Serial no.	Model no. or year
One (1) spot welder	Pyramid	X012345A	1961

(b) OBLIGATION SECURED.

Debtor, intending to be legally bound, hereby grants to Bank a Security Interest in said Collateral, in order to secure the payment of: (1) said note(s); (2) all costs and expenses incurred in the collection of same and enforcement of Bank's rights hereunder; (3) all future advances made by Bank for taxes, levies, insurance and repairs to or maintenance of said Collateral; (4) all other money heretofore or hereafter advanced by Bank to or for the account of Debtor at the option of Bank, and all other present or future, direct or contingent liabilities of Debtor to Bank of any nature whatsoever; and (5) interest on (2), (3), and (4).

(c) PURCHASE-MONEY TRANSACTION.

Debtor warrants and agrees that:

[ ] (a) Debtor will immediately use the entire proceeds of said borrowing, together with such additional funds of Debtor as may be necessary, to pay the purchase price of the above specifically described Collateral and for no other purpose.

check (a) (b) as applicable

[ ] (b) Debtor hereby authorizes Bank to disburse the proceeds of said borrowing directly to the seller of the above specifically described Collateral and/or the insurance agent or broker for insurance thereon.

(d) INSURANCE.

Debtor will at all times keep the Collateral insured in such form, in such companies, in such amounts and against such risks as may be acceptable to Bank with provisions satisfactory to Bank for payment of all losses thereunder to Bank as its interest may appear, and, if required, to deposit the policies with Bank; any sums received by Bank in payment of losses under said policies may, at Bank's option, be applied on the account of any amount owing hereunder whether or not the same is then due and payable, or may be delivered to Debtor by Bank for the purposes of repairing or restoring said Collateral. Debtor hereby assigns to Bank any return or unearned premiums which may be due upon cancellation of any such policies for any reason whatsoever and directs the insurers to pay Bank any amounts so due. Bank is hereby appointed Debtor's Attorney in Fact to endorse any draft or check which may be payable to Debtor in order to collect such return or unearned premiums or the benefits of such insurance.

(e) DEFAULT.

Debtor shall be in default hereunder upon failure to pay when due any amount payable hereunder or under said promissory note(s) or upon failure to observe or perform any of Debtor's other agreements herein contained, or if any warranty or statement by Debtor herein, or furnished in connection herewith is false or misleading, or if proceedings in which Debtor is alleged to be insolvent or unable to pay Debtor's debts as they mature, are instituted by or against Debtor under any of the provisions of the Bankruptcy Law or any other law, or if Debtor makes an assignment for the benefit of creditors, or if Bank in good faith believes its prospect of payment or performance is impaired. Thereupon, all sums secured hereby shall become immediately due and payable at Bank's option without notice to Debtor, and Bank may proceed to enforce payment of the same and to exercise any or all of the rights and remedies provided by the Uniform Commercial Code (Pa.) as well as all other rights and remedies possessed by Bank. Whenever Debtor is in default hereunder, Debtor, upon demand by Bank, shall assemble the Collateral and make it available to Bank at a place reasonably convenient to both parties.

Problem 3-5. One year after entering into the prototype transaction Apex incorporates a subsidiary to handle its printing business. Without notifying Austin State Bank, Apex transfers the bookbinder to the subsidiary in return for 100 shares of the subsidiary's corporate stock. After the transfer, does the bank have an enforceable security interest in (a) the bookbinder, or (b) the 100 shares? See UCC 9-203(3); 9-306(1), (2). Would your answer be different if the bank's loan officer knew about the transfer but said nothing?

Problem 3-6. Assume that when Apex and Austin State Bank enter into the prototype transaction, the bank, through oversight, fails to have Apex sign the security agreement. When reviewing the loan file later in the year, a bank officer notes the omission. She asks you to prepare a memorandum (a) analyzing the status of the bank's security interest, and (b) advising the bank on what steps it should now take to protect its interest. In the light of the following material, advise the bank officer. (You should take this opportunity to review the general introduction to Code analysis set out at p. 1 supra.)

1. Statutory Provisions

UCC 9-105(1)(*l*):

In this Article unless the context otherwise requires: . . .
(*l*) "Security agreement" means an agreement which creates or provides for a security interest; . . .

UCC 9-203(1)(a):

. . . [A] security interest is not enforceable against the debtor or third parties with respect to the collateral and does not attach unless:
    (a) The collateral is in the possession of the secured party pursuant to agreement, or the debtor has signed a security agreement which contains a description of the collateral. . . .

UCC 9-402(1):

(1) A financing statement is sufficient if it gives the names of the debtor and the secured party, is signed by the debtor, gives an address of the secured party from which information concerning the security interest may be obtained, gives a mailing address of the debtor and contains a statement indicating the types, or describing the items, of collateral. A financing statement may be filed before a security agreement is made or a security interest otherwise attaches. . . . A copy of the security agreement is sufficient as a financing statement if it contains the above information and is signed by the debtor. . . .

2. Official Comments

UCC 9-203. Official Comments

3. One purpose of the formal requisites stated in subsection (1)(a) is evidentiary. The requirement of written record minimizes the possibility of future dispute as to the terms of a security agreement and as to what property stands as collateral for the obligation secured. . . .
5. The formal requisite of a writing stated in this section is not only a condition to the enforceability of a security interest against third parties, it is in the nature of a Statute of Frauds. . . .

UCC 9-402. Official Comments

2. This section adopts the system of "notice filing" which proved successful under the Uniform Trust Receipts Act. What is required to be filed is not, as under chattel mortgage and conditional sales acts, the security agreement itself, but only a simple notice which may be filed before the security interest attaches or thereafter. The notice itself indicates merely that the secured party who has

filed may have a security interest in the collateral described. Further inquiry from the parties concerned will be necessary to disclose the complete state of affairs. Section 9-208 provides a statutory procedure under which the secured party, at the debtor's request, may be required to make disclosure. . . .

3. Drafting History

Spring 1950 UCC Proposed Final Draft:

> 9-204(1): Except [if the collateral is in the possession of the lender] a security interest is not enforceable against a debtor or his creditors or purchasers from him unless there is a writing signed by the debtor providing for a security interest or an assignment and containing a description of the collateral. . . .
>
> 9-403(1): A financing statement is sufficient if it is signed by the debtor and the secured lender, gives an address of the secured lender from which information concerning the security interest may be obtained, gives a mailing address of the debtor and contains a statement that the secured lender has or intends to have a security interest in collateral of the kind or kinds listed. . . .
>
> [There is no definition of "security agreement" in this 1950 Draft.—EDS.]

1952 UCC 9-105, 9-203, 9-204, 9-402:

> 9-105(1) (h): "Security agreement" means an agreement which creates or provides for a security interest;
>
> 9-203(1): A security interest is not enforceable against the debtor or third parties unless
>
> (a)   the collateral is in the possession of the secured party; or
> (b)   the debtor has signed a security agreement which contains a description of the collateral. . . .
>
> 9-204(1): A security interest cannot attach until an agreement is made that it attach and value is given and the debtor has rights in the collateral. . . .
>
> 9-402(1): A financing statement is sufficient if it is signed by the debtor and the secured party, gives an address of the secured party from which information concerning the security interest may be obtained, gives a mailing address of the debtor and contains a statement indicating the types, or describing the items, of property covered. . . .

4. Pre-Code Law

Uniform Conditional Sales Act, Sec. 6:

> The conditional sales contract or copy shall be filed. . . . It shall not be necessary to the validity of such conditional sales contract, or in order to entitle it to be filed, that it be acknowledged or attested. . . .

Uniform Trust Receipts Act, Secs. 2, 5 & 13:

> Sec. 2(2). A writing [designating the goods, documents or instruments concerned, and reciting that a security interest therein remains or will remain in, or has passed to or will pass to, the entruster] signed by the trustee, and given in or pursuant to such a transaction, is designated in this act as a "trust receipt." No further formality of execution or authentication shall be necessary to the validity of a trust receipt.
>
> Sec. 5. Between the entruster and the trustee the terms of the trust receipt shall, save as otherwise provided by this act, be valid and enforceable. . . .
>
> Sec. 13(1). Any entruster undertaking or contemplating trust receipt transactions . . . is entitled to file a statement, signed by the entruster and trustee, containing:
>
> (a) a designation of the entruster and the trustee, and of the chief place of business of each within this state, if any; . . .
>
> (b) a statement that the entruster is engaged, or expects to be engaged, in financing under trust receipt transactions the acquisition of goods by the trustee; and
>
> (c) a description of the kind or kinds of goods covered or to be covered by such financing.

1 G. GILMORE, SECURITY INTERESTS IN PERSONAL PROPERTY, 466-467 (1965): "Under all chattel mortgage and conditional sales acts the basic document required to be filed was the security agreement itself—the mortgage or the conditional sale contract. The chattel mortgage acts usually insisted on more or less elaborate formalities of execution. In addition they not infrequently required the mortgagee to file, along with the mortgage, affidavits that the mortgage was given for a fair consideration and that the mortgagee was acting in good faith and with no intention to hinder, defraud or delay the creditors of the mortgagor. These self-serving affidavits in which the mortgagee testified to his own virtue reflected the deep-rooted nineteenth century suspicion that a mortgage on personal property was in all probability a species of fraudulent conveyance. The earliest conditional sales filing statutes dated from the end of the nineteenth century and such legislation continued to be enacted over a thirty- or forty-year period until all but a dozen or so states had imposed a filing requirement. These acts typically dispensed with the formalities of execution and the accompanying affidavits characteristic of the chattel mortgage acts; we may conclude that the fraudulent conveyance idea had gradually lost its hold on the legal imagination and that the elaborate formalities had proved to be not so much deterrents to fraud as devices for the entrapment of the pure in heart."

See also Pacific Metal Co. v. Joslin, 359 F.2d 396 (9th Cir. 1966), at p. 223 infra.

5.   *Court Decisions*

Consider the following court opinions. What weight should they be given? See UCC 1-102(2)(c): "The underlying purposes and policies of this Act are . . . (c) to make uniform the law among the various jurisdictions." Note the reasoning of the courts and the authority cited. To what extent do the courts themselves rely on the prior court decisions? To what extent does or should the context in which the issue arises make a difference?

AMERICAN CARD CO. v. H.M.H. CO.
97 R.I. 59, 196 A.2d 150, 1 UCC Rep. 447 (1963)

[handwritten margin note: Held: financing stm't doesn't itself create a security interest]

CONDON, Chief Justice. . . . The sole question for our determination is whether the superior court erred in holding that UCC 9-203 requires in a case of this kind a written security agreement between the debtor and the secured party before a prior security interest in any collateral can attach. The claimants, Oscar A. Hillman & Sons, a copartnership, contend that a separate agreement in writing is not necessary if the written financing statement which was filed contains the debtor's signature and a description of the collateral. In support of that position they point out that UCC 9-402 recognizes that a security agreement and a financing statement can be one and the same document. They further argue that "under the unique circumstances that exist in this case" the minimum requirements of UCC 9-203 are satisfied by the agreed statement of facts and by exhibits A, B, and C appended thereto. [These exhibits are not reproduced in the reported opinion.—EDS.]

[handwritten margin note: no line about being secured by a s. interest]

Those circumstances may be summarized as follows. On February 21, 1962 the debtor corporation executed a promissory note in the sum of $12,373.33 payable to claimants. On March 14, 1962 the corporation as debtor and claimants as secured parties signed a financing statement form provided by the office of the secretary of state and filed it in that office in accordance with UCC 9-402.

On July 2, 1962 Melvin A. Chernick and George F. Treanor were appointed co-receivers of the debtor corporation. On October 6, 1962 claimants duly filed their proof of debt and asserted therein a security interest against certain tools and dies of the debtor which were mentioned in the financing statement as collateral. Finally, there is in addition to the agreed statement of facts testimony of claimants' agent who attempted to collect the debt. He testified that the treasurer of the debtor corporation admitted the inability of the debtor to pay the debt and agreed to the execution of the promissory note and to the designation of the tools and dies as collateral security therefor.

The claimants argue that the code requires no " 'magic word,' no precise, formalistic language which must be put in writing in order for a security interest to be enforceable." And they further argue that "the definition of a security agreement indicates, the question of whether or not a security interest is 'created or provided for' is a question of fact which must be decided upon the basis of the words and deeds of the parties." They rely on the definition of "agreement" in UCC 9-105(1)(h) [see 1972 UCC 9-105(1)(*l*)] for support of this latter contention.

Upon consideration of those provisions of the code, we are of the opinion that they are not decisive of the special problem posed in the instant case. The receivers contend here, as they did successfully before the superior court, that the controlling section of the code is, in the circumstances, UCC 9-203(1)(b) [see 1972 UCC 9-203(1)(a)] and that in order to establish a security interest in any collateral the secured party must show that "the debtor has signed a security agreement which contains a description of the collateral. . . ." They concede that such a signed agreement may serve as a financing statement if it also contains the requirements thereof, but they deny that a financing statement, absent an agreement therein, can be treated as the equivalent of a security agreement.

The pertinent language of UCC 9-402 in this regard is, "A copy of the security agreement is sufficient as a financing statement if it contains the above information and is signed by both parties." In other words, while it is possible for a financing statement and a security agreement to be one and the same document as argued by claimants, it is not possible for a financing statement which does not contain the debtor's grant of a security interest to serve as a security agreement.

In our opinion there is merit in the receivers' contention, and since the financing statement filed here contains no such grant it does not qualify as a security agreement. One of the prerequisites to the perfection of a security interest is stated in Bankers Manual on the Uniform Commercial Code, §8.6, at page 123, as follows: "Security Agreement. It is equally obvious that there must be an agreement between the parties as to the security interest." . . .

In an article by one of the editors of the manual [Craig, Accounts Receivable Financing: Transition from Variety to Uniform Commercial Code], it is stated . . . . : "The financing statement does not of itself create a security interest. An agreement in writing signed by the debtor 'which contains a description of the collateral' is required." 42 B.U.L. Rev. 187, 189 (1962). In the absence of any judicial precedent this commentary on the code is worthy of consideration in the solution of the question here.

The financing statement which the claimants filed clearly fails to qualify also as a security agreement because nowhere in the form is there any evidence of an agreement by the debtor to grant claimants a security interest. As for the testimony of the claimants' agent upon which they also rely to prove the intention of the debtor to make such a grant, our answer is that his testimony is without probative force to supply the absence of a required security agreement in writing. Therefore the trial justice did not err in holding as she did that the financing statement and the evidence before her did not prove the existence of a security agreement within the contemplation of the language of the statute.

The claimants' appeal is denied and dismissed, the decree appealed from is affirmed, and the cause is remanded to the superior court for further proceedings.

H: opp of
Ame:
security
int is
created

NOLDEN v. PLANT RECLAMATION (IN RE AMEX-PROTEIN DEVELOPMENT CORP.)
504 F.2d 1056, 15 UCC Rep. 286 (9th Cir. 1974)

PER CURIAM. . . . Plant Reclamation had sold equipment to the bankrupt on open account, but on October 16, 1972, substituted a promissory note for the open account indebtedness and caused a financing statement to be signed and filed. The parties intended to create a security interest in the property sold as collateral for the note, and the Referee [now called a "bankruptcy judge"— EDs.] so found.

The promissory note included the following line: "This note is secured by a Security Interest in subject personal property as per invoices." The words "subject . . . as per invoices" were handwritten in an otherwise typewritten sentence; the testimony before the Referee established that such words were added by an officer of the bankrupt in order to tie the security interest to the personal property that had been sold to the bankrupt by Plant Reclamation. The invoices referred to in the promissory note were the only ones submitted by Plant Reclamation.

The financing statement named Plant Reclamation as the secured party and recited that it covered the following types or items of property:

1—Dorr Oliver 100 Sq. Ft Vacuum Filter
1—Chicago Pheumatic [sic] Vacuum Compression
1—Stainless Steel Augar and Drive
1—Nichols Micro 7" dryer
1—Tolhurst Centerfuge [sic] 26 inch.

I. DID THE PROMISSORY NOTE 'CREATE OR PROVIDE FOR' A SECURITY INTEREST?

This issue turns on whether there has been compliance with the following pertinent sections of the California Commercial Code which govern the creation and enforcement of a security interest. . . . [The court sets out UCC 9-105(1)(h), 1-201(37), and 9-203 of the 1962 official text. UCC 9-105(1)(h) is renumbered as 9-105(1)(*l*) in the 1972 official text.]

The Referee denied the claim of Plant Reclamation on the single ground that no security interest had been 'granted' pursuant to the language of the promissory note, as a result of which there had been a failure to comply with the 'creates or provides for' requirement of UCC 9-105(1)(h) [see 1972 UCC

9-105(1)(*l*)]. The Referee concluded: "Creative words do not exist in the note before me. The language relied upon is passive, descriptive and informative, much like a financing statement; it is not active or creative; it does not grant or provide for. . . ." [The court concludes that it is free to examine the legal conclusion of the Referee because the facts were not in dispute.]

UCC 9-105(1)(h) defines a security agreement as one which 'creates or provides for' a security interest. The Referee found the above-quoted words to be synonymous with the word 'grant' and therefore to require active language. A fair reading of the statute, however, will not bear such a restrictive interpretation.

It is a matter of basic statutory construction that statutes are to be given 'such effect that no clause, sentence or word is rendered superfluous, void, contradictory, or insignificant.' . . . In addition, absent persuasive reasons to the contrary, statutory words are to be given their ordinary meanings.

UCC 9-105(1)(h) nowhere uses the word 'grants' nor is that word a synonym for either 'creates' or 'provides for' or for all of the quoted words together.

Webster's Third New International Dictionary (3d ed. 1965) defines 'create' as a transitive verb with the following meanings inter alia:[1] "1: to bring into existence . . . ; 2: to cause to be or to produce by fiat or by mental, moral, or legal action . . . ; 3: to cause or occasion. . . ."

'Provide' is defined as a transitive verb with the following meanings inter alia: "2a: to fit out or fit up . . . ; 3: stipulate . . ." and as an intransitive verb with the following meanings inter alia: "1a: to take precautionary measures: make provision—used with *against* or *for* . . . ; 2: to make a proviso or stipulation. . . ."

'Grant' is defined as a transitive verb with the following meanings inter alia: "1a: to consent to carry out for a person: allow, accord . . . ; 2: give, bestow, confer. . . ."

Thus the requirement of UCC 9-105(1)(h) may be satisfied not only when a security interest is caused to be or brought into existence, but also when provision or stipulation is made therefor.

No magic words or precise form are necessary to create or provide for a security interest so long as the minimum formal requirements of the Code are met. See . . . Evans v. Everett, [infra p. 130]. This liberal approach is mandated by an expressed purpose of the secured transaction provisions of the Code. . . . [The court cites from the Comment to UCC 9-101.]

The court in In re Center Auto Parts, 6 UCC Rep. 398 (C.D. Cal. 1968) upheld the validity of a promissory note as a security agreement by reading the two together. The promissory note merely recited that, "This note is secured by a certain financing statement," and the court found that such was

---

1. Webster's New International Dictionary (2d ed. 1939) lists as synonyms for 'create' the words 'make, build, produce, fashion, invent, originate.'

sufficient to 'create or provide for' a security interest within the meaning of UCC 9-105(1)(h).

A similar result was reached in a case involving the North Carolina version of the UCC, Evans v. Everett, supra, wherein the debtor gave a promissory note which recited: "This note is secured by Uniform Commercial Code financing statement of North Carolina" and wherein a similarly worded financing statement was thereafter filed. The court found that since a security agreement could serve as a financing statement there was no sound reason why the converse should not be true. The court held that the financing statement before it qualified as a security agreement. . . .

Other cases . . . have reached a like result and . . . support the position taken here. . . .

The cases relied upon by the trustee and cited by the Referee are not persuasive. Shelton v. Erwin, [472 F.2d 1118 (8th Cir. 1973),] dealt with the contention that an automobile bill of sale or a title application therefor or both together adequately set forth the intent of the parties to create or provide for a security interest and did in fact create or provide for same under pertinent Missouri statutes. In finding no security agreement, the court simply reaffirmed the principle that a single piece of paper—here the title application and later certificate of title were being treated as a financing statement—could not serve as a security agreement without containing the requirements for such. There was not, as here, two documents; a promissory note which provided for a security interest and a financing statement which gave notice of it.

Shelton, together with other cases relied upon by the trustee, stem from the ruling in American Card Company v. H.M.H. Co., [p. 126 supra], and therefore share its infirmities. There the court found that a financing statement which did not contain a 'grant' of a security interest could not also serve as a security agreement. There is no support in legislative history or grammatical logic for the substitution of the word 'grant' for the phrase 'creates or provides for.' This case has been subject to harsh criticism, see G. Gilmore, Security Interests in Personal Property §11.4, at 347-348 (1965); 6D Bender's Uniform Commercial Code Service 2-1680, and it cannot be relied upon as dispositive in the instant case.

Accordingly, the promissory note herein qualifies as a security agreement which by its terms 'creates or provides for' a security interest. . . .

NOTES & QUESTIONS

1. *Distinguishing cases.* Is the following case distinguishable from *American Card* and *Amex-Protein*?

EVANS v. EVERETT, 279 N.C. 352, 183 S.E.2d 109, 9 UCC Rep. 769 (1971): On receiving a loan Debtor executed a promissory note payable to *no!*

Creditor with the notation: "This note is secured by Uniform Commercial Code financing statement of North Carolina." On the following day financing statements were properly filed in the state offices. Each financing statement asserted that the "statement covers the following types or items of collateral" and the description of the collateral ended with the statement "same securing note for advanced money to produce crops for the year 1969." Debtor signed no other document in connection with the loan. On default, Creditor brought suit to enforce the note against Debtor and to recover the value of the crops from the purchasers of the harvested crops. *Held,* Debtor granted to Creditor an enforceable security interest by the financing statement.

2. *Holdings.* The court in In re Bollinger Corp., 614 F.2d 924, 28 UCC Rep. 289 (3d Cir. 1980) comments as follows on the *Amex-Protein* case: "The Ninth Circuit . . . echoed criticism by commentators of the *American Card* rule. . . . It concluded that as long as the financing statement contains a description of the collateral signed by the debtor, the financing statement may serve as the security agreement and the formal requirements of [UCC 9-203(1)(a)] are met." Is this what the *Amex-Protein* court holds?

no, said promissory note could qualify as security agreement.

6. Commentators

The following excerpts are taken from two works frequently cited by courts. How much weight should be given to these commentaries? What authority do the authors cite?

1 G. GILMORE, SECURITY INTERESTS IN PERSONAL PROPERTY
346-348 (1965)

Article 9 distinguishes not only between "security interest" and "security agreement" but between "security agreement" and "financing statement." When a security interest is perfected by filing, the document which is placed on record is referred to as a "financing statement." Confusingly, and unnecessarily, the formal requisites of the security agreement (§9-203) and the formal requisites of the financing statement (§9-402) are not the same. . . .

There is a sensible reason for the distinction between "security agreement" and "financing statement." Under the "notice filing" system which Article 9 adopts, the document placed on record need be only a skeletonic statement that the parties intend to engage in future transactions: the strengths and weaknesses of notice filing in general and of the Article 9 version of notice filing in particular are hereafter discussed. Normally the parties to a security transaction will evidence their agreement in a written document which will contain a great deal more than the notice required in the §9-402

financing statement; instead of filing, for example, the whole corporate indenture for record, Article 9 requires only a one-page "financing statement,"
although §9-402 also provides that a copy of the "security agreement" may be
filed as a financing statement if it complies with the §9-402 formal requisites
(two signatures, addresses, and so on).

There is no sensible reason for the discrepancies between the formal requisites of §9-203 and §9-402. [See, however, 1972 UCC texts of these sections—Eds.] With respect to signatures, §9-203 seems to be right: the debtor's
signature on a document binding him to liability is obviously essential; there
seems to be no reason for the secured party's signature to be required on either
"agreement" or "statement." The addresses are needed in the document which
is filed for record and, for simplicity's sake, might as well be included in the
underlying "agreement." There is no excuse for the failure of the two sections
to mesh with respect to the description requirement.

In American Card Co. v. H.M.H. Co. [p. 126 supra] the discrepancies
between §9-203 and §9-402 led the Rhode Island court to an unfortunate
decision. To secure a debt, H.M.H. agreed to give the card company a security interest in certain tools and dies. The card company filed a financing
statement which complied in all respects with the §9-402 requirements. In an
equity receivership, the card company was denied status as a secured creditor
on the ground that the debtor had not signed a "security agreement" in addition to the financing statement. The court noted that a security agreement, if
executed, could have been filed as a financing statement (if it met the additional requirements of §9-402) but concluded that the reverse was not true: "it
is not possible for a financing statement which does not contain the debtor's
grant of a security interest to serve as a financing statement [Professor Gilmore
misquotes the original!—Eds.]." Certainly, nothing in §9-203 requires that the
"security agreement" contain a "granting" clause. The §9-402 financing statement contained all that was necessary to satisfy the §9-203 statute of frauds as
well as being sufficient evidence of the parties' intention to create a security
interest in the tools and dies. No doubt the court would have upheld the
security interest if the debtor had signed two pieces of paper instead of one.
The §9-402 provision that a short financing statement may be filed in place of
the full security agreement was designed to simplify the operation. The Rhode
Island court gives it an effect reminiscent of the worst formal requisites holding
under the nineteenth century chattel mortgage acts.[5]

NOTES & QUESTIONS

1. *Financing statement alone as security agreement.* Does Professor Gilmore suggest that the financing statement alone is sufficient to meet the requirements
for an enforceable security interest? An attached interest?

5. The case is also reminiscent of litigation arising under the Uniform Trust Receipts Act and
Factor's Lien Acts, debating the question whether a formal requisite under those statutes was the
execution of security documents in addition to the document filed for record.

2. *Weight of draftmen's opinion.* Professor Gilmore was a draftsman of the first official text of Article 9. Does this fact give his opinion any additional authority? Compare the criticism by the draftsmen themselves of the use of the treatise of Professor Samuel Williston, draftsman of the Uniform Sales Act, as authority. Braucher, The Legislative History of the Uniform Commercial Code, 58 Colum. L. Rev. 798, 809 ("delegation to private persons of essentially legislative power"). See also the remarks by Professor Llewellyn reproduced in the General Introduction at p. 4 supra.

J. WHITE & R. SUMMERS, HANDBOOK OF THE LAW UNDER THE UNIFORM COMMERCIAL CODE
904-905 (2d ed. 1980)

Section 9-203 requires a "security agreement," a term defined in 9-105 as "an agreement which creates or provides for a security interest." The conjunction of 9-203 and 9-105 calls for two independent inquiries. The *court* must first resolve, *as a question of law,* whether the language embodied in the writing objectively indicates that the parties may have intended to create or provide for a security interest.[13] If the language crosses this objective threshold,[14] that is, if the *writing* evidences a possible secured transaction and thus satisfies the statute of frauds requirement, then the *fact-finder* must inquire whether the parties actually intended to create a security interest.[15] Parol evidence is admissible to inform the latter,[16] but not the former, inquiry.[17]

13. A few cases suggest that 9-203 requires merely a writing—not a written agreement. This view in effect eliminates the objective inquiry. See Kreiger v. Hartig, 11 Wash. App. 898, 900-901, 527 P.2d 483, 485, 15 UCC 938, 940-941 (1974); see also Clark v. Vaughn, 504 S.W.2d 550, 14 UCC 501 (Tex. Civ. App. 1974). In our opinion this position is incorrect.

14. . . . . [T]his objective threshold should not be high. . . . Many courts concur. See, e.g., In re Amex-Protein Development Corp., 504 F.2d 1056, 1058, 15 UCC 286, 290 (9th Cir. 1974) (citing "provide for" language of §9-105, court concludes Code requirements would be satisfied "not only when a security interest is caused to be or brought into existence, but also when provision or stipulation is made therefor"); Komas v. Small Business Administration, 71 Cal. App. 3d 809, 816, 139 Cal. Rptr. 669, 672, 22 UCC 550, 554 (1977) ("It is sufficient if the parties use language which leads to the conclusion that it was the intention of the parties that a security interest be created"); In re Truckers Int'l. Inc., 17 UCC 1337, 1341 (Bktcy. W.D. Wash. 1975) ("some indication that an agreement has been entered into"). See also Weinberg, [Toward Maximum Facilitation of Intent to Create Enforceable Article Nine Security Interests, 18 B.C. Indus. & Com. L. Rev. 1 (1976)] at 11 ("9-203 . . . intended to require those types of writings which could function qua statute of frauds to provide minimum evidence of a possible security interest and a minimum safeguard against fraudulent or mistaken claims of secured status").

Yet courts often confuse the objective and subjective components of the written-agreement inquiry. See e.g. Kreiger v. Hartig, 11 Wash. App. 898, 903, 527 P.2d 483, 486, 15 UCC 938, 942 (1974) ("Whether a writing is or is not a security agreement is a question of fact. We hold that the trial court properly considered parol evidence in finding the parties intended that the application and the title certificate to the truck would create a security interest.")

15. In re Metzler, 405 F. Supp. 622, 625, 19 UCC 276, 280 (N.D. Ala. 1975): "The fundamental requirement of meeting of the minds is inherent in such agreements, as it is in all contracts. Without a contract there can be no security interest." Some courts have focused on the debtor's intention at the time of contract formation. See id.: "The burden is on the creditor to establish the intention. . . . The question is what did the debtor agree to?"

NOTES & QUESTIONS

1. What is the source of authority in the statutory text for the authors' opinions? Compare UCC 2-201.

2. How would the authors resolve the issue in *American Card*? *Evans v. Everett*? *Amex-Protein*?

D.   PERFECTION AND PRIORITIES

To determine whether Austin State Bank has a perfected security interest in 'Apex's bookbinder you must examine whether the security interest has attached and whether some act to publicize the security interest to third parties has been taken. UCC 9-303(1) provides:

> (1) A security interest is perfected when it has attached and when all of the applicable steps required for perfection have been taken. Such steps are specified in Sections 9-302, 9-304, 9-305 and 9-306. If such steps are taken before the security interest attaches, it is perfected at the time when it attaches.

The usual way to publicize the security interest is to file a financing statement as directed by UCC 9-302(1). In the prototype transaction, Austin State Bank filed a financing statement on January 2 before the security interest attached, so that the bank's interest became perfected when the last prerequisite for attachment was met.

In this section we look at how a secured party perfects its security interest and the priority that perfection gives the secured party. Although the overview of Article 9 set out at the beginning of this chapter distinguishes the perfection of an interest from priority of claims, in practice the question of perfection arises when priority is in dispute. The following cases and problems therefore necessarily deal with the two matters together.

---

16. This conclusion follows from the definition of "agreement" in 1-201(5) [1-201(3)—EDs.]. See In re Lockwood, 16 UCC 195, 200 (Bktcy. D. Conn. 1974) ("parol evidence is admissible to reveal the actual negotiations of the parties in arranging the transaction and any supplemental oral discussions of the parties which demonstrate their true intention and understanding of the transaction;" better reading of the case is that lease per se passes objective threshold and parol evidence is admissible to flesh out intent).

17. See In re Delta Molded Products, Inc., 416 F. Supp. 938, 942, 20 UCC 795, 801 (N.D. Ala. 1976) ("Section 9-203 being in the nature of a statute of frauds, parol evidence is not admissible to establish the statutory requirements"); see also In re E. F. Anderson & Son, Inc., 12 UCC 567, 571 (Bktcy. M.D. Ga. 1973) (unattached list of collateral results in ineffectiveness of security agreement; despite clear indication of intended collateral on certificates of title, "[e]quity will reform an instrument but it will not make one"). See also Weinberg, supra note [14], at 17 (on exclusion of parol evidence to establish bare promissory note as security agreement: "Article Nine should be read as requiring that the writing evidence a possible secured transaction").

Problem 3-7. In the prototype transaction set forth at p. 112 supra Austin State Bank files a financing statement with the secretary of state of Texas. Texas has adopted the second alternatives of both subsections (1) and (3) of UCC 9-401.[5]

(a) Has the bank filed in the proper office in order to perfect its security interest?

(b) Would the bank have filed in the proper office if Texas had adopted alternative 1 or 3 of UCC 9-401?

(c) If under Texas real estate law the bookbinder is considered a fixture where should the bank file? See UCC 9-313 and the materials on fixtures in Chapter 7.

(d) Assume that two years after the bookbinder is delivered in Austin, Apex decides to move it to one of its branch offices in Amarillo, Texas. If the bank agrees to the move, must it file a new financing statement in order to have a continuing perfected security interest? See UCC 9-401(3). Would your answer be different if Apex did not inform the bank of the move or if the move is made despite the bank's disapproval?

Problem 3-8. The financing statement in the prototype transaction (Form 3-1) gives the names and addresses of the debtor and the secured party, describes the collateral as "printing equipment," and is signed by both parties.

(a) Is the description of the collateral sufficient so that the bank has a perfected security interest? See UCC 9-402(1), 9-110. Is there a different description you would recommend?

(b) If the secured party has failed to sign the financing statement will it still be effective?

(c) If the name of the debtor has been given as "Apex Publishers" rather than "Apex Publishing Co., Inc." will the filing be effective? See UCC 9-402(8). Will it make a difference that the company uses "Apex Publishers" as a trade name? See UCC 9-402(7).

(d) If, as is likely, a lawyer will not be present when a financing statement is filled in, what instructions, if any, should he or she give the client for completing the form?

Problem 3-9. Six months after entering into the prototype transaction Apex approaches Southwest Finance Company for a working capital loan. By filing with the Texas secretary of state's office a prescribed form requesting copies of all financing statements on which Apex is listed as debtor, the finance company discovers the Austin State Bank financing statement (Form 3-1). The finance company writes a letter to the bank requesting information about

5. Note that we have assumed that Texas law governs because all the acts of the parties took place in Texas. To support this assumption we must look to UCC 1-105 and 9-103. UCC 1-105(2) of the 1972 official text makes a cross reference to 9-103 on questions of perfection. UCC 9-103(1) covers ordinary goods, such as the bookbinder in the prototype, and paragraph (b) of that subsection points to the jurisdiction "where the collateral is when the last event occurs on which is based the assertion that the security interest is perfected or unperfected." Here, no matter what act is the "last event" it takes place in Texas. See also UCC 9-401(4).

the present status of the Apex loan and asks for a copy of the security agreement. The bank's officer asks you whether she must comply with this request. Advise her. See UCC 9-208, 9-407.

knowledge of prior interest doesn't matter, only 1st to perfect by filing does

IN RE SMITH
326 F. Supp. 1311, 9 UCC Rep. 549 (D. Minn. 1971)

LARSON, District Judge. On or about April 14, 1969, one Bruce A. Smith purchased a 1968 Plymouth automobile from Southtown Chrysler in Minneapolis, Minnesota. At that time he executed a conditional sales contract which was assigned by the seller to the First National Bank of Minneapolis. Neither the seller nor assignee filed a financing statement evidencing the security interest.

no financing stmt

In July of 1969 Community Credit Co. lent Mr. Smith money. Mr. Smith at that time executed a chattel mortgage on the Plymouth automobile in favor of the lender. The lender filed a financing statement evidencing the chattel mortgage on July 14, 1969, with the Hennepin County Register of Deeds. At the time of this transaction Community Credit Co. had actual knowledge of the unperfected security interest of the First National Bank of Minneapolis in the automobile.

Bruce A. Smith was duly adjudicated a bankrupt on May 7, 1970, after the filing of a voluntary petition in bankruptcy. The trustee in bankruptcy is given the power of a perfect lien creditor by Section 70(c) of the Bankruptcy Act [see 1978 Bankruptcy Code §544(a); UCC 9-301(3)]. He therefore takes priority over and is entitled to avoid the unperfected security interest of the First National Bank of Minneapolis.

rule

Pursuant to the order of the Referee in Bankruptcy the automobile was sold to Community Credit. The sale proceeds are held by the trustee subject to the claim of security interest by Community Credit.

The trustee, however, chose to exercise the option made available to him by Section 70(e)(2) of the Bankruptcy Act [see Bankruptcy Code §551]. That provision permitted him to preserve the Bank's interest for the benefit of the estate and to assert it against the subsequent lien taken by Community Credit.

There is no dispute that the Bank's security interest is not good against the trustee in bankruptcy. Since it was not perfected either by possession or filing, it remains subject to the rights of the trustee as perfected lien creditor. The trustee by preserving the Bank's interest and asserting it for the benefit of the estate steps into the shoes of the Bank. His rights are determined by what position the Bank would have been in had there been no bankruptcy proceedings.

The situation presented is one involving conflicting security interests in the same collateral. Community Credit holds a security interest perfected by filing. The Bank's interest is prior in time but is unperfected either by filing or possession. It is conceded by all parties that Community Credit as holder of the perfected security interest would prevail if it had not had actual knowledge of the Bank's prior unperfected interest. Hence the issue raised before the Referee in Bankruptcy and which now faces this Court is whether actual knowledge on the part of Community Credit of the Bank's prior interest prevents it from achieving priority which would have otherwise been obtained by being the first to file. The Referee answered this question in the affirmative and gave priority to the Bank's lien.

The portion of the Minnesota Uniform Commercial Code which governs this situation is [1962 UCC 9-312(5)].

> In all cases not governed by other rules stated in this section (including cases of purchase money security interests which do not qualify for the special priorities set forth in subsections (3) and (4) of this section), priority between conflicting security interests in the same collateral shall be determined as follows:
>
> (a)   In the order of filing if both are perfected by filing, regardless of which security interest attached first under [1962 UCC 9-204(1); see 1972 UCC 9-203(1), (2)] and whether it attached before or after filing;
>
> (b)   In the order of perfection unless both are perfected by filing, regardless of which security interest attached first under [1962 UCC 9-204(1)] and, in the case of a filed security interest, whether it attached before or after filing; and
>
> (c)   In the order of attachment under [1962 UCC 9-204(1)] so long as neither is perfected.

This provision nowhere makes lack of knowledge (good faith) a requirement for obtaining priority. The statute on its face provides for a race to the filing office with actual knowledge of a prior unperfected security interest apparently being irrelevant if one perfects first by filing. Such an approach by the Uniform Commercial Code would clearly be a change in the pre-existing law. Under precode commercial law, actual notice of an earlier unperfected interest in the property would prevent the second interest from obtaining priority. This was true even if the second interest was perfected first by filing.

The change would be one effected by omission rather than an affirmative statement of change. It is the absence of any reference to knowledge or good faith which raises the presumption that it is not relevant. There is no positive statement in UCC 9-312(5) that knowledge of the earlier interest has no bearing on priority. Under these circumstances, a conclusion that knowledge is not a factor in establishing priorities under UCC 9-312(5) is predicated on the underlying assumption that the omission of any reference to knowledge was a deliberate one. The Referee in Bankruptcy refused to make that assumption. He came, in fact, to the opposite conclusion, namely, that the absence of any reference to knowledge was unintentional on the part of the Code draftsmen. Hence, the instant controversy is *casus omissus* and must be interpreted in light of the common law. As was previously noted, the common law made good faith a critical factor in achieving priority.

The Referee, in reaching his decision that the omission was unintentional, relied heavily on Professor Grant Gilmore's interpretation of the drafting history of UCC 9-312(5). 2 Gilmore, Security Interests in Personal Property §34.2 at 898-902 (1965). Professor Gilmore acknowledges that Article 9 appears to have discarded good faith as a factor in determining priorities under UCC 9-312. However, he makes an argument that the result is not clearly an intentional and deliberate one on the part of the draftsmen. Professor Gilmore's analysis fairly questions whether or not the elimination of the good faith provision was a calculated one on the part of the draftsmen of the UCC. However, this Court feels that the Referee in Bankruptcy's reliance on that analysis to imply a good cause provision in UCC 9-312(5) is misplaced.

It is true that Professor Gilmore suggested implying a good cause provision as one way of approaching UCC 9-312(5). To the contrary he also pointed out that there were some good reasons for disregarding knowledge and creating a race to file situation. One is the protection of the integrity of the filing system. Gilmore, at 901-902. It is desirable that perfection of interests take place promptly. It is appropriate then to provide that a secured party who fails to file runs the risk of subordination to a later but more diligent party. In this regard it should be pointed out that filing is of particular importance with respect to notice to other parties. It is agreed that where the later party has actual notice there is no need to rely upon a filing to notify him of a prior interest. The problem, however, cannot be analyzed in this narrow context. Some parties may rely on the record in extending credit and obtaining a security agreement in collateral. Although they will prevail over the unperfected prior interest in time if a dispute arises, it is entirely possible that they wanted to avoid the dispute altogether. In other words, they may not have relied on ultimately prevailing in the event of a dispute but they may have relied on the complete absence of a prior interest perfected or otherwise out of which a dispute could arise. The only way this kind of record expectation can be protected is by prompt perfection of all security interests.

Professor Gilmore also recognizes the fact that a good faith requirement creates evidentiary problems. "[T]he presence or absence of 'knowledge' is a subjective question of fact, difficult to prove. Unless there is an overwhelming policy argument in favor of using such a criterion, it is always wise to discard it and to make decision turn on some easily determinable objective event—as, for example, the date of filing." Gilmore, at 902. The only way to effectively produce the above result is to make "knowledge" irrelevant and rely solely on perfection to establish priority.

Finally, Professor Gilmore admits that Example 2 in the official comment to UCC 9-312(5) seems to indicate that the apparent result was intended. It reads as follows insofar as relevant: "Example 2. A and B make non-purchase money advances against the same collateral. The collateral is in the debtor's possession and neither interest is perfected when the second advance is made. Whichever secured party first perfects his interest (by taking possession of the collateral or by filing) takes priority and it makes no difference whether or not he knows of the other interest at the time he perfects his own. . . . Subsections (5)(a) and (5)(b) both lead to this result. It may be regarded as an adoption, in this type of situation, of the idea, deeply rooted at common law, of a race of diligence among creditors. . . ." The comment is not directly in point because it deals with knowledge at time of perfection and not at the time of attachment. Subsections (5)(a) and (5)(b), however, give priority whether perfection is before or after attachment. Thus, if attachment came after perfection, knowledge at time of perfection would also mean knowledge at time of attachment. Presumably Example 2 would control in that situation also (although it is not certain since under Example 2's facts, attachment was clearly prior to perfection). This conclusion is supported by Example 1. "Example 1. A files against X (debtor) on February 1. B files against X on March 1. B makes a non-purchase money advance against certain collateral on April 1. A makes an advance against the same collateral on May 1. A has priority even though B's advance was made earlier and was perfected when made. *It makes no difference whether or not A knew of B's interest when he made his advance.* . . ." (Emphasis added.) This example makes clear that once priority has been achieved by being the first to file, that priority will not be destroyed as to an advance made with the knowledge that a second party has made a prior advance secured by a perfected security interest in the same collateral. This is the case, apparently, even if it is the first advance made under the prior perfected agreement. Similar treatment should be accorded any interest which attached after filing.

It can be seen from the foregoing that Professor Gilmore's position is not an unequivocal one. Furthermore, Professor Gilmore himself admits that the Code Comment to UCC 9-312(5) tends to indicate that the drafters of the code were aware and intended that knowledge be irrelevant in determining priorities under that section. Under these circumstances this Court feels that the conclusion of the Referee in Bankruptcy that good faith should be read into UCC 9-312(5) is unwarranted.

There are some other practical reasons why this Court feels constrained to reverse the Referee in Bankruptcy. First of all, there are other commentators who have argued that the elimination of the good faith provision was intentional. See Felsenfeld, Knowledge as A Factor in Determining Priorities Under the Uniform Commercial Code, 42 N.Y.U. L. Rev. 246, 248-250 (1967).

Secondly, the assumption of most of the commentators has been that UCC 9-312(5) operated without regard to knowledge of the perfecting party of a prior unperfected security interest. See Coogan, Hogan, Vagts, Secured Transactions Under the UCC 177. The Minnesota Code Comment referring to UCC 9-312(5) says: "Notice of a prior security interest does not invalidate a subsequent interest which is otherwise entitled to priority under this subsection. . . . This changes prior Minnesota law as to security interests in the nature of chattel mortgages and conditional sales, since subsequent mortgagees under prior law had the burden of proving 'good faith' (i.e., lack of notice) as against prior mortgagees or conditional vendors whose mortgages or conditional sales contracts are unfiled. . . ." It is clear that the assumption of the Minnesota legislature when they adopted the code was that it changed prior law.

Finally, all the cases which have dealt with the problem indicate by holding or dicta that knowledge is irrelevant to the operation of UCC 9-312(5). Bloom v. Hilty, 427 Pa. 463, 234 A.2d 860 (1967). . . .

The attitude of the commentators and the weight of recorded decisions clearly indicated that knowledge could be disregarded in the operation of UCC 9-312(5). The instant situation is evidence that there has been reliance on the apparent meaning of the statute as it has been interpreted by commentators and the courts.

To permit the decision of the Referee in Bankruptcy to stand would be to disrupt substantially expectations under UCC 9-312(5). Furthermore, it would create a split in authority and destroy the uniformity the code seeks to achieve. This is not to say that if the current interpretations were clearly contrary to the intent of the drafters that a split in authority would not be appropriate. That, however, is clearly not the situation presented. The only individual who seriously asserts that the elimination of a good faith requirement was unintentional is Professor Gilmore and his position is not an unequivocal one.

Under the circumstances this Court cannot permit to stand a decision which goes against the weight of authority and reasonable expectations under the statute. The decision of the Referee in Bankruptcy must therefore be reversed.

HANNA, THE EXTENSION OF PUBLIC RECORDATION
31 Colum. L. Rev. 617, 618-619, 623-624, 635-637 (1931)

An examination of the realities behind the recording requirements shows the futility of treating the recording problem abstractly and of determining in general whether recording statutes are desirable. Recording requirements must be tied to specific types of transactions, and this necessitates an independent examination of the relation of such requirements to particular security devices. The desirability of particular recording requirements must be ascertained by regarding and weighing, so far as possible, the interest such statutes are intended to protect and the interest adversely affected. As a correlative inquiry one should consider what prevailing practices tend to diminish the significance of records in respect to the interests in question.

The value of a particular recording statute depends on the risk which subsequent purchasers run if the security transaction is not made public, the risk to which creditors are exposed, the opportunities offered a person for the perpetration of fraud in respect to his property, and the existence of economic and business conditions or practices which perform the function of recording statutes or otherwise tend to diminish the risks indicated. These conditions or practices may vary greatly in different communities and to the extent of that variation suggest a question as to the desirability of the same sort of recording requirements in all states. . . .

Reliable figures are wholly lacking upon which any estimate of the desirability of the extension of recording requirements [to accounts receivable and trust receipts financing] can be based. There are no figures giving any hint as to the ratio of the total number of transactions in various business fields compared to the number filed for public record. Likewise unavailable are any statistics dealing with the cost of the recording and filing systems, the absolute and relative use to which these systems are put, or the relative effectiveness of the recording systems as compared to unofficial methods of creditor protection. The difficulty of compiling statistics along most of these lines cannot be overestimated, but it might be possible for a statistical inquiry to shed some light on the relative amount of fraud practiced in states requiring the recording of conditional sales and in states having no such requirement. Another line of investigation might compare commercial practices in the United States in the security fields where registration is required with conditions in a country such as Germany in which there are no recording provisions in similar circumstances. Unfortunately in this article I cannot report the results of any such comprehensive inquiries. . . .

A leading credit association sent out in 1925 a questionnaire to a list of 500 commercial concerns and 100 banks, well distributed geographically. Replies were received from 362 commercial concerns and 61 banks. The results of the questionnaire was a nearly unanimous condemnation of the practice of secret assignments of accounts receivable and a practically unanimous expression of belief in the extension of the registration requirements to such transactions. An investigation made by the writer in the summer of 1929, while inconclusive in many respects, demonstrated clearly the interesting fact that if a questionnaire is sent to a list, selected at random, of persons extending merchandise or financial credit, in which inquiries are made of the correspondent as to whether he favors extending the recording requirements, he will reply in the affirmative. On the contrary, when the specific business situation to which the recording extension will apply is discussed with him personally, he will generally indicate an opposition to this particular enlargement of the public registration practices. For example, in a questionnaire answered by 44 large banks, less than one-third indicated that in extending financial credit they regarded either visible merchandise or other assets. The replies were practically unanimous that credit was extended on the basis of financial statements, supplemented by business references or personal acquaintance. In response to the specific question, approximately three-fourths stated that the major basis of credit was the financial statement.

Moreover, a clear majority of financial institutions making loans on a security basis informed me in their replies that they did not file their transactions generally for public record, that they did not examine the public records before extending credit, nor did they rely upon some agency which made such an examination. Nevertheless, they voted by a small majority in favor of the recording of both trust receipts and assignments of book accounts, and by a three-to-one majority indicated their belief that the filing requirements for chattel mortgages and conditional sales should be continued.

The results of an inquiry answered by approximately eighty institutions extending merchandise credit were in substantial agreement with the replies from those who extended financial credit, except that in reply to the inquiry as to the major basis of credit, the answers indicated a greater relative reliance on business references, trade and agency reports. The correspondents, whose business involved the extension of merchandise credit, showed by their tabulated replies an even more decided support for the Commissioners' filing proposals than did the replies of the financial institutions. In opposition to these conclusions, I have in my files letters from and memoranda of interviews with a large number of representatives of finance companies and other business institutions whose volume of transactions indicates that they are collectively the most significant lenders of credit in the United States on the security of both trust receipts and book accounts. . . .

If one may make a summary statement in respect to the proposals for extending filing requirements, it is that creditors are not actively in favor of new legislation. There is no feeling that serious credit problems demand solution through remedial statutes. Important creditors are insiders. For these, public records have no utility. Small creditors obviously would not seek filing offices before rendering various services or extending minor items of credit. In the circumstances it seems unnecessary to increase the cost of business and enlarge the number of public office-holders by making filing a condition of protecting assignees of book accounts and holders of trust receipts.

NOTES & QUESTIONS

1. *Notice filing.* The authors of a leading hornbook suggest that the question of whether a public filing system is really necessary was not asked by the Code draftsmen. J. White & R. Summers, Handbook of the Law under the Uniform Commercial Code 919 n.95 (2d ed. 1980). In fact, several heated but soon forgotten debates took place with respect to the need for filing notice of security interests in accounts receivable and consumer goods. An early survey of the issues with respect to public recording of accounts-receivable financing arrangements is set out in the Hanna excerpt supra. See also Dunham, Inventory and Accounts Receivable Financing, 62 Harv. L. Rev. 588, 610-613 (1949). See generally Baird, Notice Filing and the Problem of Ostensible Ownership, 12 J. Legal Stud. 53 (1983) (notice-filing system serves interests of secured creditors but is of virtually no assistance to unsecured creditors; filing does not give notice of security interests, but the system does form the basis of priority rules that sort out property claims).

2. *Exceptions to notice filing.* Although filing is used to give notice to potential third-party claimants to collateral, Article 9 makes a number of exceptions to notice filing:

(a) Possession. Transfer of possession to the secured party perfects a security interest. UCC 9-302(1)(a), 9-305. Taking possession away from the debtor is thought to be the functional equivalent of notice: a potential creditor will be put on notice that the debtor may not have full ownership rights in property not in his possession. But is possession the functional equivalent? Several recent analyses suggest that perfection by possession is inefficient. Phillips, Flawed Perfection: From Possession to Filing Under Article 9 (pts. 1 & 2), 59 B.U.L. Rev. 1 at 54, 209 (1979); Coogan, Article 9—An Agenda for the Next Decade, 87 Yale L.J. 1012, 1030-1053 (1978) (recommending that possession be eliminated as a means of perfection).

A moment's reflection suggests that the pledge is suitable only for a limited number of types of collateral. In most secured transactions the secured party leaves the collateral in the hands of the debtor both because the debtor must use the property to generate sums to repay the secured party and because the secured party does not wish to assume the costs and responsibilities of taking possession of the collateral. To leave the collateral with the debtor does, of course, mean that the secured party takes the risk that the debtor will use the collateral in ways not contemplated by the secured party when the transaction was entered into. These counterbalancing costs may explain why the pledge is now associated primarily with commercial paper, understood broadly to include investment securities, negotiable instruments, documents of title, and letters of credit.

(b) Automatic perfection. The Code provides for automatic perfection without filing for certain transactions because they are either noncommercial, short-term, or isolated transactions. A secured party with a security interest in consumer goods need not file in order to perfect the interest, although filing would be required if he wishes to have priority should the debtor sell the collateral to another consumer. UCC 9-302(1)(d), 9-307(2). Temporary perfection is also given when instruments or documents are returned to the debtor for business purposes. UCC 9-302(1)(b), 9-304(4), (5). As we shall see below, perfection will also continue for a limited period of time when the collateral is moved from one state to another. UCC 9-103(1)(d).

(c) Inadequate filing. A secured party who relies upon filing in order to perfect his interest may be protected even when the filing cannot give third parties notice. The interest is perfected, for example, when the financing statement is turned in to the filing officer; a subsequent clerical mistake in the filing will not affect perfection. UCC 9-403(1). A potential creditor may also be unable to find out who the secured party is from the public files because an assignment by the original secured party does not have to be recorded, UCC 9-302(2), and subsequent changes in the use of collateral may make an original filing inappropriate because the secured party is not required to make a new filing. UCC 9-401(3). A particularly difficult problem arises when the debtor changes its name or corporate structure because the Code provides that a filing may continue to be effective although a potential creditor of the newly-named entity may be unable to discover the security interest. UCC 9-402(7).

3. *Knowledge of the security interest.* A secured party who fails to perfect by notice filing or by a functional equivalent such as taking possession of the collateral, runs the risk of having his security interest subordinated to a third

party's claim to the collateral. To what extent should the third party's knowledge of the unperfected security interest "estop" the third party? See generally, Felsenfeld, Knowledge as a Factor in Determining Priorities Under the Uniform Commercial Code, 42 N.Y.U. L. Rev. 246 (1967). Note that the Code's general definition section sets out elaborate definitions of *notice, knowledge,* and the giving and receiving of notice and knowledge. UCC 1-201(25)-(27).

Article 9 generally plays down the effect of knowledge.

(a) Lien creditor. Under the 1972 text of UCC 9-301(1)(b) a lien creditor has priority over an unperfected security interest whether or not he knows of the interest. Until the 1972 amendments, however, a lien creditor with knowledge of any unperfected security interest was subordinated to the secured party. The reason given for the change was that the former section "was completely inconsistent in spirit with the rules of priority between security interests, where knowledge plays a very minor role."

(b) Buyer in ordinary course. A buyer in ordinary course of goods subject to a security interest takes free of that interest even if he knows of it. The buyer will not take free of the interest, however, if he knows not only that it exists but that the sale is prohibited by the security agreement. UCC 9-307(1), 1-201(9); see also 9-301(1)(c). Note, however, that different rules apply to purchasers of chattel paper and instruments. UCC 9-308, 9-309.

(c) Competing secured party. UCC 9-312 makes no explicit reference to a competing secured party's knowledge. Professor Grant Gilmore has questioned whether the omission was intentional. 2 G. Gilmore, Security Interest in Personal Property §34.2 (1965). Professor Gilmore's doubts, however, did not persuade the courts that a subsequent secured party who perfects a security interest with knowledge of an earlier unperfected interest should be subordinated. See In re Smith, supra p. 136. The explicit elimination in 1972 of the knowledge clause in UCC 9-301(1)(b) should put to rest Professor Gilmore's doubts.

4. *Policy of UCC 9-402(7).* UCC 9-402(7) provides:

> (7) A financing statement sufficiently shows the name of the debtor if it gives the individual, partnership or corporate name of the debtor, whether or not it adds other trade names or names of partners. Where the debtor so changes his name or in the case of an organization its name, identity or corporate structure that a filed financing statement becomes seriously misleading, the filing is not effective to perfect a security interest in collateral acquired by the debtor more than four months after the change, unless a new appropriate financing statement is filed before the expiration of that time. A filed financing statement remains effective with respect to collateral transferred by the debtor even though the secured party knows of or consents to the transfer.

BURKE, THE DUTY TO REFILE UNDER SECTION 9-402(7) OF THE REVISED ARTICLE 9, 35 Bus. Law. 1083, 1085-1086 (1980): "The policy arguments applicable to the refiling issue in the name change context can be readily marshalled. Those who would argue for a refiling rule point out that if a search under the debtor's current name would not reveal the filing made under the superseded name, the purpose of the Code's filing rule is defeated. The financing statement serves as notice to no one of the existence of the security interest, and secret liens, so despised by the Code, are sanctioned. The secured creditor ought to keep his filing current even if it means policing the debtor to discover the existence of a name change. When the secured creditor has actual knowledge of the name change, there can be no excuse for his conduct in deliberately allowing competing interests to be misled because of the stale filing.

"The arguments against requiring a refiling are threefold. First, the Code's expressed policy is to test the filing requirements by the conditions that existed when the security interest was created and not by the debtor's subsequent conduct over which the secured creditor has no control. Second, under the 1966 text of article 9, there is no mechanism available to the secured creditor to permit a new financing statement to be filed where a name change occurs if the debtor will not cooperate by signing a new financing statement or an amendment to the stale financing statement. [Cf. 1972 UCC 9-402(2).— EDS.] Third, a refiling requirement would impose an undue policing burden on a secured creditor, particularly where the credit extension does not involve continuing contact between the debtor and the secured creditor. After deals are on the books, they are administered by white collar clerks without the aid of lawyers, and it is rare for lawyers to be able to rely on laymen to note a change of name from the transmittal of payment or other incidental correspondence, or to organize more aggressive investigations of the question. On the other hand, the problem of search looks very different from the point of view of those searching the public records who ought to make reasonable efforts to be aware of existing filings. A searching creditor can avoid being misled by a name change and should be thus in a better position to avoid being misled by a name change and should be compelled to exercise reasonable diligence to avoid the conflict in the first place. Moreover, the need for awareness of prior security interests because of later financing will be far less frequent than would be a need for original financers to worry about refiling following possible changes of name and the like."

5. *Other filing systems.* A number of other commercial registers and filing systems may exist in any particular jurisdiction. Article 9 now coordinates fixture filings with real property records. UCC 9-401(1), 9-402(6). Other filing systems, such as incorporation or assumed name files, are not coordinated. Should they be? See In re Triple A Sugar Corp., 3 B.R. 240, 28 UCC Rep. 1197 (Bankr. D. Me. 1980) (when corporation changes its name it would not be unreasonable to require cross-indexing and notice to secured parties before recording in corporate name index).

Problem 3-10. Assume that the law of Texas requires a financing statement to be filed with both the secretary of state and with the county office where the collateral is located and that in the prototype transaction Austin State Bank failed to file in the county office. Two years after the bookbinder is delivered Apex borrows $10,000 from Southwest Finance Company and grants Southwest a security interest in the bookbinder. During negotiations Apex tells Southwest that it has granted the Bank a security interest in the bookbinder but Southwest does not check any financing statement office, nor does it request any information from the Bank. Southwest itself files a financing statement in all the proper offices. Does Southwest's security interest have priority over the Bank? See UCC 9-401(2), 9-208, 9-312.

Problem 3-11. Assume that at the time of the prototype transaction Apex is a sole proprietorship owned by Samuel Clemens and operated under the trade name "Apex Publishers." The debtor on the financing statement is listed as Samuel Clemens and the financing statement is filed under that name. Several years later Clemens transfers the business including the bookbinder to a partnership he has formed with his twin brother and the trade name is amended to "Apex Publishing Co." The bank knows of the transfer but does not amend the financing statement or file a new one. Six months later a creditor of the partnership obtains a judgment and delivers a writ of execution to the sheriff, who levies on the bookbinder. (Under Texas law the execution lien arises when the sheriff levies.) As between the bank and the creditor who has priority? See UCC 9-301, 9-306, 9-402(7).[6] Would it make any difference if the bank could show that the judgment creditor knew at the time she extended credit to the partnership that the bookbinder had been owned by Samuel Clemens before the formation of the partnership?

Problem 3-12. Assume that Austin State Bank submits to the secretary of state's office a properly completed financing statement together with the prescribed fee. Due to a "computer error" in that office the financing statement is filed under the name "Papex Publishing Co., Inc." Two years after the statement is filed Southwest Finance Company lends $10,000 to Apex, takes a security interest in the bookbinder, and files a financing statement that is properly indexed. Before making the loan Southwest checked with the secretary of state's office and was informed Apex was not listed as debtor on any filed financing statements. See UCC 9-407. Southwest did not otherwise know of the bank's security interest.

(a) Between the Bank and Southwest who has priority in the bookbinder? See UCC 9-403(1), 9-312; 9-407, Comment 1; In re Royal Electrotype Corp., 485 F.2d 394, 13 UCC Rep. 183 (3d Cir. 1973) (secured party does not bear risk of improper indexing by filing officer; pre-Code law of Pennsylvania changed).

(b) Would your answer be different if before Southwest checked the files the bank had learned that the financing statement had been misfiled?

(c) Does the subordinated party have recourse against the filing officer or

6. Texas, like most states, has an Assumed Name Act that would require Samuel Clemens and the partnership to file a statement setting out the assumed name and the full name and residence of each proprietor or partner. Tex. Bus. & Com. Code §§36.01-36.26 (Vernon Supp. 1984).

the state for any losses? See UCC 9-407; Hudleasco, Inc. v. State, 90 Wis. 2d 1057, 396 N.Y.S.2d 1002, 22 UCC Rep. 545 (Ct. Cl. 1975) (inaccurate certification not discretionary act so state is liable).

Problem 3-13. In the prototype transaction the financing statement was filed on January 2, the note and security agreement were signed on January 9, the cashier's check was issued on January 9, and the bookbinder was sent from Houston to Austin on January 19, where it was installed and began production on January 23.

(a) Assume that Linotype had obtained a judgment against Apex the previous November for supplies that Apex had not paid for. On January 19, when the bookbinder arrived at Apex's premises, Linotype obtained a writ of execution and delivered it to the sheriff with directions to levy on the bookbinder. As between Austin State Bank and Linotype, who has priority to the bookbinder? Do you need additional information? See UCC 9-301.[7]

---

7. An unsecured creditor may reach the debtor's rights in the collateral even if a security agreement prohibits involuntary transfer or makes them an event of default. UCC 9-311 states:

> The debtor's rights in collateral may be voluntarily or involuntarily transferred (by way of sale, creation of a security interest, attachment, levy, garnishment or other judicial process) notwithstanding a provision in the security agreement prohibiting any transfer or making the transfer constitute a default.

How this section operates in practice, however, is often difficult to determine. See S. Riesenfeld, Cases & Materials on Creditors' Remedies and Debtors' Protection 206-208 (3d ed. 1979).

A first problem is that state law is not always clear as to what procedures a secured party may use to assert priority over a lien creditor. Texas law, for example, does not address the issue directly. Compare N.Y. Civ. Prac. Law §5239:

Proceeding to determine adverse claims

> Prior to the application of property or debt by a sheriff or receiver to the satisfaction of a judgment, any interested person may commence a special proceeding against the judgment creditor or other person with whom a dispute exists to determine rights in the property or debt, by serving a notice of petition upon the respondent, the sheriff or receiver, and such other person as the court directs, in the same manner as a notice of motion. . . . The court may vacate the execution or order, void the levy, direct the disposition of the property or debt, or direct that damages be awarded. . . . The court may permit any interested person to intervene in the proceeding.

A second problem concerns the effect of a sheriff's sale of the collateral on the secured party's security interest: does the purchaser take free of the security interest? Texas court rules do address this problem:

> Goods and chattels pledged, assigned or mortgaged as security for any debt or contract, may be levied upon and sold on execution against the person making the pledge, assignment or mortgage subject thereto; and the purchaser shall be entitled to the possession when it is held by the pledgee, assignee or mortgagee, on complying with the conditions of the pledge, assignment or mortgage. [Tex. Civ. P. Rules Ann. R. 643 (Vernon 1967).]

Some courts, however, suggest that pre-Code rules continue to govern this issue. See Maryland Natl. Bank v. Porter-Way Harvester Mfg. Co., 300 A.2d 8, 11 UCC Rep. 843 (Del. 1972)

(b) Assume that Austin State Bank files its financing statement on Monday, February 2, rather than on January 2. If Linotype had the sheriff actually levy on the bookbinder on January 29 will the bank or Linotype have priority in the bookbinder? See UCC 9-301(2).[8]

Problem 13-14. One year after the prototype transaction Apex agrees with ABM to trade in the bookbinder for a new model with technological improvements. Apex reports the transaction in its annual audited accounts sent to Austin State Bank. The bank does nothing. Does the bank have a security interest in either the old or the new bookbinder? Is it a perfected interest? See UCC 9-306, 9-307.

Will the bank have an attached and perfected security interest if:

(a) Apex has exchanged the bookbinder for a printing press?

(b) Apex has exchanged the bookbinder for a Matisse painting to be hung in the Apex business office?

(c) Apex has sold the bookbinder for cash and used the cash to purchase the new bookbinder, printing press, or painting?

Problem 3-15. Assume that in September before the transaction Apex began negotiations with Southwest Finance Company for a working capital loan. Although no agreement was reached at that time, Apex signed a financing statement covering "inventory and equipment," and the finance company filed it with the Texas Secretary of State. In February, after the prototype transaction, the finance company made a loan of $10,000, and Apex signed a security agreement covering "all inventory and equipment now owned." As between bank and the finance company, who has priority to the bookbinder? See UCC 9-312(4), (5). (Assume first that neither secured party has a purchase money security interest. Afterwards, consider what effect such an interest has on the general priority rule in 9-312(5). We return to these rules in greater detail in Chapter 5.)

(purchaser takes free of security interest, which attaches only to the proceeds). Does the UCC resolve this question so that reference to non-Code law is improper? See UCC 9-201, 9-306.

8. In many jurisdictions there may be non-Code statutory provisions that provide rules for calculating time periods. In Texas, for example, §2.04 of the Code Construction Act provides:

(a) In computing a period of days, the first day is excluded and the last day is included.

(b) If the last day of any period is a Saturday, Sunday, or legal holiday, the period is extended to include the next day which is not a Saturday, Sunday, or legal holiday.

(c) If a number of months is to be computed by counting the months from a particular day, the period ends on the same numerical day in the concluding month as the day of the month from which the computation is begun, unless there are not that many days in the concluding month, in which case the period ends on the last day of that month. [Tex. Rev. Civ. Stat. Ann. art. 5429b-2 (Vernon Supp. 1984).]

Problem 3-16. Assume that prior to the loan from Austin State Bank ABM had leased the bookbinder to Apex on a short-term lease. Although the lease agreement did not provide Apex an option to purchase the bookbinder, ABM and Apex subsequently agree that Apex may purchase the bookbinder in its possession if Apex obtains financing. Austin State Bank provides the financing as in the prototype. The sales contract with ABM and the bank's security agreement are signed on January 9 but a financing statement is not filed until Monday, January 19. In the meantime, however, a judgment creditor of Apex has the sheriff levy on the bookbinder on January 15. As between the Bank and the judgment creditor, who has priority in the bookbinder? See UCC 9-301, 9-305. When does Apex have rights in the collateral? When does Apex become a debtor?

Note: Multistate Transactions (UCC 9-103)

When a secured transaction involves contacts with several different states the parties will wish to know what law governs their transaction and where to file in order to perfect the security interest. We have already called your attention to UCC 9-103, which provides at least some answers to these questions. The draftsmen of the 1972 text rewrote and reorganized this section to meet extensive criticism of the 1962 text. In their effort to clarify several troubling issues the draftsmen were aided by the almost universal adoption of the Code within the United States. They were also assisted by the increasing acceptance of certificate-of-title legislation for motor vehicles. See 1 G. Gilmore, Security Interests in Personal Property 595-631 (1965); Coogan, The New UCC Article 9, 86 Harv. L. Rev. 477, 529-558 (1973).

As you read the 1972 text of UCC 9-103 you should note two important features. First, you will quickly discover that the section is organized by types of property. For each type there is a different basis for determining what is the applicable law and where a secured party must file to perfect a security interest. To perfect a security interest in *ordinary goods* (a classification you have not yet encountered) the secured party must determine the *situs* or location of the goods, while to perfect an interest in *mobile goods* (or accounts) the debtor's location is the relevant factor. Second, you will see that UCC 9-103 determines the governing law only for issues of perfection and the effect of perfection or nonperfection. The 1962 text used the ambiguous term *validity* rather than *perfection*. The revised text makes clear that UCC 9-103 applies when third-party rights might be affected, but leaves other issues to the general conflict-of-laws rules set out in UCC 1-105(1). Thus disputes over enforceability, attachment, and proceedings on default are left to the general rules on "reasonable relation" to a chosen law or an "appropriate relation" to the forum found in UCC 1-105.

In the following Problems we ask you to study the conflicts rules in UCC 9-103(1); in Chapter 7 we will examine the effect of other subsections. Of the many complexities in UCC 9-103(1) perhaps the most mysterious is the concept of *last event*, found in paragraph (b). In his analysis of this concept, Mr. Coogan suggests that the only events of perfection recognized by the Code are the acts constituting attachment and publicity (e.g., filing). Coogan, supra, at 537-544. The following analysis suggests a different conclusion: "If a security interest attaches to collateral and the additional step of filing or possession necessary to perfect it is not taken, the law of the jurisdiction in which the collateral then is tells us that the security interest is unperfected. If an appropriate filing or the taking of possession occurs while the collateral is still in that jurisdiction, the law of that jurisdiction now tells us that this last event has perfected the security interest. But if the filing occurs in another state, the law of the jurisdiction in which the collateral remains tells us that the security interest is still unperfected. If the collateral then moves into the geographic reach of a jurisdiction where there is an appropriate filing, the law of that jurisdiction tells us that this last event [i.e., the crossing of the state boundary—EDS.] has perfected the security interest." Kripke, The "Last Event" Test for Perfection of Security Interests Under Article 9 of the Uniform Commercial Code, 50 N.Y.U. L. Rev. 47, 48-49 (1975). Will the Coogan or Kripke analysis lead to the more sensible results in practice?

Problem 3-17. Assume that Apex and Austin State Bank enter into the prototype transaction but that ABM supplies the bookbinder from its plant in Chicago, Illinois, rather than from its Houston plant. ABM ships the bookbinder from Illinois on January 19 but it does not arrive in Austin until January 24. The bank has filed a financing statement in Texas on January 2 but does not file a financing statement in Illinois. On January 26 Apex without the bank's knowledge turns the bookbinder over to a supplier in satisfaction of a past-due obligation. Does the bank have priority to the bookbinder? See UCC 9-103(1)(b), (1)(c); 9-301(1)(c). Would your answer be different if the bank's security interest was not a purchase money interest?

Problem 3-18. Assume that at the time it enters into the prototype transaction Apex has a branch office for distribution in Denver, Colorado.

(a) Without informing the bank, Apex directs ABM to send the bookbinder to the Denver branch. ABM supplies the bookbinder from its Chicago plant. Three weeks later Apex files a petition in bankruptcy. Can the trustee in bankruptcy avoid the bank's security interest? See UCC 9-103(1)(b), (1)(c); 9-301(1)(b). Would your answer be different if the bankruptcy petition is filed six months after delivery to the Denver branch?

(b) The same facts as in (a) except that ABM first delivers the bookbinder from its Chicago plant to Apex's plant in Austin in order to test the equipment. After seven days of tests ABM redelivers the bookbinder to Denver. Three weeks later Apex files a bankruptcy petition. May the trustee avoid the bank's interest? See UCC 9-103, Comment 3.

Problem 3-19. The Austin State Bank and Apex enter into the transaction described in the prototype. Assume that several years later Apex transfers the ABM bookbinder to Colorado for use at its branch office. The officer in charge of the Apex account at the Austin State Bank knows of the bookbinder's transfer and does not object. The bank, however, does not give written consent to the transfer and does not file a financing statement in Colorado. Several months later a judgment creditor of Apex obtains a writ of execution and has the sheriff in Colorado levy on the bookbinder. Is there anything the subordinate party can do? Would your answers be different if there was no lien creditor and instead Apex has sold the bookbinder to a used-equipment dealer in Colorado several months after the bookbinder arrives in Colorado?

E. DEFAULT

No respectable creditor likes to see its debtor default. Unfortunately debtors do default and creditors must plan for this contingency. The default provisions in Part 5 of Article 9 seek to minimize the loss to the secured party and at the same time protect the debtor from overreaching. The following materials present some of the problems that arise on default of the commercial debtor. Chapter 8 will explore problems of default by a consumer.

To appreciate fully the importance of the Article 9 default procedure requires you to understand how an unsecured creditor enforces a claim when the debtor cannot be persuaded to perform voluntarily. Suppose, for example, that ABM had sold the bookbinder to Apex on unsecured credit, payment to be made 30 days after installation. If Apex does not pay at the time it agreed to do so ABM will probably go to great lengths to work out an arrangement rescheduling the debt. One remedy ABM will not have, however, is the right to enter Apex's premises to repossess the bookbinder. Instead, ABM will have to procure and enforce a judgment against Apex for the amount owed.

To obtain a judgment ABM will follow the ordinary court procedures for commencing an action. If Apex has a defense, a right to set off, or a counterclaim it will file an answer to ABM's complaint and there may be a trial. It is possible, however, that Apex will not dispute the claim and will allow a default judgment to be entered. The judgment will recite that it is "ordered and adjudged" that ABM recover from Apex the amount of the debt together with court costs.

Before judgment is entered ABM may be able to take advantage of prejudgment remedies designed to assure that there will be property available to satisfy a judgment. A writ of attachment, for example, may be issued by the court directing the sheriff to take possession of sufficient Apex property to assure satisfaction of a subsequent judgment. Apex in turn may be able to recover possession by posting a bond. The traditional prejudgment procedures have been revised in recent years in light of constitutional standards of due process in order to provide debtors notice and a prompt hearing. In many jurisdictions these provisional remedies will be available only in unusual circumstances, as, for example, when Apex appears likely to disappear with the bookbinder.

The entry of judgment by itself will not automatically assure ABM of payment. It is necessary to have the judgment entered on the judgment docket and then have the court clerk issue a writ of execution directing the sheriff to take possession (levy on) Apex's property, including the bookbinder, although ABM is free to ignore the bookbinder in favor of other Apex property. Frequently the sheriff will ask ABM (the judgment creditor) to help identify property available for execution. The sheriff will be cautious: state laws frequently exempt household items and tools of the debtor's trade from creditors' claims; moreover, the sheriff will not want to get involved with third-party claimants.

Once the property is taken by the sheriff, the sheriff will sell it in accordance with local procedures. These will require formal publicity of some sort. Because the purchaser at a sheriff's sale will usually take subject to third-party claims, the amount bid may be a fraction of the market value of the property sold. Indeed, in many jurisdictions, not only will the judgment creditor be able to bid at the sheriff's sale but it may be the only bidder. From the proceeds of the sale the sheriff will deduct his fee and return the remainder to the court clerk, who will apply the proceeds to ABM's judgment and return the surplus, if any, to Apex.

Even after satisfaction of the judgment, ABM runs the risk that the legal action taken against Apex will precipitate its bankruptcy and that the judgment will be avoided in order to treat equally other creditors of the financially-failing debtor. See Bankruptcy Code §547(b) and Chapter 4.

Assuming, however, that Apex is not recalcitrant and that there are no third-party claimants who intervene, ABM will find that this state-provided debt collection procedure works smoothly and relatively inexpensively. Nevertheless, as the following materials illustrate, ABM would find that taking a security interest saves time and expense and gives greater protection in bankruptcy.

1. Options on Default

Problem 3-20. The Austin State Bank and Apex enter into the transaction described in the prototype. Apex subsequently runs into financial difficulty. For several months in the spring of 1983, Apex makes its installment payments on the bookbinder three to seven days late. On the last late payment the bank officer in charge of the Apex account orally expresses concern to the president of Apex about its financial condition. In August 1983 Apex fails to make its monthly installment payment, and the bank officer consults you about possible legal action against the company. Advise her.

SPILLERS v. FIRST NATIONAL BANK OF ARENZVILLE
81 Ill. App. 3d 199, 400 N.E.2d 1057, 28 UCC Rep. 884 (1980)

WEBBER, J. . . . The background, as revealed in the record, indicates that petitioner on March 14, 1977, borrowed $25,000 from respondent and gave a judgment note therefor. The purpose of the loan was to purchase a crane which was pledged as collateral and petitioner added to the crane a set of *collateral* concrete forms which were about 2 years old at the time.

The note was for six months' duration and at the end of that time respondent demanded payment. None was made and the duration, by agreement, was extended for 30 days. At the end of that extension, no payment having been made, respondent placed the note in judgment on December 13, 1977. This judgment was confirmed on January 27, 1978, and thereafter respondent brought citation proceedings to enforce it.

Apparently as a result of the citation proceedings, petitioner turned the crane and the forms over to respondent who proceeded to sell them. One of the principal issues in this appeal is the nature and timeliness of the notice given to *issue:* petitioner of the sales of the collateral.

On March 7, 1978, petitioner's attorney received a letter from respondent's attorney stating that respondent had received a bid of $15,000 for the crane and it would be sold "[T]en days from the receipt of this notice . . . as per our agreement of February 2, 1978." Petitioner replied to this by submitting an offer of $16,000 for the crane through a corporation owned and operated by him. Respondent replied to this offer by asserting three conditions: (1) that a cashier's check for $16,000 be tendered within four days; (2) that petitioner's concrete forms be tendered to respondent at the time the crane was picked up; and (3) that petitioner sign a waiver of any and all rights in the crane, including the right to object to the sale and to exercise any right of redemption. Plaintiff felt unable to meet these conditions and all negotiations and communications between the parties then ceased.

Respondent on April 22, 1978, sold the crane to the $15,000 bidder without making any further efforts to secure other bids. Five days later this bidder sold the crane to an equipment dealer in Aledo, Illinois, named Henderson. The price of this sale does not appear in the record. On November 3, 1978, Henderson sold the crane for $27,500 to a contractor in Iowa, named Hall. At trial on May 4, 1979, Hall testified that the crane was worth all he had paid for it and that he had it for sale at a price of $35,000.

Respondent next proceeded to sell the concrete forms. One bid was received from a contractor who had his own forms mixed in with petitioner's forms on a job site. Another bid, $500 higher, was received from another contractor but was afterwards withdrawn because that bidder was unable to determine which of the intermingled forms he was bidding on. Respondent then sold the forms for $6,120 to the other bidder. It is uncontroverted that petitioner knew of the impending sale of the forms generally, but had no specific knowledge until later.

After both sales had been consummated, the crane and the forms, a deficiency of approximately $6,500 existed on the judgment. Respondent collected this through various postjudgment proceedings. In the same cause, petitioner on October 13, 1978, filed a petition for damages against respondent in which he alleged that the sales of the crane and the forms were not commercially reasonable within the meaning of the Commercial Code. After a bench trial, the circuit court found that the sales were commercially reasonable and dismissed the petition for damages. This appeal followed. We reverse.

A preliminary question to be answered is whether this transaction is governed by the Commercial Code. UCC 9-501(5) provides as follows:

> When a secured party has reduced his claim to judgment the lien of any levy which may be made upon his collateral by virtue of any execution based upon the judgment shall relate back to the date of the perfection of the security interest in such collateral. A judicial sale, pursuant to such execution, is a foreclosure of the security interest by judicial procedure within the meaning of this section, and the secured party may purchase at the sale and thereafter hold the collateral free of any other requirements of this Article.

The Official Comments to this section read in part as follows: "The second sentence of the subsection (i.e., (5)) makes clear that a judicial sale following judgment, execution and levy is one of the methods of foreclosure contemplated by subsection (1); such a sale is governed by other law and not by this Article. . . ." UCC 9-501.

The Illinois Comments on UCC 9-501 in referring to subsection (5) have this to say: "The last sentence of Official Comment 6 makes explicit what is implicit in this Section—that a judicial sale following judgment, execution and levy is governed by other law, not by this Article. However, if a secured party repossesses collateral and also reduces his claim to judgment (whether concurrently or not) and if repossession involves taking possession of collateral in any way other than pursuant to an execution issued following a judgment, his repossession and disposition of the collateral will probably be subject to the requirements of this Part." Ill. Ann. Stat., ch. 26, para. 9-501, at 320-321 (Smith-Hurd (1974)).

We find that the Illinois Comment quoted above accurately states the law and a plain reading of the statute leads inevitably to such a result. Judgment, execution and levy are ancient procedures in the law and are governed by their own statute which dates from the earliest days of this State. The Act of 1872 . . . has survived virtually unchanged for over 100 years, and is most explicit in its terms. The veriest tyro at the bar can recognize an execution sale.

On the other hand, if the procedure employed does not follow the dictates of chapter 77, it necessarily falls within the ambit of chapter 26, paras. 9-501 et seq. The secured judgment creditor has his choice: chapter 77 or chapter 26. The existence of the judgment is only the first step along either road. If the creditor elects chapter 77, he must then proceed to obtain a writ of execution, a levy and a sale. If he elects chapter 26, the latter are not involved and the existence of the judgment is immaterial. He may proceed with chapter 26 with or without a judgment.

In the instant case, respondent had already reduced his claim to judgment, but there is nothing in the record remotely resembling an execution sale under chapter 77. The petitioner turned the collateral over to the respondent who proceeded to make the sales on its own. No execution writ was ever delivered to a sheriff or other officer; no such officer ever advertised a sale; no such officer ever reported a sale. The instant case is clearly a disposition of collateral after default under UCC 9-503 . . . notwithstanding the claim had already been reduced to judgment. *Held.*

[The court then concluded that (1) respondent had failed to notify petitioner of "all and every" proposed private sale as required by UCC 9-504(3); (2) failure to give notice bars any deficiency; (3) petitioner's petition was sufficient to allow the court to review the judgment by confession even though the petition did not fully comply with procedural formalities; (4) the petitioner's right to damages is cumulative to the barring of the deficiency if he established on remand that a proper valuation of the collateral is in excess of the total debt.—EDS.]

Reversed and remanded with directions.

NOTES & QUESTIONS

1. *Definition of default.* The UCC does not define *default.* Should the draftsmen have made an attempt? Note that Article 9 focuses on the agreement creating the security interest and not on the obligation secured.

For a statutory definition of *default* see Uniform Consumer Credit Code §5.109 (1974):

> An agreement of the parties to a consumer credit transaction with respect to default on the part of the consumer is enforceable only to the extent that:
> (1) The consumer fails to make a payment as required by agreement; or
> (2) the prospect of payment, performance, or realization of collateral is significantly impaired; the burden of establishing the prospect of significant impairment is on the creditor.

This provision was drafted with the consumer debtor in mind. To what extent is the formulation adequate or appropriate in the commercial context?

2. *Judgment or cognovit notes.* The Illinois Civil Practice Act deals specifically with the judgment note known in other jurisdictions as a "cognovit"

note. See Ill. Ch. 100, §50(3) ("any person for a debt bona fide due may confess judgment by himself or attorney duly authorized, without process"). The Illinois statute was amended in 1979 to prohibit a judgment note in a "consumer transaction" as defined by the statute. Following a federal district court decision holding that garnishment invoked in a proceeding on a judgment note violated the due process clause of the fourteenth amendment, local court rules in at least some Illinois circuit courts were amended to require the judgment to be confirmed after service of process.

The United States Supreme Court upheld the constitutionality of the cognovit note in D. H. Overmyer Co. v. Frick Co., 405 U.S. 174 (1972) (a business corporation that signed a cognovit note with the advice of counsel "voluntarily, intelligently, and knowingly waived the rights it otherwise possessed to pre-judgment notice and hearing, and . . . did so with full awareness of the legal consequences"). The court in *Overmyer* indicated, however, that it might reach a different conclusion if there was unequal bargaining power or overreaching.

The Federal Trade Commission has defined as an unfair credit practice any use of a cognovit or confession of judgment term in a consumer credit transaction. 16 C.F.R. §444.2(a)(1) (1985). State legislation may also limit the use of these terms. The Uniform Consumer Credit Code §3.306, for example, prohibits a consumer from authorizing a party to confess judgment on a claim arising out of a consumer credit transaction. The UCC is neutral. See UCC 3-112(1)(d).

One commentator has summarized the business use of cognovit notes as follows: "The use of cognovit clauses by lenders and installment sellers seems to serve three classes of business purposes. First, the clauses can be so written as to facilitate debt-collection by including waivers of: procedural defects in the resulting judgment, the right of appeal from the resulting judgment, the right of inquisition, and the right to notice. Given such strictly written clauses, the process of debt-collection by judgment becomes an all but automatic process and presumably allows the economics of efficiency to lower the cost of credit. Second, it is possible — and indeed it is the practice in some states — to write the cognovit clause in such a way as to allow entry of the confession of judgment *before* any default in payment. This leaves the need only for execution to be levied upon the debtor's property once the actual default in payment occurs. Thus the creditor has what amounts to a judgment lien on the property of the debtor for the life of the obligation. This device is often used in place of collateral from the debtor to secure his debt. The third purpose served by cognovit notes is that they can be used to retain personal jurisdiction over out of state debtors after they have left the state in which the note was signed or whose law governs the note." Note, Cognovit Judgments: Some Constitutional Considerations, 70 Colum. L. Rev. 1118, 1130 (1970). See generally Hopson, Cognovit Judgments: An Ignored Problem of Due Process and Full Faith and Credit, 29 U. Chi. L. Rev. 111 (1961).

3. *Practical considerations: the business workout.* Note the court's reference in

Spillers to the 30-day extension. Did the secured party seek to enforce the judgment note immediately after the extension expired? Creditors are not always in a hurry to enforce legal rights; frequently they will negotiate with the debtor to adjust the underlying obligation. See Role, The Business Workout—A Primer for Participation Creditors, 11 UCC L.J. 183 (1978). If creditors in a particular industry or locality usually seek an adjustment before commencing legal action or before repossessing collateral under the UCC, is failure to seek adjustment a violation of the Code's good faith requirement (UCC 1-203)? Does the custom become a term of the contract (UCC 1-205)?

4. *Legal alternatives on default.* What legal alternatives do the parties have after default? The UCC contemplates that the parties may go to court rather than use self-help repossession. See UCC 9-501(5) and Official Comment 6; see also UCC 9-507(2). A judicial action theoretically might seek (a) judgment on the underlying obligation, followed by issuance of a writ of execution, levy, and a judicial sale; (b) judicial foreclosure of the security interest; or (c) a judgment in a replevin action whereby the secured party obtains possession of the collateral. In *Spillers,* what did the secured party seek? Why would a secured party ever choose to go to court rather than pursue self-help repossession under the UCC? See generally J. White & R. Summers, Handbook of the Law Under the Uniform Commercial Code §26-4 (2d ed. 1980).

What if the secured party repossesses and rather than promptly selling the collateral seeks a judgment on the underlying obligation? Does the UCC eliminate the "election of remedies" doctrine? *No ≠ cumulative*

5. *Role of the lawyer on default.* Note the role of attorneys in the *Spillers* case. How would you evaluate their performance both before and during litigation? What should the role of lawyers be when the original transaction has broken down?

6. *Notice and waiver: default and acceleration.* Does the UCC require the secured party to give notice of default or notice of acceleration of the underlying obligation? To what extent may a duty to give notice, if it exists, be waived in the security agreement or promissory note embodying the underlying obligation?

FULTON NATIONAL BANK v. HORN
239 Ga. 648, 238 S.E.2d 358, 22 UCC Rep. 1302 (1977)

Hill, Justice. Sidney Horn executed a note and security agreement to the Fulton National Bank granting the bank a security interest in a vehicle. Horn got behind in his payments and the bank had his automobile repossessed. Horn recovered the car four days later and then brought this tort action against the bank for wrongful repossession without notice and wrongful retention of the vehicle. The bank's motion for summary judgment was granted by the trial court. . . .

The crucial provision of the agreement states: "In the event of a default, any of the Liabilities [any indebtedness owed the bank, whether due or to become due] may, *at the option* of the Bank and *without demand or notice* of any kind, be *declared,* by Bank, and thereupon immediately shall become due and payable and Bank may take possession of or retain and sell or otherwise dispose of the Collateral or any part thereof, charge Borrower's deposit accounts with the amount of the Liabilities or any part thereof, and exercise from time to time any and all rights and remedies available to it under this agreement, any written instrument relating to any of the Liabilities or Collateral and any applicable law." (Matter in brackets and underlining added.)

The Court of Appeals construed this provision as requiring the bank to give notice of acceleration before it could repossess. . . .

In Lee v. O'Quinn, 184 Ga. 44, 190 S.E. 564 (1937), there was a contract of purchase of land and a promissory note. The contract provided that in the event of default the creditor "may at once declare" the entire balance of the purchase price due and payable. The note provided that in the event of default "at the option of the holder" the principal sum shall forthwith become due. However, the contract recited that the note provided that in event of default the unpaid balance shall become due "at once" and "without further notice or action." The recital did not mention the creditor's option. The court in division one of the opinion held that the recital in the contract as to what the note provided could not prevail over what the contract and note actually provided. In division two, the court (reading the words "may . . . declare" and "at the option of the holder") held that under the provisions of the note and contract in order for there to be acceleration the creditor must take some affirmative action evidencing his intention to take advantage of the right of acceleration and that the exercise of the option to declare the balance due could not take place in the creditor's mind but must be communicated to the debtor or manifested by some affirmative act sufficient to constitute notice of election such as filing suit for the entire debt.

In White v. Turbidy, 227 Ga. 825, 183 S.E.2d 363 (1971), the promissory note secured by deed to secure debt provided that in event of default the entire principal and accrued interest "shall, at the option of the holder, without notice to the [maker], become due. . . ." Citing Lee v. O'Quinn, supra, the court held that where the holder of a note has an option to declare acceleration, acceleration occurs only upon declaration thereof by the holder and notification thereof to the debtor. The court in *White* restricted Lee v. O'Quinn unnecessarily. *Lee* held that where the creditor has an option to declare the unpaid balance due, the exercise of that option must be communicated to the debtor or manifested by affirmative act constituting notice of election. White v. Turbidy appears to have referred only to the communication and not to have given effect to the "without notice" provision in the note there under consideration. . . .

Where the parties agree that in the event of default the creditor "may declare" acceleration, the exercise of the option to declare acceleration must be communicated to the debtor or manifested by some affirmative act sufficient to constitute notice to the debtor of acceleration, Lee v. O'Quinn, supra, but where the parties agree that in the event of default the creditor "may declare" acceleration "without notice" to the debtor, Lee v. O'Quinn is not applicable and, according to the agreement, notice of declaration of acceleration need not be communicated to the debtor.

The Court of Appeals erred in this case . . . by failing to give effect to the words agreed to by the parties: "without demand or notice of any kind." Moreover, under the terms of the agreement here in issue, the bank had the right to "exercise . . . any . . . rights . . . available to it under this agreement . . ." and thus it had the right to repossess independently of its right to accelerate. There being no agreed requirement of notice attached to the right to repossess, notice was not required prior to repossession. . . . UCC 9-503. Thus notice prior to repossession was not required in this case, any issue of fact as to whether notice was received would not be material, and thus the trial court did not err in sustaining the defendant's motion for summary judgment.

NOTES & QUESTIONS

1. *Acceleration of installment notes.* The black letter rule is that contracts to pay money in installments are breached one installment at a time, but when a promissory note is used, it is customary to include an acceleration clause. These clauses may permit a holder or maker to accelerate installment payments at his option, or may provide for automatic acceleration on the occurrence of a specified event such as nonpayment of an installment. Although it might be argued that an acceleration clause renders the note nonnegotiable because it is not payable at a definite time, the UCC explicitly states that acceleration clauses do not make the note nonnegotiable. UCC 3-109(1)(c).

2. *Acceleration clauses in security agreements.* A security agreement that sets out the debtor's obligation may also provide for acceleration upon default. In the absence of an acceleration clause the black letter rule applies. If the security agreement is accompanied by a promissory note, an acceleration clause in one or both documents will be given effect by reading the two documents together, although a holder in due course of the note may not be bound by a clause contained only in the security agreement. UCC 3-119.

3. *Option to accelerate at will (UCC 1-208).* UCC 1-208 provides that when a holder has the option to accelerate payment at will he has this power only "if he in good faith believes that the prospect of payment or performance is impaired." The party against whom the power is to be exercised, however, has the burden of establishing lack of good faith. See UCC 1-201(8) (definition of "burden of establishing"). Does UCC 1-208 apply to any of the following clauses?

(a) Upon failure of the maker to make payment of an installment when due, the holder shall have the right to declare the entire principal balance and all accrued interest immediately due, payable, and collectible without notice.

(b) Upon failure of the maker to make an installment payment, the entire principal balance and all accrued interest shall be due immediately without notice.

(c) This note shall be in default if for any reason the holder of this note deems himself insecure. In such event the holder may immediately and without notice declare the entire balance of this note due and payable together with all expenses of collection by suit or otherwise, including reasonable attorney's fees.

(d) Debtor shall be in default if Secured Party deems himself insecure. On default Secured Party may declare the entire balance of Debtor's obligations due and payable.

(e) At Secured Party's option, Debtor shall be in default if he dies. On default Secured Party may declare the entire balance of Debtor's obligations due and payable.

2.   Repossession

Problem 3-21. Assume that two years after entering into the prototype transaction Apex defaults on its obligation to Austin State Bank. An officer of the bank has decided to use self-help by repossessing the bookbinder. To avoid any possible liability for wrongful repossession the officer consults you about the steps he and his agents should take when repossessing the bookbinder. Advise him.

STONE MACHINERY CO. v. KESSLER
1 Wash. App. 750, 463 P.2d 651, 7 UCC Rep. 135 (1970)

Evans, Chief Judge. Plaintiff Stone Machinery brought this action in Asotin County to repossess a D-9 Caterpillar Tractor which plaintiff had sold to defendant Frank Kessler under conditional sales contract. Service of process was not made on the defendant but plaintiff located the tractor in Oregon and repossessed it. The defendant then filed an answer and cross-complaint in the Asotin County replevin action, alleging that the plaintiff wrongfully and maliciously repossessed the tractor, and sought compensatory and punitive damages under Oregon law. Trial was to the court without a jury and the court awarded defendant compensatory damages in the sum of $18,586.20, and punitive damages in the sum of $12,000 on defendant's cross-complaint.

The operative facts are not in serious dispute. Defendant Kessler purchased, by conditional sales contract, a used D-9 Caterpillar Tractor from the plaintiff Stone Machinery, for the sum of $23,500. The unpaid balance of

$17,500 was to be paid in monthly installments, with skip payments. The defendant's payment record was erratic and several payments were made late. However, payments of $3600 on March 29, 1966, and $1800 on July 18, 1966, put the contract payments on a current basis. The payment due on August 10, 1966 was not made and, on September 7, 1966, plaintiff's credit manager, Richard Kazanis, went to the defendant's ranch in Garfield, Washington, and demanded payment of the balance due on the contract or immediate possession of the tractor. At this time defendant had made payments on the purchase price totaling $17,200, including the trade-in. The defendant was unable to make full payment, or any payment at that time, and informed Mr. Kazanis that he would not relinquish possession of the tractor to him at that time, or at any time in the future, in the absence of proper judicial proceedings showing his right to repossess, and that "someone would get hurt" if an attempt was made to repossess without "proper papers." At that time the defendant informed Mr. Kazanis that he, the defendant, expected to be awarded a contract by the U.S. Bureau of Fisheries to do some work with the D-9 at their installation on the Grande Ronde River near Troy, Oregon, and that he would then be able to pay on the tractor.

On September 13, 1966, the plaintiff instituted this action in Asotin County, Washington, but the sheriff was unable to locate the tractor in that county. Thereafter, the plaintiff instituted another action in Garfield County, but the sheriff was unable to locate the tractor in that county. The evidence indicates that on September 24 Kessler took the tractor to Oregon to work the bureau of fisheries job.

On September 27, 1966, Mr. Kazanis, by use of an airplane, located the tractor on the Grande Ronde River, west of Troy, Wallowa County, Oregon. He then contacted the sheriff of Wallowa County and requested him to accompany them in the repossession of the tractor to prevent any violence by the defendant. The sheriff agreed to meet with Mr. Kazanis at Troy, Oregon, and on September 27, 1966, Mr. Kazanis in his private car, plaintiff's mechanic in a company pickup, and the plaintiff's truck driver in the company lo-boy truck, left Walla Walla, and the following morning met the Wallowa County Sheriff at Troy, where the sheriff was shown a copy of the conditional sales contract. The sheriff confirmed previous legal advice plaintiff had received that the plaintiff had the right to repossess the tractor (although not by the use of force) and thereupon the sheriff, in his official sheriff's car, followed by Mr. Kazanis in his private car, the mechanic in the pickup, and the truck driver in the lo-boy, proceeded to the scene where the defendant was operating the D-9 tractor in the Grande Ronde River approximately 7 miles west of Troy, pursuant to contract with the U.S. Bureau of Fisheries.

Upon arriving at the scene the sheriff, accompanied by Mr. Kazanis, walked to the edge of the river and motioned the defendant, who was working with the tractor in the river, to bring the tractor to shore. The sheriff was in uniform and wearing his badge and sidearms. The sheriff informed the defendant that the plaintiff Stone Machinery had a right to repossess the tractor, and stated, "We come to pick up the tractor." The defendant asked the sheriff if he had proper papers to take the tractor and the sheriff replied, "No." The defendant Kessler protested and objected to the taking of the tractor but offered no physical resistance because, as he testified, "he didn't think he had to disregard an order of the sheriff." The plaintiff's employee then loaded the tractor on the lo-boy and left for Walla Walla, Washington.

Within a few days the tractor was sold to a road contractor at Milton-Freewater, Oregon, for the sum of $7447.80 cash, on an "as is" basis. The sale price represented the balance due on the contract, plus the plaintiff's charges for repossession.

Plaintiff's first assignments of error are directed to the following findings of the trial court:

"XII. That the plaintiffs actions in repossessing the defendant's tractor on September 28, 1966, and the actions of the Wallowa County Sheriff, in aid of the plaintiffs, amounted to constructive force, intimidation and oppression, constituting a breach of the peace and conversion of defendant's tractor.

"XIV. That the plaintiffs failed to show just cause or excuse for the wrongful act of repossession of the defendant's tractor on September 28, 1966.

"XV. That the wrongful act of repossession, done intentionally on September 28, 1966, was malicious and was so wanton and reckless as to show disregard for the rights of the defendant, Frank Kessler."

Defendant Kessler's cross-claim is predicated on the theory that Stone Machinery Company committed a tort in Oregon. To resolve this question we must look to Oregon law. . . .

Retaking possession of a chattel by a conditional seller, upon the default of the buyer, is governed by UCC 9-503:

> Secured party's right to take possession after default. Unless otherwise agreed a secured party has on default the right to take possession of the collateral. In taking possession a secured party may proceed without judicial process *if this can be done without breach of the peace* or may proceed by action. . . . (Italics ours.)

Defendant Kessler was admittedly in default for nonpayment of the August and September contract installments. By the terms of the above statute Stone Machinery had the right to take possession of the tractor without judicial process, but only if this could be one without a breach of the peace. The question is whether the method by which they proceeded constituted a breach of the peace.

No Oregon cases have been cited which define the term "breach of peace" so we must look to other authority. In 1 Restatement of Torts 2d, §116 (1965), the term is defined as follows: "A breach of the peace is a public offense done by violence, or one causing or likely to cause an immediate disturbance of public order."

In the case of McKee v. State, 75 Okl. Cr. 390, 132 P.2d 173, breach of peace is defined (headnote 9, 132 P.2d 173), as follows: "To constitute a 'breach of the peace' it is not necessary that the peace be actually broken, and if what is done is unjustifiable and unlawful, tending with sufficient directness to break the peace, no more is required, nor is actual personal violence an essential element of the offense. . . ."

In the instant case it was the sheriff who said that he had no legal papers but that "we come over to pick up this tractor." Whereupon, the defendant Kessler stated, "I told him I was resisting this; there was an action started and I wanted to have a few days to get money together to pay them off." At this point defendant Kessler had a right to obstruct, by all lawful and reasonable means, any attempt by plaintiff to forcibly repossess the tractor. . . . Had the defendant offered any physical resistance, there existed upon both the sheriff and plaintiff's agents a duty to retreat. . . . However, confronted by the sheriff, who announced his intention to participate in the repossession, it was not necessary for Kessler to either threaten violence or offer physical resistance. As stated by the court in Roberts v. Speck, 169 Wash. 613 at 616, 14 P.2d 33 at 34 (1932), citing from Jones on Chattel Mortgages (4th ed.), §705: "The mortgagee becomes a trespasser by going upon the premises of the mortgagor, accompanied by a deputy sheriff who has no legal process, but claims to act *colore officii,* and taking possession without the active resistance of the mortgagor. To obtain possession under such a show and pretence of authority is to trifle with the obedience of citizens to the law and its officers."

Acts done by an officer which are of such a nature that the office gives him no authority to do them are *"colore officii."* See 7A Words & Phrases Perm. Ed. at 296. . . .

In the case of Beneficial Finance Co. of Tulsa v. Wiener, 405 P.2d 691 (Okl. 1965), the mortgagee sought to repossess furniture from the mortgagor after default in payment. The mortgagee accompanied a constable who had legal papers issued by the wrong court. The court said: ". . . A mere illegal taking or wrongful assuming of right to personal property constitutes 'conversion' and no further step is necessary to perfect right of action therefor. . . . The only restrictions upon the mode by which the mortgagee secures possession of the mortgaged property, after breach of condition, are that he must act in an orderly manner and without creating a breach of the peace, and must not intimidate by securing the aid of an officer, who pretends to act *colore officii.*"

In the instant case, when the sheriff of Wallowa County, having no authority to do so, told the defendant Kessler, "We come over to pick up this tractor," he was acting *colore officii* and became a participant in the repossession, regardless of the fact that he did not physically take part in the retaking. Plaintiff contends that its sole purpose in having the sheriff present was to prevent anticipated violence. The effect, however, was to prevent the defendant Kessler from exercising his right to resist by all lawful and reasonable means a nonjudicial take-over. To put the stamp of approval upon this method of repossession would be to completely circumvent the purpose and intent of the statute.

We hold there is substantial evidence to support the trial court's finding that the unauthorized actions of the sheriff in aid of the plaintiff amounted to

H_1:

constructive force, intimidation and oppression constituting a breach of the peace and conversion of the defendant's tractor.

Appellant Stone Machinery next assigns as error the finding by the trial court that the tractor had a fair market value of $24,900 when repossessed.

The testimony as to fair market value for witnesses permitted to testify as experts took a wide range. One reason for this variance was due to the difference of opinion among the witnesses as to the condition of the tractor at the time of repossession. However, one witness, Thurston Storey, who had been an earth-moving contractor for 21 years, during which time he had purchased a total of 12 Caterpillar Tractors, and who owned four Caterpillar Tractors of an earlier model at the time of testifying, and who was a mechanic who did his own repair work, testified that the D-9 tractor in question was in excellent condition, and placed its fair market value at $25,000, less $100 for the repair of one piston.

This estimate of value was to some extent supported by exhibit 5, which is Stone Machinery's 1967 spring catalog, advertising the sale of used tractors. The catalog contains pictures of tractors, together with their selling price. A tractor testified to as being similar to the D-9 tractor in question, but of a year-later model, is listed in the catalog with a selling price of $25,500. This same tractor was examined by Mr. Storey, who found its condition to be "good" but not as good as the Kessler tractor.

Appellant Stone Machinery attacks the competency of Mr. Storey to testify as an expert on value. A review of the testimony relating to value leads this court to the conclusion that appellant's objection goes more to the weight of the testimony of Mr. Storey rather than to the admissibility of his testimony. The weight to be given to the testimony of a witness is peculiarly within the province of the trial court. There is substantial evidence to support the trial court's finding that the fair market value of the tractor in question was $24,900 at the time of repossession. . . .

H_2:

Plaintiff's final assignment of error relates to the trial court's award of punitive damages. The Oregon law regarding punitive damages has recently been set forth in the case of Douglas v. Humble Oil & Refining Co., 445 P.2d 590 (Or. 1968): "As a general rule, punitive damages will be allowed only when the proof supports a finding that the defendant acted with improper motives or with willful, wanton, or reckless disregard for the rights of others. . . . We held recently that it is only in those instances where the violation of societal interests is sufficiently great and of a kind that sanctions would tend to prevent that the use of punitive damages is proper. 'Regardless of the nomenclature by which a violation of these obligations is described (grossly negligent, willful, wanton, malicious, etc.), it is apparent that this court has decided that it is proper to use the sanction of punitive damages where there has been a particularly aggravated disregard . . .' of the rights of the victim. Noe v. Kaiser Foundation Hospitals, Or., 435 P.2d 306 (1967)." . . .

Defendant Kessler was in default of his contract and had announced his intention to resist any attempted nonjudicial repossession. The words used in announcing his intention, namely, "someone would get hurt," were of such a nature as to justify the presence of a sheriff during any attempt at peaceable repossession although, as we have already held, this did not justify participation by the sheriff in the process of repossession. However, the fact that the sheriff did undertake to act *colore officii* in the repossession was not, under the circumstances, sufficient to support a finding that the plaintiff thereby displayed a particularly aggravated disregard for the rights of Kessler, within the meaning of Douglas v. Humble Oil & Refining Co., supra.

Judgment for compensatory damages is affirmed. Judgment for punitive damages is reversed.

NOTES & QUESTIONS

1. *Constitutionality of self-help repossession.* In the early 1970s the courts reviewed the constitutionality of many traditional creditors' remedies, including self-help repossession and disposition by secured creditors relying on UCC 9-503 and 9-504. The review was based on the due process clause of the fourteenth amendment of the federal constitution. Most of the cases involving UCC 9-503 concluded that there was no state action. Although the Supreme Court did not specifically address the issue, its decision in Flagg Brothers, Inc. v. Brooks, 436 U.S. 149 (1978) (UCC 7-210 authorizing foreclosure of warehousemen's lien does not involve state action), seems to support the conclusions of the lower courts. If there is state action it appears that the repossession provisions of Article 9 do not meet the due process requirements of a prompt hearing by a judicial officer. The focus would then be on whether there had been a valid waiver in the security agreement of this constitutional protection. Commentary on due process and self-help repossession, which was extensive at the time, has since died out. The leading case remains Adams v. Southern California First National Bank, 492 F.2d 324, 13 UCC Rep. 161 (9th Cir. 1973), *cert. denied,* 419 U.S. 1006 (1974).

In the coming years the debate may now shift to interpretation of state constitutional provisions. Sharrock v. Dell Buick-Cadillac, Inc., 45 N.Y.2d 152, 379 N.E.2d 1169, 408 N.Y.S.2d 39 (1978), held that the statutory right of a garageman to foreclose his possessory lien for repair and storage charges violated the New York constitution because it deprived the owner of a motor vehicle of a significant property interest without providing an opportunity to be heard. Some lower courts in New York subsequently concluded that the *Sharrock* reasoning would extend to UCC 9-503 and 9-504. See Crouse v. First Union Bank, 448 N.Y.S.2d 329, 33 UCC Rep. 1170 (App. Div. 1982).

2. *Breach of the peace.* Would there be a "breach of the peace" if the sheriff appears in uniform but says nothing? See Walker v. Walthall, 588 P.2d 863, 25 UCC Rep. 918 (Ariz. Ct. App. 1978) (*held,* over dissent, a breach of peace). Does the presence of a police officer constitute "state action" so that the repos-

session is unconstitutional as a taking of property without due process? The majority opinion in *Walker* suggests that proper notice and a hearing are necessary when a police officer participates in the repossession.

For a slightly more detailed definition of breach of the peace, see Uniform Consumer Credit Code §5.112 ("only if possession can be taken without entry into a dwelling and without the use of force or other breach of the peace"). What values does this section protect? Are these values ones that should be protected in the commercial context as well?

3. *Repossession by court action.* If a secured party cannot use self-help repossession he may seek to take over the collateral by a replevin or claim-and-delivery action. State rules governing these actions are subject to the due process requirements of the fourteenth amendment. Most of these rules have been revised in recent years to comply with the constitutional requirements. See Fuentes v. Shevin, 407 U.S. 67 (1972) (prejudgment replevin); Mitchell v. W. T. Grant Co., 416 U.S. 600 (1974) (La. sequestration); North Georgia Finishing, Inc. v. Di-Chem, Inc., 419 U.S. 601 (1975) (garnishment).

4. *Debtor's criminal liability.* Would the debtor in *Stone Machinery* have violated the following criminal statute?

§32.33.   Hindering Secured Creditors

(a)   For purposes of this section:

   (1)   "Remove" means transport, without the effective consent of the secured party, from the state in which the property was located when the security interest or lien attached.

   (2)   "Security interest" means an interest in personal property or fixtures that secures payment or performance of an obligation.

(b)   A person who has signed a security agreement creating a security interest in property or a mortgage or deed of trust creating a lien on property commits an offense if, with intent to hinder enforcement of that interest or lien, he destroys, removes, conceals, encumbers, or otherwise harms or reduces the value of the property.

(c)   For purposes of this section, a person is presumed to have intended to hinder enforcement of the security interest or lien if, when any part of the debt secured by the security interest or lien was due, he failed:

   (1)   to pay the part then due; and

   (2)   if the secured party had made demand, to deliver possession of the secured property to the secured party. [Texas Penal Code Ann. §32.33 (Vernon Supp. 1984)]

5. *Debtor's remedies for violation by creditor.* The court in *Stone Machinery* treated the debtor's crosscomplaint as a tort action. Was the court suggesting that violation of UCC 9-503 was a tort? Could the debtor have relied upon UCC 9-507(1)? Is UCC 9-507(1) exclusive?

6. *Calculation of damages.* How are the damages for conversion calculated

in *Stone Machinery*? If a secured party is owed $800 and the collateral has fair market value of $1,000 at the time of repossession, should the debtor recover $200, or $1,000, or some other figure if a court later determines that the secured party repossessed wrongfully? If the secured party later disposes of the collateral for $1,100, should the debtor recover an extra $100?

If the secured party had properly repossessed and disposed of the collateral what would the debtor receive? Is the secured party penalized for wrongful repossession? Should punitive damages always be available in wrongful repossession cases no matter what the state of mind of the secured party or its agent? Does the secured party lose any claim to repossession expenses? After wrongful repossession must the secured party still dispose of the collateral or may the secured party argue its conversion gives it the right to retain the property? May the debtor redeem the property?

7. *Punitive damages.* UCC 1-106 states that the general UCC goal is to compensate an aggrieved party and that penal damages may not be had "except as specifically provided by this Act or by other rule of law." UCC 9-507(1) provides a remedy for debtors but it does not mention penal damages. Should one draw the negative inference that penal damages are excluded for violations of Part 5 of Article 9?

8. *Evidence of value.* Note the care taken in *Stone Machinery* to put into evidence testimony as to the fair market value of the equipment repossessed. If there was a publication of average sale prices of used equipment how would you introduce this publication into evidence? Is the evidence hearsay? The Federal Rules of Evidence provide the following exception to the hearsay rule: "Market reports, commercial publications. Market quotations, tabulations, lists, directories, or other published compilations, generally used and relied upon by the public or by persons in particular occupation." Rule 803(17). See also UCC 2-723. Would a publication of average sale prices of used equipment fall within this exception? For an example of careful trial preparation, see Atlas Construction Co. v. Dravo-Doyle Co., 3 UCC Rep. 124, 130-132 (Pa. C.P., Allegheny Co., 1965).

9. *Protection by contract.* To what extent may the secured party protect itself from attacks on its repossession procedures by including clauses in the security agreement? Is the following clause enforceable: "On default, the secured party may repossess the collateral and may make use of such force as may be necessary to enter upon, with or without breaking into debtor's premises in order to repossess the collateral"? See Hileman v. Harter Bank & Trust Co., 174 Ohio St. 95, 186 N.E.2d 853 (1962); UCC 9-501(3). Would a contract clause that defines "breach of the peace" as limited to threats of personal injury be enforceable? Would a clause permitting the secured party to use a sheriff in repossessing be an effective waiver of debtor's constitutional rights?

10. *Notice and waiver: repossession.* Must a secured party give the debtor notice of repossession? To what extent may a duty to give notice, if it exists, be waived before or after default? See Uniform Conditional Sales Act, Sec. 17:

Sec. 17. Notice of Intention to Retake. Not more than forty nor less than twenty days prior to the retaking, the seller, if he so desires, may serve upon the buyer personally or by registered mail a notice of intention to retake the goods on account of the buyer's default. The notice shall state the default and the period at the end of which the goods will be retaken, and shall briefly and clearly state what the buyer's rights under this act will be in case they are retaken. If the notice is so served and the buyer does not perform the obligations in which he has made default before the day set for retaking, the seller may retake the goods and hold them subject to the provisions of Sections 19, 20, 21, 22 and 23 regarding resale, but without any right of redemption.

3. Disposition

Problem 3-22. Having repossessed the bookbinder following Apex's default, Austin State Bank now wishes to dispose of it. To avoid any possible liability for improper disposition, the bank officer in charge of the Apex account consults you about the steps the bank should take. Advise the officer. (For a useful summary of possible pitfalls, see Panel, Impact of 1972 Revisions on Secured Financing Transactions under UCC Article 9, 33 Bus. Law. 2491, 2546-2550 (1978).)

HALL v. OWEN CITY STATE BANK
370 N.E.2d 918, 23 UCC Rep. 267 (Ind. Ct. App. 1977)

ROBERTSON, Chief Judge. Defendant-appellant, Howard Hall (Hall) brings this appeal from an adverse judgment by the trial court, sitting without a jury, in an action by Owen County State Bank (Bank) for judgment on three promissory notes executed by Hall. . . .

The relevant facts of this case show that sometime in late 1971, Hall and his son-in-law, Allan Reed, began a trucking business under the name of H & R Trucking Company. In order to finance the needed trucking equipment, it was necessary for Hall and Reed to apply for loans from the Bank. The Bank granted loans aggregating approximately $56,000.00 in return for promissory notes and a security interest in the equipment purchased with the loan proceeds.

All went well until late 1973 or early 1974 when the business began to fail and Hall and Reed became delinquent in their monthly installments on the notes. At one point in the spring of 1974, one Bank Officer, Lewis Cline, testified he called on Hall at his home to discuss the delinquent loan payments and that Hall stated he could not afford to make any more payments, that he "washed his hands" of the entire matter and did not want to be bothered any more, and that the Bank should thereafter talk with Reed.

The Bank then contacted Reed on numerous occasions concerning the delinquent loans and an attempt was made to restructure the payment schedule. However, Reed was unable to make the payments required under the new schedule and the Bank, on June 8, 1974, sent a letter to Reed demanding possession of the collateral, which consisted of two tractor-trailer rigs. On Sunday, June 30, 1974, Reed delivered both tractors and both trailers to the Bank's parking lot without any prior notice to the Bank. He returned the next morning, Monday, July 1, to surrender to the Bank the keys to the trucks.

voluntary turning over

Robert Ingalls, a used car and truck dealer in the area, was in the Bank on Monday morning and noticed the trucks in the parking lot. He inquired as to whether the equipment was for sale, and upon receiving an affirmative response, began to negotiate with Bank officers for the purchase of the equipment. Later that day, the negotiations ended with a take-it or leave-it offer for that day only of $25,000 in cash for all four units.

After deciding to accept the offer, the Bank notified Reed, who was at Hall's residence in Gosport, by telephone and Reed returned to the Bank. Bank officers explained the terms of the sale to him, and explained that the proceeds of the sale were less than the amount due on the notes. Reed agreed that Ingalls' offer was fair and endorsed the truck titles without objection. Ingalls then paid the $25,000.00 to the Bank and the Bank credited the entire amount, without any deductions for expenses, to the amount due on the notes.

On June 9, 1975, the Bank filed its action against Hall and Reed for the amount still due under the notes. Default judgment was rendered against Reed and he has not joined in this appeal. Hall filed his answer, certain affirmative defenses, and a counterclaim against the Bank for compensatory and punitive damages. The trial court found in favor of the Bank and against Hall and awarded judgment against Hall in the sum of $2,328.25 in principal and interest and $500.00 in attorneys' fees. Hall then timely perfected this appeal.

deficiency actn

trial ct: Bank

The trial court stated in its findings that Hall had waived his right to notice of sale and that he was therefore estopped to assert any lack of notice. This finding is based on the meeting between Hall and Lewis Cline in which Hall allegedly stated that he "washed his hands" of the whole matter and directed the Bank to deal exclusively with Reed. . . .

. . . [T]here is a split of authority [under the 1962 UCC] as to whether or not the debtor may waive notice of sale after default. . . .

issue

Although it has been argued that UCC 1-103 brings in the common law of waiver and estoppel so as to allow a waiver by the debtor after default, we feel that the general provisions of UCC 1-103 are supplanted by the specific language in UCC 9-501(3) prohibiting any waiver. Furthermore, Indiana has not adopted the 1972 amendments to the UCC proposed by the Commissioners on Uniform State Laws which would amend UCC 9-504(3) to allow the debtor to sign after default a renunciation of his rights to notification. Finally, we find very persuasive as to the policy behind UCC 9-501(3) the following portion of Official Comment 4 to UCC 9-501: "The default situation offers great scope for overreaching; the suspicious attitude of the courts has been

policy for notification

grounded in common sense. Subsection (3) of this section contains a codification of this long standing and deeply rooted attitude: the specified rights of the debtor and duties of the secured party may not be waived or varied except as stated."

Although there are persuasive arguments in favor of allowing a waiver of rights by the debtor after default, we feel the better interpretation of UCC 9-501(3), and that which is more in line with the policy of UCC 9-504 to protect the rights of the debtor, is that the non-waiver provision of UCC 9-501(3) applies both before and after default. We therefore hold that UCC 9-501(3) does not allow a waiver by the debtor of his right to reasonable notification under UCC 9-504(3). . . .

Hall further argues that the trial court erred in its findings of fact that sufficient notice was sent by the Bank to Hall. Although the trial court's findings do not specifically state that sufficient notification was sent by the Bank, its Finding Number 14 implies that the trial court felt the notice sent to Reed was sufficient to bind Hall due to their relationship as partners.

There seems to be no doubt that the sale of collateral in this case should be classified under the UCC as a private sale rather than a public sale. The only notice requirement for a private sale under UCC 9-504(3) is that the secured party give "reasonable notification" to the debtor "of the time after which" the sale or disposition will be made. There is no formal step by step procedure which the secured party must follow, and there are no rigid time limits which must be obeyed. This type of procedure for sale of collateral after repossession is a rejection of the formal notice and sale requirements of the Uniform Conditional Sales Act which was the law in this state (and in many other states) prior to the enactment of the UCC in 1963. According to Official Comment 1 to UCC 9-504, the intent of the drafters of the UCC in this section was to encourage private sales through normal commercial channels. The drafters recognized the traditionally dismal results of the sheriff's public auction at the courthouse door and hoped that informal private sales through the regular course of business would "result in higher realization on collateral for the benefit of all parties."

The term "reasonable notification" is not specifically defined in the UCC. In UCC 1-201(26), the following definition of "notifies" is given:

A person "notifies" or "gives" a notice or notification to another by taking such steps as may be reasonably required to inform the other in ordinary course whether or not such other actually comes to know of it.

Under this definition, the test is not whether or not the debtor receives the notice, but only whether the secured party made a good faith effort and took such steps as a reasonable person would have taken to give notice. Accordingly, most courts have held that there is no absolute requirement under UCC 9-504 that the debtor actually received notice.

The word "send," which is found in UCC 1-201(38), is defined in such a manner as to imply that the notice must be in writing. While some courts have indeed held that only a written notice will suffice under UCC 9-504, there is also authority to the contrary. We feel that a rigid rule of law mandating a written notice in all cases conflicts with the general tenor of the UCC to reject strict procedural requirements and we would therefore read UCC 1-201(38) in conjunction with UCC 1-201(26) so as to impose upon the secured party the duty of taking reasonable steps to notify the debtor. The fact that the notice was oral instead of written should not invalidate that notice as a matter of law but should instead be one of the factors considered in deciding whether or not the notice was reasonable.

Although no definition of "reasonable notification" is contained in the UCC itself, Official Comment 5 to UCC 9-504 contains this definition: " 'Reasonable notification' is not defined in this Article; at a minimum it must be sent in such time that persons entitled to receive it will have sufficient time to take appropriate steps to protect their interests by taking part in the sale or other disposition if they so desire."

At least one state has grafted onto this definition, as a matter of law, a minimum number of days' notice needed to make the notice reasonable. De-Lay First National Bank & Trust Co. v. Jacobson Appliance Co., 196 Neb. 398, 243 N.W.2d 745, 19 UCC Rep. 994 (1976) (three days). Again, however, we must reject that line of thinking as being contrary to the basic purposes of the UCC. Although we feel that any case involving a very brief notice to the debtor should be closely scrutinized by the trial court, we also feel that the length of time of the notice should be included as one component in the decision as to whether reasonable notification was given by the secured party.

On the facts of this case, we feel the conclusion is inescapable that the Bank was required to send reasonable notification of the sale to Hall and that the Bank failed to do so.

Although H & R Trucking Company was named on the note and security agreement as debtor, the complaint filed by the Bank named Hall and Reed individually as defendants and did not name the partnership. Furthermore, Hall apparently signed the note in his individual capacity thereby making himself personally liable. UCC 3-403(2)(b). Therefore, he would fall within a definition of debtor under UCC 9-105(1)(d) and would be entitled to reasonable notification under UCC 9-504(3).

It is uncontested that no written notice of the sale was ever sent to Hall. The record shows that the bank official who telephoned Hall's house on the date of sale did not remember speaking to Hall or even if Hall was present at that time. More importantly, the notice was given only hours before the sale and Hall testified that he did not receive any notice until after the sale was completed. We feel that the notification sent by the Bank was insufficient to allow Hall to protect his interest in the collateral. We therefore hold that the Bank failed to send the reasonable notification required under UCC 9-504(3). . . .

Having decided that the Bank failed to send reasonable notification to Hall under UCC 9-504(3), the question arises as to the effect of such a failure. It appears that there are no Indiana cases dealing with this question.

③ does insuff notice bar
recovery of deficiency?

The cases decided in other states are hopelessly divided on the question as to whether the secured party should be barred from recovering a deficiency judgment from the debtor when there has been insufficient notice of the disposition of collateral after repossession. In addition to these courts, it seems that the commentators are also in disagreement on this question. From the language of UCC 9-504, it appears that the drafters of the UCC either did not consider this question or else decided to leave the question open. At least one notable authority has stated that the drafters indeed failed to consider this issue.

ⓐ arg. 1
(against barring deficiency)

It has been argued that because UCC 9-504(2) and UCC 9-502(2) specifically give the secured party a right to collect any deficiency and because there is no language in UCC 9-504 to indicate that a creditor should be barred from a deficiency, the courts should have no authority to supply such a sanction. In contrast, the language of UCC 2-706, which allows the seller of goods to resell those goods after breach by the buyer and collect damages from the buyer (much like a repossession sale and suit for deficiency judgment) strongly implies that notice to the buyer in that case is a condition precedent to the recovery of damages.

ⓑ arg 2:
policy of UCC ⇒
to bar for formality against intent

It can also be argued that the adoption of a rule which strictly bars a deficiency judgment in cases of faulty notice contravenes the intent and purpose of the UCC. First of all, as stated above, the drafters of the UCC intended to do away with rigid rules of law designed to govern in all situations in favor of more fluid guidelines which allow a case by case analysis. It was hoped that this procedure would allow parties to reach the merits of each case instead of becoming entangled in procedural technicalities: "Article 9 imposes few formal requirements and relies instead on the general obligation of commercial reasonableness. It was hoped that Article 9 default litigation would reach, and be decided on, the merits of the case without being deflected either by the debtor's allegations of a technical defense or the secured parties' demonstration of equally technical compliance with formalities." 2 Gilmore, Security Interests and Personal Property §44.9.4, at 1264 (1965).

Furthermore, the policy of the UCC as expressed in UCC 1-106 is to allow full recompense to an aggrieved party by a liberal application of the remedies provided in the UCC and to avoid the assessment of penal damages, unless such damages are expressly allowed by the UCC or other law.[10] It would seem that no automatic denial of a judgment for the remaining portion of a debt would amount to a rejection of that policy. The Nebraska Supreme Court, in rejecting a strict rule barring deficiency judgments because of insufficient notice, also felt that such a rule would be unduly punitive: "No sound

---

10. By this, we do not mean to imply that punitive damages should never be allowed in this type of situation. We are merely stating that punitive damages have no place in the normal commercial transaction, including most repossessions, just as such punitive damages have no place in the normal breach of contract suit. However, as stated in UCC 1-106 where the debtor can plead and prove the facts necessary to support some other theory, an award of punitive damages might be appropriate. Such circumstances might include a situation where the debtor can clearly show that the secured party is intentionally and maliciously violating the rights of the debtor. . . .

PUNITIVES

policy requires us to inject a drastic punitive element into a commercial context." Cornett v. White Motor Corp., 190 Neb. 496, 501, 209 N.W.2d 341, 344, 13 UCC Rep. 152 (1973).

Probably the most persuasive argument for allowing a secured party to proceed with an action for a deficiency judgment is the fact that the UCC has already provided the debtor with a remedy in UCC 9-507. Under the latter section, if a secured party is not proceeding properly, the debtor may either restrain the creditor from proceeding further, or may recover from him any loss that the debtor may have suffered due to the secured party's failure to comply with the provisions of Article 9. Further protection is afforded under UCC 9-507 to the debtor in a consumer transaction in that a minimum damage figure is set out, which roughly equals the interest charge plus 10% of the cash price of the goods. In addition, under the provision of §5-103 of the Uniform Consumer Credit Code, IC 1971, 24-4.5-5-103, the debtor is not liable for any deficiency where the secured party elects to repossess goods which had a price of $1100.00 or less and which were a part of a consumer credit sale.

Some rather persuasive arguments have also been advanced in favor of barring deficiency judgments in all cases where the secured party does not proceed properly. Such a rule would seem to be easier to apply, might bring about more uniform results and could possibly force creditors to be more careful in giving notice to debtors. Furthermore, there is nothing in the language of the UCC to suggest that the remedy provided in UCC 9-507 was intended to be an exclusive remedy. UCC 1-103 brings traditional common law into play, such as equitable principles and principles of justice and fair play, which should suggest that a creditor should not be allowed a deficiency judgment when he breaks the law: "The rule and requirements are simple. If the secured creditor wishes a deficiency judgment he must obey the law. If he does not obey the law, he may not have his deficiency judgment." Atlas Thrift Company v. Horan, 27 Cal. App. 3d 999, 104 Cal. Rptr. 315, 11 UCC Rep. 417, 426 (1972).

It must also be considered that by failing to take proper steps to notify the debtor, the secured creditor can effectively deprive the debtor of his right to redeem the collateral under UCC 9-506 and his right to protect his interest by procuring bids or buyers at any private or public sale that is held.

After considering both the cases and policy arguments on this issue, we feel that the better rule of law would allow the secured creditor a right to an action for a deficiency judgment notwithstanding a failure to send proper notice under UCC 9-504(3). In addition to the reasons cited above, we feel that the UCC should function on the premise that the majority of commercial transactions are carried out in good faith. In those cases in which the secured creditor has not complied with the appropriate notice provisions, or has otherwise not proceeded in good faith, it is better to adopt a more flexible standard which will allow the secured party to recover the damages caused by the debtor's breach, but which will also allow protection to the debtor on a case-by-case basis. The debtor is provided a remedy in UCC 9-507 and we see no reason to attach a further penalty to the creditor by declaring an automatic forfeiture of his right of a deficiency judgment.

A majority of the cases allowing the creditor to proceed in an action for a deficiency under these circumstances have ruled that the creditor before recovering his judgment, must rebut the presumption that the collateral was at least equal in value to the amount of the debt. We think that this is a sound policy, for in cases where the debtor was not notified of an impending sale, the creditor should be in a much better position to prove the value of the collateral at the time of the disposition. See Universal C.I.T. Credit Corp. v. Rone, 248 Ark. 665, 453 S.W.2d 37, 7 UCC Rep. 847 (1970). Furthermore, it seems fundamentally unfair to put the burden of showing the value of collateral after it has been repossessed and sold upon a debtor who has received insufficient notice of the disposition. We hold, therefore, that when a secured creditor disposes of collateral without proper notice under UCC 9-504(3), he must then prove, in his action for a deficiency judgment, that the reasonable value of the collateral at the time of the sale was less than the amount of the debt.

In meeting the burden outlined above, the creditor may not merely rely on the value which he received from the repossession sale. . . . Universal C.I.T. Credit Corp. v. Rone, 248 Ark. 665, 669, 453 S.W.2d 37, 39-40 (1970).

Furthermore, the secured party may not rely solely on testimony of his credit manager or his other employees as to their opinions of the fair value of the collateral. Instead, the creditor must introduce other additional credible objective evidence of value. . . .

Hall also contends that the trial court's finding that the sale of collateral was conducted in a commercially reasonable manner is not supported by sufficient evidence and is contrary to law, and that its finding that the value of the collateral at the time of sale did not exceed $25,000 is also not supported by sufficient evidence. We shall consider these issues together.

The UCC does not give a specific definition of a commercially reasonable sale of collateral. UCC 9-504(3) states that the disposition, whether by sale or otherwise, "may be as a unit or in parcels and at any time and place and on any terms, but every aspect of the disposition including the method, manner, time, place and terms must be commercially reasonable." Some examples of a commercially reasonable sale are given in UCC 9-507(2). . . . However, it is also specifically provided that this is not an exclusive list of commercially reasonable dispositions.

Because the statutory definition of a commercially reasonable sale is vague, and because a judgment as to whether or not a sale was reasonable will generally depend upon the circumstances of each particular case, many courts have held this to be a question of fact. . . . We also feel that whether a sale was held in a commercially reasonable manner is a question of fact. We further agree with the decisions holding that the secured creditor has the burden of showing, as a part of his burden of proof in an action for a deficiency judgment, that the sale or disposition was performed in a commercially reasonable manner. . . .

Certainly one of the most important factors to be weighed in deciding whether or not a disposition or sale was commercially reasonable will be the price received by the secured party. In cases where a fair sale price was received, the debtor will have suffered no injury and normally will have no complaint (except, perhaps, in cases where the debtor would have been able to find alternate financing and redeem the collateral). In cases where a fair sale price was not received, the other items to be considered will generally be relevant to the extent that they may have prevented a fair price or contributed to an unfair price.

It is expressly provided in UCC 9-507, however, that the sale price is not the only item to be considered. . . .

The above provision gives recognition to the fact that only on rare occasions will a repossession sale bring the highest bids or the highest value for the collateral and therefore such sales could always be vulnerable to attack by a showing that a higher price might have been obtained under different circumstances. This means that a secured creditor may not be held liable to the debtor or be deprived of a deficiency judgment when the secured party has, in good faith, conducted a commercially acceptable sale or disposition, even where a low sale price is received. . . .

However, even though a low sale price itself is insufficient to overturn a sale, closer scrutiny will generally be given sales in which there is a _substantial_ difference between the sale price and the fair value to determine whether there were legitimate causes for the low price such as a depressed or non-existent market, or whether the low price was caused by the secured party's failure to proceed in a commercially reasonably manner.

One relevant factor to be considered in determining whether the sale price was reasonable may be the price received by the buyer of the collateral in a subsequent sale. A showing that the collateral was sold only a short time later, after little or no reconditioning or cleaning, at a substantially or disproportionately higher price may strongly imply that the secured party failed to receive a fair price for the collateral. . . .

Another factor which may be relevant is whether the collateral is sold on a retail or wholesale market. It is certainly true that a retail sale of goods will in most cases command a much higher price. However, a retail sale will usually generate considerably more expenses, such as reconditioning expenses, advertising expenses and sales commissions, insurance costs, etc., and usually will take much longer to consummate. This in turn may result in higher storage expenses and a higher interest accrual under the original obligation. Therefore, a sale to a dealer on the wholesale market will probably be the more reasonable approach in most cases. Sales to a dealer also seem to be suggested by UCC 9-504 and the Official Comments to that section (which suggest that a private sale will be preferable in many cases) and also by Official Comment 2, to UCC 9-507. [The court quotes from the comment.— Eds.]

While we feel that in most cases a sale or disposal of collateral to a dealer or on a wholesale market or auction will be commercially reasonable, the answer to this question will generally depend upon the circumstances of each particular case and will therefore be a question of fact for the factfinder in most cases.

Other factors to be considered in deciding whether a sale was commercially reasonable include the number of bids received or solicited, particularly in a private sale. While we would not hold sales invalid as a matter of law where only 1 or 2 bids were received, such sales must receive the closest scrutiny and should be declared invalid where there is evidence of collusion, self-dealing, or bad faith. In addition, the time and place of the sale must be such that they are reasonably calculated to bring a satisfactory turnout of bidders, particularly in the case of a public sale. In deciding whether or not the disposition of collateral was accomplished in a commercially reasonable manner all of the relevant factors should be considered together. . . .

In attacking the trial court's findings as not being supported by sufficient evidence and as being contrary to law, Hall carries a heavy burden on appeal. The decision of the trial court will be sustained on appeal, when being attacked as not being supported by sufficient evidence, when there is substantial evidence of probative value to support its findings. Furthermore, we will neither weigh the evidence, nor judge the credibility of witnesses and we cannot substitute our judgment for that of the trial court. . . . Finally, it is only where the evidence is without conflict and can lead to but one conclusion and the trial court has reached an opposite conclusion, that the decision of the trial court will be set aside on the grounds that it is contrary to law. . . .

Hall advances four arguments in support of his contention that the sale was not conducted in a commercially reasonable manner. First, the value of the collateral exceeded the sale price of $25,000.00. Next, the Bank as seller was unfamiliar with the equipment it was selling and with the value of the equipment. Third, the Bank failed to publish notice of the sale and failed to contact any purchasers other than the ultimate purchaser. Finally, there was no appraisal of the collateral before the sale.

We feel that the evidence produced by the Bank, although minimal, was sufficient to carry its burden of proof as to the value of the collateral so as to rebut the presumption that the collateral was at least equal in value to the outstanding debt and was sufficient to sustain the trial court's finding that the value of the collateral did not exceed $25,000.00.

One of the witnesses called by the Bank was Robert Ingalls, who was the original purchaser of the collateral and who was an experienced used car and truck dealer in Spencer. Ingalls testified that he had trouble selling the equipment and that Reed, Hall's partner, had been trying to sell the equipment for some weeks prior to the Bank's repossession, but had been unsuccessful. He further testified that the trucks were not roadworthy when he bought them, that they would not have passed state inspection, and that $25,000.00 was the full value of the equipment.

The Bank also called as a witness James Roemer who was General Manager of Indiana Truck Center, a large truck dealership in Indianapolis. Roemer testified that his dealership had purchased three pieces of the collateral (two tractors and one trailer) from another dealer that had purchased the equipment from Ingalls. Although Roemer had purchased these three pieces for $23,000.00, he testified that after spending over $5,400.00 to recondition the equipment, he sold them at retail, for only $30,500.00.

The trial judge received testimony, from experienced truck dealers, that the equipment was not in good shape, that $25,000 was a fair price under the circumstances, and that the equipment was eventually sold at retail, after substantial reconditioning and after passing through three dealers, for a sum not substantially greater than the original sale price. While there was other credible evidence which tended to show a higher value of the collateral, we cannot say that the finding of the trial court was supported by insufficient evidence and we must therefore affirm that finding.

Hall further contends that the sale of the collateral was not reasonable because no appraisal of the equipment was made and because the Bank officials conducting the sale were unfamiliar with the equipment. However, Hall has failed to explain how an appraisal of the equipment could have been of any possible benefit in this case. We would agree that an appraisal might be a prerequisite to a commercially reasonable sale of some types of goods, but we do not feel that used trucks would necessarily fall into that category.

In his argument that the sale was unreasonable because the Bank employees were not familiar with the equipment Hall relies on the case of Liberty National Bank & Trust Co. v. Acme Tool Division of Rucker Co., 540 F.2d 1375, 19 UCC Rep. 1288 (10th Cir. 1976). The *Rucker* case, however, concerned the sale of an oil rig by the Bank's attorney, who was totally unfamiliar with oil rigs and with auctions of such rigs and who had taken no steps to prepare the rig for auction. In addition, the purchasers at the auction, who paid $42,000.00 for the rig, sold the rig shortly thereafter for over $77,000, even though there had been no change in the market. Finally, the Circuit Court in that case was affirming the trial court's finding of fact that the sale was not commercially reasonable. We feel that the *Rucker* case is distinguishable on its facts in that the Bank employees conducting the sale in this case were experienced in selling repossessed cars and trucks, and one employee, Evans, testified he had previously worked for a used car and truck dealer for six years. Furthermore, the trial court in this case, unlike the trial court in *Rucker,* made a finding of fact that the sale was commercially reasonable.

Hall also argues that the sale was improper because the Bank failed to publish notice of the sale and because there was only one bid made. However, the sale in this case was a private sale to a dealer, not a public sale, and we see no reason to require public advertisement or publication in the case of a private sale.

The case of Atlas Construction Co. v. Dravo Doyle Corp., 3 UCC Rep. 124, 114 Pitt. L.J. 34 (Pa. C.P. 1965), is cited by Hall in support of his argument that the sale should be voided because the Bank failed to solicit more than one bid. Although the court in that case ruled that a repossession sale of a crane was not commercially reasonable because of the low sale price and because only one bid was made, this was a case in which the jury made the finding of fact that the sale was not commercially reasonable. Furthermore, the creditor in *Dravo Doyle* was a dealer in cranes and yet did not attempt to solicit any further bidding from any of its customers. The debtor in that case had also produced a witness who testified that he would willingly have paid between five and eight thousand dollars more for the crane had he been given the opportunity to bid.

We agree with Hall that any private sale of collateral in which only one bid is received or solicited is highly questionable and should be closely scrutinized by the trial court. However, under the rather distinctive facts of this case, we cannot hold that the trial court erred in finding the sale to be commercially reasonable and we cannot say that the sale was improper as a matter of law.

The Bank had no prior notice as to when the equipment would be returned or in what condition it might be, but instead found the equipment in its parking lot on a Monday morning. The Bank therefore had no opportunity to solicit any bids before the day of the sale. The equipment was in need of repairs, as it had been used for some time in a failing business. That same morning, a reputable used car and truck dealer approached the Bank's loan officers and made a bid for the trucks. After several hours of negotiations with those officers, he made a take-it or leave-it offer of $25,000.00, good only for that day. This offer was particularly attractive in that the Bank was able to apply the entire sale price against the outstanding debt, without deduction for any expenses, such as insurance, transportation and storage charges, cleanup and repair charges, advertising expense and sales expenses or commissions (Roemer of Indiana Truck Center testified that his salesmen received a 25% commission on their sales). Although the equipment was later resold by other dealers at a profit, none of the subsequent dealer-purchasers sold the equipment for a disproportionate profit. Furthermore, there was evidence that Reed had been unable to find a buyer for the equipment for several weeks prior to the repossession. He made no objection when the Bank informed him of Ingalls' bid and willingly returned to the Bank to endorse the titles.

Finally, we find most persuasive the fact that there is evidence of nothing but good faith conduct on the part of the Bank. There is no evidence in the record of any collusion or under-handed dealing by the Bank. Reed in his deposition stated that he had no criticism of the manner in which the Bank conducted the sale and Hall also stated that he did not feel that the Bank had cheated him in any way and that his only criticism was that the Bank had not given him sufficient time to sell the trucks himself.

As to his claim for punitive damages, Hall contends that the trial court's finding that the Bank did not act in a willful and malicious manner is not supported by sufficient evidence and is contrary to law. Hall further argues that the trial court also erred by refusing to allow testimony concerning damages to his credit rating caused by the Bank's actions as an element in his claim for punitive damages.

Damage to Hall's credit rating would more properly be an element of compensatory damages rather than punitive damages. In any event, as was stated above, there was no evidence introduced at trial to even remotely suggest any malicious or bad faith conduct on the part of the Bank. While it might be argued that some of the Bank's employees may have displayed some errors in judgment in their conduct of the sale, such conduct falls far short of the standard to be used in awarding punitive damages. . . . We can find no error in the trial court's rulings.

Bank wins big.

Judgment affirmed.

NOTES & QUESTIONS

1. *Pre-Code law on disposition.* The pre-Code uniform acts included the following provisions.

Uniform Conditional Sales Act, Sec. 19:

> Sec. 19. Compulsory Resale by Seller. If the buyer does not redeem the goods within ten days after the seller has retaken possession, and the buyer has paid at least fifty per cent of the purchase price at the time of the retaking, the seller shall sell them at public auction in the state where they were at the time of the retaking, such sales to be held not more than thirty days after the retaking. *10–30 day* The seller shall give to the buyer not less than ten days' written notice of the sale, either personally or by registered mail, directed to the buyer at his last known place of business or residence. The seller shall also give notice of the sale by at least three notices posted in different public places within the filing district where the goods are to be sold, at least five days before the sale. If at the time of the retaking $500 or more has been paid on the purchase price, the seller shall also give notice of the sale at least five days before the sale by publication in a newspaper published or having a general circulation within the filing district where the goods are to be sold. The seller may bid for the goods at the resale. If the goods are of the kind described in Section 8 [railroad equipment or rolling stock], the parties may fix in the conditional sale contract the place where the goods shall be resold.

Uniform Trust Receipts Act, Sec. 6(3):

> 3.   (a) After possession taken, the entruster [secured party] shall, subject to Subdivision (b) and Subsection 5, hold such goods, documents or instruments with the rights and duties of a pledgee.
>   (b) An entruster in possession may, on or after default, give notice to the trustee [debtor] of intention to sell, and may not less than five days after the serving or sending of such notice, sell the goods, documents or instruments *5* for the trustee's account, at public or private sale, and may at a public sale himself become a purchaser. The proceeds of any such sale, whether public or private, shall be applied (i) to the payment of the expenses thereof, (ii) to the payment of the expenses of re-taking, keeping and storing the goods, documents, or instruments, (iii) to the satisfaction of the trustee's indebtedness. The trustee shall receive any surplus and shall be liable to the entruster *secured party doesn't get a windfall* for any deficiency. Notice of sale shall be deemed sufficiently given if in writing, and either (i) personally served on the trustee, or (ii) sent by postpaid ordinary mail to the trustee's last known business address.

(c) A purchaser in good faith and for value from an entruster in possession takes free of the trustee's interest, even in a case in which the entruster is liable to the trustee for conversion.

The official comments to UCC 9-504 indicate that the Code adopts the more flexible approach of the Trust Receipts Act. Do you agree with this choice?

2. *Notice and waiver: disposition.* If notice is so important because it allows debtor to protect its interest by redemption or by finding bidders, why doesn't the UCC require that the debtor *receive* notice? For problems a secured party may face when trying to prove it sent notice, see Leasing Associates, Inc. v. Slaughter, 450 F.2d 174 (8th Cir. 1971) (insufficient evidence showing that letter was stamped, addressed, and posted by regular U.S. mail).

3. *To whom must notice be given?* Must a secured party give notice of a proposed disposition to the guarantor of the debtor's obligation? Must a secured party who took the security interest by assignment give notice to an assignor who agreed to repurchase the obligation if the original debtor should default? See Norton v. The National Bank of Commerce, 240 Ark. 143, 398 S.W.2d 538, 3 UCC Rep. 119 (1966) (assignor who agreed to repurchase must be, given notice as a "debtor" under UCC 9-105(1)(d)). Must the secured party give notice to other secured parties claiming the same collateral? (Compare 1972 UCC 9-504(3) with 1962 UCC 9-504(3).)

4. *Strict foreclosure (UCC 9-505).* Subject to rules protecting consumers in specified cases, a secured party may choose to keep the collateral and forgo any deficiency. UCC 9-505. May a debtor force strict foreclosure on a secured party who keeps repossessed collateral for a long period of time without giving notice of a proposed disposition?

5. *Redemption (UCC 9-506).* In order to exercise his statutory right to redeem, how much must a debtor tender to the secured party? Notwithstanding the comment to UCC 9-506, Professor Gilmore has suggested that it is not clear that a debtor must pay the entire debt in order to redeem. 2 G. Gilmore, Security Interests in Personal Property 1198-1199 (1965). Do you agree?

6. *Other foreclosure proceedings.* To what extent should the doctrines and rules that govern other foreclosure proceedings—e.g., execution sales or judicial foreclosure of real property mortgages—be applied by analogy to foreclosure of personal property security interests? Consider, for example, the relevance of UCC 2-706 (seller's resale). To what extent is a breaching buyer in the same position as a defaulting debtor? If they are not in a similar situation with similar interests to be protected to what extent should the court in the *Hall* case have considered the relevance of UCC 2-706 when considering the consequence of failing to give notice?

7. *Consequences of commercially unreasonable disposition.* Should the UCC be amended to provide an explicit rule on the consequence of the secured party's failure to send reasonable notice or to dispose of the collateral in a commercially reasonable manner? Does UCC 9-507(1) provide an answer? Is the secured party's failure to act in a commercially reasonable manner a tort, such as conversion?

CHAPTER 4

The Impact of Insolvency Proceedings

It is often said that the acid test of a security interest is whether it will survive bankruptcy. In its narrowest sense this aphorism focuses on whether a security interest is perfected. As we learned in the last chapter, an unperfected security interest may be avoided by the debtor's trustee in bankruptcy. Even if a security interest is perfected, however, bankruptcy proceedings may have a profound effect on the secured party. The secured party is automatically stayed from enforcing the interest when bankruptcy proceedings are commenced. In addition, the trustee may avoid the perfected security interest if he can show, for example, that it was a preferential transfer or a fraudulent conveyance. More dramatically, a secured party may be forced to accept a modification of his claim in cases where a debtor is reorganized rather than liquidated. Indeed, the impact of the Bankruptcy Code on security interests is so great that one commentator has asked whether the security interest, like contract, is dead. See Coogan, The New Bankruptcy Code: The Death of Security Interest?, 14 Ga. L. Rev. 153 (1980).

The following materials introduce some basic bankruptcy law concepts. Specific topics such as the right of the seller to reclaim goods and the survival of the floating lien (a security interest in fluctuating collateral, such as inventory or accounts) are examined in later chapters. Although we do not study state law provisions for the administration of insolvent estates, you should note that these options exist, such as statutes providing for assignments for the benefit of creditors or for receiverships. These state law remedies may affect a secured party's interest. See generally S. Riesenfeld, Cases and Materials on Creditors Remedies and Debtors Protection 466-502 (3d ed. 1979); V. Countryman, Cases and Materials on Debtor and Creditor 181-259 (2d ed. 1974).

A. INTRODUCTION

Article I, Section 8 of the United States Constitution grants Congress the power "[t]o establish . . . uniform Laws on the subject of Bankruptcies throughout the United States." Pursuant to this power Congress enacted the Bankruptcy Reform Act of 1978, Title I of which is codified as the Bankruptcy Code in Title 11 of the United States Code. The 1978 Code replaced the Bankruptcy Act of 1898, which had been extensively amended in the 80 years since its enactment, especially by the Chandler Act of 1938, which expanded the rehabilitation and reorganization chapters. In 1970 Congress appointed the Commission on Bankruptcy Laws, whose 1973 Report precipitated extensive Congressional hearings ultimately leading to the adoption of the 1978 legislation. Most substantive provisions of the 1978 Act came into force on October 1, 1979, but the act allowed for a transition period of five years for some of its administrative provisions. A 1984 statute made far-ranging amendments both to the administrative and substantive provisions of the bankruptcy legislation. The Bankruptcy Code has also been supplemented by detailed Bankruptcy Rules and Official Forms promulgated by the United States Supreme Court. These rules came onto force July 1, 1983.[1]

The Bankruptcy Reform Act includes four titles. In addition to the substantive provisions in Title I there are provisions in the other titles that govern the reorganized bankruptcy court system, make conforming amendments to nonbankruptcy laws, and regulate the transition from the old Bankruptcy Act to the new Bankruptcy Code.

Proceedings under the Bankruptcy Code are designed either to liquidate or reorganize an insolvent person or entity.[2] Liquidation, or "straight" bankruptcy, is governed by Chapter 7; reorganization takes place in Chapter 11 proceedings. A special form of reorganization for individuals with regular income is governed by Chapter 13. Each of these proceedings is subject to the general definitions and administrative provisions in chapters 1, 3, and 5. BC 103.

The commonly stated goals of bankruptcy proceedings are "(1) equality of distribution among creditors, (2) a fresh start for debtors, and (3) economi-

---

1. The Bankruptcy Reform Act was enacted November 6, 1978. Pub. L. No. 95-598, 92 Stat. 2549 (1978). The legislative history is collected in A. Resnick & E. Wypinski, Bankruptcy Reform Act of 1978: A Legislative History (1979); Collier on Bankruptcy (L. King 15th ed. 1979), Appendix Vols. 2 & 3. For a summary of the legislative history, see Klee, Legislative History of the New Bankruptcy Law, 28 De Paul L. Rev. 941 (1979); Kennedy, Foreword: A Brief History of the Bankruptcy Reform Act, 58 N.C.L. Rev. 667 (1980). The most important congressional reports on the bankruptcy legislation are H.R. Rep. No. 95-595 (1977) and S. Rep. No. 95-989 (1978). There was no conference committee report on the final text so considerable weight is given to the final statements of the sponsors in the House and Senate. The Report of the Commission on Bankruptcy Laws was published in H.R. Doc. No. 93-137 (1973).

The Bankruptcy Amendments and Federal Judgeship Act of 1984 was signed by the President on July 10, 1984. Pub. L. 98-353, 98 Stat. 333 (1984). There are no Senate or House reports for this act; House Conference Report No. 98-882 does not contain a joint explanatory statement. See 1984 U.S. Code Cong. & Ad. News 576 (statements by legislative leaders).

2. The Bankruptcy Code defines *entity* to include *person*. BC 101(14), (33). There are separate definitions of *corporation* and *governmental unit*. BC 101(8), (24). There are also references to *individual, partnership, estate,* and *trust.* You must be very careful to read each substantive provision to see which category is covered. Note in passing that the Bankruptcy Code avoids personal pronouns in order to remain nonsexist. Cf. UCC 1-102(5)(b).

cal administration." 1 Report of the Commission on the Bankruptcy Laws of the United States 75 (1973). At different times particular goals are given more or less weight, but the general trend has been to increase the opportunities of debtors to begin afresh.

The 1978 Act provided for bankruptcy courts with broad jurisdiction to hear bankruptcy matters but did not give the judges (known as referees before 1973) lifetime tenure or protection against reductions in salary. In Northern Pipeline Construction Co. v. Marathon Pipeline Co., 458 U.S. 50 (1982), the Supreme Court found that bankruptcy judges appointed under Article I of the Constitution had too much jurisdiction without sufficient independence. The 1984 bankruptcy legislation purports to resolve the constitutional issue by vesting primary responsibility for bankruptcy matters in the federal district courts with possible reference of many matters to the bankruptcy judges, who remain Article I judges without lifetime tenure. 28 U.S.C.A. §157 (1985).

Another omnipresent figure in bankruptcy proceedings is the trustee in bankruptcy. When a debtor's estate is to be liquidated a trustee is appointed to collect and liquidate property in the estate for distribution to the creditors with unsecured claims. BC 321-326, 701-704. The trustee in other words acts primarily for the benefit of the unsecured creditors in liquidation proceedings and, although he may be authorized to carry on the business of the estate for a limited time, the primary duty is to wind up the affairs of the estate. In Chapter 11 reorganization proceedings, on the other hand, a trustee will usually not be appointed unless fraud or mismanagement is suspected. Instead, most of the trustee's powers and duties are vested in the debtor, who remains in possession. BC 1107. In Chapter 13 proceedings there is a trustee, but his role is more limited. One of his more important duties is to distribute the payments made by a debtor under a confirmed plan. BC 1302, 1303.

Although obviously no bankruptcy proceeding could commence without one, the debtor plays a relatively minor role in liquidation proceedings under Chapter 7. The debtor must turn over control of the property in the estate to the trustee and cooperate with the trustee in the liquidation. The debtor may assert exemptions in the proceedings. BC 522. Unless there are objections from a creditor or the trustee, the result of the proceedings is that the individual debtor will be discharged and the creditor with an unsecured claim will receive a pro rata share of the liquidated estate. BC 523, 524, 726, 727.

The debtor in a Chapter 11 reorganization plays a far more significant role in the proceedings. The debtor in possession continues to operate the business and has the right to submit the initial proposed plan of reorganization. The plan, if approved by the different classes of claims and interests and if confirmed by the court, adjusts the claims and interests in the debtor and its property with the object of continuing a business that is economically more valuable as a going concern than it would be if dismembered in a liquidation.

Although a trustee is appointed in a Chapter 13 proceeding to work with the debtor, the debtor may continue to administer his assets and business to the exclusion of the trustee as to most matters. BC 1302-1304. The debtor has the exclusive right to prepare a plan to adjust or extend the time for payment of debts in order to increase the amount creditors receive over what they would in a liquidation proceeding and at the same time to allow the honest debtor to readjust his financial commitments to a more realistic level. Only an individual with regular income may file a Chapter 13 petition. If the debtor's plan is confirmed by the court and the debtor completes the payments provided for by the plan, then the debtor will be discharged. BC 1327, 1328.

Most bankruptcy proceedings begin with the debtor filing a voluntary petition with the bankruptcy court. The filing of the petition constitutes an order for relief. BC 301. Creditors in some instances may initiate involuntary proceedings by filing a petition under Chapter 7 or 11. If a creditor commences an involuntary case the court may either dismiss the petition or order relief, but until the order is entered the debtor may continue to administer his assets and business. BC 303. In any case, the filing of the petition automatically operates as a stay of actions by creditors that would dissipate the estate. BC 362.

Whether voluntary or involuntary, the petition will state under which chapter (7, 11, or 13) the petitioner seeks relief. There are detailed rules on who may be a debtor under each of these chapters. BC 109. Most of the rules deal with debtor classes subject to special regulation, such as railroads, insurance companies, financial institutions, farming, and charitable organizations. A case beginning in one chapter, however, may later be converted to another chapter. BC 706, 1112, 1307; see also BC 348. Many attempts to reorganize under Chapter 11, for example, in fact end up in liquidation in Chapter 7 proceedings.

At the time the case is commenced the debtor must file a list of creditors, a schedule of assets and liabilities, a schedule of current income and expenditures, and a statement of his financial affairs. BC 521(1). Soon afterwards a meeting of creditors is held to examine the debtor on his affairs and to elect a trustee, if necessary. BC 341, 702. A creditor may file a proof of claim, which is defined as a right to payment or equitable relief (if it includes a right to payment). BC 101(4), 501. A claim will be allowed unless a party in interest objects. BC 502. Claims are divided into secured and unsecured claims. BC 506. A secured party with an Article 9 security interest, for example, has a secured claim. If the secured party is undersecured (e.g., the debtor owes $9,000 and the value of the collateral is $6,000) the secured party has both a secured and an unsecured claim (a $6,000 secured claim and a $3,000 unsecured claim). As we shall see below, the valuation of claims is important in bankruptcy proceedings.

The commencement of the case automatically creates an estate. The estate is comprised principally of all the legal or equitable interests of the debtor in property wherever located. BC 541. Contract clauses purporting to terminate automatically a debtor's interest in property on insolvency are not given effect. BC 541(c), 365(e). The estate will also include the proceeds of property of the estate and interests acquired by the estate. As we shall see below, the trustee may also recover property for the estate by avoiding certain precommencement transactions. If a person other than the debtor has possession of property of the estate that person must turn over the property to the trustee. BC 542, 543. The trustee may abandon the property if it is a burden to the estate or is of inconsequential value. BC 554. From the property of the estate will be taken property the debtor may claim as exempt. BC 522.

In Chapter 7 cases the trustee liquidates the estate for the benefit of creditors with allowed unsecured claims. Distribution of the liquidated estate is made pro rata to these claimants, although the Bankruptcy Code gives priority to specified expenses and claims such as those of employees and taxing authorities. BC 507, 726. Under principles of equitable subordination the court may subordinate a claim in the distribution. BC 510. A case is closed after the estate is fully administered and the trustee is discharged. BC 350.

For most individual debtors in Chapter 7 proceedings the object is to receive a discharge, which releases the debtor from personal liability for prebankruptcy obligations and enjoins creditors from seeking recovery of discharged obligations. BC 524. For specified causes a court may deny a debtor a discharge entirely or for a particular obligation. BC 523, 727. A debtor may reaffirm a dischargeable debt but only after steps are taken to ensure that the debtor is informed of his right to discharge and the effect of a reaffirmation. BC 524.

In proceedings under Chapters 11 and 13 the estate is administered and distributions are made pursuant to the court-approved plan. On confirmation of the plan the debtor is discharged from prepetition obligations and is required instead to carry out the substituted obligations stated in the plan. BC 1141, 1328. An individual debtor may be denied a discharge but the grounds for denial of discharge are more limited than in a liquidation case.

B. EFFECT OF BANKRUPTCY ON SECURITY INTERESTS

The following notes summarize the effect of bankruptcy proceedings on a secured party whose collateral has become part of an estate administered under Bankruptcy Code Chapter 7, 11, or 13. Parts C and D of this chapter look more closely at the modification of the secured party's right to enforce his security interest and the power of the trustee to avoid the security interest.[3]

3. For further reading, see Coogan, The New Bankruptcy Code: The Death of Security Interest?, 14 Ga. L. Rev. 153 (1980); Kennedy, Secured Creditors Under the Bankruptcy Reform Act, 15 Ind. L. Rev. 477 (1982); Orr & Klee, Secured Creditors Under the New Bankruptcy Code, 11 UCC L.J. 312 (1979); White, The Recent Erosion of the Secured Creditor's Rights Through Cases, Rules and Statutory Changes in Bankruptcy Law, 53 Miss. L.J. 389 (1983).

1.   Chapter 7

The traditional rule has been that discharge of the debtor in a bankruptcy proceeding affected only the personal liability of the debtor and did not prohibit the secured party from enforcing the security interest against the collateral. The secured party, therefore, only lost the right to claim a deficiency against the debtor. If the secured party was fully secured he did not have to file a claim or otherwise participate in the bankruptcy proceedings. Only if the secured interest was challenged or undersecured was the secured party likely to participate.

Virtually all commentators and courts assumed that the 1978 Bankruptcy Code adopted the traditional rule. For authority they cited, inter alia, BC 522(c), which provides that exempt property is not liable for any debt of the debtor except when that property is subject to a lien that has not been avoided. They also quote the following language from the House and Senate Reports: "The bankruptcy discharge will not prevent enforcement of valid liens. The rule of Long v. Bullard, 117 U.S. 617 (1886), is accepted with respect to the enforcement of valid liens on nonexempt property as well as exempt property." H.R. Rep. No. 95-595 at 361; Sen. Rep. 95-989 at 76. At least one court, however, has challenged the accepted wisdom. In In re Ray, 26 B.R. 534 (Bankr. D. Kan. 1983) the bankruptcy judge held that where a secured party had not participated in the bankruptcy proceeding it was enjoined from taking any in rem action against the collateral following the debtor's discharge. The court relied primarily on the language in BC 524(a), which stated that "[a] discharge . . . (2) operates as an injunction against the commencement . . . of an action, the employment of process, or any act, to collect . . . *from property of the debtor.*" (emphasis added)

The question raised by the *Ray* court has been resolved by a 1984 amendment to the Bankruptcy Code that deleted the phrase "from property of the debtor" in BC 524(a)(2). Note, however, that the *Ray* court's reasoning is consistent with the basic concept that the security interest is created by an ancillary contract that depends on the principal obligation. If the debtor's obligations are discharged what remains to be secured?

2.   Chapter 11

Members of a class of claims do not have to accept a proposed reorganization plan unless a majority in number and two-thirds in amount of the allowed claims accept the plan. BC 1126. Each secured claim will probably be in a separate class (BC 1122(a)) so the consent of a secured party appears to be necessary before a plan modifying the security interest can be confirmed. There are exceptions, however, to the rule requiring creditor consent, and in certain circumstances a plan can be forced upon a creditor by what is known graphically as a cramdown. First, a class that is not impaired is deemed to have accepted the plan. BC 1124, 1126(f). Second, a court may confirm a plan if it does not "discriminate unfairly" and is "fair and equitable." BC 1129(b)(1). To be fair and equitable for a class of secured claims the plan must meet the standards of BC 1129(b)(2)(A):

> With respect to a class of secured claims, the plan provides—
> (i)   (I) that the holders of such claims retain the liens securing such claims, whether the property subject to such liens is retained by the debtor or transferred to another entity, to the extent of the allowed amount of such claims; and
> (II) that each holder of a claim of such class receive on account of such claim deferred cash payments totaling at least the allowed amount of such claim, of a value, as of the effective date of the plan, of at least the value of such holder's interest in the estate's interest in such property;
> (ii)   for the sale, subject to section 363(k) of this title, of any property that is subject to the liens securing such claims, free and clear of such liens, with such liens to attach to the proceeds of such sale, and the treatment of such liens on proceeds under clause (i) or (iii) of this subparagraph; or
> (iii)   for the realization by such holders of the indubitable equivalent of such claims.

In effect, this provision gives the secured party absolute priority in the sense that until paid, no person with a claim junior to his may be paid. For further information on how the cramdown provisions work, see Blum, The "Fair and Equitable" Standard for Confirming Reorganizations Under the New Bankruptcy Code, 54 Am. Bankr. L.J. 165 (1980); Klee, All You Ever Want to Know About Cramdown Under the New Bankruptcy Code, 53 Am. Bankr. L.J. 1233 (1979); Pachulski, The Cramdown and Valuation Under Chapter 11 of the Bankruptcy Code, 58 N.C.L. Rev. 925 (1980).

3.   Chapter 13

The rights of secured parties in Chapter 13 proceedings are analogous to those in Chapter 11. A Chapter 13 plan may modify the rights of secured parties other than those with claims secured only by a security interest in the debtor's principal residence. BC 1322(b)(2). A court shall confirm the plan if the conditions of BC 1325(a)(5) are met:

> (5)   with respect to each allowed secured claim provided for by the plan—
> (A)   the holder of such claim has accepted the plan;
> (B)   (i) the plan provides that the holder of such claim retain the lien securing such claim; and
> (ii) the value, as of the effective date of the plan, of property to be distributed under the plan on account of such claim is not less than the allowed amount of such claim; or
> (C)   the debtor surrenders the property securing such claim to such holder.

For a discussion of how this cramdown provision works, see Bowman & Thompson, Secured Claims under Section 1325(a)(5)(B): Collateral Valuation, Present Value, and Adequate Protection, 15 Ind. L. Rev. 569 (1982).

CHRYSLER CREDIT CORP. v. VAN NORT (IN RE VAN NORT)
9 B.R. 218 (Bankr. E.D. Mich. 1981)

David H. PATTON, Bankruptcy Judge. This matter is before the Court to resolve a controversy arising from a dispute between the debtors, Keith and Susan Van Nort, and Chrysler Credit Corporation over the valuation of an automobile. Valuation is necessary because Chrysler Credit has objected to confirmation of the debtors' Chapter 13 plan on the ground that the amount to be distributed to it on account of its allowed secured claim is less than the value of its security interest in the vehicle. The hearing required by the Code [BC 1324] has been held. The facts material to the issue in this matter are not disputed.

Chrysler Credit is a secured creditor of the debtors, having been granted a security interest in their 1977 Plymouth Volare as part of a contractual arrangement through which it finances purchases from automobile dealerships. Under this arrangement Chrysler Credit will in certain instances require, as a condition of its agreement to provide financing, that the selling dealer agree to repurchase the vehicle in the event it is repossessed from the purchaser. Such an agreement was in effect with regard to the Van Norts' Volare.[2]

Appraisal of the vehicle established that it had a wholesale value of approximately $2,000.00 and a retail value some $800.00 to $1,000.00 higher, based on what the vehicle would bring if sold through normal commercial channels. The proposed plan provides for the payment of $2,900.00 to Chrysler Credit. It is the Van Norts' position that this amount adequately compensates Chrysler Credit for the value of its secured claim. Chrysler Credit disputes this valuation of its claim and argues that the plan should not be confirmed over its objection. The issue is whether in these circumstances the plan can be confirmed.

---

2. In pertinent part, the "Vehicle Financing and Repurchase Agreement" provides:

"3. REPURCHASE OBLIGATION. We [the dealership] agree to purchase from you [Chrysler Credit] . . . and to pay to you in cash the repurchase price computed in accordance with . . . this Agreement if you have repossessed the Vehicle . . . and tendered delivery to us. . . .

"4. REPURCHASE PRICE. The repurchase price which shall be paid with respect to a Repossessed Vehicle shall be an amount equal to the total of unpaid installments on the related Contract on the date of the repurchase plus (i) all reasonable expenses of your employees or agents incurred in connection with the repossession of the Repossessed Vehicle and (ii) the cost of transporting the Repossessed Vehicle in excess of 300 miles, less (i) the unearned portion of the finance charge computed on the date of payment of the Repurchase Price on the basis of the Rule of 78, (ii) the unearned portion of the insurance premium included in the Contract, if any . . . and (iii) the amount, if any, of the Damage Adjustment. . . ."

The criteria for confirmation of a Chapter 13 plan are contained in §1325 of the Code. Under this section a plan which provides for payments to the holder of a secured claim can be confirmed over the objection of that creditor if the creditor retains its lien and "the value, as of the effective date of the plan, of property to be distributed under the plan on account of such claim is not less than the allowed amount of such claim." BC 1325(a)(5)(B). This language has been interpreted to mean that a Chapter 13 plan can be confirmed with regard to a secured creditor where "the plan provides that the secured creditor retain its lien and be paid the value of its collateral as of the effective date of the plan." In re Lum, 1 B.R. 186, 1 C.B.C.2d 95, 96 (Bankr. E.D. Tenn. 1979). Since the lien requirement is not in dispute,[4] the main inquiry must be whether the collateral value of Chrysler Credit's interest is greater than the proposed payment under the plan.

The equation established in §1325(a)(5)(B)(ii) requires a determination of the value of Chrysler Credit's secured claim. In §506(a) it is stated that when a claim is secured by a lien on property it is secured only to the extent of the value of the creditor's interest in the estate's interest in the property. BC 506(a). Value is not defined. Chrysler Credit argues that the second sentence of §506(a) requires that its right to recourse against the selling dealer must be taken into account in determining such value. That sentence states: ". . . value shall be determined in light of the purpose of the valuation and of the proposed disposition or use of such property, and in conjunction with any hearing on such disposition or use or on a plan affecting such credit's interest." BC 506(a). This language, however, must be viewed in the context of the concern of Congress, revealed by legislative history, with the situation sometimes created under pre-Code law in which a creditor who had taken a position on valuation at an early stage of a bankruptcy case was adversely affected at later stages of the proceeding if forced to adhere to that position.[5] In a valuation necessitated by the need to determine whether payments to be made to the holder of a secured claim under a proposed Chapter 13 plan satisfy the requirements of §1325(a)(5)(B)(ii), the focus of inquiry must be on the interests that section is designed to protect, and valuation must be made with regard to those interests.[6]

Under §1325 Chrysler Credit is entitled to protection of the value of its allowed secured claims. Under §506(a) that claim is limited to the creditor's interest in the estate's interest in the property subject to the lien. In [§101(31)] "lien" is defined to mean a "charge against or interest in property to secure

---

4. Paragraph 2(c) of the proposed plan provides: "Holders of . . . secured claims shall retain the lien securing such claims until payment of their allowed claim."

5. S. Rep. No. 989, 95th Cong., 2d Sess. 68 (1978), 1978 U.S. Code Cong. & Ad. News 5787; 124 Cong. Rec. H 11,111 (daily ed. Sept. 28, 1978); S 17,428 (daily ed. Oct. 6, 1978). . . .

6. This focus is again revealed in the legislative history. See, e.g., H.R. Rep. No. 595, 95th Cong., 1st Sess. 356 (1977), 1978 U.S. Code Cong. & Ad. News 5787. It also seems consistent with the valuation procedures contemplated under §57(h) of the prior Act and Bankruptcy Rule 306(d).

payment of a debt or performance of an obligation." [BC 101(31).] The interest which must be protected is therefore the interest the creditor has in the
property as collateral. To do more would protect not only the creditor's right
to realization of the value of property in which he has a security interest when
his ability to realize that value is modified in a proceeding under the bankruptcy statute, but would also give the creditor at least a measure of the value
of its debt in excess of that amount. Under §506(a) partially secured claims
against a debtor are divided, resulting in secured and unsecured claims. The
interests a creditor may have arising from the unsecured portion of his claim
are dealt with elsewhere in §1325. [The court cites BC 1325(a)(4) in the
margin. See also BC 1325(b).—Eds.] The interest protected by §1325(a)(5) is
the right a creditor has to realize the value of certain property—the property
subject to its lien.

Based on this analysis the value which must be determined is the collateral value. This is the value which Chrysler Credit could realize from the
property if it foreclosed its lien and disposed of the property in a commercially
reasonable manner. The fact that it might obtain more than the amount
through the operation of a recourse agreement does not entitle it to a higher
valuation for its secured claim. . . . This is equally true where for other reasons
a particular item of collateral may bring an amount higher than its market
value if disposed of by a creditor. What must be protected is the right to
realize an amount *from the property* subjected to a lien equivalent to what could
be realized by selling it through established commercial channels. . . . While a
particular item or type of property may have a value to a particular creditor
greater than what would be realized in a reasonable commercial disposition
such value does not represent collateral value protected by §1325(a)(5). BC
1325, 506(a), [101(31)].

The value which Chrysler Credit could expect to receive from the liquidation of its security through commercial channels is the wholesale value. . . .
This value can be established through appraisal, as it was in this case, or by
reference to listings of automobile sources.[8] The time for valuation is the time
of the filing of the petition. . . . At that time the wholesale value of the Van
Norts' Volare was approximately $2,000.00. This is the amount of Chrysler
Credit's allowed secured claim and the minimum amount which must be
distributed for the plan to be confirmed over its objection. BC 1325(a)(5).

The $2,900.00 to be distributed under the proposed plan on account of
this secured claim therefore exceeds the amount of such claim. However, the
payment is to be made over a four (4) year period[9] and must be discounted to

---

8. In [In re American Kitchen Foods, Inc., 2 B.C.D. 715, 20 UCC Rep. 238 (Bankr. Me.
1976)], Judge Cyr enunciated a standard for collateral valuation based on "commercial reasonableness," stating, "the value of . . . collateral is equatable with the net recovery [realizable] from
its disposition as near as may be in the ordinary course of business." 2 B.C.D. at 720, 722 [20 UCC
Rep. at 254]. In this case the ordinary course of business would seem to be a quiet resale to a
knowledgeable professional buyer, the type of sale which produces a wholesale price.

9. The question whether cause exists for a four (4) year payment period is not at issue at this
time. See BC 1322(c).

reflect its present value on the effective date of the plan. . . . If the $900.00 by which the proposed payment exceeds the allowed secured claim represents a sufficient adjustment for the discount, or viewed another way, provides a rate of interest high enough to adequately compensate Chrysler Credit for the fact that it will realize the value of its security over a four (4) year period, then §1325(a)(5)(B) is satisfied and the plan can be confirmed. . . .

If $2,000.00 is taken as the principal amount, the proposed plan provides for the payment of 11.25% simple interest. This rate is greater than the prevailing rate required by Michigan law and represents a realistic effort to provide Chrysler Credit with an amount close to true present value.[11] In this Chapter 13 context and in view of the small amounts involved, a long controversy regarding interest is not justified.[12] It is the Court's conclusion that §1325(a)(5) is satisfied and the plan can be confirmed despite Chrysler Credit's objection. . . .

NOTES & QUESTIONS

1. *Valuation: the secured claim.* BC 506(a) provides:

> (a) An allowed claim of the creditor secured by a lien on property in which the estate has an interest . . . is a secured claim to the extent of the value of such creditor's interest in the estate's interest in such property . . . and is an unsecured claim to the extent that the value of such creditor's interest . . . is less than the amount of such allowed claim. Such value shall be determined in light of the purpose of the valuation and of the proposed disposition or use of such property, and in conjunction with any hearing on such disposition or use or on a plan affecting such creditor's interest.

As of what time is the valuation of the secured claim to be determined? Does BC 1325 require that the value of the secured claim be determined as of the time the debtor filed the petition or as of "the effective date of the plan"? When is the effective date of the plan? If the latter date is the proper date, what about the depreciation in value of the collateral between the time the petition was filed and the plan's effective date? What would be the result if the Van Norts had filed a Chapter 7 petition? A Chapter 11 petition?

2. *Valuation: present value and discount rate.* The court in *Van Nort* had to compare the value of the secured claim and the value of the payments to be made to the secured party. To determine the value of the installment payments to be made over four years the court had to calculate the present value

---

11. This conclusion is based in part on application of techniques utilized in the post-Code cases in this area. . . . In re Lum, supra. While methods of the sort utilized in these cases have the attractive feature of assuring a predictable result, they do not seem sufficiently related to the objective of providing collateral value to the creditor as to warrant adoption at this time. Until such a method emerges, a case by case evaluation seems necessary.

12. "The controlling concept is one of fundamental fair play." *American Kitchen Foods,* supra.

of those installments. The court notes that $2,000 set aside at 11.25% simple interest would yield $2,900, the sum proposed in the plan. Has the court made a proper calculation of present value? To answer this question requires some understanding of the concepts of present value and discounting.

The concepts of present value and discounting are based on the simple proposition that a dollar to be paid to you in one year's time is worth less than a dollar paid today because you could invest today's dollar and at the very least earn interest for a year. You therefore would not pay a full dollar in return for a promise to repay the dollar in one year. Instead, you would calculate how much you would have to set aside today to ensure that this sum, plus earnings on this sum, will equal one dollar in one year's time. The amount you set aside today is the present value of the one dollar to be paid next year. The rate used to calculate the earnings on this sum is the discount rate.[4] How should the discount rate be selected? Possible alternatives include the rate of interest set out in the original agreement, the legal rate, the rate of return earned by the creditor on all investments of like kind, and the amount earned on investments in the money market. For a more elaborate explanation of discounting to present value, see A. Alchian & W. Allen, Exchange & Production: Competition, Coordination and Control 144-154 (2d ed. 1977).

Note that an allowed claim normally will not include unmatured interest. BC 502(b)(2). Interest is allowed, however, when a secured claim is less than the value of the collateral: indeed, the holder of the secured claim may include not only interest but also reasonable fees, costs, or charges provided by the security agreement. BC 506(b).

3. *Valuation: depreciation.* The opinion in In re Lum, referred to in cryptic n.11 of the *Van Nort* case, suggests that the monthly payments must meet the "adequate protection" standard in BC 363, presumably because the debtor will use the collateral during the period of the plan. Payments at least equal to depreciation were therefore required to protect the secured party. Should the *Van Nort* court have also inquired into depreciation? How does one choose the rate of depreciation?

Note that normally payments pursuant to a Chapter 13 plan must be made within three years, although with court approval the period may be extended to as long as five years. BC 1322(c), 1329(c).

4. *Valuation: the BC 1111(b) election.* If the debtor is in Chapter 11 proceedings a secured creditor may choose either (1) to hold an allowed secured claim equal to the value of the debt or, if undersecured, the value of the collateral (i.e., a secured claim as measured by BC 506); or (2) to have an allowed secured claim equal to the entire claim (the BC 1111(b) election). As a result of making this an 1111(b) election the creditor will alter the "indubi-

---

4. In figures, the following formula may be used to determine the present discounted value of a fixed sum to be delivered at a future date: $p(1 + r) = A$, where p is the present value, r is the rate of interest, and A is the fixed sum to be paid. Example: the present value of $100 to be delivered in one year at a discount interest rate of six percent is $94.30; i.e., $94.3 (1 + 0.06) = 100$.

table equivalent" he must receive under the plan and will take the risk of appreciation or depreciation of the collateral.

An illustration may help you understand the effect of the election. Assume a creditor has a claim of $10,000 and the collateral is valued at $8,000. Under BC 506 the creditor has a secured claim of $8,000 and an unsecured claim of $2,000. After a BC 1111(b) election the creditor has a $10,000 secured claim and no unsecured claim. If the collateral then appreciates in value, the creditor may ultimately receive the full $10,000; if it depreciates, however, the creditor may possibly recover no more than the value of the collateral.

5. *A secured party with an unsecured claim.* The creditor in *Van Nort* apparently was undersecured and therefore had an unsecured claim. A 1984 amendment to BC 1325 introduced subsection (b), which limits the power of a court to confirm a plan over the objection of a holder of an unsecured claim. The objecting creditor must receive, as of the effective date of the plan, distributions equal in value to the amount of the creditor's claim or the plan must provide for distribution of all of the debtor's projected disposable income to creditors. If the Van Norts had been in Chapter 7 proceedings, on the other hand, the creditor would receive on its unsecured claim the same pro rata distribution that other unsecured creditors receive. An unsecured creditor therefore would usually prefer to have his debtor file under Chapter 13. The creditor may not, however, force the debtor to proceed in Chapter 13: the creditor may not bring an involuntary case under Chapter 13 and only the debtor may convert from a Chapter 7 to a Chapter 13 proceeding. BC 303(a), 706(c).

C. MODIFICATION OF THE SECURED PARTY'S RIGHT TO ENFORCE A SECURITY INTEREST

A secured party whose debtor files a petition in bankruptcy will suddenly find that the alternatives available under state law have been modified. The principal modification is that the secured party is automatically stayed from repossessing the collateral or creating, perfecting, or enforcing the security interest. BC 362(a)(3), (a)(4). Moreover, subject to some limitations, the trustee may use and even sell the collateral. BC 363. A secured party who already has possession of the collateral may have to turn it over to the trustee if the trustee is authorized to use it or if the debtor can exempt the property. BC 542.

If the trustee is authorized to operate the debtor's business he may be unable to obtain credit unless he can offer new creditors security interests in collateral subject to existing security interests. After notice and a hearing, the court may authorize the granting of a senior or equal security interest to the new creditor but only if the existing secured party is given adequate protection and the trustee cannot obtain credit otherwise. BC 364.

An after-acquired property clause in a security agreement will not be given effect as to property acquired by the estate after the commencement of bankruptcy proceedings. However, a perfected security interest in collateral will cover proceeds of the collateral acquired by the estate unless the court orders otherwise "based on the equities." BC 552.

We cannot overemphasize the practical importance to the secured party of these Bankruptcy Code provisions, especially BC 362-365.

1. Automatic Stay (BC 362)

The secured party may request the lifting of the stay under BC 362(d), which states:

> (d) On request of a party in interest and after notice and a hearing, the court shall grant relief from the stay provided under subsection (a) of this section, such as by terminating, annulling, modifying, or conditioning such stay—
>
> (1)   for cause, including the lack of adequate protection of an interest in property of such party in interest; or
> (2)   with respect to a stay of an act against property under subsection (a) of this section, if—
>   (A)   the debtor does not have an equity in such property; and
>   (B)   such property is not necessary to an effective reorganization.

The court must hold a hearing on the secured party's request within 30 days, and unless the court continues the stay it will be lifted automatically. At the hearing the secured party has the burden of showing that the debtor has no equity, but the party opposing relief has the burden as to all other matters. As BC 362(d) indicates, the court has considerable flexibility in the relief it can grant. To provide adequate protection for the secured party's interest the court may require the trustee to make periodic cash payments, provide an additional or replacement lien, or grant any relief that gives the secured party the "indubitable equivalent" of his interest in the collateral. BC 361. If the secured party does not request the lifting of the stay it continues as to acts against the property until the collateral is no longer part of the bankruptcy estate and as to all other acts until the case is closed, dismissed, or a decision is made as to discharge of the debtor. BC 362(c).

2. Use, Sale, or Lease of Collateral (BC 363)

The trustee may use, sell, or lease collateral (other than cash collateral) in the ordinary course of business without notice or a hearing. Notice and a hearing are necessary, however, if the trustee wishes to use or dispose of the collateral outside of the ordinary course of business. Use of cash collateral requires either the secured party's consent or a court order issued after notice and a hearing.

Notwithstanding these provisions, a secured party may request a court to prohibit the trustee from acting or to condition the trustee's use or disposition on the provision of adequate protection. The trustee has the burden of proof on this issue, and the standards and methods for providing adequate protection are the same as those applicable in hearings on the lifting of the automatic stay. When proceeding under BC 363, however, the trustee must read the statutory language with care. BC 363(a), for example, defines *cash collateral* but not *ordinary course of business*. Nor, because of the special definition of *after notice and a hearing,* is a hearing always necessary. BC 102(1). *(if not requested timely, or insufficiently timely notice properly given?)*

If collateral is sold the security interest will continue to be effective against the purchaser unless the trustee complies with BC 363(f). This section provides:

> (f) The trustee may sell property under subsection (b) or (c) of this section free and clear of any interest in such property of an entity other than the estate, only if—
>
> (1)   applicable nonbankruptcy law permits sale of such property free and clear of such interest;
> (2)   such entity consents;
> (3)   such interest is a lien and the price at which such property is to be sold is greater than the aggregate value of all liens on such property;
> (4)   such interest is in bona fide dispute; or
> (5)   such entity could be compelled, in a legal or equitable proceeding, to accept a money satisfaction of such interest.

A secured party, of course, may request the court to provide adequate protection if the trustee proposes to sell the collateral free and clear of the security interest. In most cases adequate protection is provided by having the security interest attach to the proceeds of the sale.

3. Need for Early Election (BC 521(2))

In a Chapter 7 proceeding a debtor must state no later than 30 days after filing a petition what he intends to do with estate property that secures consumer debt. He must, in other words, state whether he will surrender the property, claim an exemption, redeem, or reaffirm the debt. Within 45 days after filing this statement the debtor must carry out his intention. BC 521(2).

INGERSOLL-RAND FINANCIAL CORP. v. 5-LEAF CLOVER CORP. (IN RE 5-LEAF CLOVER CORP.)
6 B.R. 463 (Bankr. S.D. W. Va. 1980)

Edwin F. FLOWERS, Bankruptcy Judge. Ingersoll-Rand Financial Corporation asks that the automatic stay imposed by 11 U.S.C. §362 be lifted to enable it

to repossess certain mining equipment owned by the Debtors in which Ingersoll-Rand claims a security interest.

A preliminary hearing on the matter was held on July 9, 1980. . . .
Conflicting evidence was offered as to the value of the equipment and the
balance of the debt owed to Ingersoll-Rand. Nonetheless, the evidence established that the Debtors did have some equity in the equipment. The Court
concluded that the equity afforded Ingersoll-Rand adequate protection pending the final hearing and ordered the automatic stay to continue in the interim. Having also heard testimony in behalf of Ingersoll-Rand that the
Debtors were delinquent on two installments, the Court cautioned the Debtors
that they could not expect secured creditors to finance their reorganization.
The Court further suggested that an appraisal of the equipment would be
helpful in establishing its fair market value.

The final hearing was held on August 5, 1980, at which time the parties
presented additional evidence to the Court and argued the law to be applied
to that evidence.

The evidence establishes that, at some time after the incorporation of the
Debtors, a considerable amount of mining machinery was purchased by them
from the assignors of Ingersoll-Rand. On January 25, 1980, Ingersoll-Rand
refinanced the various debts of the three Debtors. New security agreements
were executed and the proper UCC filings were made to perfect the security
interests. This refinancing resulted in eight separate accounts with Ingersoll-
Rand—four owed by 5-Leaf Clover, three by J & J Motors, and one owed by
W & C Coal—representing thirty-seven different pieces of equipment. The
secured status of Ingersoll-Rand is not disputed. The parties stipulated at the
preliminary hearing that Ingersoll-Rand had validly perfected its liens well
before the Chapter 11 petitions were filed by the Debtors.

The evidence offered by Ingersoll-Rand and the Debtors varies as to the
balance due on the eight accounts. Counsel for Ingersoll-Rand proffered a
schedule of accounts which reflects a total close-out balance due, using the
interest rebate Rule of 78s, of $701,074.30 on August 5, 1980, the date of the
final hearing. The Debtors' accountant testified that the close-out balance on
May 15, 1980, again using the Rule of 78s, was $654,300.55. To aid in com-
parison of the two amounts, the Court must adjust the Debtors' May 15 figure,
adding the interest accrued daily from May 15 to August 5, or $322.27 per
day for 82 days. This produces an August 5 close-out balance of $680,726.69.
Thus, there is a slight disparity of some $20,000 between the Debtors' figures
and those of Ingersoll-Rand. No evidence was offered to otherwise reconcile
the two amounts.

On the other hand, the evidence as to the value of the equipment varies
greatly between the parties. The equipment was appraised at the request of
Ingersoll-Rand on July 31 and August 1, 1980, by a representative of Phillips
Machine Service in Beverley, West Virginia. The total fair market value of all
of the equipment was estimated at $762,400. The Debtors' accountant testified
that the book value of the equipment on the Debtors' account was approxi-

mately $982,332 on May 15, 1980. Although an appraisal was made on behalf of the Debtors, the Court did not receive competent evidence of that appraisal. Counsel for the Debtors attempted to introduce the appraisal, not by testimony of the appraiser, but through the hearsay testimony of a witness who was not qualified as an expert on the fair market value of the equipment. That testimony must therefore be excluded. Moreover, the Court gives greater weight to the presumably independent appraisal submitted by Ingersoll-Rand than to the testimony of the Debtors' accountant of the book value. Thus, the Court accepts the figure of $762,400 as the one more likely to reflect the fair market value.

The amount of equity accumulated by the Debtors ranges from approximately $61,325 to $81,674, depending upon whether the Court uses the balance due reported by the Debtors or that proffered by Ingersoll-Rand. In either case, the equity provides a small cushion of protection to the Creditor.

The Debtors contend that the equity cushion, regardless of its size, provides adequate protection to Ingersoll-Rand pending confirmation of the Debtors' plans, which will include payments to Ingersoll-Rand, a secured creditor. On the other hand, Ingersoll-Rand argues that although the equity may provide a "cushion," a creditor's interests are not adequately protected by a cushion of equity which is rapidly decreasing in amount. It contends that it is entitled to the maintenance of the cushion at a constant level, which can be achieved only by regular payments to it by the Debtors.

"Adequate protection" is not defined in BC 362, nor is it defined in section 361 of the Bankruptcy Code, which merely offers methods of providing adequate protection. See BC 361(2)-(3). The legislative history of section 361 clearly reflects the intent of Congress to give the courts the flexibility to fashion the relief in light of the facts of each case and general equitable principles. H.R. Rep. No. 95-595, 95th Cong., 1st Sess. 339 (1977), 1978 U.S. Code Cong. & Ad. News 5787.

Case law under the Bankruptcy Code has held that adequate protection under section 361 can be provided by an equity cushion. . . . However, at least one court has recognized that the equity cushion can be dissipated: "Adequate protection . . . requires, at a minimum, a periodic and careful surveillance of the facts and circumstances calculated to avoid dissipation of whatever protection the cushion affords." In re Pitts, 2 B.R. 476, 478-479 (Bankr. C.D. Cal. 1979). Thus, at some point, the diminishing cushion will no longer provide adequate protection for the secured creditor.

The Court is in agreement that the equity cushion adequately protects creditors' interests—up to a point. Equity provides adequate protection so long as the creditor may foreclose upon the collateral and realize an amount sufficient to fully cover the balance due on the debt. This does not mean, however, that the creditor must wait until there is no equity before it is entitled to a lifting of the stay to foreclose on the property. Although a debtor may have equity in the collateral, where regular payments are not being made that equity decreases over a period of time as the accrued interest increases the balance due on the debt and accumulating depreciation decreases the value of the property. In this circumstance, the equity decreases at a rate determined by combining the interest and depreciation rates. Thus, the equity reaches zero at the point in time at which the debt balance and the market value converge, or are equal. Conversely, the equity ratio can be kept constant by payment of both the interest and depreciation to the creditor.

The UCC dictates a rule of commercial reasonableness in disposition of collateral to satisfy a debt. UCC 9-504(3). The time required to make a commercially reasonable disposition of the collateral will vary according to the nature of the collateral and the condition of the market in which it will be sold. The secured creditor should be permitted to proceed against the collateral when full recovery becomes impaired—the time at which the process of collateral disposition should commence to enable the creditor to realize an adequate amount from the secured property to satisfy the debt. The creditor is minimally entitled to assure its own protection by having a reasonable period of time in which to sell the collateral at the highest price attainable. The value of the collateral is further decreasing even while the creditor is attempting to sell it. To require the creditor to wait until the collateral's value equals the lien attaching to it before foreclosure and sale is permitted does not adequately assure the creditor that the debt can be fully covered. At that point, the creditor is reduced to "quick sale" tactics, attempting to sell as soon as possible to offset the decline in the collateral's value. Thirty to sixty days would be necessary to assure disposition in a commercially reasonable fashion of the kind of equipment serving as security for the debt to Ingersoll-Rand. In this instance, Ingersoll-Rand is entitled to a sixty-day period of time to establish its statutory responsibilities without further impairment of its opportunity for a full recovery.

At the same time, in permitting the continuation of the stay until the impairment date is reached, the debtor is afforded some time to accumulate cash from its operations. During this time the debtor typically is making no payments to the creditor on the secured debt—were it otherwise, the creditor likely would not be before this Court seeking relief from the automatic stay. In the instant case, the Debtors failed to pay installments due in May, June and July. The debtor may postpone and continuously advance the impairment date by regular payments which at least equal the combined depreciation and interest on the debt. In this manner the equity ratio will be maintained at the appropriate level. If the debtor is unable to do so, the automatic stay will be lifted to permit the creditor to repossess the collateral and dispose of it in satisfaction of the debt. The Court believes this to be a fair and balanced result which satisfies the intent of Congress evidenced in sections 361 and 362 of the Bankruptcy Code. H.R. Rep. No. 95-595, 95th Cong., 1st Sess. 339 (1977); S. Rep. No. 95-989, 95th Cong., 2d Sess. 52-54 (1978), 1978 U.S. Code Cong. & Ad. News 5787.

While the Debtors have offered no direct evidence of the necessity of the equipment for reorganization, circumstantial evidence permits the Court to conclude that without the collateral an effective reorganization of the Debtor is not likely. That conclusion is not dispositive of the issues raised in this proceeding. However necessary such property is to their reorganization, the Debtors are not entitled to the use of the equipment absent adequate protection to Ingersoll-Rand. While the Bankruptcy Code contemplates the continued use and possession of property during the bankruptcy proceedings, it does not require secured creditors to finance the reorganization. The impairment rule helps implement this principle.

The application of the impairment rule to the instant case dictates that the Debtors commence payment to Ingersoll-Rand. The equity of the Debtors ranges from approximately $61,326 to $81,674. Ingersoll-Rand offered testimony to establish a depreciation rate of 2.2%, or approximately $25,000 per month. The Debtors presented evidence of a different amount of depreciation taken by them, based upon the varying depreciable lives of the equipment. It is impossible for the Court to otherwise compute the Debtors' depreciation rate from the evidence proffered. Thus, the only competent evidence on the matter is the unrefuted depreciation rate offered by Ingersoll-Rand. This is accepted by the Court as reasonable.

The contract interest rate of $322.27 per day on the unpaid balance totals approximately $10,000 per month. Again, this evidence was introduced by Ingersoll-Rand and was not contradicted by the Debtors. Combining the depreciation and interest rates, the Debtors' equity is deteriorating at a rate of $35,000 per month. Thus, their equity will reach the zero point in somewhat less than sixty days, the figures used having been established as of August 5, 1980, or one month ago.

Accordingly, the principle here adopted by the Court requires that the Debtors must make payment in the amount of $35,000 to Ingersoll-Rand to provide adequate protection to this secured creditor and to not impair the likelihood of full recovery on its debt. The Debtors will be permitted fifteen days from the entry of the order accompanying this Memorandum to make such payment to Ingersoll-Rand. The payments will thereafter continue on a monthly basis until confirmation of the Debtors' plans which may make other provisions to satisfy appropriate portions of the Code. E.g., BC 1124. If the Debtors are unable to make the payment within fifteen days, the stay will be lifted and the mining equipment must be relinquished to Ingersoll-Rand for disposition in some fashion in satisfaction of the debts owed it by the Debtors.

NOTES & QUESTIONS

1. *Valuation of obligation: rule of 78s.* To calculate how much interest has been earned by a creditor in order to determine the amount to be refunded upon prepayment many states have adopted by statute the rule of 78s or the "sum of the digits" formula. The formula has been explained as follows: "Under this method, allocation of finance charges is made as follows: First, the

numbers of the months of credit term are added. For example: In a twelve-month credit, we add the numbers 1 through 12, arriving at a sum of 78. Second, the finance charge is allocated to each month of the credit by multiplying it by a fraction, the numerator of which is the number of the specific month in reverse chronological order and the denominator of which is the sum of the numbers of the period of the credit. For example: For a twelve-month credit in which the finance charge is $6, the charge allocable to the first month is 12/78 × $6, and the charge allocable to the second month 11/78 × $6. If any part of the principal is prepaid, the creditor is required to refund to the debtor the 'unearned' portion of the finance charge." Jordan & Warren, Disclosure of Finance Charges: A Rationale, 64 Mich. L. Rev. 1285, 1288 n.5 (1966). Why did Ingersoll-Rand apply the rule of 78s to determine its secured claim? Why did the court recompute the debtors' calculation of the amount owed Ingersoll-Rand to include interest up to its final hearing on August 5? See BC 502(b)(2), 506(b).

2. *Valuation of equipment.* The court in *5-Leaf Clover* refers to the appraisal of the fair market value of the equipment. Is "fair market value" the correct standard of valuation? How does the expert appraiser determine this value? As of what time should this value be determined?

Is the following description of the "capital budgeting decision" relevant?

"As in valuing the corporate enterprise itself, the capital budgeting decision entails (1) estimating the returns that can be expected to be realized from the investment over time, and (2) discounting those projected returns to present value. The investment can be viewed as acceptable if the present value of the estimated returns equals or exceeds the cash outlay required to finance it, and on the same basis the investment can be compared with the available alternatives. To illustrate simply, assume that a firm is considering the purchase of a new machine costing $18,000 with a useful life of 5 years, at the end of which time its value will be zero. The new machine is expected to add $5,600 after taxes to the firm's annual income throughout the 5-year period. Under the present-value method of evaluation, we first discount the expected cash inflows of $5,600 per year at an appropriate discount rate—say $10%—to establish the present value of those inflows. The result is then compared with the required outlay of $18,000 in order to determine whether the investment has a positive net present value. Resorting to [a Table: Present Value of Annuity of $1, Received at End of Each Year], it turns out that the present value of the anticipated inflows is $21,224 (3.79 × $5,600). Since the investment thus has a net present value of $3,224 ($21,224-$18,000), it is acceptable and the outlay should be made. In effect, if we are able to estimate the future returns of an investment project, if we know its out-of-pocket cost, and if an appropriate rate of discount is given (the word 'if' being repeated for emphasis), management's decision problem can be resolved easily. A management bent on maximizing the value of the enterprise should accept all investment projects having a positive net present value, because the effect of such acceptance is to replace cash assets with tangible assets of greater worth. Obviously, management should reject all projects having a negative net present value.

Finally, if two 'acceptable' projects are for some reason mutually exclusive, a choice between them can be made by comparing their present values relative to their required cash outlays." V. Brudney & M. Chirelstein, Cases and Materials on Corporate Finance 42 (2d ed. 1979).

3. *Violation of stay.* As enacted in 1978, BC 362 did not state what the consequences were when a creditor failed to observe the automatic stay. Courts regularly concluded, however, that any action taken contrary to the stay was void and the party taking such action was in contempt of court. See Stacy v. Roanoke Memorial Hospitals (In re Stacy), 21 B.R. 49 (Bankr. W.D. Va. 1982) (debtor has no right of action to enforce stay; court may punish violation of stay as contempt pursuant to authority of 28 U.S.C. §1481; actions and violations of stay are void; punitive damages payable to debtor only available in "clear and urgent instances"). The 1984 bankruptcy legislation repealed 28 U.S.C. §1481 and amended BC 362 by adding subsection (h), which provides: "an individual injured by any willful violation of a stay provided by this section shall recover actual damages, including costs and attorneys' fees, and, in appropriate circumstances, may recover punitive damages." Bankruptcy Rule 9020 governs criminal contempt proceedings.

4. *Use of collateral (BC 363).* The debtors in *5-Leaf Clover* presumably were authorized to use the equipment by virtue of BC 363(c)(1), which states:

> If the business of the debtor is authorized to be operated under section 721, 1108, or 1304 of this title and unless the court orders otherwise, the trustee may enter into transactions, including the sale or lease of property of the estate, in the ordinary course of business, without notice or a hearing, and may use property of the estate in the ordinary course of business without notice or a hearing.

BC 1108 authorizes the trustee to operate the debtor's business unless the court orders otherwise. In most Chapter 11 cases the debtor in possession will have these powers of the trustee. BC 1107.

Problems

Austin State Bank and Apex enter into the prototype transaction set out at p. 112 supra. Early on the morning of April 6, 1983, an officer of Austin State Bank contacts you. She informs you that Apex will file a voluntary petition in bankruptcy in federal court the next morning. She has no official notice of this but assures you that her source is completely reliable. She indicates that the petition is not a complete surprise: she knows that Apex has been struck by employees for the last two months, and has been aware of that company's failing financial health during this period because of her close monitoring of the Apex account. Believing that pressure will only further impair prospects of repayment, the bank has not wished to place further pressure on Apex. The officer also states that there is an unpaid balance on the Apex note of "something like" $30,000. She says she has arranged to have a truck pick up the bookbinder from Apex's plant later that day. She estimates that "with luck" proceeds from the disposition of the bookbinder will leave a deficiency of between $5,000 to $10,000 after all costs of repossession, attorney's fees, and other costs are paid.

Problem 4-1. Assume Apex has not yet filed a bankruptcy petition. Is Apex in default on its obligation to the bank? If the security agreement does not authorize repossession under these circumstances, how would you revise it to protect the secured party? What are Apex's rights?

Assume in problems 4-2 through 4-8 that Apex is in default on its obligation to the bank.

Problem 4-2. Assume the bank repossesses the bookbinder on April 6, but, notwithstanding the "completely reliable" source, Apex does not file a voluntary bankruptcy petition. May the bank dispose of the bookbinder? What rights does Apex have?

Problem 4-3. Assume that on April 7 Apex does file a voluntary petition under Chapter 7 of the Bankruptcy Code. BC 301. (For the applicability of Chapters 1, 3, and 5 to Chapter 7 see BC 103.)

(a) Is the bookbinder part of Apex's bankruptcy "estate"? BC 541. Would it make a difference whether or not the bank has repossessed the bookbinder before the bankruptcy petition is filed?

(b) Must the bank file a "proof of claim"? BC 501, 502, 506. If not required to file a proof of claim, should the bank do so anyway?

(c) To what extent does the bank have a "secured" claim? BC 506. To what extent does it have an "unsecured" claim?

Problem 4-4. Assume the bank repossesses the bookbinder on April 6 and the following day Apex files a petition under Chapter 7.

(a) May the bank dispose of the bookbinder after the petition has been filed? BC 362.

(b) If the bank cannot legally dispose of the bookbinder but does so anyway, what sanctions are there for the bank's actions? BC 362.

(c) If the bank does not dispose of the bookbinder, may it keep possession or must it return the bookbinder to Apex (or its trustee in bankruptcy)? BC 542, 543.

(d) If the bank must return the bookbinder but does not do so, what sanctions are there for the bank's actions? BC 542, 543.

(e) If the bank does return the bookbinder, does Apex (or its trustee) have the right to use it? BC 363, 361, 721.

Problem 4-5. Would it make any difference to your answers to the previous two problems that Apex only owed $20,000 on the note and the expected proceeds of a disposition of the bookbinder are $25,000 to $30,000?

Problem 4-6. Would any of your answers to the previous problems be different if Apex had filed a voluntary petition under Chapter 11? BC 109, 1107, 1108, 1111.

Problem 4-7. Is Apex eligible to file a voluntary petition under Chapter 13? BC 109. If Apex was a sole proprietorship rather than a corporation, could the sole proprietor file a petition under Chapter 13? If Apex can file a petition under that chapter would any of your answers to the previous problems be different? BC 1303, 1304, 1305, 1322(b)(2), 1325(a)(5).

Problem 4-8. Assume that Apex has a checking account at the bank and that on April 6 there is $7,000 in the account.

(a) On April 6, before the petition in bankruptcy is filed, may the bank rightfully set off the amount in the account (i.e., the amount it owes to Apex) against Apex's obligation on the note secured by the bookbinder? BC 553.

(b) On April 8, after the petition in bankruptcy is filed, may the bank rightfully set off the amount in the Apex account against Apex's obligation? BC 362.

(c) If the bank may rightfully set off the amount in the account against Apex's obligation, what effect does this set off have on the bank's attempt to obtain and dispose of the bookbinder?

(d) After the petition in bankruptcy is filed may Apex draw on the account? Would it make a difference if Apex issued the checks for postpetition obligations only? BC 363, 361, 549.

D.   AVOIDANCE POWERS OF THE TRUSTEE IN BANKRUPTCY

The trustee in bankruptcy is given authority to avoid certain prepetition transfers. *Transfer* is defined broadly enough to include the creation of a security interest. BC 101(48). A secured party, therefore, must be aware of the trustee's avoidance powers, which include: BC 544(a), giving the trustee the rights and powers of a "hypothetical lien creditor" of the debtor; BC 544(b), giving the trustee the right to avoid transfers held by actual unsecured creditors; BC 545, giving the trustee the power to avoid certain state-created statutory liens; BC 547, giving the trustee power to avoid transfers that are made soon before the commencement of bankruptcy and that give the transferee a preference; and BC 548, giving the trustee power to avoid fraudulent transfers. Any transfer that is avoided is preserved for the benefit of the estate. BC 551.

1.   BC 544(a): The "Strong Arm" Clause

BC 544(a)(1) states:

> (a) The trustee shall have, as of the commencement of the case, and without regard to any knowledge of the trustee or of any creditor, the rights and powers of, or may avoid any transfer of property of the debtor or any obligation incurred by the debtor that is voidable by—

(1)   a creditor that extends credit to the debtor at the time of the commence-
      ment of the case, and that obtains, at such time and with respect to such
      credit, a judicial lien on all property on which a creditor on a simple
      contract could have obtained such a judicial lien, whether or not such a
      creditor exists.

This provision is commonly referred to as the *strong-arm* clause. The Bankruptcy Code provision restates, with important clarifications, the content of
§70c of the Bankruptcy Act of 1898.

The principal significance of the clause for secured creditors is that the
trustee may avoid a security interest that is not perfected at the commencement of a bankruptcy case. The trustee has the rights and powers, as defined
by state law, of a creditor with a judicial lien, whether or not such a creditor
actually exists. In most instances the relevant state law will be UCC 9-301. A
UCC Article 9 lien creditor has a judicial lien within the meaning of the
Bankruptcy Code. BC 101(30). The lien creditor has priority over an unperfected security interest. UCC 9-301(1)(b). Although the Bankruptcy Code
speaks of the transfer being "voidable" by a judicial lien creditor, this has been
read to include the subordination provided in UCC 9-301.

The operation of BC 544(a) is illustrated in the following example. Apex
grants Bank a security interest on January 9. Bank does not file a financing
statement. Apex files a petition in bankruptcy on January 30. Apex's trustee
may avoid the Bank's unperfected security interest under BC 544(a) and
Bank's claim would be reduced to an unsecured claim. If Bank files the financing statement on January 29 its perfected security interest is immune from the
strong-arm clause although, as we shall see, it might be subject to attack by
the trustee under other provisions of the Bankruptcy Code.

There is an important exception to the strong-arm clause for the benefit
of a purchase money security interest that is granted immediately before bankruptcy proceedings commence. UCC 9-301(2) gives the purchase money secured party priority over an intervening lien creditor if the secured party
perfects his interest within ten days after the debtor receives possession of the
collateral. The Bankruptcy Code recognizes this exception when an unperfected purchase money security interest exists at the commencement of the
case. BC 546(b) states that BC 544 does not apply when a general state law
like UCC 9-301(2) gives the security interest priority over an intervening
creditor. BC 362(b)(2) provides an exception to the automatic stay in cases
covered by BC 546(b) so that the secured party may file a financing statement
even after a bankruptcy case has commenced. The secured party must, of
course, file to perfect his interest within ten days after the debtor receives
possession.

2.   *BC 544(b): Trustee as Successor to Unsecured Creditors*

BC 544(b) states:

The trustee may avoid any transfer of an interest of the debtor in property or any
obligation incurred by the debtor that is voidable under applicable law by a

creditor holding an unsecured claim that is allowable under section 502 of this title or that is not allowable only under section 502(e) of this title.

Section 70e of the Bankruptcy Act is the predecessor of this provision. Unlike its predecessor, however, BC 544(b) does not give the trustee the rights of secured creditors whose interests can be avoided.

Under pre-UCC statutes a secured creditor who failed to record promptly the appropriate documents, ran the risk that his interest would be subordinate to or voidable by "gap creditors." For example, in many jurisdictions if a judgment creditor of the debtor levied on the collateral before the secured creditor recorded his interest, the judgment creditor would be able to avoid the secured creditor's interest. Some jurisdictions defined the protected class of gap creditors to include those who extended credit before recording without the need to obtain a judgment or to levy execution. When there was a provision like BC 544(b) in effect a trustee who could find such a gap creditor would be subrogated to that creditor's right to avoid the creditor's interest. This right to subrogation was made all the more important by the notorious case of Moore v. Bay, 284 U.S. 4 (1931), in which the Supreme Court held that the entire secured interest was avoided, rather than just the amount equal to the gap creditor's claim. It was therefore conceivable that a million-dollar secured claim could be avoided by a bankruptcy trustee who could find a $5 gap creditor. The secured claim would be reduced to an unsecured claim and the collateral would become part of the bankruptcy estate. Despite extensive debate, the Bankruptcy Code continues the rule of Moore v. Bay.

A creditor with an Article 9 security interest will be concerned with BC 544(b) principally in cases where non-UCC law provides that an unsecured creditor may avoid the security interest. Such a law will include, for example, a fraudulent conveyance statute, although the Bankruptcy Code itself permits the trustee to avoid fraudulent conveyances directly under BC 548. Perhaps the most likely state law used by the trustee will be the law governing bulk transfers, set out in UCC Article 6. A debtor who makes a bulk transfer covered by that article and does not give the required notice to creditors will find that the transfer was "ineffective." UCC 6-105.

3. BC 545: Statutory Liens

BC 545 collects several discrete bankruptcy rules on state statutory liens. If a statutory lien falls within the four classes of liens within this section the trustee may avoid the lien and leave the creditor with an unsecured claim. The section is the successor of §67b and c of the Bankruptcy Act.

BC 545(1) includes liens that first arise when the debtor's financial situation becomes so straitened that bankruptcy or state insolvency proceedings are likely. These state statutes in effect give preferences to particular classes of creditors by giving them liens on property. One stated goal of bankruptcy legislation, however, is to treat creditors equally except to the extent that the bankruptcy legislation itself provides for priorities. The language of the bankruptcy laws, therefore, suggests suspicion of state legislation creating liens that first become effective on a debtor's insolvency. BC 545(1) authorizes the trustee to avoid these liens.

BC 545(2) also grants the trustee power to avoid state statutory liens that are "unperfected" on the date the bankruptcy petition is filed. The case of In re Saberman, 3 B.R. 316 (Bankr. N.D. Ill. 1980), illustrates the operation of BC 545(2). AAA made certain improvements to the debtor's residence and completed the work on May 5, 1978. AAA, however, did not file a mechanics' lien under the Illinois Mechanics' Lien Act until January or February 1980, by which time the debtor had filed a petition under Chapter 13 of the Bank-ruptcy Code. Under Illinois law an inchoate mechanics' lien arises on substan-tial completion of the work. When a notice of the lien is filed perfection relates back to the date the lien arose. The Illinois statute provides:

> No contractor shall be allowed to enforce such lien against or to the prejudice of any other creditor or incumbrancer or purchaser, unless within four months after completion, . . . he shall either bring suit to enforce his lien therefor or shall file in the office of the recorder of deeds of the county in which the building, erection or other improvement to be charged with the lien is situated, a claim for lien. . . . Such claim for lien may be filed at any time after the contract is made, and as to the owner may be filed at any time after the contract is made and within two years after the completion of said contract. . . .

The bankruptcy court held that because AAA had not filed within four months of completing its work its lien would not be prior to a bona fide purchaser and therefore AAA's claim was unsecured by virtue of BC 545.

BC 545(3) and (4) authorize the trustee to avoid statutory liens for rent or distress for rent.

The principal problem for secured creditors raised by BC 545 is whether UCC 9-306(4)(d) (security interest in cash proceeds upon the debtor's insol-vency) creates a statutory lien within the meaning of BC 545. We take up this problem in Chapter 6.

4.   BC 547: Preferences

The power of the trustee to avoid a debtor's prepetition transfers that "prefer" one creditor over others will most interest secured parties. BC 547 continues, with several significant modifications, the policy of §60 of the Bankruptcy Act. This policy is to discourage the dismemberment of a financially troubled debtor that might occur if the most aggressive and least accommodating credi-tors are permitted to keep payments made immediately before bankruptcy. Note that the common law does not adopt this policy: outside of bankruptcy a debtor may prefer one creditor over another unless a transfer of property is fraudulent.

The heart of BC 547 is subsection (b), which sets out the following five elements of a preferential transfer:

(1)   the transfer of property by a debtor to or for the benefit of a credi-
        tor;
(2)   on account of antecedent debt owed by the debtor;
(3)   made while the debtor was insolvent;
(4)   made within 90 days before the filing of the petition (or one year,
        when the transferee is an "insider");
(5)   enabling the transferee to receive more than he would in a Chapter
        7 case.

Unlike its predecessor, BC 547 eases the trustee's burden by creating a presumption that a debtor was insolvent during the 90 days immediately preceding the date the petition was filed. BC 547(f); see also 547(g).

As was noted earlier, the granting of the security interest is a transfer of a
property interest under the general definition of *transfer*. BC 547(e) defines
when the transfer is deemed to take place for purposes of determining whether
the transfer is on account of an antecedent debt and whether it was made
within the 90-day or one-year suspect period before the commencement of the
case. When a security interest is involved the two basic rules are: (1) the
transfer is deemed to take place when it attaches if the secured party perfects
the security interest within ten days after attachment; and (2) the transfer is
deemed to take place on the date of perfection if the security interest is not
perfected within ten days of attachment. BC 547(e)(2)(A), (2)(B). In other
words, if Apex grants Bank an enforceable security interest in its equipment on
January 12 and Bank properly files a financing statement on January 18, the
transfer is deemed to take place on January 12. If the Bank does not perfect its
interest until January 25, the transfer is deemed to take place on January 25.
If the transfer is deemed to take place at the time of attachment on January 12
then, assuming that the debt also arises at the time of attachment, there will be
no transfer on account of an antecedent debt, and the trustee will not be able
to avoid the transfer as a preference. Even if the transfer is deemed to take
place on January 25 the trustee must still prove the other elements of BC
547(b).

If a transfer is found to be a preference under subsection (b), it still may
be saved if it falls within the exceptions set out in subsection (c). The case set
out below explores several of these exceptions. In Chapter 6 we examine perhaps the most interesting of the exceptions, that for security interests in accounts and inventory. See BC 547(c)(5).

5.   *BC 548: Fraudulent Transfers*

The Bankruptcy Code gives a trustee the power to avoid a fraudulent transfer
made within one year of the filing of the bankruptcy petition. The standards
for determining when a transfer is fraudulent are carried forward from the
provisions of §67d of the Bankruptcy Act and are similar to the standards

codified in the Uniform Fraudulent Conveyances Act (1918). Two basic tests
are used: (1) a transfer with intent to hinder, delay, or defraud any entity, and
(2) a transfer for less than a reasonably equivalent value in an exchange that
leaves the debtor insolvent, with an unreasonably small business capital, or
with a debt beyond the debtor's ability to pay. BC 548(a). The transferee who
gave value in good faith has a lien on the property transferred to the extent of
the value given to the debtor. BC 548(c). Chapter 8 of these materials examines fraudulent conveyance law in more detail.

BELFANCE v. BANCOHIO/NATIONAL BANK (IN RE McCORMICK)
5 B.R. 726 (Bankr. N.D. Ohio 1980)

H. F. WHITE, Bankruptcy Judge. The Trustee filed a complaint to recover
$647.48 from BancOhio/National Bank, a creditor of the debtor. The trustee
alleges that the debtor made the payment on an antecedent debt within 90
days prior to the filing of his petition for relief under the Bankruptcy Code.
Further the trustee claims that the debtor was insolvent and the payment
resulted in the creditor receiving a greater percentage of payment of its debt
than other creditors.

The trial was held and this Court makes the following finding of fact and
law.

FINDING OF FACT

1. On November 27, 1979 the debtor, Kevin Michael McCormick, filed
a voluntary petition in Bankruptcy under Chapter 7 of Title 11, United States
Code.

2. BancOhio/National Bank was scheduled as a secured creditor with a
claim in the amount of $6,500.00. The security was scheduled as a 1975
Pontiac Transam which the debtor valued at $3,000.00.

3. City Loan was scheduled as a secured creditor with a claim in the
amount of $2,200.00. The security was scheduled as a stereo which the debtor
valued at $250.00. All other creditors of the debtor were scheduled as unse-
cured creditors with claims totaling $1,528.73.

4. The debtor's total scheduled assets amount to $3,835.00, which in-
cludes the car valued at $3,000.00.

5. Kathryn Belfance was appointed interim trustee and serves as trustee
as provided for under BC 702(d) of the Bankruptcy Code. [If a trustee is not
elected at the meeting of the creditors the interim trustee serves as trustee.—
EDS.]

6. On January 8, 1980 the trustee agreed to the application and order to
abandon the 1975 Pontiac to BancOhio/National Bank as the automobile had

a probable value of $2,950.00 and the amount claimed due and owing by BancOhio was $4,446.26.

7. BancOhio took the automobile as security for an installment loan it made to the debtor in 1978. Installments on said loan were payable on the 15th of each month in the amount of $219.16.

8. The debtor's last three payments of $219.16 were made on August 16, 1979, September 19, 1979, and October 15, 1979. No payment was made in November 1979.

9. BancOhio/National Bank presented no evidence to rebut the presumption, under BC 547(f), of the debtor's insolvency on and during the 90 days preceding the filing of the petition for relief.

10. The original loan and security interest was made in 1978.

ISSUES

1. Has the trustee proven the elements necessary to void a transfer as a preference under BC 547(b)?

2. Is BancOhio/National Bank entitled to claim a setoff under BC 553?

3. Are the installment payments made by the debtor excepted under BC 547(c)(2) from treatment as voidable preferences?

DISCUSSION OF LAW

The trustee had filed a complaint to recover the amount of three installment payments of $219.19 each, which the debtor made to BancOhio on August 16, 1979, September 19, 1979, and October 15, 1979 pursuant to an automobile loan contract signed in 1978.

In her complaint the trustee alleges that the installment payments are voidable preferences under BC 547(b). In its answer, BancOhio maintains that the payments are not avoidable because they did not diminish the debtor's estate as required by BC 547(b)(5). BancOhio argues alternatively that it may claim the payments as a setoff under BC 553 and that the payments also fall within the scope of BC 547(c)(2), which excepts certain transfers made within the ordinary course of business from avoidance as a preference.

To recover property under the preference avoidance provisions of the code, the trustee must show that the allegedly preferential transfer meets specific criteria. The transfer must have been made to or for the benefit of a creditor, in payment of an antecedent indebtedness, while the debtor was insolvent and must have occurred within ninety days prior to the filing of the bankruptcy. The payment must have enabled the creditor to receive more than it would have received in a liquidation proceeding under the Bankruptcy Code, had the payment not been made. These requirements are enumerated in BC 547(b) which provides as follows:

(b) Except as provided in subsection (c) of this section, the trustee may avoid any transfer of property of the debtor—

    (1) to or for the benefit of a creditor;

    (2) for or on account of an antecedent debt owed by the debtor before such transfer was made;

    (3) made while the debtor was insolvent;

    (4) made—

        (A) on or within 90 days before the date of the filing of the petition; or

        (B) between 90 days and one year before the date of the filing of the petition, if such creditor, at the time of such transfer—

            (i) was an insider, and

            (ii) had reasonable cause to believe the debtor was insolvent at the time of such transfer, and

    (5) that enables such creditor to receive more than such creditor would receive if—

        (A) that case were a case under chapter 7 of this title;

        (B) the transfer had not been made; and

        (C) such creditor received payment of such debt to the extent provided by the provisions of this title.

[The preamble and para. (4)(B) of BC 547(b) were amended in 1984.—Eds.]

As applied to the matter before the Court, section 547(b) subsections (4)(A) and (5) require the trustee to prove that the debtor made the payments within the ninety-day preference period and that BancOhio received more than it would otherwise have received had the payments not been made. If the trustee fails to establish these elements, the Court cannot sustain the complaint to avoid the transfer.

The first of the disputed payments is not a preference, since the debtor did not make that payment within the ninety-day period preceding the date of filing his petition in bankruptcy. The preference period began on August 26, 1979, ninety days prior to the November 27, 1979 filing. The debtor had already made his car payment several days earlier on August 16, 1979. The Court must therefore overrule the complaint of the trustee to recover the amount of the August 16, 1979 payment.

However, the court will sustain the complaint of the trustee to recover the amount of the payments made on September 19, 1979 and October 15, 1979, since these payments meet the requirements of BC 547(b)(4)(A).

The debtor while insolvent paid these installments within the ninety-day preference period. The payments enabled BancOhio to receive more than it would have received had it been paid only in the liquidation proceedings according to the provisions of the Code.

BancOhio argues to the contrary and asserts that since the Bankruptcy Code provides for the payment of secured creditors in liquidation proceedings, it received no more than it otherwise would have received had the payments not been made. The thrust of this defense is that the payments did not diminish the estate and therefore fail to satisfy the requirement of BC 547(b)(5). BancOhio maintains that as a secured creditor it could not have been preferred.

However, this assumption is incorrect since BancOhio is only partially secured. Its status as a secured creditor is determined by BC 506(a) which provides as follows:

> (a) An allowed claim of a creditor secured by a lien on property in which the estate has an interest, or that is subject to setoff under section 553 of this title, is a secured claim to the extent of the value of such creditor's interest in the estate's interest in such property. . . .

Under BC 506(a), BancOhio has a secured claim for only $2,950.00, the value of its collateral, and an unsecured claim of $1,496.25, the balance of the debt, per application and order of abandonment—finding No. 6. In liquidation, BancOhio would have received payment on this unsecured claim only on a pro-rata basis with other unsecured creditors. If the two car payments made on September 19, 1979 and October 15, 1979 were credited to the unsecured balance on the debtor's account, BancOhio received more than it would have received on a pro-rata basis with other unsecured creditors, who have as yet received no dividends at all.

The Court must assume, in the absence of proof to the contrary, that the payments were credited towards the unsecured portion of the debt, since this course of action would comport with standard business practice. Consequently, one must conclude that BancOhio received greater payment on its unsecured claim than other unsecured creditors and that the transaction satisfies the requirements of BC 547(b)(5). The Court must therefore sustain the complaint of the trustee to recover the amount of the September 19, 1979 and October 15, 1979 payments.

BancOhio maintains alternatively that it is entitled to a setoff under BC 553. A setoff does not occur automatically, however, and BancOhio offered no proof that it had taken the necessary steps to effectuate a setoff. Consequently BancOhio's claim to a setoff also fails.

In Baker v. National City Bank of Cleveland, 511 F.2d 1016 (6th Cir. 1975), the Sixth Circuit Court of Appeals held that a setoff must be accompanied by some act of consummation and by clear proof that the party claiming setoff actually exercised the right. A mere declaration of an intent to setoff retrospectively does not establish a setoff.

The Court in Baker provided that three steps must be taken to accomplish a setoff. There must first have been a decision to exercise the right to setoff, a subsequent action which completes the setoff, and finally, a record which verifies that the action has been taken, such as a bookkeeping entry or a copy of a telegram to the depositor indicating that a setoff has been made.

UCC 4-303 also deals with the right to setoff. These provisions describe a series of actions after which an instrument drawn against an account is deemed impervious to a setoff, notice, stop order, or other legal process. Comment 5 following UCC 4-303 indicates that an item to be charged against a customer account cannot be frozen out by a setoff until "the setoff is actually made." The setoff does not arise automatically merely because the bank and the debtor have mutual debts, but only occurs when there has been a deliberate, overt action demonstrating that the bank has exercised its right to setoff.

In the matter before this Court BancOhio furnished no proof that such a deliberate, overt action was taken. The debtor paid his monthly installments by checks which were then charged against his checking account. The transactions were entirely ordinary and as a matter of course. No setoff was ever intended or actually made.

BancOhio also maintains that the car payments fall within BC 547(c)(2) which allows certain transfers made in the ordinary course of business to be excluded from the scope of the trustee's avoiding powers.

Section 547(c)(2) provides that the trustee may not avoid a transfer

> (2) to the extent that such transfer was—
>   (A) in payment of a debt incurred in the ordinary course of business or financial affairs of the debtor and the transferee;
>   (B) made not later than 45 days after such debt was incurred;
>   (C) made in the ordinary course of business or financial affairs of the debtor and the transferee; and
>   (D) made according to ordinary business terms.

[BC 547(c)(2) was amended in 1984 by the insertion of "by the debtor" after "incurred" in para. (A) and the deletion, with consequent renumbering, of para. (B).—Eds.] An otherwise preferential transfer must satisfy all four elements of BC 547(c)(2) to qualify for the exception. In the matter before the Court elements (A), (C), and (D) are present, but element (B) is not. . . .

[The court concluded that the debt was "incurred" in 1978 when the debtor undertook the legal obligation to repay the loan rather than when each installment fell due. The trustee therefore could avoid the payments made on September 19 and October 15.—Eds.]

In the case of In the Matter of Peter L. Duffy, 3 B.R. 263, 6 B.C.D. 88 (Bkrtcy. S.D.N.Y 1980) the court aptly stated the policy considerations which underline the matter presently before this Court. While the *Duffy* opinion deals with the meaning of "new value" under sections 547(a)(2) and 547(c)(1) rather than with the phrase "after the debt was incurred" with which we are herein concerned, the *Duffy* rationale applies nonetheless to the similar facts in the instant matter.

The court in *Duffy* found a $400.00 check to a car rental agency cashed within ninety days of bankruptcy to be an avoidable transfer and rejected the creditor's argument that a forbearance to act upon the right to reclaim the leased vehicle insulates the payment from avoidance as a preference. The

court stated as follows: "The basic concept underlying bankruptcy legi
and of particular significance in dealing with preference is the fund
goal of equality of distribution. See House Report No. 595, 95th Cong. 1st
Sess. 177, 178 (1977). . . . In the instant case a forbearance by Avis from
repossessing the rented vehicle does not enhance the value of the estate. The
debtor's continued right to drive the rented vehicle is not an asset of benefit to
creditors that could reasonably offset the diminution of the estate."

The consequences of the transfer in *Duffy* parallel those in the matter
before the Court. BancOhio received preferences in the amount of $438.32 (the
amount of the September 19, 1979 and October 15, 1979 payments), yet gave
no new consideration, performed no service which could conceivably augment
the estate for the benefit of all creditors. No policy considerations justify extending the exceptions of section 547(c) to insulate the type of transactions at
issue here. The Court must therefore allow the complaint of the trustee to
recover the amount of the September 19, 1979 and October 15, 1979 payments as avoidable preferences.

Problems

Austin State Bank and Apex enter into the prototype transaction set out
at p. 112. Assume, however, that at the time the bank extends credit, the
bank's officers know that Apex was in weakened financial health. The bank
pays the full price of the bookbinder directly to the supplier (ABM) but requires Apex to pay the bank 25 percent of the $60,000 purchase price in cash
and to sign a note for the $45,000 balance. With the transaction thus modified,
the bank is willing to finance the acquisition because (1) it has had a long
standing relationship with Apex and regards Apex's management as basically
sound; (2) it believes that the equipment, as part of a broader modernization
program, will enhance Apex's profitability; (3) the interest rate obtained is
highly favorable; and (4) it deems its security adequate.

As in the prototype, the financing statement is filed on January 2, the
note and security agreement are signed on January 9, and the bookbinder is
delivered on January 19 and begins production on January 23. Notwithstanding the bank's optimism, however, Apex files a voluntary petition under
Chapter 7 on January 21.

Problem 4-9. May Apex's trustee avoid the bank's security interest? BC
544, 547.

Problem 4-10. Assume that the bank files the financing statement on
January 29 rather than on January 2.
(a) Did the bank violate the automatic stay? BC 362(b)(3), 546(b).
(b) May Apex's trustee avoid the bank's security interest? BC 362, 544,
546, 547. Would your answers be different if the bank's interest is not a purchase money interest?

Problem 4-11. Assume that on January 20 an unsecured creditor with a judgment against Apex obtains a writ of execution and on the same day the sheriff levies on the bookbinder. May the trustee avoid the lien creditor's interest? BC 547, 550, 551. What if the sheriff does not levy execution until January 23?

Problem 4-12. Assume that the bank files the financing statement on January 29 and that a judgment creditor has the sheriff levy execution on the bookbinder on January 20. What are the respective rights of the bank, the unsecured creditor, and Apex's trustee?

Problem 4-13. Assume that when installed the bookbinder is a fixture under Texas law. The bank files, however, on the assumption that the collateral is equipment. May the trustee avoid the bank's security interest? BC 544, 547; UCC 9-313.

E.   EXCURSUS: WHY SECURED CREDIT?

In recent years there has been increased interest in the theoretical justification and explanation of secured credit and bankruptcy proceedings. Interest in economic analysis of legal rules and the redrafting of the Bankruptcy Act have encouraged re-examination of many basic concepts and principles. To give you a flavor of the questions asked and the approaches taken in this recent literature we offer the following summary of a law review article written by Professors Jackson and Kronman. Among other readily-available articles you might consult, see Jackson, Bankruptcy, Non-Bankruptcy Entitlements, and the Creditors' Bargain, 91 Yale L.J. 857 (1982); Schwartz, Security Interests and Bankruptcy Priorities: A Review of Current Theories, 10 J. Legal Stud. 1 (1981); White, Efficiency Justifications for Personal Property Security, 37 Vand. L. Rev. 473 (1984).

For readings that examine the normative justifications for bankruptcy proceedings from a broader prospective, see I Report of the Commission on Bankruptcy Laws of the United States, ch. 3 (A Philosophical Basis for a Federal Bankruptcy Act) (1973); Shuchman, An Attempt at a "Philosophy of Bankruptcy," 21 U.C.L.A. L. Rev. 403 (1973). See also Eisenberg, Bankruptcy Law in Perspective, 28 U.C.L.A. L. Rev. 953 (1981); Harris, A Reply to Theodore Eisenberg's *Bankruptcy Law in Perspective,* 30 U.C.L.A. L. Rev. 327 (1982); Eisenberg, *Bankruptcy Law in Perspective:* A Rejoinder, 30 U.C.L.A. L. Rev. 617 (1983).

JACKSON & KRONMAN, SECURED FINANCING AND PRIORITIES AMONG CREDITORS
88 Yale L.J. 1143, 1161-1178 (1979) [Summary]

1. *General justification of legal rules.* A legal rule is justified, Professors Jackson and Kronman argue, when parties regulated by the rule would have freely contracted for the substance of that rule if the transaction costs and freerider problems had not made it difficult and expensive to contract. In this article the authors seek to justify the legal rule that permits a debtor to grant a security interest in his property to one creditor and thereby give that creditor a prior claim to the property over the claims of other creditors if the debtor should default on his obligations.

2. *Specific explanation of secured credit: monitoring.* The explanation for secured credit focuses on the role of the security interest in reducing the costs to a creditor of monitoring a debtor in order to reduce the risk of the debtor's misbehavior. This risk arises because a debtor has an incentive to increase the riskiness of a loan once the interest rate of a loan has been established. By increasing the riskiness beyond that anticipated by the lender, the debtor obtains something for nothing.

The lender has an incentive, therefore, to monitor the debtor's conduct or to require the debtor to assume responsibilities for providing the lender with information by which he can assess the implications of the debtor's conduct. The amount expended on monitoring will depend on the cost of monitoring and the magnitude of the risk of misbehavior.

A security interest decreases the lender's risk by making it more likely that the loan will be repaid on the debtor's insolvency and by reducing the cost of monitoring, because the lender will now only have to focus on the collateral rather than on all the debtor's assets.

Granting a security interest to one creditor, however, will increase the risk of debtor misbehavior for other creditors. A debtor will grant one creditor a security interest if the savings in interest charged by this first creditor is greater than the increased interest charged by other creditors. Other creditors might increase the interest charged by less than the savings from the secured transaction because they are able to monitor more efficiently. To obtain this advantage the debtor will be willing to share the premium with all the creditors to induce them to agree that the first creditor will have priority.

Even if the debtor is prohibited from granting a security interest the creditors will benefit by agreeing among themselves that creditors with lower monitoring costs will subordinate their claims to the other creditors in the event of the debtor's insolvency.

3. *Secured credit rules justified.* The legal regime of secured transactions is therefore justified because creditors and borrowers freely contracting with each other would agree to that regime.

4. *Explanation of secured credit predicts existing patterns.* The authors' theory

also explains existing patterns of behavior. The authors observe that trade creditors do not take security interests while institutional lenders do. This pattern would be predicted by their theory because trade creditors have lower monitoring costs: they make short-term loans in smaller amounts and have access to more detailed information about the debtor and his industry.

5. *Fairness arguments irrelevant.* Considerations of fairness do not require adoption of a rule that all creditors must share equally in a debtor's property if he becomes insolvent. Because creditors are free to contract with whomever they want on any terms they agree to, there is no reason based on considerations of fairness to favor a rule of creditor equality over a rule whereby a debtor can rank creditor claims. Fairness arguments are usually made in connection with arguments that secret liens and preferential transfers should be unenforceable. But fairness arguments are not relevant to criticism of secret liens and preferential transfers, which should be invalid for the economic reason that otherwise creditors would increase the interest charged to cover the risk that such transactions might occur.

NOTES & QUESTIONS

1. *Freedom to contract.* At various points in their argument the authors rely on the assumption that parties enter voluntarily into contracts. Would you rebut their reasoning if you could show that many creditors and debtors are not free to contract voluntarily because of legal and practical constraints? Usury laws, for example, may establish the maximum rates a creditor may charge. Debtors may be unable to bargain on an equal footing with creditors or may not have sufficient information about credit alternatives.

2. *Causes of nonperformance.* A creditor is concerned with the risk that the debtor will not perform his obligation. What are the potential causes for nonperformance? The authors focus on potential debtor misbehavior: engaging in acts that increase the riskiness of the loan once the loan agreement has fixed an interest rate reflecting a lower risk. What about risks of poor management, management turnover, changing competitive structure of the industry, changing technology, general regional decline, increasing energy costs, changing laws? How does a creditor deal with these risks? Is collateral relevant to any of these risks? Does a creditor protect against these risks by increasing the interest rate charged?

3. *Monitoring.* What are specific monitoring acts that a creditor might use? Would research about a potential debtor before an agreement is reached be considered a monitoring cost? Would such research decrease postagreement monitoring costs? Should such research be "amortized" over the life of an agreement? What if an agreement is not reached?

4. *Alternatives to monitoring.* The authors suggest monitoring is necessary to deal with debtor misbehavior. Are there any alternatives to monitoring? Would any of the following devices serve as substitutes?

(a)   Insurance
(b)   Promise of guarantor or surety
(c)   Contract provisions prohibiting "misbehavior"
(d)   Long-term contracts with provision for periodic renegotiation of the interest rate
(e)   Higher initial interest rate to reflect risk of misbehavior
(f)   Specialized monitoring agencies similar to those that already collect information about debtors (e.g., Dun & Bradstreet)
(g)   Creation of a portfolio of loans to spread the risk

Regarding insurance, Professors Jackson and Kronman comment as follows: "Conceivably, a creditor might choose to protect himself against the possibility of debtor misbehavior by procuring third-party insurance. There are two reasons, however, why this does not impinge on the incentives to monitor and thus does not affect the results concerning the utility of secured financing. First, engaging a third-party insurer may be inefficient because it will be too costly to transmit enough information to the insurer to set his rates in a way that reflects the risk of debtor misbehavior. . . . The second and more important reason is that *insuring* against the danger of debtor misbehavior does nothing, by itself, to reduce the likelihood of its occurrence—insurance merely shifts the risk of misbehavior from the creditor to a third-party insurer. Even if a third-party insurer is able to bear this risk more cheaply than the creditor himself, there are likely to be cases in which it will be cost-justified actually to reduce the risk of debtor misbehavior by monitoring of one sort or another. . . . Thus, even supposing the creditor does procure third-party insurance, we would expect him to monitor up to the point where he would be insuring only against risk that could not be efficiently eliminated. In addition, the creditor's risk may not be insurable at all unless some monitoring is undertaken." Jackson & Kronman at 1150 n.36.

5. *Creditor monopoly.* If creditors have different monitoring costs, why don't debtors always choose the creditor with the most efficient monitoring costs? Are you persuaded by the following explanation offered by Professors Jackson and Kronman: "It might seem that the debtor should borrow all of his funds from the single creditor with lowest monitoring costs. There are, however, other reasons for a debtor to prefer some lenders for certain kinds of loans. See note 61 infra (financially sophisticated institutional lenders may be preferred over trade creditors even though trade creditors have lower monitoring costs). In addition, there may be situations in which it is desirable to have several creditors able to bid on a particular type of loan. Cf. note 99 infra (ability to exploit informational advantage gained by prior experience with debtor may be weakened by ensuring that competing creditors enjoy same advantage)." Jackson & Kronman at 1158 n.55.

6. *Fungibility of creditors and debtors.* The authors assume free competition and the fungibility of creditors and debtors. In practice, there has not always been free competition between creditors. Commercial banks have had the

advantage of deposits for which the banks have had to pay low maximum rates; finance companies have had to raise funds from more expensive sources, including the commercial paper market and loans from the banks themselves. On the other hand, banks are usually subject to much more stringent regulation than finance companies, especially with respect to the types of loans that can be made. Similarly, there are commercial debtors and consumer debtors, large debtors and small debtors, experienced debtors and inexperienced debtors. Do any of these distinctions make any difference to the argument presented by the authors?

7. *Equal distribution and bankruptcy.* If, for whatever reason, it was decreed that all creditors must share equally in a bankrupt debtor's estate, what would be the probable consequence for secured transactions?

8. *Further comment.* For detailed analysis of monitoring and other explanations of secured financing, see Schwartz, Security Interests and Bankruptcy Priorities: A Review of Current Theories, 10 J. Legal Stud. 1 (1981) (see especially pp. 9-14, comments on monitoring); Schwartz & Wilde, Imperfect Information in Markets for Contract Terms: The Examples of Warranties and Security Interests, 69 Va. L. Rev. 1387 (1983).

CHAPTER 5

Equipment Financing: Variations on the Prototype

In this chapter we look at how one might restructure the prototype transaction set out in Chapter 3 at p. 112. In the prototype the buyer (Apex) arranges for financing from its bank (Austin State Bank) and the seller (ABM) receives the full purchase price at the time of the sale. By contrast, in the following three variations it is the seller or supplier that initially extends credit to the party acquiring the equipment.

In the first variation the supplier merely sells to the buyer on *unsecured* credit. As the text in Part A explains, the legal questions raised by this variation are complex. Under certain conditions the supplier may reclaim the goods sold from the buyer. Although the right to reclaim resembles the secured party's right to repossess, the supplier's right is governed by both Article 2 and Article 9. For the first time, therefore, we study the intricate relationship of Article 9 to the rest of the Code. A fuller discussion is set out in Chapter 8.

In the second variation the supplier sells the equipment on secured credit by retaining an Article 9 security interest in the goods sold. As you have already learned, the retained interest is a *purchase money security interest* (PMSI) (UCC 9-107), which gives the seller the potential of having priority over even more claimants than a secured party with a non-purchase money security interest. Although the PMSI has antecedents in pre-Code conditional sales legislation, Article 9 now integrates this interest into its general regulation of secured transactions. The materials in Part B explore the history and theory of this special priority.

In the third and final variation the supplier *leases* the equipment, a variation that has become popular in recent years primarily because of federal tax benefits. Although the basic fact pattern is usually simple, the number of parties may rapidly multiply and their roles may become more sophisticated. Whether simple or complex the personal property lease remains governed by the common law of bailments, which has not been codified in most jurisdictions and which leaves unanswered a number of important legal questions. Part C examines the relation of the Code to these rules.

219

ile the description of each of the three variations may suggest that
o parties are usually involved, in practice the supplier will usually
ce the credit extended by using the obligation of the buyer or lessee as
ral. In Code terminology, the secured sale or lease agreement is *chattel*
the obligation of the buyer on unsecured credit is an *account*. The chattel
paper and account may either be used as collateral to secure a loan from the
supplier's lender or be sold to a financing agency with or without recourse to
the supplier. In either case, Article 9 will govern the second financing transaction (UCC 9-102(1)(b)). Chapter 6 examines in greater detail the relation
between the first and second financing transactions, i.e., the transactions between the supplier and buyer or lessee and between the supplier and its lender.

Who ultimately finances the acquisition of equipment will turn on nonle-
gal issues. There is no *legal* reason why the acquisition and financing take one
form rather than another. Transactions within an industry, however, frequently follow regular patterns, which market competition undoubtedly
shapes. A good attorney should recognize the patterns and be sensitive to the
feasible legal variations for his client's secured transactions.

A. SUPPLIER AS UNSECURED SELLER

A seller who sells goods on open account is an unsecured creditor. To collect
what is owed by the buyer he must bring a court action, obtain judgment, and
have the sheriff levy execution. The unpaid seller, in other words, cannot
merely reclaim the goods sold. At common law and under the Uniform Sales
Act, however, there were several important exceptions to this general statement. While the goods sold remained in the seller's possession he had a *seller's
lien* (U.S.A. §§54-56). While the goods were in transit the seller had a right to
stop delivery to the buyer, a right commonly referred to as *stoppage in transitu*
(U.S.A. §§57-59). This lien and right to stop delivery were lost, however, when
the buyer obtained possession. To reclaim the goods once the buyer received
them required the seller to show some form of fraud or misrepresentation on
the part of the buyer. If fraud or misrepresentation could be shown the seller
could rescind the contract and recover the goods. The buyer took the goods
subject to the right to reclaim; in most jurisdictions the buyer's lien creditors
were subordinate to seller's claim. See, e.g., Oswego Starch Factory v. Lend-
rum, 57 Iowa 573, 10 N.W. 900 (1881). A bona fide purchaser from the buyer,
on the other hand, usually took the goods free from the seller's right to reclaim.

Article 2 of the Code recognizes these pre-Code seller's rights: a seller
may refuse delivery to an insolvent buyer except for cash (UCC 2-702(1)) and
may cancel the contract and keep goods in his possession if the buyer repudiates his obligation to pay (UCC 2-703(a), (f)). A seller may stop delivery while
the goods are in transit (UCC 2-705). If the buyer received the goods while

insolvent the seller who sold on unsecured credit may reclaim the goods if he meets certain conditions (UCC 2-702(2)). Where the seller did not agree to extend credit but delivered the goods without receiving cash (by taking a check, for example) the seller may also reclaim the goods (UCC 2-507(2), 2-511(3)).

Unfortunately, the seller who seeks to exercise these Article 2 rights will discover that they may be subject to third parties' claims through the defaulting buyer. UCC 2-702(3) explicitly lists the classes of third parties who take priority over the seller who sold to a buyer on unsecured credit. These same claimants have implicit priority under UCC 2-507(2) where the seller delivers possession to the buyer but did not agree to give credit. Good faith purchasers clearly have priority; less clearly, lien creditors do not.

Litigation under the Code has focused on the seller's right to reclaim under UCC 2-702(2). The most common scenario has presented the seller who seeks to reclaim goods from the buyer's trustee in bankruptcy. Prior to 1966 UCC 2-702(3) explicitly subjected the seller's right to the rights under UCC 2-403 of a *lien creditor* (a term not defined in Article 2; cf. UCC 9-301(3)). UCC 2-403 is less than clear; subsection (4) refers the reader to Article 9. In 1966 the UCC was amended by deletion of the UCC 2-702(3) reference to *lien creditor*, with a statement that implies that the seller should prevail over the lien creditor.[1] Many jurisdictions, however, have not adopted this amendment. In any case it was not clear under the Bankruptcy Act of 1898 that this state statutory reclamation right, triggered as it was by the buyer's insolvency, was enforceable in bankruptcy because it was a lien that operated to prefer some creditors. See Bankruptcy Act §67c; In re Federal's, Inc., 553 F.2d 509, 17 UCC Rep. 407 (6th Cir. 1977) (UCC 2-702 not invalid statutory lien). The Bankruptcy Code has now resolved doubts about the seller's right to reclaim by explicitly validating the right vis-à-vis the buyer's trustee in bankruptcy, in language, however, that differs in deceptively slight ways from UCC 2-702(2) (BC 546(c)).

Outside of bankruptcy the unpaid seller will be concerned with Article 9 in at least two ways. First, the seller's rights may be "security interests arising solely under [Article 2]" and therefore also be subject to Article 9 by virtue of UCC 9-113. Second, the competing third-party claimant may be a secured

---

1. In Report No. 3 (1966), the Permanent Editorial Board gave the following explanation for recommending the deletion of the phrase "or lien creditor" from UCC 2-702(3): "Reason for Change: The cross-reference is confusing, since the only reference to 'rights of a lien creditor' found in Section 2-403 is a further cross-reference to Articles 6, 7 and 9, and the relevance of those Articles is not apparent. In re Kravitz, 278 F.2d 820 (3d Cir. 1960), held that the pre-Code law of Pennsylvania was carried forward by the Code, that under that law a defrauded seller was subordinated to a lien creditor who extended credit to the buyer after the goods were delivered to him, and that the buyer's trustee in bankruptcy as an 'ideal lien creditor' had the rights of such a lien creditor. The result in Pennsylvania is to make the right of reclamation granted by this section almost entirely illusory. In most states the pre-Code law was otherwise, and the right of reclamation seems to be fully effective. . . . Six states have resolved the problem by deleting the words 'or lien creditor' from this section, and there seems to be no other practicable route to uniformity among the states."

party claiming an interest in the goods by virtue of an agreement with the buyer granting the party an after-acquired property clause or a purchase money security interest. The question will then be whether the normal priority rules of Article 9 are affected by the rules in Article 2. These questions will be taken up in detail in Chapter 8.

B.   SUPPLIER AS SECURED CREDITOR

Problem 5-1. Apex wishes to purchase a bookbinder from ABM, which agrees to finance the transaction. ABM retains a security interest in the book-binder to secure repayment of the credit extended. You are asked to prepare the necessary documentation. Review the documents in the original prototype transaction set out in Chapter 3. What changes will have to be made? (For an example of a conditional sale form, see 5 Uniform Laws Annotated, Uniform Commercial Code Forms and Materials, Form 9:1625 (R. Henson & W. Davenport eds. 1968).)

1.   The Conditional Sale

Many older attorneys and judges still refer to the contract by which a seller agrees to extend credit to be secured by a security interest in the good sold as a *conditional sale.* The draftsmen of Article 9 deliberately avoided using the term except to note that the conditional sale is now integrated into the uniform secured transaction regulated by Article 9 (UCC 9-102(2)). The Code repeals special conditional sales acts and supersedes doctrines peculiar to the conditional sale. Pre-Code conditional sales forms may continue to be used but when there are legal questions about the transaction the form must be translated into Code terminology and be interpreted in accordance with the provisions of Article 9.

The key to the conditional sale is the thought that the seller retains title to the goods sold until the buyer fulfills the condition of making the payments agreed to. From this conceptual wellspring several consequences were said to flow logically. If the condition was met, the contractual terms were fulfilled and title passed to the buyer. If it was not met the seller had several alternatives. He could treat the contract as at an end, take back "his" goods, and retain installment payments already made. Alternatively, on default he could sue the buyer to recover a deficiency but in so doing he recognized that the buyer had title to the goods. The seller could not, therefore, both repossess the goods and recover a deficiency because the actions would be taken pursuant to mutually exclusive assumptions about who had title.

Although many countries continue to rely on the concept of title-retention, Article 9 sweeps aside the role of title. UCC 9-202 disclaims any reliance on title for the purposes of Article 9. The definition of *security interest* in UCC 1-201(37) notes that a seller who purports to retain title will have only an Article 9 security interest. In effect, the Code draftsmen argued that particular rules, such as the election of remedies, should evolve from policy decisions rather than from conceptual necessity.

The Code, of course, also integrates the conditional sale with chattel mortgages and other pre-Code secured transaction legal forms. This uniform regulation greatly simplifies issues such as whether it is necessary to file and, if so, what and where. The following case illustrates the benefits of this simplification and uniformity.

PACIFIC METAL CO. v. JOSLIN
359 F.2d 396 (9th Cir. 1966)

DUNIWAY, Circuit Judge. Pacific Metal Company, an Oregon corporation, a creditor of Edsco Manufacturing Co., bankrupt, appeals from a decision of the District Court for the Western Division of Washington. We affirm.

The facts are stipulated. Pacific sold certain machinery to Edsco under a conditional sale contract. The machinery was delivered to and used by Edsco at Vancouver, Clark County, Washington. The contract was duly and regularly filed, as a conditional sale contract, in the office of the County Auditor of Clark County. It is valid under the laws of Oregon. Before using the form of contract for sales in Washington, Pacific obtained the opinion of Washington counsel that the form would be valid as a conditional sale contract in that state. It used the form in reliance upon that opinion. Both Pacific and Edsco believed that the contract in question was valid and enforceable, and intended that it should be. If the contract is not valid, it is because of a mistake of law on the part of Pacific and Edsco.

Edsco's trustee asserted, and the court held, that the conditional sale was void as against the trustee. The contract is not valid as a conditional sale in Washington, but is valid as a chattel mortgage. The reason is that the contract permits both repossession and a deficiency judgment, under the following language:

a. The portion appearing in Sec. 5(a), dealing with repossession, and reading as follows: ". . . in which event Purchaser shall remain bound for and shall and does agree to pay to Seller the balance remaining unpaid, with interest thereon in accordance with the provisions hereof. . . ."

b. The portion appearing in Sec. 5 reading as follows: "All rights and remedies of Seller shall be and are cumulative and not alternative."

The Washington Supreme Court has held that such provisions render the contract invalid as one of conditional sale, and its recording as a conditional sale ineffectual. It may still be valid against creditors, as a chattel mortgage, if recorded as such. . . . That court has said that the rule is one of law, not a mere rule of construction. . . . Pacific concedes that this is the Washington law. It sought to have the contract reformed, based upon a mutual mistake of law, by striking the language that we have quoted. This the referee and the trial court refused to do.[1]

The court rested its decision on Pacific's failure to comply with the appropriate recording statute. Washington has separate statutes for recording conditional sale contracts (R.C. Wash. §63.12.010) and chattel mortgages (R.C. Wash. §61.04.020). Admittedly, the latter statute was not complied with; no affidavit of good faith accompanied the contract, as that statute requires. Thus, considered as a chattel mortgage, the contract is void against the trustee, who stands in the shoes of creditors.

The section dealing with conditional sale contracts reads, in part (§63.12.010):

> Sale absolute unless contract filed—Exceptions. All conditional sales of personal property . . . containing a conditional right to purchase, where the property is placed in the possession of the vendee, shall be absolute as to all bona fide purchasers . . . and subsequent creditors, whether or not such creditors have or claim a lien upon such property, unless within ten days after the taking of possession by the vendee, a memorandum of such sale . . . shall be filed in the auditor's office of the county, wherein, at the date of the vendee's taking possession of the property, the vendee resides.

The filing was within the time and with the officer specified, but, as filed, the contract was invalid on its face, as a contract of conditional sale.

Pacific asserts that the contract was subject to an equity of reformation, which would make it valid, that creditors (and the trustee in bankruptcy, who represents them) are not bona fide purchasers, and that therefore the contract can be reformed as against the trustee. The argument is appealing, but the law of Washington appears to be to the contrary, and the trial judge, himself an experienced Washington lawyer, so held.

The Statute makes the sale absolute as to creditors as well as bona fide purchasers. And the Washington court has refused to permit reformation in order to validate a filing under it as against creditors, Malott v. General Machinery Co., 19 Wash. 2d 62, 141 P.2d 146 (1943), "because an instrument

---

1. It is doubtful whether a valid ground for reformation has been shown. Nowhere does it appear that the parties did not intend to use the language in question. And the Washington court has said: "[I]t is now the law of this jurisdiction that the use of certain words in the contract between the parties must be held to lead to certain legal consequences, even though the parties may not have intended such a result." Investment Service v. La Londe, 63 Wash. 2d at 838-839, 389 P.2d at 416. However, the trial court did not rest the decision on this ground, and we do not further consider it.

cannot be reformed so as to affect the rights of innocent third parties." (19
Wash. 2d 62, 65, 141 P.2d 146, 148). There, the mistake was an erroneous
statement, in the contract, of the date of delivery of possession, so that it
appeared on the face of the contract that the recording was late. Actual delivery was within the prescribed ten days, and reformation was sought to show
the correct date. Pacific would distinguish the case on the ground that it
involved a failure to comply with filing requirements, while here those requirements were complied with, but the contract itself was defective. We cannot
follow the distinction. In either case, a creditor examining the filed contract
could conclude that, as to him, the sale was absolute. And, in *Malott*, it was to
avoid defeating creditors' rights that the court declined to decree information.
We find no Washington case to the contrary.

Affirmed.

NOTES & QUESTIONS

1. *Attorney's liability.* Should the attorneys in *Pacific Metal* who advised on
the status of the contract under Washington law be liable to the losing party?
Should the Oregon attorneys be excused because the case turned on an interpretation of Washington laws? Should the attorneys be excused because of the
confused state of pre-Code security law? If the UCC applied in *Pacific Metal*
and the attorneys advised their client to file in the wrong office should they be
excused? For a discussion of the attorney's liability for negligence in preparing
or recording security document, see Annot., 87 A.L.R.2d 991 (1965) (attorney
is liable for damages resulting from failure to exercise reasonable care or skill
of attorneys of ordinary skill and ability; client's contributory negligence is a
defense).

2. *Election of remedies.* Is it clear as a matter of policy that a secured party
in a conditional sale should be permitted both to repossess the goods sold and
to recover a deficiency?

When the Washington legislature adopted the UCC it introduced the
following nonuniform amendment to UCC 9-501(1):

> Notwithstanding any other provision of this Code, in the case of a purchase
> money security interest in consumer goods taken or retained by the seller of such
> collateral to secure all or part of its price, the debtor shall not be liable for any
> deficiency after the secured party has disposed of such collateral under [UCC 9-
> 504] or has retained such collateral in satisfaction of the debt under [UCC 9-
> 505(2)].

The Uniform Consumer Credit Code (1974 ed.) also denies a creditor regulated by its provisions the right both to repossess and to recover a deficiency
where relatively expensive consumer goods are involved (UCCC §5.103).

3. *Vestigial role of title in secured transactions.* Although the UCC disclaims
any interest in title for resolving disputes, the location of title continues to be

important for secured transactions where non-Code law is involved. For example, title may be important in sales tax, property division, antitrust, conversion, or criminal law cases. Residual rules set out in UCC 2-401 may be of some help in these cases.

4. *The conditional sale in bankruptcy.* The pre-UCC conditional sale had a considerable advantage over a chattel mortgage if the debtor became bankrupt. The property sold under a conditional sales contract was not the property of the debtor and therefore was not a part of the debtor's estate in a liquidation or reorganization proceeding under the 1898 Bankruptcy Act. In re Lake's Laundry, Inc., 79 F.2d 326 (2d Cir.), *cert. denied,* 296 U.S. 622 (1935). With the adoption of the UCC the question arose as to whether a bankruptcy court must continue to recognize the distinction when applying the Bankruptcy Act. In an important decision excerpted below, Judge Friendly held that the distinction should no longer be recognized by bankruptcy courts. If the question were to arise under the Bankruptcy Code how would it be resolved? See BC 541.

FRUEHAUF CORP. v. YALE EXPRESS SYSTEM (IN RE YALE EXPRESS SYSTEM, INC.), 370 F.2d 433, 436-438 (2d Cir. 1966): "This judicially developed doctrine that a creditor's right to reclamation is dependent on who has 'title' to the property, has not gone unchallenged. See generally Coogan, Hogan & Vagts, Secured Transactions Under the Uniform Commercial Code 978-980 (1963). It is not inappropriate to note that the decision in In re Lake's Laundry, [79 F.2d 326 (2d Cir. 1935)], was reached only over the dissent of Judge Learned Hand. With his usual keen insight he stated: 'It seems to be a barren distinction, though indubitably true, that title does not pass upon a conditional sale; "title" is a formal word for a purely conceptual notion; I do not know what it means and I question whether anybody does, except perhaps legal historians. The relations resulting from conditional sales are practically the same as those resulting from mortgages; I would treat them as the same when we are dealing with the reorganization of the debtor's property.' 79 F.2d 326, 328-329. Judge Hand postulated that the reorganization court should be able, in the exercise of its equitable discretion, to refuse the conditional vendor's request to reclaim property held by the trustee.

"Perhaps the distinction drawn by the majority in In re Lake's Laundry between conditional sales agreements and other security arrangements, was defensible at the time, in light of the important consequences that the various commercial laws of the states attached to the particular form of the security agreement. But the body of commercial law has not stood still. It has made great and progressive strides, and 47 states, the District of Columbia, and the Virgin Islands have now enacted the Uniform Commercial Code. UCC 9-202 declares the policy of Article 9 of the Code stating that '[e]ach provision of this Article with regard to rights, obligations and remedies applies whether title to collateral is in the secured party or in the debtor.' In short, it does not matter whether the security agreement is in the form of a chattel mortgage or a conditional sales contract. In either case, the secured party has the right upon default by the debtor to take possession of the collateral (UCC 9-503) and to sell, lease or otherwise dispose of it, applying the proceeds to the indebtedness (UCC 9-504).

"Even more relevant to our particular inquiry is the Official Comment to UCC 9-507: '[A] power [to control the manner of disposition of the debtor's property] is no doubt inherent in a Federal bankruptcy court, and perhaps in other courts of equity administering insolvent estates. Traditionally it has not been exercised where the secured party claimed under a title retention device, such as a conditional sale or a trust receipt. See In re Lake's Laundry, Inc., 79 F.2d 326 (2d Cir. 1935) and the remarks of Clark, J., concurring, in In re White Plains Ice Service, Inc., 109 F.2d 913 (2d Cir. 1940). But since this Article adopts neither a "title" nor a "lien" theory of security interests (see Section 9-202 and Comment thereto), the granting or denying of, for example, petitions of reclamation in bankruptcy proceedings should not be influenced by speculations as to whether the secured party had "title" to the collateral or "merely a lien." '

"The 'Official Comments' of the Code are, of course, not binding on a federal court which is in the process of exercising its equitable discretion in a reclamation proceeding. But, they are powerful dicta for the Code is 'well on its way to becoming a truly national law of commerce,' and is, therefore, as we have noted, a most appropriate source of federal law. United States v. Wegematic, 360 F.2d 674, 676 (2d Cir. 1966). We would indeed be myopic if we failed to recognize the revolution in commercial law that the Uniform Commercial Code has occasioned in the states. It would be incongruous for the federal courts, historically the leaders in the development of the law, to continue to employ anachronistic distinctions to determine whether a creditor is entitled to redeem property held by the trustee when the overwhelming number of states have succeeded in bringing their laws more into line with commercial reality. . . ."

---

5. *Title retention elsewhere in the world.* Sellers in many non-United States jurisdictions may secure repayment of credit extended to their buyers by retaining title to the goods sold. The sellers' interest frequently has the same priorities over third-party claimants that a secured party with a perfected security interest would have under the Uniform Commercial Code. See generally Pennington, Retention of Title to the Sale of Goods under European Law, 27 Intl. & Comp. L.Q. 277 (1978). For a case where the validity of such an interest was questioned by the trustee in bankruptcy of a United States debtor, see Imperial Chemical Industries Ltd. v. Slaner (In re Duplan Corp.), 455 F. Supp. 926, 24 UCC Rep. 965 (S.D.N.Y. 1978) (foreign seller shipped yarn from the Netherlands to a South Carolina buyer under contract reserving title until payment and making English law the governing law; trustee of bankrupt buyer avoids seller's interest, which is held to be unperfected under South Carolina law).

2.   The Purchase Money Security Interest

Although the conditional sale has been integrated in the Uniform Commercial Code with other pre-Code security devices, the UCC continues to recognize special priorities where the secured party is a seller. The Code does this by providing exceptional rules for the purchase money security interest, which exists when the seller takes or retains a security interest (UCC 9-107(a)). Article 9 extends the definition of the interest also to include cases where a financing agency provides value to a buyer for the purchase of goods (UCC 9-107(b)). When you examined the prototype transaction in Chapter 3, therefore, you were looking at a purchase money interest. Here we explore in greater detail the operation of the special purchase money rules and the reasons for the super-priorities.

Problem 5-2. The Austin State Bank and Apex enter into the transaction described in the prototype. Assume, however, that the Austin State Bank files its financing statement on January 30 rather than January 2. Assume also that on January 20 a creditor of Apex, who has a $4,000 judgment against Apex following a dispute over a payment for supplies, obtains a writ of execution that is executed by the sheriff. Who will have priority as to the bookbinding machine? See UCC 9-301. What, if any, additional information do you need?

Problem 5-3. The Austin State Bank and Apex enter into the prototype transaction. Assume, however, that unknown to the bank, Apex had granted in 1979 a security interest to the Texas Commercial Finance Company in other Apex equipment and "all after-acquired equipment." The finance company promptly filed with the Texas Secretary of State a properly completed financing statement that listed "equipment" as collateral. Between Bank and Finance Company who will have priority to the new bookbinder? See UCC 9-312(4). What, if any, additional information do you need? Would your answer be different if the two secured parties had security interests in inventory rather than equipment? See UCC 9-312(3).

Problem 5-4. Assume Austin State Bank agrees to finance only $30,000 of the bookbinder's purchase price. To avoid losing the sale ABM agrees to extend $10,000 credit to Apex with Apex to pay the remainder of the purchase price in cash. Both the bank and ABM take a security interest in the bookbinder to secure repayment of the credit extended. The bank properly files a financing statement on January 2, and Apex signs the bank's security agreement on January 9. ABM properly files a financing statement on January 1, and Apex signs the ABM security agreement on January 10. At the time of signing these documents the bank and ABM each knew of the other's plan to take a security interest. Between the bank and ABM who has priority to the bookbinder? See UCC 9-312(4), (5). What, if any, additional information do you need? If you were planning the transaction for either the bank or ABM, what steps might you take to avoid conflict? See UCC 9-316.

Problem 5-5. Two years after the Austin State Bank and Apex enter into the prototype transaction, Apex, without the consent of the bank, exchanges the bookbinder with Pecos Printing Co. for a small printing press and a $5,000 promissory note. Pecos had acquired the press from Printing Equipment Corp., which had retained a properly perfected security interest to secure payment of the purchase price. At the time of the exchange with Apex, Pecos has not fully paid for the press and does not obtain permission to exchange the press for the bookbinder. As between the bank and Printing Equipment Corp. who has priority as to (a) the bookbinder, (b) the printing press, and (c) the promissory note?

INTERNATIONAL HARVESTER CREDIT CORP. v. AMERICAN NATIONAL BANK
296 So. 2d 32, 14 UCC Rep. 19, 85 A.L.R.3d 1015 (Fla. 1974)

[The District Court of Appeal certified the following question to the state supreme court: "Under Florida Statute 679.312(4) and (5) [1962 UCC 9-312(4) and (5)—Eds.], does a party with a security interest in after-acquired property take priority over a party with a purchase money security interest which was not perfected within ten days after the debtor took possession of the collateral?"]

DEKLE, Justice. . . . Concerning the second question regarding "after-acquired property" as to security priorities, we are in agreement with the district's majority position in recognizing the earlier creditor's priority of security in after-acquired property (unless the required financing statement has been timely filed on such subsequent purchase). UCC 9-312(4). However, we differ with the district majority and agree with Acting Chief Justice Rawls that this priority security protection to the earlier creditor must be limited to the debtor's equity in the after-acquired property. This position is consistent with contractual constitutional requirements and equitable principles. The new seller's contract rights with his purchaser and any ownership retained in the property sold must be respected; moreover, it would be an invidious preference to the earlier creditor-bank without so much as a showing that there was a compelling public interest or purpose served by such arbitrary requirement of outright priority to the earlier creditor in the total after-acquired property.

The contention is made that to restrict the prior creditor's priority in the after-acquired property to the debtor's equity therein renders meaningless the requirement for filing a financing statement. We do not think so. There really are no conflicting security interests in this situation. That security interest retained by the subsequent seller in the after-acquired property never passes to the buyer-debtor and thus never becomes subject to the earlier creditor's claim of security interest in such after-acquired property. On the other hand, the earlier (perfected) creditor does have his security in that interest which is after-acquired by his debtor.

In this respect we note that the statute grants the priority in the *debtor's* after-acquired property; it refers to the respective security "interest" as being thereby affected. The debtor, while acquiring the physical property, only acquires an interest therein under a credit sales contract; it is this interest only then which is "after-acquired" and thereby subject to the earlier security right. The remainder is upon credit from the new creditor who often also retains title thereto. It would be abhorrent to equity and justice that the earlier creditor should acquire the subsequent *creditor's* property or "interest" in this manner. Upon principles of equity and in the avoidance of unjust enrichment, the limitation to the debtor's equity in after-acquired property appears to be the better and more logical rule. We would accordingly agree with Acting Chief Judge Rawls in this respect.

The "new value" section of the code, UCC 9-108, urged by petitioners, is not invoked in the circumstances *sub judice*. The earlier secured creditor, respondent, stands upon its original contract and not upon "new value."

Logical and traditional equitable reasons preclude a result which would allow the bank as mortgagee to subject the after-acquired farm equipment as its collateral, while not changing its position and giving no "new value" because of the later sale of equipment; consequently, the bank was not misled by the failure of the seller of the equipment to record his purchase money security.

To give the prior creditor the seller's retained interest in such property simply because of such seller's failure to record and to permit the original creditor to replevin the sold equipment would be to give such earlier creditor a windfall not favored by the code (see UCC 9-108 and Comment) contrary to established principles. . . .

Our viewpoint regarding a limitation (to the buyer's equity) of the security of the earlier creditor, allows a just result to such creditor and yet is consistent with constitutional requirements as to the subsequent seller. . . .

We accordingly modify the district court holding as to question 2 to the extent of limiting the priority allowed by the commercial code to the first (perfected) creditor (absent timely filing) to the extent of that creditor's debtor's equity in the after-acquired property under whatever contract it was purchased, preserving to the new seller his retained interest in such after-acquired property. [The court holds, in other words, that the residual priority rule in UCC 9-312 (5) gives the secured party with an after-acquired property clause priority only as to the common debtor's equity.—Eds.]

CARLTON, Chief Justice (dissenting). . . . Two reasons are given by the majority for the conclusion reached—unspecified "contractual constitutional requirements" and "equitable principles." As to the constitutional requirements, I am aware of no constitutional provision which prohibits the Legislature from giving priority to one valid security interest which is perfected according to statute over another valid security interest, whether the priority interest is the one first created or the second. If there are such constitutional provisions, they must certainly call for the invalidation of our recording statutes concerning interests in real property. Under these statutes, a conveyance of real property which is first recorded takes precedence over a prior conveyance which is recorded second.

As to "equitable principles," when there are competing security interests in the same property and the property is insufficient to satisfy both debts, *any* priority to either creditor is, in a sense, inequitable. The filing system for security interests which is established by the Code, however, generally lessens any inequitable results by providing that one who contracts for a security interest in property with *notice* of a *prior* perfected security interest in the same property takes second priority. That is exactly the situation we are presented with here, and I see nothing inequitable in granting the prior creditor the preference clearly provided in the Code. In fact, the second creditor in this instance could have gained for his security interest a priority over an earlier security interest of which he had notice. All the second creditor had to do, under a special exception in the Code, was file his security agreement within ten days. He didn't do this, so I see nothing inequitable in the Code provisions giving priority to the first creditor—who did all that was required by the Code to protect his interest.

I surmise that the real reason underlying the answer given by the majority . . . is a general aversion to security interests in after-acquired property. Such security interests are, however, a common and often necessary tool of modern financing. Note that the Legislature intended the Code to be interpreted so as "to permit the continued expansion of commercial practices through custom, usage and agreement of the parties."

The Uniform Commercial Code specifically recognizes the validity of security interests in after-acquired property, with some restrictions on their use. UCC 9-108, 9-204. The Code does not limit security interests in after-acquired property to an interest in only the debtor's "equity." . . .

Pre-Code Florida law also recognized the validity of security interests in after-acquired property, with no such restriction limiting them to a debtor's "equity" in his property. . . .

As to Article 9 of the Code, there are certain important general concepts—some of which are sweeping changes from pre-Code law—which underlie the entire theory of the Article. Our majority opinion totally rejects or ignores these concepts, witness the following passage: ". . . The debtor, while acquiring the physical property, only acquires an interest therein under a credit sales contract; it is this interest only then which is 'after acquired' and thereby subject to the earlier security right. The remainder is upon credit from the new creditor who often also retains title thereto. . . ."

First, under the Code, a buyer of property under a credit sales contract does not acquire an "interest" in the property; he acquires the property. (Otherwise, how could even a *subsequent* creditor ever obtain a security interest in anything but the debtor's "equity"?) It is the *seller* of the property that retains only a *security interest*. See UCC 2-401(1). There are certain provisions in the Code which allow a buyer and seller to specify how and when title passes—for particular purposes wherein the question of title is relevant; but the concept of title is *totally irrelevant* under Article 9 of the Code dealing with secured transactions. UCC 9-202 specifically provides:

> Each provision of this chapter with regard to rights, obligations and remedies applies *whether title to collateral is in the secured party or in the debtor.* (Emphasis supplied.)

Also, UCC 1-201(37) defines "security interest" as follows:

> "Security interest" means an interest in personal property or fixtures which secures payment or performance of an obligation. *The retention or reservation of title by a seller of goods notwithstanding shipment or delivery to the buyer (Section 2-401) is limited in effect to a reservation of a "security interest."* . . . (Emphasis supplied.)

Second, there is no difference between the relationship of a buyer and seller under a sales contract giving rise to a security interest and the relationship of any other debtor and creditor under any type of security. As evidenced by UCC 1-201(37) and 9-102(2), the Code recognizes only a single form of contractual lien on personal property—a "security interest."

Third, the majority opinion fails to recognize the fact that the owner of a purchase money security interest may be someone *other than the seller*. UCC 9-107. A third party who advances money used to purchase personal property and who takes a security interest in that property has a purchase money security interest; but it is still only a "security interest," the same as the seller would have—it is not "title." A purchase money security interest may also be assigned to a third or fourth party, without losing its character as such. (This is the situation before us.) Only a "security interest" is assigned, however—not "title."

There is only one relevant distinction between the security interest a creditor obtains in equipment he sells and any other security interest he obtains in any other collateral for any other loan. The sole distinction is that the Code gives a special preference to purchase money security interests through an exception to the general rules establishing the priorities between conflicting security interests.

The clear and specific language of the Code provisions outlining these priorities leads me to conclude that the only logical answer to the [question certified] is an unqualified, unconditional "yes." . . .

UCC 9-312(5)(a) states the general rule regarding priority of security interests which are perfected by filing (as both of these are). . . .

In this case, if the general rule were applicable, the security interest in after-acquired property would take priority over the purchase money security interest, because it was filed first. There is, however, an exception to the general rule, provided by UCC 9-312(4), which is applicable to this situation. The exception is that, "A purchase money security interest . . . conflicting security interest in the same collateral. . . ."

If this exception is effective, a purchase money security i~ ity over a prior security interest in the debtor's after-acquirec the order of filing is irrelevant.

Subsection (4), however, goes on to provide that the exce effective, ". . . if the purchase money security interest is perfected filed] at the time the debtor receives possession of the collateral or   ~en days thereafter."

In the case sub judice, the purchase money security interest was not filed within ten days. The exception of subsection (4), therefore, did not take effect. No other exception is applicable, so the general rule of subsection (5)(a) applies. Since the general rule applies, the security interest first-filed—the interest in the debtor's after-acquired property—has priority. . . .

NOTES & QUESTIONS

1. *Legislative overruling.* The Florida legislature overruled *International Harvester* in 1978 by adding a sentence to both UCC 9-312(3) and (4) stating that failure to follow the requirements of these subsections means priority is to be determined under UCC 9-312(5). Fla. Stats., Laws of 1978, ch. 78-222.

2. *The court's rationale.* If one accepts the court's reasoning in *International Harvester* in what cases will UCC 9-312(4) apply? What incentive is there for the purchase money secured party to file within ten days? What is the effect of the court's reasoning if the purchase money secured party is competing with a lien creditor? See UCC 9-301(2), 9-311. Are all purchase money secured parties covered by the court's decision or only the traditional conditional seller who retains title? See UCC 9-107. Does the court overlook UCC 9-312(5)? Are there implications for UCC 9-312(3)?

The court also suggests that it would be inequitable to give priority to the prior secured party who did not rely and who is therefore unjustly enriched. Do you agree? Did the prior secured party give any consideration for the after-acquired property clause? Was there anything the conditional seller could have done to comply with the UCC? As a practical matter is the first secured party likely to be misled by the failure of the conditional seller to file in a timely manner?

The rationale of *International Harvester* was followed in Smith v. Atlantic Boat Builder Co., 356 So. 2d 359, 24 UCC Rep. 783 (Fla. Dist. Ct. App. 1978). In this later case employees who had worked on construction of debtor's vessels and water crafts claimed priority over a bank with an after-acquired property clause. The court found that the liens for labor on vessels were not maritime liens but liens governed by Article 9. Because plaintiffs did not have possession of the vessels they could not rely on UCC 9-310. Nor could they tain the argument that the bank was estopped. Nevertheless, the court held that given the rationale of *International Harvester* the debtor was subject to the laborer's lien on the boats in its possession and the bank's after-acquired property interest in debtor's vessels was therefore subject to this lien. Sound?

3. *The purchase money security interest in bankruptcy.* The Bankruptcy Code recognizes the super-priority of the purchase money security interest for some purposes. Notwithstanding the automatic stay, a secured party with a purchase money security interest may perfect his interest after the bankruptcy petition has been filed and take priority over the strong arm of the trustee in bankruptcy (BC 362(b)(3), 546(b), 544(a)). Compare the ten-day period allowed all security interests under the preference provision of BC 547(e).

A number of jurisdictions recently have adopted a nonuniform Code amendment to extend the ten-day grace period to 20 days. Given the ten-day period provided by the Bankruptcy Code what effect will these nonuniform amendments have? What reasons would you give for such an amendment?

JACKSON & KRONMAN, SECURED FINANCING AND PRIORITIES AMONG CREDITORS
88 Yale L.J. 1143, 1161-1178 (1979) [Summary]

Note: A summary of an earlier part of this article appears at the end of the last chapter. The excerpt summarized below examines the justification for the rules that govern priorities among secured creditors, including the rule that gives the purchase money security interest super-priority.

1. *All parties would agree on "first in time, first in right" priority.* Although creditors' claims against a common debtor could be ranked *inter se* in a number of different ways, "first in time, first in right" is the rule that secured creditors would prefer. If a debtor had the power to grant priority to any later creditor the first creditor would charge a rate of interest that an unsecured creditor would charge in order to reflect the possibility of being subordinated. The rule granting priority to the earlier creditor is justified, therefore, because it provides a solution that creditors and debtors would agree to if the transaction costs of reaching agreement were not so high.

2. *All parties would agree on PMSI exception.* Purchase money security interests are an exception to the general rule of "first in time, first in right," but the special exception for these interests can be justified because freely contracting creditors and debtors would not only agree to the general rule but would also agree to the exception.

3. *PMSI and after-acquired property.* Purchase money priority is linked logically with after-acquired property clauses by which a security interest includes not only existing property of the debtor but also property the debtor subsequently acquires. After-acquired property clauses are justified because they

after a change
~ can charge
lower interest

save transaction costs (e.g., the cost of preparing new security agreements) when the creditor and the debtor want property that turns over rapidly to/*inventory* serve as collateral. The traditional explanation that an after-acquired property clause decreases the risk for the first creditor because he will have a larger pool of assets to look to if the debtor defaults overlooks the increased risk to subsequent creditors who will be subordinate to the interest of the first credi- *is* tor. Any savings in the interest charged by the first creditor, therefore, will be *Honesty* offset by the increased interest charged by subsequent creditors. *good law?*

4. *PMSI and situational monopoly.* The purchase money priority is a device for alleviating the "situational monopoly" of a creditor who has a security agreement with an after-acquired property clause. The creditor with such a clause has a competitive advantage when his debtor seeks additional funds. The first creditor will have lower monitoring costs and will be able to offer loans at a lower interest rate than other potential creditors. In other words, the first creditor need only incur the additional costs of monitoring the new collateral while potential creditors must monitor all the debtor's property to guard against collusion between the debtor and the first creditor. Collusion is likely because the debtor can bribe the first creditor to tolerate the debtor's misbehavior (using funds in a higher-risk venture than that anticipated when the interest rate was fixed), which injures only the subsequent lender.

5. *PMSI and transaction costs.* A purchase money priority blunts the situational monopoly of a creditor with an after-acquired property clause, but the clause still results in the saving of transaction costs. A creditor and a debtor in theory, therefore, might agree to contract using different combinations of clauses. Parties are aware of the difference, however, between (1) a contract with an after-acquired property clause and a purchase money provision subordinating the first creditor's interest to a subsequent purchase money interest, and (2) a contract with an after-acquired property clause, no purchase money provision, and a lower price term: the second contract is almost certain to be more expensive to negotiate.

6. *PMSI and tracing.* The purchase money priority is limited to cases where a subsequent creditor can identify collateral a debtor acquires with the credit extended by the subsequent creditor. This "tracing" rule is explicitly stated in UCC 9-107 and is justified on the following basis: suppose a subsequent creditor makes a working capital loan (e.g., to be used for wages, rent, and utilities) and is given priority in assets acquired by the debtor after the working capital loan is made. The first creditor runs the risk that the working capital will not generate an increase in the value of the debtor's assets commensurate with the amount of the loan to which the first creditor is now subordinate. If, for example, a working capital loan of $1,000 increases the value of the debtor's assets by only $800, the first creditor must absorb the "loss." The effect would be the same as having a rule of "last in time, first in right." It was shown earlier, however, that creditors would not agree to this rule.

2

NOTES & QUESTIONS

1. *First in time, first in right.* Professors Jackson and Kronman argue that the rule of "first in time, first in right" is necessary in order "to capture the special efficiencies that secured financing makes possible." Would a system that had a "last in time, first in right" basic rule refute their reasoning? The system of rules governing maritime liens purports to adopt this latter maxim within each class of liens. See generally G. Gilmore & C. Black, The Law of Admiralty 783-817 (2d ed. 1975); Varian, Rank and Priority in Maritime Liens, 47 Tul. L. Rev. 751 (1973). Note that Professors Gilmore and Black suggest that this rule of priority in maritime lien law is subject to so many exceptions that it may be evidence for the proposition that an inefficient legal rule will be eroded gradually by the exceptions because the cases supposedly governed by the inefficient rule will be worth litigating. See Priest, The Common Law Process and the Selection of Efficient Rules, 6 J. Legal Stud. 65 (1977).

2. *Mechanics' liens.* Throughout this excerpt the authors justify the legal rules on the ground that the parties, acting as economic persons maximizing their welfare, would contract for the rule in the absence of legal compulsion and therefore transaction costs are saved by adopting the rule. Would this reasoning validate a rule giving mechanics who repair collateral priority over prior secured parties for the value of the services rendered? Would secured parties agree to such a rule? Is this what UCC 9-310 does? We take up the question of nonconsensual liens created by state statute in Chapter 7.

3. *After-acquired property clauses.* The authors make the point that the validity of after-acquired property clauses is logically linked to purchase money priority. They justify the clauses on the ground that there are savings in transaction costs. Does this justification extend not only to accounts and inventory but also to equipment financing? In the prototype transaction set out in Chapter 3 why did the parties agree to an after-acquired property clause? The authors of the excerpt conclude that in the absence of transaction costs the decrease in the cost of credit from a secured party with an after-acquired property clause would be "exactly offset" by the higher cost of credit charged by unsecured creditors whose loans would be riskier because of the after-acquired property clause. Is this plausible?

4. *Limits to the validity of after-acquired property clauses.* Are there any instances where the law should be paternalistic even if this means ignoring what the parties might otherwise agree to? Is UCC 9-204(2) (ten-day limit on after-acquired consumer goods) an example of such a rule? Would the authors concede this exception for consumer goods on the ground that the transactions in which they are used as collateral are not "voluntary"?

5. *Situational monopoly by contract.* Should a contract clause forbidding the debtor to grant a security interest in the same collateral to another creditor be enforceable? If such a clause were enforceable, would the secured party be worried about the problem of purchase money secured parties?

6. *Valuing situational monopoly.* The authors suggest that in the absence of a compulsory purchase money priority rule, parties would not choose a contract that has both an after-acquired property clause and a clause that refused recognition of purchase money priority. Although a debtor might be able to obtain a lower interest rate the contract would be more expensive to negotiate. Would the market determine this rate if such clauses were available? If it is possible that any creditor at all might prefer this option can the authors justify the purchase-money preference on the ground that the legal rule is the same as that which would result from parties freely contracting with each other?

7. *Why secured credit?* Review the summary of the excerpt from the authors' article reproduced in Chapter 4, p. 215 supra. Does the argument for having security interests at all assume the "first in time, first in right" argument made in the summary set out above? If so, does this assumption make any difference to the argument in the earlier excerpt?

3.   Excursus: The Financing Buyer

There are occasions when a seller will turn to a potential buyer for financing. The seller may, for example, need the financing to acquire the equipment to be sold or the component parts to be assembled into the equipment. Like any other creditor, the buyer may secure repayment of the credit extended by taking a security interest in the equipment or the components while this collateral remains in the seller-debtor's hands. Several authors, including Professors Jackson and Kronman, whose article on secured party priorities is set out above, have asked whether the financing buyer should receive the super-priority accorded the purchase money secured party. See Jackson & Kronman, A Plea for the Financing Buyer, 85 Yale L.J. 1 (1975).

The legal analysis of the financing buyer's rights is complicated by the rights accorded the financing buyer under the sales provisions of Article 2. Once the goods sold have been "identified" the buyer may reclaim them from an insolvent seller if certain conditions are met. UCC 2-501, 2-502. Unfortunately, not only are the conditions virtually impossible to meet but this reclamation right is subject to the claims of third parties. UCC 2-402. As a result, in practice Article 2 has given no help to the financing buyer.

If the financing buyer turns to Article 9 he will come up against the need to trace the use to which the seller put the credit extended in order to show a purchase money security interest. UCC 9-107(b). Tracing will require careful and potentially extensive monitoring. Even if the buyer can trace, he will have no purchase money interest in the value added to the purchased equipment by labor because the purchase money interest extends only to goods.

On the assumption that the financing buyer is functionally equivalent to the purchase money secured party, Professors Jackson and Kronman suggest the following alternate amendments to the UCC:

The financing buyer may be elevated to parity with the purchase money lender in two ways. The first would simply be to abolish the strict tracing requirement of §9-107(b) by deleting the words "if such value is in fact so used." Although the elimination of the §9-107(b) tracing requirement may be desirable, it is also certain to be controversial.

A more conservative solution would be to add a new subsection (c) to §9-107, based in large part on the September 1949 draft of §8-105(3)(b), which would read as follows:

> A security interest is a "purchase money security interest" to the extent that it is . . .
>
> (c) taken by a buyer who makes advances to a seller to enable the seller to manufacture, assemble or process goods for the buyer during the period of one year following the advance, and the collateral securing the advance consists of (i) materials acquired after the advance has been made which are necessary for the manufacture, assembly or processing of the contract goods, and (ii) goods manufactured, assembled, or processed after the advance has been made which could be used to satisfy the contract (whether or not in a deliverable state).[147]

No further change in the Code would be necessary; the new subsection would give the financing buyer a purchase money security interest in the goods he had contracted for, thereby making him eligible for the special priority of §9-312(3). In this way, the financing buyer would be endowed with the rights, and charged with the duties, of a purchase money lender. [Jackson & Kronman, A Plea for the Financing Buyer, 85 Yale L.J. 1, 35-37 (1975).]

Problem 5-6. Assume that the bookbinder in the prototype transaction is itself a prototype to be built by ABM following designs suggested by Apex, which involves the incorporation of a laser unit that speeds the sealing of the binding process. ABM's research and development funds are otherwise committed so Apex lends ABM $20,000 to develop the prototype. ABM grants Apex a security interest in the "prototype/laser bookbinder," and Apex promptly files a financing statement in the proper office describing the collateral as "bookbinder." Much to the surprise of Apex, within 10 days after these documents are signed ABM files a petition under Chapter 11 of the Bankruptcy Code. At this time ABM has in its possession all the bookbinder com-

---

147. The proposed section limits the priority to materials received or manufacturing steps taken after the advance of the money. This is to ensure that the financing buyer is, indeed, a "financing," and not merely a prepaying buyer. The ordinary prepaying buyer does nothing to allow the manufacturer to move forward in the completion of the contract, and should not receive a special priority in the completed goods.

The relevant test should be, not the strict tracing requirement itself, but rather a test that looks to see if the financing money has actually been used in a manner that arguably enabled the debtor to progress towards completion of its contract with the financing buyer. This test is, itself, a kind of "tracing" requirement. It looks to any manufacturing steps taken after the receipt of the money from the financing buyer that further the production of goods that are for, or arguably could be for, the financing buyer. The existence of such a continuing manufacturing process signals that the money has been used in an "enabling" sense for that contract. The equities that attach to the purchase money lender, as a consequence, also attach here. Cf. Chrysler Corp. v. Adamatic, Inc., 59 Wis. 2d 219, 241-242, 208 N.W.2d 97, 108 (1973).

ponents with the exception of the laser unit, which was to be provided by a *not yet delivered*
small tool maker. The bankruptcy trustee informs Apex that he will challenge
its claim to the components and that in any case First National Bank of
Houston has informed him that it has a perfected security interest in ABM's
"equipment and inventory." Advise Apex on its prospects of recovering the
bookbinder components. *4) Apex can trace, get priority b/c P#SI?*

C. SUPPLIER AS LESSOR

In this third variation on the prototype transaction ABM, the supplier, leases
rather than sells the bookbinder to Apex. Apex obtains possession and use of
the bookbinder while ABM receives installment payments in the form of rent.
At the end of the lease term Apex has the obligation to return the equipment
to ABM.

For pedagogical reasons we have kept this variation simple. As noted at
the beginning of the chapter, in practice where long-term leases are involved
the supplier is unlikely to bear the final burden of extending credit. The
financing lease may become sophisticated, with numerous parties playing
more and more specialized roles. The excerpt set out at the end of this section
should suggest some of the complexity involved.

A business may prefer to lease equipment rather than purchase it for a *reasons to lease rather than purchase*
number of reasons. Apart from cases where a lessee only needs the equipment ①
for a short term the most important reason for leasing is usually that the tax ②
benefits are greater than for purchasing. Federal income tax rules with respect
to depreciation rates and investment credits have allowed lenders with large
taxable incomes to purchase equipment for lease to users who are unable to
take full advantage of the incentives. The lender-lessor who obtains the tax
advantages will usually share the benefit with the lessee so that the cost of
leasing may end up being less than buying.

Other reasons for leasing are frequently mentioned, although close analysis suggests at least some are illusory. The accounting treatment of leases—
which is far from uniform and continues to be much debated—has been
thought to encourage leasing because the transaction traditionally has been
mentioned only in footnotes to the balance sheet so that financial formulae
such as debt-to-equity ratios would not be affected. It is difficult to believe,
however, that investment analysts with any sophistication would be misled. A
business or a municipality may also be able to lease in situations where it is not
authorized to borrow, as in situations where prior loan agreements restrict
further borrowing or government regulations prohibit further purchasing. It
would seem that this loophole would be quickly closed by appropriate amendments to boilerplate provisions in loan agreements or regulations. A more solid

③ reason is that a business may wish to avoid the risk that the equipment will become obsolete or otherwise not operate for its full expected life.

The law governing the rights and obligations of parties to a lease of personal property is now in a state of flux. Because the widespread leasing of equipment is a relatively recent phenomenon the Uniform Commercial Code gives minimal guidance in this area. Courts must resort to the common law of bailment, which was elaborated in a financially less sophisticated age and remains undeveloped on important points in many jurisdictions. There have been recent suggestions that the resulting confusion should be resolved by new legislation, perhaps by amendment to the UCC. See Mooney, Personal Property Leasing: A Challenge, 36 Bus. Law. 1605 (1982).

The present version of the UCC is not completely silent with respect to leasing. The 1972 amendments authorize a lessor to file a financing statement specifying that it refers to a lease transaction. UCC 9-408. If it is later determined that the undertaking was really a disguised secured transaction the financing statement will be treated as properly filed from the date of original filing. On this issue the Code gives less guidance, although it is clear that its policy is to apply Article 9 to transactions that are functionally equivalent to secured transactions. See UCC 1-201(37), 9-102(2).

Further reading: Equipment Leasing—Leveraged Leasing (B. Fritch & A. Reisman 2d ed. 1980); R. Contino, Legal and Financial Aspects of Equipment Leasing Transactions (1979); Coogan, Leases of Equipment and Some Other Unconventional Security Devices: An Analysis of UCC Section 1-201(37) and Article 9, 1973 Duke L.J. 909 (1973).

FMA FINANCIAL CORP. v. PRO-PRINTERS
590 P.2d 803, 25 UCC Rep. 950 (Utah 1979)

MAUGHAN, Justice. . . . On June 19, 1974, defendant John Galanis sold certain printing equipment to the plaintiff, FMA Financial Corporation (hereafter "FMA"). On that same day, FMA arranged to lease the equipment back to Galanis for 60 months at $577.75 per month. The printing equipment cost FMA $21,114.53, and the lease payment totaled $34,665. FMA filed a financing statement with the Secretary of State, noting thereon that the property was being leased to Galanis.

With FMA's approval, Galanis assigned the lease to defendant Pro-Printers, Inc., on September 5, 1974. Certain officers of Pro-Printers, Inc., including Galanis and Jerry DeTurk, individually executed guaranty agreements at FMA's request.

Pro-Printers was unable to make the lease payments for January, 1976 and thereafter. On March 19, 1976, Jerry DeTurk requested plaintiff to repossess the equipment, which it did in April. Plaintiff appraised the equipment at $10,250 on its repossession report; four months earlier, a consultant hired by Pro-Printers had appraised the equipment at between $15,000 and $17,000.

The equipment was stored in a garage by Interwest Business Equipment Company for eight months and finally purchased by Interwest for $4,500 in the fall of 1976. In addition to Interwest, two other used equipment dealers were asked by FMA to bid on the equipment in October of 1976. One of the dealers testified he offered a "ridiculously low" bid of $2,400 because he didn't want the equipment; the other dealer bid $3,000, with the intent to resell the equipment for a profit. FMA gave defendants no notice of the private sale of the equipment.

Testimony at trial indicated FMA routinely offers its lease customers an oral option to purchase the leased equipment at the end of the lease. Galanis testified he had negotiated a total of approximately $75,000 worth of leases with FMA, and with each lease he was given the option to purchase the property at the end of the lease term for a "minimal fee," usually between 10 and 15 percent of the original cost to FMA. The equipment in the case at bar was listed by FMA as having a "residual due" of $2,129, which represented the approximate purchase price to defendants at the end of the lease period. The "residual value" of the printing equipment was almost exactly 10 percent of the equipment's cost to FMA, and was approximately 6 percent of the total lease payments.

FMA preliminarily asserts that because the written lease agreement makes no mention of an option to purchase, and contains an "integration" clause stating that the written lease contains the entire agreement between the parties, defendants should not be allowed to vary the written terms with parol evidence of an option to purchase. However, FMA's officers admitted at trial they offered lessees the option to purchase leased equipment as a matter of course in their business; thus rendering the alleged integration clause ineffective.

FMA's first major contention is, the lease is a "true lease," and not one intended as a secured sale, as the district court found. If FMA is correct, the provisions of Article 9 of the UCC on the disposition of repossessed collateral have no application to its actions, and it is entitled to a deficiency judgment for the stipulated amount.

The broad scope of Article 9 is given in UCC 9-102: "Except as otherwise provided . . . , this chapter applies (a) *to any transaction (regardless of its form) which is intended to create a security interest* in personal property . . ." (emphasis added). Therefore, if a transaction in the form of a lease is actually intended to be a sale, reserving in the "lessor" a security interest, it falls under the ambit of Article 9. UCC 1-201(37) provides in relevant part:

> Whether a lease is intended as security is to be determined by the facts of each case; however, *(a) the inclusion of an option to purchase does not of itself make the lease one intended for security, and (b) an agreement that upon compliance with the terms of the lease the lessee shall become or has the option to become the owner of the property for no additional consideration or for a nominal consideration does make the lease one intended for security.*

The question of whether a lease is intended for security has been litigated in numerous courts, and it is apparent this question must be "determined by the facts of each case;" nevertheless, if the lease is accompanied by an option to purchase, the code furnishes a "rule" which can be applied in determining the nature of the transaction. The code states that a "nominal" consideration for an option to purchase *does* make the lease one intended for security. Much of the case law on this subject understandably deals with the question of what is nominal consideration. In wrestling with this problem, courts have focused on three tests: (1) compare the option price with the original list price or cost of the property; (2) compare the option price with "sensible alternatives;" (3) compare the option price to the fair market value of the property at the time the option is to be exercised.

Although the parties on appeal dispute which of the above tests is most often applied, and which test this Court should adopt, we note that careful review of the cases reveals many courts analyze the purchase option under all three tests. We believe it unwise to restrict our analysis of the problem to one specific test, in view of the fact that all three tests are somewhat related, and each can offer insight into the nature of the transaction which is being examined.

Turning to the facts before us, the option to purchase could be exercised by defendant for approximately $2,130, which is 10 percent of the original cost to FMA, and only 6 percent of the total lease payments. Most courts using this test have concluded that purchase option which is 10 percent or less of the lessor's cost is nominal. In addition, such a small purchase option, when compared with the total lease payments of over $34,000, would logically leave the lessee in this case with no sensible alternative but to purchase the equipment. The testimony was undisputed that "the printing equipment had a useful economic life of at least ten to fifteen years." It is difficult to imagine the lessee would not have obtained outright ownership of the equipment for such a small sum where the equipment still had years of useful life. The third test, which compares the option price to the fair market value of the equipment at the time the option is to be exercised, is most relevant in determining whether the option price is nominal. If the price bears a resemblance to the fair market value of the equipment, the lease payments were in fact designated to be compensation for the use of the property, and the option price is not nominal. Here, no testimony exists concerning the projected fair market value of the equipment at the end of the lease. Instead, the testimony believed by the district court was that the option to purchase could be exercised by the lessee for approximately 10 percent of FMA's cost, regardless of the market value of the equipment.

We believe, under these circumstances, the option price was nominal; according to the code, the lease is therefore intended for security and is subject to the provisions of Article 9 secured transactions. . . .

[The court concluded that the plaintiff had failed to comply with the Article 9 default provisions and held that the lower court had properly denied plaintiff any deficiency judgment.]

C.   Supplier as Lessor

NOTES & QUESTIONS

Do
PROB

1. *Law governing the "true" lease.* If the court in *Pro-Printers* had determined that the transaction was indeed a "true" lease not subject to Article 9, what rights and obligations would the lessor and the lessee have had? For a discussion of the consequences of default on a true lease, see DeKoven, Proceedings After Default By the Lessee Under a True Lease of Equipment, in P. Coogan, W. Hogan, D. Vagts & J. McDonnell, Secured Transactions Under the Uniform Commercial Code, ch. 29B (1984).

2. *Identifying the "true" test.* After careful study of the background and relevant legislative text Peter Coogan suggests the following formula for determining whether a lease is a disguised secured transaction: "Is Lessee Required to Return the Leased Item at a Time when It Has a Not Insubstantial Value, or in the Alternative, to Purchase It at Its Reasonably Estimated Market Value or to Pay Reasonable Rent for Its Continued Use? These Estimates May Be Made as of the End of the Lease When Values Are More Easily Determinable, or at the Time of the Original Transaction—They Then Show Intent as of That Time." Coogan, Leasing and the Uniform Commercial Code, in Equipment Leasing—Leveraged Leasing 824 (B. Fritch & A. Reisman 2d ed. 1980).

3. *Filing of true leases.* Is the answer to the difficulty of distinguishing leases from disguised secured transactions a requirement that notice of all leases also be filed? Should there be exceptions to such a filing requirement for short-term and consumer leases? Does UCC 9-408 in effect adopt the above proposal?

4. *Leases in bankruptcy proceedings.* If a lease transaction is determined in a bankruptcy proceeding to be a disguised Article 9 secured transaction the lessor-secured party will have an unperfected security interest in the leased goods that may be avoided by the lessee-debtor's trustee by using the strong-arm clause (BC 544(a)(1)) unless the lessor has taken the sensible precaution of filing a financing statement (UCC 9-408). If, on the other hand, the lease is a true lease the lessor may be able to reclaim "its" goods when the lessee files a bankruptcy petition, but this right is subject to the right of the lessee's trustee to assume or reject the lease (BC 365).

Problem 5-7. ABM agrees to lease the bookbinder to Apex for ten years at an annual rental of $5,000 instead of making the installment sale set out in the prototype transaction, where Apex signed a five-year note for $54,489. At the end of this term Apex has the option to extend the lease year by year at an annual rental of $2,000. The bookbinder has an estimated useful life of 20 years. You are asked to prepare the necessary documents. Review the original prototype transaction set out in Chapter 3. What changes will have to be made? For an example of a lease form, see 5 Uniform Laws Annotated, Uniform Commercial Code Forms and Materials, Form 9:1650 (R. Henson & W. Davenport eds. 1968).

Problem 5-8. Assume that ABM is willing to sell the bookbinder, which has an estimated useful life of 20 years, to Apex for $45,000. ABM, however, is willing to consider any of the following alternatives. Would any of these create a security interest subject to Article 9? Do you need any additional information?

    (a) a lease for three years at $5,000 per year, with no option to purchase; *true lease*

    (b) a lease for 20 years at $3,200 per year, with no option to purchase;

    (c) a lease for five years at $10,600 per year, with an option to purchase the bookbinder for $1,000 at the end of the lease term;

    (d) a lease for five years at $8,000 per year, with an option to purchase for $15,000 at the end of the lease term;

    (e) a lease for five years at $8,000 per year, with an option to renew the lease for one-year terms at $1,000 per year;

    (f) a lease for five years at $5,000 per year, with an option at any time during the lease term to purchase the equipment for $45,000, subject to a credit of 75 percent of the rental payments already made.

Does it make any difference under any of these proposals who is responsible for maintaining, insuring, or paying taxes on the bookbinder? Would it make any difference if Apex (the lessee) has the option to terminate the lease at any time?

Problem 5-9. Several years after the prototype transaction, in which Austin State Bank financed the purchase of the ABM bookbinder, Apex leased a second bookbinder from Equipment Leasing Ltd. (ELL). Within three months of this lease Apex filed a petition under Chapter 7 of the Bankruptcy Code. ELL wishes to reclaim the second bookbinder. The trustee in bankruptcy argues that the lease is a disguised security agreement and ELL's interest should be avoided as an unperfected security interest. Austin State Bank also claims the second bookbinder under the terms of the security agreement entered into in the prototype transaction. What are the priorities of the parties to the second bookbinder?

Problem 5-10. In December of 1976, Marhoefer Packing Co., Inc., of Muncie, Indiana, entered into negotiations with Reiser, a Massachusetts based corporation engaged in the business of selling and leasing food processing equipment, for the acquisition of a Vemag Model 3007-1 Continuous Sausage Stuffer. Reiser informed Marhoefer that the units could be acquired by outright purchase, conditional sale contract, or lease. Marhoefer ultimately acquired a sausage stuffer from Reiser under a written "lease agreement."

The lease agreement provided for monthly payments of $665.00 over a term of 48 months. The last nine months' payments, totaling $5,985.00, were payable upon execution of the lease. If at the end of the lease term the machine was to be returned, it was to be shipped prepaid to Boston or similar destination "in the same condition as when received, reasonable wear and tear resulting from proper use alone excepted, and fully crated." The remaining terms and conditions of the agreement were as follows:

1. Any state or local taxes and/or excises are for the account of the Buyer.
2. The equipment shall at all times be located at
       Marhoefer Packing Co., Inc.
       1500 North Elm & 13th Street
       Muncie, Indiana
    and shall not be removed from said location without the written consent of Robert Reiser & Co. The equipment can only be used in conjunction with the manufacture of meat or similar products unless written consent is given by Robert Reiser & Co.
3. The equipment will carry a 90-day guarantee for workmanship and materials and shall be maintained and operated safely and carefully in conformity with the instructions issued by our operators and the maintenance manual. Service and repairs of the equipment after the 90-day period will be subject to a reasonable and fair charge.
4. If, after due warning, our maintenance instructions should be violated repeatedly, Robert Reiser & Co. will have the right to cancel the lease contract on seven days' notice and remove the said equipment. In that case, lease fees would be refunded pro rata.
5. It is mutually agreed that in case lessee, Marhoefer Packing Co., Inc., violates any of the above conditions, or shall default in the payment of any lease charge hereunder, or shall become bankrupt, make or execute any assignment or become party to any instrument or proceedings for the benefit of its creditors, Robert Reiser & Co. shall have the right at any time without trespass, to enter upon the premises and remove the aforesaid equipment, and if removed, lessee agrees to pay Robert Reiser & Co. the total lease fees, including all installments due or to become due for the full unexpired term of this lease agreement and including the cost for removal of the equipment and counsel fees incurred in collecting sums due hereunder.
6. It is agreed that the equipment shall remain personal property of Robert Reiser & Co. and retain its character as such no matter in what manner affixed or attached to the premises.

In a letter accompanying the lease, Reiser added two option provisions to the agreement. The first provided that at the end of the four-year term Marhoefer could purchase the stuffer for $9,968.00. In the alternative, it could elect to renew the lease for an additional four years at an annual rate of $2,990.00, payable in advance. At the conclusion of the second four-year term, Marhoefer would be allowed to purchase the stuffer for one dollar.

Marhoefer never exercised either option. Approximately one year after the Vemag stuffer was delivered to its plant, it ceased all payments under the lease and shortly thereafter filed a voluntary petition in bankruptcy. On July 12, 1978, the trustee of the bankrupt corporation applied to the bankruptcy court for leave to sell the stuffer free and clear of all liens on the ground that the "lease agreement" was in fact a lease intended as security within the meaning of the UCC and that Reiser's failure to perfect its interest as required by Article 9 rendered it subordinate to that of the trustee. You are counsel for Reiser. What is your response to the trustee?

FRITCH & SHRANK, LEVERAGED LEASING, IN EQUIPMENT LEASING—LEVERAGED LEASING*
215-223 (B. Fritch & A. Reisman 2d ed. 1980)

Two developments by the 1950's and 1960's led directly to the emergence of leveraged leasing as a widely used financing mechanism for capital equipment acquisition. First was the development of affirmative tax incentives, expressly designed by the 1954 Code to stimulate private investment in personal property via accelerated methods of depreciation, investment tax credits and special rules permitting faster depreciation than would be dictated by strict adherence to useful life expectations. These income tax reductions produced substantial economic incentives for investment in capital equipment even by persons who had no use for the equipment themselves. Second was the issuance in 1963 by the United States Comptroller of the Currency of interpretive ruling 3400,[2] which specifically authorized national banks to own and lease personal property. Rule 3400, together with similar authorizations for state chartered banks, which were rapidly adopted, encouraged commercial banks, usually subject to maximum income tax rates and already involved in commercial financing, to take advantage of the tax incentives.

The commercial banks, eventually joined by finance companies, and a little later by some nonfinancial industrial corporations with disposable cash and large income tax obligations, soon turned to the theory of the lever to make available to equipment users a new financial tool. Since leveraging permits an investor to acquire full ownership of an item of equipment without paying its full cost, the ensuing tax benefits are magnified in comparison with the total amount of money put to risk. In fact, when the tax credits (i.e., deductions from actual taxes payable) plus earnings from the investment of taxes postponed (e.g., through accelerated depreciations offsetting unrelated income) plus anticipated residual value are considered in the aggregate, theoretical yields on dollars invested can be 30, 40, or even 50 percent annually on an after-tax basis.

Few lessees, of course, will tolerate such returns to their sources of financing, but they will tolerate fairly substantial yields (10 to 20 percent on an

---

* For a summary of developments since the publication of this book see its Supplement 39-53 (1983). Most of the developments have been in the tax treatment of leases.—Eds.

2. 12 C.F.R. §7.3400 (1979). This original ruling has now been replaced by a more detailed one.

after-tax basis) if the benefits of the rest of the potential yields are transferred to them in the form of reduced rentals. This is the single most attractive aspect of leveraged leasing.

Let us take a simple hypothetical example:

A lessee who normally has to pay 10 percent annually to borrow $1 million to purchase a fleet of trucks can, by entering into a leveraged lease, reduce its effective annual cost by 2 percent.

A commercial bank purchases the trucks by investing $200,000 in cash and borrowing the remaining $800,000 at 10 percent per annum on a non-recourse basis from one or more insurance companies.

Taxes saved by an immediate realization of a 10 percent investment tax credit, plus even modest earnings on tax dollars saved from depreciation deductions during the early years of the lease (without giving any weight to the ultimate residual value of the trucks), will return to the investor substantially more than its initial $200,000 investment (even taking into account its tax obligations on the rentals after the depreciation deductions are exhausted). It thus needs to collect nothing more from the lessee than is necessary to service the non-recourse debt.

The aggregate rentals over the lease term, therefore, need not exceed the $800,000 debt, plus annual interest beginning at $80,000. Instead of paying interest beginning at $100,000, the lessee pays an effective initial "interest" cost of $80,000—8 percent instead of 10 percent.[4] The benefit to the lessee is more pronounced if it is not itself in a position to use the tax benefits, for example, if it expects to enjoy no taxable income in the near future or is not a United States taxpayer or has recently purchased so much depreciable equipment that it has exhausted substantially all of its taxable income.

In addition to reducing financing costs for lessees, leveraged leasing permits a multimillion-dollar item of equipment to be financed in a single lease transaction via several sources of funds instead of the single source typical in non-leveraged transactions. It thus spreads the credit risk among several investors with different priorities. . . .

STRUCTURE OF A TYPICAL LEVERAGED LEASE TRANSACTION

The typical leveraged lease transaction, assuming any leveraged lease can be called typical, involves six groups of parties: the owner or equity participants, the owner trustee, the lenders, the secured or indenture trustee, the manufacturer or supplier, and the lessee. There may also be a guarantor of the lessee's undertaking.

4. This so-called "inherent loss" transaction is purely hypothetical. Most leveraged leases produce some positive cash return to the owners, apart from yields produced by tax savings and postponements. Under current Internal Revenue Service regulations, in fact, no private federal income tax ruling that such a transaction constitutes a true lease and that the lessor is deemed to be the true owner entitled to the tax benefits of ownership will be issued unless the lessor can demonstrate a "reasonable" return on its investment apart from tax considerations. . . .

Owner participants are usually one or more commercial banks, bank affiliates, leasing companies, or finance companies who desire to acquire title to capital equipment, initially to obtain the tax benefits of ownership and ultimately to realize an additional return from disposition of the equipment. For reasons discussed below, the owner participants often do not take legal title to the property directly, but instead appoint a trustee, generally a commercial bank (the "owner trustee") to hold legal title for their benefit. The owner participants contribute to the trust the amount of their investment, generally at least 20 percent (but occasionally as high as 50 percent) of the acquisition cost, which may include such expenses as legal costs for themselves and the lenders, printing expenses, and any commissions payable to a third party for arranging the transaction.

Concurrently with receipt of the owner participants' investments, the owner trustee borrows the balance of the purchase price (plus expenses also being financed) by issuing its promissory notes, loan certificates, or bonds to the third group of parties, the lenders, usually in a private placement. Unless an exemption from registration is available under the Securities Act of 1933, which occurs, for example, when the debt is guaranteed by the United States, public debt placement is extremely expensive and generally avoided.

The debt incurred by the owner trustee is without recourse to the institution acting as owner trustee or to the general assets of the owner participants; the purchasers of the debt instruments agree to look exclusively to the rentals under the lease for repayment and, upon default, to their security interest or mortgage in the equipment and the other assets constituting the trust estate.

Because an assignment of the lease and a security interest or mortgage in the property is invariably created for the benefit of the lenders to secure repayment of the borrowings, the lenders generally appoint a second trustee, called a "secured" or "indenture" trustee, to act for them in holding the security interests.

The owner trustee, immediately upon receipt of the investments from the owner participants and borrowings from the lenders, (a) purchases the equipment from the manufacturer or supplier pursuant to an underlying construction or purchase agreement, the rights under which are assigned by the lessee to the owner trustee; (b) pays the expenses being financed in the transaction; and (c) leases the equipment to the lessee.

The term of the lease is usually identical to the amortization period of the debt, with monthly, quarterly, or semi-annual lease payments due on, or on the day immediately preceding, each day on which a payment of interest or of principal and interest is due on the debt, but occasionally the lease term survives the final debt maturity date by a year or two in order to produce additional cash flow for the benefit of the owner participants.

Since the lenders do not enjoy recourse to the general assets of the owner participants, it is evident that the financial merits of the transaction rest entirely upon the creditworthiness of either the lessee or a seventh party to the transaction who agrees in some manner to guarantee the lessee's undertakings. The guarantees generally fall into three categories.

Most often the guarantor is a parent or affiliate of the lessee, e.g., a major United States oil company doing its shipping through a foreign subsidiary that acquires use of vessels under a "bareboat charter" (the maritime equivalent of a net lease), or a group of public utilities jointly owning a thinly capitalized fuel storage company, or a foreign nation owning virtually all the outstanding stock of its national airline.

A second source of guarantees is an unrelated private business enterprise such as a major customer of the lessee willing to support the lessee's obligations because it is the principal consumer of the products to be manufactured or transported by the leased equipment, or a commercial bank of which the lessee is a major customer. (In the latter case, the guarantees often take the form of unconditional letters of credit issued by the bank for the account of the lessee.)

A third common source of credit support is a government agency such as the United States Export-Import Bank, or the U.S. government itself. Under the Title XI[6] program the government is authorized to guarantee up to 75 percent of the "actual cost" (as defined by the Maritime Administration pursuant to the Merchant Marine Act)[7] of constructing a United States built, owned, and documented vessel (as defined in the Act) built under the Government's Construction Differential Subsidy program, or 87.5 percent of the "actual cost" of a vessel built without subsidy.

In recent years, principally to save some expenses and reduce the cast of characters, the separate functions of the owner trustee and the indenture trustee have been combined in a single institution which, pursuant to a trust agreement with the owner participants as settlors, agrees to hold legal title to the equipment and to receive the rentals and other payments under the lease for the benefit, first of the lenders and, second, of the owner participants.

Two problems occasionally arise when a single trustee is proposed. First, some people see a conceptual problem in either creating or perfecting a mortgage or security instrument when both the "debtor" and the "secured party" appear as the same entity acting as trustee under the same instrument. This, however, has not prevented single-trustee instruments pertaining to U.S. registered aircraft from being recorded with the Federal Aviation Administration, or ship mortgages showing the same person as both mortgagor and mortgagee from being recorded under the United States Ship Mortgage Act, or financing statements with the same entity acting as both debtor and secured party from being recorded under the UCC.

Occasionally a mortgage or UCC financing statement will describe the status of the trustee-mortgagee as that of "agent" of the lenders, to distinguish its other role as trustee under a trust formed by the owner participants.

A theoretical concern has also been raised from time to time that a third person receiving a purported assignment of the mortgaged property from the dual trustee might be held to have acquired good title to the exclusion not only of the owner participants' interests, but also those of the lenders on

6. 46 U.S.C. §§1271-80 (1975, Supp. 1980).
7. 46 U.S.C. §1274(b) (1975, Supp. 1980).

grounds that the trustee made its transfer wearing both its owner and its mortgagee hats, even though the trustee was empowered only to transfer subject to the existing security interest. It seems safe to say however, that, if a proposed transferee is, or ought to be, aware of the trust, the law of most states would impose upon such transferee the duty to inquire into the extent of authority given the trustee with which it is dealing and such transferee would be held to have constructive notice of restrictions contained in the trust instrument.[8]

The second and more serious problem raised by the dual trustee is the concern often expressed by institutional lenders and commercial banks that such a relationship produces an inherent conflict of interest. Can a trustee faithfully serve two masters whose interests do not always coincide?

The potential conflict is probably most acute during a foreclosure following default by the lessee and is suggested by this dilemma: Should the trustee sell the equipment for cash in an amount sufficient only to retire the debt (thereby leaving the owner participants unsatisfied) or is it obligated to sell the equipment for a higher price even if the price is payable in installments over several years? If it chooses the second course, enough proceeds will be generated to satisfy both sets of beneficiaries if the new buyer fully performs. But suppose the new buyer defaults, returning equipment substantially less valuable than it had been earlier. Has the trustee breached its fiduciary duty to the lenders who are supposed to enjoy a priority above the owner participants?

It is sometimes suggested that the problem can be avoided by permitting the trustee to resign one of its roles when a default occurs, but it is highly unlikely that the investors will be able to find another entity willing to step in as lenders' or owners' trustee principally to become party to litigation. Troubled by these problems, some commercial banks decline to serve as joint trustee, and some lending institutions and owners insist upon a division of the trustee functions between separate banks.

8. A. Scott, The Law of Trusts §297.4 (3d ed. 1967).

CHAPTER 6

Accounts Receivable and Inventory Financing

In this chapter we turn from financing the acquisition of equipment, as illustrated by the prototype transaction and its variants, to general business financing secured by accounts receivable and inventory.

A lender who agrees to finance a borrower's business operations with the borrower's accounts receivable and inventory as collateral typically contemplates entering into a continuing relationship. He will probably plan to make periodic loans to the borrower and will take a security interest in existing and after-acquired accounts receivable, inventory, or both. The amount of the loan outstanding at any one time will usually vary with the value of the collateral, which both parties assume will turn over as inventory sold is replenished from proceeds and new accounts receivable are substituted for those that have been paid. This constant turnover has been likened to the Heraclitean stream, which remains a stream despite the constant flow of individual water molecules. The security interest in this fluctuating mass of accounts receivable and inventory is commonly known as a "floating lien."

For students who are unfamiliar with these specialized patterns of financing, the materials in Part A of this chapter will provide an introduction to the business background. Part B reviews the Article 9 provisions that comprise the basic legal elements of the floating lien, most of which have already been introduced in other contexts. Parts C and D then go on to examine specific problems that arise when inventory and accounts receivable, including chattel paper, are used as collateral. A brief final section, Part E, concludes with a study of the validity of the floating lien in bankruptcy.

A. THE BUSINESS BACKGROUND[1]

REISMAN, WHAT THE COMMERCIAL LAWYER SHOULD KNOW ABOUT COMMERCIAL FINANCE AND FACTORING
79 Com. L.J. 146, 148-151 (1974)

FACTORING [SALE OF ACCOUNTS RECEIVABLE]

The term "factor" stems from the Latin verb "facio" and literally means "he who does things." It originally referred to an agent for a property owner, following the Roman practice of entrusting property management to others. Modern factoring originated in the nineteenth century with sales agents who represented U.S. and European textile mills. Due to slowness of transportation and communication in those days, the sales agent's function gradually began to include receiving and shipping goods, guaranteeing credit worthiness, billing and handling collections for his client's customers. With improvements in technology, towards the beginning of the twentieth century, the mills developed their own sales and shipping organizations but continued to subscribe to the factor's financial services. The bulk of factoring activity is still in textiles and allied fields, although the percentage of volume from other industries has been increasing, including household furnishings, toys, lumber, electronics, and plastic and metal products. In addition, the principal offices and operating offices of factors are no longer located mainly in New York City but are now in principal cities throughout the United States.

The factor's size, volume, resources and extensive credit files enable it to frequently approve larger orders and credit concentrations for the client's existing customers, and to extend quickly substantial credit lines to new customers for whom the client may not have adequate credit information. The factor's volume also enables it to hire more sophisticated and experienced credit personnel, with appropriately greater salaries, than could many of its clients. . . .

Both factoring and receivable financing usually involve open account terms ranging from thirty to ninety days with or without discounts. Generally, unacceptable receivables would involve a portfolio which is heavily dependent upon one or two customers, longer datings, consignment or guaranteed sales, contras and additional requirements of installation, completion, servicing or other performance under a contract.

It should be noted that in factoring, unlike receivable financing, the client's customers are notified on their invoices that their accounts have been

---

1. For further reading on business background, see L. Moskowitz, Modern Factoring and Commercial Finance 1-6 (1977); D. Robinson, Accounts Receivable and Inventory Lending 5-14 (1977); C. Phelps, Accounts Receivable Financing as a Method of Securing Business Loans (2d ed. 1962).

purchased and are payable to the factor on the due dates. This is necessary, not only from a legal viewpoint, [but also] because direct contact with the customer is often required to obtain current credit information, as well as to control collections and available lines of credit.

There are two elements which determine the factor's compensation. The first is the commission for the factor's credit checking, collection, bookkeeping and risk taking services. This commission ranges from 3/4 of 1% to 2% of the amount of the purchased receivables, depending upon the average number of invoices and credit memoranda that have to be processed, average amount of each invoice, the projected volume of business, usual credit terms to customers and the projected loss experience and credit risk assumed. For those clients who require advance payments prior to the average maturity date of invoices purchased, there is an additional charge on advances at a rate which usually ranges from two and one half to three and one half per cent over the prime rate.

Any accurate cost comparison of factoring must take into account the savings produced by elimination of the client's credit and collection functions, bad debt losses, the ledgering of accounts receivable and other costs incidental to operating a company credit department.

Factors generally divide their clients into two basic categories, wholesale and retail. A wholesale client would typically sell its product to a manufacturer or distributor who either integrates the product into another item (e.g., a sale of yarn to a textile manufacturer) or resells the product to the retailer (e.g., a sale of shoes to a jobber or wholesaler). A retail client would generally sell a finished product to a retail outlet (e.g., the sale of shoes to a shoe store). Sales of retail clients would usually have relatively small dollar amounts per invoice, greater quantity of paper work and a higher cost of handling, thus resulting in a higher factoring commission than for a wholesale client. Since factors, who are computerized, can perform these functions much more economically and efficiently, retail factoring is assuming greater and greater importance with a relatively low commission structure. . . .

Frequently, a client's bank, the client and the factor will enter into a three-party arrangement under which the client assigns to the bank all moneys payable by the factor to the client under the factoring contract (which is generally referred to as the "credit balance"). This enables the client to borrow a greater amount of funds from its bank on the security of the factor's credit balances, than might ordinarily be available, and at a lower interest rate than the client is currently paying—another offset to the cost of factoring. . . .

ACCOUNTS RECEIVABLE FINANCING

The common denominator of most commercial finance companies is that they make loans on a revolving basis in proportion to the volume of accounts receivable assigned as collateral. New advances are made as receivables are created. Repayments are made through collections from customers. The flexibility of this kind of arrangement means that the client has available on request the funds it needs when it needs them. The need to become involved in periodic renegotiation or clean ups of short term loans is eliminated.

Unlike factoring, with accounts receivable financing the client simply borrows against collateral. Any additional services rendered are advisory. The client retains the functions and risks of credit and collection, and continues to bear the expense of supporting this activity.

Although the client's accounts are assigned to the finance company, its customers are not made aware of this or notified. They continue to make direct payment to the client. However, the client is obligated to turn over all collections to the finance company in the form received unless collections are sent by customers directly to a lock box controlled by the finance company.

Typically, accounts receivable financing involves setting a rate of advance which may range from seventy to eighty five per cent of the face amount of the acceptable accounts receivable, depending upon the nature, quality and terms of the pledged receivables. Unacceptable accounts for purposes of the borrowing base might be those sixty to ninety days delinquent or where [there] are contras, disputes, offsets and the like.

The major source of loss in commercial financing is fraud and finance companies have many procedures to minimize such losses. The typical receivable fraud involves a client who, for one reason or another, has reached the limit of his normal borrowing availability, is in a financial bind and is reluctant to approach his lender for an over advance. This usually begins by the assignment of anticipated accounts receivable when the goods are not yet ready for shipment, it proceeds to the assignment of spurious accounts as to which there is a purchase order but not even work in process and balloons into the assignment of completely fictitious accounts as to which there is not even a purchase order. [In some instances, remittances from customers are intercepted and frequently not turned over to the financier but deposited in the company's bank account.]

Accordingly, although [UCC 9-205] has abolished the rule of Benedict v. Ratner [268 U.S. 353 (1925)] that there must be an exercise of dominion over collateral in order for a security interest to be valid, the commercial finance company still wants to know that the collateral is in existence. It gets the original check to be sure that real customers are paying the account, requests for verifications are sent out in the client's name to customers directly from the commercial finance company and periodically the finance company auditors will appear at the client's premises to verify its receivable agings, books and records. These aspects of the control of collateral distinguish the finance company from the lender who takes a security interest merely for additional comfort. . . .

As a result of these higher handling costs, the smallest annual sales volume which will be financed by a major commercial finance company is in the area of \$300,000 to \$500,000. The other end of the scale often reaches into eight figure amounts. Interest is charged on a daily basis only for that part of the loan availability which is actually in use and is in the neighborhood of about six percent over the prime rate. The pricing in each situation is competitive and based on such criteria as the client's present financial condition and prospects, evaluation of the collateral available in relation to expected loan requirements and the time and expense required to maintain up-to-date collateral information. In actuality, this rate is not much greater than what would be paid to a bank after compensating balances and drawing down unneeded funds under a loan in a fixed amount, and certainly in the long run is much cheaper than giving up equity in a growing business. The actual dollar cost and not the per annum rate should be compared. The interest cost is further minimized by borrowing only when and for the time funds are needed, as well as by the immediate application of the proceeds of customer checks, after clearance, against the loan balance. It must also be noted that, by being able to generate cash from its accounts receivable prior to maturity, the client can take advantage of savings in other areas such as trade discounts on purchases of inventory, as well as other profit-making opportunities.

Many banks, including the very largest, often engage in lending participations with commercial finance companies. The banker provides a portion of the loan funds, and the finance company provides not only the balance, but assumes responsibility for all administrative and supervisory details as well. As a result the bank's rate is lower than that of the finance company, with the consequence that the mix of rates produces a lower net rate for the client.

INVENTORY FINANCING

Inventory is sometimes described as the garbage pail of the balance sheet. The reason for this is that research and development costs, work in process, packaging and shipping materials, obsolete merchandise, returned goods, scrap and other items of dubious value are often included in inventory figures in the balance sheet.

For the above reasons, as well as the difficulty in controlling inventory and its diminution in value on a forced sale basis, most commercial finance houses seldom make inventory loans except in conjunction with factoring or accounts receivable financing. Typically, these loans are made to accommodate a seasonal build up or in conjunction with opening letters of credit to finance the importation of merchandise.

Inventory loans are secured primarily by raw materials or finished goods. New advances are based upon a fixed minimum percentage of the cost of such acceptable inventory and are on a revolving basis, so that the maximum loan availability will change directly in proportion to the amount of acceptable inventory on hand. Generally, any such advances will be in the neighborhood of twenty to forty per cent of cost, depending upon the quality and nature of the inventory. Repayment of the inventory loan is obtained from the proceeds of accounts receivable as goods are sold.

Some commercial finance companies do engage in floor planning of large ticket items for distributors and retailers, such as automobiles, trucks and electrical appliances. However, this type of inventory is fast moving and requires close controls. The reported cases are replete with instances in which such inventory disappeared or where there was double financing resulting in conflicting security interests or rights of third parties. The classic inventory fraud was the "Great Salad Oil Swindle" in the early nineteen sixties. Banks and insurance companies advanced substantial sums to a commodity speculator on trust receipts which turned out to represent ninety percent water and only ten percent vegetable oil. The resulting losses exceeded one hundred million dollars.

When a finance company does extend inventory loans, it will investigate whether the inventory is fresh, frequency of turnover, condition, quality, maintenance and care. Consideration must also be given to the danger of obsolescence, whether it is high style or subject to fads, the percentage of finished goods and liquidation value. Work in process has practically no liquidation value, for it requires an additional investment to complete the fabrication into saleable finished goods. The finance company may also require an appraisal of liquidation value by an outside professional appraiser.

The inventory lender will generally require periodic reporting of the quantity and types of inventory. Filings will be made under the UCC unless warehouse receipts from a public warehouse company are delivered as security. The services of outside field warehousing companies may also be utilized as an additional protective device.

NOTES: LEGAL BACKGROUND

The pre-Code law governing the transactions described above can be summarized briefly with the following paragraphs. For further background reading the indispensable source is 1 G. Gilmore, Security Interests in Personal Property chs. 2, 4-8 (1965). Professor Gilmore suggests that the development of legal devices validating the use of inventory as collateral was one of the great legal controversies of the nineteenth century. Although some cases struggled with the validity of after-acquired property clauses, most addressed the issue as one of fraud. These latter cases suggested that to grant a mortgage in inventory was a fraudulent conveyance because the mortgagor might mislead third parties into thinking that he was owner of unencumbered property by his continuing possession and sale of the inventory. Id. at 39-47.

1. *Factor's lien.* The "factor" as a commission agent who sold goods for a number of principals was a prominent figure in the distribution of goods, especially textiles, in the nineteenth century. The role of the factor changed

over time, however, and the twentieth-century factor made advances to manufacturers and looked to their inventory and accounts for security. In 1911 New
York enacted a statute validating the factor's lien, but it was not until the
1940s that other states began adopting factor's lien statutes. Although these
later statutes followed the substance of the New York act there was no attempt
to adopt a uniform text: all the statutes covered inventory but in many only
the inventory of manufacturers was included. All the statutes required the
factor to publicize his interest, usually by the posting of signs on the premises
of the debtor.

2. *Accounts-receivable financing.* Coinciding with the enactment of the factor's lien acts was the proliferation of accounts-receivable statutes in the 1940s
and 1950s. Spurred on by court decisions that raised doubts about the efficacy
of financing arrangements using accounts receivable as security (Benedict v.
Ratner, 268 U.S. 353 (1925); Corn Exchange Natl. Bank & Trust Co. v.
Klauder, 318 U.S. 434 (1943)), these statutes validated financing arrangements where accounts receivable were purchased by the creditor or were used
as collateral, especially arrangements where the creditor left the debtor to
collect from the account debtors who would not be informed of the assignment
of the account (non-notification financing). There was no attempt to enact a
uniform law and there was fierce debate about whether filing notice of the
financial arrangement should be required. Many of the earlier statutes validated the arrangement without a public notice requirement, but the later
statutes opted for publication. Before the widespread adoption of the UCC in
the 1960s almost 40 jurisdictions had adopted accounts-receivable statutes in
some form.

3. *Inventory financing: trust receipt.* For the dealer in consumer durable
goods, especially the automobile, the trust receipt financing device was
adapted from the import trade. The dealer and creditor would enter into a
general financing agreement, notice of which would be filed, followed by a
specific agreement (trust receipt) as goods were acquired from the manufacturer. The creditor (the entruster) would pay the manufacturer for the goods
but give the debtor (the trustee) possession for the purpose of resale. When the
debtor sold the goods the proceeds would be turned over to the creditor to
satisfy the loan for the acquisition of the goods. The National Conference of
Commissioners on Uniform State Laws (NCCUSL) promulgated a Uniform
Trust Receipts Act in 1933. Although the act, drafted by Karl Llewellyn, was
criticized as highly technical it was adopted by 38 states before the NCCUSL
withdrew it as work on the UCC began.

4. *The field warehouse.* To avoid legal restrictions on the use of inventory as
collateral, lenders and borrowers developed the field warehouse. In a typical
arrangement a lender would hire a professional warehouse company to establish a "warehouse" on the borrower's premises and to control the borrower's
access to inventory stored in the warehouse. The warehouse itself might consist
only of a segregated area posted with signs; the guard might be a former
employee of the borrower hired by the warehouseman. The legal validity of
the field warehouse depended on the law of pledge: the lender was secure

because he had possession of the inventory through the warehouseman. (This might be implemented by the lender taking possession of documents of title issued by the warehouseman.) Much pre-Code litigation challenged the extent of the warehouseman's control in particular cases, but there was no pre-Code legislation directed generally at field warehouses.

B.   CONCEPTUAL COMPONENTS OF THE "FLOATING LIEN"

The common law has had great conceptual difficulty recognizing an enforceable lien in a fluctuating mass of inventory and accounts receivable. Pre-Code statutes (factor's lien acts, accounts-receivable statutes) validated this increasingly popular form of financing pattern but the legislation was nonuniform, had ambiguous definitions as to scope, and left important questions unanswered. The UCC sweeps aside these pre-Code problems and fully legitimates the floating lien. The Code affirmatively validates after-acquired property and future advance clauses (UCC 9-204) and reaffirms the secured party's right to proceeds (UCC 9-306). It clarifies the priority rules (UCC 9-312) and rejects the former legal requirement that a debtor account for the use or disposition of collateral and proceeds on penalty of having the security interest avoided as fraudulent (UCC 9-205). Notice filing, which allows a single original filing to be effective even as to subsequent transactions, greatly simplifies the paperwork (UCC 9-302, 9-303).

Professor Gilmore has noted that legitimating the floating lien was the most controversial feature of Article 9. He writes: "The case against the floating lien . . . consists usually of two principal points: (1) the availability of a floating lien on all present and future assets will leave nothing to satisfy the claims of unsecured creditors and will consequently tend to dry up the sources of such credit; (2) the law should protect a necessitous borrower against himself by refusing to allow him to encumber all the property he may ever own in order to secure a present loan. . . . The position taken in defense [of the Article 9 provisions] is that it has long been true under precode law that, under one or another of the available 'devices' and if appropriate steps are taken to promote liens on after-acquired property from 'equitable' to 'legal,' all of a debtor's present and future property can be encumbered with valid, enforceable liens. . . . Therefore, rather than pretend, on the level of legal fiction, that things cannot be done which in fact and law can be done, sound analysis requires that the floating lien be recognized as valid and then cut down to size in situations where its unlimited and unrestricted application might lead to undesirable or unjust results." 1 G. Gilmore, Security Interests in Personal Property 359-360 (1965). See also UCC 9-204, Comments 2-5.

The following materials focus on three major conceptual components of the floating lien: after-acquired property, future advances, and proceeds.

1.   After-Acquired Property (UCC 9-204(1))

UCC 9-204(1) states simply that "a security agreement may provide that any or all obligations covered by the security agreement are to be secured by after-acquired collateral." If the parties agree to an after-acquired property clause the secured party's security interest will attach automatically when the debtor acquires rights in the new property without the need to sign another security agreement. Moreover, with the exception of a special rule for consumer goods (UCC 9-204(2)), the Code does not distinguish between different types of collateral so the clause may be used for both inventory financing and equipment financing.

The Code draftsmen explain in Comment 2 to UCC 9-204 the policy for recognizing the after-acquired property clause: "This Article accepts the principle of a 'continuing general lien.' It rejects the doctrine—of which the judicial attitude toward after-acquired property interests was one expression—that there is reason to invalidate as a matter of law what has been variously called the floating charge, the free-handed mortgage and the lien on a shifting stock. . . . The widespread nineteenth century prejudice against the floating charge was based on a feeling, often inarticulate in the opinions, that a commercial borrower should not be allowed to encumber all his assets present and future, and that for the protection not only of the borrower but of his other creditors a cushion of free assets should be preserved. That inarticulate premise has much to recommend it. This Article decisively rejects it not on the ground that it was wrong in policy but on the ground that it was not effective. In pre-Code law there was a multiplication of security devices designed to avoid the policy: field warehousing, trust receipts, factor's lien acts and so on. The cushion of free assets was not preserved. In almost every state it was possible before the Code for the borrower to give a lien on everything he held or would have. There have no doubt been sufficient economic reasons for the change. This Article, in expressly validating the floating charge, merely recognizes an existing state of things." The background to the after-acquired property clause is traced in greater detail in Cohen & Gerber, The After-Acquired Property Clause, 87 U. Pa. L. Rev. 635 (1939).

Several other justifications have been given for recognizing the validity of after-acquired property clauses. The traditional reason given is that a secured party desires the clause to enlarge the pool of collateral securing the debtor's obligation, which in turn decreases the risk of nonperformance. It has been suggested, however, that the decreased risk to the secured party will increase the risk to other creditors, who can look only to a smaller pool of assets, and they will increase correspondingly the cost of credit to the debtor. Jackson & Kronman, Secured Financing and Priorities Among Creditors, 88 Yale L.J.

1143, 1166-1167 (1979). These authors suggest that a more persuasive reason for the clause is to save transaction costs, a justification with special significance for inventory and accounts financing because of the considerable paperwork that would otherwise be necessary if a new security agreement had to be signed each time the debtor acquired an item of inventory or an account.

Problem 6-1. Retailer grants Finance Company a security interest in "inventory and equipment kept at Retailer's store in Oakland, California" to secure loans made by Finance Company to Retailer. A financing statement covering "inventory and equipment" was filed promptly with the California secretary of state. One year later Retailer moved its store from Oakland to San Francisco with the consent of Finance Company. After the move Retailer acquired new inventory and new equipment. Six months later Retailer filed a petition in bankruptcy. The trustee in bankruptcy argues that Finance Company has a claim only to inventory items and equipment in Retailer's possession at the time the security agreement was signed. Should this argument prevail? Would your answer be different if the security agreement covered "inventory and equipment" while the financing statement claimed "inventory and equipment presently owned and after-acquired"?

Problem 6-2. On January 1 Manufacturer grants Bank a security interest in "all manufacturing equipment now owned or hereafter acquired" to secure a term loan from Bank. Bank promptly files in the proper office a financing statement covering "equipment." On June 1 Manufacturer acquires a lathe. Following financial reversals Manufacturer files a petition under Chapter 11 of the Bankruptcy Code on July 1. As debtor in possession Manufacturer acquires a drill press on August 1.

(a) Does Bank have a security interest in the lathe? When is the interest "transferred" to Bank under BC 547(e)? Can the manufacturer "avoid" the security interest? See BC 547.

(b) Does Bank have a security interest in the drill press? See BC 552(a): "Except as provided in subsection (b) of this section, property acquired by the estate or by the debtor after the commencement of the case is not subject to any lien resulting from any security agreement entered into by the debtor before the commencement of the case." [Subsection (b) is reproduced at p. 281 infra.—Eds.]

(c) Assume the lathe and drill press are part of Manufacturer's inventory and that Bank has a security interest in Manufacturer's "inventory now owned or hereafter acquired." Would your answers to the above questions change? (We will study the effect of BC 547(c)(5) at the end of the chapter.)

2. Future Advances (UCC 9-204(3))

UCC 9-204(3) provides that "[o]bligations covered by a security agreement may include future advances or other value whether or not the advances or value are given pursuant to commitment (subsection (1) of Section 9-105)." A lender who looks to accounts as collateral, for example, will regularly recompute the debtor's obligation by liquidating the prior loan and extending a new loan calculated with reference to the value of the current pool of acceptable accounts.

Two related issues have dominated discussion of the future advance clause. A first question concerns the extent to which an original security agreement must specifically contemplate the future advance. "Dragnet clauses," which purport to catch all obligations owed by the debtor to the secured party no matter how they arise, are frequently referred to in this debate. The second question concerns the priority of the future advance over third-party obligations that arise after the original transaction but before the future advance. The addition of UCC 9-312(7) in 1972 attempts to clarify this problem. This provision states in part: "If future advances are made while a security interest is perfected . . . the security interest has the same priority for the purposes of subsection (5) with respect to the future advances as it does with respect to the first advance."

Note that the financing statement does not require the parties to indicate the obligation secured. A future advance clause will not, therefore, be recorded. To discover the amount secured, a debtor's potential creditor will have to rely on the debtor's financial documents and the indirect formal procedure of UCC 9-208.

FRIEDLANDER v. ADELPHI MANUFACTURING CO.
5 UCC Rep. 7 (N.Y. Sup. Ct. 1968)

CRISONA, J. In this special proceeding pursuant to CPLR 5239 petitioner Adelphi Manufacturing Co., Inc. seeks to vacate an execution levy made by respondent Sheriff of the City [of New York] against the equipment and inventory of Security Blueprint Corporation (hereinafter referred to as the debtor) upon the ground that petitioner has a prior security interest and is entitled to immediate possession.

The debtor is engaged in the business of offset printing and reproductions. On November 22, 1966, petitioner and debtor entered into a security agreement covering, in addition to a stated indebtedness of $24,000, ". . . any other indebtedness or liability of the Debtor to the Secured Party, direct or indirect, absolute or contingent, due or to become due, now existing or hereafter arising, including all future advances or loans which may be made at the option of the Secured Party. . . ." The agreement further provided that the secured party would have the right to immediate possession of the collateral in the event of a default. On November 23, 1966, pursuant to Article 9 of the Uniform Commercial Code, petitioner filed a financing statement with the register of Queens County. A further agreement was entered into between petitioner and the debtor on November 2, 1967, consolidating all the then existing loans and providing for additional advances. The debtor admittedly is in default under the agreements.

On August 4, 1967, respondent Adelphi obtained a judgment against the debtor in the sum of $1,965.35. The judgment was docketed on October 21, 1967. On November 28, 1967, the sheriff levied, pursuant to an execution issued on September 26, 1967, on the property of the debtor including the collateral under the security agreement.

The type of security agreement here involved is specifically authorized by UCC 9-204. In fact, this type of floating lien was permitted under pre-Code case law relating to mortgages to secure future advances. . . . There is no doubt that petitioner is entitled to priority with respect to the original loan since his security interest was perfected before respondent Adelphi obtained its judgment against the debtor (UCC 9-301; Matter of Iselin & Co. v. Burgess & Leigh, 52 Misc. 2d 821). Therefore, petitioner was entitled, by virtue of the security agreement and UCC 9-503, to immediate possession, without judicial process, of the collateral upon the debtor's default. . . . The only question yet unanswered is the extent of the petitioner's priority, i.e., whether petitioner is entitled to priority for advances made after respondent obtained its judgment against the debtor and issued execution to the sheriff (see [N.Y.] Practice Commentary to UCC 9-204 by Homer Kripke).

A perfected security interest takes priority over all unfiled and unperfected interests "including the rights of judgment creditors who thereafter issued execution, since the liens of such creditors are perfected only by the issuance of execution pursuant to CPLR 5202 (subdiv. [a])." . . . Since in the instant case execution was issued prior to the second advance, the extent of the petitioner's priority is, generally stated, dependent upon whether successive loans against the same collateral create separate security interests or only one which attaches and becomes perfected with the first loan (see 2 Gilmore, Security Interests in Personal Property §35.1 et seq.; Coogan, Article 9 of the Uniform Commercial Code: Priorities among Secured Creditors and the "Floating Lien," 72 Harv. L. Rev. 838; Coogan & Gordon, The Effect of the Uniform Commercial Code upon Receivables Financing—Some Answers and Unresolved Problems, 76 Harv. L. Rev. 1529). The single security interest concept finds support in pre-Code case law. In Ackerman v. Hunsicker (85 N.Y. 43) the court stated: "The doctrine that a party who takes a mortgage to secure further optional advances, upon recording his mortgage, is protected against intervening liens, for advances made upon the faith and within the limits of the security, until he has notice of such intervening lien, and that the recording of the subsequent lien is not constructive notice to him, has, we think, been generally accepted as the law of the State. . . ."

There is no provision in the Uniform Commercial Code tending to negative the one security interest approach and, in fact, UCC 9-201 contains the general language that "a security agreement is effective according to its terms between the parties, against purchasers of the collateral and against creditors."

The time of perfection of the security interest thus becomes crucial in determining its priority over or subordination to a lien. Three interrelated sections of the Code are pertinent. UCC 9-303(1) provides, inter alia, that: "A security interest is perfected when it has attached and when all of the applicable steps required for perfection have been taken. . . . If such steps are taken before the security interest attaches, it is perfected at the time when it attaches."

A security interest attaches when there is "agreement . . . that it attach and value is given and the debtor has rights in the collateral" (UCC 9-204(1) [1972 UCC 9-203(1)(c)]). A person gives "value" for rights if he acquires them "(a) in return for a binding commitment to extend credit; . . . (d) generally, in return for any consideration sufficient to support a simple contract" (UCC 1-201(44)).

Although in the instant case there was no binding commitment to extend credit, petitioner clearly gave "value" for his security interest when he made the first advance (UCC 9-204(1)(d)[sic]; see 2 Gilmore, supra, at 937; for an opposing view, see Coogan & Gordon, supra, 76 Harv. L. Rev. 1529, 1550). The security interest having attached and become perfected with the first advance may thereafter vary as to the amount by partial payment of the loan or by future advances but each such act does not create a new separate security interest. As one commentary points out: ". . . to what extent is the lienor harmed by being subordinated to legitimate future advances (obligatory or voluntary) made under an existing loan agreement? We have hypothesized successive loans on April 1 and May 1 with a lien attaching on April 15. If the lienor has the machinery sold, he will succeed in reaching the debtor's equity in the machinery (its value less the April 1 loan, if we have no other interests to worry about). If he delays the sale until after May 1, he will still reach the debtor's equity, but that will now have been diminished by the May 1 loan. However, the debtor's assets have not been depleted: the May 1 advance balances the diminution of his equity in the machinery. The lienor will now receive less from the sale of the machinery than he would have received before May 1, but his chance of collecting his claim from the debtor's remaining assets (which now include the May 1 advance) is as good as ever; presumably it is better than ever since the debtor now has a new supply of working capital. Our lienor is a judgment lienor and thus by hypothesis a creditor who was originally unsecured. He does not seem to be unduly prejudiced by subordination to the subsequent advance if he chooses to wait before having the property sold or throwing the debtor into bankruptcy." (2 Gilmore, supra, at 939.)

Thus petitioner is entitled to priority for the full amount of the loans provided, however, that the second advance was made in good faith and was not simply a method, as respondent Adelphi contends, of depriving respondent of its right to collection of its judgment. That issue cannot be decided solely upon the papers submitted on this proceeding and accordingly is referred to the Honorable Samuel S. Tripp, special referee of this court, to hear and report with his findings and recommendations. If it appears that the second advance was made in bad faith, then the further issue of which of the loans were made after respondent Adelphi delivered execution to the sheriff is also referred to the honorable special referee.

Accordingly, the levy is vacated and petitioner is adjudged to have the right of possession and sale of the equipment and inventory of the debtor. The balance of the motion is held in abeyance pending the return of the special referee's report. . . .

NOTES & QUESTIONS

1. *1972 amendment.* How would *Friedlander* be decided under 1972 UCC 9-301(4)? Would the secured party have priority if he learned of the sheriff's levy ten days after the levy and three weeks later he made an optional advance to debtor? What if the secured party did not know of the levy and two months later made an optional advance to the debtor? Would it make any difference if the lien creditor knew that future advances might be made to the judgment debtor by a secured party? Note that the 45-day period was chosen to conform with the Federal Tax Lien Act of 1966. We will examine the tax legislation in Chapter 7.

2. *Use of future advance clauses.* Note the collateral (equipment *and* inventory) used in *Friedlander.* Would a secured party financing the purchase of equipment want to include a future advance clause in its security agreement with the debtor even if future advances were not contemplated? See the security agreement set out in the prototype transaction in Chapter 3.

One commentator suggests several prerequisites of future advance lending will be used. "First, of course, the borrower must be in a sufficiently risky financial position so that the lender demands security; he must be unable to get his loan except on a secured basis. Second, the law must make valuable property available as collateral. . . . Third, the lender must be unwilling to make his loan except bit by bit, and the borrower must be able to make use of the loan in this form. For example, the manufacturer of textiles whose production involves a number of time-consuming interrelated steps may be able to take advantage of a future advances loan. Fourth, the collateral must be, or must be capable of becoming, valuable enough to cover the entire sum of advances." Comment, Priority of Future Advances Lending Under the Uniform Commercial Code, 35 U. Chi. L. Rev. 128, 129-130 (1967). Does equipment financing fall within this commentator's framework?

3. *One or many security interests.* The court in *Friedlander* refers to the debate by distinguished commentators on whether under the 1962 UCC successive loans against the same collateral create separate security interests or only one. One commentator summarizes several points made in the debate as follows:

"1. Since the future advances agreement seems analogous to the after-acquired property clause, which, under [UCC 9-204(1)], creates a series of security interests as the debtor obtains rights in the collateral, the future advances relationship, like the after-acquired property clause, should create a series of security interests as well. To avoid conceptual inconsistency, then, a discrete interests view should be adopted.

"In reply to this argument a distinction between the concept of old rights in new collateral and the concept of new rights in old collateral may be drawn. There is, therefore, no conceptual inconsistency when differing priority rules which embody these different concepts are used in differing situations. Even though under UCC 9-204(1) a series of security interests arises as the debtor acquires rights in the collateral it does not follow that the secured party's interest in after-acquired property will be subordinated to the interest of intervening secured or lien creditors, since the debtor acquires rights in his collateral subject to the rights of the secured party. Just because collateral is acquired in lumps, then, does not mean that rights in that collateral must be also.

"2. Under [UCC 9-203(1)] a security interest cannot attach until "value is given;" UCC 1-201(37) states that a security interest "secures payment or performance of an obligation." Thus, each time the debtor becomes obligated to repay the lender—and new obligations are being created with every advance—a new security interest is created to secure performance of his obligation. Therefore, a series of discrete security interests is created.

"In reply it may be said that UCC [9-203(1)] and 1-201(37) speak only to the creation of security interests, not their extent. There is nothing inconsistent between these sections and the opposing single interest view of the security interest. One may grant that an obligation is created when value is given, and merely add that the security interest, once created to secure payment or performance of an obligation, may continue to grow as more obligations fall under its protection. A series of obligations does not preclude a single, mushrooming security interest which grows to embrace those obligations." [Comment, Priority of Future Advances Lending Under the Uniform Commercial Code, 35 U. Chi. L. Rev. 128, 137-139 (1967).]

How does the 1972 UCC resolve this conceptual question? See UCC 9-301(4), 9-307(3), 9-312(7). Does the conceptual debate get at the underlying policies of Article 9, such as the encouragement of future advance arrangements?

4. *Need for future advance clause in original agreement.* In which of the following cases does the secured party have a perfected security interest securing the future advance? Assume that the original security interest is perfected by filing a financing statement.

(a) The original security agreement includes a future advance clause. A future advance is made, at which time debtor signs another security agreement granting a security interest in the same collateral.

(b) The original security agreement includes a future advance clause but debtor does not sign another security agreement when the future advance is made.

(c) There is no future advance clause in the original security agreement but when the future advance is made debtor signs another security agreement.

(d) There is no future advance clause in the original security agreement, and when the future advance is made debtor does not sign another security agreement.

Would the filing of a new financing statement at the time of the future advance make a difference in your answer to any of the above?

KIMBELL FOODS, INC. v. REPUBLIC NATIONAL BANK
557 F.2d 491, 23 UCC Rep. 177 (5th Cir. 1977), *aff'd,* 440 U.S. 715, 26 UCC Rep. 1 (1979)

[O.K. Supermarkets, Inc. executed three security agreements and financing statements to Kimbell. The first, in August 1966, secured a $20,000 promissory note from Kimbell Foods, Inc. This agreement was entered into to enable O.K. to expand to a new location by delaying a balance owing to Kimbell. The collateral listed included supermarket equipment and fixtures and "[a]ll goods, wares and merchandise and any and all additions or accessions thereto." In April and November of 1968, O.K. executed the remaining security agreements and financing statements to secure a $27,000 promissory note from Kimbell. The note was issued to delay payment of a balance owing Kimbell so O.K. could pay off a debt owing to Associated Grocers. The collateral for these two agreements was again specifically identified equipment normally used in a supermarket and "[a]ll goods, wares, merchandise and stock in trade and accessions." Each of the security agreements was duly filed, and no termination statement was filed on any of the agreements. Each of the security agreements included the provision that "said security interest also being given to secure the payment of all other indebtedness at any time hereafter owing by Debtor to Secured Party as well as the discharge of all obligations imposed upon Debtor hereunder."

On February 2, 1969, O.K. borrowed $300,000 from Republic National Bank of Dallas. The Small Business Administration guaranteed 90 percent of this loan. On February 18, 1969, Republic filed with the secretary of state of the State of Texas a security agreement and financing statement executed by O.K. to Republic granting it a security interest in all of the debtor's machinery, fixtures, equipment, inventory, and all additions and accessions thereto. When O.K. defaulted on this note the SBA paid Republic 90 percent of the outstanding indebtedness, some $252,313.93, and on January 21, 1971, Republic assigned to the SBA 90 percent of the note and financing statement.

When Republic made its loan, O.K. owed Kimbell $24,893.10 on the 1968 note for $27,000. O.K. paid off this note from the Republic loan proceeds. Thus both the 1966 note and the 1968 note between O.K. and Kimbell had been satisfied. O.K. still, however, owed Kimbell $18,390.93 on open account for inventory purchases. After February 12, 1969, O.K. paid Kimbell $18,390.93 against that debt—payments Kimbell credited to O.K.'s oldest outstanding balances. O.K. kept on making inventory purchases from Kimbell on open account until January 15, 1971. By then the balance of O.K.'s account with Kimbell was $18,258.57. On January 15, 1971, Kimbell filed suit in Texas courts to recover that amount and, on January 31, 1972, obtained a judgment for $24,445.37—$18,258.57 principal, $1,186.80 interest and $5,000 attorneys' fees.]

By agreement there was a bulk sale of the fixtures, equipment, and inventory of three O.K. stores and both the SBA and Kimbell claimed priority in the $86,672 of proceeds. The appellate court first considered whether Kimbell had a security interest securing the open account.]

Gee, Circuit Judge. . . . We must first determine whether the district court properly held that Kimbell's security agreements securing the 1966 and 1968 notes did not cover the advances Kimbell made to O.K. on open account. The security agreements provide that the security interest also secures the payment of future indebtedness between the parties. Texas law countenances such so-called "dragnet clauses." See UCC 9-204(5) [1972 UCC 9-204(3)]. Acknowledging this apparent approval of future advance clauses, the district court ruled that the future advance clause did not operate in this case. It relied on pre-Code Texas cases and UCC cases from other jurisdictions to restrict the application of the future advance clause to future debts clearly contemplated by the parties. So reasoning, it ruled that in this case the parties meant the security agreements to cover only the notes for which they were executed, not later purchases on open account. We view the transactions differently.

Although the district court correctly stated the law of Texas, it arrived at the wrong conclusion in light of Texas' application of its law. Texas courts do not recognize the application of a future advance clause unless the future advance to be secured was "reasonably within the contemplation of the parties to the mortgage at the time it was made." Wood v. Parker Square State Bank, 400 S.W.2d 898, 901 (Tex. 1966). . . . Consistent with this view, in Texas a future advance clause in a mortgage does not secure a subsequent debt from the debtor to a third party acquired from the third party by the mortgagee. See *Wood*, supra. In circumstances similar to those at bar, however, Texas courts have hinted that future advance clauses will be effective. In *Wood*, for example, the Texas Supreme Court remarked that: "The more reasonable construction of this general language [a future advance clause] is that it referred to obligations directly arising between Lincoln Enterprises [the original debtor] and respondent bank [the original lender], i.e., where Lincoln became obligated to the bank as the maker of an obligation, or became liable in a secondary capacity in favor of the bank." . . . In light of this evidence we conclude that in Texas a further extension of credit to the debtor by the lender is deemed future indebtedness reasonably contemplated by the parties when they execute a future advance clause.

The district court concluded that the parties did not intend the future advance clause to cover purchases on open account because the security agreements were intended to cover only the amounts loaned under a promissory note. In reaching this conclusion, however, the district court ignored two important factors: the parol evidence rule and Texas' treatment of future advance clauses in analogous situations. The district court admitted testimony by

Harold Kindle, the president of O.K., about the subjective intention of the parties when they executed the 1966 and 1968 notes, security agreements and financing statements. Although his testimony was equivocal, the district court understood him to say that the parties intended each transaction to be separate and distinct. Admission of such testimony was error. The language of the contract, unless ambiguous, represents the intention of the parties. The intent deduced from this objective matter, not the parties' subjective understandings, is controlling. . . . Testimony as to O.K.'s subjective intent in receiving the future advance clause was a classic violation of the parol evidence rule and clearly inadmissible.

The district court compounded this error by failing to consider the truest test of the parties' intention, the words of the contract clearly providing that the security agreement should cover future indebtedness. In Estes v. Republic National Bank, 462 S.W.2d 273 (Tex. 1970), the Texas Supreme Court upheld the applicability of a future advance clause despite the debtor's claim of an oral agreement that the deed of trust containing the future advance clause was intended as a separate transaction not to extend to other indebtedness between the parties. In the absence of some evidence that the "dragnet clause" was placed in the contract by mutual mistake, the court found that the clause clearly and unequivocally stated the intention of the parties for the land to secure the debtor's other loans from the bank. See also *Wood,* supra. In light of the *Estes* and *Wood* cases, the district court improperly discarded these future advance clauses.

The district court also relied on the circumstances surrounding the 1966 and 1968 loans in finding that the parties treated each loan as a separate and distinct agreement for a specific, nonrecurring purpose and to determine that the later inventory purchases were unrelated. Examining the documents and the circumstances surrounding their execution, we find nothing that negates the parties' statement that the security agreements cover the inventory purchases on account.

The 1966 promissory note was entered into to free O.K.'s current cash flow to purchase fixtures for a new store and to allow O.K. to buy opening inventory from Kimbell on credit. At least in part, then, the 1966 security agreement contemplated the purchase of inventory on credit. The security agreement states that it is given "to secure an advance of goods, wares and merchandise and does not include a preexisting debt." Under these circumstances we cannot say that later inventory purchases on credit by O.K. were "unrelated" to the 1966 security agreement or involved future advances "not of the same class" so as to negate the applicability of the future advance clause, as the district court held. See 401 F. Supp. at 325-326.

Again in 1968, O.K.'s promissory note allowed it to delay payment on its open-account purchases so as to free current cash flow to pay off a debt owed Associated Grocers, Inc. The 1968 security agreement and financing statements were again related to Kimbell's inventory advances on open account to

O.K.[8] Although the notes, security agreements and financing statel
executed in response to special factual circumstances, those circumsu
not necessarily inconsistent with giving the future advance clauses
agreements their plain meaning . . . holding that Kimbell's 1966 ar.
security agreements and financing statements covered its later advar.
inventory to O.K. on open account. . . .

NOTE

Professor Grant Gilmore comments as follows on the enforceability of
"dragnet" clauses: "However 'covered by the security agreement' is to be
read, [UCC 9-204(3)] should certainly not be taken to overrule the so-called
'dragnet' cases under pre-Code law. Legitimate future advance arrangements
are validated under the Code, as indeed they generally were under pre-Code
law. This useful device can, however, be abused; it is abused when a lender,
relying on a broadly drafted clause, seeks to bring within the shelter of his
security arrangement claims against the debtor which are unrelated to the
course of financing that was contemplated by the parties. In the dragnet cases,
the courts have regularly curbed such abuses: no matter how the clause is
drafted, the future advances, to be covered, must 'be of the same class as the
primary obligation . . . and so related to it that the consent of the debtor to its
inclusion may be inferred.' The same tests of 'similarity' and 'relatedness,'
vague but useful, should be applied to [UCC 9-204(3)]." 2 G. Gilmore, Security Interests in Personal Property 932 (1965). Are you persuaded?

Problem 6-3. Debtor grants Bank a security interest in his accounts to
secure periodic loans to be made to him by the Bank. The security agreement
and the financing statement both indicate that Bank will not permit Debtor to
have total outstanding loans of more than $100,000 at any one time. The
parties subsequently agree formally to increase this amount to $150,000, but
no change is made in the financing statement. Soon after the agreement
Debtor goes bankrupt owing $140,000 to Bank. Can the trustee in bankruptcy
successfully attack the validity of Bank's security interest?

Problem 6-4. Manufacturer and Retailer enter into an agreement under
which Manufacturer supplies goods on secured credit. The security agreement
provides that "[t]he security interest in Retailer's inventory shall cover any
and all obligations of whatever kind owed by Retailer to Manufacturer and
shall include obligations owed by Retailer to any subsidiary or affiliate of

---

8. O.K.'s failure to demand a termination statement under UCC 9-404(1) after paying off
the 1968 note also tends to discredit the claim that the security agreements applied only to the
1966 and 1968 notes.

Manufacturer." Manufacturer promptly files a financing statement in the proper office describing the collateral as "Inventory, now owned or hereafter acquired, supplied by Manufacturer or any of its subsidiaries or affiliates."

(a) Subsidiary, a corporation wholly-owned by Manufacturer, supplies goods to Retailer. Does Manufacturer have a perfected security interest securing this obligation? Does Subsidiary?

(b) Subsidiary assigns its claim against Retailer to Manufacturer. Does Manufacturer have a perfected security interest securing this obligation? What if the security agreement provides only that "[t]he security interest shall cover any and all obligations of whatever kind owed by Retailer to Manufacturer"?

3.   Proceeds (UCC 9-306)

We have already examined most of the rules governing proceeds:

1. Attachment. UCC 9-306(2) provides that a security interest continues in identifiable proceeds of collateral notwithstanding disposition of the collateral. This security interest will automatically attach to the proceeds unless the parties otherwise agree. UCC 9-203(3).

2. Perfection. If the security interest in the original collateral was perfected the security interest in the proceeds will automatically be perfected for ten days and will continue to be perfected if the secured party meets the conditions of UCC 9-306(3).

3. Priorities. The general priority rule is that the date of filing or perfection as to the original collateral is also the date of filing or perfection as to proceeds. See UCC 9-312(6). Special priority rules are set out to govern cases where one of the secured parties had a purchase money security interest in the original collateral. UCC 9-312(3), (4).

Where collateral consists of inventory the secured party usually will explicitly authorize the sale or other disposition of the collateral in the ordinary course of business. Even if he does not do so the interest will usually be cut off by UCC 9-307(1). As a result the secured party will be particularly concerned that the security interest continue in the proceeds as a perfected interest with the same priority as in the original inventory. The proceeds will usually be "cash proceeds" (money, checks, deposit accounts, and the like), chattel paper, or accounts. These proceeds may in turn be used to acquire new inventory— proceeds of proceeds.

A major priority problem occurs where another secured party makes a direct claim to accounts receivable. Prior to the 1972 amendments some commentators argued that an inventory financer should have priority over the receivables financer because the former appears earlier in the distribution cycle. Others objected that such a rule would be difficult to apply and would discourage receivables financing. Some even argued that receivables financers

should always prevail because in practice these financers were more important. The 1972 amendments resolve the debate by granting priority under the
general rule that the first to file or to perfect prevails. UCC 9-312(5).

The 1972 amendments also clarify the problem of priority where an inventory financer competes for proceeds with a purchase money secured party.
The original secured party, if properly notified, is subordinated with respect
both to the new inventory and to cash proceeds received by the debtor before
he delivers the inventory to a buyer; the original secured party prevails as to
all other proceeds. UCC 9-312(3). This rule thus differs from UCC 9-312(4),
which states that the purchase money secured party has priority as to proceeds
where the original collateral is property other than inventory.

Problem 6-5. To secure repayment of a loan Dealer grants Bank a security interest in its inventory of mobile homes. Bank files a financing statement
with the secretary of state describing the collateral as "mobile home inventory." Dealer subsequently sells a mobile home to Homer, who trades in a
used mobile home in partial payment, gives a check for the remaining down
payment, and signs a note and security agreement for the balance of the
purchase price. Bank first learns of the sale two weeks later.

(a) Does Bank have a perfected security interest in the used mobile
home?

(b) Does Bank have a perfected security interest in the check while it is in
Dealer's possession?

(c) Does Bank have a perfected security interest in the note and security
agreement? (The note and security agreement together constitute chattel paper. UCC 9-105(1)(b).)

(d) If Homer had signed only a note without a security agreement would
Bank have a perfected security interest in the note?

(e) If Dealer deposits the check in a special deposit account maintained
at Bank for proceeds will Bank have a perfected security interest in the deposit
account? See UCC 9-104(l).

(f) If Dealer, instead of depositing Homer's check with Bank, uses the
check as part payment for the purchase of another mobile home for its inventory will Bank have a perfected security interest in the new mobile home?

(g) If Dealer, instead of depositing the check with Bank, indorses the
check to Supplier in payment of the purchase of an adding machine will Bank
have a perfected security interest in the adding machine?

Problem 6-6. In 1961 Debtor purchased a tractor truck from Mack and
granted Mack a security interest in the truck to secure the purchase price.
Mack promptly perfected its interest by filing a financing statement as required by local law but did not indicate on the statement that the security
interest covered proceeds.

In March, 1964, Debtor granted Prudential a security interest in the same truck. The financing statement filed by Prudential at this time claimed proceeds.

In June, 1964, Debtor traded in the truck as part payment applied to the purchase of a new truck bought from United. United retained a security interest in the new truck to secure the remaining purchase price and United assigned the interest to C.I.T., a finance company, which perfected this interest by filing a financing statement in July, 1964. Collision insurance was taken out on the new truck in an amount equal to the "actual cash value of the vehicle at the time of loss" and C.I.T. was listed as loss payee in the policy.

In August, 1964, the new truck was demolished, leaving only an undetermined salvage value. Soon thereafter the Debtor informed United about Mack's security interest in the old truck and, at United's insistence, Debtor assigned his interest in the insurance payout to United.

What claims do Debtor, Mack, Prudential, United, and C.I.T. have in (a) the old truck, (b) the new truck, and (c) the insurance payout? As to each of these items, what is the ranking of priorities? Assume, first, that the 1962 UCC applies and then reconsider in the light of the 1972 amendments.

Problem 6-7. Austin State Bank finances the purchase of a bookbinder by Apex, and Apex grants the bank a security interest in the bookbinder to secure repayment of the loan. Three months after the purchase Apex discovers a latent defect in the bookbinder that Apex alleges reduces its value by $10,000. Apex brings an action against ABM, the seller, for breach of express and implied warranties. If Apex does recover from ABM what part of the recovery can the bank claim under its security agreement?

UNIVERSAL C.I.T. CREDIT CORP. v. FARMERS BANK
358 F. Supp. 317, 13 UCC Rep. 109 (E.D. Mo. 1973)

WEBSTER, District Judge. . . . Gerald W. Ryan, doing business as Ryan-Chevrolet and Olds Co., a proprietorship, operated an automobile dealership in Portageville, Missouri. On or about June 18, 1968, Ryan entered into an agreement with plaintiff [C.I.T.] for wholesale financing, commonly known as floor plan financing. Under the terms of this agreement, plaintiff from time to time advanced funds to pay the manufacturer's invoice on new automobiles, acquiring a security in such automobiles. As each automobile was sold by Ryan, he was required to remit plaintiff's advance. These remittances were in the form of checks drawn on Ryan's checking account at defendant's bank. The financing statements filed in New Madrid County reflect the security interest in the proceeds of the sale of the automobiles. Proper filing is not disputed.

Toward the end of 1969, plaintiff decided for reasons of policy, but primarily because it had not been supplied with current financial statements, to terminate the floor plan arrangement. Ryan was notified that the floor plan would be terminated December 31, 1969.

Sometime after 3:00 P.M. on January 15, 1970, Ryan had a conversation with Richard L. Saalwaechter, President of defendant bank. Ryan told Saalwaechter that he was being put out of the business by plaintiff since plaintiff had revoked the floor plan, and that he wanted to be sure that the bank got paid. He said "let C.I.T. be last—they put me out of business." Ryan discussed his debt to the bank on a demand promissory note. He told Saalwaechter that he wanted the bank to be safe on its loan. Ryan asked Saalwaechter to debit his account and credit the bank with $12,000 from his checking account. Saalwaechter than verified Ryan's checking account and determined that there was a balance of $16,340.00. When Saalwaechter suggested that Ryan write a check to the bank, Ryan told him that he preferred that the bank run a debit against the account because C.I.T. was after him and he didn't know what they could do to him. Ryan further told Saalwaechter that C.I.T. had checks out, and that he wanted to make a cash withdrawal to keep C.I.T. from getting its checks. Thereupon, although the bank's business day had closed at 3:00 P.M., Saalwaechter debited Ryan's account in the amount of $12,000. The next morning, January 16th, Ryan came to the bank and made a cash withdrawal of $3,100.00. Saalwaechter testified that he had no knowledge that any of Ryan's checks to C.I.T. were in the bank until after the debit and the withdrawal.

The funds in dispute derive from the sale by Ryan of six motor vehicles. In some cases, a trade-in was involved with which we are not concerned. In each case, Ryan received a check from the purchaser in payment of the cash portion of the deal. Each check was deposited in Ryan's account with defendant bank and he received full credit therefor. Each automobile sold and the proceeds thereof were subject to plaintiff's security interest. The checks representing the proceeds of the six automobiles sold by Ryan were all deposited on or prior to January 15, 1970 and aggregate $18,112.44.

Ryan executed and delivered to plaintiff five checks pursuant to the security agreement representing remittances for sums advanced by C.I.T. on account of such automobiles pursuant to the security agreement. These checks were deposited by plaintiff in its bank January 13, 1970. . . . [T]he five Ryan checks in controversy were received by defendant bank on January 15, [1970] during banking hours. . . .

At some time on the afternoon of January 16, 1970, the bank discovered that there were insufficient funds with which to pay the five checks presented by plaintiff for payment, the bank having debited Ryan's account for $12,000 and Ryan having withdrawn $3,100 earlier that morning. Payment was refused and the checks were returned by mail through channels. . . .

It is not disputed that plaintiff had a continuously perfected security interest in six automobiles and their proceeds. (See UCC 9-306(3).) Ryan sold separately each of these automobiles and deposited the amount received on each sale in his checking account at the defendant bank. Funds from other sources were deposited in the checking account prior to and contemporaneously with such deposits. Numerous checks were issued on the account between the time of the first and last sale. Plaintiff contends that the defendant bank was not entitled to debit Ryan's checking account in the amount of $12,000 on January 15, 1970, relying upon UCC 9-306(2), which provides:

> Except where this Article otherwise provides, a security interest continues in collateral notwithstanding sale, exchange or other disposition thereof by the debtor unless his action was authorized by the secured party in the security agreement or otherwise, and also continues in any *identifiable* proceeds including collections received by the debtor. (Emphasis supplied.) [1972 UCC 9-306(2) makes stylistic amendments.—EDS.]

Defendant contends that the proceeds from the sales of the six automobiles were not "identifiable" within the meaning of UCC 9-306(2). Defendant argues that when the proceeds were deposited and thereby commingled with other funds in Ryan's account and thereafter substantial withdrawals were made exceeding the amount of the deposited proceeds, the proceeds completely lost their identity. No Missouri case defines the term "identifiable" as used in this section. It is provided in UCC 1-103 that all supplemental bodies of law continue to apply to commercial contracts except insofar as displaced by the particular provisions of the Uniform Commercial Code. Applying UCC 1-103, this court concludes that proceeds are "identifiable" if they can be traced in accordance with the state law governing the transaction. Missouri has recognized in an analogous situation—suits to impose a constructive trust—that special funds may be traced into commingled funds. Perry v. Perry, 484 S.W.2d 257 (Mo. 1972). The mere fact that the proceeds from the sales of the six automobiles were commingled with other funds and subsequent withdrawals were made from the commingled account does not render the proceeds unidentifiable under Missouri law. As the court said in Perry v. Perry: ". . . where a defaulting trustee has first commingled the trust funds with his own and then paid them out in satisfaction of his own debts, it will be presumed that the payment was made from his own contribution to the commingled fund, 'and not out of the trust money,' so that whatever is left is the money for which he is accountable in his fiduciary capacity. . . ." Perry v. Perry, 484 S.W.2d 257, 259 (Mo. 1972).

Before tracing the proceeds, it is necessary to decide whether under the circumstances in this case the defendant bank was entitled to debit Ryan's checking account if the account contained proceeds from the sales of the six automobiles. Comment 2(c) to UCC 9-306 provides: "Where cash proceeds are covered into the debtor's checking account and paid out in the operation of the debtor's business, recipients of the funds of course take free of any claim which the secured party may have in them as proceeds. What has been said relates to payments and transfers in ordinary course. *The law of fraudulent con-*

veyances would no doubt in appropriate cases support recovery of proceeds by a secured party from a transferee out of ordinary course or otherwise in collusion with the debtor to defraud the secured party." (Emphasis supplied.) There are no Missouri cases on point. However, Missouri has long recognized that one indicia of a fraudulent conveyance is a transaction outside the usual course of doing business. Bank of New Cambria v. Briggs, 236 S.W.2d 289, 291 (Mo. 1971). In Missouri, "fraud, like any other *fact,* may be established by circumstantial evidence [and] [t]here are circumstances which have come to be recognized as indicia or badges of fraud, one of which circumstances alone may not prove fraud, but may warrant an inference of fraud, especially where there is a concurrence of several indicia of fraud." Id. Ryan told Saalwaechter that plaintiff had revoked the floor plan and that he wanted the bank to be safe on its loan. Ryan asked Saalwaechter to debit his account. When Saalwaechter suggested that Ryan write a check to the bank, Ryan indicated that he preferred the bank run a debit against the account and further informed Saalwaechter that he had issued checks to plaintiff and wished to keep plaintiff from collecting on the checks. All of these events, including the debit to Ryan's account, transpired after the close of business on January 15, 1970. These facts clearly show that the debit of Ryan's account was not in the ordinary course of business. Although, as indicated above, there are no Missouri cases directly on point, this court concludes that the Missouri courts would not, under these circumstances, permit the defendant bank to retain the amount debited outside the usual course of business and thereby defeat the security interest of plaintiff in the identifiable proceeds of the sale of the six automobiles.

Support for this conclusion is also found in the law governing a bank's right of set-off. As a general rule an account constituting a general deposit is subject to the bank's right of set-off. . . . An exception to that general rule is that a bank is not entitled to a set-off where it has "sufficient knowledge of facts relating to the interests of others in the account as to put the bank on inquiry to ascertain the trust character of the account." Northern Insurance Co. v. Traders Gate City National Bank, 186 S.W.2d 491, 497 (Mo. Ct. App. 1945). . . . The *Northern Insurance Co.* case indicates that the bank's knowledge of the "trust character" of a deposit can be shown by indirect evidence or by showing that the bank would have sufficient information to put it on inquiry as to the trust character of the deposit. 186 S.W.2d at 498. The bank's knowledge that Ryan had floor plan financing with plaintiff, that Ryan had issued checks to plaintiff which Ryan did not want collected by plaintiff, and Ryan's insistence that the bank run a debit against his account, coupled with the communication of such facts after banking hours, were sufficient to put the bank on inquiry as to the possible trust character of all or part of the funds deposited in Ryan's account. Moreover, it is disputable whether the bank, even absent knowledge of the above facts, would be entitled to a set-off. In Associates Discount Corp. v. Fidelity Union Trust Co., 268 A.2d 330, 7 UCC Rep. 1350 (N.J. Super. 1970), a bank set off part of an account of one of its debtors which contained proceeds in which another party held a continuously perfected security interest. The defendant relied on UCC 9-104(i) which provides: "[T]his Chapter does not apply . . . (i) to any right of set-off. . . ." In response to the defendant's argument that it was entitled to the right of set-off, the court said: "This section, however, cannot mean that a general creditor, as the bank is here with respect to the funds in question, may abrogate a perfected security interest simply by having a right to an opportunity for a set-off. All this section means is that a right of set-off may exist in a creditor who does not have a security interest." 268 A.2d at 332. The bank then contended that it was entitled to a set-off in the account in the absence of actual knowledge on its part that the funds in the account were subject to a security interest. The defendant relied on cases decided prior to the adoption of the Uniform Commercial Code in New Jersey. In response, the court said: "However, these cases, if applicable, are subject to the superior authority of the Legislature which, by enacting the Uniform Commercial Code, continued a plaintiff's security interest in the identifiable proceeds of sales of the collateral. UCC 9-306(2)." Id.

This court's final task is to trace the proceeds of the sales of the six automobiles to determine if they were taken by the bank when it debited Ryan's account after the close of business on January 15, 1970. As indicated above, Perry v. Perry, 484 S.W.2d 257, 259, stated the general rule that in tracing commingled funds it is presumed that any payments made were from other than the funds in which another had a legally recognized interest. This is commonly referred to as the "lowest intermediate balance" rule. Restatement of Trusts, Second, §202, Comment j provides in pertinent part:

> j. Effect of withdrawals and subsequent additions. Where the trustee deposits in a single account in a bank trust funds and his individual funds, and makes withdrawals from the deposit and dissipates the money so withdrawn, and subsequently makes additional deposits of his individual funds in the account, the beneficiary cannot ordinarily enforce an equitable lien upon the deposit for a sum greater than the lowest intermediate balance of the deposit. . . .

Illustration 20 to Comment j is as follows: "A is trustee for B of $1,000. He deposits this money together with $1000 of his own in a bank. He draws out $1500 and dissipates it. He later deposits $1000 of his own in the account. He [B] is entitled to a lien on the account for $500, the lowest intermediate balance." Comment j, Illustration 20, Restatement of Trusts §202 at 544 and Restatement of Trusts, Second, §202 at 451. The situation in the instant case differs from Comment j and the Illustration in one respect. We have not one, but six, separate deposits of funds of a "trust character" spanning a period of nearly a month, during which time a substantial number of withdrawals and deposits of other funds were made in the account. Comment m to the Restatement of Trusts, Second, §202 at 453 provides:

m. *Subsequent additions by way of restitution.* Where the trustee deposits trust funds in his individual account in a bank, and makes withdrawals from the deposit and dissipates the money so withdrawn, and subsequently makes additional deposits of his individual funds in the account, *manifesting an intention to make restitution of* the trust funds withdrawn, the beneficiary's lien upon the deposit is not limited to the lowest intermediate balance.

Where the deposit of trust funds and of his individual funds was *in an account in the name of the trustee as such, and not in his individual account,* and he withdraws more than the amount of his individual funds, and subsequently deposits his individual funds in the account, the beneficiary's lien upon the deposit is not limited to the lowest intermediate balance since the new deposit will be treated as *made by way of restitution of the trust funds previously withdrawn.* (Emphasis supplied.)

Thus, individual funds subsequently deposited to a trust account by the trustee are presumed to be by way of restitution. Perry v. Perry, 484 S.W.2d 257, 259. Subsequent deposits by the trustee to his own account, on the other hand, are not so treated unless the trustee "manifests an intention to make restitution." No such manifestation of intent was shown in this case. Therefore, subsequent deposits of funds not relating to the proceeds from the sales of the six automobiles in Ryan's individual d/b/a account will not be treated as made by way of restitution of trust funds previously withdrawn.

However, each deposit of the proceeds of the sales of the six automobiles will be treated as additions to the trust fund, and the lowest intermediate balance theory will be followed.

It was stipulated at trial that the following deposits were received by Ryan from the sale of the six automobiles and their proceeds in which plaintiff held a continuously perfected security interest:

	Vehicle	Serial no.	Purchaser	Date of deposit	Amount
1.	1969 Chev.	866578	Campbell	12–19–69	$5,700.00
2.	1970 Olds.	217371	Faulkner	12–20–69	4,125.00
3.	1969 Chev.	890453	Hunter	1–09–70	1,599.94
4.	1970 Chev.	138013	Carlisle	1–12–70	2,237.50
5.	1970 Olds.	160314	Rone	1–15–70	2,700.00
6.	1970 Chev.	141638	Hendricks	1–15–70	1,750.00

The court has examined the banking records of the Ryan account and finds that the identifiable proceeds in which plaintiff held a continuously perfected security interest on January 15, 1970 prior to the bank's $12,000 debit entry was $11,429.11. This amount may be traced according to the following summarization:

Date	"Proceeds" deposited	End balance	"Proceeds" remaining in account
12-18-69		$ 710.74	
12-19-69	(1) 5,700.00	9,100.58	5,700.00
12-20-69	(2) 4,125.00	9,709.90	*9,709.90
12-24-69		6,201.41	*6,201.41
1-02-70		4,715.30	*4,715.30
1-09-70	(3) 1,599.94	11,987.65	6,315.24
1-12-70	(4) 2,237.50	15,426.72	8,552.74
1-14-70		6,979.11	*6,979.11
1-15-70	(5) 2,700.00		
	(6) 1,750.00	16,340.00	11,429.11

* Lowest Intermediate Balance

On January 15, 1970, the bank debited against the Ryan account checks aggregating $516.65 and in addition made the $12,000 debit entry in its favor. The $12,000 debit entry was made at 3:00 P.M. after the close of business. It may, therefore, be inferred that the checks aggregating $516.65 were received prior thereto in the ordinary course on January 15, 1970 during banking hours. The pro forma balance prior to the $12,000 debit entry was, therefore, $15,823.35. Subtracting from this amount the "proceeds" remaining in the account ($11,429.11), the amount which the bank was entitled to debit was $4,394.24. Accordingly, plaintiff is entitled to recover from the bank the excess amount debited, or $7,605.76. That amount is identified as proceeds in which plaintiff had a perfected security interest, and plaintiff is entitled to recover this amount, together with interest at 6% from October 26, 1970, the filing date of the complaint. The Clerk will enter judgment in favor of plaintiff on Count II in accordance with this Memorandum. . . .

MAXL SALES CO. v. CRITIQUES, INC. (IN RE CRITIQUES, INC.)

29 B.R. 941, 36 UCC Rep. 1778 (Bankr. D. Kan. 1983)

[On August 31, 1981, Critiques, Inc. executed a $12,000.00 note and security agreement to Maxl. The security agreement listed inventory, furniture, fixtures, equipment, accounts receivable, intangibles and any proceeds thereof as collateral. On September 2, 1981, Maxl caused a UCC-1 financing statement to be filed with the Kansas secretary of state. It described the collateral as inventory, furniture, fixtures, equipment, accounts receivable, and intangibles but it did not list proceeds, and the proceeds box was not checked.

Critiques, Inc. ceased doing business on or about November 14, 1981. At this time there was a principal balance due on the note of $4,607.66. On December 14, 1981, Judge Walton appointed a receiver to operate the debtor and hold in trust any net revenue from said operation. The receiver took possession of the debtor's premises on January 1, 1982 and liquidated all of the debtor's inventory in a public sale together with specially purchased inventory to which Maxl made no claim. Gross sales were $130,992.55, expenses were $86,739.77, and net revenue was $44,252.78. The receiver commingled the proceeds of preexisting inventory and specially purchased inventory into one bank account. Maxl was able to trace $119,790.99 of the $130,992.55 in gross proceeds of the sale as proceeds of inventory subject to its security interest. Maxl offered no evidence regarding the amount of cash proceeds received by the debtor within ten days before the bankruptcy petition was filed.]

Benjamin E. FRANKLIN, Bankruptcy Judge: . . . Maxl and the trustee are at odds over who has priority to the proceeds of Maxl's collateral securing the $12,000.00 note. Maxl contends that it has priority by virtue of a perfected security interest in said proceeds, and that it is therefore entitled to reclamation. The trustee contends that Maxl's interest is unperfected and that his interest is therefore superior by virtue of the "strong arm clause" in 11 U.S.C. §544.

The perfection of security interests in proceeds is governed by UCC 9-306. [The court quotes UCC 9-306(1)-(3).] . . . Here Maxl sufficiently demonstrated that it could trace the cash proceeds and identify how much of the gross proceeds were attributable to its security interest under the $12,000.00 note. Thus, Maxl complied with UCC 9-306(3)(b) and its security interest in the proceeds was duly perfected.

However, when the debtor is involved in an insolvency proceeding, a creditor's perfected security interest in proceeds is limited by UCC 9-306(4), which states:

(4) In the event of insolvency proceedings instituted by or against a debtor, a secured party with a perfected security interest in proceeds has a perfected security interest only in the following proceeds:

(a)   in identifiable non-cash proceeds and in separate deposit accounts containing only proceeds;

(b)   in identifiable cash proceeds in the form of money which is neither commingled with other money nor deposited in a deposit account prior to the insolvency proceedings;

(c)   in identifiable cash proceeds in the form of checks and the like which are not deposited in a deposit account prior to the insolvency proceedings; and

(d)   in all cash and deposit accounts of the debtor, in which proceeds have been commingled with other funds, but the perfected security interest under this paragraph (d) is

(i)   subject to any right of set-off; and

(ii) limited to an amount not greater than the amount of any cash proceeds received by the debtor within ten days before the institution of the insolvency proceedings less the sum of (I) the payments to the secured party on account of cash proceeds received by the debtor during such period and (II) the cash proceeds received by the debtor during such period to which the secured party is entitled under paragraphs (a) through (c) of this subsection (4).

Here the filing of the bankruptcy petition constituted an "insolvency proceeding" within the meaning of UCC 9-306(4). Insolvency proceeding is defined in UCC 1-201(22) as follows:

> "Insolvency proceedings" includes any assignment for the benefit of creditors or other proceedings intended to liquidate or rehabilitate the estate of the person involved.

Thus, UCC 9-306(4) applies to limit Maxl's perfected security interest in proceeds.

Specifically, UCC 9-306(4)(c) and (d) apply herein because Maxl had a perfected security interest in identifiable cash proceeds that were commingled with other cash and deposited in a bank account by the receiver, prior to the filing of the bankruptcy petition. UCC 9-306(4)(c) and (d) eliminate a secured party's rights in identifiable but commingled cash proceeds except to the extent that the debtor received any cash proceeds within ten days before the institution of the insolvency proceedings. Matter of Guaranteed Muffler Supply Co., Inc., 1 B.R. 324, 329, 29 UCC Rep. 285 (Bankr. N.D. Ga. 1979). The secured party's right to claim or trace identifiable cash proceeds pursuant to UCC 9-306(3) does not survive in the event of insolvency proceedings and when such identifiable cash proceeds have been commingled with other money or deposited in a bank account. . . . Also see In re Gibson Products of Arizona, 543 F.2d 652, 655 (9th Cir. 1976), *cert. denied,* 430 U.S. 946 (1977) where the court, citing 2 G. Gilmore, Security Interests in Personal Property §45.9, at 1340 (1965), stated: ". . . The intent was to eliminate the expense and nuisance of tracing when funds are commingled and to limit the grasp of secured creditors to the amount received during the last ten days before insolvency proceedings, which, the draftsmen assumed, would usually be less than the same creditor could trace if he had a grip on the entire balance deposited over an unlimited time."

Here the debtor ceased doing business on November 14, 1981, and the receiver completed all sales by June 8, 1982. The bankruptcy petition was filed on September 7, 1982. Clearly no cash proceeds were received by the debtor or the receiver within ten days before September 7th. Moreover, even if the December 14, 1981 appointment of the receiver could be construed as an "insolvency proceeding" there is no evidence that any cash proceeds were received by the debtor within the 10-day period before the appointment of the receiver. In fact, the debtor ceased doing business a full month before the receiver was appointed.

The Court therefore finds that Maxl's perfected security interest in the proceeds was virtually eliminated pursuant to UCC 9-306(4) because of the debtor's bankruptcy and because the receiver, in good faith, commingled Maxl's cash proceeds with all other cash proceeds. Maxl's interest is therefore inferior to the trustee's interest as an ideal lien creditor under 11 U.S.C. §544 and Maxl is not entitled to reclaim the proceeds of the inventory securing the $12,000.00 note.

NOTES & QUESTIONS

1. *"Commingled" and "identifiable" proceeds.* Consider the following interpretation of 1962 UCC 9-306(4)(d): "The general definition of 'proceeds' in UCC 9-306(1) cannot be transplanted into UCC 9-306(4) shorn of its statutory freight. The statute divides 'proceeds' into two categories, 'identifiable' and 'commingled,' i.e., nonidentifiable proceeds, and alters the reach of a perfected security interest, depending upon whether the proceeds are identifiable or nonidentifiable. (Compare UCC 9-306(4)(a), (b), (c) with 9-306(4)(d).) UCC 9-306(4)(d) deals only with nonidentifiable cash proceeds. If the cash proceeds could be 'identified,' i.e., had not been commingled, the secured party would have a perfected security interest in the whole fund under UCC 9-306(4)(b), just as he did in pre-Code days, without any of the limitations imposed by UCC 9-306(4)(d). Under the Code scheme, the secured creditor also has a perfected security interest under subsection (d) when he cannot identify his proceeds in the commingled fund, as long as he can show that some of his proceeds were among those in the commingled fund." Arizona Wholesale Supply Co. v. Itule (In re Gibson Products), 543 F.2d 652, 656, 19 UCC Rep. 1281, 1285-1286 (9th Cir. 1976), *cert. denied,* 430 U.S. 946 (1977). Do the 1972 amendments compel a different interpretation? Do you agree with the interpretation?

2. *Proceeds of collateral in bankruptcy proceedings.* In the *Critiques* case, if the receiver had not sold the inventory but had turned it over to the trustee in bankruptcy, who had then sold it, would Maxl have had a secured claim to the proceeds? See BC 552(b):

> (b) Except as provided in sections 363, 506(c), 522, 544, 545, 547, and 548 of this title, if the debtor and an entity entered into a security agreement before the commencement of the case and if the security interest created by such security agreement extends to property of the debtor acquired before the commencement of the case and to proceeds, product, offspring, rents, or profits of such property, then such security interest extends to such proceeds, product, offspring, rents, or profits acquired by the estate after the commencement of the case to the extent provided by such security agreement and by applicable nonbankruptcy law, except to the extent that the court, after notice and a hearing and based on the equities of the case, orders otherwise.

3. *UCC 9-306(4)(d) as a preferential transfer.* If UCC 9-306(4)(d) does grant a security interest in all debtor's cash and deposit accounts received within 10 days of the bankruptcy petition is there a preferential transfer for bankruptcy purposes? The court in *In re Gibson,* note 1 supra, held that there was a preferential transfer under §60 of the Bankruptcy Act to the extent the secured party could not trace the proceeds of collateral into the commingled account. Does BC 547 change this result?

4. *UCC 9-306(4) as an invalid statutory lien.* Under BC 545(1) a bankruptcy trustee may avoid a statutory lien to the extent it first becomes effective against the debtor upon the debtor's insolvency or when an insolvency proceeding is commenced against the debtor. Does UCC 9-306(4) first become effective upon the debtor's insolvency? Compare the UCC and Bankruptcy Code definitions of insolvency and insolvency proceedings. UCC 1-201(22), (23); BC 101(29). Is the difference significant? See Countryman, Code Security Interests in Bankruptcy, 75 Com. L.J. 269, 274 (1970).

Problem 6-8. Finance Company makes periodic loans to Dealer, who grants Finance Company a security interest in his inventory and proceeds to secure repayment. Finance Company perfects this interest. Under this financing arrangement Dealer deposits proceeds in an account with Bank in which he is to deposit only proceeds and from which he is to withdraw only to turn over the proceeds to Finance Company. On March 1 Finance Company makes a loan of $20,000. Dealer, however, is in financial difficulty and he begins to deposit proceeds in his personal account at Bank. In March, Dealer makes the following deposits to and withdrawals from his account:

	Deposit/Withdrawal	*Closing balance*
March 1	[account has no proceeds]	$ 8,000
2	+ $5,000 proceeds	13,000
4	− $4,000 payroll payment	9,000- *SP, 4s*
5	− $3,000 payment to Finance Co.	6,000 *2P 4s*
8	+ $5,000 proceeds	11,000 *7P 4S*
9	− $2,000 lease payment	9,000 *7P 2S*
10	+ $5,000 proceeds	14,000 *12 P 2s*
11	− $1,000 utilities payment	13,000 *12P 1S*

(a) On March 12 a judgment creditor of Dealer obtains judicial process attaching the bank account. To what extent will Finance Company have priority over the lien creditor?

(b) On March 12 Dealer files a bankruptcy petition. To what extent is Finance Company's claim secured by the bank account?

(c) Bank holds Dealer's demand note for $10,000. After Dealer files the bankruptcy petition Bank wishes to set off the $10,000 against the account. To what extent will Finance Company be affected by Bank's claim to set off? See UCC 9-306(4)(d)(i); BC 362, 506, 553.

C. INVENTORY FINANCING

Assume your client wishes to establish a retail business that sells office and home furniture. The client has approached a finance company to work out a financing arrangement in which the finance company would make periodic loans secured by your client's inventory. The client asks you to review the proposed arrangement from a legal perspective. Being well-trained you begin your review by answering the five basic questions posed at the beginning of Chapter 3, where we first introduced Article 9 secured transactions.

1. **Scope.** Article 9 clearly covers security interests in inventory.[2] UCC 9-102(1)(a) states that Article 9 applies to any transaction intended to create a security interest in goods, and UCC 9-109(4) defines *inventory* as a subcategory of *goods*. Your client's stock of office and home furniture clearly falls within this definition of inventory: they are goods "held by a person who holds them for sale or lease or to be furnished under contracts of service or if he has so furnished them, or if they are raw materials, work in process or materials used or consumed in a business."

To grant a security interest in your client's inventory is also to make a "bulk transfer" within the meaning of UCC Article 6. That Article, however, explicitly excludes from its coverage both the grant of a security interest in

2. California, of course, is an exception to this broad statement. In a nonuniform amendment California restricts the use of inventory as collateral:

§9-102(4). Notwithstanding anything to the contrary in this [Article], no nonpossessory security interest, other than a purchase money security interest, may be given or taken in or to the inventory of a retail merchant held for sale, except in or to inventory consisting of durable goods having a unit retail value of at least five hundred dollars ($500) or motor vehicles, house trailers, trailers, semitrailers, farm and construction machinery and repair parts thereof, or aircraft. . . . The phrase "purchase money security interest" as used in this [sub-section] does not extend to any after-acquired property other than the initial property sold by a secured party or taken by a lender as security as provided in Section 9107. This [sub-section] does not apply to the inventory of a person whose sales for resale exceeded 75 percent in dollar volume of his total sales of all goods during the 12 months preceding the attachment of the security interest. . . .

For a critical analysis of the reasons behind the California legislation, see Summers, Security Interests in a Retail Merchant's Inventory: California Amends the Uniform Commercial Code, 16 Stan. L. Rev. 149, 154-159 (1963) (amendment codifies judicial hostility to unpublicized security interests; author urges repeal).

Subsection (4), as reproduced above, was repealed as of July 1, 1985. Calif. Laws 1984, ch. 1197. The new legislation liberalizes the use of inventory as collateral although there continue to be restrictions where a merchant sells inventory primarily to consumers.

inventory and the repossession of the inventory on default. UCC 6-103(1), (3); see also 9-111. Article 6 is designed to protect creditors of a retail business when the proprietor of the business transfers a "major part" of his inventory out of the ordinary course of trade. The transfer is ineffective against any creditor of the transferor unless notice of the transfer is given in the time and manner prescribed by the statute. Some pre-Code bulk transfer laws applied to "bulk mortgages." The Code draftsmen excluded the inventory financing arrangement because Article 9 provides for notice to creditors and it would be burdensome to require compliance with two different notice requirements.

2. **Attachment.** The three prerequisites for attachment set out in UCC 9-203(1)—security agreement, value, rights in collateral—apply to inventory financing. In addition, the security agreement will normally include both an after-acquired property clause and a future advance clause because the parties contemplate revolving loans and inventory turnover. It will not be necessary to have an explicit clause claiming proceeds because the security interest will continue automatically in the proceeds.

3. **Perfection.** In most cases a secured party, such as your client's finance company, will perfect a security interest in inventory by filing a financing statement following the rules on what, when, and where to file that we have already studied. Several financing patterns, however, involve special rules on perfection and it is possible your client's business will be structured in such a way as to call into play these rules.

(a) Inventory may be in the hands of a bailee that has issued negotiable or nonnegotiable documents of title. To perfect an interest in goods held by an issuer of a negotiable document, such as a terminal warehouse receipt, the secured party must perfect an interest in the document itself, either by filing or by taking possession of the document. UCC 9-304(1), (2); 9-305. Where the bailee has issued only a nonnegotiable document the secured party may perfect its security interest by filing as to the goods, notifying the bailee of its interest, or having the document issued in its name. UCC 9-304(3). See p. 299 infra.

(b) A retailer may sell goods for a supplier under a *consignment agreement* by which the retailer acts as agent for the supplier and has the option of returning unsold inventory. Because the retailer appears to own the consigned goods, special rules require the supplier to publicize the arrangement or run the risk that his ownership interest in the goods will be subordinate to the claims of the retailer-consignee's creditors. In most cases the supplier will file an Article 9 financing statement to publicize the consignment arrangement. UCC 2-326(3); 9-114; 9-408. See p. 304 infra.

4. **Priority.** A secured party with a security interest in inventory will find that many of the priority rules are familiar. A perfected interest will be protected from the claims of unsecured creditors, lien creditors, or buyers not in the ordinary course of business. UCC 9-201, 9-301. As for purchasers who buy inventory from a retailer in the ordinary course of business, the secured party will lose its security interest either because it explicitly authorizes sales in order

to generate funds to repay the loan or because the purchaser takes free of the interest by operation of law. UCC 9-306(2), 9-307(1). Presumably your client will be authorized to sell furniture in the ordinary course of business.

Several classes of competing secured parties pose special priority problems for an inventory financer such as your client's finance company:

a. A subsequent purchase money financer may take priority over the finance company's security interest in after-acquired inventory if the purchase money financer complies with the requirements of UCC 9-312(3):

> (a) the purchase money security interest is perfected at the time the debtor receives possession of the inventory; and
> (b) the purchase money secured party gives notification in writing to the holder of the conflicting security interest if the holder had filed a financing statement covering the same types of inventory (i) before the date of the filing made by the purchase money secured party, or (ii) before the beginning of the 21 day period where the purchase money security interest is temporarily perfected without filing or possession (subsection (5) of Section 9-304); and
> (c) the holder of the conflicting security interest receives the notification within five years before the debtor receives possession of the inventory; and
> (d) the notification states that the person giving the notice has or expects to acquire a purchase money security interest in inventory of the debtor, describing inventory by item or type.

Analogous rules govern priority between an inventory financer and a supplier who provides goods to the debtor under a consignment arrangement. UCC 9-114. See discussion at p. 309 infra.

b. A financer of the debtor's accounts receivable may claim the proceeds from the sale of inventory. As noted above in the discussion of proceeds (see p. 270 supra), priority between a financer of inventory and a financer of accounts receivable will be determined by the general rule that gives priority to the secured party first to file or perfect. UCC 9-312(5). Where the accounts receivable take the form of chattel paper (e.g., a conditional sales contract) or instruments (e.g., notes or checks) there are more detailed rules for determining priority between an inventory financer claiming the chattel paper or instruments as proceeds and a financer to whom these proceeds have been assigned. UCC 9-308, 9-309. Moreover, if an inventory item is returned by a customer special rules determine priority in the returned good. UCC 9-306(5).

5. **Default.** There are no special Article 9 rules governing the secured party's repossession and disposition of inventory if the debtor should default. For a description of the difficulties a secured party faces when liquidating inventory see In re Zsa Zsa Ltd., 352 F. Supp. 665 (S.D.N.Y. 1972), aff'd, 475 F.2d 1393 (2d Cir. 1973) (disposition of inventory of an insolvent cosmetics business commercially reasonable although public auction of inventory in lots brought only 10 cents on the dollar).

Problem 6-9. Star Furniture agrees with Finance Company to enter into a long-term financing arrangement under which Finance Company would make periodic loans, repayment of which is to be secured by a security interest in Star Furniture's inventory of office and home furniture. As attorney for Finance Company you are asked to draw up an appropriate security agreement. Review the documentation in the prototype transaction set out at the beginning of Chapter 3. What changes will have to be made? For an example of an inventory financing form see 5 Uniform Laws Annotated, Uniform Commercial Code Forms and Materials, Form 9:1750 (R. Henson & W. Davenport eds. 1968).

Problem 6-10. Finance Company and Star Furniture enter into a financing arrangement under which Finance Company agrees to provide periodic loans, repayment of which is secured by a security interest in all Star Furniture's inventory of furniture now owned or after-acquired. Finance Company properly perfects its security interest by filing a financing statement. Star Furniture subsequently borrows additional sums from Bank for the purchase of a new line of office furniture and grants Bank a security interest in this new inventory. Bank promptly perfects its security interest by filing a financing statement claiming "inventory and proceeds." Before Star Furniture takes possession of any of the new line of office furniture Bank sends a letter to Finance Company stating "We have taken and plan to take a security interest in all Star Furniture's inventory and accounts receivable now owned or hereafter acquired." Finance Company, however, does not receive the letter until after Star Furniture receives the new inventory. Several months later Star Furniture defaults on its obligations to both Finance Company and Bank. You are asked to advise Bank on the following points:

(a) Does Bank have priority as to the new line of furniture received by Star Furniture before Finance Company received the notice from Bank?

(b) Does Bank have priority as to the furniture received by Star Furniture after Finance Company received the notice from Bank?

(c) After receiving the first shipment of the new line of furniture, Star Furniture and Customer signed a conditional sales contract for the sale of a suite of office furniture. At the time of signing Customer made a down payment of $500 and traded in some old office furniture. Star Furniture deposited the $500 in a deposit account at Bank in which only proceeds were deposited. The used furniture traded in is still in Star Furniture's warehouse and the conditional sales contract is in Star Furniture's files. Does Bank have priority as to any of this property?

KINETICS TECHNOLOGY INTERNATIONAL CORP. v. FOURTH NATIONAL BANK
705 F.2d 396, 36 UCC Rep. 292 (10th Cir. 1983)

SEYMOUR, Circuit Judge. Kinetics Technology International Corporation (KTI) brought this diversity action seeking damages for an alleged conversion of goods by Fourth National Bank of Tulsa (the Bank). The Bank admits taking possession of the goods from the custody of a third party, Oklahoma

Heat Transfer Corporation (OHT), but claims a right to the goods arising under the Oklahoma version of the Uniform Commercial Code. . . .

OHT, now defunct, was a manufacturer specializing in constructing heat exchangers to specifications supplied by its customers. On May 25, 1977, the Bank issued OHT a line of credit for $600,000, taking a security interest in OHT's inventory. On June 1, the Bank filed a financing statement covering, inter alia, "[a]ll inventory now or hereafter owned by the Debtor." . . .

KTI is a company that designs and supplies process furnaces for the refinery and petrochemical industry. On August 18, 1977, it entered into a contract with OHT under which OHT was to build eight furnace economizers to KTI's specifications, in part from materials supplied by KTI, and in part from materials supplied by OHT. KTI was to ship to OHT certain specially designed and manufactured goods consisting of finned tubes, castings, fittings, and anchors (hereinafter referred to as the KTI Goods). OHT was to build eight box units (hereinafter referred to as the Box Units) from materials out of OHT's inventory, and then install the KTI Goods into the Box Units, resulting in eight completed furnace economizers. KTI agreed to make progress payments to OHT at various stages in the process. The purchase order form, supplied by KTI, provided that title to goods delivered to OHT by KTI would remain in KTI. Title to goods acquired by OHT from other sources for use in the KTI contract would pass to KTI upon the first progress (or other) payment made by KTI to OHT. KTI did not file under the UCC.

KTI procured the goods specified in the contract (the KTI Goods), and had them delivered to OHT. Delivery was complete by January 25, 1978. OHT began work on the contract. During this time, OHT's financial situation deteriorated, and it became necessary to seek additional financing from the Bank. The Bank agreed to make additional loans (separate from the line of credit), secured in part by specified accounts receivable of OHT. A loan was made to OHT on January 10, 1978, secured by the progress payments specified in the KTI-OHT contract. The Bank instructed KTI to make the first two progress payments directly to the Bank.

OHT's work on the contract reached the point at which OHT was entitled to the first two progress payments, a total of $42,600. Both payments, which KTI made on January 10 and January 19, 1978, were received by the Bank. OHT began work on the Box Units, but prior to their completion OHT management determined that the business' financial state could not support continued operation. On January 27, OHT shut down, and on January 30, OHT's management delivered the plant keys to the Bank. At that time, the Bank took possession and control of the plant where OHT's inventory, the Box Units, and the KTI Goods were located.

[KTI demanded the surrender of the Box Units and the KTI Goods, but the Bank refused on the strength of its security interest in OHT's inventory. KTI filed suit for conversion. After a trial to the bench, the court found that KTI was entitled both to the KTI Goods and to the Box Units.]

The Bank's argument for reversal is based on its status as a holder of a perfected security interest in OHT's inventory. The Bank asserts that both the

KTI Goods and the Box Units were inventory collateral in OHT's hands, to which the Bank was entitled when OHT defaulted on the line of credit. The Bank contends that KTI's interest in the Box Units and in the KTI Goods amounted only to an unperfected security interest over which the Bank's perfected security interest had priority. KTI argues that the Bank's security interest was ineffective as to the goods at issue because, under the contract, KTI retained title and ownership rights in the KTI Goods and acquired title and ownership rights in the Box Units when it made the progress payments. . . .

I.   BANK SECURITY INTEREST IN THE KTI GOODS

The Bank's claim to the KTI Goods is based on its perfected security interest in OHT's inventory. The Bank argues that when KTI had the KTI Goods delivered to OHT and OHT began work on the contract, the goods became inventory for the purposes of the Bank's security interest. The Bank insists that KTI's rights in the KTI Goods at most amounted to a retained, unperfected security interest. KTI bases its claim on its ownership of the goods as evidenced by the title retention clause in the contract, arguing that OHT was in the position of a bailee. Thus, KTI asserts, the goods were never part of OHT's inventory,[2] and therefore never became subject to the Bank's security interest. . . .

In order for the Bank's security interest to include the KTI Goods and be enforceable, it must have attached to the goods. UCC 9-203(1) . . . The issue here is whether OHT had sufficient rights in the collateral. . . . The parties' disagreement is centered on whether OHT was a mere bailee of the KTI Goods, or instead had a greater property interest in them.

The phrase "rights in the collateral" is not defined in the UCC. The Code clearly does not require that a debtor have full ownership rights. See, e.g., UCC 9-112. The Seventh Circuit has said that the requirements of "rights in the collateral" illustrates the general principal that " 'one cannot encumber another man's property in the absence of consent, estoppel, or some other special rule.' " In re Pubs, Inc., 618 F.2d 432, 436 (7th Cir. 1980). . . .

In Amfac Mortgage Corp. v. Arizona Mall, 127 Ariz. 70, 618 P.2d 240 (Ct. App. 1980), the debtor Mall had contracted with a third party for the construction of a shopping mall. The contract specified that the contractor would obtain the needed materials, and that title to the materials would pass to the Mall upon satisfaction of various conditions, including payment. Amfac loaned money to the Mall, taking a security interest in all materials to be incorporated in the Mall. The contractor acquired the materials and had

2. The record shows that OHT believed these goods belonged to KTI and were not part of OHT's inventory. OHT had in fact reported to the Bank that there were goods in its plant that belonged to KTI. Additionally, no loans on the line of credit were made by the Bank after OHT received the KTI Goods. There is thus no question of a loan having been made in reliance on the KTI Goods as collateral.

them delivered, but prior to their incorporation and before any payments were made by the Mall to the contractor, the enterprise folded. Amfac brought an action to recover the unincorporated steel. The court, in deciding whether the Mall had had sufficient rights in the steel for Amfac's security interest to attach, stated that a debtor acquires sufficient rights when the debtor obtains possession of collateral pursuant to an agreement with the seller or manufacturer. Possession with contingent rights of ownership was held to be sufficient with or without payment on the contract. . . .

Thus, it is clear that for a security interest to attach, a debtor must have some degree of control or authority over collateral placed in the debtor's possession. The Oklahoma Supreme Court, in a case factually similar to the case before us, has said that the requisite authority exists "where a debtor gains possession of collateral pursuant to an agreement endowing him with any interest other than naked possession." Morton Booth Co. v. Tiara Furniture, Inc., 564 P.2d 210, 214 (Okla. 1977). But see Chrysler Corp. v. Adamatic, Inc., 59 Wis. 2d 219, 208 N.W.2d 97, 104 (1973) (bailee's possessory interest for limited purpose of repair not sufficient "rights in the collateral"). The *Morton Booth* definition strongly supports the Article Nine purpose of promoting certainty in commercial loan transactions. See UCC 9-101, Official Comment. Otherwise, if a debtor received collateral from a third party under an agreement giving the debtor authority to exercise any outward indicia or manifestations of ownership or control, a would-be creditor could easily be misled into making a loan under an ineffective security agreement. For example, in *Morton Booth*, the debtor, Tiara, contracted to build gun cabinets from materials supplied primarily by Morton Booth, and then sell the completed products to Morton Booth. Tiara, a furniture manufacturer, subsequently sought and received financing from the Small Business Association, giving the participating banks a security interest in Tiara's present and after-acquired inventory, which apparently consisted of the same types of materials that were supplied it by Morton Booth. See 564 P.2d at 211. Had the court found that Tiara lacked sufficient "rights" in the Morton Booth-supplied collateral for the banks' security interest to attach, the banks' claim to the goods upon Tiara's default would have been defeated by the sort of hidden-title subterfuge the Code was intended to prevent.

This reason for the *Morton Booth* result is supported by another feature of Article Nine. In this context, buyers such as Morton Booth and KTI finance a debtor's operation by supplying materials rather than money with which to buy materials. Such a buyer-lender could easily protect itself from after-acquired property creditors of its contractor by filing an Article Nine purchase money security interest in the goods supplied by it to the contractor, as well as those purchased or otherwise identified in the contract by the contractor. See UCC 9-107, 9-312(3).[3] Requiring buyers such as KTI to take this additional

3. . . . Under UCC 9-312(3), the holder of a perfected purchase money security interest in inventory enjoys priority over conflicting security interests in the same inventory if the holder

step—done easily and at minimal cost—thoroughly advances the Code policy of providing notice and certainty to inventory lenders.

In accordance with *Morton Booth Co.*, we conclude contrary to the district court that the Bank's perfected security interest in OHT's collateral attached to the KTI Goods.

II.   SALE OF GOODS BY OHT

Notwithstanding our conclusion that the Bank held a valid, enforceable security interest both in the KTI Goods and in the materials supplied under the contract by OHT, KTI may still recover if it bought the goods from OHT as sanctioned by the Code before the plant was closed. Under the UCC, a security interest generally "continues in collateral, notwithstanding sale, exchange, or other disposition," UCC 9-306(2), and "is effective . . . against purchasers of the collateral," UCC 9-201. However, there are several exceptions to this general rule, two of which are pertinent to the case at bar. First, a buyer of collateral will take free of a security interest where the sale by debtor "was authorized by the secured party in the security agreement or otherwise." UCC 9-306(2). Second, "[a] buyer in ordinary course of business . . . takes free of a security interest created by his seller even though perfected. . . ." UCC 9-307.

Under UCC 9-306(2), "a purchaser . . . of collateral takes free of a security interest *whenever the debtor is authorized by the secured party to dispose of the collateral.*" Poteau State Bank v. Denwalt, 597 P.2d 756, 759 (Okla. 1979) (emphasis in original). Authorization may be either explicit or implied. Id. at 759-760. The Bank's security agreement provided that OHT "may sell its inventory in the ordinary course of business."[5] Charles Hyde, who serviced the OHT account for the Bank, testified that the Bank generally had allowed OHT to enter into contracts with its customers and to sell inventory without the Bank's supervision or permission. The only restriction placed upon OHT was that when the Bank made the supplementary loans to OHT secured by specific OHT accounts receivable, including the KTI progress payments, the customers involved were instructed to make their account payments directly to the Bank. Hyde also testified that the Bank knew OHT "did some of their jobs with customer-supplied materials." From his point of view "it was a blessing when they [did], because it eliminated some bank borrowing needs."

Comment, "Bailment for Processing": Article Nine Security Interest or Title Retention Contract? 61 Or. L. Rev. 441, 452-454 (1982) (arguing that such transactions are in effect buyer-financing devices intended to secure performance of contract and should be treated as Article Nine secured transactions).

5. The requirement in the Bank's security agreement that a sale by OHT must be in the ordinary course of its business is identical to UCC 9-307 which provides that a "buyer in the ordinary course of business" takes free of a third party's security interest in the goods. The Bank points out in its brief on appeal that the similarity of this language is no coincidence.

The trial court found that the Bank permitted OHT to sell inventory to customers without restriction so long as the sale was in the ordinary course of business. It further found that OHT sold the Box Units in the ordinary course. The court concluded as a matter of law that the transaction was an authorized sale of goods under UCC 9-306(2), and that KTI was therefore entitled to the Box Units free of the Bank's security interest.

The Bank contests as clearly erroneous the trial court's finding that a sale occurred in the ordinary course of business. Initially, we must determine if in fact a sale occurred. We must then decide whether any such sale was in the ordinary course of OHT's business and hence was authorized.

UCC 9-105(3) incorporates the definition of "sale" found in UCC 2-106. There, a "sale" is defined as "the passing of title from the seller to the buyer for a price (Section 2-401)." UCC 2-106(1). UCC 2-401 provides:

> Each provision of this Article with regard to the rights, obligations and remedies of the seller, the buyer, purchasers or other third parties applies irrespective of title to the goods except where the provision refers to such title. Insofar as situations are not covered by the other provisions of this Article and matters concerning title become material the following rules apply:
>
> (1) *Title to goods cannot pass under a contract for sale prior to their identification to the contract (Section 2-501),* and unless otherwise explicitly agreed the buyer acquires by their identification a special property as limited by this act. . . . *Subject to these provisions and to the provisions of the Article on Secured Transactions (Article 9), title to goods passes from the seller to the buyer in any manner and on any conditions explicitly agreed on by the parties.* (Emphasis added).

Thus, there are two requirements that must be met before title can pass within the meaning of UCC 2-106(1): the goods must be identified to the contract, and the parties must agree on when title passes.[6]

Under UCC 2-501, goods become identified to the contract as follows:

> The buyer obtains a special property and an insurable interest in goods by identification of existing goods as goods to which the contract refers even though the goods so identified are non-conforming. . . . *Such identification can be made at any time and in any manner explicitly agreed to by the parties. In the absence of explicit agreement identification occurs*
>
> (a) when the contract is made if it is for the sale of goods already existing and identified;
>
> (b) *if the contract is for the sale of future goods . . . when goods are shipped, marked, or otherwise designated by the seller as goods to which the contract refers. . . .* (Emphasis added).

The contract between OHT and KTI did not set out the time and manner in which identification of the goods to the contract would occur. Therefore, iden-

---

6. If the parties do not otherwise agree, "title passes to the buyer at the time and place at which the seller completes his performance with reference to the physical delivery of the goods." UCC 2-401.

tification occurred if OHT "marked, or otherwise designated" the goods as those "to which the contract refers." Id. OHT began fabrication of the Box Units from materials purchased by OHT or supplied out of OHT's inventory, and continued work on them until the plant was shut down. The trial court found that the Box Units, as well as the KTI Goods, were identified to the contract by the time the Bank took possession of them on January 30th. "[T]he general policy is to resolve all doubts in favor of identification," UCC 2-501(1) Official Comment 2, and "there is no requirement in [UCC 2-501] that the goods be in a deliverable state or that all of the seller's duties with respect to the processing of the goods be completed in order that identification occur," id. Official Comment 4. There is ample evidence in the record to support the trial court's conclusion that the Box Units and the KTI Goods had been identified to the contract.

With respect to passage of title, the contract between KTI and OHT specified that title to the KTI Goods would remain in KTI, and that title to goods procured by OHT for the contract would "pass to Purchaser on . . . any progress or other payment made by [KTI] to [OHT]." Payments were made by KTI on January 10, 1978, and on January 19. Accordingly, we hold that a sale of goods as defined by the UCC had occurred by the time the Bank seized the Box Units and the KTI Goods, the goods having been identified to the contract and title having passed for a price.[7] . . .

The remaining question is whether the sale was in the ordinary course of OHT's business. The Bank argues strenuously that it was not, pointing out that OHT was exclusively a build-to-order metal fabrication shop that did not sell materials out of its stock but only sold finished goods built to the customer's specifications. The Bank then asserts that at the time any sale would have had to occur, the eight KTI furnace economizers were only "nuts and bolts," not completed goods. Therefore, the Bank concludes, there was no sale in the ordinary course of OTH's business.

The Bank's argument fails because when the sale occurred, KTI was not buying "nuts and bolts" or sheet steel out of OTH's inventory; it was buying eight heat economizers that had been identified to the contract. OHT's business consisted of custom fabricating steel pursuant to the terms of contracts with its customers. KTI contracted to buy custom-made goods from OHT, as was OHT's regular practice. The contract for sale was thus in the ordinary course. This was not a contract for sale of raw materials by OHT, which would not have been in OHT's ordinary practice, but was instead a contract for sale that typified OHT's business. So long as the goods were designated as those to be incorporated into KTI's eight furnace economizers, it is irrelevant that the fabrication was not complete.

7. As we have noted, title to the KTI Goods remained at all times in KTI. Nevertheless, OHT had "rights in the collateral" sufficient to support the grant to the Bank of a security interest in the KTI Goods. When both the KTI Goods and the Box Units became identified to the contract for the purchase of the eight heat economizers and the progress payments were made, we believe a "sale" of the eight heat economizers occurred within the meaning of the Code.

Because this was a sale in the ordinary course of OHT's business, and, as such, was authorized by the Bank's security agreement, KTI took the goods free of the Bank's security interest.[8] UCC 9-306(2). . . . Accordingly, we hold that KTI was entitled to the KTI Goods and the Box Units under UCC 9-306(2). We therefore affirm the trial court's conclusion that the Bank's actions constituted a conversion of the KTI Goods and the Box Units. . . .

NOTES & QUESTIONS

1. *The financing buyer.* Reconsider the discussion of the financing buyer set out at p. 237 supra. In what ways does KTI's position differ from that of a buyer who agrees to finance the manufacture of goods it buys by making a loan?

2. *Rights of seller's creditors against sold goods.* Consider the relevance of UCC 2-402 to the *KTI* case. Under this section the buyer of goods runs the risk that the seller's creditors will have a prior claim to the goods if they are left in the seller's possession. For many centuries legal rules have developed to protect creditors from secret claims to property where a debtor has *ostensible ownership* by virtue of his unfettered possession of the property. The parties to an unpublicized sale where the seller retains possession may have intended to mislead the seller's creditors. Fraudulent conveyance law has developed remedies to protect these creditors. But the parties to the sales contract may have had commercially reasonable reasons for leaving the goods with the seller, such as the inability of the buyer to take immediate delivery or to arrange for immediate carriage. Common law rules in most states incorporate a rebuttable presumption of fraud; thus a buyer will have priority over the seller's creditors if the buyer shows that the seller's retention was for a commercially reasonable purpose. Some states, however, continue to apply a "fraud-in-law" approach that subordinates the buyer to the seller's creditors. UCC 2-402 refers the reader to these common law rules and in subsection (2) amends the fraud-in-law rule to provide a limited "commercially reasonable" exception. Does UCC 2-402 apply to KTI? Is the reference to "unsecured creditors" in subsection (1) relevant? Is the cross-reference to Article 9 in subsection (3)(a) relevant?

For a further note on fraudulent conveyances see p. 405 infra.

3. *Processing raw materials.* A dealer or user of finished goods may find it costs less to produce the finished product if he buys the raw materials and hands them over to a manufacturer for processing. "Raw materials," of course, may include everything from the unfinished Box Units in *KTI* to minerals and agricultural products. For a general analysis of the legal problems that arise in

---

8. The foregoing analysis indicates that even if this were not an "authorized sale" under UCC 9-306(2), KTI would have taken the Box Units free of the Bank's security interest as a buyer in ordinary course under UCC 9-307(1).

the relationship between the parties, see Harrington, A Caveat for Commodity Processing Industries: Insolvent Processors' Creditors vs. Putative Owners of Raw Materials, 16 UCC L.J. 322 (1984).

An important recent case is In re Medomak Canning Co., 25 UCC Rep. 437 (Bankr. D. Me.), aff'd, 588 F.2d 818 (1st Cir. 1978). Underwood, a producer of New England baked beans and brown bread, agreed to deliver ingredients to Medomak for processing, including canning, and as part of the same agreement agreed to purchase a specified minimum number of cases of the finished product. Underwood agreed to pay a "net differential rate per unit," which the court found to represent a negotiated fee for the processing. When Medomak filed a Chapter XI bankruptcy petition it held ingredients and packaging materials supplied by Underwood, as well as undelivered cases of unlabeled finished cans. The bankruptcy court found that there had been a bailment of the ingredients so that Underwood, the bailor, retained title to the raw materials and finished product. Underwood, which had made no attempt to file an Article 9 financing statement, therefore prevailed over both Medomak, as debtor-in-possession, and Medomak's financer, which had a perfected security interest in Medomak's inventory. Sound?

4. *Commingling.* When the owner of raw materials hands them over to a processor for finishing there is the additional potential problem that the processor may commingle the materials with other materials supplied by others or owned by the processor himself. UCC 9-315 sets out priority rules for the different claimants to the commingled mass or final product. The best commentary on this section remains 2 G. Gilmore, Security Interests in Personal Property 845-856 (1965).

TANBRO FABRICS CORP. v. DEERING MILLIKEN, INC.
39 N.Y.2d 632, 385 N.Y.S.2d 260, 350 N.E.2d 590, 19 UCC Rep. 385 (1976)

BREITEL, Chief Judge. In an action for the tortious conversion of unfinished textile fabrics (greige goods), plaintiff Tanbro sought damages from Deering Milliken, a textile manufacturer. Tanbro, known in the trade as a "converter," finishes textile into dyed and patterned fabrics. The goods in question had been manufactured by Deering, and sold on a "bill and hold" basis to Mill Fabrics, also a converter, now insolvent. Mill Fabrics resold the goods, while still in Deering's warehouse, also on a bill and hold basis, to Tanbro.

Deering refused to deliver the goods to Tanbro on Tanbro's instruction because, although these goods had been paid for, there was an open account balance due Deering from Mill Fabrics. Deering under its sales agreement with Mill Fabrics claimed a perfected security interest in the goods.

At Supreme Court, Tanbro recovered a verdict and judgment of $87,451.68 for compensatory and $25,000 for punitive damages. The Appellate Division, by a divided court, modified to strike the recovery for punitive damages, and otherwise affirmed. Both parties appeal.

The issue is whether Tanbro's purchase of the goods was in the ordinary *ISSUE:* course of Mill Fabrics' business, and hence free of Deering's perfected security interest.

There should be an affirmance. Mill Fabrics' sale to Tanbro was in the ordinary course of business, even though its predominant business purpose was, like Tanbro's, the converting of greige goods into finished fabrics. All the Uniform Commercial Code requires is that the sale be in ordinary course associated with the seller's business (UCC 9-307(1)). The record established that converters buy greige goods in propitious markets and often in excess of their requirements as they eventuate. On the occasion of excess purchases, converters at times enter the market to sell the excess through brokers to other converters, and converters buy such goods if the price is satisfactory or the particular goods are not available from manufacturers. Both conditions obtained here.

Tanbro and Mill Fabrics were customers of Deering for many years. Goods would be purchased in scale on a "bill and hold" basis, that is, the goods would be paid for and delivered as the buyers instructed. When the goods were needed, they were delivered directly where they were to be converted, at the buyers' plants or the plants of others if that would be appropriate. Pending instructions, the sold and paid for goods were stored in the warehouses of the manufacturer, both because the buyers lacked warehousing space and retransportation of the goods to be processed would be minimized.

Mill Fabrics, like many converters, purchased greige goods from Deering on credit as well as on short-term payment. Under the sales notes or agreements, all the goods on hand in the seller's warehouse stood as security for the balance owed on the account. Tanbro was familiar with this practice. It was immaterial whether or not particular goods had been paid for. If the goods were resold by Deering's customers, Deering obtained for a period a perfected security interest in the proceeds of resale for the indebtedness on the open account (UCC 9-306(2), (3)).

Deering's sales executives advised Tanbro that it had discontinued production of a certain blended fabric. Upon Tanbro's inquiry, the Deering sales executives recommended to Tanbro that it try purchasing the blended fabric from Mill Fabrics, which Deering knew had an excess supply. Ultimately, Tanbro purchased from Mill Fabrics through a broker 267,000 yards at 26 cents per yard. Tanbro paid Mill Fabrics in full.

During October and November 1969, approximately 57,000 yards of the blended fabric was released by Deering on Mill Fabrics' instructions and delivered to a Tanbro affiliate. There remained some 203,376 yards at the Deering warehouse.

In early January of 1970, Tanbro ordered the remaining fabric delivered to meet its own contractual obligation to deliver the blended fabric in finished state at 60 cents per yard. Deering refused.

By this time Mill Fabrics was in financial trouble and its account debit balance with Deering at an unprecedented high. In mid-January of 1970, a meeting of its creditors was called and its insolvency confirmed.

As noted earlier, under the terms of the Deering sales agreements with Mill Fabrics, Deering retained a security interest in Mill Fabrics "property" on a bill and hold basis, whether paid for or not. This security interest was perfected by Deering's continued possession of the goods (UCC 1-201(37); 9-305). Tanbro argued that if it had title by purchase its goods were excluded from the security arrangement which was literally restricted to the "property of the buyer," that is, Mill Fabrics. In any event, unless prevented by other provisions of the code, or the sale was not unauthorized, Tanbro took title subject to Deering's security interest.

Under the code (UCC 9-307(1)) a buyer in the ordinary course of the seller's business takes goods free of even a known security interest as long as the buyer does not know that the purchase violates the terms of the security agreement. As defined in the code (UCC 1-201(9)) "a buyer in ordinary course" is "a person who in good faith and without knowledge that the sale to him is in violation of the ownership rights or security interest of a third party in the goods buys in ordinary course from a person in the business of selling goods of that kind but does not include a pawnbroker. 'Buying' may be for cash or by exchange of other property or on secured or unsecured credit and includes receiving goods or documents of title under a preexisting contract for sale but does not include a transfer in bulk or as security for or in total or partial satisfaction of a money debt." Critical to Tanbro's claim is that it purchased the goods in the ordinary course of Mill Fabrics' business and that it did not purchase the goods in knowing violation of Deering's security interest.

Under the code whether a purchase was made from a person in the business of selling goods of that kind turns primarily on whether that person holds the goods for sale. Such goods are a person's selling inventory. (UCC 1-201(9); 9-307(1); Official Comment, at para. 2). Note, however, that not all purchases of goods held as inventory qualify as purchases from a person in the business of selling goods of that kind. The purpose of UCC 9-307 is more limited. As indicated in the Practice Commentary to that section, the purpose is to permit buyers "to buy goods from a dealer in such goods without having to protect himself against a possible security interest on the inventory" (Kripke, Practice Commentary, McKinney's Cons. Laws of N.Y., Book 62 1/2, Uniform Commercial Code, §9-307, p. 491, para. 1). Hence, a qualifying purchase is one made from a seller who is a dealer in such goods.

A former Mill Fabrics' employee testified that there were times when Mill Fabrics, like all converters, found itself with excess goods. When it was to their business advantage, they sold the excess fabrics to other converters. Although these sales were relatively infrequent they were nevertheless part of and in the ordinary course of Mill Fabrics' business, even if only incidental to the predominant business purpose. Examples of a nonqualifying sale might be a bulk sale, a sale in distress at an obvious loss price, a sale in liquidation, a sale of a commodity never dealt with before by the seller and wholly unlike its usual inventory, or the like. . . .

The combination of stored, paid for goods, on a hold basis, and the retention of a security interest by Deering makes commercial sense. Mill Fabrics' capacity to discharge its obligation to Deering was in part made possible because it sold off or converted the goods held at the Deering warehouse. Mill Fabrics, as an honest customer, was supposed to remit the proceeds from resale or conversion to Deering and thus reduce, and eventually discharge its responsibility to Deering. Thus, so long as it was customary for Mill Fabrics, and in the trade for converters to sell off excess goods, the sale was in the ordinary course of business. Moreover, on an alternative analysis, such a sale by Mill Fabrics was therefore impliedly authorized under the code if its indebtedness to Deering was to be liquidated (see Official Comment to UCC 9-307, para. 2; . . .).

All UCC 9-307(1) requires is that the sale be of the variety reasonably to be expected in the regular course of an ongoing business. . . . This was such a case.

Hempstead Bank v. Andy's Car Rental System (34 A.D.2d 35) stands for no contrary principle. Rightly or wrongly, it was there held as a matter of law, unlike the situation here, that the selling of used rental cars was not in the ordinary course of business for an auto rental company. . . . It may be significant that the used cars were in no sense an "inventory" of a sales business, but the capital inventory of a leasing company, usually subject to extended term financing. . . .

[Affirmed.]

NOTES & QUESTIONS

1. *Commentary on* Tanbro. Following the *Tanbro* decision there was extensive law review commentary. See Kripke, Should Section 9-307(1) of the Uniform Commercial Code Apply Against a Secured Party in Possession? 33 Bus. Law. 153 (1977) (case wrong as a matter of sound commercial policy); Birnbaum, Section 9-307(1) of the Uniform Commercial Code versus Possessory Security Interests—A Reply to Professor Homer Kripke, 33 Bus. Law. 2607 (1978); Dolan, The Uniform Commercial Code and the Concept of Possession in the Marketing and Financing of Goods, 56 Tex. L. Rev. 1147 (1978).

2. *Buyer in ordinary course—"Good Faith."* Commercial Credit Corporation financed Dover Motors, an American Motors dealership, under a floor-plan arrangement. On September 27, 1967, the Sherrocks, partners in another American Motors dealership, agreed with Dover Motors to purchase two new 1969 model automobiles. The two dealers agreed that, although payment would be made by transfer of funds on the same day, delivery would be delayed for "a couple of days after October 1st." On October 2, 1968, while making a periodic check of Dover's floor, Commercial Credit learned that

Dover was selling cars "out of trust." On October 4, Commercial Credit repossessed Dover's entire stock of new automobile inventory, including the two Sherrock vehicles. The Sherrocks brought an action against Commercial Credit for damages arising from the seizure of the two automobiles. The lower court found that, although the Sherrocks were honest in fact, they did not act "in a commercially reasonable manner."

The Sherrocks appealed on the ground that the trial court applied the Article 2 definition of "good faith" (UCC 2-103(1)(b)) instead of the general definition of "good faith" in Article 1 (UCC 1-201(19)). The Delaware Supreme Court reversed the trial court. Sherrock v. Commercial Credit Corp., 290 A.2d 648, 10 UCC Rep. 523 (Del. 1972). The court stated:

"Article 2 of the Code concerns itself with the rights and obligations of buyer and seller, one to the other. Here we are concerned with the rights and obligations of buyer and secured creditor, one to the other—a transaction expressly controlled by Article 9.

"The course to be followed in arriving at the definition of 'good faith' within the meaning of Article 9 is charted clearly in the Code. There is no room for judicial interpretation. In our view, an application of an Article 2 definition to an Article 9 transaction is unwarranted by anything in the Code for the following reasons: (1) UCC 9-105(4) provides that 'Article 1 contains general definitions and principles of construction and interpretation applicable throughout this Article;' there is no similar reference to Article 2 as a source for any definition applicable to Article 9. (2) As noted, UCC 9-307 expressly refers to UCC 1-201(9) for the definition of 'buyer in the ordinary course of business.' (3) The 'Definitional Cross References' in the Delaware Study Comment refer to specific sections of Article 1 for definitions of terms found in UCC 9-307, including a reference to UCC 1-201 for the definition of 'buyer in ordinary course of business;' there is no similar reference to Article 2. (4) There is an express limitation in Article 2 of the definitions contained in Article 2, including the UCC 2-103(1)(b) definition of 'good faith' here involved.[2]

"We find no basis anywhere for the conclusion that the drafters of the Code intended to make it permissible to 'cross over' to Article 2 for the definition of the term 'good faith' as incorporated by reference in Article 9." 290 A.2d at 650-651, 10 UCC Rep. at 526-527.

---

2. In the 1962 Official Text of the American Law Institute, National Conference of Commissioners on Uniform State Laws, the drafters of the Uniform Commercial Code comment on "good faith" in Note 19 under UCC 1-201 as follows: ". . . 'Good Faith,' whenever it is used in the Code, means at least what is here stated [i.e., honesty in fact]. In certain Articles, by specific provision, additional requirements are made applicable. See, e.g., Secs. 2-103(1)(b), 7-404. To illustrate, in the Article on Sales, Section 2-103, good faith is expressly defined as including in the case of a merchant observance of reasonable commercial standards of fair dealing in the trade, so that throughout that Article wherever a merchant appears in the case an inquiry into his observance of such standards is necessary to determine his good faith." It would thus appear that the draftsmen of the Uniform Commercial Code meant the definition of "good faith" set forth in UCC 2-103(1)(b) be limited to the specific Article in which it appears: Sales Article 2 only.

A dissenting opinion argued that the Sherrocks had failed to comply with the usages of automobile dealers dealing with each other and therefore did not fit within the definition of "buyer in ordinary course of business" (UCC 9-307(1)).

[handwritten: Sherrocks are BIOC so take free v sec. interest]

1. Inventory in Possession of a Bailee

P. HUNT, C. WILLIAMS & G. DONALDSON, BASIC BUSINESS FINANCE: A TEXT
296-298 (1974)

BORROWING AGAINST INVENTORY COVERED BY WAREHOUSE RECEIPTS

Under this well-established method, physical custody of the goods is placed in the hands of a warehousing company which, at the direction of the borrower, issues a warehouse receipt made out in favor of the lender. As custodian of the goods, the warehousing firm releases them only upon the instructions of the lender. Properly handled, the warehousing arrangement gives the lender firm control over the collateral. Much of the moral risk inherent in other kinds of inventory financing, where physical control of the goods is left with the borrower, is avoided. . . .

Warehousing arrangements are of two major types—public and field. In the case of public warehouses the goods are brought to the warehouses for storage—for example, wheat moved into the public grain warehouses that dot the skylines of farm belt towns and cities. Lenders have long looked with favor on the public warehouse receipt security arrangement, and it has worked well from the borrower's viewpoint in the case of commodities that can be left undisturbed in the warehouse for long periods of time—such as whiskey being aged or wheat stored after harvest awaiting processing into flour. *[handwritten: Public]*

Yet, many firms have their own storage facilities convenient to their manufacturing facilities or markets and want to avoid the trouble and expense of moving inventory to and from the warehouseman's facilities. Further, they wish to add to and draw from warehoused stocks frequently or continuously. To meet such needs, several warehousing firms offer a field warehousing service. Under a field warehouse arrangement the warehousing firm leases storage facilities of the borrower and posts signs to signify that goods stored therein are in its exclusive custody, to be used as security. Commodities are put in the custody of the warehousing firm, which issues warehouse receipts covering these segregated goods in the name of the lender. We should make clear that the warehousing firm performs only a warehousing function, making it possible for banks or other lending organizations to advance loans against the security of the goods covered by the warehouse receipt. Under the typical field warehouse receipt loan, the lender advances a percentage of the value of the *[handwritten: reasons fr private ware-hous]* commodities covered by the warehouse receipt. When the borrowing firm wants to withdraw goods for processing or sale, it arranges with the lender to pay down that portion of the loan advanced against the particular goods involved, and the lender authorizes the warehouseman to release the goods to the borrower by surrendering the warehouse receipts.

The field warehousing arrangement is a highly ingenious method of facilitating the extension of credit and has come into widespread use in recent decades. One of the first industries to make heavy use of field warehousing was the California food-canning industry. The typical canner's manufacturing operation was highly seasonal, but sales were spread through the year. Customarily, the canner had a large investment in finished goods at the end of the canning season. The field warehousing arrangement permitted the canners to get substantial bank credit against the collateral of the canned goods and yet fill shipment orders through the year with minimum inconvenience and expense.

Over the years, field warehousing has been used for a wide variety of commodities, including such items as coal in hopper cars on a railroad siding (locked switches into the main railroad line were in the control of the field warehouseman), logs in a mill pond, and watch movements stored in a large file cabinet.

In the foregoing paragraphs . . . note the implicit confidence in the integrity and competence of the field warehousing companies. Our confidence reflected the general attitude of banks and other lenders toward the field warehouse receipts of well-known warehousing companies. It is also interesting to note that a basic commodity such as soybean oil, used in a variety of important products, and for which there is an active market, has the characteristics that make for valuable collateral—as we had listed them.

These basic considerations—widespread confidence in field warehouse companies and the validity of their receipts and confidence in the security value of basic commodities like soybean oil—help to explain how 51 companies and banks lost many millions of dollars in credit extended against field warehouse receipts for soybean and other vegetable oils that proved nonexistent. The total inventory shortage discovered in the wake of the failure of the presumed owner, Allied Crude Vegetable Oil Refining Corporation, in late 1963, was reported to be 1,854 million pounds of oil with a stated value of $175 million.[7] Incorrect or fraudulent warehouse receipts had served as the basis for what appears to have been well over $100 million of credit. The proceeds of insurance and payments from the parent company of one of the warehousing firms, American Express Company, significantly cut the gross losses but net losses were huge. Altogether the "Great Salad Oil Swindle" stands as one of the worst of all times and one especially striking because of the

---

7. The figures quoted here are from Norman C. Miller's The Great Salad Oil Swindle (New York: Coward McCann, Inc., 1965).

nature of the major victims, sophisticated and prominent business, financial, and commercial banking firms.

A Field Warehouse Arrangement [3]

Willard operated as a livestock order buyer. For a commission he would locate cattle desired by a potential buyer, purchase the cattle, and deliver them to the buyer. In most cases after Willard purchased the cattle he brought them to his farm, where they were sorted, dipped, vaccinated, and worked before they were shipped to the buyer.

Starting in 1973, the bank financed a small percentage of Willard's cattle purchases. To secure these loans, the bank held a perfected security interest in Willard's equipment, farm products, and all his livestock. In June of 1975, Collateral Control established a warehouse on Willard's property to secure and control the financed cattle for the benefit of the bank.

To obtain financing, Willard notified Collateral Control's bonded agent, who resided on the warehouse premises, that certain incoming cattle were to be stored in the warehouse. The agent filled out a receiving record, noting the approximate weight of the cattle received, the sex, the number of head unloaded, the number of the lot where the cattle were to be held, the date of receipt, and the declared value of the cattle. Willard delivered this report to the bank's agricultural loan officer, who, after reviewing the record, calculated the market value of the cattle and then loaned Willard 80 percent of that amount. Collateral Control then issued and mailed to the bank a nonnegotiable warehouse receipt representing the financed cattle.

A letter of instructions from the bank dated January 21, 1980, governed the release of receipted cattle from the field warehouse. The letter authorized Collateral Control to deliver cattle from the warehouse, provided that it forward to the bank upon each delivery a warehouse release and a check in payment of the delivered cattle. The letter read in part:

"Until you receive from us a written revocation or amendment of the following instructions, this letter will constitute your authority to deliver from your warehouse #2494 to Vance Willard d/b/a/ Fremont Cattle Company upon its request, property stored therein and covered by your non-negotiable Warehouse Receipt, now or hereafter issued to the undersigned provided: . . .

"(2) That not later than the close of business that day during which any property is delivered, you will forward to us your regular form of Warehouse

---

3. The following statement of a field warehouse arrangement is taken from Fremont Natl. Bank & Trust Co. v. Collateral Control Corp., 724 F.2d 1410, 37 UCC Rep. 1267 (8th Cir. 1983) (field warehouseman liable to bank for misdelivery when it released cattle and returned check to debtor rather than deliver check to bank).

Release in duplicate listing the quantity and kind and value of the property delivered. That you attached to the above Warehouse Release a check that will be tendered to your Bonded Agent by Vance Willard payable in our favor in an amount equal to 100 percent of the declared value of the property delivered under this authorization. We will sign and forward the original Warehouse Release to your office, retaining the duplicate for our file."

NOTES & QUESTIONS

1. *Perfection of inventory kept in a field warehouse.* In the arrangement set out above does the bank have a perfected security interest in the cattle? The facts state that in 1973, before setting up the field warehouse, the bank had a perfected security interest in all Willard's livestock, presumably by virtue of a security agreement and a filed financing statement. Does the creation of the field warehouse change the status of the security interest? If the filed financing statement lapsed would the bank have a perfected security interest?

If Collateral Control had issued a negotiable document of title to the order of the bank would any of your answers to the above questions change? Note that most lenders take nonnegotiable receipts because they are more convenient and because the lenders are not concerned about marketing the receipts. The convenience of a nonnegotiable receipt lies in the need to release the inventory in varying lots. A warehouseman rightfully releases goods covered by a negotiable receipt only on surrender of the receipt, which means that if the goods to be released are fewer in number than the amount specified in the receipt the receipt must be surrendered and a new receipt issued. It is easier to have a nonnegotiable document issued and then have the warehouseman release the goods pursuant to the lender's delivery instructions.

2. *Buyer of inventory held in field warehouse.* Will the buyer of the cattle take free of Bank's security interest? UCC 9-301(1)(c), 9-307(1).

3. *Impact of the UCC on field warehousing.* Until 1956, drafts of the UCC required secured parties using field warehouses to perfect their interests by filing. Field warehousemen criticized the requirement and at their urging it was dropped. The ease with which a lender is able to perfect a security interest in a fluctuating mass by simply filing a financing statement, however, has encouraged perfection by filing: the secured party thus avoids the risk that a court may later find the field warehouse arrangement ineffective because the party did not take possession from the debtor on whose premises the warehouse was set up.

Field warehousing continues, however, as a way of monitoring the debtor's purchase and disposition of inventory. Under the legal rules governing warehousemen's liability, the warehousemen will in effect guaranty the receipt and continuing existence of the inventory. See generally McGuire, The Impact of the UCC on Field Warehousing, 6 UCC L.J. 267 (1974) (steady decline in use of field warehouses).

2. *Financing Inventory with Trust Receipts (Floor Planning)*

P. HUNT, C. WILLIAMS & G. DONALDSON, BASIC BUSINESS FINANCE: A TEXT
298 (1974)

BORROWING AGAINST INVENTORY COVERED BY TRUST RECEIPTS

A long-established method of borrowing against inventory that has continued under the Uniform Commercial Code involves the use of trust receipts. Lending arrangements under trust receipts typically involve three parties: for example, the manufacturer of automobiles, the automobile dealer, and the commercial bank lending to the dealer. If a shipment of cars to the dealer is to serve as security, the manufacturer transfers title to the cars and receives payment for them from the lending bank. The lending bank, in turn, delivers custody of the cars to the borrowing dealer under a trust receipt agreement, which specifies what the borrower may do with the cars. In the case of finished goods held for resale, such as the automobiles on the premises of the dealer, the agreement will provide that the goods may be sold but that the borrower will use the proceeds from sale promptly to pay off the loan.

The goods in trust should be specifically identified in the trust receipt, and the lender must devote reasonable care to policing the agreement to insure that the borrower carries out his responsibilities under the trust agreement. The fact that the borrower can put the material into process or sell it, as the trust agreement specifies, before he makes settlement with the lender can be a major convenience to the borrower, but it also involves risk to the lender. Accordingly, the moral standing and reputation for integrity of the borrower are particularly important to the lender considering a trust receipt financing arrangement—more so than in the case of warehouse receipt financing.

The trust receipt device has been heavily used by distributors and retailers of new automobiles and of major equipment and appliance items, who borrow to finance their working inventories of these items. Since the trust receipts must specifically identify the security, new trust receipts must be prepared as the borrower adds and disposes of particular items of inventory. The problem of specific identification and the burden of paper work in trust receipt financing makes the trust receipt an awkward or unsuitable device for securing highly diverse, fast-moving, or hard-to-identify inventory such as work in process.

NOTES & QUESTIONS

1. *Documentation of a floor plan.* A typical floor plan arrangement—in which the collateral is placed on the floor or premises of the financed dealer—may include the following documents:

(a) Agreement between the lender and the dealer. The lender will agree to finance the purchase of inventory items from the supplier and the dealer will grant a security interest in each item to secure all obligations owed to the lender. The parties may also agree that the dealer will transfer the sales proceeds (e.g., chattel paper) to the lender. For an example of this basic agreement, see 5 Uniform Laws Annotated, Uniform Commercial Code Forms and Materials, Form 9:1765 (R. Henson & W. Davenport eds. 1968).

(b) Financing statement. The description in the financing statement should cover inventory both presently owned and after-acquired.

(c) Agreement between lender and supplier. This agreement provides for payment by the lender for inventory items sold to the dealer by a supplier. The agreement may provide for a *letter of credit:* the supplier may send to the lender a draft drawn on the lender together with invoices, documents of title, or other certificates. UCC Article 5 governs letters of credit. See Chapter 18.

(d) Dealer's letter of authorization. This letter to the supplier states that dealer agrees to have the lender pay for the inventory that the dealer orders from the supplier.

(e) Trust receipt security agreement. Following the pre-Code pattern the dealer may sign a separate promissory note and security agreement as it receives each lot of inventory. These documents will provide evidence of outstanding obligations and will help identify inventory items subject to the lender's security interest. These separate agreements are not legally necessary, however, because the master security agreement (see (a) supra) will have an after-acquired property clause.

2. *Proceeds of floor-planned inventory.* When the dealer sells inventory acquired under a floor plan the dealer will frequently receive at least part-payment in the form of chattel paper, such as a conditional sales contract signed by the consumer buyer. The profit to be made from holding this chattel paper is usually very attractive. The floor-plan lenders may charge a favorable interest rate on the floor-plan loan in order to get the dealer to agree to transfer the chattel paper to the lender. In any event, the lender expects to be repaid from the sale proceeds of the item financed, and a dealer who does not pay off the loan as the item is sold is said to sell "out of trust," a reference to pre-Code law under which the lender *entrusted* the inventory to the dealer.

3. Consignments

The true consignment is an agency relationship. The owner of goods, usually a manufacturer or wholesaler, delivers the goods to the consignee, usually a dealer who sells to the ultimate consumer. The consignee is authorized to sell the goods but the consignor retains title and may retain control over such matters as advertising and the price at which the goods are to be sold. The consignee is not obligated to pay for the goods until they are sold to a customer, at which time he collects and remits the proceeds, less the agreed commission, to the consignor. Sale of the goods transfers title directly from the consignor to the customer.

Under pre-Code law priority between competing claims to the consigned goods was decided by determining who had title to the goods. Unless the transaction was deemed a disguised conditional sale, the consignor had title and the consignee did not have an interest in the goods that his creditors could reach by attachment or execution. Moreover, the consignor could reclaim *his* goods from the consignee's trustee in bankruptcy. To protect creditors who might rely on the consignee's ostensible ownership of the inventory, some jurisdictions encouraged consignors to post notices of the consignment.

The Uniform Commercial Code, which downplays the importance of title, provides special rules for consignment transactions. Unless the parties intend to create a security interest, as they would if the transaction is a disguised conditional sale, the consignor's reservation of title is not a security interest. UCC 1-201(37). But whether a true or security consignment the arrangement is subject to the provisions of UCC 2-326, which assimilates the consignment to a "sale or return" and thus subjects the consignor's ownership interest in the goods to the claims of the consignee's creditors while the goods are in the consignee's possession. The consignor may avoid this result, however, by publicizing the consignment or by showing that most of the consignee's creditors know of the consignment. As a practical matter, the consignor will publicize by filing an Article 9 financing statement. UCC 2-326(3)(c), 9-408. The following case and notes explore the interplay between UCC 2-326 and Article 9.

STAR FURNITURE WAREHOUSE, INC. v. MARCOLY
32 B.R. 423, 37 UCC Rep. 113 (Bankr. W.D. Pa. 1983)

Joseph L. COSETTI, Bankruptcy Judge. This matter arises on a Petition for Reclamation filed by Star Furniture Warehouse, Inc. ("Star").

The facts are not in dispute. The Debtors were experiencing financial problems and desired to conduct a "going out of business sale." With the knowledge of their secured creditor, National Bank of the Commonwealth ("Bank"), the Debtors on or about September, 1982 entered into a consignment agreement with Star in which certain merchandise was consigned to the Debtors for floor samples and display. If a customer wished to purchase consigned merchandise, payment was forwarded to Star, who shipped directly to the customer. Nevertheless, the Bank claims a properly filed security interest in inventory, including after acquired inventory.

Star argues that UCC 9-312(3) does not apply because Star and the Bank do not claim conflicting security interests. Star claims that these floor samples are not property of the estate under BC 541. Star argues that these goods were not "delivered to a person for sale" under UCC 2-326(3). Star relies on Walter E. Heller & Co. v. Riviana Foods, Inc., 648 F.2d 1059 (5th Cir. 1981). That case involved a warehouseman who had no authority to sell the items, did not sell the items and was never invoiced or billed for any of the goods stored in the warehouse. The case is distinguishable from the facts here. In the present case the goods were delivered to the Debtors as floor samples and invoices were issued. The Debtors maintain a place of business wherein they deal in goods of the kind involved, under a name other than the person making the delivery (Star). UCC 2-326 provides in relevant part:

(3) Where goods are delivered to a person for sale and such person maintains a place of business at which he deals in goods of the kind involved, under a name other than the name of the person making delivery, then with respect to claims of creditors of the person conducting the business the goods are *deemed* to be on sale or return. *The provisions of this subsection are applicable even though an agreement purports to reserve title to the person making delivery* until payment or resale *or uses such words as "on consignment" or "on memorandum."* (Emphasis supplied).

[Subsection (3) goes on to provide:

However, this subsection is not applicable if the person making delivery

    (a)   complies with an applicable law providing for a consignor's interest or the like to be evidenced by a sign, or

    (b)   establishes that the person conducting the business is generally known by his creditors to be substantially engaged in selling the goods of others, or

    (c)   complies with the filing provisions of the Article on Secured Transactions (Article 9).

    —Eds.]

The Court finds equity to be on the side of Star. However, the provisions of the statute clearly deem the goods to be on sale or return and subject to claims of creditors while in the hands of the Debtor in Possession, unless the consignor (1) evidences its interest by a sign, (2) establishes that the Debtor here is generally known by creditors to be substantially engaged in selling the goods of others, or (3) files the appropriate financing statement.

Because the Bank had extended credit long before this shipment by Star and had knowledge of the consignment by Star to the Debtors, Star asks the Court to rely on GBS Meat Industry Pty. Ltd. v. Kress-Dobkin Co., 474 F. Supp. 1357 (D.W.D. Pa. 1979) and Newhall v. Haines, 10 B.R. 1019 (D. Mont. 1981) and not hold that the Bank is secured. Star argues to do so would contravene the intent of the statute, which is to give notice of "secret" liens.

These cases would appear to hold that as to a secured party with knowledge, a consignor should prevail. Absent the intervention of a bankruptcy that may be true but in this case that analysis would not give priority to Star but to the Debtor in Possession under BC 544(a)(1) and (2). BC 544 gives the Debtor in Possession a perfected interest in the goods superior to that of Star. Although the Court is convinced that this transaction was intended to be a consignment, Star did not protect its interest by placing a sign at the site, by

[Margin annotations: "Words alone serve" — "adequate notice will save — make still a consignment so that consignor (or) creditor can't reach"]

establishing that all of the Debtors' creditors generally knew Star was substantially engaged in selling the goods of others or by filing a financing statement. Star is therefore not perfected and the dispute is now between Bank and the Debtor in Possession. With respect to the relative priorities of these two parties, the Bank's knowledge of the consignment is not relevant. It is not disputed that the Bank perfected a security interest in all inventory and after acquired property of the Debtors prior to the filing of the bankruptcy petition. The Court therefore holds that the Bank has a security interest in these goods.

This Opinion does not preclude the Debtor in Possession or Star from asserting that substantially all of the inventory in the possession of the Debtors was consigned by Star to the Debtors and was known by all of the Debtors' creditors to be substantially selling consigned goods. That issue was not litigated at the hearing.

An appropriate Order will issue.

WINSHIP, THE "TRUE" CONSIGNMENT UNDER THE UNIFORM COMMERCIAL CODE, AND RELATED PECCADILLOES
29 Sw. L.J. 825, 846-848 (1975)

There is no consensus on a test, but the field has been ably surveyed from different vantage points by Professor Hawkland and Mr. Richard Duesenberg. These tests are easily stated. Professor Hawkland suggests the following functional test: whether the parties use the consignment as a concession to dealers who are unwilling to assume the risk of finding a market for the goods (a consignment intended as security) or use the device as a price-fixing arrangement (a "true" consignment). [See, e.g., Hawkland, Consignment Selling Under the Uniform Commercial Code, 67 Com. L.J. 146 (1962).] Duesenberg proposes that the test should be whether or not consignor and consignee establish in word and deed that they stand in relation to each other as principal and agent. [See Duesenberg, Consignments Under the UCC: A Comment on Emerging Principles, 26 Bus. Law. 565 (1970).] Professor Hawkland relies heavily on legislative history for his test. He notes that initially section 1-201(37) made all consignments "security interests." The provision had to be changed because "the price-fixing consignment is patently not a security transaction and obviously would not fit easily, if at all, under some of the provisions of Article 9." . . . Duesenberg questions the source and rationale of Hawkland's test. A consignment (agency, bailment) relationship may be set up not only to permit consignor to fix prices but also, for example, to control the quality of marketing and after-sale services offered by the consignee. He finds nothing in the Code wording or legislative history which indicates that price-fixing rather than agency relations in general were excluded from the scope of article 9 by the 1957 amendments. Duesenberg points out that many of the article 9 provisions, especially the default rules in part 5, are written for the debtor whose "indebtedness" is secured rather than for the consignee-agent who by definition is not indebted for the price of the goods. On more general policy grounds he argues that Hawkland's distinction will subject so many consignment marketing arrangements to all of article 9's provisions that it will discourage a legitimate marketing device worked out freely by consignor and consignee.

One advantage of the Hawkland test is its simplicity. The general agency test suggested by Duesenberg requires not only careful drafting but also continual policing by consignor for fear that a court, looking at the numerous incidents of an agency relationship, will find that the consignment arrangement is no longer a true agency relationship and, therefore, subject to article 9. By focusing on one incident of the relation between the parties the test proposed by Hawkland allows the parties to determine from the beginning whether their marketing arrangement will be subject to articles 2 and 9.

A test proposed by Professor Gilmore may resolve some of the conflicting considerations raised by Hawkland and Duesenberg. [See 1 G. Gilmore, Security Interests in Personal Property 337-340 (1965).] Professor Gilmore suggests that the distinction should turn on whether or not the consignee has the right to return unsold goods. If the consignee is absolutely liable for the price of the "consigned" goods, with no right to return the goods unsold, then the consignor's reserved claim to the goods should be treated as a security interest subject to all the provisions of article 9; otherwise the relevant article 2 provisions should apply. In any case, he rejects a distinction based on the subjective intent of the parties.

NOTES & QUESTIONS

1. *Debtor's rights in consigned goods.* If a transaction falls within the scope of UCC 2-326(3) it is deemed a *sale or return.* UCC 2-326(2) provides that goods held on sale or return are subject to the buyer's creditors while the goods are in his possession. Does the consignee have sufficient rights in consigned goods so that he is able to grant another creditor a security interest in them? Would your answer be different if the transaction does not fall within the scope of UCC 2-326(3) because the supplier files a financing statement under paragraph (c)?

2. *Complying with UCC 2-326(3).* If the consignor complies with one or more of the forms of publicity set out in UCC 2-326(3) the transaction is not deemed a sale or return and therefore is not governed by UCC 2-326(2). Does this mean that the consignor has priority over all the consignee's creditors? These creditors could be deemed to be on notice because of the publicity given the consignment arrangement. What if, however, a creditor has actual knowledge of the consignment arrangement but the consignor cannot show that appropriate publicity has been given under UCC 2-326(3)?

3. *Notice to a consignee's inventory financer (UCC 9-114).* If Star Furniture had filed a financing statement as authorized by UCC 9-408 would it have had priority over National Bank? Does UCC 2-326(3)(c) *require* Star Furniture to file the financing statement? UCC 9-114 assimilates Star Furniture to the supplier of goods who retains a purchase money security interest. Both suppliers will have their interests subordinated to a prior inventory financer with an after-acquired property clause unless they give this financer additional notice beyond the filing of a financing statement. UCC 9-114(1), 9-312(3).

4. *Code treatment of consignments and leases.* Contrast the way the UCC treats consignments with its treatment of leases (see p. 239 supra). If a transaction is a "true" lease Article 9 does not apply, and there is no equivalent of UCC 2-326. If a transaction is a "true" consignment, on the other hand, UCC 2-326 does apply and will usually require the supplier to comply with Article 9 filing requirements and the special notice requirements of UCC 9-114. Is there any justification for this different treatment? See generally Coogan, Leases of Equipment and Some Other Unconventional Security Devices: An Analysis of UCC Section 1-201(37) and Article 9, 1973 Duke L.J. 909 (1973).

D. ACCOUNTS RECEIVABLE FINANCING

Assume your client has invested in a retail business that sells office and home furniture. Finance Company agrees to provide financing with your client's accounts receivable—defined broadly to include accounts, chattel paper, and instruments—serving as collateral to secure repayment of the periodic loans Finance Company will extend to your client. Your client asks you to review the proposed arrangement with Finance Company from a legal perspective.

Before you answer the five basic secured-transactions questions you will want to keep in mind two preliminary matters: (a) the different forms the accounts receivable will take, and (b) the distinction between the initial sale or lease between your client and his customer and the subsequent loan transaction between your client and Finance Company.

As to the forms of accounts receivable, you will have to keep business and Code terminology straight. Your client explains that when he sells furniture he may (1) give his good customers short-term unsecured credit, (2) accept unsecured promissory notes, (3) have buyers sign a conditional sales contract, or (4) take checks in payment. More recently he has begun to lease furniture and takes (5) a lease form signed by the lessees. In Code terminology these proceeds will be accounts, chattel paper, or instruments—or contract rights in jurisdictions where the 1962 official text is in force. The proceeds may also be characterized more generally as intangibles or semi-intangibles.

The most simple form to understand is the account. You may have studied in your Contracts class the rights of the assignee of contract obligations and the defenses available to the contract party whose obligations were assigned. See UCC 2-210, 9-318. The other forms of proceeds may be considered accounts that have been "paperized," i.e., the obligations represented by the account are embodied in the paper. As you know from your study of promissory notes in Chapter 1, you deal with the obligations embodied in a negotiable instrument by dealing with the paper itself; prior claims and defenses may be cut off by negotiation of the paper. Chattel paper may be considered as quasi-negotiable, sharing attributes of both the account and the fully negotiable instrument. (After your study you may conclude that there has been an evolution from abstract contract rights towards paper rights. See Clark, Abstract Rights versus Paper Rights under Article 9 of the Uniform Commercial Code, 84 Yale L.J. 445 (1975).)

When analyzing the proposed receivables financing arrangement you will also want to distinguish clearly between two interrelated transactions: the initial sale or lease transaction between your client and his customer (Transaction 1), and the subsequent loan transaction between your client and Finance Company (Transaction 2). If your client, for example, has his customer sign a conditional sales contract for the purchase of office furniture your client will perfect his security interest in the furniture following the rules for perfecting a security interest in goods. The conditional sales contract happens to be chattel paper but for your client this is irrelevant in Transaction 1. When, however, your client borrows from Finance Company he is transformed from a secured party to a debtor; in this second transaction he will secure his obligation to repay the loan with his receivables, including the conditional sales contract (chattel paper). Finance Company will perfect its security interest following the rules applicable to each type of receivable, which in the case of chattel paper will be to file a financing statement or to take possession of the paper.

Keeping these preliminary distinctions clearly in mind you might analyze Article 9's application to your client's proposed receivables financing arrangement:

1. **Scope.** With limited exceptions Article 9 governs the use of accounts receivable—accounts, chattel paper, and instruments—as collateral. UCC 9-102(1)(a), 9-104(f). Article 9 goes further, however, because its provisions also apply to the sale of accounts or chattel paper. UCC 9-102(1)(b). In other words, if Finance Company agreed to act as factor (see the discussion on the business background set out at the beginning of the chapter) it would purchase your client's accounts and chattel paper but would still be an Article 9 secured party. As the Official Comment to UCC 9-102 notes, "[c]ommercial financing on the basis of accounts and chattel paper is often so conducted that the distinction between a security transfer and a sale is blurred." The draftsmen decided, therefore, to have the same rules govern the conceptually distinct transactions. Only with respect to the distribution of any surplus following default does the distinction make a difference. UCC 9-502(2); see the *Major's Furniture* case infra. This solution should be compared with the UCC treatment of "true" and "security" leases and consignments. See pp. 239 & 309 supra.

2. **Attachment.** The usual rules governing attachment in UCC 9-203 will apply. Repeal of a provision of the 1962 official text stating that the debtor has no rights in an account "until it comes into existence" makes no substantive change in the law. 1962 UCC 9-204(2)(d). Remember that the 1972 official text's definition of "account" incorporates the prior text's definition of "contract right" insofar as the latter term included contracts for the sale or lease of goods and for the rendering of services. As a result, your client will have rights in an account when he enters into an unsecured contract to sell or lease furniture to a customer.

3. **Perfection.** Each form of your client's receivables must be considered separately to determine the applicable rules for perfection:

a. A security interest in accounts may be perfected only by filing a financing statement. UCC 9-302(1); but see 9-302(1)(e) (automatic perfection when "an assignment of accounts which does not alone or in conjunction with other assignments to the same assignee transfer a significant part of the outstanding accounts of the assignor").

b. A security interest in chattel paper may be perfected either by filing or by having the secured party take possession of the chattel paper. UCC 9-304(1), 9-305.

c. A security interest in instruments may be perfected only by the secured party taking possession. UCC 9-305; but see 9-304(4), (5) (automatic perfection for limited time).

If your client has a multistate business, Finance Company must consult the special rules of UCC 9-103(3) and (4) to determine how to perfect its security interest in accounts and chattel paper. In the case of accounts and nonpossessory security interests in chattel paper these rules lead to the law of the state where your client has his place of business or chief executive office. If Finance Company takes possession of the chattel paper the law of the state where the chattel paper is located will govern.

4. **Priority.** To sort out priority issues you must remember to distinguish Transaction 1, in which your client sells or leases furniture to a customer, and Transaction 2, in which your client borrows from Finance Company and uses the receivables that arose in the first transaction as collateral for this second transaction. After Transaction 1 but before Transaction 2, your client's priority with respect to the furniture will be determined by the rules already studied. UCC 9-201, 9-301, 9-306, 9-307, 9-312. After your client assigns the receivables to Finance Company, however, you will have to distinguish between claimants against the receivables serving as collateral for Transaction 2 and claimants to the furniture sold or leased in Transaction 1.

Consider first Finance Company's priority with respect to the receivables: if the company perfects its security interest in the receivables it will have priority over your client's unsecured creditors, subsequent lien creditors, and subsequent secured parties who perfect their security interest in the receivables by filing. UCC 9-201, 9-301, 9-312. As for subsequent purchasers of the receivables, including secured parties who perfect by taking possession of chattel paper or an instrument, Finance Company's interest will be subordinated to the claims of purchasers who are the equivalent of the buyer in ordinary course. Thus Finance Company's interest is subject to the rights of a subsequent financer who purchases the chattel paper or instruments for new value and who takes possession of the chattel paper or instruments in the ordinary course of his business. UCC 9-308; see also 9-309 (protection of holders "in due course" of negotiable instruments, documents, and investment securities).

Next consider Finance Company's position with respect to competing claimants to the furniture serving as collateral for Transaction 1. The key Code provision is UCC 9-302(2):

> If a secured party assigns a perfected security interest, no filing under this Article is required in order to continue the perfected status of the security interest against creditors of and transferees from the original debtor.

The Official Comments give the following illustration of this provision: "Buyer buys goods from seller who retains a security interest in them which he perfects. Seller assigns the perfected security interest to X. The security interest, in X's hands and without further steps on his part, continues perfected against *Buyer's* transferees and creditors. If, however, the assignment from Seller to X was itself intended for security (or was a sale of accounts or chattel paper), X must take whatever steps may be required for perfection in order to be protected against *Seller's* transferees and creditors." (Emphasis in original.) In other words, if your client perfects his security interest in the furniture by filing a financing statement Finance Company will have priority over the customer's unsecured creditors, lien creditors, subsequent secured parties, and purchasers.

Finally, consider the extent to which Finance Company may be affected by the defenses or claims your client's customer may have against your client that might arise, for example, from Transaction 1 itself or from other transactions between your client and that particular customer. At the time your client and his customer enter into Transaction 1 the customer may agree not to assert any defense or claim against an assignee, such as Finance Company. If the agreement is embodied in a promissory note these defenses or claims will be cut off by negotiation under the law of negotiable instruments set out in UCC Article 3. If the agreement is part of a sale or lease contract UCC 9-206 makes the agreement enforceable with limited exceptions. UCC 9-206(1) ("Subject to any statute or decision which establishes a different rule for buyers or lessees of consumer goods . . ."). If the customer does not agree to waive these defenses or claims then Finance Company takes the assigned account or chattel paper subject to any defenses or claims arising from Transaction 1 and any other offset the customer could assert against your client that accrues before Finance Company notifies the customer of the assignment. UCC 9-318.

5. **Default.** Again you must distinguish between default in Transaction 1 and default in Transaction 2. If your client defaults on his obligation to Finance Company then the latter may take possession of any proceeds to which

it is entitled and may notify your client's customers that they are to make subsequent payments directly to Finance Company. UCC 9-502(1). If Finance Company has a right of recourse against your client for any deficiency, as it normally would if the receivables secure a loan, Finance Company must collect the receivables in a "commercially reasonable manner" and account to your client for any surplus. UCC 9-502(2). If the customer has not defaulted on his obligations in Transaction 1, however, Finance Company may not proceed against the furniture purchased by the customer.

If, on the other hand, your client does not default but the customer in Transaction 1 does, the Code provides limited guidance. It is clear that if Finance Company holds an instrument or chattel paper issued by the defaulting customer Finance Company has a duty to preserve rights against prior parties. UCC 9-207. But beyond this straightforward rule the Code is less than clear. It does not state clearly, for example, who may proceed against the defaulting customer and any collateral securing his obligation. See Wadsworth v. Yancy Brothers Co. at p. 322 infra. Your client and Finance Company may agree, of course, on who may act. They may also agree to have your client indemnify Finance Company against a customer's default by repurchasing, for example, any account or chattel paper when the customer defaults (a "recourse" agreement).

If Transaction 2 between your client and Finance Company was a sale of accounts and chattel paper rather than a pledge of this collateral, Finance Company is owner and can retain any surplus from collection. When chattel paper is involved Finance Company will also have a security interest in the furniture sold or leased in Transaction 1.

Problem 6-11. Star Furniture agrees to grant Finance Company a security interest in the accounts receivable generated by the sale of office and home furniture to secure repayment of periodic loans to be made by Finance Company. As attorney for Finance Company you are asked to draw up an appropriate security agreement. Review the documentation in the prototype transaction set out in Chapter 3. What changes will have to be made? For an example of an accounts receivable financing form, see 5 Uniform Laws Annotated, Uniform Commercial Code Forms and Materials, Form 9:1100 (R. Henson & W. Davenport eds. 1968). See also the following analysis of a hypothetical accounts receivable financing agreement.

MILLER, TAKING A LOOK AT THE COMMERCIAL FINANCE CONTRACT
65 A.B.A.J. 628, 628-630 (1979)

The rapid expansion of collateralized lending for business purposes in recent years has required many lawyers to look at commercial finance contracts for the first time, and they have been uniformly horrified.

Like many other standardized forms, the commercial finance agreement is a product of evolution and has tended to accumulate layers of boilerplate without the deletion or modification of outmoded clauses. The document is not engraved in stone, however, and it may be useful for lawyers to know which clauses ought to be scrutinized most closely, which are more susceptible to change, and which the lender is likely to be more adamant about retaining. . . .

When a borrower submits a receivables financing contract to an attorney for review, the finance company already will have completed its field audit and obtained the approval of its loan committee. Typically the loan agreement will call for a percentage advance against receivables (usually 80 percent) for which the client will pay a specified rate. Since these terms have been mutually agreed to by both borrower and lender, there should be no problem. But from then on the going may be sticky. The standard contract gives the lender all sorts of rights and powers, most of which never have to be employed but which are required to ensure access to the collateral in the event of default and to help protect against fraud, which is the largest single cause of losses in commercial finance.

The first paragraph of the [hypothetical] agreement, for example, states that the lender will act as the borrower's "sole source of financing." The intent is, however, that the lender will be the sole source of secured financing for receivables and other assets that may be covered by the contract. The contract is not intended to preclude the borrower from obtaining funds from other sources—real estate mortgages, long-term loans from insurance companies, public money, bank lines of credit, private loans, or any other type of financing. It would be appropriate for the borrower's attorney to request that the language be adjusted to the specific situation.

The next paragraph notes that the receivables are security for loans and for any other obligations of any kind that the borrower "may now or at any time hereafter owe to the lender." If there are any other obligations to the lending institution that are not intended to be covered by the collateral, it is important to note the exceptions or otherwise express the limitation.

We now come to the paragraph that contains the most important clause in the financing contract. It is one that bothers attorneys most but is least susceptible to revision. One key portion reads like this: "At the time of the assignment of receivables, we shall advance to you, upon your request but at our discretion, a sum up to 80 per cent of the net amount of receivables to us." There are three key phrases in this clause. An attorney might well begin to question it by asking, "Since my client negotiated for an 80 per cent advance, why don't you just say 80 per cent? Does the hedge mean that you might decide to advance 70 per cent, or 60 per cent, or 20 per cent?"

The answer is yes—that is precisely what it means. But go even further and ask about the phrase "at our discretion." "Does this mean that you don't have to make any advances?" Again the answer is yes! And whatever percentage the lender decides to advance at its discretion, the amount will be against "acceptable" receivables, yet nowhere does the contract define what is acceptable.

The next clause goes on in the same vein: "As additional receivables are assigned by you to us, we may advance additional sums." This paragraph is the guts of a receivables financing agreement. If you recognize how the financing mechanism operates, you will see why the lender will strongly resist any softening of the language.

An audit is made at the inception of a financing arrangement. Receivables are examined, aged, and checked against shipping receipts. On confirmation, the lender stipulates that the receivables are acceptable. But once the initial advance is made and collection of the receivables progresses, sales create new receivables and within a period of weeks there may have been a complete turnover of receivables. The new receivables may not be of the same quality as the old, and prudence may dictate that the lender reduce advances to a lower percentage. A borrower might, for example, begin to make a larger percentage of sales on consignment, a receivable that is not acceptable security.

The lender's initial evaluation also takes into account the over-all financial condition of the borrower as well as the quality of the collateral. If this condition should worsen, it might be prudent to continue making advances. A serious breach of the agreement, such as failure to turn over collections or the assignment of fraudulent receivables, also would be a ground for discontinuing advances.

Nevertheless, a borrower's attorney must be concerned that the lender may put his client out of business by withholding advances. Should the lender misuse its powers, of course, it would be liable and subject to a very good lawsuit. But that is small comfort to a borrower who would rather be operating a business than engaging in litigation. This situation poses a dilemma, because the commercial finance company will be adamant and will resist any changes in this language.

The best recommendation is that the borrower's attorney should advise clients to make sure of the lender. . . .

Once the secured lender is assured the right of access to the collateral and the prerogative of deciding which assets are acceptable as security, you can expect much more flexibility with respect to other parts of the contract.

Another clause typically found in the contract provides that the borrower "shall not allow any discount, credit, or allowance to be issued to a customer without prior consent" of the lender. This clause is invoked only when a financing goes sour and can be modified by the borrower's attorney so that the borrower can do business in its customary manner. I suggest that it be altered to read that the borrower continue these normal business practices unless notified to the contrary by the lender.

Most lenders also seek to "retain the right at all times of notifying customers that receivables have been assigned to us, and to collect such receivables directly in our own name." There also is wording to the effect that the lender shall have the right at any time to take possession of the client's books and records and remove them from the borrower's premises. Both of these clauses are intended to cover "disaster" situations, and the borrower could get some relief by providing that these actions can be taken only "upon default."

The contract also contains a number of other "disaster" clauses. For example, the assignment of "power of attorney" to an officer of the lending company with authorization to open mail, endorse bills of lading, and so forth, is obviously intended for use only in extreme events, such as a liquidation. This language is negotiable and can be adjusted, so that these powers also are exercisable only in the event of default.

One of the more baffling portions of the contract concerns the interest charges. You may find it expressed in this manner: "Our interest charge is to be an amount equal to 1/24.40 of 1 per cent on the net balance due us at the close of each day." If the fraction is expressed as a decimal, it is even more confusing. This daily percentage is usually determined by dividing the simple annual interest rate by 360. It is traditional in commercial finance to calculate interest on a 360-day year rather than 365 days. The origin of the practice is lost in antiquity, but it does give the lender a slight edge.

The daily percentage will change if the prime rate changes since the annual interest is set at a certain percentage over prime. It is essential, therefore, that the contract specify how the prime rate is to be determined. If the prime rate of a particular bank is to be the guide, the contract should say so. Generalities such as "the prevailing prime rate" or the "New York prime rate" should be avoided.

The contract may require "reports of certified public accountants satisfactory to the lender" and "periodic confirmation of receivables." If the borrower does not routinely obtain certified statements, alteration of this clause may be in order. Or, if an accounting firm is already retained by the client, then advance agreement should be sought from the finance company that the accountant is satisfactory and acceptable. Fidelity bonds on certain employees also may be called for by the contract. Unless the specific employees and amounts are listed, this clause should also be stricken.

Termination clauses deserve close scrutiny because most finance contracts are written for a term of one year or more and are self-renewing unless terminated within a specified period. When the financing relationship is mutually satisfactory, contracts may run on for many years, but there certainly should be some reasonable means of termination after the initial period.

Finally, there is the question of personal guarantees that most finance companies require of the principal owners. These requirements may seem excessive in a collateralized arrangement, but they are not merely arbitrary.

Fraud is the primary cause of commercial finance losses. In fact, given the absence of fraud, it is rare that a commercial finance company will take a loss. Personal gurantees are a means of keeping fraud at a minimum. They also help to maximize the liquidation value of collateral. If a borrower goes into bankruptcy, it is vital that the principal remains available to assist the lender in the liquidation. Spurious disputes over receivables can be held in check and, if inventories are involved, sale by the principal will generally bring a higher value than liquidation by an auctioneer. Since the personal guarantees have these benefits as primary objectives, it may be possible to set some dollar limitation on the guarantees.

Problem 6-12. Manufacturer grants Bank a security interest in its "accounts receivable" to secure repayment of a loan made to it by Bank. Bank promptly files a financing statement covering "accounts" and stamps all Manufacturer's account books and invoices with the statement "Subject to Bank's security interest." Six months later Manufacturer files a petition for reorganization under Chapter 11 of the Bankruptcy Code.

(a) Does Bank have a secured claim as to accounts and chattel paper that come into existence after the signing of the security agreement but before the filing of the bankruptcy petition?

(b) Does Bank have a secured claim as to a contract to sell goods entered into before the petition but which Manufacturer carries out after the petition?

Problem 6-13. Owner agrees to pay Contractor $100,000 for specified construction work, payment to be made as construction progresses. Before beginning the construction work Contractor borrows $60,000 from Bank and assigns his contract with Owner as collateral.

(a) What terminology does the Code use to describe Owner, Contractor, and Bank? See UCC 9-105, 9-318.

(b) Is the assignment excluded from the coverage of Article 9? See UCC 9-104(f).

(c) If Contractor signs a security agreement but Bank does not file a financing statement is Bank's security interest perfected? See UCC 9-302(1)(e).

(d) Assume that Contractor has outstanding accounts with a face value of $700,000 but all except the assigned account result from work completed more than 60 days before the assignment and are classified as dubious. Is Bank's security interest in the assigned account perfected? See UCC 9-302(1)(e) and Comment 5.

(e) Contractor fails to complete the construction work and defaults on his loan payments to Bank. To what extent may Bank enforce the assigned account against Owner? See UCC 9-318.

(f) Contractor runs into financial difficulties and Bank asks Owner to make future progress payments directly to it. By false representations as to the progress made, Contractor persuades Owner to make several progress payments to Bank. Contractor fails to complete the construction work and defaults on his loan payments to Bank. Owner learns of the misrepresentations. May Owner recover the payments made to Bank? See UCC 9-318; Michelin Tires (Canada) Ltd. v. First Natl. Bank, 666 F.2d 673, 32 UCC Rep. 657 (1st Cir. 1981).

(g) May Owner prohibit assignment of the account by a contract term to that effect? See UCC 9-318(4).

Problem 6-14. As security for the repayment of periodic loans Star Furniture grants Finance Company a security interest in all its inventory, accounts, and chattel paper then owned or thereafter acquired. Finance Company has filed in the proper office a financing statement covering inventory, accounts, and chattel paper. Star Furniture subsequently has sold a living room suite to Customer.

(a) Assume the sale to Customer was on unsecured credit. Star Furniture, without informing Finance Company, assigns the account to Bank as security for a loan from Bank. Neither Finance Company nor Bank informs Customer of its claims to the account. As between Finance Company and Bank, which lender has priority in the account? Would your answer be different if Bank informed Customer of its interest in the account before Finance Company gave any notice to Customer? What if the account is sold to Bank rather than used as collateral?

(b) Assume that Customer has signed an installment sales contract. Star Furniture, without informing Finance Company, assigns the chattel paper to Bank as security for a loan. Bank takes possession of the chattel paper. As between Finance Company and Bank, which lender has priority in the chattel paper? Would your answer be different if Finance Company has given new value to Star Furniture for the chattel paper but has left the chattel paper in the hands of Star Furniture? What if Star Furniture had sold the chattel paper to Bank rather than using it for collateral? See UCC 9-108, 9-308.

(c) Assume that Customer has signed a promissory note made payable to the order of Star Furniture. Star Furniture, without informing Finance Company, transfers the note to Bank by indorsement and delivery as collateral for a loan. As between Finance Company and Bank, which lender has priority in the note? Would your answer be different if Star Furniture delivered but did not indorse the note to Bank? What if Bank had bought the note rather than taking it as collateral for a loan? See UCC 9-309.

FELDMAN v. FIRST NATIONAL CITY BANK (IN RE LEASING CONSULTANTS, INC.)
486 F.2d 367, 13 UCC Rep. 189 (2d Cir. 1973)

JAMESON, District Judge. Respondent-Appellant, First National City Bank (Bank), appeals from an order of the district court affirming, on a petition for review, the order of a referee in bankruptcy directing the Bank to turn over to the Petitioner-Appellee, George Feldman, Trustee in Bankruptcy (Trustee) of Leasing Consultants, Incorporated (Leasing) the proceeds from the sale of equipment which had been leased by Leasing, located in New York, to Plastimetrix Corporation, located in New Jersey. The leases covering the equipment had been assigned to the Bank as security for a loan to Leasing.

The district court held, 351 F. Supp. 1390, on the basis of stipulated facts, that the perfection by the Bank by filing and possession in New York of its security interest in the lease/chattel paper was not a perfection of the Bank's security interest in Leasing's reversionary interest in the leased property, located in New Jersey. Consequently, the Trustee's lien was held superior to the Bank's unperfected security interest in the leased equipment. . . .

In March and June of 1969 Leasing entered into eight leases with Plastimetrix covering heavy equipment. The leased equipment was at all relevant times located in New Jersey. Leasing filed financing statements with the Secretary of State of the State of New Jersey covering each transaction, each statement bearing the legend: "This filing is for informational purposes only as this is a lease transaction."

On December 15, 1969 Leasing entered into a "Loan and Security Agreement" with the Bank for the financing of its business of purchasing and leasing equipment. The agreement provided in part for the assignment of a "continuing security interest in the lease(s) and the property leased" as collateral security for advances and loans not to exceed 80% of aggregate unpaid rentals.

Pursuant to the security agreement Leasing borrowed money from the Bank in December, 1969 and February, 1970 and assigned as collateral security the eight Plastimetrix leases, each assignment covering all moneys due or to become due under the lease and the "relative equipment" described in the lease. The lease documents were delivered to the Bank.

On December 30 and 31, 1969 the Bank filed financing statements against Leasing with the Secretary of State of New York and the Registrar of the City of New York, Queens County, where Leasing had its principal place of business.[1] No financing statements were filed by the Bank in New Jersey; nor did the Bank take possession of the leased equipment.

On October 14, 1970 Leasing was adjudicated bankrupt. . . . On October 30, 1970 Plastimetrix filed a petition under Chapter XI of the Bankruptcy Act. . . .

[With the consent of Leasing's Trustee, Bank sold its interest in the leases and equipment for $60,000. Both Trustee and Bank claimed the proceeds. They agreed to submit the following question to the court: "Was the Bank required to file a financing statement against the Bankrupt with the Secretary of State of New Jersey in order to perfect a security interest in the leases assigned to it and the equipment leased thereunder by the Bankrupt to Plastimetrix?"]

Based on the stipulation of counsel, the [district court] assumed that the agreements between Leasing and Plastimetrix were "true leases" and not "conditional sales agreements" or devices intended to create only a security interest. Accordingly the court found that the Bank acquired "a security interest in both the right to receive rental payments under the lease and in the reversionary interest in the underlying equipment."

1. The financing statement covered "continuing security interest in leases and any and all rents due and to become due thereunder, including all related equipment described therein, chattel paper represented thereby, accounts receivable therewith and proceeds arising therefrom."

The court held, and the parties agree, that the leases themselves were "chattel papers" (UCC 9-105(1)(b)) and that the Bank's security interest in chattel paper was perfected by filing financing statements in New York and taking possession of the leases. UCC 9-304(1), 9-305, and 9-102(1).

The court held further: "By contrast, the machines themselves constituted 'equipment' located in New Jersey and hence, for perfection purposes, came within the scope of the New Jersey requirements." The Bank having failed to perfect its interest in the reversion in New Jersey, the court concluded that the Trustee "—a lien creditor within the meaning of UCC 9-301(3)—has priority over an unperfected security interest under UCC 9-301(1)(b)."

Emphasizing the distinction between rights under the chattel paper and reversionary interest in the equipment, the court quoted from Professor Levie as follows: "In one situation the purchaser of a security agreement may have an advantage over the purchaser of a lease. Where [he] purchases equipment leases, he takes only an assignor's interest in the equipment itself. If [he] wishes to be secured by an interest in the goods as well, he must obtain a security interest . . . [in the goods] and perfect it." Levie, Security Interests in Chattel Paper, 78 Yale L.J. 935, 940 (1969).[4]

The district court concluded: "The distinction between the rights represented by the lease and those represented by the reversionary interest in the equipment is a real one, supported by logic and precedent. To ignore the distinction contributes neither to clarity nor uniformity under the Uniform Commercial Code. Moreover, it may mislead third party creditors. The simple solution for a bank in the situation of petitioner is to file notices as to its interest in the reversion in accordance with the law of the state where the equipment is located." . . .

In contending that the filing and physical possession of the lease instruments in New York were sufficient to cover the leased equipment located in New Jersey, appellant argues that the "reversionary interest" of Leasing is "an intangible interest sited at Leasing's domicile in New York, and not in New Jersey." If the reversionary interest in the equipment were characterized as a "general intangible," the Bank's security interest in the equipment would have been perfected when it filed with the New York Department of State and in the county in which Leasing had a place of business. UCC 9-103(2), 9-401(1)(c) [see 1972 UCC 9-103(3)—Eds.].

---

4. The court continued: "Practical considerations support this conclusion. The property leased was heavy manufacturing equipment. A potential creditor observing these complicated and non-portable machines should be entitled to believe that he could discover all non-possessory interests by consulting the files in the state where the equipment is located. The equipment was obviously of great value; the New Jersey files revealed only that the lessee held it under a lease. Since the lease agreement required each piece of equipment to have a plate affixed indicating that it was the 'property' of the lessor, judgment creditors of the lessor might assume that its reversionary interest in the equipment was of substantial value. Not being alerted to the diminution in value which would be affected by the creditor's security interest, they might then, for example, attach the lessor's interest, relying on an apparently unencumbered and valuable reversionary interest."

The policies of the Code, however, militate against such an interpretati\ We agree with the district court that the reversionary interest is an interest\ "goods" rather than an interest in intangibles, and that to perfect the security interest in the reversionary interest in the equipment it was necessary to file a\ financing statement in New Jersey where the equipment was located. UCC 9-102(1), 9-302, 9-401(1)(c).

Obviously the leased property itself is "goods." We conclude, as did the district court, that the future reversionary interest is likewise an interest in goods, whether it represents "equipment" or "inventory" collateral. The drafters of the Code classified collateral mainly according to the nature or use of the underlying entity, rather than the character of its ownership at any given time. Significantly, the examples of "general intangibles" given in the Official Comment to UCC 9-106 are all types of property that are inherently intangible. And several Code sections and comments suggest that a collateral interest in "goods" remains such even when the goods are leased. See UCC 9-103(2); 9-109(4) and Official Comment 3; 9-304(3); UCC 9-109, N.Y. Practice Commentary 2 (McKinney 1964) (Kripke).

We conclude accordingly that if the instruments were "true leases," the security interest in the leased equipment was not perfected because of the failure of the Bank to file financing statements in New Jersey.[8] . . .

[Remanded to reconsider effect of the parties' stipulations.]

NOTES & QUESTIONS

1. *Lease as a disguised conditional sale.* If the leases in *In re Leasing* were disguised conditional sales contracts they would have created Article 9 security interests in the goods. UCC 1-201(37); see the discussion at p. 239 supra. Review the introductory note to accounts receivable financing and consider the following questions.

(a) Before assigning the "lease" to the bank, how would Leasing perfect its security interest in the equipment "leased" to Plastimetrix? What must Leasing or the bank do to continue this perfected security interest in the equipment after Leasing assigns the "lease" to the bank? See UCC 9-302(2); 9-405. Note that this perfected interest protects Leasing and the bank from claims made by Plastimetrix creditors and not Leasing creditors.

(b) After the assignment of the "lease" to the bank, what steps must the bank take to perfect its security interest in the "lease" and thereby protect

8. Appellant alternatively contends that since "Leasing had assigned all of its interest in the machinery and equipment to the Bank" it had preferential rights to the equipment under "the law of bailment leases" regardless of the Code provisions. The assignment of the equipment from Leasing to the Bank, however, was expressly made "as security for any and all obligations of [Leasing] to the Bank under and pursuant to the Loan and Security Agreement. . . ." This assignment clearly created a security interest in the Bank and made the requirements of Article 9 applicable to the Bank's interest in the equipment. UCC 9-102(1)(a).

itself against the claims to the "lease" of Leasing's creditors? Note that the lease will be chattel paper whether or not it is a true or security lease.

2. *Lease as a "true" lease.* At the end of the lease term a lessee in a true lease transaction has an obligation to return the leased goods. The court in *In re Leasing* struggles with how the bank must perfect its interest in this "reversionary interest," and assumes that the bank was granted a security interest in the reversion by the security agreement and not by the mere assignment of the lease. In other words, the lease does not include the reversionary interest. Do you agree? Does a lease term requiring the lessee to return the equipment at the end of the term necessarily incorporate the reversionary interest? If you consider the rules on perfection as being designed to give notice to creditors, whose creditors (Leasing's or Plastimetrix's) should be given notice of the reversionary interest? Where would these creditors be more likely to look (New York or New Jersey) to discover whether there was a reversionary interest subject to a security interest? For a critical analysis of the text case see Note, In re Leasing Consultants, Inc.: The Double Perfection Rule for Security Assignments of True Leases, 84 Yale L.J. 1722 (1975).

3. *Further reading.* Jackson, Embodiment of Rights in Goods and the Concept of Chattel Paper, 50 U. Chi. L. Rev. 1051 (1983); Boss, Lease Chattel Paper: Unitary Treatment of a "Special" Kind of Commercial Specialty, 1983 Duke L.J. 69; Levie, Security Interests in Chattel Paper, 78 Yale L.J. 935 (1969), reprinted as ch. 28 in 1C P. Coogan et al., Secured Transactions Under the Uniform Commercial Code (1963, 1984).

WADSWORTH v. YANCEY BROTHERS CO.
423 So. 2d 1343, 34 UCC Rep. 1072 (Ala. 1982)

JONES, Justice. Appellant Bill Wadsworth appeals from an adverse judgment entered in an action by Yancey Brothers to recover a deficiency from the sale of a repossessed D-8-H Caterpillar tractor after Wadsworth defaulted on the conditional sales contract for which the tractor was collateral. . . .

Debtor raises the issue whether, after debtor's default under a security agreement and creditor's repossession and sale of the collateral, creditor must allege and prove, as part of its prima facie case, ownership of the contract at the time it repossesses and sells the collateral as a prerequisite to its right of action against debtor for a deficiency balance. A secondary issue (or perhaps the primary issue restated), essential to the disposition of this appeal, is whether failure of creditor to give notice to debtor of the assignment of chattel paper, with recourse, altered debtor's obligation to the original creditor under the contract, where, after default for nonpayment, the creditor repossesses and sells the collateral prior to the reassignment of the contract to the original assignor. . . .

In May of 1978, Wadsworth and Yancey began negotiations for Wadsworth's purchase of the D-8-H tractor. After a one-month rental period under a "buy-try" agreement, which applied the rental payments to the tractor's purchase price, the parties consummated a "conditional sale security agreement" on July 26, 1978, listing a purchase price of $97,926.50 (repair costs and finance charges included). Shortly thereafter, the contract was assigned by Yancey to the First National Bank of Chicago,[1] and later reassigned to Yancey by the bank. The reassignment stamped on the back of the chattel paper bears no date. . . .

[Wadsworth defaulted, and Yancey repossessed the tractor without objection from Wadsworth. Yancey ultimately submitted the high bid in a public sale and brought an action to recover the deficiency.]

While the complete agreement is not set out, the record discloses that Yancey and the First National Bank of Chicago had a standing arrangement whereby Yancey made its own collections and took whatever steps it deemed necessary to protect its "with recourse" rights. Yancey's suit for deficiency was filed in February, 1980, and resulted in a jury verdict, and judgment entered thereon, for $22,000.00. . . .

Under the facts of this case, given the "with recourse" assignment by Yancey to the bank without notice to Wadsworth, what are the respective rights of Yancey and Wadsworth upon Wadsworth's default for non-payment? . . .

Yancey's brief, in support of the trial court's ruling states: "The transaction [between Yancey and the bank] is one of chattel paper which has its explanation in the Uniform Commercial Code; however, Appellee submits that the Uniform Commercial Code does not alone govern the immediate question before the Court in that the common law and the agreement of Yancey and the financial institution govern this question. [See UCC 1-103.] The Uniform Commercial Code defines the term chattel paper and limits its treatment . . . to the problem of perfection. The Uniform Commercial Code does not govern the rights of the 'debtor' of the chattel paper transaction and the 'secured party' of a chattel paper transaction. As a matter of fact, the Uniform Commercial Code (and its Alabama counterpart) expressly allows for different possibilities of collection methods including anticipated repossession from the original debtor by either the 'debtor' of the chattel paper or the 'secured party' of the chattel paper. This is evidenced by UCC 9-207(1). . . .

"The first . . . was the transaction in which [Wadsworth] granted to [Yancey] a security interest in [the tractor]. This transaction was evidenced by a conditional sales contract which is clearly governed by the Uniform Commercial Code. See UCC 9-102(2). The second security transaction was one in which Yancey gave a security interest in certain property to the financial

---

1. Whether the original assignment by Yancey to the bank was an outright sale or a transfer for security is not clear in the record. Admittedly, if the bank were a party to these proceedings, claiming, for example, the right of repossession as against Yancey, the true nature of the assignment, of course, would be material in determining the rights and obligations of the parties. As later discussed under part III of the opinion, however, whether the assignment was a sale or a transfer for security is immaterial as between Yancey and Wadsworth.

institution in the nature of chattel paper, that is, Yancey had an obligation from Wadsworth to pay a sum of money under the conditional sales contract. This obligation was secured by Wadsworth's equipment. To obtain financing, Yancey borrowed money from the financial institution and gave as its collateral a security interest in the obligation due from Wadsworth and the security for that obligation [is] referred to under the present law as 'chattel paper.' . . .

"[The UCC] governs the validity of a sale of chattel paper, but the Code itself understands that the right of collection from the original debtor is a matter to be left to the discretion and agreement of the chattel paper debtor and the chattel secured party. UCC 9-207(1) points out this understanding in the Code." [Presumably Yancey's attorney is referring to Yancey ("chattel paper debtor") and the bank ("chattel secured party"). What terminology would you use?—Eds.]

While we are persuaded to the ultimate conclusion of Yancey's position, we find that Yancey's argument proceeds on a flawed premise.[2] As noted earlier, the record, gleaned from Yancey's own evidence, is in conflict with respect to the nature of the assignment by it to the bank. This conflict reappears in Yancey's brief. At one point, counsel for Yancey indicates that the chattel paper was transferred as security for borrowed money, and, at another point, he refers to the transaction as a sale, thus treating the assignment as a separate secured transaction.

The initial flaw in Yancey's argument is its failure to recognize that both transactions are indeed governed by the UCC. UCC 1-103 makes clear that the general law of contract has not been abrogated by the UCC, and while those general principles are to be kept in mind, the priority of secured parties is governed entirely by Article 9 of the UCC. See, specifically, UCC 9-102(1)(b) (sale of chattel paper); UCC 9-102(2) (transfer for security of chattel paper); UCC 9-105(1)(a) (definition of account debtor), -(1)(b) (definition of chattel paper), -(1)(d) (definition of debtor); UCC 9-308 (priority of rights after outright sale of chattel paper); UCC 9-318 (rights of account debtor upon assignment); UCC 9-502 (collection rights of secured party); and UCC 9-504(5) (subrogation rights of chattel paper debtor).

Without detailing the substance of each of these sections, we believe that these sections, with accompanying Comments, clarify the status of the parties and define their rights and obligations under the facts before us.

The problem we find with the "two secured transactions" analysis is that the "second transaction" would have the legal effect of severing the assignor's interest; and the assignor could no longer act in its own right under the authority of the assigned contract. On the other hand, if the assignment to the bank was a mere pledge of the collateral for a concurrent or pre-existing debt,

---

2. Recognizing that counsel are rarely offended by criticism when they win, we, nonetheless, should be careful to point out that our "nit-picking" process is not intended as criticism. Indeed, we commend both counsel for their diligence and ingenuity in the treatment of this novel issue. Rather, we chose the process of countering Appellees' various contentions as a convenient vehicle for our analysis and treatment of the issues presented.

as opposed to an outright sale of the chattel paper, the pledgor never lost its status as a secured party. UCC 9-504(5).

While the distinction between the transfer for security of chattel paper and the outright sale of chattel paper may be of great materiality under other varying factual situations, it is a distinction without a difference in the instant case. See footnote 1, supra.

If we interpret the record as supporting an outright sale, then, there is *if a sale* ample evidence to support the conclusion that Yancey was acting in an agency relationship on behalf of the bank for the collection from the account debtor, and for its further activity in the repossession and sale of the collateral upon default. In addition to the explicit agreement with respect to collections, the conduct of the parties amply supports the agency authority of Yancey to perform all acts consistent with the holder's interest as a secured party.

If, on the other hand, we interpret the evidence as amounting to a trans- *if a transfer* fer for security, then, Yancey was acting in its own behalf as a secured party in *for security* its repossession and sale of the collateral. That is to say, if Yancey's assignment was in the nature of a pledge of the chattel paper as security for a debt and not a sale of the chattel paper, Yancey's status as a secured party remained unaltered; and its rights to collect the payment, repossess upon default, sell the property, and sue for deficiency, if any, are all governed by the applicable sections of the UCC.

Finding no error in the trial court's refusing to grant Wadsworth's motion for directed verdict, we affirm the judgment.

TORBERT, Chief Justice (concurring specially). I agree that the decision of the trial court should be affirmed, but I would address the issue differently.

The majority correctly identifies the central issue in this case: "[W]hat are the respective rights of Yancey and Wadsworth upon Wadsworth's default for non-payment?" In undertaking an analysis of these rights it is important to conceptualize the transactions clearly. There are, in fact, two security transactions involved in this case. First, Yancey Brothers, the seller, became a secured party in relation to the equipment sold to Wadsworth, the debtor/purchaser. Second, upon the transfer of its security agreement to the Bank, the Bank became a secured party with Yancey Brothers being its debtor. While the Bank's security interest in the chattel paper or in the collateral itself certainly would make it an interested party on repossession or disposition of the collateral, I find no statutory authority for cutting off the seller's rights on return or repossession of the underlying collateral.

The appellant argues that Yancey no longer owned the chattel paper at the time of the repossession, while the appellee maintains that the transfer to the Bank was not a sale but merely a transfer for security. The Uniform Commercial Code recognizes that it is not always necessary to distinguish these two transactions: "Commercial financing on the basis of accounts . . . and chattel paper is often so conducted that the distinction between a security transfer and a sale is blurred, and a sale of such property is therefore covered by [Article IX] whether intended for security or not. . . . The buyer then is treated as a secured party, and his interest as a security interest." Official Comment 2, UCC 9-102. The UCC does not directly address the issue of the rights of the holder of chattel paper in the underlying collateral. However, the Alabama version of the UCC does make explicit provisions for those situations in which the seller/assignor repossesses the underlying collateral:

> If a sale of goods results in an account or chattel paper which is transferred by the seller to a secured party, and if the goods are returned to or are repossessed by the seller or the secured party, the following rules determine priorities: . . . (b) An unpaid transferee of the chattel paper has a security interest in the goods against the transferor. [UCC 9-306(5)(b).]

Because of the operation of UCC 9-306(5)(b), on return of the goods to the seller, the holder of chattel paper has a security interest in the underlying collateral which is superior to the interest of the seller.

This approach adequately protects the secured parties regardless of whether the transaction is an absolute sale or an assignment for security of the chattel paper. In either case, following the "transfer" of the chattel paper, on repossession or return of the goods to the seller, the bank/secured party has an interest in the collateral superior to that of the seller/secured party. Again, however, the seller's interest is not completely cut off. The Comments indicate that the nature of the seller's interest in the collateral will depend upon the agreement between the seller and the bank: "In cases of *repossession by the dealer* and also in cases where the chattel was returned to the dealer by the voluntary act of the account debtor, the dealer's position may be that of a mere custodian; he may be an *agent for resale,* but without any other obligation to the holder of the chattel paper; he may be obligated to repurchase the chattel, the chattel paper or the account from the secured party or to hold it as collateral for a loan secured by a transfer of the chattel paper or the account." Official Comment 4, UCC 9-306 (emphasis added).

In the case before us, I would hold that Wadsworth has no right or standing to raise an issue as to the nature of the relationship between Yancey Brothers and the Bank. As between these parties it appears that there is no dispute involving the action taken to dispose of the collateral and that the UCC provides adequate protection of their conflicting interests in the event of a dispute. Thus, I would affirm the trial court's judgment.

Problem 6-15. Case, a manufacturer of farm equipment, sells its equipment to Island Equipment Company pursuant to a wholesale financing and security agreement under which Case retains a security interest in the equipment it sells to Island and is granted a security interest in all of Island's inventory, repossessions, and returns to secure the purchase price of the Case equipment. Case files with the secretary of state a financing statement covering "farm equipment inventory, including returns and repossessions." In the ordinary course of its business Island sells a Case tractor-loader to Farmer, who signs a retail installment contract. Island assigns Farmer's contract to Borg-Warner, which took possession of the contract and promptly files with the local county office a financing statement covering "chattel paper and farm equipment." Farmer subsequently defaults. Borg-Warner repossesses the tractor-loader and returns it to Island's place of business. Soon afterwards Island defaults on its obligation to Case. Case asks you whether it has a prior claim to the repossessed tractor-loader. Advise Case. See UCC 9-306(5).

Problem 6-16. Finance Company finances the purchase of Dealer's motorhome inventory through a floor plan arrangement. Finance Company files in the proper office a financing statement covering the inventory. Dealer enters into a fraudulent scheme with Salesman, an employee, to "sell" a motorhome to Salesman by a conditional sales contract signed by Salesman. The motorhome stays on Dealer's sales lot and Dealer agrees to make the payments for Salesman. Dealer then sells the conditional sales contract to Bank, which pays Dealer cash and takes possession of the contract form. After several monthly payments Salesman (i.e., Dealer) defaults on the installment sales contract. Both Finance Company and Bank claim the motorhome, which has never left the sales lot. Which lender has priority?

MAJOR'S FURNITURE MART, INC. v. CASTLE CREDIT CORP.
602 F.2d 538, 26 UCC Rep. 1319 (3d Cir. 1979)

GARTH, Circuit Judge. This appeal requires us to answer the question: "When is a sale—not a sale, but rather a secured loan?" The district court held that despite the form of their Agreement, which purported to be, and hence was characterized as, a sale of accounts receivable, the parties' transactions did not constitute sales. Major's Furniture Mart, Inc. v. Castle Credit Corp., 449 F. Supp. 538 (E.D. Pa. 1978). No facts are in dispute, and the issue presented on this appeal is purely a legal issue involving the interpretation of relevant sections of the Uniform Commercial Code as enacted in Pennsylvania, and their proper application to the undisputed facts presented here.

The district court granted plaintiff Major's motion for summary judgment. Castle Credit Corporation appeals from that order. We affirm.

Major's is engaged in the retail sale of furniture. Castle is in the business of financing furniture dealers such as Major's. Count I of Major's amended complaint alleged that Major's and Castle had entered into an Agreement dated June 18, 1973 for the financing of Major's accounts receivable; that a large number of transactions pursuant to the Agreement took place between June 1973 and May 1975; that in March and October 1975 Castle declared Major's in default under the Agreement; and that from and after June 1973 Castle was in possession of monies which constituted a surplus over the accounts receivable transferred under the Agreement. Among other relief sought, Major's asked for an accounting of the surplus and all sums received by Castle since June 1, 1976 which had been collected from Major's accounts receivable transferred under the Agreement. . . .

The provisions of the June 18, 1973 Agreement which are relevant to our discussion provide: that Major's shall from time to time "sell" accounts receivable to Castle (¶1), and that all accounts so "sold" shall be with full recourse against Major's (¶2). Major's was required to warrant that each account receivable was based upon a written order or contract fully performed by Major's.[3] Castle in its sole discretion could refuse to "purchase" any account (¶7). The amount paid by Castle to Major's on any particular account was the unpaid face amount of the account exclusive of interest[4] less a fifteen percent "discount"[5] and less another ten percent of the unpaid face amount as a reserve against bad debts (¶8).[6]

Under the Agreement the reserve was held by Castle without interest and was to indemnify Castle against a customer's failure to pay the full amount of the account (which included interest and insurance premiums), as well as any other charges or losses sustained by Castle for any reason (¶9).

In addition, Major's was required to "repurchase" any account "sold" to Castle which was in default for more than 60 days. In such case Major's was obligated to pay Castle "an amount equal to the balance due by the customer on said Account plus any other expenses incurred by Castle as a result of such default or breach of warranty, less a rebate of interest on the account under the 'Rule of the 78's'. . . ."[7] Thus essentially, Major's was obligated to repurchase

---

3. The parties do not dispute that their rights are governed by the law of Pennsylvania. UCC 9-105, classifies the accounts receivable which are the subject of the agreement as "chattel paper."

4. According to Major's brief, the "face amount" of its customers' installment payment agreements included (1) the retail cost of the furniture purchased (amount financed), (2) the total amount of interest payable by the customer over the life of the customer's installment payment agreement, and (3) insurance charges.

5. The 15% "discount" was subsequently increased unilaterally by Castle to 18% and thereafter was adjusted monthly to reflect changes in the prime rate. . . .

6. It becomes apparent from a review of the record that the amount which Castle actually paid to Major's on each account transferred was the unpaid face amount exclusive of interest *and* exclusive of insurance premiums less 28% (18% "discount" and 10% reserve)..

In its brief on appeal, Castle sets out the following summary of the transactions that took place over the relevant period. It appears that the face amount of the accounts which were "sold" by Major's to Castle was $439,832.08, to which finance charges totalling $116,350.46 and insurance charges totalling $42,304.03 were added, bringing the total amount "purchased" by Castle to $598,486.57. For these "purchases" Castle paid Major's $316,107. Exclusive of any surplus as determined by the district court Castle has retained $528,176.13 which it has received as a result of customer collections and repurchases by Major's. Collection costs were found by the district court to be $1,627.81.

7. The Rule of 78 is "the predominant method used to determine refunds of unearned finance charges upon prepayment of consumer debts." Hunt, The Rule of 78: Hidden Penalty for Prepayment in Consumer Credit Transactions, 55 B.U.L. Rev. 331, 332 (1975). That article points out that the Rule of 78 allocates a disproportionately large portion of finance charges to the early months of a credit transaction which produces a hidden penalty for prepayment, although the extent of the penalty diminishes as the term of the debt nears expiration. [For more detail on the rule of 78, see p. 199 supra.—EDS.]

a defaulted account not for the discounted amount paid to it by Castle, but for a "repurchase" price based on the balance due by the customer, plus any costs incurred by Castle upon default.

As an example, applying the Agreement to a typical case, Major's in its brief on appeal summarized an account transaction of one of its customers (William Jones) as follows:

A customer [Jones] of Major's (later designated Account No. 15,915) purchased furniture from Major's worth $1700.00 (or more). [Some transactions involved cash down payment to Major's, but this is not at issue in the law suit.—EDS.] [H]e executed an installment payment agreement with Major's in the total face amount of $2549.88, including interest and insurance costs. . . . Using this piece of chattel paper . . . Major's engaged in a financing transaction with Castle under the Agreement. . . . Major's delivered the Jones' chattel paper with a $2549.88 face amount [to] Castle together with an assignment of rights. Shortly thereafter, Castle delivered to Major's cash in the amount of $1224.00. The difference between this cash amount and the full face of the chattel paper in the amount of $2549.88, consisted of the following costs and deductions by Castle:

1. $180.00 discount credited to a "reserve" account of Major's.
2. $300.06 "discount" (actually a prepaid interest charge).
3. $30.85 for life insurance premium.
4. $77.77 for accident and health insurance premium.
5. $152.99 for property insurance premium.
6. $588.27 interest charged to Jones on the $1700 face of the note (App. 73a No. 15,915).

Thus, as to the Jones' account, Castle received and proceeded to collect a piece of chattel paper with a collectible face value of $2549.88. Major's received $1224.00 in cash. [Brief of Appellee at 5-6.]

As we understand the Agreement, if Jones in the above example defaulted without having made any payments on account, the very least Major's would have been obliged to pay on repurchase would be $1,700 even though Major's had received only $1,224 in cash on transfer of the account and had been credited with a reserve of $180. The repurchase price was either charged fully to reserve or, as provided in the Agreement, 50% to reserve and 50% by cash payment from Major's (¶10). In the event of bankruptcy, default under the agreement or discontinuation of business, Major's was required to repurchase all outstanding accounts immediately (¶13). Finally, the Agreement provided that the law of Pennsylvania would govern and that the Agreement could not be modified except in writing signed by all the parties. (Apparently, no objection has ever been made to Castle's unilateral modification of the discount rate. . . . That issue is not before us.)

Under the Agreement, over 600 accounts were transferred to Castle by Major's of which 73 became delinquent and subject to repurchase by Major's. On March 21, 1975, Castle notified Major's that Major's was in default in failing to repurchase delinquent accounts. . . . Apparently to remedy the default, Major's deposited an additional $10,000 into the reserve. After June 30, 1975, Major's discontinued transferring accounts to Castle. . . . On October 7, 1975 Castle again declared Major's in default. . . .

Major's action against Castle alleged that the transaction by which Major's transferred its accounts to Castle constituted a financing of accounts receivable and that Castle had collected a surplus of monies to which Major's was entitled. We are thus faced with the question which we posed at the outset of this opinion: did the June 18, 1973 Agreement create a *secured interest* in the accounts, or did the transaction constitute a *true sale* of the accounts? The district court, contrary to Castle's contention, refused to construe the Agreement as one giving rise to the sales of accounts receivable. Rather, it interpreted the Agreement as creating a security interest in the accounts which accordingly was subject to all the provisions of UCC Article 9. It thereupon entered its order of June 13, 1977 granting Major's motion for summary judgment and denying Castle's motion for summary judgment. . . .

Castle on appeal argues (1) that the express language of the Agreement indicates that it was an agreement for the sale of accounts and (2) that the parties' course of performance and course of dealing compel an interpretation of the Agreement as one for the sale of accounts. Castle also asserts that the district court erred in "reforming" the Agreement and in concluding that the transaction was a loan. In substance these contentions do no more than reflect Castle's overall position that the Agreement was for an absolute sale of accounts. . . .

Our analysis starts with UCC Article 9 which encompasses both *sales of* accounts and *secured interests* in accounts. Thus, the Code "applies . . . (a) to any transaction (regardless of its form) which is intended to create a security interest in . . . accounts; and also (b) to any sale of accounts. . . ." UCC 9-102. The official comments to that section make it evident that Article 9 is to govern *all* transactions in accounts. Comment 2 indicates that, because "[c]ommercial financing on the basis of accounts . . . is often so conducted that the distinction between a security transfer and a sale is blurred," that "sales" as well as transactions "intended to create a security interest" are subject to the provisions of Article 9. Moreover, a "security interest" is defined under the Act as "any interest of a buyer of accounts." UCC 1-201(37). Thus even an outright buyer of accounts, such as Castle claims to be, by definition has a "security interest" in the accounts which it purchases.

Article 9 is subdivided into five parts. Our examination of Parts 1-4 reveals no distinction drawn between a sale and a security interest which is relevant to the issue on this appeal. However, the distinction between an outright sale and a transaction intended to create a security interest becomes highly significant with respect to certain provisions found in Part 5 of Article 9. That part pertains to default under a "security agreement."

The default section relevant here, which distinguishes between the consequences that follow on default when the transaction *secures an indebtedness* rather than a *sale*, provides:

A secured party who by agreement is entitled to charge back uncollected collateral or otherwise to full or limited recourse against the debtor and who undertakes to collect from the account debtors or obligors must proceed in a commercially reasonable manner and may deduct his reasonable expenses of realization from the collections. *If the security agreement secures an indebtedness, the secured party must account to the debtor for any surplus,* and unless otherwise agreed, the debtor is liable for any deficiency. But, *if the underlying transaction was a sale of accounts* or chattel paper, *the debtor is entitled to any surplus* or is liable for any deficiency *only if the security agreement so provides.* [UCC 9-502(2) (emphasis added).]

Thus, if the accounts were transferred to Castle *to secure Major's indebtedness,* Castle was obligated to account for and pay over the surplus proceeds to Major's under UCC 9-502(2), as a debtor's (Major's) right to surplus in such a case cannot be waived even by an express agreement, UCC 9-501(3)(a). On the other hand, if a *sale of accounts* had been effected, then Castle was entitled to all proceeds received from all accounts because the June 18, 1973 Agreement does not provide otherwise.

However, while the Code instructs us as to the consequences that ensue as a result of the determination of "secured indebtedness" as contrasted with "sale," the Code does not provide assistance in distinguishing between the character of such transactions. This determination, as to whether a particular assignment constitutes a sale or a transfer for security, is left to the courts for decision. UCC 9-502, Comment 4. It is to that task that we now turn. . . .

Castle contends that because the June 18, 1973 Agreement expressly refers only to "sales" and "purchases" that the parties intended a true "sale" of accounts and not a security transfer. However, it has been held in Pennsylvania, as it has elsewhere, that "Courts will not be controlled by the nomenclature the parties apply to their relationship." . . .

The comments to UCC 9-502(2) (and in particular Comment 4) make clear to us that the presence of recourse in a sale agreement without more will not automatically convert a sale into a security interest. Hence, one of Major's arguments which is predicated on such a *per se* principle attracts us no more than it attracted the district court. The Code comments however are consistent with and reflect the views expressed by courts and commentators that "[t]he determination of whether a particular assignment constitutes a [true] sale or a transfer for security is left to the courts." UCC 9-502, Comment 4. The question for the court then is whether the *nature* of the recourse, and the true nature of the transaction, are such that the legal rights and economic consequences of the agreement bear a greater similarity to a financing transaction or to a sale. . . .

Hence it appears that in each of the cases cited [e.g., In re Joseph Kanner Hat Co., 482 F.2d 937 (2d Cir. 1973)], despite the express language of the agreements, the respective courts examined the parties' practices, objectives, business activities and relationships and determined whether the transaction was a sale or a secured loan only after analysis of the evidence as to the true nature of the transaction. We noted earlier that here the parties, satisfied that there was nothing other than the Agreement and documents bearing on their relationship . . . submitted to the court's determination on an agreed record. The district court thereupon reviewed the Agreement and the documents as they reflected the conduct of the parties to determine whether Castle treated the transactions as sales or transfers of a security interest. In referring to the extremely relevant factor of "recourse"[12] and to the risks allocated, the district court found: "In the instant case the allocation of risks heavily favors Major's claim to be considered as an assignor with an interest in the collectibility of its accounts. It appears that Castle required Major's to retain all conceivable risks of uncollectibility of these accounts. It required warranties that retail account debtors—e.g., Major's customers—meet the criteria set forth by Castle, that Major's perform the credit check to verify that these criteria were satisfied, and that Major's warrant that the accounts were fully enforceable legally and were 'fully and timely collectible.' It also imposed an obligation to indemnify Castle out of a reserve account for losses resulting from a customer's failure to pay, or for any breach of warranty, and an obligation to repurchase any account after the customer was in default for more than 60 days. Castle only assumed the risk that the assignor itself would be unable to fulfill its obligations. Guaranties of quality alone, or even guarantees of collectibility alone, might be consistent with a true sale, but Castle attempted to shift all risks to Major's, and incur none of the risks or obligations of ownership. It strains credulity to believe that this is the type of situation, referred to in Comment 4, in which 'there may be a true sale of accounts . . . although recourse exists.' When we turn to the conduct of the parties to seek support for this contention, we find instead that Castle, in fact, treated these transactions as a transfer of a security interest." 449 F. Supp. 538, 543.

Moreover, in looking to the conduct of the parties, the district court found one of the more significant documents to be an August 31, 1973 letter written by Irving Canter, President of Castle Credit, to Major's. As the district court characterized it, and as we agree: "This letter, in effect, announces the imposition of a floating interest rate on loans under a line of credit of $80,000 per month, based upon the fluctuating prime interest rate. The key portion of the letter states: 'Accordingly, your volume for the month of September cannot exceed $80,000. Any business above that amount will have to be paid for in October. I think you'll agree that your quota is quite liberal. The surcharge for the month of September will be 3% of the principal amount financed which

---

12. Gilmore, in commenting on the Code's decision to leave the distinction between a security transfer and a sale to the courts, would place almost controlling significance on the one factor of recourse. He states: "If there is no right of chargeback or recourse with respect to uncollectible accounts and no right to claim for a deficiency, then the transaction should be held to be a sale, entirely outside the scope of Part 5. If there is a right to charge back uncollectible accounts (a right, as §9-502 puts it, of 'full or limited recourse') or a right to claim a deficiency, then the transaction should be held to be for security and thus subject to Part 5 as well as the other Parts of the Article." 2 Gilmore, Security Interests in Personal Property §44.4, at 1230. Here, of course, the Agreement provided Castle with full recourse against Major's.

is based upon a 9 1/2% prime rate. On October 1, and for each month thereafter, the surcharge will be adjusted, based upon the prime rate in effect at that time as it relates to a 6 1/2% base rate. . . .' This unilateral change in the terms of the Agreement makes it obvious that Castle treated the transaction as a line of credit to Major's—i.e., a loan situation. Were this a true sale, as Castle now argues, it would not have been able to impose these new conditions by fiat. Such changes in a sales contract would have modified the price term of the agreement, which could only be done by a writing signed by all the parties." 449 F. Supp. 538, 543.

It is apparent to us that on this record none of the risks present in a true sale is present here. Nor has the custom of the parties or their relationship, as found by the district court, given rise to more than a debtor/creditor relationship in which Major's debt was secured by a transfer of Major's' customer accounts to Castle, thereby bringing the transaction within the ambit of UCC 9-502. To the extent that the district court determined that a surplus existed, Castle was obligated to account to Major's for that surplus and Major's' right to the surplus could not be waived, UCC 9-502(2). Accordingly, we hold that on this record the district court did not err in determining that the true nature of the transaction between Major's and Castle was a secured loan, not a sale. . . .

E.   THE "FLOATING LIEN" IN BANKRUPTCY

If you reconsider BC 547 and the materials in Chapter 4 on preferential transfers in the light of what you now know about inventory and receivables financing you should be concerned with whether a bankruptcy trustee may attack these forms of financing as preferential transfers. Assume Finance Company makes periodic loans against Star Furniture's inventory and receivables. As Star Furniture acquires individual items of inventory and individual accounts Finance Company will have a security interest in these items by virtue of its after-acquired property clause. If there is a transfer of property for bankruptcy purposes when Star Furniture acquires these items it will be a transfer on account of an antecedent debt (i.e., the last advance by Finance Company). If the other elements of a preferential transfer are met Star Furniture's trustee in bankruptcy may avoid the transfer. BC 547(b); see 547(e)(3) ("a transfer is not made until the debtor has acquired rights in the property transferred").

But does the floating lien contravene the policies underlying the Bankruptcy Code's preferential transfer provision? The transfer will not be secret because Finance Company will have publicized its security interest by filing a financing statement well before the petition in bankruptcy. Nor, absent further facts, will the transfer be a last-minute grab by Finance Company to get more than it would receive in bankruptcy.

Before the 1978 Bankruptcy Reform Act there was considerable debate about whether the UCC floating lien would survive an attack by a bankruptcy trustee under §60 of the Bankruptcy Act, the predecessor of BC 547. Numerous commentators suggested that the trustee would succeed in avoiding these liens. Case law, however, supported the secured creditors. DuBay v. Williams, 417 F.2d 1277 (9th Cir. 1969); Grain Merchants of Indiana, Inc. v. Union Bank & Savings Co., 408 F.2d 209 (7th Cir. 1969). After these cases the concern was that the secured creditors had won too sweeping a victory and that it might be taken away by legislative amendment. In particular, the creditors acknowledged that an undersecured creditor might improve its position immediately before bankruptcy if it persuaded the debtor either to increase inventory by acquiring it from unsecured suppliers or, alternatively, to generate receivables by selling at a substantial discount. A committee of the National Bankruptcy Conference reviewed this problem and reported in 1970 that §60 should be revised to protect the floating lien subject to a formula that allowed the bankruptcy trustee to avoid "improvement in position." National Bankruptcy Conference Report, reprinted in H.R. Rep. No. 95-595 at 204-219 (1977).

The Bankruptcy Code adopts the approach of the National Bankruptcy Conference. A UCC floating lien on inventory and receivables may be saved from avoidance by BC 547(c)(5):

> (c) The trustee may not avoid under this section a transfer—. . .
>
>   (5)   that creates a perfected security interest in inventory or a receivable or the proceeds of either, except to the extent that the aggregate of all such transfers to the transferee caused a reduction, as of the date of the filing of the petition and to the prejudice of other creditors holding unsecured claims, of any amount by which the debt secured by such security interest exceeded the value of all security interests for such debt on the later of
>
>   (A)(i)   with respect to a transfer to which subsection (b)(4)(A) of this section applies, 90 days before the date of the filing of the petition; or
>
>   (ii)   with respect to a transfer to which subsection (b)(4)(B) of this section applies, one year before the date of the filing of the petition; or
>
>   (B)   the date on which new value was first given under the security agreement creating such security interest; . . .

See also BC 547(a) (definitions of *inventory* and *receivables*).

This special Bankruptcy Code provision resolves many of the interpretive questions that arose under the Bankruptcy Act.

(a) It had been argued that a transfer would be deemed to take place for the purposes of the preference provision when the creditor filed a financing statement, despite the fact that the debtor had not yet acquired any rights in after-acquired inventory or receivables. Section 60a(2) provided that a transfer was deemed to take place "when it became so far perfected that no subsequent lien upon such property obtainable by legal or equitable proceedings on a simple contract could become superior to the rights of the transferee." When the financing statement is filed, it was argued, the transfer is "so far perfected" because the secured party's security interest attaches automatically to after-acquired inventory and receivables so that no subsequent lien creditor can take priority under state law. BC 547(e)(3) resolves this argument by providing that "a transfer is not made until the debtor has acquired rights in the property transferred."

(b) It was also suggested that inventory and receivables should be considered a mass or unit (i.e., the Heraclitean river) that is transferred at the time of original financing even if individual items that make up the mass or unit are not yet in existence. It may still be contended that BC 547(e)(3) does not negate this argument if "the property transferred" is defined by state law and that law accepts this "mass" concept. (Does Article 9 treat inventory as a mass?)

(c) Support for the validity of floating liens in bankruptcy was also found in the "substitution" doctrine: there is no preference if new collateral is substituted for old collateral because the release of the security interest from the old collateral is a contemporaneous exchange of value. This doctrine, however, only works if one applies a relaxed standard of substitution, because rarely is a financing arrangement set up so that one can trace the substitution of new inventory or accounts for liquidated inventory or receivables.

(d) It was sometimes suggested that UCC 9-108, which purports to define when after-acquired property is acquired with "new value" (i.e., no antecedent debt), would be effective in bankruptcy. Most commentators, however, questioned whether under the supremacy clause of the United States Constitution this state law provision would be given effect in a federal bankruptcy proceeding.

(e) It was also suggested that inventory and receivables acquired by the debtor after the secured party's last advance were merely proceeds of pre-advance inventory and receivables. In effect, this suggestion is yet another variation on the substitution doctrine and suffers from the practical difficulty of having to trace the proceeds. (Does BC 547(e)(3) rebut this proceeds argument?)

Further reading: Mann & Phillips, Floating Liens as Preferential Transfers under the Bankruptcy Reform Act, 85 Com. L.J. 7 (1980); Kronman, The Treatment of Security Interests in After-Acquired Property under the Proposed Bankruptcy Act, 124 U. Pa. L. Rev. 110 (1975); Countryman, Code Security Interests in Bankruptcy, 75 Com. L.J. 269, 275-280 (1970).

Problem 6-17. Finance Company makes periodic loans to Star Furniture secured by the latter's accounts receivable. On April 1 Star Furniture files a bankruptcy petition. Star Furniture owes Finance Company $60,000 on the date of the petition; 90 days before the petition it had owed $100,000. In which of the following cases may Star Furniture's bankruptcy trustee recover a preferential transfer from Finance Company?

	Value of receivables	
	90 days before petition	*Date of petition*
(a)	$120,000	$70,000
(b)	120,000	50,000
(c)	80,000 20,000	50,000
(d)	80,000	30,000

(e) What if in case (c) the value of the receivables had dropped to $20,000 one month before the petition and during that last month Star Furniture, at Finance Company's urging, held a "going out of business sale" at which it sold furniture at cost?

Problem 6-18. Bank lends $100,000 to Manufacturer, which grants Bank a security interest in all its equipment then owned or subsequently acquired. Bank perfects its interest by filing a financial statement. On May 1 Manufacturer replaces some worn-out machines with new machines. The new machines cost $20,000, against which the supplier credits $5,000 for the trade-in of the old machines. On June 1 Manufacturer files a bankruptcy petition. Ninety days before the petition Manufacturer's equipment had a value of $80,000; on the date of the petition the equipment has a value of $95,000. At all relevant times Manufacturer owes $100,000. May Manufacturer's bankruptcy trustee avoid any part of Bank's claim?

Problem 6-19. Manufacturer grants Finance Company a security interest in its inventory to secure repayment of a loan. Finance Company perfects this interest. On November 1 Manufacturer files a bankruptcy petition. Ninety days before the petition Manufacturer owed Finance Company $60,000 and had on hand $40,000 worth of raw materials provided by unsecured suppliers. During the 90 days Manufacturer's employees processed the raw materials into finished inventory worth $70,000. On the date of the petition Manufacturer still owes Finance Company $60,000. May Manufacturer's bankruptcy trustee avoid any part of Finance Company's secured claim? See BC 547(c)(5) ("to the prejudice of other creditors holding unsecured claims").

CHAPTER 7

The Scope of Article 9

Some of the most interesting and difficult secured transactions problems arise in transactions that are regulated both by Article 9 and by some other statutory or common law regime. This chapter and Chapter 8 explore several such transactions.

A. THE PLEDGE

We have already touched on the pledge in Chapter 3 when introducing the concept of perfection by possession as a substitute for filing a financing statement. See Notes, p. 142 supra; see also the discussion of the field warehouse, p. 301 supra. Here we take up the subject again to consider the extent to which the Article 9 "possessory security interest" is governed by common law pledge rules, other UCC articles, and non-Code regulatory law.

EVANS v. STOCKTON & HING (IN RE SOUTHWEST RESTAURANT SYSTEMS INC.)
607 F.2d 1243, 27 UCC Rep. 536 (9th Cir. 1979), *cert. denied*, 444 U.S. 1081 (1980)

law firm w/ retaining lien doesn't get §9

ELY, Circuit Judge. . . . Prior to 1975, Charles G. Harris ("Harris"), John H. Greer, Jr. ("Greer"), and Harvey G. McElhanon, Jr. ("McElhanon") were each 1/3 owners of Southwest Restaurant Systems, Inc. ("the debtor corporation"). In 1972, Harris and Greer first secured the services of the law firm of Stockton & Hing with respect to an arbitration hearing. The law firm was paid in full for its services shortly after the hearing.

In May of 1973, Harris and Greer retained Stockton & Hing for other legal proceedings. In September of 1973, with an unpaid balance of approximately $10,000 owing to the law firm, Mr. Robert Ong Hing instructed Harris and Greer to deliver to the law firm their stock certificates, Nos. 3 and 2, respectively, which represented their ownership shares in the debtor corpora-

337

tion. These certificates were, in fact, deposited with Stockton & Hing with the apparent understanding that the stocks would be held as security for payment of attorneys' fees, both owing and to be incurred in the future. The certificates, however, were never endorsed by Greer or Harris. At the present time, Stockton & Hing claim that Harris and Greer owe the law firm in excess of $67,000 for legal services rendered.

On October 14, 1975, the Bankruptcy Court approved the Trustee's Plan of Reorganization for the debtor corporation under Chapter X. The sale and distribution Order provided that after payment of claims and administrative costs, any sums remaining would be distributed pro rata to the stockholders, less any amounts found due the corporation from the stockholders by reason of loans, indebtedness, or liabilities. The Order also provided that any "liens on stockholder interest that existed prior to cancellation of said stock shall, if valid and enforceable against the Trustee, all attach . . . to the proceeds of said escrow and other assets in the hands of the Trustee. . . ."

The debtor corporation secured a judgment against Greer in the amount of $350,000 in December of 1975. Judgment against Harris, also in favor of the corporation, was rendered in March, 1977, for a sum in excess of $455,000. Neither judgment was satisfied.

In May, 1977, the Bankruptcy Court authorized the interim distribution to stockholders pursuant to the October Order of sale and distribution. Because the unsatisfied judgments against Harris and Greer exceeded their pro rata shares as shareholders, these two received no distribution proceeds. Stockton & Hing objected, contending that the law firm should receive 2/3 of the distribution proceeds because of its lien rights in the Harris and Greer stock interests. The Bankruptcy Court rejected the contention that the law firm's lien was not subject to the offsets against Harris and Greer. On August 19, 1977, the District Court affirmed the Bankruptcy Court, holding that Stockton & Hing's interest was an attorney's retaining lien that was subject to the above-described offsets. Stockton & Hing appeal. . . .

The characterization of Stockton & Hing's interest with respect to the stock in the debtor corporation is a key issue. . . . Throughout these proceedings, the law firm of Stockton & Hing has contended that its interest in Harris' and Greer's stock is a perfected security interest under Article 9 of the Uniform Commercial Code, as adopted by Arizona. The law firm claims that its security interest was perfected in September of 1973 when the stock certificates were delivered by Harris and Greer to the firm. Stockton & Hing points out that a security interest may be perfected in Arizona by taking possession of the collateral. See UCC 9-305.

We reject the contention, however, that Stockton & Hing's interest in the stock constitutes a perfected security interest under Article 9. UCC 9-104(c) specifically excludes common law liens for services from the scope of Article 9: "This Article does not apply . . . [t]o a lien given by statute or other rule of law for services or materials. . . ."

Traditionally, attorneys' liens are of two types: specific charging liens, and general possessory or retaining liens. A charging lien attaches to the particular fund or other property created or secured through the attorney's efforts. A possessory or retaining lien, on the other hand, enables the attorney to retain a client's records or other property until the client pays for all of the legal fees owing to the attorney. See Restatement of Security §62(b) and Comment (j); Restatement 2d of Agency §464(b); Adams, George, Lee, Schulte & Ward, P.A. v. Westinghouse Electric Corp., 597 F.2d 570 (5th Cir. 1979). . . .

Arizona case law has focused exclusively upon attorneys' charging liens. . . . While Arizona law has not addressed the question of attorney retaining liens, we presume that Arizona will follow the Restatement. . . . As indicated above, the Restatement recognizes an attorney's general possessory lien, as security for amounts due, on papers and other chattels that come into an attorney's possession. Thus, we find that Stockton & Hing's interest in the stock certificates is properly characterized as an attorney's retaining lien. Except under circumstances not here applicable, the possessor lienor generally "has only a privilege of retention without the power of sale and without the privilege of foreclosure. . . ." Restatement of Security §72(1) and Comment a. . . .

As noted above, the Bankruptcy Court cancelled the outstanding stock of the debtor corporation in October of 1975, and substituted a pro rata right to share in the distribution proceeds, subject to offset. According to the Restatement of Security §66 Comment a: "Where . . . as a result of action by public authority a chattel is substituted in the hands of the lienor for a chattel upon which a lien exists, the lienor has the privilege of retaining the substituted chattel." Thus, we agree with the District Court's conclusion in this case that "when the October 14th order cancelled the debtor corporation's stock, Stockton & Hing retained a possessory lien on the new bundle of rights accorded Greer and Harris."

It is clear, however, that Greer and Harris had no right to moneys in the distribution, for their pro rata shares were more than offset by the unsatisfied judgments the debtor corporation claimed against them. There is little dispute that the Bankruptcy Court was authorized to alter the rights of the stockholders under Chapter X reorganization plans. 11 U.S.C. §616(1). Additionally, there is no question but that the court could offset the judgments of the debtor corporation against Greer and Harris in ordering the distribution. Because Stockton & Hing's retaining lien does not give the law firm an interest greater than that of Greer and Harris, we affirm the District Court's conclusion that the law firm was not entitled to any part of the distribution proceeds.

[Affirmed.]

NOTES & QUESTIONS

1. *Pledge and possessory liens.* Division I of the Restatement of Security (1941) includes two chapters on personal property as security. Chapter 1 (§§1-58) deals with pledges, while Chapter 2 (§§59-81) restates rules on possessory liens. A pledge is defined as a security interest "created by a bailment for the

purpose of securing the payment of a debt or the performance of some other duty," while a possessory lien is "the privilege of retaining a chattel . . . until some demand of the bailee against the bailor has been satisfied" in cases where the bailment was not intended to create a security interest. Restatement §§1, 59. In an introductory note to the scope of Chapter 2 the American Law Institute distinguishes the possessory lien from the pledge by noting that the powers of a lienor are generally less than those of a pledgee. In particular, except as permitted by statute, the lienor has only the right to retain possession and may not foreclose the lien. Id. §72. Statutory regulation of specific possessory liens is also far more common than in the case of pledges. Among the classes of creditors with common law possessory liens are artisans, carriers, warehousemen, landlords, hotelkeepers, attorneys, bankers, factors, and agisters.

2. *Attorney's liens.* As the court in the *Southwest Restaurant* case notes, the Restatement of Security distinguishes an attorney's general possessory lien from his charging lien. Section 62(b) states that the attorney has the general possessory lien "as security for the general balance due him for professional services and disbursements, upon the papers and other chattels of his client, which came into his possession in his professional capacity." Comment *b* to this section states that the attorney is allowed this lien as compensation "for the high degree of fidelity and responsibility he is bound to assume towards his client." The Restatement does not restate the law with respect to the charging lien because the lien is not a possessory lien. The charging lien exists as a charge against a judgment obtained for a client or money received for a client in a professional capacity to secure payment of the attorney's fees. Not all states recognize these common law rules. See Academy of California Optometrists, Inc. v. Superior Court, 51 Cal. App. 3d 999, 124 Cal. Rptr. 668 (1975) (California does not recognize common law retaining lien and attempt to create lien by contract void as contrary to attorney's ethical duties to client, which require return of papers to client upon withdrawal).

3. *Who may have possession: debtor.* Although a secured party may take possession of collateral through a third party agent or bailee, it may not appoint the debtor as its agent. See UCC 9-205 ("This section does not relax the requirements of possession where perfection of a security interest depends upon possession of the collateral by the secured party or by a bailee"); 9-205, Comment 6; 9-305, Comment 2. The common law did recognize, however, a continuing security interest if the pledgee surrendered the collateral to the pledgor for "a temporary and limited purpose." UCC 9-304(5) preserves this doctrine in a more limited form to allow lenders to release commercial paper or goods to the borrower in order to liquidate them and pay off the loan. A similar exception to the general rule requiring the debtor to give up possession is set out in UCC 9-304(4), which validates "day loans" to stockbrokers. Lenders have maintained the long-standing practice of making loans to brokers at the beginning of the day with the expectation that the loans would be liquidated within 24 hours. The loans are secured by investment securities held by

the brokers for delivery to customers. UCC 9-304(4) automatically perfects the lender's security interest for 21 days without the lender having to take possession. (The 1977 amendments exclude investment securities from this subsection.) See UCC 9-304, Comment 4.

4. *Who may have possession: third parties.* It is quite clear that a secured party may take possession of collateral through third parties, including agents and bailees. Two situations in particular have caused controversy:

(a) Attempts to grant a security interest in property held in escrow have been the subject of several important law suits. See Stein v. Rand Construction Co., 400 F. Supp. 944, 16 UCC Rep. 1150 (S.D.N.Y. 1975) (delivery of certificate of deposit to attorney, who acted as escrow agent, did not perfect security interest when both debtor and secured party used attorney for some legal work and debtor continued to receive interest; in any event escrow agent does not act as agent for either party); In re Copeland, 531 F.2d 1195, 18 UCC Rep. 833 (3d Cir. 1976) (escrow agent a "bailee with notice" within meaning of UCC 9-305 because escrow arrangement gives potential creditors notice of possible security interests).

(b) There has also been debate about whether notice by a subsequent creditor to a secured party that has possession of the collateral will perfect the later creditor's security interest. Several commentators suggest that a pledgee may be a bailee within the meaning of that term in UCC 9-305. See, e.g., 1 G. Gilmore, Security Interests in Personal Property 440 (1965) (citing pre-Code cases). At least one recent case, however, questions this conclusion. In re Kontaratos, 10 B.R. 956, 31 UCC Rep. 1124 (Bankr. D. Me. 1981) (pledgee may not be forced to act as bailee). See also 1978 UCC 8-313(1)(h) (transfer of interest in investment security).

5. *Pledge of insurance policies and deposit accounts.* UCC 9-104 excludes a number of secured transactions from the scope of Article 9, including the use of insurance policies and deposit accounts as collateral except when they are proceeds of other collateral. UCC 9-104(g), (*l*); 9-306(1). Consumer debtors, however, frequently pledge life insurance policies and bank passbooks by delivering the policies or passbooks to the creditor. Comment 7 to UCC 9-104 explains that "[s]uch transactions are often quite special, do not fit easily under a general commercial statute and are adequately covered by existing law." Presumably the reference to existing law is to the common law of pledge. Both the insurer and the depositary institution may try to limit by contract the right of the customer to assign their rights. Should these contract limitations be given effect? Is it significant that these entities frequently make loans to policyholders or depositors? Are you persuaded that the exclusion of these transactions is desirable?

6. *Pledge of investment securities (UCC Art. 8).* Before the 1977 amendments to Articles 8 and 9 a secured party could perfect a security interest in investment securities (instruments) only by taking possession of a certificate representing the securities. 1972 UCC 9-304(1). The 1977 amendments transfer the rules governing creation and perfection of security interests in investment secu-

rities to Article 8, although Article 9 continues to govern as to issues on which Article 8 is silent. A secured party attaches and perfects its interest by "transfer" to the secured party or his agent. 1978 UCC 8-313, 8-321. For securities represented by certificates the secured party will usually perfect by taking possession of the certificate. Revised Article 8, however, also provides rules for the transfer of interests in uncertificated securities by registration of the security interest with the issuer, a financial intermediary, or a third party. 1978 UCC 8-313(1). In any event, filing a financing statement will not be effective.

The amendments to Article 8 were inspired by the flood of paperwork and the consequent delays the securities industry encountered in the late 1960s. The principal solution to the problem is to recognize the uncertificated investment security. In their zeal to solve the paper crunch, however, the drafters of the amendments did not always keep in mind the needs of lenders who take investment securities as collateral. See Steadman, The Lender in the Certificateless Society, 26 Bus. Law. 623 (1971). After working through Problem 7-2 infra you should ask yourself whether it is necessary to remove security interests in investment securities, whether certificated or uncertificated, from the ambit of Article 9.

Further reading: Aronstein, Haydock & Scott, Article 8 *Is* Ready, 93 Harv. L. Rev. 889 (1980); Coogan, Security Interests in Investment Securities Under Revised Article 8 of the Uniform Commercial Code, 92 Harv. L. Rev. 1013 (1979); Aronstein, Security Interests in Securities: How Code Revision Reflects Modern Security-Holding Practices, 10 UCC L.J. 289 (1978).

7. *Federal securities legislation and the pledge of investment securities.* The overlap of federal securities legislation and Article 9 arises in two contexts: the initial transfer of the security interest to the secured party and, after default, the disposition of the investment securities by the secured party.

(a) A lender who discovers that the borrower made misrepresentations or otherwise acted fraudulently with respect to stock pledged as collateral may seek to recover damages under the antifraud provisions of the securities legislation. Securities Act of 1933, §17(a), 15 U.S.C. §77q(b) (1982); Securities Exchange Act of 1934, §10(b) and rule 10b-5, 15 U.S.C. §78j(b) (1982), and 240 C.F.R. §10b-5 (1984). It has been held that a pledge may be an "offer or sale" for the purposes of §17(a). See Rubin v. United States, 449 U.S. 424 (1981). Although there is a split of authority, it has also been held that a pledge may be a "purchase or sale" within the meaning of §10(b). See Mallis v. FDIC, 568 F.2d 824 (2d Cir. 1977), *cert. dismissed,* 435 U.S. 384 (1978).

(b) If the debtor defaults the secured party will dispose of pledged investment securities and the question will arise whether this disposition is subject to the registration provisions of the Securities Act of 1933. Debate focuses on whether the secured party is an "underwriter" within the meaning of §2(11) and therefore not exempted from registration by §4(1) and rule 144 (private offering exemption). 15 U.S.C. §§77b(11), d(1) (1982); 17 C.F.R. 240.144 (1984). See SEC v. Guild Films Co., 279 F.2d 485 (2d Cir. 1960) (banks considered "underwriters" when they should have known immediate foreclosure was almost inevitable).

8. *Rights and duties of secured party in possession (UCC 9-207).* A secured party that takes collateral into its possession holds the property subject to the statutory duty of care set out in UCC 9-207, which itself is an elaboration of Restatement of Security §§17, 18. If the secured party fails to act with reasonable care he is liable for any harm caused. UCC 9-207(3); cf. Restatement §20.

Problem 7-1. Tom agrees to lend Dick $6,000, to be repaid in six months. Following the advice of Harry, an attorney consulted professionally on this matter by both Tom and Dick, Dick agrees to secure repayment by delivering a $10,000 certificate of deposit (set out below) to Harry in escrow, with the understanding that Harry will release it to Tom if the loan is not repaid or return it to Dick if the loan is paid. On February 15 Tom makes the loan and Dick delivers the certificate to Harry. At the same time Dick signs both a promissory note and a financing statement but does not sign a security agreement. On February 26 Tom files the financing statement, which describes the collateral as "instruments," with the secretary of state. On May 1 Dick files a voluntary petition in bankruptcy. Dick's trustee in bankruptcy consults you as to what rights, if any, the trustee has in the certificate of deposit. Advise him. See UCC 9-104(1), 9-105(1)(e), 3-104, 3-805, 8-102(1).

CERTIFICATE OF DEPOSIT
Arlington National Bank   No. 38988

Arlington National Bank has received on deposit the sum of ten thousand and xx/100 dollars ($10,000) and on December 15, 1988 will pay to Richard Roe this sum, together with interest at the rate of 12 1/2 percent per annum, upon surrender of this certificate.

December 15, 1985   /s/   *James Coleman*
                                                                  (Authorized Official)

Problem 7-2. Debtor borrows $100,000 from Bank and signs a security agreement granting Bank a security interest in his 100 shares of ABC stock.

(a) Assume the shares are represented by a certificate (i.e., they are *certificated securities,* UCC 8-102(1)). How does Bank attach and perfect the security interest? See UCC 9-105(1)(i), 9-302(1)(f), 8-321, 8-313.

(b) Assume the shares are *uncertificated securities.* How does the Bank attach and perfect its security interest? See UCC 8-321, 8-313.

(c) Assume that after Bank perfects a security interest in the shares Debtor finds a finance company willing to lend money to Debtor and to take as collateral a junior security interest in the shares. How should the finance company perfect its security interest? See UCC 8-321, 8-313. Does your answer depend on whether the shares are certificated or uncertificated?

(d) Assume that after Bank perfects a security interest in the shares a judgment creditor of Debtor seeks to levy execution on the shares. How does the creditor levy execution? See UCC 8-317. As between Bank and the judgment creditor, who has priority to the shares? See UCC 8-321.

(e) Assume that after Bank perfects a security interest in the shares Debtor purports to sell the shares to Purchaser, who is not informed of Bank's security interest. As between Bank and Purchaser, who has priority to the shares? Does your answer depend on whether the shares are certificated or uncertificated?

(f) Assume that three months after Bank perfects its interest in the shares ABC declares a three-for-one stock split and delivers to Debtor a certificate for 200 ABC common shares. Debtor does not inform Bank about the stock split. Soon afterwards Debtor files a petition in bankruptcy. As between Bank and Debtor's trustee, who has priority to the 200 ABC common shares?

(g) Assume that Debtor defaults on the loan from Bank. Without notice to Debtor, Bank transfers the shares to itself for the fair market value prevailing on that day and seeks to recover the resulting deficiency from Debtor. Advise Debtor on what liabilities, if any, it has for the deficiency. See UCC 8-321(3).

Problem 7-3. Debtor borrowed $25,000 from Bank and delivered to Bank as collateral a certificate for 1,000 ABC shares with a fair market value at that time of $40 per share. Soon after this transaction the market value of ABC shares began a steady decline in value. When the market price reached $30 per share Debtor requested that Bank sell the shares but Bank refused. When the market price fell to $22 Debtor again asked Bank to sell and again Bank refused. Several months later, when the market price had fallen to $16, Bank sold the shares, applied the proceeds to the underlying obligation, and demanded the deficiency from Debtor.

(a) What are Debtor's rights and obligations? See UCC 9-207, 9-507.

(b) Would your answer be different if the security agreement included the following clause: "Bank shall exercise reasonable care in the custody and preservation of the collateral and shall be deemed to have exercised reasonable care if it takes such action for that purpose as the undersigned shall reasonably request in writing, but no failure to comply with any such request and no omission to do any such act requested by the undersigned shall be deemed a failure to exercise reasonable care." See UCC 1-102(3), 9-207, 9-501(3).

(c) Would your answer be different if the ABC corporation was a close corporation and the fair market value figures set out above were calculated on the basis of isolated sales?

FINANCE CO. OF AMERICA v. HANS MUELLER CORP.
(IN RE AUTOMATED BOOKBINDING SERVICES, INC.)
471 F.2d 546, 11 UCC Rep. 897 (4th Cir. 1972)

SOBELOFF, Senior Circuit Judge: Finance Company of America (FCA) and
Hans Mueller Corporation (HMC) had conflicting security interests in a bookbinding machine sold by HMC to Automated Bookbinding Services, Inc., a
Maryland corporation who later became bankrupt. This litigation was instituted to determine which secured party had priority in the binder after the
debtor's bankruptcy, and is to be decided under Article 9 of the Uniform
Commercial Code.

The referee in bankruptcy ruled in favor of FCA's claim. On a petition for
review of the referee's order, the District Court awarded the right to possession
of the binder to HMC. For the reasons set forth in this opinion we reverse and
reinstate the referee's original order. . . .

The technical intricacies of the Uniform Commercial Code necessitate a
rather particularized recital of the facts that gave birth to the present controversy. This is required for a proper perspective of the issues.

On November 20, 1968, Automated Bookbinding Services, Inc., for brev-
ity hereafter called the bankrupt, executed an installment note payable to the
order of FCA in the amount of $151,267.75. A chattel mortgage security
agreement was entered into to secure the obligation, which covered all the
bankrupt's equipment that was listed in the agreement. FCA properly filed a
financing statement on November 21, 1968, in Anne Arundel County, Maryland, which covered the bankrupt's after-acquired property as well as its present equipment, UCC 9-204(3) [1972 UCC 9-204(1)], thereby perfecting its
security interest in the collateral, UCC 9-302(1), 9-303(1).

The bankrupt contracted with HMC on January 30, 1970, to purchase a
new bookbinder. A valid security agreement was entered into and HMC retained a valid purchase money security interest in the machine, UCC 9-
107(a).

The cash price under the contract was $84,265 with an installation
charge of $2,160, making a total price of $86,425. Additional terms of the
contract provided for a cash down payment at the time of the order of
$6,442.50, cash before delivery of $6,442.50, and a trade-in allowance on an
old binder of $22,000. This left a balance of $51,540, which was secured by
HMC's purchase money security interest.

Fifteen cases of component parts for the binder were sent from Europe,
under a negotiable bill of lading, to the order of Rohner, Gehrig & Co.,
HMC's shipping agents. The shipment arrived in New York on May 18, 1970.
On May 22, 1970, after receiving the bankrupt's second payment of $6,442.50,
HMC mailed an invoice to the bankrupt identifying the binder's parts by
particular description and serial numbers and providing for payment of the
balance of $51,562.50 in cash upon completion of the installation.

The shipper, Rohner, Gehrig & Co., upon HMC's instructions, directed Hemingway Transport, Inc., a common carrier, to pick up the 15 crates from dockside in New York and to deliver them, together with two additional crates of component parts, to the bankrupt in Maryland. All these crates arrived at bankrupt's plant in Maryland on several dates between May 26, 1970, and June 2, 1970.

Pursuant to its January 30 agreement with the bankrupt, HMC sent two employees to the bankrupt's plant to install the binder. The installation began on May 27, 1970. It is not clear from the record when installation was completed, but it was finished not earlier than June 13 nor later than June 19. The bankrupt acknowledged delivery and satisfactory completion of installation on June 18.

HMC filed a financing statement in Anne Arundel County, Maryland, to perfect its purchase money security interest in the binder on June 15. The bankruptcy filing occurred on February 24, 1971. . . .

This case presents the single issue of which of the two secured creditors, FCA or the purchase money security interest holder HMC, is entitled to the binder. Under UCC 9-312(4), purchase money security interest holders are generally given priority in cases such as this. The referee held that the bankrupt received possession of the binder on June 2, when the last crates were delivered, and since HMC's June 15 filing came more than 10 days after the debtor received possession, HMC lost its UCC 9-312(4) priority. The volume of adjudication in this special area is scanty. Disposition of the case therefore requires a close analysis of the Code and its provisions.

The District Court ruled in favor of HMC's claim on two alternative grounds. First, the court held that the debtor did not receive possession on June 2, when the delivery was completed, but rather some time between June 13 and 19, when HMC completed its installation. Possession did not occur, according to the District Court, until the tender of delivery terms the bankrupt bargained for with HMC were completed (UCC 2-503, 2-507). The District Court's reasoning continued that since installation was a tender of delivery term and occurred June 13, at the earliest, HMC's June 15 filing perfected its purchase money security interest within 10 days after the debtor received possession of the collateral. Therefore, the District Court concluded, HMC's purchase money security interest retained its UCC 9-312(4) priority.

In its alternative holding the District Court ruled in favor of HMC's claim based upon the third sentence of UCC 9-103(3) [of the 1962 UCC].[6]

---

6. (3) If personal property other than that governed by subsections (1) and (2) is already subject to a security interest when it is brought into this State, the validity of the security interest in this State is to be determined by the law (including the conflict of laws rules) of the jurisdiction where the property was when the security interest attached. However, if the parties to the transaction understood at the time that the security interest attached that the property would be kept in this State and it was brought into this State within thirty days after the security interest attached for purposes other than transportation through this State, then the validity of the security interest in this State is to be determined by the law of this State. *If the security interest was already perfected under the law of the jurisdiction where the property was when the security interest attached and before*

The court was of the view that HMC had perfected its security interest while the goods were still in New York, not through filing but through taking possession of the crates, UCC 9-303(1), 9-305. Under UCC 9-103(3) HMC's already perfected security interest continued perfected in Maryland until September, 1970, and the June 15 filing was well within the allotted time for filing.

We think the District Court erred in both alternative holdings. The bankrupt received possession on June 2, when the crates arrived, and completion of tender of delivery terms is irrelevant to when possession occurs under the Code.

Additionally, the comity provisions of UCC 9-103(3) were not intended to allow a perfection in one state to continue in another when the parties knew and agreed to transfer the collateral to the second state within 30 days.

HMC's claim of priority under UCC 9-312(4), as a purchase money security interest holder, depends on how the word "possession," used in that section, is to be defined. Because assuming HMC's interest was not perfected when the bankrupt received possession, perfection would have to occur within 10 days after the bankrupt obtained possession in order for HMC's interest to take priority.

We reject the District Court's holding that possession was received by the bankrupt when the tender of delivery terms of HMC and the bankrupt were completed, between June 13 and 19. Such an approach confuses the Article 2 tender of delivery concept with the Article 9 notion of possession.

"Possession" is one of the few terms employed by the Code for which it provides no definition. The Code's general purpose is to create a precise guide for commercial transactions under which businessmen may predict with confidence the results of their dealings. In defining "possession" we must be guided by these considerations as well as by the underlying theories unique to Article 9.

Under pre-code law, a security interest became invalid if the debtor was allowed uncontrolled dominion over the collateral. Exercise of such ostensible ownership could perpetrate fraud on potential creditors who, not being able to know of the creditor's security interest, would think the collateral belonged to the debtor.

In contrast, creditors today can learn of pre-existing security interests through the filing provisions of the Code and a debtor's use of the collateral is no longer considered fraudulent, UCC 9-205. Filing is required, with certain exceptions, to perfect the security interest, so that creditors may learn of the pre-existing interest. "Possession" is used throughout Article 9 in establishing

---

being brought into this State, the security interest continues perfected in this state for four months and also thereafter if within the four months period it is perfected in this State. The security interest may also be perfected in this State after the expiration of the four month period; in such case perfection dates from the time of perfection in this State. If the security interest was not perfected under the law of the jurisdiction where the property was when the security interest attached and before being brought into this State, it may be perfected in this State, in such case perfection dates from the time of perfection in this State. (Italics added.)

the filing scheme, in permitting debtors to retain use of collateral, and in providing perfection through means other than filing, such as through the secured party's taking possession. The ostensible ownership exercised through possession is demonstrated through simple physical control. One who controls the collateral possesses it, and leads others to believe it is his. Gilmore, a draftsman of Article 9, explains: " 'Receives possession' is evidently meant to refer to the moment when the goods are physically delivered at the debtor's place of business—not to the possibility of the debtor's acquiring rights in the goods at an earlier point by identification or appropriation to the contract or by shipment under a term under which the debtor bears the risk." 2 Gilmore, Security Interests in Personal Property 787 (1965).

Pre-code security law defined possession as meaning physical control.[12]

Tender of delivery is a sales concept, employed by Article 2, which binds a buyer and seller to contractual conditions. It affects their rights against each other. It would be a serious error to allow those private conditions to affect the carefully defined rights of creditors under Article 9.

Secured parties are required, in most cases, to file a financing statement in order to perfect their security interest. To define "possession" as requiring completion of tender of delivery terms would permit a secured creditor to delay performance of a tender of delivery term, and thereby avoid the filing requirement indefinitely. Even if a debtor would have use of the collateral he would not be deemed to have "possession," under the District Court's analysis, and purchase money security interest holders filing after complying with a tender of delivery term, at any future date, would still be entitled to the UCC 9-312(4) priority. Such a result would frustrate the purpose of Article 9 and could not have been intended by the drafters.[14]

To summarize, possession under UCC 9-312(4) is not dependent upon completion of tender of delivery terms which affect only the buyer and seller of the goods. Since the last of the binder parts were delivered to the bankrupt, in their crates, on June 2, possession of the collateral was received on that date. HMC's failure to file its financing statement until June 15, more than 10 days later, causes it to lose its favored position under UCC 9-312(4) and entitles FCA to the binder. . . .

The District Court's alternative holding was that HMC obtained a perfected security interest in New York, when the binder's component parts were identified to the contract, UCC 9-204 [of the 1962 Code; see 1972 UCC 9-

12. "[A] person who is in possession of a chattel is one who . . . has physical control of a chattel with intent to exercise such control in his behalf, or otherwise than as a servant on behalf of another. . . ." Restatement of the Law of Security (1941) at 6. In Casey v. Cavaroe, 96 U.S. 467, 21 L. Ed. 779 (1877), a leading case defining possession in the security interest context, the term was understood to mean control. . . .

14. Brodie Hotel Supply, Inc. v. United States, 431 F.2d 1316 (9th Cir. 1970), is cited by HMC to stand for the proposition that mere physical control doesn't constitute possession under UCC 9-312(4). But *Brodie* is inapposite, being a case where the debtor had physical control *before* the goods were sold to him by the holder of the purchase money security interest and before the security agreement was entered into. Since HMC had contracted for the sale with the bankrupt on January 30, and entered into a security agreement, the bankrupt was in possession from June 2, when it received physical control of the collateral.

203(1)(b)], the debtor having received rights in the collateral, since HMC was in possession of the component parts at that time, UCC 9-305. That interest continued perfected in Maryland, according to the District Court.

The third sentence of UCC 9-103(3) provides that a perfected security interest continues perfected for four months if the collateral is moved into another state. Under UCC 9-305 a secured party can perfect his security interest by taking possession of the collateral. HMC urges that we hold it acquired a perfected security interest under UCC 9-305 and that that perfected security interest continued for four months in Maryland. We reject this argument on several grounds.

First, it is not clear to us that the taking of possession, spoken of in UCC 9-305, can be effectuated by merely not relinquishing control. HMC had not relinquished control of the binder to the bankrupt at the time it sent the bankrupt the May 22 notice. The binder never had left HMC's control. We are not certain that this is what UCC 9-305 means by the secured party taking possession. Perhaps the secured party must take possession from the debtor, who has possession, in order to demonstrate the ostensible ownership which indicates the perfected security interest to other potential creditors. This issue need not be decided, since ample grounds exist upon which we base our reversal of this alternative holding.

When HMC gave the binder to the common carrier in New York in late May, it relinquished possession of the machine. UCC 9-305 allows possession by the creditor to perfect his interest ". . . only so long as possession is retained." The common carrier issued a non-negotiable bill of lading naming the bankrupt as consignee. Under UCC 9-305 collateral held by a bailee, such as the common carrier, under a non-negotiable document is considered to be in the possession of the secured creditor only from the time the bailee receives notice of the secured creditor's interest. No evidence was presented to show that the carrier received such notice. Therefore, HMC's UCC 9-305 perfection, if it existed at all, didn't "continue" when the binder was removed from New York to Maryland.

A third ground for rejecting applicability of UCC 9-103(3) is predicated upon an understanding of the interrelation of the various parts of that section. Even if HMC acquired a perfected security interest under UCC 9-305, the continuation didn't take place under UCC 9-103(3). The second sentence of UCC 9-103(3) compels our conclusion. When the parties, such as HMC and the bankrupt, agreed and knew that the collateral would be transported to the second state within 30 days, for use there, "the validity of the security interest in this State [the second state, Maryland in the instant case] is to be determined by the law of this State [Maryland]." We should interpret the term "validity" as meaning the "perfection,"[15] so that the perfection must have occurred in Maryland in order for HMC to have perfected its security interest.

---

15. "The second sentence of §9-103(3) provides that, when goods are in State A at the time a security interest attaches but are intended to be kept in State B (and in fact brought into State B for use within thirty days after attachment), State B will apply its own law to determine the 'validity' of the security interest. *In this context there is no conceivable reason for differentiating between*

Analysis of the underlying policy of UCC 9-103(3) supports our reading and conclusion. The section was designed to protect secured parties whose debtors absconded with their collateral.[16] When the secured party *knows* where the collateral is to be taken, and that the transfer will take place within the short period of 30 days after the security interest attached, there is no reason or justification for allowing the secured party (HMC) to delay filing in the second state (Maryland).

The section's underlying policy provides an even stronger basis for rejecting the District Court's holding that the 4-month grace period of UCC 9-103(3)'s third sentence applied to HMC. As explained above, the section was designed to protect creditors from absconding debtors. A secured party is allowed four months to find the debtor and collateral, and file in the new state, without losing the original perfection accorded him in the first state. This protection is certainly not required where a secured party, such as HMC, itself transferred the collateral to another state pursuant to a contract with the debtor. HMC knew where the collateral was. The general Code requirement to perfect through filing in Maryland should have been met.

We are further of the view that in a situation such as this, where the creditor who was in possession shipped the goods to the debtor in another state, pursuant to a non-negotiable bill of lading, the UCC 9-305 perfection does not apply to allow the creditor's perfected interest to continue in the second state. When a secured party takes possession of the goods, it knows where they are located. The UCC 9-305 perfection lasts only as long as possession is retained by the secured party. When possession is surrendered, the perfection ceases. Therefore, when a secured party itself transfers the goods to a second state, with the debtor as consignee under a non-negotiable bill of lading, it should follow the Code's strict filing scheme to perfect, before relinquishing control to the debtor. A UCC 9-305 perfection is not the type of

---

'validity' and 'perfection': that differentiation makes sense only when the goods were initially expected to remain in State A and the parties contracted with reference to that state's law: in such a case, if the goods are subsequently removed to State B, it is entirely sensible to provide (as §9-103(3) does) that 'validity' continues to be governed by State A law although 'perfection' (after the four-month delay) becomes a matter of State B law. But when the goods were at all times intended for use in State B, then both validity and perfection should be State B matters; indeed the case for making State B law govern initial perfection is even stronger than the case for making it govern validity. Since the second sentence of §9-103(3) is crystal-clear on the validity point, it would be difficult to explain why the following sentence on perfection should take an apparently inconsistent position." (Italics added.) 1 Gilmore at 629.

16. Comment 7 to UCC 9-103(3) reads in part: "Subsection (3) proceeds on the theory that not only the secured party whose collateral has been removed but also creditors of and purchasers from the debtor in this state should be considered. The four month period is long enough for a secured party to discover in most cases that the collateral has been removed and to file in this state: thereafter, if he has not done so, his interest, although originally perfected in the state where it attached, is subject to defeat here by those persons who take priority over an unperfected security interest. . . ." See also Weintraub, Choice of Law in Secured Personal Property Transactions: The Impact of Article 9 of the Uniform Commercial Code, 68 Mich. L. Rev. 684, 712-714 (1970).

perfection that UCC 9-103(3) was designed to allow to continue for the 4-month grace period in such a situation.

Since the 4-month grace period of protection is not necessary in such a case, the Code could not have intended that it apply. HMC was not faced with the difficult task of finding a debtor who had fled with its collateral. It knew where the debtor was and where the collateral was. Indeed, HMC itself transported the collateral to Maryland.

UCC 9-103(3) was designed to protect creditors against debtors' moving the collateral, not to allow secured parties a 4-month exemption from filing under all circumstances.

Since the UCC 9-103(3) 4-month grace period from filing was designed to protect secured parties from debtors absconding with the collateral, it does not apply to HMC, a secured party, who knowingly transferred the collateral, pursuant to a non-negotiable bill of lading.

For all the reasons stated above . . . the judgment of the District Court is reversed.

NOTES & QUESTIONS

1. *Choice of law: party autonomy.* In *Automated Bookbinding* would it have made any difference if the security agreement had provided that the law of New York "shall govern the rights, duties and remedies of the parties" and HMC had filed a properly completed financing statement in New York on January 30, 1970? See UCC 1-105.

What if HMC and debtor agreed that German law applied and German law gives automatic priority over third parties to a seller who retains title to secure payment of the purchase price? See Pennington, Retention of Title to the Sale of Goods Under European Law, 27 Intl. & Comp. L.Q. 277 (1978); Imperial Chem. Ind. Ltd. v. Slaner (In re Duplan Corp.), 455 F. Supp. 926, 24 UCC Rep. 965 (S.D.N.Y. 1978) (retention of title by foreign seller in contract stipulating that foreign law applied is only unperfected security interest).

2. *Choice of law: what law should govern?* The Restatement (Second) of Conflict of Laws (1969) includes provisions (§§251-256) governing the choice of law for security interests in personal property. The Introductory Note to these sections of the Restatement, published in 1971, states that notwithstanding the UCC the Restatement rules based on case law still have validity. Does the adoption of the 1972 amendments to Article 9 eliminate the need for the Restatement rules?

For a discussion that puts UCC 9-103 into historical perspective, see Juenger, Nonpossessory Security Interests in American Conflicts Law, 26 Am. J. Comp. L. (Spec. Supp.) 145 (1978), reprinted in 84 Com. L.J. 63 (1979). See also p. 149 supra.

COOGAN, THE NEW UCC ARTICLE 9, 86 Harv. L. Rev. 477, 533-534 (1973): "From the point of view of general conflicts theory, one may question why the revised Code focuses on the location of this type of collateral [ordinary goods] for perfection purposes, rather than on the relation of the transaction to the enacting state or on the location of the debtor. To be sure, using a test as potentially vague as the 'appropriateness' of the transaction's relation to the enacting state would clearly be unworkable; certainty and predictability are too important in the area of secured transactions, which are often carefully thought out in advance by professional people who need to know the applicable law before they act. However, it is more difficult to decide whether the rule chosen by the draftsmen for localizable collateral is preferable to one based on the debtor's location. Large multistate corporations are unlikely to borrow locally against local collateral, and national lenders and other creditors can most easily look to the records in the state where such a corporation has its chief executive office. Of course, the largest of such corporations are in any event probably less likely to seek credit secured by personal property than are more moderate sized multistate companies. And although these latter companies may do business in several states, they may sometimes deal with local lenders and local creditors who may need to know whether locally situated collateral is or is not subject to a security interest.

"However, even though a local search may be of some value with regard to debtors that are moderate sized multistate companies, the information yielded by such a search will be limited indeed. It will be of no value as to accounts, general intangibles, and mobile equipment, because filing as to such collateral must under revised 9-103(3) be made in the jurisdiction where the debtor has his chief place of business. And, since under revised 9-312(3) a security interest in accounts may take priority over even a perfected security interest of the financer who claims accounts as proceeds of inventory, a local search as to inventory will be of limited value. This means that a local search pursuant to paragraph (1)(b) will be sufficient, as a practical matter, largely with respect to local *equipment* only and, even then, solely in those instances where the equipment is not mobile within the meaning of subsection (3), is not subject to a title certificate statute under subsection (2), and has been in its present jurisdiction at least 4 months and thus is not subject to local perfection in another jurisdiction under the rule of paragraph (1)(d). . . . Even in these limited instances, moreover, where the local state has adopted statewide filing, checking in the capital of the local state may in practice be no easier than checking in the appropriate filing office in the state where the debtor has his executive office. Ideally, to meet these difficulties, perhaps all UCC filings will one day be made at a national center and will be available for instantaneous inspection at any one of a myriad of computer terminals connected to a master computer's memory. But such a system was not one of the choices available to the Review Committee; and whether the Committee's choice of a location-of-collateral rule is preferable to a location-of-debtor rule for localizable collateral is a broad question upon which final judgment will have to await further explication of the remaining provisions of section 9-103."

B.   MOTOR VEHICLES

Twentieth century commercial law owes much to the motor vehicle—cars, trucks, trailers, mobile homes, airplanes, etc.—and most of the legal concepts studied in these materials could be illustrated with cases involving disputes over them. Here we pause to consider some special legal problems commonly associated with motor vehicles: liens to secure repair bills, certificate-of-title statutes, and rules on the applicable state's law.[4]

1.   Artisan's Liens and the Motor Vehicle

Anyone who has had to face payment of a car repair bill has probably wondered what would happen if the bill was not paid. One answer, both at common law and under statutes adopted in most states, is that the person performing the repair has a lien on the car to secure payment for the repairs. The common law lien is a possessory lien similar to the attorney's general lien, discussed earlier in this chapter. The statutory lien need not be as limited as that of the common law: it may provide for filing notice of the lien, surrender of possession, and the right to foreclose the lien. Unless the statute explicitly repeals the common law lien it is possible that a jurisdiction may recognize both statutory and common law artisan's liens. See Peavy's Service Center, Inc. v. Associates Financial Service Co., 335 So. 2d 169, 20 UCC Rep. 538 (Ala. Ct. App. 1976) (Alabama recognizes both common law and statutory lien.)

Article 9 excludes from its coverage liens "given by statute or other rule of law for services or materials except as provided in Section 9-310 on priority of such liens." UCC 9-104(c). UCC 9-310 states:

> When a person in the ordinary course of his business furnishes services or materials with respect to goods subject to a security interest, a lien upon goods in the possession of such person given by statute or rule of law for such materials or services takes priority over a perfected security interest unless the lien is statutory and the statute expressly provides otherwise.

Note that this section is limited to "possessory" liens. Professor Gilmore suggests that introduction of this limitation in the 1956 text was unexplained. 2 G.

---

4. Motor vehicles have also figured prominently in the case law and academic literature on repossession and disposition of collateral. Empirical research into the practices of creditors who repossess automobiles provides a wealth of data unavailable for most other commercial law topics. See White, Consumer Repossessions and Deficiencies: New Perspectives from New Data, 23 B.C.L. Rev. 385 (1982); Shuchman, Condition and Value of Repossessed Automobiles, 21 Wm. & Mary L. Rev. 15 (1979); Shuchman, Profit on Default: An Archival Study of Automobile Repossession and Resale, 22 Stan. L. Rev. 20 (1969); Comment, 3 Conn. L. Rev. 511 (1971); Note, 27 Stan. L. Rev. 1081 (1975).

Gilmore, Security Interests in Personal Property 880 (1965). The limitation may, however, lead to unexpected results. See the *Peavy* case, supra (statutory lien not possessory, therefore amendment to statute subordinating lien to perfected security interest not relevant to UCC 9-310, which is limited to possessory liens).

2 G. GILMORE, SECURITY INTERESTS IN PERSONAL PROPERTY
876-879 (1965)

[Where the security interest antedates the artisan's lien] the conceptual basis for giving priority to the security interest is the ancient slogan: first in time is first in right. The mortgagee, conditional vendor or whatnot has a property interest which cannot be—or ought not to be—diverted or diluted without his consent. In the usual case the mortgage or contract will have been recorded, so that the point can be made that the lienor either knew or ought to have known of its existence.

The arguments for giving priority to the lien tend to become more diffuse and scattered. No doubt the underlying policy justification is the thought that the lienor, through the services or materials which he has furnished, has increased the value of the property; it would be giving the holder of the security interest an unjustifiable windfall to allow him to claim the property, thus improved, while the serviceman remains unpaid. A comparable line of argument is traditionally used to explain the rule of maritime law under which contract liens are said to rank in the inverse order of creation, the most recent lien having priority over earlier liens; the maritime law analogy is not infrequently referred to in the opinions. The facts of a case will occasionally give the lie to the idea that the mortgagee or vendor has in fact received any benefit from the lienor: the amount of the repair bill alone may exceed the value of the property as repaired. But a court which is sympathetic to the "benefit conferred" argument can either overlook the fact that no real benefit was conferred in a particular case, on the theory that a good rule should be maintained even though it works an occasional injustice, or, in an outrageous case, rephrase the rule in terms of the "reasonable value" of the work done; here, as throughout the whole range of quasi-contractual or quantum meruit recovery, it will remain forever unclear whether "value" means the cost of the services to the lienor or the increased market value (if any) of the property.

If the mortgagee or vendor has properly filed or recorded his security agreement, he will of course make the constructive notice argument, pointing to the fact that the usual chattel mortgage or conditional sales act purports to give complete protection once its requirements have been complied with. Courts which are sympathetic to the lienor have not found the argument insuperable. The garageman or the livery stable keeper (depending on the vintage of the case) is not, such a court will say, the sort of person who consults, or can be expected to consult, records. He is a small businessman, ignorant of the law; furthermore he is in no position to refuse his services pending an elaborate search of the records in all the counties (or states) where a valid filing might possibly be found. Although the analogy is not often expressly made, such courts treat the constructive notice argument in this context in somewhat the same way that it is treated in cases of buyers in ordinary course of trade of inventory subject to security agreements which purport to restrict the dealer's liberty of sale.

It might be said that the approaches just described meet the policy issue head-on and resolve it in accordance with economic and social theories which appeal to the court. A more common approach, however, ducks the policy issue and purports to give priority to the lienor by finding that the holder of the security interest has, in some more or less fictional sense, consented to the making of repairs or improvements and thereby waived the priority of lien to which he would, it is assumed, otherwise be entitled. . . .

Problem 7-4. Bank financed Consumer's purchase of a new car. Consumer granted Bank a security interest in the car and had this interest noted on the certificate of title. Consumer has an accident and, without consulting Bank, takes the car to Mechanic for repairs. Bank learns of the accident while the car is still in the possession of Mechanic. Worried that Consumer may default on his payments Bank asks you whether Mechanic will have a lien against the car that will take priority over its security interest. Your research reveals the following:

(a) Prior to the adoption of the Certificate of Title Act in 1939 courts in your jurisdiction uniformly held that the holder of a recorded chattel mortgage had priority over a mechanic's lien.

(b) Courts construing the Certificate of Title Act held that a secured party's liens noted on a certificate of title had priority over a mechanic's lien. The legislation adopting the Uniform Commercial Code, however, explicitly repeals the sections of the Certificate of Title Act construed by the courts.

(c) The Uniform Commercial Code, enacted in your jurisdiction in 1966, includes UCC 9-310. There are no court decisions construing this section in your jurisdiction.

(d) The Mechanic's Lien Act, enacted in 1874 and not repealed by the 1966 legislation adopting the UCC, includes the following two sections:

> Section 1. Mechanic's Liens. Whenever any vehicle shall be repaired with labor and material, or with labor and without furnishing material by any mechanic, artisan, or other workman in this state, such mechanic, artisan, or other workman is authorized to retain possession of said vehicle until the amount due on same for repairing by contract shall be fully paid off and discharged. In case no amount is agreed upon by contract, then said mechanic, artisan, or other workman shall retain possession of such vehicle until all reasonable, customary and usual compensation shall be paid in full.

> Section 2. Other Liens not Affected. Nothing in this Title shall be construed or considered as in any manner impairing or affecting the right of parties to create liens by special contract or agreement, nor shall it in any manner affect or impair other liens arising at common law or in equity, or by any statute of this state, or any other liens not treated of under this Title.

(e) This Mechanic's Lien Act has been construed by courts to grant priority to an existing chattel mortgage over the lien of a mechanic. None of these court decisions, however, is later than 1958.

What advice do you give to Bank as to priorities?

Would your advice be different if Mechanic made a claim for $1,000 but the market value of the car was increased through his labor by only $600? Would you change your advice if Mechanic returned the car to Consumer with the understanding that his lien continued? What if Mechanic returned the car but then repossessed it?

2.   *The UCC and Certificate-of-Title Acts*

Most states now have some form of certificate-of-title legislation that requires a secured party to have its security interest in a motor vehicle noted on the certificate. Although all the legislation has the same objective of providing a definitive document setting out title to and encumbrances on a motor vehicle, the language of the statutes varies considerably. Problems coordinating the texts arise in several different contexts: What rules govern perfection and priority of security interests? Which state's law is applicable when a motor vehicle moves to a different state? Are interests cut off if the debtor entrusts the motor vehicle to a merchant who sells the vehicle to a good faith purchaser? The following case and excerpt from Professor Coogan's article explore the first two of these questions; the last question is deferred until Chapter 10.

Article 9 provides that to perfect a security interest in a motor vehicle, unless it is part of a dealer's inventory the secured party must comply with the certificate of title statute. This compliance is deemed to be the equivalent of filing a financing statement; to file a financing statement instead has no effect. The procedure for perfection and the duration and renewal of perfection are governed by the certificate-of-title legislation but "in other respects" the security interest is subject to Article 9. UCC 9-302(3), (4).

BOLDUAN v. NORMANDIN (IN RE WESTERN LEASING, INC.)
17 UCC Rep. 1369 (Bankr. D. Or. 1975)

SULLIVAN, Bankruptcy Judge. . . . On August 14, 1974, Donald Riddell, who was the President and a chief officer of Western Leasing, Inc. and Western

Truck Sales, Inc., which are both in bankruptcy, sold to Frank S. Morris Leasing (FSM) a freightliner highway tractor for $14,000 on a conditional sales contract. . . . Approximately two days later, the plaintiffs purchased the vendor's interest in the truck for $12,000 cash, which was paid at the time, and Mr. Riddell after executing an assignment with full recourse provision in the contract, physically delivered the contract to the Bolduans. . . .

Mr. Riddell testified that Western Truck Sales was formed principally for tax purposes to enable Western Leasing Inc. to take advantage of a favorable depreciation schedule. Mr. Riddell was the principal officer of both corporations and in this capacity it was his practice to sell equipment owned by Western Leasing, Inc. on conditional sales contracts executed in the name of Western Truck Sales, Inc. It was also his practice to discount these contracts to third parties such as the Bolduans on a recourse basis in the name of Western Truck Sales, Inc. and to retain possession of the title certificates on the equipment without any change in the registration as a result of the assignment of the contract to the third parties. Mr. Riddell collected the payments on the trucks from the purchasers, made payments to the assignees of the purchase contracts until shortly before bankruptcy and, when necessary, repossessed the trucks and resold them. . . .

The issue in this case is whether the transfer to the Bolduans of the vendor's interest in the conditional sales contract, which in fact was sold to the Bolduans for a fair and present consideration, was perfected.

The plaintiffs, as a principal contention among other things, argue that under UCC 9-305 and 9-302(1)(a) delivery to them of the contract of sale for the truck was sufficient to perfect the transfer and that there is no requirement that a financing statement be filed or that registration of the transfer be noted on the certificate of title.

The trustee argues that by virtue of UCC 9-102(1)(b) and 9-302(3) and ORS 481.412(2)[1] of the Motor Vehicle Code, perfection of a buyer's rights to a contract of sale of a motor vehicle against the trustee is governed by the filing and registration provisions of ORS 481.410[2] and that because the Bolduans as purchasers of the contract failed to have the Department of Motor

---

1. Oregon Revised Statute 481.412(2) states: "The provisions of this chapter that require the application for and notation on certificates of title of security interests in vehicles is the exclusive means of perfecting such interests and when the security interest has been so noted, it shall constitute perfection of the security interest and the rights of all persons in the vehicle shall be subject to the provisions of the Uniform Commercial Code."—EDS.

2. Oregon Revised Statute 481.410 provides: "Creation, satisfaction or assignment of security interest in vehicle. (1) If, after a certificate of title is issued, a security interest is created in the vehicle described in the certificate, the owner, or lessor, if there is a lease, shall sign, and enter the date, in an application space provided on the back and deliver the certificate to the person in whom the security interest was created who, within 30 days thereafter, shall sign and present the certificate with a fee of $2 to the division. In the event a prior security interest holder is in possession of the certificate of title the owner or lessor, as the case may be, shall sign and may arrange for direct delivery by the prior security interest holder to the division. The division shall, upon receiving the certificate and fee, issue a new certificate of title, note such change upon its records in order of priority and mail the certificate to the security interest holder first named on the certificate.

Vehicles substitute their name on the truck title as the holder of a security interest, the transfer of the contract had not been perfected. Alternatively, the trustee argues that ORS 481.410(3) requires the transfer to a buyer of the contract of sale to be perfected by the filing of a financing statement under the Oregon provisions of the Commercial Code and that the Bolduans failed to accomplish the required filings. As a consequence of either or both arguments, the trustee claims a right to the contract and to the truck under UCC 9-301(1)(b) and Section 70c of the Bankruptcy Act as a lien creditor having an interest prior to the unperfected interest of the Bolduans. [See BC 544(a)(1).—Eds.].

I find that, contrary to the trustee's position, the physical transfer of the contract of sale from Western to the Bolduans was sufficient under UCC 9-305 to perfect the Bolduans' interest in the contract as buyer regardless of whether the underlying interest in the trucks securing the contract had been perfected either by the buyer or the seller. Specifically, I find that the contract of sale, which is secured by the truck, constitutes chattel paper within the meaning of UCC 9-105(1)(b), that the perfection as between the immediate parties to the transfer of the chattel paper is governed by Oregon's version of the Commercial Code even though the underlying security interest in the truck is governed by the Motor Vehicle Code, and that the registration provisions of the Motor Vehicle Code do not pre-empt the applicable provisions of the Commercial Code governing the perfection of the buyer's interests in chattel paper which is secured by a motor vehicle.

UCC 9-102(3) makes the distinction between a security interest in a secured obligation and the secured obligation itself, and expressly applies the provisions of the Commercial Code to the security interest even though the underlying secured obligation is expressly excluded from coverage by the Commercial Code. This distinction is necessarily incorporated into UCC 9-104, which spells out those subject matter areas such as landlord liens which are completely excluded from coverage by the Commercial Code, and UCC 9-302(3)(b) which spells out those subject matter areas such as motor vehicles

---

"(2) Upon satisfaction of a security interest in a vehicle for which a certificate of title has been issued, the security interest holder affected, if in possession of the certificate of title, shall sign and date a release on the certificate and deliver it to the security interest holder next named, if any, otherwise to the lessor or, if none, to the owner. In the event the security interest holder affected is not in possession of the certificate he shall execute and date a release of his interest and deliver it to the person entitled thereto who shall promptly deliver it to the holder of the certificate of title. Within 30 days after the date of the release, the holder shall present the certificate of title and release, with a fee of $2, to the division. The division thereupon shall note the change upon its records and issue a new certificate of title to the first security interest holder then named, if any, otherwise to the lessor or, if none, to the owner.

"(3) A security interest holder or lessor may, without the consent of the owner, assign his interest in a vehicle to a person other than the owner without affecting the interest of the owner or the validity or priority of the interest, but a person without notice of the assignment is protected in dealing with the security interest holder or lessor as the holder of the interest until the assignee files in accordance with [UCC 9-101 to 9-507].

"(4) A person who violates any provision of this section commits a Class C traffic infraction."—Eds.

within which there is a partial exclusion as to perfection from the Commercial Code. Regardless of whether there is a partial or a complete exclusion of subject matter, there is a clear intention in UCC 9-102(3) to carry into all exclusionary provisions the distinction between a security interest in a secured obligation and the secured obligation itself and to apply all provisions of the Commercial Code to the interests arising by reason of the sale of chattel paper. This distinction is further refined into the Commercial Code's definition of chattel paper contained in UCC 9-105(1)(b), and is built upon in the other rules governing the perfection of a sale of chattel paper contained in UCC 1-201(37), 9-102(1)(b), and 9-305, and the seller's collection activities which are authorized by UCC 9-205.

The trustee makes two basic arguments against the application of the perfection by possession provisions of UCC 9-305 to chattel paper involving a motor vehicle. These arguments must be rejected.

The trustee's first argument is that ORS 481.412(2) pre-empts the Commercial Code provisions authorizing perfection by delivery of possession to the buyer of chattel paper involving security interests in motor vehicles. This argument must be rejected because of the language of this section. Although Chapter 481 requires registration where new security interests are created and where there is a vertical assignment between existing security holders, nothing in ORS 481.412(2) or in related sections of the Motor Vehicle Code affirmatively requires the registration of a horizontal assignment of an existing security holder's interest to a third party who prior to the transaction had no interest in the vehicle. ORS 481.412(2) does not itself create the requirement of registration but rather makes "the provisions of this chapter which require" registration of security interests the "exclusive means of perfecting such interests." A sale of chattel paper by definition involves the transfer of a preexisting security interest and does not in itself create a security interest in the collateral and for this reason is not governed by ORS 481.410. Thus, there is no language anywhere in the Motor Vehicle Code which overrules the Commercial Code concept of UCC 9-102(3) distinguishing between chattel paper and the security interest contained in the chattel paper. As a result, the words "security interests in vehicles" in ORS 481.410(2) must be understood as not including the interest transferred when chattel paper is sold.

The trustee's second argument is based upon ORS 481.410(3), which states that a person without notice of an assignment of a security holder's interest is protected in "dealing" with the security holder as the holder of the interests "until the assignee files in accordance with" the Commercial Code. The trustee argues that this section requires a filing of a financing statement to perfect a buyer's interest in chattel paper, or alternatively that because of UCC 9-302(3)(b) which [prescribes] the Commercial Code mode of perfection as to motor vehicles is itself a part of the Commercial Code, registration under Motor Vehicle Code therefore is required to perfect a buyer's interest in chattel paper. The first alternative argument must be rejected because ORS 481.410(3) does not affirmatively mandate either filing or registration as a means of perfection, but only affords special protection where a person is dealing with a security holder prior to a filing under the UCC. The second alternative argument must be rejected because the trustee's circle of reasoning is broken by the fact that UCC 9-302(3)(b) logically does not overrule the distinction of UCC 9-102(3) between chattel paper and the security interest contained in the chattel paper and the requirement that these interests be treated separately. If anything ORS 481.410(3) reinforces the argument that the Commercial Code in all respects governs the interests involved in the sale of chattel paper.

ORS 481.410(3) is a special protection provision which is an addition to other similar special protection provisions contained in the Commercial Code, such as UCC 9-318(3) and 9-307. All of these sections provide a special defense to persons who "deal" with secured property under certain circumstances such as a buyer of the collateral from a dealer, or a person who without notice of an assignment pays the obligation secured by the collateral. The special protection provisions cited complement each other, apply according to their terms and do not cancel out the provisions of the Commercial Code governing perfection in circumstances not governed by the special protection provisions. Unless a person has grounds to claim the special protection of these sections, the other applicable provisions governing perfection must prevail.

In anticipation of an argument by the trustee that he qualifies for the special protection provided in ORS 481.410(3), I must find that a trustee in bankruptcy is not a person who "deals" with the security interest holder within the meaning of the section and that even if he were such a person, the protection granted by this section can only be the protection otherwise afforded to a trustee in bankruptcy under the Commercial Code. Since the Commercial Code itself would not allow a trustee in bankruptcy to prevail over a buyer of chattel paper who perfects by obtaining possession of the paper, the special protection of the Motor Vehicle Code would not require a contrary result.

Although not necessary to the ruling in the present case, the special protection of ORS 481.410(3) should probably be regarded as a companion to ORS 481.412(1)[3] imposing the perfection requirements of the Commercial Code upon financiers who finance motor vehicles constituting inventory and to ORS 481.015(3) which defines a "dealer." Where a conflict arises between an inventory financier and a purchaser of chattel paper over their rights to the chattel paper or to repossessed collateral in the hands of a dealer involving motor vehicles, the special protection provision of ORS 481.410(3) would appear to resolve any doubts as to the application of UCC 9-306(5)(d) and 9-308, respectively. Where a conflict develops between a buyer and a financier

---

3. Oregon Revised Statute 481.412(1) states: "The provisions of this chapter which require application for and notation on certificates of title of the interests of security interest holders do not apply as to holders of security interests in vehicles constituting inventory. The provisions of [UCC 9-302(3)(b), (4)] do not apply to security interests in vehicles constituting inventory and provisions of the Uniform Commercial Code controlling filing and perfection of security interests in inventory apply to the rights of all persons in such vehicles."—EDS.

of a motor vehicle, the special protection afforded by UCC 9-318(3) and 9-307 would govern under the proper circumstances and would not be reduced by the special protection provision in ORS 481.410(3) of the Motor Vehicle Code. . . .

Based upon the provisions of the pre-trial order, and the above findings, the plaintiff is declared to be the owner of whatever rights the bankrupt had to the truck in question and it is unnecessary to decide the questions presented by the alternative arguments. The trustee should be required to deliver to the plaintiffs the title certificate involved.

NOTES & QUESTIONS

1. *Uniform certificate of title legislation.* The Uniform Motor Vehicle Certificate of Title and Anti-Theft Act (1955) has had limited success: only ten states have adopted it. Its provisions with respect to recording a secured party's interest on the certificate of title, however, are typical of certificate of title legislation. Uniform Act §§20-25. Like most such acts the uniform law does not apply to vehicles "owned by a manufacturer or dealer and held for sale." Id. §2(a)(2). When the Act does cover a transaction, such as the sale of a car by a dealer to a customer, the Act's procedure for perfecting a security interest is exclusive. Section 25 states:

> The method provided in this act of perfecting and giving notice of security interests subject to this act is exclusive. Security interests subject to this act are hereby exempted from the provisions of law which otherwise require or relate to the [[recording] [filing] of instruments creating or evidencing security interests. . . .]

Does this language mean that the UCC rules on attachment, priority, and foreclosure do not apply? See also Uniform Act §1(k) ("A security interest is 'perfected' when it is valid against third parties generally, subject only to specific statutory exceptions.").

2. *Federal law: security interests in aircraft.* UCC 9-104(a) excludes from Article 9's coverage security interests "subject to any statute of the United States, to the extent that such statute governs the rights of parties to and third parties affected by transactions in particular types of property." The Comment to that section calls attention, inter alia, to the Federal Aviation Act, which establishes a nationwide recording system of "[a]ny conveyance which affects the title to, or any interest in, any civil aircraft of the United States." 49 U.S.C. §1403 (1976). The UCC Comment goes on to suggest that Article 9 will continue to govern security interests in aircraft to the extent the federal act is silent. Thus the draftsmen presumably intended the UCC priority and foreclosure rules to apply. There is growing case law to support this position. See In re Gary Aircraft Corp., 681 F.2d 365, 34 UCC Rep. 722 (5th Cir. 1982)

(Federal Aviation Act does not preempt state law on priorities; buyer of airplane in ordinary course of business takes free of security interest under UCC 9-307(1)).

Compare the *Western Leasing* case with Feldman v. Chase Manhattan Bank, N.A., 368 F. Supp. 1327, 13 UCC Rep. 1133 (S.D.N.Y. 1974), *rev'd on other grounds*, 511 F.2d 468 (2d Cir. 1975). Leasing Consultants leased an airplane to Devcon for 60 months with no option to purchase. Soon afterwards Leasing Consultants borrowed from Chase and to secure repayment granted the bank a security interest in the Devcon lease by a written "chattel mortgage and security agreement" and a separate written assignment. Chase took possession of the lease document and recorded the chattel mortgage with the FAA Aircraft Registry in Oklahoma City. At no time was the Devcon lease or its assignment recorded. Leasing Consultant subsequently filed a bankruptcy petition. The trustee in bankruptcy sought to avoid Chase's security interest under the strong-arm clause (Bankruptcy Act §70c; see BC 544(a)). *Held,* summary judgment for trustee affirmed because federal act requires recording of assignment of right to receive rentals in order to perfect the security interest. Can *Western Leasing* be distinguished?

Problem 7-5. Equipment Distributors sells a truck to User. User signs an installment note for the purchase price and gives Equipment Distributors a security interest in the truck to secure the note. Equipment Distributors has its lien noted on the certificate of title and retains possession of the original certificate. The same day Equipment Distributors assigns User's note and security agreement to Lender, who takes possession of the note and security agreement. Lender does not take possession of the certificate of title nor does he have the assignment noted on the original certificate. Soon afterwards User files a bankruptcy petition. His trustee in bankruptcy argues that Lender's interest is avoidable because of the failure to note his interest on the certificate of title. Assume that the Uniform Motor Vehicle Certificate of Title and Anti-Theft Act is in force in the relevant jurisdiction. Can trustee avoid Lender's interest? What are Lender's rights if Equipment Distributors also files a bankruptcy petition?

Section 22 of the Uniform Act states:

> (a) A lienholder may assign, absolutely or otherwise, his security interest in the vehicle to a person other than the owner without affecting the interest of the owner or the validity of the security interest, but any person without notice of the assignment is protected in dealing with the lienholder as the holder of the security interest and the lienholder remains liable for any obligations as lienholder until the assignee is named as lienholder on the certificate.
>
> (b) The assignee may, but need not to perfect the assignment, have the certificate of title endorsed or issued with the assignee named as lienholder, upon delivering to the Department the certificate and an assignment by the lienholder named in the certificate in the form the Department prescribes.

3. *The Interstate Movement of Vehicles: the Applicable Law*

Determining which state's law governs the "validity" of security interests in motor vehicles that move from one jurisdiction to another has been exquisite torture under the 1962 Code. The 1972 revision of UCC 9-103 attempts to clarify the relevant rules. Subsection (2) addresses specifically the question of the applicable law when at least one jurisdiction has a certificate of title statute.

(2)   Certificate of title

(a) This subsection applies to goods covered by a certificate of title issued under a statute of this state or of another jurisdiction under the law of which indication of a security interest on the certificate is required as a condition of perfection.

(b) Except as otherwise provided in this subsection, perfection and the effect of perfection or non-perfection of the security interest are governed by the law (including the conflict of laws rules) of the jurisdiction issuing the certificate until four months after the goods are removed from that jurisdiction and thereafter until the goods are registered in another jurisdiction, but in any event not beyond surrender of the certificate. After the expiration of that period, the goods are not covered by the certificate of title within the meaning of this section.

(c) Except with respect to the rights of a buyer described in the next paragraph, a security interest, perfected in another jurisdiction otherwise than by notation on a certificate of title, in goods brought into this state and thereafter covered by a certificate of title issued by this state is subject to the rules stated in paragraph (d) of subsection (1).

(d) If goods are brought into this state while a security interest therein is perfected in any manner under the law of the jurisdiction from which the goods are removed and a certificate of title is issued by this state and the certificate does not show that the goods are subject to the security interest or that they may be subject to security interests not shown on the certificate, the security interest is subordinate to the rights of a buyer of the goods who is not in the business of selling goods of that kind to the extent that he gives value and receives delivery of the goods after issuance of the certificate and without knowledge of the security interest.

(Note that if subsection (2) does not apply then the applicable law is determined by looking to subsections (1) or (3) of UCC 9-103.)

COOGAN, THE NEW UCC ARTICLE 9
86 Harv. L. Rev. 477, 544-550 (1973)

In a connoisseur's list of the most confusing and frustrating problems arising under Article 9, there would surely be a case or two involving a multistate situation and one or more certificate of title statutes. Such statutes are built on the hope that a certificate of title may be able to control property interests in highly mobile goods like automobiles, wherever they may be. Unfortunately, however, not all states have certificate of title laws, much less the same laws, and persons have been known to obtain by fraudulent means two or more certificates of title for a vehicle, on only one of which a security interest was properly noted. When the goods are moved from a certificate state to a non-certificate state or vice versa, and when a number of secured parties or a succession of purchasers enters the picture, perplexities are bound to arise. Revised subsection (2) of 9-103 attempts valiantly to cover the principal situations that may arise. By posing a series of hypotheticals about automobiles, one can test whether the new version succeeds in being reasonably clear and comprehensive.

1. Protection of Nonprofessional Buyers.—One major policy decision should be kept in mind with regard to the rules of revised subsection (2): *all* of its provisions are subject to the protection afforded nonprofessional buyers by paragraph (d). . . .

The purpose of this overriding protection for the nonprofessional buyer is obvious. This is the class of buyer least able to protect itself. Officers issuing a certificate of title will not always be able to know all the parties who have security interests in other states and will not always be meticulous about either contacting them or listing them on the certificate. Moreover, sellers may transfer fraudulent certificates. Nevertheless, the issuing state has a strong interest in insuring that its certificates will be trusted by those most likely to rely upon them. The professional buyer, on the other hand, is presumed to know the practices of his trade and to be on the alert for the possible existence of security interests whose actual existence is not disclosed.

2. Priority Where the Security Interest Is Not Perfected in the Removal State.—Subsection (2) of revised section 9-103 makes clear which rules govern when an automobile in which an unperfected security interest exists in one state [i.e., the "removal state."—Eds.] is removed to another state where a perfected security interest is created. Suppose that *S-1* has an attached and enforceable but unperfected security interest in an automobile situated in *X*. The vehicle is then brought into *Y*, and a certificate is there issued noting a security interest in favor of *S-2*. By virtue of *Y*'s version of existing and revised paragraph 9-302(3)(b), which makes filing unnecessary to perfect a security interest in goods covered by a certificate of title statute, *S-2*'s security interest is thereby perfected without more.

It might be thought obvious that *S-2*'s perfected interest prevails over *S-1*'s temporally prior but unperfected interest. Yet it is not absolutely clear that the priority rules of Part 3 of revised Article 9, as enacted by *Y*, are intended to cover competing interests when multistate elements are present; one might read them as governing purely domestic transactions only. In any event, revised paragraphs 9-103(2)(a) and (b) make it fairly clear that *S-2* does win. Paragraph (a) states that subsection (2) of 9-103 "applies to goods covered by a certificate of title issued under a statute of this state or of another jurisdiction. . . ." Paragraph (b) provides that "perfection and the effect of perfection . . . are governed by the law (including the conflict of laws rules) of the jurisdiction issuing the certificate. . . ." Since on the facts given, Y was the only state to issue a certificate, paragraph (b) seems to make it plain that the priority rules under Part 3 of Y's revised Article 9 do in fact apply to this multistate situation; therefore, S-2's perfected security interest has priority over the unperfected interest of S-1.

3. Priority Where Both Security Interests Are Perfected but Only One is Perfected by Notation on a Certificate of Title. . . . [The author's discussion of this point is omitted because it is less relevant with the wider adoption of certificate of title legislation. Readers are urged to study the close analysis in the original.—EDS.]

4. Priority Where Both Security Interests Are Perfected by Notation on a Certificate of Title.—Where the holder of a security interest in the original state and the holder of a security interest in the state to which the goods have been removed have both perfected by notation on a certificate of title, the analysis required by paragraph (b) of subsection (2) is a variation of that given above. Suppose that S-1's security interest was perfected by notation on a certificate issued in X. The automobile comes into Y and S-2 perfects by notation on a certificate issued in Y which neither shows S-1's interest nor warns that the automobile may be subject to security interests not shown on the certificate.[161] A preliminary difficulty in resolving the question of which secured party has priority is determining whether subsection (2) of 9-103 applies at all: paragraph (a) of subsection (2) provides that this subsection applies only to goods covered by *a* certificate of title—but here the automobile is ostensibly covered by *two* certificates. The best solution is probably to read "a" to mean "at least one," as logicians do, so that subsection (2) will apply. For if it does not apply, one consequence will be that a nonprofessional buyer will not be protected against S-1 if the buyer purchases the automobile in state Y in reliance on the Y certificate; such a result seems unintended.

Once having decided this much, the potential difficulty in applying paragraph (b) to the *dual* certificate situation, with regard to rights other than those of a nonprofessional buyer, is that it states that "perfection and the effect of perfection or nonperfection of the security interest are governed by the law (including the conflict of laws rules) of the jurisdiction issuing *the* certificate . . . ." (Emphasis added). Therefore, in order to make sense out of the provision, we must carefully read paragraph (b) twice, once as if the phrase "the certificate" meant the certificate issued in X, and once as if it meant the certificate issued in Y. For convenience, reading the provision first to apply to the certificate issued in X, our analysis is similar to that undertaken above where S-1 perfected through notation in state X and S-2 perfected through

161. Note that the special protection afforded nonprofessional *buyers* by revised 9-103(2)(d) does not apply to other "purchasers" (even if also nonprofessional) as that term is defined by the Code. . . .

filing in state Y. That is, the effect of S-1's perfection in state X through notation on the certificate issued there, unless S-1 surrenders that certificate, is to leave him perfected for at least 4 months after the goods have been removed, and thereafter "until the goods are registered in another jurisdiction." Even if registration in the other jurisdiction takes place within the 4-month grace period during which S-1 is absolutely protected unless he surrenders his certificate, S-1 will have priority as the first to perfect.

Where the analysis, though not the result, differs from that where S-2 perfects by filing is either when S-1 has surrendered his certificate or when the 4-month period has expired and the automobile has been registered in a jurisdiction other than X. In that event, paragraph (b) tells us that the automobile is no longer "covered by the certificate of title" *issued in X*. However, rather than being remitted to the provisions of subsection (1) on localizable goods or subsection (3) on mobile equipment and inventory as we were before in this situation, we must now make our second reading of paragraph (b) to see if its provisions apply to "the" certificate issued to S-2 in state Y. Since that certificate is still effective, the result of our second reading is that the law of Y governs the existence and effect of perfection—so long as the reference to a state's law is taken to mean its domestic law—and thus S-2 wins because S-1 has not obtained a proper certificate in Y.

Problem 7-6. Bank finances Debtor's purchase of a new car, and to secure repayment Debtor granted Bank a security interest in the car. Bank has the lien noted on the certificate of title issued by State A and takes possession of this certificate. Soon afterwards Debtor obtains a "clean" State A certificate of title by submission of a forged affidavit. The same day Debtor takes the car to State B.

(a) Within a week after taking the car from State A Debtor sells the car to Dealer in State B. The car still has State A license plates, and Debtor has made no attempt to obtain a State B certificate of title or to register the car in State B. Can Bank recover the car from Dealer? See UCC 9-103(2), 9-306, 9-307.

(b) Assume the same facts as in (a) except that Debtor sells the car to Consumer for its fair market value. Can Bank recover the car from Consumer? See UCC 9-103(2), 9-306, 9-307.

(c) The week after taking the car from State A Debtor registers the car in State B and obtains a State B certificate of title by submitting to the State B authorities the "clean" State A certificate. Debtor then sells the car to Dealer in State B. Can Bank recover the car from Dealer? See UCC 9-103(2)(b), (d).

(d) Assume the same facts as in (c) except that Debtor sells the car to Consumer for its fair market value. Can Bank recover the car from Consumer? See UCC 9-103(2)(d).

(e) Five months after taking the car from State A Debtor sells the car to Dealer in State B. The car still has State A license plates and Debtor has not registered the car in State *B* or obtained a State *B* certificate of title. Can Bank recover the car from Dealer? See UCC 9-103(2)(b). What would be the result if the car was nonmobile equipment not subject to a certificate of title statute? See UCC 9-103(1)(b), (d). What if the car was mobile equipment not subject to a certificate of title statute? See UCC 9-103(3).

(f) Assume the same facts as in (e) except that Debtor sells the car to Consumer. Can Bank recover the car from Consumer? See UCC 9-103(2)(b), (d).

Problem 7-7. Finance Company finances Debtor's purchase of a new car. Debtor grants Finance Company a security interest in the car and the lien is noted on the certificate of title issued by State *A*. Soon afterwards Thief steals the car and takes it to State *B*. On submission of a forged certificate of title purportedly issued by State *A,* Thief obtains a certificate of title issued by State *B* in his name. He also registers the car in State *B* and obtains State *B* license plates. Thief then sells the car to Purchaser, who pays the fair market value. Finance Company seeks to replevy the car from Purchaser. Should Finance Company succeed? See UCC 9-103, 9-306, 9-307, 2-403. Assuming the Uniform Act applies in both states, what is the effect of the certificate of title legislation?

C.   REAL PROPERTY AND FIXTURES

Article 9 regulates personal property secured transactions but explicitly excludes from its coverage "the creation or transfer of an interest in or lien on real estate." UCC 9-104(j). It is clear, therefore, that the granting of a mortgage in real property is not covered by Article 9.

The simplicity of this approach is complicated, however, by two factors. First, a note secured by a real estate mortgage may be used as collateral just as chattel paper may be used as collateral. If only the note (instrument) is pledged it appears that Article 9 would govern this second secured loan transaction. Does it make a difference that the note is secured by a real estate mortgage? To answer this question requires reconciling UCC 9-102(3) with 9-104(j). A second complication arises because the division of property into real and personal interests is not absolute: fixtures ("realty, with a chattel past, and a hope of chattel future") may be governed by both bodies of law. Real property law defines when goods become so related to particular real estate that they become fixtures but Article 9 does provide perfection and priority rules for fixtures. UCC 9-313. These fixture rules proved to be some of the most controversial in the article, especially among real estate practitioners, and were extensively revised in 1972 to make them more acceptable.

1.   Real Property

RUCKER v. STATE EXCHANGE BANK

355 So. 2d 171, 23 UCC Rep. 1020 (Fla. Dist. Ct. App. 1978).

MILLS, Acting Chief Judge. The issue raised by this appeal is whether a real estate mortgage securing a promissory note becomes a secured transaction under Article 9 of the Uniform Commercial Code when it is assigned, along with the note, as collateral for a bank loan. . . .

On 17 April 1974, South 41 Corporation (South 41) purchased seventy-five acres of land from Harrell and gave Harrell a note secured by a purchase money mortgage. On 18 April, South 41 deeded the land to Rucker subject to the mortgage.

On 7 May and 9 July, Harrell obtained loans of $24,000.00 and $5,000.00 from Exchange Bank and assigned the South 41 note and mortgage to it as collateral for the loans. The Exchange Bank promptly recorded the assignment and gave notice of the assignment to South 41. It did not give notice to Rucker. It did not perfect a security interest.

On 23 July, Rucker mortgaged the land to Land Bank and paid to Harrell the entire sum due on the South 41 note and mortgage. Although Rucker obtained a satisfaction from Harrell, which she promptly recorded, she did not ascertain if the mortgage had been assigned by him nor did she demand that he surrender the mortgage to her.

On 2 January 1975, Harrell defaulted in the payment of the loans which were then due the Exchange Bank and no payment was made on the South 41 note and mortgage. The Exchange Bank brought foreclosure proceedings against Rucker based on the South 41 mortgage held by it. The trial court entered a judgment in favor of Exchange Bank; and Rucker and Land Bank appeal. . . .

UCC 9-102(3) provides:

> (3) The application of this Article to a security interest in a secured obligation is not affected by the fact that the obligation is itself secured by a transaction or interest to which this Article does not apply.

Amended Comment 4 under this section states: "The owner of Blackacre borrows $10,000 from his neighbor, and secures his note by a mortgage on Blackacre. This Article is not applicable to the creation of the real estate mortgage. Nor is it applicable to a sale of the note by the mortgagee, even though the mortgage continues to secure the note. However, when the mortgagee pledges the note to secure his own obligation to X, this Article applies to the security interest thus created, which is a security interest in an instrument even though the instrument is secured by a real estate mortgage. This Article leaves to other law the question of the effect on rights under the mortgage of delivery or non-delivery of the mortgage or of recording or non-recording of an assignment of the mortgagee's interest. See Section 9-104(j). But under Section 3-304(5) recording of the assignment does not of itself prevent X from holding the note in due course."

UCC 9-104(j) provides:

> This Article does not apply . . .
>
> (j)   except to the extent that provision is made for fixtures in Section 9-313, to the creation or transfer of an interest in or lien on real estate, including a lease or rents thereunder.

Coogan, Kripke and Weiss state: "The status under article 9 of the assignment of a note secured by a real estate mortgage has been widely discussed in New York and was among the subjects that the New York financial bar wanted clarified by legislation. The title companies in New York have insisted that for 'mortgage warehousing'—the situation in which a mortgage banker or broker makes a real estate mortgage loan and pledges the mortgage to a bank until he finds a permanent mortgagee—not only must the note (or bond) and mortgage be delivered and the assignment of the mortgage recorded under real estate law, but a financing statement with respect to the transaction must also be filed under article 9. Insofar as we understand the argument of the title companies, it rests on two separate bases:

"(a) The persons demanding clarification argue that, even though section 9-104(j) excludes from the Code the transfer of an interest in or lien on real estate, the matter is not clear because of three facts: the real estate mortgage is itself personal property, presumably a general intangible; the pledge of the note is expressly brought under article 9 by section 9-102(3); and Official Comment 4 to that section specifically states that article 9 is applicable to the security interest created in the note and mortgage.

"(b) Another argument is that the note and the real estate mortgage together are something more than they are separately. Just as a note and chattel mortgage together constitute a new form of collateral to which the Code applies the title 'chattel paper' and for which it sets forth special rules, so the note and real estate mortgage together may constitute a 'general intangible,' which is defined to include all personal property not otherwise classified. If either of the arguments is sound, a security interest in the mortgage could be perfected only by filing.

"We are satisfied that this view is unduly fearful. The clear intent of section 9-104(j) to exclude transfers of liens on real estate would be completely nullified if the argument were accepted that the lien, as a form of wealth, is personal property, a security interest in which is subject to article 9. Likewise, we feel that the argument that a note and real estate collateral could, in combination, be a general intangible under the Code is inconsistent with the fact that, when the Code intended to give special status to a combination of this nature (the chattel paper case), it expressly provided for it. If the theory advanced by the title companies were sound, it would apparently drag back into the Code all the other matters excluded by section 9-104, when transferred with a note for which they were collateral. There is, in our opinion, no danger that a court could read the statute in any such fashion. Because of the express language of section 9-104(j), we do not feel that Official Comment 4 to section 9-102 should cause any real confusion or doubt, but there can be no objection to a revision by the Permanent Editorial Board of the sentence that has been called into question, and we recommend this measure." [Coogan, Kripke & Weiss, The Outer Fringes of Article 9: Subordination Agreements, Security Interests in Money and Deposits, Negative Pledge Clauses, and Participation Agreements, 79 Harv. L. Rev. 229, 270-271.] . . .

At the time Coogan, et al. [wrote their article] . . . , Comment 4 read as follows: "An illustration of subsection (3) is as follows: The owner of Blackacre borrows $10,000 from his neighbor, and secures his note by a mortgage on Blackacre. This Article is not applicable to the creation of the real estate mortgage. However, when the mortgagee in turn pledges this note and mortgage to secure his own obligation to X, this Article is applicable to the security interest thus created in the note and the mortgage. Whether the transfer of the collateral for the note, i.e., the mortgagee's interest in Blackacre, requires further action (such as recording an assignment of the mortgagee's interest) is left to real estate law. See Section 9-104(j)." Comment 4 was amended in 1966 and the 1966 Amendment is set forth above. [The court is incorrect: the amended Comment was adopted in 1962.—Eds.] As stated in In re Bristol Associates, Inc., 505 F.2d 1056 (3d Cir. 1974): "The changes in wording produced two effects. First, deletion of the references to mortgages distinguishes between the pledge of a note, a separate and distinct contract, and the underlying real estate mortgage. Where a promissory note and mortgage together become the subject of a security interest, only that portion of the package unrelated to the real property is now covered by section 9-102. Second, the added language makes explicit that the promissory note itself falls within the scope of Article 9 by virtue of its status as an instrument. . . ."

A broad reading of UCC 9-104(j) which would exclude the real estate mortgage here from Article 9 is consistent with the views of authorities in the commercial field and is not inconsistent with the language used by the legislature.

"Where language is susceptible of two reasonable meanings, a court, in the commercial field, should choose that interpretation which comports with current universal practice in the business world." In re Bristol Associates, Inc., supra. Generally, the banking industry in Florida does not consider real estate mortgages as covered by Article 9. Rather, it considers that its interest in a real estate mortgage is protected by recording the assignment as required by Section 701.02, Florida Statutes (1975).[4] The recording of the assignment gives constructive notice of its interest in the mortgage to the world.

---

4. Section 701.02 states that:

(1) No assignment of a mortgage upon real property or of any interest therein, shall be good or effectual in law or equity, against creditors or subsequent purchasers, for a valuable consideration, and without notice, unless the same be recorded according to law.

We hold, therefore, that the assignment of a real estate mortgage securing a promissory note as collateral for a bank loan is not a secured transaction under Article 9 of the Uniform Commercial Code because it is specifically excluded by UCC 9-104(j).

There is good reason for doing this. If the court were to hold that a real estate mortgage assigned as collateral comes under Article 9, the status of all such mortgages would be called into question. This would generate considerable litigation. Undertaking to file all outstanding security interests in such mortgages would be time consuming and expensive. Chaos would result. We must not burden the business world with further chaos. We must not burden either the consumer or the business world with additional financial burdens.

In the case before us, as the Exchange Bank properly recorded the assignment of the mortgage from Harrell, Rucker satisfied the mortgage at her peril because she was on constructive notice of Exchange Bank's interest. In addition, when Rucker satisfied the mortgage she did not require that the mortgage be surrendered to her nor did she determine if it had been assigned by Harrell. . . . We affirm the judgment [foreclosing the mortgage].

NOTES & QUESTIONS

1. *Commentary on* Rucker. Evaluate the following analysis of the *Rucker* decision.

The outcome reached on the facts in the *Rucker* case is correct but the court's reasoning is hopelessly confused. This can be illustrated by considering the following cases and remembering basic principles—the most important of which is that a mortgage is a nullity unless it secures an obligation.

Case 1. Debtor makes a note payable to the order of Lender. Lender negotiates the note to Bank. Debtor pays Lender on maturity. Promptly after this payment Bank demands payment. Debtor must pay again. UCC 3-305, 3-603.

Case 2. Debtor makes a note payable to the order of Lender and also signs a security agreement granting Lender a security interest in heavy equipment. Lender sells his chattel paper to Bank: Lender indorses the note, signs a written assignment of the security agreement, and delivers the papers to Bank. On maturity Debtor pays Lender and promptly afterwards Bank demands payment. Debtor must pay again. UCC 3-305, 3-603.

Case 3. The same facts as in Case 2 but Lender does not indorse and deliver the note to Bank. If Lender surrenders the note to Debtor on payment at maturity Debtor will be discharged on the instrument and underlying obligation. UCC 3-603, 3-802. Without possession of the note Bank cannot be a

---

(2) The provisions of this section shall also extend to assignments of mortgages resulting from transfers of all or any part or parts of the debt, note or notes secured by mortgage, and none of same shall be effectual in law or in equity against creditors or subsequent purchasers for a valuable consideration without notice, unless a duly executed assignment be recorded according to law. . . .[—Eds.]

holder, let alone a holder in due course. UCC 1-201(20), 3-602, 3-603. Without an obligation to be secured the security interest in the equipment is a nullity.

Case 4. Debtor makes a note payable to the order of Lender and also signs a mortgage agreement granting Lender a mortgage of real property. Lender sells the secured note to Bank: Lender indorses the note, signs a written assignment of the mortgage, and delivers the papers to Bank. On maturity Debtor pays Lender and promptly afterwards Bank demands payment. Debtor must pay again.

Case 5. The same facts as in Case 4 but Lender, rather than selling the note to Bank, assigns and delivers the note and mortgage as collateral securing repayment of a loan from Bank. The result does not change: Debtor must pay again.

Although the facts in *Rucker* are more complicated, they can be reduced to the simple outline in Case 5. True, the original Debtor (South 41) deeded the land to Rucker "subject to" the mortgage and Rucker did not become a party to the note.[5] But the holder of the note (Bank) may foreclose the mortgage if the note is not paid by the original Debtor. Although not personally obligated to do so Rucker has an incentive to pay South 41's note in order to avoid the possibility that the mortgage on her land will be foreclosed. Rucker does not satisfy the obligation, however, by paying Harrell and failing to demand surrender of the note.

For a different analysis of the *Rucker* case, see Note, Security Interests in Notes and Mortgages: Determining the Applicable Law, 79 Colum. L. Rev. 1414 (1979). See generally Bowmar, Real Estate Interests as Security Under the UCC: The Scope of Article Nine, 12 UCC L.J. 99 (1979).

2. *Real property interests.* The *Rucker* case involves a mortgage but similar questions concerning Article 9's scope may arise in a great variety of real property interests when the interests are part of the collateral used in a second transaction. Consider, for example, the lessor who assigns as collateral his right to rental payments, the tenant who assigns his leasehold interest, the vendor who assigns his right to payments under a real estate contract, or the landlord who assigns his interest in security deposits.

Perhaps the best known of the cases discussing the application of Article 9 to these interests is In re Bristol Associates, Inc., 505 F.2d 1056, 15 UCC Rep. 561 (3d Cir. 1974), cited by the *Rucker* court. To secure repayment of a loan Bristol Associates assigned to Bank as collateral its interest as lessor of store premises. Bank did not file a financing statement or otherwise record the assignment. Bristol Associates subsequently filed a petition under Chapter XI of the Bankruptcy Act. The court held that the assignment of the lease as security fell outside Article 9 and therefore could not be avoided under §70c of the Bankruptcy Act, the trustee's strong-arm clause [see BC 544(a)]. In reach-

---

5. For a discussion of the difference between a mortgagor's transfer of real property "subject to" the mortgage and an "assumption" of the mortgage by the transferee, see G. Osborne, G. Nelson & D. Whitman, Real Estate Finance Law 250-255 (1979).

ing this conclusion the court noted, inter alia, that the document that embodies a lease of real property is not an *instrument* and that therefore Article 9's treatment of promissory notes should not be applied to an assignment of a lease.

3. *Landlord's lien.* UCC 9-104(b) explicitly excludes the landlord's lien from the scope of Article 9. The common law recognizes the lien, however, and many states have adopted statutes codifying or supplementing the common law. A lease may contain language that also grants the landlord a security interest in the tenant's personal property. Is such a consensual grant covered by Article 9? Does the exclusion mean that Article 9's rules on priority are not relevant when the landlord claims a lien on the tenant's property that is subject to a security interest? See UCC 9-201. Compare the explicit rule for other liens in UCC 9-310, discussed at p. 353 supra.

4. *Mortgages under the Uniform Land Transactions Act.* Article 3 of the Uniform Land Transactions Act (1975) sets out uniform rules for secured transactions involving real property. The approach, structure, and language of this uniform law closely follows Article 9. (This is not altogether surprising because one of the draftsmen was Professor Allison Dunham, who also served as a draftsman of Article 9.) In particular, the uniform act provides a simple, unified structure and downplays the role of "title" in determining attachment and priorities. There has not been a great deal of commentary on the act. See Comment, Secured Transactions under Article 3 of the Uniform Land Transactions Act, 1976 Wis. L. Rev. 899.

Problem 7-8. Realtor sold a house and lot to Consumer, who signed an installment note and mortgage deed to secure the purchase price. The mortgage was recorded. Needing working capital, Realtor obtained a loan from Bank and used Consumer's note as collateral. Bank took possession of the note and mortgage deed but did not record an assignment of the mortgage.

(a) Assume that Consumer defaults on the note. What are Bank's rights?

(b) Assume that Realtor subsequently files a petition in bankruptcy. Can Realtor's trustee in bankruptcy avoid Bank's interest in the note and mortgage? See UCC 9-102(3), 9-104(j).

Problem 7-9. In 1982 Rental Associates leased store premises to Bon-Bon Department Store for a 12-year period. In 1984 Rental Associates borrows $1,000,000 from Bank and assigns its interest in the lease to Bank as collateral. Bank does not file a financing statement or make any other public record of the assignment. Rental Associates continues to collect the rent. The following year Rental Associates files a petition for reorganization under Chapter 11 of the Bankruptcy Code. Bank files a petition with the bankruptcy court requesting that rental payments be made directly to it. Rental Associates argues that Bank's interest is unperfected and therefore voidable. How should the bankruptcy court rule?

Problem 7-10. On July 1, 1984, Landlord leases store premises to Dealer for a period of three years. The lease agreement grants a "lien" to Landlord in all Dealer's inventory and equipment kept on the leased premises to secure performance of Dealer's obligations under the lease. Landlord does not file an Article 9 financing statement. In November, 1984, Dealer obtains a loan from Bank and grants Bank a security interest in its inventory and equipment to secure repayment of the loan. Bank files a financing statement in the proper office. In January, 1986, Dealer fails to make a rental payment to Landlord or an installment payment on the note issued to Bank. Both Landlord and Bank declare Dealer to be in default and both claim the inventory and equipment. You represent Bank. What arguments do you make? See UCC 9-102, 9-104(b), 9-310. Assume the following statute is in force:

> All persons leasing or renting any residence, storehouse, or other building, shall have a preference lien upon all property of the tenant or of any subtenant of such tenant in such residence, storehouse, or other building, for the payment of rents due and to become due provided that in order to secure the lien for rents that are more than six (6) months due, it shall be necessary for the person leasing or renting any storehouse or other building that is used for commercial purposes, to file in the office of the county clerk of the county in which such storehouse or such other building is situated, a sworn statement of the amount of rent due, itemized as to the months for which it is claimed to be due, together with the name and address of the tenant and/or subtenant, a description of the rented premises, the date on which the rental contract began and that on which it is to terminate, verified by the person claiming such lien, his agent or attorney, and such statement when so verified shall be recorded by the county clerk in a book to be provided for such purpose. No lien for rent more than six (6) months past due upon any storehouse or other building rented for commercial purposes shall be valid as against bona fide purchasers or unsecured or lien creditors of said tenant and/or subtenant, unless said statement shall be verified, filed, and recorded as above provided. The lien for rents to become due shall not continue or be enforced for a longer period than the current contract years, it being intended by the term 'current contract years' to embrace a period of twelve (12) months, reckoning from the beginning of the lease or rental contract, whether the same be in the first or any other year of such lease or rental contract.

2. Fixtures

Assume your client plans to sell a new drill press to a local manufacturer and will extend credit to the buyer and retain a security interest in the press to secure payment. He asks you to prepare the necessary paperwork. In answer to your questions he informs you that the press will be bolted to the manufacturer's factory floor by bolts imbedded in a concrete slab. Suspecting that there is a "fixture problem" you review Article 9's regulation of fixtures, as revised in 1972. Your answers to the five basic secured-transactions questions might take the following form.

1. **Scope.** UCC 9-102(1)(a) expressly includes security interests in fixtures within the scope of Article 9. Fixtures are a subcategory of "goods": they

are goods that have "become so related to particular real estate that an interest in them arises under real estate law." UCC 9-105(1)(h), 9-313(1)(a). The Code provides little further guidance. "Ordinary building materials incorporated into an improvement" cannot be fixtures. UCC 9-313(2). On the other hand, property may be a fixture even if its removal would cause material injury to the freehold. UCC 9-313(8). As for the non-Code definitions of *fixtures,* most authors would agree that the case law even within a single jurisdiction is often unsettled. See R. Brown, The Law of Personal Property ch. 16 (W. Raushenbush 3d ed. 1975) (confusion results from failure to distinguish the different contexts in which the issue is raised).

2. **Attachment.** The general rules on attachment and enforcement also apply to security interests in fixtures. The security agreement must contain a description of the fixture sufficiently specific so that it can be reasonably identified. UCC 9-110, 9-203(1)(a). The real property equivalent of a security interest (an "encumbrance") may also apply to fixtures if the encumbrancer complies with the real property rules. UCC 9-105(1)(g), 9-313(3). In other words, if a mortgage claims an interest in fixtures the attachment and enforceability of this interest will be determined by looking to real property law.

3. **Perfection.** A secured party may perfect a security interest in a fixture either by filing a financing statement in the personal property UCC files or by making a fixture filing, which is the filing of a special financing statement in the office where a mortgage on the real estate would be filed or recorded. UCC 9-313(1)(b). The fixture financing statement differs from the usual form by setting out the additional information required by UCC 9-402(5). The financing statement will be indexed in the real property records under the names of the debtor, owner of record of the real property, and, if required by local law, also of the secured party. UCC 9-403(7). The advantage of a fixture filing is that the secured party has priority over a greater number of potential claimants.

If there is any doubt about the classification of the property, the safest course is to make both a fixture filing and a regular UCC filing. Consider the consequences of guessing wrong: (a) if the collateral is not a fixture a fixture filing will not perfect the interest; (b) if the collateral is a fixture but the secured party makes a regular UCC filing then although the interest is perfected it will not give priority over several significant real property interests.

4. **Priorities.** The 1972 amendments to the UCC 9-313 priority rules make several significant concessions to real estate interests. Symbolically, the amendments adopt a residual rule that an encumbrancer or nondebtor owner of real estate has priority over an Article 9 secured party, thus reversing the residual rule of the 1962 Code. UCC 9-313(7). More narrow, but politically very significant, is the new rule giving lenders with a construction mortgage priority over creditors who finance the acquisition of fixtures to be installed during construction. UCC 9-313(1)(c), (6).

Unless the competing interest is a construction mortgage, however, a creditor with a security interest in a fixture may have priority over real property interests if he falls within one of four categories set out in subsection (4).

Two categories require the creditor to have made a fixture filing. If the creditor makes a fixture filing he will have priority over subsequent encumbrancers or owners. UCC 9-313(4)(b). As for existing real property interests, only a creditor with a purchase money security interest promptly perfected by a fixture filing will have priority—and even this priority is lost, as noted above, to a lender with a construction mortgage. UCC 9-313(1)(c), (4)(a), (6).

Even if the creditor has not made a fixture filing, he may still have priority over some classes of other claimants. If he perfects an interest in "readily removable factory or office machines" or "readily removable replacements of domestic appliances which are consumer goods" before these goods become fixtures, he will have priority over any prior or subsequent encumbrancer or owner of the real estate. UCC 9-313(4)(c). The creditor who perfects his interest by any means authorized by Article 9 will also prevail over subsequent creditors who obtain a lien on the real property by legal or equitable proceedings. UCC 9-313(4)(d). As with security interests in personal property, this latter rule is significant primarily because it protects the creditor from the bankruptcy trustee's strong-arm attack. BC 544(a)(1); UCC 9-313, Comment 4(c).

5. **Default.** If the debtor defaults, a secured party with priority over all real property interests may remove the fixture even if removal causes physical injury to the real property. The secured party must reimburse the real property interest holders for this injury and, if demanded, must give adequate security before removing the fixture. UCC 9-313(8). See also UCC 9-501(4), which authorizes a secured party to proceed with his rights and remedies under real property law rather than under Article 9.

CORNING BANK v. BANK OF RECTOR
265 Ark. 68, 576 S.W.2d 949, 26 UCC Rep. 1367 (1979)

FOGLEMAN, Justice. . . . The controversy involves grain bins which, at least at the time of the trial, were located on real estate on which The Bank of Rector held a mortgage dated May 17, 1976, and properly filed for record on the same day. Appellant [Corning Bank] contends that its financing statement and security agreement (a single instrument) dated March 17, 1976, covering the bins, made its security interest superior to the lien of the mortgage to appellee. The financing statement and security agreement contained no description of any real property and no indication whether the property described was located on, or to be located on, any real estate. This statement was filed in the office of the Circuit Court Clerk of Clay County on March 19, 1976, where financing statements are filed only by the name of the debtor. Since there was no land description in the instrument, it was not noted or recorded in any deed, mortgage, release deed or miscellaneous record book in that office. It was filed in the Uniform Commercial Code file.

The financing statement and security agreement upon which appellant relies refers to the property described as goods. The instrument, according to appellant, contains a covenant that the Pooles would not sell, exchange, lease or otherwise dispose of the "goods" or any of the debtor's rights therein, without the written consent of appellant. It also contained the following clauses: "Debtor, upon demand by secured party, shall assemble the goods and make them available to secured party at a place reasonably convenient to both parties." "Until default hereunder, debtor shall be entitled to possession of the goods and to use and enjoy the same." There was also a provision that the property would be retained at the place of business of Greenway Elevator Co. at P.O. Box 94, Greenway, Arkansas.

The critical issues in this case, according to appellant, are whether the property involved is a fixture and whether a "fixture filing" was required to preserve the priority of appellant's security interest. The chancellor held that each of the grain bins consisted of a floor, roof and sides and that they constituted buildings, were "permanent property" and a part of the real estate. He also held that there was nothing on file to put appellee on notice of appellant's security interest. We cannot say that the chancellor erred.

Under the Uniform Commercial Code, goods are fixtures when they become so related to the real estate that an interest in them arises under real estate law. UCC 9-313(1)(a). Unless the facts are undisputed and reasonable minds could only reach one conclusion, the question whether particular property constitutes a fixture is sometimes one of fact only, but usually is a mixed question of law and fact. . . .

In reviewing the evidence on this question, we are aided in our understanding of it by photographs reproduced by appellee. W.J. Hurst, whose occupation is selling and erecting grain bins similar to those involved, had inspected these bins. He appears to have been the only witness on the question whether the bins were fixtures. According to him: a bin, the size of these, would require a "12-foot deep footing" and four to six inches of concrete over the balance of the surface; the bins, which have dimensions of 22 feet by 21 feet and a capacity of 7,000 bushels, are constructed on this foundation from side sheets 34 inches wide and 79 inches long; they are attached to the foundation by steel bolts and nuts; it would take three days to construct these bins; a bin can be removed from the foundation by removing the nuts from the bolts with a crescent wrench and the motor attached to the bins can be removed in the same way; the motor and a three-phase fan are detachable and can be changed readily; the bins can be removed and put in a truck and hauled away (leaving only a concrete slab with bolts sticking up) but it is not practical to do so, and special equipment, similar to house moving equipment, would be required; the bins could not be moved without being completely disassembled; a house could be removed "by the same token;" and the bins can be "taken down in reverse order in which they are erected." Hurst knew of two bins that had been moved, but they were on sand and wired to the ground, not set in concrete.

In Ozark v. Adams, 73 Ark. 227, 83 S.W. 920, we reiterated the basic rules for determining whether an article remains a chattel or becomes a fixture. They are: (1) real or constructive annexation to the realty in question; (2) appropriation or adaptation to the use or purpose of that part of the realty with which it is connected; and (3) the intention of the party making the annexation to make a permanent accession to the realty, this intention being inferred from the nature of the chattel, the relation and situation of the party making the annexation, the structure and mode of annexation and the purpose for which the annexation has been made. A consideration of the various facts in this case seems to support a finding that the property in question was intended to be a permanent accession to the land and therefore it became a fixture. The person making the annexation was the owner of the realty; the realty was being used as a grain storage facility and the chattels in question were grain storage bins; the bins were assembled and erected on the realty and this installation involved the pouring of a concrete slab with bolts imbedded in it. The inference is strong, where the party attaching the "fixture" is the owner of the soil, that it was intended to become a part of the soil and not a removable fixture, and to overturn it, there must be strong evidence of a contrary intention manifested by some act or circumstance. . . .

If we can assume from the record before us that, at the time the security agreement was executed, the bins had not been assembled or placed on the lands described in the mortgage to appellee, the decision in this case turns upon the effect of the filing by appellant as notice to appellee. In this case, we consider UCC 9-313 as controlling.

In this connection, we do not consider the fact that appellee's mortgage was taken and recorded in reliance upon a title opinion based upon an abstract which was made prior to the date of the filing of appellant's security agreement. In any event, appellee caused an examination of the records to be made by an abstractor on the day after its mortgage was filed. The issue does not turn upon the information appellee had. It depends upon what a proper search would have disclosed.

The abstractor did not find appellee's security agreement because it was not filed or recorded in the real estate records. The abstractor testified that, if the document had contained a legal description, he would have found it. The only description relied upon by appellant as a land description was the statement that the property would be located at the Greenway Elevator Company at Greenway, Arkansas, which, as we have pointed out, was identified only by a post office box number. We do not consider this as a sufficient key to identification of real estate to meet Uniform Commercial Code requirements.

The description was sufficient only if it reasonably identified the real estate. UCC 9-110. The test is whether the description made possible the identification of the real estate. Commentary, UCC 9-110. . . . In a financing statement filed as a fixture filing, the description of the real estate must be sufficient to have given constructive notice of a real estate mortgage under the law of this state if it had been included in a mortgage of the real estate described. UCC 9-402(5). This description did not meet this test. It is true that a real estate mortgage will not be held void for uncertainty, even as to third persons, where the description used in the mortgage furnishes a key whereby one, aided by extrinsic evidence, can ascertain what property is covered. . . . The name and address of the mortgagor would hardly furnish that key, particularly when the address is a post-office box number. To be sufficient, the description must make reference to something *tangible* by which the property can be located. . . . This requirement was not met.

On the basis of the evidence before him, the chancellor was justified in holding that appellant's collateral was goods which were, or were to become, fixtures, so that, in order to establish the priority of its security agreement, a "fixture filing" must have been made in the office where a mortgage on real estate would be filed or recorded, before the interest of a subsequent encumbrancer is placed of record. UCC 9-313(1)(b), (4)(b). There is no indication that appellant complied or attempted to comply with the requirements for a "fixture filing." There was no recitation in the instrument that it was to be filed for record in the real estate records and it did not contain a description of the real estate sufficient to give constructive notice of a mortgage of the real estate. UCC 9-402(5). Thus, the circuit clerk was not called upon to index the instrument as he would have if it had been a real estate mortgage. UCC 9-403(7).

We do not regard appellant's argument that its priority was established under UCC 9-313(5) as having any merit. That section provides that a security interest, whether or not perfected, has priority over the conflicting interest of an encumbrancer or owner of the real estate where the encumbrancer or owner has consented in writing to the security interest. Appellant takes the position that Poole was both encumbrancer and owner. He was not the encumbrancer. The Bank of Rector was. An encumbrancer is one who holds a burden, charge or lien on property or an estate to the diminution of the value of the fee, but which does not prevent the passing of the fee by conveyance. Webster's New International Dictionary, 2d Ed. See also, Black's Law Dictionary 620, 908 (DeLuxe 4th Ed.). Since The Bank of Rector did not give its consent, appellant did not have priority over that bank's interest as an encumbrancer.

Appellant also contends that a "fixture filing" was not necessary because "trade fixtures" are not actually fixtures as contemplated by the Uniform Commercial Code. We cannot see how these bins can be classified as "trade fixtures," and removable from the realty as such. It is commonly accepted that trade fixtures are articles erected or annexed to realty by a *tenant* for the purpose of carrying on a trade, and removable by him during his term (provided the removal does not affect the essential characteristics of the article removed or reduce it to a mass of crude materials) upon grounds of public policy and because, from the nature of the tenure, they are not presumed to have been annexed with the intention of making them permanent additions to the realty. . . . Poole was not a tenant, and from the testimony of Hurst, the bins could have been removed only by reducing them to a mass of crude materials.

Appellant has failed to demonstrate error in the decree, so it is affirmed.

NOTES & QUESTIONS

1. *1972 amendments.* The 1972 amendments to Article 9 made extensive changes in UCC 9-313. The most important changes were (1) to provide for a special form of fixture filing to ensure that searchers in the real estate records would discover security interests in fixtures, and (2) to give construction mortgages priority over all security interests in fixtures, even purchase money security interests. For discussion of these and other changes, see Coogan, The New UCC Article 9, 86 Harv. L. Rev. 477, 483-505 (1973); Panel, A Look at the Work of the Article 9 Review Committee, 25 Bus. Law. 307, 314 & 317 (1970).

2. *Defining* fixtures. The *Corning Bank* court applies an "intent" test to determine whether the grain bins are fixtures. Some courts use an "institutional" test which asks "whether the chattel is permanently essential to the completeness of the structure or its use." In re Park Corrugated Box Corp., 249 F. Supp. 56, 58 (D.N.J. 1966). Thus under this test lighting equipment and seats would be fixtures in a building used as a theater. How would you apply the institutional test to the facts in *Corning Bank*? Given the different contexts in which classification of property comes up—conveyance, inheritance, taxation, etc.—is it necessary or desirable to have a universal test?

3. *Accessions.* UCC 9-314 provides priority rules to govern conflicting claims to accessions, i.e., goods installed or affixed to other goods. These priority rules follow the format of the 1962 official text of UCC 9-313 on fixtures, which is not surprising because fixtures can be described as accessions to real property. The 1972 amendments to Article 9 did not revise UCC 9-314, however, probably because there has been very little litigation involving accessions. See generally Nickles, Accessions and Accessories under Pre-Code Law and UCC Article 9, 35 Ark. L. Rev. 111 (1981).

Problem 7-11. Huge Manufacturing Company obtains a loan of $120,000,000 from National Bank to build a new factory. To secure the loan HMC executes a real estate mortgage granting National Bank a mortgage in the land, factory building, and all appurtenances and fixtures then owned or thereafter acquired. The bank records the mortgage in the proper local real estate office.

(a) HMC purchases on credit a drill press from American Business Corp. for installation in the new factory. HMC grants ABC a security interest in the drill press to secure payment of the purchase price. Before the press is installed

ABC makes a fixture filing in the proper local real estate office. As between National Bank and ABC who has prior claim to the drill press? See UCC 9-313(4)(a), (6).

(b) HMC purchases on credit some word processing equipment from ABC for use in the new factory. To secure payment ABC retains a security interest. Before the equipment is delivered ABC files a financing statement in the Article 9 personal property files. As between National Bank and ABC who has prior claim to the word processing equipment? See UCC 9-313(4)(c), (6).

(c) Soon after HMC purchases the drill press and word processing equipment in the preceding transactions the company files a bankruptcy petition. Among HMC's trustee in bankruptcy, National Bank, and ABC, who has prior claim to the press and equipment? See UCC 9-313(4)(d); BC 544.

(d) HMC defaults on its payments to ABC for the drill press and the word processing equipment. ABC determines that it will cost $10,000 to repair the factory building if it removes the press but only $100 to rewire the electricity if it removes the word processing equipment. May ABC repossess these items over the protests of National Bank? See UCC 9-313(8).

Problem 7-12. Bank finances Manufacturer's purchase of a bookbinder, and Manufacturer grants Bank a security interest in the bookbinder to secure repayment. Bank perfects its interest by filing a financing statement covering "bookbinder." Several years later Manufacturer purchases from Supplier a glue-drying unit that, when attached to a bookbinder, speeds production. Supplier retains a security interest in the unit to secure payment of the purchase price and files a financing statement covering "glue-drying unit" seven days after installation.

(a) Manufacturer subsequently defaults on both loans. Between Bank and Supplier who has prior claim to the bookbinder and glue-drying unit? See UCC 9-314.

(b) Manufacturer subsequently files a bankruptcy petition. Among Bank, Supplier, and Manufacturer's trustee in bankruptcy, who has prior claim to the bookbinder and glue-drying unit?

(c) Manufacturer subsequently defaults on his payments to Supplier but not on his obligation to Bank. It will cost $400 to remove the glue-drying unit because the bookbinder will have to be rewelded. May Supplier repossess the unit?

D. THE FEDERAL TAX LIEN

The Internal Revenue Code provides for a lien on the existing and after-acquired property of any person who fails to pay a federal tax after demand.

26 U.S.C. §§6321-6323 (1982). See excerpts reprinted at p. 385 infra. The lien will usually arise on assessment, which is an administrative act that requires no publicity. To prevail over "any purchaser, holder of a security interest, mechanic's lienor, or judgment lien creditor," however, the government must file a tax lien notice in a public file. To be effective against such persons with an interest in personal property, the lien notice is filed in a single state office as designated by the state law where the delinquent taxpayer resides or, in the absence of a state-designated office, in the federal district court for the district where he resides. Although the Internal Revenue Code adopts the principle that publicity is required to "perfect" a federal tax lien it does not fully coordinate the tax filing rules with the Article 9 scheme.[6]

The present tax lien provisions were revised in 1966 to take into account the concepts and terminology of the Uniform Commercial Code. In particular, the 1966 amendments subordinated the tax lien to claims of secured parties with a floating lien in a taxpayer's inventory or accounts. 26 U.S.C. §6323(c), (d) (1982).

Unfortunately, the language of the tax statute does not completely conform to that of the UCC and does not explicitly deal with several important practical problems: it refers, for example, to a "judgment lien creditor" rather than the UCC "lien creditor." Moreover, the tax statute does not include rules explicitly dealing with purchase money security interests or claims to proceeds that arise after a tax lien notice is filed. Fortunately, in 1976 the Internal Revenue Service issued regulations that clarify most of these ambiguities and fill many of the lacunae. Treas. Reg. §§301.6321 et seq.

Further reading: B. Clark, The Law of Secured Transactions under the Uniform Commercial Code, ch. 5 (1980); Plumb & Wright, Federal Tax Liens (2d ed. 1972).

AETNA INSURANCE CO. v. TEXAS THERMAL INDUSTRIES, INC.
591 F.2d 1035, 26 UCC Rep. 179 (5th Cir. 1979)

PER CURIAM: This interpleader action requires resolution of three competing claims to the insurance proceeds due Texas Thermal Industries, Inc. (TTI) after its insured inventory was destroyed in a fire. The principal claimants are (1) the Small Business Administration (SBA), which bases its claim to the proceeds upon a UCC security interest in the inventory, accounts receivable, machinery and equipment of TTI, (2) the Internal Revenue Service, which is

---

6. Several uniform state laws provide some consistency on where federal tax lien notices are filed. With respect to personal property the Uniform Federal Tax Lien Registration Act (approved in 1966) requires a filing for corporations and partnerships to be made centrally, while a filing for individuals is to be made in a local office where the taxpayer resides. The Uniform Federal Lien Registration Act (approved in 1978) has similar requirements but covers both tax and nontax federal liens. Twenty-one states have adopted the former act; seven have incorporated the latter into their legislation.

asserting various federal tax liens against all property interests belonging to TTI, and (3) Eileen Markman, to whom TTI assigned its right to receive a portion of the insurance fund.

The case was submitted to the District Court upon an agreed statement of facts. The District Court entered findings of fact and conclusions of law, reported at 436 F. Supp. 371, and held that the SBA was entitled to the entire fund. We affirm.

The SBA interest stems from two loans made by the Citizens Bank of Kilgore, Texas, in participation with the SBA, to TTI. The loans, in the amounts of $200,000 and $150,000, were disbursed on January 5, 1973, and June 15, 1973, respectively. Collateral for these loans consisted of a security interest in and to all inventory, accounts receivable, machinery, and equipment of TTI. Financing statements were filed with the County Clerk of Gregg County, Texas, on January 15, 1973, and June 21, 1973.[1]

The loan authorization issued by the SBA on both loans required that TTI obtain hazard insurance on the mortgaged collateral with loss-payee endorsements in favor of Citizens Bank and the SBA. On October 2, 1973, Aetna Insurance Company issued a hazards insurance policy to TTI, with loss-payee endorsements in favor of Citizens Bank and the SBA. Under the second loan authorization, TTI was also required to maintain 500 units of finished goods inventory under a bonded warehouse arrangement. A large portion of this inventory was destroyed in a warehouse fire on December 18, 1973.

On April 25, 1974, Citizens Bank assigned both the $200,000 note and the $150,000 note, as well as its interest in the secured collateral, to the SBA. As of June 24, 1974, the $150,000 note had a balance of $109,885.16 plus accrued interest from that date. As of September 24, 1974, the $200,000 note had a balance of $190,437.85 plus accrued interest.

The federal tax liens asserted by the IRS stem from a number of tax liabilities incurred by TTI and assessed between September 3, 1973 and August 5, 1974. The first filing of notice of any of these federal tax liens did not occur until December 17, 1973—well after the Citizens Bank/SBA security interests had been perfected. According to the agreed statement of facts, there remains an outstanding assessed balance of $42,744.48 plus interest.

Eileen Markman's claim to the insurance proceeds stems from a loan of $16,000 she made to TTI shortly after the fire to help pay immediate expenses and maintain the business as an operating concern. As an inducement for the loans and as security for its repayment, on December 27, 1973, TTI executed an assignment of $11,000 of its rights to receive proceeds under the Aetna policy to Eileen Markman. . . .

[The insurance fund was deposited] into the Registry of the Court in an interpleader action. . . .

(1) The first issue to be decided is the relative priority as between the

---

1. Both the security agreements and the financing statements indicated that the security interests extended to proceeds of the secured collateral.

federal tax liens and the contractual SBA liens asserted under Texas law. The principal statutory provisions governing federal tax liens are Sections 6321-6323 of the Internal Revenue Code, 26 U.S.C. §§6321-6323. Section 6321 provides that a lien shall arise in favor of the United States upon all property and property rights of any taxpayer to the extent of any tax liability which that taxpayer neglects or refuses to pay after demand. By virtue of §6322, this lien arises automatically on the date of assessment. Section 6323, as over-hauled by the Federal Tax Lien Act of 1966, speaks to priority conflicts and subordinates the federal tax liens created under §§6321 and 6322 to certain competing private or nonfederal liens. Of particular importance to this case are subsections (a) and (h)(1). The former provides that a federal tax lien imposed by §6321 is not valid as against the holder of a security interest until proper notice of the federal lien has been filed. 26 U.S.C. §6323(a). "Security interest" is defined by §6323(h)(1) in the following terms:

> The term "security interest" means any interest in property acquired by contract for the purpose of securing payment or performance of an obligation or indemnifying against loss or liability. A security interest exists at any time (A) if, at such time, the property is in existence and the interest has become protected under local law against a subsequent judgment lien arising out of an unsecured obligation, and (B) to the extent that, at such time, the holder has parted with money or money's worth.

Notice of any of the federal tax liens in this case was not filed until December 17, 197[3] while the SBA security interests were perfected with the filing of the financing statements on January 5 and June 15, 1973. Thus, by the explicit terms of §§6323(a) and (h)(1), the federal tax liens in this case are not valid as against the SBA liens, provided the SBA's secured interest in proceeds encompasses insurance proceeds.

The appellants however contend that despite the provisions of §6323, the SBA liens are not prime because they are not "choate." They base their argument on the long-established principle of federal common law governing priority conflicts between nonfederal or private liens or obligations and federal claims for the collection of debts owing the United States that only "choate" nonfederal liens prime competing federal claims.[4] In a series of cases between 1950 and 1963, the Supreme Court applied this choateness doctrine to questions of priority involving federal tax liens and evolved the following test: in order for a nonfederal lien to prevail over a later filed federal tax lien, the "identity of the lienor, the property subject to the lien, and the amount of the lien" must be established as of the date of filing of notice of the tax lien.[5] Appellants argue that the SBA liens do not satisfy that choateness test.

4. See generally Kennedy, The Relative Priority of the Federal Government: The Pernicious Career of the Inchoate and General Lien, 63 Yale L.J. 905 (1954).
5. See, e.g., United States v. Pioneer American Ins. Co., 374 U.S. 84 (1963); United States v. New Britain, 347 U.S. 81 (1953); see generally Coogan, The Effect of the Federal Tax Lien Act of 1966 upon Security Interests created under the Uniform Commercial Code, 81 Harv. L. Rev. 1369, 1375-1380 (1968).

That may or may not be the case, but Congress has spared us the necessity of engaging in the metaphysical analysis necessary to answer the question. As the Treasury increased its reliance upon the tax lien as a method for collecting outstanding taxes, and as the financing world increasingly relied upon security interests in inventory and accounts receivable, the harshness of the choateness rule and the vagaries of its application in the tax lien context caused increasing confusion and generated increasing criticism. The Federal Tax Lien Act of 1966, as codified at 26 U.S.C. §6323, represented a response to the problem. The purpose of the Act was, at least in large part, to "conform the lien provisions of the internal revenue laws to the concepts developed in [the] Uniform Commercial Code."[6] We therefore conclude, and hold, that whatever role the "choateness" rule of federal common law may play in other contexts, it has been supplanted by the provisions of §6323 with respect to tax lien priority questions as to which that statute provides an unambiguous federal law answer. Cf. Slodov v. United States, 436 U.S. 238, 256-258 (1978). Since §6323 specifically subordinates federal tax liens to security interests— such as those asserted by the SBA—that are perfected under the U.C.C. provisions of state law prior to the filing of the tax lien, the SBA liens have priority, regardless whether they are "choate" or not under formerly applicable common law principles.[8]

[The court then held that the SBA security interest extended to the insurance fund as "proceeds" under UCC 9-306(1). Because the SBA's prior lien was more than the insurance fund there was nothing to be divided between the IRS and Eileen Markman.]

Internal Revenue Code, 26 U.S.C. §§6321-6323 (1982)

§6321. Lien for taxes

If any person liable to pay any tax neglects or refuses to pay the same after demand, the amount (including any interest, additional amount, addition to tax, or assessable penalty, together with any cost that may accrue in addition thereto) shall be a lien in favor of the United States upon all property and rights to property, whether real or personal, belonging to such person.

§6322. Period of lien

Unless another date is specifically fixed by law, the lien imposed by section 6321 shall arise at the time the assessment is made and shall continue until the liability for the amount so assessed (or a judgment against the taxpayer arising out of such liability) is satisfied or becomes unenforceable by reason of lapse of time.

6. H.R. Rep. No. 1884, 89th Cong., 2d Sess. 1 (1966).
8. The parties have not argued the applicability of R.S. 3466, 31 U.S.C. §191 [31 U.S.C.A. §3713 (1983)—EDS.], which states that in settling the affairs of certain insolvents "the debts due to the United States shall be first satisfied," and [we] therefore have no occasion to consider its interaction with the Federal Tax Lien Act of 1966.

§6323.   *Validity and priority against certain persons*

(a) Purchasers, holders of security interests, mechanic's lienors, and judgment lien creditors.—The lien imposed by section 6321 shall not be valid as against any purchaser, holder of a security interest, mechanic's lienor, or judgment lien creditor until notice thereof which meets the requirements of subsection (f) has been filed by the Secretary or his delegate. . . .

(c) Protection for certain commercial transactions financing agreements, etc.—

(1)   In general.—To the extent provided in this subsection, even though notice of a lien imposed by section 6321 has been filed, such lien shall not be valid with respect to a security interest which came into existence after tax lien filing but which

(A)   is in qualified property covered by the terms of a written agreement entered into before tax lien filing and constituting—

(i)   a commercial transactions financing agreement,

(ii) a real property construction or improvement financing agreement, or

(iii) an obligatory disbursement agreement, and

(B)   is protected under local law against a judgment lien arising, as of the time of tax lien filing, out of an unsecured obligation.

(2)   Commercial transactions financing agreement.—For purposes of this subsection—

(A)   Definition.—The term "commercial transactions financing agreement" means an agreement (entered into by a person in the course of his trade or business)—

(i)   to make loans to the taxpayer to be secured by commercial financing security acquired by the taxpayer in the ordinary course of his trade or business, or

(ii) to purchase commercial financing security (other than inventory) acquired by the taxpayer in the ordinary course of his trade or business;

but such an agreement shall be treated as coming within the term only to the extent that such loan or purchase is made before the 46th day after the date of tax lien filing or (if earlier) before the lender or purchaser had actual notice or knowledge of such tax lien filing.

(B)   Limitation on qualified property.—The term "qualified property," when used with respect to a commercial transactions financing agreement, includes only commercial financing security acquired by the taxpayer before the 46th day after the date of tax lien filing.

(C)   Commercial financing security defined.—The term "commercial financing security" means

(i)   paper of a kind ordinarily arising in commercial transactions,

(ii) accounts receivable,

(iii) mortgages on real property, and

(iv) inventory.

    (D) Purchaser treated as acquiring security interest.—A person who satisfies subparagraph (A) by reason of clause (ii) thereof shall be treated as having acquired a security interest in commercial security. . . .

    (d) 45-day period for making disbursements.—Even though notice of a lien imposed by section 6321 has been filed, such lien shall not be valid with respect to a security interest which came into existence after tax lien filing by reason of disbursements made before the 46th day after the date of tax lien filing, or (if earlier) before the person making such disbursements had actual notice or knowledge of tax lien filing, but only if such security interest—

    (1) is in property
        (A) subject, at the time of tax lien filing, to the lien imposed by section 6321, and
        (B) covered by the terms of a written agreement entered into before tax lien filing, and
    (2) is protected under local law against a judgment lien arising, as of the time of tax lien filing, out of an unsecured obligation. . . .

    (h) Definitions.—For purposes of this section and section 6324—

    (1) Security interest.—The term "security interest" means any interest in property acquired by contract for the purpose of securing payment or performance of an obligation or indemnifying against loss or liability. A security interest exists at any time
        (A) if, at such time, the property is in existence and the interest has become protected under local law against a subsequent judgment lien arising out of an unsecured obligation, and
        (B) to the extent that, at such time, the holder has parted with money or money's worth. . . .

    (i) Special rules.—

    (1) Actual notice or knowledge.—For purposes of this subchapter, an organization shall be deemed for purposes of a particular transaction to have actual notice or knowledge of any fact from the time such fact is brought to the attention of the individual conducting such transaction, and in any event from the time such fact would have been brought to such individual's attention if the organization had exercised due diligence. An organization exercises due diligence if it maintains reasonable routines for communicating significant information to the person conducting the transaction and there is reasonable compliance with the routine. Due diligence does not require an individual acting for the organization to communicate information unless such communication is part of his regular duties or unless he has reason to know of the transaction and that the transaction would be materially affected by the information.

NOTES & QUESTIONS

1. *Priority as to proceeds.* The tax statute is silent about the rights of a delinquent taxpayer's secured creditor when collateral is disposed of and proceeds are received after a tax lien notice is filed. The court in *Aetna Insurance*

assumes that because the secured party would prevail over the tax lien as to the original collateral (inventory) it would prevail as to proceeds. But can there be a security interest in these proceeds when they did not "exist" at the time the tax lien notice is filed? See I.R.C. §6323(h)(1); PPG Industries, Inc. v. Hartford Fire Ins. Co., 531 F.2d 58, 18 UCC Rep. 569 (2d Cir. 1976) (not to give priority to secured party would penalize party responsible for existence of fund).

2. *Priority of federal government's nontax claims: R.S. 3466.* The federal government may claim priority to the property of a person indebted to the government under the general priority rule of 31 U.S.C.A. §3713 (1983) (formerly 31 U.S.C. §191; R.S. 3466):

§*3713.   Priority of Government claims*

(a)(1) A claim of the United States Government shall be paid first when—
(A)   a person indebted to the Government is insolvent and—
    (i)   the debtor without enough property to pay all debts makes a voluntary assignment of property;
    (ii)   property of the debtor, if absent, is attached; or
    (iii)   an act of bankruptcy is committed; or
(B)   the estate of a deceased debtor, in the custody of the executor or administrator, is not enough to pay all debts of the debtor.

(2) This subsection does not apply to a case under title 11 [i.e., the Bankruptcy Code—Eds.].

(b) A representative of a person or an estate (except a trustee acting under title 11) paying any part of a debt of the person or estate before paying a claim of the Government is liable to the extent of the payment for unpaid claims of the Government.

To prevail over the federal government's claim an interest or lien arising under state law must be "choate": the lienor, the amount of the lien, and the property subject to the lien must be identified and certain. While a security agreement with a future advance clause or an after-acquired property clause will not meet the test of choateness, it is likely that an Article 9 security interest in existing property securing an ascertainable obligation will do so even though the United States Supreme Court has not delivered a definitive opinion. See United States v. Vermont, 377 U.S. 351 (1964) (court has not decided whether "prior specific and perfected lien" prevails over R.S. 3466). Note that the section does not apply in bankruptcy proceedings and that BC 507(a)(6) gives certain tax claims only limited priority over *unsecured* claims.

3. *Law applicable to government as secured lender.* When the federal government acts as lender and by contract obtains a lien or security interest, what law governs priority between this government lien and other liens? In United States v. Kimbell Foods, Inc., 440 U.S. 715, 26 UCC Rep. 1 (1979) the Supreme Court held that federal law governed the priority issue but that, in the absence of a need to protect federal interests by a uniform priority rule, the

courts should adopt state law as the appropriate federal rule for determining priority. An incidental result of this approach is that the choateness doctrine does not apply to state law claims competing with the federal lien or security interest. If the federal government's security interest should be subordinated under a state's version of Article 9, can the government turn to R.S. 3466 and attack the competing state interest as inchoate? See United States v. S.K.A. Associates, 600 F.2d 513, 27 UCC Rep. 262 (5th Cir. 1979) (nondiscriminatory state law adopted as federal rule even if debtor is insolvent).

Problem 7-13. Manufacturer borrows money from the Bank for working capital and to secure repayment grants Bank a security interest in a drill press. At the time of the loan, unknown to the Bank, the Internal Revenue Service has assessed Manufacturer for arrears in its federal income tax payments.

(a) Assume Bank does not file a financing statement. Does the tax lien have priority over Bank's security interest? See I.R.C. §§6321, 6322, 6323(a), (h).

(b) Assume that Manufacturer signs the security agreement and that a financing statement is promptly filed. Two weeks later the IRS files a tax lien notice. Does the tax lien have priority over Bank's security interest? See I.R.C. §6323(a), (h).

(c) Assume that Manufacturer signs the security agreement, the IRS files a tax lien notice, and five days later Bank files a financing statement. Does the tax lien have priority over Bank's security interest? See I.R.C. §6323(a), (h). Would your answer be different if Bank's interest was a purchase money security interest? See Rev. Rul. 68-57 (the IRS "will consider that a purchase money security interest . . . valid under local law is protected even though it may arise after a notice of Federal tax lien has been filed" despite silence of statute).

(d) Assume that at the time of the original loan Bank agrees to make future advances to be secured by the drill press. Manufacturer signs the security agreement and Bank files the financing statement before the filing of the tax lien notice. Without knowledge of the tax lien Bank makes an additional loan to Manufacturer 30 days after the tax lien notice has been filed. Will Bank have priority over the tax lien to the extent of this additional loan? I.R.C. §6323(d); UCC 9-301(4). Would your answer be different if Bank had known of the tax lien at the time of the disbursement?

(e) Assume that Manufacturer signs a security agreement with an after-acquired property clause that grants Bank a security interest in all after-acquired equipment. A financing statement is filed, the tax lien is then filed, and 30 days later Manufacturer purchases new equipment. Does the Bank have priority over the tax lien? I.R.C. §6323(a), (d), (h).

Problem 7-14. Finance Company enters into an accounts receivable financing agreement with Dealer whereby Finance Company agrees to make monthly loan disbursements to be secured by Dealer's accounts receivable. A financing statement is properly filed. This arrangement has been in operation several years when the Internal Revenue Service assesses Dealer for unpaid federal taxes and files a tax lien notice.

(a) Finance Company makes no subsequent disbursements but claims Dealer's accounts, which arose within 46 days from the filing of the tax lien notice. Does Finance Company have priority over the I.R.S. to these accounts? See I.R.C. §6323(c)(1), (2)(B). Does it matter whether Finance Company learns of the tax lien notice before the 45 days elapse?

(b) Finance Company learns of the tax lien notice but makes a further disbursement within 30 days of the filing of the tax lien notice. Does Finance Company have priority in Dealer's accounts to the extent of this subsequent disbursement? See I.R.C. §6323(c)(1), (2)(A). Would your answer be different if Finance Company did not know of the tax lien at the time of disbursement?

E. SUBROGATION RIGHTS OF THE SURETY

Assume Prime Contractor agrees with Owner to construct a factory building. The contract requires Prime Contractor to obtain a *performance bond* and a *payment bond* issued by a surety company. The performance bond assures Owner that the surety will complete construction if Prime Contractor fails to do so. The payment bond is a similar assurance that laborers and suppliers will be paid if Prime Contractor fails to do so; Owner is interested in this assurance because unpaid "materialmen" may have a lien on Owner's improved property. Assume also that Owner agrees to make progress payments as construction progresses but that he may retain a percentage of the payments until satisfactory completion.

If Prime Contractor defaults before completing construction the surety company will be obligated under the performance and payment bonds. On completing performance and making payment the surety company will be subrogated under general suretyship principles to (1) the rights of the creditors of Prime Contractor, (2) the rights of setoff or recoupment of Owner, and (3) the claims of materialmen, including any liens they may have. The surety company will also succeed to any claims Prime Contractor may have against Owner. These subrogation rights arise under the law governing suretyship discussed in Chapter 2. As additional security the surety company may also require Prime Contractor to assign to it the contractor's claims against Owner.

Assume Prime Contractor has cash flow problems and in order to borrow working capital his bank informs him he will need collateral. His contract with Owner represents a potential source of repayment to the bank. As we learned in Chapter 6 the construction contract is an *account* in Code terminology and its use as collateral is governed by Article 9. UCC 9-106; cf. 9-104(f). To perfect a security interest in the account the bank usually has to file a financing statement. UCC 9-302(1); but see 9-302(1)(e).

What happens if Prime Contractor now fails to complete construction under his contract with Owner and defaults on his loan repayment to his bank? As a secured party the bank will claim from Owner any unpaid progress payments and other funds owing to Prime Contractor. The surety company, however, will also claim these sums either on a theory of subrogation or a theory of assignment by contract. Does Article 9 resolve the priority between the claims of the secured lender and surety?

NATIONAL SHAWMUT BANK v. NEW AMSTERDAM CASUALTY CO.
411 F.2d 843, 6 UCC Rep. 441 (1st Cir. 1969)

COFFIN, Circuit Judge. In the summer of 1962, Anderson Bros., Inc., a general contractor, entered into three construction contracts with the United States Air Force for work at Otis Air Force Base in Massachusetts and Dow Air Force Base in Maine. As required by the Miller Act, 40 U.S.C. §270a et seq., Anderson Bros., Inc. applied to the appellee (surety) for payment and performance bonds. Contained in the application for the bonds was an assignment to the surety ". . . of earned monies that may be due or become due under said contract. . . ." This assignment to the surety was not recorded under the Uniform Commercial Code.

Subsequent to the posting of payment and performance bonds on two contracts, Anderson Bros., Inc. obtained a line of credit from appellant National Shawmut Bank (the Bank).[1] As collateral for the loans an assignment of ". . . all monies due and which shall hereafter become due from the United States . . ." was made to the Bank. A financing statement covering this assignment was filed in compliance with UCC Article 9, and notice of the assignment was given to the United States as required by the Assignment of Claims Act, 31 U.S.C. §203 (1964). However, no written notice was given to the surety even though such notice was required by this Act.

In the spring of 1963 the construction contracts were terminated by the United States because of Anderson's default. The surety completed the work as it was obligated to do under the bonds. The cost of completion was approximately $97,000.

As of the date of termination of the contracts, earned progress payments totaled $44,202.05. Both the surety and the Bank seek to satisfy their respective claims from this fund.

In December of 1964 a complaint was filed by the Bank naming the surety as defendant in the District Court for the District of Massachusetts. The

---

1. Between October 19, 1962, and January 9, 1963, the bank made loans to Anderson Bros., Inc. totaling $63,260 of which there remains $37,477 outstanding and unpaid.

case was tried to the court without a jury and on September 27, 1968, the district court dismissed the complaint and ordered judgment for the defendant surety. The Bank brings this appeal.

The critical question which this appeal raises is one which has been, and continues to be, the cause of some uncertainty in the wake of enactment of Article 9 of the Uniform Commercial Code (UCC). It is: to what extent, if any, does the doctrine of subrogation survive the passage of Article 9 of the UCC?

Our effort will be to see what subrogation means in the transaction before us, to see what extent Article 9 is devised to deal with such a transaction, and to apply relevant case law. Subrogation is an old term, rooted in equity, and semantically stemming from words meaning "ask under." Today we use the parallel phrase, "stand in the shoes of." The equitable principle is that when one, pursuant to obligation—not a volunteer, fulfills the duties of another, he is entitled to assert the rights of that other against third persons.

In this case there is confusion because the tendency is to think of the surety on Miller Act payment and performance bonds as standing in the shoes only of the entity it "insures"—the contractor. So long as this one-dimensional concept prevails, logic compels the surety to be assessed as merely one of the contractor's creditors, and to be subject to the system of priorities rationalized by the Uniform Commercial Code. But the surety in cases like this undertakes duties which entitle it to step into three sets of shoes. When, on default of the contractor, it pays all the bills of the job to date and completes the job, it stands in the shoes of the contractor insofar as there are receivables due it; in the shoes of laborers and material men who have been paid by the surety— who may have had liens; and, not least, in the shoes of the government, for whom the job was completed.

This unique accumulation of subrogation rights serves to induce a function that is neither ordinary insurance nor ordinary financing. The business of a construction contract surety is not one of ordinary insurance, for the risk is not actuarially linked to premiums, nor is there a pooling of risks. . . . Neither is the business one of ordinary financing, for while the surety extends its credit to the owner (the government), as the ultimate guarantee that the job will be done, this is a credit that may either never have to be drawn upon or, if it is drawn upon at all, will in all likelihood be overdrawn. That is, if a contractor defaults, "payment" of the credit depends upon the surety's competence in economically finishing what somebody else has started. In this hermaphroditic situation, the "security" for the surety is not the fee but a compound of its confidence in the contractor and the opportunity to prevent or minimize its ultimate loss by its right to salvage the debacle by its own performance. Assuming that its confidence is misplaced, the surety receives very little from the contractor but the right to complete the job. Unlike a bank, it does not face specific requests for funds which it is able to link to suitable collateral with subsequent requests determined by assessment of current management and currently available additional security. In case of default, the bank takes its security; the surety must go ahead and perform.

All of this, we think, is relevant background to an interpretation of the Uniform Commercial Code as applied to the kind of security interest at issue. We commence by saying that appellant makes a respectable argument based on the Code. At best, however, we deem the Code not compelling and, on balance, not focused or directed to the surety's problem. To begin with, we have the exculpatory general principle that "Unless displaced by the particular provisions of this chapter, the principles of law and equity . . . shall supplement its provisions." UCC 1-103. As we shall see, the Massachusetts Supreme Judicial Court gives impressive weight to this canon in French Lumber Co., Inc. v. Commercial Realty & Finance Co., 346 Mass. 716, 719, 195 N.E.2d 507 (1964).

Going on to specifics, we note the definition of "security interest" in UCC 1-201(37) as "an interest in personal property or fixtures which secures payment or performance of an obligation . . . [and which] includes any interest of a buyer of accounts . . . or contract rights. . . ." [1972 UCC omits "contract rights" but broadens the definition of "account" to include most contract rights. See 1972 UCC 9-106.—Eds.] Neither clause seems to fit the construction contract surety. What secures its payment is really the opportunity, on default, to finish the job and apply any available funds against its cost of completion. This kind of right does not readily settle under the rubric of "personal property" or "fixtures." Nor does the surety easily fit the description of a "buyer of . . . contract rights." We make a similar comment about UCC 9-102(1)(a) which applies the Code "to any transaction . . . which is intended to create a security interest in personal property or fixtures including . . . contract rights; and . . . (b) to any sale of . . . contract rights." While one may strain to say that the right to finish a job in an emergency and thus minimize damages is a contract right, we think it is not the kind of independently valuable asset that such synonyms as "goods, documents, instruments, general intangibles, [and] chattel paper" suggest.

There are other hurdles. UCC 9-102(2) requires "security interests" to be "created by contract." In this case the real security is not the assignment of accounts receivable—which could be, failing the completion of performance, set off by the government—but the eventual right to be in the shoes of the government upon job completion. This is not "created by contract" but rather by the status, resulting from a contract, inhering in a surety, quite independently of the expressed terms of the contract. . . .

We add to this our difficulties with UCC 9-106 which defines "[a]ccount" as "any right to payment . . . not evidenced by an instrument" and "[c]ontract right" as "any right to payment under a contract not yet earned by performance." As to the former, when the contractor defaults, there is no right to payment, see infra. As to the latter, we think of a right to receive payments from one who continues with the performance (as rents receivable by a landlord), rather than a right conditioned on performance by the transferee of the "right."

We have, finally, the historic fact of the rejection of a proposed UCC 9-312(7) to the Code which would have provided that "A security interest which secures an obligation to reimburse a surety . . . secondarily obligated to complete performance is subordinate to" a later lender which perfects its security interest. We report the comments of the Editorial Board in the margin.[4] Contrary to appellant's argument, we do not feel that this signaled an admission by surety companies that theirs was a "security interest" within the meaning of the Code, but simply that they had won the battle to defend the preserve of subrogation. The cases cited by the Board would seem to underscore this conclusion.

If analysis were not enough, we think that case law is. Perhaps the most significant case, not cited by appellant or its amicus is French Lumber Co., Inc. v. Commercial Realty & Finance Co., Inc., 346 Mass. 716, 195 N.E.2d 507 (1964). For we deem our source of substantive law as governed by Erie R. Co. v. Tompkins, 304 U.S. 64 (1938), and there has been no suggestion that this is a proper case for the devising of a rule of federal common law. In that case the lumber company financed the purchase of an automobile through Ware Trust Company (Ware) which filed a financing statement under the UCC. The lumber company then pledged its equity in the automobile to Commercial Realty which also filed a financing statement under the UCC. The lumber company defaulted on its obligations and Ware sought to foreclose on its note. However, the lumber company was able to refinance its obligation through Associates Discount Corporation (Associates) which gave a note for amounts due to Ware in exchange for cancellation of its security interest. The lumber company defaulted again and Associates repossessed the automobile and sold it at public auction. Commercial Realty claimed the proceeds of the sale by virtue of its recorded security interest. Of course, Associates would have had a priority if it could have succeeded to Ware's security interest which it could have done through assignment. However, no assignment was made.

Nevertheless, the Massachusetts Supreme Judicial Court held that Associates prevailed by virtue of its subrogation to the rights of Ware. In reaching this conclusion the court remarked: "No provision of the Code (UCC) pur-

---

4. "The Surety Companies' representatives convincingly took the position that subsection (7) as it stands is a complete reversal of the case law not only of the Supreme Court of the United States but also of the highest courts of most of the states. . . .

"Under the cited case law, the surety's rights come first as to the funds owing by the owner unless the surety has subordinated its right to the bank. Subsection (7) of the Code as written would reverse the situation and give the bank priority in all cases.

"Under existing case law, both the contractor and the bank are in a position to bargain with the surety which may or may not be willing to subordinate its claim. Under subsection (7) as written in the Code the surety company would have nothing to bargain about." Uniform Laws Annotated, Uniform Commercial Code, Official Draft, Text and Comments, at 773, 777 (1952); Uniform Laws Annotated, Uniform Commercial Code, Changes in Text and Comments, at 25-26 (1953).

ports to affect the fundamental equitable doctrine of subrogation." 346 Mass. at 719, 195 N.E.2d at 510.

Appellant's effort at argument to distinguish *French* on its facts does not persuade us that the Massachusetts court would take any different view here of the non-displacement of equitable subrogation by the Code.[5] Appellant argues that the surety in the case before us could have perfected a filing under UCC 9-312. But in *French* the refinancing party could similarly have taken an assignment of a prior recorded security interest. That it did not do so did not affect its rights as a subrogee.

Finally, the Bank asserts that even if the surety may claim as a subrogee, the Bank has a superior claim in equity. This is so, according to the Bank, where earned progress payments are involved and where the surety has benefitted from the contractor's application of the loan proceeds to contracts bonded by the surety.

The position espoused by the Bank originated in cases where earned progress payments had been paid to an assignee bank and the surety was attempting, after the default of the contractor, to recover the amounts paid. . . .

Here the payments were earned but unpaid prior to the contractor's default. Prior to default, the contractor had the right to assign progress payments and had the Bank received payment, it could not (absent circumstances amounting to fraud) have been divested by the surety. But upon default, the surety which is obligated to complete the work steps into the shoes of the government—not of the contractor which on default has forfeited its rights. It is subrogated not only to the right of the government to pay laborers and materialmen from funds retained out of progress payments . . . but also to the government's right to apply to the cost of completion the earned but unpaid progress payments in its hands at the time of default. . . . The Massachusetts Supreme Judicial Court has specifically recognized that a mere assignee of a contractor, such as appellant here, receives the right to moneys due the latter subject, however, to the dominant right of the owner to recoup the damages suffered by default. . . .[8]

Our analysis has centered on the interpretation of the Code and of the doctrine of subrogation as developed by the cases. We have found no basis for injecting other general equitable or policy considerations. We are unmoved by the claims of either the Bank or the surety to inherently superior status. The Bank loan undoubtedly helped minimize the surety's cost of completion. But

---

5. It is true that in *French Lumber* Ware had filed a financing statement under the UCC, and therefore, all subsequent lienors were on notice of the existence of a prior security interest. This, however, does not aid the bank in distinguishing *French Lumber*, for here the bank knew of the existence of the surety. And even if the bank had no actual notice, it might well be held, at least in a Miller Act case, to constructive notice of the surety's existence. . . .

8. It was suggested by the amicus bank that, since the government had no right to withhold payment until default, the surety had no rights to the earned but unpaid progress payments at the time of default. This ignores the fact that what the surety succeeded to was the government's right to recoup after default.

completion by the surety was necessary to preserve the fund which is here in issue. The surety could concededly have avoided this litigation by perfecting its filing, but so could the Bank by making inquiry of the arrangements between contractor and surety. It may well be—although we express no opinion—that to subject sureties to the filing requirements of the Code would improve and rationalize the system of financing public contracts. But equitable subrogation is too hardy a plant to be uprooted by a Code which speaks around but not to the issue.

On Petition for Rehearing. [National Shawmut Bank's petition for rehearing questioned the court's interpretation of the *French Lumber* case.]

PER CURIAM. . . . Petitioner's first argument is that whereas here subrogation is a substitute for a security interest, in *French Lumber* subrogation was employed as an adjunct of general equity principles. This purported distinction is in fact a comparison of the two entirely separate concepts of function and rationale. In both cases subrogation served as a substitute for a security interest, and in both cases the substitution is justified by the invocation of general equity principles. Indeed, subrogation is a creature of equity, and therefore always arises as an adjunct of equitable principles.

Petitioner's second argument is that since all three lenders in *French Lumber* had recorded their security interests under the Code, that case involved subrogation within the Code. The important point is, however, that but for subrogation the third lender would have been subordinated to the second lender. In *French Lumber* subrogation was used to override the priorities of the Code—possibly exerting more force than here where, arguably at least, the surety's interests are not covered by Article 9 of the Code.

Finally, petitioner asserts that the third lender in *French Lumber* was a "volunteer" and not entitled to subrogation rights. The general rule is that a mere volunteer is not entitled to subrogation. That fact would not, of course, bar the Massachusetts Supreme Judicial Court from holding otherwise. But, in fact, the third lender does not fall under the volunteer doctrine, which refers to gratuitous or quasi-contractual undertakings. The third lender's rights, as did the surety's here, arose because of its contractual obligations.

Petition for rehearing denied.

NOTES & QUESTIONS

1. *Federal construction contracts.* Two federal statutes are important when the federal government enters into construction contracts. The Assignment of Claims Act, 31 U.S.C. §3727 (1982), authorizes the assignment to a financial institution of moneys due under a contract with the federal government. The Act seeks to stimulate private financing of public projects. The Miller Act, 40 U.S.C. §§270a-270d (1982), requires a prime contractor to obtain performance and payment bonds. The performance bond is obviously for the direct

benefit of the United States. The payment bond, on the other hand, is only of indirect benefit because unpaid laborers and suppliers do not have liens on United States property; the bond presumably encourages careful work by assuring materialmen they will be satisfied.

2. *Payments already made to assignee.* If the federal government had already made progress payments directly to National Shawmut Bank could the surety company recover these payments from the bank? May the government recover these payments upon default by Anderson Bros.? If not, will the surety company be in any better position than the United States government, to whose rights the surety is subrogated?

What if the government had made payments to the bank by mistake when the progress payment was not yet due? May the government recover the payment? What if the payment had been made because of a fraudulent representation by Anderson Bros. that progress had been made? See UCC 9-318(1).

3. *Analysis of surety's priority.* For an analysis that questions the result of *National Shawmut* on both policy and theoretical grounds, see Dauer, Government Contracts, Commercial Banks, and Miller Act Bond Sureties—A Question of Priorities, 14 B.C. Ind. & Com. L. Rev. 943 (1973).

Problem 7-15. Builder enters into a construction contract with Municipality and provides both a performance and payment bond, with Alpha Surety Company as surety. The construction contract provides for progress payments based on the percentage of work completed, subject to a percentage retained pending completion. In his contract with Alpha, Builder assigns the proceeds of the construction contract to Alpha as security for reimbursement if Alpha should have to perform or to pay pursuant to the bonds. Before completion of construction Builder files a bankruptcy petition. Alpha completes construction and claims the sum retained by Municipality pending completion. Builder's trustee in bankruptcy argues that Alpha only has an unperfected security interest in this fund, which the trustee can avoid under BC 544. Is the trustee correct?

CHAPTER 8

Exceptions to the General Rules of Article 9

Article 9 is a tightly-drawn statute with a simple and unified structure designed to provide practical answers to practical problems. Perhaps in the drafting of no other article of the Code is the influence of practicing lawyers so clearly evident. As we shall see in the following chapters, the style of Article 9 stands in marked contrast to the open-ended provisions in Article 2, which governs sales. This transition chapter explores the extent to which the approaches of the two articles may be reconciled.[1] Part A examines the extent to which the Code's general principles, such as good faith or unconscionability, govern the performance of Article 9 obligations or change the normal priority rules. Part B focuses on the specific exceptions to Article 9's unified structure for transactions involving consumers and farmers, and Part C returns to a topic introduced in Chapter 5, the rights and relative priority of a seller with an Article 2 security interest.

A. GENERAL UCC PRINCIPLES PERMITTING FLEXIBILITY

1. General Equitable Principles (UCC 1-103)

The Code provides that the principles of law and equity supplement its provisions unless "displaced" by the particular provisions of the Code (UCC 1-103;

---

1. In an important law journal article that examines transactions governed by both Articles 2 and 9 the authors conclude: "Read literally and peremptorily, the Code solutions vacillate in an almost schizophrenic manner, resulting from the apparent inattention to the relation of Article 9 to Article 2. Yet read sensibly, with an understanding not only of the scheme of Article 9 but also of the nature of the underlying Article 2 transaction, the structure adapts. The Uniform Commercial Code, even in Article 9, is sufficiently open-textured that it can be interpreted, in the common law tradition, as a 'case-law Code' of vital importance to a continuously changing world." Jackson & Peters, Quest for Uncertainty: A Proposal for Flexible Resolution of Inherent Conflicts Between Article 2 and Article 9 of the Uniform Commercial Code, 87 Yale L.J. 907, 985-986 (1978).

Comment 1 to this section refers to "explicitly displaced"). The following materials explore the extent to which the Code displaces the law governing fraudulent conveyances and the law of equitable liens. Focus on these two bodies of law should not suggest, however, that other equitable principles, such as estoppel and waiver, do not also apply to Article 9. In Chapter 7, for example, we encountered in the *National Shawmut Bank* case the doctrine of equitable subrogation. See generally Summers, General Equitable Principles Under Section 1-103 of the Uniform Commercial Code, 72 Nw. U.L. Rev. 906, 919-923 (1978).

MEYER v. GENERAL AMERICAN CORP.
569 P.2d 1094, 22 UCC Rep. 525 (Utah 1977)

ELLETT, C. J. . . . . Meyer loaned $12,000 to General American Corporation (hereinafter referred to as "GAC") for the purpose of providing operating capital for their mining operation and to purchase a D-9 caterpillar that was necessary to the business. GAC executed promissory notes and a security agreement, giving Meyer a security interest in the caterpillar as collateral for the loan. A financing statement was not filed. On May 1, 1974, Terra Corporation (hereinafter referred to as "Terra") loaned $2,000 to GAC in return for GAC's promissory note and a security interest in the caterpillar. A financing statement was filed by Terra with the Secretary of State on October 25, 1974. On July 8, 1974, Terra loaned an additional $500 to GAC, canceled the $2,000 promissory note and received in exchange GAC's Bill of Sale for the caterpillar. [At this time the caterpillar was worth between $20,000 and $25,000 according to the evidence before the trial court.] The following day, July 9, 1974, Terra sold the caterpillar for $2,500 to McCurtain and gave him a Bill of Sale. McCurtain did not take possession of the machine, however; it was delivered to Wheeler Machinery Company who billed Terra for storage charges. Meyer subsequently learned of these conveyances through a mine employee who operated the machine and initiated suit against GAC on October 11, 1974. A Writ of Attachment was issued on that date and later filed with the county clerk on October 18, 1974. When McCurtain learned of the attachment, he intervened in this suit, and it came to trial on July 22, 1976. The court, sitting without a jury, entered judgment in favor of Meyer, and found that the Bill of Sale given to Terra by GAC was void for failure of fair consideration and lack of good faith; and further, that the subsequent sale from Terra to McCurtain was void for the same reasons. Both transactions were declared void under the Utah Fraudulent Conveyance Act. The court further held that Meyer's Writ of Attachment was valid and that she was entitled to levy execution on the caterpillar.

McCurtain appeals this decision, claiming the following errors:

(1) That the evidence submitted does not support a finding that McCurtain's purchase was void under the Utah Fraudulent Conveyance Act, and

(2) That as a purchaser, taking from a party holding a duly perfected security interest, his interest has priority over Meyer's unperfected security interest and that the proper priorities should have been resolved under the Utah Uniform Commercial Code.

The applicable sections of Utah Fraudulent Conveyance Act are discussed below:

> *25-1-4, U.C.A., 1953 as amended [Uniform Fraudulent Conveyance Act §4]*
>
> Every conveyance made, and every obligation incurred, by a person who is, or will be thereby rendered, insolvent is fraudulent as to creditors, without regard to his actual intent, if the conveyance is made or the obligation is incurred without a fair consideration.

Both the statute and case law interpreting the statute make it clear that subjective or actual intent to defraud are *not* elements of a fraudulent conveyance claim. Meyer is obligated to show only (1) that she was a creditor of GAC; (2) that GAC was insolvent at the time the conveyance was made to Terra; and (3) that the conveyance was not given for a "fair consideration."

The promissory note entered into evidence is adequate to prove Meyer's status as a creditor; indeed, there was no dispute in the lower court as to this fact.

> *25-1-2, U.C.A., 1953 as amended [U.F.C.A. §2(1)]*
>
> A person is insolvent when the present fair salable value of his assets is less than the amount that will be required to satisfy his probable liability on his existing debts as they become absolute and matured.

The level of insolvency necessary to meet the statute requirement is not insolvency in the bankruptcy sense but merely a showing that the party's assets are not sufficient to meet liabilities as they become due.

The record shows that McCurtain's own witness, a broker-dealer, testified that there was no market for the GAC stock and there had not been a market for a long time. Market inactivity is one indication of a failing financial condition. The record also shows that Meyer loaned the $12,000 to GAC *because* of GAC's insolvent condition, and she further testified that she made a personal examination of GAC's books wherein it was disclosed that the liabilities exceeded the assets. She also testified that GAC had failed to make payments on her loan. . . .

The evidence, when considered as a whole, is sufficient to prove the insolvent condition of GAC at the time the conveyance was made to Terra. Insolvency alone, however, does not justify a finding that the conveyance is fraudulent unless it was made without a fair consideration. Fair consideration is defined by statute as requiring that the conveyance be made for both a "fair equivalent" *and* in "good faith."

[The court cites 25-1-3, U.C.A., 1953 as amended [U.F.C.A. §3], which reads as follows:

> Fair consideration is given for property, or obligation,
>
> (1) When in exchange for such property, or obligation, as a fair equivalent therefor, and in good faith, property is conveyed or an antecedent debt is satisfied; or
>
> (2) When such property, or obligation, is received in good faith to secure a present advance or antecedent debt in amount not disproportionately small when compared with the value of the property or obligation obtained.—Eds.]

Fair equivalent has been deemed to mean "such a price as a capable and diligent businessman could presently obtain for the property after conferring with those accustomed to buy such property." [Utah Assets Corporation v. Dooley Bros., 92 Utah 577, 70 P.2d 738, 742 (1937).] In First Security Bank v. Vrontikis, [490 P.2d 1301], it was determined that 13% of the property's proven worth was not a fair equivalent. The Dooley test indicates that retail, not wholesale value is the measure; and McCurtain, himself, testified: "I had the tractor sold for $20,000 so that establishes a pretty good value." Expert testimony produced by McCurtain also set the caterpillar's value between $20,000 and $25,000.

McCurtain paid $2,500 for this machine which is grossly disproportionate to the real value and supports the trail court's finding of failure of fair consideration. . . .

To support the good faith requirement, McCurtain relies on his status as a bona-fide purchaser under 25-1-13, U.C.A., 1953 as amended [not taken from U.F.C.A.]:

> The provisions of this chapter shall not be construed to affect or impair the title of a purchaser for a valuable consideration, unless it appears that such purchaser had *previous notice* of the fraudulent intent of his immediate grantor, or of the fraud rendering void the title of such grantor. (Emphasis added.)

It is notice, not knowledge, that the purchaser must have, and it need not be actual notice—constructive notice is sufficient to defeat the purchaser's claim. Constructive notice can occur when circumstances arise that should put a reasonable person on guard so as to require further inquiry on his part. Here, McCurtain admitted that the purchase price was "unusual" and that he bought the caterpillar sight unseen because of its low price. He also testified that he knew the caterpillar could be sold for a much higher value—approximately 10 times what he paid for it, in fact. This circumstance alone is sufficient to put the purchaser on notice that the transaction may be tainted and that other parties are likely to be involved.

Other indicia of fraud—failure of Terra to deliver the caterpillar to McCurtain, failure of McCurtain to take steps to protect his interest, and the attempt made by the parties to keep the transactions "secret" from Meyer (GAC was unresponsive to her telephone and written requests concerning the status of her loan and the collateral)—are enough to justify the court's findings.

Under the evidence as presented, the trial court committed no error in holding that the conveyance from GAC to Terra and, subsequently, to McCurtain, was void.

McCurtain argues that the Utah Uniform Commercial Code, not the Utah Fraudulent Conveyance Act, should have been applied to find his interest superior to that of Meyer because of the priority sections of Article 9 (Secured Transactions). An examination of the history of the Uniform Commercial Code in Utah indicates that the adoption of the UCC was intended to supersede certain legislation in effect at that time. Specific laws were expressly repealed, including Sections 25-2 through 25-4, U.C.A., 1953. [The repealed sections regulated bulk transfers, leases and sales of livestock, and marketing wool.—Eds.] Section 1 of Title 25, was *not* repealed, however, indicating that the legislature intended to retain the Utah Fraudulent Conveyance Act in full force and effect as a protection against the kind of double financing engaged in here that might work an unjust result against an innocent party because of a strict application of the priorities established in the new statute.

When a conveyance is found void under the Utah Fraudulent Conveyance Act, it is treated as if the transaction never took place at all; hence, it is not necessary to reach the question of priorities under Article 9 of the Utah Uniform Commercial Code since the security agreement cannot be held to exist if the conveyance from which the security interest arose is void from its inception. The importance of the UCC should not be disregarded, however, and we feel it would not be remiss to discuss its application to the instant case since it is our opinion that Meyer would still prevail under the UCC as well as the Utah Fraudulent Conveyance Act.

The scope of Article 9 extends to all transactions intending to create a security interest and the general rule is that the first to file *or* to perfect his interest has priority over other creditors, with some exceptions. Filing always perfects a security interest once it has attached, but some perfections can occur *without* filing. It is necessary to distinguish between the two.

Filing is required to perfect a security interest unless it falls within one of the stated exceptions. Perfection occurs when the interest has "attached" and all the other requirements (filing) are met. . . .

Only a buyer in the ordinary course of business may take free of both a perfected and an unperfected interest. A buyer in ordinary course is described in UCC 1-201(9) as follows: ". . . a person who in good faith . . . buys in ordinary course *from a person in the business of selling goods of that kind.* . . ." (Emphasis added.) In the instant matter, the evidence shows that Terra was *not* in the business of selling caterpillars so McCurtain fails to qualify as a buyer in the ordinary course of business under this definition. For this reason, the perfection requirement becomes paramount.

Meyer obtained an attachment against the property and the writ was properly filed on October 18, 1974. At that time, she became a lien creditor, and by law, lien creditors take priority over any unperfected security interest. Terra filed a financing statement with the Secretary of State which perfected its security interest in the collateral, but this was not done until October 26, 1974 (after Meyer's lien was filed). Therefore, on the date Meyer became a lien creditor, Terra was in possession of an *unperfected* security interest, which, by operation of the statute was inferior to Meyer's status as a lien creditor.

Another approach through Article 9 would still give Meyer priority over all other parties. When Meyer loaned $12,000 to GAC for the express purpose of purchasing a caterpillar, she became a purchase money lender, thereby creating a preferred purchase money security interest. The definition of a purchase money interest is found in UCC 9-107, and reads as follows: "A security interest is a 'purchase money security interest' to the extent that it is . . . (b) taken by a *person who by making advances* or incurring an obligation *gives value to enable the debtor to acquire rights in or the use of collateral* if such value is in fact so used." (Emphasis added.) The loan to purchase a caterpillar that was used to enable GAC to use the machine in its mining operation is a transaction which falls squarely within this category.

Some purchase money interests are given preferential treatment in Article 9. Filing is not required to perfect a purchase money security interest in consumer goods and in some farm equipment [1962 UCC 9-302(1)(c), (d)]. Whether certain machinery is classified as "equipment" or "consumer goods" depends primarily on the principal use to which it is put. The caterpillar in this case is "equipment" rather than "consumer goods," because it was used primarily in GAC's mining business. It, therefore, falls outside the exceptions allowed in the statute and must be filed in order to perfect. However, UCC 9-312(5)(a) still gives the priority to the purchase money security interest if filed first, providing both competing interests file, and it then takes priority regardless of when attachment occurs. This section, applied to the matter before this Court, gives Meyer priority because the Writ of Attachment, protecting her rights in the purchase money interest, was filed prior in time to Terra's financing statement.

Notwithstanding the foregoing analysis, Terra's perfected security interest in the caterpillar does not automatically extend to protect McCurtain as a purchaser of that same collateral. To allow such a far-reaching consequence would work a disadvantage to other creditors so as to defeat the purpose of Article 9 which is to put the public on notice as to all existing interests in the collateral and to permit an orderly procedure whereby subsequent creditors can move their priorities to a more favored position when another secured party who perfected first releases its interest in the collateral.

Of course it is possible for a secured party to *assign* its interest to a third party by complying with the provisions of UCC 9-405. There is nothing in the record before us, however, to indicate that such a proper assignment of the security interest was made by Terra to McCurtain. The claim for priority on this ground would not stand because of failure to follow the proper statutory procedure. McCurtain, therefore, is nothing more than an unsecured creditor whose claim is inferior to that of Meyer, a lien creditor.

It appears that both the Utah Uniform Commercial Code and the Utah Fraudulent Conveyance Act would support the judgment of the court below in this instance, and we find no error in the trial court's ruling. The judgment is affirmed with costs to Meyer.

NOTES & QUESTIONS

1. *The law governing fraudulent conveyances.* Utah is one of 24 states that have adopted the Uniform Fraudulent Conveyance Act (1918). The uniform act and the statutes and common law rules governing fraudulent conveyances in other jurisdictions are usually traced back to the Elizabethan statute, 13 Eliz., ch. 5 (1571) (debtor who conveys personalty to obstruct creditors from collecting on their judgments subject to criminal sanctions and the transfer declared void) and to Twyne's Case.

TWYNE'S CASE, 76 Eng. Rep. 809 (Star Ch. 1601). "Pierce was indebted to Twyne in four hundred pounds, and was indebted also to C. in two hundred pounds. C. brought an action of debts against Pierce, and pending the writ, Pierce being possessed of goods and chattels of the value of three hundred pounds, in secret made a general deed of gift of all his goods and chattels real and personal whatsoever to Twyne, in satisfaction of his debt; notwithstanding that Pierce continued in possession of the said goods, and some of them he sold; and he shore the sheep, and marked them with his own mark: and afterwards C. had judgment against Pierce, and had a fieri facias directed to the Sheriff of Southampton, who by force of the said writ came to make execution of the said goods; but divers persons, by the command of the said Twyne, did with force resist the said sheriff, claiming them to be the goods of the said Twyne by force of the said gift; and openly declared by the commandment of Twyne, that it was a good gift, and made on a good and lawful consideration. And whether this gift on the whole matter, was fraudulent and of no effect by the said Act of 13 Eliz. or not, was the question."

The court held that the transaction was fraudulent, noting numerous signs of fraud: e.g., the donor continued in possession and continued to use the goods as his own; it was done in secret; it was done pending the writ; and the deed had a clause claiming the transfer was bona fide, which was not customary.

The case is still frequently cited as the source of the doctrine of ostensible ownership and for its discussion of evidence which establishes a presumption of fraud ("badges of fraud"). See generally G. Glenn, Fraudulent Conveyances and Preferences (rev. ed. 1940).

2. *Fraudulent conveyances and the UCC.* The Uniform Commercial Code does not deal comprehensively with fraudulent conveyances but several sections govern special situations.

(a) A seller who has "ostensible ownership" of property left in his hands by the buyer is governed by UCC 2-402(2), which refers to non-Code state law for rules on whether a creditor of a seller may treat the seller's retention of possession as fraudulent. UCC 2-402(2) limits these non-Code rules, however, by explicitly validating retention "in good faith and current course of trade by a merchant-seller for a commercially reasonable time after a sale or identification."

(b) Article 6 sets out rules on bulk transfers. The article covers transfers out of the ordinary course of business of a major part of the inventory by an enterprise whose principal business is the sale of inventory (UCC 6-102). Failure to give notice of the transfer to creditors renders it "ineffective" against any creditor of the transferor (UCC 6-105). Good faith purchasers from the transferee, however, take free of the defect (UCC 6-110).[2]

3. *Fraudulent conveyances and the Bankruptcy Code.* The Bankruptcy Code includes a fraudulent conveyance provision modeled on the Uniform Act (BC 548). Under this provision the trustee may avoid fraudulent conveyances made within one year before the bankruptcy petition is filed. The trustee may also avoid transfers that a creditor holding an unsecured claim might avoid under state fraudulent conveyance law if the trustee can find such a creditor (BC 544(b)). Because state statutes of limitation for fraudulent conveyance actions are typically longer than the one year provided by BC 548, the trustee may find that his only way to attack a fraudulent transfer is to proceed under BC 544(b).

Several significant recent cases explore the argument of trustees that pre-petition foreclosure sales were fraudulent conveyances of debtor's interests under BC 548. Compare Durrett v. Washington Natl. Ins. Co., 621 F.2d 201 (5th Cir. 1980) (foreclosure sale as invalid fraudulent transfer) with In re Madrid, 725 F.2d 1197 (9th Cir. 1984) (foreclosure sale valid).

4. *Enforcement of creditors' rights.* In most jurisdictions a creditor whose debtor has made a fraudulent conveyance may choose either to have the conveyance set aside and proceed on his claim against the debtor or to have execution levied on the property notwithstanding the fraudulent transfer and defend any action brought by the transferee to determine title (e.g., by a replevin action). The Uniform Fraudulent Conveyance Act (UFCA) sets out these alternatives in §§9 & 10:

---

2. Article 6, for reasons not altogether clear, has attracted considerable attention from the bar in recent years. A committee of the American Bar Association has published a proposed revision. There was sharp disagreement within the committee on whether to repeal the article or to strengthen it by broadening its coverage and clarifying its enforcement provisions. See generally Hawkland, Proposed Revisions to U.C.C. Article 6, 38 Bus. Law. 1729 (1983) (an article summarizing the background and proposed changes; accompanied by two related articles by practitioners).

Sec. 9.   Rights of Creditors Whose Claims Have Matured

(1) Where a conveyance or obligation is fraudulent as to a creditor, such creditor, when his claim has matured, may, as against any person except a purchaser for fair consideration without knowledge of the fraud at the time of the purchase, or one who has derived title immediately or mediately from such a purchaser,

    (a)   Have the conveyance set aside or obligation annulled to the extent necessary to satisfy his claim, or

    (b)   Disregard the conveyance and attach or levy execution upon the property conveyed.

(2) A purchaser who without actual fraudulent intent has given less than a fair consideration for the conveyance or obligation, may retain the property or obligation as security for repayment.

Sec. 10.   Rights of Creditors Whose Claims Have Not Matured

Where a conveyance made or obligation incurred is fraudulent as to a creditor whose claim has not matured he may proceed in a court of competent jurisdiction against any person against whom he could have proceeded had his claim matured, and the court may,

    (a)   Restrain the defendant from disposing of his property,

    (b)   Appoint a receiver to take charge of the property,

    (c)   Set aside the conveyance or annul the obligation, or

    (d)   Make any order which the circumstances of the case may require.

What relevance, if any, do these provisions have on the analysis in the *Meyer* case?

5. *Secured transactions and fraudulent conveyances.* If Debtor grants secured party a security interest in collateral with a value of $100,000 to secure an obligation of $5,000 has there been a fraudulent transfer? See UFCA §§3(b), 4 and 9(2). Given that other creditors may reach Debtor's equity by judicial process (UCC 9-311), what might be "fraudulent" about overcollateralization? Is it the fear that the secured party will not protect Debtor's surplus in a foreclosure sale? If there really is a surplus and Debtor is informed of the sale won't Debtor himself solicit outside bidders? See Quinn v. Dupree, 157 Tex. 441, 303 S.W.2d 769 (1957) (debtor may secure debts with his property provided that no more property is transferred than is "reasonably necessary" to secure the debt). See also S. Riesenfeld, Cases & Materials on Creditors' Remedies and Debtors' Protection 402 (3d ed. 1979).

WARREN TOOL CO. v. STEPHENSON
11 Mich. App. 274, 161 N.W.2d 133, 5 UCC Rep. 1017 (1968)

[Stephenson Industries needed tooling in order to fulfill a contract with Highway Products, Inc. and accepted the bid of Warren Tool Company to perform the tooling. Warren wanted assurance it would be paid. Stephenson Industries

wrote a letter to its bank "requesting that upon presentation for deposit of Highway Products, Inc. checks in payment of the above purchase orders, you (the Bank) agree upon collection of such funds to pay (Warren) its proportionate share based on invoices received and accepted by us." Stephenson Industries informed Warren of the contents of the letter. Warren provided the tooling, and Highway issued a check to Stephenson Industries. Officers of Stephenson Industries did not deposit the check with the bank but instead obtained payment and distributed the check proceeds to one of the officers and his brother-in-law. Soon afterwards Stephenson Industries declared bankruptcy. Warren brought an action against the officers claiming an equitable lien on the check proceeds. From an adverse judgment in the lower court Warren appealed.]

LEVIN, Presiding Judge. . . . Pomeroy provides the most authoritative general statement of the applicable law: "The doctrine [of equitable lien] may be stated in its most general form, that every express executory agreement in writing, whereby the contracting party sufficiently indicates an intention to make some particular property, real or personal, or fund, therein described or identified, a security for a debt or other obligation, or whereby the party promises to convey or assign or transfer the property as security, creates an equitable lien upon the property so indicated, which is enforceable against the property in the hands not only of the original contractor, but of his heirs, administrators, executors, voluntary assignees, and purchasers or encumbrancers with notice. Under like circumstances, a merely verbal agreement may create a similar lien upon personal property." 4 Pomeroy's Equity Jurisprudence §1235, at 696 (5th ed.).

In this context, then, an equitable lien arises from an agreement that both identifies property and evidences an intention that such property serve as security for an obligation. The rule, as stated by Pomeroy, is well supported by both Federal and State authorities and finds expression in several Michigan cases which paraphrase Pomeroy's statement. . . .

In *Wright, Christmas* and *Trist,* the court spoke indiscriminately of equitable assignments and equitable liens as if they were interchangeable concepts. They are not, and it is this merging of concepts which appears to have led to a great deal of the confusion we find in the cases. The early State and English precedents relied on in *Wright, Christmas* and *Trist* largely concerned property in the hands of a third party and the effect to be given an order upon the third party for payment to the claimant. In such a case it is understandable that, with a view to protecting the holder of the property against claims that he has failed to follow instructions, the courts have required greater clarity of expression than where the dispute is solely between the parties to the agreement themselves. It is similarly understandable that, where the property is in the hands of a third party, the courts have thought in terms of assignment rather than lien. We also note that many of the cases cited in *Wright, Christmas* and *Trist* were suits between contending lien claimants. . . .

We also note the equitable assignment and the equitable lien have different histories, which may well explain both the differences in results reached and in the explanations of those results by the courts reaching them. The doctrine of equitable lien is a rule of substantive law, grounded on equitable principles, which recognizes or declares a security interest based upon the agreement or, in certain kinds of cases not here relevant, the relationship of the parties, even though such security interest is imperfect and may be given only limited priority where the rights of third parties have intervened. 4 Pomeroy's Equity Jurisprudence (ch. 7, §1233, et seq.), at 691, et seq. . . . The origin of the *equitable assignment* is procedural rather than substantive. It is an outgrowth of equity's enforcement of nonnegotiable choses in action, expectancies and other interests which common-law courts originally would not enforce. . . . 4 Pomeroy's Equity Jurisprudence §1270, at 787; 1 Gilmore, Security Interests in Personal Property §7.3, at 200.

It does appear there is authority for the view that a distinction is to be drawn between an order on a future fund which operates as an equitable *assignment* and a mere promise to appropriate an existing or future fund, or to give an order on such a fund (4 Pomeroy's Equity Jurisprudence §1283a, at 813; . . .). Unfortunately, all the authorities have not recognized the inapplicability of these principles in a case where a claim of equitable *assignment* is not asserted, the duties of a holder of the fund are not involved, the rights of third parties have not intervened, and other equitable considerations are present justifying the recognition of an equitable lien.

. . .[T]he life of the equitable lien is not dependent on words of conveyance or the use of particular phraseology, and an agreement indicating an intention that identified property shall secure a debt is sufficient. Merely because the operative language may fail as an equitable assignment does not preclude the court from finding the requisite intention to designate particular property as security for a debt, or from declaring that the particular property has been subjected to an equitable lien. The doctrine being one of substantive law, the claimant of an equitable lien must, of course, satisfy the court that, in equity and good conscience, he is entitled to the lien.

We return to the transactions between Stephenson Industries and the plaintiffs. It is contended that under the letters to the Bucyrus bank and to Warren Tool, Stephenson Industries was as free as before to withhold deposit of the Highway check in the bank. We are asked to look upon the letters as, at most, a courtesy without consequence.

We entertain a different view. The plaintiffs insisted upon obtaining meaningful security before they would do any work. They accepted the letter to the Bucyrus bank on the understanding that that objective had been achieved, that plaintiffs' economic interest as well as Stephenson Industries' image would be protected. The letters specifically named the Highway orders by number and the amounts due on those orders; they set out that Stephenson Industries owed a designated amount to plaintiffs and that the obligation was to be satisfied upon deposit of the Highway checks and payment by the bank of the proceeds of such checks. To this point the defendants concur, but here they assert that no security interest arose even when the Highway check was received by Stephenson Industries, and that none could arise until Stephenson Industries elected to deposit the check in the bank. The argument carries small weight logically and none equitably.

Where the parties agree that a clearly identified fund secures an obligation, that agreement gives rise to a lien upon the fund. The cases tell us that the nonexistence of the fund at the time of the agreement is not necessarily consequential. The lien attaches not later than when the fund comes into existence or comes under the control of the promisor who has charged it with that obligation. The promisor takes the fund in accord with the agreement, "as trustee as soon as he gets a title to the thing." Barnes v. Alexander, [232 U.S. 117, 121 (1914)]. It would not matter that Stephenson Industries failed expressly to promise to deposit the check, for, having agreed that a specific fund, the proceeds of the Highway check, would serve as security for the obligation, it necessarily took the check, which evidenced the right to the fund, subject to the obligation to make that deposit. . . .

Pomeroy similarly reports that the doctrine of equitable lien "was introduced for the sole purpose of furnishing a ground for the specific remedies which equity confers, operating upon particular identified property, instead of the general pecuniary recoveries granted by courts of law. It follows, therefore, that in a large class of executory contracts, express and implied, which the law regards as creating no property right, nor interest analogous to property, but only a mere personal right and obligation, equity recognizes, *in addition to the personal obligation,* a peculiar right over the thing concerning which the contract deals, which it calls a 'lien,' and which, though not property, is analogous to property, and by means of which the plaintiff is enabled to follow the identical thing, and to enforce the defendant's obligation by a remedy which operates directly upon that thing." 4 Pomeroy's Equity Jurisprudence §1234, at 695. (Emphasis supplied by author.) . . .

Although it was not argued, we believe ourselves obliged to consider whether the doctrine of equitable lien survived the enactment of Article 9 of the Uniform Commercial Code. UCC 9-203 provides that a nonpossessory security interest is not enforceable against the debtor or third parties, unless the debtor has signed a security agreement which contains a description of the collateral.

The letter to the bank signed by Stephenson Industries is, of course, a writing signed by the debtor and it describes the collateral. Whether the letter is a security agreement—defined in UCC 9-105 as "an agreement which creates or provides for a security interest"—is, of course, fundamentally the same question already dealt with in this opinion.

The official comment to UCC 9-203 suggests that the equitable mortgage may be passe. That comment appears, however, to be directed to a parol agreement, or one which, unlike the letter here, does not otherwise comply with the relatively simple requirements of UCC 9-203.

We also note Professor Gilmore acknowledges that "the author, in his capacity as treatise writer, would like to suggest that, in his earlier capacity as Comment writer for Article 9, he overshot the mark. In our discussion of the term 'security interest,' we made the point that . . . the courts would have to continue to find this way through the jungle of 'equitable liens;' that there will be security interests 'within this Article' as well as 'interests in property which secure obligations' which are outside the Article. It may be predicted that the Statute of Frauds of §9-203 will be no more successful than any other Statute of Frauds has ever been in making hard problems go away and that doing away with the 'equitable mortgage' will not be as easy as the §9-203 Comment suggests." 1 Gilmore, Security Interests in Personal Property §11.4, at 345, 346 (1965).

Elsewhere Professor Gilmore states: "Article 9, for all its comprehensiveness, is a statute drafted to regulate certain well-known or institutionalized types of financing transactions. It is fair enough to say that a transaction which sets out to be one of those types should conform to the Article 9 rules or fall by the wayside. But beyond the area of institutionalized transaction, there stretches a no-man's land, in which strange creatures do strange things. For these strange things there are no rules; it makes no sense to measure them against the rules which professionals have developed for professional transactions. The best that can be done is to let the courts pick their way from case to case, working out their solutions ad hoc and ad hominem." Gilmore, supra, §11.2, at 336, 337.

We are so persuaded. The parties here did not profess to establish a security good against the world, or indeed beyond their own relationship. It was an unconventional security arrangement, one good only between the plaintiffs and Stephenson Industries and those who might have knowledge thereof. There is no reason to require that the compact before us be governed by provisions principally designed to achieve clearer perfection and to determine competing priorities of security devices daily employed in commerce.

NOTES & QUESTIONS

1. *Other equitable doctrines: marshaling.* If on default First Bank has a security interest in Debtor's equipment and inventory while Second Bank has a subordinated security interest only in the equipment, must First Bank proceed to liquidate the inventory before repossessing and disposing of the equipment? See Shedoudy v. Beverly Surgical Supply Co., 100 Cal. App. 3d 730, 161 Cal. Rptr. 164, 28 UCC Rep. 1181 (1980) (marshaling ordered where senior secured party protected from risk of loss); UCC 9-311, Comment 3. What if First Bank has a security interest in Debtor's equipment and inventory while Second Bank is an unsecured creditor? See generally Labovitz, Marshaling Under the UCC: The State of the Doctrine, 99 Banking L.J. 440 (1982).

2. *Equitable liens in bankruptcy.* Several Supreme Court decisions in the early decades of the 20th century protected the interests of creditors from being avoided as preferential transfers by recognizing doctrines of "relation back" or "pocket liens." In Sexton v. Kessler, 225 U.S. 90 (1912), for example, the court protected creditors who had left "pledged" securities in the hands of the debtor until just before the debtor's bankruptcy. The court accepted the theory that the original transaction had created an equitable lien and the later taking of possession had given the creditors a legal interest that related back to the earlier date. See also Martin v. Commercial National Bank, 245 U.S. 513 (1918) (secured transaction not preferential transfer because under Georgia law the date of transfer was the date the mortgage was executed, not the date of the recording).

In 1938, Congress attempted to overrule these decisions by amending §60 of the Bankruptcy Act, the predecessor to BC 547. The amendment deemed a transfer to take place when no creditor of, nor bona fide purchaser from, the debtor could acquire rights in the property superior to the transferee. Congress intended to overrule the *Sexton* and *Martin* cases by this formula. Thus a mortgagee who did not promptly record his interest in real property could no longer rely on a last-minute recording, because until he recorded the mortgage a bona fide purchaser of the property would take free of his interest. An unintended consequence, however, was that the amendment put in jeopardy inventory financing, which necessarily involves the sale of inventory free of the secured party's security interest. Since a bona fide purchaser of inventory could cut off the secured party's interest under state law, that interest was not sufficiently "perfected" to be protected from attack under §60. Accounts-receivable financing was subject to similar attacks. In Corn Exchange National Bank & Trust Co. v. Klauder, 318 U.S. 434 (1943), the Supreme Court found a nonnotification accounts-receivable financing scheme to be "unprotected" because under Pennsylvania law, unless notice was given to the account debtor, a subsequent purchaser of the account would take priority.

Congress responded to this problem by amending §60 in 1950 to eliminate the bona fide purchaser test. The new test for determining when a transfer took place was when the interest was so perfected that a hypothetical "lien upon such property obtainable by legal or equitable proceedings on a simple contract could [not] become superior to the rights of the transferee" (§60a(2)). To avoid returning to the pre-1938 situation the 1950 amendment introduced a provision to abolish equitable liens: "the recognition of equitable liens where available means of perfecting legal liens have not been employed is hereby declared to be contrary to the policy of this section" (§60a(6)). Notwithstanding this provision some courts continued to recognize equitable liens. See Porter v. Searle, 228 F.2d 748 (10th Cir. 1955) (equitable lien arising from promise to execute a chattel mortgage agreement becomes perfected on refusal of debtor to carry out the agreement).

The Bankruptcy Code of 1978 eliminates the specific reference to equitable liens. The Gilmore Committee report of 1970 noted that "the ambiguous provisions of §60a(6) on so-called equitable liens, which were necessary when §60 was redrafted in the late 1940's, no longer served any function, for the reason that Article 9 has turned the 'equitable lien' against which §60a(6) was directed into 'unperfected security interests' which the trustee can in any case set aside." H.R. Rep. No. 595, 95th Cong., 1st Sess. 204, 209 (1977).

What is the present status of equitable liens in bankruptcy? Consider In re Washington Communications Group, Inc., 10 B.R. 676, 31 UCC Rep. 280 (Bankr. D.D.C. 1981):

Lender, a British citizen, loaned money to a publishing firm. At the time the loan was made Lender was not represented by an attorney. The Borrower's attorney prepared the loan agreement, which granted Lender a security interest in a newsletter on child care. No financing statement was filed. The Borrower's attorney later stated in an affidavit that he believed "the legal components of the right to publish a newsletter are so various and intangible" that the UCC was not appropriate and the "only practicable form of security interest" was an equitable lien. The attorney denied that he represented that the loan agreement was recordable. Borrower later declared bankruptcy and Lender sought to establish a secured claim. Lender argued that the Bankruptcy Code recognized equitable liens under the broad definition of "security interest" (BC 101(43)), which is broader than the UCC definition, and by the deliberate omission of §60a(6) of the Bankruptcy Act. Although recognizing "that there is every indication that equitable liens arising from well-established doctrines such as equitable subrogation may well survive a trustee's right [of avoidance]" the Court found in this case no fraud or wrongdoing sufficient to find an equitable lien or to impose a constructive trust.

3. *Further reading.* See Nickles, Rethinking Some U.C.C. Article 9 Problems, 34 Ark. L. Rev. 1, 41-71 (1980) (supports continued recognition of equitable lien doctrine).

2. Good Faith (UCC 1-203)

Parties to a contract governed by the UCC are subject to "an obligation of good faith in its performance or enforcement" (UCC 1-203). Good faith means "honesty in fact" in the conduct or transaction concerned (UCC 1-201(19)). Article 2 imposes an additional obligation on merchants to observe "reasonable commercial standards of fair dealing in the trade" (UCC 2-103(1)(b), 2-104). These definitions apply "unless the context otherwise requires." A similar obligation is set out in Restatement (Second) of Contracts §205 (1981) and the Uniform Consumer Credit Code §1.110 (1974).

Article 9 includes only a few explicit references to "good faith": UCC 9-206(1), 9-208(2), 9-318(2), 9-401(2), 9-504(4)(b). In addition, several provisions incorporate by reference the good faith standard. See, e.g., the reference to "buyers in ordinary course" (UCC 9-307(1)) and to purchasers of instruments, documents, and securities (UCC 9-309). The following materials explore the scope and impact of the principle of good faith on the obligations and priorities of parties to a secured transaction.

THOMPSON v. UNITED STATES
408 F.2d 1075, 6 UCC Rep. 20 (8th Cir. 1969)

[The Federal Housing Administration (FHA) held security interests in property owned by the Thompson partnership. The security interest in the real property was perfected by filing the appropriate documents in the real estate records. There was no attempt to perfect the security interest in the personal property. The partnership defaulted and the FHA brought a foreclosure action. More than four months following the default the partnership executed a security agreement granting to the Thompson corporation (owned by the partners) a security interest in the same furniture covered by FHA's security interest. The Thompson corporation perfected this security interest by filing a financing statement in the appropriate office and then brought an action to have its security interest declared superior to that of the FHA. From an adverse decision in the district court, the Thompson corporation appealed.]

BRIGHT, Circuit Judge. . . . The government would sustain the court's conclusion and would justify its priority on UCC 9-401(2). It contends that the recording of the deed of trust in the Pulaski County real estate records and the knowledge by the corporation of the after-acquired property clause in that instrument brings its interest within the protective ambit of UCC 9-401(2). It is suggested that the filing by the government's predecessor in interest [the original lender whose interest was guaranteed by the FHA—Eds.] was made in good faith though in an improper place and is effective against any person having knowledge thereof.

No Arkansas authority has been advanced by the government to support this proposition and the applicability of UCC 9-401(2) in the present case is not clear in any of the jurisdictions now embracing the Code. The government's argument is weakened by the fact that the deed of trust covering after-acquired property, which was filed in the real estate records, did not qualify as a financing statement under the Code because it was not signed by both the debtor and the secured party. UCC 9-402(1) (1962) [see 1972 UCC 9-402(1)]. Furthermore, there was apparently no attempt to comply with Code filing requirements relating to personal property. See Official Comment 5 to UCC 9-401. We feel it to be unnecessary for purposes of the present controversy to determine what interpretation is to be given UCC 9-401(2) under Arkansas law.

The Thompson corporation, relying on UCC 9-312(5) and 9-301(1)(a) argues that, since its interest was the first to be perfected under the Code, it takes priority over the security interest created by the deed of trust even though it had actual knowledge of this interest. But there was more than "actual knowledge" of the government's interest. Vance Thompson and his children, as partners, assumed the deed of trust and regulatory agreement [the terms of the FHA guaranty agreement as determined in accordance with rules promulgated in the Code of Federal Regulations; see, e.g., 24 C.F.R. Part 200 (1984)] and they now seek to avoid that obligation through the use of a transaction with the Thompson family corporation.

By entering into a security agreement with each other, the Thompson partnership and the Thompson corporation were required to each exercise good faith in the enforcement of the security agreement on the furniture. To attempt to enforce that security agreement against the government, in our judgment, would be an act of extreme bad faith on the part of those members of the Thompson family who are affiliated with both the partnership and the corporation and particularly on the part of Vance Thompson, who dominated and acted for both business entities. UCC 1-203, which reads: "Every contract or duty within this Act imposes an obligation of good faith in its performance or enforcement,"[14] prevents the Thompson corporation from enforcing the security agreement against the government. In the regulatory agreement, Vance Thompson and his adult sons, as members of the partnership, had agreed that they would not, without the approval of the FHA Commissioner, encumber any of the mortgaged property or permit the encumbrance of any such property. The execution of the security agreement with the corporation was a breach of the regulatory agreement. The relationship between the Thompson partnership and the Thompson corporation is so close that the corporation must be charged with participation in the partnership's breach of the regulatory agreement.

We hold that UCC 1-203 permits the consideration of the lack of good faith by the Thompson entities toward the government to alter priorities which otherwise would be determined under Article 9. See French Lumber Co. v. Commercial Realty & Finance Co., 346 Mass. 716, 195 N.E.2d 507 (1964); Felsenfeld, Knowledge as a Factor in Determining Priorities under the Uniform Commercial Code, 42 N.Y.U.L. Rev. 246, 276 (1967); Coogan, Article 9 of the Uniform Commercial Code: Priorities Among Secured Creditors and the "Floating Lien," 72 Harv. L. Rev. 838, 859 (1959). . . . This seems to be in accord with the intention of the framers of the Code, as noted in the Official Comment to UCC 1-203: "This section sets forth a basic principle running throughout this Act. The principle involved is that in commercial transactions good faith is required in the performance and enforcement of all agreements or duties. . . . The concept, however, is broader than any of these illustrations and applies generally, as stated in this section, to the performance or enforcement of every contract or duty within this Act. . . ."

The simple fact is that Vance Thompson, in particular, in his domination of both the partnership and the corporation used these entities to breach the provisions of the regulatory agreement. His actions and the actions of the

14. "Good faith", as defined in the Code, means "honesty in fact in the conduct or transaction concerned." UCC 1-201(19).

Thompson corporation could well have been tortious interferences in the contract rights of the government. . . .

Under the circumstances of this case, good faith would require the members of the Thompson family and any of its business entities to observe and abide by these contractual agreements, and, under UCC 1-203, the trial court was clearly correct in determining that the government was entitled to prevail in respect to this furniture.

NOTES & QUESTIONS

1. *General obligation of good faith.* First Bank did not file an amended financing statement notwithstanding its knowledge that Debtor had changed its name and had then granted Second Bank a security interest in the same collateral. Debtor declares bankruptcy and its trustee argues that First Bank's security interest is unperfected because it had failed to act in good faith, citing UCC 1-203. Should the trustee's argument succeed? See UCC 9-402(7); In re Triple A Sugar Corp., 3 B.R. 240, 28 UCC Rep. 1197 (Bankr. D. Me. 1980) (debtor's argument fails because no statutory or contractual duty on creditor to refile under Maine law).

[margin handwritten: NO... only for collateral acquired 4 mths after new filing]

2. *Indirect application of good faith standard.* First Dealer sells two new cars to Second Dealer but is allowed to retain possession of the cars for several days. Bank, as the floor-planning financer of First Dealer, discovers that its debtor has been selling cars subject to its security interest, including the two sold to Second Dealer, without accounting for the proceeds. Bank brings a replevin action. Second Dealer argues that it takes free of Bank's security interest as a buyer in ordinary course, citing UCC 9-307(1). The trial court finds that Second Dealer acted honestly but not in a commercially reasonable manner. Will Bank be able to recover the cars? Sherrock v. Commercial Credit Corp., 290 A.2d 648, 10 UCC Rep. 523 (Del. 1972) (higher standard of UCC 2-103(1)(b) not applicable).

[handwritten: GOOD FAITH]

GENERAL INSURANCE CO. OF AMERICA v. LOWRY
570 F.2d 120, 23 UCC Rep. 1058 (6th Cir. 1978)

[The trial court made the following finding of facts (412 F. Supp. 12, 13-14):

1. Prior to January 14, 1972, plaintiff General Insurance Company of America issued surety bonds on which George A. Hyland, Edward F. Lowry and C. M. Dingledine were indemnitors. Pursuant to obligations credited by such bonds the plaintiff paid out various sums of money for which it sought indemnity from the named indemnitors.

2. On January 14, 1972, a cognovit note in the sum of $564,566.79 was executed by the three named indemnitors. Twelve items of collateral security

[margin handwritten: against signors; no defenses will be allowed — authorize attorney to confess judgmt]

were given to secure such promissory note. For purposes of this litigation, only one such is of any significance. Item III in the list of collateral securities is stated to be "shares of common stock owned by Edward F. Lowry in Pico, Inc., an Ohio corporation." On the same date the above indemnitors executed a Memorandum Agreement (Plaintiff's Exhibit 1) which contained the following language: "Hyland, Lowry and Dingledine each agree that he will do no act which will reduce or impair the security listed and that each will cooperate in the preparation and execution of the instruments necessary to perfect the security."

3. Subsequently on October 12, 1972, and on July 3, 1973, other notes were executed by the indemnitors and in each instance Item III of the collateral security was a pledge of shares of common stock owned by Edward F. Lowry in Pico, Inc. (Plaintiff's Exhibits 2 and 3). At no time were the shares of stock ever delivered to the plaintiff and no further written agreement regarding such shares was ever executed by the defendant.

4. Throughout these proceedings defendant was represented by attorney Jacob Myers, both as an individual practitioner and as President and sole shareholder in Kusworm & Myers Company, LPA. Mr. Myers attended the meeting of January 14, 1972, examined the documents signed by his client and actively represented defendant Lowry throughout the time involved in this litigation. Subsequent meetings of the parties were held in July, 1972, September, 1972, and May, 1973. Mr. Myers attended the meetings of September 27, 1972, and May 8, 1973, but did not attend the meeting in July of 1972. Other than a letter in January of 1972 from counsel for plaintiff to Mr. Myers requesting delivery of the shares of stock, no other written demand for such shares was ever made by plaintiff's counsel.

5. On January 8, 1974, Edward Lowry executed a promissory note to Kusworm & Myers Company, LPA, in the sum of $12,555.65 (Joint Exhibit I). To secure such note defendant Lowry likewise signed an agreement pledging 19 shares of stock in Pico Development Company, Inc. to Kusworm & Myers Company, LPA, (Joint Exhibit IV) and endorsed at the appropriate place Certificate No. 4 of Pico Development Company (Joint Exhibit II). The stock was subsequently transferred on the books of such company to the name of Kusworm & Myers Company, LPA, and Jacob Myers individually had knowledge of the agreements that had been signed, the reference to the stock in Pico Development Company and the fact that such shares had not been transmitted to plaintiff. The note signed by Edward Lowry to Kusworm & Myers Company, LPA, was given for a valuable consideration, to-wit: attorney fees rendered and to be rendered by both Kusworm & Myers Company, LPA, and Jacob Myers.

7. Pursuant to preliminary injunction issued by this court on June 26, 1975, physical possession of 19 shares of Pico Development Company still remain with Jacob A. Myers, conditioned upon an injunction against sale, assignment, transfer, hypothecation or other disposition without prior approval of this court.]

PHILLIPS, Chief Judge. . . . In diversity cases, federal courts must apply the law of the State as pronounced by its highest court. See Erie R.R. v. Tompkins, 304 U.S. 64 (1938). We conclude that because of the peculiar circumstances involved in this case, the Supreme Court of Ohio would uphold the imposition of an equitable lien notwithstanding the priority provisions of UCC 9-312. We reach this conclusion based upon two considerations.

First, UCC 1-203 provides: "Every contract or duty within this Act imposes an obligation of good faith in its performance or enforcement." UCC 1-201(19) defines good faith as "honesty in fact in the conduct or transaction concerned." . . . In Thompson v. United States, 408 F.2d 1075, 1084 (8th Cir. 1969) [p. 414 supra], the Eighth Circuit held that the good faith provision of the UCC "permits the consideration of the lack of good faith . . . to alter priorities which otherwise would be determined under Article 9."

The district court emphasized that this case involves the attorney for one of the parties, not a disinterested creditor attempting to protect his commercial interests. We agree with the district court that the record discloses facts which do not meet the good faith standards of the Uniform Commercial Code.

Second, an equitable lien was created by appellants in favor of appellee. In 1913, the Supreme Court of Ohio dealt with facts strikingly similar to the present suit. In Klaustermeyer v. The Cleveland Trust Co., 89 Ohio St. 142, 105 N.E. 278 (1913), each member of the Board of Directors of Euclid Avenue Trust Company loaned $5,000 to the company when the trust company began having financial difficulties. Stock owned by the company was to be delivered to the directors as security for each member of the [Board not then indebted to the company. The assets of the trust company were assigned by the] Board of Directors of Euclid Avenue Trust for the benefit of creditors to the Cleveland Trust Company before the stock was delivered to Klaustermeyer, one of the board members. The Supreme Court of Ohio held that Klaustermeyer had an "equitable lien on the securities in possession of the Euclid Avenue Trust Company, which were assigned and transferred to the Cleveland Trust Company. . . ." 89 Ohio St. at 144, 105 N.E. at 279. In holding that the trust company had a duty to deliver the securities to Klaustermeyer, the court said: "In modern times the doctrine of equitable liens has been liberally extended for the purpose of facilitating mercantile transactions, and in order that the intention of the parties to create specific charges may be justly and effectually carried out. Bispham's Principles of Equity (8 ed.), Section 351. What good conscience requires, equity should require, and while we are able to find no adjudicated case upon parallel facts, we are persuaded from the nature of the transaction, the relations and the rights of the parties, good conscience and sound morals among men in everyday business, that Klaustermeyer should have his lien for his loan." 89 Ohio St. at 153, 105 N.E. at 282.

We disagree with appellants' argument that the enactment of the Uniform Commercial Code overruled *Klaustermeyer* and eliminated equitable liens in all situations. UCC 1-103 states in pertinent part: "Unless displaced by the particular provisions of this Act, the principles of law *and equity* . . . shall supplement its provisions." (emphasis added).

Discussing the doctrine of equitable liens and citing *Klaustermeyer,* the Ohio Court of Appeals held in Syring v. Sartorius, 28 Ohio App. 2d 308, 309-310, 277 N.E.2d 457, 458 (1971): "The doctrine may be stated in its most general form that *every* express executory agreement in writing whereby a contracting party sufficiently indicates an intention to make some particular property, real *or personal,* or fund, therein described or identified, *a security for a debt* or other obligation, or whereby the party promises to convey, assign, or transfer the property as security, creates an equitable lien upon the property so indicated, which is enforceable against the property in the hands not only of the original contractor, but of his purchasers or encumbrancers with notice. Under like circumstances, a merely verbal agreement may create a similar lien upon personal property. The doctrine itself is clearly an application of the maxim 'equity regards as done that which ought to be done.' Cf. Klaustermeyer v. Cleveland Trust Co., 89 Ohio St. 142, 105 N.E. 278." (emphasis added). . . .

Construing Texas law, the Fifth Circuit implicitly found that the existence of an equitable lien does not conflict with Article Nine of the UCC. See Citizens Co-Op Gin v. United States, 427 F.2d 592, 695-696 (5th Cir. 1970). Other Circuits construing various state laws have recognized the doctrine of equitable liens. . . .

We, therefore, are convinced that the Ohio Supreme Court, if it were deciding this case, would follow its earlier opinion in *Klaustermeyer,* holding that General Insurance Company is entitled to an equitable lien on the Pico stock in possession of appellant Myers.

3. Unconscionability (UCC 2-302)

Although it is unnecessary to introduce the general concept of unconscionability it is important to remember that the concept is codified in UCC 2-302 and that the statutory text must be construed with close attention to its wording as well as its "reason." The text states:

Sec. 2-302. Unconscionable Contract or Clause

(1) If the court as a matter of law finds the contract or any clause of the contract to have been unconscionable at the time it was made the court may refuse to enforce the contract, or it may enforce the remainder of the contract without the unconscionable clause, or it may so limit the application of any unconscionable clause as to avoid any unconscionable result.

(2) When it is claimed or appears to the court that the contract or any clause thereof may be unconscionable the parties shall be afforded a reasonable opportunity to present evidence of its commercial setting, purpose and effect to aid the court in making the determination.

See also Uniform Consumer Credit Code §5.108 (1974); Restatement (Second) of Contracts §208 (1981). Does UCC 2-302, concerning sales contracts, have any relevance to secured transactions? The following cases explore this question.

WILLIAMS v. WALKER-THOMAS FURNITURE CO.
350 F.2d 445, 2 UCC Rep. 955 (D.C. Cir. 1965)

J. Skelly WRIGHT, Circuit Judge: Appellee, Walker-Thomas Furniture Company, operates a retail furniture store in the District of Columbia. During the period from 1957 to 1962 each appellant in these cases purchased a number of household items from Walker-Thomas, for which payment was to be made in installments. The terms of each purchase were contained in a printed form contract which set forth the value of the purchased item and purported to lease the item to appellant for a stipulated monthly rent payment. The contract then provided, in substance, that title would remain in Walker-Thomas until the total of all the monthly payments made equaled the stated value of the item, at which time appellants could take title. In the event of a default in the payment of any monthly installment, Walker-Thomas could repossess the item.

The contract further provided that "the amount of each periodical installment payment to be made by [purchaser] to the Company under this present lease shall be inclusive of and not in addition to the amount of each installment payment to be made by [purchaser] under such prior leases, bills or accounts; *and all payments now and hereafter made by [purchaser] shall be credited pro rata on all outstanding leases, bills and accounts* due the Company by [purchaser] at the time each such payment is made." (Emphasis added.) The effect of this rather obscure provision was to keep a balance due on every item purchased until the balance due on all items, whenever purchased, was liquidated. As a result, the debt incurred at the time of purchase of each item was secured by the right to repossess all the items previously purchased by the same purchaser, and each new item purchased automatically became subject to a security interest arising out of the previous dealings.

On May 12, 1962, appellant Thorne purchased an item described as a Daveno, three tables, and two lamps, having total stated value of $391.10. Shortly thereafter, he defaulted on his monthly payments and appellee sought to replevy all the items purchased since the first transaction in 1958. Similarly, on April 17, 1962, appellant Williams bought a stereo set of stated value of $514.95.[1] She too defaulted shortly thereafter, and appellee sought to replevy all the items purchased since December, 1957. The Court of General Sessions granted judgment for appellee. The District of Columbia Court of Appeals affirmed, and we granted appellants' motion for leave to appeal to this court.

Appellants' principal contention, rejected by both the trial and the appel-

---

1. At the time of this purchase her account showed a balance of $164 still owing from her prior purchases. The total of all the purchases made over the years in question came to $1,800. The total payments amounted to $1,400.

late courts below, is that these contracts, or at least some of them, are unconscionable and, hence, not enforceable. In its opinion in Williams v. Walker-Thomas Furniture Company, 198 A.2d 914, 916 (1964), the District of Columbia Court of Appeals explained its rejection of this contention as follows:

"Appellant's second argument presents a more serious question. The record reveals that prior to the last purchase appellant had reduced the balance in her account to $164. The last purchase, a stereo set, raised the balance due to $678. Significantly, at the time of this and the preceding purchases, appellee was aware of appellant's financial position. The reverse side of the stereo contract listed the name of appellant's social worker and her $218 monthly stipend from the government. Nevertheless, with full knowledge that appellant had to feed, clothe and support both herself and seven children on this amount, appellee sold her a $514 stereo set.

"We cannot condemn too strongly appellee's conduct. It raises serious questions of sharp practice and irresponsible business dealings. A review of the legislation in the District of Columbia affecting retail sales and the pertinent decisions of the highest court in this jurisdiction disclose, however, no ground upon which this court can declare the contracts in question contrary to public policy. We note that were the Maryland Retail Installment Sales Act, Art. 83 §§128-153, or its equivalent, in force in the District of Columbia, we could grant appellant appropriate relief. We think Congress should consider corrective legislation to protect the public from such exploitive contracts as were utilized in the case at bar."

We do not agree that the court lacked the power to refuse enforcement to contracts found to be unconscionable. In other jurisdictions, it has been held as a matter of common law that unconscionable contracts are not enforceable.[2] While no decision of this court so holding has been found, the notion that an unconscionable bargain should not be given full enforcement is by no means novel. In Scott v. United States, 79 U.S. (12 Wall.) 443, 445, 20 L. Ed. 438 (1870), the Supreme Court stated: ". . . If a contract be unreasonable and unconscionable, but not void for fraud, a court of law will give to the party who sues for its breach damages, not according to its letter, but only such as he is equitably entitled to. . . ." Since we have never adopted or rejected such a rule, the question here presented is actually one of first impression.

Congress has recently enacted the Uniform Commercial Code, which specifically provides that the court may refuse to enforce a contract which it finds to be unconscionable at the time it was made. UCC 2-302. The enactment of this section, which occurred subsequent to the contracts here in suit, does not mean that the common law of the District of Columbia was otherwise at the time of enactment, nor does it preclude the court from adopting a similar rule

2. Campbell Soup Co. v. Wentz, 172 F.2d 80 (3d Cir. 1948); Indianapolis Morris Plan Corporation v. Sparks, 132 Ind. App. 145, 172 N.E.2d 899 (1961); Henningsen v. Bloomfield Motors, Inc., 32 N.J. 358, 161 A.2d 69, 84-96; 75 A.L.R.2d 1 (1960). Cf. 1 Corbin, Contracts §128 (1963).

in the exercise of its powers to develop the common law for the District of Columbia. In fact, in view of the absence of prior authority on the point, we consider the congressional adoption of UCC 2-302 persuasive authority for the following rationale of the cases from which the section is explicitly derived.[5] Accordingly, we hold that where the element of unconscionability is present at the time a contract is made, the contract should not be enforced.

Unconscionability has generally been recognized to include an absence of meaningful choice on the part of one of the parties together with contract terms which are unreasonably favorable to the other party.[6] Whether a meaningful choice is present in a particular case can only be determined by consideration of all the circumstances surrounding the transaction. In many cases the meaningfulness of the choice is negated by a gross inequality of bargaining power.[7] The manner in which the contract was entered is also relevant to this consideration. Did each party to the contract, considering his obvious education or lack of it, have a reasonable opportunity to understand the terms of the contract, or were the important terms hidden in a maze of fine print and minimized by deceptive sales practices? Ordinarily, one who signs an agreement without full knowledge of its terms might be held to assume the risk that he has entered a one-sided bargain.[8] But when a party of little bargaining power, and hence little real choice, signs a commercially unreasonable contract with little or no knowledge of its terms, it is hardly likely that his consent, or even an objective manifestation of his consent, was ever given to all the terms. In such a case the usual rule that the terms of the agreement are not to be questioned should be abandoned and the court should consider whether the terms of the contract are so unfair that enforcement should be withheld.[10]

----

5. See Comment, UCC 2-302 (1962). Compare Note, 45 Va. L. Rev. 583, 590 (1959), where it is predicted that the rule of UCC 2-302 will be followed by analogy in cases which involve contracts not specifically covered by the section. Cf. 1 State of New York Law Revision Commission, Report and Record of Hearings on the Uniform Commercial Code 108-110 (1954) (remarks of Professor Llewellyn).

6. See Henningsen v. Bloomfield Motors, Inc., supra Note 2; Campbell Soup Co. v. Wentz, supra Note 2.

7. See Henningsen v. Bloomfield Motors, Inc., supra Note 2, 161 A.2d at 86, and authorities there cited. Inquiry into the relative bargaining power of the two parties is not an inquiry wholly divorced from the general question of unconscionability, since a one-sided bargain is itself evidence of the inequality of the bargaining parties. This fact was vaguely recognized in the common law doctrine of intrinsic fraud, that is, fraud which can be presumed from the grossly unfair nature of the terms of the contract. See the oft-quoted statement of Lord Hardwicke in Earl of Chesterfield v. Janssen, 28 Eng. Rep. 82, 100 (1751): ". . . [Fraud] may be apparent from the intrinsic nature and subject of the bargain itself; such as no man in his senses and not under delusion would make. . . ."

8. See Restatement, Contracts §70 (1932); Note, 63 Harv. L. Rev. 494 (1950). See also Daley v. People's Building, Loan & Savings Assn., 178 Mass. 13, 59 N.E. 452, 453 (1901), in which Mr. Justice Holmes, while sitting on the Supreme Judicial Court of Massachusetts, made this observation: ". . . Courts are less and less disposed to interfere with parties making such contracts as they choose, so long as they interfere with no one's welfare but their own. . . . It will be understood that we are speaking of parties standing in an equal position where neither has any oppressive advantage or power. . . ."

10. See the general discussion of "Boiler-Plate Agreements" in Llewellyn, The Common Law Tradition 362-371 (1960).

In determining reasonableness or fairness, the primary concern must be with the terms of the contract considered in light of the circumstances existing when the contract was made. The test is not simple, nor can it be mechanically applied. The terms are to be considered "in light of the general commercial background and the commercial needs of the particular trade or case."[11] Corbin suggests the test as being whether the terms are "so extreme as to appear unconscionable according to the mores and business practices of the time and place." 1 Corbin op. cit. supra note 2.[12] We think this formulation correctly states the test to be applied in those cases where no meaningful choice was exercised upon entering the contract.

Because the trial court and the appellate court did not feel that enforcement could be refused, no findings were made on the possible unconscionability of the contracts in these cases. Since the record is not sufficient for our deciding the issue as a matter of law, the cases must be remanded to the trial court for further proceedings. . . .

DANAHER, Circuit Judge (dissenting). The District of Columbia Court of Appeals obviously was as unhappy about the situation here presented as any of us can possibly be. Its opinion in the *Williams* case, quoted in the majority text, concludes: "We think Congress should consider corrective legislation to protect the public from such exploitive contracts as were utilized in the case at bar."

My view is thus summed up by an able court which made no finding that there had actually been sharp practice. Rather the appellant seems to have known precisely where she stood.

There are many aspects of public policy here involved. What is a luxury to some may seem an outright necessity to others. Is public oversight to be required of the expenditures of relief funds? A washing machine, e.g., in the hands of a relief client might become a fruitful source of income. Many relief clients may well need credit, and certain business establishments will take long chances on the sale of items, expecting their pricing policies will afford a degree of protection commensurate with the risk. Perhaps a remedy when necessary will be found within the provisions of the "Loan Shark" law, D.C. Code §§26-601 et seq. (1961).

I mention such matters only to emphasize the desirability of a cautious approach to any such problem, particularly since the law for so long has allowed parties such great latitude in making their own contracts. I dare say there must annually be thousands upon thousands of installment credit transactions in this jurisdiction, and one can only speculate as to the effect the decision in these cases will have.

11. Comment, UCC [2-302].
12. See Henningsen v. Bloomfield Motors, Inc., supra Note 2; Mandel v. Liebman, 303 N.Y. 88, 100 N.E.2d 149 (1951). The traditional test as stated in Greer v. Tweed, 13 Abb. Pr., N.S., at 429, is "such as no man in his senses and not under delusion would make on the one hand, and as no honest or fair man would accept, on the other."

test for unconscionability

I join the District of Columbia Court of Appeals in its disposition of the issues.

NOTES & QUESTIONS

1. *Nonjudicial decisions on unconscionability.* In his study of unconscionability Professor Arthur Leff concluded that the approach of the *Williams* case allows judges to impose values by their decisions that no legislature would vote to impose. Leff, Unconscionability and the Code—The Emperor's New Clause, 115 U. Pa. L. Rev. 485, 557-558 (1967). Several nonjudicial attempts have been made to address specific clauses that have been found unconscionable by courts. See UCCC §§3.302, 3.303 (1974).

2. *Justification for the Add-On Clause.* The following argument has been made in favor of "add-on" clauses like the one found in *Williams*. Are such arguments relevant to a court considering a claim of unconscionability?

EPSTEIN, UNCONSCIONABILITY: A CRITICAL REAPPRAISAL, 18 J. Law & Econ. 293, 307 (1975): "Although agreements of this kind can, and have, been attacked on unconscionability grounds, they made good sense in the cases to which they apply. One of the major risks to the seller of personal property is that the goods sold will lose value, be it through use or abuse, more rapidly than the purchase price is paid off. The buyer can, and quite often does, have a 'negative' equity in the goods. The seller, therefore, who takes back a security interest only in the goods sold, runs the real risk that repossession of the single item sold will still leave him with a loss on the transaction as a whole, taking into account the costs of interest and collection. One way to handle this problem is to require the purchaser of the goods to make a larger cash down payment, but that, of course, is something which many buyers, particularly those of limited means, do not want to do. Another alternative is for the buyer to provide the seller with additional collateral; yet here the best collateral is doubtless in goods sold by the seller to the buyer. Other goods already in the possession of the buyer may be of uncertain value, and they may well be subject to prior liens. Again, they may be of a sort that the seller cannot conveniently resell in the ordinary course of his business. Even if the goods are suitable collateral for the loan, it could take a good deal of time and effort for the seller to determine that fact. The 'add-on' clause allows both parties to benefit from the reduction in costs in the setting up of a security arrangement."

3. *Evidence of commercial context.* UCC 2-302(2) allows parties a reasonable opportunity to present evidence as to the commercial setting of a questioned contract or clause. What kind of evidence is relevant? How is the evidence to be collected? Consider the 1968 Federal Trade Commission study of installment credit practices in the District of Columbia (the jurisdiction in which the

Williams case arose). The elaborate study found that most of the higher gross margin of low-income market retailers was offset by higher expenses for personnel, advertising, bad debt losses, insurance, and legal and professional fees. Net profits were not markedly higher for low-income market retailers than for general market retailers, whether measured as a percentage of sales or of owner equity. FTC, Economic Report of Installment Credit and Retail Sales Practices of District of Columbia Retailers (March 1968). Is the study relevant to the questioned clause in *Williams*? Is it reasonable to expect parties to finance and carry out such studies?

4. *Application of UCC 2-302 in Article 9.* Most courts that have addressed the issue have refused to apply UCC 2-302 to secured transactions. See Hernandez v. S.I.C. Finance Co., 79 N.M. 673, 448 P.2d 474, 5 UCC Rep. 1151 (1968) (by its terms does not apply to secured transactions); Bornstein v. Metal-Built Products, Inc. (In re Metal-Built Products, Inc.), 28 UCC Rep. 1077 (Bankr. E.D. Pa. 1980); but see Penney v. First National Bank, 385 Mass. 715, 433 N.E.2d 901, 33 UCC Rep. 433 (1982) (court upholds repossession clause but applies test of unconscionability). What arguments might be made in support of the applicability of UCC 2-302 to Article 9? Does it make any difference that the secured obligation arose out of a sales transaction?

IN RE ELKINS-DELL MANUFACTURING CO.
253 F. Supp. 864, 3 UCC Rep. 386 (E.D. Pa. 1966)

Joseph S. LORD, III, District Judge. . . . [This case involves] a narrow but important question of bankruptcy law and administration: May and, if so, should a referee in bankruptcy refuse to enforce a security agreement between a creditor and the bankrupt which the referee finds unconscionable? . . .

[Elkins-Dell, the bankrupt] and Fidelity America Financial Corporation entered into a loan agreement in October, 1959. Fidelity was to advance money to the bankrupt against an assignment of accounts receivable. In January, 1960, an involuntary bankruptcy petition was filed, and after an unsuccessful attempt at an arrangement, Elkins-Dell was adjudicated a bankrupt in May, 1960.

The agreement was, to say the least, somewhat one-sided. Fidelity was to advance 75% of the value of accounts assigned to it, but was obligated to take only "such Accounts of [Elkins-Dell] which, in the sole and unlimited discretion of [Fidelity], may be acceptable to [Fidelity] and to pay therefor." The bankrupt, on the other hand, promised that it would neither "negotiate for nor borrow any form of money whatsoever from any source other than [Fidelity] without the written consent of [Fidelity] first obtained" and that it would neither "sell or assign any accounts to any person, firm or corporation other than [Fidelity]; nor sell, dispose of, or in any way, hypothecate any assets, without the written consent of [Fidelity] first obtained." The bankrupt, in other words, had the obligation to finance only through Fidelity, but Fidelity had the power to refuse to supply the bankrupt with funds. This arrangement, the referee concluded, "spelled ruin to the bankrupt. . . ."

Fidelity also reserved the power to direct the Post Office to deliver all the bankrupt's mail to it, to receive and open such mail and "to dispose of all mail addressed to [the bankrupt]." The bankrupt promised not to "request an extension from or a composition with creditors" or to "file a Voluntary Petition in Bankruptcy, or for an Arrangement or Reorganization or the appointment of a Receiver or make an Assignment for the Benefit of Creditors; without the written consent of [Fidelity] first obtained." Fidelity got the power to veto a suspension of the bankrupt's business, for that, too, required Fidelity's prior "written consent." It had the unilateral power to change the terms of the contract merely by giving notice of the change by certified mail. Such a change could be vetoed by the bankrupt if it expressed its disagreement in writing within five days, and there is no evidence of any attempts to change any of the terms.

The interest rate was 1/23 of 1% per day (more than 15.8% per year) on the total unpaid balance of any amount loaned, but in any event a minimum of $500. per month, plus 5/23 of 1% on check collections. The interest rate would have been usurious, except for the Pennsylvania statute which precludes a corporation from raising the defense of usury. 15 P.S. §2852-313.

Pursuant to the agreement, substantial advances of money were made to the bankrupt, and during October, November and December, 1959, substantial collections were made by Fidelity on the accounts assigned. At the end of December, Fidelity was still owed about $28,536 (cents omitted throughout). No loans were made thereafter. By the date the involuntary petition was filed, collections on accounts had reduced the balance due to about $14,061. . . . [A hearing was held before the referee in bankruptcy.]

The referee concluded, to use his language in Elkins-Dell, that each of these agreements "is so one-sided in favor of Fidelity, drives so hard a bargain and is so overreaching as to be unenforceable in a court of conscience." . . . He relied largely on Campbell Soup Co. v. Wentz, 172 F.2d 80 (3d Cir. 1948), which held that equity would not enforce an unconscionable contract. Campbell Soup had succeeded in obtaining an agreement with a carrot grower which included a provision excusing Campbell from accepting carrots under certain circumstances, but did not permit the grower to sell rejected carrots anywhere else. When Campbell sued for specific performance, the court found that "the sum total of its provisions drives too hard a bargain for a court of conscience to assist." 172 F.2d at 84. In the instant contracts, there is a provision comparable to the one which the court found in *Campbell* to be "the hardest." Id. at 83. That is the provision allowing Fidelity to pick and choose what accounts it would accept but precluding the bankrupts from going elsewhere to find funds. There are, in addition, other provisions, outlined above, which the referee found onerous and oppressive. . . .

[The court concludes that a bankruptcy court, as a court of equity, may inquire into the conscionability of a claim and apply federal law standards of conscionability.]

As a matter of federal law, the *Campbell Soup* case indicates that unconscionability is a valid defense in equity. 172 F.2d at 81-82. But [Manufacturers' Finance Co. v. McKey, 294 U.S. 442 (1935)] suggests a persuasive reason for exercising this equitable discretion more cautiously in bankruptcy. *McKey* rests heavily on the exclusiveness of the remedy in the equity court. Proceeding from the premise that "in an action at law against the receivers the court would have been bound to enforce the contract under review strictly in accordance with its terms," the opinion concludes that "the rule is not otherwise where plaintiff . . . is obliged to submit the determination of his strictly legal rights to a chancery court because it has plenary control of the remedy." 294 U.S. at 451. . . .

[In *Campbell Soup* the court] denied the aid of equity to the plaintiff, thus leaving it to pursue the available remedy at law. Plaintiff, in other words, was left with some place to go. It could vindicate its legal rights in a legal forum. Equity, therefore, could afford the luxury of not specifically enforcing the legal rights without impairing their viability at law.

The bankruptcy court is, of course, the exclusive forum in which Fidelity could press its claim. While some of the provisions of the instant contracts are of dubious validity under Pennsylvania law and public policy, it is not suggested that the essential and operative terms of the contracts, or the contracts as wholes, are invalid. Because of the exclusiveness of the remedy in bankruptcy, it does not follow inexorably that what was soup for Campbell is sauce for Fidelity. Although unconscionability would be legitimate reason to disallow a claim in a proper case, convincing proof of the inequitable conduct of the claimant is necessary to warrant the exercise of that power. . . .

We turn to a consideration of how the power of the referee to disallow a claim for unconscionability ought to be exercised, and particularly, what standard should be employed to determine whether a contract is so unconscionable as to be unenforceable in bankruptcy.

Unconscionable contracts are a genus, of which there is more than one species. One variety of unconscionable contract is very much like contracts of adhesion (which are becoming increasingly difficult to make stick). It usually involves a party whose circumstance, perhaps his unworldliness or ignorance, when compared with the circumstances of the other party, make his knowing assent to the fine-print terms fictional. Courts have frequently found in these circumstances the absence of a meaningful bargain. See 3 Corbin, Contracts §559, at 270-271 (1960). Another species concerns what is basically economic duress. In the absence of a general mandate to review the adequacy of consideration, there has sometimes been a review of the economic positions of the parties and a finding that the position of one was so vulnerable as to make him the victim of a grossly unequal bargain. To be sure, these two types of situations sometimes overlap, but the latter is substantially the case of the bankrupts here. We are not dealing with a fictional assent but a genuine assent by businessmen to terms which, the trustees assert, ought not to be countenanced. . . .

To hold these contracts unenforceable on their face would probably be to impose a judicially invented but economically dysfunctional morality upon knowledgeable contracting parties. It might jeopardize the availability of receivables financing for those for whom factoring is the only practicable way of securing capital. It would be to add a risk of unenforceability to the other risks inherent in such financing. The invocation of the economic duress species of unconscionability has most often been questioned on the ground that refusal to enforce a contract because of it has deleterious economic consequences. See, e.g., Note, Unconscionable Business Contracts: A Doctrine Gone Awry, 70 Yale L.J. 453 (1961). It is those consequences we wish to avoid.

The argument can be made that this is not just a case of excessive interest rates. Here a factor entered into agreements which by their terms tied the bankrupts to it as their sole source of funds without giving any assurance whatever that the funds would be forthcoming. Even indulging the assumption that the provision giving Fidelity "sole and unlimited discretion" to reject any accounts the bankrupts sought to assign would be construed judicially to allow only the exercise of a reasonable discretion, that would be little solace to the bankrupts in their quest for financial viability. They could not assign their accounts to anyone else anyway, and even if they could despite the express provisions to the contrary, the contract terms made the bankrupts' rights to assign them elsewhere so cloudy and their positions so risky that it is difficult to conceive that any other avenues of credit would be open to them. Far from furthering the policy favoring the prevention of business failures, this argument goes, Fidelity's conduct in these two cases contravened it. There would thus be no substantial economic interest served in allowing it the fruits of these transactions.

We have made this argument at length because it deserves full consideration. We are unable to accept it, however, for two reasons. First, whether or not these agreements had the effect of closing off the bankrupts' other sources of credit, the fact is that at least some factors apparently view this type of contract as a necessary form of protection to insure that they have the opportunity to lend money on accounts that are collectible. If these provisions are held unenforceable in bankruptcy, which is, after all, where at least some such borrowers end up, lenders are likely to substitute another form of protection, perhaps higher interest or more selective choice of borrowers. It is therefore a dangerous oversimplification to distinguish the interest rates from the other contract terms.

Secondly, that these arguments are in effect more detrimental than helpful to borrowers is an economic judgment which we are not well-equipped to make. This is precisely the kind of problem that the legislature, either federal or state, would be far better able to deal with than the courts. . . .

We are left, then, on the one hand, with the mandate to screen claims for inequitable conduct, the harsh terms of these contracts, and the "fundamental purpose of the Bankruptcy Act . . . to secure an equitable distribution of the bankrupt's assets among his unsecured creditors," 4 Collier, Bankruptcy ¶67.12[5], at 129 (14th ed. 1964), and, on the other, with the economic dubiousness and institutional difficulty inherent in judicially refusing to enforce the otherwise valid agreements. Certainly, the present records are singularly inadequate to enable a court to decide so perplexing an issue. As evidence on the issue of unconscionability, they contain only the contracts themselves. The contracts appear to be the products of dealings by a lender with borrowers in acute financial distress. But the contracts cannot tell us whether those dealings resulted in imposition on the bankrupts or merely justified precautions on the part of the factor. Given the interest in commercial certainty, the exclusiveness of the creditor's equitable remedy in bankruptcy, and the knowledgeability of the borrower where economic duress is the basis of the asserted unconscionability, to prove unconscionability there must be a showing, not only that the terms of the contract are onerous, oppressive, or one-sided, but also that the terms bear no reasonable relation to the business risks. This is a showing that depends on the commercial environment and cannot be made from the face of a contract alone.

We think, therefore, that the referee acted precipitously in refusing to enforce these contracts. He viewed the question solely as a matter of law, to be judged from "the terms of the contract, which speaks for itself." . . . In that view, he was in error. Even in the context of an unconscionable sales contract, which the Uniform Commercial Code permits the courts to refuse to enforce in whole or in part, UCC 2-302(1), the parties are "afforded a reasonable opportunity to present evidence as to its commercial setting, purpose and effect to aid the court in making the determination."[4] UCC 2-302(2). . . . The commercial context would be at least as relevant in these cases, where the varying risks make the objective ascertainment of the value of the consideration exchanged a seemingly more hazardous task. . . .

We therefore find it incumbent to prolong the termination of this lengthy litigation still further by remanding these cases to the referee for prompt and thorough factual hearings on unconscionability. . . . The ultimate question for the referee will be whether these contracts were, in the light of all the circumstances, reasonable commercial devices. Among the issues which may be explored at these hearings, and which may enter into the determination, are the financial positions of the bankrupts at the time the agreements were entered into; the extent to which agreements of this kind are customary among lenders like Fidelity; the extent to which Fidelity's contracts vary with and reflect anticipated risks; the availability of other credit to the bankrupts, both at the

4. We do not accept the invitation of the trustees to hold UCC 2-302 applicable to agreements other than sales contracts. Cf. Note, 45 Va. L. Rev. 483 (1959). In view of the disposition we make of these cases, it is unnecessary to reach that question.

time and after they entered into these agreements; the extent to which the various provisions were enforced by Fidelity or influenced the bankrupts' business conduct, particularly their ability to secure other funds; whether the terms of these contracts facilitated commerce by making funds available where they otherwise would not be or impeded commerce by precluding access to other sources of funds; and the effects of holding these contracts unenforceable in bankruptcy on the future financing of similar businesses in need of funds. . . .

NOTES & QUESTIONS

1. *Bankruptcy courts as courts of equity.* It has long been recognized that bankruptcy courts sit as courts of equity. See Bankruptcy Act of 1898, §2a; Bank of Marin v. England, 385 U.S. 99 (1966); Pepper v. Litton, 308 U.S. 295 (1939). Drawing on this tradition the Bankruptcy Code provides that a bankruptcy court "may issue any order, process, or judgment that is necessary or appropriate to carry out the provisions of this title." BC 105(a).

2. *Equitable subordination.* The Bankruptcy Code also provides that a bankruptcy court may subordinate one claim to another "under principles of equitable subordination." BC 510(c). The legislative comments on this latter provision state: "It is intended that the term 'principles of equitable subordination' follow existing case law and leave to the courts development of this principle. To date, under existing law, a claim is generally subordinated only if the holder of such claim is guilty of inequitable conduct, or the claim itself is of a status susceptible to subordination, such as a penalty or a claim for damages arising from the purchase or sale of a security of the debtor. The fact that such a claim may be secured is of no consequence to the issue of subordination. However, it is inconceivable that the status of a claim as a secured claim could ever be grounds for justifying equitable subordination." H.R. Debate, 124 Cong. Rec. 32350, 32398 (1978). Would BC 510(c) be relevant in *Elkins-Dell?*

3. *Unconscionable transactions between businessmen.* A survey of recent appellate cases dealing with unconscionability suggests the following generalizations. Appellate cases in which the issue of unconscionability is argued are relatively rare. Although much public attention has been given to consumer cases, in fact a majority of the reported cases deal with transactions between merchants. In almost all of these the courts dismissed the claim of unconscionability relatively quickly without special hearings. Those cases where a clause or contract is found unconscionable almost always involve farmers or small merchants—although by no means are all farmers and small merchants successful when they claim unconscionability! Most of the opinions examine the claim of unconscionability in the context of dispute over terms in contracts for sale that (a) disclaim warranties, (b) limit remedies, or (c) permit the termina-

tion or cancellation of long-term contracts, such as a franchise arrangement or supply contract of long standing. Despite the comment to UCC 2-302 ("the principle of [this section] . . . is not the disturbance of allocation of risks because of superior bargaining"), most courts mention the relative bargaining power when either striking down or upholding a clause in a contract between merchants. There are virtually no cases, other than *Elkins-Dell,* where business debtors challenge a security agreement as unconscionable.

B. SPECIAL UCC RULES FOR CONSUMERS AND FARMERS

1. Consumers and Consumer Goods

After considerable debate the sponsors of the Uniform Commercial Code decided Article 9 should not regulate consumer credit transactions in detail.[3] Nevertheless, a number of Code provisions supply special rules when a consumer is involved: UCC 9-109(1) (definition of *consumer goods*); 9-204(2) (limiting rights in after-acquired consumer goods); 9-206(1), 9-302(1)(d), 9-307(2), 9-401(1) (special protection and priority rules); 9-504(3), 9-505(1), 9-507(1) (consumer rights on default).

Some of these special rules have survived attacks on the constitutional grounds of equal protection ("not rational classification") and due process (perfection without notice). See Personal Thrift Plan v. Georgia Power Co., 242 Ga. 388, 249 S.E.2d 72, 25 UCC Rep. 310 (1978) (upholds constitutionality of UCC 9-302(1)(d)).

3. Professor Grant Gilmore has described as follows the drafting history with respect to consumer transactions: "The original drafting scheme had contemplated a thorough coverage of the special problems involved in the field of consumer finance, along the lines of the Retail Installment Selling Acts which have been widely enacted since approximately 1940. Early drafts contained provisions regulating the form of contract to be used in consumer goods transactions, invalidating clauses under which a consumer waived defenses against an assignee of his contract, and so on. Most of the consumer protective provisions were eliminated from the final draft, although a few curious traces remain. The motives which led to the decision to abandon the consumer to his fate were mixed: some of those who took part in the debate felt that the consumer provisions were 'social legislation,' inappropriate in a general codifying statute; others felt that the provisions unfairly discriminated against banks and finance companies engaged in consumer finance; still others felt that the provisions were so weak that they gave merely an illusion of protection and would be ineffective to curb abuses believed to exist. The controversy over the consumer question was one of the most violent in the history of the Code's drafting. The decision to abandon the field was no doubt wise in view of the demonstrated impossibility of arriving at a satisfactory solution. The upshot was that, although the 'security' aspect of consumer goods transactions (for example, filing) continued within the coverage of the Article, the intention to regulate abuses was expressly disclaimed; a statutory Note was included [after UCC 9-203(4)] to make the point that the regulatory provisions of Retail Installment Selling Acts, small-loan legislation and the like should not be repealed when the Article is enacted." 1 G. Gilmore, Security Interests in Personal Property 293-294 (1965). Do you agree with the draftsmen's judgment?

UNION NATIONAL BANK v. NORTHWEST MARINE, INC.

62 Erie Co. L.J. 87, 27 UCC Rep. 563 (Pa. C.P. 1979)

[On June 12, 1973, The Union National Bank of Pittsburgh (UNB) made a loan in the amount of $8,000.00 to Peter and Doreen Paffen to enable them to purchase a 1966 33-foot Chris-Craft Cavalier. The Paffens used the entire proceeds of the loan to purchase the boat, which they bought to use primarily for personal or family purposes. At the time the loan was made, the Paffens duly executed, sealed and delivered to UNB a Consumer Goods and Equipment Note and Security Agreement. A financing statement was not recorded.

On September 7, 1973, Northwest Marine, Inc. took the boat as a trade-in from the Paffens, to whom it gave credit of $7,000 on the purchase price of a new boat. At that time, Northwest did not know that the boat was subject to a security interest in favor of UNB. On September 7, 1973, the Paffens owed UNB a balance in excess of $7,000.00 on the Note and Security Agreement. Peter Paffen gave Northwest a document called a Warranty of Seller.

Subsequently, Northwest sold the boat for $7,000 to a purchaser, who bought it for personal or family purposes. Northwest did not turn over any proceeds of the sale to UNB.

On August 9, 1974, the Paffens defaulted on their note to UNB. They owed UNB a balance of $8,166.74, with unearned interest totaling $1,178.88 and the payoff figure totaling $6,987.82. On August 9, 1974, the Paffens executed, sealed, and delivered to UNB another Consumer Goods and Equipment Note and Security Agreement, dated August 9, 1974. UNB did not know, and the Paffens did not tell the bank that they no longer owned the boat.

The Paffens defaulted on the August 9, 1974 note. UNB recovered a judgment against the Paffens but was unable to collect.]

DWYER, P. J. . . . The essential problem to resolve is whether the motorboat in the hands of the Paffens was a "consumer good."

[The court quotes UCC 9-109(1):

Goods are
(1) "consumer goods" if they are used or bought for use primarily for personal, family or household purposes; . . .

and 9-302(1)(d):

(1) A financing statement must be filed to perfect all security interests except the following: . . .
(d) a purchase money security in consumer goods; but filing is required for a motor vehicle required to be registered; and fixture filing is required for priority over conflicting interests in fixtures to the extent provided in Section 9-313.]

The defendant's position is that a 33-foot motorboat is not a consumer good, and that the draftsmen of the Uniform Commercial Code did not intend that expensive motorboats be treated the same as refrigerators or televisions for the purposes of dispensing [with] the filing of the security agreement [financing statement—EDS.] by the secured party; i.e., the plaintiff lending institution in instant case. Indeed, there is compelling reason for treating ordinary household goods differently from expensive motorboats. The concept of a consumer good indicates the "using up" or "wasting away" or consumption of the consumer good to the extent that a second lending institution would unlikely be willing to advance money to the owner of the readily depreciable consumer good and take a security interest therein. This court is of the opinion that the defendant is correct in these views.

This court finds that a 33-foot boat is a good of substantial magnitude relative to the ordinary concept of consumer goods and should be treated differently under UCC 9-302. Indeed, in Pennsylvania, a motorboat would seem to be more similarly classified in the status of a motor vehicle rather than to the category of consumer goods for two reasons.

With respect to the purchase price, motorboats and motor vehicles are much more similar than motorboats and most of the other items properly classified as consumer goods. Secondly, and more importantly, motorboats are required to be licensed in Pennsylvania as are motor vehicles. The latter licensure requirement being expressly recited in UCC 9-302(1)(d), which requires filing security agreements for motor vehicles that need to be licensed. See Section 485 of the Motorboat Law which requires the registration of motorboats in Pennsylvania. 55 PS §485.

The only possible qualitative difference between a motor vehicle and a motorboat is that only the former requires a certificate of title. This court is of the opinion that the Legislature should give serious consideration to requiring such certificates for motorboats.

While it appears that the Pennsylvania Legislature probably committed an oversight in drafting UCC 9-302(1)(d), thereby ignoring the special problem created by motorboats, this gap is probably best filled by interstitial lawmaking by the court until the Legislature takes the opportunity to fill the void.

It is enigmatic why in UCC 9-302(1)(c) [1962; deleted by 1972 UCC revisions—EDS.] the Legislature differentiates farm equipment by requiring the filing of a security agreement for said equipment if the purchase price of said equipment is in excess of $2,500.00, but conferring automatic perfection on said equipment with a purchase price under $2,500.00. At the same time the Legislature, in effect, lumps together all consumer goods, regardless of the purchase price.

Similarly, our sister state of Maryland differentiates consumer goods for the purpose of perfection and priorities under its adopted version of the Code on the following basis: "A financing statement must be filed to perfect all security interests except the following: . . . (d) A purchase money security interest in consumer goods having a purchase price not in excess of $500.00. . . ." Md. Ann. Code art. 95B, §9-302(1).

UCC 9-302, which exempts all purchase money security interests in consumer goods without purchase price restrictions, is an anomaly that presents

[handwritten margin notes: "fear of secret liens", "on high value items"]

dangers in secured transactions. Under this section, which creates secret liens, a lending institution could loan money against an expensive yacht, taking a security interest therein, unaware that another institution has a prior secret lien against the yacht, courtesy of UCC 9-302's automatic perfection of security interests in *all* consumer goods.

With respect to the even more basic issue raised by the defendant as to whether a motorboat is a consumer good, our research indicates a dearth of case law, in Pennsylvania or otherwise, addressing the issue. The sole appellate law in Pennsylvania on this issue is the case of Atlas Credit Corp. v. Dolbow, 193 Pa. Super. 649; 165 A.2d 704 (1960), in which the Superior Court held, without comment, that a motorboat of the value of almost $6,000.00, which was purchased by two farmers for their personal pleasure, was "consumer goods" for the purpose of an application of UCC 9-507(1). . . .

We feel that it would be inequitable to allow the plaintiff in instant case to recover a judgment based on the facts presented in the hereinabove set forth stipulation.

From reading of the Superior Court's reported Opinion in the *Atlas* case, this court is of the opinion that the Superior Court had no reasons before it to be alerted to the possible problems that have developed over the years by the vast number of boats that are now in use by the public, the vast territories covered by many of these boats in their travels and the confusion and unfairness that now exists by classifying boats as "consumer goods." We therefore hold that the boat in question in the instant case is not a consumer good and will find for the defendant.

In Gray v. Grunnagle, 423 Pa. 144, 152 (1966), our Supreme Court . . . said: "Ratio est legis anima; mutata legis ratione mutatur et lex. Reason is the soul of the law; the reason of the law being changed, the law is also changed."

[The court granted defendant's motion for summary judgment.]

NOTE & QUESTION

Definition of consumer goods. Note that UCC 9-109(1) focuses on the intended use of the specific purchaser. Compare the definition of *consumer product* in the Magnuson-Moss Warranty Act ("normally used for personal, family, or household purposes") (15 U.S.C. §2301 (1982)). Would reference to *normal use* provide greater certainty in the proper classification of goods in Article 9?

CORONADO v. BEACH FURNITURE & APPLIANCE, INC. (IN RE CORONADO)
7 B.R. 53 (Bankr. D. Ariz. 1980)

William A. SCANLAND, Bankruptcy Judge. The debtors, through their attorney, filed a motion to avoid a non-purchase money security interest under 11

U.S.C. §552(f)(2) in the following property: (1) Maytag Automatic Washer; (1) Chest; (1) Night stand; (1) T-Bird Triple Dresser & Mirror, and (2) 900 Bunk beds. The debtors had bought all of the items except the washer under a security agreement dated December 20, 1978, from Beach Furniture and Appliance, Inc. No financing statement was filed. The washer was purchased under a security agreement dated November 3, 1979, and the words "Rewrite: (2) 900 Bunk beds complete T-Bird triple dresser & mirror 4530 chest, nitestand" were listed together with a description of the Maytag washer in the section providing for a description of the goods. No financing statement was filed. The debtors had made the monthly payments required under the December 20, 1978, security agreement, and had made payments under the consolidated security agreement of November 3, 1979.

The debtors' attorney first points out that UCC 9-107 defines a purchase money security agreement. . . . He cites a leading case, In re Manuel, 507 F.2d 990 (5th Cir. 1975). In this case the Fifth Circuit held, under circumstances similar to the matter before this Court, that the statutory requirements of a purchase money security interest require that such interest be in the item purchased, and the purchase money security interest cannot exceed the price of what is purchased in the transaction wherein the security interest is created, if the vendor is to be protected despite the absence of filing. The Court voided a security interest in all items made under a prior security agreement and expressly stated they did not express a view as to whether there was a valid purchase money security interest in a subsequent purchase of a TV set. The prior purchase and the balance due thereunder were consolidated in the security agreement taken on the later purchase of the TV set.

Beach's attorney argues in a supplemental memorandum in opposition to the motion to avoid the lien that A.R.S. §44-6002 (1956 Supp. eff. 1979), gets around the problem raised in In re Manuel, supra. This section provides that a contract, i.e., security agreement, may provide for a consolidation of subsequent purchases with one or more previous purchases. This section, however, does provide that the goods purchased under the previous contract may be security for the goods purchased under the subsequent contract, "but only until such time as the total payments under the previous contract or contracts is fully paid."

A careful review of the Parties' Exhibit No. 2, which is dated November 3, 1979, shows that the Plaintiff-Buyer gave the Defendant-Seller a security interest in the washing machine as well as the household items previously purchased. This agreement provides that the buyer shall make twenty-four consecutive monthly payments of $65.81 each, commencing November 15, 1979. This security agreement does not meet the requirements of A.R.S. §44-6002 (1956 Supp.) as there is no provision in the security agreement for the surrendering of the security interest by the seller in the household furnishings first purchased by the debtor upon full payment of that purchase price. A reading of this security agreement shows that the seller retained a security interest in the household furnishings until all items, including the washing machine, had been fully paid. It is clear to this Court that the seller, Beach

Furniture and Appliance, Inc., does not have a purchase money security agreement in the household furnishings, and if it desired to take a security interest in these items at the time of the sale of the washing machine, it would have to file a financing statement as required by UCC 9-302. . . .

The interesting question now arises as to whether or not the seller, Beach Furniture and Appliance, Inc., has a valid security interest in the washing machine. One case touching upon this point is In re Brouse, 6 UCC Rep. 471 (Bankr. W.D. Mich. 1969). In this case the bankruptcy judge followed the reasoning of In re Manuel and found that there was no purchase money security interest in previously purchased items. However, . . . a Michigan statute in the Mich. Retail Installment Sales Act, M.C.L.A. §445.861(c), which provides for an allotment of monthly payments to prior and subsequent purchases[,] resolves the problem concerning the validity of the security interest in the washing machine. The bankruptcy judge admitted that the computation of the amounts due on one item would be very complex, but that this special Michigan statute resolved the problem.

The problem here is that the security agreement dated November 3, 1979, provides for twenty-four monthly payments of $65.81 each, and there is no apportionment of this monthly payment to the purchase price of the furniture sold under the prior security agreement nor to the purchase price of the washer sold under the latter security agreement. The debtor or any other person examining this security agreement would not be able to determine how much of the total purchase price would have to be paid before he would get clear title to the washing machine. In re Mulcahy, [3 B.R. 454 (Bankr. S.D. Ind. 1980)], discusses this problem. In *Mulcahy,* a buyer had purchased certain living room furniture under a retail installment contract or security agreement. Thereafter, the Mulcahys obtained financing from the Morris Plan for the purchase of certain bedroom furniture under a security agreement from a different seller. He also gave the Morris Plan a security agreement on both living room furniture and bedroom furniture. The Court held that clearly the security agreement to Morris Plan, in considering the question of whether it was a loan as distinguished from payment of a purchase price, clearly was invalid as to the living room furniture, citing many cases. They applied the general rule that if consumer goods secure any price other than their own and there is no formula for application of payments, the security interest in those goods is non-purchase money. Counsel for the parties had indicated at pretrial conferences that the complaint to avoid the lien was only to extend to the living room furniture. The Bankruptcy Court accepted the stipulation as being a settlement in regards to holding the security interest in this furniture valid. This court discusses an Indiana statute which allows cross-collateralization and provides that payments made shall be applied first to the payment of the debt first arising. They cite Williams v. Walker-Thomas Furniture Company [p. 420 supra] which held unconscionable a security agreement that permitted a seller to retain a security interest in all furniture sold at different times until complete payment of the purchase price. The Court said the formula enables

purchaser to keep consumer goods he has paid off free from the cross-colla-
teralization agreement. It also, however, provides a means for determining
precisely what price each of the items in question secures.

In the instant case, the debtor had no way of obtaining title to the furniture unless or until he paid the full purchase price not only of the furniture but
also of the washer. This Court finds that there is no way that the debtor could
have determined how much he would have to pay in order to obtain clear title
to the washer. The security agreement makes no provision for the release of
any collateral except upon full and complete payment of the entire purchase
price of the consolidated security agreement and is therefore unconscionable.
This Court finds that as a matter of law the Seller-Plaintiff does not have a
valid purchase money security agreement in any of the furniture or the washer
purchased and described in the security agreement of November 3, 1979, and
that such security agreement in such furniture and washer is void. . . .

NOTES & QUESTIONS

1. *After-acquired collateral.* Why doesn't the secured party in *Coronado*
merely provide in the original security agreement that debtor's after-acquired
consumer goods shall secure the repayment obligation? See UCC 9-204(2).

2. *Truth in lending and after-acquired property.* Federal Truth-in-Lending legislation requires disclosure of credit terms to potential debtors. 15 U.S.C.
§1601 (1982). Among matters that must be clearly set forth is the security
interest. As of April 1, 1982, Regulation Z requires creditors to disclose in an
initial disclosure statement "the fact that the creditor has or will acquire a
security interest in the property purchased under the plan, or in other property identified by item or type" (12 C.F.R. §226.6(c) (1984); see also
§226.18(m)). Prior to April of 1982 the disclosure requirement was much more
extensive and made specific reference to after-acquired property. "If after-
acquired property will be subject to the security interest, or if other or future
indebtedness is or may be secured by any such property, this fact shall be
clearly set forth in conjunction with the description or identification of the type
of security interest held, retained or acquired." 12 C.F.R. §226.8(b)(5) (1980).
A great deal of litigation focused on whether a statement that the security
interest extended to after-acquired property, without mention of the ten-day
limitation in UCC 9-204(2), satisfied the requirements of Regulation Z. See
Tinsman v. Moline Beneficial Finance Co., 531 F.2d 815 (7th Cir. 1976)
(clause without reference to ten-day limit did not satisfy Reg. Z). Do these
cases survive the amendment of the regulation?

3. *Federal Trade Commission regulations.* FTC rules now define as an unfair
credit practice the inclusion in a consumer credit transaction of a term granting a nonpossessory security interest in household goods other than a purchase
money security interest. 16 C.F.R. §444.2(a)(4) (1985). Failure to comply with

the rule is an unfair act or practice within the meaning of Section 5 of the Federal Trade Commission Act.

4. *Bankruptcy Code 522(f)(2).* BC 522(f)(2) permits a debtor to avoid a nonpossessory, nonpurchase-money security interest in specified property if the security interest impairs the debtor's right to exempt the property under BC 522(b). There has been considerable litigation over whether this provision is unconstitutional because it takes the secured party's property retrospectively without due process. In United States v. Security Industrial Bank, 495 U.S. 70 (1982), the Supreme Court avoided the constitutional issue with respect to security interests created before enactment of the Bankruptcy Reform Act on November 6, 1978, by reading BC 522(f)(2) as not applying retroactively. What about secured party's interest in *Coronado?*

5. *Exemption statutes.* State exemption statutes, sometimes mandated by constitutional provisions, define the property of the debtor that is exempt from judicial process. These statutes are designed to protect debtors and their families from destitution. In most jurisdictions attempted waivers by debtors of their exemption rights are construed narrowly. See Hernandez v. S.I.C. Finance Co., 79 N.M. 673, 448 P.2d 474, 5 UCC Rep. 1151 (1968) (grant of security interest in exempt property an enforceable present waiver).

Problem 8-1. Standard House Trailer, Inc., sells a house trailer to Debtor, who signs a conditional sales agreement for a total price, including the finance charge, of $15,000. The expected life of the trailer is 20 years. Standard does not file a financing statement. Soon after the purchase Debtor declares bankruptcy. Advise Debtor's trustee on whether he can avoid Standard's security interest. See UCC 9-109(1), 9-302(1)(d). Assume that the certificate of title legislation in the state in which Debtor resides has the following definition of *vehicles* governed by that statute: "*vehicle* means a device in, upon, or by which a person or property is or may be transported or drawn upon a highway." Is this statute relevant?

Problem 8-2. Doctor purchases a window air conditioner unit from Seller and grants Seller a security interest in the unit to secure the price. At the time of the purchase Doctor checks a box on the written security agreement indicating that she plans to use the unit "for personal, family, or household purposes." Seller installs the unit in Doctor's house. One month later Doctor decides to re-install the unit in her office at a nearby clinic. She does not inform Seller of the re-installation. Seller has not filed a financing statement. Does Seller have a perfected security interest in the air conditioner? See UCC 9-302, 9-401(3), 9-313.

Problem 8-3. Debtor, a resident of Dallas, purchases a home computer from Discount Store and grants the store a security interest in the computer to secure the price. Discount Store files a financing statement listing the collateral as "home computer" with the Dallas County clerk's office. Six months later Debtor's employer transfers Debtor to its branch office in Oklahoma City, and two months after the move Debtor sells the computer to a colleague there. Soon after this sale Discount Store discovers that Debtor has moved out of the state and no longer has the computer. What, if anything, should Discount Store do? See UCC 9-103, 9-307, 9-401(3)

[handwritten margin notes: "depends which selected here. Buyer father subj. to sec. int. (see 9-103)" "Is this filing sufficient" "—not. buyer—ord course — is "casual buyer"]

Problem 8-4. Professor buys an electric typewriter from Dealer in order to type the manuscript of a book. Dealer retains a security interest in the typewriter to secure the purchase price and files a financing statement in the proper office. To raise cash Professor subsequently sells the typewriter to Retailer, who deals in new and used typewriters. Retailer then sells the typewriter to Consumer for cash. (a) Does Consumer take the typewriter subject to Dealer's security interest? See UCC 9-306, 9-307. (b) If Consumer sells the typewriter to Neighbor does Neighbor take free of Dealer's security interest in the typewriter? See UCC 9-306, 9-307.

[handwritten margin notes: "only had months to keep perfect see 9-103(b) Debtor's locat'n governs (e) 4 mths" "Continuous perfectn"]

[handwritten: ") cg? buyer - ord course _ this seller §NO]

Problem 8-5. Following Debtor's default, Debtor asks Seller to repossess the refrigerator that has served as collateral for the sale price. The cash price for the refrigerator was $520 and the time-price differential was $80. Before default Debtor had paid $325 in installments. At the time it repossessed the refrigerator Seller indicated on its books that the refrigerator was worth $250. Although Seller subsequently attempted to dispose of the refrigerator the only offers it received were below $250 so Seller decided to wait to see if the market for used refrigerators improved. Six months after repossession Seller sold the refrigerator for $200. Seller now sues Debtor for a deficiency of $75, storage fees of $60, and repossession costs of $25. Advise Debtor on his obligations. See UCC 9-504, 9-505.

Problem 8-6. Following Debtor's default Finance Company repossesses the washing machine that had served as collateral for its loan to Debtor. Finance Company disposes of the collateral in a private sale for $200 but gives Debtor no notice of the disposition. Finance Company sues Debtor for a deficiency of $150 and proves that the used washing machine had a fair market value of $200 and that its procedures for disposition were in accordance with the reasonable usages of sellers of used appliances. Debtor counterclaims for the "statutory penalty" of UCC 9-507(1), which would more than offset Finance Company's claim for a deficiency. As judge, how would you rule on the counterclaim? See UCC 9-504, 9-507(1).

Problem 8-7. You are asked to prepare the brief for the secured party on the appeal from the following bankruptcy case. What points will you make?

IN RE JOHNSON, 13 UCC Rep. 953 (Bankr. D. Neb. 1973). HFC claims a security interest in the following collateral described in the security agreement: "All of the household and consumer goods . . . now or hereafter

located in or about the premises constituting the mortgagor's residence . . . ."
The financing statement described the collateral simply as "consumer goods."

"I agree with the contention of bankrupt that: . . . 'The after acquired property clause in question grants the lender upon default by the debtor an unfair and overreaching collection device, one he is not entitled to as a matter of law because of the express prohibitions contained in [UCC 9-204(2)]. By purporting to take a security interest in "all household and consumer goods now or hereafter located on borrower's premises," the creditor is falsely misrepresenting to the client the true extent of the collateral. Upon default, the creditor can represent to the debtor its authority for repossessing everything of value owned by the debtor. The value of such a clause as a collection tool is infinite. . . . The only reason for its existence is to coerce the debtor to continue payments on fear of repossession or to allow the repossession of additional collateral which would then satisfy any deficiency.'

"HFC in the secured transaction with the bankrupt did not act in good faith as required under UCC 1-203 or in other words, with honesty in fact as required under UCC 1-201(19) when it purported to take a security interest in consumer goods acquired more than ten days after value was given. This is because HFC had no legitimate reason for taking such a security interest and did so for whatever the language would be worth as against an unsophisticated defaulting debtor. I so hold.

"A knotty problem is what remedy should follow from the absence of good faith. The bankrupt submits that the absence of good faith entails unconscionability under UCC 2-302 and hence this court should grant the major remedies provided for therein—namely to refuse to enforce the entire security agreement.

"I have great difficulty in holding a statutory provision located in Article 2 dealing with sales is directly applicable to a transaction governed by Article 9 dealing with secured transactions. Even so, the Bankruptcy Court is a court of equity and may apply equitable principles and contrive new remedies in appropriate situations. There is no reason therefore that the Bankruptcy Court cannot apply any appropriate remedy including those in UCC 2-302. And under the circumstances, I agree with bankrupt and hold that the appropriate remedy here is to refuse to enforce the security agreement in toto."

Problem 8-8. You are legislative assistant to Senator Humperdink. The Senator has asked you for your comments on the following proposed legislation, which is designed to require the use of understandable language and meaningful sequence in consumer agreements.

1. Every written agreement to which a consumer is a party wherein the money, property, or service that is the subject of the transaction is primarily for personal, family, or household purposes must be:
   (a) Written in nontechnical language and in a clear and coherent manner, using words with common and everyday meanings, and

   (b)   Appropriately divided and captioned by its various sections.

2. Any creditor or seller who fails to comply with the foregoing provisions shall be liable to a consumer who is a party to a written agreement governed by the provisions thereof in an amount equal to the sum of any actual damages sustained plus fifty dollars ($50.00). The total class action penalty against any such creditor or seller shall not exceed ten thousand dollars ($10,000). These penalties may be enforced only in a court of competent jurisdiction, but not after both parties to the agreement have fully performed their obligations under such agreement, nor against any creditor or seller who attempts in good faith to comply with this section. This subdivision shall not apply to agreements involving amounts in excess of fifty thousand dollars ($50,000).

3. A violation of the provisions of this section shall not render any such agreement void or voidable nor shall it constitute:

   (a)   A defense to any action or proceeding to enforce such agreement; or
   (b)   A defense to any action or proceeding for breach of such agreement.

Advise Senator Humperdink. See (A.B.A.) Committee on Regulation of Consumer Credit, Report: Plain Language Legislation, 35 Bus. Law. 297 (1979).

2.   Farmers and Farm Products

Farmers, as well as consumers, are singled out for special treatment in Article 9, such as the rules in UCC 9-109(3) (definition of *farm products*), 9-203(1)(b) (security agreement covering crops), 9-307(1) (sale of farm products does not cut off security interest), 9-312(2) (priority where new value secured by crops), 9-401(1) (local filing), and 9-402(1), (3) (financing statement covering crops). The most important rule is that a sale of farm products does not cut off a nonconsenting secured party's interest.

   The 1972 amendments cut back on the special provisions for farmers. The 1962 Code had included additional provisions: UCC 9-204(2)(a) (when debtor acquires rights in crops), 9-204(4)(a) (after-acquired crops), 9-302(1)(c) (automatic perfection for low-cost farm equipment), and 9-307(2) (buyer of low-cost farm equipment).

UNITED STATES v. HEXT
444 F.2d 804, 9 UCC Rep. 321 (5th Cir. 1971)

WILKEY, Circuit Judge: The United States brought suit under the jurisdictional grant of 28 U.S.C. §1345 alleging conversion of 578 bales of cotton in which it held a security interest. Named as defendants were Walter A. Hext, Sr., (Hext), the grower of the cotton, the W. A. Hext & Sons Gin Co., Inc. (the Gin Co.), a corporation wholly owned by Hext which ginned and marketed the cotton, Harlingen Compress Co. (Harlingen), a warehouse company which stored the cotton, and Marshall & Marshall (Marshall), a cotton brokerage firm through whom the cotton was marketed. A default judgment was entered against Hext and the Gin Co., both of whom were insolvent. After trial to the court, the District Judge, based on stipulated facts, depositions, and oral testimony, found Harlingen and Marshall liable to the United States and entered judgment against them in the amount of $15,650.13, plus interest, from which Harlingen and Marshall appeal. For reasons hereinafter stated we reverse the judgment of the trial court. . . .

The Farmers Home Administration (FHA) is an agency of the United States Department of Agriculture which, among other things, engages in the financing of farming operations as authorized by the Bankhead-Jones Farm Tenant Act [7 U.S.C. §§1941-1947]. In 1961-62 the FHA loaned Walter A. Hext, a cotton farmer, a total of $38,720.00 to finance his farming operations for 1962. In order to provide security for the loan, Hext granted a chattel mortgage on his forthcoming cotton crop to the FHA. The mortgage was duly recorded. Hext, as the FHA knew when it made the loan, in addition to being a cotton farmer, was also in the cotton ginning business as the sole owner of the W. A. Hext and Sons Gin Co., Inc. The FHA was aware when it financed Hext's cotton crop that, after harvesting, the cotton would be ginned and marketed by Hext through his own ginning company. The Gin Co., in addition to processing the cotton grown by Hext, also ginned and marketed cotton produced by a number of other farmers in the area.

After ginning, the Gin Co. transported the cotton to the Harlingen Compress Co., where the cotton was compressed and stored. Harlingen issued negotiable warehouse receipts covering each bale of cotton received. These negotiable receipts were retained by the Gin Co.[4]

In order to market the cotton the Gin Co. contracted with Marshall & Marshall, known in the cotton trade as a "spot broker" or "selling agent." At the Gin Co.'s direction Harlingen sent Marshall samples cut from each bale of cotton warehoused. Marshall displayed these samples, received offers to purchase from buyers who inspected the samples, and transmitted the offers to the Gin Co. The Gin Co. then told Marshall that the offers were either accepted or rejected, and Marshall communicated this information to the buyers. If an offer were accepted, Marshall prepared an invoice and draft and sent them to the Gin Co. The Gin Co. then forwarded the invoice, draft, and the warehouse receipts covering the cotton sold through banking channels to the buyer. When the draft was honored by the buyer the purchase price was credited to the Gin Co.'s account at its bank. In due course the buyers presented Harlingen with the warehouse receipts and shipping instructions, with which Harlin-

---

4. According to stipulation of the parties, some of the warehouse receipts covering the 578 bales in question were made out in the name of "W. A. Hext" and some were merely issued to the gin in blank. The testimony indicates that whether or not the receipts bore the name of the individual farmer depended upon the evidently fortuitous circumstance of whether or not the truck manifest covering the cotton delivered to the warehouse indicated the name of the farmer from whom the gin had received the cotton. In any event, the warehouse always delivered the receipts to the Gin Co., which in accordance with trade practice retained them until the cotton was sold to a buyer.

gen complied. Neither Harlingen nor Marshall had any actual knowledge of the FHA's security interest.

As the Gin Co. received payment for the cotton from the buyers, it in turn paid the various farmers who had produced it.[5] In the case of the 578 bales of cotton grown by Hext himself, however, the money received for the cotton remained in the Gin Co. account. At the end of the season Hext was unable to make full payment on the loan, defaulting in the amount of $18,139.07. . . .

[The United States brought suit against Marshall and Harlingen, alleging conversion. The trial court rendered judgment for the United States. On appeal, the appellate court held that federal rather than state law controlled and the applicable federal rule would be guided by the principles of the UCC.]

Having determined to look to the Uniform Commercial Code as a source for fashioning federal law applicable to the rights of the parties in this case, we now proceed to examine the facts and circumstances surrounding the transactions here involved in light of the Code's provisions.

The record establishes that the custom and practice in the cotton trade in Texas is for the individual cotton farmer to sell his cotton to a gin.[23] The gin in turn gins the cotton, arranges for storage pending sale, markets the cotton by placing samples with a selling agent, and sells the cotton to buyers who make offers to the gin after examining the samples. Warehousemen, selling agents and buyers all deal with the gin and not with the individual farmer, and indeed frequently do not even know the identity of the individual farmer who originally raised the cotton.[24] In the usual transaction the gin that deals with a farmer who has mortgaged his cotton to the FHA protects itself and satisfies the loan by issuing its checks in payment for the cotton jointly to the farmer and the FHA.[25]

---

5. Some of the farmers were paid for their cotton at the time it was delivered to the gin. In the case of most, however, payment was not effected until after the cotton was sold by the gin and the purchase price credited to the gin's account.

23. The record is unclear as to the precise nature of the typical transaction between the farmer and the gin. Evidently the farmer is sometimes paid outright for his cotton at the time he delivers it to the gin. Perhaps more frequently, payment by the gin to the farmer is not made until after the cotton is marketed. The farmer may or may not be consulted as to the acceptability of a particular offer to buy the cotton. In any event, the farmers apparently permit the gins to warehouse, market, and sell the cotton, and to keep possession of the negotiable warehouse receipts evidencing the cotton, pending sale. All parties appear to deal with the transaction between the farmer and the gin as a sale to the gin. Indeed, the Government in its complaint in the instant case alleged that Hext individually *sold* the cotton here in question to the Gin Co. . . .

24. Each bale of cotton ginned is given a tag number by the gin. The warehousemen and others deal with the gin and identify the cotton by this tag number and by the warehouse receipt number given each bale by the warehouse. The gin appears to be the only party who has an accurate record of which bale comes from which farmer. There was testimony on behalf of Harlingen that it knew the name of the individual farmer only about 40% of the time, and then only because the truck manifest pursuant to which the cotton was delivered to the warehouse by the gin happened to list some farmers' names.

25. As a matter of practice, the FHA further protects its security by sending each season to the gins in the area a list of the farmers in whose crops it holds a security interest. As the trial judge observed, in the instant case this protection was of no value to the FHA because the cotton it financed on this occasion was raised by the gin operator himself.

As the trial judge astutely noted, the problem in the instant case arose because of the fact that Hext, the farmer to whom the FHA provided financing, also operated his own gin company, and rather than transferring payment received by the Gin Co. for the 578 bales of cotton raised by him individually to the Government at the time the cotton was sold, he simply waited until the end of the season and at that time paid the Government the amount then remaining in the Gin Co. account. As related previously, the FHA knew when it loaned money to Hext that Hext operated a gin, and intended to gin his own cotton therein and market it just as he did the cotton received from other farmers, i.e., through the Gin Co.

[The court quotes UCC 9-306(2).]

The trial judge held as a matter of law that the Government's action vis-à-vis Hext did not amount to consent to sale of the mortgaged cotton in the manner here accomplished. Appellants urge that this determination was error. However, assuming *arguendo* that the holding of no consent was correct, it is apparent that in terms of UCC 9-306(2) the sale was not "authorized" by the secured party so as to terminate the security interest in the cotton. Thus, unless some other section of Article 9 "otherwise provides," the Government's security interest continued after the cotton was sold by the Gin Co. . . .

[The court quotes UCC 9-307(1) and 1-201(9).]

Under the UCC 1-201 definition, it is clear that the Gin Co. was in the business of selling cotton and that the buyers of the cotton in question here were buyers in the ordinary course of business. Nor is there any doubt that ordinarily ginned cotton is in the category of "farm products" referred to by UCC 9-307(1). However, in order for the FHA's security interest to continue in the cotton by virtue of the exception from UCC 9-307(1) pertaining to buyers of farm products, the farm products must be bought "from a person engaged in farming operations."[29]

In our view, the record establishes that the buyers of the cotton here involved bought from the Gin Co., and not from Hext himself. They did not therefore purchase from a person engaged in farming operations within the meaning of UCC 9-307(1).[30] It is true that Hext himself as the grower of the

29. The exception from the effects of ordinary course buying under UCC 9-307(1) for persons who buy from farmers has been criticized as unwarranted on the ground that no reasonable basis exists for treating modern agricultural operations differently from other types of businesses. See Comment, "Farm Products" under the UCC—Is a Special Classification Desirable?, 47 Texas L. Rev. 309 (1969); Coogan & Mays, Crop Financing and Article 9: A Dialogue with Particular Emphasis on the Problems of Florida Citrus Crop Financing, 22 U. Miami L. Rev. 13, 18-23 (1967); 2 G. Gilmore, Security Interests in Personal Property §26.10, at 707, §26.11, at 714 (1965). While there would appear to be considerable merit to the critics' position, no state has yet amended its Code to remove the Farm Products exemption from UCC 9-307(1). The preference generally given to agricultural financers is thus still universally accepted in the operation of the commercial law of secured transactions. The Review Committee for Article 9 of the Uniform Commercial Code has similarly questioned the soundness of the Farm Products exemption and recommended its removal from the Code as an optional amendment. The Permanent Editorial Board, however, deleted the Committee's recommendation. See Final Report, Appendix, at 208-209.

30. Indeed, the cotton may not even be a farm product since in order to be such, under UCC 9-109(3) it must be "in the possession of a debtor engaged in raising . . . or other farming

cotton was engaged in farming operations, was at the same time the sole owner of the Gin Co., and for other purposes might thus be regarded as the alter ego of the Gin Co. From the point of view of the buyers, however, in light of the general trade practice of buyers in dealing with the gins as the owners of the cotton being marketed, we do not think that the buyers here can be regarded as buying from a person engaged in farming operations when they purchased cotton from the W. A. Hext and Sons Gin Co., Inc.

Similarly, Marshall and Harlingen, although not buyers, dealt in the ordinary course of their businesses with gin companies and not with individual farmers. To the extent that they were dealing with Hext personally here, they were dealing with him qua gin owner, and not qua farmer. Nevertheless, as will be seen, their liability for conversion depends upon whether or not the actual buyers of the cotton took subject to the security interest under UCC 9-306(2) or free of the security interest under UCC 9-307(1).

Even though a cotton buyer purchases in the ordinary course of business from a gin, which is in the business of selling cotton (and not engaged in farming operations), the buyer would not ordinarily take free of a security interest in the cotton created by a farmer who had sold the cotton to the gin. UCC 9-307(1) requires that in order for the buyer to purchase unencumbered by such a prior lien, the security interest in question must have been *"created by his seller."* Thus, the fact that mortgaged cotton is sold by a farmer-debtor to a gin and then by the gin in the ordinary course of business to a buyer, does not, in the normal transaction, extinguish the security interest. But in the instant case Hext, the farmer who created the security interest, was the sole owner of the Gin Co. which sold the cotton to the buyer, *and this state of affairs was known to the secured party at the time the security interest was created.*

We think this situation is directly analogous to one where a secured party takes a security interest in goods purchased by the debtor as consumer goods or equipment, knowing the debtor to be in the business of selling goods of that kind, and the debtor then puts the goods in his inventory and sells them to a buyer in ordinary course. Professor Gilmore has suggested that in such a situation the buyer should take free of the security interest under the provisions of UCC 9-307(1).[33] We agree. In the instant case, the FHA took a security interest in goods (the 578 bales of cotton) as farm products, knowing that the debtor had the capability of transferring them in the category of inventory and selling them in the ordinary course of his gin business. The buyers of the cotton thus took free of the security interest and could not themselves be sued by the Government for conversion.[34] This conclusion in turn determines the issue of

---

operations." The Gin Co., not Hext individually, was in possession of the negotiable warehouse receipts evidencing the cotton and the gin was not engaged in farming operations.

33. [G. Gilmore, 2 Security Interests in Personal Property, §26.8, at 699-700 (1965).]

34. The same result would obtain under Article 7 of the Code if the transactions here be viewed as involving the purchase of negotiable documents of title (warehouse receipts) rather than the purchase of the cotton itself. See UCC 9-309. Article 7, in UCC 7-503(1), requires that the holder of a negotiable warehouse receipt obtains "no right in goods against a person who before issuance of the [receipt] had . . . a perfected security interest in them" unless the secured party

whether Marshall and Harlingen who dealt with the cotton as intermediaries between the Gin Co. and the buyers can be liable for conversion.

Section 233(1) of the Restatement (Second) of Torts, cited to us by the Government as authority to be followed in determining the federal rule of conversion applicable to this case, provides: ". . . one who as agent or servant of a third person disposes of chattel *to one not entitled to its immediate possession* in consummation of a transaction negotiated by the agent or servant, is subject to liability for a conversion to another who, as against his principal or master, is entitled to the immediate possession of the chattel." (Emphasis supplied). Ac-

---

either (a) entrusted the goods "to the bailor or his nominee with actual or apparent authority to . . . store" them or with power of disposition under UCC 9-307; or (b) "acquiesced in the procurement by the bailor or his nominee of any document of title." Under this section it is clear that in the circumstances of the instant case the cotton was entrusted to the possession of Hext (the bailor) and that he had apparent authority to store the cotton with Harlingen. Further, as we have held supra, Hext had power of disposition of the cotton under UCC 9-307(1). As Professor Gilmore has pointed out: "The cross reference to §9-307 [in §7-503(1)] means . . . that there is nothing a secured party can do to protect himself against the contingency of a fraudulently procured document with respect to collateral which is inventory held by a debtor for sale . . . (G. Gilmore, 2 Security Interests in Personal Property §25.4, at 666 (1965).)

Finally, under UCC 7-503(1)(b) it is clear that the Government must in this case be found to have "acquiesced" in the procurement of the warehouse receipts by Hext. As Comment 1 to UCC 7-503 states: "A . . . mortgagor [cannot] defeat any rights of a . . . mortgagee which have been perfected under the local law merely by wrongfully shipping or storing a portion of the crop or other goods. However, 'acquiescence' by the [mortgagee] does not require active consent under subsection (1)(b) and knowledge of the likelihood of storage or shipment with no objection or effort to control it is sufficient to defeat his rights as against one who takes by 'due' negotiation of a negotiable document." In the circumstances here, it simply could not be credibly maintained that the Government had no knowledge of the likelihood that the cotton would be stored after harvesting. For the reasons indicated above, under Article 7 the buyers of the negotiable warehouse receipts evidencing the cotton here in question clearly would be held entitled to possession of the cotton as against a prior secured party. For an indication that a contrary result would obtain if the warehouse receipts in question had been non-negotiable, see Funk, Trust Receipt vs. Warehouse Receipt—Which Prevails When They Cover the Same Goods, 19 Bus. Law. 627 (1964); compare, Lofton v. Mooney, 452 S.W.2d 617 (Ky. 1970); see generally Annot., 21 A.L.R.2d 1339 (1968). Since the buyers here were entitled to immediate possession by virtue of the negotiation to them of the warehouse receipts, Marshall could not be liable as a converter for in good faith facilitating the transfer to them. See text, infra. However, the same reasoning would not necessarily apply to Harlingen who, after all, was the issuer of the negotiable warehouse receipts by virtue of which the buyers were entitled to priority over the Government's security interest. Nevertheless, Harlingen is otherwise protected from conversion liability by UCC 7-404 which provides:

> A bailee who in good faith including observance of reasonable commercial standards has received goods and delivered or otherwise disposed of them according to the terms of the document of title or pursuant to this Article is not liable therefor. This rule applies even though the person from whom he received the goods had no authority to procure the document or to dispose of the goods and even though the person to whom he delivered the goods had no authority to receive them.

As the Comment to UCC 7-404 explains: "The section states explicitly what is perhaps an implication from the old acts that the common law rule of 'innocent conversion' by unauthorized 'intermeddling' with another's property is inapplicable to the operations of commercial carriers and warehousemen, who in good faith and with reasonable observance of commercial standards perform obligations which they have assumed and which generally they are under a legal compulsion to assume."

cepting this as an authoritative statement of the law (and none of the other authorities cited by the parties are to the contrary), it is at once apparent that Harlingen and Marshall, to the extent they acted, in good faith and without actual knowledge of the Government's interest, as agents of the Gin Co. by facilitating the sale of the cotton to the buyers, cannot be liable as converters since the cotton was not transferred "to one not entitled to its immediate possession." Rather, since the buyers took free of the Government's security interest under UCC 9-307(1), they were entitled to immediate possession, and the acts of Harlingen and Marshall in facilitating the transfer to them were thus not tortious. The Government thus has no valid claim against appellants Harlingen and Marshall. The judgment of the District Court must therefore be reversed.

NOTES & QUESTIONS

1. *Agricultural lenders.* "The chief proponent of the present rule [in UCC 9-307(1)] preserving the security interest in farm products is the federal government and it fought the committee's efforts [Review Committee for Article 9] to make the change. The federal government always has an ace to play in these struggles by threatening to enact its own legislation to give it what it deems desirable. Much farm credit, perhaps the majority of it, is supplied by the federal government, and an alternative threat is to withhold this credit if the climate for lending is unfavorable." Hawkland, The Proposed Amendment to Article 9 of the UCC—Part I: Financing the Farmer, 76 Com. L.J. 416, 420 (1971).

Among the federal agencies active in agricultural finance are:

(a) Farmers Home Administration (FHA), an agency of the Department of Agriculture, which makes and insures loans to farmers and ranchers pursuant to the terms of the Consolidated Farm & Rural Development Act, 7 U.S.C. §§1921-1996 (1982).

(b) Commodity Credit Corporation (CCC), an agency and instrumentality within the Department of Agriculture, which makes loans for price support, farm storage, warehouse storage, and farm facilities. 15 U.S.C. §§714-714p (1982).

(c) Federal intermediate credit banks, part of the federal farm credit system, which make funds available to production credit associations (PCAs), cooperatives owned by the farmers, which in turn make operating loans to members. 12 U.S.C. §§2001-2260 (1982) (see especially §§2071-2079).

2. *Law applicable to federal agriculture loans.* In United States v. Crittenden, 440 U.S. 715, 26 UCC Rep. 1 (1979) (usually known by the name of the companion case, United States v. Kimbell Foods, Inc.), the Supreme Court held that federal law governed priority between the FHA and a party claiming a mechanic's lien for repairs to the tractor securing the FHA loan. The

court went on to hold, however, that the content of the federal priority rule should be taken from state law because there was no need to protect federal interests by a national rule. The court noted that the federal regulations governing FHA lending activities did not expressly provide a priority rule. On remand, the Fifth Circuit held that the mechanic's lien had priority under Georgia's mechanic's lien statute and UCC 9-310. 600 F.2d 478, 27 UCC Rep. 298 (5th Cir. 1979).

3. *Documents of title.* In Chapter 10 we examine in greater detail the law governing documents of title. Note here that the use of negotiable documents permits buyers to deal with the paper rather than the cotton itself. The buyers may resell the cotton by negotiating the document or they may borrow using the document as collateral by delivering it to the secured party. UCC Article 7, Part 5, provides rules on transfer and negotiation of documents of title. For agricultural goods stored prior to shipment in interstate commerce, see United States Warehouse Act, 7 U.S.C. §§241-372 (1982).

Problem 8-9. Debtor, a cotton farmer, also owns and operates a cotton gin under the name of Cotton Gin Company where he gins his own cotton and that of his neighbors. With a loan from Local Bank, Debtor purchases furniture to be used in an office in Debtor's home, where he operates the company and keeps his farm records. To secure repayment of the loan Debtor grants Local Bank a security interest in the furniture. What steps should Local Bank take to perfect its security interest? See UCC 9-303, 9-302, 9-401, 9-402, 9-107, 9-109.

Problem 8-10. Rancher grants Bank a security interest in his cattle to secure repayment of a loan. The security agreement prohibits Rancher from selling the cattle without the Bank's prior written consent. Four times in a three-year period Rancher sells some of his cattle without asking for the written consent but with the knowledge of the Bank. Rancher then sells some cattle to Dealer, who in turn sells them to Meatpacker. Dealer fails to pay for the cattle and Rancher defaults on his bank loan. Bank seeks to replevy the cattle in the hands of Meatpacker. What arguments can you make on behalf of Meatpacker? Is Meatpacker's case stronger if you can show that neither Bank nor any other local financer insists on written consents? See UCC 9-306, 9-307(1), 9-301(1)(c).

Problem 8-11. Farmer sells wool to Wool Co. and retains a security interest in the wool to secure the purchase price. The security interest is perfected by filing. Without Farmer's knowledge Wool Co. warehouses the wool and receives a nonnegotiable warehouse receipt issued in the name of Lender. Wool Co. gives the receipt to Lender to secure a loan from Lender. Neither Lender nor the warehouseman knows of Farmer's security interest. Wool Co.

then defaults on both loans. Between Farmer and Lender who has prior claim to the wool? See UCC 9-304, 9-305, 9-312, 7-502, 7-503, 7-504.

C.   THE OVERLAP OF ARTICLES 2 AND 9

In addition to Article 9 security interests, the Code provides for security interests in other articles. These security interests arise by operation of the statute and do not involve the voluntary secured financing we have been studying in the last six chapters. Article 4, for example, provides that if a bank allows a customer to draw against an item presented for collection the bank will have a security interest in the item until it is paid (UCC 4-208). Article 2 refers explicitly to security interests in UCC 2-505 and 2-711(3), and other sections of Article 2 give sellers and buyers rights and obligations functionally similar to those created in Article 9.

The provisions of Article 9 apply to these special security interests but are subject to special exceptions. UCC 4-208(3) makes the bank's interest subject to the provisions of Article 9 except that no security agreement is necessary to make the interest enforceable, no filing is necessary to perfect the interest, and the interest has priority over conflicting security interests in the item and its proceeds.

How Article 2 security interests relate to Article 9, however, poses more difficult problems. UCC 9-113 subjects security interests "arising solely under [Article 2]" to the provisions of Article 9 except that no security agreement is necessary, no filing is required, and the default provisions of Article 2 apply. As a result, holders of these interests are subject to the priority rules of Article 9 when their claims conflict with those of other parties.

UCC 9-113 presents two major difficulties: how to identify security interests that arise solely under Article 2 and how to apply the priority provisions to competing claims. The section does offer some help with the identification of Article 2 security interests. The section's text in effect limits these interests to those where the buyer "does not have or does not lawfully obtain possession of the goods." The comments to UCC 9-113 suggest some of the Article 2 provisions the draftsmen had in mind. Determining priorities, however, requires close examination of the language of Article 2.

The following materials examine the rights of a seller to reclaim goods for which he has not been paid. UCC 2-702(2) codifies the reclamation rights of a seller who has extended unsecured credit to an insolvent buyer. UCC 2-702(3), however, subjects this right to the claims of specified third parties and provides a cross-reference to UCC 2-403, which itself is a priority provision. If this reclamation right is an Article 2 security interest there is an obvious problem:

how to reconcile the Article 2 priority provisions with the comparable provisions in Article 9 that would be applicable because of UCC 9-113.

The same questions arise when a seller delivers goods to a buyer who does not pay on delivery as agreed. UCC 2-507(2) provides that the buyer's right to retain or dispose of the goods is conditional on making the payment due. Is the seller's right to reclaim the goods an Article 2 security interest? Will the seller's right to reclaim be cut off by third party claimants? UCC 2-507 gives even less guidance than UCC 2-702.

JACKSON & PETERS, QUEST FOR UNCERTAINTY: A PROPOSAL FOR FLEXIBLE RESOLUTION OF INHERENT CONFLICTS BETWEEN ARTICLE 2 AND ARTICLE 9 OF THE UNIFORM COMMERCIAL CODE
87 Yale L.J. 907, 925-930 (1978)

. . . [If] the fraudulent sale creates a security interest "arising solely under" Article 2, however, the authority to reclaim under Article 2 may be undermined by Article 9. If section 9-113 applies in full force once the buyer is in possession, then his possession is irreversible, because the seller's security interest is invalid without a written security agreement and is subject to Article 9 rules on default and liquidation of contract goods now characterized as collateral.

Why should an interest that is never characterized by Article 2 as creating a "security interest" fall into the snares of section 9-113? The definition of a security interest in Article 1 is expansive. It encompasses any "interest in personal property . . . which secures payment or performance of an obligation," without regard to consensual designation or distinguishing features of form. As noted earlier, the common law seller's lien and right of stoppage in transit, neither of which is labeled a "security interest" in Article 2, do fall within section 9-113. The conditional sale, although denominated a security interest in section 2-401, is a normal Article 9 security interest rather than one "arising solely under" Article 2. Although the reference to a security interest in section 2-505(1), concerning documentary reservations, and in section 2-711(3), concerning buyers' possessory liens, happens to fit both Article 2 and Article 9, this identity of language is surely fortuitous. To the extent that reclamation rights are analogous to seller's liens, the fact that Article 2 does not characterize them as "security interests" cannot insulate them from section 9-113. The drafting pattern of Article 2 emphasizes the consequences rather than the labeling of commercial relationships. [A seller] cannot be spared the travails of Article 9 simply because sections 2-507 and 2-702 speak to rights rather than to security interests.

Justice Braucher offers two other reasons for differentiating reclamation rights from security interests: "First, a right to rescind is a right to undo the transaction—to reclaim the goods as a substitute for the price—not a right to 'secure' payment of the price as required by the definition of 'security interest'; under section 2-702(3), successful reclamation 'excludes all other remedies.' Second, any such security interest is not the result of a transaction 'intended to create a security interest' and is not 'created by contract' within the meaning of section 9-102, which defines the scope of Article Nine on secured transactions." The second suggestion seems plainly wrong: if a security interest arises "solely" under Article 2, by definition it is *not* the result of a transaction "intended to create a security interest," nor is it "created by contract." Section 9-113 is an alternate route into Article 9, which bypasses the requirements of section 9-102. By necessary implication, section 9-102 is superseded whenever section 9-113 applies.

The proposition that a right to rescind cannot be a security interest is more plausible, but it, too, is ultimately unpersuasive. It is not inconsistent with the idea of a security interest, as section 9-505 recognizes that one remedy for a secured party may be the return and retention of secured property. Moreover, as section 9-113(c) expressly acknowledges, the rights upon default preserved by Article 2 differ from the constellation of rights existing in Article 9. In the transactions to which section 9-113 applies, where the seller's right is to withhold delivery or to stop goods in transit or to retain control through documents, the seller's remedy is to retain or to retrieve the contract goods. It is true that in all of these cases the seller's remedy of retention is not doctrinally, although it may be practically, his exclusive remedy. Yet in every respect other than exclusivity, the seller's right to reclaim under a cash sale or a fraudulent sale closely resembles the interests that are otherwise characterized as security interests "arising solely" under Article 2 and are incorporated in Article 9 through section 9-113. And whatever may be obscure about section 9-113, it does manifest an intention to cover at least some transactions in which some buyers temporarily receive possession, of which they may then be divested.

The critical language in section 9-113 is contained in the statement that there may be security interests arising solely under Article 2 in which the debtor "does not have or does not lawfully obtain possession of the goods." Under either alternative, the hybrid security interest is valid without the normal security agreement and is perfected without a financing statement. If, on the other hand, the debtor obtains unfettered possession, the normal Article 9 requirements for validation and perfection govern even under section 9-113. The seller reclaiming under section 2-507 or 2-702 appears to be a prime candidate to assert a claim that the buyer-debtor did not "lawfully obtain possession;" indeed, no other claim founded in Article 2 seems to come close. As Justice Braucher pointed out, a right of reclamation routinely arises as a result of behavior that is impliedly fraudulent, even though intent to deceive is not an express prerequisite of the seller's cause of action. "Unlawful" possession must refer principally to fraudulent conduct by the [buyers] of this world, since outright theft entitles [a buyer's supplier] to a claim in conversion rather than to a security interest.

STOWERS v. MAHON (IN RE SAMUELS & CO., INC.)

510 F.2d 139, 16 UCC Rep. 577 (5th Cir. 1975), *rev'd*, 526 F.2d 1238, 18 UCC Rep. 545 (1976), *cert. denied*, 429 U.S. 834 (1976)

[The following facts are taken from the majority opinion of a three-judge panel. 510 F.2d at 143-144. On rehearing before the Fifth Circuit sitting en banc the majority of the circuit court adopted per curiam the dissenting opinion reproduced below.—Eds.]

[Samuels & Co., Inc., is a Texas meatpacking firm that purchases, processes, and packages meat and sells the meat within and without the State of Texas. Since 1963 Samuels' operations, including its cattle purchases, have been financed on a weekly basis by C.I.T. Corporation. To secure its financing, C.I.T. has properly perfected a lien on Samuels' assets, inventory and all after-acquired property, including livestock that is from time to time purchased for slaughter and processing.

From May 12 through May 23, 1969, the appellants, 15 cattle farmers, delivered their cattle to Samuels. Although the sellers did not receive payment for the sale simultaneously with delivery of the cattle, checks were subsequently issued to the sellers. On May 23, 1969, before these checks had been paid, C.I.T., believing itself to be insecure, refused to advance any more funds to Samuels for the operation of the packing plant. On that same day Samuels filed a petition in bankruptcy. Since C.I.T. refused to advance more funds, even though apparently aware that there were unpaid checks outstanding, the appellants' checks issued in payment for cattle were dishonored by the drawee bank.

Because of the fungible nature of the cattle, the beef has long since been butchered and processed and sold through the normal course of business. The proceeds from the cattle sales have been deposited with the trustee in bankruptcy pending the outcome of this litigation. The issues in this case concern the priority of interest in these proceeds between a creditor of the debtor, which holds a perfected security interest in the debtor's after-acquired property, and a seller of goods to the debtor. Since the sellers have not been paid, they claim a superior right to the deposited proceeds and argue that they are now entitled to payment out of these proceeds. The finance corporation, on the other hand, contends that the sellers are merely unsecured creditors of the bankrupt and are not entitled to a prior claim to the funds, and alternately that the finance corporation qualified as a good faith purchaser of the cattle and is therefore immune to the sellers' claims of nonpayment.]

GODBOLD, Circuit Judge (dissenting). . . . This case raises one primary question: under the Uniform Commercial Code as adopted in Texas, is the interest of an unpaid cash seller in goods already delivered to a buyer superior or subordinate to the interest of a holder of a perfected security interest in those same goods? In my opinion, under Article Nine, the perfected security interest is unquestionably superior to the interest of the seller. Moreover, the perfected lender is protected from the seller's claim by two independent and theoretically distinct Article Two provisions. My result is not the product of revealed truth, but rather of a meticulous and dispassionate reading of Articles Two and Nine, and an understanding that the Code is an integrated statute whose Articles and Sections overlap and flow into one another in an effort to encourage specific types of commercial behavior. The Code's overall plan, which typically favors good faith purchasers,[2] and which encourages notice filing of nonpossessory security interests in personalty through the imposition of stringent penalties for nonfiling, compels a finding that the perfected secured party here should prevail. . . .

I. RIGHTS UNDER UCC 2-403

My analysis begins with an examination of the relative rights of seller and secured party under UCC 2-403(1).

UCC 2-403 gives certain transferors power to pass greater title than they can themselves claim. UCC 2-403(1) gives good faith purchasers of even fraudulent buyers-transferors greater rights than the defrauded seller can assert. This harsh rule is designed to promote the greatest range of freedom possible to commercial vendors and purchasers.

The provision anticipates a situation where (1) a cash seller has delivered goods to a buyer who has paid by a check which is subsequently dishonored, UCC 2-403(1)(b), (c), and where (2) the defaulting buyer transfers title to a Code-defined "good faith purchaser." The interest of the good faith purchaser is protected *pro tanto* against the claims of the aggrieved seller. UCC 2-403(1); 2-403, Comment 1. The Code expressly recognizes the power of the defaulting buyer to transfer good title to such a purchaser even though the transfer is wrongful as against the seller. The buyer is granted the *power* to transfer good title despite the fact that under UCC 2-507 he lacks the *right* to do so.

The Code definition of "purchaser" is broad, and includes not only one taking by sale but also covers persons taking by gift or by voluntary mortgage, pledge or lien. UCC 1-201(32), (33). It is therefore broad enough to include an Article Nine secured party. UCC 1-201(37); 9-101, Comment; 9-102(1), (2). Thus, if C.I.T. holds a valid Article Nine security interest, it is by virtue of that status *also* a purchaser under UCC 2-403(1). . . .

---

2. See, e.g., UCC 2-403; 3-302, 3-305; 6-110; 7-501; 7-502; 8-301, 8-302; 9-307; 9-309.

While I shall discuss in detail infra, the implications of C.I.T.'s security interest under Article Nine and under other Article Two provisions, I here note that C.I.T. is the holder of a perfected Article Nine interest which extends to the goods claimed by the seller Stowers.

Attachment of an Article Nine interest takes place when (1) there is agreement that the interest attach to the collateral; (2) the secured party has given value; and (3) the debtor has rights in the collateral sufficient to permit attachment. UCC 9-204(1) [1972 UCC 9-203(1)].

(1) *The agreement:* In 1963, Samuels initially authorized C.I.T.'s lien in its after-acquired inventory. The agreement between these parties remained in effect throughout the period of delivery of Stowers' cattle to Samuels.

(2) *Value:* At the time of Stowers' delivery, Samuels' indebtedness to C.I.T. exceeded $1.8 million. This pre-existing indebtedness to the lender constituted "value" under the Code. UCC 1-201(44).

(3) *Rights in the collateral:* Finally, upon delivery, Samuels acquired rights in the cattle sufficient to allow attachment of C.I.T.'s lien. The fact that the holder of a voluntary lien—including an Article Nine interest—is a "purchaser" under the Code is of great significance to a proper understanding and resolution of this case under Article Two and Article Nine. The Code establishes that purchasers can take from a defaulting cash buyer, UCC 2-403(1). Lien creditors are included in the definition of purchasers, UCC 1-201(32), (33). A lien *is* an Article Nine interest, UCC 9-101, Comment; 9-102(2); 9-102, Comment. The existence of an Article Nine interest presupposes the debtor's having rights in the collateral sufficient to permit attachment, UCC 9-204(1) [see 1972 UCC 9-203(1)(c)]. Therefore, since a defaulting cash buyer has the power to transfer a security interest to a lien creditor, including an Article Nine secured party, the buyer's rights in the property, however marginal, must be sufficient to allow attachment of a lien. And this is true even if, *arguendo,* I were to agree that the cash seller is granted reclamation rights under Article Two. . . .

If the Article Nine secured party acted in good faith, it is prior under UCC 2-403(1) to an aggrieved seller. Under the facts before us, I think that C.I.T. acted in good faith. The Code good faith provision requires "honesty in fact," UCC 1-201(19), which, for Article Two purposes, is "expressly defined as . . . reasonable commercial standards of fair dealing." UCC 1-201, Comment 19; 2-103(1)(b). There is no evidence that C.I.T. acted in bad faith in its dealings with Samuels, or that Stowers' loss resulted from any breach of obligation by C.I.T. There is no claim that the 1963 security agreement was the product of bad faith. The lender's interest had been perfected and was of record for six years when Stowers' delivery to Samuels occurred. There is no suggestion that the $1.8 million debt owing from Samuels to C.I.T. was the result of bad faith or of a desire to defeat Stowers' $50,000 claim. There is no claim that C.I.T. exercised or was able to exercise control over Samuels' business operations. There is no evidence that C.I.T. authorized or ordered or suggested that Samuels dishonor Stowers' check. There is no contention that

C.I.T.'s refusal to extend credit on May 23, the date Samuels filed a voluntary petition in bankruptcy at a time when it owed C.I.T. more than $1.8 million, was violative of an obligatory future advance clause. The Code's good faith provision requires "honesty in fact," UCC 1-201(19); it hardly requires a secured party to continue financing a doomed business enterprise.

The majority deny that C.I.T. acted in good faith because, they claim, the lender had "intimate" knowledge of Samuels' business operations. The majority's source of information on the scope of C.I.T.'s knowledge is a little puzzling. The Referee in Bankruptcy found only that "C.I.T. knew or should have known of the manner by which the bankrupt bought livestock . . . on a grade and yield basis." . . . This factual finding was affirmed by the District Court which reversed the Referee and upheld C.I.T.'s priority over Stowers. . . . Neither the Referee nor the District Court found, nor have the parties alleged, that C.I.T.'s knowledge of Samuels' business extended to knowledge of the debtor's obligation to third party creditors.

However, even if evidence had established that C.I.T. knew of Samuels' nonpayment and of Stowers' claim, C.I.T.'s status as an Article Two good faith purchaser would be unaffected. Lack of knowledge of outstanding claims is necessary to the common law BFP, and is similarly expressly required in many Code BFP and priority provisions. See, e.g., UCC 3-302; 6-110; 8-301, 8-302; 9-301(1)(b) [but see 1972 UCC 9-301(1)(b)]. But the Code's definition of an Article Two good faith purchaser does not expressly or impliedly include lack of knowledge of third-party claims as an element. The detailed definition of the Article's counterpart of the common law BFP requires only honesty in fact, reasonable commercial behavior, fair dealing. And this describes precisely C.I.T.'s dealings with Samuels: during the period May 13-22—the time when the bulk of Stowers' cattle were delivered and the time of the issuance of the NSF checks—C.I.T.'s advances to Samuels totalled $1 million. The advances were curtailed on May 23 because of Samuels' taking voluntary bankruptcy at a time when its indebtedness to C.I.T. was enormous. The decision to terminate further funding was clearly reasonable. It was also fair, and honest, and, as the majority have failed to grasp, was not the cause of Stowers' suffering. As I note infra in my analysis of rights under Article Nine, the Sellers' loss was avoidable through perfection of their security interests in the cattle. If they had perfected, they would not only have been prior to C.I.T. as an Article Nine lender, UCC 9-312, but also protected against C.I.T. as an Article Two purchaser, UCC 9-201. As it happens, Stowers did not perfect. I believe the sellers cannot now be permitted to force an innocent, if prosperous, secured creditor to shoulder their loss for them.

II.   RIGHTS UNDER UCC 2-507

The majority opinion devotes much of its concentration and energy to an analysis of the sellers' "reclamation right" under UCC 2-507 and 2-702. Relying on an expansive reading of these Sections, the opinion concludes that a cash seller whose right to payment is frustrated through a check ultimately dishonored can "reclaim" proceeds of goods delivered to the buyer despite an interim third-party interest, and despite a year-long delay in seeking reclamation. I am unable to accept this reading of Code policy and requirements.

Although the Code expressly grants a credit seller the right and power to reclaim goods from a breaching buyer, the right is triggered only by specific and limited circumstances; it can be asserted only if an exacting procedure is followed; and the right can never be asserted to defeat the interests of certain third parties who have dealt with the defaulting buyer. UCC 2-702(2), (3). There is no Code Section expressly granting a similar reclamation right to a cash seller.

The seller's remedies upon breach are enumerated in UCC 2-703. These provisions do not include or suggest a right or power in a cash seller to recover goods already delivered to a breaching buyer. Nevertheless the courts have read a reclamation right into the Code. It is this judicially-confected right to reclaim goods in which the majority's reclamation analysis is grounded. However, the majority take the reclamation right beyond anything intimated by the Code or heretofore permitted by courts recognizing a cash seller's reclamation right.

The cash seller's right to reclaim has been drawn from the language of UCC 2-507(2) and UCC 2-507, Comment 3. I note, first, that the remedy granted by UCC 2-507(2) is one of seller against buyer, see In re Helms Veneer Corp., 287 F. Supp. 840 (W.D. Va. 1968). It does not concern rights of seller against third parties. UCC 2-507, Comment 3 explains that the seller's rights under UCC 2-507 must "conform with the policy set forth in the bona fide purchase section of this Article," i.e., with UCC 2-403. As I have noted above, under this provision the rights of an aggrieved cash seller are subordinated to those of the buyer's good-faith purchasers, including Article Nine lenders such as C.I.T. Thus, the Code provisions supporting a cash seller's reclamation right expressly preclude recovery by Stowers as against C.I.T. See UCC 2-507(2); 2-507, Comment 3; 2-702(2), (3). . . .

Moreover, those courts which have permitted reclamation under UCC 2-507 have invariably adhered to UCC 2-507, Comment 3's express requirement that demand for return be made within ten days after receipt by the buyer or else be lost. See [In re Helms Veneer Corp., supra] . . .

In the instant case, demand was not made within ten days or ten weeks; it came a full year after delivery to Samuels. The majority excuse this gross noncompliance by finding that the sellers' failure was the product of innocent error, and, in any event, was not required since the "purpose" of the demand rule—protection of purchasers of the delivered goods—was served through C.I.T.'s alleged intimate knowledge of Samuels' business operations.

The Code's ten-day provision is an absolute requirement. There is no exception in the Code Sections or Comments, express or implied, to the statutory period. I would be hesitant to read any extension into a statute of limitations clear and unambiguous on its face, and particularly unwilling to allow an extension some 36 times greater than the statutory maximum. My reluctance is all the greater where the right at issue is not granted by the Code but is rather the product of judicial interpretation of a Comment, which, whatever grant of power it may suggest, expressly limits that right to a ten-day life.

The spirit in which the rule was broken seems to me irrelevant. Even conceding that Stowers' noncompliance occurred in absolute good faith, it was nonetheless noncompliance. Mistake of law does not constitute excuse of mistake.

C.I.T.'s apocryphal intimate knowledge of Samuels' business operations is, I believe, also irrelevant to a determination of the validity of Stowers' claim. The majority find the purpose of the ten-day rule to be one of notice to third parties that a claim exists. I have somewhat greater difficulty than my brothers in pinpointing the purpose of the ten-day rule. But I am convinced that the goal is not one of protection or notice to third-party purchasers, for their rights are secure under the Code as against the aggrieved seller even if demand is timely made. UCC 2-507, Comment 3; 2-702(3). The Code does not condition the purchasers' rights on a lack of knowledge of the seller's interest. With or without knowledge, the purchaser rests secure. I am therefore forced to conclude that the ten-day rule serves some function other than notifying third-party takers, and, consequently, that even if C.I.T. knew of Stowers' claim, the sellers' obligation under the ten-day rule would not have been excused. And even if knowledge by the purchaser suspended the sellers' duty to make a timely demand, the record in this case is devoid of any hint that C.I.T. knew of Samuels' breach and Stowers' reclamation right.

Moreover, UCC 2-507 and 2-702 speak of a right to reclaim goods. Neither provision grants a right to go after proceeds of those goods. Where a right or interest in proceeds is recognized by the Code it is recognized expressly. See, e.g., UCC 9-306. The right granted by UCC 2-507 is narrowly defined. I am unwilling to imply an extension to such a short-lived and precisely drawn remedy.

Finally, even if there were a right to reclaim proceeds, even if the right had been timely exercised, and even if it could have been exercised despite the transfer of interest to C.I.T., Stowers would have taken subject to C.I.T.'s perfected Article Nine interest. See UCC 9-201, 9-301, 9-306, 9-312. See also my discussion of C.I.T.'s rights and interest under Article Nine, infra.

III. RIGHTS UNDER UCC 2-511

The majority opinion states that C.I.T.'s interest cannot be found superior to Stowers' because such a finding would violate UCC 2-511's prohibition on penalizing a seller for accepting as payment a check which is ultimately dishonored. I believe the majority have misconstrued the scope and significance of UCC 2-511.

Like UCC 2-507, UCC 2-511 concerns claims of the seller as against the buyer. See UCC 2-511(3), 2-511, Comment 4. On its face it does not affect the rights of third parties taking from the defaulting buyer. Moreover, and more important, the seller is not here "penalized" for taking an N.S.F. check. Such loss as Stowers suffered is the direct result of his failure to comply with Code provisions which, once followed—and regardless of Stowers' acceptance of Samuels' check—would have made his interest invulnerable to claims by C.I.T. See, e.g., UCC 9-107; 9-201; 9-301; 9-312(3), (4).

IV.   RIGHTS UNDER ARTICLE NINE

I am also unable to agree with the majority's conclusion that, under the Code, Stowers' interest is different from and greater than a security interest. Similarly, I disagree with the theory that by virtue of Stowers' power under Article Two, C.I.T.'s security interest is subject to defeat since it (1) could not attach because the debtor's rights in the collateral were too slight to permit attachment and (2) was subject to defeat even if it attached because a security interest collapses if the debtor's right to the property is extinguished. The majority's result is achieved only by ignoring or circumventing the plain meaning of Article Nine and Article Two.

Prior to the enactment of the Uniform Commercial Code, seller and buyer could agree that, despite buyer's possession, title to goods sold was to remain in the seller until he was paid. Such a reservation of title under the "cash sale" doctrine would defeat not only a claim to the goods by the defaulting buyer, but also the claims of lien creditors of the buyer, for the buyer's naked possession could give rise to no interest to which a lien could attach.

However, the U.C.C. specifically limits the seller's ability to reserve title once he has voluntarily surrendered possession to the buyer: "Any retention or reservation by the seller of the title (property) in goods shipped or delivered to the buyer is limited in effect to a reservation of a security interest." UCC 2-401(1). See also UCC 1-201(37). The drafters noted the theory behind this provision: "Article [Two] deals with the issues between seller and buyer in terms of step by step performance or non-performance under the contract for sale and not in terms of whether or not 'title' to the goods has passed." UCC 2-401, Comment 1.

The majority opinion interprets UCC 2-401(1) as applying only to "credit" sales, and of no effect where the parties have contracted a "cash" sale. However, the Code provision speaks of "any reservation of title." It does not on its face apply solely to credit sales. There is no authority under the Code for the majority's restrictive interpretation. Numerous courts have, in fact, applied UCC 2-401 to cash sales. . . . I have been unable to find even one case suggesting that UCC 2-401 applies only to credit sales.

If the majority were correct, the Section would be merely definitional, for a credit sale is but a sales transaction in which the seller reserves a security interest. However, UCC 2-401 is not definitional. It is operational and concerns the effect of transfer of possession under a sales contract upon any reservation of title. Neither law nor logic leads me to believe that UCC 2-401 is correctly interpreted to exclude cash sales.

The majority also suggests that Stowers' interest cannot be characterized as a security interest subject to Article Nine requirements and priorities since, the majority conclude, such interests must be "consensual." While it is true that many interests governed by Article Nine are consensual, UCC 9-102; 9-102, Comment, the Code clearly subjects Article Two security interests arising not by consent but by operation of law to Article Nine. See UCC 2-401(1); 9-113; 9-113, Comment 2. See also UCC 2-326; 9-114; 9-102, Comment 1.

Since Stowers' interest upon delivery of the cattle to Samuels was limited to a security interest subject to Article Nine, UCC 2-401(1); 9-113, the validity of C.I.T.'s Article Nine interest becomes crucial. If C.I.T. is the holder of a perfected Article Nine interest in the collateral claimed by Stowers through its unperfected UCC 2-401 interest, C.I.T.'s interest will prevail over Stowers', UCC 9-312(5).

The majority assert that C.I.T. cannot claim an interest in the cattle because Samuels' interest was too slight to permit attachment. See UCC 9-204(1) [1972 UCC 9-203(1)(c)]. As I noted in my discussion of rights under UCC 2-403, this argument ignores the significance of UCC 2-403(1) and UCC 1-201(32), (33). The Code anticipates a situation where the interest of an unpaid cash seller who has delivered goods to a breaching buyer is subordinated to the interest of "purchasers" of the buyer. Lien creditors are included in the definition of "purchasers;" in order that there *be* lien creditors, the buyer's interest must be great enough to allow attachment. Therefore, however Samuels' interest upon delivery of the cattle is defined, and however slight or tenuous or marginal it was, it was necessarily great enough to permit attachment of a lien, including C.I.T.'s Article Nine interest.

The majority find that even if attachment occurred, C.I.T.'s interest would be defeated by Stowers' reclamation. The theory behind this argument is that the rights of the Article Nine secured party are at best coextensive with the rights of the debtor; if the debtor loses his rights, the security interest too is lost.

Upon nonpayment Samuels lost the right to retain or dispose of the property, but the Code recognizes that the breaching buyer had the power to encumber, despite nonpayment, so long as he retained possession. UCC 2-403(1); 1-201(32), (33). In the instant case, this power arose as a result of Stowers' delivery, and it did not terminate while the goods remained in Samuels' hands. The whole point of Article Nine is the continuity of perfected security interests *once they have properly attached*, despite subsequent loss of control or possession of the collateral by the debtor. UCC 9-201. Article Nine does not except an unpaid cash seller from this overall plan. In fact it specifically provides a means for him to perfect and become prior to previous perfected security interests. UCC 9-312(3), (4).

To hold that a reclaiming seller is given the power to sweep away a security interest which was able to attach only as a direct and Code-approved result of his voluntary act of delivery to the buyer would require ignoring the meaning and interplay of Article Two and Article Nine. Article Two recognizes the continuous vitality and priority of an Article Nine interest over the rights of an aggrieved seller. See UCC 2-403(1); 2-507, Comment 3; 2-702(3). It would be error to believe that a proper analysis of Article Nine could require the extinction of an identical Article Nine interest in the very circumstances specified by Article Two as triggering the priority of lienor over seller. See UCC 2-403(1); 2-507(2); 2-507, Comment 3; 2-702(2), (3); 9-102; 9-107(a); 9-312(3), (4).

Any seeming unfairness to Stowers resulting from the Code's operation is illusory, for the sellers could have protected their interests, even as against C.I.T.'s prior perfected interest, if they had merely complied with the U.C.C.'s purchase-money provisions. UCC 9-107, 9-312(3), (4). The Code favors purchase-money financing, and encourages it by granting to a seller of goods the power to defeat prior liens. The seller at most need only (1) file a financing statement and (2) notify the prior secured party of its interest before delivery of the new inventory. The procedure is not unduly complex or cumbersome. But whether cumbersome or not, a lender who chooses to ignore its provisions takes a calculated risk that a loss will result.

In the instant case Stowers did not utilize UCC 9-312's purchase-money provision. The sellers never perfected. Thus, in a competition with a perfected secured party they are subordinated, and, in this case, lose the whole of their interests. See UCC 9-201, 9-301, 9-312(5).

NOTES & QUESTIONS

1. *Legislative response.* Legislatures at both the federal and state levels ultimately overturned the result in the *Samuels* case. Congress amended the Packers & Stockyards Act, 7 U.S.C. §196 (1982), to create a trust for "cash sellers":

> (b) All livestock purchased by a packer in cash sales, and all inventories of, or receivables or proceeds from meat, meat food products, or livestock products derived therefrom, shall be held by such packer in trust for the benefit of all unpaid cash sellers of such livestock until full payment has been received by such unpaid sellers. . . . Payment shall not be considered to have been made if the seller receives a payment instrument which is dishonored. . . .
>
> (c) For the purpose of this section, a cash sale means a sale in which the seller does not expressly extend credit to the buyer.

The Texas legislature also adopted the following provision (Agric. Code §148.026):

> (a) To secure all or part of the sales price, a person who sells cattle, sheep, goats, or hogs for slaughter has a lien on each animal sold and on the carcass of

the animal, products from the animal, and proceeds from the sale of the animal, its carcass, or its products.

(b) A lien under this section is attached and perfected on delivery of the livestock to the purchaser without further action. The lien continues as to the animal, its carcass, its products, and the proceeds of any sale without regard to possession by the party entitled to the lien.

See generally Tex. Agric. Code Ann. §148.021-148.028 (Vernon 1982). Does this legislative response suggest that the attempt to unify all security devices and priority rules goes too far in that it ignores different financing patterns or "transaction-types"?

2. *Time within which seller must act.* A supplier who sells on unsecured credit may demand the return of the goods sold within the time limits set out in UCC 2-702(2) ("within ten days after [buyer receives goods]" or no limit if the buyer made a written misrepresentation of solvency to the seller within three months of delivery). If the insolvent buyer declares bankruptcy BC 546(c) requires the unpaid seller to make a written demand "before ten days after receipt." In bankruptcy there is no exception when the buyer has made a written misrepresentation of solvency, although the seller's claim may not be discharged by the bankruptcy proceeding because of the misrepresentation. BC 523(a)(2).

A "cash" seller may reclaim the goods from his buyer under UCC 2-507(2), but that provision does not include a specific time limit. Comment 3 states that the ten-day limit of UCC 2-702(2) also applies to the cash seller. Most courts have agreed with the comment. Compare Szabo v. Vinton Motors, Inc., 630 F.2d 1, 29 UCC Rep. 737 (1st Cir. 1980) (demand by seller who took check must be made within ten days after buyer received the goods rather than ten days after learning that the check had been dishonored) with Burk v. Emmick, 637 F.2d 1172, 29 UCC Rep. 1489 (8th Cir. 1980) (as between seller and buyer ten-day period does not apply).

3. *Reclaiming seller's rights in bankruptcy.* A supplier who sold goods on unsecured credit will be able to reclaim the goods from a bankrupt buyer if the seller complies with BC 546(c). For an argument, which most courts have found unpersuasive, that this bankruptcy provision is not exclusive, see Mann & Phillips, Section 546(c) of the Bankruptcy Reform Act: An Imperfect Resolution of the Conflict Between the Reclaiming Seller and the Bankruptcy Trustee, 54 Am. Bankr. L.J. 239 (1980).

What are the rights of the "cash" seller in bankruptcy proceedings? Does BC 546(c) also apply to this seller? If not, will the buyer's trustee be able to avoid the seller's claim under the strong-arm clause of BC 544(a) or under the avoidance power of BC 545 as a statutory lien?

Problem 8-12. Several years after the prototype transaction set out in Chapter 3, Apex agrees to purchase from ABM a glue-drying heating element that was made to be bolted to the bookbinder purchased in the prototype. ABM delivers the heating element on June 1. Apex, in accordance with the sales agreement, mails a check for the purchase price to ABM on delivery of the heating element to Apex. Apex draws the check on its general account with Austin State Bank, which still has a security interest in the bookbinder. Because there are insufficient funds in the account the bank dishonors the check when it is presented for payment on June 8. ABM is informed of the dishonor on June 12. May ABM reclaim the heating element? Will ABM have priority to the attachment over the bank's claim to the same attachment as an accession to the bookbinder covered by the original security agreement? If Apex files a petition in bankruptcy on June 14, who will have the priority in the heating element?

Problem 8-13. Assume that Austin State Bank agrees to finance only 80 percent of the cost of the bookbinder. ABM agrees, nevertheless, to give Apex 90 days' unsecured credit for the remainder of the purchase price but before agreeing has checked with Dun & Bradstreet, which informed ABM that Apex had had some cash flow problems in the last year because of difficulties in expanding the readership of *Texas Commerce*. ABM also examined an unaudited balance sheet and income statement for Apex's financial year ending September 30, 1980. These documents showed a ratio of current assets to current liabilities of 1:2, shareholders' equity of $25,000, and a net profit after taxes of $10,000. As in the prototype, ABM delivers the bookbinder to Apex on January 19.

(a) On January 29 the president of Apex informs ABM by telephone that a creditor had just obtained a judgment for $45,000, which Apex is unable to satisfy. The president indicates that Apex is contemplating a reorganization under the Bankruptcy Code. May ABM reclaim the bookbinder? What if the president called on February 5?

(b) Assume that on January 27 the judgment creditor has the sheriff levy execution on the bookbinder. May ABM reclaim it from the sheriff?

(c) Assume that on January 29 Apex files a petition under Chapter 11 of the Bankruptcy Code. May ABM reclaim the bookbinder?

PART III

Sales Transactions

Read the sales opinions in any volume of the UCC Reporting Service and you will find farmers selling grain to dealers, grocers selling to customers, lumber merchants selling lumber to city developers, manufacturers selling built-to-order turbines to sophisticated business firms, or dealers selling mobile homes to young couples, for whom the purchase may be the most significant investment of their life. The problem facing the draftsman of sales legislation is to develop rules that take into account the great diversity of transactions.

Karl Llewellyn's solution to the draftsman's dilemma was to draft rules that allowed courts to use their "situation sense." The late Dean Mentschikoff described the approach as follows:

> The most important drafting concept rests on the belief that relative certainty and uniformity of construction depend on the court's perception of the situation represented by the rule and the reason the rule was adopted, and that proper construction follows the reason and is limited or extended by it. The attempt, therefore, has been to draft rules so that both the situation being covered and its reason tend to appear on the face of the language, and to keep the language reasonably open-ended. [Mentschikoff, Highlights of the Uniform Commercial Code, 27 Mod. L. Rev. 167, 170 (1964).]

A more critical commentator concludes:

> It is suggested here that the animating theory of Article II is that law is immanent. The law job is to search it out. There is thus no need for a legislature to create law. The central focus, as in all the writings of the realists, is on courts. Article II is a document whose thrust is not so much to put law on the statute books as it is to coerce courts into looking for law in life. [Danzig, A Comment on the Jurisprudence of the Uniform Commercial Code, 27 Stan. L. Rev. 621, 635 (1975).]

Chapter 8 has introduced some of the ways that Article 2 provides flexibility by means of general rules, such as those governing good faith and unconscionability. The following chapters examine Article 2 more systematically. As you read the materials you should ask whether the article provides adequate guidance for the efficient resolution of disputes arising out of the great variety of sales transactions.

CHAPTER 9

Contract Formation and Contract Terms

Most of the topics discussed in this chapter will appear to be familiar. First year contract law courses introduce the legal rules governing offer and acceptance, the statute of frauds, and parol evidence. You may even have studied the relevant UCC sections in detail. This chapter reviews most of these topics but focuses on aspects that are peculiarly commercial.

Except to review the "battle of the forms" (UCC 2-207), we will not study in detail the Code rules on offer and acceptance. You should, however, read UCC 2-204 to 2-210. Note that these sections do not codify the rules of offer and acceptance in a systematic fashion. The Code text assumes that the reader knows the common law rules and sets out exceptions where the draftsmen thought the rules had gone off the track. For example, UCC 2-205 assumes the reader knows the general Anglo-American rule that offers are revocable unless consideration has been given for an option contract: the section proceeds to provide an exception to this rule where the offer is made by a merchant in a writing that states that it will be held open. As suggested by UCC 2-204, the general thrust of the Code rules is to encourage courts to enforce agreements that parties intend to be binding, notwithstanding gaps and ambiguities that pre-Code courts found to be fatal.

A. INTRODUCTION: SCOPE OF ARTICLE 2

One of the most intellectually interesting—and difficult—questions you will encounter in commercial practice is whether or not certain borderline transactions fall within the scope of Article 2. Logically, these questions will arise very early in your analysis. Because they are difficult, however, we defer our study of scope problems until we examine them in the context of particular Article 2 provisions and policies. The five Problems are inserted at this point only to

465

whet your appetite. You should return to them after studying the following chapters.

UCC 2-102 states that Article 2 applies to *transactions* in *goods* unless the context otherwise requires. Although most of the specific sections in Article 2 refer only to sales or contracts for sale, use of the word "transaction" in UCC 2-102 suggests a broader application. The definitions of *sale* and *contract for sale* in UCC 2-106(1) focus on the passing of title for a price. As we note in Chapter 10, however, Article 2 downplays the role of title in sales transactions. It might only be a small step to read the word *transaction* broadly and the clause "unless the context otherwise requires" narrowly.

A transaction must also involve goods before Article 2 is applicable. UCC 2-105(1) defines *goods* to include "all things . . . movable at the time of identification to the contract for sale." This section goes on to provide specific rules for troublesome cases: choses in action, for example, are excluded, but growing crops are included. UCC 2-107 deals with cases on the borderline between real and personal property.

In any event, even if Article 2 does not govern by its terms, there are numerous comments throughout the Code that encourage the use of UCC rules by analogy where the logic of the rule is applicable. After giving numerous examples of purposive interpretation taken from pre-Code court opinions, Comment 1 to UCC 1-102 concludes that "the application of the [UCC] language should be construed narrowly or broadly, as the case may be, in conformity with the purposes and policies involved." Comment 2 to UCC 2-313 (express warranties), which is also frequently cited, notes that the statutory text is limited to contracts for sale but stresses that the section leaves the question of whether warranties exist in other transactions to developing case law "with the intention that the policies of this Act may offer useful guidance in dealing with further cases as they arise."

The Restatement (Second) of Contracts puts the matter broadly: "The profound impact of the Code on the law of contracts has sometimes resulted in the statement of rules applicable to contracts generally that are derived by analogy from rules laid down in the Code for contracts for the sale of goods." Restatement of Contracts (Second) Introduction (1981). See also Murray, Under the Spreading Analogy of Article 2 of the Uniform Commercial Code, 39 Fordham L. Rev. 447 (1971); Note, The Uniform Commercial Code as a Premise for Judicial Reasoning, 65 Colum. L. Rev. 880 (1965).

Problem 9-1. Having lost the contract to maintain the county roads Dehahn agrees orally to sell his equipment and a 52-acre gravel pit to Innes for $35,000. The parties make no attempt to evaluate the items sold, although the equipment's blue book value at the time of the agreement is $30,000. Before taking delivery several weeks later, Innes inspects the equipment and discovers it is rusty. Innes promptly writes Dehahn that "I am not going to take the truck and bulldozer because they are not in A-1 condition as you promised."

State law provides that contracts for the sale of real property are unenforceable unless in writing. May Dehahn recover the purchase price of the equipment and gravel pit from Innes? See UCC 1-206, 2-105(1), 2-107, 2-201.

Should you divide the transaction into two transactions, one for the equipment and one for the gravel pit, or should you apply the law applicable to the "predominant factor" of the transaction? Where goods and services are mixed, many courts apply the predominant factor test. See Bonebrake v. Cox, 499 F.2d 951, 14 UCC Rep. 1318 (8th Cir. 1974) (predominant factor test applied to sale and installation of used bowling equipment where some goods were defective and installation not completed). On the other hand, some courts have been willing to apply the UCC to the "goods" portion of a transaction. See Foster v. Colorado Radio Corp., 381 F.2d 222, 4 UCC Rep. 446 (10th Cir. 1967) (sale of radio station included license, goodwill, real estate, and equipment; UCC damage provisions applied to buyer's failure to take delivery of the equipment).

Problem 9-2. ABC Inc. owns and manages several restaurants in Texas. John Senior owns all the common shares of ABC. Senior agrees in writing to sell the business to Bill Brazen by transferring all the common shares. One week before the transfer is to take place Brazen announces that he will not go through with the purchase. The only reason he gives is that one of the creditors of ABC objects to the transfer. What remedies, if any, does Senior have under the UCC? See UCC 2-105, 8-102, 8-301 to 8-321. See also UCC 6-102, 6-103.

Note: *Sale of Goods, Sale of Assets, and Sale of Securities*

UCC 2-105(1) explicitly excludes investment securities (Article 8) from the definition of *goods*. The last paragraph of Comment 1 notes the express exclusion but adds that "[i]t is not intended by this exclusion, however, to prevent the application of the particular section of this Article by analogy . . . when the reason of that section makes such application sensible and the situation involved is not covered by (Article 8)." The Comment cites Agar v. Orda, 264 N.Y. 248 (1934), which is also cited in Comment 1 to UCC 1-102. In *Agar* the buyer of corporate shares refused to accept the seller's tender of share certificates, and the seller brought an action for the price. At common law an action for the price would lie, and no distinction would be made as to the remedy between goods and choses in action, including corporate shares. The Uniform Sales Act changed the remedy to permit only an action for damages, but the act explicitly excluded shares from its coverage (U.S.A. §156). The *Agar* case applied the new Uniform Sales Act rule by analogy, rather than the old common law, in order to retain a uniform solution to the problem of remedies and to apply what the court thought was a better rule.

In the context of this problem Article 8 provides its own puzzles. Are shares of a close corporation's securities within UCC 8-102's definition? Are there any provisions in Article 8 on seller's remedies?

If Article 2 remedies should be applied by analogy to Article 8 investment securities, should state and federal regulations of their sale and distribution be applied by analogy to the sale of goods? See Securities Act of 1933, 15 U.S.C. §§77a-77aa (1982); Securities Exchange Act of 1934, 15 U.S.C. §§78a-78kk (1982); Uniform Securities Act (1956). Federal regulation relies primarily on disclosure requirements but state legislation may authorize a state administrator to review the fairness of the securities' proposed distribution. Why should the sale of securities be subject to special regulations when the sale of goods is not?

When the owner of a business sells 100 percent of the stock in a corporation holding title to the business assets, courts are divided on the applicability of the federal securities laws. Compare Frederiksen v. Poloway, 637 F.2d 1147 (7th Cir. 1981) with Golden v. Garafalo, 678 F.2d 1139 (2d Cir. 1982); and see generally Seldin, When Stock Is Not a Security: The "Sale of Business" Doctrine Under the Federal Securities Laws, 37 Bus. Law. 637 (1982).

Problem 9-3. Equipment Leasing Corp. (ELC) enters into a written "equipment lease agreement" with Data Processing, Inc. (DPI) to "lease" to DPI data processing equipment for five years at an annual rental of $1,400. Under the agreement DPI has the right to the exclusive use of the equipment and the obligation to maintain it, and pay all taxes incident to its use. The agreement includes the following clause in bold face type: "ELC makes no warranty express or implied with respect to the leased equipment." At the time the written agreement is signed the parties orally agree that at the end of five years DPI has the option to buy the equipment for $200; if it does not exercise the option it must promptly return the equipment to ELC, which usually gives such options to its customers. The cost of the equipment, if purchased from a retailer for cash, is $5,200. In a subsequent dispute between DPI and ELC about the quality of the equipment, is the UCC applicable? See UCC 2-102, 2-106, 2-316. Would your answer be different if the parties included the following clause in their contract: "The parties explicitly agree that this is not a lease transaction"?

Note that you might conclude that the UCC is applicable because (1) the transaction is a true sale disguised as a lease; (2) the lease is a "transaction in goods" within the scope of Article 2 by virtue of UCC 2-102; or, (3) although not directly applicable, the UCC warranty provisions should apply by analogy. On the other hand, of course, you might conclude that the UCC is not applicable at all. If so, what law then governs?

For a discussion of leases and secured transactions see Chapter 5. On this problem generally see Farnsworth, Implied Warranties of Quality and Non-Sales Cases, 57 Colum. L. Rev. 653, 655-660 (1957); Note, Disengaging Sales

Law from the Sale Construct, A Proposal to Extend the Scope of Article 2 of the UCC, 96 Harv. L. Rev. 470 (1982).

Problem 9-4. *S* is a manufacturer of trucks incorporated in Delaware with its head office in Pennsylvania; *B* is a trucking company incorporated in Oklahoma with its head office in Oklahoma. *S* and *B* sign a written agreement in Oklahoma in which *S* sells to *B* ten trucks manufactured at *S*'s plant in Ohio and delivered to *B*'s branch office in Codeland. The trucks are used in Codeland, Oklahoma, and Louisiana. Four and one-half years after delivery of the trucks *B* brings an action against *S* in a federal district court in Codeland claiming damages for breach of the implied warranty of merchantability with respect to two of the trucks. Assume that Codeland has a nonuniform five-year statute of limitations and that all other jurisdictions have the Code's standard four-year statute of limitations. Should *B*'s action be dismissed because it was brought too late? See UCC 1-105, 2-725.

Does the language of UCC 1-105 permit a court to apply the "center of gravity" or "governmental interest" analysis characteristic of modern conflict of laws analysis? The present language of this section can be traced to the desire of the Code draftsmen to make the UCC applicable to as many transactions as possible. Many commentators in the early 1950s were very critical of the draftsmen's approach, but the policy issue has become moot because of the almost universal adoption of the UCC. Is this drafting history relevant to how the section should be interpreted today? See generally Comment, Conflicts of Law and the Appropriate Relations Test of Section 1-105 of the UCC, 40 Geo. Wash. L. Rev. 797 (1972). See also Restatement (Second) of Conflict of Laws §§6, 191 (1969).

Problem 9-5. Dairy Mart operates a chain of franchised convenience stores. In November, 1973, Dairy Mart agreed with Zapatha that it would grant him a franchise to operate a Dairy Mart store and license him to use the Dairy Mart trademark and its "confidential" merchandising methods. Dairy Mart would provide the store and equipment and would pay the rent and utility bills. In return Dairy Mart would receive a franchise fee, to be computed as a percentage of the store's gross sales. Zapatha would pay for the starting inventory and maintain a minimum stock of salable merchandise thereafter. It was estimated that 30 percent of the inventory would be supplied by Dairy Mart. Zapatha would also be responsible for paying the wages of employees, related taxes, and any sales taxes. The termination provision allowed either party, after 12 months, to terminate the agreement without cause on 90 days' written notice. If it terminated the franchise without cause Dairy Mart agreed to repurchase the salable merchandise inventory at retail price, less 20 percent.

In November, 1977, Dairy Mart presented a new and more detailed franchise agreement to Zapatha for execution. The agreement required Zapatha to keep his store open for longer periods of time and reserved to Dairy Mart the option to relocate a franchisee to a new location. Zapatha refused to sign this agreement and Dairy Mart promptly gave him written notice of termination, effective in 90 days. The notice indicated that Dairy Mart was prepared to purchase the Zapatha salable inventory.

Zapatha comes to you for advice. He explains that a Dairy Mart representative read and explained to him the termination provision of the 1973 agreement. He had understood every word of the provision but he interpreted it to mean that Dairy Mart could terminate the agreement only for cause. He did not consult an attorney at that time although advised to do so by a Dairy Mart representative. The Dairy Mart representative indicated, however, that the terms of the contract were not negotiable.

Is this agreement subject to the UCC? Is the termination clause unconscionable? Was the exercise of the termination option done in good faith? If the UCC does not apply, are the Article 2 concepts of unconscionability and good faith applicable by analogy? See UCC 1-201(19), 1-203, 2-103(1)(b), 2-302.

Note: Franchise Arrangements

Franchising is a method of distributing goods or services. Recent analyses distinguish two forms: The United States Department of Commerce, for example, distinguishes between the traditional "product and trade name franchising" and "business format franchising." U.S. Department of Commerce, Franchising in the Economy, 1978-1980 (1980). In product and trade name franchising the franchisor, who is usually a manufacturer, grants a franchise to a distributor for the distribution of the franchisor's trademark products in a way that allows the buying public to identify the products with the franchisor. Product and trade name franchising is typical for manufacturers of motor vehicles, farm implements, tires and bicycles, gasoline service stations, and bottlers and distributors of soft drinks and beer. Under business format franchising, a franchisor licenses a franchisee to operate under the franchisor's trademark or trade name subject to a prescribed marketing and operations plan, complete with detailed operating manuals and quality control. This form is common to volume food retailers, drugstores, hotels and motels, fast food restaurants, and business service systems. Although business format franchising may be more familiar, the traditional form has in recent years accounted for three-fourths of the franchises sold. In both forms the principal advantage is that financial and managerial resources of the franchisor may be spread further. See Rollinson, Alternatives to Franchising, 1980 Ariz. St. L. Rev. 505.

Recently both the federal and state governments have enacted rules to regulate the franchise arrangement. The Federal Trade Commission (FTC), pursuant to its power to proscribe unfair trade practices (Sec. 5 of the Federal

Trade Commission Act), has promulgated a Rule on Disclosure Requirements and Prohibitions Concerning Franchising and Business Opportunity Ventures, 43 Fed. Reg. 59614 (1978), codified in 16 C.F.R. part 436 (1984). In much the same way the federal securities legislation regulates the marketing of securities, the FTC regulates the relation by requiring the franchisor to make detailed disclosures, especially where the franchisor makes any representation as to the franchisee's potential earnings. Although the FTC controls where state law conflicts with its provisions, the rule does not otherwise pre-empt state regulation. More than one-half of the states have enacted legislation to regulate the franchise arrangement. Although some states require only disclosure, others require registration or proscribe specified unfair practices. See generally G. Glickman, Franchising (1978); Note, Regulation of Franchising, 59 Minn. L. Rev. 1027 (1975). For a detailed discussion of the relation between automobile manufacturers and their dealers, see S. Macaulay, Law and the Balance of Power: The Auto Manufacturers and Their Dealers (1966).

Commentators have identified a number of alleged problems to which the distribution relation gives rise. Potential franchisees may be induced to enter into a franchise arrangement by fraud or misrepresentation, and the operation of the franchise may involve claims of unfair allocation of goods or restrictions on marketing. Termination of franchises may involve claims of acting without good cause. Once entered into, a franchise gives the franchisor greater bargaining power because it usually controls supplies and has the power to terminate the franchise.

The Uniform Commercial Code does not regulate the franchise arrangement in detail, if at all.[1] Courts nevertheless have looked to the Code for guidance in resolving disputes between parties to a franchise arrangement, especially those arising from termination. See, for example, Corenswet, Inc. v. Amana Refrigeration, Inc., 594 F.2d 129, 26 UCC Rep. 301 (5th Cir. 1979) (contract clause empowering the manufacturer to terminate distributorship contract "at any time and for any reason" did not contravene UCC's good faith and unconscionability standards).

B.   STATUTE OF FRAUDS; CONCEPT OF "MERCHANT"

The statute of frauds for sales transactions is set out in UCC 2-201. The statute requires a writing sufficient to indicate a contract when the price for the sale of goods is $500 or more. If a party fails to produce a writing he may not enforce

---

1. Indeed, with relatively few exceptions (see, e.g., 2-208, 2-209, 2-306, 2-612) the Code fails to articulate principles primarily directed to regulating long-term multiple transaction relationships.

the contract unless he shows that the transaction falls within an exception to the statute. The Code lists exceptions in UCC 2-201(2) and (3), and courts may recognize non-Code exceptions based on general principles such as estoppel (UCC 1-103). Even if a party satisfies the statute of frauds by producing a writing or establishing an exception he must still prove the terms of the contract, which need not appear in the writing. The contract will not be enforced, however, for more than the written quantity.

We have already encountered the concept of the statute of frauds in Chapter 3 when we studied the requirements for an enforceable security agreement set out in UCC 9-203. See also UCC 1-206, 8-319. Here we review the statute as codified in Article 2 and focus on an exception for certain transactions "between merchants" (UCC 2-104(1) and (3); 2-201(2)), which was added by the Code to the traditional formulation of the statute of frauds. It has given rise to considerable litigation.

DECATUR COOPERATIVE ASSN. v. URBAN
219 Kan. 171, 547 P.2d 323, 18 UCC Rep. 1160 (1976)

HARMAN, Commissioner. This action was brought to obtain possession of 10,000 bushels of wheat allegedly purchased under an oral contract, or alternatively, for damages for failure to deliver the wheat. The primary issue is whether the alleged seller, a farmer, was a "merchant" within the meaning of the uniform commercial code so as to remove the oral contract from operation of the statute of frauds. A secondary issue is whether the seller was equitably estopped from relying on the statute of frauds as a defense to an action on the oral contract.

Appellant, The Decatur Cooperative Association, commenced this action August 24, 1973, by filing its petition against appellee, Franklin Urban, alleging an oral purchase of 10,000 bushels of wheat from Urban on July 26, 1973, at $2.86 per bushel and a repudiation by him of the agreement on August 14, 1973. Other facts were alleged which will be noticed later. Urban answered, denying the alleged purchase and raising the defense of the statute of frauds. Urban also moved for summary judgment.

For the purpose of ruling on the request for summary judgment the parties stipulated to the facts, which we summarize. Appellant is a corporation which has been in existence since 1953. It owns and operates a grain elevator and its principal business is the purchasing of wheat and other grains from area farmers which it markets to larger regional elevators and grain dealers. During the fiscal year ending March 31, 1973, appellant purchased grain from about 500 farmers and sold grain to four regional elevators.

Appellant has a well-established policy of never speculating on the price of grain. Therefore, as soon as it purchases grain from a farmer or farmers amounting to one train carload or about 2000 bushels, it places a phone call to a terminal elevator and orally sells the grain to that elevator at the prevailing price. Thereafter, a written confirmation of sale is sent by the terminal elevator to the cooperative. This procedure is a well-established and well-known method of handling and marketing grain in Decatur county, Kansas. Appellant has a general manager and an assistant manager to run its daily operations, each of whom is authorized to enter into sales contracts on behalf of the cooperative.

Appellee Urban is a resident of Decatur county and was a member of the cooperative throughout the year 1973. He has been engaged in the wheat farming business for about twenty years. He owns about 2,000 acres of his total farmed acreage of 2,320 acres. About 1,200 acres are broken out and farmable while the remaining acreage is unbroken and devoted to pasture. In the year 1974 appellee had approximately 500 acres sown in wheat. Appellee also owns a cow herd of about 200 head. He is engaged solely in the farming business, although he has in the past done some custom harvesting of wheat and other grains. He has sold wheat and other grains, which he raises, to the appellant cooperative and to other elevators in the area since 1966 and has sold livestock through area sale barns.

On July 26, 1973, appellee was in St. Francis, Kansas, on his way to Colorado to do some custom wheat harvesting. While in St. Francis he placed two phone calls to the cooperative. On the first call he requested to speak to the assistant manager but was told he was not available. Later that afternoon appellee placed a second call to the cooperative office and did reach the assistant manager. As a result of this second call, appellant contends the parties entered into an oral contract whereby appellee agreed to sell to the cooperative 10,000 bushels of wheat at $2.86 per bushel, to be delivered on or before September 30, 1973. Appellee denies that any contract of sale was made during this phone call and he has never admitted by pleading, testimony or otherwise that a sale agreement was reached during the call. The total cash value of the wheat alleged to have been sold was $28,600.00.

During the phone conversation there was discussion of a written memorandum of sale to be prepared and sent to appellee later. It is appellant's practice to send a signed written confirmation of sale to the seller immediately after oral conversations and appellant did in fact send such a confirmation to appellee. This confirmation was signed by appellant's assistant manager and was binding as against appellant. Appellee received the confirmation within a reasonable time, read it, and gave no written notice of objection to its contents within ten days after it was received.

Early in the morning of July 27, 1973, in reliance on the alleged oral contract of sale, appellant placed a phone call to Far-Mar-Co., a regional terminal elevator in Kansas City, Missouri, and sold the wheat for $3.46 per bushel, the cooperative to pay freight and other charges. During the latter part of July and early part of August of 1973, the price of wheat rose substantially.

On August 13, 1973, appellee notified appellant that he would not deliver the wheat. The price of wheat at the cooperative on that date was $4.50 per bushel.

Upon the foregoing the trial court made the following findings:

"1. The Court finds that under the provisions of [UCC 1-206] that the amount of the contract price exceeded $5,000.00 and that under that statute the oral agreement was void for lack of being signed by the parties to be bound thereby to-wit, the defendant, and that the supposed contract is void under the provisions of that statute.

"2. The term 'Merchant' is defined under provisions of [UCC 2-104] and it is the finding and conclusion of this Court that such term is not applicable to the parties to this action, particularly the defendant, Franklin Urban.

"3. [The Court also finds that] a farmer, whether he be large, intermediate or small is not a merchant under the facts of this case and that by reason thereof the provisions of [UCC 2-201] are not applicable to this case in so far as the defendant is concerned."

The court sustained Urban's motion for summary judgment and Decatur Cooperative has appealed. . . . [The court holds that UCC 1-206 is not applicable because the sale of wheat is the sale of "goods" within the meaning of UCC 2-105, thus UCC 2-201 is the relevant statute of frauds.]

We turn now to the more difficult issue—the court's invalidation of the alleged oral contract pursuant to our statute of frauds applicable to certain contracts for the sale of goods.

UCC 2-201 provides in pertinent part:

Formal Requirements; Statute of Frauds

(1) Except as otherwise provided in this section a contract for the sale of goods for the price of $500 or more is not enforceable by way of action or defense unless there is some writing sufficient to indicate that a contract for sale has been made between the parties and signed by the party against whom enforcement is sought or by his authorized agent or broker. A writing is not insufficient because it omits or incorrectly states a term agreed upon but the contract is not enforceable under this paragraph beyond the quantity of goods shown in such writing.

(2) Between merchants if within a reasonable time a writing in confirmation of the contract and sufficient against the sender is received and the party receiving it has reason to know its contents, it satisfies the requirements of subsection (1) against such party unless written notice of objection to its contents is given within 10 days after it is received.

Under subsection (2) a "merchant" is deprived of the defense of the statute of frauds as against an oral contract with another merchant if he fails to object to the terms of a written confirmation within ten days of its receipt. The issue presently here is whether or not appellee is, under the facts, also a "merchant." If he is not, UCC 2-201 acts as a bar to the enforcement of the alleged contract. UCC 2-104 contains the following definitions:

(1) "Merchant" means a person who deals in goods of the kind or otherwise by his occupation holds himself out as having knowledge or skill peculiar to the practices or goods involved in the transaction or to whom such knowledge or skill may be attributed by his employment of an agent or broker or other intermediary who by his occupation holds himself out as having such knowledge or skill. (3) "Between merchants" means in any transaction with respect to which both parties are chargeable with the knowledge or skill of merchants.

[The court then sets out the text of Official Comments 1 and 2 (first para.) to UCC 2-104.]

From the foregoing it appears there are three separate criteria for determining merchant status. A merchant is (1) a dealer who deals in the goods of the kind involved, or (2) one who by his occupation holds himself out as having knowledge or skill peculiar to the practices or goods involved in the transaction, even though he may not actually have such knowledge, or (3) a principal who employs an agent, broker or other intermediary who by his occupation holds himself out as having knowledge or skill peculiar to the practices or goods involved in the transaction (see 1 R. Anderson, Uniform Commercial Code §2-104:4, at 220 (2d ed. 1970)). Professionalism, special knowledge and commercial experience are to be used in determining whether a person in a particular situation is to be held to the standards of a merchant.

The few courts which have considered the question whether a farmer, with experience similar to that in the case at bar, is a merchant under the statute of frauds provision in the UCC have divided on the issue. . . .

In our opinion the facts here disclose that appellee neither "deals" in wheat, as that term is used in UCC 2-104, nor does he by his occupation hold himself out as having knowledge or skill peculiar to the practices or goods involved in the transaction. The concept of professionalism is heavy in determining who is a merchant under the statute. The writers of the official UCC comment virtually equate professionals with merchants—the casual or inexperienced buyer or seller is not to be held to the standard set for the professional in business. The defined term "between merchants," used in the exception proviso to the statute of frauds, contemplates the knowledge and skill of professionals on each side of the transaction. The transaction in question here was the sale of wheat. Appellee as a farmer undoubtedly had special knowledge or skill in raising wheat but we do not think this factor, coupled with annual sales of a wheat crop and purchases of seed wheat, qualified him as a merchant in that field. The parties' stipulation states appellee has sold only the products he raised. There is no indication any of these sales were other than cash sales to local grain elevators, where conceivably an expertise reaching professional status could be said to be involved.

We think the trial court correctly ruled under the particular facts that appellee was not a merchant for the purpose of avoiding the operation of the statute of frauds pursuant to UCC 2-201(1) and (2).

This brings us to the second point of the appeal—not ruled upon by the trial court—whether appellee is equitably estopped to assert the statute of frauds as a defense. UCC 1-103 provides that certain principles of law and equity, including estoppel, unless displaced by the particular provisions of the uniform code, shall supplement its provisions.

Appellant pleaded in its petition, and the parties stipulated the facts pertinent thereto, its immediate disposition of the wheat it thought it had purchased from appellee and contends that because appellee knew, or reasonably should have known because of his special relationship as a member of appellant, that it would sell the wheat immediately, he is estopped to assert the statute of frauds as a defense to enforcement of the oral contract. . . .

Courts have taken differing positions as to whether a party may be equitably estopped to assert the statute of frauds as a defense (see Annot., Promissory Estoppel As Basis For Avoidance of Statute of Frauds, 56 A.L.R.3d 1037). One line of cases holds that to allow the concept of estoppel to preclude assertion of the statute of frauds as a defense to an oral contract would defeat the purpose of the statute. . . .

A substantial number of courts, however, hold that the doctrine of promissory estoppel may render enforceable any promise upon which the promisor intended, or should have known, that the promisee would act to his detriment, and which is indeed acted upon in such a manner by the promisee, where application of the statute of frauds to that promise would thus work a fraud or a gross injustice upon the promisee (Annot., supra, §6[a], at 1060-1063; 73 Am. Jur. 2d, Statute of Frauds §565, at 202-204). Courts in this line of cases bottom their reasoning on the general equity principle that the statute of frauds was enacted to prevent fraud and injustice, not to foster or encourage it, and a court of equity will not ordinarily permit its use as a shield to protect fraud or to enable one to take advantage of his own wrong. This court has long been committed to the principles enunciated in the last sentence and on that basis has applied the doctrine of estoppel to cases wherein the statute of frauds would otherwise be applicable as a defense. . . .

Before the doctrine of promissory estoppel can be invoked in a case involving the statute of frauds the promisee must first show by competent evidence that a valid and otherwise enforceable contract was entered into by the parties (3 Williston on Contracts §533A, at 802-803 (W. Jaeger 3d ed. 1957)). The conduct of the promisor must be something more than a mere refusal to perform the oral contract, since any party to an oral contract unenforceable under the statute of frauds has that right, and the exercise of the right of nonperformance is no more a fraud than a breach of any other contract (37 C.J.S. Frauds, Statute of §247, p.755). And the promisee must show the facts of the case and the conduct of the promisor justifying application of the doctrine. . . .

Recapitulating, appellant's theory is it changed its position in reliance upon appellee's conduct; that appellee was or reasonably should have been aware of its practices in the particular type of situation; that appellant bound itself in the transaction and it would be unjust and a fraud upon appellant to permit appellee to speculate and profit on a risen market at appellant's expense. From the facts pleaded and placed before the trial court by stipulation it is clear appellant was entitled to invoke the doctrine of promissory estoppel so as to bar application of the statute of frauds and to have an evidentiary hearing upon disputed matters in connection with that issue. The summary judgment denying that right was improperly entered and it must be and is hereby reversed and the cause remanded for further proceedings accordingly.

Reversed and remanded.

NOTES & QUESTIONS

1. *Merchants and Article 2.* Why the draftsmen included special rules for merchants in Article 2 comes out clearly in the following excerpt from the Report & Second Draft: The Revised Uniform Sales Act (1941) prepared by Karl Llewellyn:

"The reasons for making this category appear in the Report, and appear again and again in the particular sections of the Draft which are expressly extended only to professional dealings between professionals.

"Such persons, in regard to such dealings, have an understanding of trade practice, habits and skills of adjustment, needs for speedy action, probable commitments, access to counsel, which make many provisions both needful and feasible for them which are neither needful nor feasible for, say, farmers or household consumers.

"Mansfield's incorporation of the law merchant into the common law was in all fields but that of Sales the incorporation of a body of law tailored directly and skillfully to the needs of merchants in their dealings with other merchants—to which body of law other men had to conform, or (as in the case of lawyers' partnerships) appropriate exceptions could be made.

"In Sales this did not occur; and such specially adapted law as merchants have received has been worked out so to speak under cover, by way of 'general' rules of supposedly 'general' application, which just happen to apply to situations in which the participation of a non-merchant approaches the unthinkable. Examples are the 'to arrive' contract, or C.I.F. But experience shows that precisely these purely mercantile rules have given the most clarity and the most satisfaction, within the whole Sales field.

"The Draft proposes to free the matter from confusion by bringing such situations out into daylight, tailoring rules to special mercantile need where there is such need, but not inflicting such rules on non-professionals, when non-professionals might be at a disadvantage under them." Id. at 38-39. See also UCC 2-104, Comment 2, which classifies the special merchant provisions in the final text.

For further study of the "merchant" provisions, see Dolan, The Merchant Class of Article 2: Farmers, Doctors, & Others, 1977 Wash. U.L.Q. 1; Newell, The Merchant of Article 2, 7 Val. U.L. Rev. 307 (1973).

Does the Code pose the issue of whether farmers are merchants, or whether *this* farmer is a merchant?

2. *UCC 1-103 and promissory estoppel.* Not all courts accept the suggestion by the *Decatur Cooperative* court that the doctrine of promissory estoppel would make a contract enforceable if the statute of frauds was not otherwise satisfied. In answer to a question certified to it by the Ninth Circuit, the Washington Supreme Court stated that applying the doctrine would circumvent the UCC, increase litigation and confusion, and decrease uniformity in the case law gloss on the Code. Lige Dickson Co. v. Union Oil Co., 96 Wash. 2d 291, 635 P.2d 103, 32 UCC Rep. 705 (1981). Are you persuaded? See generally Restatement (Second) of Contracts §139 (1981).

3. *Usage of trade and the statute of frauds.* If a trade association adopts and publishes rules that state that agreements between members shall be enforceable even if there is no written memorandum, should a court enforce an oral agreement between two association members? What if the association rule is not published? What if the rule is not formally adopted but observed in practice by association members? See UCC 1-205.

4. *The statute of frauds and contract modification.* UCC 2-209(3) requires that the statute of frauds must be satisfied "if the contract as modified is within its provisions." The section goes on to state that an attempted modification that does not satisfy the statute may operate as a waiver. UCC 2-209(4). Under certain circumstances a party may retract a waiver of an executory portion of the contract. UCC 2-209(5). Can there be waiver, however, if the original contract includes a clause prohibiting amendments to contractual obligations unless the amendments are set out in a signed writing?

Problem 9-6. Roberts Fiber Co. agreed orally with Anderson to purchase Anderson's cotton production at 32 cents a pound. The following day Roberts sent a confirmation form, prepared by Roberts, which included the following clause:

> Buyer agrees to purchase and take delivery from Seller, and Seller agrees to sell and deliver to Buyer, all the acceptable cotton produced during the crop year 1973 on the following acreage, and none other:

No. of acres	Farm no.	County	Allotment in name of	Projected yield
4,222		Calhoun	Various	500 lbs/acre

Anderson planted the acreage the following month but refused to deliver the cotton after harvesting. Roberts brought suit to enforce the contract. On appeal, what result? See UCC 2-201, 2-204, 2-306. May either party introduce evidence to prove that shortly after planting the parties had orally agreed that the maximum quantity under the contract would be one million pounds? Suppose that following this oral agreement Anderson contracted elsewhere for the sale of an additional one million pounds? See UCC 2-201, 2-209.

Problem 9-7. Jim manufactures cane chairs and distributes them through numerous handicraft outlets. In the last two years he and his assistant have sold almost 600 chairs a year, although he sold no more than 50 through any one outlet. Sam, owner of Leisure Time Furniture, meets with Jim and allegedly orders 200 cane rocking chairs for delivery in three months. There is no written document evidencing the alleged agreement. Soon after their talk Jim orders 50 percent more cane than usual and hires an additional part-time worker. He also turns down several possible orders from handicraft outlets. At the end of one month he sends 40 rockers to Sam, who accepts them but has not yet paid for them. Two weeks later, Jim telephones Sam to ask for delivery instructions for the next lot of rockers. Sam, however, denies that he had ordered additional rockers. His explanation of their first conversation is that he had merely inquired about the total number of rockers that Jim could supply if Sam should order them.

You represent Sam, who tells you the above story. What questions, if any, will you ask him? What would you advise him to do? If you bring legal action and you suspect Sam will perjure himself, what steps should you take?

With respect to your obligations as an attorney who suspects perjury, consider the following rules taken from A.B.A., Model Rules of Professional Conduct (1983):

Rule 3.3.   Candor Toward the Tribunal

(a)   A lawyer shall not knowingly:
      (1)   make a false statement of material fact or law to a tribunal;
      (2)   fail to disclose a material fact to a tribunal when disclosure is necessary to avoid assisting a criminal or fraudulent act by the client; . . .
      (4)   offer evidence that the lawyer knows to be false. If a lawyer has offered material evidence and comes to know of its falsity, the lawyer shall take reasonable remedial measures.
(b)   The duties stated in paragraph (a) continue to the conclusion of the proceeding, and apply even if compliance requires disclosure of information otherwise protected by Rule 1.6.
(c)   A lawyer may refuse to offer evidence that the lawyer reasonably believes is false. . . .

Rule 1.6.   Confidentiality of Information

(a)   A lawyer shall not reveal information relating to representation of a client unless the client consents after consultation, except for disclosures that are impliedly authorized in order to carry out the representation, and except as stated in paragraph (b).

(b) A lawyer may reveal such information to the extent the lawyer reasonably believes necessary:
(1) To prevent the client from committing a criminal [or fraudu-
lent] act that the lawyer reasonably believes is likely to result in
imminent death or substantial bodily *harm* [or in substantial injury to the financial interests or property of another]; *or*
[(2) to rectify the consequences of a client's criminal or fraudulent
act in the furtherance of which the lawyer's services had been
used; . . .]
(2) to establish a claim or defense on behalf of the lawyer in a
controversy between the lawyer and the client, to establish a
defense to a criminal charge or civil claim against the lawyer
based upon conduct in which the client was involved, or to
respond to allegations in any proceeding concerning the lawyer's representation of the client. . . .
[(4) to comply with other law.]

Note: Bracketed material appears in 1982 Final Draft but was deleted when
the text was adopted in 1983. Italicized material was added in 1983.

COMMENT, THE STATUTE OF FRAUDS AND THE BUSINESS COMMUNITY: A RE-APPRAISAL IN LIGHT OF PREVAILING PRACTICES
66 Yale L.J. 1038, 1039-1040, 1064-1065 (1957)

Although the conflicting evaluations of the Statute of Frauds are chiefly attributable to different basic assumptions concerning business practice, writers
have made little attempt to discover what contractual practices businessmen
actually follow. To fill this empirical gap, the Yale Law Journal consulted ten
firms in the New Haven area and then composed a Questionnaire which was
distributed to 200 Connecticut manufacturers.[6] One hundred seventy manufacturers were selected from eleven of the state's major industries, while the
remaining thirty were chosen from miscellaneous fields. Within each industry
the firms in the sample were selected at random, except that wholly-owned
subsidiaries were excluded.[7] Eighty-seven, or forty-six per cent of the 188 still

6. The Questionnaire is reprinted in full in the Appendix [to the Comment] . . . Although the
results of the ten interviews were accorded great weight in constructing the Questionnaire, the
data presented represents solely the responses to the Questionnaire itself. And to prevent bias,
none of the interviewees was sent a Questionnaire.
7. The sample of 200 firms was taken from the Directory of Connecticut Manufacturers and
Mechanical Establishments (1954), a compilation of all Connecticut manufacturers. The number
of firms selected from any one industry was roughly proportionate to the total number of firms
listed in that industrial category. The sample of 200 was comprised of the following types of
manufacturers: primary metals (A), 10 firms; fabricated metals (B), 20; instruments and clocks
(C), 10; electrical equipment (E), 20; furniture and fixtures (F), 10; miscellaneous manufacturing
industries (I), 30; leather goods (L), 10; machinery (M), 20; paper (P), 20; rubber (R), 20; stone,
clay and glass products (S), 10; and lumber and wood products (W), 20. The code letter following
each industrial group will be used throughout to designate a reference to that particular industry.

solvent and traceable businesses responded to the Questionnaire.[8] Information was solicited concerning the degree of adherence to the Statute's requirements, the attitude of the manufacturer toward the legal enforceability of oral and written agreements, and the action which he usually takes in the event of a failure to honor an agreement. . . .

[The study concludes:] . . . Business practice usually complies with the requirements of the Statute of Frauds. The average manufacturer ordinarily reduces his own commitments to writing and receives written promises from the parties with whom he deals. But manufacturers' transactions probably are characterized by signed memoranda because the parties deem it sound business practice to have written records, and not because they are concerned with the legal enforceability of their promisors' obligations under the Statute of Frauds. This conclusion is bolstered by the findings that 1) 90% of the manufacturers never turn to the courts in the event of a breach; 2) the manufacturers' practice of obtaining written records is not changed for orders of special goods or for orders below the value of $500, even though the customer can be legally held to such orders in the absence of a signed memorandum; 3) even those manufacturers who request written memoranda from their customers are frequently willing to commence production on the basis of an unenforceable oral order, thus sacrificing the certainty of a legally binding promise for business expediency; 4) most manufacturers are willing to rely on an oral acceptance of their revision of an order, even though the customer is not legally obligated to accept goods conforming to the revised terms; and 5) the manufacturer is frequently satisfied with an oral acknowledgment from a supplier, and does not request a written acknowledgment to ensure the existence of legal rights in case the supplier fails to deliver.

Thus, it seems proper to conclude that business practice would not be modified if the Statute of Frauds were repealed and oral promises were made legally binding. The businessman would still want written records irrespective of their legal value; for the reduction of commitments and agreements to

8. The returned Questionnaires (hereinafter cited as Questionnaires) are on file in Yale Law Library.

Five firms had become insolvent and seven others were untraceable. The 87 manufacturers responding represent all the industries in the original sample of 200, but the percentage of responses from each industrial group varies from 20% (leather goods) to 74% (electrical equipment). The number of responses from each industry, together with the number of solvent and traceable firms in that industry to which the Questionnaire was sent, is as follows: Industry A, 6 of 10; B, 11/20; C, 5/8; E, 14/19; F, 3/10; I, 11/28; L, 2/10; M, 10/20; P, 7/18; R, 8/18; S, 5/10; and W, 5/17. See note 7 supra for explanation of the above code letters. Where relevant, later footnotes analyze the practices of each industry to determine whether unequal representation of the various industries biases the figures for the total sample.

It could be argued that the figures are biased because the very fact that a manufacturer responds is indicative of his business practices, and thus the sampling answering the Questionnaire is not truly random with respect to the questions asked. It is possible, for example, that the sample is biased in favor of firms which are used to transacting business by mail and therefore would have responded as a matter of course. . . . However, a disproportionately large number of responses might have come from manufacturers who are dissatisfied with the lack of protection which present law affords their oral agreements and are thus desirous of aiding any effort to re-evaluate the worth of the Statute of Frauds. Thus, no conclusion can readily be drawn as to the sample's bias in these respects.

writing contributes to a smoother working business organization and eliminates the uncertainties and confusion which may accompany agreements involving only the spoken word. Accordingly, the only effect which repeal of the
Statute of Frauds would have for the business community would be to allow
an additional, and limited, class of promisees access to the courts in the event
of a breach.

The majority of businessmen answering the Questionnaire does not believe that this class of promisees should have legal rights, especially when the
potential plaintiff has not performed in reliance upon the oral promise.
Eighty-eight per cent of the manufacturers expressed the opinion that the law
should not enforce an oral promise if the suing party has not performed. The
explanation for this aversion to the intervention of the law may be found in the
nature of the business transaction which is marked by an oral promise. Since
businessmen usually give and obtain promises evidenced by signed memoranda, a transaction not following this pattern obviously constitutes an exception to standard business practice. And the fact that many manufacturers will
not insist upon written confirmation of an oral order if the customer is known
to them, and known to be reliable, indicates that the promisee will make this
exception, if at all, when dealing on a personal, informal basis with a party
with whom he has regularly carried on business. This conclusion is also supported by the greater prevalence of oral promises in the transactions of small
manufacturers than in those of large ones, for the opportunities of the small
manufacturer to do business under such conditions that the contracting parties
will gain personal knowledge of each other are of course far greater. Businessmen who have dealt informally for a considerable period of time may not feel
the need to possess documents signed by the obligated party or to have the
latter's oral promise legally enforceable. And if the parties do want the law to
supervise their transactions, it seems fair to assume that they will reduce their
respective commitments to writing. For only 12% of the manufacturers never
require a written confirmation of their customer's oral orders, thus indicating
that an overwhelming majority of the manufacturers will request a signed
memorandum at least in those cases where they desire legal protection. Under
these circumstances, it seems doubtful whether any interest would be served by
making oral promises legally enforceable, especially when there has been no
action in reliance. The parties do not want such a law, and there is no reason
why it should be forced upon them.

NOTES & QUESTIONS

1. *Empirical studies.* For a comment on empirical research into commercial
transactions, see Shuchman, Empirical Studies in Commercial Law, 23 J.
Legal Ed. 81 (1970).

2. *The Code draftsmen and empirical research.* Despite their interest in business
practice the Code draftsmen conducted no systematic field research while

drafting the provisions of the UCC. For a reasoned, if not wholehearted, defense of the draftsmen, see W. Twining, Karl Llewellyn and The Realist Movement 313-320 (1973). Professor Twining suggests that the draftsmen did do some research, did find much relevant information from reading appellate opinions, and did learn from the comments of members of the Code's sponsoring institutions (the American Law Institute and the National Conference of Commissioners on Uniform State Laws). Moreover, when drafting general commercial legislation it may only be necessary to have "a reasonably accurate picture of standard practices" rather than detailed information about each specific type of transaction. Given the limited resources available to the draftsmen, one may question the feasibility of conducting empirical research. Are you persuaded?

Consider also the following comment by Professor Gilmore: "We overrate the results that can be achieved by hiring a team of specialists and having a survey made. The bigger the problem to be investigated, the longer the survey takes, the more it costs and the more doubtful the results. The task of a statute like the Code is to state basic principles under which business transactions can be carried out. This task does not require a scientific knowledge of each business fact—even if such knowledge were conceivably available, which it is not. 'Science' performs miracles; we worship the controlled experiment of the laboratory man and think that salvation lies in applying his methods to everything we do. What we get, outside the laboratory, is an illusion of certainty. In the drafting of statutes a draftsman who is aware of the possibility of human error and walks cautiously is infinitely to be preferred to a pseudo-scientist who knows he has the truth. I am not an advocate of happy ignorance. What was needed—and achieved—in the drafting of the Code was a good working knowledge of the facts of business life.[2]" Gilmore, The Uniform Commercial Code: A Reply to Professor Beutel, 61 Yale L.J. 364, 365-366 (1952).

C. PAROL EVIDENCE; CONCEPT OF "USAGE OF TRADE"

Having concluded that there is an enforceable agreement because the parties intend to be bound and the statute of frauds has been satisfied, a court must still determine what the terms of the contract are. As you have learned in your general study of contract law, courts are directed by the parol evidence rule to

2. My disclaimer of "scientific" methods of investigation is by no means an acceptance of Beutel's implied charges that little or no effort was made to discover the true nature of things. On the contrary. No Article of the Code reached anything like final form without having undergone the intensive scrutiny of people—both lawyers and operating men—who were intimately acquainted with the area of business practice and law involved. [Gilmore]

give preference to written statements of these terms over prior or contemporaneous oral statements. Although the Code carries forward a version of the parol evidence rule, the draftsmen clearly intended to reject some of the strict interpretations courts had given it. See UCC 2-202, comment 1. This approach is consonant with a modern trend among courts and commentators that was already in progress at the time of the Code's formulation, and that was subsequently carried a good deal further. See 3 A. Corbin, Contracts, §§573-596 (rev. ed. 1960);[2] Restatement (Second) of Contracts, §§209-223 (1981). It will be considerably easier for merchants to introduce evidence of the commercial context within which the transaction took place under the Code's rule. UCC 2-202(a). In the following case we explore the rule's scope in a mercantile setting.[3]

COLUMBIA NITROGEN CORP. v. ROYSTER CO.
451 F.2d 3, 9 UCC Rep. 977 (4th Cir. 1971)

BUTZNER, Circuit Judge. Columbia Nitrogen Corp. appeals a judgment in the amount of $750,000 in favor of F. S. Royster Guano Co. for breach of a contract for the sale of phosphate to Columbia by Royster. Columbia defended on the grounds that the contract, construed in light of the usage of the trade and course of dealing, imposed no duty to accept at the quoted prices the minimum quantities stated in the contract. . . . The district court excluded the evidence about course of dealing and usage of the trade. . . . The jury found for Royster on [the contract claim]. . . . We hold that Columbia's proffered evidence was improperly excluded and Columbia is entitled to a new trial on the contractual issues. . . .

Royster manufactures and markets mixed fertilizers, the principal components of which are nitrogen, phosphate and potash. Columbia is primarily a producer of nitrogen, although it manufactures some mixed fertilizer. For several years Royster had been a major purchaser of Columbia's products, but Columbia had never been a significant customer of Royster. In the fall of 1966, Royster constructed a facility which enabled it to produce more phos-

---

2. Corbin's masterful writings on the parol evidence rule are among the classics of American legal scholarship. Students may also find helpful Corbin, The Parol Evidence Rule, 53 Yale L.J. 609 (1944), particularly its section contrasting the purposes and effects of the parol evidence rule and the statute of frauds.

3. The Code's rule does not in so many words distinguish mercantile and nonmercantile settings. Although trade usage and course of dealing are liable to be far more significant in the former, the Code rule is also thought by some to improve the position of consumers. See Broude, The Consumer and the Parol Evidence Rule: Section 2-202 of the Uniform Commercial Code, 1970 Duke L.J. 881.

phate than it needed in its own operations. After extensive negotiations, the companies executed a contract for Royster's sale of a minimum of 31,000 tons of phosphate each year for three years to Columbia, with an option to extend the term. The contract stated the price per ton, subject to an escalation clause dependent on production costs.[2]

Phosphate prices soon plunged precipitously. Unable to resell the phosphate at a competitive price, Columbia ordered only part of the scheduled tonnage. At Columbia's request, Royster lowered its price for diammonium

2. In pertinent part, the contract provides: "Contract made as of this 8th day of May between Columbia Nitrogen Corporation, a Delaware corporation, (hereinafter called the Buyer) hereby agrees to purchase and accept from F. S. Royster Guano Company, a Virginia corporation, (hereinafter called the Seller) agrees to furnish quantities of Diammonium Phosphate 18-46-0, Granular Triple Superphosphate 0-46-0, and Run-of-Pile Triple Superphosphate 0-46-0 on the following terms and conditions.

"*Period Covered by Contract*—This contract to begin July 1, 1967 and continue through June 30, 1970, with renewal privileges for an additional three year period based upon notification by Buyer and acceptance by Seller on or before June 30, 1969. Failure of notification by either party on or before June 30, 1969, constitutes an automatic renewal for an additional one-year period beyond June 30, 1970, and on a year-to-year basis thereafter unless notification of cancellation is given by either party 90 days prior to June 30 of each year.

Products Supplied Under Contract	Minimum Tonnage Per Year
Diammonium Phosphate 18-46-0	15,000
Granular Triple Superphosphate 0-46-0	15,000
Run-of-Pile Triple Superphosphate 0-46-0	1,000

"Seller agrees to provide additional quantities beyond the minimum specified tonnage for products listed above provided Seller has the capacity and ability to provide such additional quantities. . . .

"*Price*—In Bulk F.O.B. Cars, Royster, Florida.

Diammonium Phosphate 18-46-0	$61.25 Per Ton
Granular Triple Superphosphate 0-46-0	$40.90 Per Ton
Run-of-Pile Triple Superphosphate 0-46-0	$ 0.86 Per Unit

"*Default*—If Buyer fails to pay for any delivery under this contract within 30 days after Seller's invoice to Buyer and then if such invoice is not paid within an additional 30 days after the Seller notifies the Buyer of such default, then after that time the Seller may at his option defer further deliveries hereunder or take such action as in their judgment they may decide including cancellation of this contract. Any balance carried beyond 30 days will carry a service fee of 3/4 of 1% per month. . . .

"*Escalation*—The escalation factor up or down shall be based upon the effects of changing raw material cost of sulphur, rock phosphate, and labor as follows. These escalations up or down to become effective against shipments of products covered by this contract 30 days after notification by Seller to Buyer. . . . "No verbal understanding will be recognized by either party hereto; this contract expresses all the terms and conditions of the agreement, shall be signed in duplicate and shall not become operative until approved in writing by the Seller."

phosphate on shipments for three months in 1967, but specified that subsequent shipments would be at the original contract price. Even with this concession, Royster's price was still substantially above the market. As a result, Columbia ordered less than a tenth of the phosphate Royster was to ship in the first contract year. When pressed by Royster, Columbia offered to take the phosphate at the current market price and resell it without brokerage fee. Royster, however, insisted on the contract price. When Columbia refused delivery, Royster sold the unaccepted phosphate for Columbia's account at a price substantially below the contract price.

Columbia assigns error to the pretrial ruling of the district court excluding all evidence on usage of the trade and course of dealing between the parties. It offered the testimony of witnesses with long experience in the trade that because of uncertain crop and weather conditions, farming practices, and government agricultural programs, express price and quantity terms in contracts for materials in the mixed fertilizer industry are mere projections to be adjusted according to market forces.[3]

Columbia also offered proof of its business dealings with Royster over the six-year period preceding the phosphate contract. Since Columbia had not been a significant purchaser of Royster's products, these dealings were almost exclusively nitrogen sales to Royster or exchanges of stock carried in inventory. The pattern which emerges, Columbia claimed, is one of repeated and substantial deviation from the stated amount or price, including four instances where Royster took none of the goods for which it had contracted. Columbia

---

3. Typical of the proffered testimony are the following excerpts:

"The contracts generally entered into between buyer and seller of materials has always been, in my opinion, construed to be the buyer's best estimate of his anticipated requirements for a given period of time. It is well known in our industry that weather conditions, farming practices, government farm control programs, change requirements from time to time. And therefore allowances were always made to meet these circumstances as they arose."

"Tonnage requirements fluctuate greatly, and that is one reason that the contracts are not considered as binding as most contracts are, because the buyer normally would buy on historical basis, but his normal average use would be per annum of any given material. Now that can be affected very decidedly by adverse weather conditions such as a drought, or a flood, or maybe governmental programs which we have been faced with for many, many years, seed grain programs. They pay the farmer not to plant. If he doesn't plant, he doesn't use the fertilizer. When the contracts are made, we do not know of all these contingencies and what they are going to be. So the contract is made for what is considered a fair estimate of his requirements. And, the contract is considered binding to the extent, on him morally, that if he uses the tonnage that he will execute the contract in good faith as the buyer. . . . "

"I have never heard of a contract of this type being enforced legally. . . . Well, it undoubtedly sounds ridiculous to people from other industries, but there is a very definite, several very definite reasons why the fertilizer business is always operated under what we call gentlemen's agreements. . . . "

"The custom in the fertilizer industry is that the seller either meets the competitive situation or releases the buyer from it upon proof that he can buy it at that price. . . . [T]hey will either have the option of meeting it or releasing him from taking additional tonnage or holding him to that price. . . . "

And this custom exists "regardless of the contractual provisions."

"[T]he custom was that [these contracts] were not worth the cost of the paper they were printed on."

offered proof that the total variance amounted to more than $500,000 in reduced sales. This experience, a Columbia officer offered to testify, formed the basis of an understanding on which he depended in conducting negotiations with Royster.

The district court held that the evidence should be excluded. It ruled that "custom and usage or course of dealing are not admissible to contradict the express, plain, unambiguous language of a valid written contract, which by virtue of its detail negates the proposition that the contract is open to variances in its terms. . . . "

A number of Virginia cases have held that extrinsic evidence may not be received to explain or supplement a written contract unless the court finds the writing is ambiguous. . . . This rule, however, has been changed by the Uniform Commercial Code which Virginia has adopted. The Code expressly states that it "shall be liberally construed and applied to promote its underlying purposes and policies," which include "the continued expansion of commercial practices through custom, usage and agreement of the parties. . . . " UCC 1-102. The importance of usage of trade and course of dealing between the parties is shown by UCC 2-202, which authorizes their use to explain or supplement a contract. The official comment states this section rejects the old rule that evidence of course of dealing or usage of trade can be introduced only when the contract is ambiguous. And the Virginia commentators, noting that "[t]his section reflects a more liberal approach to the introduction of parol evidence . . . than has been followed in Virginia," express the opinion that [earlier Virginia cases] no longer should be followed. Va. Code Ann. §8.2-202, Va. Comment. . . . We hold, therefore, that a finding of ambiguity is not necessary for the admission of extrinsic evidence about the usage of the trade and the parties' course of dealing.

We turn next to Royster's claim that Columbia's evidence was properly excluded because it was inconsistent with the express terms of their agreement. There can be no doubt that the Uniform Commercial Code restates the well established rule that evidence of usage of trade and course of dealing should be excluded whenever it cannot be reasonably construed as consistent with the terms of the contract. Division of Triple T Service, Inc. v. Mobil Oil Corp., 60 Misc. 2d 720, 304 N.Y.S.2d 191, 203 (1969), aff'd mem., 311 N.Y.S.2d 961 (1970). Royster argues that the evidence should be excluded as inconsistent because the contract contains detailed provisions regarding the base price, escalation, minimum tonnage, and delivery schedules. The argument is based on the premise that because a contract appears on its face to be complete, evidence of course of dealing and usage of trade should be excluded. We believe, however, that neither the language nor the policy of the Code supports such a broad exclusionary rule. UCC 2-202 expressly allows evidence of course of dealing or usage of trade to explain or supplement terms intended by the parties as a final expression of their agreement. When this section is read in light of UCC 1-205(4), it is clear that the test of admissibility is not whether the contract appears on its face to be complete in every detail, but whether the proffered evidence of course of dealing and trade usage reasonably can be construed as consistent with the express terms of the agreement.

The proffered testimony sought to establish that because of changing weather conditions, farming practices, and government agricultural programs, dealers adjusted prices, quantities, and delivery schedules to reflect declining market conditions. For the following reasons it is reasonable to construe this evidence as consistent with the express terms of the contract:

The contract does not expressly state that course of dealing and usage of trade cannot be used to explain or supplement the written contract.

The contract is silent about adjusting prices and quantities to reflect a declining market. It neither permits nor prohibits adjustment, and this neutrality provides a fitting occasion for recourse to usage of trade and prior dealing to supplement the contract and explain its terms.

Minimum tonnages and additional quantities are expressed in terms of "Products Supplied Under Contract." Significantly, they are not expressed as just "Products" or as "Products Purchased Under Contract." The description used by the parties is consistent with the proffered testimony.

Finally, the default clause of the contract refers only to the failure of the buyer to pay for delivered phosphate. During the contract negotiations, Columbia rejected a Royster proposal for liquidated damages of $10 for each ton Columbia declined to accept. On the other hand, Royster rejected a Columbia proposal for a clause that tied the price to the market by obligating Royster to conform its price to offers Columbia received from other phosphate producers. The parties, having rejected both proposals, failed to state any consequences of Columbia's refusal to take delivery—the kind of default Royster alleges in this case. Royster insists that we span this hiatus by applying the general law of contracts permitting recovery of damages upon the buyer's refusal to take delivery according to the written provisions of the contract. This solution is not what the Uniform Commercial Code prescribes. Before allowing damages, a court must first determine whether the buyer has in fact defaulted. It must do this by supplementing and explaining the agreement with evidence of trade usage and course of dealing that is consistent with the contract's express terms. UCC 1-205(4), 2-202. Faithful adherence to this mandate reflects the reality of the marketplace and avoids the overly legalistic interpretations which the Code seeks to abolish.

Royster also contends that Columbia's proffered testimony was properly rejected because it dealt with mutual willingness of buyer and seller to adjust contract terms to the market. Columbia, Royster protests, seeks unilateral adjustment. This argument misses the point. What Columbia seeks to show is a practice of mutual adjustments so prevalent in the industry and in prior dealings between the parties that it formed a part of the agreement governing this transaction. It is not insisting on a unilateral right to modify the contract.

Nor can we accept Royster's contention that the testimony should be excluded under the contract clause: "No verbal understanding will be recognized by either party hereto; this contract expresses all the terms and conditions of the agreement, shall be signed in duplicate, and shall not become operative until approved in writing by the Seller." Course of dealing and trade usage are not synonymous with verbal understandings, terms and conditions. UCC 2-202 draws a distinction between supplementing a written contract by consistent additional terms and supplementing it by course of dealing or usage of trade. Evidence of additional terms must be excluded when "the court finds the writing to have been intended also as a complete and exclusive statement of the terms of the agreement." Significantly, no similar limitation is placed on the introduction of evidence of course of dealing or usage of trade. Indeed the official comment notes that course of dealing and usage of trade, unless carefully negated, are admissible to supplement the terms of any writing, and that contracts are to be read on the assumption that these elements were taken for granted when the document was phrased. Since the Code assigns course of dealing and trade usage unique and important roles, they should not be conclusively rejected by reading them into stereotyped language that makes no specific reference to them. Indeed, the Code's official commentators urge that overly simplistic and overly legalistic interpretation of a contract should be shunned. [The court quotes in a footnote UCC 1-205, Comment 1.]

We conclude, therefore, that Columbia's evidence about course of dealing and usage of trade should have been admitted. Its exclusion requires that the judgment against Columbia must be set aside and the case retried. . . .

NOTES & QUESTIONS

1. *The importance of usage of trade.* The UCC distinguishes an "agreement" from a "contract." An agreement includes not only the dickered terms but also terms implied from usage of trade, the course of dealing in prior transactions between the parties, and the course of performance of the agreement in question. UCC 1-201(3), 1-205, 2-208. An agreement is not always legally enforceable in strict accordance with its terms. For example, the parties may not have satisfied the statute of frauds; the parol evidence rule may exclude evidence of prior or contemporaneous oral agreements; or terms of the agreement may be struck down because they are unconscionable. A contract, therefore, is the total legal obligation resulting from an *enforceable* agreement. UCC 1-201(11).

The UCC assumes that parties understand that practices followed in their course of dealing or as a usage of their trade will be observed in every transaction they enter into with each other unless they otherwise agree. By emphasizing the role of course of dealing and usage of trade the draftsmen hoped to resolve disputes in accordance with businessmen's reasonable expectations. They also hoped to provide flexibility in the Code rules by allowing the continued expansion of commercial practices without impediment from antiquated legal rules. UCC 1-102(2)(b). For a discussion of the draftsmen's theory and how it has been treated by the courts, see Kirst, Usage of Trade and Course of Dealing: Subversion of the UCC Theory, 1977 U. Ill. L.F. 811. See also Murray, The Realism of Behaviorism Under the Uniform Commercial Code, 51 Ore. L. Rev. 269, 276 (1972) (need for "a more precise and fair identification of the actual or presumed assent of the parties . . . [requires] empirical verification of the specific circumstances surrounding the 'deal' ").

2. *Usage of trade in summary judgment.* The existence and scope of a usage of trade are to be proved as facts but the interpretation of a written statement of usages is for the court to decide. UCC 1-205(2). If a party can find an expert to testify as to a usage that "explains, supplements or qualifies" the terms of the agreement, will the party be able to avoid summary judgment because there is a disputed fact issue? See also UCC 2-202(a). Does UCC 1-205(4) permit a court to exclude proposed testimony regarding a usage that contradicts express terms, or does the section say merely that a court must admit the testimony into evidence and weigh it in the light of the express terms? When hearing a motion for summary judgment may a judge consider the relevance of the proffered evidence? Thus in *Columbia Nitrogen* should the court have excluded the evidence because it was not relevant to the *type* of long-term contract in that case? Note that if a party can avoid summary judgment he will be able to increase his leverage on the other party to settle. The parties in *Columbia Nitrogen,* for example, settled their dispute for a substantial sum approximately one week before retrial. C. Corman, Commercial Law Cases and Materials 54 (1976).

3. *Merchant juries.* The 1941 Report and Second Draft of the Revised Uniform Sales Act proposed to institutionalize the finding of mercantile facts through merchant experts. Sections 59 to 59-D of the 1941 draft provide a procedure "to accomplish speedy and competent determination of questions of fact which fall within the field of special merchants' knowledge rather than of general knowledge." By these provisions, either party in a sales dispute between merchants is empowered to submit specially the following questions of mercantile fact to "a special sworn expert tribunal":

(a) The effect on the terms or conditions of the sale or contract to sell, of mercantile usage, or of the usage of a particular trade;
(b) The conformity or non-conformity in quality, routing, or any other mercantile aspect of any delivery, to the duties or conditions resting on the seller, and the measure of the discrepancy, if any; and whether any defect in performance has been substantial;
(c) The mercantile reasonableness of any action by either party, the mercantile reasonableness of which is challenged;
(d) Any other issue which requires for its competent determination special merchants' knowledge rather than general knowledge. [§59(1).]

The procedures for demand, selection, hearings, and determination are set out. Although the parties initiate the submissions to the merchant experts, the trial court retains control of the proceedings. The court settles the issues of mercantile fact to be submitted, selects the experts if the parties fail to do so, and presides at the hearing. Although a unanimous finding by the experts may be received in evidence in the particular dispute, a Comment notes that the procedure is not designed to build precedent since "[t]he *fixing* of trade practice and standards is believed to be properly a task for associations." The proposal was soon dropped without comment. Should it have been?

4. *Published trade standards.* Foxco is a manufacturer of knitted fabrics with its principal place of business in New York City. Fabric World is engaged in the retail fabric business and operates a chain of stores in a number of states, including Alabama where it has its headquarters. Fabric World orders from Foxco 12,000 yards of "first quality" fabric. In litigation about the quality standards the fabric must meet, Foxco introduces into evidence the "Standards for Finished Knitted Fabrics" published by the Knitted Textile Association, an association of over 1,500 members. The standards provide that certain types and amounts of flaws are permissible in "first quality" fabric. Foxco is a member of the association; Fabric World is not a member and was not aware of the published standards. *Held,* on appeal, the standards were properly admitted into evidence under UCC 1-205(2), (3), and 2-202. Foxco Industries, Ltd. v Fabric World, Inc., 595 F.2d 976 (5th Cir. 1979). Excerpts from *Foxco* dealing with remedial issues appear infra at p. 591.

5. *Usage of trade and the new entrant.* HMT planned to grow and market for the first time processing potatoes used in the making of potato chips. Blue Bell knew of HMT's proposed entrance into the market, and during the summer of 1970 negotiated a contract for the sale of 100,000 cwt. sacks to be delivered between May 17 and July 17, 1971. The contracts were signed in October, 1970, on behalf of HMT by Hoffman, who had over 20 years' experience in the processing potato industry, but who had only been hired a few weeks before the signing. Because of a decline in demand for Blue Bell products in May through July of 1971 Blue Bell's needs were severely reduced. After prorating its demand among its suppliers, Blue Bell took only 60,105 cwt. sacks from HMT. HMT sued Blue Bell for breach of contract. Blue Bell offered testimony that "because the contracts are executed eight or nine months before the harvest season, the custom in the processing potato industry is to treat the quantity solely as a reasonable estimate of the buyers' needs based on their customers' demands and the growers' ability to supply based on the anticipated yield for the delivery period." *Held,* on appeal, evidence of the custom was admissible to explain the quantity figures; there was no error in the trial court's refusal to give the following instruction:

> A party to a contract is not bound by a custom or usage in the trade or industry unless such party has knowledge, either actual of constructive, of such custom or usage. A party cannot be held to have constructive knowledge of such custom unless it is of such general and universal application *and he has been engaged in such industry for such period of time that he may be conclusively presumed* to know of it. [Court's emphasis.] [Heggblade-Marguleas-Tenneco, Inc. v. Sunshine Biscuit, Inc., 59 Cal. App. 3d 948, 131 Cal. Rptr. 183, 19 UCC Rep. 1067 (1976).]

The case is cited with apparent approval, Restatement (Second) of Contracts, §222, Reporter's Note, comment 6 (1981).

Problem 9-8. California Concrete Corp. (CCC) entered into a written agreement with Building Contractors, Inc. (BCI) in which CCC agreed to supply BCI with "approximately 70,000 cubic yards" of concrete during a specified six-month period at $24.60 per cubic yard. Among other terms the agreement included a clause stating: "No conditions that are not incorporated in this contract will be recognized." During the six months BCI ordered only 20,000 cubic yards, which was all it needed for its construction work. CCC brings an action to recover profits lost by BCI's alleged breach. BCI seeks to introduce testimony that it is generally understood by contract suppliers and contractors that the quantity stipulated in a contract for concrete is not mandatory upon either party and that both quantity and price terms are subject to renegotiation. Should BCI be permitted to introduce this testimony into evidence? See UCC 1-205, 2-201, 2-202, 2-306. Apart from parol evidence problems, is such an agreement an enforceable contract? See UCC 2-204, 2-209, 2-305.

D. CONTRACT FORMATION; SUPPLEMENTARY TERMS

Parties may agree to be bound but omit a specific term either inadvertently or intending to fill it in at a later time. Part 3 of Article 2 sets out a number of provisions to fill these gaps. For example, parties may intend to enter into an enforceable contract but leave the price term open. UCC 2-305(1) states that in most such cases "the price is a reasonable price at the time for delivery." Similar provisions fill gaps in delivery and payment terms. UCC 2-307 to 2-310. Some general principles are also stated for output and requirements contracts (UCC 2-306) and for contract provisions that leave performance of some obligation at the option of one of the parties (UCC 2-311). These statutory terms incorporate standards designed to represent what the parties would have agreed on if they had not left the gap. To allow maximum flexibility these sections make frequent reference to "reasonableness" and "good faith."

The more gaps to be filled, of course, the less likely that parties have agreed to be bound. The following case explores the difficulty of determining whether there has been an agreement when a payment term has been left unresolved.

SOUTHWEST ENGINEERING CO. v. MARTIN TRACTOR CO.
205 Kan. 684, 473 P.2d 18, 7 UCC Rep. 1288 (1970)

FONTRON, Justice. This is an action to recover damages for breach of contract. Trial was had to the court which entered judgment in favor of the plaintiff. The defendant has appealed.

Southwest Engineering Company, Inc., the plaintiff, is a Missouri corporation engaged in general contracting work, while the defendant, Martin Tractor Company, Inc., is a Kansas corporation. . . .

We glean from the record that in April, 1966, the plaintiff was interested in submitting a bid to the United States Corps of Engineers for the construction of certain runway lighting facilities at McConnell Air Force Base at Wichita. However, before submitting a bid, and on April 11, 1966, the plaintiff's construction superintendent, Mr. R. E. Cloepfil, called the manager of Martin's engine department, Mr. Ken Hurt, who at the time was at Colby, asking for a price on a standby generator and accessory equipment. Mr. Hurt replied that he would phone him back from Topeka, which he did the next day, quoting a price of $18,500. This quotation was re-confirmed by Hurt over the phone on April 13.

Southwest submitted its bid on April 14, 1966, using Hurt's figure of $18,500 for the generator equipment, and its bid was accepted. On April 20, Southwest notified Martin that its bid had been accepted. Hurt and Cloepfil thereafter agreed over the phone to meet in Springfield on April 28. On that date Hurt flew to Springfield, where the two men conferred at the airfield restaurant for about an hour. Hurt took to the meeting a copy of the job specifications which the government had supplied Martin prior to the letting.

At the Springfield meeting it developed that Martin had upped its price for the generator and accessory equipment from $18,500 to $21,500. Despite this change of position by Martin, concerning which Cloepfil was understandably amazed, the two men continued their conversation and, according to Cloepfil, they arrived at an agreement for the sale of a D353 generator and accessories for the sum of $21,500. In addition it was agreed that if the Corps of Engineers would accept a less expensive generator, a D343, the aggregate price to Southwest would be $15,000. The possibility of providing alternative equipment, the D343, was suggested by Mr. Hurt, apparently in an attempt to mollify Mr. Cloepfil when the latter learned that Martin had reneged on its price quotation of April 2. It later developed that the Corps of Engineers would not approve the cheaper generator and that Southwest eventually had to supply the more expensive D353 generator.

At the conference, Mr. Hurt separately listed the component parts of each of the two generators on the top half of a sheet of paper and set out the price after each item. The prices were then totaled. On the bottom half of the sheet Hurt set down the accessories common to both generators and their cost. This handwritten memorandum, as it was referred to during the trial, noted a 10 per cent discount on the aggregate cost of each generator, while the accessories were listed at Martin's cost. The price of the D353 was rounded off at $21,500 and D343 at $15,000. The memorandum was handed to Cloepfil while the two men were still at the airport. We will refer to this memorandum further during the course of this opinion. [The memorandum had a handprinted notation at the top left-hand corner: "Ken Hurt, Martin Tractor, Topeka, Caterpillar."—Eds.]

On May 2, 1966, Cloepfil addressed a letter to the Martin Tractor Company, directing Martin to proceed with shop drawings and submittal documents for the McConnell lighting job and calling attention to the fact that applicable government regulations were required to be followed. Further reference to this communication will be made when necessary.

Some three weeks thereafter, on May 24, 1966, Hurt wrote Cloepfil the following letter [with heading and addresses omitted.—EDS.]:

May 24, 1966

Dear Sir:

Due to restrictions placed on Caterpillar products, accessory suppliers, and other stipulations by the district governing agency, we cannot accept your letter to proceed dated May 2, 1966, and hereby withdraw all verbal quotations.

Regretfully,

/s/ *Ken Hurt*

Ken Hurt, Manager
Engine Division

On receipt of this unwelcome missive, Cloepfil telephoned Mr. Hurt who stated they had some work underway for the Corps of Engineers in both the Kansas City and Tulsa districts and did not want to take on any other work for the Corps at that time. Hurt assured Cloepfil he could buy the equipment from anybody at the price Martin could sell it for. Later investigation showed, however, that such was not the case.

In August of 1966, Mr. Cloepfil and Mr. Anderson, the president of Southwest, traveled to Topeka in an effort to persuade Martin to fulfill its contract. Hurt met them at the company office where harsh words were bandied about. Tempers eventually cooled off and at the conclusion of the verbal melee, hands were shaken all around and Hurt went so far as to say that if Southwest still wanted to buy the equipment from them to submit another order and he would get it handled. On this promising note the protagonists parted.

After returning to Springfield, Mr. Cloepfil, on September 6, wrote Mr. Hurt placing an order for a D353 generator (the expensive one) and asking that the order be given prompt attention, as their completion date was in early December. This communication was returned unopened.

A final effort to communicate with Martin was attempted by Mr. Anderson when the unopened letter was returned. A phone call was placed for Mr. Martin, himself, and Mr. Anderson was informed by the girl on the switchboard that Martin was in Colorado Springs on a vacation. Anderson then placed a call to the motel where he was told Mr. Martin could be reached. Martin refused to talk on the call, on learning the caller's name, and Anderson was told he would have to contact his office.

Mr. Anderson then replaced his call to Topeka and reached either the company comptroller or the company treasurer who responded by cussing him and saying "Who in the hell do you think you are? We don't have to sell you a damn thing."

Southwest eventually secured the generator equipment from Foley Tractor Co. of Wichita, a company which Mr. Hurt had one time suggested, at a price of $27,541. The present action was then filed, seeking damages of $6,041 for breach of the contract and $9,000 for loss resulting from the delay caused by the breach. The trial court awarded damages of $6,041 for the breach but rejected damages allegedly due to delay. The defendant, only, has appealed; there is no cross-appeal by plaintiff. . . .

[The trial court found, inter alia, that an agreement had been reached on April 28, and that it included additional terms not noted in the memorandum of that date: Southwest was to install the equipment; Martin was to deliver the equipment to Wichita; Martin was to assemble and supply submittal documents within three weeks. The appellate court affirmed the trial court's conclusion that the memorandum of April 28 satisfied the requirements of UCC 2-201.]

In a pre-trial deposition, Mr. Hurt, himself, deposed that "we agreed on the section that I would be quoting on, and we come to some over-all general agreement on the major items." At the trial Hurt testified he did not wish to change that statement in any way.

Hurt further testified that in his opinion the thing which stood in the way of a firm deal was Martin's terms of payment—that had Southwest agreed with those terms of payment, so far as he was concerned, he would have considered a firm deal was made. Mr. Hurt acknowledged while on the stand that he penned the memorandum and that as disclosed therein a 10 per cent discount was given Southwest on the price of either of the generators listed (depending on which was approved by the Corps of Engineers), and that the accessories common to both generators were to be net—that is, sold without profit.

It is quite true, as the trial court found, that terms of payment were not agreed upon at the Springfield meeting. Hurt testified that as the memorandum was being made out, he said they wanted 10 per cent with the order, 50 per cent on delivery and the balance on acceptance, but he did not recall Cloepfil's response. Cloepfil's version was somewhat different. He stated that after the two had shaken hands in the lobby preparing to leave, Hurt said their terms usually were 20 per cent down and the balance on delivery; while he (Cloepfil) said the way they generally paid was 90 per cent on the tenth of the month following delivery and the balance on final acceptance. It is obvious the parties reached no agreement on this point.

However, a failure on the part of Messrs. Hurt and Cloepfil to agree on terms of payment would not, of itself, defeat an otherwise valid agreement reached by them. [The court quotes UCC 2-204(3).]

The official UCC Comment is enlightening: "Subsection (3) states the principle as to 'open terms' underlying later sections of the Article. If the parties intend to enter into a binding agreement, this subsection recognizes that agreement as valid in law, despite missing terms, if there is any reasonably certain basis for granting a remedy. The test is not certainty as to what the parties were to do nor as to the exact amount of damages due the plaintiff. Nor is the fact that one or more terms are left to be agreed upon enough of itself to defeat an otherwise adequate agreement. Rather, commercial standards on the point of 'indefiniteness' are intended to be applied, this Act making provision elsewhere for missing terms needed for performance, open price, remedies and the like. The more terms the parties leave open, the less likely it is that they have intended to conclude a binding agreement, but their actions may be frequently conclusive on the matter despite the omissions."

The above Code provision and accompanying Comment were quoted in Pennsylvania Co. v. Wilmington Trust Co., 39 Del. Ch. 453, 166 A.2d 726, where the court made this observation: "There appears to be no pertinent court authority interpreting this rather recent but controlling statute. In an article entitled 'The Law of Sales In the Proposed Uniform Commercial Code,' 63 Harv. L. Rev. 561, 576, Mr. Williston wanted to limit omissions to 'minor' terms. He wanted 'business honor' to be the only compulsion where 'important terms' are left open. Nevertheless, his recommendation was rejected (see note on p. 561). This shows that those drafting the statute intended that the omission of even an important term does not prevent the finding under the statute that the parties intended to make a contract." (166 A.2d at 731, 732.)

So far as the present case is concerned, UCC 2-310 supplies the omitted term. This statute provides in pertinent part:

> Unless otherwise agreed
> (a) payment is due at the time and place at which the buyer is to receive the goods even though the place of shipment is the place of delivery; . . .

In our view, the language of the two Code provisions is clear and positive. Considered together, we take the two sections to mean that where parties have reached an enforceable agreement for the sale of goods, but omit therefrom the terms of payment, the law will imply, as part of the agreement, that payment is to be made at time of delivery. In this respect the law does not greatly differ from the rule this court laid down years ago. . . .

We do not mean to infer that terms of payment are not of importance under many circumstances, or that parties may not condition an agreement on their being included. However, the facts before us hardly indicate that Hurt and Cloepfil considered the terms of payment to be significant, or of more than passing interest. Hurt testified that while he stated his terms he did not recall Cloepfil's response, while Cloepfil stated that as the two were on the point of leaving, each stated their usual terms and that was as far as it went. The trial court found that only a brief and casual conversation ensued as to payment, and we think that is a valid summation of what took place.

Moreover, it is worthy of note that Martin first mentioned the omission of the terms of payment, as justifying its breach, in a letter written by counsel on September 15, 1966, more than four months after the memorandum was prepared by Hurt. On prior occasions Martin attributed its cancellation of the

Springfield understanding to other causes. In its May 24 letter, Martin ascribed its withdrawal of "all verbal quotations" to "restrictions placed on Caterpillar products, accessory suppliers, and other stipulations by the district governing agency." In explaining the meaning of the letter to Cloepfil, Hurt said that Martin was doing work for the Corps of Engineers in the Kansas City and Tulsa districts and did not want to take on additional work with them at this time.

The entire circumstances may well give rise to a suspicion that Martin's present insistence that future negotiations were contemplated concerning terms of payment, is primarily an afterthought, for use as an escape hatch. Doubtless the trial court so considered the excuse in arriving at its findings. . . .

The defendant points . . . [to] the May 2 letter, as interjecting a new and unacceptable term in the agreement made at Springfield. ". . . We are not prepared to make a partial payment at the time of placing of this order. However, we will be able to include 100% of the engine-generator price in our first payment estimate after it is delivered, and only 10% will have to be withheld pending acceptance. Ordinarily this means that suppliers can expect payment of 90% within about thirty days after delivery."

It must be conceded that the terms of payment proposed in Southwest's letter had not been agreed to by Martin. However, we view the proposal as irrelevant. Although terms of payment had not been mutually agreed upon, UCC 2-310 supplied the missing terms, i.e., payment on delivery, which thus became part of the agreement already concluded. In legal effect the proposal was no more than one to change the terms of payment implied by law. Since Martin did not accept the change, the proposal had no effect, either as altering or terminating the agreement reached at Springfield. As the Michigan Court of Appeals said in American Parts v. American Arbitration Assn., 8 Mich. App. 156, 154 N.W.2d 5: ". . . Surely a party who has entered into an agreement cannot change that agreement by the simple expedient of sending a written 'confirmation' containing additional or different terms. . . . " (p. 174, 154 N.W.2d at 15.) Neither, may we add, will an extraneous proposal which materially alters the original agreement, be included unless agreed to by the other party. (Application of Doughboy Industries, Inc., 17 A.D.2d 216, 233 N.Y.S.2d 488.) . . .

[Affirmed.]

NOTES & QUESTIONS

1. *Promissory estoppel.* Is the doctrine of promissory estoppel relevant in the *Southwest Engineering* case?

2. *Contract to bargain.* For an argument that the UCC should be read to make "contracts to bargain" enforceable, see Knapp, Enforcing the Contract to Bargain, 44 N.Y.U. L. Rev. 673 (1969). Professor Knapp argues that businessmen may reach a point in negotiations when "they regard themselves as bound to each other to the extent that neither can withdraw for an 'unjusti-

fied' reason, and yet still free enough that neither will be compelled to perform if—after good faith bargaining—actual agreement cannot be reached." Id. at 685. He suggests that UCC 2-204(3) could be read to support the contract to bargain. Would this concept be relevant in *Southwest Engineering?* Note that UCC 1-203, which imposes an obligation of good faith, refers only to the performance or enforcement of a contract or duty covered by the UCC and therefore does not govern precontract negotiations.

3. *General contract law.* The new Restatement has adopted the Code's position that open terms are merely evidence of a lack of intention to conclude a bargain and that the test of certainty is a reasonably certain basis for fashioning a remedy. Restatement (Second) of Contracts §33 (1981).

E.   BATTLE OF THE FORMS; ARBITRATION

More ink has probably been spilled in the debate over the meaning of UCC 2-207 (additional terms in acceptance or confirmation) than over any other provision of Article 2. All contracts students know that the traditional common law required acceptances to be the mirror image of the offer; any modification or addition turned the acceptance into a counteroffer that the original offeror had to accept before there was a contract. On the assumption that most persons in this situation believed that a contract had been formed notwithstanding the variance, the Code draftsmen set out to make the "agreement" enforceable and to provide rules for determining which terms became part of the contract. To judge by the continuing litigation UCC 2-207 has not provided the final solution to this problem, commonly known as the battle of the forms.

MARLENE INDUSTRIES CORP. v. CARNAC TEXTILES, INC.
45 N.Y.2d 327, 380 N.E.2d 239, 408 N.Y.S.2d 410, 24 UCC Rep. 257 (1978)

GABRIELLI, Judge. This appeal involves yet another of the many conflicts which arise as a result of the all too common business practice of blithely drafting, sending, receiving, and filing unread numerous purchase orders, acknowledgments, and other divers forms containing a myriad of discrepant terms. Both parties agree that they have entered into a contract for the sale of goods; indeed, it would appear that there is no disagreement as to most of the essential terms of their contract. They do disagree, however, as to whether their agreement includes a provision for the arbitration of disputes arising from the contract.

Petitioner Marlene Industries Corp. (Marlene) appeals from an order of the Appellate Division which, one Justice dissenting, affirmed a judgment of

Supreme Court denying an application to stay arbitration. There should be a reversal and arbitration should be stayed, for we conclude that the parties did not contract to arbitrate.

The dispute between the parties, insofar as it is relevant on this appeal, is founded upon an alleged breach by Marlene of a contract to purchase certain fabrics from respondent Carnac Textiles, Inc. (Carnac). The transaction was instituted when Marlene orally placed an order for the fabrics with Carnac. Neither party contends that any method of dispute resolution was discussed at that time. Almost immediately thereafter, Marlene sent Carnac a "purchase order" and Carnac sent Marlene an "acknowledgement of order." Marlene's form did not provide for arbitration; it did declare that it would not become effective as a contract unless signed by the seller, and that its terms could not be "superceded by a[n] unsigned contract notwithstanding retention." Carnac's form, on the other hand, contained an arbitration clause placed in the midst of some 13 lines of small type "boilerplate." It also instructed the buyer to "sign and return one copy of this confirmation." However, neither party signed the other's form. When a dispute subsequently arose, Carnac sought arbitration, and Marlene moved for a stay.

The courts below have denied the application to stay arbitration, the Appellate Division reasoning that "as between merchants where 'a writing in confirmation of the contract and sufficient against the sender is received and the party receiving it has reason to know its contents' written notice of objection should be given within 10 days after it is received" (59 A.D.2d 359, 360, 399 N.Y.S.2d 229, 231, quoting UCC 2-201(2)). Since Marlene had retained without objection the form containing the arbitration clause, the court concluded that Marlene was bound by that clause. We disagree.

This case presents a classic example of the "battle of the forms," and its solution is to be derived by reference to UCC 2-207, which is specifically designed to resolve such disputes. The courts below erred in applying UCC 2-201(2) for that statute deals solely with the question whether a contract exists which is enforceable in the face of a Statute of Frauds defense; it has no application to a situation such as this, in which it is conceded that a contract does exist and the dispute goes only to the terms of that contract. In light of the disparate purposes of the two sections, application of the wrong provision will often result in an erroneous conclusion. As has been noted by a recognized authority on the code, "[t]he easiest way to avoid the miscarriages this confusion perpetrates is simply to fix in mind that the two sections have nothing to do with each other. Though each has a special rule for merchants sounding very much like the other, their respective functions are unrelated. Section 2-201(2) has its role in the context of a challenge to the use of the statute of frauds to prevent proof of an alleged agreement, whereas the merchant rule of section 2-207(2) is for use in determining what are the terms of an admitted agreement" (Duesenberg, General Provisions, Sales, Bulk Transfers and Documents of Title, 30 Bus. Law. 847, 853).

UCC 2-207(2) is applicable to cases such as this, in which there is a consensus that a contract exists, but disagreement as to what terms have been included in that contract. UCC 2-207(1) was intended to abrogate the harsh "mirror-image" rule of common law, pursuant to which any deviation in the language of a purported acceptance from the exact terms of the offer transformed that "acceptance" into a counter-offer and thus precluded contract formation on the basis of those two documents alone (see Poel v. Brunswick-Balke-Collender Co., 216 N.Y. 310, 110 N.E. 619 (1915)). Under UCC 2-207(1), however, an acceptance containing additional terms will operate as an acceptance unless it is "expressly made conditional on assent to the additional or different terms." Having thus departed from the common-law doctrine, it became necessary for the code to make some provision as to the effect upon the contract of such additional terms in an acceptance. Subsection (2) was designed to deal with that problem.

Before continuing, we would note that the section speaks of both acceptances and written confirmations. It is thus intended to include at least two distinct situations: one in which the parties have reached a prior oral contract and any writings serve only as confirmation of that contract; and one in which the prior dealings of the parties did not comprise actual formation of a contract, and the writings themselves serve as offer and/or acceptance. In either case, the writing or writings may contain additional terms, and in either case the effect of such additional terms under the code is the same. Thus, on this appeal, since the prior discussions of the parties did not reach the question of dispute resolution, it is unnecessary to determine whether those discussions rose to the level of contract formation, or whether no contract was created until the exchange of forms.[3] Therefore, whether Marlene's form is an offer and Carnac's an acceptance, or whether both are mere confirmations of an existing oral contract, the result in this case is the same, and that result is dependent upon the operation of UCC 2-207(2).

UCC 2-207(2) provides that any additional terms in an acceptance or a written confirmation are to be considered merely proposals for additions to the contract, and that such terms normally will not become a part of the contract unless expressly agreed to by the other party. As with many sections of the code, however, there is a special provision for merchants [UCC 2-207(2)]:

> (2) The additional terms are to be construed as proposals for addition to the contract. Between merchants such terms become part of the contract unless:
>   (a)   the offer expressly limits acceptance to the terms of the offer;
>   (b)   they materially alter it; or
>   (c)   notification of objection to them has already been given or is given within a reasonable time after notice of them is received.

The parties to this dispute are certainly merchants, and the arbitration clause is clearly a proposed additional term, whether Carnac's form be consid-

---

3. It should be noted that in some cases, there may be no prior oral agreement, and the terms of the forms utilized may be so divergent as to preclude contract formation in the absence of further action upon the part of the parties (cf. UCC 2-207(3)). This is not such a case.

ered an acceptance of an oral or written offer or a written confirmation of an oral agreement. As such, it became a part of the contract unless one of the three listed exceptions is applicable. We hold that the inclusion of an arbitration agreement materially alters a contract for the sale of goods, and thus, pursuant to UCC 2-207(2)(b), it will not become a part of such a contract unless both parties explicitly agree to it.

It has long been the rule in this State that the parties to a commercial transaction "will not be held to have chosen arbitration as the forum for the resolution of their disputes in the absence of an express, unequivocal agreement to that effect; absent such an explicit commitment neither party may be compelled to arbitrate." . . . [The court cites four cases, only one of which deals with textiles—EDS.] The reason for this requirement, quite simply, is that by agreeing to arbitrate a party waives in large part many of his normal rights under the procedural and substantive law of the State, and it would be unfair to infer such a significant waiver on the basis of anything less than a clear indication of intent (see Matter of Riverdale Fabrics Corp. [Tillinghast—Stiles Co.], 306 N.Y. at 289, 118 N.E.2d at 104-105; Siegel, New York Practice §588, at 835).

Since an arbitration agreement in the context of a commercial transaction "must be clear and direct, and must not depend upon implication, inveiglement or subtlety . . . [its] existence . . . should not depend solely upon the conflicting fine print of commercial forms which cross one another but never meet" (Matter of Doughboy Indus. [Pantasote Co.], 17 A.D.2d 216, 220, 233 N.Y.S. 488, 493). Thus, at least under this so-called "New York Rule" (Squillante, General Provisions, Sales, Bulk Transfers and Documents of Title, 33 Bus. Law, 1875, 1881), it is clear that an arbitration clause is a material addition which can become part of a contract only if it is expressly assented to by both parties (see Matter of Doughboy Indus. [Pantasote Co.], supra; accord: Frances Hosiery Mills v. Burlington Indus., 285 N.C. 344, 204 S.E.2d 834; see also, Duesenberg, General Provisions, Sales, Bulk Transfers, and Documents of Title, 30 Bus. Law. 847, 853). Applying these principles to this case, we conclude that the contract between Marlene and Carnac does not contain an arbitration clause; hence, the motion to permanently stay arbitration should have been granted.

Accordingly, the order appealed from should be reversed, with costs.

NOTES & QUESTIONS

1. *Subsequent cases.* Given *Marlene* as a precedent, how should the following cases be resolved? Is UCC 2-207(3) relevant?

(a) After entering into an oral agreement to purchase yarn, Buyer signs Seller's confirmation-of-order form with knowledge that it contained an arbitration clause that the parties apparently had not agreed upon earlier. Thereafter, Buyer receives and retains without objection six additional confirmation-of-order forms identical to the first. In a dispute arising out of one of these later transactions must Buyer submit to arbitration?

(b) After arranging orally for sale and purchase by Seller and Buyer of textured polyester tissue faille, Broker sent sales note setting out the terms of the transaction and providing for arbitration of any controversy arising out of the transaction. The note also stated that duplicate copies were sent simultaneously to Seller and Buyer and "acknowledgement of sale by either party shall bind both parties to all of the terms and conditions set forth herein unless written notice of objection to the contents shall be made within ten days after receipt of the sales note." Subsequent sales between these parties followed the same pattern and used the same form. After four transactions that raised no problems Buyer refused delivery of goods in a fifth transaction on the ground that the goods were substandard. Must this issue be submitted to arbitration?

2. *Arbitration practice in the textile trade.* In Houston, A Barrier to Arbitration in the Textile Industry, 34 Arb. J. 9, June 1979, the author suggests that the *Marlene* decision undermines the long-standing practice in the textile trade of submitting disputes to arbitration. The article provides details of the arbitration practices and rules of various trade associations that make up the textile industry. Is this evidence relevant to the issue before the *Marlene* court? If one court finds that arbitration is customary in a particular trade is a later court bound by this finding? May a judge take judicial notice of such a custom?

3. *Separability of arbitration agreements.* The doctrine of separability distinguishes between the enforceability of arbitration clauses and the other terms of the contract in which the arbitration clause is contained. If a party claims that he was fraudulently induced to enter into a contract with an arbitration clause, for example, the doctrine suggests that you must first determine if there is an enforceable arbitration agreement and, if so, whether its terms require submission of the alleged fraud to an arbitrator. In Prima Paint Corp. v. Flood & Conklin Manufacturing Co., 388 U.S. 395 (1967), the Supreme Court accepted the separability doctrine for transactions governed by the Federal Arbitration Act, 9 U.S.C. §§1-14 (1982). For an analysis that accepts the separability doctrine and argues that UCC 2-207 does not apply to the separate arbitration clauses because Article 2 only applies to "transactions in goods," see Furnish, Commercial Arbitration Agreements and the Uniform Commercial Code, 67 Calif. L. Rev. 317, 348 (1979). Do you agree?

4. *The UCC and arbitration.* The UCC does not deal explicitly with procedures for resolving disputes, such as arbitration or mediation. (But see UCC 2-515.) Does the Code, however, implicitly affect arbitration agreements? Compare Collins, Arbitration and the Uniform Commercial Code, 41 N.Y.U. L. Rev. 736 (1966) (UCC may not require the arbitration agreement to be in writing, may have abolished the doctrine of separability, and may require arbitrators to apply the Code) with Bernstein, The Impact of the Uniform Commercial Code on Arbitration, 42 N.Y.U. L. Rev. 8 (1967) (written in response to Collins, "not to praise him, but to bury him"). See also the article

by Professor Furnish, supra Note 3. Whether or not the UCC does affect arbitration, should the Code have paid more attention to evidentiary and procedural questions?

5. *Commercial arbitration.* See generally G. Goldberg, A Lawyer's Guide to Commercial Arbitration (1977); Mentschikoff, Commercial Arbitration, 61 Colum. L. Rev. 846 (1961).

6. *Llewellyn's "type-transaction" and the Code.* Llewellyn expressed at times the view that courts must develop a "situation sense" for the "type-transaction" involved in commercial disputes. Most answers would be clear to a court that had such an understanding. Do the cases in this chapter present "type-transactions" specific to the textile trade, fertilizer trade, or forward contracts in agriculture? If not, what are the "type-transactions" they do present? Do Code provisions such as UCC 2-207, 2-202, and 2-201 allow or encourage courts to discern "type-transactions?" Do the opinions in this chapter show any facility for doing so?

Problem 9-9. Itoh submits to Jordan a purchase order for a specified quantity of steel coils. In response, Jordan promptly sends its acknowledgement form. On the face of Jordan's form the following statement appears: "Seller's acceptance is expressly conditional on buyer's assent to the additional or different terms and conditions set forth on the reverse side. If these terms and conditions are not acceptable, buyer should notify seller at once." One of the terms on the reverse side of Jordan's form is the following arbitration clause:

> Any controversy arising under or in connection with the contract shall be submitted to arbitration in New York City in accordance with the rules then obtaining of the American Arbitration Association. Judgment on any award may be entered in any court having jurisdiction. The parties hereto submit to the jurisdiction of the federal and state courts in New York City and notice of process in connection with arbitral or judicial proceedings may be served upon the parties by registered or certified mail, with the same effect as if personally served.

After the exchange of documents, Jordan delivers and Itoh pays for the steel coils. Itoh never expressly assents or objects to the additional arbitration term in Jordan's form. A dispute subsequently arises as to the quality of the steel coils. Do the parties have an enforceable agreement for arbitration?

CHAPTER 10

Seller's Obligations

If the parties enter into an enforceable agreement for the sale of goods the seller is under a general obligation to transfer and deliver the goods while the buyer must accept and pay for them (UCC 2-301). Unless otherwise agreed these obligations are concurrent conditions: tender of delivery is a condition to the buyer's duty to accept and to pay; tender of payment is a condition to the seller's duty to tender delivery (UCC 2-507(1), 2-511(1)). How the parties are to perform these obligations is determined by their contract and by the provisions of Part 5 of Article 2 (Performance).

The following materials focus on the seller's obligation to transfer and deliver. In Chapter 11 we will examine the rules governing the buyer's duty to accept the goods and in Part IV we will explore how payment by the buyer can be made (Chapters 15 & 16) and how the seller may decrease the risk of nonpayment (Chapter 18).

A. SELLER'S OBLIGATION TO TENDER AND DELIVER

The Uniform Commercial Code provides three different sets of suppletory rules defining the seller's obligation to deliver.

(1) The Code provides gap-filling rules to complete the agreement where the parties are silent. Thus, if they do not agree on a place for delivery, UCC 2-308(a) specifies that it is to be the seller's place of business. See also UCC 2-307 (presumption that goods are to be tendered in one lot), 2-309 (reasonable time for shipment or delivery), 2-311(2) (arrangements for shipping at the option of seller).

(2) Alternatively, the parties may have agreed to shipment or delivery terms using symbols, such as F.O.B. or C.I.F., to summarize their obligations. In UCC 2-319 to 2-325 the Code restates the obligations to which the parties

have agreed. These provisions do not fill gaps in the parties' agreement but spell out the content of their agreement.

(3) A third set of Code provisions amplifies the rules on how contract delivery obligations are to be performed. See UCC 2-503 (general rules on tender of delivery), 2-504 (shipment by seller).

Although delivery in most consumer sales transactions is across the counter, delivery in many commercial transactions involves shipment. The Code distinguishes *shipment* and *destination* contracts. In a shipment contract the seller is required or authorized to arrange transportation of the goods to the buyer but he is not required to deliver to a particular destination. Obviously even in a shipment contract the seller must tell the carrier where to deliver the goods. What makes the sales contract a shipment contract is that it *does not* require the seller to deliver at that destination. To carry out his obligation under a shipment contract the seller must take the steps set out in UCC 2-504. A sales contract that *does* require the seller to deliver at a particular destination is a destination contract and the seller agrees to tender the goods at this destination in accordance with UCC 2-503(3). The terms of the sales contract will determine the seller's obligation. Frequently these contract terms are capsulized in trade terms like "F.O.B. seller's plant" or "C.I.F. buyer's port." In the absence of agreement the Code presumes that the contract is a shipment, rather than a destination, contract. See UCC 2-503, Comment 5.

The opinion in Droukas v. Divers Training Academy, Inc., 375 Mass. 149, 376 N.E.2d 548 (1978), illustrates the operation of the delivery provisions. Buyer in Massachusetts bought marine engines from a seller in Florida. The seller agreed to arrange shipping but the parties did not agree that the seller would deliver the engines in Massachusetts. The court concluded that the transaction involved a shipment contract, that the seller performed his delivery obligation in Florida, and that the seller had therefore not supplied goods in Massachusetts so as to come within the state's long-arm statute. As a result, in a warranty dispute buyer could not obtain jurisdiction in Massachusetts over the seller.

Commercial transactions also sometimes involve the transfer of bailed goods or the delivery of documents of title instead of the goods themselves. Special rules govern seller's tender and delivery obligations in these cases. See UCC 2-503(4), (5).

HARLOW & JONES, INC. v. ADVANCE STEEL CO.
424 F. Supp. 770, 21 UCC Rep. 410 (E.D. Mich. 1976)

Feikens, District Judge. This is an action in contract, brought by the seller, Harlow and Jones, Inc. (hereinafter "Harlow"), against the buyer, Advance Steel Co. (hereinafter "Advance"), to recover damages and costs for an alleged breach of an agreement to purchase 1000 tons of imported European steel.

Defendant denies liability, claiming that the shipment of steel was late and was therefore properly rejected under the contract. . . .

In late June, 1974, Robert Stewart, president of Advance, had several telephone conversations with a William VanAs, an independent steel broker who is authorized to solicit orders on a commission basis from customers in the Great Lakes area on behalf of Harlow. During these conversations, VanAs informed Stewart of the availability of some 5000 metric tons of cold-rolled steel which Harlow could import from a West German mill for shipment during September-October, 1974. On July 2, 1974, Stewart advised VanAs that he was interested in purchasing 1000 tons of this shipment. The terms of the transaction were recorded by VanAs on his worksheet of July 2, 1974, and later that same day were relayed by VanAs to Carl Greve, president of Harlow.

On July 9, 1974, Greve mailed to Stewart a sales form, S-2373, confirming a sale of 1000 metric tons of cold-rolled steel, with shipment from a European port during September-October, 1974. That same day, Greve placed an order with Centro Stahlhandel GmbH for the 1000 tons and included a copy of its sales form to Advance. Stewart received Harlow's confirmation form but never signed or returned the enclosed copy as requested. On July 19, 1974, Stewart prepared a worksheet for the transaction in question, and on the basis of the worksheet prepared and mailed Advance's purchase order, B-04276, containing the same quantities, specifications (with minor revisions), and shipping dates as Harlow's confirmation form. Advance's purchase order was received by Harlow on July 25, 1974, but was never signed or returned.

The steel was shipped from Europe on three separate vessels. Approximately 214 tons were shipped on the M.S. Federal Lakes in September, 1974, and arrived in Detroit in October, 1974. Another 195 metric tons were shipped on the M.S. Ermis in October, 1974, and arrived in Detroit in early November, 1974. These two shipments were accepted and paid for by Advance. The balance of the steel was shipped from Antwerp on November 14, 1974, and arrived in Detroit on November 27, 1974. In a letter to Harlow dated October 29, 1974, Advance rejected this third shipment because of "late delivery." In a letter dated November 7, 1974, Harlow rejected Advance's cancellation and denied that a delay had yet developed which would justify Advance's action.

Further exchanges of correspondence ensued, with each party reaffirming its position that the other had breached its responsibilities under the contract. After arrival, the steel was warehoused in Detroit for a time and eventually sold at a loss by Harlow to other buyers, including Advance.

Harlow has taken the position throughout these proceedings that its sales confirmation form S-2373 of July 9, 1974 was an offer which defendant accepted by mailing back Advance purchase order form B-04276 on July 19, 1974. . . . Under this construction of the evidence, the terms of Harlow's S-2373 form would control. Specifically, there are a host of fine print terms on the back of this document which state that all delivery dates are approximate, contingent upon timely delivery by Harlow suppliers, and qualified by disclaimers of liability for "force majeure," acts of God, labor strikes, etc.[2]

Though no delivery date in fact appears on Harlow's S-2373, the form does specify a shipment date of "September-October, 1974." Harlow produced testimony from VanAs, Greve, and two disinterested local steel importers who all agreed that, according to an accepted steel importing trade usage, shipment in September-October means delivery in October-November. Since delivery here of the final shipment occurred before the end of November, Harlow contends that its shipping obligations were met and that Advance improperly and prematurely rejected this shipment on October 29. Harlow also sought to establish that the delay in shipment past the end of October was caused by bad weather, a Canadian pilot strike, and an accident in the Welland Canal— all contingencies which Harlow claims were unanticipated and beyond its control.

Advance takes the position that Harlow's sales form S-2373 was an offer which Advance rejected shortly after its receipt through a series of oral communications with VanAs. Stewart testified that he telephoned VanAs some time between July 9 and July 22 and informed him that he could not accept the boilerplate disclaimers regarding delivery on the back of Harlow's sales form and that VanAs had told him to just circle the objectionable terms and return the form. Stewart also testified to a second conversation with VanAs during this period in Stewart's office during which Stewart circled certain terms on the back of Harlow's S-2373 form and wrote on the front "delivery no later than October 31;" VanAs was reported to have said, "fine, no problem."

Advance contends that it had good reason to be concerned about the shipping dates. According to the testimony of Stewart and others, the market

2. *5. Delivery*

(a) All delivery dates are approximate and not guaranteed.

(b) Time of delivery is indicated on the basis of a corresponding promise of delivery by our suppliers. We shall not be responsible in case of delays or failure to deliver on the part of our suppliers, unavailability of shipping space, changes of sailing schedules and/or diversion of steamer while in transit.

(c) If force majeure, acts of God, labor disturbances, or other causes beyond our control should result in delays or nondelivery on our part, or on the part of our suppliers, or of the manufacturers, we shall not be liable, and the buyer agrees to accept delivery within a reasonable time after the aforementioned circumstances cease to exist and correspondingly extend time of delivery. Any extra expenses incurred because of any delays or failure of buyer in accepting delivery shall be for buyer's account.

(d) "Force majeure" shall include fire, strikes, breakdown of machinery or accidents of any kind, any delay in, interference with or inability to obtain transportation, inability to obtain suitable insurance or any license or permit now or hereafter required; Municipal, State, Federal or any government action, regulation or prohibition effecting the production, transportation, sale or delivery of, any of the goods affected by this contract; the present or any subsequent war conditions or any development thereof or any new outbreak of war, loss, destruction, or detention of ship; embargo; failure for any reason whatsoever of subcontractors, carriers, manufacturers or Seller's vendors to perform any contract relating to the goods hereby sold; or any and all causes beyond Seller's control.

for steel was high and unstable during the summer and fall of 1974, and in any purchase of imported European steel, time was therefore of the essence. Having rejected the shipping terms contained in Harlow's sales form S-2373 for this reason, Advance argues that its purchase order B-04276, sent on July 22, 1974, was a counter-offer which Harlow accepted by making two partial shipments in October. Under this analysis, the terms of Advance's purchase order B-04276 would control. B-04276 contains a shipment date of "Sept-Oct 74," and further specifies that a failure to ship within this time allows Advance to cancel the order without notice.[3] Since these terms of shipment were bargained for and crucial in Advance's view, and since the balance of the steel was not in fact shipped until November 14, Advance argues that its rejection of this last shipment was fully justified under the contract.[4]

Each party has sought to establish that the terms of this agreement are governed by the provisions of its own contract form. This is certainly understandable, since both S-2373 and B-04276 provide ample disclaimers of liability for late shipment and delivery. But in taking these respective positions, both Harlow and Advance have misread the evidence. The court finds that an oral contract for the purchase of steel was formed before either party began sending or receiving written contract forms.

The court finds that an agreement to purchase the 1000 tons of European steel was made through the several telephone conversations between Stewart and VanAs during the week of July 2, 1974. Greve testified that much of the steel importing business is conducted by phone and that oral contracts are often made in this way and then later confirmed in writing. This method of contract formation is also recognized by the UCC 2-204(1). [The court quotes UCC 2-204(1).]

The conduct of the parties here indicates a common understanding that the sale had been arranged as of July 9, 1974. Harlow apparently assumed such an understanding, since on July 9, 1974, it mailed an order to its German supplier for the 1000 tons and included the size and grade specifications which Advance had given to VanAs. Harlow's S-2373 form sent that same day could hardly be an offer to Advance then, especially since Harlow styled it as a sales confirmation form and never followed up on Advance's failure to sign and return it as requested.

3. This order not valid unless acknowledged and accepted immediately. If the material is not shipped on or before the time specified herein, the purchaser has the privilege of cancelling without notice.

4. During July, 1974, plaintiff and defendant negotiated two other contracts for the purchase of steel. The first was initiated by Advance's purchase order form B-04242, mailed July 15, 1974, to which Harlow responded with its sales form S-2386 on July 17, 1974. The second agreement was formed on the basis of Advance's purchase order B-4304 sent on July 23, 1974, and Harlow's sales form S-2391 mailed on July 30, 1974. These two transactions were completed without dispute or mishap. Both parties have construed these transactions as a course of dealing which can be used to explain their conduct in this case. The court finds that both of these transactions occurred either subsequent to or contemporaneously with the transaction here in question and thus do not constitute a course of dealing as defined in UCC 1-205. The evidence relating to these other contracts is therefore irrelevant.

Advance's conduct also corroborates the existence of an oral contract as of July 9. Advance has always taken the position that VanAs had at least apparent authority to negotiate contracts on behalf of Harlow, and this was apparently Stewart's understanding at the time of his telephone conversation with VanAs in early July, 1974. Stewart having indicated to VanAs during these conversations not only Advance's interest in purchasing 1000 tons of steel but also the various size and grade specifications and shipping dates which Advance wanted, it becomes difficult to accept his testimony that Advance had made no firm commitment to purchase at this point.

Advance's conduct upon receiving Harlow's confirmation form does not undercut the court's conclusion that an oral contract had already been negotiated at this point. Even if believed, Stewart's testimony indicates only an objection to S-2373's boiler-plate terms regarding delivery and does not show any disagreement with Harlow's assertion in the cover letter to this form that a contract for the purchase of steel had already been agreed upon. It is worth noting that VanAs flatly denies the assertion that Stewart ever informed him that delivery was to be made by October 31, and VanAs denies that he ever agreed to any such modification of Harlow's sales confirmation. Stewart did not remember ever having mailed to Harlow the copy of S-2373 with Advance's written notation for delivery by October 31. Moreover, the purchase order form B-04276 which Advance did eventually send to Harlow on or about July 22, 1974, was admittedly prepared in reference to Harlow's sales form, yet contains no indication that delivery was to be made by this date.

Even though it is difficult to identify the exact point at which a binding contract was formed, that does not prevent the court from finding that an agreement was in fact made during the series of telephone conversations conducted by the parties between July 2 and July 9, 1974. UCC 2-204(2) speaks directly to this point. [The court quotes UCC 2-204(2).] The fact that shipping and delivery terms were not completely ironed out during oral negotiations is likewise unimportant. [The court quotes UCC 2-204(3) and 2-311(1).]

Having found that a contract to purchase the steel in question was made initially on an oral basis, the written forms sent by both parties must be construed as confirmatory memoranda. In order to determine the specifics of a contract formed in this manner, UCC 2-207(3) provides for an integration of the parties' confirmations. . . . [The court quotes UCC 2-207(3) and Comment 6 to UCC 2-207.] There is in this case a substantial agreement between the confirmation forms of the parties. The forms contain the same price terms, weight and grade specifications (with one minor exception), and the same shipment date of September-October, 1974.

More important, and largely ignored by the parties throughout these proceedings, both forms specify a "C.I.F." shipping term. This provision renders the contract a shipment as opposed to a destination contract. UCC 2-320. Practically speaking, this means that the seller himself is not required to ship or deliver the goods under the terms and dates otherwise provided; rather, the seller is obliged to make a proper contract with his carrier for timely shipment or delivery, and having made such a contract, title and risk of loss pass to the buyer. [The court quotes UCC 2-320(2) and Official Comment 1 to UCC 2-320.]

An argument could be made that the inclusion of a C.I.F. shipment term in this contract supports defendant's position that Harlow was the defaulting party. Under UCC 2-320, transfer of title under a C.I.F. contract is made to depend solely on the seller's provision for timely shipment through his carrier. Advance has continually emphasized that shipment was in fact late by two full weeks. Advance argues that the bad weather, pilot strike and canal accident described by plaintiff's witnesses were never linked to the delay of this shipment and that Harlow did not do all that it reasonably could have to ensure shipment by October 31. Harlow therefore breached its duties under UCC 2-320, and title to the steel in question, in Advance's view, never passed.

This argument would appear to be Advance's best ground for escaping liability under the contract. Yet the court is unpersuaded. There is a further provision of the UCC governing performance under a C.I.F. shipment contract, UCC 2-504—a provision which effectively undercuts defendant's reliance on the delay in shipment.

UCC 2-504. *Shipment by Seller*

Where the seller is required or authorized to send the goods to the buyer and the contract does not require him to deliver them at a particular destination, then unless otherwise agreed he must

    (a)   put the goods in the possession of such a carrier and make such a contract for their transportation as may be reasonable having regard to the nature of the goods and other circumstances of the case; and

    (b)   obtain and promptly deliver or tender in due form any document necessary to enable the buyer to obtain possession of the goods or otherwise required by the agreement or by usage of trade; and

    (c)   promptly notify the buyer of the shipment.

Failure to notify the buyer under paragraph (c) or to make a proper contract under paragraph (a) is a ground for rejection only if material delay or loss ensues.

The key provision here is the final part of this section, which requires a "material delay" before a buyer can reject a C.I.F. contract on the basis of late shipment. Official Comment 6 makes this point even clearer: "6. Generally, under the final sentence of the section, rejection by the buyer is justified only when the seller's dereliction as to any of the requirements of this section in fact is followed by material delay or damage. It rests on the seller, so far as concerns matters not within the peculiar knowledge of the buyer, to establish that his error has not been followed by events which justify rejection."

Was there, then, a material delay in this case which would justify Advance's rejection of October 29? The court holds there was not. Though not shipped until November 14, 1974, the steel in question did arrive in Detroit on November [27], 1974 and the court accepts the testimony of Harlow and the several expert witnesses it produced, all of whom related that under a recognized trade usage, a shipment term of September-October implies delivery by October-November. Cast in this light, the record indicates that any delay in shipment was cured by timely delivery and that Advance therefore acted prematurely in repudiating the agreement.

There is no universal formula for determining when a delay in shipment becomes material, and UCC 2-504 makes no attempt to elaborate on what is meant by a "material delay." The issue of materiality must depend in each case upon the particular circumstances involved. In this case, there is ample evidence to conclude that it was delivery, not shipment, which primarily concerned Advance, and it is upon this basis that a finding of immaterial delay is made.

Advance's own letter of cancellation, dated October 29, 1974, states that the shipment in question was rejected for "late delivery." Advance's subsequent letter to Harlow, dated November 13, 1974, likewise cites "late delivery" as the reason for cancellation. Stewart's testimony regarding his objections to and attempted modifications of Harlow's sales form S-2373 further corroborates his concern over delivery dates, not shipment dates. Nor was this apparent emphasis on arrival time unusual in the context of this transaction. As one local steel importer testified, you cannot sell imported European steel to a local manufacturer or processor until it arrives from Europe.

Neither party has been able to cite to the court a past case dealing with the situation here presented—where a seller has breached a contractual shipment term but still managed to make timely delivery. However, the court through its own research has uncovered one such case, and it appears to provide some authority for the court's analysis. Val Decker Packing Co. v. Armour and Co., 184 N.E.2d 548 (Ohio Ct. of Comm. Pl. 1967), aff'd, Ohio App., 177 N.E.2d 401, involved a contract for the sale of a truckload of dressed hogs under which the seller was obliged to arrange for a carrier and to ship by "11 P.M. 12/26/56." The contract contained a provision for "C.A.F." shipment, a term with the same legal effect as the C.I.F. term involved in this case. See Ohio's Revised Code §§1315.19 and 1315.20; see also Val Decker Packing Co. v. Armour and Co., 177 N.E.2d 401, 403 (American Meat Packers "Trade and Term Definitions," Art. 6). In a confirmatory memorandum to the seller, defendant buyer made it clear that prompt delivery was its primary concern: "Note: Please show on bill of lading in large size, bright colored print or crayon that Western Pork Packers, Inc. desire to unload these hogs not later than 3:30 P.M., Friday, 12/28 and as much sooner as possible." Val Decker Packing Co. v. Armour and Co., supra at 549. The hogs were in fact not shipped until 12:25 P.M. December 27, 1956, and due to unforeseen weather and mechanical breakdowns with the truck, did not arrive at buyer's place of business until December 31, at which point they were rejected.

Defendant buyer sought to justify its rejection by arguing that the C.A.F. term contained in the contract required timely shipment before title to the goods passed, and since the shipment was late, buyer had "materially breached" the agreement and therefore prevented title from passing. The court in *Val Decker* rejected this argument, finding that delivery time, not shipment time, was the primary concern of the parties and that a delay in shipment was therefore not of such material importance as to justify buyer's cancellation of the order. . . .

Admittedly, *Val Decker Packing Co.* was decided under Ohio's own case law and former commercial statutes, not under the Uniform Commercial Code, but this only demonstrates that UCC 2-320 and 2-504 have not really departed from nor modified traditional contract doctrine regarding shipment contracts. A material delay in shipment has traditionally been required before a buyer under a C.I.F. agreement is allowed to cancel his order, and a merely technical delay or a delay which is later cured by timely delivery has never by itself justified cancellation, since this would, in effect, work a penalty or a forfeiture upon the seller.

Advance argues with some merit that its conduct should not be judged in hindsight but rather in the context of the circumstances presented at the time of rejection. Advance points out that at that point in time, shipment was not likely until well into November, and considering the usual 30-day transit time, this would mean delivery in December. Advance contends that a decision had to be made at that time, in order to preserve its rights under the contract, and the fact that subsequent events proved Advance wrong in its expectations provides no basis for finding an unjustified cancellation. A good faith judgment to cancel, in Advance's view, is all that can reasonably be expected.

This argument is unpersuasive. The court has no real reason to doubt Advance's good faith in concluding by October 29, 1974, that the steel in question would not, in all likelihood, be delivered until December, but the court finds that Advance had other means, short of cancellation, to protect itself in that event. UCC 2-609 outlines the proper and more reasonable course of conduct for a buyer in defendant's position:

UCC 2-609. *Right to Adequate Assurance of Performance*

(1) A contract for sale imposes an obligation on each party that the other's expectation of receiving due performance will not be impaired. When reasonable grounds for insecurity arise with respect to the performance of either party the other may in writing demand adequate assurance of due performance and until he receives such assurance may if commercially reasonable suspend any performance for which he has not already received the agreed return.

(2) Between merchants the reasonableness of grounds for insecurity and the adequacy of any assurance offered shall be determined according to commercial standards.

(3) Acceptance of any improper delivery or payment does not prejudice the aggrieved party's right to demand adequate assurance of future performance.

(4) After receipt of a justified demand failure to provide within a reasonable time not exceeding thirty days such assurance of due performance as is adequate under the circumstances of the particular case is a repudiation of the contract.

Advance here never demanded adequate assurances from Harlow. Advance's letter of October 29, 1974, indicates a total repudiation of the contract, not a mere temporary suspension of performance.

Had Advance taken the course prescribed by UCC 2-609, Harlow would have had the opportunity to effect a timely delivery and so cure any delay in shipment. In light of this available remedy, Advance's outright rejection of the contract on October 29, 1974 was unjustified. No delay at all, either in shipment or delivery, had in fact occurred at that point, and no material delay would have occurred had Harlow been permitted to effect delivery by November 31[30!—Eds.], 1974.

Accordingly, the court holds that Advance breached the contract by improperly and prematurely rejecting shipment. Harlow's subsequent resale of the steel is authorized by UCC 2-703(d) and was made in a commercially reasonable manner. Under UCC 2-706, Harlow may therefore recover the difference between the resale price and the contract price, together with any incidental damages incurred. Harlow produced evidence showing that a net loss of $105,954.40 was taken on the resales, and that storage and handling costs of $2,607.22 were also incurred. The total is $108,561.62, and Harlow is entitled to a judgment for that amount together with costs.

NOTES & QUESTIONS

1. *"C.I.F." and documentary transactions.* Given the use of the C.I.F. term by the parties in *Harlow & Jones,* is UCC 2-320(4) relevant? If that provision was applicable, seller would perform its contract obligation to buyer by arranging for shipment in accordance with UCC 2-504 and by tendering documents of title rather than the goods. With the documents the buyer can obtain delivery of the goods from the carrier or can sell the goods by negotiating the documents. The tender of documents may be made through customary banking channels (UCC 2-308(c)) but the documents must conform strictly with the terms of the sales contract (UCC 2-504(b)). See also UCC 2-503(5). Chapter 18 will explore documentary transactions in detail.

2. *Material delay in documentary transactions.* Granted that buyer erred in cancelling the contract on October 29, would buyer have been justified in cancelling the contract on November 2? What is a material delay (UCC 2-504) in the context of a documentary transaction? Does the steel trade's understanding of September/October shipment as requiring October/November delivery change the character of this contract as a shipment contract? Does it represent a situation, under UCC 2-320(4), where the parties have "otherwise agreed"? See the remarks of Llewellyn at p. 560 infra.

3. *Substituted performance (UCC 2-614).* Would UCC 2-614(1) excuse the seller in *Harlow & Jones* if it could show that the delay in shipment was caused by bad weather, the pilot strike, and the canal accident?

4. *Assurance of performance* (*UCC 2-609*). The court suggests that the buyer in *Harlow & Jones* should have made a written demand for assurance of performance in accordance with UCC 2-609. What specifically should the buyer demand to assuage its concerns, and what response by the seller would provide adequate assurance? What are the consequences to buyer if he is wrong about whether he has reasonable grounds for insecurity or about whether the seller's response is adequate?

5. *Installment contract* (*UCC 2-612*). The seller in *Harlow & Jones* had the 1,000 tons of European steel shipped in several different vessels. Was it authorized to do so? See UCC 2-307. If separate shipments are authorized, is the contract an installment contract governed by UCC 2-612? If so, has either seller or buyer breached under UCC 2-612(2) or (3)?

Note: Trade Delivery Terms

UCC 2-319 to 2-325 codify the parties' undertaking when they use symbols (F.O.B., C.I.F., etc.) to express their agreement on delivery of the contract goods. These trade terms have developed from trade usage, especially in international trade. Notwithstanding the UCC definitions, trade organizations sometimes restate the meanings of these terms in trade association publications. Perhaps the most important of these restatements are the "Incoterms" codified by the International Chamber of Commerce (ICC) for international trade. The ICC first published these terms in 1936 and revises them periodically to reflect changes in trade usage. The latest revision was published in 1980 (ICC Publication No. 350). Major United States trade associations have announced that they will observe the 1980 Incoterms in preference to the American Foreign Trade Definitions—Rev. 1941, a restatement that many of the same associations had prepared. If the Code definition conflicts with the understanding in a particular trade which should prevail?

Compare the definitions of F.O.B. in UCC 2-319 with the following ICC restatement of "F.O.B. (named port of shipment)":

Incoterms (No. 350, 1980)

FOB means "Free on Board." The goods are placed on board a ship by the seller at a port of shipment named in the sales contract. The risk of loss of or damage to the goods is transferred from the seller to the buyer when the goods pass the ship's rail.

A. The seller must:

1. Supply the goods in conformity with the contract of sale, together with such evidence of conformity as may be required by the contract.

2. Deliver the goods on board the vessel named by the buyer, at the named port of shipment, in the manner customary at the port, at the date or

within the period stipulated, and notify the buyer, without delay, that the goods have been delivered on board.

3. At his own risk and expense obtain any export licence or other governmental authorization necessary for the export of the goods.

4. Subject to the provisions of articles B.3 and B.4 below, bear all costs and risks of the goods until such time as they shall have effectively passed the ship's rail at the named port of shipment, including any taxes, fees or charges levied because of exportation, as well as the costs of any formalities which he shall have to fulfil in order to load the goods on board.

5. Provide at his own expense the customary packing of the goods, unless it is the custom of the trade to ship the goods unpacked.

6. Pay the costs of any checking operations (such as checking quality, measuring, weighing, counting) which shall be necessary for the purpose of delivering the goods.

7. Provide at his own expense the customary clean document in proof of delivery of the goods alongside the named vessel.

8. Provide the buyer, at the latter's request and expense (see B.6), with the certificate of origin.

9. Render the buyer, at the latter's request, risk and expense, every assistance in obtaining a bill of lading and any documents, other than that mentioned in the previous article, issued in the country of shipment and/or of origin and which the buyer may require for the importation of the goods into the country of destination (and, where necessary, for their passage in transit through another country).

B. The buyer must:

1. At his own expense, charter a vessel or reserve the necessary space on board a vessel and give the seller due notice of the name, loading berth and delivery dates to the vessel.

2. Bear all costs and risks of the goods from the time when they shall have effectively passed the ship's rail at the named port of shipment, and pay the price as provided in the contract.

3. Bear any additional costs incurred because the vessel named by him shall have failed to arrive on the stipulated date or by the end of the period specified, or shall be unable to take the goods or shall close for cargo earlier than the stipulated date or the end of the period specified and all the risks of the goods from the date of expiration of the period stipulated, provided, however, that the goods shall have been duly appropriated to the contract, that is to say, clearly set aside or otherwise identified as the contract goods.

4. Should he fail to name the vessel in time or, if he shall have reserved to himself a period within which to take delivery of the goods and/or the right to choose the port of shipment, should he fail to give detailed instructions in time, bear any additional costs incurred because of such failure, and all the risks of the goods from the date of expiration of the period stipulated for delivery, provided, however, that the goods shall have been duly appropriated to the

contract, that is to say, clearly set aside or otherwise identified as the contract goods.

5. Pay any costs and charges for obtaining a bill of lading if incurred under article A.9 above.

6. Pay all costs and charges incurred in obtaining the documents mentioned in articles A.8 and A.9 above, including the costs of certificates of origin and consular documents.

In 1980 the ICC published a new term, "Free Carrier (named point)," which was developed to meet the needs of modern transport, especially the rapidly expanding use of containers. The seller's obligations are similar to those where an F.O.B. term is used except that the seller completes delivery when he puts the goods into the custody of the carrier at the specified point. Should the Code be amended to incorporate a definition of this term? Should the draftsmen have codified the trade terms in UCC 2-319 to 2-325?

Problem 10-1. On August 14 Rancher informs Dealer that he has 103 head of cattle for sale. After inspecting the cattle Dealer agrees to pay 61 cents per pound for the cattle, the weight to be determined by weighing on Dealer's trucks with 3 percent off for shrinkage. As a down payment Dealer gives Rancher his check for $1,000, with the notation "103 cattle." The parties do not agree on the time for delivery. Dealer does not come with his trucks during the month of August and Rancher is unable to reach him by telephone. On September 1 Rancher asks you what he should do. Advise Rancher. See UCC 2-308, 2-309, 2-310, 2-503, 2-507, 2-609, 2-610.

Problem 10-2. On February 1, 1981, Manufacturer agrees with Canner to sell and install new canning equipment. On March 1, 1981, Manufacturer delivers equipment to Canner's factory and completes installation on April 1, 1981. In early 1985 Canner discovers the installed equipment is rebuilt rather than new equipment. On March 15, 1985, Canner brings an action against Manufacturer for breach of warranty. Manufacturer moves to dismiss the action as untimely under the four-year statute of limitations in UCC 2-725. Should Manufacturer's motion be granted?

Problem 10-3. Supplier and Exporter agree in writing that Supplier will supply Exporter with "95,000 pallets at $9.95 each, FAS Port, Norfolk, Virginia." Supplier delivers the pallets to the independent terminal in Norfolk designated by Exporter. Several days later the terminal operator sends Supplier a bill for port, transfer, and facility charges. Supplier protests to Exporter that it is not responsible for these charges under their sales contract. Exporter replies that Supplier is required to pay these charges by virtue of the custom in the port of Norfolk and refuses to reimburse Supplier. Supplier is unaware of this custom but on inquiry finds several shippers who state that the custom is as stated by Exporter. Supplier informs you that Exporter's agent had told him during negotiations that Exporter would bear these costs. Advise Supplier on whether he should bring an action against Exporter for breach of contract. See UCC 1-205, 2-202, 2-319.

B. TRANSFER OF TITLE

One of the most fundamental innovations of the UCC is its downgrading of the role of "title" in commercial transactions. We have already seen in Part II that title is immaterial in secured transactions governed by Article 9 (UCC 9-202). A similar approach is taken in Article 2. The official comment to UCC 2-101 notes: "The arrangement of the present article is in terms of contract for sale in the various steps of its performance. The legal consequences are stated as following directly from the contract and action taken under it without resorting to the idea of when property or title passed or was to pass as being the determining factor. The purpose is to avoid making practical issues between practical men turn upon the location of an intangible something, the passing of which no man can prove by evidence and to substitute for such abstractions proof of words and actions of a tangible character." (See also UCC 2-401.) It was this iconoclastic approach to title that Professor Samuel Williston, draftsman of the Uniform Sales Act of 1906, found "the most objectionable and irreparable feature" of Article 2, and it weighed heavily in his recommendation that the UCC should not be adopted. Williston, The Law of Sales in the Proposed Uniform Commercial Code, 63 Harv. L. Rev. 561, 566-572 (1950).

Despite his admiration for the work of Williston, Karl Llewellyn, principal draftsman of the UCC, consistently attacked the use of the "lump concept" of title to solve practical problems. As early at 1930 he wrote in his casebook on the law of sales:

"Lump-concept thinking moves in terms of *wide* premises. Decide that on specific facts 'title' is in either B or S; and you can then proceed to draw a dozen conclusions, as to risk, price, rules of damages, levy by creditors, etc; among the dozen will be the one deciding the case in hand. . . . The advantages of narrow-issue thinking and concepts are obvious. First, they make possible a neater description of what has happened. The meaning of the case is always clearer when one knows and states exactly what issue was decided, *as well as* what *ratio decidendi* was expressed; and . . . the *ratio decidendi* will have clearer outline if the court has occupied itself with study of the narrow issues and differentiation of other narrow issues. Secondly, the policy aspects of the narrow issues come in for observation and study, under narrow-issue thinking. . . . The narrow issues that arise on questions 'of title' are largely questions involving the allocation of a great number of distinct risks; risk of destruction; risk of disposing of the goods (can S have price, or only damages?); risk of being able to cover in the event of non-delivery; time and place of measure of damages; risk of S's insolvency (B opposing S's creditors); risk of S's or B's dishonesty or bad faith (attempted fraudulent resale to a third party). Each of these risk problems raises policy-questions all its own; different facts have different significance in regard to the different questions—as a matter of sense. Narrow-issue thinking leads to weighing these differences as a matter of sense, in order to see whether similar differences should follow, in law." K. Llewellyn, Cases and Materials on the Law of Sales 565 (1930). Llewellyn's approach to title illustrates his general approach to legal thinking and his more specific argument that the law of sales had developed "Through Title to Contract and a Bit Beyond" (15 N.Y.U. L.Q. Rev. 159 (1938)).

Article 2 does not avoid title altogether. *Sale* continues to be defined as "the passing of title from the seller to the buyer for a price" (UCC 2-106(1)). The seller normally gives his buyer a warranty of title (UCC 2-312). Specialized transactions, such as sales on approval, still refer to title (UCC 2-326, 2-327). To provide guidance for these provisions UCC 2-401 sets out a residual rule for determining the location of title.

To the extent that property notions continue to play a role, however, they are usually given a distinctive name to avoid confusion with the general concept of title. A seller who purports to retain a property interest in goods sold reserves a "security interest" (UCC 1-201(37), 2-401(1)). Identification of existing goods gives a buyer an "insurable interest" and a "special property" in the goods that permits him to insure the goods or to recover prepaid goods from an insolvent seller (UCC 2-501, 2-502).

The following notes and problems explore how the remnants of title continue to play a role in sales transactions.

1. Residual Rule on Title (UCC 2-401)

UCC 2-401 sets out the residual rules on the location of title to govern when a specific Code provision refers to title. Subject to several mandatory rules, the parties may agree *explicitly* on when title passes. In the absence of an explicit agreement the rule most generally applicable refers to completion of seller's obligation with reference to "physical delivery" of the goods (UCC 2-401(2)). This reference to "objective" facts may limit to some extent a judge's discretion. While the Code provision explicitly applies only when Article 2 sections refer to title courts frequently refer to the rules and UCC 2-401 to resolve non-Code questions, such as responsibility for sales tax or insurance.

2. Power to Transfer Title (UCC 2-403)

A *purchaser* acquires all title bargained for that his transferor had or had power to transfer (UCC 2-403(1), 1-201(32), (33)). If the transferor had no title because, for example, he is a thief or a bailee, he can transfer no title. If the transferor took from someone with no title he acquires no title and therefore can transfer no title.

If the transferor has full unencumbered title he can transfer this good title to a purchaser. While the UCC provides this general rule you must refer to non-Code law for the rules on how much title a transferor has. The Code in other words does not tell you that a thief acquires no title, nor does it provide a general rule for when a transferee acquires "voidable title."

The law of "good faith purchase" provides a series of exceptions to the general rule that a transferor can transfer no better title than he himself has.[1] Pre-Code law held that a wrongful transfer of a chattel clothed the transferee with "voidable" title in certain circumstances. A transferee who held voidable title (as opposed to "void," or *no* title) could in turn transfer *good* title to a bona fide purchaser for value. It was necessary, in analyzing situations, to characterize *two* transfers. First, one considered the transfer from A to B to determine whether B received voidable title or no title at all. If B received *no* title, then the "general" rule would apply downstream, and no transferee from B would ever obtain good title to the property. But if the transfer clothed B with *voidable* title it was necessary to determine whether subsequent transfers resulted in a transferee who qualified as a good faith purchaser. Since a good faith purchaser has a title good even as against the original owner, he may therefore transfer to anyone the rights he has—a form of "shelter rule."

When drafting UCC 2-403 the draftsmen assumed the reader would know this pre-Code form of analysis. Although the Code does not define when a person has voidable title it does deal explicitly with several fact patterns frequently litigated under pre-Code law. Thus a person who deceived his transferor as to his identity may transfer good title to a good faith purchaser for value (UCC 2-403(1)(a)). Pre-Code cases sometimes distinguished between persons deceived in face-to-face transactions and those deceived by false communications. The Code resolves the uncertainty in the case law with a simple rule. Of course if a purchaser from someone with voidable title does not meet the standards of good faith or value he will receive only the voidable title his transferor had.

UCC 2-403(2) also permits a transferor to transfer better title than he has:

> Any entrusting of possession of goods to a merchant who deals in goods of that kind gives him power to transfer all rights of the entruster to a buyer in ordinary course of business.

See also UCC 2-403(3) (definition of *entrusting*).

---

1. It is essential to distinguish the *power* to transfer good title from the *right* to transfer good title. As the following discussion illustrates, a seller may have no right to sell a good because, for example, the legally-recognized owner has not explicitly authorized him to do so. But the seller may nevertheless have the power to transfer good title so that the original owner no longer has an enforceable claim to the good.

Most of the disputes under these provisions of UCC 2-403 are between two innocent persons. Both parties may have dealt with the same wrongdoer but invariably the wrongdoer is not a viable defendant. Legal rules must therefore allocate the loss between these innocent parties, and because these parties have not bargained with each other the rules are analogous to tort rules. Can the results under UCC 2-403 be justified on the ground that they are efficient? Is an entruster to a merchant who deals in goods of the kind entrusted, for example, better able to protect against the risk of that merchant's wrongdoing than a buyer from that merchant? What steps would an entruster or buyer have to take to protect himself?

You should also pause to compare these rules on good faith purchase with the rules on negotiability of commercial paper studied in Chapter 1. Have goods become "negotiable?" Should they become negotiable? At the end of his career Professor Grant Gilmore suggested that the UCC draftsmen misread history when they increased protection of the good faith purchaser. Gilmore, The Good Faith Purchase Idea and the Uniform Commercial Code: Confessions of a Repentant Draftsman, 15 Ga. L. Rev. 605 (1981); cf. Gilmore, The Commercial Doctrine of Good Faith Purchase, 63 Yale L.J. 1057 (1954).

Problem 10-4. Andy owned a rare buffalo head nickel. He left it with Ted, a dealer in rare coins, for an appraisal. Ted, without consulting Andy, sold the nickel to Ben. Ben exchanged the nickel with Charles for a Roman coin. Charles then sold the nickel back to Ted in satisfaction of a debt owed by Charles to Ted. Soon afterwards Ted sold the nickel to Ed for cash but Ed did not take delivery in order to allow Ted to clean the coin. While Ted still had possession Andy demanded the return of the nickel. Is Andy entitled to the coin? See UCC 2-402, 2-403.

3.   Warranty of Title (UCC 2-312)

The seller warrants to his buyer that he is conveying good title, is making a rightful transfer, and is delivering the goods free from any undisclosed security interest or other lien (UCC 2-312(1); see also 2-312(3)). Comment 1 to this section suggests that the UCC abolishes the pre-Code "warranty of quiet possession" that protected a buyer against colorable third-party claims to the goods.

The Code provides no explicit remedies for breach of this warranty. If the buyer is sued by a third party he may be able to "vouch in" the seller so that the seller may take over conduct of the defense and be bound by the result (UCC 2-607(5)).

The warranty of title assumes that sellers are in a better position to evaluate the risk of defects in title, to protect against third-party claims, and to estimate potential damages. It also assumes reasonable buyers expect that sellers make this warranty unless the warranty is specifically disclaimed (UCC 2-312(2)). How does one evaluate the accuracy of these assumptions?

Problem 10–5. Smith, a gun dealer, sold an antique pistol to Brown for $10,000. Soon after Brown took possession of the pistol the police confiscated it on the complaint of Jones, who claimed that it had been stolen from him. What recourse, if any, does Brown have against Smith? See UCC 2-312.

(a) Would your answer be different if Smith was an antique dealer who had never sold an antique gun before? What if Smith was a private gun collector?

(b) If at the time the gun was confiscated it had a fair market value of $12,000, how much should Brown be able to recover? See UCC 2-711 to 2-715.

(c) If Jones ultimately could not prove his ownership and the police returned the gun to Brown, would Brown have any recourse against Smith?

(d) If the police had acted five years after Brown took possession of the pistol would your answer be different? See UCC 2-725.

(e) If Smith sold the gun "as is" has he disclaimed the warranty of title? UCC 2-312(2); cf. UCC 2-316(3)(a).

4. Certificates of Title

Motor vehicles are frequently subject to state certificate of title legislation. There is a Uniform Motor Vehicle Certificate of Title & Anti-Theft Act (1955) that, though it has been adopted in only ten states, is similar in concept to the law in a great majority of states. The relation of such legislation to UCC Article 2 raises difficult questions that are complicated further by the almost inevitable presence of a secured party whose interests are governed by Article 9. You should review the introduction to this topic set out in Chapter 7 at p. 356 supra.

A basic issue is the purpose of certificate of title legislation. One purpose, as suggested by the title of the uniform act, is to protect against theft. Is it also designed to protect a person who entrusts his car to a used car dealer so that the dealer can solicit offers? Should a distinction be made between the sale of new and used cars? Should it make a difference that almost without exception buyers and their financers do not wait for clear title before paying for a car?

GODFREY v. GILSDORF
86 Nev. 714, 476 P.2d 3, 8 UCC Rep. 316 (1970)

THOMPSON, Justice. . . . This is a replevin action to recover possession of a used automobile. It was commenced by the seller, Godfrey, against the buyer, Gilsdorf, who had purchased the vehicle from a used car dealer to whom the seller had entrusted it for sale. The facts are stipulated. Godfrey was the registered owner of a 1967 Toyota. The legal owner was Commercial Credit Corporation who held title as security for the balance ($1,187.03) of a debt owing it by Godfrey. Godfrey removed the license plates and certificate of registration from the car and delivered the vehicle for sale to a used car dealer, Auto Center. Gilsdorf saw the car at Auto Center and arranged to buy it. He made a down payment of $300, signed a car purchase order, and received possession of the Toyota to which was affixed the pink copy of the statutory Dealer's Report of Sale. He then borrowed $1,600 from Allstate Credit Corporation, gave a chattel mortgage as security, and inquired of Allstate whether he should get the title certificate. Allstate advised him not to worry about it since Auto Center would mail the certificate to Allstate directly. Gilsdorf then delivered Allstate's draft for $1,600 to Auto Center together with his personal check for $726.50 and received in return the green copy of Dealer's Report of Sale. He submitted the latter document to the Motor Vehicle Department and was issued license plates and a registration certificate as allowed by N.R.S. 482.400(2) and 482.215.

Meanwhile, Godfrey noticed that his car was not on the Auto Center lot and made inquiry. He was told that the car was sold and payment would be forthcoming when the check cleared the bank. The money was never paid him. Auto Center ceased doing business. Several weeks later Godfrey paid his debt to Commercial Credit ($1,187.03) and received the title certificate to the Toyota. The value of the car when delivered to Auto Center was $2,550 and its reasonable rental value was $150 per month.

When this replevin action was commenced Godfrey obtained possession of the car by resort to the provisional remedy of claim and delivery. . . . Gilsdorf, the defendant, had used the car for eight months. The complaint requested alternative relief, delivery of the car or its value in case delivery could not be had, and damages for its unlawful detention. . . . Gilsdorf, by counterclaim, sought to compel Godfrey to transfer the title certificate to him.

The seller, Godfrey, plaintiff below and appellant here, insists that title to a motor vehicle can only be transferred in accordance with the motor vehicle licensing and registration law, and not otherwise. That law requires the legal owner (in this instance Commercial Credit Corporation) and the transferee (Allstate Credit Corporation who financed a major portion of the purchase for Gilsdorf) to write "their signatures with pen and ink upon the certificate of ownership issued for such vehicle, together with the residence address of the transferee, in the appropriate spaces provided upon the reverse side of the certificate." N.R.S. 482.400. Thereafter, one of them must deliver the certificate of title to the Department of Motor Vehicles. N.R.S. 482.426. Since the purpose of the statute is to provide a fast and simple way to determine ownership and to prevent fraud and theft, strict compliance is essential. Exceptions should not be allowed, for to do so would frustrate the realization of an important legislative purpose and policy. This contention carries considerable force and may not lightly be cast aside.

On the other hand, the buyer Gilsdorf, defendant below and respondent here, urges that the entrustment provisions of the Uniform Commercial Code, UCC 2-403(2), (3) create an estoppel against the seller to assert title to the car. Moreover, he argues that the buyer, in these circumstances, acquired the automobile free of the security interest of Commercial Credit Corporation. UCC 9-307. In persuasive fashion he presses the following. The seller entrusted his car to a merchant who deals in cars and, in the words of the UCC "gave him the power to transfer all rights of the entrustor to a buyer in the ordinary course of business." UCC 2-403(2). Gilsdorf was a "buyer in the ordinary course of business." UCC 1-201(9). He bought a used car from a person in the business of selling used cars, and bought it in good faith without knowledge of the ownership rights of a third party, Commercial Credit Corporation. He arranged immediate financing for the car and paid cash to the dealer. He inquired as to title and was assured by the dealer and by Allstate who financed the purchase for him, that title would be taken care of by having the dealer send it to Allstate. He had the car registered in his name and paid for the license plates. Finally, the buyer stresses the fact that the seller set in motion the chain of events which led to the sale of the car and should bear the loss incurred from the misconduct of the dealer whom he selected. We turn to resolve these opposing views.

1. The licensing and registration provision of the vehicle code are essentially police regulations and strict compliance with them appears to be the prevailing view. . . . The underlying policy and purpose of that regulatory scheme are best promoted by such a view. It does not follow, however, that those purposes are subverted by the application of an estoppel theory to a business transaction falling within the entrustment provisions of the UCC. As we see it, the relevant provisions of the two codes can exist side by side with meaning given to each and without doing violence to either, and we should so construe them. . . .

When the used car dealer sold the Toyota to Gilsdorf, the Commercial Credit Corporation enjoyed a perfected security interest in that vehicle, to-wit, legal title. At that point, the purchaser, under the entrustment provisions of UCC 2-403(2), acquired only the rights of the entruster-seller subject to the security interest of Commercial Credit. At least, such appears to be the case if we look only to UCC 2-403(2). However, sections of the UCC found elsewhere, particularly UCC 2-103(1)(d) defining "seller," and UCC 9-307, may be construed to mean that the buyer took the car free of the perfected security interest of Commercial Credit. We need not resolve this problem in the case at hand since the seller, Godfrey, paid off his debt to Commercial Credit, and acquired the ownership certificate before filing suit. Thus, we are concerned only with the propriety of applying an estoppel against the seller to achieve the purposes of UCC 2-403(2), (3). . . .

In summary, we find, as did the court below, that Godfrey entrusted the car to a merchant who deals in cars. The merchant was empowered to transfer

Godfrey's rights to a buyer in the ordinary course of business and did so. We conclude that the principle of estoppel precludes Godfrey from asserting his later acquired title against Gilsdorf who purchased in good faith, for value and without notice of the then existing security interest of Commercial Credit Corporation. . . .

NOTES & QUESTIONS

1. *Certificate of title legislation.* Section 14(e) of the Uniform Certificate of Title Act provides that "[a] transfer by an owner is not effective until the provisions of this Section [execution of assignment, execution of application for new certificate, and mailing or delivery to Department] have been complied with." Would the court in *Godfrey* have reached a different result if the uniform act governed?

2. *Usage of trade.* Assume it could be shown that buyers of new and used cars usually take delivery of the cars before receiving a certificate of title and that dealers usually handle the paperwork. Of what relevance is this evidence? See Fuqua Homes, Inc. v. Evanston Building & Loan Co., 52 Ohio App. 2d 399, 370 N.E.2d 780 (1977) (purchaser of new car protected from claim of dealer's floor plan lender; "[t]o require the purchaser or [his] financier to receive clear title before paying would stop the free flow of commerce and impede established commercial practices in motor vehicle transactions").

3. *Priority of perfected security interest.* If Godfrey had not paid off Commercial Credit Corp., how should the court have resolved the priority conflict between Commercial Credit Corp. and Gilsdorf? Did Godfrey err in paying off the secured party?

Problem 10-6. Smith leaves his 1982 Volare with Rick's Repair Shop for minor repairs. Unknown to Smith, Rick operates a used car business on the same premises. That afternoon Rick sells the Volare to Brown for its fair market value. Brown takes immediate delivery of the car. When he asks about the certificate of title Rick promises that he will handle the paperwork and have the secretary of state mail the certificate to Brown. Assuming that the following legislation is in effect may Smith, who still has the certificate of title, recover the car from Brown?

Uniform Certificate of Title Act §14.

(a) If an owner transfers his interest in a vehicle, other than by the creation of a security interest, he shall, at the time of the delivery of the vehicle, execute an assignment and warranty of title to the transferee in the space provided therefor on the certificate or as the Department prescribes, and cause the certificate and assignment to be mailed or delivered to the transferee or to the Department.

(b) The transferee shall, promptly after delivery to him of the vehicle, execute the application for a new certificate of title in the space provided therefor on the certificate or as the Department prescribes, and cause the certificate and application to be mailed or delivered to the Department. . . . (e) A transfer by an owner is not effective until the provisions of this Section have been complied with; however, an owner who has delivered possession of the vehicle to the transferee and has complied with the provisions with this Section requiring action by him is not liable as owner for any damages thereafter resulting from operation of the vehicle.

Problem 10-7. Thief steals a car from Owner in State *A*. He brings it to State *B* where he obtains a certificate of title in his name. He then sells the car to Consumer by assigning the certificate of title. Consumer obtains a new certificate of title. As between Owner and Consumer, who has a superior claim to the car? Would your answer be different if the purchaser in State *B* was a used car dealer?

C. DOCUMENTS OF TITLE

A document of title is "[a] document which in the regular course of business or financing is treated as adequately evidencing that the person in possession of it is entitled to receive, hold and dispose of the document and the goods it covers" (UCC 1-201(15)). The most common documents of title are the bill of lading (Forms 10-1, 10-2 at p. 546 supra) and the warehouse receipt (Forms 10-3, 10-4 at p. 546 supra), both of which are issued by professional carriers or warehousemen to evidence the bailment of goods with them and to set out the terms of the bailment contract (UCC 1-201(6), (45)). We examine documents of title here because of their relevance to the seller's delivery obligations and because of the contrast they provide to the title problems we have just been exploring. In Chapter 18 we will study how these documents are used in documentary transactions in which the seller retains control of the goods until the buyer pays for them. For additional commentary on documents of title, see R. Henson, Documents of Title Under the Uniform Commercial Code (1984) and R. Riegert & R. Braucher, Documents of Title (3d ed. 1978).

A document of title may be negotiable or nonnegotiable. A document which by its terms states that the bailed goods are to be delivered to bearer or to the order of a named person is a negotiable document; all other documents used in domestic trade are nonnegotiable (UCC 7-104(1)). Where a bailee issues a nonnegotiable document he must deliver the goods to the person named in the document; the document itself does not represent the goods and need not be surrendered when the bailee delivers them according to his contractual obligations. The person entitled to delivery may transfer this right just as he may assign an ordinary contract claim. When the right is assigned the transferee acquires "the title and rights which his transferor had or had actual authority to convey" (UCC 7-504(1)). A negotiable document, on the other hand, is like Article 3 commercial paper in that the bailee's obligation is merged into the document itself. A holder may therefore transfer rights in the bailed goods by transferring the document. The bailee must deliver the goods to the holder of the document, who should surrender it on delivery.

Most of the rules of transfer and negotiation of a negotiable document are analogous to Article 3 rules (UCC 7-501, 7-502). Negotiation of an order document, for example, requires indorsement and delivery; only delivery is necessary to negotiate a bearer document. If the document is *duly* negotiated to a holder who purchases it for value and in good faith without notice of any defense against it or claim to it, the holder acquires rights equivalent to an Article 3 holder in due course (UCC 7-501(4); 7-502). This means that a transferee may acquire greater rights than his transferor had. Due negotiation is a more restricted concept, however, than negotiation governed by Article 3: it must be in the regular course of business or financing and does not include transactions in which the document is taken in settlement or payment of a money obligation (UCC 7-501(4); see also Comment 1 to this section).

Documents of title play an important role in the marketing and financing of goods. Goods stored in a warehouse or delivered to a carrier may be transferred by delivering the documents without having to move the goods. Similarly, as we saw in Part II, documents of title may be used as collateral to secure loans by physically delivering the document to the secured party (UCC 9-304(2), 9-305). This permits borrowers to obtain financing while the goods are stored.

Several problems recur: documents may be issued when goods have not been received by the bailee; the bailor may not have title to the bailed goods; the goods may be lost, damaged, or destroyed while in the hands of the bailee; the bailee may deliver these goods to a person not entitled to delivery. The following cases explore some of these problems.

As the following materials will illustrate, federal law plays a much larger role in this area than in other areas covered by the UCC. The Federal Bills of Lading Act of 1916 (Pomerene Act) governs interstate and export shipments by common carriers. 49 U.S.C. §§81-124 (1982). UCC Article 7 covers intrastate and some import shipments. The federal act follows closely the Uniform Bills of Lading Act, which has been superseded by Article 7. Ocean bills of lading covering both exports and imports to the United States are governed by the Harter Act, 46 U.S.C. §§190-195 (1982) (requiring the issuance of bills and restricting clauses limiting liability), and the Carriage of Goods by Sea Act, 46 U.S.C. §§1300-1315 (1982) (bills of lading subject to state regulation of carriage). The United States Warehouse Act applies to receipts covering agricultural goods stored for interstate or foreign commerce. 7 U.S.C. §§241-273 (1982) (see especially §§258-262).

LINEBURGER BROS. v. HODGE
212 Miss. 204, 54 So. 2d 268 (1951)

ALEXANDER, Justice. Separate bills were filed against the Federal Compress & Warehouse Company, a corporation, by E. S. Vancleve, J. R. Hodge, and E. A. Bates & Company, a partnership, each praying for a mandatory injunction against the defendant to compel delivery of cotton held by the defendant to them as purchasers and holders of the warehouse receipts covering the number of bales of cotton held respectively by each of the complainants, or in the alternative for the value of the cotton thereby represented. The total number of bales is twenty-four, Vancleve claiming nine, Hodge six, and E. A. Bates & Company nine.

It is adequately shown that all of the cotton was grown and ginned by Lineburger Brothers, B. C. Lineburger, J. G. Outlaw and F. A. Little, and stolen by one J. V. Carr from a gin where the cotton had been processed and tagged. This asportation occurred at night and was conducted with the aid of a truck driver who was not a regular employee of Carr. Early the next morning Carr carried the cotton to the defendant warehouse, and, after weighing, had the receipts issued in three fictitious names and delivered to him. Carr took the receipts to nearby towns and sold the cotton, so identified, to the three complainants in separate lots. The purchasers gave their separate checks to Carr who procured payment by endorsing them respectively in the names of the three fictitious persons. He then disappeared and has not since been located.

As stated, the three buyers filed their separate bills against the warehouse. The gin company was not made a party. Upon application of the planters or owners, they were allowed to intervene and claim the cotton. From a decree dismissing the petition of the intervenors, absolving the warehouse of negligence in the issuance of the receipts, and awarding title to the respective warehouse receipts to the purchasers with full rights to claim the cotton thereby represented, after paying storage charges to the warehouse, the planters, or owners, appeal. . . .

We approach, then, the rights of the appellants, the planters and owners. As heretofore stated, they had given Carr no authority to take and haul away any of this cotton. Specific instructions, including the time and identity of cotton to be so hauled, were always given, and Carr knew this. It is immaterial whether the warehouse knew of this limitation upon Carr's authority. It is sufficient that this limitation was understood between Carr and appellants. Here there was no dispute, and it is without question that the taking by Carr, under all the circumstances, was larceny, and that the receipts were fraudulently obtained. . . . We repeat that the gin is not a party here and the test of the right of the owners must depend on whether this cotton was under any circumstances entrusted to Carr by permission and knowledge of the owners.

We find that the cotton was not so entrusted to Carr, and since the cotton was in fact stolen and the receipts fraudulently obtained, the defense of apparent authority, although available to the warehouse, does not aid the claim of the purchasers of the receipts.

It was held in Unger v. Abbott, 92 Miss. 563, 46 So. 68 (1908), that the rule caveat emptor applies against the claim of an innocent purchaser of warehouse receipts who purchased them from the owner's servant who had been sent with cotton to a compress company with instructions to have it weighed and to bring the receipts back to the owner, but who, contrary to his authority and instructions, took the receipts in his own name and sold them.

If it be observed that this case was decided prior to our statutes upon Warehouse Receipts, [adopting the Uniform Warehouse Receipts Act], attention is directed to Section 5051 [U.W.R.A. §40], which is as follows: "A negotiable receipt may be negotiated: . . . (b) By any person to whom the possession or custody of the receipt has been entrusted by the owner, if, by the terms of the receipt, the warehouseman undertakes to deliver the goods to the order of the person to whom the possession or custody of the receipt has been entrusted, or if at the time of such entrusting the receipt is in such form that it may be negotiated by delivery."

We look next at Section 5052 [U.W.R.A. §41]: "A person to whom a negotiable receipt has been duly negotiated acquires thereby: (a) Such title to the goods as the person negotiating the receipt to him had or had ability to convey to a purchaser in good faith for value, and also such title to the goods as the depositor or person to whose order the goods were to be delivered by the terms of the receipt had or had ability to convey to a purchaser in good faith for value, and . . . ."

Section 5058 [U.W.R.A. §47] is also in point. It is as follows: "The validity of the negotiation of a receipt is not impaired by the fact that such negotiation was a breach of duty on the part of the person making the negotiation, or by the fact that the owner of the receipt was induced by fraud, mistake, or duress to entrust the possession or custody of the receipt to such person, if the person to whom the receipt was negotiated, paid or a person to whom the receipt was subsequently negotiated, paid value therefor, without notice of the breach of duty, or fraud, or mistake or duress."

Appellees cite for support Weil Bros., Inc. v. Keenan, 180 Miss. 697, 178 So. 90. Here there was an interpleader suit filed by the warehouse. The testimony disclosed that the receipts had been entrusted to one Spencer by the owner, and were misappropriated by the former. After recognizing that one, especially a trespasser, cannot convey a better title than he has, the Court found that the receipts had been entrusted to the thief and an innocent purchaser was protected. . . .

Our statutes do not go so far as those of some other states in protecting a bona fide purchaser of negotiable receipts in cases where the receipts had been stolen. . . . Since such receipts were not negotiable at common law, their negotiability is to be measured by our statutes.

We hold, therefore, that neither the cotton nor the receipts had been entrusted to Carr by the owners and that the latter are not estopped to set up their claim to the cotton as against the several appellees who purchased the receipts. . . .

The assertion wants no support that the statutes referred to were designed to insure the negotiability of warehouse receipts and to facilitate commerce in the market places where cotton is brought and sold. The innocent purchaser of a negotiable receipt is guaranteed an assurance without which the traffic could not be conducted. Yet, such assurance must take into account the older principle that an owner of cotton may not be divested of title by a trespasser or a thief. In order to strike a just balance between these two concepts the statutes were enacted. The buyer must still beware lest he is buying receipts which have been fraudulently obtained for cotton which has been stolen. We need not analyze the statutes to divine whether the owner, who has voluntarily clothed another with indicia of ownership or entrusted him with possession of receipts, is barred of recovery from an innocent purchaser by principles of estoppel or pursuant to the rule that where two innocent persons must suffer from a fraud, he who reposes confidence in the fraudulent agent must suffer. It is enough that the statute recognizes title in the innocent purchaser who has bought receipts from one to whom they have been entrusted by the owner.

Here, as in all such cases, one of two innocent persons must suffer the loss. The thief has stolen or fraudulently obtained property from someone. We hold that the unlawful act was committed against the owners and that the title to the cotton remains in them. As stated in Unger & Co. v. Abbott, "(The appellees) are to be condoled with for their loss by this swindle; but their misfortune can not affect the right of (the appellants) to have (their) cotton. . . . 'Caveat emptor' applies." [92 Miss. 563, 46 So. 68 (1908).]

The cause will be reversed and decree awarded to the appellants for the cotton, and the Federal Compress & Warehouse Company is directed to hold the same to the order of appellants, but without storage charges thereon. . . .

NOTES & QUESTIONS

1. *When a document of title confers no rights.* UCC 7-503(1), perhaps one of the most intricate sections in the entire UCC, provides:

> (1) A document of title confers no right in goods against a person who before issuance of the document had a legal interest or a perfected security interest in them and who neither
>
> > (a)   delivered or entrusted them or any document of title covering them to the bailor or his nominee with actual or apparent authority to ship, store, or sell or with power to obtain delivery under this Article (Section 7-403) or with power of disposition under this Act (Sections 2-403 and 9-307) or other statute or rule of law; nor
> >
> > (b)   acquiesced in the procurement by the bailor for his nominee of any document of title.

What would be the result in *Lineburger* under UCC 7-503(1)? Was the receipt in *Lineburger* negotiable or nonnegotiable? (See UCC 7-104). Does UCC 7-503 apply to nonnegotiable documents?

2. *Comparison of UCC 2-403, 3-302, 7-501.* You are now in a position to compare the "negotiability" of goods, commercial paper, and documents of title. To what extent do the relevant Code rules differ as to (a) good faith, (b) value, (c) notice, (d) "due" negotiation or transfer? To what extent can these distinctions be explained by the differences in the nature of the items transferred or the parties who typically deal in them? See Warren, Cutting Off Claims of Ownership Under the Uniform Commercial Code, 30 U. Chi. L. Rev. 469 (1963); see also Dolan, Good Faith Purchase and Warehouse Receipts: Thoughts on the Interplay of Articles 2, 7, and 9 of the UCC, 30 Hastings L.J. 1 (1978).

Problem 10-8. Consider the following variations on the *Lineburger* case.

(a) Lineburger grows and gins cotton. Without express authority Carr, an employee of Lineburger, sells the cotton to Hodge, a cotton dealer who does not know of Carr's lack of authority. May Lineburger replevy the cotton from Hodge?

(b) Lineburger grows and gins cotton. Without express authority Carr delivers the cotton to Federal Warehouse, which does not have notice of Carr's lack of authority, and the warehouse issues negotiable documents of title to the order of Carr. Carr indorses the documents and delivers them to Hodge for cash. Between Lineburger and Hodge, to whom should Federal Warehouse deliver the cotton? Would your answer be different if Carr was the manager of Lineburger's cotton gin?

(c) Lineburger delivers its ginned cotton to Federal Warehouse and the warehouse issues negotiable documents of title to Lineburger's order. Without authority Carr indorses the documents in Lineburger's name and delivers them to Hodge for cash. Between Lineburger and Hodge, to whom should Federal Warehouse deliver the cotton? See UCC 7-502(2). Would your answer be different if the documents were payable to bearer? Would your answer be different if Hodge merely promised to pay for the documents in 30 days? What if Hodge paid only 80 percent of the fair market value of the cotton?

(d) Lineburger sells its ginned cotton to Hodge, and Hodge makes a promissory note payable to the order of Lineburger for the purchase price. Without authority Carr indorses the promissory note in Lineburger's name and delivers the note to Bates for cash. Between Lineburger and Bates, to whom should Hodge make payment on the promissory note? Would your answer be different if the note had been indorsed in blank by Lineburger? Would your answer be different if Bates merely promised to pay for the note in 30 days? What if Bates paid only 80 percent of the face value of the note?

Problem 10-9. On January 15 Farmer delivers 5,000 bushels of corn to Grain Elevator for storage and receives a nonnegotiable warehouse receipt in his name, issued by Grain Elevator. On June 1 Farmer purports to sell the grain to Dealer by a written contract. Farmer delivers the warehouse receipt to Dealer at the time the contract is signed, and one week later Dealer mails a notice of this transfer to Grain Elevator. On June 15 Grain Elevator files for bankruptcy. Was the corn "delivered" to Dealer? Who is the "owner" of the grain? See UCC 2-309, 2-401, 2-503, 7-104, 7-504.

ROUNTREE v. LYDICK-BARMANN CO.
150 S.W.2d 173 (Tex. Civ. App. 1941)

SPEER, Justice. . . . The record before us conclusively shows that plaintiff [Lydick-Barmann Co.] has its office and domicile at 2611 West Seventh Street, in Fort Worth, Texas, that defendant [Rountree] is a common carrier of interstate freight, under the rules and regulations of the U.S. Interstate Commerce Commission, and the regulations of such Motor Freight Lines as that operated by defendant. That the shipment was received by defendant at the time alleged and it issued its bill of lading therefor, which on its face was captioned, "Uniform Motor Carrier Straight Bill of Lading—Original—Not Negotiable—Domestic." The bill acknowledged receipt of the freight from plaintiff at its street address in Fort Worth, Texas, "Consigned to Lydick-Barmann Company (plaintiff), destination 616 Street, Louisiana City, Little Rock County, Ark. State. Notify Crone Company." The bill of lading described the merchandise, was signed by both plaintiff and defendant, acting through their respective agents, and was endorsed in blank by plaintiff. The undisputed evidence further shows that plaintiff has no office or agent at the street address in Little Rock, as given in the bill of lading. The merchandise was delivered to Crone Company. Because of this delivery by defendant the plaintiff lost the value of its goods, shown to be $129.50.

We do not believe that plaintiff's right of recovery is dependent upon whether or not the bill of lading under which the shipment moved was a shipper's order billing. It is clear that if it was a shipper's order contract, which would obligate the defendant (the carrier) not to deliver the merchandise until the endorsed bill of lading was produced and delivered to him, and delivery was made as in this case, without obtaining the bill, there would be liability. As we view it, we need not determine whether or not it was a shipper's order contract, although under one count in plaintiff's pleadings, it is claimed to be such. In support of this contention, one of plaintiff's officers testified that when defendant's agent called for the freight, he was informed that plaintiff had "an order notify shipment for him." The agent furnished the blank bill of lading that was used; the plaintiff endorsed the bill of lading and attached a draft on Crone Company for the purchase price of the merchandise, and sent both to a Little Rock bank for collection and delivery of the bill of lading; the draft was not paid; and both were returned to plaintiff. The bill of lading, as above indicated, contained the words, "Notify Crone Company." The word "notify" in bills of lading is only required by the U.S. ICC Act, in shipper's order contracts. The rules also require that "straight" billing contracts be printed on white paper and that "Shipper's Order" contracts be printed on yellow paper. See "National Motor Freight Classification No. 3," issued February 21st, 1938, pages 149A and 152A, introduced in evidence by defendant. The bill in this case was printed on yellow paper, and was endorsed by the shipper, which is only required in "Shipper's Order" bills of lading. Upon the other hand, the "Classification Rules" referred to provide that straight bills shall read: "Consigned to" some person, firm or corporation (plaintiff in this case) while a shipper's order bill of lading is required, among other things, to provide for the name and address of the consignor, and consigned to "the order of" the person, firm or corporation named as consignee. As stated above, we find it unnecessary to discuss in detail the nature and effect of the two classes of bills of lading executed in shipments of interstate freight.

The undisputed facts in this case entitled plaintiff to recover, as we view the law applicable. The defendant insists that the bill of lading under which the shipment moved was a straight bill. It has all of the elements of such, except that it was on yellow and not white paper, and contains the expression, "Notify Crone Co." These are elements of a shipper's order bill. They do not destroy the fact that it could be properly classed as a straight bill.

Defendant urges under proper assignments that the term "notify Crone Co." was equivalent to the expression, "Consigned to" a named person "in care of" another, as is often used in straight bills. Our courts have held that when a bill names the consignee "in care of" another person, such other person is held to be the named agent of the consignor for delivery of the merchandise, and that delivery to that person is delivery to the consignee. . . . We have not been cited to any case, nor from an independent search have we found where any court has construed the two expressions as synonymous. It is perceivable why, if one is directed to deliver an article to another in care of one named, that delivery to the latter would be compliance with the contract, but the same course of reasoning would not produce the same result when instructions are given to deliver to a certain person, notifying another. This conclusion is emphasized by the fact that the word "notify" as used in a bill of lading is only required when a shipper's order contract is made. In formulating the respective requisites of bills of lading, some significance must be given to the requirement that a shipper's order bill must contain the word "notify."

For purposes of this appeal, we are construing the bill of lading in this case as a straight bill. The goods were consigned by plaintiff to itself, at Little Rock, Ark. [The Federal Bills of Lading Act, 49 U.S.C. §§81-124 (1982)] Sec. 82, provides: "A bill in which it is stated that the goods are consigned or destined to a specified person is a straight bill." When goods are so shipped the carrier is bound by the provisions of Section 88 of the same Code, which reads: "A carrier, in the absence of some lawful excuse, is bound to deliver goods upon a demand made either by the consignee named in the bill for the goods or . . . ." The carrier is justified in making delivery, under Section 89, to, "(a)

A person lawfully entitled to the possession of the goods, or (b) the consignee named in a straight bill for the goods." If delivery is made by the carrier under any other conditions than those provided, and the consignor suffers a loss on account thereof, the carrier is liable. . . .

It is conceded by defendant that this was a straight bill of lading; that he delivered the goods to Crone Company, named in the bill as the party to be notified. In this way, defendant earnestly insists that he has performed his contract of shipment. . . .

Defendant's contention that he had "literally" and "definitely" carried out the terms of the written contract between the parties, is based upon what we believe to be an erroneous hypothesis—that delivery of the shipment to Crone Company, named as the one to be notified, was delivery to the consignee named in the bill of lading, which was the contract of shipment. Lydick-Barmann Co. (plaintiff) was the consignee in the contract. It was likewise the consignor. It was the owner of the merchandise at all times and was entitled to possession at destination. The fact that consignee had no office or place of business at Little Rock, rendering it impossible for defendant to make physical delivery of it then and there, presented no insuperable difficulty. Defendant had consignor's—consignee's—street address at Fort Worth, Texas, and when defendant found that it could not deliver the freight to the consignee, as he had promised to do, immediate notice should have been given to the consignor. It was not sufficient for defendant to choose to deliver the goods to some one else not entitled to possession. . . .

[Affirmed.]

NOTES & QUESTIONS

1. *Article 7 and misdelivery.* The court in *Rountree* applies the Federal Bill of Ladings Act. If the UCC governed, would the result be the same? See UCC 7-303, 7-403, 7-404.

2. *Negotiable documents and misdelivery.* If the court in *Rountree* had found the document to be negotiable would the result have been different? Section 88 of the Federal Act states:

> A carrier, in the absence of some lawful excuse, is bound to deliver goods upon a demand made either by the consignee named in the bill for the goods, or if the bill is an order bill, by the holder thereof, if such a demand is accompanied by—
>
> (a) An offer in good faith to satisfy the carrier's lawful lien upon the goods;
>
> (b) Possession of the bill of lading and an offer in good faith to surrender, properly indorsed, the bill which was issued for the goods, if the bill is an order bill; and
>
> (c) A readiness and willingness to sign, when the goods are delivered, an acknowledgment that they have been delivered, if such signature is requested by the carrier. . . .

Problem 10-10. Koreska, an Austrian manufacturer of paper, sells 10,000 reams of copying paper to Parker, a buyer in New York. Koreska delivers the paper in four large packages to United, a carrier, for carriage from Austria to New York. United issues a negotiable bill of lading naming Koreska's New York collecting agent, a bank, as the party to whose order the paper is consigned and requiring the carrier to give an arrival notice to Parker. United delivers the paper to Parker without requiring him to surrender the bill of lading. Parker does not pay Koreska for the paper. If the UCC applies, will Koreska be able to hold United responsible for this delivery? See UCC 7-303, 7-403. Will the UCC be applicable? Should United be permitted to show that there is a trade custom that permits a carrier to deliver without requiring surrender of the bill of lading?

D. RISK OF LOSS

Under pre-Code law it was the party who had title to goods who bore the risk that the goods might be lost, stolen, damaged, or destroyed. Title is a legal abstraction, however, rather than a physical fact. Accordingly, judges were free to manipulate the concept in deciding particular cases, and thus considerable uncertainty resulted. The draftsmen of the Code responded to the situation by abandoning title as a determinant and fashioning instead in UCC 2-509 and 2-510 a set of narrower rules directed to particular factual situations.

> *Situation:* if there is an absence of breach (UCC 2-509, caption); and if the contract requires or authorizes the seller to ship the goods by carrier (UCC 2-509(1), preamble); and if it does not require him to deliver them at a particular destination (UCC 2-509(1)(a), first clause); and whether or not the shipment is under reservation (UCC 2-509(1)(a), last clause), then
> *Rule:* the risk of loss passes to the buyer when the goods are duly delivered to the carrier (UCC 2-509(1)(a)).

The draftsmen also articulated the underlying policy in the comments. Comment 3 to UCC 2-509, for example, states: "The underlying theory of this rule is that a merchant who is to make physical delivery at his own place continues meanwhile to control the goods and can be expected to insure his interest in them. The buyer, on the other hand, has no control of the goods and it is extremely unlikely that he will carry insurance on goods not yet in his possession." By articulating these more specifically defined rules and the reasons for them, the Code draftsmen thought they would provide greater guidance for merchants and courts. To judge by the relatively few appellate court opinions on risk of loss problems, they succeeded.

A. M. KNITWEAR CORP. v. ALL AMERICA EXPORT-IMPORT CORP.

41 N.Y.2d 14, 359 N.E.2d 342, 390 N.Y.S.2d 832, 20 UCC Rep. 581 (1976)

COOKE, Judge. The issue in this action is whether a seller of goods performed in accordance with its agreement, by loading the goods into a container supplied by the buyer and by notifying the buyer of such loading, so as to shift thereby the risk of loss of the goods to the buyer. We answer this question in the negative and thereby affirm the holding of the Appellate Division.

In June of 1973, the buyer, All America Export-Import Corp., placed an order with the seller, A. M. Knitwear Corp., for several thousand pounds of yarn. The buyer used its own purchase order form, dated June 4, 1973, and typed thereon a description of the goods, a statement that partial shipments would be accepted, a description of how to mark the cartons, the quantity in pounds, and the dollar amount of the order. In addition, at the place on the buyer's form where the words "Ship Via" are printed, the buyer typed the instructions: "Pick Up from your Plant to Moore-McCormak Pier [sic] for shipment to Santos, Brazil." Further, in the price column on the form, the buyer typed: "FOB Plant per lb. $1.35" (underlining in original). However, left blank by the buyer was the place on the form where the letters F.O.B. are printed and space is provided for the entry of F.O.B. terms.

In support of its contention that it had fully performed when the goods were loaded in the container, seller quotes from an examination before trial of the buyer's vice-president, who stated:

"*Q:* What about the second order?

"*A:* After the first order was completed, Mr. Lubliner said he has more on hand.

"I said 'What do you mean by hand? Do you have again at the pier?'

"He says 'No. I have the same type of merchandise in my warehouse.' He says 'I could make you a similar offer, the same amount of cartons, 352 cartons. I do not know the weight. The weight may vary, at the same price.'

"I said, 'Okay,' We bought it. I accepted it.

"He asked me, what should I do.

"I said, 'As you know, most of the goods being shipped to South America is being containerized. I have to order a container or a trailer, whatever is the simplest expression. And then in turn you will have to put it into the container.'

"Mr. Lubliner, said, 'This is no problem. Just send down the container. I will try to help you.' "

In preparation for shipping the goods to South America, the buyer phoned International Shipper's Co. of New York, a customs house broker and freight forwarder, and a third-party defendant in this action, to arrange for a local truckman to pick up and deliver the goods to the pier. International Shippers engaged a local truckman, Ability Carriers, Inc., another third-party defendant in this action, which as part of its services picked up an empty container from the Moore-McCormack Lines.

On Friday, June 22, 1973, the local truckman deposited the empty container adjacent to premises located at 57 Thames Street, Brooklyn, New York. There is some dispute between the parties involving, in part, whether these were the seller's premises since Bogart Knitwear, Inc. (apparently related to the seller corporation), another third-party defendant, occupies these premises, but it need not be discussed, since it is not material to our analysis. It is sufficient to say that the container was delivered to the seller for loading.

On Monday, June 25, 1973, the seller had the goods loaded in the container and, on the same day, notified the buyer that the loading had been completed. The buyer then advised its freight forwarder to have the local truckman pick up the loaded container and deliver it to the Moore-McCormack pier. At around 8:00 P.M. that evening, prior to the arrival of the local truckman engaged by the buyer's freight forwarder, an individual driving a tractor arrived at the Thames Street premises where the container was located and hooked up the trailer containing the loaded container to his tractor. The tractor driven by this individual had no descriptive markings thereon or anything to identify its owner. Before leaving the premises, the driver signed a bill of lading, but the signature was indecipherable. It appears that this individual was a thief and had stolen the goods.

Sometime after June 25, the buyer delivered to the seller a check dated July 2, 1973 in the sum of $24,119.10 in payment for the goods loaded in the container. Payment on the check was thereafter stopped by the buyer, apparently when it was learned that the goods had not been received, and the seller brought an action against the buyer to recover payment for the goods.

At Special Term, both the seller and the buyer moved for summary judgment. That court found that the seller's undertaking was to load the goods in deliverable condition into the carrier's container and that, by doing so and notifying the buyer, delivery was made in conformity with the agreement of the parties. Special Term thus determined that the risk of loss of the goods had passed to the buyer and granted the seller's motion for summary judgment.

The Appellate Division reversed Special Term and granted the buyer's motion for summary judgment, on the basis that there was neither physical delivery to the carrier nor delivery within the meaning of the Uniform Commercial Code. Both courts relied on UCC 2-401(2) and UCC 2-509, but the Appellate Division also relied on the holding in Avisun Corp. v. Mercer Motor Frgt., 37 A.D.2d 517, 321 N.Y.S.2d 658 (1971). We affirm the order of the Appellate Division which granted the buyer's motion for summary judgment.

Although the seller contends that the F.O.B. term on the buyer's form did not have its ordinary meaning, the Uniform Commercial Code provides that, unless otherwise agreed, the term F.O.B. at a named place "even though used only in connection with the stated price, is a delivery term" (UCC 2-319(1)). Where the term F.O.B. the place of shipment is used, as in this case with the term F.O.B. plant, the code provides that the seller must ship the goods in the manner provided in UCC 2-504 and "bear the expense and risk of putting them into the possession of the carrier" (UCC 2-319(1)(a)).

With respect to shipment by the seller, the code provides that where the seller is "required or authorized" to send the goods, but not required to deliver them to a particular destination, then "unless otherwise agreed" the seller must "put the goods into the possession of . . . a carrier" (UCC 2-504(a)). Further, with respect to the risk of loss, the code provides that where the contract requires or authorizes the seller to ship the goods by carrier "if it does not require him to deliver them at a particular destination, the risk of loss passes to the buyer *when the goods are duly delivered to the carrier*" (UCC 2-509(1)(a); emphasis added). The risk of loss provision is, however, "subject to contrary agreement of the parties" (UCC 2-509(4)). Although the seller contends that UCC 2-509 is not applicable because the agreement between the parties does not "require" the seller to "ship the goods by carrier," it should be noted that the section applies where the seller is "required or authorized" to ship the goods by carrier and is thus applicable here.

The effect of the provisions of the Uniform Commercial Code may be varied by agreement, with exceptions not applicable here (UCC 1-102(3)). Furthermore, the provisions relevant to this action provide that the requirements set forth therein apply "unless otherwise agreed" or "subject to contrary agreement of the parties," though the absence of these words in the specific provisions was not intended to imply that the effect of such provisions may not be varied by agreement (UCC 1-102(4)). In this respect, the Official Comment to one provision states that "[c]ontrary agreement can also be found in the circumstances of the case, a trade usage or practice, or a course of dealing or performance" (Official Comment 5, UCC 2-509; see also UCC 1-205).

Despite the provisions of the code which place the risk of loss on the seller in the F.O.B. place of shipment contract until the goods are delivered to the carrier, here the seller contends that the parties "otherwise agreed" so that pursuant to its agreement, the risk of loss passed from the seller to the buyer at the time and place at which the seller completed physical delivery of the subject goods into the container supplied by the buyer for that purpose. In support of this contention, the seller alleges that the language of the purchase order "Pick Up from your Plant" is a specific delivery instruction and that the language "FOB Plant per lb. $1.35," which appears in the price column, is a price term and not a delivery term. Further support for the seller's contention is taken from the fact that the space provided in the buyer's own purchase order form for an F.O.B. delivery instruction was left blank by the buyer. Thus, the seller contends its agreement with the buyer imposed no obligation on it to make delivery of the loaded container to the carrier.

As often happens in commercial transactions, the parties to this action did not prepare an extensive written agreement, but merely made an arrangement that, under normal circumstances, would have been entirely satisfactory. The intervention of a wrongdoer who stole the goods that were the subject of the agreement forces the court to determine who should bear the loss resulting from the theft. In this respect, although the seller argues that only to the extent that the agreement is silent should the code apply, it should be noted that the underlying purpose and policy of the code is "to simplify, clarify and modernize the law governing commercial transactions" (UCC 1-102(2)(a)). To this end, the code provides a framework for analyzing a variety of commercial transactions.

The seller's contention, that the parties intended the F.O.B. term as a price term and not a delivery term, conflicts with the code provision that states that the F.O.B. term is a delivery term "even though used *only* in connection with the stated price" (UCC 2-319(1); emphasis added). That the F.O.B. term was not inserted in the space provided for such an expression in the buyer's own purchase order form does not require a determination that the F.O.B. term was intended as a price term, since the drafters of the code recognized that the term F.O.B. will often be used in connection with the stated price. Thus, the place where the term F.O.B. was typed on the buyer's form is not sufficient to suggest that the parties intended a price term, particularly when one considers that the relevant code provision was specifically intended to negate the decisions which treated this term as "merely a price term" (Official Comment 1, UCC 2-319).

Since the term "FOB Plant" was a delivery term, the risk of loss was on the seller until the goods were put into the possession of the carrier—unless the parties "otherwise agreed" or there was a "contrary agreement" with respect to the risk of loss. In this respect, the holding in Avisun v. Mercer Motor Frgt., cited by the Appellate Division, is illustrative. There, the question was whether the defendant carrier was liable as bailee for goods that were loaded in its trailer but were stolen before it arrived to pick them up. The Appellate Division there determined that until the acceptance of the goods by the defendant carrier, there was no bailment and that making available a vehicle for (37 A.D.2d at 518, 321 N.Y.S.2d at 659-660) "possible temporary storage" was not an "acceptance." The seller contends that the *Avisun* case has no relevance to this case because it involves the issue as to when a bailment arises as a matter of law. The seller's interpretation is, however, too limited. The *Avisun* case is relevant here because in the same sense that loading the trailer was not an "acceptance" of a bailment by the carrier, the loading of the container by the seller is not "delivery" to the carrier for purposes of the code, unless the parties so agree.

With respect to the agreement of the parties, the seller contends that the statements in the affidavits of the parties and a portion of an examination before trial of the buyer's vice-president manifest that the parties intended that the seller's performance would be complete when the goods were loaded into the container and the buyer was notified thereof. That this was the agreement of the parties is, according to the seller, further suggested by the fact the buyer issued a check, the payment of which was subsequently stopped, in payment for the goods.

The issuance of the check by the buyer gives little support to the seller's view. The making of payment is as consistent with the buyer's expectation that delivery had been made to the proper carrier as it is with the seller's contention that payment was made because the buyer considered the seller's performance to be completed upon loading the container.

With respect to the seller's contention as to the meaning of the statements of the buyer's vice-president, the seller has a formidable task in trying to prove that the parties did not intend the ordinary meaning of the term "FOB Plant," i.e., delivery to the carrier. Although the only written expression in the transaction was the buyer's purchase order form on which the buyer typed the F.O.B. term, if the seller did not agree to this term, the seller should have expressed its disagreement after it received the purchase order form. For example, the seller should have indicated that the term "FOB Plant" was merely a price term and not a delivery term (see, e.g., 5 McKinney's Forms, UCC 2-319, Form 1) or that the risk of loss was on the buyer after loading (cf. 5 McKinney's Forms, UCC 2-319, Form 2). The code anticipates that a written confirmation by a party may state terms additional to, or even different from, those offered and agreed upon, which terms, depending on certain factors, may become part of the contract (see UCC 2-207). Yet here the seller did not seek to modify the F.O.B. term typed on the buyer's purchase order, but apparently relied on its own understanding of the agreement.

The provisions of the code with respect to risk of loss are subject to the "contrary agreement" of the parties (UCC 2-509(4)). In this respect, the Official Comment states that " '[c]ontrary' is in no way used as a word of limitation and the buyer and seller are left free to readjust their rights and risks . . . in any manner agreeable to them" (Official Comment 5, UCC 2-509). It is, however, a recognized principle that "if the parties have made a memorial of the bargain . . . the law does not recognize . . . their intent, unless it is expressed in, or may fairly be implied from, their writing" (4 Williston on Contracts §600A, at 286 (W. Jaeger 3d ed. 1957)). It has also been established that when words have a well-understood meaning the courts are not permitted to search for the intent of the parties. . . . The term "FOB Plant" is well understood to require delivery to the carrier and does not imply any other meaning. If a contrary meaning was intended, an express statement varying the ordinary meaning is required. The statements made by an officer of the buyer and the other circumstances of this case are not enough to show that the term did not mean what it does in ordinary commercial transactions. One of the principal purposes of the code is to simplify, clarify and modernize the law governing commercial transactions (UCC 1-102(2)(a)). To allow a commonly used term such as F.O.B. to be varied in meaning, without an express statement of the parties of an intent to do so, would not serve that purpose.

Accordingly the order of the Appellate Division which granted the buyer's motion for summary judgment should be affirmed, with costs.

Note: Liability of Insurers and Bailees

The UCC rules, of course, allocate the risk of loss primarily between the seller and the buyer. In practice neither party may bear the ultimate burden because of the presence of insurance or the responsibility of a carrier or warehouseman.

Rules on when insurance against a risk is effective may not conform with the UCC rules allocating the risk. The Standard Fire Policy, for example, has a commonly used rider (Building and Contents Rider, Form No. 4) that covers inventory, including goods "sold but not removed," contained in buildings occupied by the insured. The policy and rider do not cover property purchased but not yet received. As a result a seller who has tendered but not yet delivered goods may have effective insurance and the buyer may have no insurance even though the risk of loss has passed to the buyer (e.g., under UCC 2-509(3)). It should be noted that both parties may have an insurable interest in the goods under UCC 2-501 or other legal rules and one or both may have policies, such as an "all risks" transportation policy, which provides broader coverage, including coverage of goods in transit.

Whether an insurance company that indemnifies its insured is subrogated to any contract claim of the insured against a third party, such as the other party to a contract for sale, is a difficult question. UCC 2-510(2) and (3), which allow a nonbreaching party to recover only to the extent of a deficiency in his insurance coverage, appear to prohibit such subrogation. The policy underlying these Code provisions, however, is not clear and has been questioned by commentators.

Liability of professional bailees has ancient roots that have not been altered significantly by codification.

UCC 7-204(1) states: "A warehouseman is liable for damages for loss of or injury to the goods caused by his failure to exercise such care in regard to them as a reasonably careful man would exercise under like circumstances but unless otherwise agreed he is not liable for damages which could not have been avoided by the exercise of such care."

In contrast to the negligence standard applicable to warehousemen, common carriers at common law were strictly liable for loss, damage, or destruction of goods bailed with them. The federal law states that a common carrier is liable for the "actual loss or injury" to the property of a person entitled to recover under the receipt of bill of lading, 49 U.S.C. §11707 (1982), and explicitly states that remedies provided under the act are in addition to remedies existing at common law. 49 U.S.C. §10103 (1982). UCC 7-309(1) also indirectly incorporates the common law standard by disclaiming any intent to change existing state law imposing liability for damages not caused by the negligence of the carrier. Although strictly liable, carriers may limit the extent of damages they must pay by the classification of goods under a tariff, which both sets the rates charged for carriage and limits the carrier's maximum liability for loss or damage. These tariffs are filed with the Interstate Commerce Commission and are a matter of public record. A shipper who wishes more coverage must declare a higher value and pay an additional fee or must arrange for insurance.

Domestic air carriers are subject to much the same regime as rail and truck carriers: strict liability subject to tariff classifications filed with the Civil Aviation Board, which sets rates and maximum liability. International air carriers are subject to the considerably less onerous liability set out in the Warsaw Convention, as revised by various Protocols.

Ocean carriers are usually governed by the standards of the Harter Act, 46 U.S.C. §§190-195 (1982) and the Carriage of Goods by Sea Act, 46 U.S.C. §§1300-1315 (1982).

Problem 10-11. On March 1, Farmer Brown agrees to sell the hay growing in his fields to Farmer Jones. It is agreed that Brown will harvest the hay and stack it in the field until Jones comes to pick it up in early June. On May 15, due to the fault of neither farmer, the haystack is destroyed by fire. Brown insists Jones must pay the agreed price. Must Jones pay? Would your answer be different if the hay is destroyed on June 10 before Jones has come for it? See UCC 2-509, 2-510, 2-709. See also 2-613.

Problem 10-12. Marina operates a full-service boat dealership. It enters into a purchase agreement with Clouser for a 19-foot boat at a price of $8,500. Clouser makes a down payment of $1,700 but leaves the boat with Marina to permit the dealership to install an engine from another boat. The following day, while the Marina's employees are testing the boat, it hits a seawall and is completely destroyed. Marina's insurance policy excludes any damage resulting from watercraft hazard but makes an exception to this exclusion for damage to any watercraft under 26 feet in length not owned by Marina. What are the rights and obligations of Marina, Clouser, and Marina's insurance company? See UCC 2-401, 2-509. Would your answer be different if motor boats are covered by certificate of title legislation and Marina has not yet delivered the certificate to Clouser?

Problem 10-13. Caudle agrees in writing to buy a house trailer from Sherrard Motors. While Sherrard is preparing the trailer for delivery Caudle is told by his employer to go immediately to its head office in another city. He tells Sherrard that he will return in several days to take possession of the trailer. Two days later the trailer is stolen from Sherrard's lot. On Caudle's refusal to pay, Sherrard brings an action for the agreed purchase price. What defenses does Caudle have to this action? See UCC 2-509, 2-510.

Problem 10-14. Pestana, a Mexican merchant, agrees to buy 64 electronic watches from Karinol, Inc., a Florida corporation. The contract states "send via air parcel post to Chetumal, Mexico" and has no clause allocating the risk of loss. Karinol delivers the goods to an air carrier. The goods are lost before arriving in Mexico. Between Pestana and Karinol, who bears the risk of loss? What result if the contract provides (a) "F.O.B. Miami"? (b) "F.O.B. Chetumal"? (c) "C.I.F. Chetumal"? If the watches are defective when delivered to the carrier, who bears the risk? See UCC 2-319, 2-320, 2-509, 2-510.

Problem 10-15. On June 30 Multiplastics agrees to sell to Arch 40,000 pounds of polystyrene plastic pellets to be manufactured specifically for Arch. Arch agrees to take delivery at Multiplastics' plant at the rate of 1,000 pounds per day after completion of production. Multiplastics completes production by July 14 but Arch refuses to take delivery because of "labor difficulties and its vacation schedule." On August 18 Multiplastics demands shipping instructions. On receiving the letter Arch promises to issue instructions but has not yet done so when Multiplastics' plant is destroyed by fire. Multiplastics' fire insurance does not cover the loss of the pellets. May Multiplastics recover the purchase price from Arch? See UCC 2-509, 2-510, 2-709.

E. EXCUSE FOR NON-PERFORMANCE

A seller is expected to carry out his bargain even if he has second thoughts about the deal he has struck and even if nonperformance is not his fault. As we shall see in subsequent chapters, he is "strictly" liable if he breaches his contractual obligations. Contractual liability, as a general proposition, is strict liability—not a "best efforts" or "negligence" standard. In exceptional circumstances, however, the seller may be excused. You have no doubt already studied the concepts of impossibility or impracticability and frustration, which are favorite topics in contract law courses. See Restatement (Second) of Contracts §§261-272 (1981).

The Uniform Commercial Code addresses these problems in UCC 2-613 to 2-616. UCC 2-615 (Excuse by failure by presupposed conditions), for example, codifies the doctrine of impracticability:

> "Except so far as a seller may have assumed a greater obligation . . . delay . . . or non-delivery . . . is not a breach . . . *if performance as agreed has been made impracticable by the occurrence of a contingency the non-occurrence of which was a basic assumption on which the contract was made.*" (Emphasis added.)

UCC 2-613 may also excuse a seller when goods identified to the contract at the time of contracting have suffered a casualty without fault of either party, and UCC 2-614 permits substitute performance, where performance in strict compliance with the contract is not possible, under certain circumstances. See also UCC 2-311(3) (delay excused if necessary cooperation of other party is not forthcoming).

For readings on this topic, see The Economics of Contract Law 122-153 (A. Kronman & R. Posner eds. 1979). See generally Posner & Rosenfield, Impossibility and Related Doctrines in Contract Law: An Economic Analysis, 6 J. Legal Stud. 83 (1977) (in absence of contract term, party who can insure against the risk more cheaply should bear the risk); Speidel, Excusable Non-Performance in Sales Contracts: Some Thoughts About Risk Management, 32 S. Car. L. Rev. 241 (1980).

TRANSATLANTIC FINANCING CORP. v.
UNITED STATES
124 U.S. App. Dec. 183, 363 F.2d 312, 3 UCC Rep. 401 (D.C. Cir. 1966)

J. Skelly WRIGHT, Circuit Judge. This appeal involves a voyage charter between Transatlantic Financing Corporation, operator of the SS Christos, and the United States covering carriage of a full cargo of wheat from a United States Gulf port to a safe port in Iran. The District Court dismissed a libel filed by Transatlantic against the United States for costs attributable to the ship's diversion from the normal sea route caused by the closing of the Suez Canal. We affirm.

On July 26, 1956, the Government of Egypt nationalized the Suez Canal Company and took over operation of the Canal. On October 2, 1956, during the international crisis which resulted from the seizure, the voyage charter in suit was executed between representatives of Transatlantic and the United States. The charter indicated the termini of the voyage but not the route. On October 27, 1956, the SS Christos sailed from Galveston for Bandar Shapur, Iran, on a course which would have taken her through Gibraltar and the Suez Canal. On October 29, 1956, Israel invaded Egypt. On October 31, 1956, Great Britain and France invaded the Suez Zone. On November 2, 1956, the Egyptian Government obstructed the Suez Canal with sunken vessels and closed it to traffic.

On or about November 7, 1956, Beckmann, representing Transatlantic, contacted Potosky, an employee of the United States Department of Agriculture, who appellant concedes was unauthorized to bind the Government, requesting instructions concerning disposition of the cargo and seeking an agreement for payment of additional compensation for a voyage around the Cape of Good Hope. Potosky advised Beckmann that Transatlantic was expected to perform the charter according to its terms, that he did not believe Transatlantic was entitled to additional compensation for a voyage around the Cape, but that Transatlantic was free to file such a claim. Following this discussion, the Christos changed course for the Cape of Good Hope and eventually arrived in Bandar Shapur on December 30, 1956.

Transatlantic's claim is based on the following train of argument. The charter was a contract for a voyage from a Gulf port to Iran. Admiralty principles and practices, especially stemming from the doctrine of deviation, require us to imply into the contract the term that the voyage was to be performed by the "usual and customary" route. The usual and customary route from Texas to Iran was, at the time of contract, via Suez, so the contract was for a voyage from Texas to Iran via Suez. When Suez was closed this contract became impossible to perform. Consequently, appellant's argument continues, when Transatlantic delivered the cargo by going around the Cape of Good Hope, in compliance with the Government's demand under claim of right, it conferred a benefit upon the United States for which it should be paid in *quantum meruit.*

The doctrine of impossibility of performance has gradually been freed from the earlier fictional and unrealistic strictures of such tests as the "implied term" and the parties' "contemplation." Page, The Development of the Doctrine of Impossibility of Performance, 18 Mich. L. Rev. 589, 596 (1920). See generally 6 Corbin, Contracts §§1320-1372 (rev. ed. 1962); 6 Williston, Contracts §§1931-1979 (rev. ed. 1938). It is now recognized that " 'A thing is impossible in legal contemplation when it is not practicable; and a thing is impracticable when it can only be done at an excessive and unreasonable cost.' " Mineral Park Land Co. v. Howard, 172 Cal. 289, 293, 156 P. 458, 460, L.R.A. 1916F, 1 (1916). Accord, Whelan v. Griffith Consumers Company, D.C. Mun. App., 170 A.2d 229 (1961); Restatement, Contracts §454 (1932); UCC 2-615, comment 3. The doctrine ultimately represents the ever-shifting line, drawn by courts hopefully responsive to commercial practices and mores, at which the community's interest in having contracts enforced according to their terms is outweighed by the commercial senselessness of requiring performance.[1] When the issue is raised, the court is asked to construct a condition of performance[2] based on the changed circumstances, a process which involves at least three reasonably definable steps. First, a contingency—something unexpected—must have occurred. Second, the risk of the unexpected occurrence must not have been allocated either by agreement or by custom. Finally, occurrence of the contingency must have rendered performance commercially impracticable.[3] Unless the court finds these three requirements satisfied, the plea of impossibility must fail.

---

1. While the impossibility issue rarely arises, as it has here, in a suit to recover the cost of an alternative method of performance, compare Annot., 84 A.L.R.2d 12, 19 (1962), there is nothing necessarily inconsistent in claiming commercial impracticability for the method of performance actually adopted; the concept of impracticability assumes performance was physically possible. Moreover, a rule making nonperformance a condition precedent to recovery would unjustifiably encourage disappointment of expectations.

2. Patterson, Constructive Conditions in Contracts, 42 Colum. L. Rev. 903, 943-954 (1942).

3. Compare UCC 2-615(a), which provides that, in the absence of an assumption of greater liability, delay or non-delivery by a seller is not a breach if performance as agreed is made "impracticable" by the occurrence of a "contingency" the non-occurrence of which was a "basic assumption on which the contract was made." To the extent this limits relief to "unforeseen" circumstances, comment 1, see the discussion below, and compare UCC 2-614(1). There may be a point beyond which agreement cannot go, UCC 2-615, comment 8, presumably the point at which the obligation would be "manifestly unreasonable," UCC 1-102(3), in bad faith, UCC 1-203, or unconscionable, UCC 2-302. For an application of these provisions see Judge Friendly's opinion in United States v. Wegematic Corporation, 360 F.2d 674 (2d Cir. 1966).

The first requirement was met here. It seems reasonable, where no route is mentioned in a contract, to assume the parties expected performance by the usual and customary route at the time of contract.[4] Since the usual and customary route from Texas to Iran at the time of contract[5] was through Suez, closure of the Canal made impossible the expected method of performance. But this unexpected development raises rather than resolves the impossibility issue, which turns additionally on whether the risk of the contingency's occurrence had been allocated and, if not, whether performance by alternative routes was rendered impracticable.[6]

Proof that the risk of a contingency's occurrence has been allocated may be expressed in or implied from the agreement. Such proof may also be found in the surrounding circumstances, including custom and usages of the trade. See 6 Corbin, supra, §1339, at 394-397; 6 Williston, supra, §1948, at 5457-5458. The contract in this case does not expressly condition performance upon availability of the Suez route. Nor does it specify "via Suez" or, on the other

4. UCC 2-614, comment 1, states: "Under this Article, in the absence of specific agreement, the normal or usual facilities enter into the agreement either through the circumstances, usage of trade or prior course of dealing." So long as this sort of assumption does not necessarily result in construction of a condition of performance, it is idle to argue over whether the usual and customary route is an "implied term." The issue of impracticability must eventually be met. One court refused to imply the Suez route as a contract term, but went on to rule the contract had been "frustrated." Carapanayoti & Co. Ltd. v. E. T. Green Ltd., [1959] 1 Q.B. 131. The holding was later rejected by the House of Lords. Tsakiroglou & Co. Ltd. v. Noblee Thorl G.m.b.H., [1960] 2 Q.B. 348.

5. The parties have spent considerable energy in disputing whether the "usual and customary" route by which performance was anticipated is defined as of the time of contract or of performance. If we were automatically to treat the expected route as a condition of performance, this matter would be crucial, and we would be compelled to choose between unacceptable alternatives. If we assume as a constructive condition the usual and customary course always to mean the one in use at the time of contract, any substantial diversion (we assume the diversion would have to be substantial) would nullify the contract even though its effect upon the rights and obligations of the parties is insignificant. Nor would it be desirable, on the other hand, to assume performance is conditioned on the availability of *any* usual and customary route at the time of performance. It may be that very often the availability of a customary route at the time of performance other than the route expected to be used at the time of contract should result in denial of relief under the impossibility theory; certainly if *no* customary route is available at the time of performance the contract is rendered impossible. But the same customarily used alternative route may be impracticable in another, as where the goods are unable to survive the extra journey. Moreover, the "time of performance" is no special point in time; it is every moment in a performance. Thus the alternative route, in our case around the Cape, may be practicable at some time during performance, for example while the vessel is still in the Atlantic Ocean, and impracticable at another time during the performance, for example after the vessel has traversed most of the Mediterranean Sea. Both alternatives, therefore, have their shortcomings, and we avoid choosing between them by refusing automatically to treat the usual and customary route as of any time as a condition of performance.

6. In criticizing the "contemplation" test for impossibility Professor Patterson pointed out: " 'Contemplation' is appropriate to describe the mental state of philosophers but is scarcely descriptive of the mental state of business men making a bargain. It seems preferable to say that the promisee *expects* performance by [the] means . . . the promisor expects to (or which on the facts known to the promisee it is probable that he will) use. It does not follow as an inference of fact that the promisee expects performance by only that means. . . ." Patterson, supra note 2, at 947.

hand, "via Suez or Cape of Good Hope."[7] Nor is there anything in custom or trade usage, or in the surrounding circumstances generally, which would support our constructing a condition of performance.[8] The numerous cases requiring performance around the Cape when Suez was closed, see e.g., Ocean Tramp Tankers Corp. v. V/O Sovfracht (*The Eugenia*), [1964] 2 Q.B. 226, and cases cited therein, indicate that the Cape route is generally regarded as an alternative means of performance. So the implied expectation that the route would be via Suez is hardly adequate proof of an allocation to the promisee of the risk of closure. In some cases, even an express expectation may not amount to a condition of performance.[9] The doctrine of deviation supports our as-

7. In Glidden Company v. Hellenic Lines, Limited, 275 F.2d 253 (2d Cir. 1960), the charter was for transportation of materials from India to America "via Suez Canal or Cape of Good Hope, or Panama Canal," and the court held performance was not "frustrated." In his discussion of this case, Professor Corbin states: "Except for the provision for an alternative route, the defendant would have been discharged, for the reason that the parties contemplated an open Suez Canal as a specific condition or means of performance." 6 Corbin, supra, §1339, at 399 n.57. Appellant claims this supports its argument, since the Suez route was contemplated as usual and customary. But there is obviously a difference, in deciding whether a contract allocates the risk of a contingency's occurrence, between a contract specifying no route and a contract specifying Suez. We think that when Professor Corbin said, "Except for the provision for an alternative route," he was referring, not to the entire *provision*—"via Suez Canal or Cape of Good Hope" etc.—but to the fact that *an alternative route* had been provided for. Moreover, in determining what Corbin meant when he said "the parties contemplated an open Suez Canal as a specific condition or means of performance," consideration must be given to the fact, recited by Corbin, that in *Glidden* the parties were specifically aware when the contract was made the Canal might be closed, and the promisee had refused to include a clause excusing performance in the event of closure. Corbin's statement, therefore, is most accurately read as referring to cases in which a route is specified after negotiations reflecting the parties' awareness that the usual and customary route might become unavailable.

8. The charter provides that the vessel is "in every way fitted for *the voyage*" (emphasis added), and the "P. & I. Bunker Deviation Clause" refers to "the contract voyage" and the "direct and/or customary route." Appellant argues that these provisions require implication of a voyage by the direct and customary route. Actually they prove only what we are willing to accept—that the parties expected the usual and customary route would be used. The provisions in no way condition performance upon non-occurrence of this contingency.

There are two clauses which allegedly demonstrate that time is of importance in this contract. One clause computes the remuneration "in steaming time" for diversions to other countries ordered by the charterer in emergencies. This proves only that the United States wished to reserve power to send the goods to another country. It does not imply in any way that there was a rush about the matter. The other clause concerns demurrage and despatch. The charterer agreed to pay Transatlantic demurrage of $1,200 per day for all time in excess of the period agreed upon for loading and unloading, and Transatlantic was to pay despatch of $600 per day for any saving in time. Of course this provision shows the parties were concerned about time, see Gilmore & Black, The Law of Admiralty §4-8 (1957), but the fact that they arranged so minutely the consequences of any delay or speedup of loading and unloading operates against the argument that they were similarly allocating the risk of delay or speed-up of the voyage.

9. UCC 2-614(1) provides: "Where without fault of either party . . . the *agreed* manner of delivery . . . becomes commercially impracticable but a commercially reasonable substitute is available, such substitute performance must be tendered and accepted." (Emphasis added.) Compare Mr. Justice Holmes' observation: "You can give any conclusion a logical form. You always can imply a condition in a contract. But why do you imply it? It is because of some belief as to the practice of the community or of a class, or because of some opinion as to policy . . . ." Holmes, The Path of the Law, 18 Harv. L. Rev. 457, 466 (1897).

sumption that parties normally expect performance by the usual and customary route, but it adds nothing beyond this that is probative of an allocation of the risk.[10]

If anything, the circumstances surrounding this contract indicate that the risk of the Canal's closure may be deemed to have been allocated to Transatlantic. We know or may safely assume that the parties were aware, as were most commercial men with interests affected by the Suez situation, see *The Eugenia*, supra, that the Canal might become a dangerous area. No doubt the tension affected freight rates, and it is arguable that the risk of closure became part of the dickered terms. UCC 2-615, comment 8. We do not deem the risk of closure so allocated, however. Foreseeability or even recognition of a risk does not necessarily prove its allocation.[11] Compare UCC 2-615, Comment 1; Restatement, Contracts §457 (1932). Parties to a contract are not always able to provide for all the possibilities of which they are aware, sometimes because they cannot agree, often simply because they are too busy. Moreover, that some abnormal risk was contemplated is probative but does not necessarily establish an allocation of the risk of the contingency which actually occurs. In this case, for example, nationalization by Egypt of the Canal Corporation and formation of the Suez Users Group did not necessarily indicate that the Canal would be blocked even if a confrontation resulted.[12] The surrounding circum-

10. The deviation doctrine, drawn principally from admiralty insurance practice, implies into all relevant commercial instruments naming the termini of voyages the usual and customary route between those points. 1 Arnould, Marine Insurance and Average §376, at 522 (10th ed. 1921). Insurance is cancelled when a ship unreasonably "deviates" from this course, for example by extending a voyage or by putting in at an irregular port, and the shipowner forfeits the protection of clauses of exception which might otherwise have protected him from his common law insurer's liability to cargo. See Gilmore & Black, supra note 8, §2-6, at 59-60. This practice, properly qualified, see id. §3-41, makes good sense, since insurance rates are computed on the basis of the implied course, and deviations in the course increasing the anticipated risk make the insurer's calculations meaningless. Arnould, supra, §14, at 26. Thus the route, so far as insurance contracts are concerned, is crucial, whether express or implied. But even here, the implied term is not inflexible. Reasonable deviations do not result in loss of insurance, at least so long as established practice is followed. See Carriage of Goods by Sea Act §4(4), 49 Stat. 1210, 46 U.S.C. §1304(4); and discussion of "held covered" clauses in Gilmore & Black, supra, §3-41, at 161. Some "deviations" are required. E.g., Hirsch Lumber Co. v. Weyerhauser Steamship Co., 233 F.2d 791 (2d Cir.), *cert. denied,* 352 U.S. 880, 77 S. Ct. 102, 1 L. Ed. 2d 80 (1956). The doctrine's only relevance, therefore, is that it provides additional support for the assumption we willingly make that merchants agreeing to a voyage between two points expect that the usual and customary route between those points will be used. The doctrine provides no evidence of an allocation of the risk of the route's unavailability.

11. See Note, The Fetish of Impossibility in the Law of Contracts, 53 Colum. L. Rev. 94, 98 n.23 (1953), suggesting that foreseeability is properly used "as a *factor* probative of assumption of the risk of impossibility." (Emphasis added.)

12. Sources cited in the briefs indicate formation of the Suez Canal Users Association on October 1, 1956, was viewed in some quarters as an implied threat of force. See N.Y. Times, Oct. 2, 1956, p.1, col. 1, noting, on the day the charter in this case was executed, that "Britain has declared her freedom to use force as a last resort if peaceful methods fail to achieve a satisfactory settlement." Secretary of State Dulles was able, however, to view the statement as evidence of the canal users' "dedication to a just and peaceful solution." The Suez Problem 369-370 (Department of State Pub. 1956).

stances do indicate, however, a willingness by Transatlantic to assume abnormal risks, and this fact should legitimately cause us to judge the impracticability of performance by an alternative route in stricter terms than we would were the contingency unforeseen.

We turn then to the question whether occurrence of the contingency rendered performance commercially impracticable under the circumstances of this case. The goods shipped were not subject to harm from the longer, less temperate Southern route. The vessel and crew were fit to proceed around the Cape.[13] Transatlantic was no less able than the United States to purchase insurance to cover the contingency's occurrence. If anything, it is more reasonable to expect owner-operators of vessels to insure against the hazards of war. They are in the best position to calculate the cost of performance by alternative routes (and therefore to estimate the amount of insurance required), and are undoubtedly sensitive to international troubles which uniquely affect the demand for and cost of their services. The only factor operating here in appellant's favor is the added expense, allegedly $43,972.00 above and beyond the contract price of $305,842.92, of extending a 10,000 mile voyage by approximately 3,000 miles. While it may be an overstatement to say that increased cost and difficulty of performance never constitute impracticability, to justify relief there must be more of a variation between expected cost and the cost of performing by an available alternative than is present in this case,[14] where the promisor can legitimately be presumed to have accepted some degree of abnormal risk, and where impracticability is urged on the basis of added expense alone.[15]

---

13. The issue of impracticability should no doubt be "an objective determination of whether the promise can reasonably be performed rather than a subjective inquiry into the promisor's capability of performing as agreed." Symposium, The Uniform Commercial Code and Contract Law: Some Selected Problems, 105 U. Pa. L. Rev. 836, 880, 887 (1957). Dealers should not be excused because of less than normal capabilities. But if both parties are aware of a dealer's limited capabilities, no objective determination would be complete without taking into account this fact.

14. Two leading English cases support this conclusion. *The Eugenia,* supra, involved a time charter for a trip from Genoa to India via the Black Sea. The charterers were held in breach of the charter's war clause by entering the Suez Canal after the outbreak of hostilities, but sought to avoid paying for the time the vessel was trapped in the Canal by arguing that, even if they had not entered the Canal, it would have been blocked and the vessel would have had to go around the Cape to India, a trip which "frustrated" the contract because it constituted an entirely different venture from the one originally contemplated. The lower court agreed, but the House of Lords (see Lord Denning's admirable treatment, [1964] 2 Q.B. at 233), "swallowing" the difficulty of applying the frustration doctrine to hypothetical facts, reversed, holding that the contract had to be performed. Especially relevant is the fact that the case expressly overruled Societe Franco Tunisienne D'Armement v. Sidermar S.P.A. (*The Massalia*), [1961] 2 Q.B. 278, where a voyage charter was deemed frustrated because the Cape route was "highly circuitous" and cost 195s. per long ton to ship iron ore, rather than 134s. via Suez, a difference well in excess of the difference in this case.

In Tsakiroglou & Co. Ltd. v. Noblee Thorl G.m.b.H., supra note 4, the difference to the seller under a C.I.F. contract in freight costs caused by the Canal's closure was £15 per ton instead of £7.10s. per ton—precisely twice the cost. The House of Lords found no frustration.

15. See UCC 2-615, comment 4: "Increased cost alone does not excuse performance unless the rise in cost is due to some unforeseen contingency which alters the essential nature of the performance." See also 6 Corbin, supra, §1333; 6 Williston, supra, §1952, at 5468.

We conclude, therefore, as have most other courts considering related issues arising out of the Suez closure,[16] that performance of this contract was not rendered legally impossible. Even if we agreed with appellant, its theory of relief seems untenable. When performance of a contract is deemed impossible it is a nullity. In the case of a charter party involving carriage of goods, the carrier may return to an appropriate port and unload its cargo . . . subject of course to required steps to minimize damages. If the performance rendered has value, recovery in *quantum meruit* relief for the entire performance is proper. But here Transatlantic has collected its contract price, and now seeks *quantum meruit* relief for the additional expense of the trip around the Cape. If the contract is a nullity, Transatlantic's theory of relief should have been *quantum meruit* for the entire trip, rather than only for the extra expense. Transatlantic attempts to take its profit on the contract, and then force the Government to absorb the cost of the additional voyage.[17] When impracticability without fault occurs, the law seeks an equitable solution, see 6 Corbin, supra, §1321, and *quantum meruit* is one of its potent devices to achieve this end. There is no interest in casting the entire burden of commercial disaster on one party in order to preserve the other's profit. Apparently the contract price in this case was advantageous enough to deter appellant from taking a stance on damages consistent with its theory of liability. In any event, there is no basis for relief.

Affirmed.

16. Appellant seeks to distinguish the English cases supporting our view. *The Eugenia,* supra, appellant argues, involved a time charter. True, but it overruled *The Massalia,* supra note 14, which involved a voyage charter. Indeed, when the time charter is for a voyage the difference is only verbal. See Carver, Carriage of Goods by Sea 256-257 (10th ed. 1957). More convincing is the argument that *Tsakiroglou & Co. Ltd.,* supra note 4, involved a contract for the sale of goods, where the seller agreed to a C.I.F. clause requiring him to ship the goods to the buyer. There is a significant difference between a C.I.F. contract and voyage or time charters. The effect of delay in the former due to longer sea voyages is minimized, since the seller can raise money on the goods he has shipped almost at once, and the buyer, once he takes up the documents, can deal with the goods by transferring the documents before the goods arrive. See *Tsakiroglou & Co. Ltd.,* supra note 4, [1960] 2 Q.B. at 361. But this difference is not so material that impossibility in C.I.F. contracts is unrelated to impossibility in charter parties. It would raise serious questions for a court to require sellers under C.I.F. contracts to perform in circumstances under which the sellers could be refused performance by carriers with whom they have entered into charter parties for affreightment. See *The Eugenia,* supra, [1964] 2 Q.B. at 241. Where the time of the voyage is unimportant, a charter party should be treated the same as a C.I.F. contract in determining impossibility of performance.

These cases certainly are not distinguishable, as appellant suggests, on the ground that they refer to "frustration" rather than to "impossibility." The English regard "frustration" as substantially identical with "impossibility." 6 Corbin, supra, §1322, at 327, n.9.

17. The argument that the Uniform Commercial Code requires the buyer to pay the additional cost of performance by a commercially reasonable substitute was advanced and rejected in Symposium, supra note 13, 105 U. Pa. L. Rev. at 884 n.205. In Dillon v. United States, 156 F. Supp. 719, 140 Ct. Cl. 508 (1957), relief was afforded for some of the cost of delivering hay from a commercially unreasonable distance, but the suit was one in which the plaintiff had suffered losses far in excess of the relief given.

NOTES & QUESTIONS

1. *Admiralty law: charter parties.* For further reading on the rights and obligations of charter parties, see G. Gilmore & C. Black, The Law of Admiralty 193-243 (2d ed. 1975).

2. *Excuse in international trade and foreign law.* Arguments about when a party to a contract is excused are made in all legal systems. See, for example, Berman, Excuse for Non-Performance in the Light of Contract Practices in International Trade, 63 Colum. L. Rev. 1413 (1963). For an interesting review of foreign law approaches to this problem, see the Appendix to the controversial District Court opinion in Aluminum Co. of America v. The Essex Group, Inc., 499 F. Supp. 53, 93-94 (W.D. Pa. 1980).

3. *Impracticability.* Would it be desirable to legislate or otherwise adopt a crude rule of thumb to determine when a seller's performance is impracticable? For example, such a rule might state that performance of a contract obligation is not impracticable unless the cost of performance has increased more than 100 percent beyond what was reasonably anticipated. See Publicker Industries, Inc. v. Union Carbide, 17 UCC Rep. 989, 992 (E.D. Pa. 1975) ("we are not aware of any cases where something less than a 100% cost increase has been held to make a seller's performance 'impracticable' ").

4. *Causation.* Showing that a particular contingency *caused* the seller's inability to perform may be difficult if there are multiple causes. For example, a producer of uranium concentrate would have to show not only the extent of unexpected production cost increases but also the causes for these increases. If production costs increase because of unexpected market shortages, new environmental regulations, and internal decisions as to production methods, the relative impact of each cause on the increased production costs must be shown. See Iowa Electric Light & Power Co. v. Atlas Corp., 467 F. Supp. 129, 23 UCC Rep. 1171 and 25 UCC Rep. 163 (N.D. Iowa 1978), *rev'd for lack of jurisdiction,* 603 F.2d 1301 (8th Cir. 1979).

5. *Foreseeability.* The court in *Transatlantic* downplays the significance of whether the contingency is foreseeable. Many other courts, however, consider foreseeability to be an important factor in their analysis. It has been suggested that the issue is germane because of the law's interest in protecting reasonable commercial expectations: if a seller is silent as to a foreseeable risk the buyer can reasonably expect the seller to bear the risk when the seller agrees to deliver goods under a contract for sale. It has also been suggested that foreseeability is relevant to determine who is able most cheaply to insure against the risk. Are you persuaded? Aren't most contingencies foreseeable, even if the likelihood of their occurrence is very remote? Do sellers' prices include, as a matter of course, some premium to insure against the likelihood of some unforeseen contingency occurring?

6. *Contract adjustment.* UCC 2-615 and 2-616 provide for allocation if the seller is able to perform at least part of his contract obligations. See White, Allocation of Scarce Resources under Section 2-615 of the UCC: A Compari-

son of Some Rival Models, 12 U. Mich. J.L. Ref. 503 (1979). See also the
options available to the buyer under UCC 2-613 when goods identified to the
contract have suffered a casualty. To what extent do these specific provisions
authorize or foreclose a court order adjusting the terms of a contract?

7. *Exculpatory Clauses.* McDonnell Douglas agreed to sell 100 jet planes to
Eastern Airlines. Because of demands made on it and its suppliers by the
United States Department of Defense for Vietnam war efforts, McDonnell
Douglas delivered the planes only after long delays. Eastern claims damages
for the delays. McDonnell Douglas responds that it was excused by the following contract clause: "Seller shall not be responsible nor deemed to be in default on account of delays in performance . . . due to causes beyond Seller's
control and not occasioned by its fault or negligence, including but not being
limited to . . . any act of government, governmental priorities, allocation
regulations or orders affecting materials, equipment, facilities or completed
aircraft, . . . failure of vendors (due to causes similar to those within the scope
of this clause) to perform their contracts . . . , provided such cause is beyond
Seller's control." If asked by Eastern whether it should pursue its claim for
damages, what would you advise the airline to do? See Eastern Air Lines, Inc.
v. McDonnell Douglas Corp., 532 F.2d 957, 19 UCC Rep. 353 (5th Cir.
1976).

Problem 10-16. Jim manufactures cane chairs that he distributes through
handicraft outlets. In the last two years he has distributed almost 600 chairs a
year with no outlet receiving more than 50 chairs. One summer in an attempt
to expand business he made 40 cane rocking chairs of a new design. At the end
of the summer he took one chair as a sample and solicited orders from furniture wholesalers and retailers. As a result he signed a written contract with
Sam, the owner of Leisure Time Furniture, to supply 100 rockers, the 40
already made to be delivered promptly and the remaining 60 in three months.
Unknown to both Sam and Jim, at the time they signed the contract a fire had
destroyed Jim's workshop and the 39 rockers stored there. On learning of the
fire Jim asks you to advise him as to his legal obligations. He tells you that to
replace his inventory of cane will increase his expenses so that the contract
with Leisure Time will no longer be profitable, that in any event he will not be
able to deliver 100 rockers in less than six months, and that he feels obligated
to give priority to his traditional outlets. Advise Jim. See UCC 2-613, 2-615,
2-616.

Problem 10-17. Associated agrees to sell 4,000 tons of cryolite to Kaiser.
Associated relies for its supply of cryolite on its contract with ICIB, an Italian
processor. Because of a strike by its workers ICIB is unable to deliver any
cryolite for a nine-month period. On making inquiries Associated learns that it
can purchase only 2,000 tons of cryolite on the open market and that these
purchases would be at a price 20 percent above the contract price agreed with
Kaiser. What are Associated's obligations? See UCC 2-615.

CHAPTER 11

Inspection, Acceptance and Rejection, Cure, and Revocation of Acceptance

In a major law review article analyzing the Code's remedial provisions, Chief Justice Ellen Peters identifies three basic options available to a non-breaching seller or buyer: he may seek (1) to "escape from the contract," (2) to require full (strict) performance, or (3) to recover damages. Peters, Remedies for Breach of Contracts Relating to the Sale of Goods Under the Uniform Commercial Code: A Roadmap for Article Two, 73 Yale L.J. 199 (1963). This chapter deals primarily with the scope of the buyer's right to call off the contract by rejecting or revoking acceptance of goods.

The buyer may have differing motives for rejecting goods. If the tender of delivery or the goods themselves are nonconforming the buyer may simply wish to escape the contract in order to obtain a conforming tender or goods. Market prices may drop or technological advances may offer less expensive or otherwise more desirable alternatives. A buyer may also wish to back out of the contract because his needs have changed between the time of contracting and the time of tender.

When a buyer should have not only the power but also the legal right to call off the contract is an issue that sharply divides most sellers and buyers. It is sometimes stated that the common law required a seller to make a "perfect" or conforming tender; anything less, unless *de minimis,* could be rejected by a buyer. Pre-Code law, whether common law or the Uniform Sales Act, was much more subtle than this statement suggests. See Honnold, Buyer's Right of Rejection, 97 U. Pa. L. Rev. 457 (1949); see also Llewellyn's comments on an early draft of Article 2 set out at p. 559 infra. The UCC nominally builds on the prior perfect tender rule, but in fact weakens it to accommodate the reasonable expectations of sellers and buyers in different kinds of transactions.

A. "TARR"

The Code's rules on tender, acceptance, rejection, and revocation of acceptance (TARR) are deceptively clear cut. The seller *tenders* the goods following the rules we explored in Chapter 10. The buyer may then *inspect* the goods to see if they conform to the contract terms. Whether or not the goods or tender conform the buyer may *accept* the goods. On acceptance the buyer becomes obligated to pay for the goods at the contract rate and may no longer reject them. Alternatively, on tender the buyer may *reject* the goods, and may do so whether or not the goods or tender conform. The buyer will be liable for damages, however, if the seller can prove the buyer rejected a proper tender of conforming goods. Even if the buyer accepts he may later *revoke acceptance* under certain restricted circumstances and may return the goods to the seller if he can show that they were nonconforming at the time of tender. These rules are set out in UCC 2-601 through 2-608, which should be read for an elaboration of the summary set out above.

A study of the case law under these Code provisions suggests, however, that these clearcut distinctions are really part of one ball of wax—or, as one commentator has put it, one ball of TARR. Whaley, Tender, Acceptance, Rejection and Revocation—The Uniform Commercial Code's "TARR"-Baby, 24 Drake L. Rev. 523 (1974). In their UCC handbook Professors White and Summers conclude that "the cases decided to date give little support to the proposition that the buyer may freely reject but only rarely revoke acceptance" and "none [of the reported cases on rejection] grants rejection on what could fairly be called an insubstantial nonconformity." J. White & R. Summers, Handbook of the Law Under the Uniform Commercial Code 297, 305 (2d ed. 1980).

To complicate matters even further Article 2 itself includes a number of provisions that qualify significantly the perfect tender rule of UCC 2-601. The right to reject is limited, for example, where tender requires a shipment contract or the contract calls for performance by installments. UCC 2-504, 2-612. Moreover, even if a buyer has the right to reject, the seller in many cases will have a statutory right to cure a defective tender. UCC 2-508.

Problem 11-1 explores the statutory framework, and the law review excerpt that follows studies the possible justifications that might underlie rules to resolve disputes that arise when a buyer seeks to walk away from the contract.

Problem 11-1. Aspen places an order for 200 pairs of Snowmass skis. There are to be 40 pairs each of 160, 170, and 180 cm. length, and 20 pairs of 140, 150, 190, and 200 cm. length. All of the skis are to be shipped in October via parcel post. In the normal course of events the skis will arrive by mid-November at the latest. In which, if any, of the following circumstances will Aspen have the right to reject or revoke acceptance of the skis?

(a) Snowmass ships only 30 pairs of 160 cm. skis. It "substitutes" 5 extra pairs of 150 and 170 cm. skis in place of the 10 pairs of 160 cm. skis. Does it matter whether industry practice would allow distributor to "vary the mix" on such orders?—Or if Snowmass had similarly substituted goods when filling Aspen's orders in previous seasons? See UCC 2-601, 2-508.

(b) In addition to the 200 pairs of skis ordered Snowmass ships 10 additional pairs of 160 cm. skis. Before the shipment arrives the market price for skis drops dramatically because of weather predictions of little snow for the forthcoming winter. Aspen wishes to reject the entire shipment but admits that the only reason it wishes to do so is the fall in market price. See UCC 1-201(19), 1-203, 2-103(1)(b), 2-601.

(c) Snowmass is late in filling the order and therefore ships the skis air freight during the first week of November. Snowmass pays the additional freight. See UCC 2-504, 2-616.

(d) Instead of one shipment, Snowmass is to make two equal shipments—one in September and one in November. In the first shipment, Snowmass makes the substitutions mentioned in (a). See UCC 2-612.

(e) Assume that the agreed assortment of skis arrives and is put on display by Aspen. The first purchaser is Hot Dog, a local ski bum. Hot Dog returns his skis about two weeks later and shows the manager of the ski department three places where the skis are delaminating. The manager quickly surveys a rack of skis and finds several pairs that seem irregular. See UCC 2-601, 2-513, 2-606, 2-607, 2-508, 2-608.

(f) In (e) assume that Aspen identifies 20 pairs of skis as suffering from "delamination of core." On that basis, Aspen notifies Snowmass that it is rejecting the entire shipment, specifying the delamination of 20 pairs. In fact, none of the skis suffers from delamination. Rather, a machine in Snowmass's plant sometimes fails to tension correctly the mask through which the ski cosmetics are applied to the skis. This results in a rippled appearance on the top and base of the ski. Cosmetic defects of this type render skis "seconds," which are accepted in the trade for 60 percent of the usual price. In addition, close inspection reveals that one ski in the entire lot has a dangerous hairline crack, which usually causes the ski to shatter if skied hard on an icy surface. Snowmass asserts that the skis have been "accepted" and that it is therefore entitled to recover the price. See UCC 2-709, 2-601, 2-513, 2-606, 2-605, 2-607, 2-608, 2-508.

(g) Suppose in (f) that Aspen's ski buyer notices the irregularities when unpacking the skis and then undertakes a closer investigation that also reveals the hairline crack. The buyer calls the manager and tells him, "Snowmass still can't seem to lick its quality control problems. What do you want me to do?" The manager tells the buyer to repackage the skis and set them aside, as he plans to meet Snowmass's regional representative in Vail later in the month. The meeting is cancelled when the sales representative gets the influenza. Snowmass first learns of the problem a month later when a second invoice is returned marked: "Rejected. Goods defective." What, if any, further facts do you wish?

(h) Suppose in (g) that Aspen's manager calls Snowmass the same day that the defects are discovered and tells Snowmass that Aspen is rejecting the goods but will hold them for 30 days pending instructions. A week later (i) Aspen tells the captain of its sponsored ski team that the team may select 20 pairs for use in training, or (ii) in reply to an inquiry from another local shop that was short on inventory, Aspen lets the shop have the skis for 20 percent off contract price and notifies Snowmass: "Skis sold for your account. Remittance enclosed net 15 percent commission and selling expenses." See UCC 2-602, 2-606, 2-604.

PRIEST, BREACH AND REMEDY FOR THE TENDER OF NONCONFORMING GOODS UNDER THE UNIFORM COMMERCIAL CODE: AN ECONOMIC APPROACH
91 Harv. L. Rev. 960, 963-968 (1978)

Once the contract is found to have been breached by a nonconforming tender, the law provides the buyer two possible remedies. He may call off the sale and return the goods to the seller, or he may keep the goods and seek damages for the nonconformity. The costs imposed by these two remedies can be classified into two categories. First, there are allocative costs—the transfer of real resources from one or both of the parties to the outside world. Freight and insurance for reshipment, administrative costs of resale, and fees for attorneys involved in dispute resolution fall into this category. Second are distributive costs, which consist of transfers of resources between the parties, as when one party recovers damages from the other. Ordinarily, the minimization of allocative costs will benefit the parties regardless of the distribution of costs between them. However, the distribution of costs will affect allocative costs because each party will strive to minimize his personal share of the joint costs, even if his effort increases joint costs. In fact, in any dispute over the interpretation of a contract, the parties will expend resources in negotiation or litigation, thereby reducing the joint value of the transaction. In the text that follows, the conditions for minimizing the allocative costs of a remedy are first analyzed apart from the effects of the distribution of costs. Then the causes and effects of the distribution of costs between the parties are analyzed separately.

1. *Minimizing Allocative Costs of the Remedy.*—A judgment awarding damages differs from a judgment returning the goods to the seller in two ways. First, to award damages, the buyer's loss from the defect must be calculated. Second, if the buyer recovers damages, he keeps the defective goods and must either adapt them for his use or dispose of them, while if the buyer returns the

goods to the seller, the seller must dispose of them. Thus, the principal allocative costs of the damage remedy are the buyer's costs of adaptation, or his costs
of disposal and cover, and the administrative cost of determining the buyer's
loss. If the buyer adapts the goods, the costs are the expenditures the buyer
must make to bring the goods into conformity with the contract or the adjustments he must make to use the nonconforming goods. If he resells the defective
goods and covers by buying other goods—which will be the more efficient
course of action if his costs of adaptation are greater than those of other firms
in the market—the costs of breach are the difference between the resale and
cover prices, plus the administrative costs to the buyer of effectuating the
resale and procuring replacement goods. A damage remedy entails the calculation of these costs—a process which requires the expenditure of resources
whether performed by a court or by the parties themselves in settlement negotiations. In addition, the calculation introduces a risk of error to the buyer and
seller, respectively, of underestimating or overestimating the buyer's loss,
which increases the cost of the damage remedy.

When the buyer is allowed to refuse the defective tender, different costs
are incurred. They include the cost of returning the goods to the seller, the cost
to the seller of reselling the defective goods, and the buyer's costs of purchasing
substitute goods, i.e., the difference between the cover and contract prices plus
the administrative costs of effectuating the purchase. If the buyer and seller
negotiate toward the efficient remedy, they would likely agree to rescission
where the sum of the costs of returning the goods is less than the total cost of
the cheaper of the damage remedies.

Although the comparison of the costs of rescission and damages appears
complicated, it can be simplified. Parties wishing to maximize the joint value
of the transaction will prefer return of the goods to damages whenever the
goods have a greater value in the seller's hands than in the buyer's. The value
of the goods in the seller's hands is their market value less the seller's costs of
retrieval and resale. The value of the goods in the buyer's hands is the greater
of (1) their market value less the buyer's costs of resale, or (2) their value to the
buyer after adaptation less the costs of adapting them. If the parties seek to
conserve costs, they might first compare the value of the defective goods to the
buyer with the market value of the goods. Where the loss from the defect is less
to the buyer than to the market, returning the goods is generally not the
cheaper remedy. If, however, the value to the buyer of the defective goods is
less than the market value, the parties would agree to return the goods to the
seller if the seller's costs of resale were lower than the buyer's by an amount
greater than the retrieval costs. If the buyer's business involves the sale of
defective as well as conforming goods, the buyer's and the seller's costs of resale
may be equivalent, so that retrieval costs tip the balance in favor of a damage
remedy. However, if the buyer is a consumer or is engaged solely in manufacturing, the value of managerial time necessary to resell the defective goods
may be substantial. Then the advantages of the original seller—superior information about potential customers for defective goods and a superior distribu-

tion system—may offset the costs of retrieval and make rescission the preferable remedy.

In many cases, the cost of calculating damages may be decisive in determining which is the more efficient remedy, especially where there is no market in goods possessing the particular defect. Since in such cases the buyer's subjective valuation is difficult to ascertain, there is great danger both of the buyer's self-serving testimony and of a failure adequately to appreciate the particular tastes of the buyer. Where the latter factor is dominant, the remedy of returning the goods to the seller is the analogue of the equitable remedy of specific performance, which is awarded in sales of land or other "unique" forms of property because the legal remedy of damages is viewed as "inadequate." . . .

The analysis thus far has ignored the distribution of the joint costs of breach between the buyer and seller. Because the choice of remedy can affect that distribution, each party may, for selfish reasons, prefer the remedy which, under the analysis so far, is less efficient. Moreover, each party may incur further allocative costs in negotiating or litigating toward the remedy which provides him the greatest personal benefit. Thus, the effects of the distribution of costs may affect not only the choice of remedy, but also the joint cost of the remedy chosen. . . .

Where the price of the goods declines after formation of the contract, the buyer has an incentive to conjure up defects or to exaggerate the materiality of real defects, and to demand rescission rather than damages, regardless of which remedy minimizes allocative costs. A similar incentive exists when the buyer realizes that he has chosen an unsuitable product. As long as the legal rules governing breach and remedy are sufficiently manipulable to offer the buyer a significant opportunity for distributional benefits, he will expend resources in negotiation or litigation in an attempt to gain them. Indeed, a rational buyer will spend nearly as much as the amount of the market price decline, discounted by his probability of prevailing in court.

Two conclusions may be drawn from this analysis. First, courts may reduce the parties' expenditures in attempts to gain distributional benefits by making legal rules certain in application. As legal rules become more certain, the probability of each party's manipulating them to his advantage decreases, and hence he is willing to spend less in such an effort. Second, the parties' expenditures in attempts to achieve private benefits sometimes may be greater than the savings achieved by choosing the remedy which otherwise would minimize allocative costs.

NOTES & QUESTIONS

1. *Illustration of the Priest analysis.* Seller agrees to sell a machine to Buyer for $100. The machine Seller tenders, however, is defective and although the market price for machines with these defects is $90 the machine is worthless for

Buyer's purposes unless it is modified. By the expenditure of $13 Buyer can modify the machine so that it is conforming and worth $100 to Buyer. Alternatively, Buyer can resell the defective machine for $90 at a cost of $4 and can purchase a conforming machine for $100 with the expenditure of $1 in transaction costs. Seller, on the other hand, can retrieve the machine and resell it for $90 at a cost of $3. Under the Priest analysis, should Buyer be permitted to reject? Would your answer be different if the machine was conforming but the market price for conforming machines had dropped to $90?

2. *Certainty of law on rejection.* Is there any doubt that Buyer in Note 1 has the right to reject under UCC 2-601? After analyzing case reports from the period 1954-1976, Professor Priest concludes that courts have resolved disputes in a way to promote economic efficiency even if this has required distortion of the Code's text. He tests this hypothesis by examining whether the facts the court treats as determinative are similar to those that would be determinative in an economic judgment. When reading the cases that follow consider whether they are consistent with Professor Priest's analysis.

3. *Llewellyn's approach.* In an early draft of Article 2 Karl Llewellyn distinguished between exact performance and mercantile performance. A merchant buyer dealing with a merchant seller did not have a right to reject mercantile performance. The draft statute defined mercantile performance as follows:

> A performance is mercantile when there is no substantial defect, that is, when—
> (i) the delivered lot is of such character as not in a material manner to increase the risks or burdens which would rest on the buyer under exact performance; and (ii) it is of such character as reasonably to meet the operating or marketing requirements of the buyer in the course of his business, in general, and where the contract looks to a particular purpose, then also in regard to that particular purpose. [NCCUSL, Report and Second Draft: The Revised Uniform Sales Act §11-A(2) (b) (1941).]

This draft text also included the following statement of policy:

> The principle of mercantile performance is that a contract between merchants calls for a performance having the expected substance, but that discrepancies are not to interfere with the flow of goods in commerce unless they are in mercantile fact material discrepancies, and unless an appropriate money-allowance against the price can give no adequate compensation for failure of exact performance. [Id. at §11-A(2)(c).]

The draft required exact performance for documentary transactions and for cases when the contract explicitly so provided. Id. at §11-A(2)(e), (f). The draft also assumed that there would be a specialized merchant tribunal to determine questions of "mercantile performance." Id. at §59.

Llewellyn's analysis of the prior case law, which he suggested supported his proposal, appeared in the Comment to Section 11-A:

"The cases before the Sales Act of 1906 were groping with little success to meet the needs of three sharply divergent situations. There was first the private consumer, or the buyer of machinery, to whom even 'minor' defects in the goods might mean either disturbance of taste or uneconomic operation. The Sales Act introduced rescission for defects, even minor defects, thus skillfully providing for this difficulty.

"There was, second, the documentary overseas contract, in which such terms as 'March shipment' or shipment 'from Glasgow' were vital to the handling of the documents in insurance, resale, or the financing transactions. It is this situation which in both England and the United States gave rise to the rule: 'In mercantile contracts time is of the essence and is part of the description, and all terms must be strictly complied with.' . . .

"There was, however, a radically different third situation. That was the situation of ordinary deliveries between merchants. In these, both expectation and practice have long recognized that exact compliance is commonly not mercantilely practicable, and deliveries are made and accepted in terms of minor variation and adjustment occurring in ordinary course and as of course. The majority cases before the Sales Act of 1906 raised one difficulty here which that Act cured: Those cases forced the buyer to either take a defective delivery as *wholly* satisfactory, or else to reject it, wholly. The Act in Section 49 met one aspect of this difficulty: it gave the *buyer* the privilege of *taking* a delivery which was adequate for use, though not up to contract, and still *claiming* his due adjustment. But it did not give the *seller*, in a deal between merchants, the *corresponding* privilege of *making* a mercantilely adequate delivery, and *making* his adjustment. The result has been a series of cases which do plain mercantile injustice by permitting, on a falling market, or after buyer's change of mind, rejection of a delivery which in all mercantile decency could be expected as of course to fill the buyer's expectations. Where sellers hire lawyers, or where they have gained sad and costly experience, the clauses in frequent use make their understanding in this matter very clear: 'five percent more or less,' '90 percent delivery guaranteed,' 'not more than 2 percent fatty acid,' 'basis middling.' Practice does the like: shipments are somewhat delayed, with regret expressed, or the buyer requests delay, and the like.

"Meantime the law of Contract has developed an explicit law of 'substantial performance,' and—what is much more important—an under-cover law of performance of substance which ranges over the whole body of Contract law, taking different surface-shape in different places. There is not only the field of building contracts. There is the development in the insurance field of a process of judicial 'construction' and of standard terms to guaranty the assured some substance, and a technique of waiver of conditions which runs directly on principles of the substance being enough. The line of cases insisting on 'reasonable' grounds of 'dissatisfaction' is part of the same drive. So is the requirement of 'mutuality' in addition to formal consideration. So is the range of tacit or constructive warranty, or the 'reasonable' reading of output or requirements contracts, or the constant implication of unexpressed counter-promise (as in

Wood v. Duff-Gordon). All of these go to getting enough substance into a contract performance to render the contract fair and intelligible, rather than a trap. The other side of the same coin has allowed the expected substance to be enough, avoiding literal reading of language, and stretching the doctrine of waiver.

"In result, there is already in operation, in the cases, and over the whole field of Contract law, an ingrained body of rulings, and an ingrained attitude, avoiding breach by nonsubstantial defect.

"But left thus unexpressed, these lines of doctrine have led to the heaping of technicality upon technicality with a resultant welter of uncertainty. It is quite impossible to keep courts from having and following the urge for sense and justice, expressed in these decisions. The hope lies rather in digging out for statement and for clear guidance the line which is fair, *and in putting clear and workable limits* on its use. This may be expected to unify, clarify, and produce a true certainty. In Sales, commercial practice makes this feasible."

To what extent does Llewellyn's method of analysis differ from Priest's? To what extent do their conclusions differ? When reading the material in this chapter consider to what extent the official text of Article 2 reflects Llewellyn's approach.

PERFORMANCE MOTORS, INC. v. ALLEN
280 N.C. 385, 186 S.E.2d 161, 10 UCC Rep. 568 (1972)

[Performance Motors sold a mobile home to Allen and retained a security interest to secure the installment note in the sum of $10,097.64 given for the balance of the purchase price. When Allen defaulted Performance Motors repossessed and disposed of the mobile home. Performance Motors then brought an action to recover the deficiency. Allen, the defendant, presented the counterclaim described below.]

[B]y way of counterclaim, defendant alleges that, prior to the execution of the note and conditional sales agreement, plaintiff, through its agents, expressly warranted and represented that said mobile home was of sound construction, free from all defects of workmanship and material, and would remain in first-class condition for a period of many years after its purchase, and further represented that plaintiff "would properly install and set up said mobile home on the lot designated by the defendant and would properly wire the same and connect the same to proper commercial outlets and would connect the septic tank by pipe leading from said mobile home;" that all such warranties and representations by plaintiff were false when made, known by plaintiff to be false, made with intent to deceive defendant and to induce her to purchase the mobile home, and in fact did deceive defendant; that in reliance upon them she purchased the mobile home and executed the note and conditional sales agreement.

Defendant further alleged in her counterclaim that plaintiff delivered said mobile home to defendant on a designated lot in Maysville, North Carolina; that plaintiff did not properly wire and connect said mobile home to commercial outlets, did not furnish the pipe and connect the same to the septic tank as a result of which plaintiff spent $75 to have the house wired and connected and $78.60 in connecting said home to the septic tank. She further alleged that the said mobile home was not well made, not free from defects in workmanship and material, and was installed incorrectly on its foundation so that it was never level; that the ceilings sagged throughout the home, the carpeting had been cut, the front door was installed out of line and refused to close properly, sofa springs were broken, plastic counter tops were chipped, cabinet doors and shelves did not function correctly, walls throughout the home became warped, bowed and loose, toilet tanks and seats were broken, door facings throughout the trailer became loose, vinyl floors were cut, scarred and installed without a proper subfloor, all heating vents protruded from their proper location, and the heating unit did not operate properly.

Defendant further alleged that, relying on plaintiff's express and implied warranties, she made a down payment of $4,000 on the mobile home and three monthly payments of $120.21 each which, when added to her expenditures for wiring and septic tank connection, total $4,514.23; that by reason of the enumerated defects the mobile home was completely unfit and unserviceable for use as a home; that defendant repeatedly notified plaintiff of the defects and was reassured that said defects would be repaired but such repairs were never made; that defendant elected before the commencement of this action, and now elects, to rescind said contract on account of plaintiff's breach of warranties, both express and implied; that defendant is entitled to recover of plaintiff $4,360.63 paid on the purchase price plus $153.60 for the wiring and septic tank connection, a total of $4,514.23, with interest from 21 December 1968. . . .

Defendant's testimony tends to show the defective conditions alleged in her counterclaim. After cataloging the defects set out in her counterclaim, she testified that the mobile home had never been leveled; that you could see the ground through the floor; that "when they were putting it up, I told those men, 'Now this is not right and I do not want it;' " that after the mobile home was installed in such fashion, she complained to the plaintiff's president continually "from September to the last of December when he hung up on me and said Happy New Year;" that she ceased making monthly payments by reason of plaintiff's failure to make the necessary repairs to place the trailer in a usable condition; that she lived in the mobile home from September to May when plaintiff repossessed it by claim and delivery. . . .

HUSKINS, Justice . . . . What remedies are available to defendant for breach of implied warranty of fitness? The answer to this question turns on whether defendant *accepted* the mobile home. This requires consideration of the Uniform Commercial Code's concept of rejection, acceptance, and revocation of acceptance.

Acceptance is ordinarily signified by language or conduct of the buyer that he will take the goods, but this does not necessarily indicate that the goods conform to the contract. UCC 2-606(1)(a). Acceptance may also occur by failure of the buyer "to make an effective rejection" after a reasonable opportunity to inspect. UCC 2-606(1)(b). Effective rejection means (1) rejection within a reasonable time after delivery or tender and (2) seasonable notice to the seller. UCC 2-602. Acceptance precludes rejection of the goods accepted and, if made with knowledge of a nonconformity, cannot be revoked because of it unless the acceptance was on the reasonable assumption that the nonconformity would be seasonably cured. UCC 2-607(2). Thus, the buyer may *revoke his acceptance* if (1) "the acceptance was on the reasonable assumption that the non-conformity would be seasonably cured," UCC 2-607(2), and (2) the non-conformity substantially impairs the value of the goods. UCC 2-608(1). Revocation of acceptance must be made within a reasonable time after the buyer discovers, or should have discovered, the ground for it . . . and it is not effective until the buyer notifies the seller of it. UCC 2-608(2). A buyer who so revokes his acceptance is no longer required to elect between revocation of acceptance on the one hand and recovery of damages for breach of implied warranty of fitness on the other. Both remedies are now available to him. UCC 2-608.

The Uniform Commercial Code does not speak of rescission, as such. We need not now decide whether a buyer may still obtain a judicial rescission of the contract by virtue of pre-Code concepts of law or equity which have not been displaced and therefore continue under the Code as an "invalidating cause" supplementing the provisions of the Code within the meaning of UCC 1-103. Assuming without deciding that rescission remains available to the buyer as a remedy by virtue of UCC 1-103, defendant's allegation of "rescission" will be given effect here as an allegation of "revocation of acceptance" since that Code concept more nearly reflects the claims asserted by the defendant. 2 R. Anderson, Uniform Commercial Code §2-711:19, at 420 (2d ed. 1971). . . .

Applying the foregoing principles to the evidence in this case, if defendant (1) made an effective rejection of the mobile home, or (2) justifiably revoked her acceptance of it, she has a right to recover "so much of the price as has been paid" plus any incidental and consequential damages she is able to prove. UCC 2-711(1), 2-715. On the other hand, if defendant did not reject but accepted the mobile home, and there has been no revocation of acceptance, she is obligated to pay the balance due on the contract price, and she is limited on her counterclaim to recovery of damages for breach of implied warranty of fitness. The measure of damages in that event is "the difference at the time and place of acceptance between the value of the goods accepted and the value they would have had if they had been as warranted, unless special circumstances show proximate damages of a different amount," UCC 2-714(2), plus incidental damages and such consequential damages as were within the contemplation of the parties. UCC 2-715. . . .

Here, defendant's evidence is insufficient to support a finding that she *rejected* the mobile home. She testified that when the mobile home was installed she told the plaintiff's agent "now this is not right and I do not want it." While this statement could have been effective as a rightful rejection, UCC 2-601(a), she did not pursue that remedy. Instead, her evidence tends to show she moved into the mobile home, all the while complaining of numerous defects—some of which plaintiff attempted but failed to correct—and made three monthly payments under the terms of the contract. She complained of the defects "continually from September to the last of December [1968] when he [plaintiff] hung up on me and said Happy New Year." Thereafter defendant made no further payments, and plaintiff made no further attempt to correct the defects or to collect the monthly payments until May 1969 when the mobile home was repossessed and sold at public auction for $9115. This evidence, considered in the light most favorable to defendant, would permit a jury to find that she initially accepted the mobile home on the reasonable assumption that plaintiff would correct the nonconforming defects and subsequently revoked her acceptance by reason of plaintiff's failure to do so. Constant complaints from September to December with cessation of payment would seem to constitute sufficient notice of revocation of acceptance. "Any conduct clearly manifesting a desire of the buyer to get his money back is a sufficient notice to revoke." 2 R. Anderson, Uniform Commercial Code §2-608:16, at 245 (2d ed. 1971). Furthermore, "[a] tender of the goods by the buyer to the seller is not an essential element of a revocation of acceptance. All that is required by the Code is a notification of revocation." Id. §2-608:18, at 246. . . .

The decision of the Court of Appeals awarding a new trial is modified to conform to this opinion and, as modified, affirmed.

NOTES & QUESTIONS

1. *Rejection versus revocation of acceptance.* Is there any reason to have two concepts, rejection and revocation of acceptance, rather than just one? How do the two concepts differ? Would the results be different in *Performance Motors* if the court found that Mrs. Allen had effectively *rejected*?

2. *Communication between the parties.* If you reread UCC 2-601—2-608 you will see numerous references to notice and communication between the parties. The Code places a premium on having each party inform the other when there has been an alleged breakdown in contract performance. Nowhere is this Code emphasis more apparent than the procedure outlined in UCC 2-609 (Right to Adequate Assurance of Performance).

Given this emphasis on communication should a court read in a notice requirement even when the Code is silent? UCC 2-705, for example, permits a seller to stop delivery of goods in transit under some circumstances but does not require the seller to notify the buyer. Should he be required to do so? See Indussa Corp. v. Reliable Stainless Steel Supply Co., 369 F. Supp. 976, 14

UCC Rep. 709 (E.D. Pa. 1974), which held that the seller in that case had a duty to notify the buyer when it stopped shipment of final installments because buyer had not paid for earlier installments. The court stated, "It appears to us that reasonable commercial standards of fair dealing would, in the circumstances of this case, require plaintiff to notify defendant of its decision to stop delivery. We are particularly influenced by consideration of (1) the ease, simplicity, and minimal expense of giving such notification, (2) the potential benefit to defendant of receiving notification, and the potential harm of not receiving notification, and (3) the absence of any reasons for the plaintiff not to give notification." 369 F. Supp. at 980; 14 UCC Rep. at 715.

As with all references to notices, you should consider to whom notice must be given, the form (written or oral) it must take, its content, the time within which it must be given, the time when it becomes effective, and the consequences of failing to give it. The *Performance Motors* court concludes that Mrs. Allen gave adequate notice of her revocation of acceptance. See UCC 2-607(3), 2-608(2). Do these provisions answer all the points set out at the beginning of the paragraph?

3. *Buyer's use of rejected goods.* Mrs. Allen lived in the mobile home from September until May. The court apparently thought this fact was important when it concluded that Mrs. Allen accepted the mobile home, although the decision does not specify on which provision of UCC 2-606(1) it was relying. The court may have thought living in the home was inconsistent with the seller's ownership and therefore an acceptance under UCC 2-606(1)(c). But isn't continued occupancy also inconsistent with the purported revocation of acceptance?

If Mrs. Allen may revoke her acceptance notwithstanding her continued use of the mobile home should Performance Motors be allowed to recover anything for the "value" she received? How should this value be measured? By the amount of depreciation between September and May? By the amount of the monthly installment payments she had been paying? By the rent she would have paid for similar housing? What would be the legal basis for Performance Motors' recovery or setoff of this value?

Continued use of the mobile home after rejection or revocation of acceptance may be "wrongful" as against Performance Motors, the seller. UCC 2-602(2)(a), 2-608(3); see also 2-606(1)(c). Presumably the seller's recovery will be measured by tort standards. What are these standards?

Following rejection or revocation Mrs. Allen has by virtue of UCC 2-711(3) a security interest in the mobile home for any payments made and any expenses reasonably incurred. That subsection states that the buyer may hold the mobile home and even resell it in like manner as an aggrieved seller under UCC 2-706. Does having a security interest also justify Mrs. Allen's use of the mobile home? See UCC 9-113, 9-207.

4. *Rescission.* As the court in *Performance Motors* notes, the Code avoids the use of "rescission." UCC 2-720 and 2-721 provide rules to protect parties from unintended losses of rights. The latter section specifically extends Article 2

remedies to parties who rescind their sales contracts for material misrepresentation or fraud. See also UCC 2-209(2). Do these statements support the court's suggestion that rescission remains available by virtue of UCC 1-103? Would there be advantages to bringing an action for fraud?

5. *Discerning "type-transactions."* Examine Llewellyn's statements appearing at p. 559 supra, and at pp. 570 & 656 infra. Does *Performance Motors* involve a "type-transaction"? If so, is the type sale to end users or consumers? Or is it a sale of a consumer product? Sale of a mobile home? Do the policies surrounding the resolution of such issues as inspection, the effect of continued use of the goods, or notification of revocation differ between sales of bulk commodities and sales of machinery to end users or consumers? Between the sale of a mobile home and sale of an automobile or TV set? Do you believe that Llewellyn's "type-transaction" is a workable concept?

B.   INSPECTION

A buyer may examine goods at different points in time. He may examine them, for example, (a) before entering into a contract for their purchase, (b) when the seller tenders the goods but before acceptance, or (c) after acceptance. As we shall see in Chapter 14, an examination of the goods before entering into a contract may both create an express warranty as to their quality and also be a disclaimer of implied warranties as to defects that the buyer sees or should have discovered. UCC 2-313(1), 2-316(3)(b). In other words, this examination helps to determine what obligations the seller must perform to satisfy the contract of sale.

A buyer, however, may also examine the goods when the seller tenders them in performance of his contractual obligations. The Code calls this examination an *inspection*. The Code expressly gives the buyer the right to inspect the tendered goods before payment or acceptance unless otherwise agreed and provides some guidelines for inspection. UCC 2-513(1); 2-606(1). The inspection must be at a reasonable time and place and be carried out in a reasonable manner, and the buyer must bear the inspection expenses unless he rejects the goods for nonconformity. The parties' contract of course may provide details or reallocate the burden of inspection expenses. See UCC 2-513.

After acceptance the buyer owns the goods and may examine or use them as he wishes. Although the buyer may no longer reject the goods he has some incentive to discover defects because he may lose his right to seek other remedies. He must notify the seller, for example, of any breach he finds or should have found within a reasonable time or he will be barred from any remedy. UCC 2-607(3)(a). The buyer may also lose his right to obtain a remedy by the statute of limitations, which begins to run from the time of breach, whether or not the buyer knows of the breach. UCC 2-725.

Problem 11-2. Dealer, a Nebraska grain merchant, agrees to sell four barge loads of No. 1 yellow corn to Miller, a Mississippi milling business. The contract includes the following delivery term: "F.O.B. Nebraska City." Dealer loads the corn in Nebraska City on June 19, and the barges arrive in Mississippi on July 7. Miller inspects the corn on July 10 and discovers that three barges contain No. 2 yellow corn.

(a) When and where does Dealer tender delivery of the corn? See UCC 2-319, 2-503, 2-504.

(b) When must the corn conform to the quality contracted for? See UCC 2-601.

(c) Must Miller pay for the corn upon tender and before inspecting it? See UCC 2-507, 2-513.

(d) Did Miller have the right to inspect the corn before shipment from Nebraska City? See UCC 2-513.

(e) May Miller wait to inspect the corn until after it arrives in Mississippi? If so, how long after arrival does Miller have to inspect? See UCC 2-513, 2-602, 2-606.

(f) Who has the burden of showing that the corn conforms at the time of tender? See UCC 2-601, 2-607. If tender takes place in Nebraska City will inspection in Mississippi supply proof that the goods were nonconforming on tender?

(g) Does Dealer have the right to inspect the corn to verify Miller's claim of nonconformity? See UCC 2-515.

(h) If you were advising Miller before he entered into the contract what advice would you give with respect to inspection?

SOO LINE R.R. v. FRUEHAUF CORP.
547 F.2d 1365, 20 UCC Rep. 1181 (8th Cir. 1977)

[Magor agreed to manufacture 500 hopper cars for Soo Line. After complaining about the numerous repairs necessary to these cars Soo Line sued Magor to recover damages from alleged breaches of warranty and negligence in the manufacture of the cars. The court's discussion of the effect of the inspection clause in the parties' contract is set out below. See p. 647 infra for other parts of the court's opinion.]

STEPHENSON, Circuit Judge. . . . At this point we must necessarily confront appellant's additional contention that the inspection clause in the contract prohibits recovery of damages. The inspection provision contained within the terms and conditions of sales states:

> All construction is subject to inspection by you or your authorized agent who may have access to any part of our plant where any of this work is in progress. Cars to be satisfactory in every respect before acceptance and final inspection and acceptance to be at our plant. Should you waive inspection, then

inspection for the Purchaser will be performed by our regular inspection forces and said inspection will constitute acceptance of the cars at our works by your Company.

Notwithstanding any other acceptance point herein called out, specified or agreed upon, the buyer agrees that final inspection will be accomplished at our plant and evidenced by a Certificate or Certificates of Inspection to be signed and delivered by your representative inspector to our Company at the time of final inspection, which Certificate will not conflict or abrogate any other terms pertaining to warranty involved herein.

Magor claims that the inspection clause should bar recovery of damages because Soo Line allegedly failed to undertake inspection of the railroad cars during the manufacturing process. We disagree. . . .

[Soo Line's assistant superintendent of its car department inspected approximately 80 completed cars and found "a significant number of defects," including defects in welding. Magor's general sales manager orally stated that the cars would be corrected and reinspected. Some defects ultimately uncovered, however, were latent and not discovered by Soo Line's superintendent. It is not apparent from the court record that Soo Line inspected the actual manufacturing process.]

Review of the language in the inspection clause indicates that a waiver of inspection by the purchaser entitled Magor to perform its own inspection and such inspection would have constituted acceptance of the railcars. In any event, the provision neither expressly provides nor even implies that a failure to exercise the right of inspection constitutes a waiver of any other contractual remedy. See generally United States v. Franklin Steel Products, Inc., 482 F.2d 400, 403-404 (9th Cir. 1973), *cert. denied,* 415 U.S. 918 (1974). When the right to inspect arises *after* the creation of the contract, as in the instant case, acceptance of goods, even with knowledge that they do not conform to the contract, may preclude rejection but it does not impair any other remedy. UCC 2-607(2). Cf. UCC 2-316(3)(b) (effect of inspection or refusal of inspection *before* entering into contract).[11] The buyer's right to recover damages for goods that have been accepted but do not conform to the contract is expressly reserved. UCC 2-714(1).

In this case the jury found that Soo Line notified Magor of the faults or defects when they were first discovered and afforded Magor the opportunity to verify and repair or replace the faults or defects at Magor's plant or another place mutually agreeable. The record amply supports the jury's finding in this respect. Accordingly, it is clear that the inspection clause in the contract does not bar liability in the instant case.

---

11. UCC 2-316, Comment 8, states that if a buyer discovers a defect or unreasonably fails to inspect goods prior to use, resulting injuries may be found to result from the buyer's action rather than proximately from breach of warranty. Nevertheless, the evidence supports the jury verdict indicating damages were directly caused by Magor's breach of warranty.

Problem 11-3. Seller agrees to manufacture an electric generator according to the specifications supplied by Buyer. The parties include in their written contract the following clause: "No later than 5 days after delivery and installation Buyer shall inspect the generator to determine if it conforms with the contract specifications. If Buyer discovers defects present in the generator at the time of delivery Buyer agrees to notify Seller in writing of the defects within five days of discovery. Seller may, at its option, repair or replace the generator or any defective part. Buyer agrees that it will not reject the generator because of any defect." Seller delivers and installs the generator. Buyer promptly inspects the generator but fails to discover a defect that causes the generator to burn out two weeks after installation. May Buyer reject or revoke acceptance of the generator? May Buyer recover damages? See UCC 2-606, 2-607, 2-608, 2-714, 2-719.

Problem 11-4. Re-examine the facts alleged in Mrs. Allen's counterclaim in Performance Motors v. Allen, p. 561 supra. Assume that the conditional sales agreement that Mrs. Allen signed contains the following clause: "Buyer admits, upon examination, that the goods are as represented by Seller and acknowledges acceptance and delivery of the goods in good condition and repair." This agreement is signed by Mrs. Allen at the dealer's lot. Following that, the mobile home is brought to Mrs. Allen's lot, and her difficulties with the seller commence. Has Mrs. Allen effectively waived a right to inspect following installation? May she justify revocation of acceptance not only on defects resulting from or occurring in the installation process, but also on defects evident on inspection of the goods at the dealer's lot? See UCC 2-601, 2-608, 2-605, 2-607, 2-513. Can seller exclude Mrs. Allen's evidence pertaining to defects on the basis of the Code's parol evidence rule? See UCC 2-202. Cf. UCC 2-316(3)(b).

Problem 11-5. Alpine Graphics (AG) purchases some specialized printing equipment from Graphic Werke (GW), a German firm. The equipment is sold "C.I.F. Denver." The contract expressly provides for September shipment so that the press can be in use for the Christmas season. When the press arrives in mid-October AG's shop foreman tells two of his employees to inspect the crate, and if it looks okay, to unpack the equipment, inspect it, and set it up for use. Later that afternoon, the employees tell the manager that they have uncrated and set up the equipment. The next day, the foreman tells his employees to run off several different "formats" to experiment with the press' versatility. In the course of these tests it becomes apparent that the press "shades" graphics unevenly. This might be due to a misalignment, which can be adjusted in a day's time, or it might be a design characteristic. At this time it is also noted that GW has not attached an accessory auto-paper feed as ordered. May AG reject and recover the price, which was paid against documents? See UCC 2-320, 2-513, 2-512, 2-601, 2-508, 2-608.

C.   CURE

The seller's right to cure, set out in UCC 2-508, has been called a "novel legal doctrine." J. White & R. Summers, Handbook of the Law Under the Uniform Commercial Code 318 (2d ed. 1980). The Uniform Sales Act did not include a provision on the right to cure, but Karl Llewellyn attempted to draw out of the case law a consistent pattern of decisions on cure of defective tender. Compare the following early draft text and commentary prepared by Llewellyn with the official text of UCC 2-508.

NCCUSL, REPORT AND SECOND DRAFT: THE REVISED UNIFORM SALES ACT (1941)

Section 42-A. (New.) *Cure of Defective Tender.* A defective tender or offer of delivery or of payment may be cured by a subsequent and proper tender or offer, provided that—

(1) the latter occurs within the time proper for performance; and

(2) the party making the defective tender gives notice that the tender or offer will be cured, or the other party has incurred no material change of position because the tender or offer made was defective; and

(3) the obligee has not reasonably resorted to cover, under Section 58; and

(4) the obligee has not within a reasonable time before the defective tender given notice to the party making the same that the conditions of the contract will be strictly insisted on.

The burden is on the party seeking to cure a tender to bring himself within this section.

Comment *on Section 42-A.* The case-law on cure of defective tender is in utter confusion, with relatively little discussion of reasons, and relatively little note taken by one decision of another.

The situations involved are of two quite diverse types.

A. The first involves a contract which has become most unwelcome to the obligee (commonly because of a severe change in the market), and involves an obligee who sits back waiting and hoping for an error in tender. In such a case errors should be curable, if they can be cured in time; it is both uncommercial and unjust to "freeze a breach" unnecessarily. Subsection 4 makes it possible for the obligee, if he wishes, to force full clarification of the situation on the first tender, by giving notice in advance that he will insist on his rights, in strictness.

The only real question is whether a time for cure, extending a reasonable time beyond the normal due-day, should be allowed when there is a sudden and unexpected insistence on technicality. Such sudden insistence can cause severe hardship. Yet it is believed that the answer to the question is: No. For (1) in overseas documentary cases, it would be clearly improper to extend the time; (2) sudden insistence on technicality no longer has the dangers, under the Draft, which have attended it under many of the cases. The mercantile performance provisions (Section 11-A) [see p. 559 supra] safeguard the seller; whereas the substitution of mercantile adequacy of tender (Section 42) [predecessor of UCC 2-507, 2-511] for the older highly technical and confused law of tender "of money" safeguards the buyer. (3) The circumstances normally giving rise to the case, to wit, a severely shifted market, make it highly desirable to clarify the situation promptly, and in the great bulk of instances they also serve to give the party tendering reasonable notice that he must be careful to stay within the time-limit.

B. The second situation involves a delinquent or hardly pressed or shifty obligor dealing with an obligee who wants not an out, but performance. Especially in regard to delivery of goods, the possible need for cover looms large. The situation is not greatly dissimilar from that under an installment contract (Section 45) [predecessor of UCC 2-612], when there is a defective delivery which upsets a buyer's safety in relying, and in thus exposing himself to business hardship if the promised future performance turns out to be inadequate. It is not proper that any rule intended to allow fair correction of a reasonable error should be so drawn as to embarrass a contract-keeper who needs assurance that his goods will be forthcoming.

The provisions of the section are believed to fit with the best mercantile practice, to clear up a confusion of the case-law, and to implement the better considered decisions.

Three cases will suffice to show the bearing of the Section. Suppose a contract for fruit, arrival draft against documents, with inspection permitted before payment (or with the question in doubt as to whether inspection is by the contract so permitted). If the collecting bank demands payment without inspection, and that is refused, a prompt retender allowing inspection on the seller's telegraphic instructions has reason to be held good. Again, if in a documentary contract the documents show minor discrepancies which are curable, but only at needless expense, an early tender to elicit whether such cure will be insisted on, has no business, of itself, to freeze a breach. On the other hand, in the case first put, if the fruit is highly perishable, or the market so fluctuating that a day's delay is of serious moment, "arrival" means arrival, and the corrected retender comes too late.

NOTES & QUESTIONS

1. *Cure and efficiency.* Consider how Professor Priest might incorporate the right to cure into his analysis excerpted at p. 556 supra. Do the following cases support the proposition that courts will construe a provision like UCC 2-508 consistently with economic efficiency?

2. *Obligation to cure.* Under both draft Section 42-A and UCC 2-508 the seller has the right to cure. Should the seller ever be under an obligation to

cure? Should the buyer ever be able to require the seller to cure absent a contract provision to that effect?

WILSON v. SCAMPOLI
228 A.2d 848, 4 UCC Rep. 178 (D.C. App. 1967)

MYERS, Associate Judge. This is an appeal from an order of the trial court granting rescission of a sales contract for a color television set and directing the return of the purchase price plus interest and costs.

Appellee purchased the set in question on November 4, 1965, paying the total purchase price in cash. The transaction was evidenced by a sales ticket showing the price paid and guaranteeing ninety days' free service and replacement of any defective tube and parts for a period of one year. Two days after purchase the set was delivered and uncrated, the antennae adjusted and the set plugged into an electrical outlet to "cook out."[1] When the set was turned on, however, it did not function properly, the picture having a reddish tinge. Appellant's delivery man advised the buyer's daughter, Mrs. Kolley, that it was not his duty to tune in or adjust the color but that a service representative would shortly call at her house for that purpose. After the departure of the delivery men, Mrs. Kolley unplugged the set and did not use it.

On November 8, 1965, a service representative arrived, and after spending an hour in an effort to eliminate the red cast from the picture advised Mrs. Kolley that he would have to remove the chassis from the cabinet and take it to the shop as he could not determine the cause of the difficulty from his examination at the house. He also made a written memorandum of his service call, noting that the television "Needs Shop Work (Red Screen)." Mrs. Kolley refused to allow the chassis to be removed, asserting she did not want a "repaired" set but another "brand new" set. Later she demanded the return of the purchase price, although retaining the set. Appellant refused to refund the purchase price, but renewed his offer to adjust, repair, or, if the set could not be made to function properly, to replace it. Ultimately, appellee instituted this suit against appellant seeking a refund of the purchase price. After a trial, the court ruled that "under the facts and circumstances the complaint is justified. Under the equity powers of the Court I will order the parties put back in their original status, let the $675 be returned, and the set returned to the defendant."

Appellant does not contest the jurisdiction of the trial court to order rescission in a proper case, but contends the trial judge erred in holding that rescission here was appropriate. He argues that he was always willing to comply with the terms of the sale either by correcting the malfunction by minor repair or, in the event the set could not be made thereby properly operative,

---

1. Such a "cook out," usually over several days, allows the set to magnetize itself and to heat up the circuit in order to indicate faulty wiring.

by replacement; that as he was denied the opportunity to try to correct the difficulty, he did not breach the contract of sale or any warranty thereunder, expressed or implied.[3]

UCC 2-508 provides:

> (1) Where any tender or delivery by the seller is rejected because non-conforming and the time for performance has not yet expired, the seller may seasonably notify the buyer of his intention to cure and may then within the contract time make a conforming delivery.
> (2) Where the buyer rejects a non-conforming tender which the seller had reasonable grounds to believe would be acceptable with or without money allowance the seller may if he seasonably notifies the buyer have a further reasonable time to substitute a conforming tender.

A retail dealer would certainly expect and have reasonable grounds to believe that merchandise like color television sets, new and delivered as crated at the factory, would be acceptable as delivered and that, if defective in some way, he would have the right to substitute a conforming tender. The question then resolves itself to whether the dealer may conform his tender by adjustment or minor repair or whether he must conform by substituting brand new merchandise. The problem seems to be one of first impression in other jurisdictions adopting the Uniform Commercial Code as well as in the District of Columbia.

Although the Official Code Comments do not reach this precise issue, there are cases and comments under other provisions of the Code which indicate that under certain circumstances repairs and adjustments are contemplated as remedies under implied warranties. In L & N Sales Co. v. Little Brown Jug, Inc., 12 Pa. D. & C. 2d 469 (Phila. County Ct. 1957), where the language of a disclaimer was found insufficient to defeat warranties under UCC 2-314 and 2-315, the court noted that the buyer had notified the seller of defects in the merchandise, and as the seller was unable to remedy them and later refused to accept return of the articles, it was held to be a breach of warranty. In Hall v. Everett Motors, Inc., 340 Mass. 430, 165 N.E.2d 107 (1960), decided shortly before the effective date of the Code in Massachusetts, the court reluctantly found that a disclaimer of warranties was sufficient to insulate the seller. Several references were made in the ruling to the seller's unsuccessful attempts at repairs, the court indicating the result would have been different under the Code.

---

3. Appellee maintains that the delivery of a color television set with a malfunctioning color control is a breach of both an implied warranty of merchantability (UCC 2-314) and of an implied warranty of fitness for a particular purpose (UCC 2-315) and as such is a basis for the right to rescission of the sale. We find it unnecessary to determine whether a set sold under the circumstances of this case gives rise to an implied warranty of fitness for a particular purpose or whether, as appellant contends, the remedial provisions of the express warranties bind the buyer to accept these same remedial provisions as sole remedies under an implied warranty.

While these cases provide no mandate to require the buyer to accept patchwork goods or substantially repaired articles in lieu of flawless merchandise, they do indicate that minor repairs or reasonable adjustments are frequently the means by which an imperfect tender may be cured. In discussing the analogous question of defective title, it has been stated that: "The seller then, should be able to cure [the defect] under subsection 2-508(2) in those cases in which he can do so without subjecting the buyer to any great inconvenience, risk or loss." Hawkland, Curing An Improper Tender of Title to Chattels: Past, Present and Commercial Code, 46 Minn. L. Rev. 697, 724 (1962). . . .

Removal of a television chassis for a short period of time in order to determine the cause of color malfunction and ascertain the extent of adjustment or correction needed to effect full operational efficiency presents no great inconvenience to the buyer. In the instant case, appellant's expert witness testified that this was not infrequently necessary with new televisions. Should the set be defective in workmanship or parts, the loss would be upon the manufacturer who warranted it free from mechanical defect. Here the adamant refusal of Mrs. Kolley, acting on behalf of appellee, to allow inspection essential to the determination of the cause of the excessive red tinge to the picture defeated any effort by the seller to provide timely repair or even replacement of the set if the difficulty could not be corrected. The cause of the defect might have been minor and easily adjusted or it may have been substantial and required replacement by another new set—but the seller was never given an adequate opportunity to make a determination.

We do not hold that appellant has no liability to appellee,[4] but as he was denied access and a reasonable opportunity to repair, appellee has not shown a breach of warranty entitling him either to a brand new set or to rescission. We therefore reverse the judgment of the trial court granting rescission and directing the return of the purchase price of the set.

Reversed.

NOTES & QUESTIONS

1. *Reasonable belief.* The *Wilson* court states: "A retail dealer would certainly expect and have reasonable grounds to believe that merchandise like color television sets, new and delivered or crated at the factory, would be acceptable as delivered and that, if defective in some way, he would have the right to substitute a conforming tender." Is UCC 2-508(2) meant to provide a right to cure, no matter how nonconforming the goods, so long as the seller

---

4. Appellant on appeal has renewed his willingness to remedy any defect in the tender, and thus there is no problem of expiration of his warranties. He should be afforded the right to inspect and correct any malfunction. If appellee refuses to allow appellant an opportunity to do so, then no cause of action can lie for breach of warranty, express or implied, and the loss must be borne by appellee.

reasonably believes that he is making a good tender? Note that there are two elements to this question, the seriousness of the nonconformity and the reasonable belief of the seller. Does subsection (2) address both elements? Can you provide alternative constructions of UCC 2-508(2)?

2. *Form of cure.* Subsections (1) and (2) of UCC 2-508 use different language to describe the form cure may take: "make a conforming delivery" and "substitute a conforming tender." Is the difference significant? Should one allow repair or replacement before the contract time for tender but only replacement after that time? What about money allowance? Note what is at stake. From the perspective of a buyer like Mrs. Kolley's father in *Wilson*, he is asked to take either (a) a repaired TV instead of a new TV, or (b) a new substitute TV of a type in which he may have lost confidence because of the defect in the TV first tendered. Would he be indifferent as between the different forms of cure? For a general assessment of the options available, see Schwartz, Cure and Revocation for Quality Defects: The Utility of Bargains, 16 B.C. Indus. & Com. L. Rev. 543 (1975).

3. *Contractual limitation of remedy.* Goods such as TV sets are customarily sold with a warranty for a limited period (e.g., 90 days), together with a limitation of the buyer's remedies under which the seller's only duty is to "repair or replace." Does this warranty bar a buyer from rejecting or revoking acceptance? Suppose the seller cannot repair? See UCC 2-719. These issues will be discussed in Chapter 14.

GAPPELBERG v. LANDRUM
666 S.W.2d 88, 37 UCC Rep. 1563 (Tex. 1984)

KILGARLIN, J. This case presents an issue previously undecided in Texas, or for that matter, any other American jurisdiction. Under the Uniform Commercial Code, does the seller have the right to cure a substantial defect by making a replacement of the product after the buyer has revoked acceptance?

On September 5, 1980, Petitioner, Nathan Gappelberg, purchased a large screen Advent television set from Respondent, Neely Landrum, doing business as The Video Station. Gappelberg gave as consideration for the new set $2,231.25 cash and was allowed a $1,500 credit on the trade-in of his old set. Gappelberg immediately experienced numerous and different problems with the new set. Landrum and Alpha Omega, the authorized repair agency, made several house calls in an effort to repair the set. On September 26, 1980, the set totally ceased operating. Gappelberg allowed the television set to be removed from his home, but refused offers to make further repairs on the set, saying he simply wanted his money and old set returned to him. Landrum felt he was in no position to return the old set, as he had promised it as a prize for a promotional sweepstakes, and offered Gappelberg another Advent as replacement. Gappelberg refused to accept the substitute, and brought suit against Landrum. . . .

The trial court found as follows:

1. Gappelberg accepted the television set without knowledge of the defects, which were discovered later;

2. Gappelberg revoked acceptance within a reasonable time after the defects were discovered and before any change in the condition of the set occurred not caused by such defects;

3. Gappelberg timely notified Landrum of his revocation; and

4. The television set's faulty convergence, thereby causing color shadowing around the screen's images; the constant projection of a red dot on one corner of the screen when the television set was in operation; and, the complete power failure of the set were each defects which substantially impaired the set.

The trial court nevertheless concluded that revocation of acceptance under UCC 2-608, was subject to a seller's right to cure under UCC 2-508.

Accordingly, the trial court rendered judgment for Landrum. The court of appeals, while affirming the judgment of the trial court, concluded that a seller did not have the right to cure by repair once there had been a revocation of acceptance, but the right to cure by replacement was not precluded. . . .

[The court quotes UCC 2-608:]

§2-608.   *Revocation of Acceptance in Whole or in Part*

(1) The buyer may revoke his acceptance of a lot or commercial unit whose non-conformity substantially impairs its value to him if he has accepted it
   (a)   on the reasonable assumption that its non-conformity would be cured and it has not been seasonably cured; or
   (b)   without discovery of such non-conformity if his acceptance was reasonably induced either by the difficulty of discovery before acceptance or by the seller's assurances.

(2) Revocation of acceptance must occur within a reasonable time after the buyer discovers or should have discovered the ground for it and before any substantial change in condition of the goods which is not caused by their own defects. It is not effective until the buyer notifies the seller of it.

(3) A buyer who so revokes has the same rights and duties with regard to the goods involved as if he had rejected them.

It will be noted that paragraph (1)(b) is applicable to this case. The only reference to cure in UCC 2-608 is in situations when the buyer knew of the defects at the time of acceptance of the goods. There is no reference to cure for our situation where Gappelberg accepted the television set without knowing of the defects. The court of appeals, in its opinion, has listed the numerous cases from other jurisdictions which hold that once a buyer properly revokes acceptance, the seller no longer has the right to cure by repair. This is likewise the conclusion of White and Summers, Handbook of the Law Under the Uniform Commercial Code 293 (2d ed. 1980), who state that revocation of acceptance is not limited by the right to cure. We do not consider paragraph (3) in UCC

2-608 as having any reference to UCC 2-508. It is more logically related to UCC 2-603 and 2-604, as UCC 2-608(3) makes absolutely no mention of seller's rights. . . .

The court of appeals in this case notes that in none of the cases in which a seller's right to cure has been denied once revocation of acceptance occurs was the buyer presented with such a generous offer as Landrum's offer to replace. The court of appeals concluded that "in the spirit of the Code," cure by replacement even in revocation situations should be authorized.

Although a rejection case, in Zabriskie Chevrolet, Inc. v. Smith, 99 N.J. Super. 441, 240 A.2d 195 (1968), the court observed that "for a majority of people, the purchase of a new car is a major investment, rationalized by the peace of mind that flows from its dependability and safety. Once their faith is shaken, the vehicle loses not only its real value in their eyes, but becomes an instrument whose integrity is substantially impaired and whose operation was fraught with apprehension." In *Zabriskie,* a new 1966 Chevrolet ceased to operate within one mile of being removed from the showroom, because of a faulty transmission. The buyer was not forced to take the Chevrolet with a different transmission in it, his faith in the whole automobile having been shaken. By the same token, Gappelberg had seen one Advent television perform, or fail to perform as the case may be, and there certainly is justification for his not wanting to go through experiences with another Advent.

Professor Wallach states, "the seller is ordinarily in a better position to maximize the return on the resale of the goods, and his disposition of the goods eliminates the storage and other incidental expenses that may be involved in the unsatisfactory transaction." G. Wallach, The Law of Sales Under the Uniform Commercial Code 9-30 (1981). This is probably the best policy reason of all denying replacement after revocation . . . the relative position of the parties. It is true that a new machine provided by Landrum could have proved perfectly free of defects. It is equally possible that such a new machine would have defects, perhaps similar to those of the old Advent or entirely different ones. No one contends that the seller's right to cure is limitless. Even Landrum, in argument, admits that a day of reckoning must come, although he earnestly contends that the three weeks in the situation at bar was not adequate time to allow cure.

We are cited no good policy reason why different rules should attain as to cure by replacement instead of cure by repair. Indeed, we cannot envision any basis for a distinction. Thus, we state that once a buyer has properly revoked acceptance of a product, the seller has neither the right to cure by repair nor by replacement. . . .

NOTE & QUESTIONS

"Wrongful" revocation. What if Gappelberg had given timely notice of his revocation but did not have substantive grounds for revocation (e.g., the "sea-

sonable" time for cure had not yet elapsed)? UCC 2-703 and 2-709(3) refer to "wrongful" revocation. What are the rights and obligations of a seller following a wrongful revocation?

Problem 11-6. Seller sells Buyer 100 carloads of Chemical Compound X, Grade 1. The terms of the sale are F.O.B. Seller's City. Upon arrival in Buyer's City, Buyer's inspection reveals an impurity that reduces the goods to Grade 2.

(a) May Seller cure by offering Buyer a 20 percent discount, the normal variance in the trade between Grade 1 and Grade 2?

(b) Would your answer be different if Seller is a manufacturer and Buyer is a wholesaler who trades in both grades? Or if Seller is a wholesaler who trades in both grades and Buyer is an end-user?

D.   INSTALLMENT CONTRACTS

As we have seen, the Code introduces a number of hedges to the rule of perfect tender. The broadest of these is the forthright adoption of a substantial performance standard with respect to installment contracts. According to UCC 2-612 a nonconformity must substantially impair the value of an installment before the buyer may reject that installment; additionally, nonconformities must substantially impair the value of the whole contract before they may be treated as a breach of the whole, rather than merely a breach of the particular installment. These exceptions to the perfect tender rule will have that much greater an impact because UCC 2-612(1) defines *installment contract* more broadly than did prior law.

Comment 6 to UCC 2-612 states in part: "Whether the non-conformity in any given installment justifies cancellation as to the future depends, not on whether such non-conformity indicates an intent or likelihood that the future deliveries will also be defective, but whether the non-conformity substantially impairs the value of the whole contract. If only the seller's security in regard to future installments is impaired, he has the right to demand adequate assurances of proper future performances but has not an immediate right to cancel the entire contract."

We have already had occasion to consider UCC 2-609 (right to adequate assurance of performance) in conjunction with Harlow & Jones, Inc. v. Advance Steel Co., at p. 513 supra. This provision plays a particularly important role in the administration of installment contracts. If UCC 2-609 represents a realistic and workable mechanism, the position taken in Comment 6 is probably wise; if the contrary is true, however, UCC 2-612 may allow chiselers to hold a nonbreaching party to a contract while performing below contract specifications on a recurrent basis. Of course, the nonbreaching party may always cancel when the cumulative nonperformance substantially impairs the value of the entire contract. Not everyone, however, will readily understand how to apply this standard, particularly if one is to disregard the future. Consider the following case and Problem.

GRAULICH CATERER INC. v. HANS HOLTERBOSCH, INC.
101 N.J. Super. 61, 243 A.2d 253, 5 UCC Rep. 440 (1968)

FOLEY, J.A.D. Plaintiff, caterers, take this appeal from a judgment for defendant rejecting plaintiff's suit sounding in contract. . . .

[Plaintiff agreed with defendant, who had received the franchise to operate the Lowenbrau beer pavilion at the 1964 World's Fair in New York, to supply meals of German food on a daily basis for at least one year. Plaintiff was to cook the meals using microwaves, a technique only recently introduced by Raytheon Corporation. The agreement was entered into after plaintiff presented sample meals satisfactory to the defendant. Under the agreement, plaintiff was to prepare each day the number of meals ordered by defendant's commissary. Although the parties expected the number of meals to fluctuate they estimated that demand the first year would be about 1,000,000 units.

On April 1 the parties signed a letter that provided, inter alia, "Our contract will contain guarantees as to the quality and specific portions to be used on each plate." A rider to the letter, signed on the same day, stated: "It is understood that this letter indicates intent only and that a detailed contract will be drawn as soon as possible which will contain complete and detailed specifications on quality and quantity of food and details of service. Such a contract will also contain the necessary protective provisions relating to cancellation in the event that quality of product or service falls below the established standards." Although the parties did not prepare the contemplated contract document the appellate court found that there was an enforceable contract, citing UCC 2-201, 2-202, and 2-204.]

In reliance on this agreement plaintiff contracted with suppliers for platters, trays and dollies, which, coupled with labor expenses, totaled $29,937 after adjustments. This sum, plus a projected profit figure of $35,950, was claimed by plaintiff as the amount of damages in its suit. . . .

The delayed and muddled opening of the Fair brought the parties into daily, and at times even hourly, contact. Postponements followed premature orders until a firm order for April 23, 1964 was placed by Mr. Leigh, an employee of Becker & Becker. Upon delivery the members of defendant's organization were stunned by the product and complained immediately that the tendered units did not, in any way, match the contract samples. Rejecting this 955-unit installment as unacceptable, defendant described the food as "bland," unpresentable, tasteless and "just wasn't the type of food that we could sell." Notwithstanding this low grade delivery, defendant, obligated to the Fair to serve food and committed in theory to the Raytheon ovens, conferred with the equally dissatisfied plaintiff in seeking to improve the quality standard of the product to the point where it would be acceptable. Plaintiff's effort to improve the quality of the units was aided by Becker and defendant's pavilion personnel manager, Mueller, as well as the special foods chef from the "VIP" section of defendant's exhibit.

The second delivery, made on April 25, 1964, was likewise unacceptable. Of the 2520 units delivered, between 500 and 700 were distributed among the employees and patrons of the exhibit for a fast reaction. The complaints in response to the food were many and varied. Defendant, describing the sources of unfavorable comment, stated that the sauerbraten was dry and the gravy, pasty and unpalatably "gooey," surrounded rather than enveloped the meat. The knockwurst platter suffered similarly, being dry and comparing unfavorably with the standards established by the samples. Generally, defendant complained that the food was simply not "German food" and as such was unacceptable for the Lowenbrau Pavilion.

Following the failure of the second delivery Holterbosch claimed that plaintiff took no further curative measures, while plaintiff protested that defendant was "not available" following the second and last delivery of April 25, 1964. Graulich stated that he was told through Becker that plaintiff's food would be unsuitable for the Lowenbrau Pavilion. Becker, affirming the nonconformity of the deliveries, denied terminating the relationship and insisted that such an act was beyond his authority as an agent.

Hellmuch Laufer, defendant's pavilion factotum, affirmed hearing Graulich verbally acknowledge Holterbosch's complaints. Laufer agreed that the second delivery was qualitatively no different than the first, stressing that plaintiff's efforts to cure the unpalatable food failed. This witness, joined by Mueller and the "VIP" chef, converted the microwave cooking area into a conventional kitchen using pot burners to successfully prepare the food served for the duration of the Fair. . . .

Giving due regard to the original trier's opportunity to observe the demeanor and to judge the credibility of the witnesses, we find as a matter of fact that the deliveries of April 23 and 25, 1964 did not conform to the samples originally presented and approved. Since warranties of sample and description are characterized as "express warranties," the "whole of the goods shall conform to the sample or model." UCC 2-313(1)(c). The "goods" to "conform" to the sample or model must be "in accordance with the obligations under the contract" UCC 2-106(2); here, to comply with the standards established by the March 17 taste-test of the samples. Any distinguishing language would be controlled by the sample as presented on March 17. Additionally, the implied warranty of fitness for purpose attaches to contracts of this type, where, as here, they are not specifically excluded. A breach of these warranties triggers a buyer's rights following seller's breach as catalogued in UCC 2-711. These remedies include but are not limited to, cancellation, UCC 2-711(1), 2-106(4), "if the breach goes to the whole of the contract." UCC 2-612(3).

UCC 2-612 discloses the rights of the parties to installment contracts:

(1) An "installment contract" is one which requires or authorizes the delivery of goods in separate lots to be separately accepted, even though the contract contains a clause "each delivery is a separate contract" or its equivalent.

(2) The buyer may reject any installment which is non-conforming if the non-conformity substantially impairs the value of that installment and cannot be cured or if the non-conformity is a defect in the required documents; but if the non-conformity does not fall within subsection (3) and the seller gives adequate assurance of its cure the buyer must accept that installment.

(3) Whenever non-conformity or default with respect to one or more installments substantially impairs the value of the whole contract there is a breach of the whole. But the aggrieved party reinstates the contract if he accepts a non-conforming installment without seasonably notifying of cancellation or if he brings an action with respect only to past installments or demands performance as to future installments.

Here, Holterbosch has the right to reject any installment that was non-conforming, provided that the nonconformity substantially impaired the value of that installment and could not be cured. UCC 2-612(2). "Cure," novel to New Jersey's jurisprudence, permits the seller to cure a defective tender through repair, replacement or price allowance if he reasonably notifies the buyer of his curative intention and, in effecting the cure, makes a timely conforming delivery. UCC 2-508(1).

The effect of the installment contract section, UCC 2-612(2), is to extend the time for cure past the contract delivery date for that nonconforming installment, provided the nonconformity does not "substantially [impair] the value of that installment" and can be cured. We find that Holterbosch was justified in rejecting Graulich's tender of the April 23 initial installment since the nonconformity of the tendered goods with the accepted sample was incurable, and thus substantially impaired the value of that installment.

Replacing considerations of anticipatory repudiation and the material injury with the test of substantial impairment, UCC 2-612, adopts a more restrictive seller-oriented approach favoring "the continuance of the contract in the absence of an overt cancellation." See Comment to UCC 2-612, para. 6; also New Jersey Study Comment, para. 2; W. Hawkland, Sales and Bulk Sales 116 (1958). To allow an aggrieved party to cancel an installment contract, UCC 2-612(3), requires (1) the breach be of the whole contract which occurs when the nonconformity of "one or more installments substantially impairs the value of the whole contract;" and (2) that seasonable notification of cancellation has been given if the buyer has accepted a nonconforming installment.

What amounts to substantial impairment presents a question of fact. Analyzing this factual question, the New Jersey commentators counsel that the test as to whether the nonconformity in any given installment justifies cancelling the entire contract depends on whether the nonconformity substantially impairs the value of the whole contract, and not on whether it indicates an intent or likelihood that the future deliveries also will be defective. Continuing, the Comment relates the intent underlying a breach to insecurity and those sections of the Code providing buyer with adequate assurance of performance, UCC 2-609, and anticipatory repudiation, UCC 2-610. More practical in its treatment of "substantial impairment," the official Comment states that "substantial impairment of the value of an installment can turn not only on the quality of the goods but also on such factors as time, quantity, assortment, and the like. It must be judged in terms of the normal or specifically known purposes of the contract." Comment to UCC 2-612, para. 4; [see] also W. Hawkland, supra, at 117.

At the Lowenbrau Pavilion on April 23, 1964 plaintiff Graulich, timely noticed of the nonconforming initial tender, gave assurance that future tenders would be cured to match the original samples. Unequivocally committed to the microwave kitchen method, defendant lent plaintiff three members of its staff in aid of this adjustment. Since plaintiff was given the opportunity to cure, there is no need to touch upon the substantiality of the initial nonconforming installment.

The second installment tender was as unsatisfactory as the first. The meat was dry, the gravy "gooey" and the complaints abundant. After the nonconforming second delivery it became apparent that eleventh-hour efforts attempting to rework and adjust the platters failed. Translating this into legal parlance, there was a nonconforming tender of the initial installment on a contract for the sale of goods; upon tender the buyer Holterbosch notified the seller Graulich of the nonconformity and unacceptable nature of the platters tendered; the failure of the cure assured by plaintiff, seller, was evidenced by a subsequently defective nonconforming delivery. The second unacceptable delivery and the failure of plaintiff's additional curative efforts left defendant in a position for one week without food. Time was critical. Plaintiff knew that platters of maximum quality were required on a daily installment basis. Because of defendant's immediate need for quality food and plaintiff's failure to cure, we find that the nonconformity of the second delivery, projected upon the circumstances of this case, "substantially impair[ed] the value of the whole contract [and resulted in] a breach of the whole." UCC 2-612(3). If the breach goes to the whole contract the buyer may cancel the whole contract. UCC 2-711(1). Accordingly, we find that Holterbosch was justified in cancelling the installment agreement signed on April 1, 1964.

Since defendant's counterclaim was withdrawn it is unnecessary to treat of the right retained by a cancelling party to press any remedy for breach of the whole contract. UCC 2-106(4).

Judgment in favor of defendant for the reasons herein stated. Costs to defendant.

Problem 11-7. On July 26, 1974, Cherwell agreed to sell "Cherco Meal" to Rytman Grain Co. by installments over an indefinite period. The contract called for shipments according to weekly instructions from Rytman, with payments to be made within 10 days after delivery.

(a) Cherwell makes all shipments requested between July 29, 1984, to April 23, 1985, but Rytman, despite reminders, falls behind on its payments. On April 23 Cherwell asks you what steps it can take to protect its interests. Advise Cherwell. In addition to UCC 2-612 re-examine UCC 2-609 through 2-611.

(b) Before Cherwell takes your advice the president of Rytman asks Cherwell's president in a telephone conversation for assurances that Cherwell would continue to deliver. Rytman's president notes that there has been a significant increase in the market price for Cherco Meal and similar products. Cherwell's president says that if past due payments are made Cherwell will deliver. Rytman promptly issues a check for all payments due before March 31. Reconsider your advice to Cherwell.

(c) Soon after sending the check Rytman's president is told by a Cherwell truck driver that the April 30 shipment will be the last Cherwell delivery. As attorney for Rytman what would you advise?

(d) After listening to your advice Rytman's president stops payment on the April 23 check and writes a letter to Cherwell demanding adequate assurance of future deliveries. As attorney for Cherwell what would you advise?

(e) Immediately after receiving the Rytman letter Cherwell's president replies in writing with a demand for immediate payment. Cherwell makes no further deliveries. As attorney for Rytman what would you advise?

(f) Thirty days after sending the letter to Cherwell demanding assurance of future deliveries, as in (d), Rytman's president writes a letter to Cherwell declaring that Cherwell has repudiated the contract. As attorney for Cherwell what would you advise?

(g) Soon after receiving the letter mentioned in (f) Cherwell brings a suit against Rytman for nonpayment of moneys due and owing for accepted deliveries of Cherco Meal. As attorney for Rytman what would you advise?

CHAPTER 12

Seller's Remedies

The principal thrust of the modern law of damages is compensation. In the field of sales contracts, it is the nonbreaching party's "expectation interest" that is to be compensated. This principle is set out in UCC 1-106(1):

> The remedies provided by this Act shall be liberally administered to the end that the aggrieved party may be put in as good a position as if the other party had fully performed but neither consequential or special nor penal damages may be had except as specifically provided in this Act or by other rule of law.

The more specific sales remedies set out in Part 7 of Article 2 must be read in the light of this general principle.

As we shall see when we look at the application of these Article 2 remedy provisions to particular problems, the seemingly clear and broad principle of UCC 1-106 rapidly degenerates into a bewildering array of refinements and exceptions. The law of sales remedies provides a fascinating insight into the tangle of half-articulated, half-reconciled viewpoints that shape much of modern law. In particular, this field has been enriched by a voluminous doctrinal history, the creativity of Karl Llewellyn, and a growing body of critical literature, written principally from an economic perspective. See Sebert, Remedies Under Article Two of the Uniform Commercial Code: An Agenda for Review, 130 U. Pa. L. Rev. 360 (1981).

This chapter focuses on the seller's options when the buyer breaches. We examine first the seller's right to call off the contract—the analog of the buyer's right to reject or revoke acceptance of nonconforming goods—by retaining or recovering possession of the goods. We turn then to the seller's closest equivalent to specific performance, i.e., the right to have a judgment for the full purchase price promised by the buyer. A third section studies the alternative formulas for monetary damages that a seller may recover. The chapter ends with a consideration of the extent to which parties may agree on remedies, including liquidated damage clauses. For useful background reading, see Harris, A Radical Restatement of the Law of Seller's Damages: Sales Act and Commercial Code Results Compared, 18 Stan. L. Rev. 66 (1965); Peters, Remedies for Breach of Contracts Relating to the Sale of Goods Under the Uniform Commercial Code: A Roadmap for Article Two, 73 Yale L.J. 199, 240-284 (1963).

A. GOODS-ORIENTED REMEDIES

UCC 2-703 includes in its general summary of the seller's remedies the right to withhold delivery or to stop delivery by a bailee. Even when the buyer has taken possession of the goods the seller may be able to recover the goods under UCC 2-507 or 2-702 if the buyer has failed to pay for them as promised. Coupled with the right of the seller to cancel the contract because of the buyer's breach, UCC 2-703(f), these remedies permit the seller to take back or keep his goods and call off the contract.

In our study of secured transactions we have already examined these remedies. In Chapter 5 we surveyed the rights of the unsecured seller (p. 220 supra), and at the end of Chapter 8 we considered when the seller's right to recover possession of goods from the buyer may be cut off by the claims of competing third parties such as purchasers (p. 449 supra). You should review these materials and then consider the following case and the notes and questions that explore the right of a seller to stop goods in transit.

BUTTS v. GLENDALE PLYWOOD CO.
710 F.2d 504, 36 UCC Rep. 545 (9th Cir. 1983)

NORRIS, Circuit Judge. The question presented by this appeal is whether Glendale Plywood Co. (Glendale) had the right to stop a shipment of plywood to Summit Creek Plywood Company (Summit Creek) after Summit Creek resold the plywood to a third party and ordered its destination changed. The district court held that, under UCC 2-705, the redirection of a shipment at the order of a buyer, without the seller's knowledge, constitutes a reshipment that cuts off the seller's right to stop the goods in transit. We affirm. . . .

Summit Creek ordered two railroad carloads of lumber from Glendale Plywood in March, 1978. On April 15, Glendale was instructed to ship the cars to "Summit Creek Forest Products, Murray, Utah." On April 17, Glendale shipped the cars. The railroad issued a [nonnegotiable] bill of lading showing Glendale as the shipper, Summit Creek as the consignee, and Summit Creek at Murray, Utah as the destination. On April 19, while the goods were in transit, Summit Creek sold its interest in the lumber to Davidson Lumber Sales (Davidson). At the request of Summit Creek, the railroad changed the waybills* to show Summit Creek as the shipper, Davidson as the consignee,

---

*A *waybill* is an instrument given connecting carriers by the original carrier. It sets out delivery instructions. According to the facts stated in the district court opinion, Glendale delivered the cars to Southern Pacific, which transferred them to Union Pacific for delivery to Summit Creek. Summit Creek, the buyer, asked Union Pacific to change the waybills. 5 B.R. 815, 32 UCC Rep. 1490 (D. Ore. 1981). The waybill itself is not a document of title. See UCC 1-201(15); R. Riegert & R. Braucher, Documents of Title 29 (3d ed. 1978) ("seems not to be a document of title at all"). Cf. "through bills of lading," UCC 7-302.—EDS.

and Davidson at Murray, Utah as the destination. Summit Creek then sold this account receivable from Davidson, and others, to Walter E. Heller Western, a factoring agent.

The railroad, following Summit Creek's instructions, sent the cars on their way to Davidson at Murray. On April 28, having learned that Summit Creek might be insolvent and before the cars had reached Murray, Glendale ordered the railroad to stop both cars. The railroad complied with Glendale's orders and Glendale then sold the lumber directly to Davidson. The lumber was delivered to Davidson at Murray on May 3.

On May 3, Summit Creek was adjudicated a bankrupt. Thereafter, Summit Creek's trustee in bankruptcy sued Glendale, claiming it had no right to stop the shipment. The bankruptcy court held for Glendale. The district court reversed, holding that Glendale was not allowed to stop the shipment and that Summit Creek, not Glendale, was entitled to payment from Davidson. Glendale appeals. The only issue on appeal is whether, under UCC 2-705, Glendale had the right to stop the shipment while it was in transit. . . .

UCC 2-705 provides that:

> (1) The seller may stop delivery of goods in the possession of a carrier or other bailee when he discovers the buyer to be insolvent (Section 2-702) and may stop delivery of carload, truckload, planeload or larger shipments of express or freight when the buyer repudiates or fails to make a payment due before delivery or if for any other reason the seller has a right to withhold or reclaim the goods.
> (2) As against such buyer the seller may stop delivery until
> (a) receipt of the goods by the buyer; or
> (b) acknowledgment to the buyer by any bailee of the goods except a carrier that the bailee holds the goods for the buyer; or
> (c) such acknowledgment to the buyer by a carrier by reshipment or as warehouseman; . . .

The dispute in this case is whether the railroad's redirection of the cars from Summit Creek to Davidson at Summit Creek's request constituted a reshipment which cut off Glendale's right to stop delivery under UCC 2-705(2)(c). The legal question we must thus decide is whether a re-routing of a shipment from a purchaser to a subpurchaser (a buyer from the original purchaser) upon the instructions of the purchaser and without the knowledge of the seller should constitute a reshipment under UCC 2-705(2)(c). We hold that it should.

The purpose of UCC 2-705(2)(c) is to protect transactions between original buyers and subpurchasers. . . . Section (2)(c) protects a subpurchaser from being affected by disputes between the buyer and the seller by ensuring that the goods he orders are delivered regardless of the financial condition of his seller (the original buyer). Whether the original seller has knowledge of the transaction between his buyer and the subpurchaser has no effect on the subpurchaser's need for protection. To read into UCC 2-705 a requirement of seller knowledge or permission for reshipment would endanger subpurchasers and discourage resale transactions of the sort conducted here.[1]

Moreover, defining reshipment as the point at which the seller's right to stop shipment ceases provides a time at which the rights of all parties are fixed. Disputes between sellers, buyers, and subpurchasers as to whether permission was ever granted or what the seller intended in his grant of permission, which would result if the seller's permission was required to reship, are avoided.

We find unpersuasive Glendale's argument that the rule we adopt today will cause sellers to demand payment before shipment in order to ensure that they will be paid. While it is true that our interpretation of UCC 2-705 gives the buyer the power, by reshipping, to cut off the seller's right to stop shipment, the seller's right to stop transit is cut off once the goods are received by the buyer in any event. In most instances the seller has not been paid at this point and still runs the risk of being unable to collect. Yet sellers have not, as a response, shipped only on a C.O.D. basis. There is no reason to believe that they will begin demanding prepayment under our interpretation of UCC 2-705(2)(c).[2]

The interpretation of UCC 2-705 adopted by the district court is consistent with the goals of predictability in commercial transactions and providing protection for buyers and sellers alike. The judgment is thus affirmed.

NOTES & QUESTIONS

1. *Responsibility of the carrier.* A carrier must deliver to the person who is entitled to the goods under the bill of lading unless excused by the provisions of UCC 7-403(1) or 7-404. In the *Butts* case, Southern Pacific issued a nonnegotiable bill of lading naming Summit Creek, the buyer, as consignee and therefore delivery had to be made to Summit Creek. UCC 7-403(1), (4). A carrier is excused, however, if it can show that the seller exercised his right to

---

1. Glendale argues that, while UCC 2-705 is designed to protect subpurchasers, the subpurchaser here needed no protection because he was able to buy the goods directly from the seller when shipment was stopped. It is true that the subpurchaser in this case was able to mitigate his damages by buying from the seller (though we do not know at what price). However, that may not be the situation in other cases, for example when the subpurchaser has already paid his seller (the buyer). To allow the seller to stop transit after the buyer has made a bargain with a subpurchaser forces the shipment to the subpurchaser to be delayed and the subpurchaser to renegotiate his deal, possibly at a higher price, through no fault of his own. Moreover, an interpretation of UCC 2-705 that would allow a seller in a rising market to stop transit of the goods and resell them to the subpurchaser at a higher price would allow the seller, merely by claiming a fear of buyer insolvency, to deprive the buyer of the benefit of an advantageous bargain with the subpurchaser. Such a result would be both inequitable and inconsistent with the goals of protection of the contractual rights of all the parties.

2. Glendale also contends that it is inequitable to establish a rule under which a buyer, without the seller's knowledge, can cut off the seller's right to stop shipment by merely shipping the goods to a third party. While it is true that a buyer can cut off the seller's right to collect by reshipment, to do so he has to sell the goods to someone else and give up the right to receive and use them. If he only has them shipped to himself at another location, his action would be a mere diversion which would not rise to the status of a reshipment, UCC 2-705 Official Comment 3, and would not cut off the seller's rights.

stop delivery under UCC 2-705 or that there was a diversion or reconsignment under UCC 7-303. When the seller notifies the carrier to stop delivery the carrier must follow this order provided that the seller gives timely notice and surrenders any negotiable document. UCC 2-705(3). If the seller's order is wrongful as to the buyer, the buyer must pursue the seller rather than the carrier because the carrier is excused under UCC 7-403(1)(d). If the carrier follows the diversion or reconsignment order of a person specified in UCC 7-303 it is also protected from an action for misdelivery. In the *Butts* case, for example, the carrier could follow Summit Creek's reconsignment if Summit Creek had possession of the nonnegotiable bill or if Summit Creek was entitled to dispose of the lumber as against Glendale. UCC 7-303(1)(c), (1)(d). The court does not state who has possession of the bill. Does Summit Creek have the right to dispose of the lumber while it is in transit? Does it matter whether Summit Creek has title to the lumber? See UCC 2-401(2).

2. *Rights of subpurchaser.* In Ramco Steel, Inc. v. Kesler (In re Murdock Machine & Engineering Co.), 620 F.2d 767 (10th Cir. 1980), the court concluded that the seller that stopped delivery had priority over the claims of a subpurchaser when the goods had been delivered to neither the original buyer nor the subpurchaser. The court noted that this conclusion was consistent with pre-Code law, citing Uniform Sales Act §62 (the right to stop delivery "not affected by any sale or other disposition of goods which the buyer may have made, unless the seller has assented thereto"). Are this case and the pre-Code law relevant to the issue in the *Butts* case?

3. *Right to stop delivery and bankruptcy.* If a buyer files a petition in bankruptcy, will goods in transit become part of the bankruptcy estate? See BC 541(a)(1) ("all legal or equitable interests of the debtor in property"). If the goods are part of the estate, will the automatic stay of BC 362 prohibit a seller from exercising his right to stop goods in transit? Consider also whether the right to stop delivery can be described as an Article 2 security interest? See UCC 9-113. If so, is the right a *lien* for purposes of the Bankruptcy Code? See BC 101(31). Under what circumstances can the trustee in bankruptcy avoid the lien? Cf. BC 546(c); UCC 2-702(2), (3).

Problem 12-1. Wholesale makes frequent sales to Grocer. On Monday, Wholesale makes the following shipments:

(a) A carload of oranges, shipped under a nonnegotiable bill of lading naming Wholesale as consignor and Grocer as consignee.

(b) A truckload of lettuce, which at Wholesale's direction is shipped under a nonnegotiable bill of lading naming Seaside Resorts, Seaside, Oregon, as consignee and Grocer as consignor.

(c) One ton of potatoes, a partial truckload, consigned to Grocer's Local Store #402.

On Tuesday, Wholesale makes the following additional deliveries:

(d) 10,000 gallons of vegetable oil evidenced by a negotiable warehouse receipt issued to Wholesale's order, indorsed by Wholesale, and forwarded through bank collection channels with a sight draft attached.

(e) 2,000 cases of fresh strawberries held by Farmers' Terminal Warehouse. Wholesale gives an oral delivery order to Warehouse Tuesday morning and on that afternoon Warehouse sends written confirmation to Grocer that it is holding the strawberries for Grocer's account.

Which of the above deliveries may Wholesale stop if it learns on Wednesday that (1) Grocer has repudiated the order in question, (2) Grocer may be unable to pay for the produce, or (3) Grocer has filed a petition in bankruptcy that morning? See UCC 2-705.

B.   RIGHT TO THE PRICE

On entering into a sales contract a seller expects to receive the price agreed on and, if the buyer should breach, presumably would prefer a money judgment for the full contract price. This is an analog to specific performance, but it is recoverable as damages in an action at law rather than pursuant to a decree of specific performance in equity. The practical effect of giving the seller an action for the price, however, is to force the goods on an unwilling buyer who may be less able than the seller to resell the goods. This may explain why sales law has traditionally limited the situations in which the seller may recover the price. UCC 2-709(1) continues this tradition:

> When the buyer fails to pay the price as it becomes due the seller may recover, together with any incidental damages under the next section, the price
> (a) of goods accepted or of conforming goods lost or damaged within a commercially reasonable time after risk of their loss has passed to the buyer; and
> (b) of goods identified to the contract if the seller is unable after reasonable effort to resell them at a reasonable price or the circumstances reasonably indicate such effort will be unavailing.

Under the comparable provision of the Uniform Sales Act (§63), the primary concern is whether title to the goods had passed. As you read the following materials you should consider whether the seller should have a right to the price in cases other than those provided for by the Code and whether manipulation of the concept of title under prior law permitted desirable additional flexibility.

Problem 12-2. Altos Computer agrees to sell 500 of its 212A modems to Standalone Supplies. The contract states that the units are to be delivered in May for $275 each, F.O.B. San Jose, freight prepaid to Beaverton, Oregon. Construction at Altos' San Jose facility delays production so in mid-May the company's San Jose manager requests Altos' Burlingame facility to fill the order from stock on hand in Burlingame. The Burlingame plant ships the modems on May 29 but due to a misunderstanding between Altos' two plants the order is shipped freight collect. The carrier's truck loses its brakes en route and the modems are totally destroyed. May Altos recover the price? See UCC 2-709, 2-319, 2-509, 2-510, 2-504.

FOXCO INDUSTRIES, LTD. v. FABRIC WORLD, INC.
595 F.2d 976, 26 UCC Rep. 694 (5th Cir. 1979)

TJOFLAT, Circuit Judge. In this diversity action Foxco Industries, Ltd. (Foxco), a Delaware corporation, following a jury trial recovered a $26,000 judgment against Fabric World, Inc. (Fabric World), an Alabama corporation, for breaching a contract to purchase certain knitted fabric goods and refusing to pay for merchandise previously purchased. . . .

Foxco is in the business of manufacturing knitted fabrics for sale to retail fabric stores and the garment industry. Foxco's principal place of business is in New York City. . . . Fabric World is engaged in the retail fabric business and operates a chain of stores in a number of states; its headquarters is in Huntsville, Alabama.

There are two seasons in the fabric industry, a spring season and a fall season. Before the beginning of each season Foxco displays for customers samples of the line of fabrics it will manufacture that season. Customer orders are accepted only from the fabric shown on display. Foxco's manufacturing operation is limited to filling these orders; no fabrics are manufactured merely to be held as inventory. There was some conflict in the testimony as to whether fabric specially knit for one customer, such as Fabric World, could be resold to another customer.

Foxco sells some of its goods to retail fabric stores through manufacturers' representatives, operating on a commission basis, who sell the lines of numerous manufacturers. Foxco furnishes each representative with samples and a price list. Larger retail store customers, such as Fabric World, are handled personally by Foxco's sales manager, Allen Feller, a salaried employee, who supervises all retail fabric store sales. He has responsibility over the approximately twenty-six manufacturers' representatives carrying the Foxco line. . . .

On April 22, 1974, Feller traveled to Huntsville to show Fabric World the new fall line. His meeting with Glenn Jameson, Fabric World's president, culminated in a written order for "first quality" goods. A dispute subsequently arose regarding the quality of the goods sent to fill the order, and Fabric World refused to pay for the portion of the goods it considered defective.

On October 21, 1974, Feller returned to Huntsville to show Jameson the line for the following spring season. Jameson voiced no complaint about the quality of the goods received pursuant to the previous April 22 order. In fact, he gave Feller a new order, in writing, for 12,000 yards of first quality fabric, at a price of $36,705, to be delivered by January 15, 1975.

A few weeks after the October 21 order was placed, the textile industry began to experience a precipitous decline in the price of yarn. Because of a drop in the price of finished goods, Fabric World wrote Foxco on November 15, 1974, and cancelled its October 21 order. Foxco immediately replied, stating that the manufacture of the order was substantially completed and that it could not accept the cancellation. On November 27, 1974, Foxco's attorney wrote Fabric World that if the goods were not accepted they would be finished and sold and Fabric World sued for the difference between the contract price and the sales price received by Foxco. On December 3, 1974, Fabric World agreed to accept the order, but threatened to return the entire shipment if it contained one flaw. Foxco, believing that it was impossible to produce an order of this magnitude without a single flaw, decided it would not ship the order (which was completed a short time later).

Fabric World established that in December 1974 the fair market value of the October order was approximately 20% less than the contract price. However, Foxco made no attempt to sell the goods from the time Fabric World cancelled the order until September 1975, when the goods had dropped 50% in value. In that month Foxco sold at a private sale without notice to Fabric World approximately 7,000 yards from the order for an average price of between $1.50 and $1.75 per yard, a total consideration of $10,119.50. By the time of trial in April 1976, Foxco had on hand about 5,000 yards of the order worth between $1.25 and $1 per yard, or about $6,250. . . .

We now turn to Fabric World's argument that, while Foxco was entitled to have the jury charged under UCC 2-708, the instruction under UCC 2-709 was improper. . . .

Fabric World maintains that the $26,000 verdict awarded to Foxco cannot be supported by the district court's instruction under UCC 2-708, allowing the difference between the market and contract price as the measure of damages. Fabric World calculates that, in view of the market price at the time the October 1974 contract was breached, the maximum amount the jury could have given Foxco under the UCC 2-708 instruction was approximately $16,000, $10,000 less than its $26,000 verdict. Accordingly, it reasons that the verdict must have been fashioned pursuant to the UCC 2-709 charge and the verdict cannot stand unless that charge was proper. As we now discuss, the jury was appropriately instructed, and Foxco's damage award must be approved.

UCC 2-703 sets out the remedies available to the seller of goods against a defaulting purchaser.

Seller's Remedies in General

Where the buyer wrongfully rejects or revokes acceptance of goods or fails to make a payment due on or before delivery or repudiates with respect to a part or the whole, then with respect to any goods directly affected and, if the breach is of the whole contract (Section 2-612), then also with respect to the whole undelivered balance, the aggrieved seller may

(a) withhold delivery of such goods;

(b) stop delivery by any bailee as hereafter provided (Section 2-705);

(c) proceed under the next section respecting goods still unidentified to the contract;

(d) resell and recover damages as hereafter provided (Section 2-706);

(e) recover damages for non-acceptance (Section 2-708) or in a proper case the price (Section 2-709);

(f) cancel.

As Fabric World correctly argues, notwithstanding UCC 2-703(d) Foxco cannot invoke UCC 2-706 in this case because, following Fabric World's breach, Foxco privately sold some of the goods without notice to Fabric World. Thus, Foxco, having elected not to pursue the relief available under UCC 2-703(a), (b), and (f), is limited to its remedies under UCC 2-703(e), i.e., either UCC 2-708 or 2-709. The district court charged the jury under both of these latter provisions, leaving to the jury the determination of which was more appropriately applicable under the facts developed at trial. Since Fabric World properly concedes that a UCC 2-708 instruction was warranted on the state of the record before the trial judge, we may reverse only if the evidence was insufficient for the jury to invoke UCC 2-709 as a measure of Foxco's damages.

When Fabric World cancelled its October 1974 order on November 15, 1974, Foxco had not yet fully completed the manufacture of the contracted-for fabric. Under UCC 2-704, a seller aggrieved by a buyer's repudiation of unfinished goods may, in the exercise of reasonable commercial judgment and in order to avoid loss, either complete the manufacture and wholly identify the goods to the contract or cease their manufacture and resell them at their salvage value. As stated in the Official Comment to this section, "1. This section gives an aggrieved seller the right at the time of breach to identify to the contract any conforming finished goods, regardless of their resalability, and to use reasonable judgment as to completing unfinished goods. It thus makes the goods available for resale under the resale section, the seller's primary remedy, and *in the special case in which resale is not practicable, allows the action for the price which would then be necessary to give the seller the value of his contract*" (emphasis added). The jury obviously decided that Foxco acted in a commercially reasonable manner when it decided to process to a conclusion the manufacture of the already substantially completed Fabric World order. Foxco was then entitled to the appropriate seller's breach of contract remedy.

UCC 2-709(1)(b), that portion of UCC 2-709 which would apply here, provides that an action for the price of goods may be maintained "if the seller is unable after *reasonable* effort to resell them at a *reasonable* price or the circumstances *reasonably* indicate that such effort will be unavailing." UCC 2-709(1)(b) (emphasis added). The Official Comment to UCC 2-709 states, in pertinent part, that: "2. The action for the price is now generally limited to those cases where resale of the goods is impracticable. . . . 3. This section substitutes an objective test by action for the former 'not readily resalable' standard. An action for the price under subsection (1)(b) can be sustained only after a 'reasonable effort to resell' the goods at reasonable price has actually been made or where the circumstances 'reasonably indicate' that such an effort will be unavailing." As was recognized in Multi-Line Manufacturing, Inc. v. Greenwood Mills, Inc., 123 Ga. App. 372, 180 S.E.2d 917 (1971), a case involving the cancellation of a contract to purchase fabric, the language of UCC 2-709(1)(b) "clearly evinces legislative intent that these matters ordinarily should be subject to determination by a jury. . . ." Id. at 373, 180 S.E.2d at 918. Thus, we will reverse only if, as a matter of law, there was no way in which the jury could find that Foxco was unable, after reasonable effort, to resell the fabric at a reasonable price or that it was reasonably clear that an effort to resell would have been fruitless.

The evidence at trial clearly established that all of Foxco's goods were specially manufactured for the customer who ordered them and that it was difficult for Foxco to resell fabric manufactured for one purchaser to another buyer. Further, it was normally very difficult to sell Foxco's spring fabric after the spring buying season had ended; the precipitous decline of the knitted fabric market presented an additional barrier to resale. It was not until the next spring buying season returned that Foxco, in September 1975, finally sold a portion of the goods identified to Fabric World's October 1974 order.

Fabric World argues that Foxco made no effort whatsoever to resell the goods during the months that intervened (between the contract breach and Foxco's eventual disposition of the fabric in September 1975) despite the presence of some market for the goods in that interim period. Thus, Fabric World concludes, the requisites of UCC 2-709(1)(b) were not satisfied. Under UCC 2-709(1)(b), however, Foxco was required only to use reasonable efforts to resell its goods at a reasonable price. From the time of Fabric World's breach to September 1975 there was a 50% decline in the market price of this material. We cannot say that the jury was precluded from finding that Foxco acted reasonably under the circumstances or that there was no reasonable price at which Foxco could sell these goods.[5] Fabric World breached its contract with Foxco, and the jury was entitled to a charge which gave Foxco the full benefit of its original bargain.[6] . . .

[Affirmed.]

---

5. Fabric World points to Cole v. Melvin, 441 F. Supp. 193, 205 n.7 (D.S.D. 1977), for the proposition that UCC 2-709(1)(b) cannot be applied in case of a plummeting market if there were some market for the relevant good. We note several points. First, Cole v. Melvin was a non-jury trial, so there was no issue whether a UCC 2-709 jury instruction was appropriate in that case. Moreover, the court noted that UCC 2-709 was inapplicable because the seller's attorney felt he could not produce evidence to support an action for the price; in the case before us Foxco presented evidence which made a UCC 2-709 jury instruction appropriate. Finally, the proposition Fabric World draws from Cole v. Melvin was dictum.

6. . . . We reject Fabric World's argument that Foxco should be denied the application of UCC 2-709 because it was barred from the UCC 2-706 remedy. See Wolpert v. Foster, 312 Minn. 526, 254 N.W.2d 348, 351-352 (1977).

NOTES & QUESTIONS

1. *Completion of unfinished goods.* The court in *Foxco* notes that the jury must have concluded that Foxco acted reasonably when it decided to complete manufacture, yet the court refers to no evidence. As attorney for Foxco what evidence would you look for? If, notwithstanding your evidence, the jury had decided that completion was unreasonable what would be the consequence?

2. *Disposition of the goods.* Was Foxco or Fabric World in a better position to dispose of the fabric? If Fabric World was in the better position, then to allow Foxco to recover the full contract price would put pressure on Fabric World to take over the resale of the fabric and thereby minimize allocative costs. (Consider what will happen to the 5,000 yards of fabric Foxco still has on hand.) If Foxco, on the other hand, can sell the fabric more efficiently, should it be allowed to recover the price? Because UCC 2-709 does not focus on this issue neither the court nor the jury in *Foxco* inquired into who was in a better position to resell. Consider the following situation: Foxco delivers the fabric to Alabama, where Fabric World effectively but wrongfully rejects. Can Foxco recover the price? Who is likely to be able to dispose of the fabric for the greatest net return?

3. *Wrongful revocation and action for the price.* Both UCC 2-703 and 2-709(3) refer to wrongful revocation of acceptance. Should a seller be forced to take back and resell goods a buyer may have allowed to depreciate? If Fabric World had accepted the fabric when delivered but had effectively (i.e., with timely notice) but wrongfully revoked acceptance in February after discovering it could not sell the fabric, would Foxco be able to recover the full contract price? Cf. Akron Brick & Block Co. v. Moniz Engineering Co., 365 Mass. 92, 310 N.E.2d 128, 14 UCC Rep. 563 (1974) (after using machine buyer returned it to seller; seller allowed to recover contract price, but court finds *no* revocation of acceptance rather than *wrongful* revocation).

4. *Applying the proceeds from the seller's sale.* Foxco sold 7,000 of the 12,000 yards. Because Foxco gave Fabric World no notice of the proposed sale the court points out that Foxco may not use UCC 2-706, which would calculate damages by subtracting the net resale proceeds from the contract price. By applying the $10,119.50 of resale proceeds to the recovery of the contract price under UCC 2-709 the court in effect uses the same formula. But if UCC 2-706 were applicable the parties might raise issues of the seller's good faith and the commercial reasonableness of the resale. Could Fabric World raise these same issues under UCC 2-709? The limited reference to resale in UCC 2-709(2) does not mention good faith, commercial reasonableness, or notice to the buyer. Should any of these requirements be read in?

C. BASIC MONETARY DAMAGE REMEDIES

The Code provides three formulas for measuring the seller's damages in cases where he cannot recover the full contract price.

(1) The seller may resell the goods and recover the difference between the contract price and the resale price if the sale is made "in good faith and in a commercially reasonable manner." UCC 2-706. The assumption underlying this formula is that the price received on an actual resale is an easy-to-prove and fairly accurate measure of the market price and therefore a suitable substitute for the market price subtrahend in the traditional damage formula allowing the seller the difference between the contract price and the market price. The draftsmen also wished to encourage resale by the seller as consistent with the expectations and practices of reasonable merchants.

(2) The Code also recognizes the traditional contract price/market price formula. UCC 2-708(1).

(3) A third formula, which allows recovery of "profit (including reasonable overhead)," is also available. UCC 2-708(2). This formula has received increasing attention in the courts and has been hailed by some commentators as the seller's primary remedy. See Childres & Burgess, Seller's Remedies: The Primacy of UCC 2-708(2), 48 N.Y.U. L. Rev. 833 (1973).

In any event, no matter what formula is used the seller may also recover incidental damages resulting from the buyer's breach. UCC 2-710.

Problem 12-3. Waterhouse, Inc. issues a written offer to purchase its common stock at $32 per share if tendered by August 22. Investor tenders her 40,000 shares on August 20, at which time the shares are traded over the counter at a low of $29.50 and a high of $31. By mistake, Waterhouse rejects Investor's tender and so informs her on September 1, at which time the OTC quotes range from $29 to $30. The following day Investor telephones a Waterhouse officer and informs him that if Waterhouse does not accept her tender she will be forced to sell her shares and bring legal action. Waterhouse again refuses to accept the tender. On September 14 Investor sells her shares to a neighbor for $26.00 a share. The OTC quotes on September 14 range from $27.50 to $28.75. How much may Investor recover from Waterhouse? See UCC 2-706, 8-107; cf. 9-504.

UCC 8-107(2) of the 1972 Official Text provides:

> When the buyer fails to pay the price as it comes due under a contract of sale the seller may recover the price
> (a) of securities accepted by the buyer; and
> (b) of other securities if efforts at their resale would be unduly burdensome or if there is no readily available market for their resale.

Does this subsection provide a remedy for Investor? For the possible application of Article 2 to investment securities, see Problem 9-2 at p. 467 supra. Note, however, that Comment 2 to UCC 8-107 concludes that "[t]he approval of these particular remedies does not constitute disapproval of other remedies that may exist under other rules of law. Section 1-103." Does the Comment exclude reference to Article 2?

C. Basic Monetary Damage Remedies

Problem 12-4. Chicago Steel, a Chicago firm, orders 200 tons of coal from Ohio Valley Coal. The contract price is $28 per ton, F.O.B. Wheeling, West Virginia, with shipment to be made in four equal lots in July, September, November, and December. In July the first lot is shipped and accepted. At this time the market price in Chicago is $27 per ton. When the second shipment arrives the market price has declined to $26 in Wheeling and $25 in Chicago. Chicago Steel rejects this shipment. Market prices continue to decline. In November Chicago Steel repudiates the contract and neither the November nor the December shipment is made. The market price is $25 in Wheeling and $24 in Chicago throughout November and December. The freight charges from Wheeling to Chicago are $1.50 per ton.

(a) What sums may Ohio Valley Coal recover in respect of each shipment? See UCC 2-708(1), 2-709, 2-710.

(b) What result if the contract provides for delivery "F.O.B. Chicago"?

(c) Under either (a) or (b), suppose that Ohio Valley Coal, having loaded the cars for the November shipment, resells them to Binghamton Rolling Mills in New York at a price of $27 per ton, F.O.B. Binghamton. The freight charges from Wheeling to Binghamton are $1 per ton. What are Ohio Valley Coal's damages? See UCC 2-708(1), 2-708(2), 2-710, 2-706.

Problem 12-5. Dunbar Molasses accepts an order for 10,000 gallons of Refined Blackstrap Syrup, #1 Commercial Grade. The contract price of the syrup is $4.00 per gallon. The variable costs of producing the syrup are $2.50 per gallon, allocable overhead is approximately $1.00 per gallon, and $0.50 per gallon is net profit. Dunbar's customer repudiates the contract at a time when the market price has fallen to $1.75 per gallon. May Dunbar recover the contract-market differential of $2.25 × 10,000 gallons? See UCC 2-708(1), 2-708(2).

NOBS CHEMICAL, U.S.A., INC. v. KOPPERS CO.
616 F.2d 212, 28 UCC Rep. 1039 (5th Cir. 1980)

HENDERSON, Circuit Judge. Koppers Company contracted with the plaintiffs, Nobs Chemical, U.S.A., Inc. (hereinafter referred to as "Nobs") and Calmon-Hill Trading Corporation (hereinafter referred to as "Calmon-Hill") to purchase 1000 metric tons of cumene.[1] Koppers breached the contract. Nobs and Calmon-Hill brought suit in United States District Court for the Southern District of Texas, and the case was tried before the court sitting without a jury.

The district court found that the plaintiffs had arranged to purchase the cumene in Brazil for $400.00 a ton and to expend $45.00 per ton for the cost

---

1. Cumene is "a colorless oily hydrocarbon . . . used as an additive for high-octane motor fuel. . . ." Webster's Third New International Dictionary 553 (1966).

of transporting the cumene to the defendant, for a total expense of $445,000.00. Koppers agreed to buy the cumene for $540,000.00. The court applied UCC 2-708(2) and determined that the plaintiffs were entitled to recover their lost profits, $95,000.00 ($540,000.00 minus $445,000.00). The district court ruled that the plaintiffs could not recover the extra $25.00 per ton they allegedly were forced to pay their Brazilian supplier when the price per ton increased because their total order with the supplier was reduced from 4,000 metric tons to 3,000 metric tons because of Koppers' breach. The court decided this lost quantity discount amounted to consequential damages and was, therefore, not recoverable.

Nobs and Calmon-Hill appeal the measure of damages applied by the district court, and, assuming it is correct, they challenge the computation of those damages. The defendant, Koppers, cross-appeals, also claiming that the district court's calculation of damages under the lost profits method was incorrect.

We first turn to the issue of whether the district court was correct in applying the lost profits measure of damages to the plaintiffs' loss.

According to UCC 2-708:

> (1) . . . the measure of damages for non-acceptance or repudiation by the buyer is the difference between the market price at the time and place for tender and the unpaid contract price together with any incidental damages provided in this Article (Section 2-710), but less expenses saved in consequence of the buyer's breach.
>
> (2) If the measure of damages provided in subsection (1) is inadequate to put the seller in as good a position as performance would have done then the measure of damages is the profit (including reasonable overhead) which the seller would have made from full performance by the buyer, together with any incidental damages provided in this Article (Section 2-710), due allowance for costs reasonably incurred and due credit for payments or proceeds of resale.

The plaintiffs urge that subsection (1) should govern in this case. Because the market value of cumene dropped to between $220.40 and $264.48 a metric ton at the time of the breach, the plaintiffs contend that they should recover the difference between the contract price ($540,000.00) and the market price (between $220,400.00 and $264,480.00), substantially more than the $95,000.00 awarded them under subsection (2). . . .

Because there does not appear to be any [Texas] law directly on point, we take the liberty of looking to those more learned on the subject of the Uniform Commercial Code. Professors White and Summers, recognizing that UCC 2-708(2) is not the most lucid or best-drafted of the sales article sections, decided that the drafters of the Uniform Commercial Code intended subsection (2) to apply to certain sellers whose losses would rarely be compensated by the subsection (1) market price-contract price measure of damages, and for these sellers the lost profit formula was added in subsection (2). One such type of seller is a "jobber," who, according to the treatise writers, must satisfy two conditions: "[f]irst, he is a seller who never acquires the contract goods. Second, his decision not to acquire those goods after learning of the breach was not commercially unreasonable. . . ." J. White & R. Summers, Uniform Commercial Code §7-10, at 228 (1972) (hereinafter cited as "White & Summers"). Nobs and Calmon-Hill clearly fit this description. The plaintiffs never acquired the goods from their Brazilian supplier, and, as White and Summers point out, an action for the purchase price or resale was therefore unavailable. See UCC 2-703, 2-704, 2-706, 2-709. See also American Metal Climax, Inc. v. Essex International, Inc., 16 UCC Rep. 101, 115 (S.D.N.Y. 1974) ("[C]ompensatory damages as provided in the contract-market formula of UCC 2-708(1) are realistic only where the seller continues to be in a position to sell the product to other customers in the market.").

The plaintiffs argue, however, that in this case the measure of damages under subsection (1) would adequately compensate them and therefore, according to the terms of subsection (1), subsection (2) does not control. This is an intriguing argument. It appears that the drafters of UCC 2-708(1) did not consider the possibility that recovery under that section may be *more than adequate*. White & Summers §7-12, at 232-233.

It is possible that the code drafters intended subsection (1) as a liquidated damage clause available to a plaintiff-seller regardless of his actual damages. There have been some commentators who agree with this philosophy. See C. Goetz & R. Scott, Measuring Sellers' Damages: The Lost-Profits Puzzle, 31 Stan. L. Rev. 323, 323-324 n.2 (1979); E. Peters, Remedies for Breach of Contracts Relating to the Sale of Goods Under the Uniform Commercial Code: A Roadmap for Article Two, 73 Yale L.J. 199, 259 (1963). But this construction is inconsistent with the code's basic philosophy, announced in UCC 1-106(1), which provides "that the aggrieved party may be put in as good a position as if the other party had fully performed" but not in a better posture. White & Summers §7-12, at 232. This philosophy is echoed in Texas case law. "The measure of damages for breach of contract is the amount necessary to place plaintiffs in a financial position equivalent to that in which it would have had [sic] if the contract had been fully performed by both parties." Little Darling Corp. v. Ald, Inc., 566 S.W.2d 347, 349 (Tex. Civ. App. 1978). Moreover, White and Summers conclude that statutory damage formulas do not significantly affect the practices of businessmen and therefore "breach deterrence," which would be the purpose of the statutory liquidated damages clause, should be rejected in favor of a standard approximating actual economic loss. White & Summers §7-12, at 232. No one insists, and we do not think they could, that the difference between the fallen market price and the contract price is necessary to compensate the plaintiffs for the breach. Had the transaction been completed, their "benefit of the bargain" would not have been affected by the fall in market price, and they would not have experienced the windfall they otherwise would receive if the market price-contract price rule contained in UCC 2-708(1) is followed. Thus, the premise contained in

UCC 2-708(1) and Texas case law is a strong factor weighing against application of UCC 2-708(1).[3]

Our conclusion that the district court was correct in applying UCC 2-
708(2) brings us to the second issue—was it error for the district court to refuse
to award the plaintiffs the additional $75,000.00, which they were required to
pay when they lost their quantity discount?

We believe the trial court was correct in declining to award the plaintiffs
the extra $75,000.00.[4] Under UCC 2-708(2), in addition to profit, the seller
may recover "incidental damages" and "due allowance for costs reasonably
incurred." The code does not provide for the recovery of consequential damages by a seller. UCC 1-106(1); Petroleo Brasileiro, S.A. v. Ameropan Oil
Corp., 372 F. Supp. 503, 508 (E.D.N.Y. 1974); cf. UCC 2-715 (buyer's remedies). "Incidental damages" are defined in UCC 2-710 as "any commercially
reasonable charges, expenses or commissions incurred in stopping delivery, in
the transportation, care and custody of goods after the buyer's breach, in
connection with return or resale of the goods or otherwise resulting from the
breach." The draftsmen's comment to the section states that the purpose is to
"authorize reimbursement of the seller for expenses reasonably incurred by
him as a result of the buyer's breach." We think it is clear that UCC 2-710 was
intended to cover only those expenses contracted by the seller after the breach
and occasioned by such things as the seller's need to care for, and, if necessary,
dispose of, the goods in a commercially reasonable manner. See Guy H. James
Construction Co. v. L. B. Foster Co., No. 17,473 (Tex. Civ. App. 1979) (cost of
replacing material in stock for resale recoverable as incidental damages);
Cesco Mfg. Corp. v. Norcross, Inc., 7 Mass. App. 837, 391 N.E.2d 270, 27
UCC Rep. 126 (Mass. App. 1979) (incidental damages awarded for storage
and moving of goods wrongfully rejected); Lee Oldsmobile v. Kaiden, 32 Md.
App. 556, 363 A.2d 270, 20 UCC Rep. 117 (1976) (commissions paid to
salesman and broker on resale, floor plan interest on cost of car between
breach of contract for sale of car and resale, and transportation expenses
recoverable as incidental damages); Harlow & Jones, Inc. v. Advance Steel
Co., [supra p. 506] (charges for storage and handling of goods after breach
recoverable as incidental damages); Neri v. Retail Marine Corp., 30 N.Y.2d
393, 334 N.Y.S.2d 165, 285 N.E.2d 311, 10 UCC Rep. 950 (1972) (proper
incidental damages include storage, upkeep, finance charges and insurance for
boat after buyer breached contract for sale); Bache & Co. v. International
Controls Corp., 339 F. Supp. 341, aff'd, 469 F.2d 696 (2d Cir. 1972) (seller can

---

3. White and Summers condition forcing the damage formula of subsection (2) on the plaintiff-seller. They would require the defendant to prove that the measure of damages in subsection
(1) would overcompensate the plaintiff. We do not find this to be a problem here, as the figures
themselves refute any contention that the market price-contract price rule is anything but overad-
equate compensation for the plaintiffs. White & Summers §7-12, at 232-233.

4. Because we find that these expenses were not recoverable under UCC 2-708(2), it is
unnecessary to decide whether the district court correctly termed these costs "consequential damages."

recover as incidental damages commissions due him as result of buyer's breach); Hudgens v. Bain Equip. & Tube Sales, Inc., 459 S.W.2d 873 (Tex. Civ. App. 1970) (expense of recovering and transporting goods not paid for awarded); cf. Industrial Circuits Co. v. Terminal Communications, Inc., 26 N.C. App. 536, 216 S.E.2d 919, 17 UCC Rep. 996 (1975) ("bill back" charges which resulted when buyer failed to order a certain quantity not allowed).

Equally as clear is the premise that this lost discount is not a "cost reasonably incurred" within the meaning of UCC 2-708(2) which has been defined as "an amount equal to what he [the seller] has expended for performance of the contract that will now be valueless." White & Summers §7-13, at 236. The extra $25.00 per ton does not fall within this definition, most obviously because it was not an expense necessary to the performance of the contract. Rather, it was simply an extra benefit the sellers did not receive from their supplier by reason of the buyer's breach.

Finally, on cross-appeal, Koppers first maintains that the district court failed to include in the damage formula the commission Calmon-Hill would have been required to pay Nobs had there been no breach. This sum, $16,200.00, claims Koppers, should have been added into the costs which would have been incurred by Calmon-Hill in performing the contract. Plugging the commission into the lost profits formula would reduce the damage award, because lost profits are computed by subtracting the cost of performance to the seller from the contract price.

Koppers' argument assumes that Nobs is not seeking its commission from Calmon-Hill because of the breach. That has not been shown. In fact, it appears that Nobs now expects a much larger percentage of the damage award than the 3% commission originally agreed upon. See Trial Transcript, at 12, 47. . . .

Affirmed.

NOTES & QUESTIONS

1. *Cumulation of Remedies.* Comment 1 to UCC 2-703 states in part: "This Article rejects any doctrine of election of remedy as a fundamental policy and thus the remedies are essentially cumulative in nature and include all of the available remedies for breach. Whether the pursuit of one remedy bars another depends entirely on the facts of the individual case." Is this comment relevant to the *Nobs* court's consideration of which subsection of UCC 2-708 should apply? What if the sellers had taken delivery of the 1,000 tons of cumene from their Brazilian supplier and had sold it, after proper notice to Koppers, for $250 per ton? Could the sellers insist on recovery under UCC 2-706? Would taking delivery of the 1,000 tons be contrary to the policy of UCC 2-704 or of a general obligation to mitigate, applicable by virtue of UCC 1-103?

2. *UCC 2-708(1) as a statutory liquidated damage provision.* It has been suggested that the UCC 2-708(1) formula can be justified only as a statutory liquidated damage provision because the contract price-market price so rarely will compensate the seller. Peters, Remedies for Breach of Contracts Relating to the Sale of Goods Under the Uniform Commercial Code: A Roadmap for Article Two, 73 Yale L.J. 199, 259 (1963). If so, then should the sellers in the *Nobs* case be allowed to recover under UCC 2-708(1) even if it yields a larger recovery than under UCC 2-708(2)?

3. *Recovery of quantity discount.* Are any of the following theories for recovery of the $75,000 quantity discount persuasive? Would allowing recovery be consistent with UCC 1-106?

(a) Sellers should recover this sum as consequential damages, which may be recovered under general contract principles, applicable by virtue of UCC 1-103, or by reading the terms *profits* or *costs* in UCC 2-708(2) to include consequential damages.

(b) Under UCC 2-708(2) the profit should be calculated on the basis of the marginal cost of the 1,000 tons rather than on the average cost per ton for the whole order placed with the Brazilian supplier.

(c) The UCC 2-708(1) formula should be used but adjusted to show the loss averted as "expenses saved." In other words, if the sellers had to purchase the 1,000 tons they would have sustained a loss when they resold the cumene on the depressed market.

Problem 12-6. Microbyte accepts an order from Western Peripherals for 100 of its TX-100 dual disk drives. The contract price is $1,600 each, a price which is competitive for similar equipment when the parties enter into the contract in January. The contract calls for delivery of 20 units per month commencing in July. When deciding to accept the order Microbyte calculates that its costs per unit will be $1,000 in variable costs and $600 of overhead, with no net profit margin.

Western Peripherals repudiates the contract in May, at which time the market price for similar equipment has fallen to $1,050 per unit. At the time of repudiation, Microbyte has already incurred $12,000 in variable costs for the first 20 units and $2,000 for the second 20 units. If the partially finished units were sold as scrap there would be a return of $5,000.

(a) Microbyte calls you immediately after Western Peripheral's repudiation. Its president asks you what remedial options are available. Advise Microbyte. See UCC 2-703, 2-704, 2-706, 2-708, 2-709.

(b) In July IBM announces a previously-feared across-the-board cut in prices of its microcomputers and accessories, and the price of equipment similar to the Microbyte disk drives moves sharply downward, reaching $900 per unit in September. Microbyte asks your advice on possible remedies in July, August, and September. What would you advise at each point in time?

TERADYNE, INC. v. TELEDYNE INDUSTRIES, INC.
676 F.2d 865, 33 UCC Rep. 1669 (1st Cir. 1982)

WYZANSKI, Senior District Judge. In this diversity action, Teradyne, Inc. sued Teledyne Industries, Inc. and its subsidiary for damages pursuant to UCC 2-708(2). Teledyne does not dispute the facts that it is bound as a buyer under a sales contract with Teradyne, that it broke the contract, and that Teradyne's right to damages is governed by UCC 2-708(2). The principal dispute concerns the calculation of damages.

The district court referred the case to a master whose report the district court approved and made the basis of the judgment here on appeal.

The following facts, derived from the master's report, are undisputed.

On July 30, 1976 Teradyne, Inc. ["the seller"], a Massachusetts corporation, entered into a Quantity Purchase Contract ["the contract"] which, though made with a subsidiary, binds Teledyne Industries, Inc., a California corporation ["the buyer"]. That contract governed an earlier contract resulting from the seller's acceptance of the buyer's July 23, 1976 purchase order to buy at the list price of $98,400 (which was also its fair market value) a T-347A transistor test system ["the T-347A"]. One consequence of such governance was that the buyer was entitled to a $984 discount from the $98,400 price.

The buyer canceled its order for the T-347A when it was packed ready for shipment scheduled to occur two days later. The seller refused to accept the cancellation.

The buyer offered to purchase instead of the T-347A a $65,000 Field Effects Transistor System ["the FET"] which would also have been governed by "the contract." The seller refused the offer.

After dismantling, testing, and reassembling at an estimated cost of $614 the T-347A, the seller, pursuant to an order that was on hand prior to the cancellation, sold it for $98,400 to another purchaser [hereafter "resale purchaser"].

Teradyne would have made the sale to the resale purchaser even if Teledyne had not broken its contract. Thus if there had been no breach, Teradyne would have made two sales and earned two profits rather than one.

The seller was a volume seller of the equipment covered by the July 23, 1976 purchase order. The equipment represented standard products of the seller and the seller had the means and capacity to duplicate the equipment for a second sale had the buyer honored its purchase order.

Teradyne being of the view that the measure of damages under UCC 2-708(2) was the contract price less ascertainable costs saved as a result of the breach . . . offered as evidence of its cost prices its Inventory Standards Catalog ["The Catalog"]—a document which was prepared for tax purposes not claimed to have been illegitimate, but which admittedly disclosed "low inventory valuations." Relying on that Catalog, Teradyne's Controller, McCabe, testified that the *only* costs which the seller saved as a result of the breach were:

direct labor costs associated with production	$ 3,301
material charges	17,045
sales commission on one T-347A	492
expense	1,800
Total	$22,638

McCabe admitted that he had not included as costs saved the labor costs of employees associated with testing, shipping, installing, servicing, or fulfilling 10-year warranties on the T-347A (although he acknowledged that in forms of accounting for purposes other than damage suits the costs of those employees would not be regarded as "overhead"). His reason was that those costs would not have been affected by the production of one machine more or less. McCabe also admitted that he had not included fringe benefits which amounted to 12% in the case of both included and excluded labor costs.

During McCabe's direct examination, he referred to the 10-K report which Teradyne had filed with the SEC. On cross-examination McCabe admitted that the 10-K form showed that on average the seller's revenues were distributed as follows:

profit	9%
"selling and administrative" expense	26%
interest	1%
"cost of sales and engineering" (including substantial research and developmental costs incidental to a high technology business)	64%

He also admitted that the average figures applied to the T-347A.

Teledyne contended that the 10-K report was a better index of lost profits than was the Catalog. The master disagreed and concluded that the more appropriate formula for calculating Teradyne's damages under UCC 2-708(2) was . . . " 'gross profit' including fixed costs but not costs saved as a result of the breach." He then stated: "In accordance with the statutory mandate that the remedy 'be liberally administered to the end that the aggrieved party may be put in as good a position as if the other party had fully performed,' [UCC 1-106], I find that the Plaintiff has met its burden of proof of damages, and has established the accuracy of its direct costs and the ascertainability of its variable costs with reasonable certainty and 'whatever definiteness and accuracy the facts permit.' Comment 1 to [UCC 1-106]." In effect, this was a finding that Teradyne had saved only $22,638 as a result of the breach. Subtracting that amount and also the $984 quantity discount from the original contract price of $98,400, the master found that the lost "profit (including reasonable overhead)" was $74,778. To that amount the master added $614 for "incidental damages" which Teradyne incurred in preparing the T-347A for its new customer. Thus he found that Teradyne's total UCC 2-708(2) damages amounted to $75,392.

The master declined to make a deduction from the $75,392 on account of the refusal of the seller to accept the buyer's offer to purchase an FET tester in partial substitution for the repudiated T-347A. . . .

1. The parties are agreed that UCC 2-708(2) applies to the case at bar. Inasmuch as this conclusion is not plain from the text, we explain the reasons why we concur in that agreement.

UCC 2-708(2) applies only if the damages provided by UCC 2-708(1) are inadequate to put the seller in as good a position as performance would have done. Under UCC 2-708(1) the measure of damages is the difference between unpaid contract price and market price. Here the unpaid contract price was $97,416 and the market price was $98,400. Hence no damages would be recoverable under UCC 2-708(1). On the other hand, if the buyer had performed, the seller (1) would have had the proceeds of two contracts, one with the buyer Teledyne and the other with the "resale purchaser" and (2) *it seems* would have had in 1976-77 one more T-347A sale.

A literal reading of the last sentence of UCC 2-708(2)—providing for "due credit for payments or proceeds of resale"—would indicate that Teradyne recovers nothing because the proceeds of the resale exceeded the price set in the Teledyne-Teradyne contract. However, in light of the statutory history of the subsection, it is universally agreed that in a case where after the buyer's default a seller resells the goods, the proceeds of the resale are not to be credited to the buyer if the seller is a lost volume seller[2]—that is, one who had there been no breach by the buyer, could and would have had the benefit of both the contracts.[3]

Thus, despite the resale of the T-347A, Teradyne is entitled to recover from Teledyne what UCC 2-708(2) calls its expected "profit (including reasonable overhead)" on the broken contract.[4]

---

2. The term "lost volume seller" was apparently coined by Professor Robert J. Harris in his article A Radical Restatement of the Law of Seller's Damages: Sales Act and Commercial Code Results Compared, 18 Stan. L. Rev. 66 (1965). The terminology has been widely adopted. . . . See Restatement (Second) Contracts §347 Comment f; J. White and R. Summers, Uniform Commercial Code, (2d ed. 1980) [hereafter "White and Summers"] §7-9, particularly at 276 first full paragraph.

3. . . . See White and Summers §7-13, particularly 284-285.

4. . . . White and Summers at 284-285 give the following suppositious case which parallels the instant case. Boeing is able to make and sell in one year 100 airplanes. TWA contracts to buy the third plane off the assembly line, but it breaks the contract and Boeing resells the plane to Pan Am which had already agreed to buy the fourth plane. Because of the breach Boeing sells only 99 aircraft during the year. White and Summers say that the right result, despite the words of UCC 2-708(2), is that Boeing recovers from TWA both the net profit and the overhead components of the TWA contract price, no credit being given for any part of the proceeds Boeing received from its sale to Pan Am.

We do not agree with the third sentence in the following Comment f to Restatement (Second) Contract §347 insofar as it indicates that a volume seller like Teradyne may recover from a defaulting buyer only the lost net profit on the original contract.

f. *Lost volume.* Whether a subsequent transaction is a substitute for the broken contract sometimes raises difficult questions of fact. If the injured party could and would have entered into the subsequent contract, even if the contract had not been broken, and could have had the benefit of

2. Teledyne not only "does not dispute that damages are to be calculated pursuant to UCC 2-708(2)" but concedes that the formula used in Jericho Sash & Door Co. v. Building Erectors, Inc., 362 Mass. 871, 286 N.E.2d 343 (1972), for determining lost profit including overhead—that is, the formula under which direct costs of producing and selling manufactured goods are deducted from the contract price in order to arrive at "profit (including reasonable overhead)" as that term is used in UCC 2-708(2)—"is permissible provided all variable expenses are identified."[5]

---

both, he can be said to have 'lost volume' and the subsequent transaction is not a substitute for the broken contract. The injured party's damages are then based on the net profit that he has lost as a result of the broken contract. Since entrepreneurs try to operate at optimum capacity, however, it is possible that an additional transaction would not have been profitable and that the injured party would not have chosen to expand his business by undertaking it had there been no breach. It is sometimes assumed that he would have done so, but the question is one of fact to be resolved according to the circumstances of each case. See illustration 16. See also Uniform Commercial Code §2-708(2)." [Emphasis added.]

Limiting the volume seller's recovery to lost net profit does not permit the recovery of reasonable overhead for which provision is specifically made in the text of UCC 2-708(2). The reason for the allowance of overhead is set forth in Vitex Mfg. Corp. v. Caribtex Corp., 377 F.2d 795, 799 (3rd Cir. 1967) [hereafter "Vitex"]: ". . . as the number of transaction[s] over which overhead can be spread becomes smaller, each transaction must bear a greater portion or allocate share of the fixed overhead cost. Suppose a company has fixed overhead of $10,000 and engages in five similar transactions; then the receipts of each transaction would bear $2000 of overhead expense. If the company is now forced to spread this $10,000 over only four transactions, then the overhead expense per transaction will rise to $2500, significantly reducing the profitability of the four remaining transactions. Thus, where the contract is between businessmen familiar with commercial practices, as here, the breaching party should reasonably foresee that his breach will not only cause a loss of 'clear' profit, but also a loss in that the profitability of other transactions will be reduced. . . ." Vitex represents the law of Massachusetts. . . .

5. We concur in the view that Massachusetts law determines whether a particular formula for calculating damages under a Massachusetts statute is permissible. Salemme v. Ristaino, 587 F.2d 81, 87 (1st Cir. 1978). But we are not certain that the Jericho court purported to declare that in every UCC 2-708(2) case the use of the formula would be permissible.

An examination of the original record in Jericho shows that the seller offered evidence of the contract price and of virtually all the expenses that were saved by him as a result of the breach, but he did not offer evidence showing separate figures for profit and for overhead. The trier of fact allowed as damages the contract price less the direct costs because "as a general principle, it may be stated that the loss will be measured by the contract price less those costs and expenses directly attributable to the performance of the contract." On appeal, the Massachusetts Supreme Judicial Court stated that "The sole question presented is whether the trial judge erred in allowing damages for 'profit (including reasonable overhead),' under [UCC 2-708(2)], in the absence of evidence showing separate figures for profit and for overhead." Inspection of the briefs reveals that that statement is not accurate. Other questions were presented. But the parties nowhere raised the issue whether the method—contract price less direct costs—which was proper as a general principle would be proper where the seller had expenses which were not direct costs (say, for example, a rental charge, or an executive officer's salary, or research expenses) which either were in excess of a reasonable amount or were not properly regarded as overhead reasonably related to the goods covered by the contract.

In light of the concession made in Teledyne's brief, we need not determine whether in a case where reasonableness of overhead was an issue the Massachusetts courts would distinguish Jericho, or would declare that if part or all of a particular item is not recoverable as "reasonable overhead" it is nonetheless recoverable as part of "the profit . . . which the seller would have made from full performance," or would permit the use of the formula and leave it to the trier of fact to decide whether the results which flowed from its application were credible.

What Teledyne contends is that all variable costs were not identified because the cost figures came from a catalog, prepared for tax purposes, which did not fully reflect all direct costs. The master found that the statement of costs based on the catalog was reliable and that Teledyne's method of calculating costs based on the 10-K statements was not more accurate. Those findings are not clearly erroneous and therefore we may not reverse the judgment on the ground that allegedly the items of cost which were deducted are unrealiable. Fed. R. Civ. P. 52(a). . . .

Teledyne's more significant objection to Teradyne's and the master's application of the *Jericho* formula in the case at bar is that neither of them made deductions on account of the wages paid to testers, shippers, installers, and other Teradyne employees who directly handled the T-347A, or on account of the fringe benefits amounting in the case of those and other employees to 12 per cent of wages. Teradyne gave as the reason for the omission of the wages of the testers, etc. that those wages would not have been affected if each of the testers, etc. handled one product more or less. However, the work of those employees entered as directly into producing and supplying the T-347A as did the work of a fabricator of a T-347A. Surely no one would regard as "reasonable overhead" within UCC 2-708(2) the wages of a fabricator of a T-347A even if his wages were the same whether he made one product more or less. We conclude that the wages of the testers, etc. likewise are not part of overhead and as a "direct cost" should have been deducted from the contract price. *A fortiori* fringe benefits amounting to 12 per cent of wages should also have been deducted as direct costs. Taken together we cannot view these omitted items as what *Jericho* called "relatively insignificant items." We, therefore, must vacate the district court's judgment. . . . [W]e remand this case so that with respect to the omitted direct labor costs specified above the parties may offer further evidence and the court may make findings "with whatever definiteness and accuracy the facts permit, but no more." *Jericho*, p. 872, 286 N.E.2d 343. . . .

3. Teledyne contends that Teradyne was required to mitigate damages by acceptance of Teledyne's offer to purchase instead of the T-347A the FET system. . . . That point is without merit.

The meaning of Teledyne's offer was that if Teradyne would forego its profit-loss claim arising out of Teledyne's breach of the T-347A contract, Teledyne would purchase another type of machine which it was under no obligation to buy. The seller's failure to accept such an offer does not preclude it from recovering the full damages to which it would otherwise be entitled. As Restatement (Second) Contracts, §350 Comment c indicates, there is no right to so-called mitigation of damages where the offer of a substitute contract "is conditioned on surrender by the injured party of his claim for breach." "One is not required to mitigate his losses by accepting an arrangement with the repudiator if that is made conditional on his surrender of his rights under the repudiated contract." 5 Corbin, Contracts 2nd (1964) §1043 at 274. . . .

Teradyne acted in a commercially reasonable manner in refusing to accept Teledyne's offer. . . .

[Judgment vacated and case remanded.]

NOTES & QUESTIONS

1. *"Profit (including reasonable overhead)."* Would it have been easier for the seller to prove its damages in *Teradyne* if the formula "contract price minus variable costs" was substituted for "profit (including reasonable overhead)" found in UCC 2-708(2)? Would the substitute formula lead to the same result?

2. *"Proceeds of resale."* The court in *Teradyne* suggests that the "proceeds of resale" clause in UCC 2-708(2) should be ignored when a lost-volume seller is involved. Not all authors agree. See Schlosser, Construing Section 2-708(2) to Apply to the Lost-Volume Seller, 24 Case W. Res. L. Rev. 686 (1973) (reads "profit" to include both the profit on the lost sale and on the resale; "proceeds of resale" would then reduce this amount only by the return on one sale).

Problem 12-7.[1]   Duffer contracts to buy from Boatyard a new boat of a specified model for the price of $12,587.40. Given the choice of making a deposit of $40 with delivery in six weeks or making a deposit of $4,250 with delivery from the manufacturer within one week, Duffer makes the larger deposit. Several days later Duffer has an emergency operation and his lawyer writes a letter to Boatyard to cancel the order. Before Boatyard receives this letter the boat is delivered by the manufacturer. Duffer now demands the return of his deposit. Boatyard asks your advice on what it should do. It informs you that four months after it received delivery it sold the boat to another buyer for the same price as that negotiated with Duffer; that while the boat remained unsold Boatyard had expenses of $674 for storage, upkeep, finance charges, and insurance; that it expected a profit of $2,579 on the sale to Duffer; and that it has agreed to pay you $1,250 in attorneys fees if the matter should go to trial. What do you advise? See UCC 2-708(2).

GOETZ & SCOTT, MEASURING SELLERS' DAMAGES: THE LOST-PROFITS PUZZLE
31 Stan. L. Rev. 323, 330-331, 346-349 (1979)

Sellers frequently advance lost-profit claims even though there exists an available market for the contract goods. These sellers claim that they have lost sales and can only be made whole by recovering the expected profits on the

1. This problem is based on the frequently-cited case of Neri v. Retail Marine Corp., 30 N.Y.2d 393, 285 N.E.2d 311, 334 N.Y.S.2d 165, 10 UCC Rep. 950 (1972). For particularly careful analysis of the case from an economic perspective, see Goetz & Scott, Measuring Sellers' Damages: The Lost-Profits Puzzle, 31 Stan. L. Rev. 323, 331-346 (1979); Goldberg, An Economic Analysis of the Lost-Volume Retail Seller, 57 So. Cal. L. Rev. 283 (1984).

breached contract. Any breach leaving a manufacturer with unfilled productive capacity or a retail seller with standard-priced goods is generally believed to result in a lost sale.

Common law courts were generally skeptical about the validity of these lost-volume claims. If the contract goods were on hand at the time for performance, the majority of courts limited the seller to market damages, reasoning that any resale adequately replaced the breached contract.

Considering the resistance of pre-Code courts, what explains the paradigmatic lost-volume claim where excess capacity or supply triggers the presumption that an entire profit was lost by the breach? Disputes involving retailers of standard-priced goods exposed an apparent anomaly: Only nominal damages are awarded when market price is equivalent to contract price. The resulting inference of undercompensation was reinforced by the gratuitous assumption that "volume sellers" have virtually unlimited profitable production capacity. . . .

Obviously, the seller's capacity to supply the breached units in addition to its actual output is a *necessary* condition for a lost-volume claim. The lost-volume presumption mistakenly assumes that excess productive capacity is also a *sufficient* condition for such an award. But the relevant issue is not whether the post-breach firm had the physical capacity to produce the breached units in addition to its actual volume, but whether it would have been profitable to do so. The validity of a lost-volume claim depends entirely on *the effect of the breach* on the seller's ability to sell to other buyers profitably. If sales to other buyers are unaffected by breach, a lost-volume claim is justified because profitable volume then declines by the full amount of the breach. Conversely, the seller loses no volume if the breach alters its costs and demand conditions so that supplying other buyers becomes newly profitable.

The replacement model demonstrates that the buyer's breach increases the profitable volume of additional sales. In other words, a seller will not have the capacity to *profitably* supply all of the breached quantity in addition to its existing sales. In fact, performance by the buyer would make some existing sales unprofitable. When a seller operates in a competitive market, it will always have more available buyers than it can profitably supply; therefore, additional sales will always make up for any breached volume. The competitive seller will always sell the same number of goods, regardless of breach. A seller with market power has a limited number of buyers willing to purchase at its profit-maximizing price. Although this seller could conceivably lower its price and discover new buyers, price cutting reduces revenues and effectively restrains the seller from capturing additional buyers at lower prices. Indeed, such a seller has "lost" a sale. Nevertheless, the seller has not lost the entire profit which that sale would have earned. By refusing the goods, the defaulting buyer no longer can resell them and thus diminish the seller's pool of potential buyers. The breach, by removing the risk that the seller may lose one of its limited noncontractual buyers, permits some expansion in the seller's market for additional sales.

Additionally, whenever the seller's production costs increase with additional sales, the buyer's breach also enables the seller to save costs on future noncontractual sales. Reduced marginal costs for other units of production lead to a further expansion in profitable output. But marginal costs for many sellers may be constant over wide ranges in output; thus the cost effect of a given breach is always an empirical question. Examining cost and demand conditions demonstrates that awarding sellers complete lost-volume profit recoveries is likely to overcompensate them. In order to mirror true losses, the new profits made possible by replacement must always offset the seller's lost-profit claims. . . .

Information about the extent of replacement is necessary for precise damage measurement. Accurately measuring those profits recaptured by a given breach requires information concerning the presence of other sellers in the market, the extent of the resale risk, and the nature of the seller's cost and market conditions. Obtaining much of this information is extremely costly. Indeed, a crucial element in the calculus—the resale risk and its probable impact on the seller's market—may be totally inaccessible.

Although information costs prohibit accurate measurement of true losses, the preceding analysis suggests that the common law presumption of total replacement is not demonstrably less accurate in assessing damages than the lost-volume presumption of no replacement for the "lost" sale. Absent empirical data, assumptions about typical cost and demand conditions necessarily limit judgments. It is initially tempting to urge that neither the lost-volume nor common law presumption is a useful rule for decision in view of their likely inaccuracy in any specific circumstances. Nevertheless, the extraordinarily high direct costs of proving true losses, and the uncertainty that error spawns, argue strongly for a legal presumption that guides results in the absence of rebutting evidence.

Examining the lost-volume litigation provides some basis for proposing a decision rule that will minimize enforcement costs. Cases raising lost-volume claims fall into three broad categories based on the markets in which the breach occurred. The first two categories—sales in commercial and commodities markets—raise strong factual parallels with the market-power and competitive models. Our analysis suggests that a presumption of replacement in cases arising under these market conditions will minimize enforcement costs. In the third category—the retail automobile market—factual circumstances make it difficult to construct efficient damage rules.

Problem 12-8. Datapoint contracts for the sale of 1,000 electronic cash registers to Amalgamated Retailers at a price of $1,000 per unit. Amalgamated is to take delivery at the rate of 100 units per month over the next ten months. During the course of negotiations Datapoint's president emphasizes that the company relies upon borrowed working capital and that it is essential for Datapoint's cash flow that payment be within ten days of delivery. In fact, ten-day payment terms are incorporated into the final contract.

Amalgamated takes delivery of only 500 units and then repudiates the contract and also fails to make timely payment for the accepted units. Datapoint brings an action to recover the unpaid purchase price of the accepted units, damages on the undelivered goods, and a claim for "interest expenses for borrowed funds," which it states to be the added borrowing cost incurred due to the lack of cash flow that had been projected from the buyer's timely payment. May Datapoint recover these interest expenses as incidental damages under UCC 2-710? May Datapoint recover these expenses as consequential damages? Do any of the other sections on seller's remedies allow for a recovery?

D. STIPULATED REMEDY TERMS

The common law distinguishes between enforceable liquidated damage clauses and unenforceable penalty clauses. Although the Uniform Sales Act was silent on the subject, the Uniform Commercial Code codifies the distinction. UCC 2-718(1) states:

> Damages for breach by either party may be liquidated in the agreement but only at an amount which is reasonable in the light of the anticipated or actual harm caused by the breach, the difficulties of proof of loss, and the inconvenience or nonfeasibility of otherwise obtaining an adequate remedy. A term fixing unreasonably large liquidated damages is void as a penalty.

Restatement (Second) of Contracts §356 sets out the common law rule in language that has been harmonized with the Code.

Both sellers and buyers may wish to stipulate in their contracts the remedies available when the other parties breach. Whether to enforce these stipulations brings into conflict two Code principles: freedom of contract (UCC 1-102(3)) and just compensation (UCC 1-106).

GOETZ & SCOTT, LIQUIDATED DAMAGES, PENALTIES AND THE JUST COMPENSATION PRINCIPLE: SOME NOTES ON AN ENFORCEMENT MODEL AND A THEORY OF EFFICIENT BREACH
77 Colum. L. Rev. 554, 554-555, 558-562, 593-594 (1977)

For more than five centuries, strict judicial scrutiny has been applied to contractual provisions which specify an agreed amount of damages upon breach of a base obligation. Although the standards determining the enforceability of liquidated damage clauses have developed novel and labyrinthine permutations, their motivating principle has remained essentially immutable. For an executory agreement fixing damages in case of breach to be enforceable, it must constitute a reasonable forecast of the provable injury resulting from breach; otherwise, the clause will be unenforceable as a penalty and the non-breaching party will be limited to conventional damage measures.

The historical genesis of this principle sheds some light on its original rationale. Relief against penalties was one of the earliest exercises of equitable interference, having developed during the fifteenth century when the common law had no adequate machinery for trying cases of fraud. At a time when legal rules permitted double recovery through the sealed penalty bond, as well as other recovery grounded in fraud, a presumption by the early equity courts that liquidated damage provisions carried an unusual danger of oppression and extortion would have seemed well justified. In addition, the promisor faced information barriers greatly increasing the risk of overestimating his ability to perform. Consequently, the equity courts apparently refused enforcement when either actual or presumptive evidence of unfairness indicated that recovery would result in an "unjust, extravagant or unconscionable quantum of damages in case of a breach."

The common law courts soon usurped and subtly altered the developing penalty rule, invalidating the agreed remedy in any case where it specified a significantly larger amount than conventional damage recovery. Applying the principle of "just compensation for the loss or injury actually sustained" to liquidated damage provisions, courts have subsequently refused enforcement where the clause agreed upon is held to be *in terrorem*—a sum fixed as a deterrent to breach or as security for full performance by the promisor, not as a realistic assessment of the provable damage. Thus, attempts to secure performance through *in terrorem* clauses are currently declared unenforceable even where the evidence shows a voluntary, fairly bargained exchange. . . .

The modern law of contract damages is based on the premise that a contractual obligation is not necessarily an obligation to perform, but rather an obligation to choose between performance and compensatory damages. Once a contemplated exchange has been negotiated, the breaching party is merely required to provide "just compensation" equal to the value of performance. The implications of this rule can be usefully illustrated through the principles of economic analysis. Generally, breach will occur where the breaching party anticipates that paying compensation and allocating his resources to alternative uses will make him "better off" than performing his obligation. As long as the compensation adequately mirrors the value of performance, this damage rule is "efficient." It induces a result superior to performance, since one party receives the same benefits as performance while the other is able to do even better. Under the current damage rule, all of these net gains from breaching are retained by the breacher—the non-breacher is in the same position as if there had been performance. In order to maintain the efficiency value of the rule, however, it is only necessary that some minimal amount of benefits are retained by the breacher in order to induce him not to perform. The allocation of the gains from breach is, therefore, largely a question of wealth transfer between the contracting parties.

Facing this conventional damage measure, contracting parties have incentives to negotiate liquidated damages clauses whenever the costs of negotiating are less than the expected costs resulting from reliance on the standard damage rule for breach. There are two primary factors which might induce the decision to negotiate:

> (1) The expected damages are readily calculable, but the parties determine that advance stipulation will save litigation or settlement costs;
> (2) The expected damages are uncertain or difficult to establish and the parties wish to allocate anticipated risks.

Of course, these factors may be present singly or in combination.

Pre-breach agreements will not be legally enforceable, however, unless two requirements coincide. First, the agreement must be a reasonable forecast of just compensation for the anticipated harm that would be caused by the breach. Second, the possible damages which might result from the breach must be uncertain and difficult to estimate. However, liquidated damages provisions have seldom been voided solely because the damages were easy to estimate. Instead, courts have considered the degree of uncertainty an influential factor in determining the reasonableness of the estimate. If the conditions inducing damage agreements are viewed on a continuum, the application of the penalty rule becomes clearer: as the uncertainty facing the contracting parties increases, so does their latitude in stipulating post-breach damages.

The threat of subsequent review clearly increases the costs of negotiating a damages clause relative to relying on the standard damages rule. Are these costs accompanied by counterbalancing advantages? The traditional justification for post-breach inquiry is prevention of "unjust" punishment to the breacher, i.e. compensation exceeding the harm actually caused. This justification has been expressed in two distinct forms. One basis for invalidation is the presumption of unfairness: liquidated damage provisions are unreasonable—a penalty—whenever the stipulated sum is so disproportionate to provable damages as to require the inference that the agreement must have been effected by fraud, oppression, or mistake. The other major basis for invalidating agreed remedies is that, since the courts set damages based upon the principle of just compensation, parties should not be allowed to recover more than just compensation from the courts through a privately concocted alternative arrangement, even one fairly negotiated.

The common theme of these decisions is that a disproportion between the stipulated and the anticipated damage justifies an inference of overcompensation. In turn, overcompensation implies either bargaining unfairness or an objectionable *in terrorem* agreement to secure performance. This line of reasoning suggests two benefits which may be expected from the current rule invalidating penalties. First, the cost of identifying unfairness may be reduced by a standard rule-of-thumb based on disproportion. Second, an enforceable *in terrorem* clause might discourage promisors from breaching and reallocating resources where changed circumstances would ordinarily create efficiency gains from this behavior. Inducing performance under these conditions is a misallocation which prevents the net social gain that would result from nonperformance.

As the efficient damages model formalized below will demonstrate, however, this analysis incorrectly assumes that, rather than negotiating out of the penalty, the promisor who is subject to an *in terrorem* clause will inevitably undertake an inefficient performance. In addition, there is no basis for the apparent assumption that the premium placed by the promisee on performance is valueless. Indeed, the market paradigm on which the compensation standard is based requires a contrary presumption; a promisee has a recognizable utility in certain *in terrorem* provisions and this utility is frequently reflected in willingness to pay a price for such clauses. . . .

The historical background of the penalty rule discloses initial judicial interference to protect against fraud and duress in a legal context where alternative, less costly, protections were not available. Subsequently invalidation was grounded on a presumption of unfairness based on indications that information barriers prevented rational assessment of the nature and extent of the risk allocations produced by the agreement. The costs of identifying unfairness in individual cases generated pressure for a rule invalidating these clauses on more precise criteria. Applying the compensation limitation to liquidated damages appeared to satisfy these wants and consequently received wide acceptance. Since the roots of the penalty rule were nourished on fairness concerns, it is not surprising that generations of lawyers have clung to the view that penalties are "bad." This notion does not withstand rigorous, dispassionate analysis. The current penalty rule does not promote end results which are any "fairer" than an enforcement rule. The behavior which requires regulation is unfairness in bargaining. The penalty rule, however, fails to mirror accurately the proscribed behavior. Consequently, the penalty rule is used as a second level control together with standard restrictions on process unfairness.

Challenging the penalty rule demonstrates that it has numerous costly effects. First, the rule denies true compensation to the promisee with non-provable idiosyncratic wants, inducing him either to protect those wants with inefficient third party insurance or to suffer exposure to inefficient breaches. Secondly, assuming that cases of non-compensable idiosyncratic value are rare, the rule produces a more significant cost by inducing review of the entire continuum of cases where liquidated damages provisions are intended to reimburse true losses which are to any extent uncertain.

The modern development of unconscionability as a unifying fairness principle presents a less costly alternative to the sweeping invalidation powers exercised under the penalty rule. With our present enhanced access to information and consequential greater accuracy in individual risk evaluation, an enforcement model which facilitates the recovery of difficult-to-prove values would appear to maximize the allocative efficiency of the contracting process.

In sum, contemporary cost-benefit analysis suggests that the traditional penalty rule is anachronistic for several reasons: (1) the efficiency costs of the rule are now apparent in the light of modern analysis; (2) the market imperfections once addressed by the rule have become empirically less important; and (3) more selective legal doctrines, such as unconscionability, have developed as remedies for those market imperfections which retain practical importance.

NOTES & QUESTIONS

1. *Alternative analysis.* Compare the Goetz-Scott analysis with the analysis of Clarkson, Miller & Muris, Liquidated Damages v. Penalties: Sense or Nonsense?, 1978 Wis. L. Rev. 351. The authors of this latter article argue that the concept of economic efficiency provides a rational basis for distinguishing between liquidated damages and penalties, and that the outcomes of court decisions follow this distinction and are therefore efficient. The authors propose the following formula for the distinction: "(1) if neither party has an opportunity or incentive covertly to induce the other party to breach, stipulated damage clauses should be freely enforced; and (2) if either party does have opportunity and might have incentive, the clauses should be enforced only if they are reasonable in relation to the damages sustained." Id. at 352.

2. *Functional equivalents of stipulated remedy term.* Are any of the following devices the functional equivalent of a liquidated damage clause?

(a) The grant of a security interest to secure performance by the other party? (See Chapter 3 on secured transactions.)

(b) A letter of credit that can be drawn on if the other party fails to perform? (See Chapter 18 on letters of credit.)

(c) A deposit of money with the other party to be returned upon performance or applied to the purchase price? See UCC 2-718(2), (3).

(d) An adjustment to the price to reflect the possibility that the other party will not perform? See Note 3 infra.

3. *Price terms and liquidated damage clauses.* When agreeing upon a price does a contract party take into consideration the possibility that the other party will not perform? Does a seller, for example, include in his asking price a sum that reflects the probability (e.g., 1 in 1,000) that the buyer will not pay for the goods contracted for (e.g., $0 rather than $1,000)? A buyer may think, however, that he has more accurate information about the probability that he will not perform and be willing to agree on a stipulated damage clause in return for a lower price. Will the parties be indifferent as between the two contract terms?

4. *Contract clauses stipulating specific performance.* Should a buyer be permitted to enforce a contract term that purports to give him the right to obtain an order of specific performance against the seller? If so, why shouldn't the seller be permitted to enforce an analogous clause requiring the buyer to accept and pay for the goods, at least where the tendered goods are conforming?

Problem 12-9. Lumber Company agrees to supply building materials to Builder. The typewritten contract includes the following term immediately above the parties' signatures: "If the Buyer breaches this contract and the enforcement thereof is turned over to an attorney, the Buyer agrees to pay, in addition to all of Seller's expenses, a reasonable counsel fee, which is hereby agreed to be thirty percent (30%) of any moneys to be collected." Builder accepts delivery of the materials but refuses to pay for them. Lumber Company brings an action to recover the contract price for the accepted goods ($8,000) and attorney's fees ($2,400). Builder admits liability for the price but disputes the attorney's fees. Builder argues that the contract provision on attorney's fees should not be enforced because (a) it is a penalty under UCC 2-718(1), and (b) it is unconscionable under UCC 2-302. He offers to show that Lumber Company's attorney spent no more than 10 hours in the collection effort and that a reasonable hourly fee for similar services in that geographical area is $80. As attorney for Lumber Company how would you respond? What further facts would you look for?

CHAPTER 13

Buyer's Remedies

A buyer potentially has three options when the seller breaches: to call off the contract, to have the contract specifically enforced, and to recover damages. We have already studied in Chapter 11 the buyer's right to cancel the contract when we examined the right to reject or to revoke acceptance of nonconforming goods. In this chapter we focus on the buyer's right to specific performance and his right to recover damages.

The buyer's options are, as you recognize, the same as the seller has when the buyer breaches. There is an intentional parallelism in Article 2 between the seller's remedies and the buyer's remedies. Not only does the same basic principle of compensating the nonbreaching party's expectation interest underlie both sets of remedy provisions but also the structure and sometimes the language of these provisions are similar. As a result, some commentators have found particularly persuasive the argument of parallel construction when the language of a remedy formula is ambiguous.

A. SPECIFIC PERFORMANCE

When a buyer does not end up with the goods, whether because the seller does not tender them or because the buyer rejects them as nonconforming, the Code gives the buyer two potential remedies. He may seek to have a court order the seller to deliver the goods, or he may bring an action to recover damages.

Recovering the goods themselves, together with any incidental damages, will usually most nearly satisfy the expectations of the buyer at the time he entered into the contract. At the time the buyer contracted he would also have expected the seller to perform without compulsion, so after the seller's breach the buyer may not be as sanguine about adequate performance by the seller. The remedy of specific performance in other words has considerable theoretical attraction but may not be satisfactory in practice.

Unlike many other legal systems, Anglo-American law does not begin with the assumption that specific performance is the primary remedy available

to a nonbreaching party. On the contrary, common law jurisdictions traditionally order specific performance only if damages cannot be calculated or are
inadequate. The Uniform Commercial Code does not break with this tradition, but it does suggest that specific performance should be more readily
available "in other proper circumstances."

The Code provides the buyer with three specific performance remedies, if
we define specific performance not in its technical sense but broadly, to include all legal ways by which the buyer may recover the promised goods from
the breaching seller:

(1) A decree of specific performance. UCC 2-716(1), (2). The following
cases and problems examine when a court will or should order the seller to
perform.

(2) A replevin action. UCC 2-716(3). The Code requires that goods be
identified and cover unavailable, but does not require the buyer to show he
has title to the goods as he usually had to under pre-Code law.

(3) An action to recover goods for which the buyer has prepaid. UCC 2-
502. This remedy is limited to cases where the seller is insolvent and will
therefore usually be subject to the overriding rules of bankruptcy law.

EASTERN ROLLING MILL CO. v. MICHLOVITZ
157 Md. 51, 145 A. 378 (1929)

Parke, J. The plaintiffs, Simon Michlovitz, Abraham Michlovitz, and David
Furman, are copartners trading as Michlovitz & Co., and carry on an extensive wholesale business in buying and selling iron, steel, and other scrap. . . .
The defendant, the Eastern Rolling Mill Company . . . is a manufacturer of
sheet steel, and its processes leave for disposal a large quantity of what is
known to the trade as "crop end scrap" and "bundled steel scrap." The first is
the ends of steel bars, which are the raw material of the industry; and the
second is the ends of steel sheets, which the defendant hydraulically compresses
into bundles for sale as scrap. The steel sheets constitute 98 per centum of the
gross money value of the corporate business, and the other two per centum is,
practically, the two kinds of scrap mentioned.

Since the defendant began operation in 1920, the defendant has exclusively disposed of this scrap to the plaintiffs. [After initial contracts for three-
month periods and one five-year period, the parties entered into contracts for
a five-year period from October 1, 1927.] By these contracts, the defendant
agreed to sell its entire accumulation of the two kinds of scrap during the
period of five years at prices to be fixed at the beginning of every quarter for
the next succeeding three months in the following manner: The plaintiffs were
to accept delivery of the scrap as it accumulated, and its price, when loaded by
defendant on gondola cars at its plant, was, (a) with respect to the pressed
bundled sheet steel scrap, $3 a ton less than what was quoted in the "Iron

Age," a trade publication, at the beginning of every quarter, as the Philadelphia market for bundled steel sheets; and (b) with respect to the crop end scrap, $3 a ton less than what was quoted in said Journal, at the beginning of every quarter, as the Philadelphia market for No. 1 heavy melting steel. . . .

No controversy of any kind arose until the death of John M. Jones, who had been the president and general manager of the defendant from its inception, and who, in these capacities, had made with the plaintiffs all the contracts for the sale of scrap to the plaintiffs. Jones died about November 1, 1927, and in the following month, under the direction of A. J. Hazlett, the new president, an effort was made to induce the plaintiffs to agree to a rescission of the contracts. The defendant's objection to the contracts was their duration and the prices, but it was willing to enter into new contracts for not over a year, upon the other terms, including the prices, of the original contracts. . . .

Since the June, 1928, deliveries, the defendant has refused to comply with its contracts, although the plaintiffs have demanded their performance, and the defendant does not question plaintiffs' willingness and ability to complete and discharge fully their obligations. Under these circumstances, and, because of the alleged irreparable loss and injury to the plaintiffs resulting from the defendant's refusal to fulfill its continuing contracts, the plaintiffs brought a bill to enforce specifically the contracts. After answer and the taking of proof by the parties in open court the chancellor decreed the relief prayed for; and this appeal raises the question of the right of the plaintiffs to relief. . . .

[I]n the court's judgment, the contracts are shown to have been fair, equal, and just at the time of their inception, when the parties, with equal knowledge and means of obtaining knowledge of all the material facts, with a common opportunity of judging their consequences, must be assumed to have contemplated and provided against all possible contingencies. Nor does the evidence prove that the enforcement of the contracts for the residue of its term would be oppressive. . . .

[T]he court as a general rule, will refuse to decree special performance in respect of chattels because damages are a sufficient remedy. This principle does not apply in all cases of chattels, so there are many exceptions to this rule, because, principally, of the inadequacy of the remedy at law in the particular case or of the special nature and value of the subject-matter of the contract. Passing by other illustrations of the exceptions to one more clearly in point, Pomeroy on Specific Performance of Contracts §15 (3d ed. 1926), puts it thus: "Again, contracts for the delivery of goods will be specifically enforced, when by their terms the deliveries are to be made and the purchase price paid in installments running through a considerable number of years. Such contracts 'differ from those that are immediately to be executed.' Their profits depending upon future events cannot be estimated in present damages, which must, of necessity, be almost wholly conjectural. To compel a party to accept damages under such circumstances is to compel him to sell his possible profits at a price depending upon a mere guess." This statement of the law is supported by the Maryland decisions. . . .

Under the cases, the right to specific performance turns upon whether the plaintiffs can be properly compensated at law. The plaintiffs are entitled to compensatory damages, and, if an action at law cannot afford them adequate redress, equity will specifically enforce the contracts, which would not impose upon the court any difficulties in enforcement, as the subject-matter of the contracts is the accumulated scrap at the plant of the defendant. The defendant relied upon the case of Fothergill v. Rowland, L.R. 17 Eq. 132 (1873), but there the contract was one whose performance involved the working of a coal mine, which required personal skill, and this with its different facts distinguishes that case from the one at bar. The goods which the parties here had bargained for were not procurable in the neighborhood, and, moreover, they possessed a quality and concentrated weight which could not be secured anywhere within the extensive region covered by the "Philadelphia Market." In addition, the delivery of the scrap at Baltimore was one of the valuable incidents of the purchase. It follows that the right to these specific goods is a consideration of great importance, and this and the difficulty of securing scrap of the same commercial utility are factors making for the inadequacy of damages.

The scrap is not to be delivered according to specified tonnage, but as it accumulates, which in the past has been at the rate of one and two, and occasionally three, carloads of scrap a day, so the quantities vary from quarter to quarter. If the plant should cease to operate or suffer an interruption, there would be no scrap accumulating for delivery under the contracts, and its deliveries would end or be lessened. Neither are the prices for the scrap constant during the period of the contracts, but change from quarter to quarter according to the quotations of two specified materials on the Philadelphia market whose quarterly prices are accepted as the standards upon which the contract prices are quarterly computed. The contracts run to September 30, 1932. By what method would a jury determine the future quarterly tonnage, the quarterly contract price, and quarterly market price during these coming years? How could it possibly arrive at any fair ascertainment of damages? Any estimate would be speculative and conjectural, and not, therefore, compensatory. It follows that the defendant's breach of its contracts is not susceptible of fair and proper compensation by damages; and that to refuse to compel the defendant to do merely what it bound itself to do, and to remit the plaintiffs to their action at law, is to permit the defendant to relieve itself of the contracts and to force the plaintiffs to sell their profits at a conjectural price. To substitute damages by guess for due performance of contract could only be because "there's no equity stirring."

The equitable remedy of specific performance is indicated by the facts and circumstances; and would seem to be authorized by [Uniform Sales Act §68]; providing as follows: "Where the seller has broken a contract to deliver *specific or ascertained goods*, a court having the powers of a court of equity may, if it thinks fit, on the application of the buyer, by its judgment or decree direct that the contract shall be performed specifically, without giving the seller the option of retaining the goods on payment of damages. The judgment or decree may be unconditional, or upon such terms and conditions as to damages, payment of the price and otherwise, as to the court may seem just."

The goods in the instant case are all of the daily by-product of the raw materials used in the manufacturing processes of a particular plant. The goods assume their distinctive form of scrap and are of a known quantity and quality when the raw material has been made into the commercial product; and they are identified by reason of their location in the plant where they were manufactured. The defendant does not perform its contracts by delivering any scrap other than that agreed upon; that is, the scrap made and accumulated by a particular manufacturer as the by-product of the operations of a specified manufacturing plant. If the contract had been for generic goods, the defendant could deliver any goods which answer to the description. The term "specific goods" is defined to mean goods identified and agreed upon at the time a contract to sell or a sale is made. [U.S.A. §76.] It is not necessarily confined to existing goods, but may embrace future goods which were unascertainable at the date of the contract, if they be so susceptible of identification and appropriation by description as to be clearly ascertainable when the contract comes to be enforced. So "specific" has been held to apply to future and unascertained goods, if they are the product of what is specific. This principle is illustrated by Howell v. Coupland [1876] 1 Q.B. Div. 258, where defendant agreed to sell plaintiff 200 tons of potatoes grown on land belonging to defendant at a particular place. At the time of the agreement, the ground had been prepared, but the potatoes had not been planted, but were put out, and should have produced the agreed quantity. Without any default of the defendant, disease reduced the crop to about 80 tons. The question was whether the defendant had performed his contract by the delivery of the 80 tons, and its solution hinged on whether this agreement for the delivery of future goods was a sale of specific goods. The court held that, inasmuch as the contract was for potatoes off specific land, it was therefore a contract for a part of a specific crop, although it was not planted at the time of the contract; and that, because the specific goods had perished without the fault of the seller, he was not bound to deliver the 200 tons, as he would have been if the sale had not been of specific goods. . . . So here the obligation is to deliver a particular chattel, not to deliver any proper chattel. The scrap becomes specific property by reason of its manufacture in a special manner, at a certain plant, by a designated manufacturer, during a given period, and for a single purchaser of the whole quantity produced; and, as soon as the scrap is made, it is ascertained goods, appropriated to the contract by force of its fulfilling the description of the chattel sold through its complete identification with the subject-matter.

Thus the property about which the parties to this appeal bargained is not an undistinguished portion of a quantity of similar goods. . . . From the time the scrap is produced and pressed into bundles, it is identified, and nothing further remains to be done to put it in condition for delivery. This scrap, and none other, is the exclusive subject-matter of the contracts. A sale of a pound of it to a third party is a breach of the contracts; and not until every pound of this scrap—and none other—is delivered to the plaintiffs, is the contract fulfilled.

Under the special circumstances of this case, the scrap sold is "specific or ascertained goods" within the meaning of [U.S.A. §68]; and the chancellor was empowered to pass the decree for specific performance. The logic of the facts leads to this conclusion, which was anticipated by eminent authority. 2 S. Williston, The Law Governing Sales of Goods §601 (2d ed. 1924); J. Benjamin, A Treatise on the Law of Sale of Personal Property 165, 1120, 1122, [apparently 6th English ed. 1920—EDS.]; Fry on Specific Performance §82 [apparently 6th ed. 1921—EDS.]; Cassinelli v. Humphrey Supply Co., 43 Nev. 208, 183 P. 523 (1919).

For the reasons given, the decree will be affirmed. Decree affirmed, with costs.

LACLEDE GAS CO. v. AMOCO OIL CO.
522 F.2d 33, 17 UCC Rep. 447 (8th Cir. 1975), *rev'd on other grounds*, 531 F.2d 942 (8th Cir. 1976)

Ross, Circuit Judge. The Laclede Gas Company (Laclede), a Missouri corporation, brought this diversity action alleging breach of contract against the Amoco Oil Company (Amoco), a Delaware corporation. It sought relief in the form of a mandatory injunction prohibiting the continuing breach or, in the alternative, damages. The district court held a bench trial on the issues of whether there was a valid, binding contract between the parties and whether, if there was such a contract, Amoco should be enjoined from breaching it. It then ruled that the "contract is invalid due to lack of mutuality" and denied the prayer for injunctive relief. The court made no decision regarding the requested damages. Laclede Gas Co. v. Amoco Oil Co., 385 F. Supp. 1332, 1336 (E.D. Mo. 1974). This appeal followed, and we reverse the district court's judgment.

On September 21, 1970, Midwest Missouri Gas Company (now Laclede), and American Oil Company (now Amoco), the predecessors of the parties to this litigation, entered into a written agreement which was designed to provide central propane gas distribution systems to various residential developments in Jefferson County, Missouri, until such time as natural gas mains were extended into these areas. The agreement contemplated that as individual developments were planned the owners or developers would apply to Laclede for central propane gas systems. If Laclede determined that such a system was appropriate in any given development, it could request Amoco to supply the propane to that specific development. This request was made in the form of a supplemental form letter, as provided in the September 21 agreement; and if Amoco decided to supply the propane, it bound itself to do so by signing this supplemental form.

Once this supplemental form was signed the agreement placed certain duties on both Laclede and Amoco. Basically, Amoco was to "[i]nstall, own, maintain and operate . . . storage and vaporization facilities and any other facilities necessary to provide [it] with the capability of delivering to [Laclede] commercial propane gas suitable . . . for delivery by [Laclede] to its customers' facilities." Amoco's facilities were to be "adequate to provide a continuous supply of commercial propane gas at such times and in such volumes commensurate with [Laclede's] requirements for meeting the demands reasonably to be anticipated in each Development while this Agreement is in force." Amoco was deemed to be "the supplier," while Laclede was "the distributing utility."

For its part Laclede agreed to "[i]nstall, own, maintain and operate all distribution facilities" from a "point of delivery" which was defined to be "the outlet of [Amoco] header piping." Laclede also promised to pay Amoco "the Wood River Area Posted Price for propane plus four cents per gallon on all amounts of commercial propane gas delivered" to it under the agreement.

Since it was contemplated that the individual propane systems would eventually be converted to natural gas, one paragraph of the agreement provided that Laclede should give Amoco 30 days written notice of this event, after which the agreement would no longer be binding for the converted development.

Another paragraph gave Laclede the right to cancel the agreement. However, this right was expressed in the following language: "This Agreement shall remain in effect for one (1) year following the first delivery of gas by [Amoco] to [Laclede] hereunder. Subject to termination as provided in Paragraph 11 hereof [dealing with conversions to natural gas], this Agreement shall automatically continue in effect for additional periods of one (1) year each unless [Laclede] shall, not less than 30 days prior to the expiration of the initial one (1) year period or any subsequent one (1) year period, give [Amoco] written notice of termination." There was no provision under which Amoco could cancel the agreement.

For a time the parties operated satisfactorily under this agreement, and some 17 residential subdivisions were brought within it by supplemental letters. However, for various reasons, including conversion to natural gas, the number of developments under the agreement had shrunk to eight by the time of trial. These were all mobile home parks.

During the winter of 1972-1973 Amoco experienced a shortage of propane and voluntarily placed all of its customers, including Laclede, on an 80% allocation basis, meaning that Laclede would receive only up to 80% of its previous requirements. Laclede objected to this and pushed Amoco to give it 100% of what the developments needed. Some conflict arose over this before the temporary shortage was alleviated.

Then, on April 3, 1973, Amoco notified Laclede that its Wood River Area Posted Price of propane had been increased by three cents per gallon. Laclede objected to this increase also and demanded a full explanation. None was forthcoming. Instead Amoco merely sent a letter dated May 14, 1973, informing Laclede that it was "terminating" the September 21, 1970, agreement effective May 31, 1973. It claimed it had the right to do this because "the Agreement lacks mutuality."

The district court felt that the entire controversy turned on whether or not Laclede's right to "arbitrarily cancel the Agreement" without Amoco having a similar right rendered the contract void "for lack of mutuality" and it resolved this question in the affirmative. We disagree with this conclusion and hold that settled principles of contract law require a reversal. . . . [The appellate court goes on to hold that the parties had entered into an enforceable requirements contract.—EDS.] Since he found that there was no binding contract, the district judge did not have to deal with the question of whether or not to grant the injunction prayed for by Laclede. He simply denied this relief because there was no contract. . . .

Generally the determination of whether or not to order specific performance of a contract lies within the sound discretion of the trial court. . . . However, this discretion is, in fact, quite limited; and it is said that when certain equitable rules have been met and the contract is fair and plain "specific performance goes as a matter of right." . . .

With this in mind we have carefully reviewed the very complete record on appeal and conclude that the trial court should grant the injunctive relief prayed. We are satisfied that this case falls within that category in which specific performance should be ordered as a matter of right. . . .

Amoco contends that four of the requirements for specific performance have not been met. Its claims are: (1) there is no mutuality of remedy in the contract; (2) the remedy of specific performance would be difficult for the court to administer without constant and long-continued supervision; (3) the contract is indefinite and uncertain; and (4) the remedy at law available to Laclede is adequate. The first three contentions have little or no merit and do not detain us for long.

There is simply no requirement in the law that both parties be mutually entitled to the remedy of specific performance in order that one of them be given that remedy by the court. . . .

While a court may refuse to grant specific performance where such a decree would require constant and long-continued court supervision, this is merely a discretionary rule of decision which is frequently ignored when the public interest is involved. . . . Here the public interest in providing propane to the retail customers is manifest, while any supervision required will be far from onerous.

Section 370 of the Restatement of Contracts (1932) provides: "Specific enforcement will not be decreed unless the terms of the contract are so expressed that the court can determine with reasonable certainty what is the duty of each party and the conditions under which performance is due."

We believe these criteria have been satisfied here. . . . [A]s to all developments for which a supplemental agreement has been signed, Amoco is to supply all the propane which is reasonably foreseeably required, while Laclede is to purchase the required propane from Amoco and pay the contract price therefor. The parties have disagreed over what is meant by "Wood River Area Posted Price" in the agreement, but the district court can and should determine with reasonable certainty what the parties intended by this term and should mold its decree, if necessary accordingly. Likewise, the fact that the agreement does not have a definite time of duration is not fatal since the evidence established that the last subdivision should be converted to natural gas in 10 to 15 years. This sets a reasonable time limit on performance and the district court can and should mold the final decree to reflect this testimony.

It is axiomatic that specific performance will not be ordered when the party claiming breach of contract has an adequate remedy at law. . . . This is especially true when the contract involves personal property as distinguished from real estate.

However, in Missouri, as elsewhere, specific performance may be ordered even though personalty is involved in the "proper circumstances." UCC 2-716(1); Restatement of Contracts §361. And a remedy at law adequate to defeat the grant of specific performance "must be as certain, prompt, complete, and efficient to attain the ends of justice as a decree of specific performance." . . .

One of the leading Missouri cases allowing specific performance of a contract relating to personalty because the remedy at law was inadequate is Boeving v. Vandover, 240 Mo. App. 117, 218 S.W.2d 175, 178 (1949). In that case the plaintiff sought specific performance of a contract in which the defendant had promised to sell him an automobile. At that time (near the end of and shortly after World War II) new cars were hard to come by, and the court held that specific performance was a proper remedy since a new car "could not be obtained elsewhere except at considerable expense, trouble or loss, which cannot be estimated in advance."

We are satisfied that Laclede has brought itself within this practical approach taken by the Missouri courts. As Amoco points out, Laclede has propane immediately available to it under other contracts with other suppliers. And the evidence indicates that at the present time propane is readily available on the open market. However, this analysis ignores the fact that the contract involved in this lawsuit is for a long-term supply of propane to these subdivisions. The other two contracts under which Laclede obtains the gas will remain in force only until March 31, 1977, and April 1, 1981, respectively; and there is no assurance that Laclede will be able to receive any propane under them after that time. Also it is unclear as to whether or not Laclede can use the propane obtained under these contracts to supply the Jefferson County subdivisions, since they were originally entered into to provide Laclede with propane with which to "shave" its natural gas supply during peak demand periods [i.e., by adding propane to the natural gas—EDS.]. Additionally, there was uncontradicted expert testimony that Laclede probably could not find another supplier of propane willing to enter into a long-term contract such as the Amoco agreement, given the uncertain future of worldwide energy supplies. And, even if Laclede could obtain supplies of propane for the affected developments through its present contracts or newly negotiated ones, it would still face considerable expense and trouble which cannot be estimated in advance in making arrangements for its distribution to the subdivisions.

Specific performance is the proper remedy in this situation, and it should be granted by the district court. . . .

NOTES & QUESTIONS

1. *Code changes to pre-Code law.* Under UCC 2-716 a judge may order specific performance when "the goods are unique or in other proper circumstances." Comment 1 to UCC 2-716 states that the Code "seeks to further a more liberal attitude" towards granting decrees of specific performance. Comment 2 goes on to suggest that an output or requirements contract involving a particular source is an example of "other proper circumstances," and that evidence that a buyer cannot cover is strong support for a decree of specific performance. Do the statute and the Comments provide judges with adequate guidance? For a general review of the aims of the Code draftsmen, see Greenberg, Specific Performance Under Section 2-716 of the Uniform Commercial Code: "A More Liberal Attitude" in the "Grand Style," 17 New Eng. L. Rev. 321 (1982).

2. *Specific performance under the Restatement (Second) of Contracts.* The court in *Laclede* quotes from the first Restatement of Contracts. The Second Restatement has revised these rules in the light of the UCC. Restatement (Second) of Contracts §§357-369 (1979). The Introductory Note to these provisions notes that the most important limitation on a court's discretion is the need to find that damages are not adequate (§359), but goes on to point out that more and more courts are finding damages to be inadequate in the cases before them. How does one determine inadequacy? Section 360 suggests the following factors: the difficulty of proving damages with reasonable certainty, of acquiring a substitute performance with the damages, and of collecting the judgment for damages from the seller. To what extent are these Restatement principles and rules of help to a judge acting under UCC 2-716?

3. *Ensuring performance.* Assume that a buyer is seriously concerned with the possibility that the seller will be unable or unwilling to perform. Which, if any, of the following devices might be enforceable or effective to ensure performance?

(a) A contract term by which the seller consents to the granting of a decree of specific performance.

(b) A contract term providing for the passage of title when the goods are identified to the contract.

(c) A security agreement granting a security interest in the goods or raw materials to be used to manufacture the goods.

(d) A performance bond by which a surety guarantees performance.

(e) A liquidated damage clause in an amount sufficient to encourage performance.

(f) Formation of a joint venture with the seller.

4. *The case for specific performance.* For a thoughtful argument in support of specific performance, see Schwartz, The Case for Specific Performance, 89 Yale L.J. 271 (1979). Professor Schwartz points out that specific performance of a contractual obligation will satisfy the compensation goal of putting the nonbreaching party in as good a position as if there had been uncompelled performance. He then suggests that damage remedies tend to undercompensate, and that there is little difference between the transaction costs generated by specific performance and damage remedies. Moreover, he argues, ordering specific performance does not unduly interfere with the "liberty interests" of breaching parties. Professor Schwartz concludes that a nonbreaching party should be able to obtain a decree of specific performance on request. For an analysis that supports the traditional restrictions on specific performance, see Kronman, Specific Performance, 45 U. Chi. L. Rev. 351 (1978).

For a discussion of specific performance as the remedy operates in other legal systems, see Dawson, Specific Performance in France and Germany, 57 Mich. L. Rev. 495 (1959).

Problem 13-1. In which of the following cases should a court order specific performance? Would replevin be more appropriate? See UCC 2-716.

(a) As he has in each of the last ten years, Farmer agrees to sell to Broker the grain to be grown on his land. Farmer later learns he can receive a greater profit from a government program that will pay him not to grow crops. Farmer repudiates the contract with Broker.

(b) Supplier agrees with Manufacturer to construct a drill press with special modifications designed to Manufacturer's specifications. After purchasing the raw materials Supplier repudiates the contract. Supplier is insolvent but not yet in bankruptcy proceedings.

(c) Dealer agrees to sell Consumer a used '79 Volkswagen convertible with all the extras. On the day for delivery Dealer refuses to hand over the car because he has another "live one" willing to pay more.

Problem 13-2. Assume that in each of the cases in Problem 13-1 the seller is willing and able to perform but the buyer refuses to take delivery. In which cases may the seller obtain a judgment requiring the buyer to accept and pay for the tendered goods? UCC 2-709.

B. DAMAGES AS TO UNACCEPTED GOODS

As was noted at the beginning of the previous part, a buyer who does not end up with the goods may choose to seek damages from the seller rather than some form of specific performance. UCC 2-711 gives the buyer two alternative damage formulas calculated on the difference between the contract price and either the price paid by the buyer in a substitute (cover) transaction or the market price. The formulas are spelled out in UCC 2-712 and 2-713. In addition to these damages the buyer may recover incidental and consequential damages in appropriate cases. UCC 2-715. Where rejected goods are in the buyer's control at least part of the buyer's claim for damages is secured by a statutory security interest in these goods. UCC 2-711(3).

The following materials examine two particularly perplexing issues raised by the Code's formulation of the buyer's remedies. One important ambiguity concerns the buyer's freedom to elect between the Code's alternative damage formulas. A second involves the question of the appropriate formula when the seller repudiates the contract prior to performance. While studying these issues you should remember that businessmen usually prefer speed, certainty, and simplicity over precision. Any evaluation of the Code's resolution of these issues must therefore consider not only a legal but also a business perspective.

Problem 13-3. On March 15 Supplier, a Texas cotton broker, agrees to sell 200 bales of grade A cotton (100,000 pounds) to Cotton Mills, a North Carolina enterprise. The contract provides a purchase price of 40 cents per pound, F.O.B. Amarillo, Texas. Supplier is to ship the cotton on September 30, freight prepaid. The freight charge for 200 bales is $100.

(a) Supplier ships 200 bales as agreed but when they arrive in North Carolina on October 7 Cotton Mills discovers that the cotton is an inferior grade and rejects the cotton. Cotton Mills decides not to purchase substitute cotton. What damages may it recover? On September 30 the market price for grade A cotton is 45¢ per pound in Amarillo and 46¢ per pound in North Carolina; on October 7 the market price increases 1¢ per pound in each market. Are Cotton Mills' reasons for not covering relevant? Would it make a difference that instead of tendering nonconforming cotton Supplier does not ship at all? See UCC 2-713.

(b) Assume that on October 15 Cotton Mills purchases from another North Carolina mill 150 bales of grade A cotton for immediate delivery at 49¢ per pound. The market price on October 15 is 47¢ per pound in Texas and 48¢ per pound in North Carolina. What damages may Cotton Mill recover? May it choose between recoveries under UCC 2-712 and UCC 2-713?

(c) Assume that Supplier repudiates the contract on August 1. On this date the spot market price is 44¢ per pound in Texas and 45¢ per pound in North Carolina; the futures market price for delivery on September 30 is 46¢ per pound and 47¢ per pound respectively. What damages may Cotton Mill recover? See UCC 2-610, 2-711.

Problem 13-4. Assume that in each of the cases in Problem 13-3 Supplier is willing and able to perform but that Cotton Mills wrongfully rejects or repudiates. What damages may Supplier recover? See UCC 2-706, 2-708.

OLOFFSON v. COOMER
11 Ill. App. 3d 918, 296 N.E.2d 871, 12 UCC Rep. 1082 (1973)

ALLOY, Presiding Justice. Richard Oloffson, d/b/a/ Rich's Ag Service appeals from a judgment of the circuit court of Bureau County in favor of appellant against Clarence Coomer in the amount of $1,500 plus costs. The case was tried by the court without a jury.

Oloffson was a grain dealer. Coomer was a farmer. Oloffson was in the business of merchandising grain. Consequently, he was a "merchant" within the meaning of UCC 2-104. Coomer, however, was simply in the business of growing rather than merchandising grain. He, therefore, was not a "merchant" with respect to the merchandising of grain.

On April 16, 1970, Coomer agreed to sell to Oloffson, for delivery in October and December of 1970, 40,000 bushels of corn. Oloffson testified at the trial that the entire agreement was embodied in two separate contracts, each covering 20,000 bushels and that the first 20,000 bushels were to be delivered on or before October 30 at a price of $1.12 3/4 per bushel and the second 20,000 bushels were to be delivered on or before December 15, at a price of $1.12 1/4 per bushel. Coomer, in his testimony, agreed that the 40,000 bushels were to be delivered but stated that he was to deliver all he could by October 30 and the balance by December 15.

On June 3, 1970, Coomer informed Oloffson that he was not going to plant corn because the season had been too wet. He told Oloffson to arrange elsewhere to obtain the corn if Oloffson had obligated himself to deliver to any third party. The price for a bushel of corn on June 3, 1970, for future delivery, was $1.16. In September of 1970, Oloffson asked Coomer about delivery of the corn and Coomer repeated that he would not be able to deliver. Oloffson, however, persisted. He mailed Coomer confirmations of the April 16 agreement. Coomer ignored these. Oloffson's attorney then requested that Coomer perform. Coomer ignored this request likewise. The scheduled delivery dates referred to passed with no corn delivered. Oloffson then covered his obligation to his own vendee by purchasing 20,000 bushels at $1.35 per bushel and 20,000 bushels at $1.49 per bushel. The judgment from which Oloffson appeals awarded Oloffson as damages, the difference between the contract and the market prices on June 3, 1970, the day upon which Coomer first advised Oloffson he would not deliver.

Oloffson argues on this appeal that the proper measure of his damages was the difference between the contract price and the market price on the dates the corn should have been delivered in accordance with the April 16 agreement. Plaintiff does not seek any other damages. The trial court prior to entry of judgment, in an opinion finding the facts and reviewing the law, found that plaintiff was entitled to recover judgment only for the sum of $1,500 plus costs as we have indicated which is equal to the amount of the difference between the minimum contract price and the price on June 3, 1970, of $1.16 per bushel (taking the greatest differential from $1.12 1/4 per bushel multiplied by 40,000 bushels). We believe the findings and the judgment of the trial court were proper and should be affirmed.

It is clear that on June 3, 1970, Coomer repudiated the contract "with respect to performance not yet due." Under the terms of the Uniform Commercial Code the loss would impair the value of the contract to the remaining party in the amount as indicated. (UCC 2-610.) As a consequence, on June 3, 1970, Oloffson, as the "aggrieved party," could then:

> (a) for a commercially reasonable time await performance by the repudiating party; or
>
> (b) resort to any remedy for breach (Section 2-703 or Section 2-711), even though he has notified the repudiating party that he would await the latter's performance and has urged retraction; . . .

If Oloffson chose to proceed under sub-paragraph (a) referred to, he could have awaited Coomer's performance for a "commercially reasonable time." As we indicate in the course of this opinion, that "commercially reasonable time" expired on June 3, 1970. The Uniform Commercial Code made a change in existing Illinois law in this respect, in that, prior to the adoption of the Code, a buyer in a position as Oloffson was privileged to await a seller's performance until the date that, according to the agreement, such performance was scheduled. To the extent that a "commercially reasonable time" is less than such date of performance, the Code now conditions the buyer's right to await performance. (See UCC 2-610, Illinois Code Comment, Paragraph (a).)

If, alternatively, Oloffson had proceeded under subparagraph (b) by treating the repudiation as a breach, the remedies to which he would have been entitled were set forth in UCC 2-711, which is the only applicable section to which UCC 2-610(b) refers, according to the relevant portion of 2-711:

> (1) Where the seller fails to make delivery or repudiates or the buyer rightfully rejects or justifiably revokes acceptance then with respect to any goods involved, and with respect to the whole if the breach goes to the whole contract (Section 2-612), the buyer may cancel and whether or not he has done so may in addition to recovering so much of the price as has been paid
>
> (a) 'cover' and have damages under the next section as to all the goods affected whether or not they have been identified to the contract; or
>
> (b) recover damages for non-delivery as provided in this Article (Section 2-713). . . .

Plaintiff, therefore, was privileged under UCC 2-610 to proceed either under subparagraph (a) or under subparagraph (b). At the expiration of the "commercially reasonable time" specified in subparagraph (a), he in effect would have a duty to proceed under subparagraph (b) since subparagraph (b) directs reference to remedies generally available to a buyer upon a seller's breach.

Oloffson's right to await Coomer's performance under UCC 2-610(a) was conditioned upon his:

(i) waiting no longer than a "commercially reasonable time;" and

(ii) dealing with Coomer in good faith.

Since Coomer's statement to Oloffson on June 3, 1970, was unequivocal and since "cover" easily and immediately was available to Oloffson in the well-organized and easily accessible market for purchases of grain to be delivered in the future, it would be unreasonable for Oloffson on June 3, 1970, to have awaited Coomer's performance rather than to have proceeded under UCC 2-610(b) and, thereunder, to elect then to treat the repudiation as a breach. Therefore, if Oloffson were relying on his right to effect cover under UCC 2-711(1)(a), June 3, 1970, might for the foregoing reason alone have been the day on which he acquired cover.

Additionally, however, the record and the finding of the trial court indicates that Oloffson adhered to a usage of trade that permitted his customers to cancel the contract for a future delivery of grain by making known to him a desire to cancel and paying to him the difference between the contract and market price on the day of cancellation. There is no indication whatever that Coomer was aware of this usage of trade. The trial court specifically found, as a fact, that in the context in which Oloffson's failure to disclose this information occurred, Oloffson failed to act in good faith. According to Oloffson, he didn't ask for this information: "I'm no information sender. If he had asked I would have told him exactly what to do. . . . I didn't feel my responsibility. I thought it his to ask, in which case I would tell him exactly what to do." We feel that the words "for a commercially reasonable time" as set forth in UCC 2-610(a) must be read relatively to the obligation of good faith that is defined in UCC 2-103(1)(b) and imposed expressly in UCC 1-203.

The Uniform Commercial Code imposes upon the parties the obligation to deal with each other in good faith regardless of whether they are merchants. The Sales Article of the Code specifically defines good faith, "in the case of a merchant . . . [as] honesty in fact and the observance of reasonable commercial standards of fair dealing in the trade." For the foregoing reasons and likewise because Oloffson's failure to disclose in good faith might itself have been responsible for Coomer's failure to comply with the usage of trade which we must assume was known only to Oloffson, we conclude that a commercially reasonable time under the facts before us expired on June 3, 1970.

Imputing to Oloffson the consequences of Coomer's having acted upon the information that Oloffson in good faith should have transmitted to him, Oloffson knew or should have known on June 3, 1970, the limit of damages he probably could recover. If he were obligated to deliver grain to a third party, he knew or should have known that unless he covered on June 3, 1970, his own capital would be at risk with respect to his obligation to his own vendee. Therefore, on June 3, 1970, Oloffson, in effect, had a duty to proceed under UCC 2-610(b) and under UCC 2-711(1)(a) and (1)(b). If Oloffson had so proceeded under UCC 2-711(1)(a), he should have effected cover and would have been entitled to recover damages all as provided in UCC 2-712, which requires that he would have had to cover in good faith without unreasonable delay. Since he would have had to effect cover on June 3, 1970, according to UCC 2-712(2), he would have been entitled to exactly the damages which the trial court awarded him in this cause.

Assuming that Oloffson had proceeded under UCC 2-711(1)(b) he would have been entitled to recover from Coomer under UCC 2-713 and 2-723, the difference between the contract price and the market price on June 3, 1970, which is the date upon which he learned of the breach. This would produce precisely the same amount of damages which the trial court awarded him. [See UCC 2-723(1).]

Since the trial court properly awarded the damages to which plaintiff was entitled in this cause, the judgment of the circuit court of Bureau County is, therefore, affirmed.

CARGILL, INC. v. STAFFORD
553 F.2d 1222, 21 UCC Rep. 707 (10th Cir. 1977)

BREITENSTEIN, Circuit Judge. This diversity jurisdiction case relates to two transactions for the sale of wheat by defendant Stafford to plaintiff Cargill. The court denied recovery on the first and allowed recovery on the second. Both parties have appealed. We affirm except as to the amount of damages recoverable from the second transaction. [The following excerpts deal only with the second transaction.—EDS.]

Cargill is a cash merchandiser of agricultural commodities. Stafford owns and operates a country grain elevator under the name "Stafford Elevator" in Campo, Colorado. . . .

On July 31 Stafford telephoned Julsonnet [an agent of Cargill]. . . . Stafford agreed to sell, and Cargill to buy, an additional 26,000 bushels of wheat. . . .

On August 21 Stafford wrote Cargill objecting to the provision of the confirmations giving Cargill an option to cancel and saying: "Thus contract void." An agent of Cargill called Stafford on August 27 and urged him to perform. Stafford insisted that the confirmations were void because of the optional cancellation provisions. Cargill continued to urge performance. After Stafford told Cargill on September 6 that he would not perform, Cargill told Stafford that the contracts were cancelled and that Stafford owed Cargill the difference between the contract prices and the September 6 price. The price of wheat rose from the end of July, reaching a high point on August 21. Stafford refused to pay and Cargill brought suit for breach of the contracts. . . .

We turn to the July 31 transaction. The parties made on the telephone an oral contract for the sale by Stafford of 26,000 bushels of wheat to Cargill. A written confirmation was received by Stafford on August 7. The confirmation was thus received within the "reasonable time" requirement of UCC 2-201(2).

Stafford's rejection of the confirmation occurred on August 21, and was not within the ten-day requirement of the statute. Ibid. . . .

The remaining question is the damages to which Cargill is entitled. The trial court awarded damages in the amount of $27,300 plus interest which was the difference in the price of wheat on September 6 over that on July 31. September 6 is the day on which Cargill acted upon Stafford's statement that he would not perform. The court gave no reason for its selection of the September 6 date. The final day for performance was September 30.

Stafford repudiated the contract by an August 21 letter which was received by Cargill on August 24. Cargill argues alternatively that, (1) it should recover the difference between the price of wheat on August 24 and on July 31, and (2) the difference between the price on September 30 when performance was due and the price on July 31.

UCC 2-711 provides that when a seller repudiates the buyer may (1) cover (buy substitute goods) and recover the difference in price, (2) recover damages for non-delivery under UCC 2-713, or sue for specific performance under UCC 2-716. Cargill has not attempted to obtain specific performance. The record contains scant, if any, evidence that Cargill covered the wheat. UCC 2-713 relates to non-delivery and provides [in sub-section (1)]:

> Subject to the provisions of this Article with respect to proof of market price (Section 2-723), the measure of damages for non-delivery or repudiation by the seller is the difference between the market price *at the time when the buyer learned of the breach* and the contract price together with any incidental and consequential damages provided in this Article (Section 2-715), but less expenses saved in consequence of the seller's breach. (Emphasis supplied.)

The basic question is whether "time when buyer learned of the breach" means "time when buyer learned of the repudiation" or means "time of performance" in anticipatory repudiation cases. See discussion in J. White & R. Summers, Uniform Commercial Code 197-202 (1972). The authors conclude, Ibid. at 201, that the soundest arguments support the interpretation of "learned of the breach" to mean "time of performance" in the anticipatory repudiation case. We agree for two reasons.

First, before the adoption of the Code in Colorado and other states, damages were measured from the time when performance was due and not from the time when the buyer learned of repudiation. See [Uniform Sales Act §67] and A. Corbin, 5 Corbin on Contracts §1053, at 309 (1964). A clear deviation from past law would not ordinarily be accomplished by Code ambiguities.

Second, UCC 2-723(1) discusses when to measure damages in a suit for anticipatory repudiation which comes to trial before the time for performance. That section says:

> [A]ny damages based on market price (Section 2-708 or Section 2-713) shall be determined according to the price of such goods prevailing at the time when the aggrieved party *learned of the repudiation.* (Emphasis supplied.)

Thus, when the Code drafters intended to base damages on the date a party "learned of the repudiation," they did so by explicit language. We conclude that under UCC 2-713 damages normally should be measured from the time when performance is due and not from the time when the buyer learns of repudiation.

To support its contention that the time when it learned of the repudiation controls Cargill cites two cases. Sawyer Farmers Coop. Assn. v. Linke, 231 N.W.2d 791 (N.D. 1975) is not helpful because the date for determination of the market price was controlled by a contract provision and not by UCC 2-713. Oloffson v. Coomer, [at p. 629 supra], is more nearly in point. There the buyer contracted in 1969 with the seller-farmer for delivery of corn in 1970. In June 1970 the seller notified the buyer that he was not planting corn because of weather conditions and would not deliver in September. The buyer refused to cover and urged performance even though he knew there would be none. The court refused to award damages based on the September price but based its award on the price of corn on the June date when the seller notified the buyer that he would not deliver. In so doing the court pointed out that there was an easily accessible market for purchase of the grain, . . . and that the words "for a commercially reasonable time" appearing in UCC 2-610(a), relating to anticipatory repudiation "must be read relatively to the obligation of good faith that is defined in UCC 2-103(1)(b) and imposed expressly in UCC 1-203."

This brings us to UCC 2-712 which provides that the buyer may "cover" by the reasonable purchase of substitute goods. A buyer is allowed to buy substitute goods so long as he does not delay unreasonably. UCC 2-713 relates to a buyer's damages for nondelivery or repudiation. The official comment to that section says: "The general baseline adopted in this section uses as a yardstick the market in which the buyer would have obtained cover had he sought that relief."

We conclude that under UCC 2-713 a buyer may urge continued performance for a reasonable time. At the end of a reasonable period he should cover if substitute goods are readily available. If substitution is readily available and buyer does not cover within a reasonable time, damages should be based on the price at the end of that reasonable time rather than on the price when performance is due. If a valid reason exists for failure or refusal to cover, damages may be calculated from the time when performance is due.

Specifically, this means that Cargill had a reasonable time after the August 24 anticipatory repudiation to cover. This reasonable time expired on September 6 when Cargill cancelled the contract. The record does not show that Cargill covered or attempted to cover. Nothing in the record shows the continued availability or nonavailability of substitute wheat. On remand the court must determine whether Cargill had a valid reason for failure or refusal to cover. If Cargill did not have a valid reason, the court's award based on the September 6 price should be reinstated. If Cargill had a valid reason for not covering, damages should be awarded on the difference between the price on September 30, the last day for performance, and the July 31 contract price.

The judgment is affirmed except for the award of damages to Cargill under the July 31 transaction. The case is remanded for determination, in the light of this opinion, of the damages recoverable by Cargill. . . .

NOTES & QUESTIONS

1. *Election of remedies.* Compare Comment 3 to UCC 2-712 ("The buyer is always free to choose between cover and damages for non-delivery under the next section") with Comment 5 to UCC 2-713 ("The present section provides a remedy which is completely alternative to cover under the preceding section and applies only when and to the extent that the buyer has not covered"). Is the latter comment consistent with the general statement made in connection with the seller's remedies: "This Article rejects any doctrine of election of remedies"? UCC 2-703, Comment 1.

2. *What constitutes repudiation.* In both *Oloffson* and *Cargill* the courts assume that the sellers had repudiated. The buyers might have used—but did not—the procedure of UCC 2-609 to provide support for an allegation that the sellers had repudiated by not providing adequate assurance of performance. UCC 2-609(4). The Code assumes, however, that repudiation may be shown by other evidence, although the Code text does not define what acts constitute repudiation. Comment 1 to UCC 2-610 suggests the following formula: "an overt communication of intention or an action which renders performance impossible or demonstrates a clear determination not to continue with performance." See also Restatement (Second) of Contracts §§250-251 (1981).

3. *Damages for anticipatory repudiation.* For an economic efficiency analysis that suggests that an aggrieved buyer should recover damages based on an actual or hypothetical purchase in the futures market at or near the date of repudiation, see Jackson, "Anticipatory Repudiation" and the Temporal Element of Contract Law: An Economic Inquiry into Contract Damages in Cases of Prospective Nonperformance, 31 Stan. L. Rev. 69 (1978). Professor Jackson concludes that this efficiency analysis is not inconsistent with the text of the Uniform Commercial Code. Id. at 98-101, 110-112.

4. *Futures contracts.* There are organized commodity and foreign exchange "futures" markets in which a party may protect itself against losses from price fluctuations by purchasing a contract to deliver goods (or take delivery of them) at a later date for a price determined now. For a description of how "hedging" works, see A. Alchian & W. Allen, Exchange and Production 131-142 (2d ed. 1977); P. Samuelson, Economics 424-425 (10th ed. 1976). An illustration of how a price term may be drafted with reference to a futures market is set out in Balfour, Guthrie & Co. v. Gourmet Farms, 108 Cal. App. 3d 181, 166 Cal. Rptr. 422, 29 UCC Rep. 1144 (1980) (farmer hedges against "fixed-price-later" contract).

BLISS PRODUCE CO. v. A. E. ALBERT & SONS, INC.
35 Agric. Dec. 742, 20 UCC Rep. 917 (1976)

This is a reparation proceeding under the Perishable Agricultural Commodities Act, 1930, as amended (7 U.S.C. §§499a et seq.). In a formal complaint received October 19, 1973 complainant [Bliss Produce Company] requested an award of reparation in the sum of $10,832.64 plus 10% interest, which is alleged to be the damages suffered by complainant in connection with respondent's failure to pay for 433,235 pounds of potatoes delivered during the first part of June, 1973, f.o.b. Arizona. . . .

On February 5, 1974 respondent [A. E. Albert & Sons, Inc.] filed an answer which included a counterclaim. In his answer respondent admitted the purchase, receipt, and debt of $10,832.64 for 433,235 pounds of potatoes. However, respondent further alleged that complainant was under contractual obligation to deliver an additional 566,765 pounds of potatoes, which is admitted to have been undelivered.

Due to complainant's breach of contract because of nondelivery of potatoes, respondent alleges he was required to repurchase the identical amount elsewhere and asked as reparation the sum of $27,402.22 as the alleged cost of cover.

[On November 7, 1972 the parties entered into a written contract for the sale and purchase of 20,000 hundredweight (2,000,000 pounds) of Arizona Kennebec potatoes. Contract terms provided for shipment of potatoes from Arizona "F.O.B., grade guaranteed to destination," during May, 1973, at $2.75 per cwt. and during June, 1973, at $2.40 per cwt., payment due in thirty days. No potatoes were shipped during the month of May and on June 1 Bliss notified Albert by letter that the potato crop yield was low due to adverse growing conditions in Arizona, but that every effort would be made to meet the contract obligations. Between June 8 and June 16 Bliss made nine shipments for a total of 433,235 pounds. Albert accepted each shipment without complaint but did not pay Bliss the invoice price of $10,832.64 for the potatoes.

Following a letter of June 7 from Bliss, which stated that Bliss would only be able to supply 10,000 cwt. because of the adverse weather, the parties agreed on June 13 to release Bliss from his obligation to deliver 10,000 cwt. in consideration for the payment by Bliss of $13,250. Notwithstanding the modification Bliss wrote Albert on June 26 to inform him that it would be necessary to prorate contract requirements due to the shortage of potatoes. The following day Albert notified Bliss that if the total contract requirements of 10,000 cwt. were not received by June 30 he would buy on Bliss' account comparable quality potatoes to fulfill the balance due under the contract. On June 28 Bliss telegramed Albert that all available sources for Arizona potatoes had been checked but due to the general potato crop failure no potatoes were available to be shipped to Albert to fulfill the contract. The following day Albert telegramed back that he was buying similar potatoes from the nearest available source and would hold Bliss liable for its failure to fulfill the contract. By an accounting dated July 9 Albert notified Bliss that North Carolina potatoes were purchased commencing on June 7, for the account of Bliss, to fulfill the contract requirements.]

The record shows that on June 26, there was correspondence notifying Albert that complainant would not be able to fully perform his contract. This language was sufficiently unequivocal to invoke the UCC 2-610 provision which deals with anticipatory repudiation and would be the earliest date that respondent would have cause to take action.

Albert relies on the cover principle in Volpe-Son & Kemelhar, Inc. v. M. R. Davis & Bros., 21 Agric. Dec. 941 (1962) to support his claim for cover and in the alternative demands damages. The requirements for cover are fourfold: 1) To make in good faith, 2) without unreasonable delay, 3) any reasonable purchase of goods, 4) in *substitution* of those due from seller. It is unchallenged that purchases were made, but whether they were in substitution of those due from the seller is debatable. From the three different price lists that respondent has submitted (Exhibits 4, 5, and 8) it appears that he has made numerous potato acquisitions pursuant to his business, commencing May 26, 1973 through June 28, 1973. Both Exhibits 5 and 8 were submitted as evidence of prices paid, but only Exhibit 8 specifies purchase quantities and prices from which cover [could] be calculated; yet, Exhibit 8's list of substituted potatoes appears to only contain invoices of potatoes bought from June 7, 1973 to June 14, 1973. Respondent has failed to list quantities of potatoes purchased subsequent to the anticipatory repudiation date of June 26, 1973, that could have been a substituted purchase of goods. The UCC 2-712 provision is specific in that its implementation is only for substituted goods. We are not impressed with respondent's reliance on Volpe's language to support a cover argument since this case was addressed solely to a damage issue—the replacement or replenishment purchase being tangential.

This is not to say that respondent is without a valid method of computing damages. UCC 2-711 stipulates a viable alternative employing UCC 2-713 which allows a recovery of damages and which was alternatively argued by respondent. The damages herein would be the difference between market price at the time the buyer learned of the breach and the contract price, less expenses saved because of the breach.

The record demonstrates the numerous correspondence between the parties relating to the weather conditions and complainant's anxieties regarding the anticipated crop reduction. On June 26 there was communication indicating the need to pro-ration and at least partially comply. It was not until June 28 that Bliss unequivocally expressed his complete inability to fulfill contract requirements.

UCC 2-713 comment No. 1 states that the prices to be used in calculating damages come from "the market in which the buyer would have obtained cover had he sought that relief." Since potatoes were unobtainable in the Arizona market because of the crop failure and respondent's purchases which it sought to use as cover were made in North Carolina, it appears that North Carolina is a reasonable market from which cover could have been obtained. According to the Federal-State Market News Service, potatoes in the North Carolina area were selling for $7.00 per hundredweight on both June 26, the anticipatory repudiation date and June 28, the unequivocal breach of contract date.

Therefore, using this figure as our benchmark, the value of the 566,765 pounds of potatoes not delivered was $39,673.55. From this amount should be subtracted the contract price of $2.40 per hundredweight or $13,602.36, leaving a balance of $26,071.19. Expenses saved because of the breach must be deducted from this figure. The record establishes that there would be a savings of $1.15 per hundredweight in transportation costs amounting to $6,517.80, yielding a net of $19,553.39.

The failure of respondent Albert to pay complainant Bliss promptly the purchase price for 433,235 pounds of potatoes is in violation of section 2 of the [Perishable Agricultural Commodities Act]. Therefore, the amount of $10,832.64 should be set off against Respondent's damages for nondelivery.

The failure of Bliss to complete delivery under the contract of 566,765 pounds of potatoes is in violation of section 2 of the Act. Reparation in the net amount of $8,720.75 should therefore be awarded to respondent against complainant [Bliss]. . . .

NOTES & QUESTIONS

1. *The Perishable Agricultural Commodities Act.* The court in *Bliss* found that the parties had violated §2 of the Perishable Agricultural Commodities Act. This section states in relevant part:

> It shall be unlawful in or in connection with any transaction in interstate or foreign commerce—. . .
> (2) For any dealer to reject or fail to deliver in accordance with the terms of the contract without reasonable cause any perishable commodity bought or sold or contracted to be bought, sold, or consigned in interstate or foreign commerce by such dealer; . . .
> (4) For any commission merchant, dealer, or broker . . . to fail or refuse truly and correctly to account and make full payment promptly in respect of any transaction in any such commodity to the person with whom such transaction is had; . . . [7 U.S.C. §499b(2), (4) (1982).]

A party who violates the act is liable to the person injured for "the full amount of damages sustained in consequence of such violation." 7 U.S.C. §499e(a). The act does not spell out how these damages are to be calculated and the Uniform Commercial Code becomes relevant because the act explicitly states that it does not "abridge or alter the remedies now existing at common law or by statute." 7 U.S.C. §499e(b).

For a classic study of the Act, see H. Hart & A. Sacks, The Legal Process: Basic Problems in the Making and Application of Law 10-75 (1958).

2. *"F.O.B., grade guaranteed to destination."* Regulations issued under the Perishable Agricultural Commodities Act provide rules of construction for some trade terms. 7 C.F.R. §46.43 (1984). These regulations define "F.O.B." as follows:

> (i) "F.o.b." (for example, "f.o.b. Laredo, Tex.," or "f.o.b. California") means that the produce quoted or sold is to be placed free on board the boat, car, or other agency of the through land transportation at shipping point, in suitable shipping condition (see definitions of "suitable shipping condition," paragraphs (j) and (k) of this section), and that the buyer assumes all risk of damage and delay in transit not caused by the seller irrespective of how the shipment is billed. The buyer shall have the right of inspection at destination before the goods are paid for to determine if the produce shipped complied with the terms of the contract at time of shipment, subject to the provisions covering suitable shipping condition. [7 C.F.R. §46.43(i).]

The regulations do not, however, define "grade guaranteed to destination." Is this last clause inconsistent with the "F.O.B." term?

LAWRENCE v. PORTER
63 F. 62 (6th Cir. 1894)

LURTON, Circuit Judge. This is an action for breach of a contract of sale brought by the buyers against the sellers for failure to deliver a large quantity of lumber according to the terms of the agreement. The lumber was to be delivered by the defendants at their mill, on vessels to be furnished by the plaintiffs, during the shipping season of 1890. As each cargo was received, the buyer was to give acceptances, payable in 90 days. After the delivery of one cargo, the defendants refused, for no sufficient reason, to deliver the remainder upon the terms of the bargain, but offered to supply the lumber needed to complete the bill at a reduction of 50 cents on each 1,000 feet, for cash on delivery over the rail of plaintiffs' vessels and at the time when delivery was required by the broken agreement. The buyers stood upon their contract, and demanded delivery upon the credit therein stipulated, and refused to take the lumber offered by the delinquent sellers on any other terms than those contained in the agreement. There was evidence tending to show that the quantity and quality of lumber contracted for, and of the dimensions designated, could not be procured at the place of delivery from others than the defendants, or at any other available market in time for shipment according to the terms of the contract; that the lumber was intended for resale at Tonawanda, N.Y.; that defendants were so informed; and that the market value of such lumber at Tonawanda, after deducting freight and hauling, was considerably above the contract price. . . .

[The circuit court held that plaintiffs had suffered no legal damage because "the defendants offered to furnish the identical articles contracted for at
a price not greater than the contract price."]

Neither the declaration nor the bill of particulars sets out or particularizes
any special damages sustained by plaintiffs. They are therefore limited to
"general damages," which, for such a breach as the one declared on, are
measured by the difference between what they had agreed to pay and the sum
for which they could have supplied themselves with lumber of the same character at the place of delivery, or if not obtainable there, then at the nearest
available market, plus any additional freight resulting from the breach. In
case of such breach, the plaintiffs are entitled only to indemnity in a sum equal
to the loss they have sustained as a consequence. Hence it results that if the
plaintiffs are able to replace the goods by others, bought at a less or equal
price at the place of delivery, or other near and available market, they have
sustained no loss, and are entitled at best to nothing more than nominal
damages. Neither the declaration nor bill of particulars alleges any inability to
pay cash, as demanded by the defendants. We do not, therefore, consider
whether special damages might not, under some circumstances, be recovered,
which were sustained by reason of the inability of plaintiffs to pay cash for
lumber to replace that which defendants had contracted to sell them on credit.
It follows that if plaintiffs were able to buy, and did not, they cannot throw
upon the defendants any special losses incident to their own failure to mitigate
the injury as far as they reasonably could. T. Sedgwick, A Treatise on the
Measure of Damages §741 (8th Ed. 1891); Marsh v. McPherson, 105 U.S. 709
(1881); Warren v. Stoddart, 105 U.S. 224 (1881).

The ground upon which the defendants refused to carry out the sale was
ostensibly their unwillingness to extend to the plaintiffs the credit of 90 days
provided for in the agreement of sale. They have not endeavored to show that
there were any circumstances which justified this breach of the agreement.
Credit is often a material element in a contract of sale, whereby the buyer is
enabled to operate upon the capital of the seller. Credit extended without
interest is, in effect, a sale at the stipulated price less the interest for the period
of credit. The damage for a breach of contract to pay money at a particular
date is the lawful rate of interest for the period of default, unless some other
penalty is imposed by the agreement. So it would seem that if the buyer, in
order to supply himself with the articles which the seller was obligated to sell,
is compelled to buy from another, and to pay cash, one element of recovery for
the breach would be interest upon his purchase for the period of credit. It is
the well-settled duty of the buyer, when the seller refuses to deliver the goods
contracted for, to do nothing to aggravate his injury. Indeed, he must do all
that he reasonably can to mitigate the loss. If the buyer could have supplied
himself with goods of like kind, at the place of delivery or other available
market, at the time the contract was broken, and neglected to do so, whereby
he suffered special damages by reason of the breach, he will not be suffered to
recompense himself for such special damage, for the reason that to that extent

he has needlessly aggravated the loss. The contention of the plaintiffs is that they could not supply themselves at the time the contract was broken with lumber of the qualities and sizes mentioned in their contract, either at the place of delivery or at any other available market; that they were not required to buy from the defendants, who were already in default; that to have bought from them would operate both to encourage breaches of contracts, and would have been a waiver of all other right of recovery for the breach of their agreement; that to have accepted the proposal of the defendants to supply them for cash at the reduced price would simply have been to substitute one contract for another, thereby enabling defendants to escape all liability for a deliberate and indefensible violation of the bargain. They therefore insist that the measure of damage was the difference between the contract price and the market value at Tonawanda, N.Y., less freights to that point; the evidence showing that the lumber was bought for resale at Tonawanda, and that defendants were informed of that purpose.

For a breach of contract of sale, the law imposes no damages by way of punishment. The innocent party is simply entitled to recover his real loss. If the market value is less than the contract price, the buyer has sustained no loss. This is axiomatic, and needs no citation of authority. If the plaintiffs could have bought at East Jordan, or at any other convenient and available market, at the time of the breach, lumber of like kinds, at the same price or a less price, it would be clear that they would have sustained no general damages. If they refused to avail themselves of such opportunity, and thereby sustained special and unusual loss, by reason of not having lumber of the kinds called for by the contract, or by being deprived of a profit resulting from a resale at Tonawanda, they could not recover such special damage, for such damage might have been avoided by replacing the undelivered lumber by other of like kinds. The fact that they could only buy from the defendants does not affect the duty of plaintiffs to minimize their loss as far as they reasonably could. The offer to sell for cash at a reduced price more than equalized the interest for 90 days, which was the value of credit. There seems to be no insurmountable objection in thus permitting a delinquent contractor to minimize his loss. The objection on the buyer to mitigate his loss, by reason of the seller's refusal to carry out such a sale, is not relaxed because the delinquent seller affords the only opportunity for such reduction of the buyer's damage. Warren v. Stoddart, 105 U.S. 224; . . .

In Warren v. Stoddart, above cited, the essential facts were these: Stoddart & Co. were publishers of an edition of the Encyclopaedia Britannica. It was a book sold only by subscription. Certain territory was assigned to the plaintiff, in which he was to have the exclusive right to sell the book on subscription. He was to have the book on a credit of 30 days, thus enabling him to deliver it to his subscribers, and obtain the means to make his own payments. Warren obtained a large number of subscriptions to Stoddart's publication. After delivering a few numbers, he ceased to canvass for the Stoddart publication, and became a canvasser for a rival edition. Thereupon

Stoddart refused to extend further credit to Warren, and demanded cash on all his orders to supply his subscribers for the Stoddart edition. Warren demanded credit, and refused to pay cash. Being unable to get the Stoddart edition from any other source, he, at great expense to himself, substituted the Scotch, or rival edition, with which he furnished his subscribers for Stoddart's edition. For the loss thus sustained he sued. After discussing the effect upon Warren's contract, because of his ceasing to canvass for Stoddart and taking up a rival work, the court proceeded to decide the case upon the second ground of defense presented, saying:

". . . The rule is that where a party is entitled to the benefit of a contract, and can save himself from a loss arising from a breach of it at a trifling expense or with reasonable exertions, it is his duty to do it, and he can charge the delinquent with such damages only as with reasonable endeavors and expense he could not prevent. . . . The course pursued by Warren was not necessary to his own protection. He might have paid Stoddart cash for the books required to fill his orders, or have allowed Stoddart to fill the orders and divide the profits of the business between them, on equitable terms. The law required him to take that course by which he could secure himself with the least damage to the defendant in error. Instead of this, he unnecessarily destroys a valuable interest of Stoddart in the business in which they were jointly engaged, and then seeks to charge him with the great expense and damage which he brought on himself in so doing. If Stoddart violated his contract with Warren in refusing to fill his orders except for cash, the measure of Warren's damages would be the interest for thirty days on the amount of cash paid on his orders. As no proof was given to show that Warren had ever paid cash for any books ordered by him, he would only be entitled, in any view of the case, to nominal damages."

The opinion in Warren v. Stoddart rests upon the theory that the buyer does not surrender or yield any right of action he may have for the breach of contract. It rests wholly upon the duty of mitigating the loss by replacing the goods by others, if they are obtainable by reasonable exertion. If this duty be such as to require him to buy from the delinquent seller; if the article can be obtained only from him, or because he offers it cheaper than it can be obtained from others, such a purchase from the seller is not the abandonment of the original contract by the substitution of another, nor would the purchase operate to the seller's advantage, save in so far as the damage resulting from his bad faith was thereby reduced. If the seller offers to sell for cash at a reduced price, or to sell for a less price than the market price, though in excess of the contract price, with the condition that it should operate as a waiver of the original contract, or of any right of action for its breach, then the buyer would not be obligated to treat with the seller, nor would the seller's offer, if rejected, operate as a reduction of damages. . . .

[T]he case of Warren v. Stoddart is controlling. The offer after the breach by the defendants to sell the lumber necessary to complete the contract was

not coupled with any condition operating as an abandonment of the contract, nor as a waiver of any right of question for damages for the breach. . . .
Judgment affirmed.

NOTES & QUESTIONS

Measure of damages. Lawrence v. Porter states the measure of damages for breach of a promise to pay money at a particular date as the "lawful rate of interest for the period of default." Modern cases involving loan commitments look more generally to the borrower's added cost of borrowing and award damages based on the difference between the contract rate and market rate of interest. In either case, the underlying assumption is that funds are freely available to the borrower at the market rate of interest. Suppose that funds are unavailable to the borrower because (1) tight credit markets are causing all lenders to severely restrict borrowing and to allocate available funds to favored customers, or (2) the borrower has suffered reverses that make him a shaky loan prospect. How do these bear on the adequacy of the traditional remedy? In Lawrence v. Porter, the buyer never argued inability to pay cash or to obtain credit from another source. Should the buyer's subjective inability to cover by obtaining credit elsewhere excuse a failure to mitigate damages? See generally C. McCormick, Handbook on the Law of Damages 140, 142-143 (1935).

Problem 13-5. Cross-Tie enters into a contract with Green Thumb Centers (GTC) to supply GTC's requirements for treated landscape timbers for the years 1983-1987. The price is $2,700 per thousand, F.O.B. Cross-Tie's plant. In 1984, GTC's requirements rise sharply and Cross-Tie hedges its own obligation by contracting with Yankton Timber. Under the Yankton-Cross-Tie contract, Yankton is to supply timbers as needed up to 100,000 timbers per month, at a price of $2,300 per thousand, F.O.B. Yankton's plant. Shortly after this contract is made, Yankton repudiates it, advising Cross-Tie that without a renegotiation of the price Yankton will not realize a profit on the contract and accordingly will not perform. Cross-Tie proceeds to send purchase orders to Yankton on a monthly basis during 1984 and the first half of 1985. In no case does Yankton perform. In each case Cross-Tie increases its own production. It then "sells" the cross-ties in question to itself at a price of $3,100 per thousand and allocates them to its performance of the Cross-Tie-GTC contract. Evidence will tend to substantiate Cross-Tie's claim that $3,100 per thousand represents its production costs, plus a reasonable markup. May Cross-Tie recover damages from Yankton under the cover formula of UCC 2-712 and, if so, how much?

C.   DAMAGES AS TO ACCEPTED GOODS

When a buyer accepts goods he becomes liable for the price whether or not the seller's tender or the goods themselves conform to the contract. UCC 2-607(1). As we saw in Chapter 11, under certain circumstances the buyer is authorized to revoke acceptance and return the goods to the seller. If the buyer may not revoke or decides to keep the goods despite the nonconformity he may still recover damages under UCC 2-714. This section includes two separate damage formulas. For "any non-conformity of tender" the buyer may recover under subsection (1) "the loss resulting in the ordinary course of events from the seller's breach as determined in any manner which is reasonable." Where the buyer claims that the seller has breached a warranty, subsection (2) provides a more specific formula: "the difference at the time and place of acceptance between the value of the goods accepted and the value they would have had if they had been as warranted, unless special circumstances show proximate damages of a different amount." This latter subsection has been the focus of most litigation but it is conceivable that the buyer may also bring a warranty claim under subsection (1). In any event, the buyer may also recover incidental and consequential damages where appropriate. UCC 2-714(3), 2-715.

Problem 13-6. Small Tool Co. agrees to manufacture and sell to Bottling Co. a machine that will cap 1,000 bottles per hour. The agreed purchase price is $20,000. When the machine is delivered it can process an average of only 700 bottles per hour. After making repairs and modifications Bottling Co. discovers that the machine still handles only 800 bottles per hour. The company decides to keep the machine and to make a claim for damages. During negotiations about the damage claims Bottling Co. tells Small Tool Co. (a) machines that can process 700 and 800 bottles per hour are available for approximately $14,000 and $16,500 respectively; (b) the cost of the repairs and modifications made by Bottling Co. is $3,000; and (c) during the month the machine was repaired and modified the company's loss of profits attributable to the absence of the machine was $1,400. The president of Small Tool Co. asks you to evaluate Bottling Co.'s claim for damages in light of the above information. What further questions would you ask Bottling Co.? What advice do you give Small Tool Co.? See UCC 2-714, 2-715.

Problem 13-7. Before entering into the transaction outlined in Problem 13-6 the president of Small Tool Co. asks you to look over the following contract term she has drafted to limit the company's liability.

> **Disclaimer.** The parties agree that the value of the bottle capping machine is $20,000 if at the time of delivery it caps 1,000 bottles an hour as agreed. If within 10 days of delivery Bottling Co. notifies Small Tool Co. the machine fails to meet

the agreed specifications Small Tool Co. may repair or modify the machine. If, after repairs, the machine caps 1,000 bottles an hour the parties agree that the value of the machine will be $20,000. If Small Tool Co. does not repair or modify the machine Bottling Co. agrees to be bound by Small Tool Co.'s determination of the fair market value of the machine, which shall not be less than $16,000. In any event, Bottling Co. waives any claim to incidental and consequential damages.

Advise the president. See UCC 2-714, 2-715, 2-718, 2-719.

MELODY HOME MANUFACTURING CO. v. MORRISON
502 S.W.2d 196, 13 UCC Rep. 1035 (Tex. Civ. App. 1973)

EVANS, Justice. Melody Home Manufacturing Company appeals from a judgment rendered on jury findings that a mobile home which it had manufactured and delivered to a retailer, and which was subsequently purchased by appellees, was defective at the time of purchase. Judgment was for the sum of $4,000.00, which represented the different between the reasonable cash market value of the mobile home at the time of purchase and the amount of its market value had it then been fit for the purpose intended. Interest at the rate of 6% was awarded from the date of purchase. . . .

As to the measure of damages, UCC 2-714(2) provides:

> The measure of damages for breach of warranty is the difference at the time and place of acceptance between the value of the goods accepted and the value they would have had if they had been as warranted, unless special circumstances show proximate damages of a different amount.

The testimony of appellee, Mrs. Morrison, and the parties' stipulation indicate that the base price for the mobile home was around $5,300.00, which with finance charges, insurance and interest made a total payment of $7,584.36. A witness for appellee, Mr. Paul Knox, testified that the reasonable cash value of the mobile home in the year and in the county where it was purchased was approximately $6,000.00 if it had been free of the described defects. One of the appellant's witnesses, A. L. St. John, a mobile home dealer, testified that in his opinion the fair market value of the mobile home at the time and place of purchase and assuming normal construction and use of good workmanship and materials was a suggested retail price of between $6,012.00 and $5,995.00. On the basis of this record, we find the trial judge was justified in concluding, as a matter of law, that the reasonable cash market value of the mobile home at the time and place purchased was $6,000.00.

Melody Home argues, however, that the proper measure of damages was the difference between the amount of $2,000.00, found by the jury to be the actual cash market value of the mobile home in question as it existed when it was purchased, and the sum of $5,300.00, the base contract price of the mobile home. . . .

Under UCC 2-714(2) the trial court properly utilized the actual cash market value of the mobile home instead of the base contract price, even though the base contract price may have been a lesser sum. See Ash v. Beck, 68 S.W. 53 (Tex. Civ. App., 1902, n.w.h.); and 51 Tex. Jur. 2d (rev.), part 1, Vol. 51, Sales 354, p. 144, footnote 9, with reference to UCC 2-714(2) wherein it stated: "It might be noted that the measure is based on 'value' rather than 'price.' Thus, if the buyer purchases for $100 a machine that would be worth $200 if it answered its warranties, but is worth only $50 as the result of a breach of warranty, the UCC provision might permit the buyer to recover $150, rather than merely $50, which would be the amount if 'price' were the criterion. See 1 Hawkland, A Transactional Guide to the Uniform Commercial Code 263." . . .

Appellees' claim for damages for breach of warranty was not waived by its acceptance and use of the mobile home, nor by the fact they did not undertake to correct the defective conditions. UCC 2-714. . . . Appellant's point of error number 8 is overruled. . . .

We are further of the opinion that the jury's finding as to the cash market value of the mobile home in question as it existed at the time it was purchased is supported by sufficient evidence and is not against the great weight and preponderance of the evidence. There was detailed testimony as to the extensive nature of the defects which rendered the trailer unfit for the purpose intended and appellees' valuation witness testified that on the basis of such defective condition his opinion of the reasonable cash market value at the time and place of purchase was $2,000.00. Appellant argues that a check list made at the time the mobile home was accepted by the dealer showed no defects or deficiencies; that the testimony reflected a number of checks being made of the appellant's mobile homes during the course of manufacturing; that no defects or deficiencies were indicated at the time Mrs. Morrison went to the dealer's store to pick out the mobile home; and that Knox's testimony indicates that most of the defects could be repaired for $200 or $300. While this testimony could be considered as bearing upon the actual cash market value of the mobile home at time of purchase, it was not conclusive and the jury was at liberty to conclude from the evidence that the market value was as stated in the opinion of Mr. Knox. We overrule appellant's points of error numbers 10, 13 and 14.

Appellant's last point is that the trial court erred in awarding interest at the legal rate from May 2, 1969, the date of purchase. Under the circumstances of this case we find the trial court was justified in awarding interest by way of damages on the difference between the value of the mobile home in its existing condition at the time of purchase and its reasonable cash market value if it had been free from defects. . . . UCC 2-715. . . . Appellant's point of error No. 17 is overruled.

The judgment of the trial court is affirmed.

NOTES & QUESTIONS

1. *Notice of breach; examination and cure.* Although not mentioned by the court in the *Melody Home* case, the Morrisons had to notify Melody Home of the defects within a reasonable time or be barred from any remedy. UCC 2-607(3)(a). Loss of remedy is drastic, but consider the position of Melody Home: if it learns that there may be a breach Melody Home may examine the mobile home to collect evidence and it may cure acknowledged defects. UCC 2-508, 2-515. Obviously Melody Home will be unable to examine or cure if it is not told there are problems. It should also be noted that the burden on the Morrisons is not great: the notice does not have to be formal as long as it lets Melody Home know that the transaction is still troublesome. UCC 2-607, Comment 4.

2. *Burden of proof.* Having accepted the mobile home the Morrisons have the burden of proving the breach. UCC 2-607(4).

3. *Value of goods as warranted.* As the *Melody Home* case illustrates, the value of the goods as warranted need not be the same as the purchase price. For a dramatic example of this point and of the buyer's difficult burden of proof, see Chatlos Systems, Inc. v. National Cash Register Corp., 670 F.2d 1304, 33 UCC Rep. 934 (3d Cir. 1982) (fair market value of computer system as warranted, rather than favorable purchase price, the appropriate value for determining amount of damages under UCC 2-714).

SOO LINE R.R. v. FRUEHAUF CORP.
547 F.2d 1365, 20 UCC Rep. 1181 (8th Cir. 1977)

STEPHENSON, Circuit Judge. This appeal concerns a contract in which Fruehauf Corporation (Magor) [a division of Fruehauf] agreed to the manufacture, sale and delivery of 500 railroad hopper cars to Soo Line Railroad Company for the approximate price of $9,750,000. Soo Line, in this diversity action initiated against Magor, claims breach of contract and negligence in the manufacture of the railcars, and the district court entered judgment based upon a jury verdict for Soo Line in the amount of $1,238,754.82. Magor appeals. . . . [W]e affirm.

Magor and Soo Line in 1967 created the contract which provided for Magor to manufacture and deliver 500 covered hopper freight railroad cars at approximately $19,500 per car according to an agreed design and detailed written specifications. . . .

Soo Line, a corporation that owns and operates substantial railroad lines and railroad cars, purchased the cars and utilized them pursuant to a long term net lease for public service in hauling grain and other dry bulk commodities. The cars were delivered in early 1968. It is undisputed that, despite an estimated 40-year useful life, the underframes developed serious and widespread cracks in the wheel structure and welds within a few months of delivery. Following both unilateral and mutual inspection of the railcars by the parties, Soo Line concluded that the cracks resulted from structural and welding defects and accordingly requested that Magor perform its obligation to repair pursuant to the warranty. However, Magor's management, claiming that the cracking derived from construction specifications required by Soo Line insisted it had no such responsibility. After Magor refused to repair the cars, Soo Line implemented its own remedial operation. The cost of repairs was $506,862.78, slightly more than $1,000 per car. Soo Line has contended, and the jury verdict reflects, that this expenditure did not fully restore the cars to totally acceptable operating condition.

On July 30, 1971, Soo Line filed its complaint claiming breach of express and implied warranties and negligence based on the structural failure of the railroad cars and Magor's refusal to accept responsibility for repair. . . .

Trial commenced on August 13, 1975, and concluded on October 2, 1975, with a jury verdict in favor of Soo Line. . . . The jury in its special verdicts awarded: $975,970 for the difference between the value of the cars as accepted and their value if built to conform to the contract specifications; $182,444 for revenue lost while the cars were undergoing repairs; and $10,084.93 for damages sustained in transporting the cars in connection with their repair.[4] The trial court adopted the answers in the special verdict and *inter alia* found that Soo Line had sustained $70,255.89, in damages resulting from spoiled ladings caused by water leakage through defective roofs of the cars. In addition, the district court concluded as a matter of law that the warranty provision in the contract was ineffective in limiting Magor's liability and entered judgment in the total amount of $1,238,754.82. Magor appeals from the denial of its post-trial motions for judgment notwithstanding the verdict or, in the alternative, for a new trial. . . .

The most significant issue in this appeal is whether either the disclaimer of liability, inspection clause or remedial limitation contained within the contract bars recovery of any or all damages arising from defective manufacture of the railroad cars. . . .We consider initially the remedial limitation upon liability arising from breach of the express warranty.

It is undisputed and the district court found that the document entitled "Terms and Conditions of Sale" is a part of the contract between Soo Line and Magor. The warranty provision appearing in this document specifically states:

> We will warrant to you (except as to items not manufactured by us) for a period of one year after date of acceptance of each of said cars that they will be free from all defects in material and workmanship under normal use and service, and that the cars will be in full conformity with the specifications referred to herein. Our obligation under this warranty shall be limited to repairing or replacing any part which is found to be defective provided we are notified of the fault or defect when it is first discovered and we are afforded an opportunity for verification, said repairs or replacement to be made at our plant or at such other place as

---

4. The jury found that 95% of the negligence could be attributed to Magor and 5% to Soo Line and awarded $699,391.71 for damages sustained as a direct result of such negligence.

may be mutually agreed upon. This warranty is expressly in lieu of all other warranties expressed or implied, and we shall not be liable for indirect or consequential damages resulting from any such defects in material or workmanship.[5]

The court eventually concluded, without articulating a particular reason, that this warranty provision was ineffective to limit Magor's liability.

In this diversity case we are, of course, applying the substantive law of Minnesota. It is clear under Minnesota law that parties to a contract may limit or alter the measure of damages recoverable, as by limiting the buyer's remedies to repair and replacement of nonconforming goods or parts. UCC 2-719(1). . . . A limited remedy to repair or replace goods which are initially defective but are promptly remedied by the seller will normally be enforceable. UCC 2-719, Comment 1.

Nevertheless, limitations on remedies and damages permissible under UCC 2-719(1) are subject to UCC 2-719(2), which states:

Where circumstances cause an exclusive or limited remedy to fail of its essential purpose, remedy must be had as provided in this chapter.[6]

The rationale underlying UCC 2-719(2) is adequately reflected by the court's statement in Jones & McKnight v. Birdsboro Corp., 320 F. Supp. 39, 43-44 (N.D. Ill. 1970): "This Court would be in an untenable position if it allowed the defendant to shelter itself behind one segment of the warranty when it has allegedly repudiated and ignored its very limited obligations under another segment of the same warranty, which alleged repudiation has caused the very need for relief which the defendant is attempting to avoid."

In applying UCC 2-719 to the facts in the instant case, we conclude that the remedial limitation contained within the contract failed of its essential purpose and is therefore unenforceable. The record reveals substantial evidence showing that the railroad cars manufactured by Magor were defective with respect to their structure and the welding of certain crucial joints which precipitated serious cracking in the underframes of the cars. . . . Even more significant is the jury's answer to question 6(b) of the special verdict form, which states that Magor did not meet its obligation to repair or replace defective parts of the railcars.[7] The jury also found, as reflected by its answer to

5. T. R. Klingel, executive vice president of Soo Line, testified that the warranties given by a manufacturer of railroad equipment are non-negotiable and that in this particular transaction the subject of the warranty never arose during the negotiations.

6. The Minnesota Code Comments reflect that UCC 2-719(2) is consistent with cases decided prior to Minnesota's adoption of the Uniform Commercial Code in 1961. Under the pre-Code law, where enforcement of a contractual remedy would have been unreasonably harsh, the Minnesota Supreme Court employed strict construction or found a waiver of remedial limitations. . . . We also note that in other jurisdictions courts applying UCC 2-719(2) have uniformly concluded that a breach by a manufacturer of a limited obligation to repair or replace defective parts caused a limited remedy to fail of its essential purpose. . . .

7. A limited remedy fails of its purpose whenever the seller fails to repair goods within a reasonable time. UCC 2-719 becomes operative when a party is deprived of its contractual remedy and it is unnecessary to prove that failure to repair was willful or negligent. See Beal v. General Motors Corp., 354 F. Supp. at 427 [p. 701 infra].

question 6(a), that Soo Line had promptly notified Magor, pursuant to the contract, of the defects and afforded Magor the opportunity to verify the defects. . . .

Based on this evidence, we conclude that the contract's limited remedy of repair failed of its essential purpose, and therefore all available Uniform Commercial Code remedies apply. See UCC 2-719(2) and 2-714. . . .

Finally, we consider the question whether Magor should be exonerated from liability for consequential damages because the contract contains a specific bar against such damages existing independently of the exclusive remedy to repair.[12] The Minnesota courts have yet to confront this issue. A federal court must, notwithstanding the absence of a controlling state decision, apply the rule it believes the courts of the state would follow. Accordingly, we conclude that the contract does not effectively bar liability for consequential damages. . . . Uniform Commercial Code remedies should be liberally administered, UCC 1-106, and a buyer when entering into a contract does not anticipate that the sole remedy available will be rendered a nullity, thus causing additional damages. In addition, the fundamental intent of UCC 2-719(2) reflects that a remedial limitation's failure of essential purpose makes available all contractual remedies, including consequential damages authorized pursuant to UCC 2-714 and 2-715. See Jones & McKnight Corp. v. Birdsboro Corp., 320 F. Supp. 39, 43-44 (N.D. Ill. 1970); Adams v. J. I. Case Co., 125 Ill. App. 2d 388, 261 N.E.2d 1 (1970) [p. 687 infra]. See generally J. White & R. Summers, Handbook of the Law under the Uniform Commercial Code §12-10, at 382 (1972).

For the reasons outlined above, we hold that neither the remedial limitation, the inspection provision, nor the disclaimer of consequential damages contained within the Soo Line-Magor contract prohibits liability arising from breach of the express warranty. Without the limiting clauses, the Uniform Commercial Code remedies apply, including those set out in UCC 2-714 which allows the buyer damages for non-conforming goods. See UCC 2-719 and 2-714. . . .

In reviewing the substance of Klingel's testimony on valuation, the measure of damages and the limits of relevancy are set by the substantive law of Minnesota. . . . Under Minnesota law, the measure of damages applicable to breach of contract is the difference between the actual value of the cars at the time of acceptance and the value they would have had if they had been as warranted. UCC 2-714(2). . . . The buyer is not limited to repair costs when repair does not completely restore the goods to the value which they would have had if built in conformity with the contract; remaining diminution in value may also be recovered. . . .

Taking into consideration the structural and welding defects existing in the cars manufactured for Soo Line by Magor, Klingel expressed the opinion

---

12. The jury awarded $262,784.82 in consequential damages, which includes $182,444 for loss of revenue and $70,255.89 for leakage claims paid to shippers.

that the reasonable market value per car was $17,500 at the most. Klingel further opined that he would probably discount the purchase price of the cars by an additional $1,000 or $2,000, which would result in a fair market value of approximately $15,500 per car.

In formulating the diminution in fair market value of the cars, Klingel properly placed reliance on the necessity for present and future repairs and the fact that even a rebuilt patched railcar would be worth less than a correctly constructed one. . . . The record reflects that approximately $1,000 per car in immediate repair costs was expended by Soo Line and that, even after implementation of the repairs, Soo Line had experienced continued maintenance costs beyond those expended for cars other than those manufactured by Magor.

Klingel also stated that a hypothetical buyer of the railcars would discount the purchase price because the buyer's financing costs would continue while the cars were out of service being repaired with no ability to generate revenue. Klingel testified that approximately $200,000 or $400 per car in interest payments would be lost without concomitant benefit during repairs. This statement, of course, may not be considered as evidence of diminution in value of the Soo Line railcars. Cost of financing is not an element of reduced market value pursuant to UCC 2-714. Nonetheless, we reject appellant's contention that this aspect of Klingel's testimony rendered inadmissible his overall opinion on the diminution in market value of the railcars. An objection that an expert's opinion is based on elements of damage not lawfully recoverable generally relates to the weight rather than the admissibility of the testimony. . . .

For similar reasons, we reject appellant's assertion that Klingel's reference to "future maintenance costs" was unduly speculative and erroneous. Klingel merely expressed an opinion on the present value of the railcars at the time of acceptance in light of known risks associated with existing defects. Soo Line had already experienced increased maintenance costs with Magor cars previously repaired. Klingel's testimony overall had sufficient probative value to outweigh the danger that it would lead the jury to assess damages on an improper basis. . . . Magor had adequate opportunity to cross-examine and refute Klingel's testimony on valuation. . . . Under these circumstances, we conclude that the trial court did not commit an abuse of discretion in the admission of Klingel's testimony concerning the diminution in market value of the railroad cars resulting from their structural failure. . . .

Affirmed.

NOTES & QUESTIONS

1. *Consequential damages: lost revenue.* Soo Line recovered $182,444 as consequential damages for revenue lost while the cars were being repaired. Are you persuaded by the following argument against this award? "The value of the cars as warranted represents the discounted value of the expected flow of net

revenues to be earned by use of the cars. Likewise, the value of the cars as accepted is an estimate based on the expected flow of revenues—a flow which is smaller because of the cost of repairs and the loss of revenues while the cars are being repaired. The difference between these two values (i.e. $975,970) already includes the $182,444 claimed as 'consequential' damages."

2. *Consequential damages: property damage.* Soo Line recovered $70,255.89 in damages for ladings spoiled by water leaking through the defective roofs. Should this amount be reduced if Magor shows that Soo Line could have avoided 40 percent of the loss by the use of tarpaulins? May Magor avoid liability if it shows that it had not foreseen that Soo Line would transport such expensive goods in the cars? See UCC 2-715(2).

CHAPTER 14

Warranty

A. INTRODUCTION[1]

Warranty law addresses a host of questions concerning the seller's obligations with respect to the quality of goods sold, which may arise either from the words or conduct of the seller in a specific transaction (express warranties) or by implication from the circumstances of the sale (implied warranties).

In studying the law governing warranties your first task is to become familiar with the types of warranties the Code recognizes, the facts necessary for their creation, and the scope of the obligation they impose once created. Second, you should consider the seller's freedom (a) to avoid or to disclaim warranty liability and (b) to limit the remedies available to the buyer when a warranty is breached. Finally, you should study the relation of the Code's scheme to other bodies of law affecting product liability and evaluate the continuing vitality of particular warranty rules, such as the traditional requirement of privity.

Several points should be borne in mind throughout your study of this chapter. The first is the long and checkered history of warranty. Lying on the borderline of tort and contract, warranty has at different times seemed more tort-like or more contractual in nature. At the time the Code was formulated no jurisdiction had yet adopted strict tort liability for defective products. Thus warranty law was under some pressure to fill this void, and the Code bears some signs of these pressures (although some more extensive proposed revisions had to be abandoned.) Yet strict liability doctrine triumphed at about the same time the Code was enacted in many jurisdictions, leaving warranty law free to develop principally economic loss issues. One continued sign of the tort heritage of warranty is the tension between warranty law as a set of suppletory provisions, providing the presumed intent of the parties in given circum-

---

1. This chapter focuses on the warranty of quality. For a brief description of the warranty of title (UCC 2-312), see p. 521 supra. You might reconsider the warranty of title after reading the following materials. To what extent is that warranty amenable to an analysis based on commercially reasonable expectations and the allocation of the risk of defects?

stances, and warranty law as a set of norms dictating minimal acceptable standards for transactions, without regard to intent. Frequently, of course, both concerns will be present, and it will not be possible to determine with certainty which is dominant.

Second, the Code's provisions governing warranty are few in number and purport to apply generally to all contracts for the sale of goods. But the types of transactions to be so governed are exceedingly diverse. There may be a tendency for the quite broad principles to produce clusters of cases centered on certain kinds of transactions ("type-transactions"?). Eventually, therefore, there may be not a law of express warranty, law of implied warranty, and law of limited remedies, but rather a law of automobile warranties, a law of bulk commodity warranties, and a law of turbine generator warranties. However, the drawbacks of such an approach are also readily noted: decisions that are correct on the facts of the transaction will distort ostensible doctrine and will prevent more promising generalizations from being discerned.

A third point to be considered is the tendency of warranty problems to defy easy pigeonholing. Although the Code's structure sets forth an intellectually clean analysis, courts' and counsels' handling of raw facts is not so fastidious. In part to give the student an accurate sense of this flavor of warranty law, the principal cases have been lightly edited and are often followed by notes drawing your attention to alternative, and sometimes superior, analyses.

Against the background of these general concerns, you need to obtain a basic knowledge of the Code provisions that address the various issues of warranty law.

Initially it must be determined whether any warranties exist in a given transaction. Another way of stating this question is whether the seller has any obligation respecting the properties of the goods, or whether the buyer is entirely at risk as to their quality.

Under the Code's structure the ultimate question of the existence of warranty involves three potential subissues. The first of these is creation of warranty. It is dealt with in three sections, UCC 2-313 (express warranties), 2-314 (implied warranty of merchantability), and 2-315 (implied warranty of fitness for a particular purpose). These sections detail the transactions in which, and circumstances under which, the respective types of warranty arise. Second, where more than one warranty is arguably present, UCC 2-317 must be consulted to determine whether the warranties are cumulative, or whether one or more is displaced. Finally, UCC 2-316 must be considered to ascertain whether there has been an effective disclaimer of warranties which might otherwise be present. These five warranty sections, however, together with the possible application of sections such as UCC 2-202 (parol evidence), 1-205 (usage of trade), and 2-302 (unconscionability), are sufficient to determine the existence of a warranty in a transaction.

A second major issue is who extends warranties to whom. At one time, warranties extended only between parties who were in privity of contract. The student is probably already familiar with the decline of this doctrine in tort law. In warranty law there has also been substantial change but the doctrine retains some vitality. With respect to the issue of vertical privity (e.g., action by buyer against manufacturer in addition to retailer) the Code is neutral. One provision, UCC 2-318, deals with issues of horizontal privity (e.g., action by buyer's husband against seller), but current privity law is usually case law, and is distinctly nonuniform.

A third set of issues relates to scope of warranty, breach and causation. Scope refers to the standard of quality a given warranty imposes and requires attention to the same sections that determine the creation of warranty. Breach and causation pose issues general to the law of contract. Although these issues are analytically separate, they are grouped together here for a practical reason: a warranty dispute begins with facts—frequently the failure of goods to perform to a given level. In such cases (more typical of goods for end use than for raw materials), a process of reasoning back is employed: if the goods can be shown to be warranted fit for a given use, then the unfitness for such use will per se suggest a breach that caused the loss. While such a process may be descriptive of initial appraisals of a situation, some of the cases in this chapter will illustrate the dangers of forgetting the distinct phases of the analysis. Many sellers strive diligently to assure that they will warrant only one or more properties of the goods they sell, and not fitness for use. In such cases, the buyer will have to establish carefully all three elements: scope, breach, and that the breach caused the loss. Even in cases where fitness for *some* end use is warranted, murky disagreements about the exact character or scope of that use may arise. Causation may also be disputed, such as where the plaintiff has relied primarily on evidence of unfitness to satisfy all three elements, and it is then suggested that this is insufficient. The alleged failure of the goods may have other causes, such as misuse. These issues tend to run into one another, are often highly factual, and require careful thought with limited statutory direction.

Finally, you must consider the remedies available to the aggrieved buyer. In part this requires only a thoughtful application of the doctrine learned in preceding chapters. But limitations of remedy are so frequently used in some warranty contexts that this chapter will give more extensive consideration both to why this is the case and the effectiveness of such limitations under both Code provisions (UCC 2-719) and other applicable law.

As you study the Code's warranty provisions remember that they address issues that have been around for many centuries. Some historical perspective should encourage a healthy skepticism that the Code's solutions are final. For provocative studies see Gilmore, Law, Logic and Experience, 3 How. L.J. 26 (1957); Hamilton, The Ancient Maxim Caveat Emptor, 40 Yale L.J. 1113 (1931); Llewellyn, On Warranty of Quality, and Society (pts. 1 & 2), 36 Colum. L. Rev. 699 (1936), 37 Colum. L. Rev. 341 (1937). The following excerpt from Llewellyn's masterful review of Anglo-American warranty cases emphasizes a point already made, the importance of identifying the type of transaction.

LLEWELLYN, ON WARRANTY OF QUALITY, AND SOCIETY
36 Colum. L. Rev. 699, 720-723 (1936)

At two poles, behind such a state of decisions [in early nineteenth century England], behind even such conditioning factors as the Exchequer's technical rigidity, lie in my guess two conceptions of that elusive figment, "The Market." The one envisages the yokel in Cheapside, the horse-trade, the wooden nutmeg, the butter-and-egg man in a metropolitan night-club, the distributing center sucking the shekels out of a commercially illiterate bunch of savages, backwoodsmen, farmers, small-towners, or foreigners, to the advance of real estate values, general prosperity, and happy days for the only people who count. The type-buyer is in such a picture often an outsider; above all, he is a man whose money is more wanted than his trade. The type-goods are there to see, at the time of dicker; let the buyer trust his eyes! Although the type-seller may be superior in understanding of the goods and of the bargain-game as a modern Armenian rug-dealer is to most of the customers he manages to acquire.

The other pole is Utopia: value to the buyer. But, more or less approaching it, there exists another view of the market: repeat orders are what a seller needs; to stand behind words, and even behind wares-without-words, is good business *for the seller*—and is therefore good policy for a court to encourage. Transactions look to future delivery; even where they do not, they look to standard quality of goods produced in mass and grade, and sold by name, brand, or description. Distribution of goods is indirect, almost as of course; a buyer has only his dealer to trust to; it is a dealer's business to know the goods he sells. As between dealers (even as between retail-dealer and consumers), standing relations mean goodwill; and goodwill is what makes the balance-sheet wax fat. Confidence, not trickery, is the basis of prosperity. The department store, in the final stages of this thinking, reaches in to partially protect even the ultimate consumer: "The customer is always right." . . .

What is essential to an understanding of the shifts which have *already* occurred in the law of seller's obligation for quality, is to see that as a given court, in its sizing up of the background situation, approximates the one or the other of the two much exaggerated over-idealizations of face-to-face and of credit markets indicated above, the decision of particular cases will differ, and the shape and growth-path of rules of law will alter. This because here, as in all bargain-law (and most of tort, and much of criminal law, and such non-bargain transaction-situations as estoppel or waiver), the court's conception of *reasonableness-in-the-circumstances* goes far toward determining its views on proper rules, *and especially toward determining its reading of fact.* Take such superficially disparate problems as when spoken or written words are to operate at all against the seller; or as to the operative effect of displaying a blue-print or a specimen or model; or as to whether a warranty of quality will be "implied" from mere sale and circumstance; and if so, how far that implied warranty carries. Common to all is a picture of the way in which dickers of this kind typically happen, and so of how the parties *ought* to have understood what was said and done. The creation of implied obligations, and the measurement of their scope, seek in the first instance to standardize what is supposedly common understanding in fact. Of course, they run beyond this; the obligation implicit, because tacit, tends ever to be followed by the obligation imposed by force and arms, but in the guise of tacit understanding. . . .

What is, however, almost regularly neglected in discussion of sales law, is that the court's background picture of transactions "of *this* type" very commonly indeed is not one merely of a "sale" or "a contract for sale" or of "express" or "implied" warranty, but rather of "a sale of produce by a farmer to a buyer," or "a sale of farm machinery to a farmer," or "an overseas documentary sale (or contract therefor)," or "a contract for sale by a city manufacturer to a small-town dealer," or "a sale of something *I* should not like to see prove dangerous to *me*." What the types are which have often enough and consistently enough moved in the background of courts' minds to justify— indeed, to require—attention to their effects as one reanalyzes the *law* of sales in its operation and true meaning, is to be found only by wrestling with the cases and with the types of transaction out of which these cases grew. In this paper particular attention is paid only to certain significant divergences which appear between primitive-mercantile, credit-mercantile, and ultimate-consumer transactions.

To put Llewellyn's comments in comparative perspective, see Kessler, The Protection of the Consumer under Modern Sales Law, Part I—A Comparative Study, 74 Yale L.J. 262 (1964).

Throughout this chapter, you should carefully consider the "type-transaction" involved in each case or problem, and the extent to which the Code allows, or requires, consideration of the transaction-type.

Note: Consumer Warranties: A Disclaimer

These course materials focus on *commercial* transactions. In the area of warranty law, however, concern for the protection of nonbusiness consumers in recent years has stimulated the development of legal rules that have superseded or supplemented the Code's warranty framework. We examine these extra-Code developments at the end of this chapter, but we emphasize here that merely to know the Code warranty rules is not sufficient to resolve questions of consumer warranty protection.

One by-product of the recent concern with consumer protection is that some of the best recent academic studies of warranty law have focused on sales to consumers. See Priest, A Theory of the Consumer Product Warranty, 90 Yale L.J. 1297 (1981); Whitford, Comment on a Theory of the Consumer

Product Warranty, 91 Yale L.J. 1371 (1982); Priest, The Best Evidence of the Effect of Products Liability Law on the Accident Rate: Reply, 91 Yale L.J. 1386 (1982); Schwartz & Wilde, Imperfect Information in Markets for Contract Terms: The Examples of Warranties and Security Interests, 69 Va. L. Rev. 1387 (1983).

B.   EXISTENCE OF WARRANTY

As the introductory materials noted, the Code provides three major forms of warranty as to quality: the express warranty (UCC 2-313), the implied warranty of merchantability (UCC 2-314), and the implied warranty of fitness for a particular purpose (UCC 2-315). The following problems and cases focus on whether a warranty exists, which necessarily introduces questions of whether the parties have agreed to an effective disclaimer that states that even if a warranty might otherwise exist the parties agree that in this transaction this warranty will not be given effect. UCC 2-316. In addition, there will be some consideration of scope, causation and breach. As you were warned, warranty cases do not stay in neat pigeonholes.

Consider in reading the materials whether there is an essential unity to the tripartite division of the Code's warranty provisions. The argument might proceed as follows:

"Warranty law protects the buyer's reasonable expectations about the quality of goods. These expectations all arise because of some 'action' taken by the seller. The seller's action may be as formal as a written statement that 'Seller warrants that this wheat is #2 Hard Red Winter Wheat.' But the seller's action need not be this express in order to stimulate a buyer's legitimate expectations as to quality. A buyer may, for example, tell a shoe salesman that he wants to buy boots for mountain climbing and indicate that he is relying on the salesman's skill to select suitable boots; even if the salesman is the strong silent type and says nothing, the buyer will expect to receive appropriate boots. On the other hand, where the salesman acts for a shoe merchant who regularly sells shoes, a buyer who just wants 'every-day' shoes may say nothing to the salesman but will expect that the shoes will be fit for walking around in even if the salesman also says nothing.

"In the last two cases the seller makes no express statement. In *all* the cases, however, the seller should know that the buyer is likely to have expectations. Warranty law in effect says these expectations are reasonable and requires the seller either to provide goods of the expected quality or to bargain with the buyer to change the expectation. The bargain may shift to the buyer the risk that the goods will not meet the anticipated quality or may provide for delivery of goods with lesser qualities. To place this burden on the seller is not a hardship: the seller may choose not to make statements or promises about the quality of the goods; he may choose not to be a professional seller of the goods; and he may choose not to sell if he is uncertain his goods will satisfy the buyer's particular needs.

"Talk of reasonable expectations can be recast in terms of risk allocation. The seller has the risk that goods will not meet a standard he expressly or impliedly says they meet unless the buyer agrees to accept the risk that they do not meet the standard. No matter how the issue is expressed, however, there is no need to accept the Code's tripartite division of warranties as anything more than a useful elaboration of the general principle." Sound?

U.S. FIBRES, INC. v. PROCTOR & SCHWARTZ, INC.
358 F. Supp. 449, 13 UCC Rep. 254 (E.D. Mich. 1972)

[Steuernagel developed a process to produce a resinated cotton pad. The process consisted of introducing a dry resin into a fluffy cotton pad, curing the resinated pads under heat, and then reducing the thickness of the pad by pressure. He persuaded Clapp and Simon to form U.S. Fibres to supply padding to various car makers. The company approached Proctor & Schwartz (P & S) to supply machinery necessary to produce the padding. Before purchase U.S. Fibres insisted on tests to see if the P & S machinery would produce padding that met Ford Motor Co. specifications. After successful tests the parties negotiated for the supply of an oven and two duo-forms with specified dimensions and capacities. Neither the oven nor the duo-forms had been used for a similar dry resin process. P & S supplied duo-forms already in existence and specially manufactured the oven, which was larger than existing P & S ovens.

After installation in January, 1966, U.S. Fibres encountered a number of problems. P & S cured early problems and paid U.S. Fibres "back charges" as compensation. In March, 1966, the parties agreed on the purchase of a second oven dryer, which was installed later that year. Again P & S had to make a number of repairs and adjustments. The earlier equipment was used through June, 1969, when it was dismantled. The later dryer was used through March, 1968. While in operation U.S. Fibres used the equipment to produce padding that varied considerably in density and that in some cases was as much as twice the density required by Ford specifications.]

KAESS, Chief Judge. This is a civil action for damages, claiming fraud, breach of express warranties, breach of implied warranty of merchantability, breach of implied warranty of fitness for a particular purpose, and negligence. . . .

The parties entered into written contracts in connection with the purchase of all of the equipment involved in this case. Each contract contained a long description of the equipment to be supplied. Included in the contract of June 10, 1965 are the following provisions:

Performance.

The herein described machine is designed to cure resin impregnated cotton batting at the rate of 1200 pounds per hour.

It should be noted that in view of the variables present affecting the capacity of the machine, no guarantee can be extended. However, the Company's standard warranty outlined later in this contract does apply. . . .

CONVEYORS

A. Carrying Conveyor

This conveyor consists of plain steel plates with 1/8″ diameter holes on 3/16″ centers. These conveyor plates have an effective width of 96″ and are attached to two runs of plain steel 8″ pitch roller chain riding on wear strips fastened to rugged steel track. Each plate has a rugged separate supporting girt and is interlocked with a special piano hinge joint. This conveyor is especially designed to hold a tolerance of ± 1/32″ across the width of the batt, based on a 30 pound per square foot compressive force.

B. Holddown Conveyor

The holddown conveyor has materials of construction as above. It is designed and fabricated so that its pitch line coincides with the pitch line of the carrying conveyor. This conveyor is designed so that it is easily adjustable through a motorized set of mechanical jacks located at the appropriate intervals on the roof along the length of the machine. . . .

GENERAL PROVISIONS

1. The Company warrants the machine against defects in materials or workmanship, but makes no other warranties, express or implied (except as set forth under "Patents") unless the word "guarantee" is used. Warranties of merchantability or of fitness for a particular purpose or arising from a course of dealing or usage of trade, are specifically excluded. The Purchaser agrees that any affirmations of fact, description of the machine or sample or model machine herein referred to, whether or not the same relate to production or capability of the machine to perform, are not the basis of this contract, unless the word "guarantee" is used in connection therewith, in which case the same shall be express warranties. . . .

No modification of this agreement shall be binding unless such modification shall be in writing, accepted by the Purchaser and approved by an officer of the Company. . . .

3. The Company's liability hereunder shall exist only if the machine is erected, started in operation and tested with the assistance of one of the Company's loaned employees, is erected in conformity with erection instructions, if any, furnished by the Company, has had normal use and service for the purpose for which it was designed, has not been subjected to misuse, negligence or accident and has not been altered or repaired by others than the Company in any respect which in the Company's judgment affects its condition or operation.

4. In the event that the machine does not conform to the provisions of this contract, the Purchaser's *exclusive remedy* shall be as follows: Purchaser may give the Company written notice of non-conformity within ninety (90) days after date

of shipment. Within ninety (90) days after the Company shall receive such notice, the Company shall have the opportunity of making the machine conform to the provisions of this contract. If the Company is unable to do so, the Company shall, upon order in writing from the Purchaser, remove the machine as soon as practicable, refund any portion of the purchase price heretofore paid and cancel the Purchaser's obligation to pay the unpaid portion of the price in full satisfaction of the Company's liability hereunder. The Purchaser shall furnish at the Purchaser's expense a means of egress for removal of the machine.

5. The Company shall repair or replace f.o.b. Company's plant any defective parts furnished hereunder upon receipt of notice from the Purchaser within one year from the date of shipment. All labor involved in the removal and/or installation of such parts shall be at the Purchaser's expense.

6. The Company shall not be liable for proximate, incidental, consequential or other damages, including, but not limited to erecting expenses and damages for loss of production or injury to person or property.

The contract of March 23, 1966 contained the same provisions, except that under Conveyors, the following provision was substituted under "A. Carrying Conveyor":

This conveyor consists of plain steel plates with $1/8''$ diameter holes on $3/16''$ centers. These conveyor plates have an effective width of $96''$ and are attached to two runs of plain steel $8''$ pitch roller chain riding on wear strips fastened to rugged steel track. Each plate has a rugged separate supporting girt and is interlocked with a special piano hinge joint. This conveyor is especially designed with a deflection tolerance of $\pm 1/32''$ across each conveyor plate. This deflection is further based on a uniformly distributed load of 30 pounds per sq. ft. . . .

Plaintiff first claims a breach of express warranty. UCC 2-313(1) provides as follows:

(1) Express warranties by the seller are created as follows:
    (a) Any affirmation of fact or promise made by the seller to the buyer which relates to the goods and becomes part of the basis of the bargain creates an express warranty that the goods shall conform to the affirmation or promise.
    (b) Any description of the goods which is made part of the basis of the bargain creates an express warranty that the goods shall conform to the description. . . .
   [(c) Any sample or model which is made part of the basis of the bargain creates an express warranty that the whole of the goods shall conform to the sample or model.]

[The court quotes only paragraphs (a) and (b). Is (c) relevant?—EDS.]

There can be no doubt that Section 1 of the General Provisions of the contract is an express warranty against defects in materials and workmanship with regard to all machinery involved in this case. The evidence shows that there was a breach of this warranty with regard to the dryer on Line I, as indicated by the following defects: (1) a left-handed oven instead of a right-handed oven; (2) failure to properly drill holes in the conveyor; (3) failure to level dryer properly; (4) lack of clutch to prevent conveyors from running at different speeds.

The evidence likewise indicates certain defects in the Line II dryer which were a breach of the express warranty given by Proctor. However, all of these defects were remedied by the defendant. In addition to the repairs, all claims for breach of the express warranty were fully settled by the defendant when it paid so-called "back charges" to the plaintiff.

The plaintiff also claims that certain descriptions in both contracts amount to express warranties. Certainly descriptions which form the basis of the bargain can be express warranties. However, all such descriptions have been negated as express warranties by Section 1 of the liability clauses, since the word "guarantee" does not appear in the clauses as required by the contracts.

Such provisions are permitted under UCC 2-316(1), which provides:

> Words or conduct relevant to the creation of an express warranty and words or conduct tending to negate or limit warranty shall be construed wherever reasonable as consistent with each other; but subject to the provisions of this Article on parol or extrinsic evidence (Section 2-202) negation or limitation is inoperative to the extent that such construction is unreasonable.

The Official Code Comments provide that: "This section is designed principally to deal with those frequent clauses in sales contracts which seek to exclude 'all warranties, express or implied.' It seeks to protect a buyer from unexpected and unbargained language when inconsistent with language of express warranty and permitting the exclusion of implied warranties only by conspicuous language or other circumstances which protect the buyer from surprise."

Thus, any description of the equipment, such as the Clause under A.— Carrying Conveyer, which provides: "This conveyor is especially designed to hold a tolerance of $\pm$ 1/32 across the width of the batt, based on a 30 pound per square foot compressive force." did not give rise to an express warranty. . . . This interpretation of the contract is fully warranted by the evidence in this case, which clearly shows that, at the time in question, we are dealing with an unproven process. At the time the first Duoform and drying oven were purchased, no one had ever used them in connection with the process which plaintiff contemplated. At the time of the original contract, in June of 1965, it was Steuernagel who thought the P&S dryer could be used to cure air flote-dry resin pads which are involved in this case.

Under these circumstances, it cannot be said that the contract provisions were unexpected by the buyer. In fact, it would have been sheer folly to warrant the performance of the machines. Thus, we do not have a situation in which the contract both gives an express warranty to the buyer and in the next breath takes it away. The provisions of the contract are consistent within the meaning of UCC 2-316(1). Therefore considering the contract as a whole, there are no express warranties beyond the express warranties against defects in materials and workmanship.

Plaintiff next claims a breach of implied warranty of fitness. UCC 2-315 provides:

> Where the seller at the time of contracting has reason to know any particular purposes for which the goods are required and that the buyer is relying on the seller's skill or judgment to select or furnish suitable goods, there is unless excluded or modified under the next section an implied warranty that the goods shall be fit for such purpose.

Whether or not this warranty arises in any individual case is basically a question of fact to be determined by the surrounding circumstances. Of course, under the above section, the buyer need not bring home to the seller the actual knowledge of the particular purpose for which the machine is intended, or his reliance on the seller's skill and judgment, if the circumstances are such that the seller has reason to realize the purpose intended. However, the buyer must actually be relying on the seller. . . .

Steuernagel admitted that he was familiar with compression drying. He stated that, in the mid-1950's, he read dry resin fiber process patents which described a compression dryer which had compression and carrying conveyor. He further admitted that these patents gave him the idea to try his air flote-dry resin process.

In 1959, at Lockport Mills, Steuernagel used a German air laying machine and a compression dryer made by Michigan Ovens to develop a dry-resin process. Steuernagel actually helped modify this drying oven. Steuernagel also worked on the amount of residence time of this drying oven. Steuernagel also worked on 1/4" pads for automotive applications. He was familiar with the compression rating of this oven. Steuernagel applied for a patent for improvements of drying ovens. He was familiar with drying ovens used by Gustin-Bacon and Allen Industries which were used to cure pads. Steuernagel also exhibited great familiarity with other types of drying ovens made by Proctor.

Steuernagel also worked for ten years for James Hunter Company, which makes dryers in direct competition with Proctor. He worked on the development of certain types of conveyor dryers. Although he denied working on a compression dryer, Steuernagel was also aware that, throughout the industry, there were numerous problems encountered with drying ovens. For example, he knew there were tracking problems with conveyors. It appears that he made a trip to see a Proctor dryer in operation and was informed of these problems prior to the order of the dryer from Proctor. In 1964, while employed at Allen Industries, Steuernagel installed a dry-resin line including a compression dryer of Allen's design.

Furthermore, Steuernagel admitted that, based on his experience at Lockport, he felt that the 30 pounds per square foot maximum pressure limitation was more than sufficient to compress the batts.

The evidence showed that the dryer involved in this case was essentially a scaled-up version of a standard 84" Proctor hold down conveyor dryer. It is obvious to the court that plaintiff bought the dryer with the hope that it would work. Oral assurances from certain Proctor personnel that they also thought it would work, or that it should work, do not change the fact that this was a high-risk venture in which no one knew what would work and what would not work.

In this case there could be no implied warranty of fitness. William Clapp and Daniel Steuernagel both had extensive experience in the area of manufacturing operations, non-woven products and textiles. It was Simon who demanded that tests be performed at Proctor before any contract was entered into. It was Steuernagel who supervised these tests at Proctor.

Thus, the evidence has established no reliance upon seller but rather that U.S. Fibres . . . relied upon [its] own judgment and skill in selecting machinery which [it] concluded would produce [its] product. The judgment and skill referred to includes Steuernagel's prior knowledge of the Gustin Bacon compression ovens, the Allen Industries compression ovens and the Michigan Oven compression ovens, all of which were utilized in the manufacture of dry, resinated batting. The reason Steuernagel was hired was to evaluate the Proctor machinery. He viewed the Standard Cotton compression oven and selected a similar oven from Proctor from among those which he knew about.

Furthermore, Clause One of the general provisions of both contracts expressly excludes a warranty of fitness. This provision was fully reviewed by plaintiff prior to signing the contracts. This clause is in conformity to the requirements of UCC 2-316, since it is in writing, conspicuous, and specifically states the word fitness.

Therefore there could be no warranty of fitness on any of the equipment involved in this case.

Plaintiff also claims a breach of implied warranty of merchantability. . . . UCC 2-314 provides:

> (1) Unless excluded or modified (Section 2-316), a warranty that the goods shall be merchantable is implied in a contract for their sale if the seller is a merchant with respect to goods of that kind. . . .
> (2) Goods to be merchantable must be at least such as
> (a)   pass without objection in the trade under the contract description; and . . .
> (c)   are fit for the ordinary purposes for which such goods are used; and
> (d)   run, within the variations permitted by the agreement, of even kind, quality and quantity within each unit and among all units involved; . . .

Here again Clause One of the general provisions of both contracts expressly excludes any warranty of merchantability. . . . UCC 2-316(2) provides:

(2) Subject to subsection (3), to exclude or modify the implied warranty of merchantability or any part of it the language must mention merchantability and in case of a writing must be conspicuous, and to exclude or modify any implied warranty of fitness the exclusion must be by a writing and conspicuous. Language to exclude all implied warranties of fitness is sufficient if it states, for example, that "There are no warranties which extend beyond the description on the face hereof."

Clause One conforms in all respects to the requirements of UCC 2-316(2). This clause was fully reviewed by plaintiff prior to signing the contract. The exclusion is in writing, is conspicuous and expressly mentions the word merchantability.

Plaintiff urges the court to strike down certain provisions of the contracts involved in this case because they are unconscionable. [The court quotes UCC 2-302(1).]

In the light of the facts and commercial background of this transaction, the contract is neither oppressive nor unfair. Both parties realized that its purpose was to allocate the risks associated with this type of transaction. When this is the case, such limitation clauses are enforced, even where one of the parties is in a superior bargaining position. K & C Inc. v. Westinghouse Electric Corporation, 437 Pa. 303, 263 A.2d 390 (1970). . . .

In view of all of these considerations, it is ordered that defendant's motion for an involuntary dismissal be, and hereby is, granted. . . .

NOTES & QUESTIONS

1. *Express warranties: "basis of the bargain."* Whereas Uniform Sales Act §12 required the buyer to show reliance on the seller's affirmation of fact or promise, UCC 2-313(1) requires the buyer to show that the seller's statement was part of the basis of the bargain. Comment 3 to UCC 2-313 suggests that the buyer need not show any particular reliance. What was the U.S. Fibres—P & S bargain? For a recent analysis that stresses the need to have a broad conception of *bargain,* see Murray, "Basis of the Bargain": Transcending Classical Concepts, 66 Minn. L. Rev. 283 (1982).

2. *Implied warranty of merchantability: existence.* For there to be a warranty of merchantability the seller must be not just a merchant (UCC 2-104) but a merchant "with respect to goods of that kind." UCC 2-314(1). Did P & S in the *U.S. Fibres* case meet this requirement? Even if P & S meets the requirements of subsection (1), can the specially manufactured or modified equipment be "merchantable" within any of the categories of subsection (2)? Note that if there is no warranty under UCC 2-314 it is unnecessary to disclaim the warranty. Does including a disclaimer clause provide evidence of the existence of a warranty?

3. *Implied warranty of fitness for a particular purpose: existence.* The *U.S. Fibres* court states that for there to be an implied warranty of fitness for a particular

purpose the buyer must actually rely on the seller's skill or judgment to furnish suitable goods. Is this what UCC 2-315 says? Should there be a reliance requirement? If P & S knew that the equipment it sold would not be suitable for the dry resin process to be used by U.S. Fibres may it remain silent even if the buyer does not rely? Is the contract doctrine of mistake relevant? See Kronman, Mistake, Disclosure, Information, and the Law of Contracts, 7 J. Leg. Stud. 1 (1978) (unless parties actually assign risk of mistake, legal rules should assign risk to cheaper information-gatherer).

4. *Samples and models.* The Uniform Sales Act provided separately for "implied warranties in sale by sample" (§16). The UCC combines sales by sample with sales by use of models, and labels the warranties as express. UCC 2-313(1)(c). Although a seller who exhibits a model paring knife may say nothing, he can reasonably expect a buyer to believe that a paring knife sold by him will conform with the characteristics of the model. Are prototypes "models" within the meaning of this section?

LEWIS v. MOBIL OIL CORP.
438 F.2d 500, 8 UCC Rep. 625 (8th Cir. 1971)

GIBSON, Circuit Judge. . . . Plaintiff Lewis has been doing business as a sawmill operator in Cove, Arkansas, since 1956. In 1963, in order to meet competition, Lewis decided to convert his power equipment to hydraulic equipment. He purchased a hydraulic system in May 1963, from a competitor who was installing a new system. The used system was in good operating condition at the time Lewis purchased it. It was stored at his plant until November 1964, while a new mill building was being built, at which time it was installed. Following the installation, Lewis requested from Frank Rowe, a local Mobil oil dealer, the proper hydraulic fluid to operate his machinery. The prior owner of the hydraulic system had used Pacemaker oil supplied by Cities Service, but plaintiff had been a customer of Mobil's for many years and desired to continue with Mobil. Rowe said he didn't know what the proper lubricant for Lewis' machinery was, but would find out. The only information given to Rowe by Lewis was that the machinery was operated by a gear-type pump; Rowe did not request any further information. He apparently contacted a Mobil representative for a recommendation, though this is not entirely clear, and sold plaintiff a product known as Ambrex 810. This is a straight mineral oil with no chemical additives.

Within a few days after operation of the new equipment commenced, plaintiff began experiencing difficulty with its operation. The oil changed color, foamed over, and got hot. The oil was changed a number of times, with no improvement. By late April 1965, approximately six months after operations with the equipment had begun, the system broke down, and a complete new system was installed. The cause of the breakdown was undetermined, but apparently by this time there was some suspicion of the oil being used. Plaintiff Lewis requested Rowe to be sure he was supplying the right kind of oil. Ambrex 810 continued to be supplied.

From April 1965 until April 1967, plaintiff continued to have trouble with the system, principally with the pumps which supplied the pressure. Six new pumps were required during this period, as they continually broke down. During this period, the kind of pump used was a Commercial pump which was specified by the designer of the hydraulic system. The filtration of oil for this pump was by means of a metal strainer, which was cleaned daily by the plaintiff in accordance with the instruction given with the equipment.

In April 1967, the plaintiff changed the brand of pump from a Commercial to a Tyrone pump. The Tyrone pump, instead of using the metal strainer filtration alone, used a disposable filter element in addition. Ambrex 810 oil was also recommended by Mobil and used with this pump, which completely broke down three weeks later. At this point, plaintiff was visited for the first time by a representative of Mobil Oil Corporation, as well as a representative of the Tyrone pump manufacturer.

On the occasion of this visit, May 9, 1967, plaintiff's system was completely flushed and cleaned, a new Tyrone pump installed, and on the pump manufacturer's and Mobil's representative's recommendation, a new oil was used which contained certain chemical additives, principally a "defoamant." Following these changes, plaintiff's system worked satisfactorily up until the time of trial, some two and one-half years later.

Briefly stated, plaintiff's theory of his case is that Mobil supplied him with an oil which was warranted fit for use in his hydraulic system, that the oil was not suitable for such use because it did not contain certain additives, and that it was the improper oil which caused the mechanical breakdowns, with consequent loss to his business. The defendant contends that there was no warranty of fitness, that the breakdowns were caused not by the oil but by improper filtration, and that in any event there can be no recovery of loss of profits in this case. . . .

Defendant maintains that there was no warranty of fitness in this case, that at most there was only a warranty of merchantability and that there was no proof of breach of this warranty, since there was no proof that Ambrex 810 is unfit for use in hydraulic systems generally. We find it unnecessary to consider whether the warranty of merchantability was breached, although there is some proof in the record to that effect, since we conclude that there was a warranty of fitness.

Plaintiff Lewis testified that he had been a longtime customer of Mobil Oil, and that his only source of contact with the company was through Frank Rowe, Mobil's local dealer, with whom he did almost all his business. It was common knowledge in the community that Lewis was converting his sawmill operation into a hydraulic system, Rowe knew this, and in fact had visited his mill on business matters several times during the course of the changeover. When the operations with the new machinery were about to commence, Lewis asked Rowe to get him the proper hydraulic fluid. Rowe asked him what kind of a system he had, and Lewis replied it was a Commercial-pump type. This was all the information asked or given. Neither Lewis nor Rowe knew what the oil requirements for the system were, and Rowe knew that Lewis knew nothing more specific about his requirements. Lewis also testified that after he began having trouble with his operations, while there were several possible sources of the difficulty the oil was one suspected source, and he several times asked Rowe to be sure he was furnishing him with the right kind.

Rowe's testimony for the most part confirmed Lewis's. It may be noted here that Mobil does not contest Rowe's authority to represent it in this transaction, and therefore whatever warranties may be implied because of the dealings between Rowe and Lewis are attributable to Mobil. Rowe admitted knowing Lewis was converting to a hydraulic system and that Lewis asked him to supply the fluid. He testified that he did not know what should be used and relayed the request to a superior in the Mobil organization, who recommended Ambrex 810. This is what was supplied.

When the first Tyrone pump was installed in April 1967, Rowe referred the request for a proper oil recommendation to Ted Klock, a Mobil engineer. Klock recommended Ambrex 810. When this pump failed a few weeks later, Klock visited the Lewis plant to inspect the equipment. The system was flushed out completely and the oil was changed to DTE-23 and Del Vac Special containing several additives. After this, no further trouble was experienced.

This evidence adequately establishes an implied warranty of fitness. Arkansas has adopted the Uniform Commercial Code's provision for an implied warranty of fitness. [The court quotes UCC 2-315]. Under this provision of the Code, there are two requirements for an implied warranty of fitness: (1) that the seller have "reason to know" of the use for which the goods are purchased, and (2) that the buyer relies on the seller's expertise in supplying the proper product. Both of these requirements are amply met by the proof in this case. Lewis' testimony, as confirmed by that of Rowe and Klock, shows that the oil was purchased specifically for his hydraulic system, not for just a hydraulic system in general, and that Mobil certainly knew of this specific purpose. It is also clear that Lewis was relying on Mobil to supply him with the proper oil for the system, since at the time of his purchases, he made clear that he didn't know what kind was necessary.

Mobil contends that there was no warranty of fitness for use in his particular system because he didn't specify that he needed an oil with additives, and alternatively that he didn't give them enough information for them to determine that an additive oil was required. However, it seems that the circumstances of this case come directly within that situation described in the first comment to this provision of the Uniform Commercial Code: "1. Whether or not this warranty arises in any individual case is basically a question of fact to be determined by the circumstances of the contracting. Under this section the buyer need not bring home to the seller *actual knowledge of the particular purpose* for which the goods are intended or of his reliance on the seller's skill and judgment, if the circumstances are such that the seller has reason to realize the purpose intended or that the reliance exists." UCC 2-315, Comment 1 (emphasis added). Here Lewis made it clear that the oil was purchased for his system, that he didn't know what oil should be used, and that he was relying on Mobil to supply the proper product. If any further information was needed, it was incumbent upon Mobil to get it before making its recommendation. That it could have easily gotten the necessary information is evidenced by the fact that after plaintiff's continuing complaints, Mobil's engineer visited the plant, and, upon inspection, changed the recommendation that had previously been made.

Additionally, Mobil contends that even if there were an implied warranty of fitness, it does not cover the circumstances of this case because of the abnormal features which the plaintiff's system contained, namely an inadequate filtration system and a capacity to entrain excessive air. There are several answers to this contention. First of all, the contention goes essentially to the question of causation—i.e., whether the damage was caused by a breach of warranty or by some other cause—and not to the existence of a warranty of fitness in the first place. Secondly, assuming that certain peculiarities in the plaintiff's system did exist, the whole point of an implied warranty of fitness is that a product be suitable for a specific purpose, and that a seller should not supply a product which is not so suited. Thirdly, there is no evidence in the record that the plaintiff's system was unique or abnormal in these respects. It operated satisfactorily under the prior owner, and the new system has operated satisfactorily after it was adequately cleaned and an additive type oil used.

While we will discuss these problems more completely in the question of causation, it may be briefly noted here that the proof shows that plaintiff's filtration system was installed and maintained in strict accordance with the manufacturer's recommendations, that this was a standard system, and that any hydraulic system has a certain unavoidable capacity to entrain air. While a "perfect" system which is run 24 hours a day might not have any air in it, in actual practice there are at least two sources of air. One is from minute leaks in "packaging glands." The other source arises from the fact that when the system is shut down, as at night and over the lunch hour, as well as for repairs, the oil drains out of the system and into the reservoir. When the system is started up again, air which has entered the system to replace the drained oil must be dissipated. This dissipation occurs by running the system for a few minutes and is affected by the capacity of the oil to rid itself of air bubbles. It is sufficient to note here that there was no evidence that the plaintiff's system was in any way unique in this respect. Thus, Mobil's defense that there was no warranty of fitness because of an "abnormal use" of the oil is not appropriate here.

[The court's discussion of causation and damages is omitted.]

Affirmed.

NOTES & QUESTIONS

Particular purpose or ordinary purpose. What is the particular purpose for which Mobil warranted its oil to be fit? Presumably the oil sold to Lewis could be used in some hydraulic systems. If so, is the oil fit for the ordinary purposes for which lubricating oil is used? Assume Mobil could show that the oil could be used in all hydraulic systems except Brand X, which has a market share of only 10 percent. Assume also that this information was known only by the manufacturer of Brand X. Would this information be relevant when determining whether there is an implied warranty in *Lewis*?

Problem 14-1. Wilson purchases a dunebuggy from Gila Desert Motors with a sticker on its front window saying "1969." At the time of purchase, Wilson signs a security agreement that also describes the vehicle as a "1969 Volkswagen dunebuggy." There are no oral discussions concerning the age of the vehicle. After the purchase, Wilson discovers that the vehicle had been reconstructed in 1969 from 1967 Volkswagen component parts and from earlier models. Gila had accepted the vehicle in trade as a 1969 vehicle before reselling it to Wilson. It had previously been licensed as a 1969 dunebuggy in another state, under the practice of that state to treat the year of reconstruction as the model year. Arizona, where Gila is located, simply accepts model years from the documentation of incoming vehicles. Wilson states that the practice of the motor vehicle departments is irrelevant and brings suit for breach of an express warranty that the vehicle is a 1969 vehicle. What result?

Problem 14-2. Doctor advises Sue that she will endanger her life if she becomes pregnant and recommends that she take an oral contraceptive manufactured by Pharmacist. Sue takes the contraceptive following the printed directions that accompany her purchase of the contraceptive. This same printed form states that the contraceptive "offers virtually 100 percent protection when taken as directed." After Sue has taken the contraceptive for a little more than one year, however, she becomes pregnant. She consults you about potential claims she might have against Doctor and Pharmacist. You discover evidence that the "gross pregnancy rate" for users of the contraceptive is 1.9 pregnancies per 100 woman-years. Does Sue have a claim for breach of an express warranty against either party and, if so, what issues will you have to prepare to deal with?

Problem 14-3. Farmer purchases SX-31 seed corn from Seller. Prior to the purchase, Farmer was shown Dealer's Spec Sheet for SX-31, which stated among other things that the seed had exceptional blight resistance, producing blight-free yields in the range of X to X + 10 bushels per acre under normal growing conditions. Farmer sows his entire field using SX-31 seed. The entire crop is destroyed by blight. Farmer now seeks to recover his loss from Seller.

(a) As Farmer's attorney, what is your advice to Farmer? If you bring suit against Seller what problems do you foresee?

(b) Suppose that the blight that destroyed the crop was a new strain, previously unknown. Does that bear on the proper result in the case?

(c) May Seller successfully assert that it has disclaimed warranty liability because it is a "trade usage" in agriculture that seed companies do not stand responsible for crop failure?

(d) May Seller successfully assert that a written disclaimer accompanying the shipment of seed should be given effect because it is a trade usage that such disclaimers accompany seed shipments and therefore are to be expected whether or not they are mentioned or incorporated in documents at the time of sale?

Problem 14-4. Bigelow, Vermont's "Outstanding Farmer of 1982," is experienced in farming, including hay-baling. In an average year Bigelow bales 18,000 to 20,000 bales. Normally the hay must be dried until the moisture level falls to 20 to 25 percent before being baled. However, Agway manufactures a product called Hay Savor, which retards the growth of mold and allows moist hay to be baled. It is so advertised. Bigelow purchases Hay Savor and sprays it on his newly mown hay. A representative of Agway visits Bigelow's farm shortly after the mowing. He looks at the hay and states that due to the Hay Savor it can now be safely baled. Bigelow does so, and the hay molds, spoils, combusts, and burns Bigelow's barn to the ground. Bigelow now sues Agway. What result?

Problem 14-5. For several years Industrial Builders has ordered *XX* brand pipe for use in its projects. The uses vary, including running hot and cold water, chemical supplies, and high-pressure steam. *XX* brand pipe had always performed well under these conditions. For its latest project Industrial again orders *XX* brand pipe from Manufacturer. The delivered pipe proves to be brittle, and Industrial judges it to be too difficult to handle and unsuitable for buried use, where shifting might fracture the pipe. May Industrial successfully resist a suit for the price of the pipe?

Suppose that the brittleness is due to a change in alloy recommended by Manufacturer's metallurgists to improve the strength of the pipe (which it does), making it more suitable for high-pressure uses. Does that affect your answer? Suppose that Industrial purchases from Distributor. How does that affect your answer?

Problem 14-6. Ice Rink receives a catalog from Equipco, which describes a resurfacing tank and gives the tank size, price, and model number. An illustration in the catalog pictures the tank with a blade extending beyond the width of the tank and showing a water-release valve located near the pushing bar, where it can be operated while pushing the tank. Ice Rink orders the tank using the model number printed in the catalog. The tank that is delivered does not have the blade and valve, although it is the size and model listed in the catalog. After trying the tank in operation, Ice Rink notifies Equipco that it is revoking its acceptance of the goods. What result in an action for the price by Equipco?

Is it pertinent to your evaluation to know whether Ice Rink has a full appreciation of the utility of the wide blade and the location of the water-release valve when it orders, or instead only discovers this when workers try to operate the equipment? Suppose that the wide blade is essential to resurfacing Ice Rink's skating rink because of the radius of the curvature of the skating surface's ends. Suppose that, absent a water-release valve that can be reached while a resurfacing tank is being pushed, it is impossible to obtain a smooth ice surface. How, if at all, will the above suppositions change the way you view Ice Rink's position?

Problem 14-7. Lewis and Sims is the successful bidder on a subcontract to install a water and sewer system for the town of North Pole, Alaska. The contract requires L & S to furnish all the necessary pipe. L & S submits to Liberty, a middleman, a purchase order for specified quantities of pipe of various sizes, all to be lined with coal tar enamel. Liberty in turn submits this order to Northwest Pipe. Liberty and Northwest both know that this pipe is for use in an Alaskan project and will be unloaded in Alaska in the winter months. The pipe is shipped and unloaded in March, when temperatures range from −27 to +6 degrees. After several thousand feet of pipe are installed it is discovered that the enamel lining has cracked and separated on the remaining pipe. Coal tar enamel lining is fragile at low temperatures and subject to damage if it receives sharp jolts or shocks at such temperatures. L & S informs Liberty that it will not accept or pay for the pipe not yet in place. What result?

Problem 14-8. Blackjack has a bad cut on the side of the front wheel of his Honda trail bike. At Central Honda he tells a salesman that he needs a new tire for his Honda. The salesman asks the model number and consults a catalog, which lists sizes for front and rear wheels. The salesman jots down the number of the rear wheel size and gets one from the storeroom. Blackjack purchases the new tire and mounts it on his bike. A week later he goes over a bump. The slightly larger size of the tire causes the front wheel to "bottom out" and seize, and he is thrown and slightly injured. The bike's frame is broken. Blackjack sues Central Honda. What result? Suppose that when Blackjack tells the salesman the model of bike he has the salesman walks over to a floor display and jots down the tire size from the rear tire of the same model. What result?

Problem 14-9. Plaintiff purchases nuts in a clear glass jar bearing this label:

PLANTERS

Dry Roasted
Mixed Nuts

No oils or sugar
used in processing

Shelled nuts are visible through the glass of the jar. Plaintiff while eating nuts from the jar bites down on an unshelled filbert, suffers extreme pain, and must pay substantial sums for dental work. Does plaintiff have a valid warranty claim against the grocery or the manufacturer? At trial the defense introduces department of agriculture standards pertaining to the grading of nuts. These standards list a number of varieties and state percentages ranging from 1 to 2.5 percent as "allowable unshelled." Are these standards helpful?

Problem 14-10. Friedman, president of Blockhead, is looking for a method of manufacturing small "wiglet" cases to complement the wig cases Blockhead is already marketing. Friedman has investigated and rejected the injection-molding process used for plastic cases. He approaches Plastic Forming Company (PFC) about the possibility of employing a cheaper process called blow-molding. In injection-molding, plastic is extruded into a mold, a method which in this case would cost about $25,000. The blow-molding process employs a cheaper mold ($5,000) and entails cheaper production costs, but it is not possible, as it is in injection molding, to produce differing wall thicknesses.

Friedman rejects PFC's first drawings for a wiglet case as too dissimilar from Blockhead's existing wig cases. He imposes four conditions on the design involving compatibility with the existing wig cases and the use of the wig case handle design. Suggestions for changing the dimensions of the handle housing, which would thicken the wall at that point, were rejected.

PFC produces 15 preproduction models, which are examined by Friedman and approved, with a few notes for minor improvements. Thereafter, several thousand wiglet cases are produced before Friedman requests that production cease. Among the reasons cited for this decision is that the wall of the case is too thin where the handle is attached, thus causing the cases to break. Blockhead asserts that PFC has breached both an express warranty that the production models will conform to the preproduction cases and implied warranties of fitness and merchantability. Evaluate Blockhead's claims.

Problem 14-11. Siemen owns and operates a sawmill. He wishes to purchase a new rip saw and contacts Alden, a saw manufacturer. Alden informs Siemen it will be at least six months until a new saw can be delivered. Alden suggests that Siemen contact Korelski, another saw mill operator, who has a spare used saw that Alden thinks might fit Siemen's purposes. Siemen calls Korelski and outlines his needs. Korelski suggests that Siemen come to Korelski's mill and examine the used saw. When Siemen arrives, Korelski shows him the saw, which is dismantled in a storage section of the mill. Korelski tells Siemen he will have to provide his own saw blades, shivs, belts, and pulleys, but that he may have the saw for $2,900. When Siemen purchases the saw and places it in operation, it proves unsatisfactory for his purposes of making pallets because it cannot saw to the required tolerances. There is some reason to believe that such a rip saw, when operated properly, can saw to such tolerances. Siemen seeks to recover the price from Korelski. What result?

C. DISCLAIMER OF WARRANTY AND LIMITATION OF REMEDY

You have already encountered in preceding materials typical disclaimer and limitation of remedy provisions. This aspect of warranty law is so important, however, that we return here to give it extended treatment. As you read these materials you must call upon your knowledge of buyer's remedies acquired in preceding chapters. The seller's aims in disclaiming warranty and limiting remedy are best understood in terms of the Code results thereby avoided.

The Code distinguishes between disclaimers of warranties and limitations of remedies. If warranty is disclaimed there is no warranty, and a seller obviously cannot breach a nonexistent warranty. On the other hand, a clause limiting a buyer's remedies has no direct effect on the existence of warranties. There may be both warranties and breaches of those warranties, but the clause will limit the remedies available to the buyer as a result of those breaches. As a practical matter, of course, the buyer may end up without a remedy under either kind of clause. Recognizing this consequence, courts have not always followed the distinction scrupulously. Warranty provisions themselves frequently combine both disclaimers and limitations of remedy.

The Code's warranty disclaimer and remedy limitation provisions give parties great freedom to shape the contours of their particular deals, but the Code does impose some restraints. When analyzing these limits it is customary to distinguish between "procedural" and "substantive" limitations. Procedural limitations are formal in nature: for instance, UCC 2-316(2) requires the use of certain words to disclaim warranties of merchantability. Substantive limitations may absolutely preclude a disclaimer or limitation of remedy.

Having noted this distinction we caution against taking it too seriously. Few Code provisions and even fewer cases in actual life can be so neatly characterized. In a related context Llewellyn once distinguished between suppletory provisions supplying the parties' supposed intent and mandatory provisions embodying legal norms not subject to variance. He then continued: "Still others, and indeed the bulk of the sections of both the Original Act and the present Draft, occupy *a position which is intermediate between these two*. They express more than presumed intention of the parties, or tacit agreement. They express the law's approach to *fairness* in the circumstances. Yet they are not designed, one by one, as iron-clad, and the parties (or the trade) are designed to be left free to modify or negate any of them." (Emphasis in the original.) Comment on Section 8, Report and Second Draft: The Revised Uniform Sales Act (1941). Although made with respect to an earlier draft of Article 2, the comment is no less pertinent to an understanding of the provisions eventually enacted.

The materials in this Part are nominally organized along the lines of the procedural/substantive distinction but we urge you to view any serious dichotomy quite skeptically. Instead, we ask that you make a careful attempt to identify *factual* characteristics of the transaction presented in each of the cases and problems that follow. Are the facts characteristic of a particular trade, status of the parties, or mode of contracting? Are they truly peculiar to the individual case, or are they likely to appear repetitively in such transactions? Is the language or conduct of the parties concerning disclaimer or limitation case-specific, type-specific, or such as might be employed in all contracts? Finally, consider the Code provisions that are said to be determinative in each case or problem. They may be phrased in quite general language. May they nonetheless be understood as directed more narrowly at particular "type-transactions," for purposes of *either* facilitation or prohibition?

1. Procedural Issues

Consider first the question of a seller's freedom to disclaim liability for express warranties. This issue focuses almost exclusively on UCC 2-316(1) and 2-202. The tension between procedural and substantive issues may be probed through discussion of the following Problems.

Problem 14-12. Buyer, a painting subcontractor on a large project, purchases several thousand gallons of paint from Manufacturer. Manufacturer states that the paint will cover with a one-coat application. The written contract, which is the seller's standard purchase order form, states in conspicuous print, however, that the paint is "warranted conforming to formula and sample, but not as to use or application." Buyer has signed the contract and asserts an express warranty of one-coat application. What result?

Problem 14-13. Seller, demonstrating a truck to Buyer, states that it is a "demonstrator" that has had light use despite its 25,000 miles. Buyer purchases the truck, the sale being evidenced on Seller's standard sales form. The truck is correctly described by model year and type, and the words *as is* are handwritten across the face of the form. A printed provision at the bottom of the form states:

This is the entire contract of the parties. Agents of the Seller have no authority to vary the terms of this agreement, except in a signed writing approved by Sales

Manager. Buyer acknowledges that there are no statements or representations made in connection with this sale upon which he has relied, except as expressly set forth in writing this agreement. All sales are final.

Buyer discovers that the truck had been owned briefly by a construction company and had been involved in an accident that twisted the frame. May Buyer recover the price?

Problem 14-14. Seller, a mobile home dealer, uses the same form as in Problem 14-13. Buyer visits the Seller's lot, and inspects a model mobile home on display. The unit is a 65-foot 1978 mobile home called Biscayne Bay. Buyer states she would like to purchase a mobile home and salesman fills in the sales form, describing the unit sold as a 1978 Biscayne Bay. A week later a model home is delivered to Buyer. The home is admittedly a 65-foot Biscayne Bay, 1978 model. Buyer refuses to accept it, however, stating that it does not conform to the model that was shown to her. (It does not: the interior arrangement and colors are different.) Same case as in Problem 14-13?

Suppose the form states

There are no express warranties made in connection with this law, except as appear on the face of this form. All models displayed are for purposes of illustration only and do not form a part of the basis of the parties' bargain.

Same case?

Suppose, in conjunction with a sale evidenced on this form, the salesman states to Buyer, "Your home will be exactly like this model, and will be delivered within the week." Same case?

Problem 14-15. Westinghouse is a supplier of turbine generators for power plants. It enters into a contract with Mid-American Power Company, under which the power company purchases two turbines rated at one-megawatt generating capacity. The contract describes the turbines as "Westinghouse series 1978-A 1-megawatt generators." It is uncontested that at all points throughout negotiation the parties understand that generators with a one-megawatt capacity are desired. The contract, which consists of a 20-page typewritten document, warrants the generators free from defects in materials or workmanship for a period of one year, disclaims in appropriate form express and implied warranty liability, and limits remedy to repair or replacement. The two generators, when installed, develop .85 and .90 megawatts, respectively. Westinghouse states that it will cooperate with Mid-American in trying to raise output and will repair any defects discovered, but states that the turbines are not warranted to generate one megawatt. May Westinghouse successfully assert this position?

We turn now to the rules on disclaimers of implied warranties set out in UCC 2-316(2) and (3). These subsections are grounded on two different theories of disclaimer: one addresses the language employed by the parties; the other the conduct or circumstances surrounding the transaction. Both (2) and (3) are related insofar as they are thought to impose principally procedural limitations: neither subsection prohibits disclaimer. In reading each of the following Problems and cases, ask as a starting point how far each subsection's procedures will ensure that the intent of the parties is respected. Again, that may be a question that does not have the same answer for all types of transactions. Note, however, that by their *terms* the subsections apply without respect to transaction type.

Problem 14-16. Trucker and Lessor enter into a "lease-purchase agreement" covering a diesel-powered truck-tractor. The agreement includes the following separate paragraph:

> No Warranty: Lessor, not being the manufacturer of the equipment nor manufacturer's agent, makes no warranty against patent or latent defects in materials, workmanship, or capacity of the equipment; no warranty that the equipment will satisfy the requirements of any law, rule, specification or contract which provides for specific machinery or operators, or special methods; all liabilities therefrom are assumed by Lessee at its sole risk and expense. No oral agreement, guaranty, promise, condition, representation related hereto and/or to said equipment are integrated herein. No modifications hereof shall be binding unless in writing signed by Lessor.

The paragraph is in the same size of type as the rest of the contract terms.

After using the truck-tractor for six months Trucker determines that it is not suitable for the long-haul use necessary to her business. Trucker consults you about the effect of the above paragraph. She admits that she had been asked to read the paragraph, she had read it, and she understood that Lessor "was trying to avoid responsibility for defects" by the paragraph. She also states that she graduated from junior college. Is any of this evidence relevant under UCC 2-316(2) or (3)? Advise Trucker.

Problem 14-17. Fairchild leases a helicopter to Maritime for one year, with an option to purchase at the end of the year. Maritime exercises the option, and the parties sign a printed purchase agreement with the following paragraph inserted by typewriter:

```
It is specifically understood and agreed by the parties that the
Aircraft is sold in an 'As is' condition. Seller makes no representation
or warranties express or implied whatsoever except Warranty of Title.
Buyer acknowledges that before entering into this Agreement he has
examined the Aircraft as fully as he desires.
```

Three months later Maritime has to make extensive repairs to the engine. Maritime consults you on the paragraph's effect on Fairchild's potential warranty liability. Advise Maritime. Consider, in particular, whether it makes any difference whether the paragraph is conspicuous.

Problem 14-18. Steelco mails inquiries to six companies, including Equipco, requesting price and delivery information about two types of cranes: a 75-ton used diesel crane with a 70-foot boom, and a 100-ton used diesel crane with a 70-foot boom. Soon afterwards Equipco contacts Steelco concerning a 75-ton steam crane with 40-foot boom. This crane has never been seen by Equipco, but the company knows its location and that it is for sale. Two inspections of the crane are made by Steelco's repair foreman and a Steelco crane operator, during which the crane is observed operating and its maneuverability and mechanical parts are examined. No test is made of its lifting capacity.

Thereafter Steelco receives a formal quotation from Equipco describing the crane as a "75 ton, 40 foot boom Brownhoist Steam Locomotive Crane." It further lists boiler and speed specifications, the manufacturing date (1942), and its serial number. The price asked is $9,950. The quotation form also contains a printed term located conspicuously on its front:

> Conditions: All quotations are for immediate acceptance. They are subject to withdrawal, change, and prior sale without notice. All equipment is subject to inspection and the descriptions are approximate and intended to serve as a guide. All orders received are binding only when they have been accepted and acknowledged by us in writing. Provisions in customer's purchase orders contrary to these conditions are not binding upon us unless accepted in writing.

A plaque on the side of the crane indicates conspicuously that the crane is rated as having 75 tons lifting capacity; the same plaque states that the crane is equipped with a 30-foot boom.

Steelco purchases the crane from Equipco. When the crane is placed in operation, it is able to lift only 15 tons. Later inquiries directed to Industrial Brownhoist, the manufacturer of the crane, disclose that the crane had originally been equipped with a curved 30-foot boom, rather than a 40-foot boom, and that as originally manufactured and equipped the crane apparently was able to lift 75 tons. Steelco asks you to evaluate whether it can recover back the price.

PERFORMANCE MOTORS, INC. v. ALLEN
280 N.C. 385, 186 S.E.2d 161, 10 UCC Rep. 568 (1972)

[We have already met Mrs. Allen and have read her sad tale about the defects in the mobile home she bought. See p. 561 supra. At that time we assumed that there was a warranty that had been breached and asked whether Mrs. Allen could reject or revoke her acceptance of the mobile home. Here we examine the assumption that there was a warranty.

The syllabus to the court's opinion reports the following testimony as to the parties' intent: Julian T. Peel, President of Performance Motors, Inc., testified that "we did not imply any warranty other than the home would be as she saw it at that time"; that the plaintiff only agreed to sell it to her "and block it up on her lot. If she had placed it in a mobile home park we would have hooked up the power and the water, but since she was putting it on a lot which had no facilities we could not do that as our people are not licensed electricians or plumbers."]

HUSKINS, Justice. . . . The security agreement signed by defendant contains the following language as part of the "provisions" printed on the reverse side of the instrument itself: "Buyer further warrants and covenants that: 1. The Buyer admits, upon examination, that the Collateral is as represented by Seller and acknowledges acceptance and delivery thereon in good condition and repair." Plaintiff contends the security agreement was intended by the parties as a final expression of their agreement and that the quoted language constitutes a waiver by defendant of all warranties and renders incompetent her testimony with respect to the defective condition of the mobile home after it was installed on defendant's lot. Admission of her testimony is assigned as error.

Plaintiff's position on this point is unsound. Obviously, the security agreement was signed by defendant at plaintiff's place of business *before* the mobile home was delivered and installed. In light of that fact, the buyer at that time could not acknowledge "delivery thereof in good condition and repair." As a part of the contract of sale, plaintiff agreed to deliver the mobile home "and block it up on her lot." Until that was done plaintiff's obligations under the contract remained unfulfilled. Defendant's testimony was competent, not to contradict the terms of a written contract, but as evidence of additional consistent terms of the sale. [The court quotes UCC 2-202(b).] Here, the evidence of both parties shows that the mobile home was to be delivered and set up on defendant's lot. Hence the security agreement was not intended "as a complete and exclusive statement of the terms of the agreement." This assignment is overruled. . . . [The court therefore concludes that there is an implied warranty of merchantability, i.e., a warranty that the mobile home would be fit as a residence.]

While there is no implied warranty when the buyer, before entering into the contract, examines the goods as fully as he desires, UCC 2-316(3)(b), and has knowledge equal to that of the seller, . . . this principle is not applicable to the facts here because the contract of sale imposed on the seller the obligation to deliver the mobile home and "block it up" on defendant's lot. Until that was properly done, fitness or unfitness for use as a home could not be ascertained by the buyer's examination and inspection of the goods on the seller's premises. Until otherwise agreed, "[w]hen the seller is required . . . to send the goods to the buyer, the inspection may be after their arrival," UCC 2-513(1); and the buyer is entitled to a reasonable time after the goods arrive at their destination in which to inspect them and to reject them if they do not comply with the contract. . . . Moreover, defendant's down payment would not impair her right to inspect following delivery. UCC 2-512(2). Here, delivery was not accomplished until plaintiff "blocked it up" on defendant's lot.

NOTE & QUESTION

Disclaimer by inspection. Reconsider the inspection clause used in the *Soo R.R.* case, set out at p. 567 supra. What did the parties wish to accomplish by that clause?

ROTO-LITH, LTD. v. F. P. BARTLETT & CO., INC.
297 F.2d 497, 1 UCC Rep. 73 (1st Cir. 1962)

ALDRICH, Circuit Judge. Plaintiff-appellant Roto-Lith, Ltd., is a New York corporation engaged inter alia in manufacturing, or "converting," cellophane bags for packaging vegetables. Defendant-appellee is a Massachusetts corporation which makes emulsion for use as a cellophane adhesive. This is a field of some difficulty, and various emulsions are employed, depending upon the intended purpose of the bags. In May and October 1959 plaintiff purchased emulsion from the defendant. Subsequently bags produced with this emulsion failed to adhere, and this action was instituted in the District Court for the District of Massachusetts. At the conclusion of the evidence the court directed verdict for the defendant. This appeal followed.

Defendant asks us to review the October transaction first because of certain special considerations applicable to the May order. The defense in each instance, however, is primarily the same, namely, defendant contends that the sales contract expressly negatived any warranties.[2] We will deal first with the October order.

On October 23, 1959, plaintiff, in New York, mailed a written order to defendant in Massachusetts for a drum of "N-132-C" emulsion, stating "End use: wet pack spinach bags." Defendant on October 26 prepared simultaneously an acknowledgment and an invoice. The printed forms were exactly the same, except that one was headed "Acknowledgment" and the other "Invoice," and the former contemplated insertion of the proposed, and the latter of the actual, shipment date. Defendant testified that in accordance with its regular practice the acknowledgment was prepared and mailed the same day. The plaintiff's principal liability witness testified that he did not know whether this acknowledgment "was received, or what happened to it." On this state of the evidence there is an unrebutted presumption of receipt. The goods were shipped to New York on October 27. On the evidence it must be found that the acknowledgment was received at least no later than the goods.

The acknowledgment and the invoice bore in conspicuous type on their face the following legend, "All goods sold without warranties, express or implied, and subject to the terms on reverse side." In somewhat smaller, but still conspicuous, type there were printed on the back certain terms of sale, of which the following are relevant:

2. The defendant also contends that the warranties, if any there might have been, were not broken. This is a question of fact with which we are not concerned.

1. Due to the variable conditions under which these goods may be trans-ported, stored, handled, or used, Seller hereby expressly excludes any and all warranties, guaranties, or representations whatsoever. Buyer assumes risk for results obtained from use of these goods, whether used alone or in combination with other products. Seller's liability hereunder shall be limited to the replace-ment of any goods that materially differ from the Seller's sample order on the basis of which the order for such goods was made.

7. This acknowledgment contains all of the terms of this purchase and sale. No one except a duly authorized officer of Seller may execute or modify con-tracts. Payment may be made only at the offices of the Seller. If these terms are not acceptable, Buyer must notify Seller at once.

It is conceded that plaintiff did not protest defendant's attempt so to limit its liability, and in due course paid for the emulsion and used it. It is also con-ceded that adequate notice was given of breach of warranty, if there were warranties. The only issue which we will consider is whether all warranties were excluded by defendant's acknowledgment.[3]

The first question is what law the Massachusetts court would look to in order to determine the terms of the contract. Under Massachusetts law this is the place where the last material act occurs. Under UCC 2-206, mailing the acknowledgment would clearly have completed the contract in Massachusetts by acceptance had the acknowledgment not sought to introduce new terms. [The court quotes UCC 2-207.]

Plaintiff exaggerates the freedom which this section affords an offeror to ignore a reply from an offeree that does not in terms coincide with the original offer. According to plaintiff defendant's condition that there should be no warranties constituted a proposal which "materially altered" the agreement. As to this we concur. See Uniform Commercial Code comment to this section, Mass. Gen. Laws annotation, supra, paragraph 4. Plaintiff goes on to say that by virtue of the statute the acknowledgment effected a completed agreement without this condition, and that as a further proposal the condition never became part of the agreement because plaintiff did not express assent. We agree that UCC 2-207 changed the existing law, but not to this extent. Its purpose was to modify the strict principle that a response not precisely in accordance with the offer was a rejection and a counteroffer. Now, within stated limits, a response that does not in all respects correspond with the offer constitutes an acceptance of the offer, and a counter-offer only as to the differ-ences. If plaintiff's contention is correct that a reply to an offer stating addi-tional conditions unilaterally burdensome upon the offeror is a binding acceptance of the original offer plus simply a proposal for the additional con-ditions, the statute would lead to an absurdity. Obviously no offeror will subsequently assent to such conditions.

---

3. Defendant also relies upon the terms of the invoice in view of the fact that it was admit-tedly received before plaintiff used the goods. Whether an invoice not received until after the goods can modify the contract raises some possible matters which we do not reach.

The statute is not too happily drafted. Perhaps it would be wiser in all cases for an offeree to say in so many words, "I will not accept your offer until you assent to the following: . . ." But businessmen cannot be expected to act by rubric. It would be unrealistic to suppose that when an offeree replies setting out conditions that would be burdensome only to the offeror he intended to make an unconditional acceptance of the original offer, leaving it simply to the offeror's good nature whether he would assume the additional restrictions. To give the statute a practical construction we must hold that a response which states a condition materially altering the obligation solely to the disadvantage of the offeror is an "acceptance . . . expressly . . . conditional on assent to the additional . . . terms."

Plaintiff accepted the goods with knowledge of the conditions specified in the acknowledgment. It became bound.[4] Whether the contract was made in Massachusetts or New York, there has been no suggestion that either jurisdiction will not give effect to an appropriate disclaimer of warranties. See UCC 2-316; New York Personal Property Law, McKinney's Consol. Laws, c.41, §152. This disposes of the October order.

With respect to the May order a different situation obtains. Here plaintiff ordered a quantity of "N-136-F," which was defendant's code number for a dry-bag emulsion. The order stated as the end use a wet bag. Accordingly, defendant knew, by its own announced standards, that the emulsion ordered was of necessity unfit for the disclosed purpose. In this bald situation plaintiff urges that the defendant cannot be permitted to specify that it made no implied warranty of fitness.

We do not reach this question. In the court below, when plainly asked to state its opposition to the direction of a verdict, plaintiff did not advance the arguments it now makes, and in no way called the court's attention to any distinction between the May and the October orders. An appellant is not normally permitted to have the benefit of a new theory on appeal. . . .

Judgment will be entered affirming the judgment of the district court.

NOTES & QUESTIONS

1. Roto-Lith *as a warranty case.* You probably remember *Roto-Lith* from your contracts course, where you no doubt concluded it badly interprets UCC 2-207. Here, however, we wish to look at *Roto-Lith* not only as a battle-of-the-forms case, but as an interesting problem involving the creation, scope, and disclaimer of warranty liability. To shape your thinking about the case, consider the following points:

(a) Read UCC 2-313, 2-314 and 2-315. As you understand *Roto-Lith,* what warranty liability would seller have if a contract was formed on the basis

---

4. It does not follow that if the acknowledgment had miscarried, plaintiff's receipt of the goods would have completed a contract which did not include the terms of the acknowledgment. We are not faced with the question of how the statute may affect the common law under such circumstances.

of the buyer's purchase order? If implied warranties did exist in this case, which of those warranties would be breached? (Note that the seller also argued that no warranty had been breached, but the court treated this as a factual issue that it need not consider: see footnote 2.)

(b) Judge Aldrich assumes that if the seller's acknowledgment is a counter-offer accepted by acceptance of the goods, then the disclaimer in the form effectively disclaims warranty liability. Do you agree?

(c) Critics of *Roto-Lith* have usually accepted Judge Aldrich's conclusion that the disclaimer provision was a "material" term, but they properly attack his reasoning that the provision results in an "expressly conditional" reply. But do you agree that the disclaimer is a material term, additional to or different from the terms of the offer? Suppose such provisions are common in the sale of adhesives. What effect would that have on the operation of the disclaimer clause? See UCC 2-207, Comments 4 and 5.

(d) Consider the risk allocation urged by the buyer in *Roto-Lith*. Do you find it surprising that the court rejected it? Re-reading seller's documentation, what risk allocation does the seller try to establish? Is this a reasonable allocation? How do the answers to this question and question (c) bear on the battle of the forms? Reread with regard to these questions Note 4 in the opinion.

2. *Trade usage and implied warranties.* To what extent do you agree with the following views?

TAYLOR, U.C.C. SECTION 2-207: AN INTEGRATION OF LEGAL ABSTRACTIONS AND TRANSACTIONAL REALITY, 46 U. Cinn. L. Rev. 419 (1977): "Difficulty also is encountered if the trade usage or prior dealing with which seller's response is consistent, is itself inconsistent with the corresponding supplementary provision of the Code. For example, this would be the situation if it were customary in the trade for warranty coverage to be limited or if such a limitation had been agreed to consistently by the parties in the past and this fact were reflected in the price term. In such a case, mechanistic application of subsection (3) would penalize the seller in an unforeseeable manner and would give the buyer a windfall neither paid for nor reasonably expected. However, such a result is not mandated necessarily by section 2-207, at least not if section 2-207 is read together with section 2-302. Subsection 2-302(1) provides:

> If the court as a matter of law finds the contract or any clause of the contract to have been unconscionable at the time it was made the court may refuse to enforce the contract, or it may enforce the remainder of the contract without the unconscionable clause, or it may so limit the application of any unconscionable clause as to avoid any unconscionable result.

"Thus, if the court finds the implied warranty term to have been unconscionable when the contract was made, application of subsection 2-302(1) would be necessary 'to avoid any unconscionable result.' Of course, one ordinarily would not think of the imposition of minimum implied warranty liability as being unconscionable. In fact, at first blush, holding any term implied in law by a specific Code section to be unconscionable would appear shocking. However, one announced purpose of section 2-302 is the 'prevention of unfair surprise,' such as is present in the instant hypothetical. This unfair surprise can be precluded by limiting the implied warranty protection when such a limitation is customary in the trade or reflects the parties' past practice. Moreover, such a result fulfills the more reasonable of the two expectations."

Note that the Code provides for both the creation of an implied warranty and for the disclaimer of an implied warranty by evidence of trade usage. UCC 2-314(3); 2-316(3)(c).

Problem 14-19. Reid purchases from Dealer a new Lincoln Continental manufactured by Ford. Two months later, after the car has been driven 1,800 miles, the wiring under the front seat starts a fire while the car is parked in Reid's garage. Within ten minutes the fire has destroyed both the car and Reid's residence. Reid brings an action against Ford for breach of an express warranty. Ford answers that the warranty document effectively limits Reid's remedy to replacement of defective parts, which at most means replacement of the car. The warranty document is set out below. How would you advise Reid as to Ford's argument?

BASIC WARRANTY

Ford Motor Company warrants to the owner each part of this vehicle to be free under normal use and service from defects in material and workmanship for a period of 24 months from the date of original retail delivery or first use, or until it has been driven for 24,000 miles, whichever comes first.

POWER TRAIN WARRANTY

In addition, Ford Motor Company further warrants to the owner each part of the engine block, head, and all internal engine parts, water pump, intake manifold, transmission case and all internal transmission parts, torque converter, drive shaft, universal joints, rear axle and differential, and rear wheel bearings of this vehicle to be free under normal use and service from defects in material and workmanship for a period of five (5) years from the date of original retail delivery or first use, or until it has been driven for fifty thousand (50,000) miles, whichever comes first.

STEERING, SUSPENSION AND WHEEL WARRANTY

In addition, Ford Motor Company further warrants to the owner each part of the suspension system, steering gear and linkage, power steering pump, road wheels, and front wheel bearings and seals of this vehicle to be free under normal use and service from defects in material and workmanship for a period of five (5) years from the date of original retail delivery or first use, or until it has been driven for fifty thousand (50,000) miles, whichever comes first.

The further warranties do not include or apply to related items such as ignition, electrical, fuel, cooling, or brake systems, engine or transmission controls or linkages, steering column, clutch assembly, shock absorbers, or load leveling system.

GENERAL WARRANTY PROVISIONS

It is a condition of all the warranties that the owner maintain this vehicle according to the maintenance schedule set forth in the Customer Maintenance Record in the Maintenance section of this Owner's Manual. It is also a condition of all the warranties that, every twelve months, the owner furnish an authorized Ford or Lincoln-Mercury dealer with evidence that these maintenance services have been performed and obtain the dealer's written certification that he has received such evidence.

All the warranties shall be fulfilled by the Selling Dealer (or if the owner is traveling or has become a resident of a different locality, by any authorized Ford or Lincoln-Mercury dealer) replacing with a genuine new Ford or Ford-Authorized Reconditioned part, or repairing at his place of business, free of charge including related labor, any such defective part.

None of the warranties shall apply to (i) tires or tubes (adjustments for them being provided by their manufacturers), or (ii) normal maintenance services (such as engine tune-up, fuel system cleaning and wheel and brake adjustments), or (iii) normal replacement of service items (such as filters, spark plugs, ignition points, wiper blades and brake linings), or (iv) deterioration, due to normal use or exposure, of soft trim, appearance items, hoses, belts or moulded rubber or rubber-like items.

The warranties herein are expressly in lieu of any other express or implied warranty, including any implied warranty of merchantability or fitness, and of any other obligation on the part of the Company or the Selling Dealer.

Problem 14-20. Toledo Edison purchases a generator from Westinghouse. After two years the turbine blades break. Westinghouse replaces the blades without charge but denies liability for Toledo Edison's claims for its additional costs to maintain normal output and for loss of demand charges for short-term energy to other utility companies. Toledo Edison brings an action to recover these damages. Westinghouse moves for summary judgment on the ground that the following contract terms limit its responsibility for consequential damages. Toledo Edison answers that the limitations are ineffective because the terms are inconspicuous and that this is a factual question, thus precluding summary judgment. The terms appear on the third page of an 18-page document; they are set out in the same size type as the rest of the document. As judge, how do you rule?

1. Warranty—Westinghouse warrants that the equipment delivered by it will be of the kind and quality described in the order or contract and will be free of defects in workmanship or material. Should any failure to conform to this warranty appear within one year Westinghouse shall upon notification correct such non-conformity, including non-conformance with the specifications, at its option, either by repairing any defective part or parts, or by making available f.o.b. the Corporation's plant, a repaired or replacement part.

This Warranty is in lieu of all warranties of merchantability, fitness for purpose, or other warranties, express or implied, except of title and against patent infringement. Correction of non-conformities, in the manner and for the period of time provided above, shall constitute fulfillment of all liabilities of Westinghouse to Toledo Edison, whether based on contract, negligence or otherwise with respect to, or arising out of such equipment.

2. Limitation of Liability—Neither party shall be liable for special, indirect, or consequential damages. The remedies of Toledo Edison set forth herein are exclusive, and the liability of Westinghouse with respect to any contract or sale or anything done in connection therewith, whether in contract, in tort, under any warranty, or otherwise, shall not, except as expressly provided herein, exceed the price of the equipment or part on which such liability is based.

2.   Substantive Issues

Thus far we have examined the limitations upon the parties' contractual freedom that are traditionally viewed as "procedural." They deal with *how* the parties must strike a deal (or document it) if it is to be given effect. Now we turn to the question of whether the Code places substantive limits on permissible types of warranty "deals."

We will consider four distinguishable issues:

(a) When does a limited remedy fail of its essential purpose?

(b) When is a limitation of consequential loss unconscionable?

(c) How does failure of essential purpose affect limitations of consequential loss?

(d) When is it appropriate to say that a disclaimer of warranty liability is unconscionable?

Although analytically separable, these issues are often muddled by the courts.

UCC 2-719(2) states:

> Where circumstances cause an exclusive or limited remedy to fail of its essential purpose, remedy may be had as provided in this Act.

This provision is new with the Code, and its language is far from self-explanatory. Courts frequently take refuge in the Official Comments: ". . . it is of the very essence of a sales contract that at least *minimum adequate remedies* be available. If the parties intend to conclude a contract for sale within this Article they must accept the legal consequence that there be at least a *fair quantum of remedy*. . . . [W]here an apparently fair and reasonable clause because of circumstances fails of its purpose or *operates to deprive either party of the substantial value of the bargain,* it must give way to the general remedy provisions of this Article." (Emphasis added.)

Invocation of catchphrases, however, is no substitute for analysis. Further, it is not clear that this is an area where the comments provide a reliable guide to construction. Application of the comments has led to some questionable outcomes and to clouded analysis even in cases where the result is probably correct.

ADAMS v. J. I. CASE CO.
125 Ill. App. 2d 388, 261 N.E.2d 1, 7 UCC Rep. 1270 (1970)

JONES, J. Plaintiff appeals from an order of the Circuit Court granting defendants' motions to dismiss his Second Amended Complaint.

The case is presented to us upon the pleadings. It appears from plaintiff's Second Amended Complaint that defendant J. I. Case Company, a corporation, is the manufacturer (and is hereinafter referred to as manufacturer), defendant Jones Farm Supply, a corporation, is the seller (and is hereinafter referred to as dealer), and plaintiff is the purchaser of a crawler loader tractor. Plaintiff's Second Amended Complaint contains five counts, each directed against both defendants and each based upon essentially the same factual allegations. In each count of the complaint the plaintiff uses language that would pertain to breach of express warranty, breach of implied warranty, manufacturer's strict liability and negligent manufacture. One count also alludes to the remedy of restitution. The prayers for relief in the several counts seek both direct and consequential damages. Each of the defendants filed its Motion to Dismiss the Second Amended Complaint. After argument the trial court entered a final order of dismissal of plaintiff's Second Amended Complaint, filing a Memorandum of Opinion which recited that plaintiff had elected to stand on his pleadings requesting involuntary dismissal with prejudice so an appeal would immediately lie. The Memorandum recited: "The Second Amended Complaint attempts to recover on a number of legal theories, some inconsistent, some barred by admitted written warranty, some by the provisions of the Uniform Code, and some by operation of law. All are intermingled in numerous counts, none of which conform to the requirements of Section 33, Subsection 2 of the Civil Practice Act. Rather than examine in detail all of the defects of the complaint, the Court will rather indicate substantial merit in most of the points raised in the two Motions to Dismiss. The Complaint is therefore subject to dismissal for numerous reasons including duplicity." . . .

Turning to the Second Amended Complaint we find that the first twelve paragraphs of Count I allege that both manufacturer and dealer are foreign corporations authorized to do business in Illinois; that manufacturer delivered the tractor to dealer for sale to the general public and it was purchased by plaintiff on March 3, 1966 for an installment price of $14,896.75, and that installment payments are current. Further, that plaintiff is an experienced operator and at all times operated the tractor in a careful and prudent manner so as to protect it and that plaintiff was engaged in a bulldozing business as a general contractor for hire at $12.00 per hour which business included performance of various types of work all of which was known to the defendants.

At the time tractor was purchased plaintiff had many jobs contracted and others promised that would keep him busy with the tractor which was known by the defendants. Plaintiff had purchased several tractors similar to the one involved from the defendants and had never experienced any serious difficulty with any of them and he completely relied upon the skill and ability of the defendants to produce and service a good satisfactory tractor of the type purchased. The tractor purchased was a defective tractor unable to do the customary work performed by plaintiff which defects were (a) radiator was defective and whenever temperature was over 75 degrees Fahrenheit the tractor would overheat so that it was dangerous to operate and (b) hydraulic system for raising and lowering the bucket was defective and would not hold the bucket up so that it was dangerous to operate the tractor. These same twelve paragraphs were adopted and alleged in the four succeeding counts of the complaint. After the first twelve paragraphs Count I continued by alleging that defendants through the use of reasonable care would have discovered the defects prior to the sale but they failed to exercise reasonable care in the manufacturing of the tractor. Plaintiff called the defects to the attention of defendants on April 19, 1966, but defendants did not correct the defects until July 17, 1967, causing plaintiff to lose 810 work hours while the tractor was in defendant's shop for which he would have received $12.00 per hour for a loss of $9720.00 and plaintiff also suffered the loss of many jobs and a loss of reputation because of his inability to perform jobs which he had contracted to do, all because of the defective tractor. Count I prays damages from the defendants in the sum of $9995.00 and costs.

Count I of plaintiff's complaint contains incomplete elements of causes of action in implied waranty, strict liability for defective manufacturing and negligence in manufacturing. None of the theories of liability are stated completely. It is not a well-pleaded count and even with the application of rules requiring liberal construction of pleadings it cannot fairly be said that defendants are informed of a valid claim under a general class of cases. We conclude that defendants' motions to dismiss Count I were properly allowed.

Count II of the Second Amended Complaint adopts and realleges the first twelve paragraphs of Count I as the first twelve paragraphs of Count II. Then follow allegations that defendants sold the tractor with a written warranty, which is set forth verbatim, and that under the terms of the warranty defendants were under a duty to correct the tractor within a reasonable time whenever it was in the shop for work, but they were wilfully dilatory in making the needed repairs, often letting said tractor "set" (sic) for weeks at a time without working on it. Further, that defendants carelessly and negligently worked on the tractor making many changes and alterations that were not needed or required and which did not correct its defective performance; that the defects in the tractor should have been corrected by defendants within a week's time but instead they kept the tractor for 810 working hours thereby causing plaintiff to lose all that time plus loss of jobs and reputation. Count II concludes with a prayer for damages in the amount of $9995.00 and costs.

The written warranty provides that it is the warranty of both the manufacturer and the dealer and binds them to repair or replace defective parts for a period of twelve months after delivery. It also provides ". . . In no event shall Dealer or Company be liable for consequential damage of any kind or nature . . ." and that ". . . This warranty is in lieu of all other warranties and conditions, express, implied, or statutory, and all other obligations or liabilities on the part of the Dealer and Company. No representative of the company has authority to change the terms of this Warranty in any manner whatsoever. . . ." The reverse side of the warranty card was signed by the plaintiff under this language: "The undersigned agree to the terms and conditions of the Warranty as set forth on the reverse side hereof."

Defendants' motions attack Count II upon the grounds that it is duplicitous, that it is insufficient in law because the written warranty expressly provides that neither dealer nor company will be liable for consequential damage of any kind or nature, and that the action is barred by the written warranty which declares it is in lieu of all other warranties and conditions, express, implied or statutory. . . .

The question of duplicity aside, the substantive allegations of Count II are that a breach of the written warranty has occurred and in compliance with the warranty the requisite repairs have been made. The crux is, however, that defendants were under a duty to make timely repairs called for by their warranty but the defendants took an inordinate amount of time in making the repairs, that they were wilfully dilatory or were careless and negligent in their work of compliance, with the result that plaintiff has suffered direct and consequential damage. Otherwise stated, having agreed to repair or replace the defective parts of the tractor there arose an implied warranty that the manufacturer and dealer would correct the defects within a reasonable time but because they were wilfully dilatory or negligent, they did not do so.

May an implied warranty be found and may consequential damages be sought despite the fact that the written warranty given at the time of sale provides it is in lieu of all other warranties, express, implied, or statutory, limits liability to that of repairs or replacement of defective parts, and negates liability for consequential damages? Defendants vigorously argue the negative of the proposition. They point out that plaintiff agreed to the terms and conditions of that warranty and placed his signature upon it to evidence the fact. They also point out that this case is governed by the Uniform Commercial Code, pertinent provisions of which authorize the restrictive provisions of warranty. They cite UCC 2-316 which authorizes exclusion or modification of warranties.

They also cite UCC 2-719(1)(a) and (b).

When tested by these Uniform Commercial Code criteria, the restrictive warranty is indeed authorized and proper. The plaintiff buyer accepted the tractor with the knowledge that the manufacturer and dealer had limited their liability to repair or replacement as they may properly do under the above sections of the Code so long as that limitation is not unreasonable. Plaintiff does not plead any coercive, fraudulent, overreaching or unconscionable sales tactics so presumably the original limitation of liability was not unreasonable and from all that appears the plaintiff made his purchase with full knowledge of the limitations. But plaintiff could not have made his bargain and purchase with knowledge that defendants would be unreasonable, or, in the words of his complaint, wilfully dilatory or careless and negligent in making good their warranty in the event of its breach. The manufacturer and the dealer have agreed in their warranty to repair or replace defective parts while also limiting their liability to that extent. Had they reasonably complied with their agreement contained in the warranty they would be in a position to claim the benefits of their stated limited liability and to restrict plaintiff to his stated remedy. The limitations of remedy and of liability are not separable from the obligations of the warranty. Repudiation of the obligations of the warranty destroy its benefits. The complaint alleges facts that would constitute a repudiation by the defendants of their obligations under the warranty, that repudiation consisting of their wilful failure or their careless and negligent compliance. It should be obvious that they cannot at once repudiate their obligation under their warranty and assert its provisions beneficial to them. Thus, the allegations of Count II of plaintiff's complaint invoke other provisions of the Uniform Commercial Code. Section 2-719(2) provides:

> Where circumstances cause an exclusive or limited remedy to fail of its essential purpose, remedy may be had as provided in this Act.

Failure of the exclusive remedy provided in the warranty is readily found in the allegation that defendants were wilfully dilatory or careless and negligent in complying with their obligations under the warranty. In considering the issue those allegations stand admitted by defendants' motions.

Provisions of the Code providing plaintiff's remedy are readily found. UCC 2-314 deals with Implied Warranty; Merchantability; Usage of Trade. Subsection (3) of that section provides:

> Unless excluded or modified (Section 2-316) other implied warranties may arise from course of dealing or usage of trade.

The Official Comment on this section states that it is to make explicit that usage of trade and course of dealing can create warranties and that they are implied rather than express warranties and thus subject to exclusion or modification under UCC 2-316. It is clear that an implied warranty for reasonably prompt and timely repairs upon breach of the express warranty may arise under this Code section. Though excluded by the written warranty as authorized in UCC 2-316, defendants' repudiation for failure to reasonably comply avoids the exclusion. The allegations of Count II that the parties had prior dealings, that the defendants knew plaintiff's business and knew of his contracts for work, and the further allegation that the repair work should take only one week are sufficient, if proven, to give rise to the implied warranty.

As to the measure of damages to which plaintiff is entitled, UCC 2-714(2) and (3) of the Code provides:

> (2) The measure of damages for breach of warranty is the difference at the time and place of acceptance between the value of the goods accepted and the value they would have had if they had been as warranted, unless special circumstances show proximate damages of a different amount.
>
> (3) In a proper case any incidental and consequential damages under the next section may also be recovered.

Plaintiff has prayed consequential damages. They may be recovered under the above section only if special circumstances show proximate damages of a definite amount. UCC 2-715(2), relating to buyers' incidental and consequential damages, provides:

> Consequential damages resulting from the seller's breach include
>
> (a) any loss resulting from general or particular requirements and needs of which the seller at the time of contracting had reason to know and which could not reasonably be prevented by cover or otherwise. . . .

The defendants call attention to the case of Keystone Diesel Engine Co. v. Irwin, 411 Pa. 222, 191 A.2d 376, in which it was held that the "special circumstances" were the communication to the seller at the time of entering into the contract of sufficient facts to make it apparent that the subsequently claimed loss of profits was within the reasonable contemplation of the parties. The court remarked that the buyer had alleged no facts which would make the seller aware that the buyer intended to hold him responsible for any loss of profits resulting from inability to use the engine there involved. Our attention is also called to Flug v. Craft Manufacturing Co., 3 Ill. App. 2d 56 (1954), a case decided prior to the adoption of the Uniform Commercial Code in which it was stated: "Before loss of profits can be used as a measure of damages, the contract should expressly or by implication from its terms contemplate such damages; the defaulting party must fairly be presumed to have understood the extent of his liability for loss of profits and to have assented thereto; and the loss of profits when used as a measure of damages should be fairly compensatory to the vendee and not unjust to the vendor. In the instant case, the only reference to any contract which might involve a loss of profits is the notation on the order which showed that the dies were being made in connection with governmental work. That is clearly not enough to establish that thereby it was expressly or by implication agreed that damages for loss of profits was in contemplation." Other Illinois cases, notably, Phelan v. Andrews, 52 Ill. 486; and Fruehauf Trailer Co. v. Lydick, 325 Ill. App. 28, hold that damages for loss of time of use of equipment arising from seller's breach may be recovered and there is no requirement that liability for such loss be contemplated by the parties at the time of the contract. In their Official Comment upon UCC 2-715(2) its framers make it clear that the "tacit agreement" test for the recovery of consequential damages is rejected. The language of that section should not be so narrowly construed as to require a prior understanding or agreement that the seller would be bound for consequential damages in the event of his breach. If that is the holding of the Keystone and Flug cases it must be rejected. The Official Comment further states that the older common-law rule which made the seller liable for all consequential damages of which he had "reason to know" in advance is followed, modified to require reasonable prevention of loss by cover or otherwise. The Code provision and the Official Comment make it clear that strictures are not to be applied to the plain meaning of the Code by adherence to what the parties have agreed or contemplated at the time of sale. Rather, each case is to be considered on its merits touching upon the issue of special circumstances arising in that particular case. In the instant case, it is alleged that the plaintiff's particular needs in his tractor business and his existing contracts were known to the defendants and that plaintiff was relying on their judgment; but notwithstanding this, the defendants were wilfully dilatory or careless and negligent in making the corrections or repairs called for in their warranty. We hold these allegations to be sufficient to show "special circumstances" required by UCC 2-714(2) and that consequential damages have resulted and may be recovered pursuant to UCC 2-715(2)(a). . . .

The order of the trial court dismissing Counts I, IV and V of plaintiff's Second Amended Complaint is affirmed. The order dismissing Counts II and III of plaintiff's Second Amended Complaint is reversed and the cause is remanded for further proceedings.

EDDY, ON THE "ESSENTIAL" PURPOSES OF LIMITED REMEDIES: THE METAPHYSICS OF U.C.C. SECTION 2-719(2)
65 Calif. L. Rev. 28, 58-64 (1977)

The analytic process proposed in the previous section may be tested by applying it to the second recurrent situation in which section 2-719(2) is presently utilized: the case of a limited repair warranty provision. Automobiles, many other consumer products, and substantial numbers of commercial and industrial products are typically sold with such a "warranty." These provisions have a number of elements: first, a carefully delineated express warranty is made; second, all other warranties, express or implied, are disclaimed; third, the remedy for breach of the express warranty is limited to a sole remedy of repair or replacement, at the seller's option; and fourth, the provision may additionally state that seller shall have no liability for consequential damages.

When carefully drafted, such a provision accords with the freedom of contract that Article Two recognizes; indeed, specific Code authority may be cited for each element of the term. Nevertheless, such clauses have been subject to a variety of attacks. Putting aside issues of personal injury, the major battles currently swirling around the limited repair warranty concern recoverability of economic loss: diminished value of the goods sold, consequential economic loss, or both.

Attempts to recover such damages usually begin with an attack upon the validity of the limited repair warranty. Here, although the courts have not always done so, it is necessary to note the Code's distinction between disclaimer of warranty and limitation of remedy. Disclaimer is governed most directly by section 2-316, which restricts itself to establishing standards for effective disclaimer of implied warranties. Although it does impose some minimal restrictions upon negation of express warranties, a carefully drawn limited repair warranty provision will have no difficulty complying with the section. In the face of the apparent validation of complying disclaimers by section 2-316, a few jurisdictions have extended tort liability to cover economic loss, and decisions elsewhere have voided disclaimers despite compliance with section 2-316. Some states have adopted nonuniform versions of section 2-316, prohibiting disclaimer of implied warranties in consumer transactions. And under the Magnuson-Moss Warranty-Federal Trade Commission Improvement Act, it will no longer be possible for those who make certain types of express warranties to disclaim at the same time an implied warranty of merchantability.

Despite these inroads, in the vast majority of commercial transactions and in a substantial number of consumer transactions, it remains possible for sellers to disclaim implied warranty liability. Thus the pressure exerted by those seeking relief for their disappointed economic expectations is shifted to the seller's attempted limitation of remedies for breach of the express warranty given.

As noted, the typical limited repair warranty embodies an exclusive remedy of repair or replacement and an exclusion of consequential damages. Section 2-719(1)(a) validates the former; section 2-719(3) the latter, unless unconscionable. Such a "repair or replace" provision not only operates equitably but also minimizes senseless economic waste. It assures that in the end the buyer will receive substantially what was bargained for—a functioning item meeting the contract description. Yet although holding the seller to this substantial performance standard, it does not impose an unrealistic standard of perfection.

For example, consider a consumer who purchases a new refrigerator. On the third day of operation a defect in the compressor becomes apparent. This defect absolutely prevents the refrigerator from operating: that is, it very substantially impairs the value of the refrigerator to the buyer. Accordingly, if the other conditions of section 2-608 are met, the buyer will normally be entitled to revoke the acceptance and tender back the refrigerator. Assuming that the seller later fixes the defective coil, the refrigerator, which sells now as a "used" refrigerator of "unknown lineage," will sell at a substantially discounted price. This discount will reflect in part societal antipathy to potential defects, including those that may have been acquired during the first ownership period. In any case, a "loss" will be imposed on the seller here that may be avoided if the seller has an option to repair the goods. The "repair or replace" warranty may thus be portrayed as a fair balancing of the interests of the two parties. Indeed, to a limited extent, the Code requires that a buyer allow a seller such opportunities: this is the precise aim of the Code's "cure" provision, section 2-508. The limited repair warranty, therefore, represents a contractual extension of the cure concept, and similar policies of "substantial performance" appear to support it.

This rosy picture of the limited repair warranty, however, rests upon at least three assumptions: that the warrantor will diligently make repairs, that such repairs will indeed "cure" the defects, and that consequential loss in the interim will be negligible. So long as these assumptions hold true, the limited remedy appears to operate fairly and, as noted above, will usually withstand contentions of "unconscionability." But when one of these assumptions proves false in a particular case, the purchaser may find that the substantial benefit of the bargain has been lost. The language of the Official Comment to section 2-719 squarely supports this proposition:

> [U]nder subsection (2), where an apparently fair and reasonable clause because of circumstances fails in its purpose or operates to deprive either party of the substantial value of the bargain, it must give way to the general remedy provisions of this Article.

With increasing frequency purchasers are raising section 2-719(2) contentions with such circumstances, and courts have displayed confusion in dealing with the arguments.

Under the analysis previously proposed, the first step is to determine the purposes served by a limited remedy. As in the case of "undiscoverable defects," however, courts have been slow to recognize the need for such analysis. Instead, while perhaps perceiving implicitly the nature of the transaction and therefore the "essential purpose" of the limited remedy, some courts have chosen to focus on such morally laden issues as the character of the defendant's conduct. Such emphasis may give rise to a rule of decision that is at the same time too narrow and too broad: too narrow because contract liability is often strict liability, with the consequence that a limited remedy may fail of its essential purpose despite the innocence of the warrantor; too broad because, conversely, the "bad" character of a contractant is not a reliable guide for the imposition of the liability in circumstances in which the parties' agreement may narrowly define the contractant's obligation. A brief examination of the cases will demonstrate both propositions.

Problem 14-21. Lankford purchases from Dealer a new Thunderbird car manufactured by Ford. Ford supplies a warranty document identical to the one set out in Problem 14-19, at p. 684 supra. A number of defects immediately begin to occur: for example, the power steering fails, and activating the safety flasher turns on the radio. Dealer repairs each defect when brought to its attention but over 18 months the car is in its shop for 45 days for 50 different defects. Lankford asks your advice as to whether it may recover from Ford for breach of an implied warranty of merchantability.

Problem 14-22. Westinghouse sells to Allegheny Power a turbine generator. The contract contains a one-year limited repair warranty. The turbine is rated at one megawatt. After the generator is installed, it malfunctions due to a defect in the turbine blades. Westinghouse replaces the blades but Allegheny suffers a substantial consequential loss while the generator is down. May Allegheny successfully argue failure of essential purpose?

Suppose that the unit fails to develop the rated capacity. Westinghouse tries to repair the unit, but despite alterations in the blades and other adjustments, the unit fails to develop its rated capacity. May Allegheny successfully argue failure of essential purpose and recover the substantial losses it suffers through lost generating capacity?

Suppose that when notified that the unit does not generate at capacity, Westinghouse refuses to do anything. Allegheny has had others attempt to get the unit up to rated capacity but to no avail. Has there been a failure of essential purpose? May Allegheny recover (a) the costs of the attempted "repair," and (b) the losses accruing from loss of generating capacity?

EARL M. JORGENSEN CO. v. MARK CONSTRUCTION, INC.
540 P.2d 978, 17 UCC Rep. 1126 (Hawaii 1975)

MENOR, J. This case arises out of a contract for the sale of some 3,468 lineal feet of sectional steel plate. The seller-appellee, Earl M. Jorgensen Co., sued the purchaser-appellant, Mark Construction, Inc., for the unpaid balance of the purchase price. Mark counterclaimed for damages allegedly resulting from Jorgensen's failure to supply material conforming to specifications. Jorgensen moved for summary judgment on the counterclaim, contending that its liabilities were limited under the contract. The trial court granted the motion, but allowed Mark to file this interlocutory appeal.

The point in dispute concerns the terms and provisions constituting the contract between the parties. More specifically, at issue is whether the limitation of liability clause asserted by Jorgensen was part of the contract, and if so, (1) whether the limitation of liability clause was unconscionable, and (2) whether Mark's remedy as provided in the contract had failed of its essential purpose. . . .

The limitation of liability provision was an essential part of Jorgensen's offer. The quotation of June 8, 1970, contained the disputed provision. So also did the quotation of July 10, 1970. Both quotations were on single sheet printed forms entitled "Quotation." The front side of each form contained a description of the quantity and type of sectional plate to be furnished, the price, the terms of payment, and the place of delivery. Both were signed by Mike Durant for Jorgensen. At the bottom of the front page appeared the following which were printed in block capital letters:

> Notice provisions printed on the reverse side hereof comprise additional terms of this contract limiting the seller's warranty obligation and excluding liability for consequential damages.

On the reverse side, among other provisions, was the following:

Limitation of Warranty Liability

> Seller hereby warrants that the material described herein conforms to specifications. Seller's liability is expressly limited to replacement of defective material or refund of purchase price to the original purchaser, at Seller's option, when material is properly worked or used within a reasonable time. In no event shall Seller be liable for any labor claims or special, indirect, consequential or other damages, whether arising under any warranty, express or implied, or otherwise, and the remedies of Buyer expressed herein are exclusive. Anything contained in prior or subsequent communications between Buyer and Seller which purports to alter this provision shall be void and is superseded by this provision. This warranty is made in lieu of all other express and implied warranties, including any implied warranty of merchantability or fitness for a particular purpose, and of any other obligations or liability on the part of Seller. Seller neither assumes nor authorizes any person to assume for it any liability not expressed herein.

Mark's purchase order made no reference whatsoever to this limitation of warranty liability provision, nor to any of the other printed provisions. . . .

We deem it sufficiently clear from the undisputed facts that the submission of the purchase order by Mark was a manifestation of its intent to accept Jorgensen's offer in all of its essential terms. Mr. Gaborno was vice-president and engineer in charge of estimating, preparing bids, and purchasing materials for Mark at the time of these transactions. The H-2 project was only one of the several construction projects Mark was engaged in at the time. There is no question about his authority to act for Mark in its transactions with Jorgensen. Mr. Gaborno used the first written quotation as a basis for preparing Mark's bid to the State. He used the second written quotation as a basis for preparing Mark's purchase order to Jorgensen. There is no assertion on his part that he was unaware of the limitation of liability and of warranty provision. There is no claim that he was misled. . . .

On the question of whether the trial court erred in failing to hold that the limitation of liability clause was unconscionable and in failing to allow an independent hearing on the issue of unconscionability, we find no error. . . .

UCC 2-719 permits the limitation of remedies to repair or refund, as well as the exclusion of consequential damages, provided that such exclusion is not unconscionable. Clauses similar to the one involved here have withstood attacks of unconscionability. . . .

Comment 1 to UCC 2-302 states the test applicable in determining unconscionability: "The basic test is whether, in the light of the general commercial background and the commercial needs of the particular trade or case, the clauses involved are so one-sided as to be unconscionable under the circumstances existing at the time of the making of the contract. . . . The principle is one of the prevention of oppression and unfair surprise . . . and not of disturbance of allocation of risks because of superior bargaining power."

It is evident from the undisputed facts that this contract was not made under circumstances involving oppression and unfair surprise. There was no great disparity between the bargaining power of the two parties. At the time of the making of the contract, Mark was conducting a multi-million dollar business, and was engaged in a number of large construction projects. Moreover, Mark was aware that at least one other company besides Jorgensen was capable of supplying it with the required sectional plates, and was not precluded from dealing with that other. Nor can Mark claim unfair surprise over the inclusion of the limitation of liability clause in the contract. Mark had the terms of Jorgensen's quotation before it at the time of the preparation of the purchase order. In sum, there simply is no evidence showing that Mark was an unwilling purchaser overreached and forced to yield to onerous terms imposed by Jorgensen. The trial court did not err in determining that the limitation of liability clause under consideration was not unconscionable. . . .

Of more significant import is Mark's contention that the limited remedy provided in the contract had failed of its essential purpose. UCC 2-719(2). It contends that the steel plates delivered to the job site by Jorgensen did not conform to contractual specifications in major respects, and that the defect in the material could not be detected until construction had actually commenced. It charges Jorgensen with having failed to render adequate assistance when requested, and points out that defective plates sent back to Jorgensen for corrective repairs were returned to Mark uncorrected. Mark urges that considering the number and nature of the defects encountered, the time constraints imposed upon it by its contract with the State, the number of men and machinery tied up for each day of delay caused by the defective material supplied by Jorgensen, and the failure of Jorgensen to perform its part of the bargain, the limited remedy provided in the contract had failed of its essential purpose and that, therefore, the limitation of liability clause should be declared void and of no effect. . . .

Limited remedies under the Code have been held to fail of their essential purpose in two basic situations.

One of these involves defects in the goods which are latent and not discoverable upon receipt of shipment and reasonable inspection. In Neville Chemical Company v. Union Carbide Corporation, 294 F. Supp. 649 (D. Pa. 1968), *vacated on other grounds,* 422 F.2d 1205 (3d Cir. 1970), [p. 704 infra] it was held that a clause limiting damages to the purchase price of the goods (resin oil) failed of its essential purpose where the defect in the goods (contamination) only was not discoverable until after the goods had been processed. See also Wilson Trading Corporation v. David Ferguson, Ltd. . . .

A limitation of remedies clause fails, in the other instance, when the seller or other party required to provide the remedy, by its action or inaction, causes the remedy to fail. . . .

Jorgensen here had warranted that the material it supplied to Mark would conform to specifications. Whether it breached this warranty is an issue in dispute. Assuming a breach, Jorgensen had nevertheless limited its liability under the contract to replacement of defective material or to refund of the purchase price. Mark alleges that the defects in the material supplied were not detectable until attempts to put the plates in place were made. Under these and the totality of the circumstances, a refund of the purchase price would have been a totally inadequate remedy. Neville Chemical Company v. Union Carbide Corporation, supra. Moreover, when the alleged defective condition of the material was called to Jorgensen's attention, it chose to attempt corrective repairs. There is a dispute as to whether the remedy provided by Jorgensen in this respect was effective. No replacement of allegedly defective material was undertaken by Jorgensen.

Whether Jorgensen breached its materials warranty, and if it did, whether Jorgensen, by its conduct, had caused Mark's contractually limited remedy to fail of its essential purpose, must depend upon the particular facts and circumstances of this case. The record reveals the existence of genuine issues of material fact, which, if resolved in Mark's favor, would entitle it to the array of remedies provided a buyer by the Uniform Commercial Code. . . .

[Reversed and remanded.]

NOTES & QUESTIONS

1. *Undiscoverable defects.* Many UCC 2-719(2) cases stress the undiscoverable nature of the defects. What exactly is meant by the assertion that the defects are not discoverable? Should the present case be distinguished from one where the defects could have been detected by an X-ray analysis of the plates on receipt by the buyer? If defects are not discoverable by the buyer, are they discoverable by the seller? In any event, why does *unavoidability* of loss control the freedom of the parties to *allocate* the loss?

2. *Legislative history.* Courts invalidating limited remedies in cases of "undiscoverable defects" sometimes rely on the language of the comment providing that neither party shall be "deprived of the substantial value of the bargain." This language, unlike the "failure of essential purpose" language immediately proceeding it, no longer appears in the statute.

A 1941 draft of the Revised Sales Act provided as follows:

§57-B (New to Sales Act) *Prohibited Contractual Modification of Remedy.* No contract to sell or sale shall so modify or negate provisions of this Part IV on Remedies and Remedial Rights as to unreasonably restrict the remedy, as,—. . . (c) by limiting the remedy to repair, replacement, or the like, when the results thereof fail, in the circumstances of the contract and breach, to give the buyer the substantial value contracted for. . . .

In *Jorgensen,* was the contract remedy a "minimum adequate remedy" to provide the buyer with "the substantial value contracted for" under the circumstances of the contract? (What are the "circumstances of the contracy?") Under the "circumstances of the breach?" And is consequential loss part of the "substantial value" bargained for?

In the same 1941 draft the preceding provision stated:

§57-A (New to Sales Act) Permissible Contractual Modifications of Remedies. In furtherance of the principles of Section 57, a particularized term of the contract may in an appropriate case—. . . (2) Between merchants, provide that consequential damages are limited or excluded, notwithstanding that they flow from defects not reasonably discoverable by the buyer, if such defects are not due to avoidable fault on the part of the seller.

The "principles" that §57-A seeks to further include the following: "The buyer's remedies are founded on the principle that his contract entitles him to rely on receiving, net, the value to him of conforming goods duly delivered for use or resale, in return for the price."

Llewellyn appears to support the following views:

(a) Generally, the effect of contract (remedies) is provided by law;

(b) but within the limits of reasonability and good faith, parties may modify remedies to suit the circumstances of a type-transaction;

(c) nonetheless, a limitation reasonable for one type-transaction may be unreasonable in another;

(d) a given transaction may be "atypical;" and

(e) For a variety of reasons, including transaction costs, the documentation of a deal may be the same, whether it is a case within (b), (c) or (d) above.

UCC 2-719(3) recognizes the propriety of limiting or excluding consequential loss when not unconscionable, and provides that limitation of such damages "for injury to the person in the case of consumer goods is prima facie unconscionable but limitation of damages where the loss is commercial is not." Although students often assume that such limitations are harsh, their frame of reference often is the consumer transaction, and is sometimes drawn from previous analysis of torts issues. The useful role that risk allocation may play is readily apparent, however, in purely commercial settings.

Problem 14-23. Wool yarn is subject to certain defects not detectable on visual inspection. These defects affect the ability of the yarn to take dyes evenly. They can be discovered, but only by dyeing a test batch of the yarn. Dyes differ somewhat, so a dye test conducted with one dye is not always conclusive as to the evenness with which another dye will take.

Mill #1 has computed its costs of inspection to be $10 per gross of spools. It has decided to forgo inspection. It sells all its wool on the following terms:

"2. No claims relating to excessive moisture content, short weight, count variations, twist, quality or shade shall be allowed if made after weaving, knitting, or processing, or more than 10 days after receipt of shipment. . . . The buyer shall within 10 days of the receipt of the merchandise by himself or agent examine the merchandise for any and all defects. . . .

"4. This instrument constitutes the entire agreement between the parties, superseding all previous communications, oral or written, and no changes, amendments or additions hereto will be recognized unless in writing signed by both seller and buyer or buyer's agent. It is expressly agreed that no representations or warranties, express or implied, have been or are made by the seller except as stated herein, and the seller makes no warranty, express or implied, as to the fitness for buyer's purposes of yarn purchased hereunder, seller's obligations, except as expressly stated herein, being limited to the delivery of good merchantable yarn of the description stated herein."

Mill #2 has computed its costs of inspection to be $4.75 per gross of spools. It sells its wool at a price out of which it pays all manufacturing costs, including inspection costs and a reserve for products liability claims.

Mill #3 has computed its cost of inspection to be $3.75 per gross of spools. However, it does not inspect, nor does it provide a reserve for claims: it deals with claims on an ad hoc basis as they arise.

Neither Mill #2 nor Mill #3 attempts to disclaim or limit liability.

Weaver #1 uses wool primarily for rough work clothes for loggers, fishermen, and the military. It is relatively indifferent to dye quality.

Weaver #2 uses wool for fine woolen goods. It never conducts its own testing, regarding it as too expensive.

Which Mill offers superior terms? Which seller is acting the "best"? Which buyer? What else would you like to know, if anything? Does the law have any interest in upsetting Mill #1's terms? Does it make any difference if Mill #2 not only inspects more cheaply than Mill #1, but also sells more cheaply? Does it make any difference if all buyers buy for essentially the same purposes and with the same quality needs? If all sellers sell upon the same terms?

The foregoing problem is drawn from Wilson Trading Corp. v. David Ferguson, Ltd., 23 N.Y.2d 398, 244 N.E.2d 685, 297 N.Y.S.2d 108, 5 UCC Rep. 1213 (1968). *Wilson* is followed in *Jorgensen,* supra. Both cases hold that the seller's limitation of remedy to return of goods and refund of price fails of its essential purpose when the goods have latent defects that cause the buyer to suffer substantial consequential loss. In both cases, however, the seller had excluded liability for consequential loss, and the *Jorgensen* court is at some pains to point out that this exclusion is not unconscionable.

If the exclusion of consequential damages is not unconscionable, it would appear that the buyer is limited to the recovery of the price or some measure

of direct damages that presumably would not exceed the price. It is remarkable, therefore, that the courts in both *Wilson* and *Jorgensen* find that the limited remedy fails of its essential purpose when the buyer suffers consequential
loss, and flatly wrong for the courts then to use the failure of essential purpose
as a basis for striking down the consequential loss exclusion. In essence, the
court's position may be reduced to a statement that it is fair to allocate consequential loss to the buyer, provided that there is no loss to allocate.

We would argue strenuously that if a court finds a clause excluding consequential loss conscionable, it should not argue the materialization of that
same loss as a ground for finding failure of essential purpose, and certainly
should not do so with the goal of thereby shifting the consequential loss back to
the seller. But there may be instances in which the limited remedy fails because a risk materializes that the parties did not allocate. In such instances, it
may be viewed as a surprising (unconscionable) construction to hold that a
general exclusion of consequential damages applies to the particular damages
that ensue. Consider the cases that follow in this light.

BEAL v. GENERAL MOTORS CORP.
354 F. Supp. 423, 12 UCC Rep. 105 (D. Del. 1973)

[Plaintiff purchased a diesel tractor from Watkins, an authorized GM dealer.
The purchase order form extended an express 24 months/24,000 miles warranty against defects in parts or workmanship, and limited GM's obligation
under that warranty to repair or replacement, at GM's option, of any defective
parts. All other warranties, express or implied, were excluded.]

STAPLETON, District Judge. . . . In his amended complaint plaintiff alleges
that this warranty was breached, specifies a host of defects, and asserts that
General Motors was unable or unwilling to repair or replace the offending
parts in such a way as to make the vehicle operable. His claim for damages
includes a claim for profits lost as a result of his inability to utilize the truck in
his business.

The major legal issue presented by defendant General Motors' motion to
strike is whether consequential damages may be recovered upon proof of a
breach of the express warranty relied upon. If as a matter of law they may not,
defendant argues, then allegations in the amended complaint which relate
only to that claim should be stricken as immaterial.

The Delaware version of the Uniform Commercial Code clearly permits
the type of limitation of remedy contemplated by this contract. [The court
quotes UCC 2-719.]

It, therefore, appears that the limitation of remedy contained in the contract is valid, and consequential damages are not recoverable unless the limitation is unconscionable or, on these facts, fails of its essential purpose. If either
situation is found "remedy may be had as provided in this Act," UCC 2-
719(2), including, [in] a proper case, consequential damages. UCC 2-714,
2-715.

The purpose of an exclusive remedy of replacement or repair of defective parts, the presence of which constitute a breach of an express warranty, is to give the seller an opportunity to make the goods conforming while limiting the risks to which he is subject by excluding direct and consequential damages that might otherwise arise. From the point of view of the buyer the purpose of the exclusive remedy is to give him goods that conform to the contract within a reasonable time after a defective part is discovered. When the warrantor fails to correct the defect as promised within a reasonable time he is liable for a breach of that warranty. Steele v. J. I. Case Co., 197 Kan. 554, 419 P.2d 902 (Kan. 1966); Seely v. White Motor Co., 63 Cal. 2d 9, 45 Cal. Rptr. 17, 403 P.2d 145 (1965). The limited, exclusive remedy fails of its purpose and is thus avoided under UCC 2-719(2), whenever the warrantor fails to correct the defect within a reasonable period.

The situation here is like that which confronted the court in Jones & McKnight Corp. v. Birdsboro Corp., 320 F. Supp. 39 (N.D. Ill. 1970). There Judge Will analyzed the problem in terms of repudiation of the seller's duties under the warranty which resulted in a failure of the exclusive remedy to achieve its purpose: ". . . Although the plaintiff-buyer purchased and accepted the machinery and equipment with the apparent knowledge that the seller had properly limited its liability to repair or replacement, and although the plaintiff does not allege any form of unconscionability in the transactions which led to the purchase, plaintiff also was entitled to assume that defendants would not be unreasonable or wilfully dilatory in making good their warranty in the event of defects in the machinery and equipment. It is the specific breach of the warranty to repair that plaintiff alleges caused the bulk of its damages. This court would be in an untenable position if it allowed the defendant to shelter itself behind one segment of the warranty when it has allegedly repudiated and ignored its very limited obligations under another segment of the same warranty, which alleged repudiation has caused the very need for relief which the defendant is attempting to avoid. If the plaintiff is capable of sustaining its burden of proof as to the allegations it has made, the defendant will be deemed to have repudiated the warranty agreement so far as restricting plaintiff's remedies, and the exclusive remedy provision of the contract will be deemed under the circumstances to have failed of its essential purpose, thus allowing plaintiff the general array of remedies under the Code."[2]

General Motors here argues that there is no failure in essential purpose because recovery by the buyer of the difference in market value of a truck free of defects and the truck actually delivered will give the buyer everything he had a right to expect under the contract. The logic urged in support of this argument is flawed, however.

---

2. The limited remedy fails of its purpose whenever the seller fails to repair the goods within a reasonable time; good faith attempts to repair might be relevant to the issue of what constitutes a reasonable time. However, since UCC 2-719(2) operates whenever a party is deprived of his contractual remedy there is no need for a plaintiff to prove that failure to repair was willful or negligent.

Defendant concedes that plaintiff is entitled to direct damages measured by market values. What is it, however, that gives him this remedy? It is clearly not the contract, for it purports to substitute a right of replacement and repair for any right to damages. Rather, the right to direct damages arises from UCC 2-714(2). But where the parties expressly provide for an exclusive remedy "in substitution for" the "measure of damages recoverable" under the Code, that remedy is the buyer's sole recourse. UCC 2-719. The direct damage remedy of UCC 2-714(2), therefore, is applicable only when the exclusive remedy provided in the contract fails of its essential purpose within the meaning of UCC 2-719(2). Under that section when such a failure occurs recourse may be had to all the remedial provisions of the Code. There is no discernible reason for limiting that recourse to selected remedial provisions as defendant apparently attempts to do. The direct damages section, UCC 2-714(2), has no greater claims to application here than does the consequential damages section, UCC 2-714(3), assuming, of course, that this is otherwise "a proper case" for consequential damages.

While this court is unable to hold that consequential damages are not recoverable in this case, neither may it be determined at this preliminary stage whether such damages will be recoverable if liability is established. . . .

The issues of what the parties had reason to know and what actions, if any, plaintiff might reasonably have taken to mitigate his damages present questions which cannot properly be answered at this stage. For present purposes it is enough to state that issues relating to the recovery of consequential damages are still in this case and that defendant General Motors' motion to strike allegations referring thereto and to strike allegations referring to "background" of the contract negotiations must be denied. . . .

NOTES & QUESTIONS

1. *Allocation of risk.* In S. M. Wilson & Co. v. Smith International, Inc., 587 F.2d 1363, 25 UCC Rep. 1066 (9th Cir. 1978) Smith agreed to manufacture a rock tunnel boring machine to be used by Wilson to drill a mine shaft. The written agreement disclaimed all warranties except an express warranty that the machine would be free of defects in material and workmanship, and limited Wilson's remedies to repair or replacement of defective parts. The agreement also excluded liability that might have resulted from the use or loss of use of the machine. The machine did not work up to the contract specifications, and despite repeated attempts Smith was unable to cure the defects. *Held,* the limited remedy failed in its essential purpose but buyer could not recover its consequential damages. On the latter point, the court stated:

"The issue remains whether the failure of the limited repair remedy to serve its purpose requires permitting the recovery of consequential damages as UCC 2-714(3) and 2-715 permit. We hold it does not. In reaching this conclusion we are influenced heavily by the characteristics of the contract between Smith and Wilson. . . . Parties of relatively equal bargaining power negotiated an allocation of their risks of loss. Consequential damages were assigned to the buyer, Wilson. The machine was a complex piece of equipment designed for the buyer's purposes. The seller Smith did not ignore his obligation to repair; he simply was unable to perform it. This is not enough to require that the seller absorb losses the buyer plainly agreed to bear. Risk shifting is socially expensive and should not be undertaken in the absence of a good reason. An even better reason is required when to so shift is contrary to a contract freely negotiated. The default of the seller is not so total and fundamental as to require that its consequential damage limitation be expunged from the contract.

"Our holding is based upon the facts of this case as revealed by the pleadings and record and is not intended to establish that a consequential damage bar always survives a failure of the limited repair remedy to serve its essential purpose. Each case must stand on its own facts."

2. *Pointless gestures; mitigation.* Consider the following argument: "In most cases, on a fair reading of the contract, it seems likely that the parties knew that the limited remedy might or might not be efficacious. And yet they also included an exclusion of consequential loss. Is it reasonable to suppose that this exclusion was meant to prevent recovery of losses accruing while repairable goods were being repaired, but to allow recovery in the more serious case when goods cannot be fixed? And if it is once admitted that the exclusion clause is effective when the goods cannot be fixed, why should it matter whether the seller tries at all? For either the goods cannot be fixed, in which case trying is a pointless gesture, or else they can be, in which case buyer should mitigate loss if it faces substantial consequential damage." Sound?

NEVILLE CHEMICAL CO. v. UNION CARBIDE CORP.
422 F.2d 1205, 7 UCC Rep. 81 (3d Cir. 1970)

ADAMS, Circuit Judge. This is an appeal from a judgment of the District Court for the Western District of Pennsylvania, entered after a jury found that Union Carbide Company (Carbide) had been negligent and breached its warranties in the sale of a certain unsaturated oil to Neville Chemical Company (Neville).

Carbide is a substantial large producer of various chemical products. One of these products is a hydrocarbon oil, used for forming resins, originally referred to as "unsaturated oil" and later called "U-171." Unsaturated oil is produced from dripolene, a product of Carbide's "cracking" operations, in which natural gas and other materials are processed into ethylene and additional commodities.

Neville is in the business of manufacturing hydrocarbon resins from products which it purchases from petrochemical companies such as Carbide. Neville produces resins at plants located at Neville Island near Pittsburgh, Pennsylvania, and Anaheim, California. It sells its resins to customers throughout the United States and parts of Canada for use in the manufacture of such items as floor tile, shoe soles, rubber matting, pigments for printing ink, paper packaging products, paint and varnish.

Over a period of fifteen years prior to the events in question, Carbide sold Neville large quantities of unsaturated oil. Carbide was aware of the particular purposes for which Neville purchased this product and knew the end uses of the resins which Neville manufactured.

By 1959, Neville was dissatisfied with the yield and color qualities of Carbide's unsaturated oil. In order to "get more money for their product" and because of Neville's dissatisfaction, Carbide instituted a program to improve the quality of its unsaturated oil. Beginning in January, 1960, it submitted to Neville several samples of refined unsaturated oil which it developed in an effort to meet Neville's requirements. None of these samples was satisfactory. In February, 1961, Carbide delivered to Neville a sample of refined unsaturated oil which Carbide called "UO-171." Neville then ordered on a trial basis and received in October, 1961, a barge shipment of approximately 300,000 gallons of this material, then designated "U-171" by Carbide. The trial shipment produced a satisfactory resin and Neville, in 1961 and 1962, purchased ten more 300,000 gallon barge lots of U-171. In February, 1963, Carbide also commenced shipment of U-171 to Neville's Anaheim plant.

After negotiations in Pittsburgh, Carbide drafted a year-to-year contract, dated February 12, 1963, to be effective October 1, 1962, by which Neville agreed to purchase from Carbide its requirements of "Resin Intermediate, U-171," "estimated to be 1,500,000 gallons per year," at "17.5 cents per gallon." The agreement was signed by Neville in Pittsburgh and then transmitted to New York where it was signed by Carbide.

Although the contract does not define "Resin Intermediate, U-171," it specifies the required maximum or minimum limits on four of its physical properties, and states that "the material is a derivative of Dripolene a by-product from Ethylene production." The four properties itemized are "Polymerizable Content," "Resin Color," "Aniline Point," and "Resin Solubility." The contract contains Carbide's warranty "to deliver to Buyer material conforming to the specifications" and an "escape clause" in the event a "change in the character of Dripolene, for any reason whatsoever, render(s) it impossible . . . for [Carbide] to produce material conforming to the specification limits. . . ." Paragraph 7, entitled "Claims," requires that notice of claims against Carbide be given "within fifteen (15) days after the receipt of such material;" provides that Neville "assumes all risk and liability for the results obtained by the use of any material . . . in manufacturing process . . . or in combination with other substances;" and provides that "No claim . . . shall be greater in amount than the purchase price of the material in respect of which such claim is made." Paragraph 9 states that the contract "contains all of the representations and agreements between the parties hereto and no warranties shall be implied."

All the U-171 sold to Neville was produced at and delivered from Carbide's Kanawha Valley facilities at Institute and South Charleston, West Virginia. Beginning January, 1963, dripolene from Carbide's Seadrift, Texas plant was imported into the Kanawha Valley by Carbide and, without Neville's knowledge, was used to produce U-171.

Without notice to Neville, but with notice to its own personnel,[1] Carbide in early June, 1963, changed its Seadrift, Texas ethylene process to permit ethyl acrylate, a chemical additive made from ethylene and used in the production of polyethylene, to be recycled into the ethylene stream, and thus into the dripolene. Prior to the change at Seadrift any ethyl acrylate was, from its first use in 1959, destroyed in the cracking furnaces before it could get into the ethylene stream. No ethyl acrylate of any significance could have survived the cracking furnace heat to which it was subjected before June, 1963. The earliest time at which ethyl acrylate could have reached any Neville plant as part of U-171 was early August, 1963.

In October, 1963, personnel at Neville's Anaheim plant began receiving serious complaints from the Flintkote Company branch in California. Flintkote used Neville's resin to make floor tile, and several of Flintkote's customers were complaining to it about an unusual, persistent and intolerable odor in the floor tile which had been manufactured from Neville's resin. Neville's President, Lee V. Dauler, immediately went to the West Coast to investigate. Thereafter, in November, 1963, he went to New York City and met with Carbide officials. Mr. Dauler advised Carbide of the Flintkote complaints and told Carbide he suspected a change had been made in U-171. A sample of the malodorous Flintkote tile was left with Carbide for analysis. Carbide did not advise Neville of the results of its analysis.

Although Neville claimed that the October, 1963 complaint was the first serious odor complaint, Neville described at least one floor-tile complaint from Flintkote before August, 1963, and conceded that before mid-July, 1963, Flintkote had asked for a "deskunking" of Neville's resin. In January, 1964, personnel at the Neville Island plant began receiving numerous complaints from customers in Eastern United States and Canada who had purchased resin made from U-171 and used it in the manufacture of shoe soling material, paper packaging products, rubber matting, pigments for printing inks, paint and varnish. There were, however, customers of Neville who used resins made from U-171 during this same period and did not complain, including Armstrong Cork, which like Flintkote used Neville resin in manufacturing floor tile.

Neville stopped purchasing U-171 after December, 1963.

Investigation by Neville and its customers established that after the various end products made with resins containing U-171 were distributed, they developed an intolerable odor which persisted for long, indeterminate periods of time. Efforts to mask or otherwise abate the odor proved fruitless.

---

1. Notice to Carbide personnel was given by a memorandum dated May 31, 1963, and circulated in the Seadrift plant, which stated that: ". . . As our knowledge of the hazards of acrylate increases, we can operate our plant at maximum profit while handling the acrylate with the care it deserves as a reactive chemical. . . . The Institute Plant, which processes our dripolene, has been alerted that the Seadrift dripolene will contain small quantities of acrylate. They have agreed to accept the material on a trial basis and will let us know if any problems arise. . . ."

During 1964, Mr. Dauler and D. W. Kelso, Vice President and Treasurer of Neville, wrote several letters to Carbide advising of the claims asserted and the litigation threatened against Neville. On July 17, 1964, Neville's counsel wrote to Carbide setting forth the number and gravity of the claims, listing each of the complaining customers, the dollar amount of each claim, and notifying Carbide of Neville's claim against it for full reimbursement of amounts paid in respect of such claims and related costs. In reply to these communications, Carbide denied any responsibility in the matter, refused to provide any information to Neville regarding the possible cause of the odor problem, and did not advise Neville of any change in its process of manufacturing U-171. Neville investigated and then settled its customers' complaints and claims.

Neville brought suit on July 20, 1965, under diversity jurisdiction, charging Carbide with negligence in allowing ethyl acrylate to enter the dripolene, and failing to notify Neville of the change, with breach of its express warranties, and with breach of the implied warranties of merchantability and fitness for a particular purpose. Neville sought to recover $696,534 it paid to settle claims asserted by customers which had purchased its resin; $128,075.40 in interest in this amount; $53,965 claimed from Neville by Liberty Mutual Insurance Company paid to Beebe Rubber Company, a customer of Neville; $281,063 it claimed was spent on technical research, settlement expenses, and disposition of defective materials; and $1,519,145 estimated loss of profits for a ten year period.

Carbide counterclaimed for the cost of merchandise which had been shipped to Neville and not paid for, and for the loss of profits sustained by it because Neville refused to accept the remaining U-171 which Neville had contracted to purchase.

The case was tried in two stages before Judge Gerald J. Weber and a jury. In the first stage, all issues as to liability were submitted to the jury on special interrogatories. In answer to 15 interrogatories, the jury found: (1) the contact with ethyl acrylate during Carbide's processing was the proximate cause of the odor which made Neville's resin unacceptable to users; (2) Carbide was negligent in delivering such material to Neville; (3) Carbide was negligent in failing to notify Neville of the change in its process; (4) there was no negligence on the part of Neville which contributed to the odor problem; (5) Neville did not assume the risk of objectionable odor; (6) Carbide did not breach its contract with Neville to supply Neville with the material agreed upon; (7) Carbide agreed to deliver material conforming to a sample labeled "UO-171" and (8) failed to do so; (9) Carbide agreed to deliver material substantially conforming to the material delivered by barge loads in 1961 and 1962 and (10) failed to do so; (11) Carbide agreed to deliver material that "had been identified by a verbal description which identified the material" and (12) did deliver such material; (13) Carbide failed to deliver material which would pass as a resin former oil without objection in the trade or was of fair average quality or which was fit for the ordinary purposes of such material in the trade; (14) Carbide had reason to know of Neville's particular purposes for the material, Neville relied on Carbide's skill and judgment, Carbide had reason to know this; and (15) Carbide failed to supply material fit for Neville's purposes.

After the jury made its findings on liability, the issues of damages were tried and the jury returned a verdict for the plaintiff in the amount of $2,151,-534. . . .

The basic question presented on this appeal is whether the District Court properly refused to grant defendant's motion for judgment notwithstanding the verdict, pursuant to Rule 50(b), Federal Rules of Civil Procedure. Such a motion may not be granted unless as a matter of law it is found that Neville failed to present a case for the jury, and a verdict in Carbide's favor should have been directed at the end of the trial.

Carbide advances the following reasons in support of its motion for judgment notwithstanding the verdict:

I. Neville failed to prove a prima facie case of causation.

II. Neville failed to prove negligence, or to establish a breach of warranty.

III. The terms of the contract between Neville and Carbide preclude liability to Neville for either breach of warranty or negligence.

IV. The damage verdict was improper because its various elements were not legally recoverable.

[The court's discussion of issues I, II, and IV has been omitted.]

Having concluded that there was sufficient evidence to support the jury's finding that Carbide was negligent and that this negligence was the proximate cause of Neville's odor problem, we must decide whether Carbide could and did insulate itself against, or limit, its liability to Neville by the contract covering the sale of the U-171. The pertinent language of the contract is as follows:

Paragraph 7

"Failure of Buyer to give notice of any claim with respect to any material delivered hereunder within fifteen (15) days after the receipt of such material shall be an unqualified acceptance of such material and a waiver by Buyer of all claims with respect thereto. Buyer assumes all risk and liability for the results obtained by the use of any material delivered hereunder in manufacturing processes of Buyer or in combination with other substances. No claim of any kind, whether as to material delivered or for nondelivery of material, shall be greater in amount than the purchase price of the material in respect to which such claim is made."

In the first sentence of Paragraph 9 of the contract, it provided: "This Agreement contains all of the representations and agreements between the parties hereto and no warranties shall be implied."

The general rule on this point established by Pennsylvania case law is that a private party may validly contract to relieve himself from liability for the consequences of his own negligent acts. . . . However, there is no doubt that the law is and perhaps always has been that "contracts against liability for negligence are not favored by the law," and will be construed strictly, with every doubt resolved against the party seeking their protection. . . . This is particularly so where such party has drafted the contract.

The question that we must address ourselves to therefore is the specificity of the language required to disclaim or limit responsibility for negligence. The Pennsylvania test for evaluating the required language is set forth in Dilks v. Flohr Chevrolet, 411 Pa. 425, 192 A.2d 682 (1963) and Employers Liability Assurance Corp. v. Greenville Business Men's Assn., 423 Pa. 288, 224 A.2d 620 (1966). After reviewing the Pennsylvania cases on exculpatory contracts, the court in *Dilks* said that (411 Pa. at 436, 192 A.2d at 688): ". . . where a person claims that, under the provisions and terms of a contract, he is rendered immune from and relieved of any liability for negligent conduct on his part or on the part of his employees, the burden is upon such person to prove (a) that such contractual provisions and terms do not contravene public policy and (b) that the provisions and terms of the contract *clearly* and *unequivocally* spell out the intent to grant such immunity and relief from liability. Absent such proof, the claim of immunity falls." . . .

The first provision on which Carbide relies to bar its liability is the fifteen day notice requirement. This requirement is manifestly unreasonable if it is construed to require that notice be given of *latent* defects which would not be discoverable until after the time specified has elapsed. The crux of the jury's finding of negligence is that Carbide shipped Neville a product knowing or having reason to know it was likely to cause an obnoxious odor after Neville processed it into resin and sold the resin to its customers. We do not agree that the time limitation for notice of claims was intended to apply in these circumstances. Such an interpretation would be inconsistent with the rule that a party is immunized from the consequences of his own negligence only by clear and unequivocal language expressing that intent.

The same result would follow under the Uniform Commercial Code. The trial court decided that the notice requirement was ineffective under UCC 1-204(1), which states that "Whenever this Act requires any action to be taken within a reasonable time, any time which is not manifestly unreasonable may be fixed by agreement." Just as a seller of tulip bulbs from Holland could not bar claims against it for defective bulbs by requiring notice before the bulbs would normally bloom, Vandenberg & Sons, N.V. v. Siter, 204 Pa. Super. 392, 204 A.2d 484 (1964), Carbide could not require notice of a defect in its chemical products at a point in time at which it was impossible to discover the defect. 294 F. Supp. at 655.

Although there is some question whether the Uniform Commercial Code is applicable to this point, since here we have a jury finding of negligence as distinguished from a mere breach of a warranty, nonetheless, there is no reason on this record to distinguish between the reasonableness of a notice requirement effective to bar recovery for contract claims and that effective to bar recovery for negligence claims. . . .

Carbide argues that the strict construction of exculpatory language is reserved for contracts of adhesion where there is a disparity in the bargaining power between the parties. This is questionable since Dilks v. Flohr Chevrolet and *Employers Liability Assurance* each involved a dispute in a commercial setting between a lessor and a business tenant. . . .

Strict construction of exculpatory clauses is also indicated by the Uniform Commercial Code which requires sellers use very specific language in order to modify or disclaim liability to purchasers for a breach of the implied warranties. The implied warranty of merchantability can be excluded or modified only by language that mentions the word "merchantability," or by the words "as is," "with all faults" or "other language which . . . makes plain that there is no implied warranty. . . ."

The clause that Carbide relies on does not include the word negligence or any of its cognates and is essentially a clause of "general import." It says that Neville assumes "all risk and liability for the results obtained by the use of any material delivered hereunder in manufacturing processes of Buyer or in combination with other substances." Neville did not clearly assume the risk of Carbide's negligence as to material which did not conform to that in the sample barge and, hence, was not "delivered hereunder." As the jury's finding established, the odor did not result from anything in Neville's processing operation nor use of the material by Neville, but was almost an inevitable reaction from the time Carbide allowed the ethyl acrylate to enter the dripolene. The clause is not appropriate to place the risk on Neville that Carbide would change its process without notifying Neville of such change, in a manner making it likely an unmerchantable resin would result.

The last sentence of paragraph 7 of the Contract, which limits claims to the return of the purchase price, is also a general disclaimer. It is not clearly and unequivocally applicable to negligence of the type present on this record. The last two sentences of paragraph 7 are complementary and we cannot say that the latter one clearly excluded what the previous one did not.

Nor can we accept Carbide's argument that paragraph 7 meant nothing if it did not limit liability for negligence under these circumstances. The provision could be an attempt to limit damages which occurred in excess of the purchase price as a result of a breach of contract. Whether it was effective for this purpose is a question we do not have to reach[25] since the jury specifically found negligence in this case. . . . [The court affirmed the trial court's denial of

---

25. Judge Weber decided that the limitation of claims to the purchase price was ineffective to limit Carbide's liability on any theory. In doing so, he relied on the rules of the Uniform Commercial Code, and the cases thereunder. He decided that under UCC 2-719 an attempt to limit recovery to the purchase price was inapplicable if there were a latent as opposed to patent defect. . . .

The latent nature of the defect, Judge Weber indicated "cause[d] an exclusive or limited remedy to fail of its essential purpose." In Zicari v. Joseph Harris Co., the Appellate Division of the New York Supreme Court held that the word "merchantability" must be used to limit liability for its breach under UCC 2-719 or 2-316. 33 A.D.2d 17, 304 N.Y.S.2d 918 (1969).

The rules of UCC 2-719 apply to limiting or altering the measure of damages recoverable under the Uniform Commercial Code and may not be directly applicable to limitation of liability for negligence.

judgment n.o.v. or a new trial with respect to all liability issues, but remanded the case on the issue of damages.]

UCC 2-719(3) expressly refers to unconscionability with respect to exclusion of consequential damages; UCC 2-316 is silent as to whether warranty disclaimers may be struck as unconscionable. Consider the following comment in a leading analysis of unconscionability. How would you answer Professor Leff?

LEFF, UNCONSCIONABILITY AND THE CODE—THE EMPEROR'S NEW CLAUSE, 115 U. Pa. L. Rev. 485, 523 (1967): "Given a careful meeting of the requirements of section 2-316 (the Code section particularly devoted to warranty disclaimers), may the more generally protective and loosely defined section devoted to general naughtiness be invoked to avoid the harsh result?

"Almost everyone seems to think so. It appears to be a matter of common assumption that section 2-302 is applicable to warranty disclaimers. I find this, frankly, incredible. Here is 2-316 which sets forth clear, specific and anything but easy-to-meet standards for disclaiming warranties. It is a highly detailed section, the comments to which disclose full awareness of the problem at hand. It contains no reference of any kind to section 2-302, although nine other sections of article 2 contain such references. In such circumstances the usually bland assumptions that a disclaimer which meets the requirements of 2-316 might still be strikable as 'unconscionable' under 2-302 seems explainable, if at all, as oversight, wishful thinking or (in a rare case) attempted sneakiness."

NOTES & QUESTION

Seed Cases. A number of cases deal with suits against seed distributors brought by farmers whose crops have failed. Sometimes the seeds have failed to germinate or are the wrong variety. It is difficult if not impossible to tell one kind of seed from another. If the "wrong" seeds are planted, this is known only when they grow—or fail to do so. Distributors universally package and sell their seeds with broad disclaimers, limitations of remedy to refund of the price, or the like. Do these cases present the same issue as any of the preceding cases?

D. PRIVITY

You no doubt already have some familiarity with issues of privity from classes in torts or products liability. In this century the doctrine has atrophied in warranty law as well as in tort, but it retains sufficient vitality to require treatment of the problems that still exist.

First, you should recall some terminology. *Vertical* privity deals with the issue of whether an action lies only against one's immediate seller or also against "upstream" parties such as distributors or the manufacturer. *Horizontal* privity deals with the issue of whether someone other than the immediate buyer may bring the action, such as the buyer's employee, spouse, guest, or even a bystander.

Second, you should recognize that the same court may relax privity requirements for some warranty theories and not for others. Thus some courts may view the extension of an express warranty directly to the buyer by someone other than the seller (for instance, by a manufacturer who extends an express warranty) as "creating" privity on that warranty. It does not follow that the same court would treat implied warranties as running from the manufacturer to the ultimate buyer. Yet *some* courts do so: when the pattern of distribution is such that the manufacturer "makes the market," through advertising, extending express warranties to buyers, and the like, these courts treat implied warranties as also being available to the buyer against the manufacturer.

Third, the kind of loss suffered may be decisive: whether, for example, the plaintiff has suffered personal injury rather than economic loss. Older historical patterns that treat some products (principally food, cosmetics, and chemicals) as different from other products also persist in some jurisdictions.

Courts do not always excel at keeping track of the state of their own doctrine in this area. There is some tendency to invoke the above factors in cases where the court views them as decisive. Otherwise, the court may speak in general, and potentially misleading, terms. You should keep in mind the possible impact of these factors whenever you evaluate a privity issue.

NOBILITY HOMES OF TEXAS, INC. v. SHIVERS
557 S.W.2d 77, 22 UCC Rep. 621 (Tex. 1977)

Pope, Justice. This is a products liability case. It presents the question of whether a remote manufacturer is liable for the economic loss his product causes a consumer with whom the manufacturer is not in privity. John Shivers used Nobility Homes of Texas, Inc., the manufacturer of a mobile home. Shivers purchased the home from Marvin Hurley, an independent retail dealer who is now out of business and is not joined as a party to this suit. Shivers's purchase contract was only with Hurley; Shivers was not in privity with Nobility Homes. The trial court, sitting without a jury, found that the mobile home was defective in both its workmanship and materials. There were no findings that these defects made the unit unreasonably dangerous or caused physical harm to Shivers or his property. The trial court did find that the mobile home was negligently constructed and not fit for the purposes for which it was sold. The trial court also found the unit's reasonable market value to be 8,750 dollars less than its purchase price. This is Shiver's economic loss,[1] it is the only damage which Shivers suffered. The trial court awarded judgment to Shivers. The court of civil appeals, with a divided court, affirmed that judgment. 539 S.W.2d 190. We affirm the judgments of the courts below.

The court of civil appeals allowed Shivers to recover his economic loss against Nobility Homes, a manufacturer with whom Shivers was not in privity. The primary basis of the court of civil appeals decision was "an implied warranty of reasonable fitness of a product as a matter of public policy." 539 S.W.2d at 194. The court of civil appeals explained, "This concept is not adverse to the jurisprudence of this state. The principle was applied over three decades ago with respect to contaminated foods . . ." in Jacob E. Decker & Sons, Inc. v. Capps, 139 Tex. 609, 164 S.W.2d 282 (1942). We do not believe that *Decker* is authority for allowing the recovery of economic loss. At the time of *Decker's* writing, the consumer had little remedy for losses caused by defective products. To compensate for this lack of remedy, *Decker* created "an implied warranty imposed by operation of law as a matter of public policy." 164 S.W.2d at 829. This remedy has been described as, "a freak hybrid born of the illicit intercourse of tort and contract." Prosser, The Assault Upon the Citadel, 69 Yale L.J. 1099, 1126 (1960). The protection of Texas consumers no longer requires the utilization of an "implied warranty as a matter of public policy." Since the *Decker* decision, Texas has adopted section 402A of the Restatement (Second) of Torts and the Uniform Commercial Code. McKisson v. Sales Affiliates, Inc., 416 S.W.2d 787 (Tex. 1967); Tex. Bus. & Comm. Code Ann. §§1.101-9.507 (1968). These adoptions furnish the user of defective products remedies which were unavailable at the time of *Decker's* writing. Today, section 402A of the Restatement (Second) of Torts and the Uniform Commercial Code rather than *Decker's* "implied warranty as a matter of public policy" should determine a manufacturer's liability.

The important issues in this case are whether section 402A of the Restatement (Second) of Torts or the implied warranties of the Uniform Commercial Code allow a consumer to recover this economic loss against a manufacturer with whom the consumer is not in privity. We hold that Shivers may not recover his economic loss under section 402A of the Restatement (Second) of Torts but may recover such loss under the implied warranties of the Uniform Commercial Code and the theory of common law negligence. Although the court of civil appeals did not discuss negligence, it was an independent basis of the trial court's judgment in favor of Shivers which the court of civil appeals affirmed.

---

1. Economic loss may be either direct or consequential. The distinction between direct and consequential economic loss has been summarized as follows: "Direct economic loss may be said to encompass damage based on insufficient product value; thus, direct economic loss may be "out of pocket"—the difference in value between what is given and received—or "loss of bargain"—the difference between the value of what is received and its value as represented. Direct economic loss also may be measured by costs of replacement and repair. Consequential economic loss includes all indirect loss, such as loss of profits resulting from inability to make use of the defective product." Note, Economic Loss in Products Liability Jurisprudence, 66 Colum. L. Rev. 917, 918 (1966).

STRICT LIABILITY ISSUE

The application of the tort doctrine of strict liability to economic loss has prompted considerable commentary. Courts of other jurisdictions are split on whether to extend strict liability to economic loss. The two leading judicial opinions are probably Santor v. A. and M. Karagheusian, Inc., 44 N.J. 52, 207 A.2d 305 (1965) and Seely v. White Motor Co., 63 Cal. 2d 9, 45 Cal. Rptr. 17, 403 P.2d 145 (1965). In *Santor,* the New Jersey Supreme Court held the purchaser of defective carpeting could sue the manufacturer, with whom he was not in privity, on either a breach of implied warranty of reasonable fitness or strict liability. In Seely v. White Motor Co., supra, the California Supreme Court rejected *Santor's* holding. The California court held that White Motor Co. breached an express warranty to Seely but condemned *Santor's* application of strict liability to economic loss. Writing for the California Supreme Court in *Seely,* Chief Justice Traynor stated: "The distinction that the law has drawn between tort recovery for physical injuries and warranty recovery for economic loss is not arbitrary and does not rest on the 'luck' of one plaintiff in having an accident causing physical injury. The distinction rests, rather, on an understanding of the nature of the responsibility a manufacturer must undertake in distributing his products. He can appropriately be held liable for physical injuries caused by defects by requiring his goods to match a standard of safety defined in terms of conditions that create unreasonable risks of harm. He cannot be held for the level of performance of his products in the consumer's business unless he agrees that the product was designed to meet the consumer's demands." 45 Cal. Rptr. at 23, 403 P.2d at 151.

Texas courts of civil appeals have consistently preferred the result of *Seely* and have held that strict liability does not apply to economic losses. A strict liability action in Texas is based upon section 402A of the Restatement (Second) of Torts. *McKisson,* supra. Section 402A requires that the defective product be, "unreasonably dangerous to the user or consumer or to his property . . ." and that the product cause, "physical harm to the ultimate user or consumer, or to his property. . . ."[5] The courts of civil appeals have correctly reasoned that the economic loss is not "physical harm" to the user or his property. As stated in Melody Home Manufacturing Co. v. Morrison, 455

---

5. In its entirety section 402A of the Restatement (Second) of Torts states:

   (1) One who sells any product in a defective condition unreasonably dangerous to the user or consumer or to his property is subject to liability for physical harm thereby caused to the ultimate user or consumer, or to his property, if
       (a) the seller is engaged in the business of selling such a product, and
       (b) it is expected to and does reach the user or consumer without substantial change in the condition in which it is sold.
   (2) The rule stated in Subsection (1) applies although
       (a) the seller has exercised all possible care in the preparation and sale of his product, and
       (b) the user or consumer has not bought the product from or entered into any contractual relation with the seller.

S.W.2d 825 (Tex. Civ. App. 1970, no writ) [p. 645 supra]: "There is a distinction between physical harm, or damage, to property and commercial loss." We agree and hold that strict liability does not apply to economic losses. There is no finding in this case that the product was unreasonably dangerous to Shivers or caused physical harm to Shivers or his property.

UNIFORM COMMERCIAL CODE ISSUES

Chief Justice Traynor stated in *Seely* that: "The law of sales has been carefully articulated to govern the economic relations between suppliers and consumers of goods. The history of the doctrine of strict liability in tort indicates that it was designed, not to undermine the warranty provisions of the sales act or of the Uniform Commercial Code but, rather, to govern the distinct problem of physical injuries." 45 Cal. Rptr. at 21, 403 P.2d at 149.

In writing about claims for economic loss, Dean Keeton has explained: "Jurisprudentially, it is difficult to understand how the Code can be ignored in dealing with such claims. Those who drafted the Code doubtless contemplated that the obligations imposed by law for commercial losses, without respect to fault, were exclusively contained in the Code." Keeton, Torts, 1971 Survey of Tex. Law, 25 Sw. L.J. 1 (1971). The Code was drafted specifically to govern commercial losses, and obviously provides the proper remedies to recover such losses.

To support a recovery for economic loss, the Uniform Commercial Code provides both express and implied warranties. Neither the Code's express warranty, UCC 2-313, nor the Texas Deceptive Trade Practices Consumer Protection Act, Tex. Bus. & Comm. Code Ann. §17.41 to .63 (Supp. 1976-1977), are before us; consequently, these remedies are not affected by this decision. The Code also provides two implied warranties—the warranty of merchantability, UCC 2-314, and the warranty of fitness, UCC 2-315. UCC 2-314's warranty of merchantability is before us. UCC 2-314 explains that a seller impliedly warrants that goods are merchantable, and that goods are merchantable if they are, "fit for the ordinary purposes for which such goods are used. . . ." UCC 2-314(2)(c). Under the terms of the Code, a manufacturer may also be a seller. The Code does not limit its definition of seller to the immediate seller of a product. Instead, the Code defines a seller as "a person who sells or contracts to sell goods." UCC 2-103(1)(d). Nobility Homes "sells or contracts to sell goods;" consequently, Nobility Homes is a seller under the Code.

Plaintiff Shivers pleaded and the trial court found that Nobility Homes breached its warranty of merchantability to Shivers by manufacturing a product which, "was unfit for the purpose for which it was purchased, to-wit, a home." Without discussion, the court of civil appeals affirmed this holding. A critical question in this case is whether Nobility Homes' implied warranty of merchantability runs to Shivers with whom Nobility Homes is not in privity.

We now hold that a manufacturer can be responsible, without regard to privity, for the economic loss which results from his breach of the Uniform Commercial Code's implied warranty of merchantability.

The Uniform Commercial Code as enacted by the Texas Legislature is neutral as to the requirement of privity. This neutrality is expressed by the Code's statement that:

> This chapter does not provide whether anyone other than a buyer may take advantage of an express or implied warranty of quality made to the buyer or whether the buyer or anyone entitled to take advantage of a warranty made to the buyer may sue a third party other than the immediate seller for deficiencies in the quality of the goods. These matters are left to the courts for their determination. Tex. Bus. & Comm. Code Ann. §2.318 (1968) [a nonuniform text of UCC 2-318—Eds.].

For the most part, the requirement of privity has been abolished in strict liability tort actions. See Prosser, The Fall of the Citadel (Strict Liability to the Consumer), 50 Minn. L. Rev. 791 (1966). There is a split among both Texas courts and courts of other jurisdictions as to whether privity should also be abolished in implied warranty actions for economic loss. In holding that the requirement of privity should be abolished in such actions, the Alaska Supreme Court explained that it is unfair to allow a consumer to recover for his physical loss against a manufacturer with whom he is not in privity but to deny the same right to a consumer who suffers economic injury. Morrow v. New Moon Homes, Inc., 548 P.2d 279 (Alaska 1976). We agree. The fact that a product injures a consumer economically and not physically should not bar the consumer's recovery. Economic loss can certainly be as disastrous as physical injury. As Justice Peter's separate opinion in *Seely* pointed out, economic loss as well as personal injury can constitute the "overwhelming misfortune" in one's life which merits redress. Today, a consumer, without regard to privity, can recover against a manufacturer whose defective product causes the consumer to suffer the slightest physical injury. It would be inconsistent to demand privity as a prerequisite to the same consumer's recovery against a manufacturer whose defective product causes the consumer to lose his entire life savings. Consequently, we hold that privity is not a requirement for a Uniform Commercial Code implied warranty action for economic loss. To hold otherwise, would encourage manufacturers to use thinly capitalized "collapsible corporations" to sell their commercially inferior products leaving no one for the buyer to sue for his economic loss. . . . Further, by holding that implied warranty remedies apply to economic injuries, we are consistent with, "the well developed notion that the law of contract should control actions for purely economic losses and that the law of tort should control actions for personal injuries." Comment, The Vexing Problem of Purely Economic Loss in Products Liability: An Injury in Search of a Remedy, 4 Seton Hall L. Rev. 145, 175 (1972).

Courts which have declined to overturn the privity requirement in warranty actions for economic loss have reasoned that economic loss is more subjective and less predictable than physical loss. These courts fear that holding manufacturers liable for economic loss imposes unlimited and unforeseeable liability upon manufacturers. These fears are justified when manufacturers are held strictly liable for economic loss under the terms of section 402A of the Restatement (Second) of Torts. But, these fears are not justified when manufacturers are held liable by the Uniform Commercial Code because the Code, itself, protects manufacturers against unlimited and unforeseeable liability. First, the Uniform Commercial Code allows manufacturers to restrict their liability by the exclusion or modification of both implied and express warranties. UCC 2-316. Second, manufacturers' liability is restricted by the very terms of the Uniform Commercial Code sections which furnish the consumer's implied warranty remedies, UCC 2-314 and 2-315.

UCC 2-314 provides an implied warranty that the goods are merchantable but only "if the seller is a merchant with respect to goods of that kind." UCC 2-314(1). UCC 2-314 also states that merchantable goods, "are fit for the ordinary purposes for which such goods are used. . . ." UCC 2-314(2)(c). The manufacturer has liability, under UCC 2-314 only if the consumer uses the goods for an ordinary purpose. If the goods are employed for a purpose other than "the ordinary purposes for which such goods are used," the manufacturer is not liable.

UCC 2-315 furnishes the consumer his second implied warranty protection. The section provides an implied warranty of fitness for a particular purpose. This implied warranty only arises where, "the seller at the time of contracting has reason to know any particular use for which the goods are required and that the buyer is relying on the seller's skill or judgment to select or furnish suitable goods. . . ." Unless the manufacturer has this specific knowledge, he is not liable upon an implied warranty of fitness for a particular purpose. The Uniform Commercial Code provisions provide a predictable definition of a manufacturer's potential liability. These provisions adequately protect a manufacturer against unlimited and unforeseeable liability.

Many manufacturers have, in fact, always paid for the consumer's economic loss. As the New York Court of Appeals stated in Randy Knitwear, Inc. v. American Cyanamid Co., 11 N.Y.2d 5, 226 N.Y.S.2d 363, 181 N.E.2d 399 (1962): "It is true that in many cases the manufacturer will ultimately be held accountable for the falsity of his representations, but only after an unduly wasteful process of litigation. Thus, if the consumer or ultimate business user sues and recovers, for breach of warranty, from his immediate seller and if the latter in turn, sues and recovers against his supplier in recoupment of his damages and costs, eventually, after several separate actions by those in the chain of distribution, the manufacturer may finally be obliged 'to shoulder the responsibility which should have been his in the first instance.' " Dean Prosser explains that this chain of actions is "an expensive, time-consuming and wasteful process, and it may be interrupted by insolvency, lack of jurisdiction, disclaimers, or statutes of limitations." Prosser, The Assault Upon the Citadel, 69 Yale L.J. 1099, 1124 (1960). Our holding avoids such wasteful litigation.

THE NEGLIGENCE ISSUE

Consumers have other remedies for economic loss against persons with whom they are not in privity. One of these remedies is a cause in negligence.

Shivers alleged negligence against the manufacturer Nobility. He asserted that Nobility was negligent in: improperly designing the frame, improperly constructing the frame, roof, paneling, bathroom fixtures, and water system; and in failing to inspect the home prior to the sale. The trial judge made findings that Nobility's negligence was a proximate cause of Shivers's damages. Nobility attacked those findings in the court of civil appeals, asserting that there was no evidence or insufficient evidence to support the findings. The court of civil appeals overruled each of those points, holding that there was some evidence to support the findings. Nobility does not challenge this separate and independent ground of recovery; consequently, we must also affirm the judgment for Shivers on the negligence point. . . .

The judgments of the courts below are affirmed.

NOTES & QUESTIONS

1. *UCC 2-318.* The Texas version of UCC 2-318, as the *Nobility* court noted, is nonuniform. Even the official UCC text, however, states three alternatives rather than a single uniform provision. The Official Comments to UCC 2-318 suggest that judges are to develop doctrine as new cases arise; in doing so they are to be guided, but not constrained, by the Code. UCC 2-313, Comment 2. If this is to be the approach, isn't the explicit delegation to the courts in the Texas version more forthright? But is it appropriate to delegate to the courts the development of these rules on risk allocation? Compare the American Law Institute's caveat to Restatement (Second) of Torts §402A, which calls attention to issues on which the Institute does not express an opinion.

2. *Vouching in (UCC 2-607(5)).* UCC 2-607(5)(a) codifies the common law doctrine of vouching in. If Customer sues Dealer for breach of warranty for which Manufacturer is ultimately responsible, then Dealer may notify Manufacturer of the action and Manufacturer will be bound by any relevant finding of fact. Manufacturer may protect itself, however, by defending the action brought by Customer. Relatively few cases of vouching in are reported; those that are reported are straight-forward. See International Harvester Co. v. TRW, Inc., 37 UCC Rep. 753 (Idaho 1983) (manufacturer bound by finding as to defect when it refused to defend initial action). See generally Bernard, Vouching to Warranties of Quality: A Legal Anachronism?, 55 U. Det. J.

Urb. L. 73 (1977) (procedure may be still useful in title or infringement cases but an anachronism for warranties of quality).

3. *Analyzing cases by jurisdiction.* As a more general law of products liability is developing, it may be more revealing to study judicial technique within a particular jurisdiction rather than to look for national uniformity. Consider, for example, subsequent Texas supreme court decisions:

(a) Mid Continent Aircraft Corp. v. Curry County Spraying Service, Inc., 572 S.W.2d 308, 24 UCC Rep. 574 (Tex. 1978): action between immediate parties to recover damages to used airplane sold "as is" caused by defect in engine; relying on *Nobility* discussion of economic loss, the court concluded that the loss was economic since damages were only to airplane and that the UCC validated the "as is" disclaimer.

(b) Signal Oil & Gas Co. v. Universal Oil Products, 572 S.W.2d 320, 24 UCC Rep. 555 (Tex. 1978): action between immediate parties to recover for physical damage to property allowed to proceed not only on warranty claim but on strict liability theory because property other than the isomax reactor purchased was damaged by fire caused by defect in reactor.

(c) Garcia v. Texas Instruments, Inc., 610 S.W.2d 456, 30 UCC Rep. 401 (Tex. 1980): employee of buyer allowed to bring action based on breach of implied warranty of merchantability against seller of concentrated sulfuric acid which caused personal injury to employee. The court noted that neither *Nobility* nor *Mid Continent* stated that strict tort liability and UCC warranty liability were mutually exclusive, while *Signal Oil* recognized that both sources provide rules for defective products. Citing UCC 2-715(2)(b), the court held that the Code permits recovery for personal injuries when an implied warranty is breached. On the question of privity, the court adopted the same rationale for not requiring privity that it had used when abolishing it in strict liability actions: the desire to minimize risks of personal injury or property damage to innocent bystanders.

See also Clark v. DeLaval Separator Corp., 639 F.2d 1320, 30 UCC Rep. 1542 (5th Cir. 1981) (concluding no privity required under Texas law for recovery of economic loss).

Texas case law is relatively orderly; you should not assume that the law of all jurisdictions is equally so.

E.   RELATION OF UCC WARRANTY LAW TO OTHER DOCTRINES

1.   Strict Tort Liability

In the *Nobility* case, we introduced §402A of the Restatement (Second) of Torts, the text of which is reproduced in n.5 at p. 714 supra. Comment *m* to that section explains its relation to the law of warranty: "The liability stated in this Section does not rest upon negligence. It is strict liability. . . . The basis of liability is purely one of tort.

"A number of courts, seeking a theoretical basis for the liability, have resorted to a 'warranty,' either running with the goods sold, by analogy to convenants running with the land, or made directly to the consumer without contract. In some instances this theory has proved to be an unfortunate one. Although warranty was in its origin a matter of tort liability, and it is generally agreed that a tort action will still lie for its breach, it has become so identified in practice with a contract of sale between the plaintiff and the defendant that the warranty theory has become something of an obstacle to the recognition of the strict liability where there is no such contract. There is nothing in this Section which would prevent any court from treating the rule stated as a matter of 'warranty' to the user or consumer. But if this is done, it should be recognized and understood that the 'warranty' is a very different kind of warranty from those usually found in the sale of goods, and that it is not subject to the various contract rules which have grown up to surround such sales.

"The rule stated in this Section does not require any reliance on the part of the consumer upon the reputation, skill, or judgment of the seller who is to be held liable, nor any representation or undertaking on the part of that seller. The seller is strictly liable although, as is frequently the case, the consumer does not even know who he is at the time of consumption. The rule stated in this Section is not governed by the provisions of the Uniform Sales Act, or those of the Uniform Commercial Code, as to warranties; and it is not affected by limitations on the scope and content of warranties, or by limitation to 'buyer' and 'seller' in those statutes. Nor is the consumer required to give notice to the seller of his injury within a reasonable time after it occurs, as is provided by the Uniform Act. The consumer's cause of action does not depend upon the validity of his contract with the person from whom he acquires the product, and it is not affected by any disclaimer or other agreement, whether it be between the seller and his immediate buyer, or attached to and accompanying the product into the consumer's hands. In short, 'warranty' must be given a new and different meaning if it is used in connection with this Section. Is is much simpler to regard the liability here stated as merely one of strict liability in tort."

Note

No matter what theoretical distinction may be recognized between strict liability and warranty, as a practical matter most litigants allege breach of warranty, strict liability, and negligence claims in the same action. There are, however, some important differences between the different causes of action that must be kept in mind.

(a) Privity. Some jurisdictions still require privity in a sales warranty action but may not do so for a tort action. See Part D supra.

(b) Notice. UCC 2-607(3)(a) requires a buyer to give notice to the seller; notice is not required for a strict liability action.

(c) Statute of limitations. UCC 2-725 provides a statute of limitations that commences to run in a warranty action when tender of delivery is made. UCC 2-725(2). A statute of limitations for tort actions may be shorter but it may not begin to run until an injury occurs.

(d) Causation. UCC 2-715(2)(b) allows recovery of damages "proximately" caused. Tort standards of causation may require a showing of "producing" cause.

Some jurisdictions have sought to reconcile differences by providing for a unitary "product liability action." See, e.g., R.C.W.A. 7.72.010 (West 1961, 1983 Supp.). The relation of these statutory schemes to the Code varies.

Problem 14-24. In January Seely entered into a conditional sales contract with Southern Truck Sales for the purchase of a truck manufactured by White Motor Company. Seely purchased the truck for use in his business of heavy-duty hauling. On taking possession of the truck Seely found that it bounced violently, an action known as "galloping." For 11 months after the purchase, Southern, with guidance from White's representatives, made many unsuccessful attempts to correct the galloping. In November, when slowing down for a turn, Seely found that the brakes did not work. The truck overturned, and Seely, who was not personally injured, had the damage repaired for $5,466.09. The following month, after paying $11,659.44 of the purchase price of $22,041.76, Seely serves notice that he will make no more payments. Southern thereafter repossesses the truck and resells it for $13,000.

Seely brings an action against Southern and White seeking (1) damages, related to the accident, for the repair of the truck, and (2) damages, unrelated to the accident, for the money he had paid on the purchase price and for the profits lost in his business because he was unable to make normal use of the truck. On what legal theory is Seely more likely to succeed?

2. Misrepresentation

As the preceding section indicates, strict tort liability will rarely be available to the plaintiff who suffers only economic loss. That is not to say that warranty law is the only string to plaintiff's bow in such cases. Where plaintiff can establish actionable misrepresentation, economic losses may be recoverable.

Consider the following hypothetical transaction: Plaintiff purchases a used car from Defendant dealer. The price of the car is $5950, including a trade-in valued at $2000. Defendant represents that the car is in "mint" condition, has been driven only 15,000 miles, and has been gone over and completely checked out by Defendant's mechanic. A car in this condition would have a market value of at least $7500. In fact, the car has been driven about 45,000 miles and was involved in an accident in which the frame was twisted. Its actual value is only about $3700. The bill of sale states that the car is sold "as is."

You may assume that, at a minimum, plaintiff would like an adjustment to the price if the true facts become known. Indeed, it is likely plaintiff would like to "undo" the transaction. But it is also quite possible that the "as is" disclaimer will be sufficient to negate implied warranty (if such liability would be held to exist in a sale of used merchandise) and that proof of an express warranty will be challenged under the parol evidence rule. Arguably there are several misrepresentations present in the transaction. May they be proved, are they actionable, and what remedies will be available?

Initially, we can dispose of the parol evidence issue. The modern view regards the rule as a substantive principle of discharge and will not block the introduction of evidence unrelated to the terms of the contract. The same statement, therefore, that if labeled a warranty might be excluded under UCC 2-316(1) and 2-202 may be admitted as a misrepresentation. Where the contract contains a merger clause, case law is divided. As with most issues associated with the parol evidence rule, it would be foolhardy to insist on particular results; minimally, however, addition of a misrepresentation theory may assist substantially in obtaining introduction of oral statements.

The tort character of the misrepresentation action dispenses with other contractual aspects of warranty actions. Notice is not required; privity of contract is not required (although the misrepresentation must have been directed to the plaintiff); and disclaimers will not usually be effective (although a properly worded disclaimer clause, and some merger clauses, may bear on the issue of the plaintiff's reliance on the statement).

However, some aspects of the misrepresentation action will sound quite familiar to the student steeped in express warranty doctrine and will require consideration of exactly the same facts. Traditional doctrine distinguishes misrepresentations of fact from opinion. This and the warranty/puffing distinction both represent another way of approaching the issue of the probability and justifiability of reliance. And with reference to reliance, it should be noted that this remains, in its pristine form, a requirement for actionable misrepresentation.

Perhaps the most important comparative aspects of misrepresentation and warranty doctrine relate to the defendant's state of mind and to the remedies available to the plaintiff. The two questions are interrelated, as the former may affect the latter.

As noted, the plaintiff's major hurdle in proceeding on an express warranty theory in the above hypothetical would be introducing evidence that the oral statements were made. The Code makes it quite clear that no intention to warrant is required. Nor is the fact that defendant honestly believed the statements to be true of any avail: warranty liability is strict liability. In contrast, a traditional requirement of misrepresentation was scienter: intent to deceive.

Gradually, this requirement has been relaxed in many jurisdictions to allow recovery premised on negligent statements, and an increasing number of jurisdictions impose liability for innocent misstatements. At this point the liability starts more closely to approach warranty liability; even those jurisdictions typically restrict the remedies available in such cases, however.

In the above hypothetical we note that plaintiff might want either to adjust the price or to avoid the transaction. The case presents no consequential damages; however, if they did exist the plaintiff would also wish to recover them no matter which of the first two options are pursued. Warranty law provides the plaintiff with all of these alternatives. Under UCC 2-714 the buyer could recover the difference between the value of the goods accepted and the value they would have had they been as warranted: $7,500 less $3,700, or $3,800. Under UCC 2-717, these same damages could be deducted from the as-yet unpaid purchase price. In either event, the buyer would have the benefit of his bargain, that is, a total value of $7,500 in exchange for an outlay of $5,950. If the buyer chooses instead to avoid the transaction, UCC 2-608 provides for that. And, in any event, in an appropriate case the buyer would be able to recover consequential damages, without reference to the course he had pursued.

Two measures of damages are commonly applied in misrepresentation cases. The first of these is a benefit of the bargain rule, which applies the same measure of damages as UCC 2-714. However, this measure is not available when the misrepresentation is innocent. If it is innocent, which most clearly approximates the scope of express warranty liability, the buyer may find that he is restricted to an out-of-pocket or restitutionary measure that seeks to return the plaintiff to his precontract financial position. Of course the most direct way to do this would be to rescind the transaction (like revocation of acceptance) and allow the buyer to recover the price while returning the goods. However, without doing this an economically similar result can be achieved by awarding the buyer the difference between the value of what he parted with and the value of what he received. In the above hypothetical, this would be $2,250 ($5,950 minus $3,700).

Pre-Code law recognized a doctrine of election of remedies. This required the plaintiff to choose between rescinding the contract or seeking damages. If the contract was avoided, then it was conceptually inconsistent to premise a damage action on the existence of the avoided contract. An essentially similar doctrine prevailed when the buyer sought purely contractual remedies for breach of warranty under sales law. As the foregoing recapitulation of Article 2 remedies illustrates, the Code has abandoned this doctrine. It would be anomalous, however, to provide more liberal remedies for cases of simple contract breaches than for those accompanied by *scienter* fraud. Accordingly, UCC 2-721 abolishes the doctrine in misrepresentation cases arising in the context of sales transactions. This provision will not alter the restriction to out-of-pocket measures when the misrepresentation is innocent, but it will mean that where it is not, the buyer's remedies will be more expansive than previously.

3. Mistake

A final extra-Code doctrine the student should consider is that of mistake. Many will recall from first-year contracts Sherwood v. Walker, 66 Mich. 568, 33 N.W. 919 (1887). Plaintiff contracted to buy a cow believed by both parties to be barren. The price was computed in relation to the cow's value as beef. Plaintiff tendered $80, according to this value, but the defendant refused delivery because the cow was then with calf. Plaintiff sought to replevy the cow; verdict for defendant.

Not all courts would follow Sherwood v. Walker: even at its best the case displays the limitations in this area of a mistake theory. Would anyone believe that the defendant, had the cow been delivered, would be successful in an action to recover the excess of the cow's value over the price, on the grounds that the parties had been mistaken?

Sherwood v. Walker is the converse of a warranty case: the goods sold have a higher value than the assumed value on the basis of which they are sold. Mistake in the exact context of a warranty case is presented in Smith v. Zimbalist, 2 Cal. App. 2d 324, 38 P.2d 170 (1934). There defendant Zimbalist, a violinist of international repute, had purchased two violins from plaintiff, a knowledgeable collector of, but not a dealer in, rare violins. The two violins were thought to be a Guarnerius and a Stradivarius and sold for a price of $8,000, of which $2,000 was paid immediately. Before further payments had been made, Zimbalist discovered that the violins were imitations worth no more than $300. Plaintiff brought an action to recover the balance of the purchase price. The court affirmed judgment for the defendant: the sale had been founded on the mutually mistaken belief of the parties that the violins were rare and valuable.

Note that the theory employed in Smith v. Zimbalist allowed the court to split the loss. Due to the procedural stance of the case, Smith still received $2,000 for violins worth $300, and since no warranty was found, Zimbalist was left without an action to protect the "benefit of the bargain" as well. The student may find it instructive to reconsider a few of the warranty problems in the preceding section and to ask what success an innocent seller would have had in each with the argument that no liability should attach because the parties were mutually mistaken.

F.   EXTRA-CODE RESPONSES TO REAL OR PERCEIVED DEFICIENCIES OF THE UCC WARRANTY SYSTEM

We have now surveyed in some detail the application of the Code's warranty system to a variety of transactions. In the preceding section, we explored the

potential effect of nonwarranty law on issues of product quality in sales transactions. No doubt along the way you have made your own assessment of the
present state of the law. In reading this section you may sharpen your evaluation by focusing on three responses to real or perceived deficiencies of the
Code. They are 1) nonuniform amendments, 2) comprehensive state warranty
enactments, and 3) federal response through the Magnuson-Moss Act.

1.   Nonuniform Amendments

A substantial number of states have enacted nonuniform amendments to the
Code's warranty provisions. Several states reject all three alternatives offered
by the Code for UCC 2-318, and in their stead may enact provisions that deal
with vertical as well as horizontal privity. Other defenses to warranty actions,
such as lack of notice, are also addressed: for instance, Massachusetts provides:

> Lack of privity between plaintiff and defendant shall be no defense in any
> action brought against the manufacturer, seller, lessor or supplier of goods to
> recover damages for breach of warranty, express or implied, or for negligence,
> although the plaintiff did not purchase the goods from the defendant, if the
> plaintiff was a person whom the manufacturer, seller, lessor or supplier might
> reasonably have expected to use, consume or be affected by the goods. A manu-
> facturer, seller, lessor or supplier may not exclude or limit the operation of this
> section. Failure to give notice shall not bar recovery under this section unless the
> defendant proves that he was prejudiced thereby. All actions under this section
> shall be commenced within three years next after the date the injury occurs.
> [Mass. Gen. Laws, ch. 106, §2-318, as amended.]

Such provisions should be considered in conjunction with the materials
both on privity and on tort doctrine. Some of the same issues (for instance,
whether actions seeking economic loss should be treated like an action for
personal injury) recur. The desire for uniformity is not per se a significant
factor in evaluating such statutes. The law in this area has long been nonuniform, and the Code's "uniform" provisions already defer to that fact.

Another frequent variation involves placing strictures on disclaimers of
warranty, limitations of remedy, or both. Again, consider the following Massachusetts section:

> §2-316A. Exception as to the Exclusion or Modification of Warranties, etc.,
> in Sales of Consumer Goods. The provisions of section 2-316 shall not apply to
> sales of consumer goods, services or both. Any language, oral or written, used by
> a seller or manufacturer of consumer goods and services, which attempts to
> exclude or modify any implied warranties of merchantability and fitness for a
> particular purpose or to exclude or modify the consumer's remedies for breach of
> those warranties, shall be unenforceable.
>   Any language, oral or written, used by a manufacturer of consumer goods,
> which attempts to limit or modify a consumer's remedies for breach of such

manufacturer's express warranties, shall be unenforceable, unless such manufacturer maintains facilities within the Commonwealth sufficient to provide reasonable and expeditious performance of the warranty obligations.

   The provisions of this section may not be disclaimed or waived by agreement. [Mass. Gen. Laws, ch. 106, §2-316A.]

   What transaction-types does this provision govern? Is there a legitimate reason for treating these differently? What is the significance of the "maintenance within the state" provision? Is it desirable for all consumer products? Is the blanket prohibition of disclaimer of implied warranties justified? Could you achieve the same results under the uniform provisions?

   A Washington amendment prohibits merchant sellers from disclaiming implied warranties in consumer sales, "except insofar as the disclaimer sets forth with particularity the qualities and characteristics which are not being warranted." R.C.W.A. 62A.2-316(4) (West 1961, 1983 Supp.).

2. Extra-Code State Law Enactments

A few states have enacted somewhat more comprehensive legislation. Sometimes these acts deal with the same issues as the nonuniform amendments discussed above but typically they are more detailed. Thus they may contain their own definitions of express and implied warranties, which must be carefully compared with the Code definitions. As is the case with the nonuniform amendments, the legislation focuses on the consumer setting. See, for example, the Texas Deceptive Trade Practices Act, which allows a plaintiff to recover for breach of warranty. Tex. Bus. & Com. Code §§17.41-17.63 (1968; Vernon Supp. 1984) (potential treble damage recovery and award of attorney's fees). Product liability legislation must also be reviewed for possible impact.

3. The Magnuson-Moss Act

Apart from the Code, the most pervasive attempt to regulate product warranties is the Magnuson-Moss Act (formally called the Magnuson-Moss Warranty-Federal Trade Commission Improvement Act, 88 Stat. 2183, 15 U.S.C §§2301-2312 (1982)). An understanding of what the Act does and does not do can most easily be gained by working through a simple set of problems. Some questions will also be posed as an aid to assessing the federal effort.

   For further commentary on the Act, see C. Reitz, Consumer Protection Under the Magnuson-Moss Warranty Act (1978); Eddy, Effects of the Magnuson-Moss Act upon Consumer Product Warranties, 55 N.C.L. Rev. 835 (1977); Note, An Empirical Study of the Magnuson-Moss Warranty Act, 31 Stan. L. Rev. 1117 (1979).

The leading decision construing the Act is Skelton v. General Motors Corp., 660 F.2d 311 (7th Cir. 1981). See Lester, The Magnuson-Moss Warranty Act: The Courts Begin to Talk, 16 UCC L.J. 119 (1983).

Problem 14-25. Consumer buys a new RCA Color TV from Stereoworld. A sales slip describes the set as a "1980 RCA XL-100." There is no other documentation of the sale.

(a) Under the Code, what warranties have been made? By whom and to whom?

(b) Under the Magnuson-Moss Act, how would you answer the same questions?

(c) Suppose the salesman states: "This set has a full one-year warranty." Or suppose that he asserts that the set is on sale because it is a floor display model when actually it is a previous return from a dissatisfied buyer. Within a week the set completely fails. What warranties have been breached under the Code? Under the Magnuson-Moss Act?

(d) Is the Magnuson-Moss Act dealing with a particular "type-transaction"? How would you describe the type-transaction?

Problem 14-26. Assume that the carton containing the RCA XL-100 also contains a large certificate that states:

> RCA, Inc., warrants this set free from defects in materials and workmanship for a period of 90 days from date of purchase. This warranty is in lieu of all other warranties, express or implied, including any warranty of merchantability. Liability for breach of this express warranty is limited to repair or replacement, at RCA, Inc.'s option, of defective parts, and in no event shall RCA, Inc., be liable for consequential loss.

Consumer has made no inquiry as to warranty coverage, and Stereoworld has made no statements.

(a) What is the effect of this certificate on the warranty liability of RCA and Stereoworld under the Code?

(b) What is the effect of the certificate under the Magnuson-Moss Act?

(c) Has either RCA or Stereoworld incurred any liability for failure to draw these warranty provisions to the attention of the consumer prior to the sale?

(d) Would your answer to (c) be any different if the purchaser was Andy's Tavern, buying the set for use in its bar?

Problem 14-27. Stereoworld displays an XL-100 on its showroom floor. A large placard next to it is headed: "Limited 90-Day Warranty." The placard reproduces the text of the warranty, as in the preceding problem. A certificate, also headed "Limited 90-Day Warranty," is packaged with each set. It also reproduces the text of the warranty, set out in the preceding problem.

(a) Assume that the set malfunctions after six weeks. Stereoworld makes several attempts to repair it, but fails to do so. Does Consumer have a remedy under the Magnuson-Moss Act? Under the Code?

(b) Assume that the purchase is by Andy's Tavern, and that during the period that the set is "down," it is necessary to rent a substitute set. May Andy's recover the amount of rentals? What provisions of the Code are relevant to answering this issue? What provisions of the Magnuson-Moss Act?

(c) Assume that upon its first malfunction the set short-circuits, and starts an electrical fire that does substantial damage to Consumer's living room. Does Consumer have an action under either federal or state law to recover this loss? Again, which provisions of the Code and the Act should be considered?

(d) Assume that the set malfunctions, but when Consumer brings the set to Stereoworld, he is told that the set can only be repaired if Consumer will ship the set prepaid to RCA's factory. Further, although parts will be provided free, Consumer will have to pay for the labor involved. What are Consumer's rights under the Code? Under the Act?

(e) Assume that the set performs adequately for a year but then starts to malfunction. It is uncontested that the normal "life" for a color TV is between five and ten years. What rights does Consumer have under the Code? Under the Act?

Problem 14-28. You are employed by the general counsel's office at RCA. The senior vice-president for marketing contacts you. She states that Sony is about to offer a "Full 90-Day Warranty" on their Trinitron sets. RCA is concerned about the potential effect on RCA's sales. You are asked what additional liabilities RCA will subject itself to if it relabels its warranty as a full warranty. You are also asked to indicate the relative liabilities that RCA would subject itself to if it decides to offer a one-year limited warranty. Also, the vice-president wants to know whether it is possible to warrant the set for 90 days and the picture tube for one year and if so, whether it is safe to label either or both warranties as "full" warranties. She states that the director of quality control has expressed concern about extending any warranty protection beyond 90 days, except for the picture tube. Consider what additional information you would regard as important in answering these questions.

PART IV

Payment Systems

In Part IV we examine the competing systems that effect payment for goods and services. Payment, of course, is as much a part of financial and investment transactions as it is of more narrowly commercial transactions. The law we examine in these chapters is therefore of very broad applicability. Because the systems in question function very efficiently on the whole, relatively few lawyers come into frequent contact with this field, which is often thought of as the most highly technical area of commercial law.

It is common knowledge that the banking industry is in the midst of a revolution. This is due in part at least to the enormously increased capacity for processing financial data that has followed on the widespread introduction of computers into the commercial world. For several decades the imminent disappearance of checks and other "paper" payment media has been predicted. Judged by the market place, however, checks have served personal and business needs well. While they now co-exist with such alternative payment systems as credit cards and electronic funds transfer systems, they are far from becoming obsolete. It would appear that paper media will be with us for many years to come.

Our initial chapter focuses on the two traditional means of effecting payment: checks and drafts. Both are negotiable instruments subject to the general principles of Article 3, which you have studied in earlier chapters. Their separate treatment here is justified on several grounds: first, the promissory note normally serves a credit function, while the check and the draft are primarily means of bringing about payment. Second, the note is a *promise* to pay, and is sometimes referred to as "two party" paper—the two parties being the maker and payee. Checks and drafts embody *orders* to pay and are referred to as "three party" paper—the three parties being the drawer, the drawee (in the case of a check, drawer's bank), and the payee. Most notes, although negotiable in form, are held by the initial payee, or are perhaps discounted or transferred once. In contrast, checks and drafts customarily pass through a number of hands in the course of collection and presentment. This creates yet a third reason for separate treatment: these instruments, unlike notes, cannot be understood in any realistic sense apart from the bank collection system. Nor can the rights and liabilities of parties to them be determined without a grasp of both the mechanical and legal aspects of bank collection. A thorough analysis of the present collection system, and the complex legal regime under which it operates, is presented in Chapter 16. Finally, perhaps the best reason for separating checks and drafts from notes is so that they can be treated at the same time, and contrasted with, competing media such as credit cards and electronic fund transfer systems (EFTS).

Chapter 17 examines recurrent problems such as NSF checks, stop orders, and forgery.

In the last chapter the student's exposure to commercial law is rounded out through consideration of documentary transactions and letters of credit. We believe these materials provide a fascinating insight into the present economy and a worthy capstone to the study of commercial law.

CHAPTER 15

Drafts and Checks as Payment Media

A. THE COMMERCIAL CONTEXT OF CHECKS AND DRAFTS

In Chapter 1 the student was introduced to the promissory note as one subspecies of negotiable instrument. In this chapter we introduce the check and the draft. The note functions in the modern economy principally as a credit medium; in contrast the check and draft act primarily as current payment media. All, however, are negotiable instruments within the scope of Article 3.

The note, check, and draft, therefore, share a basic conceptual unity. Checks and drafts must meet the same "formal requisites" as notes in order to be negotiable within Article 3, and the same principles of transfer and negotiation apply. Like notes, checks and drafts may be issued in either bearer (as in "pay to the order of cash") or order form (as in "pay to the order of Safeway"). The same rules as to the form of special and blank indorsements apply. The concepts of holder, holder in due course, and real and personal defenses are shared by all three instruments. So too are the basic principles of contractual liability on the instrument, warranty liability incident to transfer and presentment, and tort liability for conversion.

Checks and drafts are today distinguished from notes by three basic characteristics. Two have already been mentioned: they serve a payment function, making it useful to treat them together with alternative payment media such as credit cards; they also require an understanding of the bank collection system. The third distinction is the different scope of the contractual liability assumed by the *drawer* of a check or draft as opposed to the *maker* of a note.

A drawer's contract, as set forth in UCC 3-413(2), is a contract of *secondary* liability, and the drawer is a *secondary party* (UCC 3-102(1)(d)). This may be easily seen in the context in which a check is usually used: Student, returning home, stops at Convenience Store. Having made a number of purchases, Student writes a check for $20.47. See Form 15-1.

FORM 15-1
Check

Compare the face of this instrument with that of the short-form promissory note at p. 13 supra. The above instrument is a demand instrument. UCC 3-108. Suppose Student stops by the same store the next evening, and Manager demands payment in cash of $20.47. Student asks whether his bank has refused to honor the check and is told that the check has not been presented— the Manager just wants cash. This request is not simply beyond the scope of Student's expectation, it is beyond the scope of Student's contractual liability on the instrument. UCC 3-413(2). Stripped of technical niceties the section says, "I'll pay you, if you let me know that my bank won't." As a matter of both law and commercial expectation, the payee or other holder of a check or draft must look first to the *drawee* of the instrument (in the above example, Seattle-First National Bank) for payment of the instrument. Only upon dishonor and any necessary notice of dishonor will the holder be able to enforce the instrument against its drawer.

Every student is familiar with the check. Drafts, however, are rarely used in consumer transactions. The contract of the drawer of a draft is exactly the same as that of the drawer of a check. In fact a check is technically merely a specialized form of draft: one that is drawn on a bank and is payable on demand. UCC 3-104(2)(b). What distinguishes *all* drafts from notes is that they represent *orders* to someone else (the drawee) to pay, rather than a primary promise to pay. Nonetheless, the drawer does make a contractual promise on the instrument by signing as drawer. That promise is conditional, however, on dishonor of the drawer's order: thus the liability is said to be *secondary*.

Drafts other than checks need not be drawn on banks, and they may be either demand instruments (sight drafts) or time drafts. The use of drafts in a commercial setting may be illustrated as follows:

Seller in City *A* sells goods to Buyer in City *B*. In most cases today, Seller would simply ship these goods to *B* and expect Buyer to pay by sending back a check in the amount of the purchase price. However, as an alternative, Seller may draw a draft in the form shown in Form 15-2.

This draft would then be forwarded, usually through the banking system, to Buyer. When Buyer honors this draft by payment, the proceeds are remitted back through the banking system to the account of Seller at Seller's bank.

Students are confused by the fact that it is the Seller, who is *owed* money, who draws the draft. In the case of a check it is invariably the Buyer, who *owes* money, who draws the check. What explains the difference? The answer is, in part, that if the instrument is honored (as in the great majority of cases), there is a difference in mechanism but not in result. The two situations are diagrammed in Figures 15-1 and 15-2.

Although the movement of the paper instrument is different, the flow of funds is the same: from Buyer, to Buyer's Bank, to Seller's Bank, to Seller. Moreover, in both cases the underlying payment obligation arising from the sale will be discharged only when the instrument is paid. In the event of dishonor, however, substantial differences in the obligations of Seller and Buyer exist. The use of drafts is most frequently encountered in the case of documentary sales transactions, which are discussed in Chapter 18.

$4,000.00   *Boston* Sept. 12   19 81

_____ At sight _____   *Pay to the*

Order of _____ Seller, Inc. _____

Four thousand and no/oo ————————— *Dollars*

Value Received and charge same to account of

                                                  Seller, Inc.

To   Buyer & Co. _____

Address   7 Flat Street, Belfast, Maine _____

                                        Andrew Seller
                                        Andrew Seller, Pres.

FORM 15-2
Sight Draft

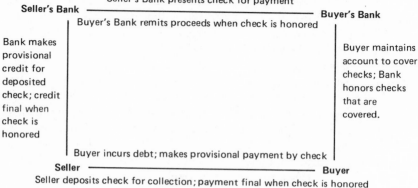

FIGURE 15-1
Payment by Check

As noted, drafts may be either demand drafts or time drafts. An example of a time draft appears in Form 15-3.

This draft will be forwarded in the same manner as the sight draft, but Buyer's Bank will in this instance make presentment of the instrument for acceptance. Buyer indicates acceptance by signing the instrument across its face. Form 15-3 shows a time draft that has already been accepted in this manner. The draft will then be presented at maturity for payment. Failure to accept the draft upon initial presentment, as well as failure to pay the draft when presented at maturity, constitutes dishonor. The use of the time draft as a financing device is also discussed in Chapter 18.

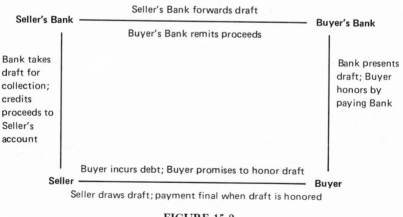

FIGURE 15-2
Payment by Draft

$4,000.00   *Boston* Sept. 12   *19* 81

_____ Ninety (90) Days after sight _____   *Pay to the*

Order of _____ Seller, Inc. _____

Four thousand and no/oo ——————————— *Dollars*

Value Received and charge same to account of

                                                        Seller, Inc.

            Buyer & Co. _____

Address   7 Flat Street, Belfast, Maine _____   *Andrew Seller*
                                                        Andrew Seller, Pres.

FORM 15-3
Time Draft

B.   DRAWEE'S LIABILITY

SABIN MEYER REGIONAL SALES CORP. v. CITIZENS BANK
502 F. Supp. 557, 30 UCC Rep. 595 (N.D. Ga. 1980)

Robert H. HALL, District Judge. Plaintiff brought this case against defendant Citizens Bank and defendant Hollis Q. Lathem, under the court's diversity jurisdiction. 42 U.S.C. §1332. In June, 1977, plaintiff received five checks, each in the amount of $20,000.00 drawn on the account of Tress Enterprises, Inc., with defendant Citizens. As a result, plaintiff released sea food it had been holding for Tress. Prior to that release, plaintiff's president, Sabin Meyer, spoke to defendant Lathem, the executive vice president of defendant Citizens, and was allegedly assured that the Tress account contained and would contain sufficient funds to cover the five post-dated checks when presented. When the checks were presented, they were returned because insufficient funds existed in the Tress account with defendant Citizens. A similar series of conversations took place between defendant Lathem and Robert Meyering, the assistant treasurer of Chase Manhattan Bank, concerning whether or not sufficient funds would exist in the Tress account to cover the checks when presented. A second attempt was made to present the checks to defendant Citizens, but the checks were again rejected since the Tress account contained insufficient funds to pay them.

The sequence of events and transactions involved in this litigation is actually very complex, but the facts material to resolving defendants' pending motion for summary judgment are quite simple. Checks numbered 178, 179, 180, 181, and 182 were drawn by Tress on Tress's account with defendant bank. The checks were for $20,000.00 each, a total of $100,000.00. No written guaranty for payment of the checks was ever made by defendants.

The theories advanced by plaintiff in this case are somewhat confused. The court is nevertheless able to dispose of the pending motion by addressing each of plaintiff's theories, as interpreted by both parties. First, the court will address whether defendants are liable on the checks themselves. The court will then address plaintiff's theory of a breach of an oral guaranty, breach of a contract of assignment, fraud, conversion, estoppel, and negligence. UCC 3-409.

Whether or not defendants are liable on the checks themselves is governed by UCC 3-409(1), which states:

> A check or other draft does not of itself operate as an assignment of any funds in the hands of the drawee available for its payment, and the drawee is not liable on the instrument until he accepts it.

If defendant bank has not, as a matter of law, accepted the checks in question, it cannot be liable on the checks themselves. What constitutes acceptance is governed by statute. "Acceptance is the drawee's signed engagement to honor the draft as presented. It must be written on the draft, and may consist of his signature alone. It becomes operative when completed by delivery or notification." UCC 3-410(1). The facts of this case reveal that there has been no written acceptance. Indeed, the checks at issue were dishonored within the meaning of UCC 3-507(1)(a) since they were returned prior to the bank's deadline of midnight of the next banking day following the banking day on which the checks were received. UCC 4-104(1)(h). See also UCC 3-102(3) and UCC 4-301(4).

Therefore, since the checks were not accepted within the meaning of the Georgia Code by defendant Citizens, defendant Citizens cannot be liable on them. Of course, the same reasoning applies to defendant Lathem, and he is also not liable on the checks themselves.

Furthermore, under any construction of the oral conversations various agents of plaintiff had with defendant Lathem as a contract between plaintiff and either or both defendants, the court cannot enforce the contract that may have resulted. If the conversations are to be construed as an oral acceptance of the drafts, the court cannot enforce the acceptance since acceptance must be in writing. UCC 3-410(1) and Ga. Code Ann. §20-401(8). If the conversations are construed as a guaranty, they are also unenforceable. Ga. Code Ann. §20-401(2). The same reasoning requires the court to find that, construed as a contract of suretyship, the conversations cannot be enforced. . . . As an oral certification of the five checks, the conversations still fail to yield an obligation binding on defendants. Since certification of payment is the same as acceptance, it is not binding unless in a writing signed by the acceptor or certifying party. UCC 3-410(1) and 3-411(1).

In the alternative the court finds that a contract of guaranty arising from the conversations is illegal and unenforceable. Regulations of the Federal Deposit Insurance Corporation found at 12 C.F.R. §332.1 forbid member banks to execute contracts of guaranty or surety. Section 20-501 of the Georgia Code provides that a "contract to do an . . . illegal thing is void." The statute does not make an illegal contract voidable at the option of the party seeking to enforce the contract. Rather, an illegal contract is utterly void. Since the pertinent legal authority is equally available to both parties to the contract, such a result is not unjust in this case. To enforce the purported oral guaranty contract would be a violation of public policy that this court will not countenance.

Another contractual theory arises under plaintiff's characterization of the subject checks as an assignment. Georgia law recognizes implicitly that a check may, in certain special circumstances, constitute an assignment of funds. UCC 3-409(1) and 3-409, comment 1. The sufficiency of given facts to establish that a check should operate as an assignment is governed by Georgia case law, and sufficient facts are hard to attain. The court finds that the facts in this case, accepting the contentions of the party opposing summary judgment as true, are insufficient to establish an assignment. "It is well settled in this State . . . that an unaccepted check drawn in the usual form, not upon any particular fund, or not using words indicating a transfer of the whole or any part of the amount standing to the credit of the drawer, does not of itself amount to an assignment of the money to the credit of the drawer." McIntire v. Rasking, 173 Ga. 746, 748, 161 S.E. 363, 364 (1931). The checks in the present case fall within the exclusion of *McIntire.* The checks in this case were in the usual form, were not accepted by the drawee, and had no words to indicate an assignment. Furthermore, and most important to the resolution of this issue, they were not drawn upon any particular or special fund within the meaning of cases such as Mid-Continent Casualty Co. v. Jenkins, 431 P.2d 349 (Okla. 1967), the case cited by plaintiff in support of its assignment theory.

By enacting the Uniform Commercial Code, the official text of which only impliedly allows raising a check to the status of an assignment, the Georgia General Assembly did not intend to displace existing state law on what facts were sufficient in order to interpret a check as an assignment. Since certification provides an easy and clear procedure under the Uniform Commercial Code to assure payment of a check, the court does not believe that raising a check to the status of an assignment should be easier under the present law than it was under the law prior to Georgia's enactment of that Code. Therefore, the difficult standard of *McIntire* applies. UCC 1-103.

Plaintiff also advances a theory of common law fraud. . . .

All representations made to which the court's attention has been called, then, were as to future events, and even if false, are not actionable under Georgia law as fraud. . . . The facts in the present cases amount to nothing more than a prediction. Given that plaintiff could have easily assured that the checks would be paid by insisting on certification, the court finds that prediction is too ephemeral a basis on which to recover on a theory of fraud.

Plaintiff also asserts a theory of estoppel as a cause of action. Estoppel, however, is not a cause of action under Georgia law. . . . Plaintiff apparently misunderstands the nature of the equitable doctrine of estoppel. Estoppel may be used to prevent a party from denying at the time of litigation a representation that was made by that party and accepted and reasonably acted upon by another party with detrimental results to the party that acted thereon. The doctrines of estoppel "are primarily negative in their operation against the party making the statement or admission, rather than creative of any new rights in the opposite party." . . . Without some proper legal cause of action, establishing all the elements of equitable estoppel will not entitle plaintiff to relief.

Finally, the court turns its attention to plaintiff's theory of negligence. Since defendant Citizens, as drawee of a check, owes no duty to plaintiff, as presenter of a check, in the absence of acceptance or certification . . . the court finds that defendant Citizens has not negligently treated the check itself. Nor was defendant Citizens negligent in failing to issue a federal operating circular as plaintiff argues. Since Citizens is not a Federal Reserve Bank, it is not required as a matter of law to issue such a circular. 12 C.F.R. §210.65. Since the check was stamped as having been refused acceptance and was returned to the Federal Reserve prior to defendant Citizens' midnight deadline, a timely notice of dishonor was given in accordance with UCC 3-508. Therefore, defendants were not liable for failing to do so.

Since under Georgia law plaintiff cannot prevail on any of the theories discussed above, the court grants defendants' motion for summary judgment as to those theories. The theory that defendants were negligent in reporting the status of the Tress checking account with defendant Citizens, however, remains. Though defendant Citizens has no duty to set aside funds to cover the checks once a representation has been made . . . the bank and its agents must exercise due care in reporting on a customer's account if they choose to so report. A factual issue remains as to whether defendant Citizens or defendant Lathem told plaintiff that there would be funds in the Tress checking account by the time the five checks were presented for payment, and whether, if so, they failed "to conform to the legal standard of reasonable conduct in the light of the apparent risk." W. Prosser, Handbook of the Law of Torts §53 (4th ed. 1971). The fact that defendant Citizens was in the process of reviewing a loan application, which if approved would have covered the checks, lends credence to this theory. There nevertheless remain grave problems with establishing the theory, and it may be necessary to prevent the issue from ultimately going to a jury or even to trial. The court is reluctant, however, to remove the issue from a jury's consideration at this time, since there is some possibility that plaintiff may be able to establish the elements of negligence and recover on that cause of action. The issue, then, of whether or not defendants were negligent in reporting the status of the Tress account is the sole remaining issue in this case.

Therefore, defendants' motion for summary judgment is granted in part and denied in part.

NOTES & QUESTIONS

1. *Certification.* What would the effect have been if Sabin Meyer had obtained certification? See UCC 3-411, 3-410, 3-413.

2. *Drawer-drawee relation.* Does *Sabin Meyer* mean that the drawee has no obligation to honor the instrument? A drawee bank's liability to the drawer when it fails to honor an instrument is treated in Section D infra. When a seller draws a sight draft upon the buyer for the purchase price of goods sold, does the holder of the draft have an action against the buyer if the draft is dishonored? Against the seller? See UCC 3-401. Does the seller have an action against the buyer?

3. *Alternatives to certification.* A bank ordinarily has no duty to certify a check for either the holder of the instrument or for the bank's own customer. Banks often resist certification: the reasons have to do with certain operational difficulties in the automated handling of such checks, which cause increased costs for the bank. These difficulties will be more fully appreciated after the student has studied the bank collection system, discussed in the next chapter. The advantage of a certified check is of course that it places the bank's liability on the check in addition to, or in the place of, the drawer's liability. An alternative is for the customer to purchase either a check that the customer's bank draws on itself (*cashier's check*) or a draft drawn by a bank on another drawee (*bank draft*). Both engage the liability of the customer's bank, although in different capacities. These instruments are discussed further in Chapter 17 in connection with stop-payment orders.

4. *Postdated checks.* The checks in *Sabin Meyer* were all postdated. Such checks are often considered suspect, but as a general rule there is nothing illegal about them. Indeed, the Code specifically recognizes their negotiability. UCC 3-114. Postdated checks may violate bad-check criminal statutes when the check writer has no intention of covering them, but this is equally true of current-dated checks. If the holder puts the check into the check collection process early a variety of potential problems are created. In Allied Color Corp. v. Manufacturers Hanover Trust Co., 484 F. Supp. 881, 28 UCC Rep. 456 (S.D.N.Y. 1980) a check postdated to December 31 was received December 14 and presented to payor bank December 18. Payor bank stamped item "paid" but held it until December 28, when it cancelled its "paid" stamp and returned the check unpaid. *Held,* complaint by payee of check stated cause of

action against payor bank for liability for failure to take timely action (pay or return) under UCC 4-302. Compare this case to Siegel v. New England Merchants National Bank, 386 Mass. 672, 437 N.E.2d 218, 33 UCC Rep. 1601 (1982), p. 834 infra. *Held,* postdated item not "properly payable" until date arrives, and customer may seek recredit to its account; however, bank may defend by setting off rights of prior holders on the check and on the transaction from which it arose, and burden is then on customer to show it has a defense good against such persons, and therefore has suffered true loss.

5. *Acceptance of drafts.* Sight drafts, like checks, are demand instruments. Although a sight draft may be presented for acceptance, the drawee has no liability on the instrument if he fails to accept, and usually would have no liability on the underlying contract. Why? Time drafts are quite different: a time draft may be drawn in the form "30 days after sight pay to the order of Jones." Presentment for acceptance is then necessary. Or it may be drawn in the form "On December 31, 1986, pay to the order of Jones," in which case presentment for acceptance is optional. The Code's rules as to necessary and optional presentment are discussed further in Section C infra. In any event, a drawee who accepts an instrument thereby makes an acceptor's contract. UCC 3-410. An acceptor's liability is primary in nature; in fact, it is the same as the liability of the maker of a note. UCC 3-413(1). We have already examined the maker's contract in Chapter 1.

C.   DRAWER'S AND INDORSER'S SECONDARY LIABILITY ON THE INSTRUMENT

The principal contract that appears on either a check or a draft is that of the *drawer* of the instrument. Its content is defined in UCC 3-413(2):

> The drawer engages that upon dishonor of the draft and any necessary notice of dishonor or protest he will pay the amount of the draft to the holder or to any indorser who takes it up. The drawer may disclaim this liability by drawing without recourse.

Many checks and most drafts will carry one or more indorsements upon them. We have briefly examined indorser's liability in Chapter 1. The Code's statutory formulation of an indorser's contract appears in UCC §3-414(1):

> Unless the indorsement otherwise specifies (as by such words as "without recourse") every indorser engages that upon dishonor and any necessary notice of dishonor and protest he will pay the instrument according to its tenor at the time of his indorsement to the holder or to any subsequent indorser who takes it up, even though the indorser who takes it up was not obligated to do so.

As noted earlier, both of these are contracts of secondary liability: each is conditioned on dishonor, any necessary notice of dishonor, and any necessary protest.[1] We shall examine the respective liabilities of drawers and indorsers of checks and drafts through a series of problems that illustrate the operation of these conditions.

1. Dishonor

Read UCC 3-507, 3-501, and 3-502, and consider the following problems:

Problem 15-1. Drawer draws a check to order of Payee, who indorses to Holder. Holder takes the check to Drawee Bank and requests certification. Drawee Bank refuses. Has the instrument been dishonored?

Problem 15-2. On the same facts Holder requests payment. Drawee Bank refuses. Has the instrument been dishonored? Suppose that Drawee Bank demands that Holder identify himself and sign a receipt for payment on the instrument. Holder refuses, and then Drawee Bank refuses payment. Is this dishonor? See UCC 3-505.

Problem 15-3. On the same facts, suppose the bank teller notices that Payee has failed to indorse the check and therefore refuses to pay it. Is this dishonor? How long, if at all, may the bank retain the check in order to verify indorsements or otherwise make inquiries as to the check? See UCC 3-505, 3-506, and 3-507.

Problem 15-4. Seller draws a sight draft on Buyer, payable to the order of Seller's bank. Seller's bank indorses without recourse and sends the draft to the Buyer's bank for presentment to Buyer. Buyer's bank telephones Buyer and asks that Buyer come to the bank and pay the draft. Is presentment necessary in this case? If Buyer fails to pay the draft that day, has it been dishonored? See UCC 3-504 and 4-210.

Problem 15-5. Seller draws a draft on Buyer payable on sight. May this draft be presented for acceptance prior to presentment for payment? Suppose the draft is payable 90 days after sight. What presentments of this instrument are necessary presentments? Suppose the draft is payable July 1, 1987. What

---

1. This is a paraphrase that clarifies the provisions' meaning. A close reading indicates that 3-413(2) speaks of notice of dishonor *or* protest, while 3-414(1) speaks of notice of dishonor *and* protest. Neither section makes clear whether "necessary" modifies only "notice of dishonor" or also "protest." This is but one of several instances of an annoying lack of parallelism between the two sections. No substantive differences are to be inferred. This is not to say that a drawer and an indorser have exactly the same scope of obligation: they do not, as we shall presently see. The differences, however, are tucked away in UCC 3-501 through 3-511, which detail the conditions of secondary liability.

presentments are necessary? What presentments are optional? For instance, must the latter draft be presented for acceptance within a reasonable time after issuance? If it is presented for acceptance and acceptance is refused, must it be presented for payment?

The foregoing problems have introduced the student to the role of presentment in the use of checks and drafts, and the relationship between due presentment and dishonor. Dishonor is the first of the conditions of a secondary party's liability. When dishonor occurs, that condition to charging either a drawer or indorser has been satisfied. However, if a necessary presentment is not duly made, the effect may not be limited to nonsatisfaction of a condition precedent in order to impose liability. Rather, the secondary party may be wholly discharged from liability, present or future. The rules with respect to discharge vary depending on whether the secondary party is a drawer or indorser. The following problems develop this issue.

Problem 15-6. Professor leaves for summer vacation on May 28. Sometime in mid-June she remembers that she has neglected to make any arrangements for the deposit of her payroll checks and calls and asks her secretary to deposit the checks to her account. Secretary is just departing for vacation. When he returns on July 5, he puts Professor's June 30 and May 31 payroll checks in the mail to Bank. Bank posts the June 30 check to Professor's account, but returns the May 31 check with the stamped notation "Returned unpaid: [✓] Stale." Has the check been dishonored? Is the university (drawer of the check) discharged? See UCC 3-501, 3-503, 3-511, 3-601, and 3-502. See also 3-802.

Problem 15-7. Spouse mails a support check to X, antedating the check 15 days to June 1. X receives the check on June 22 and on the 25th indorses it to Landlord for past due rent. Landlord puts the check in her desk drawer and deposits it to her account on July 5. On July 10 Landlord receives a notice that the item has been returned marked "account closed." Spouse replies that he closed the account on June 30 when he moved to a new job. Is Spouse discharged on the instrument? Is X? Is either or both discharged on the underlying obligation? See UCC 3-501, 3-511, 3-503, 3-601, 3-502, and 3-802.

2.   Notice of Dishonor

A further condition of secondary liability is that any necessary notice of dishonor must be given. The purpose of this is to allow a secondary party who must pay to initiate steps to protect himself and in turn recover from parties who may be liable to him.

Consider a situation where Drawer has drawn a check to the order of *H1* and the check has then been indorsed in turn to *H2, H3,* and *H4. H4* deposits the check in his bank account, which in turn forwards it for presentment to Drawer's bank. Drawer's bank stamps the check "Insufficient Funds" and returns it to *H4*'s bank. *H4*'s bank in turn notifies *H4* that the item has been returned, and provisional credit that has been given will be charged back against *H4*'s account. The manner in which all this transpires within the bank collection system and the special duties and time limits applicable to banks will be considered in the next chapter. In this chapter our focus is primarily on the actions of parties outside the banking system.

Reread the drawer's and indorser's contracts that appear in UCC 3-413(2) and 3-414. These sections indicate the correctness of our common understanding of rights on a dishonored check: any indorser who makes good the check (takes it up) may sue the drawer or any prior indorser. Thus *H4* has a cause of action against the drawer, *H1, H2,* and *H3.* On the other hand, *H1* has an action only against the drawer, and the drawer has no action against subsequent indorsers.

This sequence of liability must be understood and kept in mind in order to apply correctly the Code's rules concerned with notice of dishonor. In addressing the problems that follow, consider UCC 3-413(2), 3-414, 3-501, 3-502, 3-508, 3-511, and 3-601.

Problem 15-8. On the above facts, assume that *H4*'s bank has both received timely notice and given timely notice to *H4.* Is any further action required before *H4* can charge *H3*? Suppose *H4* calls *H3* the same day but *H4* makes no effort to contact *H2, H1,* or Drawer—all of whom are strangers to *H4,* who has dealt only with *H3. H3* turns out to be insolvent. May *H4* now sue the other parties on the instrument? Suppose *H4* has made a reasonable effort to locate these parties, but to no avail—may he sue them if he later finds them?

Problem 15-9. It is common in the above situation for Drawer's bank to give notice to Drawer that the bank has returned a check drawn on his account. If the bank has done so in the above situation, how will that alter your answer to Problem 15-8?

Problem 15-10. Suppose that Drawer knowingly drew the check against insufficient funds, or had entered a stop order against the check. Is it still necessary to give notice of dishonor to Drawer? To the indorsers?

Problem 15-11. *H3,* who has received no notice of dishonor, takes up the check from *H4.* He sues *H2, H1* (neither of whom received timely notice of dishonor), and Drawer, who drew the check against a closed account, received notice from his previous bank, and is now insolvent. Are *H2* and *H1* liable?

3. Protest

Protest is a means of certifying dishonor and, if so specified in the protest, also giving notice of dishonor. See UCC 3-509. Protest is necessary to charge a drawer and indorsers only when a draft (which includes a check, see UCC 3-104(2)) is on its face drawn or payable outside the United States. UCC 3-501(3). Protest is sometimes used when instruments for large amounts are dishonored, as a matter of conservative practice and to simplify proof. Because the Code provides sufficiently similar status to pertinent bank or trade notations or records, the practice is rarely encountered. See UCC 3-510.

A final topic that requires comment is the so-called qualified indorsement, when an indorser signs "without recourse." A typical situation arises when a person holds order paper. To negotiate the paper, the holder must indorse it. However, it does not follow that the person indorsing wishes to add his credit to that of the drawer or prior indorsers. Negotiating the instrument, without assuming contractual liability, may be accomplished by adding the words "without recourse."

The Code also recognizes the practice of *drawing* without recourse. UCC 3-413(2). As we saw in part B, the drawee of an instrument has no liability until it is accepted. If the drawer draws without recourse, the payee therefore holds an instrument upon which *no one* is liable. What is the utility of such an instrument?

Problem 15-12. Consider the following business contexts:

a. Claims Agent for Insurance Company settles claims by the company's policyholders. Agent does so by drawing without recourse a draft upon Insurance Company, in the amount of the agreed settlement, "payable through" Bank in the city where Insurance Company's home office is located. See UCC 3-120.

b. Petroleum "Landman" is in the business of leasing mineral interests for a major oil company. When a surface owner signs a lease Landman pays by drawing a draft in the same manner as Agent in a., with the oil company as drawee.

Problem 15-13. What is the result in Problem 15-12 if Landman signs the draft "Major Oil Company, Harvey Landman"? See UCC 3-403. Is this result satisfactory? May the problem be avoided by greater clarity? Suppose Claims Agent signs preprinted drafts that state

> Insurance Company, Drawer
>
> By _____
>
> Authorized Claims Agent

See UCC 3-403, 3-118.

D. BANK-CUSTOMER RELATIONSHIP

We have seen in the preceding materials that a drawer only engages to pay the draft if it is dishonored by the drawee. The drawee has no liability on the instrument, but in all but exceptional cases the drawee *will* honor the instrument. A simple reason for this is the fact that dishonor of a draft may well subject the drawee to liability to the drawer. To repeat, this is not liability on the instrument; it is a consequence of a contractual relationship between the drawer and drawee.

In the case of a merchant's draft on Buyer, Buyer generally has promised to honor drafts in a certain form or amount. This promise is a term of the sales contract. If Buyer dishonors a properly drawn draft (that is, one drawn in compliance with the terms of the contract), he will thereby breach the sales contract. Although neither the drawer nor any holder may sue the drawee on the instrument, Seller will have an action on the contract. If Seller has discounted the draft in the meantime, Seller may have to pay a holder of the draft to fulfill his drawer's contract.

Although you probably do not give much thought to the nature of your relationship with the bank where you maintain a checking account, the same principles apply. In essence, your checking account represents an agreement by which you lend money to the bank. In exchange for the use of your funds, the bank agrees not only to repay the money to you on demand, but also to allow you to draw orders on the bank directing payment to someone else. To facilitate the process, the bank provides you with a standard form of order, your checkbook. By using the bank's standard form you enable machine-processing of the checks you draw. The intricacies of the high-speed techniques employed by modern banks, and the problems they create, are the subject matter of the next chapter.

The discussion above describes the basic aspects of a checking account relationship. Other features may be added by agreement of the parties, such as the bank's offer of interest-bearing accounts. It may also agree to pay orders drawn even though they exceed the amount you have lent (read, in common parlance, "deposited with") the bank or, coversely, may have you agree to pay interest on such overdrafts. It may impose a charge for each check you draw and a substantial charge for any check that creates an unauthorized overdraft. The bank usually will impose a fee for any check that it returns upaid, or for what banks often regard as the "privilege" of stopping payment on a check.

Given that the bank-customer relationship is contractual in nature, where are the terms of this contract to be found? In part, they are set forth in the Code, particularly in Article 4, Part 4, Relationship Between Payor Bank and Its Customer. Like the rest of Article 4, these provisions may be varied by agreement. UCC 4-103. The most common instance of "variation by agreement" is found in the fine print covering the front and back of the signature card one signs when an account is opened.

FIRST NATIONAL BANK v. LA SARA GRAIN CO.
646 S.W.2d. 246, 34 UCC Rep. 1277 (Tex. App. 1982)

GONZALEZ, Justice. This case primarily involves the question of a Bank's liability, when it pays checks and allows withdrawals on less than the required number of signatures. In April, 1975, Plaintiff-appellee, La Sara Grain Company, opened a checking account at the First National Bank of Mercedes, Texas, Defendant-appellant. La Sara gave the Bank a corporate resolution requiring the signatures of two persons to sign all its checks. Over a three and a half year period, the Bank honored La Sara's checks with only one signature. La Sara brought suit against the Bank alleging negligence, breach of warranty, breach of contract, fraud and under the Deceptive Trade Practices Act. . . .

The relevant facts are as follows: La Sara is a Texas Corporation engaged in the business of buying and selling grain. Upon the death of La Sara's General Manager in 1974, La Sara discovered that the General Manager had utilized corporate funds for his personal use. Harold Jones was hired [as] General Manager and in April of 1975, La Sara opened a checking account with the Bank. It provided the Bank with a corporate resolution that specified that any two of four individuals listed in the resolution were authorized to sign checks. Jones was one of the four. (A copy of this resolution is attached to this opinion as an appendix "A".) The Bank was also provided with a signature card. Sometime during the circulation of the signature card between the four individuals, the card was altered or changed to strike out the requirement of two signatures and to require only one signature. (A copy of this card is also attached to this opinion as appendix "B"). The record is not clear whether the corporate resolution or the signature card was furnished to the Bank first or if they were furnished at the same time. The record does show, however, that La Sara's bookkeeper was the last one to sign the signature card and he testified that when the card was presented to him, it provided for only one signature.

During the next three and a half years, (from April 9, 1975 to the Fall of 1978), in contravention of the corporate resolution but in keeping with the signature card, several hundred checks were drawn and paid by the Bank on La Sara's account with only Jones' signature. Also during this time, several checks marked "for deposit only" with La Sara listed as the payee were deposited into Jones' personal account. In some instances the deposits were split with a portion going into La Sara's account and a portion going into Jones' personal account. Without a corporate resolution, Jones also borrowed money from the Bank in the name of La Sara with some of these proceeds also being split between the two accounts. Each month the Bank sent the customary bank statements to La Sara.

In the Fall of 1978, Jones was fired by La Sara because of suspected dishonesty. After an audit it was determined that La Sara had lost approximately Three Hundred Forty-Two Thousand Seven Hundred Ninety Dollars and 69/100 ($342,790.69). In June, 1979, La Sara sued the Bank, Fidelity and

Deposit Company of Maryland, and others. . . . The president of the Bank testified that the Bank filed the corporate resolution in the bookkeeping department and filed the signature card in the check file where it was kept for comparison of signatures on the checks. From the beginning, the Bank acted as if only one signature was required on all transactions. It allowed Jones to split deposits, make withdrawals and make loans at the Bank in La Sara's name solely on his signature. Jones was not the only La Sara employee to have access to the monthly statements from the Bank. Other employees reconciled these monthly statements and during the time in question, accountants prepared financial statements and federal income tax returns.

"The relationship between a bank and its depositor is that of debtor and creditor with title to the deposited funds passing to the bank. . . . The bank is under the duty of disbursing the funds on deposit in accordance with the directions of the depositor. . . . In suits against a bank to recover deposits, the burden of proving payment under authority from the depositor is on the bank." Mesquite State Bank v. Professional Invest. Corp., 488 S.W.2d 73, 75 (Tex. 1977). Also, 9 Tex. Jur. 3d Banks §149, at 122 (1980) states: "The relationship between banker and depositor is a voluntary one of contractual nature. . . ." Therefore, there can be no question but that the corporate resolution established the terms of this contractual relationship.

Generally, the signature card is merely a vehicle or a tool utilized by a Bank to ensure that the signatures on the checks correspond to those of the signature card. If a corporate resolution and a signature card on the same account are in variance with one another regarding the requisite number of signatures, the resolution prevails. Therefore, at the time the Bank account was open, the Bank impliedly warranted and agreed with La Sara that all transactions between La Sara and the Bank would require at least two of the four authorized signatures.

Generally, whenever the Bank pays checks on less than the required number of signatures, the Bank is liable on the theory of negligence, breach of contract, or under the Uniform Commercial Code. However, the Bank can escape liability in some situations under the theory of lack of consideration, the depositor's failure to examine statements and notify the Bank under common law, or under the U.C.C. provisions, where there is no loss or damage to the depositor, or under the defense of acquiescence in or notification of payment, estoppel or waiver of the signature requirement. 7 A.L.R. 4th 655 (Annot.). . . .

BANK'S LIABILITY UNDER UCC 4-406

[The court quotes UCC 4-406(1)-(4) with emphasis on the following sections:

> (1) When a bank sends to its customer a statement of account . . . the customer must exercise reasonable care and promptness to examine the statement and items to discover his unauthorized signature or any alteration. . . .

(4) Without regard to care or lack of care of either the customer or the bank a customer who does not within one year from the time the statement and items are made available to the customer (subsection (1)) discover and report his unauthorized signature or any alteration on the face or back of the item . . . is precluded from asserting against the bank such unauthorized signature or indorsement or such alteration.]

UCC 1-201(43) defines an unauthorized signature as:

"Unauthorized" signature or indorsement means one made without actual, implied or apparent authority and includes a forgery.

Applying this section to UCC 4-406, it is obvious that Jones' signature on a check standing alone, would be made without actual, implied or apparent authority to sign La Sara's checks. The only authorized signatures on La Sara would be a signature containing the name of the corporation plus two signatures of the four persons named in the resolution. The trial court made findings of fact and conclusions of law to the contrary. We believe that since UCC 4-406(4) endeavors to provide finality that is important for the security of banking instructions, the better view is, and we hold as a matter of law, that when a bank honors a check or withdrawal on less than the required number of signatures, the signature is an unauthorized signature within the meaning of UCC 4-406(4). . . . Therefore, it was error for the trial court to hold to the contrary.

BANK'S LIABILITY UNDER BREACH OF CONTRACT

During the period in question, La Sara never complained to the Bank of any irregularities. They led the Bank to believe that everything regarding their account was in order. The record shows that persons other than the General Manager had access to and reconciled the bank monthly statements. Not only did other persons reconcile these monthly statements but accountants prepared financial statements and income tax returns for the period in question.

By its silence, did La Sara waive the two signature requirement? Did La Sara cloak the General Manager with apparent authority to transact business in its name with only his signature? Who should bear the loss: The Bank because of its failure to compare the signature card with the corporate resolution or La Sara because it hired the dishonest employee and allowed this conduct to continue for three and a half years? . . .

In Calvin Coal Co. v. First Nat. Bank of Bastrop [a pre-Code case—
EDS.], the coal company opened a bank account and advised the Bank that
two signatures were required on all checks. The Bank honored many checks
with only one signature. For five years the coal company made no objections
to the Bank. The coal company brought suit against the Bank for the amount
that had been wrongfully paid out. The Bank defended on the grounds that
twenty-seven statements have been sent to the bank along with the cancelled
checks and no objections to any of these items were made. For this reason, the
Bank argued the coal company could not recover on the doctrine of estoppel
and limitations.

The case was tried to a jury and the trial court directed a verdict in favor
of the Bank. The Appeals Court affirmed the judgment and said: "It is urged
by appellant that . . . the bank violated this contract (two signature requirement) and the coal company is entitled to recover regardless of whether it was
negligent in not examining the bank's statements and canceled checks and
vouchers. It is also urged that the delivery of the passbook, statements, and
canceled checks and vouchers to Jenkins did not constitute notice to the coal
company, because Jenkins was personally interested in concealing his improper withdrawals from the account. These contentions we do not think are
sound. . . . A most casual examination of the books of the bank would show
that the two-signature rule was not followed invariably, and a checking over of
any one of the 27 statements covering a period of over five years would have
brought forth the information that Jenkins was not following this practice. . . .
The course of business actually followed during practically the entire period,
being at variance with the original two-signature check instructions, clearly
constituted a waiver of that requirement. . . . [If] the other directors of the
corporation were kept in ignorance of the state of the account . . . it was due to
no fault of the bank, but to the lax business methods of the coal company. It
was clearly the duty of the coal company to have the bank account checked
within a reasonable time and to determine and report any irregularities . . . we
think a clear case of estoppel is presented." 286 S.W. at 903.

We believe that the rationale in *Calvin Coal* is consistent with the rule now
codified in UCC 4-406. It is apparent, then, that as in *Calvin Coal*, estoppel has
been clearly established. Therefore, La Sara is precluded from recovery under
any breach of contract theory.

BANK'S LIABILITY UNDER NEGLIGENCE THEORY

The trial court found that the Bank had actual knowledge of the unauthorized change or alteration of the signature card from a dual to a single
signature requirement. There is no evidence to support this finding. The trial
court also found constructive knowledge on the Bank's part. However, there is

no evidence of what a reasonably prudent bank would have done under similar circumstances. . . . Having failed to establish a primary element of its negligence cause of action, recovery cannot be had on this theory. . . .

The judgment of the trial court is reversed and rendered.[2]

APPENDIX A

THE FIRST NATIONAL BANK
OF MERCEDES, TEXAS

At a meeting of the Board of Directors of the _____ LA SARA GRAIN COMPANY _____

(Name of Corporation)

held at its office in the City of _____

on ____ April 9, 1975 ____, pursuant to due notice, at which a quorum of the Board was pres-
(Date)

ent, on motion, duly seconded, the following resolutions were unanimously adopted:

RESOLVED, That the following officer or officers of this Corporation,

Name	Signature	Title
O. S. Wyatt, Jr.		President
Harold Jones		Vice President
E. C. Thomas		Secretary/Treasurer
Salome Saenz		Bookkeeper

or ____ any two of them ____ be hereby authorized to sign the name of this Corporation, drawn on or in
(Any one, or any two of them as desired)

favor of the First National Bank of Mercedes, Texas, including checks payable to the order, for whatever purpose, of the officer or officers signing same.

RESOLVED, also that said Bank be furnished with a certified copy of these resolutions, and is hereby authorized to deal with the officers hereinabove named under said authority unless and until it be expressly notified to the contrary by this Corporation, and said Bank shall at all times be protected in recognizing as such officer or officers so named until notified in writing by registered mail of any change and Resolution of Board of Directors directing a change of officer or officers.

This is to certify that the above is true and correct extract from the minutes of the meeting of the Board of Directors of this Corporation, held ____ April 9, 1975 ____, at which said Resolution was
(Date)

adopted by the Board of Directors, and at a regular meeting of said Board of Directors.

Witness my hand and the seal of the Corporation.

O. S. WYATT, JR.   President.   E. C. THOMAS   Secretary.

(SEAL)

2. On appeal, the Texas Supreme Court reversed the court of appeals and affirmed the trial court's award of actual damages. The supreme court concluded that Jones' signature was an "unauthorized signature" within the meaning of UCC 4-406(4) but that the bank could not claim the protection of UCC 4-406 because it had not paid the checks in good faith as required by UCC 4-406(1) and 1-203. The bank lacked good faith because it knew from the signature card on file that one signature was insufficient. 27 Tex. Sup. Ct. J. 382 (1984).—EDS.

APPENDIX B

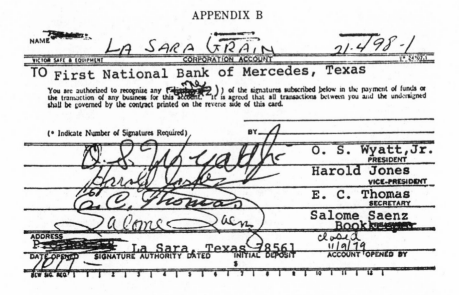

NAME ____ LA SARA GRAIN ____ 21.498-1

CORPORATION ACCOUNT

TO First National Bank of Mercedes, Texas

You are authorized to recognize any (   )) of the signatures subscribed below in the payment of funds or the transaction of any business for this account. It is agreed that all transactions between you and the undersigned shall be governed by the contract printed on the reverse side of this card.

(* Indicate Number of Signatures Required)   BY

O. S. Wyatt,Jr.
                                                     PRESIDENT
Harold Jones
                                                     VICE-PRESIDENT
E. C. Thomas
                                                     SECRETARY
Salome Saenz
                                                     Bookkeeper

ADDRESS   closed
            La Sara, Texas 78561   11/9/79
DATE OPENED SIGNATURE AUTHORITY DATED INITIAL DEPOSIT ACCOUNT OPENED BY

NOTES & QUESTIONS

1. *The* "properly payable" *item.* The key concept of the bank-customer relationship is the "properly payable" item. See UCC 4-401, 4-104(1)(i). The definition in UCC 4-104 mentions specifically only "availability of funds." What the definition does not mention are some matters of more fundamental importance: that the item is to be paid in accordance with the drawer's "true" order. Thus a check with a forged drawer's signature is not properly payable: it is not the *true* drawer's order at all. A check with a forged *necessary* indorsement is not a properly payable item because it has not been paid in accordance with the drawer's true order. An altered item is properly payable only according to its original tenor. With the exception of the last matter, which is indicated clearly by UCC 4-401(2)(a), the Code leaves the student to glean these fundamental propositions from the air. The consequence of the above items not being properly payable is that the bank has no authority to charge the drawer's account. If the bank pays, it pays with its own funds. The ability of the bank to shift this risk, and the ultimate placement of loss, are dealt with in Chapter 17.

2. *Overdrafts.* The one aspect of the properly-payable concept dealt with by UCC 4-104's definition is the availability of funds. However, UCC 4-401 makes clear that a bank may charge to its customer's account an item that is otherwise properly payable, even though it creates an overdraft (i.e., funds are *not* available). Payment of checks drawn against insufficient funds is therefore at the payor bank's option.

3. *Duty to examine bank statements.* In the principal case, the checks in question were not properly payable, but the drawer's behavior over the course of

several years precluded it from recovering from its bank the sums that had been improperly charged to its account. UCC 4-406 provides instances in which a customer may become liable for items that are not normally properly payable to its account. All of these instances involve situations such as in the *La Sara* case, where examination of its bank statements by the customer would have alerted the customer to a pattern of wrongdoing and enabled it in turn to alert its bank. This rule, and some related rules in Article 3 that reallocate risk, are treated in more detail in Chapter 17.

4. *Variation by agreement.* The Code's most general statement concerning variation by agreement is found in UCC 4-103(1):

> (1) The effect of the provisions of this Article may be varied by agreement except that no agreement can disclaim a bank's responsibility for its own lack of good faith or failure to exercise ordinary care or can limit the measure of damages for such lack or failure; but the parties may by agreement determine the standards by which such responsibility is to be measured if such standards are not manifestly unreasonable.

The difference between a provision that "sets a standard" and a provision that "disclaims . . . failure to exercise ordinary care" is not a bright-line distinction. Tension therefore exists as to the extent that banks' attempts to limit liability should be given effect.

5. *Contract defenses.* When banks vary the Code's rules, they usually purport to do so on the basis of their contract with their customer. Thus a signature card may state that the account is subject to the bank's rules and regulations. As a practical matter, banks vary considerably in the number of their rules and regulations, how often they change them, and whether they adhere to them. If the basis of the relationship is contract, are there not traditional bases for objecting to ad hoc attempts to vary or impose new terms? Consider possible objections to the signature card contract.

6. *Primacy of collection system rules.* Federal reserve regulations, clearing house rules, and other agreements integral to the check collection system may have a binding effect on parties who have neither assented to them nor have knowledge of them. This topic is considered in the immediately following chapter.

CHAPTER 16

The Bank Collection System

One important function of commercial banks is to facilitate the payment of current obligations. The following materials explore how the traditional paper-based collection system works and what law regulates the system. The final two sections of the chapter contrast this traditional system with the development of credit cards and electronic fund transfer systems.

A. THE COLLECTION PROCESS

Although the holder of a check may present it to the drawee bank for payment over the counter, far more often the check will be deposited in his bank, to be forwarded for payment through the bank collection system. The *depositary* bank will often send the check to an *intermediary* bank, which in turn may forward it to a *presenting* bank. (These three banks are also known as *collecting* banks.) The presenting bank will present the check to the *payor* bank (the drawee on the check) for payment. The payor bank frequently will settle provisionally for an item through book entries and eventually will pay the item—by not reversing these entries. The payor bank may pay, however, with a remittance instrument (for example, a check drawn on another bank) that it will send back through the collection system by way of *remitting* banks back to the depositary bank. In any one day, of course, a bank handles numerous items and plays all these different roles in the collection process.

Checks are not the only payment instruments collected through the bank collection system. Banks may, for example, collect payment of negotiable or nonnegotiable drafts drawn on nonbanks. The depositary bank forwards a draft, just as it does a check, through intermediary banks until it reaches the last bank in the collection chain, which will then present the draft to the drawee for payment or acceptance. If these drafts are accompanied by documents they are *documentary drafts,* and the presenting bank will surrender the documents to the drawee upon payment.

UCC Article 4 regulates the collection of *items,* a classification that in-

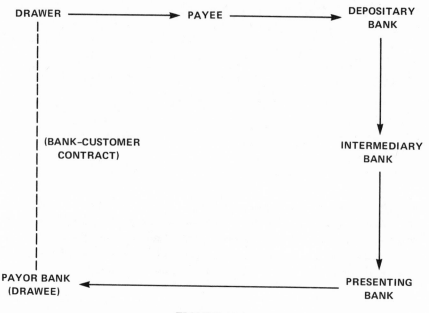

FIGURE 16-1

cludes "any instrument for the payment of money even though it is not negotiable" (UCC 4-104(1)(g)). Checks are *demand* items, also commonly known as
cash items. Banks handle these in volume, following routines with the assumption that most cash items will be paid in the ordinary course. Documentary
drafts, on the other hand, must be handled individually, and banks do not
assume they will be paid. Most of the Article 4 rules apply to the collection of
items generally, but they are most relevant to demand or cash items. Part 5 of
Article 4 sets out special rules for the collection of documentary drafts, which
we will examine in Chapter 18.

   The structure of the collection system is illustrated in Figure 16-1 and by
the following examples of various transactions.[1]

   Example 1. In payment for a book sold to him by a colleague, Peter
Winship draws a check on his account with Texas Commerce Bank payable to
the order of J. P. Riquelme for $9.75. Riquelme also has an account at Texas
Commerce Bank. He indorses the check "J. P. Riquelme, T.C.B. acct.
#4264010" and deposits it at the bank for credit to his account. At the end of
its banking day (3:00 P.M.) Texas Commerce Bank sorts the check as an "on
us" item, credits Riquelme's account, and debits Winship's account. The

---

   1. For a more detailed description of the journey that a check takes from issue to final
payment, see M. Mayer, The Bankers 125-162 (1974). See also Malcolm, How Bank Collection
Works—Article 4 of the Uniform Commercial Code, 11 How. L.J. 71 (1965).

check never leaves the bank premises in the settlement process and no cash changes hands. Although Winship's account may be debited with the amount of the check at the time of the settlement, Riquelme will not be allowed to withdraw the $9.75 until the opening of the bank's second banking day after deposit. Because Riquelme's credit is good, however, the bank may permit him to withdraw the amount before this time.

Note that Riquelme could probably have cashed the check at the bank by presenting it over the counter at Texas Commerce Bank. The teller probably would check both accounts to see if there were sufficient funds to protect the bank. Given the small amount, it is unlikely that the bank would not have paid cash.

A nonbank may also cash the check; some convenience stores attract customers by offering to cash their checks, but third-party checks drawn on nonbusiness accounts are much less likely to be cashed. Nonbanks will protect themselves by knowing their customers and by requiring them to indorse their personal checks, thereby adding an indorsement obligation to that of the drawer. Note, however, that when a convenience store cashes a check it does not *pay* the check; it takes it by negotiation and must in turn deposit it with its bank for collection.

Example 2. To pay for a pair of jogging shoes, Winship draws a check on his account with Texas Commerce Bank for $35.81, payable to Luke's Locker. Luke indorses the check with a rubber stamp marked "For Deposit Only, Pay to the order of Republic National Bank, Previous Endorsements Guaranteed, Luke's Locker, 172-078-0." At the end of its banking day, on the day of deposit, Republic National Bank provisionally credits the account of Luke's Locker, stamps the item with the date and the indorsement "Republic National Bank, Dallas, Texas, Pay Any Bank—P.E.G., " and places the item with other "city" or "clearinghouse" items. The following morning Republic National Bank sends all the checks drawn on Texas Commerce Bank, together with a "cash letter" in the form of an adding machine tape, to the central Dallas clearinghouse, where a Texas Commerce Bank representative will exchange items drawn on Republic National Bank for those drawn on Texas Commerce Bank. Clearinghouse rules determine when and how the total daily balances between Republic National Bank and Texas Commerce Bank are to be settled. When Texas Commerce Bank receives the Winship check it will be handled in a similar manner to an "on us" check. Unless Texas Commerce Bank chooses not to honor the check (because, for example, there are insufficient funds in the Winship account) it will do nothing, and the provisional credit given Republic National Bank at the time the checks were exchanged will become final. Assuming nothing goes wrong, Luke's Locker should be able to withdraw this amount sometime on the third banking day after deposit.

If there were insufficient funds in Winship's account, Texas Commerce Bank might honor the check, thereby creating an overdraft, or it might dishonor the check. To dishonor effectively it must return the item or send notice of dishonor to the presenting bank (Republic National Bank in this case) before midnight of the next banking day after it receives the check (*its midnight deadline*). Republic National Bank then charges back the amount of the dishonored check to the Luke's Locker account. If Luke's Locker has already withdrawn the provisional credit, Republic National Bank will have a claim against Luke's Locker and will have given "value" for the purpose of determining whether it is a holder in due course of the check.

Example 3. To pay for some international trade law books Winship draws a check for $74.50 on his account with Texas Commerce Bank payable to the order of "United Nations Publications." The U.N. indorses the check with the stamped notation "Pay to the order of Chemical Bank, U.N. Revenue Producing Activities Account, U.N. Publications" and deposits it in the New York midtown branch of Chemical Bank. The branch provisionally credits the U.N. account, stamps the check with the date and the indorsement "Chemical Bank Midtown," and forwards the check on the same date to a central sorting office for collection. After identifying those items to be collected through the Federal Reserve Bank in Dallas, Chemical Bank stamps the check "Chemical Bank, New York, Pay Any Bank" and forwards the check to the Dallas Federal Reserve Bank.[2] When the Federal Reserve Bank in Dallas receives the check three days later it provisionally credits the Federal Reserve Bank in New York for the account of Chemical Bank with the amount of the check and debits the Texas Commerce Bank account for the same amount. On the same day the Dallas Federal Reserve Bank presents these items directly to Texas Commerce Bank. On receiving the checks, Texas Commerce Bank verifies that there are sufficient funds in Winship's account, stamps the check "paid," and debits Winship's account. As in the case of the "city" check in Example 2, Texas Commerce Bank finishes these steps by its midnight deadline and finally pays the check by not promptly reversing the provisional debit to its account at the Federal Reserve Bank. The U.N. may withdraw the amount of the Winship check when the payment becomes final and Chemical Bank has had a reasonable time to learn that the settlement is final. In practice, a bank such as Chemical Bank uses an availability schedule that estimates the length of time it takes for an item to be collected from different parts of the country.

Note: Sources of Law Governing Bank Collection

The primary state law governing bank collections is UCC Article 4, supplemented by consistent provisions of Article 3. The predecessor of Article 4 was the Bank Collection Code, published in 1929 as a model act by the American Bankers Association and adopted in 19 states. Early drafts of the

2. Chemical Bank could forward the check to the Federal Reserve bank in its own federal reserve district (New York), but reserve bank operating circulars or bulletins authorize sending a check directly to a Federal Reserve bank in another district. 12 C.F.R. §210-4(a) (1984).

bank collection rules for the planned Uniform Commercial Code failed to please the banking community. Revisions made to satisfy the banks drew the charge from one commentator that Article 4 was "vicious class legislation." Nevertheless, there was little opposition in state legislatures, and its text has been adopted with very few nonuniform amendments. More recently, the Permanent Editorial Board of the UCC has appointed a 3-4-8 committee to recommend changes to these particular articles of the Code to cope with technological developments. In 1977 the ALI (American Law Institute) and NCCUSL (National Conference of Commissioners of Uniform State Laws) adopted a revised Article 8 to regulate uncertificated investment securities. Even more recently, drafts of a New Payments Code have been circulated. The impact of credit cards and electronic fund transfer systems on bank collection will be examined in the final sections of this chapter.

Much of the content of Article 4 is subject to agreements that vary or derogate from its terms. The concept of *agreement* is defined broadly to include "Federal Reserve regulations and operating letters, clearing house rules, and the like . . . whether or not specifically assented to by all parties interested in items handled" (UCC 4-103(2)). The agreement may not disclaim a bank's responsibility for its own lack of good faith or negligence, nor may it limit the measure of damages for bad faith conduct or negligence. It may, however, fix standards defining a bank's responsibility, as long as these standards are "not manifestly unreasonable" (UCC 4-103(1)).

The Federal Reserve Board has issued Regulation J (Collection of Checks and Other Items and Transfers of Funds), which regulates the collection of items through the Federal Reserve banks. 12 C.F.R. Part 210 (1984). Part A of Regulation J deals with collection of demand items and documentary drafts; Part B governs wire transfers. Individual Federal Reserve banks in the 12 districts of the federal reserve system issue operating circulars or bulletins that provide greater detail on collection within the individual district. The following case provides some background to the relation between these federal rules and UCC Article 4.

COMMUNITY BANK v. FEDERAL RESERVE BANK OF SAN FRANCISCO
500 F.2d 282 (9th Cir. 1974), *modified,* 525 F.2d 690 (1975), *cert. denied,* 419 U.S. 1089 (1974)

SNEED, Circuit Judge. On June 21, 1972, the Board of Governors of the Federal Reserve System unanimously approved changes in Regulation J, 12 C.F.R. §210, which governs the collection of checks and other items by Federal Reserve Banks. Appellant State Banks, who are neither members of nor affiliated with the Federal Reserve System, object to the amendments to Regulation J insofar as they affect nonmember and non-affiliated payor banks.

Briefly stated, the changes in Regulation J affect both the *time* and *manner* in which payor banks must settle for demand items presented for collection by Reserve Banks. Prior to the amendments, payor banks became accountable if they failed to settle for demand items before midnight of the banking day of receipt, and settlements made earlier could be revoked prior to the midnight deadline. The amendments to Regulation J advance the settlement *time* to the *close* of the banking day of receipt, and only if settlement is made prior to this time may it be revoked before midnight of the banking day [next following the day] of receipt.* The amendments also affect the manner in which settlement may be made by eliminating drafts drawn on other banks as permissible forms of settlement.[1]

Appellants attack the amendments to Regulation J on two broad grounds. First, they urge that the changes are inconsistent with the time and manner of settlement provisions contained in the California Commercial Code, which they contend should govern the operations of nonmember banks chartered under the laws of the State of California. Second, they argue that, to the extent that they attempt to bind payor banks which are not members of the Federal Reserve System, the amendments to Regulation J exceed the power conferred on the Board under the Federal Reserve Act.

Appellant State Banks' application for a preliminary injunction was denied by the district court on October 10, 1972, and on February 8, 1973, the court entered summary judgment in favor of appellees. We affirm.

Our consideration of the issues presented in this appeal will begin with a brief description of the check collection process and the effects of the amendments to Regulation J on this process. We will then turn to a more detailed examination of the provisions of the California Commercial Code and Regulation J to determine if the amendments to the regulation give rise to a federal-state conflict in the area of banking regulation. Finally, finding no such conflict, we will consider whether Regulation J as amended exceeds the scope of authority conferred on the Board by the Federal Reserve Act.

---

* [We will study these time limits in detail later in this chapter. The following summary may help you to understand the court's abbreviated discussion—a discussion not helped by the apparently inadvertent omission of the bracketed clause. Before the 1972 amendments to Regulation J a payor bank that received a check in the midmorning had until midnight of that day to settle for the check with the bank that presented the check for payment. Under a system called "deferred posting," the payor bank is permitted to settle provisionally by listing appropriate entries in the books of the two banks. The payor bank then has until its "midnight deadline" to ratify or revoke this provisional settlement. Unless it is revoked, the settlement became final. *Midnight deadline* is a term of art: it means "with respect to a bank . . . midnight on its next banking day following the banking day on which it receives the relevant item or notice or from which the time for taking action commences to run, whichever is later" (UCC 4-104(1)(h)). Following the amendments to Regulation J a payor bank has to settle provisionally by the end of its banking day (e.g., 2:00 P.M.; see UCC 4-107) rather than midnight, but it may still revoke up to midnight of the next banking day.—EDS.]

1. Prior to the amendments, the time and manner of settlement provisions of Regulation J and the California Commercial Code were virtually identical. [The California Commercial Code in turn is identical with Article 4 on the matters relevant to this opinion.—EDS.]

I. BACKGROUND

Approximately 25 billion checks were collected by banks in 1972; of these, eight billion, or roughly one-third, were handled by Federal Reserve Banks. The Reserve Banks provide check collection services for member banks and affiliated nonmember banks which maintain a certain balance with a Reserve Bank;[2] neither the members nor the affiliated nonmembers, however, are required to use the services of the Reserve Banks to collect checks which have been presented to them.

To handle the increased volume of checks, Federal Reserve and other large banks now use computer-controlled, highspeed electronic sorters which are capable of handling 1000 checks per minute. For this purpose, "Magnetic Ink Character Recognition" (MICR) units are pre-printed on each check. The first group of four digits in the MICR number encoded on the bottom of each check designates the Federal Reserve district, territory, and relationship to the local Federal Reserve office.[3] Each of the appellant State Banks encode their checks with a MICR number that begins with "12," which indicates that they are located in the district of the Federal Reserve Bank of San Francisco. The consequence of this is that checks which are drawn on appellants may be presented by a member or affiliated nonmember bank for collection through the Federal Reserve system.

When checks are presented to a Reserve Bank for collection, settlement is made on the basis of a deferred-payment schedule. This schedule is, with one important exception, based on the amount of time usually required for the Reserve Bank to collect items of a similar type. Since checks drawn on banks in the same city may usually be collected on the same day, same-day credit is passed to the depositor. Checks drawn on the banks in other cities having Federal Reserve offices may usually be collected the following day; accordingly, one-day credit is passed to the depositor. Two-day credit is passed when the check is drawn on banks located within the same Federal Reserve territory but outside of a Reserve office city. The exception exists because, while three days may be required to collect checks drawn on banks outside of the Reserve territory and not located in an office city,[4] two-day credit is the maximum length of deferment for any check presented to a Reserve Bank for collection.[5] Thus, in this latter situation the Reserve Bank pays for a check on the basis of

2. See 12 U.S.C. §342. [Under the Monetary Control Act of 1980 (94 Stat. 140) nonmember banks may use the federal reserve collection system upon payment of the fees prescribed by the Federal Reserve System.—EDS.]

3. In addition, the numerator of the fraction located on the upper right-hand portion of appellants' checks represents the Federal Reserve routing number.

4. The three days include: (1) one day to process the item at the Reserve Bank of first receipt and transmit it to the Reserve Bank for the area in which the payor bank is located; (2) one day for the item to be processed by the second Reserve Bank and transmitted to the payor bank; and (3) one additional day to receive the remittance.

5. Federal Reserve Operating Circular No. 1.

the deferred-payment schedule one day before that check is actually collected; this effectively generates a one-day, interest-free loan to the bank involved. The total amount of such loans is known as Federal Reserve "float." Aggravating the problem of delay in the process of settlement is the practice of some payor banks to settle by means of drafts drawn on other banks.[6]

To alleviate these problems, the amendments to Regulation J (1) advance the time within which payor banks must settle for checks presented for collection by Reserve Banks, and (2) eliminate the use of bank drafts as permissible forms of settlement by requiring settlement to be immediately-available funds. The resulting acceleration of the process, in turn, enables the Reserve Bank in some instances to pass earlier credit to the depositor bank. From the vantage point of the Federal Reserve, the changes are particularly desirable in that they tend to reduce the problem of "float."

II.   STATE LAW

We now turn to a consideration of whether the amendments to Regulation J are, as the appellants insist, in conflict with the pertinent provisions of the California Commercial Code. . . .

Two principal California Commercial Code provisions governing the time in which a payor bank must settle when presented with a check for collection are affected by the amendments to Regulation J. UCC 4-302 makes a payor bank accountable if it retains an item beyond midnight of the banking day of receipt without settling for it, and UCC 4-301 allows the payor banks to revoke a provisional settlement if such revocation is made before the midnight deadline. [UCC 4-104(1)(c), (h); 4-107.]

Section 210.9(a)(1) of the amended Regulation J, however, makes a payor bank accountable if it fails to settle for demand items before the close of its banking day of receipt, and Section 210.12(a) provides that only if settlement has been made by this time may the payor bank revoke prior to midnight of the banking day [next following the banking day] of receipt.

Taken this far, Regulation J quite obviously is in conflict with the above provisions of state law. The conflict disappears, however, in light of the flexibility provided in UCC 4-103. Subsection (1) of this provision permits variation of the Code's provisions by agreement, and subsection (2) provides that "Federal Reserve regulations and operating letters, clearing house rules, and the like, have the effect of agreements . . . whether or not specifically assented to by all parties interested in the items handled."

Appellants contend that UCC 4-103(2) does not operate to make Federal Reserve regulations binding on nonmember, payor banks. We disagree. The legislative history behind the language of subsection (2), which elevates Fed-

---

6. A draft on the remitting bank itself is not permissible because it would merely substitute for the original item another item on the same payor. [UCC 4-211(1)(a).]

eral Reserve regulations to the status of agreements, "whether or not specifically assented to by all parties interested in the items handled," makes clear that it may be applicable to nonmember payor banks. The California Commercial Code Comment indicates that, under prior California law, clearinghouse rules "did not govern the rights of a *drawer* and *payee* who were not members of the clearinghouse and who did not contract with express reference to those rules." (emphasis added). The reference to the rights of drawers and payees under "prior California law" suggests that the Code has changed this result. That this change effected by the Code is *not* limited to drawers and payees is indicated by the breadth of the following comment of the Senate Fact Finding Committee: "Subdivision 2 apparently changes the rule insofar as it applies between *parties* who are not members of the clearinghouse." (emphasis added). Sixth Progress Report to the Legislature by the Senate Fact Finding Committee on the Judiciary: Part I, The Uniform Commercial Code 87.

The Report of the New York Law Revision Commission contains an even stronger indication that UCC 4-103(2) is- applicable to nonmember, payor banks which affiliate themselves with the Federal Reserve's check collection process: "Federal Reserve Regulations and operating letters now operate as 'agreements' between the Federal Reserve Banks and banks using the Federal Reserve facilities for collection, and clearinghouse rules now operate of course as agreements among member banks and banks clearing through banks that are members of the clearinghouse association. *They are similarly effective as agreements binding on other banks, and their customers, whenever a claim of agency and subagency can be made out connecting the remote bank, and its customer, with the banks that are parties to the agreement,* and the agency includes, as a term of the agreement binding the remote party, the power to adhere to that agreement on behalf of the remote principal. Explicit agreement is sometimes difficult to spell out, however. Section 4-103(2) postulates an implied assent as a rule of law." (emphasis added). 2 Report of the New York Law Revision Commission for 1955: Study of the Uniform Commercial Code 1262-1263. The "claim of agency or subagency" referred to in the Report, which constitutes the necessary predicate for Federal Reserve regulations to be binding on nonmember banks, is readily established by the current voluntary use of MICR members by appellants.

As mentioned above, each of appellants encode their checks with the number "12," which indicates that they are located in the 12th Federal Reserve district. Obviously, if this number is merely removed, appellants' checks cannot be electronically processed. If, however, it is replaced by appropriate symbols, the checks may be electronically processed and collected outside of the Federal Reserve system.

That elimination of the Federal Reserve routing numbers is commercially feasible is demonstrated by the current practices of nonpar banks. Since Reserve Banks are prohibited by statute from paying an exchange fee, 12 U.S.C. §342, checks drawn on nonpar banks cannot be collected through the Federal Reserve system. Nonpar banks replace the Federal Reserve routing number on the lower left-hand portion of their checks with the number "9." This enables the checks of nonpar banks to be electronically processed even though the MICR number begins with a "9" and even though it does not contain a number referring to any Federal Reserve office. A somewhat similar system as an alternative to the use of Federal Reserve routing numbers is available to appellants. The fact that nonmember banks may find it less commercially advantageous than utilizing the Federal Reserve routing number does not militate against this conclusion.

In sum, appellants are not required to include the Federal Reserve routing number on their checks, and so long as they continue to use this number, the "claim of agency or subagency" referred to in the Report of the New York Law Revision Commission exists, and the terms of Regulation J are binding upon them because of the operation of UCC 4-103(2). . . .

[The court goes on to hold that (1) there is no conflict between the UCC and the federal regulation as to the manner in which payor banks must settle for demand items, and (2) the Federal Reserve Board had authority to issue Regulation J as amended.]

NOTES & QUESTIONS

1. *Regulation J.* Since the *Community Bank* case the Federal Reserve Board has simplified the language of Regulation J. See 45 Fed. Reg. 68633 (Oct. 16, 1980). The regulation and operating circulars have a binding effect on all persons interested in an item collected through the federal reserve system. Section 210.3 provides:

§*210.3   General provisions*

(a)   General. Each Reserve Bank shall receive and handle items in accordance with this subpart, and shall issue operating circulars governing the details of its handling of items and other matters deemed appropriate by the Reserve Bank. The circulars may, among other things, classify cash items and noncash items, require separate sorts and letters, and provide different closing times for the receipt of different classes or types of items.

(b)   Binding effect. This subpart and the operating circulars of the Reserve Banks are binding on the sender of an item, on each collecting bank, paying bank, and nonbank payor, to which a Reserve Bank (or a subsequent collecting bank) presents or sends an item, and on other parties interested in the item, including the owner.

The provisions of Regulation J and the operating circulars prevail over inconsistent state law.

2. *Regulation J: payment and return of cash items.* After the 1980 amendments, the sections relevant to the *Community Bank* case read:

§210.9 Payment

(a) Cash items. A paying bank becomes accountable for the amount of a cash item received directly or indirectly from a Reserve Bank, at the close of the paying bank's banking day on which it receives[3] the item if it retains the item after the close of that banking day, unless, prior to that time, it pays for the item by:

(1) Debit to an account on the Reserve Bank's books;

(2) Cash; or

(3) In the discretion of the Reserve Bank, any other form of payment.

The proceeds of any payment shall be available to the Reserve Bank by the close of the Reserve Bank's banking day on the banking day of receipt of the item by the paying bank. If the banking day of receipt is not a banking day for the Reserve Bank, payment shall be made on the next day that is a banking day for both the Reserve Bank and the paying bank.

§210.12 Return of cash items

(a) Recovery of payment. A paying bank that receives a cash item directly or indirectly from a Reserve Bank, other than for immediate payment over the counter, and that pays for the item as provided in §210.9(a) of this subpart, may recover the payment if, before it has finally paid the item, it:

(1) Returns the item before midnight of its next banking day following the banking day of receipt; or

(2) Takes any other action to recover the payment within the times and by the means provided by State law.

The rules or practices of a clearinghouse through which the item was presented, or a special collection agreement under which the item was presented, may not extend these return times, but may provide for a shorter return time.

B. THE DEPOSITARY BANK; COLLECTING BANKS

All banks other than the payor bank are collecting banks. The depositary bank is the first bank in the collection system. UCC 4-105(a). When the bank is the drawee on the check deposited, the depositary bank will also be the payor bank. If the depositary bank has multiple branches and the deposited check is drawn on an account at another branch, the bank as a whole is

---

3. A paying bank is deemed to receive a cash item on its next banking day if it receives the item:

(1) On a day other than a banking day for it; or

(2) On a banking day for it, but

  (i) After its regular banking hours;

  (ii) After a "cut-off hour" established by it in accordance with State law; or

  (iii) During afternoon or evening periods when it is open for limited functions only.

considered both the depositary and payor bank, even though for some purposes the branches may be treated as separate banks. UCC 4-106. Unless it is also a payor bank, the depositary bank has the same rights and duties as any other collecting bank.

To appreciate fully the status of the collecting bank you must understand that it is both a transferee of an item and an agent or subagent for the purposes of collection. When a customer deposits a check for collection he is transferring a negotiable instrument. If the customer indorses the check "Pay X Bank," and delivers it to the bank, the bank is an Article 3 holder of a negotiable instrument and as a holder it has the same rights as any other holder to enforce the instrument against the parties to it. Article 4 adds several rules to supplement the rules on negotiation and holder status that we have already studied in Article 3. See UCC 4-102(1) (in case of conflict Article 4 governs Article 3 provisions). UCC 4-205 authorizes the depositary bank to supply the missing indorsement of its customer, so if the customer has failed to indorse a check when depositing it the depositary bank may become a holder by indorsing it to itself. Special rules on when banks give value are set out in UCC 4-208 and 4-209. If the bank makes an advance against the item either in actual funds or by giving its customer the right to draw against a provisional credit, the bank has given value for the purposes of holder in due course status (UCC 4-208, 4-209). Moreover, when the check is transferred in the collection process the transferor makes warranties similar to, but not identical with, the UCC 3-417 warranties (UCC 4-207).

The depositary bank and other collecting banks are not only transferees of items but also the agent or subagent of the customer. UCC 4-201(1) states that "[u]nless a contrary intent clearly appears . . . the bank is an agent or sub-agent of the owner of the item." The subsection goes on to make clear that the depositary bank is governed by the rules of Article 4 even if it has purchased the item, as it does when it "discounts" the item. Much pre-Code litigation turned on whether the depositary bank purchased an item or merely acted as an agent for collection. UCC 4-201 resolves this issue in favor of agency status. The bank customer, in other words, is the owner of the item deposited and bears the risk that the item will be lost or destroyed in the collection process and also the risk that the drawee bank will not pay. At the same time, however, the customer rather than the collecting bank has the benefit of the insurance provided by the Federal Deposit Insurance Corporation. This is important when the payor bank has finally paid an item but the depositary bank has not yet received the proceeds at the time the payor bank fails.[4]

As agents, the depositary bank and other collecting banks must use ordinary care when taking steps to collect an item. UCC 4-202 states this general

---

4. The F.D.I.C. is governed by the Federal Deposit Insurance Act, 15 U.S.C. §§1811-1831 (1982). Note that before final payment by the drawee or payor bank the customer initiating the collection process is not protected by the insurance.

standard, noting that a bank is liable only for its own negligence and not for acts of other collecting banks. In general, action taken by a depositary or other collecting bank in accordance with special rules of Article 4, rules of the federal reserve system, clearing house rules, and general banking use is prima facie the exercise of ordinary care.

If a collecting bank fails to use ordinary care it will be liable to its customer for damages. The bank may not disclaim responsibility for its own negligence but it may provide standards in the contract with its customer by which to measure this responsibility. UCC 4-103(1). Damages are limited, however, by UCC 4-103(5), which states:

> The measure of damages for failure to exercise ordinary care in collecting an item is the amount of the item reduced by an amount which could not have been realized by the use of ordinary care, and where there is bad faith it includes other damages, if any, suffered by the party as a proximate consequence.

Part 2 of Article 4 sets out specific rules for the collection process. Steps taken to collect must be taken seasonably, usually before a bank's midnight deadline. Certain actions that were disputed in pre-Code law are explicitly authorized: a depositary bank is authorized, for example, to send an item directly to a payor bank. UCC 4-204. Certain forms of remittance are explicitly made acceptable. A remitting bank, for example, may settle with a collecting bank by sending a check drawn on another bank, a cashier's check drawn on itself when it is a member of the same clearing house as the collecting bank, or a bank check when the item being settled for was drawn on a nonbank (e.g., an insurance company settlement draft drawn on the company by an agent). If the remitting bank has an account with the collecting bank, settlement may also be by an authorized charge to that account. UCC 4-211(1). If an item is dishonored or lost in collection the depositary bank must promptly notify its customer or return the item. UCC 4-202, 4-301, 4-302.

BOWLING GREEN, INC. v. STATE STREET BANK & TRUST CO.
425 F.2d 81, 7 UCC Rep. 635 (1st Cir. 1970)

Coffin, Circuit Judge. On September 26, 1966, plaintiff Bowling Green, Inc., the operator of a bowling alley, negotiated a United States government check for $15,306 to Bowl-Mor, Inc., a manufacturer of bowling alley equipment. The check, which plaintiff had acquired through a Small Business Administration loan, represented the first installment on a conditional sales contract for the purchase of candlepin setting machines. On the following day, September 27, a representative of Bowl-Mor deposited the check in defendant State Street Bank and Trust Co. The Bank immediately credited $5,024.85 of the check against an overdraft in Bowl-Mor's account. Later that day, when the

Bank learned that Bowl-Mor had filed a petition for reorganization under Chapter X of the Bankruptcy Act, it transferred $233.61 of Bowl-Mor's funds to another account and applied the remaining $10,047.54 against debts which Bowl-Mor owed the Bank. Shortly thereafter, Bowl-Mor's petition for reorganization was dismissed and the firm was adjudicated a bankrupt. Plaintiff had never received the pin-setting machines for which it contracted. Its part payment remains in the hands of defendant Bank.

Plaintiff brought this diversity action to recover its payment from defendant Bank on the grounds that the Bank is constructive trustee of the funds deposited by Bowl-Mor. In the court below, plaintiff argued that Bowl-Mor knew it could not perform at the time it accepted payment, that the Bank was aware of this fraudulent conduct, and that the Bank therefore received Bowl-Mor's deposit impressed with a constructive trust in plaintiff's favor. The district court rejected plaintiff's view of the evidence, concluding instead that the Bank was a holder in due course within the meaning of UCC 4-209 and 3-302, and was therefore entitled to take the item in question free of all personal defenses. [307 F. Supp. 648 (D. Mass. 1969).]

Plaintiff's appeal challenges the conclusion of the district court in three respects. First, plaintiff maintains that the Bank has not met its burden of establishing that it was a "holder" of the item within the meaning of UCC 1-201(20), and thus cannot be a "holder in due course" within the meaning of UCC 4-209 and 3-302. Second, plaintiff argues that the Bank's close working relation with Bowl-Mor prevented it from becoming a holder in good faith. Finally, plaintiff denies that defendant gave value within the meaning of UCC 4-209 for the $10,047.54 which it set off against Bowl-Mor's loan account.

Plaintiff's first objection arises from a technical failure of proof. The district court found that plaintiff had endorsed the item in question to Bowl-Mor, but there was no evidence that Bowl-Mor supplied its own endorsement before depositing the item in the Bank. Thus we cannot tell whether the Bank is a holder within the meaning of UCC 1-201(20), which defines holder as one who takes an instrument endorsed to him, or to bearer, or in blank. But, argues plaintiff, once it is shown that a defense to an instrument exists, the Bank has the burden of showing that it is in all respects a holder in due course. This failure of proof, in plaintiff's eyes, is fatal to the Bank's case.

We readily agree with plaintiff that the Bank has the burden of establishing its status in all respects. UCC 3-307(3), on which plaintiff relies to establish the defendant's burden, seems addressed primarily to cases in which a holder seeks to enforce an instrument, but Massachusetts courts have indicated that the policy of UCC 3-307(3) applies whenever a party invokes the rights of a holder in due course either offensively or defensively. . . . The issue, however, is not whether the Bank bears the burden of proof, but whether it must establish that it took the item in question by endorsement in order to meet its burden. We think not. The evidence in this case indicates that the Bank's transferor, Bowl-Mor, was a holder. Under UCC 3-201(1), transfer of an instrument vests in the transferee all the rights of the transferor. As the Official

Comment to UCC 3-201 indicates, one who is not a holder must first establish the transaction by which he acquired the instrument before enforcing it, but the Bank has met this burden here.

We doubt, moreover, whether the concept of "holder" as defined in UCC 1-201(20) applies with full force to Article 4. Article 4 establishes a comprehensive scheme for simplifying and expediting bank collections. Its provisions govern the more general rules of Article 3 wherever inconsistent. UCC 4-102(1). As part of this expediting process, Article 4 recognizes the common bank practice of accepting unendorsed checks for deposit. See C. Funk, Banks and the UCC 133 (2d ed. 1964). UCC 4-201(1) provides that the lack of an endorsement shall not affect the bank's status as an agent for collection, and UCC 4-205(1) authorizes the collecting bank to supply the missing endorsements as a matter of course.[3] In practice, banks comply with UCC 4-205 by stamping the item "deposited to the account of the named payee" or some similar formula. Funk, supra at 133. We doubt whether the bank's status should turn on proof of whether a clerk employed the appropriate stamp, and we hesitate to penalize a bank which accepted unendorsed checks for deposit in reliance on the Code, at least when, as here, the customer himself clearly satisfies the definition of "holder." UCC 4-209 does provide that a bank must comply "with the requirements of section 3-302 on what constitutes a holder in due course," but we think this language refers to the enumerated requirements of good faith and lack of notice rather than to the status of holder, a status which UCC 3-302 assumes rather than requires. We therefore hold that a bank which takes an item for collection from a customer who was himself a holder need not establish that it took the item by negotiation in order to satisfy UCC 4-209.

Plaintiff's second objection arises from the intimate relationship between Bowl-Mor and the Bank, a relationship which plaintiff maintains precludes a finding of good faith. The record shows that the Bank was one of Bowl-Mor's three major creditors, and that it regularly provided short term financing for Bowl-Mor against the security of Bowl-Mor's inventory and unperformed contracts. The loan officer in charge of Bowl-Mor's account, Francis Haydock, was also a director of Bowl-Mor until August 1966. In the five months before the transaction in question, the Bank charged $1,000,000 of Bowl-Mor's debt to the Bank's reserve for bad debts. However, the record also shows that the Bank continued to make loans to Bowl-Mor until September 12.

The Bank was also aware of the underlying transaction between Bowl-Mor and the plaintiff which led to the deposit on September 26. During the week prior to this transaction, Bowl-Mor had overdrawn its checking account with the Bank to meet a payroll. In order to persuade the Bank to honor the overdraft, officials of Bowl-Mor contacted Haydock and informed him that a

---

3. See also UCC 4-105(a), which defines "depositary bank" in terms of transfer rather than negotiation, and UCC 4-206, which speaks of transfer between banks. For the difference between transfer and negotiation, compare UCC 3-201 with UCC 3-202(1).

check for $15,000 would be deposited as soon as plaintiff could obtain the funds from the Small Business Administration. The district court found, however, that the Bank was not aware that the directors of Bowl-Mor had authorized a Chapter X petition or that Bowl-Mor officials planned to file the petition on September 27.

On the basis of this record, the district court found that the Bank acted in good faith and without notice of any defense to the instrument. The Code defines "good faith" as "honesty in fact," UCC 1-201(19), an essentially subjective test which focuses on the state of mind of the person in question. The Code's definition of "notice," UCC 1-201(25), while considerably more prolix, also focuses on the actual knowledge of the individuals allegedly notified. Since the application of these definitions turns so heavily on the facts of an individual case, rulings of a district court under UCC 3-302(1)(b) and 3-302(1)(c) should never be reversed unless clearly erroneous. In this case, the evidence indicated that Bowl-Mor had persevered in spite of long-term financial ill health, and that the event which precipitated its demise was the withdrawal of financial support by another major creditor, Otis Elevator Co., on the morning of September 27, after the deposit of plaintiff's check. Thus, at the time of deposit, the Bank might reasonably have expected Bowl-Mor to continue its shambling pace rather than cease business immediately. The findings of the district court are not, therefore, clearly erroneous.

Plaintiff, however, urges us to adopt the "objective" standard of good faith promulgated in Jones v. Approved Bancredit Corp., 256 A.2d 739 (Del. Sup. Ct. 1969), which held that a finance company could not as a matter of law be a holder in due course of a consumer installment note which it discounted for a closely affiliated construction company. We doubt whether *Approved Bancredit* represents the law in Massachusetts. In a similar case, Universal C.I.T. Credit Corp. v. Ingel, 347 Mass. 119, 196 N.E.2d 847 (1964), the consumer sought to introduce evidence concerning the credit company's knowledge of previous complaints concerning the payee's performance. The Supreme Judicial Court held that such evidence was properly excluded because it did not establish that the credit company had notice of the payee's fraud. 347 Mass. at 125, 196 N.E.2d 847. While this decision is not squarely addressed to good faith, it indicates to us that Massachusetts continues to look to the facts of the individual case rather than applying an "objective standard" based on the general business dealings between the transferor and transferee of an instrument.

We note, moreover, that the balance of convenience on which the Delaware Court relied in *Approved Bancredit* inclines in a different direction when the instrument is a check rather than a consumer note. A consumer who executes a note often has no way of investigating the honesty of the person with whom he deals and his only realistic remedy in the event of breach is to withhold payment. A bank or finance company, on the other hand, will find it relatively easy to check the honesty and competence of those who regularly present consumer paper for discounting. When the instrument is a check, however, the equities are quite different. The check is the major method for transfer of funds in commercial practice. The maker, payee, and endorsers of a check naturally expect it will be rapidly negotiated and collected. Even companies which, like Bowl-Mor, are tottering on the brink of financial collapse will continue to deposit checks for collection during each business day. The wheels of commerce would grind to a halt if the bank became "constructive trustee" of these items at the first whiff of insolvency. We therefore see no sufficient reason not only to adopt the objective standard but also to extend it to a commercial bank accepting a check.

This brings us to plaintiff's final argument, that the Bank gave value only to the extent of the $5,024.85 overdraft, and thus cannot be a holder in due course with respect to the remaining $10,047.54 which the Bank credited against Bowl-Mor's loan account. Our consideration of this argument is confined by the narrow scope of the district court's findings. The Bank may well have given value under UCC 4-208(1)(a) when it credited the balance of Bowl-Mor's checking account against its outstanding indebtedness. . . . But by that time the Bank knew of Bowl-Mor's petition for reorganization, additional information which the district court did not consider in finding that the Bank acted in good faith and without notice at the time it received the item. We must therefore decide whether the Bank gave value for the additional $10,047.54 at the time the item was deposited.[5]

Resolution of this issue depends on the proper interpretation of UCC 4-209, which provides that a collecting bank has given value to the extent that it has acquired a "security interest" in an item. In plaintiff's view, a collecting bank can satisfy UCC 4-209 only by extending credit against an item in compliance with UCC 4-208(1). The district court, on the other hand, adopted the view that a security interest is a security interest, however acquired. The court then found that defendant and Bowl-Mor had entered a security agreement which gave defendant a floating lien on Bowl-Mor's chattel paper. Since the item in question was part of the proceeds of a Bowl-Mor contract, the court concluded that defendant had given value for the full $15,306.00 at the time it received the deposit.

With this conclusion we agree. UCC 1-201(37) defines "security interest" as an interest in personal property which secures payment or performance of an obligation. There is no indication in UCC 4-209 that the term is used in a

---

5. Defendant suggests that we can avoid the analytical problems of UCC 4-209 by simply holding that the Bank's inchoate right to set off Bowl-Mor's outstanding indebtedness against deposits, as they were made constituted a giving of value. See Wood v. Boylston National Bank, 129 Mass. 358 (1880). There are, however, some pitfalls in this theory. First, under prior law a secured creditor could not exercise its right of set-off without first showing that its security was inadequate. Forastiere v. Springfield Institution for Savings, 303 Mass. 101, 104, 20 N.E.2d 950 (1939). Second, although the Uniform Commercial Code forswears any intent to change a banker's right of set-off, UCC 4-201 does change the presumption that a bank owns items deposited with it. This presumption played a role under prior law in assessing the bank's rights against uncollected commercial paper. Compare [the *Wood* case] with Boston-Continental National Bank v. Hub Fruit Co., 285 Mass. 187, 190, 189 N.E. 89 (1934) and American Barrel Co. v. Commissioner of Banks, 290 Mass. 174, 179-181, 195 N.E. 335 (1935).

more narrow or specialized sense. Moreover, as the official comment to UCC 4-209 observes, this provision is in accord with prior law and with UCC 3-303, both of which provide that a holder gives value when he accepts an instrument as security for an antecedent debt. . . . Finally, we note that if one of the Bank's prior loans to Bowl-Mor had been made in the expectation that this particular instrument would be deposited, the terms of UCC 4-208(1)(c) would have been literally satisfied. We do not think the case is significantly different when the Bank advances credit on the strength of a continuing flow of items of this kind. We therefore conclude that the Bank gave value for the full $15,306.00 at the time it accepted the deposit.

We see no discrepancy between this result and the realities of commercial life. Each party, of course, chose to do business with an eventually irresponsible third party. The Bank, though perhaps unwise in prolonging its hopes for a prospering customer, nevertheless protected itself through security arrangements as far as possible without hobbling each deposit and withdrawal. Plaintiff, on the other hand, not only placed its initial faith in Bowl-Mor, but later became aware that Bowl-Mor was having difficulties in meeting its payroll. It seems not too unjust that this vestige of caveat emptor survives.

Affirmed.

NOTES & QUESTIONS

1. *Supplying customer's indorsement (UCC 4-205)*. If a depositary bank supplies its customer's indorsement in accordance with UCC 4-205, what form should the indorsement take? Are the following indorsements effective?

    (a)   "credited to the account of the payee herein named, Depositary Bank"

    (b)   "for deposit only, Depositary Bank"

2. *Restrictive indorsements*. Restrictive indorsements, such as the phrases, "for collection," "for deposit," or "pay any bank," are defined by UCC 3-205. UCC 3-206 spells out the effect of these indorsements. The depositary bank must pay or apply any value given consistently with the indorsement. If the payee's indorsement includes the notation "for deposit only," for example, the depositary bank must credit the payee's account and should not pay any other person the amount of the item. In the same case, however, the intermediary banks are not affected by a restrictive indorsement of any person other than an immediate transferor. UCC 3-206(2), (3); 3-419(4). When the holder of an restrictively indorsed instrument is paid in a manner inconsistent with the indorsement the payor's liability is not discharged, UCC 3-603(1)(b), and the depositary bank that allows the proceeds of an item to be paid inconsistent with the terms of the indorsement may be liable to the owner in conversion. UCC 3-419(3).

Consider the following problem: Marine Midland accepts for collection a check payable to Proctor Construction without Proctor's indorsement. Marine

Midland supplies the indorsement "credited to the account of the payee herein named" and wires the amount of the check to Proctor's account at another bank. Is the indorsement a restrictive indorsement? If so, does Marine Midland comply with the restriction? When the drawee fails to pay the check is Marine Midland a holder? Marine Midland v. Prince, Miller, Evans & Flowers, 57 N.Y.2d 220, 441 N.E.2d 1083, 34 UCC Rep. 1207 (1982).

3. *Value (UCC 3-303, 4-208, 4-209)*. Under UCC 4-208 and 4-209 a depositary bank gives value when it permits its customer to draw against uncollected items. For criticism of these Code provisions consider the following excerpt.

ROSENTHAL, NEGOTIABILITY—WHO NEEDS IT?, 71 Colum. L. Rev. 375, 384-385 (1971): "If the depositary bank were to grant credit to the payee by allowing withdrawals before collection, and if it were to do this in reliance upon its knowledge of the *drawer*'s financial standing or reputation, there might be good reason to protect the depositary bank in this fashion. Typically, however, the depositary bank pays no attention to the identity of the drawer; in fact, it does not even know whether the drawer's signature is genuine. It will often allow or refuse to allow withdrawals against the check before collection solely on the basis of its relations with and knowledge of the creditworthiness of its own customer, the payee. If payment is stopped, and the depositary bank cannot recover its advances by charging the amount back against the payee's account, but is permitted to hold the drawer liable, the bank receives a windfall: in such cases, it picks up the liability of the drawer, which by hypothesis it had not counted upon when it made its decision to allow withdrawals before collection.

"The fact that the depositary bank would not normally be relying upon the drawer's credit may be seen in the improbable combination of circumstances that have to coincide for the drawer's liability to matter. First, the bank's customer, the payee, must have allowed his account to drop to the point at which some of his withdrawals cannot be charged against other funds in the account but must be regarded as advances against the uncollected check. Second, the payee must be insolvent, or at least his assets must not be readily amenable to collection.

"Third, the drawer has to be solvent and available, and his signature genuine. Fourth, the check must be dishonored. Finally, for the doctrine to make any ultimate difference, the drawer must have a legitimate defense on the check that is good against the payee, but is not of a type that can be asserted against a holder in due course. Only if all of these elements coincide is the bank's position improved by virtue of its becoming a holder in due course. It must therefore be a rare case indeed in which the bank's decision to extend credit before the check is collected can be regarded as having been made in reliance upon its ability to cut off the defenses of the drawer. Neither banks specifically, nor commerce in general, seem to need the rule declaring the bank to be a holder in due course. Where the bank relies entirely on the identity and credit of the payee in allowing withdrawals, it should shock no one's conscience if the bank were limited to the payee as a source of reimbursement."

4. *Notice and good faith of depositary bank.* If a depositary bank knows of its customer's financial difficulties and has refused in the past to permit the customer to draw against uncollected items, will it be able to meet the standards of notice and good faith when claiming holder-in-due-course status if it subsequently honors a check drawn against an item that ultimately is not paid?

LUFTHANSA GERMAN AIRLINES v. BANK OF AMERICA N.T.S.A.
478 F. Supp. 1195, 27 UCC Rep. 1067 (N.D. Cal. 1979), *aff'd*, 625 F.2d 835, 31 UCC Rep. 1426 (9th Cir. 1981)

SCHWARZER, District Judge. Plaintiff Lufthansa German Airlines brought suit to recover $63,081.98 which, it alleged, was wrongfully charged back to its account by defendant Bank of America. Plaintiff and defendant have filed cross motions for summary judgment.

On June 15, 1978, Novo International Airfreight Corporation issued a check in favor of plaintiff in the amount of $63,081.98. The check was drawn on First Pennsylvania Bank and Trust Company in Philadelphia. The next day, June 16, plaintiff endorsed the check and deposited it in the Union Square branch of the Bank of America ("Bank"). The check was endorsed by the Bank on the same day and transferred to the Federal Reserve Bank ("FRB") of San Francisco.

On June 19, 1978, the FRB in Philadelphia received the check and transferred it to the First Pennsylvania Bank. Two days later, on June 21, 1978, that bank dishonored the check for insufficient funds and returned it to the FRB in Philadelphia.

On the day it received the dishonored check, the FRB in Philadelphia informed the FRB in San Francisco by telephone that the item had been returned for insufficient funds. The San Francisco FRB in turn called the Bank's returned item section, also on June 21, 1978, to inform it of the check's dishonor. In conformity with Federal Reserve Operating Circular #2, the FRB notified the Bank of (1) the amount of the dishonored check; (2) the reason for the nonpayment; (3) the date of the Federal Reserve cash letter; (4) the name of the maker; and (5) the American Banking Association ("ABA") routing numbers of all endorsers preceding the FRB. The FRB did not inform the Bank of the branch in which the check had initially been deposited. On June 26, 1978, five days after receiving notice from Philadelphia and notifying the Bank, the FRB in San Francisco received the check. On the same day, at the 3:00 P.M. clearings, the check was returned to the Bank's returned item section. On the next day, June 27, 1978, according to the Bank, plaintiff was notified that the check had been dishonored. Plaintiff claims this notification did not occur until a day later, June 28, 1978, and the Court will assume, for the purposes of the motion, that plaintiff is correct.

A collecting bank's right to charge back its depositor's account where a check has been dishonored is governed by UCC 4-212 [as enacted in California—EDS.] which provides in relevant part:

> If a collecting bank has made provisional settlement with its customer for an item and itself fails by reason of dishonor, suspension of payments by a bank or otherwise to receive a settlement for the item which is or becomes final, the bank may revoke the settlement given by it, charge back the amount of any credit given for the item to its customer's account or obtain refund from its customer whether or not it is able to return the item *if by its midnight deadline or within a longer reasonable time after it learns the facts it returns the item or sends notification of the facts.* (Emphasis added)

In this case, the Bank received timely notice of dishonor from the Philadelphia FRB on June 21 but did not notify Lufthansa until June 28. The issue is whether it sent notification "by its midnight deadline or within a longer reasonable time after it learn[ed] the facts." If it did not, it was not entitled to charge back against Lufthansa.

UCC 4-104(1)(h) defines "midnight deadline" as "midnight on [the] next banking day following the banking day on which [the bank] receives the relevant item or notice or from which the time for taking action commences to run, whichever is later." This section contains a potential ambiguity. If the words "whichever is later" were read to modify receipt of notice separately from receipt of the item, a bank would be under no duty to notify its customer until it had actually received the check, regardless of its having received prior notice. Such an interpretation would make notice largely irrelevant and therefore would run contrary to the scheme underlying these rules. Moreover, it would make surplusage of the provision of UCC 4-212 allowing a bank reasonable time after it learns facts to return the item or send notification. If the bank were always permitted to wait until it received the dishonored item, it would never need additional time to learn facts necessary to give notice to its depositor. The reasonable and practical interpretation of UCC 4-104(1)(h), therefore, would fix the midnight deadline at midnight of the day following the later of (1) the day of receipt of the item or of notice, or (2) the day from which the time for taking action begins to run.

Inasmuch as the Bank received notice of dishonor on June 21, its notification to Lufthansa on June 28 was untimely under the first branch of the midnight deadline definition. The question therefore is whether under the circumstances of this case the time for taking action began to run on a day subsequent to June 21.

Lufthansa concedes that the midnight deadline is extended "in unusual situations where the bank was unable to act by its midnight deadline through no fault of its own," citing The Law of Bank Checks by Henry J. Bailey (4th ed. 1969). It argues, however, that inasmuch as the notice of dishonor given the Bank was sufficient, conforming to the requirements of UCC 3-508, this was not an unusual situation. But the Code by its terms does not require notice of dishonor to include information sufficient to enable the collecting bank to make a timely charge back. Although there is a logical connection between notice of dishonor to the collecting bank and notice of charge back to that bank's customer, the provisions of UCC 3-508 and 4-212 do not dovetail. The open-ended language of the latter defers the midnight deadline until the collecting bank "learns the facts." The only reasonable interpretation of the latter language would seem to be that the duty to notify the customer arises only after the bank has learned facts sufficient to enable it to do so.[1]

The difficulty in this case is that the notice of dishonor from the Philadelphia FRB did not identify the branch in which the check had been deposited. Without that information the Bank could not determine the identity of the customer whose account had been credited. Lufthansa contends, therefore, that since the delay in giving notice was due solely to the Bank's failure to use a procedure to identify the branch of deposit, it should be attributed to the Bank's fault.

That argument, however, ignores the fact that the practice of the banking industry, approved by the Federal Reserve Board, is normally to limit banks operating branches to a single routing number. As the pamphlet "Routing Numbers Specifications and Guides," issued by the joint ABA/FRB Routing Number Task Force, explains, the purpose of routing numbers is to identify the endpoint in the collection process. Since in the usual case banks process items for collection centrally and not at their separate branches, routing numbers should not be used to identify branches (p. 7). Accordingly, the major banks in the San Francisco area, as well as elsewhere, use a single routing number for all branches and offices in the particular area. See American Bankers Association Key to Routing Numbers 1978 (60th ed.) p. K-40.

The purpose of the limitation on the number of numbers, as explained by the ABA/FRB task force, was not to serve the convenience of individual banks, but to enhance the operation of the payment system of the banking industry. The limitation was adopted as a result of a joint industry-FRB effort. Under these circumstances it would be inappropriate to hold the Bank liable for having failed to employ separate routing numbers for its branches.

The Court concludes therefore that the Bank's obligation to give notice did not arise until June 26 when, having received the returned check, it learned facts sufficient to enable it to give notice to Lufthansa. Inasmuch as the check was not returned until the 3:00 P.M. clearings on that day, it was received after closing and is therefore deemed to have been received on June 27. UCC 4-107. Lufthansa was notified not later than June 28 in compliance

1. Lufthansa suggests without citation of authority that the Bank might have been under a duty to make inquiries upon receipt of the notice of dishonor on June 21 so as to enable it to learn the necessary facts and give notice to its depositor promptly. The Commercial Code affords no basis for the imposition of such a duty and the Court is aware of no authority on the point.

with the midnight deadline under UCC 4-212, as well as within a reasonable time as prescribed by that section.

For the reasons stated defendant's motion for summary judgment must be granted and plaintiff's motion denied.[2]

NOTES & QUESTIONS

1. *Tracing the route of an item.* When faced with a check collection case you should trace with care the route the item has taken from the date of issue. Consider the following chronology of the check in the *Lufthansa* case. Does the court report sufficient facts so that you can verify compliance with the applicable rule on timely and proper action?

(a) June 15. Novo issues check payable to Lufthansa and drawn on First Pennsylvania Bank & Trust in Philadelphia (First). (Who receives the check and where is it delivered? Relevant?)

(b) June 16. Lufthansa indorses check and deposits it with Union Square branch of the Bank of America. Is Lufthansa under any time limit in the collection process? See UCC 3-304(3)(c) and 3-503(2)(a).

(c) June 16. Bank of America indorses the check and transfers it to the Federal Reserve Bank of San Francisco (FRB-SF). Timely? Under what provision?

(d) June 19. FRB in Philadelphia receives the check and transfers it to First. Did FRB-SF and FRB-Philadelphia act in a timely manner? Under what provision?

(e) June 21. First dishonors for insufficient funds and returns the check to FRB-Philadelphia. Did First act with sufficient promptness?

(f) June 21. FRB-Philadelphia telephones FRB-SF. What authority is there for telephone notice?

(g) June 21. FRB-SF telephones Bank of America's returned-item section. Proper?

(h) June 26. FRB-SF receives check and returns it after 3:00 P.M. to Bank of America's returned-item section. Did *both* Federal Reserve banks act with sufficient promptness?

(i) June 27 or 28. Bank of America notifies Lufthansa.

The *Lufthansa* case focuses on the timeliness of the last step, (i). What if a bank earlier in the collection cycle has not given timely or proper notice?

2. *Liability of Federal Reserve banks.* Regulation J provides that a Reserve Bank acts only as the sender's agent and not as agent or subagent of any other "owner or holder" of the item. The regulation then limits the Reserve Bank's liability as the sender's agent to cases where the bank lacks good faith or fails to exercise ordinary care. 12 C.F.R. §210.6(a)(1) (1984).

---

2. Regrettably the memoranda and arguments submitted by the Bank were of little help in the decision of this matter. The court would like to think that, especially in a matter such as this involving questions important to its operation, the Bank would have the resources, capability and desire to provide the court with more assistance than it did here.

Problem 16-1. Customer, payee of a check issued by Buyer, deposits the check with Bank. Bank credits Customer's account with the amount of the check and promptly forwards the check directly to Payor Bank. While the check is on its premises but before final payment Payor Bank becomes insolvent and the Federal Deposit Insurance Corporation takes over the bank. What should Customer do?

Problem 16-2. Payee deposits a check to his order in First Bank without indorsement. First Bank sends the check for collection but does not supply Payee's indorsement. In the meantime First Bank permits Payee to draw against the uncollected item. Drawer of the check stops payment because he alleges that Payee fraudulently induced him to enter into the underlying sales transaction. The check is returned unpaid to First Bank. What rights does First Bank have against Drawer and Payee?

Problem 16-3. Guarantor of loan from State Bank draws a check payable to Debtor with instructions that the check is to be used to liquidate the loan. In the presence of Guarantor, Debtor indorses the check "Pay Any Bank, Debtor." Before delivering the check to State Bank, Debtor cancels "Pay Any Bank" by crossing out the words. State Bank pays the proceeds of the check to Debtor. When the bank later demands payment of the loan Guarantor claims that State Bank has not complied with the restrictive indorsement. Evaluate Guarantor's claim. UCC 3-205, 3-208, 4-203.

Problem 16-4. Customer deposits with Second Bank three checks drawn to his order for $1,000, $2,000, and $3,000 respectively. Before these checks are finally paid Customer draws a check for $2,500, which Second Bank honors. If the check for $1,000 is not honored on presentment because the drawer claims he was induced to issue it by Customer's misrepresentations what rights does Second Bank have against the drawer of the check? Does it matter whether either of the other two checks has been paid? Does it matter whether Customer has drawn against the uncollected items as of right? Does it matter whether Customer has sufficient funds from other sources in his account to cover the amount of the dishonored check? UCC 4-208, 4-209.

Problem 16-5. Merchant deposits with National Bank a check payable to his order. National Bank gives Merchant provisional credit for the amount of the check and Merchant withdraws the full amount of the check. The check is dishonored and returned to National Bank. Without notifying Merchant, National Bank charges back the amount of the dishonored check against Merchant's account. Has National Bank acted properly? UCC 4-202, 4-212(1) and (4); see also 4-103(5). Would it make any difference if the deposit agreement stated "Customer is hereby given notice of and consents to the Bank's retention of the right to setoff, without any notice to Customer, mutual debts, and/or obligations of an ascertained amount by way of deduction of this account or by way of application of payments from this account"?

C. THE PAYOR BANK

The check collection process ends with presentment to the payor bank (the drawee). In the normal course of events the payor bank will promptly pay most checks. As we learned in the last chapter, however, a drawee is not obligated to pay the check until he accepts it. UCC 3-409. In the case of checks, acceptance takes the form of certification, usually by stamping a signed note of certification on the check, as was explained in Chapter 15 at p. 739 supra. A bank has no obligation to certify the check, however, unless it has agreed with its customer (the drawer) to do so. UCC 3-411. As a result, unless it certifies the check the payor bank will not be liable on the check if it should decide not to pay it. The bank may, of course, be liable to its customer on its bank-customer contract for not paying in accordance with the customer's order, but it will not be liable on the check.

A payor bank becomes accountable on final payment of a check. UCC 4-213(1) sets out four ways in which payment may become final:

(1) payment in cash;
(2) settlement without reserving the right to revoke settlement or without having the right to revoke under a statute, clearing house rule, or agreement;
(3) completion of the process of posting the item to the customer's account (UCC 4-109); and
(4) provisional settlement and failure to revoke in a manner permitted by statute (including UCC 4-301), clearing house rule, or agreement.

If the bank takes any of these steps it will be accountable for the face amount of the check. In the usual case, final payment automatically firms up provisional settlements between the collecting banks. A payor bank may, however, pay by a remittance instrument. UCC 4-211.

A payor bank also becomes accountable for the amount of the check when it fails to follow the procedures and time limits set out in UCC 4-301 and 4-302 for dishonoring the check.

The following cases explore these Code provisions.

KIRBY v. FIRST & MERCHANTS NATIONAL BANK

210 Va. 88, 168 S.E.2d 273, 6 UCC Rep. 694 (1969)

GORDON, Justice. On December 30, 1966, defendant Margaret Kirby handed the following check to a teller at a branch of plaintiff First & Merchants National Bank:

	Check
NEUSE ENG. AND DREDGING CO.	Number _____
	68–728
	514

12–29–1966

Pay to the
order of ___ William J. Kirby & Margaret Kirby ___ $ 2,500.00

___ Twenty-Five Hundred – – – – – – – – – – – – – – – – – ___ Dollars

FIRST & MERCHANTS
NATIONAL BANK
Virginia Beach, Virginia　　　NEUSE ENG. & DREDGING CO.
. . . 0514. . . 0728　　　　　　/s/　W. R. Wood

The back of the check bore the signatures of the payees, Mr. and Mrs. Kirby.

　　Mrs. Kirby, who also had an account with the Bank, gave the teller the following deposit ticket.[1]

The teller handed $200 in cash to Mrs. Kirby, and the Bank credited her account with $2,300 on the next business day, January 3, 1967. The teller or

---

1. The handwriting in the upper-left portion of the deposit ticket corresponds with Mrs. Kirby's handwriting on the back of the check. The record does not indicate what persons added the other handwritten information on the ticket. The symbol "68-728-514" [sic] designates a check drawn on First & Merchants by a depositor who has an account with a branch of that Bank in the Norfolk-Virginia Beach area. The word following the symbol is "partial."

another Bank employee made the notation "Cash for Dep." under Mr. and Mrs. Kirby's signatures on the back of the Neuse check.

On January 4 the Bank discovered that the Neuse check was drawn against insufficient funds. Instead of giving written notice, a Bank officer called Mr. and Mrs. Kirby on January 5 to advise that the Bank had dishonored the check and to request reimbursement. Mr. and Mrs. Kirby said they would come to the Bank to cover the check, but they did not. On January 10 the Bank charged Mrs. Kirby's account with $2,500, creating an overdraft of $543.47.

On January 18 the Bank instituted this action to recover $543.47 from Mr. and Mrs. Kirby. At the trial a Bank officer, the only witness in the case, testified:

> Q. Did you cash the check [the Neuse check for $2,500.00] before you credited this deposit [the deposit of $2,300 to Mrs. Kirby's account]?
> A. Yes, sir.
> Q. So the bank, in effect, cashed the check for $2,500.00 and then gave the defendant a credit of $2,300.00 to their [sic] account and gave them [sic] $200.00 in cash?
> A. Correct. . . .
> Q. So you cashed the check for $2,500.00?
> A. Yes, sir.

The trial court, sitting without a jury, entered judgment for the plaintiff First & Merchants, and the defendants Mr. and Mrs. Kirby appeal. The question is whether the Bank had the right to charge Mrs. Kirby's account with $2,500 on January 10 and to recover from Mr. and Mrs. Kirby the overdraft created by that charge ($543.47).

UCC 4-213 provides:

> (1) An item is finally paid by a payor bank when the bank has done any of the following, whichever happens first:
> (a) paid the item in cash. . . .

So if First & Merchants paid the Neuse check in cash on December 30, it then made final payment and could not sue Mr. or Mrs. Kirby on the check except for breach of warranty.[4]

---

4. As shown by the quotation in the text, UCC 4-213, which deals with bank deposits and collections, provides without qualification that a payor bank's payment of an item in cash is final. The Code recognizes, however, that a bank may recover a payment when a presenter's warranty is breached, e.g., when an indorsement is forged. UCC 3-417(1), 4-207(1). And under the established law before adoption of the Uniform Commercial Code, a bank could also recover a payment in case of fraud or bad faith on the part of the person receiving the payment. 3 Paton's Digest of Legal Opinions, Overdrafts §4:1 (1944). In this case there is no evidence of breach of a presenter's warranties or of fraud or bad faith.

Unlike UCC 4-213, UCC 3-418, which deals with commercial paper generally, implies that

When Mrs. Kirby presented the $2,500 Neuse check to the Bank on December 30, the Bank paid her $200 in cash and accepted a deposit of $2,300. The Bank officer said that the Bank cashed the check for $2,500, which could mean only that Mrs. Kirby deposited $2,300 in cash.

And the documentary evidence shows that cash was deposited. The deposit of cash is evidenced by the word "currency" before "2,300.00" on the deposit ticket and by the words "Cash for Dep." on the back of the check.[5] The Bank's ledger, which shows a credit of $2,300 to Mrs. Kirby's account rather than a credit of $2,500 and a debit of $200, is consistent with a cashing of the Neuse check and a depositing of part of the proceeds. We must conclude that First & Merchants paid the Neuse check in cash on December 30 and, therefore, had no right thereafter to charge Mrs. Kirby's account with the amount of the check.

The trial court apparently decided that Mr. and Mrs. Kirby were liable to the Bank because they had indorsed the Neuse check. But under UCC 3-414(1) an indorser contracts to pay an instrument only if the instrument is dishonored. And, as we have pointed out, the Bank did not dishonor the Neuse check, but paid the check in cash when Mrs. Kirby presented it.

As a practical matter, the contract of an indorser under UCC 3-414(1) does not run to a drawee bank. That contract can be enforced by a drawee bank only if it dishonors a check; and if the bank dishonors the check, it has suffered no loss.

The warranties that are applicable in this case are set forth in UCC 3-417(1) and 4-207(1): warranties made to a drawee bank by a presenter and prior transferors of a check. Those warranties are applicable because Mrs. Kirby presented the Neuse check to the Bank for payment. UCC 3-504(1); Bunn, Snead & Speidel, An Introduction to the Uniform Commercial Code §3.4(B) (1964). And those warranties do not include a warranty that the drawer of a check has sufficient funds on deposit to cover the check.

The rule that a drawee who mistakenly pays a check has recourse only against the drawer was firmly established before adoption of the Uniform Commercial Code:

"The drawer of a check, and not the holder who receives payment, is primarily responsible for the drawing out of funds from a bank. An overdraft is an act by reason of which the drawer and not the holder obtains money from the bank on his check. The holder therefore in the absence of fraud or express understanding for repayment, has no concern with the question whether the

---

payment of an instrument is final only in favor of a holder in due course or a person who has changed his position in reliance on the payment. First & Merchants neither relied on UCC 3-418, nor based its right to recover on an assertion that Mr. and Mrs. Kirby were not holders in due course and did not change their position. See UCC 3-307 and comment. Moreover, insofar as UCC 3-418 and 4-213 conflict, UCC 4-213 prevails. UCC 4-102(1).

5. Since no dollar amount was inserted after "checks" on the deposit ticket, the notation "6-28-728-514 [sic] partial" was apparently inserted to identify the source of the currency being deposited. See n.1 supra.

drawer has funds in the bank to meet the check. The bank is estopped, as against him, from claiming that by its acceptance an overdraft occurred. A mere mistake is not sufficient to enable it to recover from him. Banks cannot always guard against fraud, but can guard against mistakes.

"It is therefore the general rule, sustained by almost universal authority, that a payment in the ordinary course of business of a check by a bank on which it is drawn under the mistaken belief that the drawer has funds in the bank subject to check is not such a payment under a mistake of fact as will permit the bank to recover the money so paid from the recipient of such payment. To permit the bank to repudiate the payment would destroy the certainty which must pertain to commercial transactions if they are to remain useful to the business public. Otherwise no one would ever know when he can safely receive payment of a check." 7 Zollman, The Law of Banks and Banking §5062 (1936). See generally 3 Paton's Digest of Legal Opinions, Overdrafts §4 (1944).

Virginia followed the same rule. . . .

Nevertheless, First & Merchants contends that under the terms of its deposit contract with Mrs. Kirby, the settlement was provisional and therefore subject to revocation whether or not the Neuse check was paid in cash on December 30.[6] It contends that in this regard the deposit contract changes the rule set forth in the Uniform Commercial Code. But in providing that "all items are credited subject to final payment," the contract recognizes that settlement for an item is provisional only until the item is finally paid. Since the deposit contract does not change the applicable rule set forth in the Uniform Commercial Code, we do not decide whether a bank can provide by deposit contract that payment of a check in cash is provisional.

Even if the Bank's settlement for the Neuse check had been provisional, the Bank had the right to charge that item back to Mrs. Kirby's account only if it complied with UCC 4-212(3) and 4-301. Those sections authorize the revocation of a settlement if, before the "midnight deadline" [see UCC 4-

6. The depositor's contract provides: "Items received for deposit or collection are accepted on the following terms and conditions. *This bank acts only as depositor's collecting agent and assumes no responsibility beyond its exercise of due care. All items are credited subject to final payment and to receipt of proceeds of final payment in cash or solvent credits by this bank at its own office.* This bank may forward items to correspondents and shall not be liable for default or negligence of correspondents selected with due care nor for losses in transit, and each correspondent shall not be liable except for its own negligence. Items and their proceeds may be handled by any Federal Reserve bank in accordance with applicable Federal Reserve rules, and by this bank or any correspondent, in accordance with any common bank usage, with any practice or procedure that a Federal Reserve bank may use or permit another bank to use, or with any other lawful means. *This bank may charge back, at any time prior to midnight on its business day next following the day of receipt, any item drawn on this bank which is ascertained to be drawn against insufficient funds or otherwise not good or payable. An item received after this bank's regular afternoon closing hour shall be deemed received the next business day.*

"This bank reserves the right to post all deposits, including deposits of cash and of items drawn on it, not later than midnight of its next business day after their receipt at this office during regular banking hours, and shall not be liable for damages for nonpayment of any presented item resulting from the exercise of this right. . . ." (Italicized language is quoted in First & Merchants' brief.)

104(1)(h)], the bank "(a) returns the item; or (b) sends written notice of dishonor or nonpayment if the item is held for protest or is otherwise unavailable for return." UCC 4-301. The Bank concedes that it neither sent written notice of dishonor nor returned the Neuse check before the "midnight deadline." So the Bank had no right to charge the item back to Mrs. Kirby's account.

For the reasons set forth, the trial court erred in entering judgment for First & Merchants against Mr. and Mrs. Kirby.

HARRISON, Justice (dissenting). I dissent from the holding of the majority that the check involved here was "cashed." It is apparent that the check of Neuse Engineering and Dredging Company was "deposited" in normal course by Mrs. Kirby, and received and accepted for deposit by the Princess Anne Plaza Branch of the First and Merchants National Bank. The same bank official, quoted by the majority, also testified:

Q. Did Margaret Kirby or William Kirby bring you a check to deposit on December 29, 1966?
A. Yes, sir, they did.
Q. Tell what happened to this particular check.
A. We received it for deposit on Friday night, the 29th. We deposited $2,300 and gave back cash, $200. . . .

(Admittedly the correct date of the deposit was Friday, December 30, 1966.)

This witness, the only one who testified in the case, was Mr. Floyd E. Waterfield, Vice President of the bank. From his testimony we learn that late on the afternoon of December 30, 1966, Mrs. Kirby, a customer of the bank with an active checking account, came into the bank with the Neuse check. Apparently she desired $200 in cash. In making out the deposit slip, $2300 was erroneously written opposite the currency line instead of opposite the check line. However, indicated in writing on the face of the deposit slip is a notation that the deposit was evidenced by a check drawn on another of the bank's branches in the Norfolk-Virginia Beach area. Also on the face of the deposit slip is shown the manner in which Mrs. Kirby obtained the $200 she wanted, i.e. by deducting $200 from the $2500 check.

This was a perfectly normal and customary banking transaction. Mrs. Kirby, as a customer of that particular branch bank, presumably could have obtained $200 by writing her personal check, or by having the bank issue and she initial a debit memorandum or charge on her account, or by having the transaction reflected on the face of the deposit slip. She and the bank teller obviously pursued the latter course, and this was entirely in order. When the books of the bank were balanced for the day's operations, the bank had a $2500 check of Neuse, which was offset or balanced against a cash withdrawal of $200, plus a tentative or provisional credit of $2300 in the Kirby checking account.

There is nothing in this record from which it could possibly be deduced that Mrs. Kirby walked into the bank and cashed the Neuse check for $2500. That is, she presented the check and demanded and received $2500 in cash, and afterwards redeposited $2300 of it in currency. This simply did not occur, and the evidence does not reflect it. While the bank officer does refer to "cashing the check," the evidence and the records of the bank show that is was not cashed, but was accepted for deposit and clearance as any other check.

The fact that the bank permitted Mrs. Kirby to withdraw $200 is of no significance. She was a customer of the bank, with a checking account. Had the withdrawal, absent the Neuse deposit, caused an overdraft, this would not have been unusual for banks permit customers to overdraw from time to time in reasonable amounts. Furthermore, at that time neither Mrs. Kirby nor the bank had reason to anticipate that the Neuse check would be dishonored because of insufficient funds.

If the check was deposited and not cashed, the next question faced is to determine the obligation of the Princess Anne Plaza Branch of the bank when the Neuse check was dishonored and returned to it because of insufficient funds. Admittedly, there is a statutory duty on the part of a bank, occupying the position of the appellee here, to send notice of dishonor.

Appellee requires, as a condition or prerequisite for the opening of an account by a depositor, that such depositor sign the written contract set forth in a footnote of the opinion. This contract in essence expressly provides that the bank, in receiving items for deposit, acts only as the depositor's collecting agent, and that such items are credited subject to final payment.

The bank here was not dealing with a stranger. It was dealing with the Kirbys—customers of the bank—with whom they had a contractual arrangement. When the Neuse check was returned, the bank promptly communicated by telephone with the Kirbys and advised them of the return of the check. The Kirbys, with whom the bank enjoyed a professional and a semi-confidential relationship, and who had designated the bank as their collecting agent, promised "they would be in to cover." The bank relied upon the agreement, and the Kirbys' express representation, and withheld taking any action pending their arrival to attend to the transaction.

Normally the bank would have charged the Neuse check to the account of the Kirbys, attached a slip to it showing that it had been returned because of insufficient funds, and mailed to them. That would have completed the transaction insofar as the bank was concerned, and the Kirbys could have taken such action against Neuse as they felt proper. In the instant case the check was not returned for the reason that the bank had permitted the Kirbys to draw on their checking account in an amount which reduced their account below the sum of $2500. The Neuse check was the bank's evidence of the obligation and therefore it could not properly be surrendered.

The purpose of prompt notification to a customer that a check deposited by him has been dishonored is two-fold: (1) So that the customer payee of the check can take prompt action against the drawer to recover, and (2) So that the customer will not draw checks on his account under the impression that his deposit, as evidenced by a dishonored check, is good, and that he has funds in the amount of the check in the bank.

The statute (UCC 4-301) in dealing with the return to a bank of an item, such as a dishonored check, expressly recognizes the possibility of the bank's handling the check pursuant to the customer's instructions. Here the customer not only contracted in writing that the bank, in receiving checks for deposit, would act as collecting agent, but, upon notification that the Neuse check had been dishonored, agreed to come to the bank and take care of the overdrawn account.

This express promise to come to the bank and cover the overdraft, made upon receipt of notification of the check's dishonor, was justification of the bank's action in withholding formal written notice of the dishonor, pending their arrival.

Under the circumstances, I am of opinion that the Kirbys are estopped by the depositor's contract that they signed, and by their actions and dealings with the bank, from availing themselves of the provisions of UCC 4-212(3) and 4-301, requiring written notice.

I would affirm the judgment of the lower court.

NOTES & QUESTIONS

1. *Branch banks.* Is UCC 4-106 (Separate Office of a Bank) relevant in *Kirby?* This section provides:

> A branch or separate office of a bank [maintaining its own deposit ledgers] is a separate bank for the purpose of computing the time within which and determining the place at or to which action may be taken or notices or orders shall be given under this Article and under Article 3.

2. *Revoking provisional settlement.* If the bank in *Kirby* had not finally paid the check, could it have revoked the provisional settlement? See UCC 4-212, 4-301. What steps would it have to take to do so? Could the bank have revoked if the back of the deposit slip had stated: "items drawn on this bank, not good at close of business day on which they have been deposited, may be charged back to depositor?"

3. *Notice of dishonor.* After concluding that the bank had not finally paid the check, the dissenting judge in *Kirby* argued that the Kirbys were estopped from requiring the bank to give written notice of dishonor before it could charge back the amount of the item. Must the bank give written notice of dishonor? UCC 4-301(1) requires a payor bank to return the item or to send *written notice* in order to revoke a provisional settlement. UCC 4-212(1) requires a collecting bank to return the item or to send *notification* in order to

charge back a provisional settlement. See also UCC 1-201(38) (definition of *send*); 3-508(3) (notice of dishonor may be either oral or written); 4-104(3) (3-508 definition of notice of dishonor incorporated into Article 4); UCC 4-302(a) (payor bank accountable if it does not pay or return the item or send notice of dishonor by midnight deadline).

4. *Final payment: reconciling UCC 3-418 and 4-213.* The *Kirby* court suggests that UCC 4-213(1) may conflict with 3-418. See n.4 supra. Can the two sections be reconciled? If UCC 3-418 applies the Kirbys would have to show either that they were holders in due course or that they had changed their position in good faith in reliance on the payment. Would they have to make a similar showing under UCC 4-213? Does UCC 4-213 merely define when payment is final, leaving UCC 4-302 to state the consequences of final payment? See the last sentence of UCC 4-213(1).

BLAKE v. WOODFORD BANK & TRUST CO.
555 S.W.2d 589, 21 UCC Rep. 383 (Ky. Ct. App. 1977)

PARK, Judge. This case involves the liability of the appellee and cross-appellant, Woodford Bank and Trust Company, on two checks drawn on the Woodford Bank and Trust Company and payable to the order of the appellant and cross-appellee, Wayne Blake. Following a trial without a jury, the Woodford Circuit Court found that the bank was excused from meeting its "midnight deadline" with respect to the two checks. Blake appeals from the judgment of the circuit court dismissing his complaint. The bank cross-appeals from that portion of the circuit court's opinion relating to the extent of the bank's liability on the two checks if it should be determined that the bank was not excused from meeting its midnight deadline. . . .

The basic facts are not in dispute. On December 6, 1973, Blake deposited a check in the amount of $16,449.84 to his account at the Morristown Bank, of Morristown, Ohio. This check was payable to Blake's order and was drawn on the K & K Farm account at the Woodford Bank and Trust Company. The check was dated December 3, 1973.

On December 19, 1973, Blake deposited a second check in the amount of $11,200.00 to his account in the Morristown Bank. The second check was also drawn on the K & K Farm Account at the Woodford Bank and Trust Company and made payable to Blake's order. The second check was dated December 17, 1973. . . .

When Blake deposited the second check on December 19, he was informed by the Morristown Bank that the first check had been dishonored and returned because of insufficient funds. Blake instructed the Morristown Bank to re-present the first check along with the second check. Blake was a cattle trader, and the two checks represented the purchase price for cattle sold by Blake to James Knight who maintained the K & K Farm Account. Blake testified that he had been doing business with Knight for several years. On other occasions, checks had been returned for insufficient funds but had been paid when re-presented.

The two checks were forwarded for collection through the Cincinnati Branch of the Federal Reserve Bank of Cleveland. From the Federal Reserve Bank, the two checks were delivered to the Woodford Bank and Trust Company by means of the Purolator Courier Corp. The checks arrived at the Woodford Bank and Trust Company on Monday, December 24, 1973, shortly before the opening of the bank for business. The next day, Christmas, was not a banking day. The two checks were returned by the Woodford Bank and Trust Company to the Cincinnati Branch of the Federal Reserve Bank by means of Purolator on Thursday, December 27, 1973.

The two checks were received by the bank on Monday, December 24. The next banking day was Wednesday, December 26. Thus, the bank's "midnight deadline" was midnight on Wednesday, December 26. UCC 4-104(1)(h). As the bank retained the checks beyond its midnight deadline, Blake asserts that the bank is "accountable" for the amount of the two checks under UCC 4-302(a). . . .

Under the Uniform Negotiable Instruments Law a payor bank was not liable to the holder of a check drawn on the bank until the bank had accepted or certified the check. Ewing v. Citizens National Bank, 162 Ky. 551, 172 S.W. 955 (1915); W. Britton, Bills and Notes §169 (1943). Because of the payor bank's basic nonliability on a check, it was essential that some time limit be placed upon the right of the payor bank to dishonor a check when presented for payment. If a payor bank could hold a check indefinitely without incurring liability, the entire process of collection and payment of checks would be intolerably slow. To avoid this problem, a majority of courts construing §136 and §137 of the Uniform Negotiable Instruments Law held that a payor bank was deemed to have accepted a check if it held the check for 24 hours after the check was presented for payment. Britton, supra, at §179. Thus, in a majority of jurisdictions, the payor bank had only 24 hours to determine whether to pay a check or return it. However, in Kentucky and a few other jurisdictions, the courts held that §136 and §137 of the Uniform Negotiable Instruments Law applied only to checks which were presented for acceptance. In Kentucky Title Savings Bank & Trust Co. v. Dunavan, 205 Ky. 801, 266 S.W. 667 (1924), the Court of Appeals held that §136 and §137 of the Uniform Negotiable Instruments Law had no application to a check which was presented for payment. Consequently, the payor bank would be liable on the check only if it held the check "for an unreasonable length of time" and could thus be deemed to have converted the check.

In order to bring uniformity to the check collection process, the Bank Collection Code was proposed by the American Bankers' Association. The Bank Collection Code was adopted by Kentucky in 1930. Under §3 of the Bank Collection Code, a payor bank could give provisional credit when a check was received, and the credit could be revoked at any time before the end of that business day. The payor bank became liable on the check if it retained the item beyond the end of the business day received. . . .

Banks had only a few hours to determine whether a check should be returned because of insufficient funds. Banks were required to "dribble post checks" by sorting and sending the checks to the appropriate bookkeepers as the checks were received. This led to an uneven workload during the course of a business day. At times, the bookkeeping personnel might have nothing to do while at other times they would be required to process a very large number of checks in a very short time. H. Bailey, The Law of Bank Checks (Brady on Bank Checks) §10.4 (4th ed. 1969). Because of the increasingly large number of checks processed each day and the shortage of qualified bank personnel during World War II, it became impossible for banks to determine whether a check was "good" in only 24 hours. The banks were forced to resort to the procedure of "paying" for a check on the day it was presented without posting it to the customer's account until the following day. See First National Bank of Elmwood v. Universal C.I.T. Credit Corp. 132 Ind. App. 353, 170 N.E.2d 238, at 244 (1960). To meet this situation, the American Banking Association proposed a Model Deferred Posting Statute. The Model Deferred Posting Statute was not adopted in Kentucky until 1956. . . .

Under the Model Deferred Posting Statute, a payor bank could give provisional credit for a check on the business day it was received, and the credit could be revoked at any time before midnight of the bank's next business day following receipt. A provisional credit was revoked "by returning the item, or if the item is held for protest or at the time is lost or is not in the possession of the bank, by giving written notice of dishonor, nonpayment, or revocation; provided that such item or notice is dispatched in the mails or by other expeditious means not later than midnight of the bank's next business day after the item was received." [Model Statute §1(1).] If the payor bank failed to take advantage of the provisions of the deferred posting statute by revoking the provisional credit and returning the check within the time and in the manner provided by the act, the payor bank was deemed to have paid the check and was liable thereon to the holder. First National Bank of Elmwood v. Universal C.I.T. Credit Corp., supra.

The Model Deferred Posting Statute was the basis for the provisions of the Uniform Commercial Code. Under UCC 4-301(1), a payor bank may revoke a provisional "settlement" if it does so before its "midnight deadline" which is midnight of the next banking day following the banking day on which it received the check. Under the Model Deferred Posting Statute, the payor bank's liability for failing to meet its midnight deadline was to be inferred rather than being spelled out in the statute. Under UCC 4-302, the payor bank's liability for missing its midnight deadline is explicit. If the payor bank misses its midnight deadline, the bank is "accountable" for the face amount of the check. . . .

Like the Model Deferred Posting Statute, the Uniform Commercial Code seeks to decrease, rather than increase, the risk of liability to payor banks. By permitting deferred posting, the Uniform Commercial Code extends the time within which a payor bank must determine whether it will pay a check drawn on the bank. Unlike the Bank Collection Code or the Uniform Negotiable Instruments Code as construed by most courts, the Uniform Commercial Code does not require the payor bank to act on the day of receipt or within 24 hours of receipt of a check. The payor bank is granted until midnight of the next business day following the business day on which it received the check.

EXCUSE FOR FAILING TO MEET MIDNIGHT DEADLINE

UCC 4-108(2) provides:

> Delay by a . . . payor bank beyond time limits prescribed or permitted by this Act . . . is excused if caused by interruption of communications facilities, suspension of payments by another bank, war, emergency conditions or other circumstances beyond the control of the bank provided it exercises such diligence as the circumstances require.

The circuit court found that the bank's failure to return the two checks by its midnight deadline was excused under the provisions of UCC 4-108. . . .

[The court then summarizes Sun River Cattle Co. v. Miners Bank of Montana, 164 Mont. 237, 521 P.2d 679, 14 UCC Rep. 1004 (1974) (breakdown of armored car and computer malfunction not excused under UCC 4-108) and Port City State Bank v. American National Bank, 486 F.2d 196, 13 UCC Rep. 423 (10th Cir. 1973) (new computer malfunction an excuse under UCC 4-108).]

The facts in this case will be examined in light of the principles set out in the foregoing cases. The basic facts found by the circuit court can be summarized as follows: a) the bank had no intention of holding the checks beyond the midnight deadline in order to accommodate its customer; b) there was an increased volume of checks to be handled by reason of the Christmas Holiday; c) two posting machines were broken down for a period of time on December 26; d) one regular bookkeeper was absent because of illness. Standing alone, the bank's intention not to favor its customer by retaining an item beyond the midnight deadline would not justify the application of UCC 4-108(2). The application of the exemption statute necessarily will turn upon the findings relating to heavy volume, machine breakdown, and absence of a bookkeeper.

The bank's president testified that 4,200 to 4,600 checks were processed on a normal day. Because the bank was closed for Christmas on Tuesday, the bank was required to process 6,995 checks on December 26. The bank had four posting machines. On the morning of December 26, two of the machines were temporarily inoperable. One of the machines required two and a half hours to repair. The second machine was repaired in one and one half hours. As the bank had four bookkeepers, the machine breakdown required the bookkeepers to take turns using the posting machines for a time in the morning. One of the four bookkeepers who regularly operated the posting machines was absent because of illness on December 26. This bookkeeper was replaced by the head bookkeeper who had experience on the posting machines, although he was not as proficient as a regular posting machine operator.

Because of the cumulative effect of the heavy volume, machine breakdown and absence of a regular bookkeeper, the bank claims it was unable to process the two checks in time to deliver them to the courier from Purolator for return to the Federal Reserve Bank on December 26. As the bank's president testified: "Because we couldn't get them ready for the Purolator carrier to pick them up by 4:00 and we tried to get all our work down there to him by 4:00, for him to pick up and these two checks were still being processed in our bookkeeping department and it was impossible for those to get into returns for that day." The validity of this claim must be considered in light of the testimony of the bank's bookkeeper who processed the two checks.

Betty Stratton was the regular bookkeeper who posted all of the accounts from "D" through "K," and she processed the two checks in question on December 26. While two posting machines were being repaired, Mrs. Stratton shared her posting machine with Garnetta Bunch, another regular bookkeeper and posting machine operator. Since the substitute bookkeeper was not processing the two checks in question and was not sharing a posting machine with Mrs. Stratton, it is difficult to see how the absence of one of the regular bookkeepers could have delayed the posting of the two checks in question.

Mrs. Stratton testified that she did not complete the posting of all the checks in the "H" through "K" accounts until after 4:00. Had it not been for the extra volume of checks to be handled and the breakdown in the posting machines, she should have completed the process of posting by 12:30 P.M. In accordance with her operating instructions, Mrs. Stratton took the two checks to Susan Williams, the bank employee with the duty of handling any checks which were to be returned because of insufficient funds. Because of the lateness of the hour, Ms. Williams and all responsible officers of the bank had left for the day. Mrs. Stratton left the two checks on Ms. Williams desk. . . . The two checks were returned to the Cincinnati branch of the Federal Reserve Bank by the regular Purolator courier on Thursday afternoon, December 27.

The increased volume of items to be processed the day after Christmas was clearly foreseeable. The breakdown of the posting machines was not an unusual occurrence, although it was unusual to have two machines broken down at the same time. In any event, it should have been foreseeable to the responsible officers of the bank that the bookkeepers would be delayed in completing posting of the checks on December 26. Nevertheless, the undisputed evidence establishes that no arrangements of any kind were made for return of "bad" items which might be discovered by the bookkeepers after the departure of the Purolator courier. The two checks in question were in fact determined by Mrs. Stratton to be "bad" on December 26. The checks were not returned because the regular employee responsible for handling "bad" checks had left for the day, and Mrs. Stratton had no instructions to cover the situation.

Even though the bank missed returning the two checks by the Purolator courier, it was still possible for the bank to have returned the checks by its midnight deadline. Under UCC 4-301(4)(b) an item is returned when it is "sent" to the bank's transferor, in this case the Federal Reserve Bank. Under UCC 1-201(38) an item is "sent" when it is deposited in the mail. 1 R. Anderson, Uniform Commercial Code §1-201, at 118-119 (2d ed. 1970). Thus, the bank could have returned the two checks before the midnight deadline by the simple procedure of depositing the two checks in the mail, properly addressed to the Cincinnati branch of the Federal Reserve Bank.

This court concludes that circumstances beyond the control of the bank did not prevent it from returning the two checks in question before its midnight deadline on December 26. . . . The circuit court erred in holding that the bank was excused under UCC 4-108 from meeting its midnight deadline. . . .

RE-PRESENTMENT OF CHECK PREVIOUSLY DISHONORED BY NONPAYMENT

On its cross-appeal, the bank argues that the circuit court erred in holding that there was no difference in the status of the two checks. The bank makes the argument that it is not liable on the first check which had previously been dishonored by nonpayment. Blake received notice of dishonor when the first check was returned because of insufficient funds. The bank claims that it was under no further duty to meet the midnight deadline when the check was re-presented for payment.

The bank relies upon the decision of the Kansas Supreme Court in Leaderbrand v. Central State Bank, 202 Kan. 450, 450 P.2d 1, 6 UCC Rep. 172 (1969). A check drawn on the Central State Bank was presented for payment on two occasions over the counter. On both occasions, the holder of the check was advised orally that there were not sufficient funds in the account to honor the check. Later, the holder deposited the check in his own account at the First State Bank. The First State Bank did not send the check through regular bank collection channels, but rather mailed the check directly to the Central State Bank for purposes of collection. The check arrived at the Central State Bank on March 21 or March 22, and the check was not returned by the Central State Bank to the First State Bank until April 5. The Kansas Supreme Court held that there was no liability under UCC 4-302 for a check which had previously been dishonored when presented for payment.

. . . The Kansas Supreme Court specifically held that UCC 3-511(4) applied to a check which was dishonored when presented for payment, stating: "While the language of [UCC 3-511(4)]—'Where a draft has been dishonored by nonacceptance'—does not refer to a dishonor by nonpayment, we think reference to the dishonor of a 'draft' 'by nonacceptance' would, a fortiori, include the dishonor of a check by nonpayment." The Kansas Supreme Court concluded that a payor bank was excused from giving any further notice of dishonor when a previously dishonored check was re-presented for payment and there were still insufficient funds in the drawer's account to cover the check. . . .

The decision of the Kansas Supreme Court in the *Leaderbrand* case has been criticized. As UCC 3-511(4) applies by its terms to a "draft" which has been "dishonored by nonacceptance," most of the criticism has been directed to the Kansas court's application of UCC 3-511(4) to a check which had been dishonored by nonpayment. As stated in B. Clark & A. Squillante, The Law of Bank Deposits, Collections and Credit Cards 71-72 (1970): "Use of this section to excuse retention under §4-302 seems questionable, since the draftsmen are saying nothing more than dishonor by nonacceptance excuses notice of dishonor by nonpayment. If a time draft is not accepted, it is a useless act to present it for payment. On the other hand, sending a check through a second or third time often yields results, since the depositor may have had time to make a deposit to his account. It is presumably for this reason that the Code draftsmen limited the excuse rule of §3-511(4) to 'nonacceptance' of 'drafts' and did not by express language indicate 'nonpayment' of 'checks.' " . . .

Two courts have refused to follow the *Leaderbrand* decision. [The court summarizes Wiley, Tate & Irby v. Peoples Bank & Trust Co., 438 F.2d 513, 8 UCC Rep. 887 (5th Cir. 1971) (UCC 3-511(4) does not apply to demand items, such as checks) and Sun River Cattle Co. v. Miners Bank of Montana, supra (follows *Wiley*). The court also notes that the pre-Code case of Kentucky Title Savings Bank & Trust Co. v. Dunavan, supra, is consistent with this reading of UCC 3-511(4).] Thus, there are ample grounds for rejecting the *Leaderbrand* opinion based upon the technical language of UCC 3-511(4). However, there are more fundamental reasons why the *Leaderbrand* decision is unsound and should not be followed in Kentucky.

The *Leaderbrand* decision is based upon the assumption that the sanctions of UCC 4-302 are applied to a failure to give timely notice of dishonor. This assumption may appear reasonable from an initial reading of UCC 4-302(a). Under that section, a payor bank is accountable for a check if it "does not pay or return the item or send notice of dishonor until after its midnight deadline." If a payor bank were excused from giving notice of dishonor, it would be plausible to argue that it was not accountable under UCC 4-302. However, this reasoning ignores the primary purpose of notice of dishonor, and it completely ignores the language of UCC 4-301.

Prior to the time that he received the first check, Blake had a contractual claim for the purchase price of the cattle. When Blake took the first check, his claim for the purchase price of the cattle was not discharged, but that claim was "suspended pro tanto" until Blake presented the check for payment. See UCC 3-802(1)(b). Furthermore, at the moment he took the check, Blake had no claim against Knight on the check itself. As drawer of the check, Knight was a "secondary party." UCC 3-102(1)(d). As a secondary party, Knight was not liable on the first check until Blake had presented the check for payment and notice of dishonor had been given. See UCC 3-501(1)(c) and (2)(b). The first check was dishonored when it was returned in a timely manner for insufficient funds. See UCC 3-507(1)(a). As soon as the first check was dishonored, Blake had a right to maintain an action on the check itself or on the underlying contract for the cattle. See UCC 3-802(1)(b); Clark & Squillante, supra, at 17. When Blake presented the check for payment, there was no need for a further notice of dishonor in order to revive the underlying contract or to make Knight liable on the check.

Even if it was unnecessary to give further notice of dishonor when the check was re-presented for payment in order to make Knight liable on the check and to revive the underlying contract, it does not follow that the bank was relieved of its obligation to meet the midnight deadline. Most opinions and commentaries have focused on UCC 4-302 which only defines the extent of the payor bank's liability for failure to meet its deadline. Whether a payor bank has met its midnight deadline for return of an item is determined by UCC 4-301, not 4-302. Under 4-301(1), a payor bank may "revoke" a provisional settlement if, before its midnight deadline, the payor bank complies with the following requirements:

(a) returns the item; or
(b) sends written notice of dishonor or nonpayment if the item is held for protest or is otherwise unavailable for return.

Written notice of dishonor is a permitted method of revoking a provisional settlement *only* if the check is unavailable for return or it is being held for protest. Otherwise, the check itself must be returned.

The relationship of UCC 4-301 and 4-302 was clearly demonstrated by the unusual facts presented in United States v. Loskocinski, 403 F. Supp. 75, 18 UCC Rep. 461 (E.D.N.Y. 1975). In the course of an armed robbery of the National Bank of North America, eleven blank cashier's checks were stolen. After forging the bank officer's signature and completing the check in the approximate sum of $99,000.00, one of the stolen checks was presented for payment to the bank by a distant bank to which it had been negotiated. The payor bank dishonored and returned this check by its midnight deadline. In the course of investigating the armed robbery, a grand jury subpoena duces tecum was served upon the bank directing it to turn over any other stolen checks which might be presented. The bank moved to quash the subpoena on the grounds that its failure to return the checks as required by UCC 4-301 would expose it to staggering liability under UCC 4-302. In support of the subpoena, the government argued that the bank could avoid liability under UCC 4-302 by giving written notice of dishonor rather than returning the checks themselves. The United States District Court for the Eastern District of New York granted the bank's motion to quash the subpoena. The district court held that the bank was under a duty to return the checks themselves unless the checks were being held for protest or were "otherwise unavailable for return." Because of the district court's doubt whether, as a matter of New York state law, the subpoena would make the checks "otherwise unavailable for return," the court held that the bank could refuse to honor the subpoena so that the checks themselves could be returned.

In the present case, both checks were available to the bank for return. Neither check was being held for protest. Consequently, the only way the bank could revoke its provisional settlement for the check was by returning the check before its midnight deadline. As notice of dishonor was not available as a means of revoking the provisional settlement, the provisions of UCC 3-511(4) excusing notice of dishonor could have no application to the case.

A practical reason also exists for rejecting the *Leaderbrand* decision. In 1972, approximately 25 billion checks passed through the bank collection process. The Federal Reserve Banks handled 8 billion checks that year. . . . An earlier study indicated that only one half of one percent of all checks were dishonored when first presented for payment. Of those initially dishonored, approximately one half were paid upon re-presentment. Leary, Check Handling Under Article Four of the Uniform Commercial Code, 49 Marq. L. Rev. 331, 333 n.7 (1965). A significant number of previously dishonored checks are paid upon re-presentment in the regular course of the check collection process. Such checks are often presented through intermediate collecting banks, such as the Federal Reserve Bank in this case. Each collecting bank will have made a provisional settlement from the bank to which it forwarded the check. In this way, a series of provisional settlements are made as the check proceeds through the bank collection process.

Under UCC 4-213(2), final payment of a check "firms up" all of the provisional settlements made in the collection process. Under UCC 4-213(1)(d), a payor bank makes final payment of a check when it fails to revoke a provisional settlement "in the time and manner permitted by statute, clearing house rule or agreement." As to items not presented over the counter or by local clearing house, this means that a payor bank is deemed to have made final payment of a check when it fails to revoke a provisional settlement by its midnight deadline. See UCC 4-213, Official Code Comment 6. In his article on check handling, Leary has described UCC 4-213 as the "zinger" section: "when provisional credit given by the payor bank becomes firm then— 'zing'—all prior provisional credits are instantaneously made firm." Leary, supra, at 361. If a payor bank was not required to meet its midnight deadline with respect to previously dishonored items, then none of the other banks involved in the collection process could safely assume that the check had been paid. Consider the problems of the depository bank. It must permit its customer to withdraw the amount of the credit given for the check when provisional settlements have become final by payment and the bank has had "a reasonable time" to learn that the settlement is final. See UCC 4-213(4)(a). The depository bank will rarely receive notice that an item has been paid. In actual practice, the depository bank will utilize availability schedules to compute when it should receive the check if it is to be returned unpaid. Leary, supra, at 345-346. If a payor bank is not bound by its midnight deadline as to previously dishonored items, then there is no way for the depository bank to know whether a previously dishonored item has been paid upon re-presentment except by direct communication with the payor bank. Such a procedure would impose an unnecessary burden upon the check collection process.

This court concludes that the circuit court was correct in holding that there was no difference in the status of the two checks.

MEASURE OF LIABILITY

The bank contends that its liability should be determined under UCC 4-103(5). The general measure of damages for failure to exercise ordinary care in handling a check in the collection process is the face amount of the check less any sum which could not have been realized even by the exercise of ordinary care. As there was never more than $1,853.32 in the K & K Farm Account at any time after December 11, 1973, the bank claims that Blake can show no actual damage resulting from the one day delay in returning the two checks. This argument ignores the fact that a payor bank is liable for the face amount of the check under UCC 4-302 when it delays returning a check beyond its midnight deadline. . . . The bank's liability for the face amount of the check is not based upon its failure to exercise ordinary care. By delaying return of the check beyond its midnight deadline, the bank is deemed to have paid the check. Having paid the check, it is therefore accountable for the face amount of the check. See UCC 4-213(1). Damages have no relevance to the concept of accountability.

There is a rational basis for imposing a different liability on payor banks than is imposed upon collecting banks. The payor bank is the only bank in the collection process in a position to know the actual state of the drawer's account, and it is the only bank in the collection process that can actually pay the check.

Deferred posting was authorized by the Bank Collection Article of the Uniform Commercial Code, and by its predecessor, the Model Deferred Posting Statute, in order to grant payor banks additional time within which to determine whether to pay a check presented for collection. If banks are no longer able to meet their midnight deadline because of new banking conditions, then the remedy of the banks is to be found in the legislature. The present statute is intended to provide a mechanical standard of easy application for determining the time of payment of checks and the liability of payor banks. Having in mind the need for prompt settlement of items in the collection process, this court is not at liberty to tinker with the present statute by judicial amendment.

When a payor bank has paid a check by failing to return the check by its midnight deadline, the bank may be entitled to relief under UCC 3-418.

Under the statute, payment of a check is final only in favor of a holder in due course or a person who has in good faith changed his position in reliance on the payment. As explained in the official comment: "If no value has been given for the instrument the holder loses nothing by the recovery of payment . . . and is not entitled to profit at the expense of the drawee; . . . If he has taken the instrument in bad faith or with notice he has no equities as against the drawee." Comment 3, Official Code Comment, UCC 3-418. In their commentary on UCC 3-418, Clark and Squillante state: "For example, if a drawee bank pays a check and then realizes that the drawer has insufficient funds in his account, that mistake is irreversible as against a holder in due course or a person who has relied on the payment. Does this mean that payment by mistake is final in favor of the original payee of a check who deposited it for collection and did not negotiate it to a holder in due course? The Code provides that the payee may himself be a holder in due course. §3-302(2). Therefore, if a payee gave value for the check and was without notice of any defense which might have been asserted by the drawer, the drawee bank is stuck. Conversely, if the payee is not a holder in due course, payment might be reversed since the payee could probably not show that he 'has in good faith changed his position in reliance on the payment.' " Clark & Squillante, supra, at 218. Neither party relies upon UCC 3-418, and there is no evidence in the record that Blake was not a holder in due course at the time he took the checks from Knight.

The bank also contends that UCC 4-302 is unconstitutional because of the different liability imposed upon payor banks and collecting banks. The record establishes that the attorney general was not notified that the constitutionality of the statute was being questioned. CR 24.03; KRS 418.075. Therefore, this court will not consider the issue. . . .

The judgment of the circuit court on the appeal is reversed with directions to enter judgment in favor of Blake for the face amount of the two checks, less a credit for any amounts which Blake may have recovered from Knight. The judgment on the cross-appeal is affirmed.

NOTES & QUESTIONS

1. *Excuse (UCC 4-108).* In Sun River Cattle Co. v. Miners Bank of Montana, 164 Mont. 237, 521 P.2d 679, 14 UCC Rep. 1004 (1974) the court rejected a payor bank's claimed excuse that it had followed ordinary operating procedures and that the delay in return of an item was caused by the breakdown of an armored truck and the subsequent malfunctioning of the computer at a check sorting center some distance from the bank. To establish an excuse under UCC 4-108(2) the court stated that the bank must show (1) a cause for the delay; (2) the cause was beyond the bank's control; and (3) the bank exercised the diligence required under the circumstances. Not having established an excuse in this case the payor bank was therefore accountable under

UCC 4-302 for the delay in settling for the item. The court suggested that it would be possible to alter the strict accountability of the payor bank by agreement, citing UCC 4-103, but noted that no such agreement was involved in this case.

2. *Liability.* In Colorado National Bank v. First National Bank & Trust Co., 459 F. Supp. 1366, 27 UCC Rep. 176 (W.D. Mich. 1978) the court held that noncompliance with a Federal Reserve Bank operating circular that required a payor bank to give notice of dishonor by wire should be treated as a failure to exercise ordinary care rather than as a failure to revoke provisional settlement in a timely fashion. As a result the payor bank—which had returned the item within its midnight deadline—was responsible only for the damages caused by its negligence and was not accountable for the item under UCC 4-213(1), 4-302. Note, however, that the bank had returned the checks through the mail before its midnight deadline.

3. *Constitutionality.* In Rock Island Auction Sales v. Empire Packing Co., 32 Ill. 2d 269, 204 N.E.2d 721, 2 UCC Rep. 319 (1965) the court held that the different measures of liability imposed on payor banks and collecting banks did not violate the equal protection clause of the United States Constitution. "Depositary and collecting banks act primarily as conduits. The steps that they take can only indirectly affect the determination of whether or not a check is to be paid, which is the focal point in the collection process. The legislature could have concluded that the failure of such a bank to meet its deadline would most frequently be the result of negligence, and fixed liability accordingly. The role of a payor bank in the collection process, on the other hand, is crucial. It knows whether or not the drawer has funds available to pay the item. The legislature could have considered that the failure of such a bank to meet its deadline is likely to be due to factors other than negligence, and that the relationship between a payor bank and its customer may so influence its conduct as to cause a conscious disregard of its statutory duty. The present case is illustrative. The defendant, in its position as a payor bank, deliberately aligned itself with its customer in order to protect that customer's credit and consciously disregarded the duty imposed upon it." 204 N.E.2d at 723, 2 UCC Rep. at 322.

Problem 16-6. Bank Leumi, the depositary bank, sends a check for collection. Jersey Bank, the payor bank, returns the check upaid because there are insufficient funds in the drawer's account. Bank Leumi sends the check through the collection system a second time. In preparing the check for representment, however, the bookkeeper makes an error when she encodes the MICR number showing the amount for which the check was drawn. The bookkeeper then corrects the error by pencil. When it receives the check on Friday, October 20, Jersey Bank decides that it will have to handle the check by hand rather than send it through its high-speed computer system. Jersey bank processes the check on Monday, October 23, and returns the check unpaid the following day because there still are insufficient funds in the account. Bank Leumi requests your advice as to whether it may hold Jersey Bank accountable for the amount of the returned check. Advise the bank.

WEST SIDE BANK v. MARINE NATIONAL EXCHANGE BANK
37 Wis. 2d 661, 155 N.W.2d 587, 4 UCC Rep. 1003 (1968)

The plaintiff (appellant herein), West Side Bank (hereinafter referred to as West Side), claims that Marine National Exchange Bank (hereinafter Marine) had made "final payment" on a check that West Side had presented to Marine and that, hence, it could no longer honor its customer's (the maker's) stop-payment order, but was accountable to West Side for the amount of the check. West Side has appealed from an order denying its motion for summary judgment.

The facts giving rise to this action are these: On Thursday, August 11, 1966, the stock brokerage firm of Paine, Webber, Jackson & Curtis (hereinafter Paine, Webber) issued a check in the amount of $262,600 drawn on Marine to one Byron Swidler. The same day Swidler deposited this check to his account at West Side. On Friday morning, West Side, through the Milwaukee clearing house, presented the check to Marine for payment. On Friday evening, Marine commenced the process of posting by sending the check (with others) through sorting and encoding machines and through the electronic computer.

As a part of the computer process, the account of the customer was charged with the item and a "paid" stamp affixed to the check. Had the conditions of the customer's account at the time of the computer run warranted it, the computer would have prepared and printed an unposted or no-account report, an overdraft report, an uncollected-funds report, or a large-item report.

The item, being for more than $500, appeared on the large-item report, but since the Paine, Webber account was not deficient in any respect, the result of the computer run was to charge the item to the customer and to stamp it "paid." On the morning of Monday, August 15, 1966, the report of the computer was submitted to the bookkeeper; and since the computer run revealed no deficiencies, and was not rejected by the computer, the item was photographed, cancelled, and filed in the Paine, Webber account. West Side contends that at this point Marine completed the "process of posting" and made "final payment," shifting responsibility for the item from the maker to the payor bank. Thereafter, at about 4:00 P.M. on Monday, August 15, Marine discovered and informed Paine, Webber that a check drawn by Swidler in the amount of $270,000 payable to Paine, Webber had been dishonored as an NSF check. Thereupon, Paine, Webber stopped payment of the check for $262,600 payable to Swidler. Upon the receipt of the stop-payment order, Marine withdrew the item from the Paine, Webber file and notified West Side that the check was being returned because of the stop-payment order. The check entries were reversed in the computer run Monday night by crediting Paine, Webber and stamping the check "payment stopped" and "cancelled in error." The check was returned to West Side at the morning exchange of the clearing house on Tuesday, August 16, 1966.

West Side's suit is brought upon the theory that the Uniform Commercial Code, which became effective in Wisconsin on July 1, 1965, provides that an item is finally paid by a payor bank and the bank is accountable therefore when it has "completed the process of posting the item to the indicated account of the drawer, maker or other person to be charged therewith." UCC 4-213(1)(c). The Trial Judge concluded that final payment had not been made and denied the motion of West Side for summary judgment.

HEFFERNAN, Justice. . . . The Uniform Commercial Code provides that, upon final payment, the payor bank shall become accountable for the amount of the item (UCC 4-213(1)(a)). Insofar as UCC 4-213 is relevant to this case it provides that an item is finally paid when the bank has "completed the process of posting the item to the indicated account of the drawer, maker or other person to be charged therewith" (UCC 4-213(1)(c)).

The "process of posting" is defined in UCC 4-109:

> The "process of posting" means the usual procedure followed by a payor bank in determining to pay an item and in recording the payment including one or more of the following or other steps as determined by the bank:
>
> (a) verification of any signature;
> (b) ascertaining that sufficient funds are available;
> (c) affixing a "paid" or other stamp;
> (d) entering a charge or entry to a customer's account;
> (e) correcting or reversing an entry or erroneous action with respect to the item.

It is upon this statute that the appellant primarily relies. It contends that the "process of posting" was completed when Marine decided to pay the item as was evinced by verification of the signature, ascertainment that there were sufficient funds to the credit of the drawer's account, charging of the account, stamping the check "paid" or "cancelled," and filing the check with the customer's file as a voucher to be returned to him. It is clear that all of these steps were carried out by Marine and that they constituted the performance of at least the first four of the steps required in the process of posting.

Marine, however, contends that until the fifth step, "correcting or reversing an entry or erroneous action with respect to the item," is considered and determined, either affirmatively or negatively, the process of posting is not completed. Marine contends that it may defer this decision until the last possible time that will allow it to make a return of the item; and only (in the absence of some other unequivocal conduct) upon its decision not to reverse the entries or upon its failure to make a timely return of the item is there final payment.

West Side contends that Marine's interpretation would minimize the effect of UCC 4-213(1)(c), and would almost completely negate the possibility of using completion of the "process of posting" as the benchmark for determining final payment. Marine's argument in essence is that, so long as time remains in which entries can be reversed (until the clearing-house deadline), a check is not finally paid under the Code. Marine contends, and the trial court agreed, that UCC 4-109(e) permitting the payor bank to reverse any entry, whether the original entry was correct or erroneous. West Side contends that this subsection permits only the correction of an error or the reversal of erroneous action.

It would appear whatever rationaliae [sic] may be offered to the contrary, and they are numerous, reason must yield to the plain meaning of the statute. No limitation is set forth in the legislation. The phrase the legislature used was "reversing an entry." Only by the most strained interpretation is it possible to glean from the face of the statute the inference that the entry must have been made in error. While the legislative intent may have been otherwise, and there is evidence that some authors prominent in the preparation of the Code concluded that only erroneous entries were intended, yet it is not within the province of this Court to seek secondary sources of legislative intent where the meaning of the statute is plain and unambiguous.

Persuasive argument for West Side's position is found in 38 Ind. L.J. 693, 717 (1962-1963), wherein the interpretation urged by Marine is discussed:

"Subsections (a), (b) and (c) set out points of time which are somewhat earlier than what has normally been considered the 'process of posting,' whereas subsection (d) is the action which has normally been held to constitute the vital determining factor. Without the detailed definition of section 4-109, subsection (d) would stand as the relevant activity of the payor for accountability under section 4-213(1)(c), however, subsection (e) of 4-109 broadens the definition of the 'process of posting' to make it almost meaningless. A payor bank, it appears, is now able to reverse an entry which was previously considered final. In other words, the payor bank can perform one of the vital steps in (a), (b), (c) or (d) and it would not be accountable since, by the plain meaning of subsection (e), it can correct or reverse an entry as it sees fit.

"Why such extreme latitude is permitted after the Code has gone to great lengths to set out a precise point of time for payor accountability is difficult to comprehend. Perhaps, in the desire to be consistent, this subsection should be read narrowly to apply *only* to erroneous entries. If it can be limited to mechanical errors of the entry, then the preciseness of section 4-213(1) will not be lost. If it is not narrowed to this point, however, the payor bank would be able to charge the account of the drawer and later reverse this charge, contending the initial entry was erroneous, since it did not realize that the drawer had insufficient funds.

"It is thus seen that the plain meaning of section 4-109 would destroy the effect of section 4-213(1)(c) and negate the effect of the Code for consistency in each section where final payment is a consideration. Perhaps, if litigation should arise under any of the final payment sections, the narrow construction would appeal to the court, but until such a time a result of such litigation is unpredictable. If limitation and clarification is not possible, the only alternative would seem to be repeal of subsection (e)."

We can only echo the sentiments expressed in the commentator's last sentence. If the interpretation that is urged by Marine, which we accept, fails to comport with the intent of the framers of the Code, there must be a resort to legislative clarification. We cannot, however reasonable West Side's argument might be, conclude that the interpretation of the trial court constitutes a deviation from the intent of the framers of the Code.

Fairfax Leary, Jr., formerly the reporter for Article 4 of the Code, writing in 49 Marq. L. Rev. 331 (1965-1966), pointed out that the "process of posting" is a combination of two diverse elements—one is the element of judgment in determining whether or not payment should be made and the other is the mechanical element of recording the item. The oral arguments of both parties to this appeal and the affidavits in support and in opposition to the motion make it clear that the computer merely records the information fed into it and only after the computerized facts are sorted and recorded do the officers and employees of the bank apply the judgment factors that culminate in the decision to pay.

The Leary article, considering the pre-judgment recording by the computer, stresses the need for the maximum time for the correction of entries and argues that this procedure is an integral part of the "process of posting." He states at page 360:

"And so one of the included steps in the process of posting includes the correction of errors and the reversal of entries. It would seem to follow, then, that the subdivision of Section 4-213(1) based on 'completion of the process of posting' would not be satisfied, until the time within which entries could be reversed had expired. So long as time remains in which entries could be reversed, it would, in view of the enumeration of 'reversal of entries' as one of the steps included in the 'process of posting,' be difficult for a court to say that the 'process of posting,' had been completed. Normally, in the non-clearings-cash-letter-for-credit-in-an-account situation this means that the process of posting is not completed until the expiration of the midnight deadline where the bank is working three shifts in its processing of checks, otherwise at the close of operations next preceding the midnight deadline."

We conclude, rejecting the constricted meaning of UCC 4-109(e) urged by the appellant, that the plain meaning of the statute permits the reversal of entries for any reason whatsoever (subject to the good-faith provisions of the Code) if made within the time limited for return of items to the clearing house.

Marine argues that, even if it were held accountable under the Code, it is exonerated from liability by reason of the clearing-house agreement to which both Marine and West Side are signatories. By-law IV, sec. 3, of the clearinghouse agreement expressly provides that unacceptable items are returnable through the exchanges on the second business day following the date they are presented at the exchange. Marine returned the Swidler check to West Side within the time limit. UCC 4-103(1) specifically provides that the effect of the Code may be varied by agreement, and UCC 4-103(2) provides that clearing-house rules have the effect of such agreements.

Fletcher R. Andrews, Dean of the School of Law at Western Reserve University, in his article, The City Clearing House: Payment, Returns, and Reimbursement, [27 Ind. L.J. 155 (1951-1952)], recognized before the adoption of the Code that clearing-house rules are strong evidence of the intention of banks regarding the time in which a decision to pay a check may be made. Dean Andrews states:

"Consequently, the only problem causing any difficulty arises when the drawee bank debits the drawer's account, and later wishes to cancel the entry, treat the check as dishonored, and return it to the presenting bank within the time stipulated by the clearing house rule. In debiting the drawer's account, the bank has performed an act which ordinarily is considered payment. But the banks, by rule, have agreed that items may be returned before a certain hour. Since payment is a matter of intent, and the parties have set down their intent in the rules of the clearing house, the solution of the problem becomes merely a matter of interpretation of the rule. . . .

"It may conceivably be argued that a [returned] . . . item means only an item which never has been charged against the drawer's account, by reason of the discovery of a shortage of funds, forgery, or the like. The argument gains in plausibility when it is recalled that checks are inspected for irregularities, omissions, forgeries, and other defects before being entered in the general ledger, and that the bookkeeper examines the state of the drawer's account before making his entry. As a consequence, the item might be regarded as 'good' or 'paid' when, after successfully completing the several tests, it is finally charged against the drawer. Yet this interpretation seems to overlook the fundamental purpose of the rule, which is to permit the banks to wait until a certain time before finally deciding whether to honor or dishonor the items presented. Had the banks wished to make the debiting of the account the last 'rite,' they could easily have said so in their rule. In the absence of a provision to that effect, the rule should be interpreted to mean that the check is not paid until the expiration of the return period." [Id. at 167, 168.]

In view of the express approval of the statutes that the Code may be waived or altered by agreement, we are compelled to hold that the clearing-house agreement supersedes any inconsistent portions of the Code, and in this instance additionally serves to expand the time in which entries may be reversed. Moreover, such modifications are within the stated purpose of the Code (UCC 1-102(2)(b)) "to permit the continued expansion of commercial practices through custom, usage and agreement of the parties."

Related to the desirability of recognizing local agreements in derogation of specific provisions of the Code is the statute's express standard that final payment is dependent not upon some objective universal standard, but upon the subjective test of "the usual procedure followed by the payor bank." (UCC 4-109.) The affidavits of Marine tend to show that no decision in respect to payment was made until a judgment was reached regarding the reversal or nonreversal of entries and that the process of posting was not completed until the time for reversal expires. The recent case of Gibbs v. Gerberich (1964), 1 Ohio App. 2d 93, 98, 203 N.E.2d 851, stressed the subjective test to be applied: "The key point in a bank's completion of the 'process of posting' is the completion of all the steps followed in the *particular* bank's payment procedure." (Emphasis supplied.)

While a motion for summary judgment does not constitute a trial by affidavit, it is apparent that the affidavits of Marine, if believed at trial, would lead to the conclusion that the exercise of judgment following the computerized phase of the posting process to determine whether or not entries should be reversed constituted an essential part of Marine's process of posting and making "final payment."

The rules of the Milwaukee County Clearing House Association, upon which Marine relies, reflect the practical problems involved in handling quantities of bank checks by mechanical or electronic devices. The use of such devices rests upon the assumption that there will be sufficient time after the mechanical processes are completed for the human factor of judgment to be exercised and upon the statistically derived conclusion that only a very small proportion of the checks in circulation will present problems that require individual treatment. It has been estimated that in 1963 the Federal Reserve System handled 4,700,000,000 items for collection and the Federal Reserve Bank of Chicago alone handled 700,000,000. The annual check volume countrywide is believed to exceed 50,000,000 a day and 13,000,000,000 a year. Fairfax Leary, Jr., in 49 Marq. L. Rev. 331, 333, 334, points out that two principles have guided the selection of rules governing the law of check collections: "One is that the rules must be suitable for a bulk processing of large numbers of checks at little cost. The second, which is a corollary of the first, is that rules to ensure a proper allocation of losses incurred in the area of the one eighth of one percent of bad items should not be so restrictive as to clog the free flow and smooth handling of the almost unanimous number of *good checks, collections in bulk, and deferred posting.*"

It would appear that the rules of the Milwaukee County Clearing House Association urged by Marine comport with these principles. Because of the tremendous volume of checks being handled, the rule recognizes that the payor bank needs a grace period following the computer phase to make the determination to pay or not to pay. Recognition of the viability of such a rule effectuates the purpose of the Code as expressed in comment to [UCC 4-101], where it was stated that one of the goals of the Code was to provide "for flexibility to meet the needs of the large volume handled and the changing needs and conditions that are bound to come with the years."

We conclude that the order of the trial court denying the appellant's motion for summary judgment must be affirmed. . . .

NOTES & QUESTIONS

1. *Final payment and the "four legals" (UCC 4-213, 4-303).* Under UCC 4-213(1) a payor bank is accountable for an item when it has finally paid. UCC 4-303, on the other hand, states that after the bank has taken certain steps with respect to an item presented for payment an attempt to require the bank to recognize any one of four types of legal actions (the four legals) will come too late to terminate the bank's right or duty to pay the item. The list of steps set out in UCC 4-303 follows closely the provisions on final payment in UCC 4-213(1). The four legals include:

(1) a customer's stop order;
(2) legal process, such as garnishment of a customer's account;
(3) setoff by the bank itself; and
(4) knowledge or notice of some event, such as death or bankruptcy, which terminates the bank's authority.

West Side involved a customer's stop order. Why didn't the court in *West Side* refer to UCC 4-303? For further discussion see Chapter 17 at p. 839 infra.

2. *The plain meaning of UCC 4-109.* Compare the *West Side* court's reading of UCC 4-109 with the comments of a subsequent opinion:

H. SCHULTZ & SONS, INC. v. BANK OF SUFFOLK COUNTY, 439 F. Supp. 1137, 1140-1141, 22 UCC Rep. 1013, 1017-1018 (E.D.N.Y. 1977): "Nor is the language of UCC 4-109(e) as plain and unambiguous as the Wisconsin court described. If the language as the Wisconsin court viewed it read merely 'reversing an entry,' there might be substance to the plain meaning argument for rejecting an otherwise clear legislative intent. However, the statute does not read 'reversing an entry.' Those words appear in a larger phrase: 'correcting or reversing an entry or erroneous action.' In the context of this larger phrase, the legislature could have contemplated several different meanings. Following a principle of parallel grammatical construction, it could have meant 'correcting an entry or reversing an erroneous action,' thereby permitting the first verb to operate on the first direct object. Under this interpretation both phrases involve elements of righting an error. 'Correcting an entry' would remedy mechanical or recording errors; 'reversing an erroneous action' would permit correction of more complex actions such as judgments over a correct signature or determination of whether sufficient funds were available.

"Another possible reading of subsection (e) would present four possible combinations of the two verbs and two direct objects: 'correcting an entry,' 'correcting erroneous action,' 'reversing an entry,' and 'reversing erroneous action.' Under this view of the language, three of the four involve concepts of 'correcting' or 'erroneous.' Only one of them, 'reversing an entry,' omits any specific reference to a prior mistake. Thus, five out of these six possible readings of subsection (e) focus upon errors, either mechanical or judgmental.

"Under these circumstances the statute cannot reasonably be read as having a plain meaning and unambiguously providing that 'error' was not the determinative factor. When the underlying policies and intent of the bank collection sections of the UCC are so clearly demonstrated by its history, see [Note, Bank Procedures of the UCC—When is a Check Finally Paid?, 9 B.C. Indus. & Com. L. Rev. 1957 (1968)], and by the Official Comments, the court should not adopt an aberrational interpretation of UCC 4-109(e) such as urged by the defendant here and adopted by the Wisconsin Supreme Court. This is particularly so when the interpretation urged by defendant would render meaningless the remaining four subsections of UCC 4-109. Furthermore, on a policy level, an enormous legislative effort would be required to substitute in the states' separate enactments of this uniform law language which would unambiguously state the clear legislative purpose."

3. *Deletion of UCC 4-109.* When it adopted Article 4 the California legislature omitted UCC 4-109 and deleted UCC 4-213(1)(c) because of complaints about the uncertainty engendered by the process-of-posting test. Should the California approach be more generally adopted?

Problem 16-7. Unishops draws a check dated November 26 on its account with Suffolk County Bank payable to H. Schultz & Sons in the amount of $40,000. Schultz deposits the check for collection on November 27 in its account at Fidelity Union Trust Co. Fidelity forwards the check to the Federal Reserve Bank of New York, which in turn forwards the check to the Suffolk County Bank. Suffolk County Bank receives the check on November 29 and on the same day photographs the check, "proves" it by examining the account, and debits Unishops' account for the amount of the check. According to the bank vice-president, the bank would not have processed the check further before sending out Unishops' monthly statement. On November 30, however, the bank learns that Unishops has filed a petition in bankruptcy. On the same day the bank gives telephone notice of dishonor to the Federal Reserve Bank in New York. Schultz asks your advice on what it should do. Advise Schultz. See UCC 4-109.

CENTRAL BANK v. PEOPLES NATIONAL BANK
401 So. 2d 14, 31 UCC Rep. 1428 (Ala. 1981)

EMBRY, J. This appeal is from a judgment in favor of plaintiff Peoples National Bank of Huntsville and against defendant Central Bank of Alabama,

N.A. in an action asserting that Central was liable to Peoples in the amount of $82,000 on account of the payment to Beth B. White of that amount when a worthless check drawn upon her account at Central was accepted by Peoples.

. . . By stipulation the parties agreed that the sole issue for determination by the trial court was the "midnight deadline" theory. Simply stated, that theory makes the depository or payor bank liable to pay the forwarding bank the amount of a check if, after presentment and receipt, the check is not returned by the midnight deadline. . . .

Peoples contends that under the midnight deadline theory Central was correctly found liable because Central failed to comply with UCC 4-302:

> . . . [I]f an item is presented on and received by a payor bank the bank is accountable in the amount of
>
> (a) a demand item other than a documentary draft whether properly payable or not if the bank, in any case where it is not also the depositary bank, retains the item beyond midnight of the banking day of receipt without settling for it or, regardless of whether it is also the depositary bank, does not pay or return the item or send notice of dishonor until after its midnight deadline. . . .

On the other hand, Central says the trial court's judgment is erroneous because, under the facts of this case, Central complied with the provisions of UCC 4-301:

> (1) Where an authorized agent for a demand item (other than a documentary draft) received by a payor bank otherwise than for immediate payment over the counter has been made before midnight of the banking day of receipt the payor bank may revoke the settlement and recover any payment if before it has made final payment (subsection (1) of Section 4-213) and before its midnight deadline it
>
> (a)   returns the item, or;
> (b)   sends written notice of dishonor or nonpayment if the item is held for protest or is otherwise unavailable for return. . . .
>
> (4) An item is returned:
> (a)   as to an item received through a clearing house, when it is delivered to the presenting or last collecting bank or the clearing house or is sent or delivered in accordance with its rules; or
> (b)   in all other cases, when it is sent or delivered to the bank's customer or transferor or pursuant to his instructions.

. . . On 18 September 1978, Mrs. Beth B. White presented the check, the subject of this litigation, to the Dunnavant's Mall Branch of Peoples National Bank of Huntsville. She was the maker of the check which was drawn on her account at the Florence branch of Central Bank. Peoples paid her the proceeds of the check and then forwarded it with a cash letter to the Federal Reserve Bank in Birmingham, which is a clearing house for the litigant banks. According to standard procedure, the Federal Reserve Bank made a provisional credit to People's account and simultaneously debited the account of Central at Florence. Both actions occurred on 20 September 1978. The check arrived at Central Bank's designated place of presentment at the Decatur Data Processing Center on 20 September 1978. This is also known as Central Computer Center, Inc. On that same date, when the check was received by that center it was stamped "processed" and debited against Mrs. White's account. That center performed the basic bookkeeping and data processing functions for the various branches of Central, including that at Florence, as well as substantially all the accounting functions of the Florence branch. However, the Florence branch did check for forgeries and make the final decision whether an item should be returned or not. On 21 September 1978, the check was delivered to the Florence branch of Central where it was determined that the endorsement of the payee, her son, was a forgery and the credit balance in Mrs. White's account was conditional and based upon "uncollected funds."

Uncollected funds are funds posted in an account based upon checks payable by, but not collected from, various other banks upon which the deposited checks were drawn. On 22 September 1978, a courier of Central took the check in question to Peoples in Huntsville. The check was returned to Central at Florence by the same courier on that same day. On 23 September 1978, Central at Florence deposited the check with the courier service for the Birmingham Federal Reserve. It was received by the latter on 25 September 1978. To return the subject check through the Birmingham Federal Reserve, acting as a clearing house, all required is that the check with a cash letter be deposited in the Federal Reserve courier service depository. Such could have been accomplished on the 22nd of September after the return of the courier from Huntsville. The check was returned by the Federal Reserve directly to Peoples after debiting Peoples reserve account in the amount of $82,000. Regulation "J," CFR 210.12, is controlling in cases where items are forwarded through the Federal Reserve System. Among other things, it provides that a paying bank shall have the right to recover payment or remittance if it ". . . takes such other action to recover such payment or remittance within such time and by such means as provided by applicable state law. . . ." The applicable state law is UCC 4-301.

As we can see from these facts, there was an attempt to make a direct return of the check and also an attempt to return it through a clearing house; each after midnight of 21 September 1978.

The pivotal determination to be made in this case is the time when the midnight deadline began to run on Central. The trial court did not reach the issue of *when* Central's midnight deadline began to run. Central contends the deadline did not begin to run until the check arrived at its Florence branch on 21 September 1978. Central says that because the trial court failed to decide the issue of when Central's midnight deadline began to run, whether upon arrival of the check at the computer center or at the Florence branch, that in the event of a reversal of the trial court upon the first two issues, as stated by it, this case should be remanded for an initial determination of the third issue by the trial court. The trial court stated those issues as follows:

1. Did the defendant abort its return of the subject item prior to effective delivery of the same on September 22, 1978?

2. Is UCC 4-106 applicable to presenting banks as well as to payor bank? An answer to this question is determinative as to whether or not a delivery to the Madison Street Branch of the plaintiff was an effective return to the presenting bank.

3. Is a computer center, which is the designated place of presentment, and which performs all the basic bookkeeping functions for a bank or a branch thereof, a 'separate bank' under UCC 4-106? An answer to this question is determinative as to whether the time for the midnight deadline began to run on September 20, 1978 or September 21, 1978.

It appears that a determination of any one of the stated issues favorable to the plaintiff would be determinative of this cause.

We cannot agree, because the trial court, though assigning erroneous reasons, arrived at the correct result in this case; therefore, its judgment is due to be affirmed. . . . We have no difficulty in making the determination about the beginning of the running of the midnight deadline. Peoples relies heavily, and rightfully so, on the case of Farmers & Merchant Bank v. Bank of America, 98 Cal. Rptr. 381, 20 Cal. App. 3d 936 (1971). Appellant contends that its Florence branch was a separate bank as defined by UCC 4-106:

§4-106.   Separate Office of a Bank

A branch or separate office of a bank is a separate bank for the purpose of computing the time within which and determining the place at or to which action may be taken or notices or orders shall be given under this Article and under Article 3.*

That being true, Central says, then of necessity, its midnight deadline did not begin to run until the check arrived at its Florence branch. We agree that the Florence branch is a separate bank for purposes of UCC 4-106. However, we cannot agree that the midnight deadline did not begin to run until the check arrived at the Florence branch. *Farmers & Merchants Bank,* supra, is strikingly similar to this case. Because we deem it controlling as precedent, we burden this opinion with an extensive quote from that case:

"The central issue before the court below was whether both the Bank of America and Farmers and Merchants were barred from returning their respective sets of checks to each other because each of them held the checks beyond the time limits prescribed by section 1013 of the Financial Code.[1] In

---

* As noted below, Alabama has not adopted the optional phrase "maintaining its own deposit ledgers."—Eds.

1. Section 1013 of the Financial Code read[s] in part: "In any case in which a bank receives, other than for immediate payment over the counter, a demand item payable by, at or through such bank and gives credit therefore before midnight of the day of receipt, the bank may have until midnight of its next business day after receipt within which to dishonor or refuse payment of such item. Any credit so given together with all related entries on the receiving bank's books, may be revoked by returning the item, or if the item is held for protest or at the time is lost or is not in

order to decide the correctness of the court's holding it becomes necessary to
determine whether the time set forth under Section 1013 begins to run when
the checks were delivered to Bank of America's Montebello computer center
(as held by the court below), or whether the statutory time begins to run after
their arrival at the Harbor-Orangewood branch, as appellant, Bank of America, urges upon us. Assuming that receipt of the checks by the Montebello
computer center was receipt by the drawee branch within the meaning of
section 1013, then the trial court correctly found that Exhibits 1-4 and 8 and
9 were not dishonored in time, since these checks were returned after midnight
of the next business day after receipt.

"Bank of America argues that the Harbor-Orangewood branch is a separate bank under section 1012 and section 1018 of the Financial Code, and that
time should run from receipt at that office and not from receipt at the Montebello computer. Section 1012 of the Financial Code provides in part: '. . . (c)
each branch or office of a bank shall be deemed a separate bank.'

"Section 1018 of the Financial Code, as in effect at the time of the transaction involved, provides in part: 'An item . . . received for collection . . . at
any other office of the same bank, shall be deemed for all the purposes of this
article as . . . payable at another bank.'

"The fact that the Harbor-Orangewood branch is a 'branch or office' and
therefore a 'separate bank' within the meaning of the above code section, in no
way negates the fact that the Montebello computer center is part of that
branch for purposes of section 1013. The testimony set forth in the facts clearly
shows that the Montebello computer center mainly performed the Harbor-
Orangewood branch's bookkeeping functions and those acts that were performed by the computer were not performed in the Harbor-Orangewood
office. Prior to the formation of the Montebello computer center, the acts
being performed by the Montebello computer were performed manually by
employees at the Harbor-Orangewood branch. All these facts tend to support
the trial court's finding that the Montebello computer was part of the Harbor-
Orangewood branch within that meaning of former section 1013 of the Financial Code.[3]

"Statutes in other cases similar to Financial Code, section 1013 have been
strictly construed[4] as to the time limit.

---

the possession of the bank, by giving written notice of dishonor, nonpayment, or revocation;
provided, that such item or notice is dispatched in the mails or by other expeditious means not
later than midnight of the bank's next business day after the item was received. For the purpose of
determining when notice of dishonor must be given or protest made under the law relative to
negotiable instruments, an item duly presented, credit for which is revoked as authorized by this
article, shall be deemed dishonored on the day the item or notice is dispatched. A bank, revoking
credit pursuant to the authority of this article, is entitled to refund of, or credit for, the amount of
the item."

3. For the purposes of this appeal, we accept the trial court's theory that receipt by the
'Erma' computer, which merely sorted out checks, was not a receipt of checks by the Harbor-
Orangewood branch.

4. See General Finance Corp. v. Central & Trust Co. 264 F.2d 869 (5th Cir. 1959); Wisner
v. First National Bank 220 Pa. 21, 68 A. 955, 17 L.R.A., N.S. 1266 (1908).

"Since the Bank of America failed to return checks 1-4, 8 and 9, and A through F before midnight of the next business day after receipt by the Montebello computer center, those checks were returned beyond the time limit of section 1013."

We think this case clearly falls within the rationale of and is factually similar to *Farmers & Merchants Bank* exemplified by the quoted paragraph beginning with the words "[T]he fact that the Harbor-Orangewood. . . ."

Under the facts of this case, we think Central Computer Center, the designated place for presentment of items for payment by Central's Florence branch, is part of that branch for purposes of UCC 4-104, 4-301, and 4-302. It follows that the midnight deadline began running when the check arrived at Central Computer Center on 20 September 1978 and expired at midnight 21 September 1978. Central would argue that the conclusion we have reached and our reliance on *Farmers & Merchants Bank* are unsound and unworkable. Central cites the "Alabama Comment" to UCC 4-106 which notes that in adopting this section defining a branch or separate office as a separate bank for the purposes stated in the section the optional language "maintaining its own deposit ledgers" following the words "separate office of a Bank" near the beginning of the section was omitted and therefore the Florence branch is a separate bank even though it does not maintain its own deposit ledgers and the midnight deadline does not begin running until the check arrives at that branch. It makes no difference that it is a separate bank; the computer is still an integral part of it. Central contends that Idah-Best, Inc. v. First Security Bank, 99 Idaho 517, 584 P.2d 1242 (1978), is controlling in this case and compels reversal. We do not agree that comparison of the facts in this case with the Supreme Court of Idaho's analysis of the facts in that case would lead us to a different conclusion than that reached by the Idaho Court. A reading of *Idah-Best* fails to show that the data processing center in that case was the designated place of presentment of a collection item as was here the case. Further, it is important to note that Idaho, unlike Alabama and California, by statute, requires that on the face of the bank checks the designated place of presentment or acceptance must be identified.

Different factual conclusions were reached by the Idaho court than those reached by the trial court and by us in this case. The following quote from *Idah-Best* will illustrate this: ". . . An analysis of the operations of the Boise data processing center shows that its functions are limited to the sorting and indorsing process typical of a collecting bank and to the transmitting of information that allows the Salt Lake City computer to keep tentative customer accounts. It is the conclusion of this court that when considered in light of the entire collection and payments process, a check's arrival at the data processing center cannot be characterized as 'presentment upon' and 'receipt by' the Hailey Branch."

Central expresses grave concern that a substantial and burdensome logistical problem will be created if local branches of Central are required to return the check on the day after its receipt at the computer center where Central has forty branches served by the computer center, some of which are located as much as 100 miles from that center. To allow this reasoning to permit the midnight deadline to begin running from time of receipt at the local branch would be to thwart the very purpose of the midnight deadline: to encourage prompt return of dishonored checks. Moreover, to permit delay of the beginning of the running of the midnight deadline would have the effect of allowing the payor bank to unilaterally decide where the deadline would begin to run by the simple device of choosing the time to forward the check to the branch. Taken to the extreme, the failure of the computer center to forward the check to the branch would never trigger the beginning of the running of the midnight deadline. This argument also ignores the fact of the present state of the art of computer capability, particularly with regard to visual communication between computer and terminals. . . .

Affirmed.

Problem 16-8. Pursuant to an "Off-Premises Presentment Request" (the Request) between the Federal Reserve Bank of Boston (Fed), First National Bank of Boston (First), and Old Colony Bank & Trust Co. (Bank), Bank employs the services of First, a member of the Federal Reserve System, to receive cash items of Bank's customers that clear through Fed. The Request is a collection agreement between Bank, Fed, and First that establishes the method and time of presentment of cash items on Bank. By the agreement Fed, upon completion of its processing functions, delivers the respective cash items in a "cash letter" to a messenger of First who calls at Fed's offices to receive the items. Fed obtains a signed receipt from First's messenger that designates the several banking institutions whose cash items have been cleared through Fed and are to be processed by First. The receipt will also specify the particular morning or afternoon cash letters received by the messenger.

Pursuant to the "Agreement for Gross Payment of Cash Letters by Non-Member Country Bank by Authority to Charge to Member Banks Reserve Account" (the Settlement Agreement), Fed advises First and Bank that Fed has charged First's reserve account with Fed with the amount of the cash letter to be delivered to Bank. Upon Fed's notice to First and Bank, Bank automatically makes settlement on all cash items clearing through Fed by accepting a debit to Bank's account with First.

Pursuant to the Request, presentment to Bank is made at the premises of First. As part of the correspondent bank relationship between First and Bank, as established by the Request and the Settlement Agreement, Bank utilizes the computer services of First to begin processing all cash items cleared through Fed and presented upon Bank for payment. Bank furnishes First with records of Bank's customers' accounts that are assimilated into First's computer system in order to post cash items to customers' accounts in daily settlements. All transactions by Bank regarding cash items, except for notices of dishonor and return, bear the date when items are sorted and coded by First.

Thereafter, all items constituting the cash letter are made ready for delivery to Bank. The cash letter is customarily received by Bank on the banking day following the day in which the cash items are processed at First's computer center. On physical receipt Bank performs the inspection and other verification steps used in determining whether to pay an item or to reverse an item previously entered by First's computer at the commencement of the posting process.

On the morning of July 12, 1976, a messenger for First calls on and receives from Fed cash items drawn on and/or payable at Bank. He then delivers the morning cash letter to the check collection department of First for further processing. Fed advises First and Bank that Fed has charged First's reserve account with the amount of the July 12 cash letter in accordance with the Settlement Agreement. Following receipt of the July 12 cash letter at First's computer center for sorting and coding, the account of Eastern Yachts, Inc. is debited for the amount of a check drawn by Eastern payable to Catalina Yachts and the check, together with all other items constituting the cash letter, are made ready for delivery to Bank on the next banking day.

The cash items contained in the July 12 cash letter are received by Bank on July 13, 1976. Bank reviews the checks on receipt and determines that Eastern's balance discloses insufficient funds. On July 14, 1976, Bank effects reversal of the debit charged by computer to Eastern's account and returns the Catalina check to Fed with notice of dishonor for insufficient funds.

Catalina brings an action against Bank on the theory that Bank did not act before its midnight deadline. Evaluate Catalina's case. See Catalina Yachts v. Old Colony Bank & Trust Co., 497 F. Supp. 1227, 32 UCC Rep. 241 (D. Mass. 1980).

D.   THE CREDIT CARD

There are at least three distinct classes of credit cards: the retail credit card issued by large retailers (e.g., Sears & Roebuck), the travel and entertainment card (e.g., American Express), and the bank credit card (e.g., Visa and Master Card). Recently banks have issued debit cards to their customers, who are able to use the cards at remote terminals to make electronic transfers from their accounts without having to go to the bank itself. Debit cards, however, are not designed for credit transactions unless the bank has agreed to extend preauthorized overdraft privileges.

The retail credit card is the simplest system to describe because it usually involves only two parties, the issuer and the customer. A retailer issues a plastic card to a customer, who then presents the card at the time of a purchase from the retailer. The customer is then billed by the retailer on a regular basis and, if the agreement with the issuer so provides, may pay the account in installments on a revolving basis.

The travel and entertainment card may be described as a tripartite arrangement between the card issuer, the cardholder, and a merchant. Two separate agreements are involved, that between the issuer and the cardholder and that between the issuer and the merchant. The issuer bills the cardholder on a regular basis and typically does not expect to grant more than short-term credit. The merchant agrees to allow the card holder to charge expenses by use of the card, and the issuer agrees to pay the merchant for the face amount of the charge slip minus an agreed discount.

A bank credit card arrangement typically includes at least four parties: the cardholder, the issuing bank, the merchant, and the merchant's bank. The cardholder agrees to repay the issuing bank for the amount the holder charges by use of the card, together with any agreed-upon credit charges. The merchant has an agreement with its bank for the purchase of the charge slips. The issuing bank and the merchant's bank are part of a bank credit card association that will provide for settlement of the charges made by the cardholder, typically without the movement of the paper slips. Thus the major difference between bank cards and travel and entertainment cards is that the bank issuing a bank card expects to extend credit. For a further description of bank credit card arrangements, see B. Clark, The Law of Bank Deposits, Collections and Credit Cards ch. 9 (rev. ed. 1981).

The legal characterization of the relation between the three or more parties involved in a bank credit card or a travel and entertainment card system has led to considerable controversy. It has been suggested that the relation involves a letter of credit, an assignment of accounts, or a direct obligation between the issuer and the merchant honoring the card. The Uniform Commercial Code does not provide a clear-cut answer but the Uniform Consumer Credit Code treats the credit card transaction as a direct obligation. UCCC §1.301(25).

There has been no comprehensive regulation of credit cards. Several federal laws regulate aspects of the issuance and use of credit cards by consumers. The Truth-in-Lending Act, as supplemented by Regulation Z issued by the Federal Reserve Board, governs the issuance of credit cards, the liability of cardholders, and the fraudulent use of credit cards. 15 U.S.C. §§1642-1645 (1982); 16 C.F.R. Part 226 (1984). The Fair Credit Billing Act regulates billing disputes, setoff, and cardholder defenses. 15 U.S.C. §1666 (1982).

For further reading, see Brandel & Leonard, Bank Charge Cards: New Cash or New Credit? 69 Mich. L. Rev. 1033 (1971); Bergsten, Credit Cards— A Prelude to the Cashless Society, 8 B.C. Indus. & Com. L. Rev. 485 (1967); Davenport, Bank Credit Cards and the Uniform Commercial Code, 1 Val. U.L. Rev. 218 (1967); Macaulay, Private Legislation and the Duty to Read— Business Run by IBM Machine, the Law of Contracts and Credit Cards, 19 Vand. L. Rev. 1051 (1966).

SCHORR v. THE BANK OF NEW YORK, N.Y.L.J., Feb. 15, 1983, at 1, col. 6 (N.Y. App. Div. 1983): Mechanic and Bank of New York (BNY) entered into a "Charge Plan Merchant Agreement" which included the following two paragraphs:

"10. On demand Merchant [i.e., Mechanic] will pay to BNY the amount paid or credited for, and will indemnify BNY against all liability, loss claims and demands whatsoever arising in connection with unqualified Sales Slips, i.e., Sales Slips and the transactions evidenced thereby in connection with which there is any dispute or defense (whether or not valid) between Merchant and Card Holder. BNY may charge any Unqualified Sales Slip to the Merchant and offset the amount of any Unqualified Sales Slip against the net proceeds due to Merchant from other Sales Slips deposited with BNY and BNY is authorized to debit Merchant's account for the amount thereof.

"13. Merchant waives notice of default or non-payment, protest or notice of protest, demand for payment and any other demand or notice in connection with any Credit Sales, Sales Slips, Credit Memo or this Agreement."

Mechanic agreed to repair the transmission of Consumer's car. Consumer used his credit card to "pay" for the repair. Mechanic deposited the credit card sales slip with BNY on February 8 and BNY credited Mechanic's account.

On March 29 Consumer sent a "cardholder dispute" form to Marine Midland Bank where he maintained his credit card account. In the form Consumer stated that the repair work had not been performed by Mechanic. Federal regulations permit a cardholder to withhold payment to the card-issuing bank for the amount in controversy but the regulations do not place a time limit within which such action must be taken. 12 C.F.R. §226.13 (1984).

Eventually BNY learned of Consumer's action and on April 15 BNY debited Mechanic's account in the amount in controversy. Mechanic brought an action against BNY on the grounds that BNY should have investigated before charging its account and that the "Charge Plan Merchant Agreement" was unconscionable because there were no time limits within which BNY had to act. *Held*, BNY acted properly in accordance with an enforceable agreement.

If Consumer had paid by check would Mechanic have been better off?

E.   ELECTRONIC FUND TRANSFER SYSTEMS

There is no generally accepted definition of electronic fund transfer systems (EFTS). The Federal Electronic Fund Transfer Act defines *electronic fund transfer* as "any transfer of funds, other than a transaction originated by check, draft, or similar paper instrument, which is initiated through an electronic terminal, telephonic instrument, or a computer or magnetic tape so as to order, instruct, or authorize a financial institution to debit or credit an account." 15 U.S.C. §1693(a)(6) (1982). State legislation and commentators, however, include many different systems within the term.

The following devices and systems are typical of EFTS.

(1) Automated Teller Machine (ATM). A bank issues to its customer a card with a personal identification number (PIN). The card may be used in an unmanned terminal to make deposits, disburse cash, and transfer funds between accounts. The card is used for transactions between the bank and the customer rather than for making payments directly to third persons.

(2) Point-of-Sale Terminal (POS). A bank issues to its customer a card that may be used in a terminal maintained at a merchant's place of business to transfer funds from the customer's bank account to the merchant's account. The merchant receives immediate payment and avoids the problem of bad checks, but he must make a substantial investment in terminal facilities. The customer pays without the need to carry cash or a checkbook but he will not be able to stop payment and he loses the float he would normally have before a check is finally paid.

(3) Telephone Transfer. By prearrangement with his bank a customer may make transfers to and from his account by telephone.

(4) Automated Clearing House (ACH). An automated clearing house is a computerized interbank transfer system used to make pre-authorized transfers to and from the accounts of bank customers. Payroll payments, for example, may be deposited to the accounts of employees by having the employer deposit with its bank the payroll data on a single magnetic tape. The bank then makes the transfers to the accounts of the employees through the ACH. The ACH, in other words, operates in much the same way as a check clearing house, with the difference that clearings are made through electronic transfers rather than through the exchange of paper. There is a National Association of Automated Clearing Houses that coordinates the activities of the regional clearing houses. The Federal Reserve Board has encouraged the development of these regional associations and has made its wire transfer facilities available to them.

(5) Bank Wire Systems. To facilitate the transfer of large dollar items between banks, several wire transfer systems have developed. Fedwire is operated by the Federal Reserve system as both a clearing house and a settlement facility. Bank Wire II is a nationwide private alternative to Fedwire. CHIPS (the Clearing House Interbank Payment System), on the other hand, is operated by the New York Clearing House Association to handle primarily international transfers of funds.

The law governing electronic fund transfer systems is fragmentary at present. The Electronic Fund Transfer Act regulates the rights of consumers who participate in such transfers. 15 U.S.C. §§1693-1693r (1982). Regulation E, issued by the Federal Reserve Board, provides further detail. 12 C.F.R. Part 205 (1984). Several states have also adopted consumer legislation to spell out the rights and obligations of parties who participate in the systems. The relations between participants in interbank transfer systems, however, are determined primarily by contract and association rules but Regulation J (Part B) provides rules for wire transfers.

The relation between these EFTS and the Uniform Commercial Code has been a troubling one for many commentators. For an early analysis, see Penney, Questions Needing Answers—Effects of EFTS on the U.C.C., 37 U. Pitt. L. Rev. 661 (1976). The Uniform New Payments Code being prepared under the auspices of the Permanent Editorial Board of the Uniform Commercial Code originally proposed to amalgamate the present paper-based rules in the UCC with rules developed specifically for electronic transfers. The first widely-circulated draft is P.E.B. Draft No. 3 (June 2, 1983). The 1978 report of Professor Hal Scott sets out the objectives of the project. H. Scott, New Payment Systems: A Report to the 3-4-8 Committee of the Permanent Editorial Board for the Uniform Commercial Code (1978) [Summary reprinted in 3 ALI-ABA Course Materials J. 6 (1978)]. The future of the UNPC is uncertain. Drafts to date have drawn substantial criticism from both the banking community and consumer interest groups. This criticism questions the need to make substantial changes in the present paper-based rules and the desirability of including consumer-protection provisions in the new codification.

For further readings, see N. Penney & D. Bauer, The Law of Electronic Fund Transfer Systems (1980); Vergari, Articles 3 and 4 of the Uniform Commercial Code in an Electronic Transfer Environment, 17 San Diego L. Rev. 287 (1980); Brandel & Olliff, The Electronic Fund Transfer Act: A Primer, 40 Ohio St. L.J. 531 (1979).

EVRA CORP. v. SWISS BANK CORP., 673 F.2d 951 (7th Cir. 1982), *cert. denied,*—U.S.—(1984): Hyman-Michaels chartered the *Pandora* for one year to carry scrap metal to Brazil. Payment was to be made by semi-monthly deposits to the shipowner's account in a Swiss bank. Hyman-Michaels usually made deposits by requesting its Chicago bank to make a wire transfer of funds through a correspondent bank in Switzerland. On April 25, 1973 Hyman-Michaels requested a wire transfer of funds for a payment due by the close of business on April 26. Because it had difficulty reaching the cable department of the correspondent bank in Switzerland the Chicago bank sent the telex message to a machine in the foreign exchange department of the correspondent bank. The correspondent failed to make the transfer of payment, and the owner of the *Pandora* cancelled the charter for nonpayment. Hyman-Michaels brought an action against the correspondent bank, which impleaded the Chicago bank. *Held,* on appeal, the correspondent bank was not liable under common law principles for the consequences of negligently failing to make the transfer. The appellate court assumed, for purposes of the case before it, that UCC Article 4 was not applicable.

Is the court correct in its assumption that Article 4 is not applicable? If Article 4 were applicable what would be the responsibility of the two banks?

CHAPTER 17

Error and Wrongdoing

Every day the banking system in the United States processes an enormous number of items. A high percentage of these are processed without incident. However, several recurring problems arise in the operation of the payment system: the drawer may not have provided sufficient funds to cover its order; the drawee may wrongfully dishonor its customer's order; or the drawer may change its mind after drawing its check and countermand payment. These basic problems arise simply from the tripartite nature of the payment order (drawer, drawee, payee). Additional complications are introduced by occasional dishonesty: an employee or other wrongdoer may forge a drawer's signature, forge an indorsement, or alter the amount of a check.

The following cases and problems will require that you synthesize all the materials you have studied thus far. For example, a check drawn on insufficient funds may raise the following issues: the drawee bank's privilege of honoring the check, or its right of charging the account of its customer; or the holder's rights against a prior indorser or against a party who has transferred the check without indorsement.

The key to understanding in this area is rigorous adherence to a systematic analysis. We will suggest below an analytical framework that will serve you well in solving negotiable instrument problems.

As a first step, you should chart the path of the instrument. What are the circumstances of its issuance and each subsequent transfer? A transfer between C and D may be made in good faith, for value, and without notice of any defense, but D may receive very limited rights because B stole the instrument and forged A's signature. Conversely, although D gives no value or has notice of a defense he may nonetheless acquire the rights of a holder in due course if C has such rights.

You should next define the exact issue being posed. Is the student to ascertain C's rights against the instrument's drawer?—or, C's rights against the transferor?

Finally, you should review the various bases for liability: contract, warranty, or conversion.

These two points, identifying the exact issue and selecting the appropriate theory of liability, are obviously closely related. Once you have identified the issue and the theory of liability you should not be diverted or confused by other factors. We stress this because the law of negotiable instruments is replete with rules yielding partial solutions: frequently *D* will have no contract action against *A* but will have a warranty action against *C*. And *A*, although not liable in contract to *C*, may be liable to *D*. The Code's system of loss allocation is elaborate. When particular rules are applied in isolation the results may seem improper but when all applicable rules are given effect the results may be more understandable.

This chapter is organized according to common events. You may find it useful to diagram these situations: forged indorsement returned unpaid, forged indorsement check paid, or forged drawer's signature returned unpaid. As you then consider the cases and problems you should apply the various theories of action and cross-action that allocate loss. An example of the resulting diagram is set out in J. White & R. Summers, Handbook on the Law under the Uniform Commercial Code 581 (2d ed. 1980).

A.   "NSF" CHECKS

For an anniversary present Winship buys a stereo from Stereo Supplies and pays by writing a check for the purchase price. Stereo Supplies deposits the check with its bank the following morning. After crediting Stereo Supplies' account the depositary bank promptly forwards the check through a collecting bank to the drawee bank. The drawee bank examines the condition of Winship's account and discovers there are insufficient funds.

The drawee bank has several options: it may honor the check and its final payment will firm up the provisional credits given in the bank collection process so that Stereo Supplies will be paid. By honoring the check the bank in effect extends a loan to Winship. UCC 4-401(1) expressly authorizes the bank to create this overdraft:

> As against its customer, a bank may charge against his account any item which is otherwise properly payable from that account even though the charge creates an overdraft.

Because Winship has other accounts with the bank and has been reliable in the past the bank may honor the check to accommodate a good customer.

In the alternative, the bank may dishonor Winship's check. If the bank and the collecting banks act seasonably the unpaid check will be returned to Stereo Supplies and the depositary bank will charge back the check to Stereo Supplies' account. Stereo Supplies may then bring an action against Winship on either the check or the obligation that is revived upon dishonor (UCC 3-

802). Absent any delay or negligence, however, Stereo Supplies will not be able to recover from either its bank (the depositary bank) or Winship's bank (the drawee bank). As we saw in the last chapter, the depositary bank is merely an agent for collection and has the right to charge back the amount of the check when it does not receive a settlement for it (UCC 4-202, 4-212). In Chapter 15 we learned that a drawee is not liable on an instrument until it is accepted such as by certification (UCC 3-409, 3-410, 3-411).

Having insufficient funds in an account is the most common reason for nonpayment of checks. A drawee bank has the option of protecting itself by refusing to honor checks drawn on these accounts. A merchant like Stereo Supplies may call a credit bureau before taking the check, record information about the drawer when cashing the check, or absorb the loss from the bad check as a cost of doing business. In addition, as illustrated in the *Williams* case set forth at p. 825 infra, it may also call on the criminal justice system to deal with someone who passes a bad check.

Compare the situation of the merchant who takes a bad check with that of a merchant who accepts a credit card or uses an electronic fund transfer device such as a point-of-sale terminal. Most merchant-bank credit charge agreements require the merchant to call the bank for approval of charges above a specified sum so that the bank may check the present status of the customer's account. The merchant will know immediately, therefore, whether or not the bank will accept the sales slip and may protect itself by not selling to a customer who has passed his credit limits. With a point-of-sale terminal the merchant will learn immediately whether he will receive payment, and the bank will be responsible for any mistake in determining the status of the customer's account.

NATIONAL SAVINGS & TRUST CO. v. PARK CORP.
722 F.2d 1303, 37 UCC Rep. 817 (6th Cir. 1983), *cert. denied,*—U.S.—(1984)

MARTIN, Circuit Judge. In this diversity action, National Savings and Trust challenges the summary denial of its claim for restitution of $74,737.25 it mistakenly paid Park Corporation on a bad check.

On January 8, 1980, Park Corporation contracted to sell some used mining equipment to DAI International Investment Corporation. The sales agent for the transaction was Garland Caribbean Corporation. As part of its down payment, DAI gave Garland a check for $75,000 drawn on its account with the plaintiff, National Savings and Trust Company. On January 16, Garland called National Savings to determine if DAI had sufficient funds in its account to cover this check. The bank said DAI did not. That same day, Garland endorsed the check over to Park Corporation. Park Corporation then sent the check to National Savings "for collection."

On January 22, Garland once again called the bank to determine if DAI had sufficient funds in its account to cover the check. Once again, the bank said DAI did not.[1] Moreover, on this occasion, the banking employee who received the inquiry went to the bank's "platform officer" and notified him not to accept any DAI checks drawn on insufficient funds. Unfortunately for the bank, the platform officer only saw checks arriving through normal banking channels and not those coming in "for collection."

DAI's check arrived at the bank that same day. However, the employee who normally processed "for collection" checks was scheduled to work in another department that day. Prior to her departure, she did manage to open the incoming mail, including the DAI check. Her supervisor then volunteered to help out by taking the DAI check to the wire room for payment. Neither employee followed the bank's standard procedure and checked DAI's account to ensure that it held sufficient funds to cover the check. Each assumed that the other had done so. As a result, the check was paid even though DAI had only $236.75 in its account.

On January 28, 1980, after discovering its mistake, National Savings asked Park Corporation to return the $75,000. Park refused and National Savings subsequently brought this lawsuit. On motion for summary judgment by the defendant, the court found for Park on the grounds that National Savings had made an improvident extension of credit and that the bank was in a better position to know the true facts and to guard against mistakes. We disagree.

The basic law of restitution in Ohio, the state whose law controls, is summarized in Firestone Rubber & Tire Co. v. Central Natl. Bank of Cleveland, 159 Ohio St. 423, 112 N.E.2d 636 (1953). The Firestone case held that money paid to another by mistake is recoverable unless the other person has changed his position in reliance on the payment. This rule applies even if the mistake was the result of negligence.

Park Corporation attempts to circumvent the holding in *Firestone* by arguing that banks are not protected by normal restitutionary principles when they pay an insufficient funds (NSF) check. There is some support for this position. See, e.g., Spokane & Eastern Trust Co. v. Huff, 63 Wash. 225, 115 P. 80 (1911); 7 Zollman, The Law of Banks and Banking §5062 (1936). Nonetheless, this rule has not been universally applied, see, e.g., Manufacturers Trust Co. v. Diamond, 186 N.Y.S.2d 917, 919 (App. Div. 1959), and Park has not cited, nor have we been able to find, any Ohio cases adopting this rule. Moreover, it is questionable whether such a doctrine, if ever in existence, would survive the subsequent enactment of the Uniform Commercial Code in Ohio and the particular provisions applicable to the facts of the present case.

Park Corporation next argues that Firestone does not control because National Savings' payment was not a mistake but rather a knowing extension of credit. Park relies heavily on the New Jersey case of Demos v. Lyons, 151 N.J. Super. 489, 376 A.2d 1352 (Law Div. 1977). The factual circumstances of

1. There is no evidence Park was ever aware of Garland's phone conversations with the bank.

Demos, however, are quite distinct from the present case. In *Demos*, the bank actually examined the customer's account, realized the customer had insufficient funds to cover the check, yet paid the check anyway. The bank did not want to embarrass its customer and it hoped that he had made a late deposit to cover the check which would appear on the next day's balance sheet. No such deposit was ever made. In our case, National Savings never intended to make good on an NSF check. The platform officer had been notified not to pay out on DAI's check. The "for collection" employees were operating under standing orders to check balances before paying a check and never to pay on an NSF check. Despite all these precautions, the check was paid. At no time, however, did the employees making the payment decision know that DAI's account had insufficient funds to cover the check.

Park's next contention is that the Uniform Commercial Code as adopted in Ohio bars restitutionary recovery for banks that pay NSF checks. This argument focuses on an apparent conflict between two provisions of the UCC, 3-418 and 4-213. UCC 3-418, which applies to all transactions involving negotiable instruments, states that "payment or acceptance of any instrument is final in favor of a holder in due course, or a person who has in good faith changed his position in reliance on the payment." Because a holder in due course is simply a special type of detrimental relier, this section is basically a codification of restitutionary principles established in *Firestone*. Official Comment 3 to this section makes clear that if there is no detrimental reliance by the payee, then recovery of payment is permitted.

Park Corporation argues that UCC 4-213 establishes a special non-recovery rule for banks which mistakenly pay a bad check. UCC 4-213(1) states that "[a]n item is finally paid by a payor bank when the bank has done any of the following, whichever happens first: (a) paid the item in cash. . . ." Park contends that "finally paid" as used in this section has the same meaning as the "payment is final" language in UCC 3-418, namely restitutionary recovery is no longer possible. Moreover, because UCC 4-213 does not have the restrictive provisions which limit coverage to holders in due course or those who detrimentally rely, Park argues that UCC 4-213 makes a bank strictly liable as soon as it pays on an NSF check.[3] Furthermore, UCC 4-102 provides that, in case of conflict between Articles 3 and 4, the provisions of Article 4 are to govern. Thus, Park argues, National Savings is barred from recovering the $75,000.

At first glance, Park's argument has a certain appeal. That is not surprising because it is based in large part on the work of White & Summers, whose treatise, Uniform Commercial Code (2d ed. 1980), is generally considered the leading authority on commercial transactions. Id. at 613-617. . . . Several courts have also reached the same conclusion. See, e.g., Kirby v. First & Merchants Natl. Bank [at p. 778 supra]. . . .

---

3. Park agrees with White & Summers, Uniform Commercial Code 617 (2d ed. 1980), that there must be a "good faith" requirement read into UCC 4-213 so that payors acting fraudulently do not benefit.

Nonetheless, opinion on the matter is by no means uniform. Other writers, see H. Bailey, Brady on Bank Checks §14.20, at 14-32 (5th ed. Supp. 1983); B. Clark, The Law of Check Deposits §5.3[3] (2d ed. 1981), and other courts, see Demos v. Lyons, 151 N.J. Super. 489, 376 A.2d 1352 (Law Div. 1977); Blake v. Woodford Bank & Trust Co. [at p. 785 supra] have argued that banks retain their restitutionary rights with respect to mistaken payment of NSF checks. Our own analysis of the Code convinces us that the latter group is correct and that UCC 4-213 does not expand the final payment doctrine to bar recovery by payor banks from payees who have not detrimentally relied. In our analysis, we rely heavily on the official Comments to UCC 3-418 and 4-213. While these comments to the Code are not part of enacted law, they are a very helpful guide to construing the meaning of Code provisions. . . .

An examination of the comments to UCC 3-418 makes clear both that this section was intended to apply to "the payment of overdrafts, or any other payment made in error as to the state of the drawer's account," Comment 2, and that restitutionary recovery was to be denied only when the payee had relied on the payment. "If no value has been given for the instrument the holder loses nothing by the recovery of the payment . . . and it is not entitled to profit at the expense of the drawee. . . ." Comment 3.

The only mention of UCC 4-213 occurs in Comment 5, where the Code drafters point out that the provisions of UCC 3-418 do not apply until payment is final as defined in UCC 4-213. This comment suggests a method for resolving the apparent conflict between UCC 3-418 and 4-213. As the court in Demos v. Lyons put it, UCC 4-213 "is oriented toward time of payment, not legal effect of payment." 376 A.2d at 1356. The purpose of UCC 4-213 is "to determine *when* settlement for an item or other action with respect to it constitutes final payment." Comment 1, UCC 4-213 (emphasis added). UCC 4-213 determines *when* the final payment rule of UCC 3-418 comes into effect, not what that rule is supposed to mean. Further support for this position comes from the remaining comments to UCC 4-213. Comment 1 states "final payment is important" because it helps determine "priorities between items and notices, stop orders, legal process and setoffs, [because it] is the 'end of the line' in the collection process, [and because it] is the point at which many provisional settlements become final." The remaining comments discuss such arcane banking matters as posting, provisional settlements, and midnight deadlines. At no point does any comment to UCC 4-213 mention the effect this section is supposed to have on the restitutionary rights of banks. Thus, it seems evident that the drafters of the Code never intended for UCC 4-213 to supersede 3-418, and we can see no reason to adopt a position contrary to that intent.

As further support for our decision, we feel obliged to note that White & Summers, the authorities most relied on for the contrary proposition, now appear to have changed their minds. Professor White, in a note written for a colleague's textbook, has recanted and now supports the view that UCC 4-213 makes no substantive change in the law of restitution as applied to banks.

See D. Epstein & J. Martin, Basic Uniform Commercial Code 514 (2d ed. 1983). Presumably the next edition of his treatise will reflect this change in thinking.

Park Corporation next contends that, even if UCC 3-418 controls, it is both a holder in due course and one who has changed its position in reliance on National Saving's payment and therefore should be allowed to retain the $75,000. We find no support in the record for either proposition. On the holder in due course issue, Park does not qualify because it did not give value for the check. It was still in possession of the machinery it had contracted to sell to DAI. Although it had promised to deliver the equipment to DAI, such an executory promise does not constitute value. UCC 3-303, Comment 3. Park Corporation is, of course, no longer required to carry out its promise because DAI has breached its agreement to pay.

As for detrimental reliance, Park contends that it paid $37,500 as a commission to Garland Corporation on the assumption that DAI's check was good. However, Park did not pay Garland until February 13, 1980, two weeks after National Savings had informed Park that it had paid the DAI check by mistake and that it wanted Park to return the money. UCC 3-418 only makes payment by the bank final in favor of someone who has "in good faith changed his position in reliance on the payment." Once aware of the insufficiency in funds, Park could not have "in good faith" paid Garland $37,500 in reliance on that check. Park also alleges it paid rent for storing the equipment and painted the equipment in reliance on the payment. There is no evidence to support these allegations.

Accordingly, the decision of the district court is reversed.

Problem 17-1. Collector gives a check to Painter for the purchase price of a painting. At the time she delivers the check to Painter, Collector does not have sufficient funds in her checking account at Payor Bank but she expects money to be deposited by the time the check is presented for payment. Painter indorses the check in blank and delivers it to Art Supplies to pay off an overdue account. Art Supplies deposits the check with First Bank, which credits Art Supplies' account and forwards the check to Second Bank for presentation to Payor Bank. When the check is presented for payment Collector's funds have not yet been deposited in her account, and Payor Bank dishonors the check. The check is returned through the collecting banks to Art Supplies. What rights does Art Supplies have against the following entities:

(a) Payor Bank? Would your answer be different if Payor Bank had delayed in returning the check beyond the time limits specified in UCC 4-302?

(b) First Bank? Would your answer be different if First Bank had not charged back Art Supplies' account before the midnight deadline specified in UCC 4-212?

(c) Second Bank? Would your answer be different if Second Bank had delayed in the return of the dishonored check?

(d) Painter?

(e) Collector?

Problem 17-2. In the fact situation outlined in the previous problem assume that, without realizing that there are insufficient funds in Collector's account, Payor Bank pays the check by not revoking a provisional settlement. May Payor Bank recover the amount of the check from:

(a) Collector? See UCC 4-401.

(b) Art Supplies? See UCC 3-418, 4-213, 4-301.

(c) First Bank?

(d) Second Bank?

(e) Painter?

If, instead of transferring the check to Art Supplies, Painter had presented Collector's check to Payor Bank over the counter and had been paid cash, could Payor Bank recover this sum?

Problem 17-3. On May 1 Retailer issues a check for $1,500 to its manager. The following day Retailer issues to its two principal suppliers checks for $2,000 and $2,500 respectively. These three checks are presented to the drawee bank on May 5 in the same batch of checks from the local clearing house. At the time of presentment Retailer has only $5,000 in its account. An officer in the bank asks you which checks it is required to honor. Advise the officer. See UCC 4-303(2) and Comment 6 to that section.

Problem 17-4. Assume in the fact situation outlined in Problem 17-1 that Payor Bank does not pay the check. Is either Collector or Painter subject to prosecution under the following criminal statute?

32.41. Issuance of Bad Check

(a) A person commits an offense if he issues or passes a check or similar sight order for the payment of money knowing that the issuer does not have sufficient funds in or on deposit with the bank or other drawee for the payment in full of the check or order as well as all other checks or orders outstanding at the time of issuance.

(b) This section does not prevent the prosecution from establishing the required knowledge by direct evidence; however, for purposes of this section, the issuer's knowledge of insufficient funds is presumed (except in the case of a postdated check or order) if:

(1) he had no account with the bank or other drawee at the time he issued the check or order; or

(2) payment was refused by the bank or other drawee for lack of funds or insufficient funds on presentation within 30 days after issue and the issuer failed to pay the holder in full within 10 days after receiving notice of that refusal.

(c) Notice for purposes of Subsection (b)(2) of this section may be notice in writing, sent by registered or certified mail with return receipt requested or by telegram with report of delivery requested, and addressed to the issuer at his address shown on:

   (1)   the check or order;

   (2)   the records of the bank or other drawee; or

   (3)   the records of the person to whom the check or order has been issued or passed.

   (d) If notice is given in accordance with Subsection (c) of this section, it is presumed that the notice was received no later than five days after it was sent.

   (e) A person charged with an offense under this section may make restitution for the bad checks. Restitution shall be made through the prosecutor's office if collection and processing were initiated through that office. In other cases restitution may, with the approval of the court in which the offense is filed, be made through the court, by certified checks, cashier's checks, or money order only, payable to the person who received the bad checks.

WILLIAMS v. UNITED STATES, 458 U.S. 279, 34 UCC Rep. 385 (1982): Justice Blackmun, writing for the majority, summarizes the facts as follows:

"In 1975, petitioner William Archie Williams purchased a controlling interest in the Pelican State Bank in Pelican, La., and appointed himself president. The bank's deposits were insured by the Federal Deposit Insurance Corporation.

"Among the services the bank provided its customers at the time of petitioner's purchase was access to a 'dummy account,' used to cover checks drawn by depositors who had insufficient funds in their individual accounts. Any such check was processed through the dummy account and paid from the bank's general assets. The check was then held until the customer covered it by a deposit to his own account, at which time the held check was posted to the customer's account and the dummy account was credited accordingly. As president of the bank, petitioner enjoyed virtually unlimited use of the dummy account, and by May 2, 1978, his personal overdrafts amounted to $55,055.44, approximately half the total then covered by the account.

"On May 8, 1978, federal and state examiners arrived at the Pelican bank to conduct an audit. That same day, petitioner embarked on a series of transactions that seemingly amounted to a case of 'check kiting.'[1] He began by opening a checking account with a deposit of $4,649.97 at the federally-in-

---

1. As the Government explains, a check kiting scheme typically works as follows: "The check kiter opens an account at Bank A with a nominal deposit. He then writes a check on that account for a large sum, such as $50,000. The check kiter then opens an account at Bank B and deposits the $50,000 check from Bank A in that account. At the time of deposit, the check is not supported by sufficient funds in the account at Bank A. However, Bank B, unaware of this fact, gives the check kiter immediate credit on his account at Bank B. During the several-day period that the check on Bank A is being processed for collection from that bank, the check kiter writes a $50,000 check on his account at Bank B and deposits it into his account at Bank A. At the time of the deposit of that check, Bank A gives the check kiter immediate credit on his account there, and on the basis of that grant of credit pays the original $50,000 check when it is presented for collection.

   "By repeating this scheme, or some variation of it, the check kiter can use the $50,000 credit originally given by Bank B as an interest-free loan for an extended period of time. In effect, the check kiter can take advantage of the several-day period required for the transmittal, processing, and payment of checks from accounts in different banks. . . ." Brief for United States 12-13.

sured Winn State Bank and Trust Company in Winnfield, La. The next day, petitioner drew a check on his new Winn account for $58,500—a sum far in excess of the amount actually on deposit at the Winn bank—and deposited it in his Pelican account. Pelican credited his account with the face value of the check, at the same time deducting from petitioner's account the $55,055.44 total of his checks that previously had been cleared through the dummy account. At the close of business on May 9, then, petitioner had a balance of $452.89 at the Pelican bank.

"On May 10, petitioner wrote a $60,000 check on his Pelican account—again, a sum far in excess of the account balance—and deposited it in his Winn account. The Winn bank immediately credited the $60,000 to petitioner's account there, and Pelican cleared the check through its dummy account when it was presented for payment on May 11. The Winn bank routinely paid petitioner's May 9 check for $58,500 when it cleared on May 12.

"Petitioner next attempted to balance his Pelican account by depositing a $65,000 check drawn on his account at yet another institution, the Sabine State Bank in Many, La. Unfortunately, the balance in petitioner's Sabine account at the time was only $1,204.81. The Sabine bank therefore refused payment when Pelican presented the check on May 17. On May 23, petitioner settled his Pelican account by depositing at the Pelican bank a $65,000 money order obtained with the proceeds from a real estate mortgage loan."

Williams was indicted for violation of 18 U.S.C. §1014, which provides:

> Whoever knowingly makes any false statement or report, or willfully overvalues any land, property or security, for the purpose of influencing in any way the action of [named financial institutions] upon any application, advance, discount, purchase, purchase agreement, repurchase agreement, commitment, or loan . . . shall be fined not more than $5,000 or imprisoned not more than two years, or both.

A divided Supreme Court reversed Williams' conviction. The majority opinion pointed out that Williams had made no "false statement" for the technical reason that "a check is not a factual assertion at all. . . . Petitioner's bank checks served only to direct the drawee banks to pay the face amounts to the bearer, while committing petitioner to make good the obligations if the banks dishonored the drafts. Each check did not, in terms, make any representation as to the state of petitioner's bank balance." In support of this statement, the court cited UCC 3-104(2)(b), 3-413(2), and 3-409(1)—UCC Article 3 having been adopted in Louisiana at the time of the prosecution. The court notes that unlike many state statutes the federal statute does not cover the deposit of checks that are supported by insufficient funds.

Four justices dissented in two vigorous opinions. Justice White notes that just because the UCC describes the check in a certain manner does not mean that a check does not also carry other representations, including the representation that there are sufficient funds in the drawer's account. Justice Marshall agrees that a check necessarily implies that there are sufficient funds but he also argues that the court's reasoning discredits the theory underlying state statutes that provide that knowingly presenting a bad check is fraud and a misrepresentation.

Note: For a classic study of the use of the criminal justice system to punish bad-check offenders, see F. Beutel, Some Potentialities of Experimental Jurisprudence as a New Branch of Social Science 193-418 (1957) and the thoughtful review by Cavers, Science Research and the Law: Beutel's "Experimental Jurisprudence," 10 J. Legal Ed. 162 (1957).

B.   WRONGFUL DISHONOR

LOUCKS v. ALBUQUERQUE NATIONAL BANK
76 N.M. 735, 418 P.2d 191, 3 UCC Rep. 709 (1966)

La Fel E. OMAN, Judge, Court of Appeals. The plaintiffs-appellants, Richard A. Loucks and Del Martinez . . . were partners engaged in a business at Albuquerque, New Mexico, under the partnership name of L & M Paint and Body Shop. . . . By their complaint they sought both compensatory and punitive damages on behalf of the partnership, on behalf of Mr. Loucks, and on behalf of Mr. Martinez against the defendants-appellees, Albuquerque National Bank and W. J. Kopp. . . .

Prior to March 15, 1962 Mr. Martinez had operated a business at Albuquerque, New Mexico, under the name of Del's Paint and Body Shop. He did his banking with defendant bank and he dealt with Mr. Kopp, a vice-president of the bank. . . . On February 8, 1962 Mr. Martinez borrowed $500 from the bank, which he deposited with the bank in the account of Del's Paint and Body Shop. He executed an installment note payable to the bank evidencing this indebtedness.

On March 15, 1962 the plaintiffs formed a partnership in the name of L & M Paint and Body Shop. On that date they opened a checking account with the bank in the name of L & M Paint and Body Shop and deposited $620 therein. The signatures of both Mr. Loucks and Mr. Martinez were required to draw money from this account. The balance in the account of Del's Paint and Body Shop as of this time was $2.67. This was drawn from this account by a cashier's check and deposited in the account of L & M Paint & Body Shop on April 18, 1962.

Two payments of $50.00 each were made on Mr. Martinez' note of February 8, 1962, or on notes given as a renewal thereof. These payments were made by checks drawn by plaintiffs on the account of L & M Paint and Body Shop. The checks were payable to the order of the bank and were dated June 29, 1962 and August 28, 1962. A subsequent installment note was executed by Mr. Martinez on October 17, 1962 in the principal amount of $462 payable to the order of the bank. This was given as a replacement of the prior notes which started with the note of February 8, 1962. . . . Mr. Martinez became delinquent in his payments on this note of October 17, 1962 and the bank sued him in a Justice of the Peace court to recover the delinquency.

As of March 14, 1963 Mr. Martinez was still indebted to the bank on this note in the amount of $402, and on that date, Mr. Kopp, on behalf of the bank, wrote L & M Paint and Body Shop advising that its account had been charged with $402 representing the balance due "on Del Martinez installment note," and the indebtedness was referred to in the letter as the "indebtedness of Mr. Del Martinez."

The charge of $402 against the account of L & M Paint and Body Shop was actually made on March 15, 1963, which was a Friday. . . . Both plaintiffs went to the bank on Monday, March 18, and talked with Mr. Kopp. They both told Mr. Kopp that the indebtedness represented by the note was the personal indebtedness of Mr. Martinez and was not a partnership obligation. Mr. Loucks explained that they had some outstanding checks against the partnership account. Mr. Kopp refused to return the money to the partnership account. There was evidence of some unpleasantness in the conversation. The partnership account, in which there was then a balance of only $3.66, was thereupon closed by the plaintiffs.

The bank refused to honor nine, and possibly ten, checks drawn on the account and dated between the dates of March 8 and 16, inclusive. . . . The checks dated prior to March 15 total $89.14, and those dated March 15 and 16 total $121.68. . . .

The case came on for trial before the court and a jury. The court submitted the case to the jury upon the question of whether or not the defendants wrongfully made the charge in the amount of $402 against the account of L & M Paint and Body Shop. The allegations of the complaint concerning punitive damages and compensatory damages, other than the amount of $402 allegedly wrongfully charged by the defendants against the partnership account, were dismissed by the court before the case was submitted to the jury. The jury returned a verdict for the plaintiffs in the amount of $402.

The plaintiffs have appealed and assert error on the part of the trial court in taking from the jury the question of (1) punitive damages, (2) damages to business reputation and credit, (3) damages for personal injuries allegedly sustained by Mr. Loucks, and (4) in disallowing certain costs claimed by plaintiffs. . . .

The plaintiffs, as partners, sought recovery on behalf of the partnership of $402 allegedly wrongfully charged against the partnership account. This question was submitted to the jury, was decided in favor of the partnership, and against the defendants, and no appeal has been taken from the judgment entered on the verdict. They also sought recovery on behalf of the partnership of $5,000 for alleged damages to its credit, good reputation, and business standing in the community, $1,800 for its alleged loss of income, and $14,404 as punitive damages.

Each partner also sought recovery of $5,000 for alleged damages to his personal credit, good standing and business standing. Mr. Martinez sought punitive damages individually in the amount of $10,000, and Mr. Loucks sought punitive damages individually in the amount of $60,000. Mr. Loucks also sought $25,000 by way of damages he allegedly sustained by reason of an ulcer which resulted from the wrongful acts of the defendants.

The parties have argued the case in their respective briefs and in their oral arguments upon the theory that the questions here involved . . . are questions of the damages which can properly be claimed as a result of a wrongful dishonor by a bank of checks drawn by a customer or depositor on the bank, and of the sufficiency of the evidence offered by plaintiffs to support their claims for damages.

Both sides quote UCC 4-402 which provides as follows:

> A payor bank is liable to its customer for damages proximately caused by the wrongful dishonor of an item. When the dishonor occurs through mistake liability is limited to actual damages proved. If so proximately caused and proved damages may include damages for an arrest or prosecution of the customer or other consequential damages. Whether any consequential damages are proximately caused by the wrongful dishonor is a question of fact to be determined in each case.

It would appear that the first question to be resolved is that of the person, or persons, to whom a bank must respond in damages for a wrongful dishonor. Here, the account was a partnership account, and if there was in fact a wrongful dishonor of any checks, such were partnership checks.

We have adopted the Uniform Commercial Code in New Mexico. In UCC 4-402, quoted above, it is clearly stated that a bank "is liable to its customer." In UCC 4-104(1)(e), entitled "Definitions and index of definitions" it is stated that:

> (1) In this Article unless the context otherwise requires . . .
> (e) "Customer" means any person having an account with a bank or for whom a bank has agreed to collect items and includes a bank carrying an account with another bank; . . .

This requires us to determine who is a "person" within the contemplation of this definition. Under part II, article I of the Uniform Commercial Code, entitled "General Definitions and Principles of Interpretation," we find the term "person" defined in UCC 1-201(30) as follows: " 'Person' includes an individual or an organization . . . ." Subsection (28) of the same section expressly includes a "partnership" as one of the legal or commercial entities embraced by the term "organization."

It would seem that logically the "customer" in this case to whom the bank was required to respond in damages for any wrongful dishonor was the partnership. The Uniform Commercial Code expressly regards a partnership as a legal entity. This is consistent with the ordinary mercantile conception of a partnership. . . .

The question of whether a wrongful dishonor is to be considered as a breach of contract or as a breach of a tort duty was apparently avoided by the drafters of the Uniform Commercial Code by using the words "wrongful dishonor." UCC 4-402, Comment 2.

We have not overlooked the fact that tortious conduct may be tortious as to two or more persons, and that these persons may be the partnership and one or more of the individual partners. 2 Rowley on Partnership §49.2J, at 278 (R. Rowley 2d ed. 1960).

The relationship, in connection with which the wrongful conduct of the bank arose, was the relationship between the bank and the partnership. The partnership was the customer, and any damages arising from the dishonor belonged to the partnership and not to the partners individually.

The damages claimed by Mr. Loucks as a result of the ulcer, which allegedly resulted from the wrongful acts of the defendants, are not consequential damages proximately caused by the wrongful dishonor as contemplated by UCC 4-402. In support of his right to recover for such claimed damages he relies upon the cases of Jones v. Citizens Bank, 58 N.M. 48, 265 P.2d 366, and Weaver v. Bank of America, 59 Cal. 2d 428, 30 Cal. Rptr. 4, 380 P.2d 644. The California and New Mexico courts construed identical statutes in these cases. The New Mexico statute . . . was repealed when the Uniform Commercial Code was adopted in 1961.

Assuming we were to hold that the decisions in those cases have not been affected by the repeal of the particular statutory provisions involved and the adoption of the Uniform Commercial Code, we are still compelled by our reasoning to reach the same result, because the plaintiffs in those cases were the depositor in the California case and the administratrix of the estate of the deceased depositor in the New Mexico case. In the present case, Mr. Loucks was not a depositor, as provided in the prior statute, nor a customer, as provided in our present case. No duty was owed to him personally by reason of the debtor-creditor relationship between the bank and the partnership.

It is fundamental that compensatory damages are not recoverable unless they proximately result from some violation of a legally-recognized right of the person seeking the damages, whether such be a right in contract or tort. . . .

Insofar as the damage questions are concerned, we must still consider the claims for damages to the partnership. As above stated, the claim on behalf of the partnership for the recovery of the $402 was concluded by judgment for plaintiffs in this amount. This leaves (1) the claim of $5,000 for alleged damage to credit, reputation and business standing, (2) the claim of $1,800 for alleged loss of income, and (3) the claim of $14,404 as punitive damages.

The question with which we are first confronted is that of whether or not the customer, whose checks are wrongfully dishonored, may recover damages merely because of the wrongful dishonor. We understand the provisions of

UCC 4-402 to limit the damages to those proximately caused by the wrongful dishonor, and such includes any consequential damages so proximately caused. If the dishonor occurs through mistake, the damages are limited to actual damages proved.

It is pointed out in the comments to this section to the Uniform Commercial Code that: ". . . This section rejects decisions which have held that where the dishonored item has been drawn by a merchant, trader or fiduciary he is defamed in his business, trade or profession by a reflection on his credit and hence that substantial damages may be awarded on the basis of defamation 'per se' without proof that damage has occurred. . . ." UCC 4-402, Comment 3.

If we can say as a matter of law that the dishonor here occurred through mistake, then the damages would be limited to the "actual damages proved." Even if we are able to agree, as contended by defendants in their answer brief, that the defendants acted under a mistake of fact in ". . . that Mr. Kopp acting on behalf of the bank thought that the money was invested in the partnership and could be traced directly from Mr. Martinez to the L & M Paint and Body Shop," still defendants cannot rely on such mistake after both Mr. Martinez and Mr. Loucks informed them on March 15 and 18 that this was a personal obligation of Mr. Martinez and that the partnership had outstanding checks. At least it then became a question for the jury to decide whether or not defendants had wrongfully dishonored the checks through mistake.

The problem then resolves itself into whether or not the evidence offered and received, together with any evidence properly offered and improperly excluded, was sufficient to establish a question as to whether the partnership credit and reputation were proximately damaged by the wrongful dishonors. There was evidence that ten checks were dishonored, that one parts dealer thereafter refused to accept a partnership check and Mr. Loucks was required to go to the bank, cash the check, and then take the cash to the parts dealer in order to get the parts; that some persons who had previously accepted the partnership checks now refused to accept them; that other places of business denied the partnership credit after the dishonors; and that a salesman, who had sold the partnership a map and for which he was paid by one of the dishonored checks, came to the partnership's place of business, and ripped the map off the wall because he had been given "a bad check for it."

This evidence was sufficient to raise a question of fact to be determined by the jury as to whether or not the partnership's credit had been damaged as a proximate result of the dishonors. This question should have been submitted to the jury. . . .

The next item of damages claimed on behalf of the partnership, which was taken from the jury, was the claim for loss of income in the amount of $1,800 allegedly sustained by the partnership as a result of the illness and disability of Mr. Loucks by reason of his ulcer. We are of the opinion that the trial court properly dismissed this claim for the announced reason that no substantial evidence was offered to support the claim, and for the further reason that the partnership had no legally-enforceable right to recover for personal injuries inflicted upon a partner.

Even if we were to assume that a tortious act has been committed by defendants which proximately resulted in the ulcer and the consequent personal injuries and disabilities of Mr. Loucks, the right to recover for such would be in him. An action for damages resulting from a tort can only be sustained by the person directly injured thereby, and not by one claiming to have suffered collateral or resulting injuries. . . .

The last question of damages concerns the claim for punitive damages. The trial court dismissed this claim for the reason that he was convinced there was no evidence of willful or wanton conduct on the part of the defendants. Punitive or exemplary damages may be awarded only when the conduct of the wrongdoer may be said to be maliciously intentional, fraudulent, oppressive, or committed recklessly or with a wanton disregard of the plaintiffs' rights. . . . Malice as a basis for punitive damages means the intentional doing of a wrongful act without just cause or excuse. This means that the defendant not only intended to do the act which is ascertained to be wrongful, but that he knew it was wrong when he did it. . . .

Although, as expressed above, we are of the opinion that there was a jury question as to whether defendants acted under a mistake of fact in dishonoring the checks, we do not feel that the unpleasant or intemperate remark or two claimed to have been made by Mr. Kopp, and his conduct, described by Mr. Martinez as having "run us out of the bank more or less," are sufficient upon which an award of punitive damages could properly have been made. Thus, the trial court was correct in taking this claim from the jury. . . .

It follows from what has been said that this cause must be reversed and remanded for a new trial solely upon the questions of whether or not the partnership credit was damaged as a proximate result of the dishonors, and, if so, the amount of such damages. . . .

NOTES & QUESTIONS

1. *The trader rule.* Prior to the UCC many jurisdictions recognized the "trader rule": if a bank wrongfully dishonored a check written by a customer who was a merchant then it was presumed that his credit and reputation were damaged and he could recover substantial damages by merely showing that the check had been dishonored wrongfully. There has been considerable debate about whether the Code retains the rule. Comment 3 to UCC 4-402, quoted by the *Loucks* court, suggests the rule has been abolished. A recent thorough study of the problem comes to the same conclusion. Davenport, Wrongful Dishonor: UCC Section 4-402 and the Trader Rule, 56 N.Y.U.L. Rev. 1117 (1981) (precedent and reason support conclusion that trader rule was abolished).

But does the language of UCC 4-402 leave room for the trader rule? The limitation to actual damages is set out in a sentence that addresses dishonors through mistake. Where the dishonor is *willful* what damages may be recovered? For a suggestion that the trader rule continues where dishonor is willful, see J. White & R. Summers, Handbook of the Law under the Uniform Commercial Code §17-4 (2d ed. 1980).

2. *Dishonor through mistake.* Even if one accepts that the distinction between mistaken and willful dishonors may lead to different damage awards, how does one know whether the bank's act is willful? Is a setoff against a customer's account in the mistaken belief that there is a legal right to do so a willful act?

Consider the following analysis: "The next question we must decide is what the word *mistake* means in the second sentence, for whether the dishonor was a mistake determines which rule applies. *Mistake* here has several possible meanings. One is anything but a knowingly wrongful dishonor. This is overly broad; even if the mistake exception was included primarily to allow courts to award punitive damages, *mistake* should not be limited to all but such deliberate dishonors. Another is that suggested in White & Summers, at 669-674, which is essentially a distinction between mistakes of law and mistakes of fact. We are not persuaded that this distinction is the proper one. The most sensible meaning is *good faith* as defined in Article 2: 'honesty in fact and the observance of reasonable commercial standards of fair-dealing in the trade.' Cf. Farmers & Merchants State Bank of Krum v. Ferguson, 605 S.W.2d 320 (Tex. Civ. App. 1980) (at least where bank is reckless, action under UCC 4-402 sounds in tort for purposes of recovery for mental anquish as consequential damages)." Elizarraras v. Bank of El Paso, 631 F.2d 366, 376-377, 30 UCC Rep. 627, 641-642 (5th Cir. 1980) (bank's failure to notify customer that interpleader action had been filed was not in good faith and subsequent dishonor was therefore not a mistake).

3. *Damages recoverable.* UCC 4-402 refers to "actual damages" and the possibility of "consequential damages." What about damages for emotional distress or punitive damages? Comment 2 to UCC 4-402 disclaims any theory (breach of contract, tort, or defamation) for the statutory cause of action. Damages for emotional distress and punitive damages are usually recoverable in tort but not contract actions. UCC 1-106 itself provides that "neither consequential or special nor penal damages may be had except as specifically provided in this Act or by other rule of law." What "other rule of law" supplements UCC 4-402?

In Yacht Club Sales & Service, Inc. v. First National Bank, 623 P.2d 464, 29 UCC Rep. 1340 (Idaho 1979) the bank had a "hold" on its cutomer's account when it received a writ of execution against an entity that had a similar name. The bank did not inform the customer and subsequently dishonored several checks drawn on the account. The court held that the customer must introduce evidence of actual damages but it need not prove an "exact dollar amount." The court also held that, notwithstanding UCC 1-106, punitive damages could be awarded by reference to common law rules of either contract or tort law applicable by virtue of UCC 1-103. Idaho law permits recovery in contract actions where there is "clear evidence of fraud, malice or oppression, or if there is other sufficient reason." Id. at 1352.

4. *Prior statute.* The court in *Loucks* refers to a New Mexico statute the UCC repealed. This pre-Code provision was drafted by the American Bankers Association and had been adopted by 24 states. It stated:

> No bank shall be liable to a depositor because of the nonpayment through mistake or error, and without malice, of a check which should have been paid unless the depositor shall allege and prove actual damage by reason of such nonpayment and in such event the liability shall not exceed the amount of damage so proved.

Is UCC 4-402 an improvement in drafting? How would you redraft the provision?

Problem 17-5. Kendall Yacht Corporation opens a deposit account with National Bank. Unknown to the bank, the corporation has never issued corporate shares. The bank deals with Larry and Linda Kendall, sole officers of the corporation, and when the corporation borrows from the bank the Kendalls personally guarantee the corporation's debt. One year after the corporate account is opened the bank receives a writ garnishing the account of a Kimbell Boatyard Corporation. Not having an account in that name and noting the similarity with the Kendall Yacht Corporation account, the bank puts a hold on the Kendall account without informing the corporation or the Kendalls. As a result, the bank subsequently dishonors checks totaling $5,000 drawn on the corporation account, even though there are sufficient funds to pay the checks if there is no hold on the account. Larry and Linda Kendall bring an action against the bank for $10,000 in actual damages and $50,000 in punitive damages. You represent the bank. What defenses will you explore?

Problem 17-6. In the previous problem, assume you discover in your research that the signature card for the Kendall Yacht Corporation includes the following clause: "Customer agrees that National Bank will not be liable for failing to honor checks drawn on Customer's account when the bank determines that more than one person are claiming the account in good faith." What is the effect of this clause?

C. WRONGFUL PAYMENT; STOP ORDERS

SIEGEL v. NEW ENGLAND MERCHANTS NATIONAL BANK
386 Mass. 672, 437 N.E.2d 218, 33 UCC Rep. 1601 (1982)

HENNESSEY, Chief Justice. We are called upon to define the respective rights of a bank and its depositor when the bank has paid a post-dated check before maturity and deducted the amount of the check from the depositor's account. Applying the Uniform Commercial Code, we conclude that the bank must recredit the depositor's account, but may then assert against the depositor any rights acquired by prior holders on either the instrument or the transaction from which it arose. In the course of this opinion, we shall describe the parties' responsibilities of proof with respect to the bank's subrogation claim. We remand for a further hearing on the question of subrogation.

The plaintiff's decedent, David Siegel, maintained a checking account with the defendant, New England Merchants National Bank. On September 14, 1973, Siegel drew and delivered a $20,000 check to Peter Peters, post-dated November 14, 1973. Peters immediately deposited the check in his own bank, which forwarded it for collection. The defendant bank overlooked the date on the check, and, on September 17, paid the item and charged it against Siegel's account. Siegel discovered the error in late September when another of his checks was returned for insufficient funds. He informed the bank that the check to Peters was post-dated November 14, and asked the bank to stop payment of the check. Later, he requested that the bank return the $20,000 to him.

When the bank refused to restore the $20,000, Siegel brought this action for wrongful debit of his account. The bank denied liability, raised defenses of waiver, estoppel, and ratification, and filed counterclaims asserting rights on the instrument and rights of subrogation. Two banks in the collecting chain became parties, one permitted to intervene as a party defendant and the other impleaded by the bank. The bank also impleaded Peters, the payee, who filed a suggestion of bankruptcy. The case was later dismissed as against the two collecting banks.

After a trial, jury-waived, the judge found that the check was post-dated by agreement between Peters and Siegel, without fraudulent purpose, and that Siegel had acted with reasonable speed to inform the bank of the error. He also found that Peters had paid no money to Siegel since receiving the check. The judge ruled that (1) the check was a negotiable instrument; (2) the check was not payable until November 14; (3) the bank was negligent in paying it before that date; (4) the bank had no right to debit Siegel's account; (5) Siegel had not waived his rights or ratified the bank's action and was not estopped from demanding the $20,000; and (6) the wrongful debit caused Siegel a loss of $20,000. He also rejected the bank's counterclaims as having no merit. He then entered judgments for Siegel against the bank in the amount of $20,000, for Siegel on the bank's counterclaims, and for the bank against Peters for $20,000. The bank appealed, and we transferred the case to this court on our own motion. We vacate the judgment and remand the case for further consideration of the bank's subrogation claims. . . .

The parties agree that the bank should not have paid the check when Peters presented it on September 14, and had no right at that time to charge it against Siegel's account. UCC 3-114, 4-401(1). . . . Their differences center instead on whether the bank's wrongful action caused Siegel any loss, so as to entitle him to damages. Siegel contends, and the judge ruled, that his loss must be $20,000 because that amount was debited from his account. The bank contends that there was no loss, because Siegel drew the check with the intention that it eventually be paid, and the bank could rightfully have charged it against his account on November 14. We believe that the drafters of the code anticipated disputes such as this, and provided a logical system for their resolution.

We begin with UCC 4-401(1), which governs bookkeeping between depositor and bank. A bank may charge any "properly payable" item against its depositor's account. Implicitly, the bank may not charge items, such as postdated checks, that are not properly payable. If the charge is unauthorized, it follows that the depositor has a valid claim to the amount of the charge by virtue of the account itself. . . .

As the bank points out, the depositor's realization of this claim may produce unjust enrichment. Even when an item is not properly payable, due to prematurity or a stop payment order, the bank's payment may discharge a legal obligation of the depositor, or create a right in the depositor's favor against the payee. See UCC 3-601(1)(a), 3-603(1), 3-802(1)(b); J. White & R. Summers, Uniform Commercial Code 542 (2d ed. 1980). If the depositor were permitted to retain such benefits, and recover the amount of the check as well, he would profit at the bank's expense. Therefore, UCC 4-407 provides that upon payment, the bank is "subrogated" to any rights prior holders may have had against the drawer-depositor, on either the check or the initial underlying transaction, and to any rights the drawer may have against the payee or other holders.[5] . . .

Thus, the code fixes the rights of the bank and the depositor by a two part adjustment. The depositor has a claim against the bank for the amount improperly debited from its account, and the bank has a claim against the depositor based on subrogation to the rights of the payee and other holders. The bank may assert its subrogation rights defensively when its depositor brings an action for wrongful debit. . . .

Here, the bank asserted a subrogation claim based on the rights of Peters, the payee.[6] Neither party, however, introduced evidence concerning Peters's rights against Siegel.[7] A question then arises as to what matters each party was obligated to prove in order to prevail.

---

5. . . . At the time a bank asserts subrogation rights, the check will of course have been paid, and prior holders will have no rights against the drawer. UCC 3-601(1)(a), UCC 3-603(1), UCC 3-802(1)(b). Therefore, we understand UCC 4-407 to refer to rights existing prior to the payment.

6. The bank waived all claims based on the rights of the collecting banks.

7. The trial judge did find that the transaction between Peters and Siegel arose out of Siegel's sale of a shopping mall to Peters, and Peters's subsequent default on payments due Siegel on notes, and that Siegel and Peters had agreed to the post-dating of the check. He also found that Peters had "made no payment to [Siegel] since he received the check, either as payment on the notes or as a repayment of the $20,000 extended by the check." The bank objects to these findings on the ground that there is no evidence in the record to support them. The bank appears to be correct on this point. In any event, the judge's findings, while they tend to suggest that the transaction was a loan, do not clearly establish either that Peters was entitled to receive the money on November 14, or that Siegel had a right to cancel the transaction before the check became due. It should be

UCC 4-403(3) provides that when the problem is one of improper payment over a stop order, the "burden of establishing the fact and amount of loss . . . is on the customer." UCC 4-403(3). Here, of course, the bank's liability is for premature payment rather than for payment over a stop order. Nevertheless, these two forms of improper payment have in common the problem of unjust enrichment, and we believe that UCC 4-403(3) is a source of useful analogy.

The rule of UCC 4-403(3), that a depositor must prove his loss, may at first seem at odds with our earlier conclusion that UCC 4-401(1) provides the depositor with a claim against the bank in the amount of the check, leaving the bank with recourse through subrogation under UCC 4-407. . . . We believe, however, that UCC 4-403(3) was intended to operate within the process of credit and subrogation established by UCC 4-401(1) and 4-407. See UCC 4-403, comment 8. When a bank pays an item improperly, the depositor loses his ability to exercise any right he had to withhold payment of the check. His "loss," in other words, is equivalent to his rights and defenses against the parties to whose rights the bank is subrogated—the other party to the initial transaction and other holders of the instrument. UCC 4-403(3) simply protects the bank against the need to prove events familiar to the depositor, and far removed from the bank, before it can realize its subrogation rights. The depositor, who participated in the initial transaction, knows whether the payee was entitled to eventual payment and whether any defenses arose. Therefore, UCC 4-403(3) requires that he, rather than the bank, prove these matters. . . .

This view of the three relevant sections of the code suggests a fair allocation of the burden of proof. The bank, which has departed from authorized bookkeeping, must acknowledge a credit to the depositor's account. It must then assert its subrogation rights, and in doing so must identify the status of the parties in whose place it claims. If the bank's subrogation claims are based on the check, this would entail proof that the third party subrogor was a holder, or perhaps a holder in due course. This responsibility falls reasonably upon the bank, because it has received the check from the most recent holder and is in at least as good a position as the depositor to trace its history.

The depositor must then prove any facts that might demonstrate a loss. He must establish defenses good against a holder or holder in due course, as the case may be. UCC 3-305, 3-306. If the initial transaction is at issue, he must prove either that he did not incur a liability to the other party, or that he has a defense to liability. Thus the bank, if it asserts rights based on the

---

noted that the mere circumstance that the transaction was a loan, and that the loan had since proved uncollectible, would not necessarily mean that the bank's premature payment had caused the depositor a loss. If the payee was unconditionally entitled to receive the loan, the risk that he would not repay it was a risk the depositor assumed in making the loan, and was not increased by the bank's action. UCC 4-407, by extending the bank's subrogation to rights on the instrument as well as to rights on the transaction, makes clear that the depositor could not recover in this situation. Thus, to defeat the bank's subrogation rights the depositor must establish a condition on the right to cash the check, an element of fraud, or some other defense good against the payee as a holder of the instrument.

transaction, need not make out a claim on the part of its subrogor against the depositor. Responsibility in this area rests entirely with the depositor, who participated in the transaction and is aware of its details. Further, the depositor must establish any consequential loss.[8]

A further hearing is necessary to determine the question of subrogation in the present case. The judge ruled that the check was a negotiable instrument, see UCC 3-114(1), and the evidence at trial fairly indicated that Peters was a holder. See UCC 1-201(20). Thus the burden, under the rules we have set out, was upon Siegel to prove a defense good against a holder of the instrument. However, the trial record makes clear that neither the parties nor the judge was proceeding with these rules in mind. Indeed, the judge excluded, at the bank's strenuous request, evidence offered by Siegel concerning the transaction between Siegel and Peters. We believe, therefore, that Siegel's executrix should have had an opportunity to present evidence that Siegel suffered a loss. . . .

In sum, Siegel had a valid claim against the bank for premature payment in the amount of the item paid, but the bank was entitled to assert the rights of prior holders on the check and on the transaction from which it arose. We vacate the judgment and remand for a further hearing to determine those rights. At the hearing, the bank must establish the status of its subrogor. Siegel's executrix must establish any defenses to liability on the instrument as well as the absence of rights or presence of defenses on the underlying transaction.

NOTES & QUESTIONS

1. *Use of postdated checks.* Why did the parties in the *Siegel* case use a postdated check? Would creating an escrow arrangement or giving a promissory note have been the functional equivalent? Could Siegel have protected himself by issuing a stop order on the check and then revoking the stop order at the time payment was due?

2. *Postdated checks: bank liability.* To what extent may a bank avoid the consequence of premature payment of a postdated check by a contract with its customer? (See UCC 1-102(3), 4-103.) Does the following clause effectively protect a bank such as the payor bank in *Siegel?* "It is agreed that Bank will

8. Several courts have harmonized UCC 4-403(3) with 4-401(1) and 4-407 in terms of shifting burdens of production and persuasion. "Simply because a bank pays a check over a stop payment order does not entitle the customer to recover damages against the bank, but it does establish a *prima facie* case for the customer. The bank must present evidence to show absence of loss, or the right of the payee of the check to receive payment. Then the customer must sustain the ultimate burden to show why there was a defense to payment of the item." Southeast First Natl. Bank v. Atlantic Telec, Inc., 389 So. 2d 1032, 1033 (Fla. Dist. Ct. App. 1980). Mitchell v. Republic Bank & Trust Co., 35 N.C. App. 101, 104, 289 S.E.2d 867 (1978). Thomas v. Marine Midland Tinkers Natl. Bank, 86 Misc. 2d 284, 290-291, 381 N.Y.S.2d 797 (Sup. Ct. 1976). Although our analysis will often have the same result as that of the cited cases, it may in some cases give greater force to UCC 4-403(3).

not be liable for any damage caused by premature payment, through accident or inadvertence, of a postdated check, whether such damages arise from dishonor of a check subsequently presented or otherwise. It is further agreed that Bank shall have all rights of a purchaser and holder in due course of a postdated check for which it pays out money or gives other value in good faith before the date of the instrument."

3. *Right to charge fee for stop payment.* The Michigan attorney general has issued several opinions defining the circumstances under which a bank may charge a fee for stopping payment. In the first opinion the attorney general concluded that a bank may not condition the exercise of the statutory right to stop payment by requiring a customer to pay a fee. Michigan Atty. Gen. Op. No. 5867, 30 UCC Rep. 1626 (April 13, 1981). A subsequent opinion concluded, however, that a bank and its customer may expressly agree that the customer is to pay a fee, subject, however, to the doctrine of adhesion contracts that make inconspicuous or unclear contractual language unenforceable. Michigan Atty. Gen. Op. No. 5947, 33 UCC Rep. 1445 (August 7, 1981). Does the following clause, in small print, satisfy these requirements? "Bank will charge a fee for implementing any stop payment order and Depositor agrees to pay such fee."

4. *Stop order as one of UCC 4-303's "four legals."* Review the *West Side Bank* case and text following, at p. 797 supra, and UCC 4-303. If a stop order is received and a reasonable time to act on it expires after the bank has taken any of the steps listed in UCC 4-303(1) then it comes too late to terminate the bank's right or duty to pay the check. May the bank nevertheless stop payment (i.e., dishonor) as an accommodation to its customer? Will the bank be liable on the instrument if it does dishonor the check? (Note that the steps listed in UCC 4-303(1) differ somewhat from the provisions of UCC 4-213(1) on final payment.) Why didn't the court in *West Side Bank* refer to UCC 4-303?

Problem 17-7. Retailer discovers that the stationery purchased from his supplier is defective and telephones his bank to stop payment on the check he gave to the supplier in payment. He informs the bank officer that the check number is 4321 and that the amount of the check is $1,210.80. In fact, the check is number 4311 and the amount of the check is $1,280.10. The bank is unable to find this check using its computer check-sorting program and pays the supplier when it presents the check for payment. Retailer protests the charge to his account. As attorney for the bank you are asked if the bank must reverse the charge. Advise the bank.

If you determine that the bank is obligated to Retailer you are asked to prepare language to be placed in the signature card or stop order form to protect the bank in the future. What language do you suggest?

Problem 17-8. Assume that in the preceding problem Retailer instead promptly submits an accurately-completed stop-order form to the bank. Inadvertently the bank pays the supplier when it presents the $1,280.10 check.

Retailer protests the charge to his account, pointing out that the defective stationery is worth no more than $300.

(a) If the bank agrees to reverse the charge to Retailer's account does it have any recourse against the supplier? See UCC 4-407.

(b) If the bank refuses to reverse the charge what rights does Retailer have against the supplier?

(c) If the bank refuses to reverse the charge what rights does Retailer have against the bank? What is the effect of the following clause in the signature card signed by Retailer when he opened the account? "Depositor agrees to indemnify and reimburse Bank for any loss, damages, costs, suits, judgments and any expenses resulting from nonpayment of any item drawn on this Account for which a stop payment order is requested. Should Bank pay an item subsequent to a request of stop payment either due to inadvertence or oversight, or if by reason of such payment other items drawn by Depositor are returned insufficient, it is expressly agreed that Bank shall in no way be held responsible or liable."

(d) Following refusal to reverse the charge the bank dishonors other checks drawn by Retailer on the account because of insufficient funds. Will Retailer be able to recover for wrongful dishonor? See UCC 4-402, 4-403.

Problem 17-9. Assume that in the preceding problem Retailer orally asks the bank to stop payment on his check to supplier. On the afternoon of the same day, four hours later, the check is presented for payment and the bank pays the check by mistake. As attorney for the bank you are asked if the bank must reverse the charge to Retailer's account. Advise the bank. See UCC 4-403(1), 4-303.

DZIURAK v. CHASE MANHATTAN BANK, N.A.
58 A.D.2d 103, 396 N.Y.S.2d 414, 21 UCC Rep. 1130 (1977), aff'd, 44 N.Y.2d 776, 377 N.E.2d 474, 406 N.Y.S.2d 474, 23 UCC Rep. 958 (1978)

COHALAN, Justice Presiding. The sole question on this appeal is whether a bank depositor to whom an "official bank check" has been issued (and by him endorsed to the order of a third party), can legally stop payment thereon, in the absence of a court order or an indemnification bond. An official bank check is commonly referred to as a "cashier's check." Trial Term held it could be stopped. We disagree. . . .

The plaintiff currently holds a judgment against the defendant Chase Manhattan Bank (Bank) in the amount of $17,000, plus interest and costs.

During the year 1973 Dziurak maintained a savings account with "Branch #40" of the Bank in the sum of $18,000. He was cozened by an acquaintance named Staveris into a proposal whereby, for $22,000 cash, he could acquire a one-third interest in a corporation whose sole asset was a going restaurant. There was nothing in writing to bind the bargain. Dziurak paid

Staveris $5,000 down. He then went to the Bank and, through the assistant manager, arranged for the proper withdrawal. He asked for a "check" to be drawn to the order of Staveris. Monaco, the assistant manager, advised him to have the check drawn to himself as payee. A further bit of advice by Monaco was for Dziurak to go to his attorney, who would instruct him how to endorse the check.

The $17,000 was transferred to the Bank's coffers and Dziurak's savings account was debited accordingly. A cashier's check was then issued to the order of "Francis A. Dziurak."

Plaintiff ignored the suggestion that he consult with his attorney. Instead he wrote on the back of the instrument "Francis Dziurak. Pay to order Mario Staveris" and delivered the item to Staveris. The latter, instead of depositing the check into the corporate restaurant account, deposited it in his own savings account.

Before he learned of Staveris' perfidy and before the cashier's check had cleared, Dziurak belatedly sought the advice of a local attorney. Very properly, the attorney advised him to try to stop payment on the cashier's check.

Back went Dziurak to the Bank. He saw Monaco and asked him if the check had cleared. It had not, but had arrived at the Bank that morning.

While plaintiff was with him, Monaco telephoned the Bank's attorney and was advised that the check could not be stopped, absent a court order. He so advised the plaintiff and while Dziurak was still with him he telephoned the plaintiff's attorney to advise him to the same effect. The attorney said he was aware that a court order could effectively produce a stop of the payment.

This action was started against the Bank after judgment was first taken against Staveris, and after execution was returned unsatisfied.

As to the law, the controlling statutes are contained in several sections of the Uniform Commercial Code (hereinafter UCC) which, in turn, are fleshed out in reported decisions of nisi prius and appellate courts.

We begin with UCC 4-403(1) ("Customer's Right to Stop Payment; Burden of Proof of Loss"):

> A customer may by order to his bank stop payment of *any item payable for his account* but the order must be received at such time and in such manner as to afford the bank a reasonable opportunity to act on it prior to any action by the bank with respect to the item described in Section 4-303. (Emphasis supplied.)

As to this section (UCC 4-403) we part company with Trial Term, which held that the $17,000 represented by the cashier's check was actually Dziurak's money and not that of the Bank. As noted in Wertz v. Richardson Heights Bank & Trust, 495 S.W.2d 572, 574 (Tex. 1973): "A cashier's check is not one payable for the customer's account but rather for the bank's account. It is the bank which is obligated on the check."

The reference in UCC 4-403 more properly fits the situation where the depositor, as drawer, issues his own check on his own bank, as drawee. Such a check can be stopped if reasonable notice is given. "A cashier's check is of a very different character. It is the primary obligation of the bank which issues it (citation omitted) and constitutes its written promise to pay upon demand (citation omitted). It has been said that a cashier's check is a bill of exchange drawn by a bank upon itself, accepted in advance by the very act of issuance" (Matter of Bank of United States [O'Neill], 243 A.D. 287, 291, 277 N.Y.S. 96, 100). This exposition of the law has been followed consistently. . . . No decisions holding to the contrary have been unearthed.

But to go on. UCC 4-303(1) ("When Items Subject to . . . Stop-Order") states, in part:

> Any . . . stop-order received by . . . a payor bank, whether or not effective under other rules of law to terminate . . . the bank's right or duty to pay an item . . . comes too late to so terminate . . . if the . . . stop-order . . . is received . . . and a reasonable time for the bank to act thereon expires . . . after the bank has done any one of the following:
> (a) accepted or certified the item.

The next section to consider is UCC 3-410 ("Definition and Operation of Acceptance"):

> (1) Acceptance is the drawee's signed engagement to honor the draft as presented. It must be written on the draft, and may consist of his signature alone. It becomes operative when completed by delivery or notification.

At this point we can refer back to annotation 5 in the Official Comment under UCC 4-403: "There is no right to stop payment after certification of a check or other acceptance of a draft, and this is true no matter who procures the certification. See Sections 3-411 and 4-303. The acceptance is the drawee's own engagement to pay, and he is not required to impair his credit by refusing payment for the convenience of the drawer."

Thus, the Bank's one signature on the instrument constitutes both a drawing and an acceptance and makes the Bank a drawer and a drawee. . . .

In the recitation of the facts, mention was made that the local attorney for the plaintiff remarked to Monaco that he was aware that a court order (presumably one of a court of competent jurisdiction) could have acted as a "stop payment" order. The statute providing for such an order is UCC 3-603. It is headnoted "Payment or Satisfaction" and, pertinently, reads:

> (1) The liability of any party is discharged to the extent of his payment . . . to the holder even though it is made with knowledge of a claim of another person to the instrument unless prior to such payment . . . *the person making the claim either supplies indemnity deemed adequate by the party seeking the discharge* or enjoins payment or satisfaction by order of a court of competent jurisdiction in an action in which the adverse claimant and the holder are parties. (Emphasis supplied.)

The fact that the attorney for the plaintiff was aware that a court order could effect a stop payment presupposes that he also knew he could file an indemnity bond to protect the Bank, since both options are included in UCC 3-603(1).

Viewed in retrospect, the Bank, as a practical matter, could quite safely have stopped payment on its cashier's check and, by interpleader, have paid the money into court. Staveris could not have established himself as a holder in due course (see UCC 3-302). But, if the Legislature laid upon a bank the onus of questioning the reason for the issuance of all cashier's checks it would destroy the efficacy of such instruments, which, for all practical purposes, are treated as the equivalent of cash. . . .

To do justice to the Bank, it is only fair to observe that the entire brouhaha was occasioned by the intransigence of Dziurak. Had he followed the advice of Monaco to consult his attorney, the situation in which the parties are now involved would have been averted. . . .

Contrary to Trial Term's opinion, the statute makes no distinction between a cashier's check presented for payment by a payee or one presented by an endorsee of the payee. . . . It engages to pay on demand to the person who presents the check unless he falls within either of the categories listed in UCC 3-603(1) (theft or restrictive endorsement).

From all that has been stated, and harsh as it may appear, it follows that the judgment must be reversed and the complaint dismissed, with costs. . . .

NOTES & QUESTIONS

1. Dziurak *case on appeal.* The New York Court of Appeal affirmed the *Dziurak* order set out above in a memorandum opinion that stated only that the issuing bank accepted the cashier's check on issuance and therefore the item was not payable for a customer's account within the meaning of UCC 4-403(1). Dziurak v. Chase Manhattan Bank, N.A., 44 N.Y.2d 776, 377 N.E.2d 475, 406 N.Y.S.2d 30 (1978). Does this mean that the court of appeals rejected the lower court's analysis based on UCC 4-303?

2. *Defenses available to bank issuing a cashier's check.* If the bank in the *Dziurak* case chooses to dishonor the cashier's check as an accommodation to Dziurak it will be liable on its contract as an *acceptor* of the check. UCC 3-413(1). As a holder, but not a holder in due course, Staveris (the indorsee) will be able to enforce this contractual liability subject to the available defenses under UCC 3-306. Does the issuing bank have any defenses? It received consideration from Dziurak (the payee) by its charge against his account; Dziurak did not obtain the check by fraud or misrepresentation. May the bank raise Dziurak's defense of fraud? See UCC 3-306(d). May the bank, in its capacity as drawer, order itself to stop payment? If so, will its stop-payment order ever be timely under UCC 4-303(1)(a)?

3. *Cashier's checks as substitute for cash.* The court in *Dziurak* suggests that cashier's checks are treated as the equivalent of cash. If so, should *any* defenses be available against a holder of a cashier's check? For a suggestion that only the defenses of forgery and alteration should be available to the issuer of cashier's checks, see Lawrence, Making Cashier's Checks and Other Bank Checks Cost-Effective: A Plea for Revision of Articles 3 and 4 of the Uniform Commercial Code, 64 Minn. L. Rev. 275 (1980) (to allow other defenses would impose costs on cashier's checks substantially similar to personal checks and would make them inefficient substitutes for cash).

4. *Personal money orders and teller's checks.* Cashier's checks, where the bank draws a check on itself payable to the order of the person designated by the customer or purchaser of the check, should be distinguished from personal money orders and teller's checks.

(a) A personal money order is like a one-shot checking account. A financial institution may sell a personal money order to a customer who fills in the name of the payee and signs the instrument as drawer; the financial institution is the drawee.

(b) A teller's check is an instrument drawn by a financial institution on its checking account at a bank to the order of a payee designated by the purchaser of the teller's check. The financial institution is the drawer of the check, the bank is the drawee, and the purchaser of the instrument is the remitter, a term used but not defined by the Code.

Given the different relations between the parties on these instruments, do different legal rules determine whether a purchaser may stop payment? If in commercial practice transferees treat these instruments as interchangeable should the rules on stopping payment be the same? See generally Note, Personal Money Orders and Teller's Checks: Mavericks Under the UCC, 67 Colum. L. Rev. 524 (1967).

Problem 17-10. On April 1 Dorsett purchases with cash the personal money order set out below from First National Bank. Together with the money order Dorsett receives a Record Copy to record the money order's details. At the bottom of the Record Copy there is a printed statement that the money order is sold on two conditions: (1) the purchaser signs his name and address after filling in a date and name of a payee, and (2) no request for a refund or a stop payment may be made to the bank unless the Record Copy is submitted with the request. Several hours after the purchase Dorsett reports to the bank that the money order had been lost or stolen and requests that payment be stopped.

On April 2 Riggins presents the money order in its blank form to White, who runs a check cashing service. On furnishing proof of his identity, Riggins inserts his name as payee and signs the money order. White pays Riggins the amount of the money order, less a fee for cashing the check.

White presents the check for payment. May he enforce the check against First National Bank? See UCC 3-603.

FORM 17-1

Personal Money Order   Personal Money Order

FIRST NATIONAL BANK
Register Check

_____ 19____

Pay to the order of _____

One hundred and fifty dollars ($150.00)

No. 19,473   Signature: _____

                     Date: _____

Problem 17-11. Assume that Dorsett purchases the money order in the preceding problem with a personal check drawn on State Bank. Dorsett promptly delivers the properly-completed money order to Harris in payment of a pre-existing debt. State Bank dishonors Dorsett's check because there are insufficient funds in his account. When Harris presents the money order to First National Bank it refuses to pay. May Harris recover from the bank? Would Harris be in a better position if First National Bank had issued a cashier's check rather than a money order?

Problem 17-12. Bryan sells a go-cart business to B & G Construction Co. on October 11. As part of the consideration for the go-carts Bryan receives a $10,000 check drawn by B & G on the Citizens National Bank, which is postdated to November 1. B & G issues a stop payment order on the check on October 19 after it has concluded that the business has been overvalued. Bryan does not know of the stop order and repeatedly attempts to obtain payment of the check from Citizens. Each time Bryan presents the check, he is told only that the account contains insufficient funds. On November 11, however, Bryan presents the check again, and Citizens' president approves payment. Citizens gives Bryan a cashier's check for $10,000 in payment of B & G's check for $10,000, and Bryan deposits the cashier's check in another bank. Bryan uses the funds for living expenses and as security for loans. Citizens now brings an action against Bryan for restitution. You represent Bryan. Advise him.

D. FORGERY

Many generations of law students have been entertained by the problem of how the law should allocate losses from forged or unauthorized signatures on negotiable instruments. The obvious answer is rarely a practical one: the forger will usually have disappeared or will be insolvent. The loss must, therefore, be allocated between more or less innocent persons. The Code's framework for dealing with this problem is summarized in the following excerpt from an opinion by Judge Everett Goldberg.*

A.   THE CODE FRAMEWORK

Perpetuating a distinction introduced into the legal annals by Lord Mansfield in the eighteenth century, the Code accords separate treatment to forged drawer signatures (hereinafter "forged checks") and forged indorsements. In general, the drawee bank is strictly liable to its customer drawer for payment of either a forged check or a check containing a forged indorsement. In the case of a forged indorsement, the drawee generally may pass liability back through the collection chain to the party who took from the forger and, of course, to the forger himself if available. In the case of a forged check, however, liability generally rests with the drawee. The patchwork of provisions from which this general allocation of liability emerges merits more detailed description.

1.   Forged Indorsements

A check bearing a forged indorsement, included in the UCC 1-201(43) definition of unauthorized signatures,[6] is not "properly payable." J. White and R. Summers, Uniform Commercial Code 559 (1972).[7] Regardless of the care

---

* Perini Corp. v. First Natl. Bank, 553 F.2d 398, 403-406, 21 UCC Rep. 929, 937-941 (5th Cir. 1977). Unfortunately, because of the length and complexity of the *Perini* opinion we have not reproduced it. For an analysis of the opinion that also sets out some of the titillating details see Baker, The *Perini* Case: Double Forgery Revisited (pts. 1-2), 10 UCC L.J. 309, 11 UCC L.J. 41 (1978). The case may be summarized as follows:

Perini maintained accounts with Brown Brothers and Morgan Guaranty Trust, and drew large numbers of checks on both accounts in the ordinary course of its construction business. Forger drew checks on these accounts, placing an unauthorized (forged) drawer's signature upon the checks. The checks were payable to the order of two companies that are probably, although not certainly, fictitious. A man claiming a connection with the companies indorsed the checks. However, the indorsement was made in an individual rather than representative capacity. Thus the checks arguably had both forged drawer's signatures and forged indorsements. The court had to determine whether the case was a true double forgery, and whether it should follow the loss allocation rules applicable to forged drawer's signatures or forged indorsements.

6. UCC 1-201(43) provides: "Unauthorized" signature or indorsement means one made without actual, implied or apparent authority and includes a forgery.

7. A check drawn to the order of the payee, i.e., an order instrument, may not be negotiated without the payee's indorsement. See UCC 3-202(1). The unauthorized indorsement by the forger does not operate as the true payee's signature. See UCC 3-404(1), which provides that "any unauthorized signature is wholly inoperative as that of the person whose name is signed unless he ratifies it or is precluded from denying it." A forged indorsement check therefore lacks the payee's indorsement and, without that necessary indorsement, may not be negotiated. See UCC 3-202(1). Negotiation is necessary to confer holder status on a check's transferee. Id. Accordingly, the transferee of a forged indorsement check does not become a holder. Only a holder or the holder's

exercised, a drawee bank is with few exceptions liable to its drawer customer for payment of such a check. See UCC 4-401.

Upon recrediting the drawer's account after payment over a forged indorsement, the drawee will seek redress against prior parties in the collection chain through an action for breach of the statutory warranty of good title. Each person who obtains payment of a check from the drawee and each prior transferor warrants to the party who in good faith pays the check that he has good title to the instrument. UCC 3-417(1)(a), 4-207(1)(a). A forged indorsement is ineffective to pass title; see UCC 3-417, Comment 3. The drawee may therefore bring a breach of warranty action against a person who presented a check bearing a forged indorsement. These warranty actions will continue up the collection chain to the party who took from the forger or to the forger himself.

Additionally, payment of a check bearing a forged indorsement constitutes conversion under UCC 3-419(1)(c). This conversion action at least provides the check's "true owner," the payee or indorsee from whom it was stolen and whose name was falsely indorsed, direct relief from the drawee. See White and Summers, supra, at 500. Without the conversion action the true owner would have to seek payment from the drawer, who might be overcautious and unaware of his right to force the drawee to recredit his account for any payment over a forged indorsement.

The danger created by forged indorsements is that the party designated by the instrument as entitled to its proceeds will appear with a claim to those proceeds after payment has been made to the malefactor. The statutory actions for improper payment, conversion, and breach of warranty of good title combine, however inartfully, to safeguard the drawer against double liability and to assure the payee of payment. The loss falls on the party who took the check from the forger, or on the forger himself.

2. Forged Checks

As opposed to diverting an intended payment to someone other than the intended recipient, forged checks present the problem of depleting the ostensible drawer's funds when he had intended no payment. The Code's treatment of forged checks, however, begins in the same place as its treatment of forged indorsements. The forgery does not operate as the ostensible drawer's signature. See UCC 3-404(1). Payment consequently is not to the ostensible drawer's order and violates the drawee bank's strict duty to charge its customer's account only for properly payable items. See UCC 4-401(1).

The Code's analysis for forged check liability not only begins with the drawee, however; it also generally ends there. The drawee's payment of a

---

agent may properly present the check for payment. See UCC 3-504(1). Thus the UCC reaffirms the general pre-Code rule that a drawee may not charge its drawer customer's accounts for payment of an order instrument bearing a forged indorsement. See White and Summers, supra, at 559. . . .

forged check is final in favor of a holder in due course or one who has relied on the payment in good faith. UCC 3-418. This final payment rule codifies and attempts to clarify the rule of Price v. Neal, 3 Burr. 1354, 97 Eng. Rep. 871 (K.B. 1762), "under which a drawee who accepts or pays an instrument on which the signature of the drawer is forged is bound on his acceptance and cannot recover back his payment." UCC 3-418, Comment 1. Prior parties in the collection chain who meet the prerequisites set out in UCC 3-418 will be immunized by its final payment rule from any liability for negligence in dealing with the forged check.

The above scheme allocating forgery losses among the various parties to the check collection process operates without regard to fault. The drawee's duty to charge its customer's account only for "properly payable" items and the warranty of title given by prior parties in the chain of transfer impose standards of strict liability.

Fault does occupy a secondary role in the UCC treatment of forgery losses. One whose negligence substantially contributes to the making of an unauthorized signature cannot assert the invalidity of that signature against a holder in due course or a drawee who without negligence pays the check. UCC 3-406. Thus the drawee can pass the loss back to a drawer or forward to a prior party in the collection chain whose negligence substantially contributed to a forgery. The complaining party's negligence will not, however, bar otherwise available recovery against a party, including a drawee, who is also negligent. Id. Additionally, while nothing in the Code precludes a bank and its customer from modifying the forgery loss rules by contract, the bank cannot enforce an agreement permitting it to act in violation of reasonable commercial standards. UCC 4-103(1).

B.   THE CODE POLICY: INCOMPLETELY GREASING THE COMMERCIAL WHEELS

In sum, the Code, while allowing for some modification on the basis of fault or agreement, sets up a system of strict liability rules allocating loss according to the type of forgery. The system uneasily rests on two policy bases. First, it incorporates an at least partially outmoded notion of the relative positions of drawee banks and prior parties in the collection chain with respect to detecting different types of forgeries. Second, it incompletely serves the notion that commerce will be facilitated by bringing to the swiftest practicable conclusion the processing of a check transaction.

As mentioned, the separate treatment given forged checks and forged indorsements harkens back to the eighteenth century decision of the King's Bench in Price v. Neal. That decision left forged check liability on the drawee on the view that, as against other parties in the line of transfer, the drawee stood in the best position to recognize the signature of the drawer, its customer.

The corollary principle for forged indorsements is that the person who takes the check from the forger—frequently, as here, the depositary bank—is in the best position to detect the bogus indorsement.

Reaffirming Price v. Neal in the final payment rule of UCC 3-418, the Code drafters recognized that the case's appraisal of relative opportunity to scrutinize drawer signatures was somewhat unrealistic in a nation where banks may handle some 60 million checks daily.[9] The contemporary pace of commerce has eroded the five senses used by bankers in the face-to-face era of Price versus Neal; little remains save the sensory activity of punching keys. While the drafters thus concluded that Price v. Neal had been drained of all its personality, they nevertheless insisted that its conclusion survives. The drafters noted that modern groundwork for the final payment rule could be found in the "less fictional rationalization . . . that it is highly desirable to end the transaction on an instrument when it is paid rather than reopen and upset a series of commercial transactions at a later date when the forgery is discovered." UCC 3-418, Comment 1. In recognition of the frenetic commerce of our time, the thrust of the UCC here and elsewhere is for speed and facility at some expense to exact checks and balances.

Leaving forged check liability on the drawee may serve well this finality policy. That policy, however, does not itself justify separate treatment for forged checks and indorsements. The concern that commercial transactions be swiftly brought to rest applies with equal force to both varieties of wrongdoing. See White and Summers, supra, at 522-523; Comment, Allocation of Losses From Check Forgeries Under the Law of Negotiable Instruments and the Uniform Commercial Code, 62 Yale L.J. 417, 459-460 (1953).

While finality viewed alone calls for equal treatment of forged checks and forged indorsements, one might still maintain that forged indorsements merit separate rules. The modern demands of commerce have as the drafters recognized, deprived drawees of any superior opportunity to detect forged drawer's signatures. Only a concern for finality therefore justifies placing forged check losses on drawee banks.

Such simple expedients as requiring identification, however, may still permit transferees of checks to provide a significant protection against forged

9. For a discussion of the volume of checks processed and the resultant interplay between the law of forgery losses and bankers' perceptions of the forgery problem, see Murray, Price v. Neal in the Electronic Age: An Empirical Survey, 87 Banking L.J. 686 (1970). We note the commentator's interesting observation that many banks do not record separately losses from forged checks and forged indorsements, contrary to the implicit assumption in the final payment rule that the two types of losses represent security breakdowns in different functions of a bank—accepting checks for deposit to its customers' accounts and paying checks drawn by its customers—which might call for different protective measures.

On the other hand, the author does suggest specific measures for protecting banks against forged check losses. The possibility remains that the separate allocation of strict liability for forged check and forged indorsement losses may act as some incentive for the development of those precautionary measures that consistent with the press of business will most effectively reduce the risk of loss from either type of forgery.

indorsements that drawees cannot. To insure such protective measures are
taken, it may be sensible to override the finality policy and to place forged
indorsements losses on the depositary bank or other party who takes from the
forger. . . .

Note: Insuring Against Forgery

The party who must bear the loss under the UCC's risk allocation rules
may be able to obtain insurance against the risk. Three types of insurance
should be noted:

1. **The Bankers Blanket Bond, Standard Form No. 24.** This form includes Clause A (employees' fidelity insurance) and Clause D (forgery and
alteration). The latter clause, as revised in 1980, states:

> (D)   Loss resulting directly from
>
> (1) Forgery or alteration of, on or in any Negotiable Instrument (except an
> Evidence of Debt), Acceptance, withdrawal order, receipt for the withdrawal of
> Property, Certificate of Deposit or Letter of Credit.
>
> (2) Transferring, paying or delivering any funds or Property or establishing
> any credit or giving any value on the faith of any written instructions or advices
> directed to the Insured and authorizing or acknowledging the transfer, payment,
> delivery or receipt of funds or Property, which instructions or advices purport to
> have been signed or endorsed by any customer of the Insured or by any banking
> institution but which instructions or advices either bear a signature which is a
> Forgery or have been altered without the knowledge and consent of such cus-
> tomer or banking institution. Telegraphic, cable or teletype instructions or ad-
> vices, as aforesaid, exclusive of transmissions of electronic funds transfer systems,
> sent by a person other than the said customer or banking institution purporting
> to send such instructions or advices shall be deemed to bear a signature which is
> a Forgery.
>
> A mechanically reproduced facsimile signature is treated the same as a
> handwritten signature.

A later provision defines *forgery* to mean "the signing of the name of another
with intent to deceive; it does not include the signing of one's own name with
or without authority, in any capacity, for any purpose." See Annotated Bankers Blanket Bond (F. Skillern ed. 1980).

2. **Depositors Forgery Bond.** Commercial enterprises other than financial institutions may insure against losses from forgery or alterations of negotiable instruments purporting to be issued by the enterprise. Insurance
covering forgery or alteration of incoming instruments is also available but is
less common.

3. **Fidelity Bond.** An enterprise may obtain individual or blanket bonds indemnifying the enterprise against losses caused by dishonest employees. The fidelity bond may be combined with the depositors forgery bond.

See generally Farnsworth, Insurance Against Check Forgery, 60 Colum. L. Rev. 284 (1960).

FIRST NATIONAL CITY BANK v. ALTMAN
3 UCC Rep. 815 (Sup. Ct. 1966), *aff'd*, 27 A.D.2d 706, 277 N.Y.S.2d 813 (1967)

TIERNEY, J. . . . . This action was brought to recover the proceeds of two checks, in the respective sums of $22,300.80 and $23,900.75, drawn on the account of J. W. Mays, Inc., a depositor in plaintiff bank, deposited in Altman's account in the Trade Bank and Trust Company, collected by said bank, and credited to Altman's account, on the ground that the signature of the drawer had been forged and the checks were not issued or drawn by J. W. Mays, Inc. nor with its authority or consent; and that payment was made by mistake, in good faith, in reliance on the endorsements of both defendants, without notice or knowledge of any defect in the instruments or in defendants' title thereto, and in the belief that the instruments had been drawn by the depositor, J. W. Mays, Inc.

Defendant Altman interposed an answer consisting of a general denial, an affirmative defense and counterclaim that plaintiff was negligent in failing to discover the forgery before making payment and that its negligence caused him to part with merchandise of the value of the checks, and an additional affirmative defense of estoppel as a result of such negligence. The answer of the Trade Bank and Trust Company consists of a general denial.

Defendant Altman is a wholesale diamond dealer. A Mr. Nieman presented himself at Altman's place of business and introduced himself as a buyer for J. W. Mays, Inc. Nieman selected a number of unset diamonds which Altman placed inside an envelope and sealed. Altman kept the diamonds. A few days later, Nieman sent a letter, on his own stationery, confirming the sale. He also enclosed a check drawn on plaintiff bank against the account of J. W. Mays, Inc., in the sum of $22,300.80, as full payment for the diamonds. Altman deposited the check in his account. Nieman then revisited Altman's place of business and selected more diamonds. The same procedure was followed, and Nieman's letter confirming the sale arrived with a check for $23,900.75, in full payment of the second group of diamonds. Altman, immediately upon receipt, deposited each check into his account at the Trade Bank. When Nieman requested delivery of the first envelope of diamonds, Altman communicated with the Trade Bank and determined that the first check had been paid defendant bank by the drawee, prior to turning over the diamonds. He turned over the second selection of diamonds several days later, but did not first ascertain that the second check had been paid, although in fact plaintiff had made payment; that same afternoon the Trade Bank notified him that plaintiff bank had given notice that both checks had been forged and that payment had been made by mistake.

Payment or acceptance of any instrument is final in favor of "a person who has in good faith changed his position in reliance on the payment" (UCC 3-418). This legal principle was long ago enunciated in Price v. Neal, 3 Burr. 1354 (1762) where it was held that a drawee who pays an instrument on which the signature of the drawer is forged is bound on his acceptance and cannot recover back his payment from a holder in due course, or a person who has in good faith changed his position in reliance on the payment.

In moving for dismissal of the complaint defendant Altman contends that the doctrine of Price v. Neal is a bar to recovery by plaintiff on either of the two forged checks herein.

The facts are clear that with respect to the first packet of diamonds, defendant Altman did not make delivery thereof until he had first ascertained that the check by which payment therefor had been made had been paid by plaintiff. Accordingly, defendant Altman, the payee of the check, does qualify as a person who changed his position in reliance on the drawee's payment. However, in all of the circumstances, the court is of the view that the issue of his good faith presents a triable issue of fact which precludes summary dismissal of the action based on the first check. . . . It has been held that the negligence of the purchaser, at the time he acquired title to the instrument, in not making inquiries which, if made, might reveal the fact of forgery, releases the drawee from the rule of Price v. Neal, and enables the drawee to recover from the purchaser the amount paid to him on the instrument (Whitney, The Law of Modern Commercial Practices §338, at 504 (2d ed. 1965)).

Inasmuch as defendant Altman did not determine that the second check had been paid by plaintiff prior to delivery of the second packet of diamonds, said defendant is not in a position to claim the status of "a person who has . . . changed his position in reliance on the payment." Therefore, the proscription against the drawee stated in the rule of Price v. Neal loses its impact and all the issues relative to plaintiff's right to recover the proceeds of the second check remain in issue.

Accordingly, the motion for summary judgment dismissing the complaint is denied. . . .

NOTES & QUESTIONS

1. *Prevention of risk.* In the *Altman* case who is in the best position to prevent the risk from occurring: Altman, the depositary bank, the payor bank, or J. W. Mays, Inc.? Who can spread the risk most effectively? Who is most likely to insure against the risk of a forged drawer's signature? Who has the

"deepest pockets"? Are any of these questions relevant to determine who should bear the loss from the fraud practiced in *Altman*?

2. *Altman's status.* Is Altman a *holder* of the forged check? For Altman to be a holder UCC 1-201(20) requires him to have possession of an instrument drawn or issued to his order. UCC 3-404(1) states that the signature of an unauthorized signer is effective as that person's signature in favor of any person who (in good faith?) takes the instrument for value. A forger of a drawer's signature can, in other words, draw an instrument to the order of Altman. If Altman is a holder is he also a *holder in due course*? Did he give value when he took the check? See UCC 3-302(1), 3-303. If Altman is a holder in due course UCC 3-418 makes payment by the drawee final without regard to whether Altman in good faith changed his position in reliance on the payment. Why should payment be final as to a nonrelying holder in due course?

3. *Liability of depositary and collecting banks for forgery of a drawer's signature.* Will the depositary bank in *Altman* be responsible to the payor bank? In the *Altman* case the depositary bank warranted that it had good title to the check and that it had no knowledge that the drawer's signature was unauthorized (UCC 4-207(1)(a), (1)(b)). Given that the forged signature is effective as that of the forger, title to the instrument can be passed in accordance with the normal rules on transfer and negotiation (UCC 3-201, 3-202, 3-404(1)). The depositary bank therefore does not breach the warranty of title. Since the bank does not know that the drawer's signature is forged there is no breach of its second warranty.

4. *Liability of Altman to the depositary bank.* When Altman deposited the check he made transfer warranties to the depositary bank and other collecting banks that are somewhat different from the presentment warranties made to the payor bank. See UCC 4-207(2)(a), (2)(b). If Altman has title to the check on the reasoning suggested in the previous notes then he does not breach a warranty of good title. On the other hand, Altman also warrants that "*all* signatures are genuine or authorized." Altman has breached this warranty. When will this breach be relevant?

5. *Negligence of person receiving final payment.* Is the *Altman* case consistent with UCC 3-418, Comment 4? "The section rejects decisions under the original Act permitting recovery on the basis of mere negligence of the holder in taking the instrument. If such negligence amounts to a lack of good faith as defined in this Act (Section 1-201) or to notice under the rules (Section 3-304) relating to notice to a purchaser of an instrument, the holder is not a holder in due course and is not protected; but otherwise the holder's negligence does not affect the finality of the payment or acceptance."

6. *Facsimile signature machines.* Many drawers issue so many checks that they use facsimile signature machines. Banks will normally require these drawers to agree to assume the risk that an unauthorized person will gain access to the machine. The court in Perini Corp. v. First National Bank, 553 F.2d 398, 21 UCC Rep. 929 (5th Cir. 1977), enforced a drawer's corporate resolution

authorizing its banks "to honor all checks, drafts or other orders of payment of money drawn in the name of Perini Corporation on its Regular Account . . . when bearing or purporting to bear the single facsimile signature of R. A. Munroe . . . said banks shall be entitled to honor and charge Perini Corporation for all such checks, . . . regardless of by whom or by what means the actual or purported facsimile signature thereon may have been affixed thereto, if such facsimile specimen resembles the facsimile specimen from time to time filed with said banks."

7. *Payor bank's insurance.* Assume that the payor bank has the insurance provided by Clause D of the Bankers Blanket Bond (see p. 850 supra). If the bank is ultimately held responsible under the UCC for the loss resulting from the forgery of its customer's signature will the bank be indemnified under the bond?

COOPER v. UNION BANK
9 Cal. 3d 123, 507 P.2d 609, 107 Cal. Rptr. 1, 12 UCC Rep. 209 (1973)

Mosk, Justice. We here consider the rights of the true owner of a negotiable instrument which has been collected and paid on a forged indorsement. The question has not previously arisen in this state under the Uniform Commercial Code, and has seldom been addressed in other jurisdictions.

The record recounts a typical tale of forgery. Plaintiff Joseph Stell, an attorney, employed one Bernice Ruff as a secretary and bookkeeper. During a period of approximately a year and one-half Ruff purloined some 29 checks intended for Stell and forged the necessary indorsements thereon. She cashed some of these checks at defendants Union Bank and Crocker Citizens National Bank and deposited the remainder (except one that was cashed elsewhere) to her personal account at the latter bank. The entire amount of such deposits was subsequently withdrawn by Ruff prior to discovery of the forgeries. Certain of the checks were forwarded to and paid by defendants Crocker Citizens National Bank, Security First National Bank, and First Western Bank and Trust Company; the remainder were drawn on payors who are not parties to this action.

Stell and his partners bring this action in conversion against both the collecting and the payor banks to recover the amounts of the instruments handled by them on the forged indorsements. The critical provision is UCC 3-419 which establishes "(1) An instrument is converted when . . . (c) it is paid on a forged indorsement." Notwithstanding this language, the superior court denied recovery on the basis of UCC 3-419, which provides:

> (3) Subject to the provisions of this Act concerning restrictive indorsements a representative, including a depositary or collecting bank, who has in good faith and in accordance with reasonable commercial standards applicable to the business of such representative dealt with an instrument or its proceeds on behalf of one who was not the true owner is not liable in conversion or otherwise to the true owner beyond the amount of any proceeds remaining in his hands.

The court concluded that all defendants in the case, including payor as well as collecting banks, qualified as representatives, had acted in good faith and in accordance with reasonable commercial standards, and had no proceeds remaining in their hands. Thus defendants were held immune from liability. The court also found that plaintiffs had been negligent in failing to discover Ruff's defalcations by April 1, 1966, approximately six months following their commencement, and that such negligence substantially contributed to the making of the subsequent forged indorsements. On this additional basis it held plaintiffs were "precluded from asserting such forgeries or lack of authorized signatures against any of the respective Defendants herein on checks presented after April 1, 1966."

We hold that the trial court relied on an erroneous interpretation of UCC 3-419 and that therefore the judgment must be reversed in part. Inasmuch as collecting banks and payor banks raise distinctive issues under UCC 3-419, the application of this section to the two categories of banks will be discussed separately.

COLLECTING BANKS

It is clear, excluding for the moment the issue of plaintiffs' negligence, that defendant collecting banks are liable for conversion unless they can establish a defense under UCC 3-419(3). A careful study of this provision, however, reveals no possible defense in this case after it becomes evident that the court below erroneously held defendant collecting banks had parted with the proceeds of the fraudulently indorsed instruments. The code, unfortunately, fails to define the word "proceeds" in the context of bank collection. Therefore, to fully comprehend the code section we must examine the concept of proceeds as it was understood prior to enactment of the code and to general theory of bank collection found elsewhere in the code and in other parts of the law.

Whether defendant depositary banks have any proceeds of the fraudulently indorsed checks remaining in their hands is resolved through a bifurcated inquiry: first, did they receive any proceeds and second, have they parted with any proceeds they may have received? Each of these queries is more complex than superficially appears. A collecting bank obviously does not receive any proceeds of an instrument unless such proceeds are forwarded to it from a payor bank. Under the dominant theory of bank collection that preexisted the code and which the code has left unchanged, however, the amounts a payor bank remits on a forged indorsement are not considered the proceeds of the instrument. The explanation for this result lies in the relationship between a payor bank and its customer, the depositor-drawer. The relationship is one of debtor and creditor: the bank is indebted to the customer and promises to debit his account only at his direction. If the bank pays, on an instrument drawn by its customer, any person other than the designated payee or a person to whom the instrument is negotiated, the bank's indebtedness to the customer is not diminished. If the bank does debit the customer's account, the customer can compel the bank to recredit the sum. Inasmuch as the full amount of the instrument remains in the account of the drawer when the bank pays on a forged indorsement, the bank manifestly does not part with the proceeds of the instrument but merely remits other funds from its own account.

General bank collection theory also instructs us that the true owner, in bringing an action against a collecting bank for conversion of a check collected on a forged indorsement, is deemed to have ratified the collection of the proceeds from the payor bank. This ratification transmutes the remittance of funds by the payor bank into an authorized act for which it may debit its customer's account.[6] In the case at bar, it appears that plaintiffs' action against defendant collecting banks constitutes such a ratification, and these banks, therefore, must be considered to have received the proceeds of the instruments.

Ratification of collection, however, does not constitute a ratification of the collecting bank's delivery of the proceeds to the wrong person. The dominant pre-code law established, on the contrary, that the proceeds were held, after collection by the collecting banks, for the benefit of the true owner. Again resorting to general banking theory, we find that the amounts a collecting bank remits to a person who transfers to the bank a check bearing a forged indorsement do not constitute the proceeds of the instrument. This result is quite clear in the case of an instrument cashed over the counter. At the time the bank takes such an instrument it has obviously not made any prior collection and, thus, has nothing that could be considered proceeds. The money paid over the counter is, consequently, the bank's own money. Upon collection of the instrument, the proceeds become merged with the bank's general funds and are therefore retained by the bank. (See Advanced ALI-ABA Course of Study on Banking and Secured Transactions under the Uniform Commercial Code 56 (1968).)

A bank that accepts an instrument for deposit likewise ultimately retains the proceeds of that instrument. Such a bank is initially considered to be an agent of the person who delivers the instrument to it for collection. When, however, the bank receives a final settlement for an item it has forwarded for collection, the agency status typically ends, and the bank becomes a mere debtor of its customer. As a mere debtor, it becomes entitled to use the proceeds as its own. . . .

It is significant that the Commercial Code does not make a collecting bank accountable to its customers for the *proceeds* of an instrument but only for "the *amount* of the item." (UCC 4-213(3); italics added.) . . . [The official comments state:] "[I]f a collecting bank receives a settlement for an item which is or becomes final the bank is accountable to its customer for the

---

6. Although courts have employed various theories in holding collecting banks liable, the theory of ratification appears to have dominated. . . . W. Britton, Handbook of the Law of Bills and Notes §147, at 422-424 (2d ed. 1961). The ratification doctrine has been firmly established in the law of California. . . .

amount of the item. One means of accounting is to remit to its customer the amount it has received on the item. If previously it gave to its customer a provisional credit for the item in an account its receipt of final settlement for the item 'firms up' this provisional credit and makes it final. When this credit given by it so becomes final, in the usual case *its agency terminates and it becomes a debtor to its customer for the amount of the item.*" (UCC 4-213, Comment 9; italics added.)

. . . [T]he parties can by mutual agreement extend the agency relationship until the amount of an instrument is received by the customer. Under such an agreement the proceeds would be maintained as a separate fund until paid over to the customer. The ordinary banking transaction, however, contains no such agreement, and it is apparent that there was none in the present case. Defendant collecting banks, on the contrary, became debtors, and the proceeds of the instruments were completely merged with the banks' own funds. The effect of this commingling is that the banks retain the proceeds of the instruments even though amounts set forth in the instruments, in the banks' own money, were remitted to Ruff. This conclusion is derived by reference to the law of constructive trusts. The cases in that area establish that money received by a bank and mingled with the bank's funds is traceable by a proper claimant into these funds. This result is unaffected by withdrawals so long as the amount of the cash on hand is not diminished below the amount of the claimant's money that has been mingled with the fund. Since it is obvious that no such severe diminution of funds occurred in the present case, defendant collecting banks must be deemed to retain the proceeds of the instruments transferred by Ruff, regardless of whether those instruments were cashed or accepted for deposit.[12]

Our conclusion that defendant collecting banks did not part with the proceeds of the instruments in making the various payments to Ruff is reinforced by several additional factors. To begin with, had the draftsmen of the Commercial Code intended to absolve collecting banks from liability by virtue of such payments, it seems probable they would have employed language more explicit than that of retaining or parting with proceeds. Instead, the words "for value" could have been employed. The collecting banks in this case

---

12. Ervin v. Dauphin Deposit Trust Co., 38 Pa. D.&C.2d 473, 3 UCC Rep. 311 (1965), arrives at this same conclusion. The court states: "When [the collecting bank] purchased or cashed the forged checks drawn on other banks it did so with its own money and then, in putting them through for collection it obtained from the drawee banks money which belongs to the plaintiff." Commentators have suggested that the *Ervin* case may stand for the rule that the collecting bank parts with the proceeds if it accepts an instrument for deposit in an account and later pays out the money in the account but does not part with the proceeds if it cashes the instrument. (Advanced ALI-ABA Course of Study on Banking and Secured Transactions under The Uniform Commercial Code 54-57 (1968) (dialogue between Professor E. Allan Farnsworth and Fairfax Leary, Jr.); Clark & Squillante, The Law of Bank Deposits, Collections and Credit Cards 143-144 (1970).) There appears to be no practical rationale for this arbitrary solution, and the *Ervin* decision clearly appears to negate it: "As far as the problem in the instant case is concerned we can find no distinction between the *cashing* of a forged check and the *accepting* of such check for deposit." (3 UCC Rep. 311, 315.)

are in a situation comparable to that of a holder in due course under the Commercial Code or a bona fide purchaser under the law of constructive trusts inasmuch as they took property and in return gave consideration to the transferor. With respect to a holder in due course or a bona fide purchaser, however, this consideration is termed "value." (UCC 3-302; . . .) The fact that different terminology is contained in UCC 3-419(3) suggests that the ambiguous language of this provision was not intended to refer to the giving of such consideration. If the draftsmen and the Legislature had intended to protect collecting banks that had merely given value for an instrument, it may be assumed they would have clearly said so.

Secondly, an examination of the law existing prior to the enactment of the Uniform Commercial Code reveals a nearly unanimous agreement among the jurisdictions that the true owner of an instrument collected on a forged indorsement could recover in a direct suit against a collecting bank even though the bank had acted in good faith and with the highest degree of care and even though it had remitted the amount of the instrument to a prior party. Since the rule had apparently operated satisfactorily, there is no reason to believe the code draftsmen or the Legislature would have wished to modify it to make direct suits extremely difficult. As discussed below, the payor bank is in effect strictly liable to the true owner if it pays an instrument on a forged indorsement. The collecting banks that handled the instrument for collection are, in turn, strictly liable to the payor bank for breach of warranty of good title. (UCC 4-207).[14] Because liability ultimately rests with the first collecting bank, it is unlikely that such a bank was intended to have a ready defense in a direct suit by the true owner. Requiring cumbersome and uneconomical circuity of action to achieve an identical result would obviously run contra the code's explicit underlying purposes "to simplify, clarify and modernize the law governing commercial transactions." (UCC 1-102(2)(a).)

Such a modification would also create a significant potential for injustice. In cases involving forged indorsements collecting banks are generally the most feasible defendants. A forger typically transfers instruments bearing forged indorsements to only one or two banks for collection. Often the banks are

---

14. [The court quotes UCC 4-207(1)(a) and notes that UCC 3-417 provides a parallel remedy against non-bank transferors of instruments.] The remedies of direct action by the true owner and of circuitous action through the payor bank are not strictly coincident inasmuch as the payor's warranty action may be barred by his failure to act in a timely fashion. UCC 4-207(4) provides: "Unless a claim for breach of warranty under this section is made within a reasonable time after the person claiming learns of the breach, the person liable is discharged to the extent of any loss caused by the delay in making claim." This proviso is of small significance with respect to forged indorsements since the forgery is rarely, if ever, discovered soon enough to prevent loss. The fact that the direct action and the circuitous action might result in different allocation of liability in one improbable situation appears insufficient to justify the diseconomy and injustice created by circuitous action. Moreover, assuming the payor bank failed to make a timely claim to the collecting bank, which failure proximately resulted in the collecting bank's payment of the amount of an instrument on a forged indorsement, and that the true owner recovered from the collecting bank in a direct action, it would appear that the collecting bank should be able to recover its loss from the payor bank, if not under the code, in an action for common law negligence or in a suit in equity to prevent unjust impoverishment.

located near the true owner. Thus it would be practical for him to bring a suit against such banks. The payors, by contrast, may be situated in many and distant states or in foreign countries, and the drawers may be equally geographically diverse. Even though the collecting banks would be ultimately liable after initial suits were brought in all the various fora, the expense and difficulty of bringing such suits would have the actual effect of freeing the collecting banks from any responsibility. The true owner would be required to shoulder the loss that should have been that of the banks, thus the banks would receive a windfall. That UCC 3-419(3) was intended to produce this unjust result is highly doubtful.

Had such substantial and controversial deviation from prior law been intended, moreover, it could be expected that the official commentary to UCC 3-419 would have so stated and would have included extensive explanation of the reasons for the change. Neither the California nor the uniform comment to this section, however, contains any such discussion. The comments, on the contrary, are brief and state that UCC 3-419(3) is merely a codification of prior decisions (UCC comment 5) and is entirely consistent with prior California law (Cal. comment 5).

The prior decisions to which the Uniform Commercial Code comment makes reference are presumably a line of cases primarily involving defendants that had acted as investment brokers and had marketed negotiable securities, remitting the consideration received to their customers. The relationships between the representatives and their customers in those cases appear to have been true agency relationships that did not merge into debtor-creditor relationships upon collection of the proceeds. Unlike the ordinary bank collection transaction, in which the collecting bank and its customer have tacitly agreed a debtor-creditor relationship will emerge upon collection, the ordinary agency transaction gives rise to no such debt when the agent receives funds intended for the principal. Such funds, instead of being mingled, must be kept separate from the agent's own funds and identified as the property of the principal. Thus, when the true agent remits the amount of an instrument to his customer, the agent actually does part with the proceeds. It is to this kind of situation, rather than to the typical bank collection transaction, that UCC 3-419(3) appears to be addressed.

Defendant collecting banks are, therefore, liable to plaintiffs for the amounts of those instruments received by them as of April 1, 1966. Plaintiffs' negligence, however, bars them from recovering for conversion of instruments received after that date. Plaintiffs do not dispute the trial court's finding that their negligence substantially contributed to the conversion of these instruments, and it appears, viewing the evidence in the light most favorable to the judgment, substantial evidence existed to justify such a finding. Stell had been retained by Ruff in 1963 because of her insolvency and because of litigation instituted against her by several creditors. She had informed Stell at that time that her financial difficulties were primarily due to considerable gambling losses she had sustained. A short time thereafter he hired her as a secretary and bookkeeper. He exercised practically no supervision over her, never reviewed the books, and never checked the bank reconciliation of deposits on the accounts she handled. Only during an annual examination made for tax return purposes by one of Stell's partners were Ruff's records reviewed, and even then, despite the suspicious absence of an entry, her accounts were accepted without checking for accuracy or veracity.

UCC 3-404 provides: "Any unauthorized signature is wholly inoperative as that of the person whose name is signed unless he ratifies it *or is precluded from denying it. . . .*" (Italics added.) The Uniform Commercial Code comment to this section adds the following explanation. "The words 'or is precluded from denying it' are retained in subsection (1) to recognize the possibility of an estoppel against the person whose name is signed, as where he expressly or tacitly represents to an innocent purchaser that the signature is genuine; *and to recognize the negligence which precludes a denial of the signature.*" (UCC 3-404, comment 4; italics added.) The preclusion language of UCC 3-404 is essentially the same as that of §23 of the Negotiable Instruments Law. . . . This language had been interpreted to provide for equitable estoppel in order to avoid an unconscionable result. We conclude that the doctrine must be invoked in the present case. Plaintiffs' negligent failure to discover Ruff's patent defalcations was directly responsible for defendant depositary banks' detrimental change of position in paying Ruff the amount of the instruments. Defendants acted entirely in good faith, and, though their conduct with respect to certain of the instruments may have fallen somewhat below reasonable commercial standards, it was not sufficiently egregious to shift the balance of the scales in plaintiffs' favor.

For the purposes of this case, therefore, plaintiffs are precluded from denying the forged signatures are operative indorsements. Ruff is then deemed to be a "holder," which the code defines as "a person who is in possession of a document of title or an instrument or an investment security drawn, issued or indorsed to him or to his order or to bearer or in blank." (UCC 1-201(20).) Good faith payment or satisfaction to the holder of an instrument discharges a party to the extent of his payment or satisfaction, even though the holder may have acquired the instrument by theft. (UCC 3-603(1).) Defendant collecting banks are thus discharged on the instruments received by them after April 1, 1966.

PAYOR BANKS

All but three of the instruments paid by defendant payor banks had been transferred for collection by collecting banks that are also parties to this suit. As indicated above plaintiffs ratified the collection of these instruments by bringing this action against the collecting banks. This ratification retroactively validates the payor banks' remission of proceeds and provides a defense to an action for conversion. With respect to these instruments, therefore, no liability exists as to any payor bank. Two of the instruments on which this action is based, however, were presented by Ruff directly to the payor, Crocker Bank. The one remaining instrument was collected through banks that are not parties to this action and was also paid by Crocker. With respect to these three instruments no ratification occurred, and we must therefore consider whether Crocker is liable for their conversion.

The conclusion of the court below that UCC 3-419(3) shields defendant payor banks from liability is erroneous.[18] Even if we assume arguendo that UCC 3-419(3) was intended to apply to payor banks, the provision would afford them no protection in cases such as this. As we stated above, the amounts a payor bank transfers to a collecting bank on a forged indorsement do not constitute the proceeds of the instrument, unless the true owner ratifies the collection. It follows that, absent such ratification, the proceeds remain in the hands of the payor bank. The payor bank is, consequently, liable for the full amount of the instrument notwithstanding UCC 3-419(3).

It is not now necessary for us to undertake an extensive analysis of the applicability of UCC 3-419(3) to payor banks. Inasmuch as the three instruments that concern us were all transferred by Ruff after April 1, 1966, plaintiffs' negligence stands as a bar to recovery. UCC 3-406 states that "Any person who by his negligence substantially contributes to a material alteration of the instrument or to the making of an unauthorized signature is precluded from asserting the alteration or lack of authority against a holder in due course or against a drawee or other payor who pays the instrument in good faith and in accordance with the reasonable commercial standards of the drawee's or payor's business."

The record contains substantial evidence to support the trial court's finding that Crocker acted in good faith and in accordance with reasonable commercial standards in handling the three instruments. Ruff held an account with Crocker, and at the time the account was opened, she had been introduced to the bank by one of its established customers. Nothing on the face of the instruments would have led the bank to suspect they were irregular in any way. A single branch of a large bank, as the testimony indicated, may handle several thousand instruments bearing third party indorsements in a single day. Considering this burden, it would be commercially unreasonable to expect payor banks to undertake foolproof efforts to verify ostensibly valid indorsements. Crocker's diligence with respect to the check received through bank collection channels is, of course, particularly evident, inasmuch as Crocker apparently received the instrument with all prior indorsements guaranteed by the collecting banks. Having acted in good faith and in accordance with rea-

18. It appears clear that UCC 3-419(3) was not intended to apply to nondepositary payor banks. The fact that the provision expressly includes depositary and collecting banks but does not mention payor banks creates a strong negative inference in this regard. The applicability of the term "representative" to nondepositary payor banks is also doubtful. It is significant that the extensive commentary in UCC 3-419 by numerous experts on the law of commercial paper apparently does not contain a single suggestion that the defense of UCC 3-419(3) is available to nondepositary payor banks. . . .

sonable commercial standards, Crocker is therefore entitled to invoke the defense of UCC 3-406.

CONCLUSION

We conclude that defendant collecting banks are liable for the amount of any instrument received by them prior to April 1, 1966. The record reveals that only 7 of the 29 misappropriated checks were received by that date, and each of them was taken for collection by defendant Union Bank. The total amount of these seven checks is $2,791.11. The judgment is therefore reversed with directions to enter judgment against Union for $2,791.11 plus the appropriate interest due on the amounts of each of the seven checks. With respect to the other defendants the judgment is affirmed.

NOTES & QUESTIONS

1. *Issuance of substitute check.* May Stell require his clients whose checks were taken by Ms. Ruff to issue new checks? If Stell has a conversion action against the collecting and payor banks, does this action necessarily imply that Stell's claim against the drawer is no longer enforceable? Stell does not have possession of the original checks. May Stell bring an action on the underlying claim when the check has not been dishonored? See UCC 3-802(1)(b). May Stell bring an action as the owner of a stolen instrument under UCC 3-804?

2. *Conversion by collecting banks.* What is the basis for the conversion action against the collecting banks? Does UCC 3-419(1)(c) apply to collecting banks? Do they pay for an instrument? Does UCC 3-419(3) establish an affirmative cause of action against collecting banks or merely a defense available to these banks? At common law true owners could recover from collecting banks in a conversion action or, in some jurisdictions, in an action for money had and received. If UCC 3-419 does not recognize a statutory conversion action against collecting banks, may a court apply the common law actions by virtue of UCC 1-103?

3. *Ratification and pleading in the alternative.* Is the *Cooper* court's holding on ratification of the collection of proceeds from the payor bank consistent with procedural rules which authorize pleading in the alternative? See Fed. R. Civ. P. 8(e)(2). If Stell sued Ruff would Stell have ratified the turning over of proceeds to Ruff and therefore be precluded for suing any of the banks?

4. *Collecting banks and UCC 3-406.* Why isn't UCC 3-406 applicable to the collecting banks in *Cooper?* Can they be holders in due course if they took an instrument with an unauthorized signature? Are they payors within the meaning of "drawee or other payor"? If UCC 3-406 had applied to the collecting banks they would not have prevailed because the court found that despite

their good faith their conduct "may have fallen somewhat below reasonable commercial standards."

5. *Payor banks and UCC 3-404.* The court in *Cooper* found that the payor bank had acted in good faith and in accordance with commercially reasonable standards. The bank could have avoided liability therefore by showing that the payee (Stell) had by his negligence substantially contributed to the forgeries and was precluded from asserting the forgeries under UCC 3-406. Could the payor bank have relied on UCC 3-404(1) and avoided all question of its own good faith and commercially reasonable actions?

MERRILL LYNCH, PIERCE, FENNER & SMITH, INC. v. CHEMICAL BANK
57 N.Y.2d 439, 442 N.E.2d 1253, 456 N.Y.S.2d 742, 34 UCC Rep. 1489 (1982)

FUCHSBERG, Judge. This appeal requires us to explore the extent to which, if at all, immunity from liability accorded a drawee bank by UCC 3-405(1)(c) may be limited by the drawee's negligence in paying checks over forged indorsements.

The section at issue, commonly referred to in commercial circles as either the "fictitious payee" or "padded payroll" rule, provides, "An indorsement by any person in the name of a named payee is effective if . . . an agent or employee of the maker or drawer has supplied him with the name of the payee intending the latter to have no such interest."

The factual context in which the case is here is undisputed. The defendant, Chemical Bank, unaware that the indorsements of the payees' name were forged, routinely paid 13 checks drawn by the plaintiff, Merrill Lynch, on its Chemical account in the aggregate sum of $115,180. The forgeries were occasioned by chicanery of a Merrill Lynch accounts payable employee who, by presenting his employer's New York check issuing department with false invoices which ostensibly represented obligations due its suppliers, caused checks to be issued to the order of these supposed creditors. The malefactor or accomplices then indorsed the names of the payees and, in face of the fact that New York addresses appeared below the payees' names, caused the checks to be deposited in California and Ohio bank accounts in names other than those to whose order they had been drawn. Seven of the checks were presented to Chemical by the Federal Reserve Bank (FRB) as collecting bank and the remainder by the depositary banks themselves. In due course, Chemical charged its Merrill Lynch account.

This suit, instituted by Merrill Lynch to recover the amount so debited, was brought on three theories. As set out in its complaint, the first was that "Chemical acted negligently and contrary to normal and accepted practices, breached its duty of good faith and failed to exercise ordinary care." Particularizing, it added that Chemical should have been alerted to the irregular nature of the checks because "the purported indorsements of the corporate payees were handwritten, and in many instances illegible," were indorsed "in blank, rather than for deposit only" and bore "second indorsements of unrelated persons or entities."[1] Reiterating the allegations of the first count, the second sounded in breach of contract and the third in conversion. In its answer, Chemical relied, among other affirmative defenses, on what, in the circumstances of this case, it took to be the exculpatory effect of UCC 3-405.

At the same time, Chemical, by way of a third-party summons and complaint, impled FRB essentially on the rationale that, if Merrill Lynch recovered, Chemical, in turn, should be made whole by FRB, which, as a collecting bank, would then have to be found in breach of its warranty of good title (UCC 4-207). FRB countered with a motion for summary judgment, premised on the position that, under UCC 3-405, "endorsement of the checks in the name of the payee thereof was sufficient and effective to transfer title to the instrument." On the same ground, Chemical thereupon cross-moved for partial summary judgment dismissing Merrill Lynch's complaint, except for the issue of staleness it had raised (see supra, n.1). Special Term denied both motions.

On appeal, the Appellate Division unanimously modified Special Term's order, on the law, by granting the motion directed to Chemical's third-party case against FRB. In so deciding, the court agreed that, under UCC 3-405, the forged indorsements were effective to transfer title to the checks. However, as to Chemical's cross motion against Merrill Lynch, the court, by a vote of 3 to 2, found that UCC 3-405 was "not available to defendant to avoid liability for its own negligence" (82 A.D.2d 772, 773, 440 N.Y.S.2d 643); on this view, it affirmed, thus relegating the issue of Chemical's negligence to trial.

On the present appeal, which brings up for review Chemical's motion against Merrill Lynch only, the appellant in the main presses the point that its alleged negligence in disregarding irregularities in the indorsements may not deprive it of the benefits of UCC 3-405 and, in the alternative, that, in any event, it was not negligent because it was under no obligation to inspect the indorsements, a duty which, it insists, was the responsibility of FRB and the depositary banks alone. . . . Chemical also advances the pragmatic argument that a contrary reading of the statute would impose what, at least for large commercial banks, would constitute an unrealistically onerous and expensive burden of inspecting an "immense volume of checks," all the more so since these checks must be "processed and paid or alternatively, returned or dishonored by midnight of the following business day." . . . Merrill Lynch, on the other hand, . . . contend[s] that UCC 3-405 will not absolve a banking institution, be it a depositary, drawee or collecting bank, from liability for its own negligence.

1. As part of the first cause of action, it was also alleged that "the checks were each paid more than six months after their date of issuance, despite the notation on their face 'Not to be cashed later than 60 days from the date of this check.' "

For the ensuing reasons, we believe that, under the circumstances of this case, Chemical's motion for partial summary judgment should have been granted.

Our analysis may well begin with the observation that UCC 3-405(1)(c) bespeaks an exception to the general rule governing the responsibility of a bank to its customers. For it is basic that ordinarily a drawee bank may not debit its customer's account when it pays a check over a forged indorsement. This is because the underlying relationship between a bank and its depositor is the contractual one of debtor and creditor, . . . implicit in which is the understanding that the bank will pay out [its] customer's funds only in accordance with the latter's instructions. . . . Thus, absent contrary instruction or legislative exception, when a drawer issues a check in the name of a particular payee, the drawee bank is to apply funds from the drawer's account to its payment only upon receiving the payee's authorized indorsement. In this perspective, a forged indorsement, since it is an unauthorized signature (UCC 1-201(43)) in and by itself would be "wholly inoperative" (UCC 3-404(1)).

It follows that, in the typical case in which payment is made on a check that is not properly payable (see UCC 4-401(1)), the payment is deemed to have been made solely from the funds of the drawee bank rather than from those of its depositor. But, when the conditions which UCC 3-405 contemplates prevail, the indorsement, though forged, is still effective, and the instrument then must be treated as "both a valuable instrument and a valid instruction to the drawee to honor the check and debit the drawer's account accordingly" (Underpinning & Foundation Constructors v. Chase Manhattan Bank, 46 N.Y.2d 459, 465, 414 N.Y.S.2d 298, 386 N.E.2d 1319).

This departure from the general rule is explained by UCC 3-405's Official Comment 4, which advises, "The principle followed is that the loss should fall upon the employer as a risk of his business enterprise rather than upon the subsequent holder or drawee. The reasons are that the employer is normally in a better position to prevent such forgeries by reasonable care in the selection or supervision of his employees, or, if he is not, is at least in a better position to cover the loss by fidelity insurance; and that the cost of such insurance is properly an expense of his business rather than the business of the holder or drawee."

Since the assumptions instinct in this rationalization are hardly indisputable, it is no surprise that the rule it supports represents a conscious choice between the traditional one, which, as we have seen, was more protective of the bank's customer, and the one in the code, which, as some commentators have bluntly acknowledged, was "a banker's provision intended to narrow the liability of banks and broaden the responsibility of their customers" (White & Summers, Uniform Commercial Code §16-8, at 639 (2d ed. 1980)). Thus, whatever, in the abstract, may have been the equities of the respective contentions of the competing commercial camps, there can be little doubt but that the outcome, so far as the adoption of UCC 3-405 is concerned, was calculated to shift the balance in favor of the bank "in situations in which the drawer's own employee has perpetrated the fraud or committed the crime giving rise to the loss" (1 W. Hawkland, A Transactional Guide to the Uniform Commercial Code 391-394 (1964)).

That this represents contemporary legislative thinking is clear from the way in which the statutory scheme evolved. Long before UCC 3-405 came into being, subdivision 3 of section 28 of the former Negotiable Instruments Law already provided that a check is "payable to bearer . . . [w]hen it is payable to the order of a fictitious or non-existing person, and such fact was known to the person making it so payable." Carrying this language to its logical limits, one might have thought that, because an instrument forged by an employee was to be treated as bearer paper, the fact of forgery had been rendered irrelevant to its negotiability.

Nevertheless, most courts, reluctant to read the statute this broadly, applied it only when the faithless employee made or drew the check himself, but not, as in the case before us now, when he had merely furnished the payee's name to the employer, for then the falsity presumably would not be "known to the person making it so payable" (Hawkland, supra). This narrow interpretation apparently fell short of the drafters' intention because the reaction, first, in 1960, was to amend section 28 of the Negotiable Instruments Law to make it explicit that knowledge to the malefactor who furnished the name was sufficient (Britton, Handbook of the Law of Bills and Notes §149, at 433-437 (2d ed. 1961)). And, secondly, by the adoption of UCC 3-405, the bearer fiction device was replaced by the more forthright effective indorsement concept (see Official Comment 1 to UCC 3-405).

The special scrutiny this legislative course demanded also highlights the fact that UCC 3-405's failure to delineate a standard of care, to which a bank itself must adhere if it is to advantage itself of this section, was no oversight. In contrast are UCC 3-406 and 4-406, which, along with UCC 3-405's "padded payroll" provision, deal with defenses which may be available to a drawee bank in forged indorsement cases.

For instance, UCC 4-406(2), which otherwise precludes a customer from asserting a claim which might have been averted but for its neglect in examining "the [bank] statement and items to discover his unauthorized signature or any alteration on an item" (subd. [1]), makes preclusion inapropos when "the customer establishes lack of ordinary care on the part of the bank in paying the item" (subd. [3]). And, similarly, UCC 3-406, which puts the onus for a forgery on a customer who "substantially contributes to a material alteration of the instrument or to the making of an unauthorized signature," still requires the bank to have paid the instrument "in good faith and in accordance with the reasonable commercial standards of the drawee's or payor's business."

It is fair to conclude, therefore, that unlike cases which fall within the foregoing sections, a drawee bank's mere failure to use ordinary care in the handling of a check whose forgery has brought it within the embrace of UCC

3-405(1)(c) will not subject it to liability (White & Summers, Uniform Commercial Code §16-8, at 639).[3]

This is not to say that, if a check is "tainted in *some other way* which would put the drawee on notice, and which would make its payment unauthorized" (Underpinning & Foundation Constructors v. Chase Manhattan Bank, 46 N.Y.2d 459, 466 (emphasis supplied)), a drawee bank may yet not be liable. For instance, a drawee bank surely is not immunized by UCC 3-405 when it acts dishonestly. In short, "a basis for liability *independent* of any liability which might be created by payment over a forged instrument alone" may very well survive (46 N.Y.2d 459, 469 (emphasis supplied)).

In contrast, without more, in the present case, it is at once clear that the irregularities on which Merrill Lynch here focuses were part and parcel of the forgeries themselves and, as the dissenters at the Appellate Division observed, "could not possibly have alerted the bank to the fact that the checks were tainted, indeed it would have been most remarkable if the drawee bank had even noticed them." (82 A.D.2d 772, 774, 440 N.Y.S.2d 643.)

Finally, Merrill Lynch's reliance on *Underpinning* is misplaced. The checks there, unlike the ones here, contained restrictive indorsements, e.g., "for deposit only," by which the maker explicitly limited deposit to the restrictive indorsers' accounts alone, failure to conform to which would create an independent cause for liability. Indeed in *Underpinning*, we are not called upon to resolve the liability of a drawee bank, but that of a depositary bank which, as the first to take the checks with the restrictive indorsements, could most readily have prevented the fraud (UCC 3-206(2); see generally Whaley, Forged Indorsements and the UCC's "Holder," 6 Ind. L. Rev. 45, 50 (1972)). Significantly, even there, we pointed out that the forgeries and disregard of the restrictions were distinct defects, one not justifying the other. Obviously, then, *Underpinning* and the present case are not akin.

Accordingly, the order of the Appellate Division, insofar as appealed from, should be reversed, with costs, and defendant Chemical's motion for partial summary judgment granted. . . .

Cooke, Chief Judge (concurring). To permit a drawee bank to avoid liability for paying a check on a forged indorsement by asserting the "fictitious payee" rule, when the bank itself may have acted negligently in paying the check, is a harsh result. Inasmuch as UCC 3-405 does not include any requirement that a bank act with ordinary care, however, I am constrained to concur in the majority's result. . . .

Questions have been raised as to the scope of UCC 3-405. It is unsettled whether it validates certain signatures for all purposes or only for the limited purpose of permitting negotiability (see Harbus, The Great Pretender—A

---

3. Because of the manifest advantages of uniformity in the law of bills and notes, we observe that other courts which have considered the matter have arrived at the same conclusion. . . .

Look at the Impostor Provision of the Uniform Commercial Code, 47 U. Cin. L. Rev. 385, 390-394; Comment, The Effect of Bank Misconduct on the Operation of the Padded Payroll Preclusion of U.C.C. §3-405, 27 U.C.L.A. L. Rev. 147, 160-161). Thus, it has been suggested that the warranty provisions of UCC 3-417 should apply (see Harbus, supra, at 390-393) and that a transferee should be denied holder-in-due-course status when an irregularity on the item's face gives notice of some defect in the instrument (see Comment, supra, at 165-170).

The central rationale of UCC 3-405 is that an employer is in the best position to institute controls to guard against employees' fraudulently obtaining checks and so should bear the loss when this occurs (see UCC 3-405, Official Comment 4). The soundness of the reasoning of this conceded " 'banker's provision' " . . . has been questioned by this court (see Underpinning & Foundation Constructors v. Chase Manhattan Bank, 46 N.Y.2d 459, 468) and commentators (see Harbus, supra; Comment, supra). Its particular hardship becomes clearer when the drawee bank is itself negligent. In a padded payroll situation such as here, the drawer may well not be negligent at all, but rather is the victim of an employee's criminal act (see Harbus, supra, at 409). Yet, the negligent bank, which in other situations may be held liable notwithstanding the drawer's negligence (see UCC 3-306, 4-406), will be totally exonerated regardless of its own carelessness because the drawer was duped by an employee (see Harbus, supra). "Th[e] principle [of Comment 4] exemplifies a reasonable commercial policy if all parties are innocent; it seems quite unfair if the bank has not acted in a commercially reasonable manner. It allows a negligent party to escape from the ordinary consequences of its negligence." (Harbus, supra, at 409.) The "rules of 3-405 [should be considered] to be first cousins of the rules in 3-406 and 4-406, and . . . a customer [should be allowed] to prove a drawee's negligence and, having proved it, to assert the forged indorsement." (White & Summers, Uniform Commercial Code §16-8, at 639.)

Plaintiff here is not attempting to controvert directly the *effectiveness* of the forged corporate indorsements for negotiating the items. Rather, it argues that the *appearance* of the indorsements was such as to put defendant on notice of the checks' irregularity. To subsume this issue within that of the effectiveness of the indorsements . . . condones cashing checks with dubious indorsements (cf. Underpinning & Foundation Constructors v. Chase Manhattan Bank, 46 N.Y.2d 459, 468, ["the drawer is thus precluded from recovering *solely* on the basis of the forgery from banks which honor the check" (emphasis added)]).

There is no sound reason why a drawee should be absolved of all duty to exercise reasonable care merely because a check was obtained by a drawer's defrauding employee. The large volume of daily business cannot explain this, inasmuch as the burden is placed on the drawee in other situations. Nor is consistency among the States a compelling reason. Two courts in this State have held that a drawee must exercise reasonable care before obtaining the protection of UCC 3-405 . . . as have courts in at least two other States. . . .

Unless displaced by the provisions of the Uniform Commercial Code, traditional principles of law and equity are expressly reserved (see UCC 1-103). On the record before this court, it cannot be said that, as a matter of law, checks bearing handwritten, often illegible, corporate indorsements in blank with third-party indorsements of unrelated persons or entities in States far removed from the payees' addresses are not such as would give notice of the item's irregularity to the drawee. This is especially true of those checks that were deposited later than the 60-day limitation printed on their fronts. Certainly, this is not a question to be resolved by Judges on a motion for summary judgment, but one that should be left to the trial court.

Construing UCC 3-405 in the same manner as UCC 3-406 and 4-406 would not shift the loss on all imposter/fictitious-payee checks to the drawee. UCC 3-405 should be recognized as the exception it is, however, and applied narrowly (see White & Summers, supra). When the indorsement is in a form that would not arouse suspicion, it would be effective to negotiate the check. If, however, the form of the imposter's or fictitious payee's indorsement is such that, under any other circumstances, it would raise a question as to the item's validity or regularity, the drawee's conduct would be scrutinized and, if found to be negligent, the drawee charged with the forged indorsement.

Having said all this, I must join the majority in reversing the order of the Appellate Division. The absence of a standard of care in UCC 3-405 must be deemed an intentional omission by the Legislature in light of its ability to include such language when it desires, as manifested by UCC 3-406 and 4-406. This court should not require ordinary care by the drawee when the Legislature has declined to do so. . . . Instead, UCC 3-405 should be amended to preclude its invocation by a drawee or other transferee who has failed to exercise due care (see Harbus, supra, at 415).

NOTES & QUESTIONS

1. *Comparing UCC 3-405 with UCC 3-404 and 3-406.* If UCC 3-405 applies, as it does in the *Merrill Lynch* case, then an indorsement is effective and subsequent transferees may be holders and holders in due course. The negligence or good faith of these transferees is not relevant: the loss must be borne by the drawer. UCC 3-404 also makes a signature effective—whether as drawer or indorser—and does not refer to a transferee's negligence or good faith. UCC 3-406, on the other hand, permits a negligent party to avoid the consequences of his negligence by showing that the limited group of persons protected by the provision have not acted in good faith or in accordance with commercially reasonable standards. As the *Girard Bank* case shows, p. 871 infra, UCC 4-406 also considers the negligence of both parties. Should there be greater coordination of these provisions? How would you redraft these sections?

2. *Bankers Blanket Bond and fictitious payees.* Before 1980 Bankers Blanket Bond Standard Form No. 24 (see p. 850 supra) included the following language: "Any check or draft (a) made payable to a fictitious payee and en-

dorsed in the name of such fictitious payee or (b) procured in a face to face
transaction with the maker or drawer thereof or with one acting as agent of
such maker or drawer by anyone impersonating another and made or drawn
payable to the one so impersonated and endorsed by anyone other than the
one impersonated, shall be deemed to be forged as to such endorsement." This
clause does not appear in the 1980 revision. The Statement of Change explains: "Language referring to the fictitious payee has been deleted . . . because the Uniform Commercial Code treats the signature as a forgery. Thus,
specific reference is unnecessary." Do you agree with this analysis? If not, does
the bond now insure against fictitious payees?

Problem 17-13. At the direction of its attorney, Fund draws a check on
its account with Trust Company payable to the order of Pitney, Hardin &
Kipp, a law firm representing a party in a pending suit against Fund. Fund
hands the check to its attorney, who is to deliver it to the law firm as part of a
settlement agreement. Without authority, however, the attorney indorses the
check as follows: "For Deposit Only: Pay Account No. 021-043478 /s/ Pitney,
Hardin, & Kipp." The attorney then deposits the check with National Bank.
The bank credits the amount of the check to the named account, which happens to be the attorney's. The attorney then closes the account and disappears.
Trust company pays the check when presented and charges Fund's account.

(a) May the Pitney firm require Fund to issue another check?

(b) May the Pitney firm recover the amount of the check from Trust
Company?

(c) May the Pitney firm recover the amount of the check from National
Bank?

(d) May Fund require Trust Company to recredit its account?

(e) May Fund recover from National Bank?

(f) If Trust Company recredits Fund's account may Trust Company recover from National Bank?

(g) Would your answer to any of the above questions differ if Fund's
attorney had delivered the check to the Pitney firm and an employee of that
firm had forged the firm's indorsement?

Problem 17-14. Forger forges the signature of Drawer on a check that
Forger draws to the order of Payee. Forger then forges the indorsement of
Payee and cashes the check at a convenience store using false identification.
The convenience store deposits the check with a depositary bank, which pres-
ents the check to the payor bank. The payor bank pays the check. When it
subsequently learns of the forgeries the payor bank asks you for advice on
whether it may recover the amount of the check from the depositary bank.
Advise the payor bank.

Problem 17-15. Southwestern Investment Co. agrees to lend Impson
$12,000 in order to permit him to purchase a truck from J. L. Williams and

James L. Wilson. It makes out a check payable to Williams and Wilson for the amount of the loan and delivers it to a man who represents himself to be J. L. Williams. Soon afterwards Impson deposits the check, which bears the payees' purported indorsements in blank, in his account at National Bank. National Bank stamps its indorsement with the notation "PEG" and sends the check to the drawee bank, which pays the check. Three months later Impson defaults on his loan repayments. When Southwestern seeks to foreclose its security interest in the truck it learns that the truck had been stolen and that no one has ever heard of Williams or Wilson. Southwestern asks you whether it has any recourse against its bank (the drawee) or the depositary bank. Advise Southwestern. See UCC 3-405(1)(a).

GIRARD BANK v. MOUNT HOLLY STATE BANK
474 F. Supp. 1225, 26 UCC Rep. 1210 (D.N.J. 1979)

BROTMAN, District Judge. This case presents intriguing questions concerning commercial paper transactions and Articles 3 and 4 of the Uniform Commercial Code. In particular, the court must determine to what extent the negligence of the drawer of a check affects the liability of a depository bank for a forged indorsement under the UCC and common law. The drawee bank has sued the depository bank on its presentment warranty and now seeks summary judgment, while the depository bank defends by asserting the drawer's negligence. The depository bank has also sued the drawer directly in a third-party claim, on which the drawer now seeks summary judgment. The court is asked to hold that certain types of negligence by the drawer, no matter how serious, will not preclude liability of a depository bank or other party taking a check bearing a forged indorsement.

I. FACTUAL AND PROCEDURAL BACKGROUND

Certain facts are not disputed by the litigants. On August 4, 1977, third-party defendant Penn Mutual Life Insurance Company issued its check numbered 377406, dated August 4, for $28,269.54 to a Morris Lefkowitz of New York City, as a return of a policy premium. The check was drawn on Penn Mutual's account at plaintiff Girard Bank in Philadelphia. The check, prepared and signed in Philadelphia, was to be sent by mail to Penn Mutual's agency in New York for distribution to Mr. Lefkowitz.

On August 5, third-party defendant Darlene Payung deposited the check in her account at Mount Holly State Bank of Mount Holly, New Jersey, the defendant and third-party plaintiff. The check bore a forgery of Mr. Lefkowitz's signature as an indorsement; the origin of the forgery is disputed. Ms. Payung also added her signature as an indorsement when she deposited the check. Mount Holly transferred the check through normal banking channels to Central Penn National Bank of Philadelphia, which then presented it for payment to the drawee and payor, Girard. Mount Holly, the depository and a collecting bank, recovered the full amount of the check from Central Penn. . . .

[The New York agency of Penn Mutual first alerted the Philadelphia office that the check had not been received by a telephone call on August 19; the agency had become aware about August 11 that the check might be missing. Girard and Mount Holly were notified that the check was missing on the 19th and froze the remaining $5600 in Ms. Payung's account, but most of the proceeds had already been withdrawn by Ms. Payung.]

It is not certain how the check was stolen and forged. Mount Holly maintains that several checks had been stolen by Penn Mutual employees prior to August 4, and that the company knew of the problem and unreasonably failed to take proper security measures. The defendant further contends that it can prove at trial that the Lefkowitz check, which was deposited at Mount Holly the day after it was drawn, was stolen by a Penn Mutual employee.

Girard has sued Mount Holly to recover on the latter's presentment warranty which it alleges was breached by the forged check. . . . Mount Holly has filed third-party complaints against Ms. Payung and Penn Mutual, while the two third-party defendants have cross-claimed against each other. Girard now seeks summary judgment against [Mount Holly] for the full amount of the check, and Penn Mutual has asked for summary judgment dismissing Mount Holly's third-party claim against it. The claims by and against Ms. Payung are not at issue here.

II.   DRAWEE'S UCC 4-207 CLAIM

A.   Choice of Law

[Citing UCC 4-102(2) the court holds that New Jersey law applies to Girard's claim against Mount Holly.]

B.   Presentment Warranty

Girard seeks recovery for Penn Mutual's breach [sic; Mount Holly] of its presentment warranty under UCC 4-207(1)(a). . . .

The forged indorsement prevented Mount Holly, the depository and collecting bank, from obtaining good title to the check, and Mount Holly therefore breached its warranty. See UCC 3-417, Comment 3; UCC 4-207, Comment 1; J. White & R. Summers, Uniform Commercial Code 510 & n.37 (1972).[2] The overriding scheme of the Code is to place liability on the person

---

2. The forged indorsement of Mr. Lefkowitz's name in blank does not convert the check into a valid bearer instrument which could allow Ms. Payung to pass good title. See UCC 3-202, 3-404(1); White & Summers, supra, at 459.

who takes from the forger, which is often the depository bank. The rationale is that this party is normally in the best position to detect the forgery and prevent the fraud. . . .

This policy is reflected throughout Articles 3 and 4 of the Code. Various sections indicate that a check bearing a forged indorsement is not "properly payable" within the terms of UCC 4-401(1). . . . That section indicates that, absent cognizable negligence on the part of the drawer, the drawee bank may not charge the drawer for a check that is not "properly payable." However, the drawee which has paid the check may seek recovery against prior banks in the collection chain for breach of presentment warranty under UCC 4-207. The depository bank may also sue the prior transferring party under a similar warranty provided in UCC 3-417. In the instant case, Mount Holly, if found liable to Girard, may be able to shift the loss back to the prior transferor, Ms. Payung. However, it is often the case that a depository bank will be unable to recover from a prior party and will ultimately bear the loss.

While the Code essentially presumes that the depository bank (or prior party) was negligent in accepting the check and should be held liable, that bank can sometimes shift the loss to the drawer or drawee if those parties were negligent. Mount Holly does not deny the applicability of UCC 4-207 here, but raises various negligence defenses under several Code provisions.

C.   UCC 4-207(4) Defense

Mount Holly first contends that it is relieved of liability on its warranty by UCC 4-207(4), which states:

> (4) Unless a claim for breach of warranty under this section is made within a reasonable time after the person claiming learns of the breach, the person liable is discharged to the extent of any loss caused by the delay in making claim.

Mount Holly argues that there is a genuine issue of material fact precluding summary judgment as to whether Girard asserted its claim within a reasonable time.

While reasonableness has been held to present a fact question, . . . the court finds there is nothing in the record to show that Mount Holly suffered a loss as the result of any delay by Girard in making its claim against Mount Holly. Mount Holly's vice president stated in his deposition that the bank was notified of a problem the morning of August 19, and immediately froze the remaining proceeds of the check. Uncontroverted evidence also indicates that Girard was first notified of the problem on August 19. Therefore any delay in Girard's noticing Mount Holly could not possibly have caused any loss since all proceeds of the check were frozen the same day Girard first learned it had a claim against Mount Holly. There is no factual issue here, and this defense can be precluded as a matter of law. . . .

874 Chapter 17. Error and Wrongdoing

D. UCC 3-405 Defense

Mount Holly next asserts that UCC 3-405 precludes Girard's warranty claim. [The court quotes UCC 3-405.] . . . The section does not explicitly place liability on the drawer; rather it renders a forged indorsement "effective," thereby precluding liability of a collecting bank on a UCC 4-207 warranty and liability of a drawee bank to its customer under UCC 4-401, thus shifting the loss to the drawer. . . . These provisions can be invoked against a drawer which has been defrauded in certain specified ways. Mount Holly believes that UCC 3-405(1)(c) is applicable here. Paragraph (1)(c) refers to the padded payroll situation where the drawer is defrauded by its employee before or during preparation of its checks. . . .

Taking Mount Holly's contentions as true, the most it could show at trial is that a dishonest Penn Mutual employee had stolen a properly prepared check. There is no evidence whatsoever indicating that an employee added Mr. Lefkowitz's name to a list of payees intending him not to receive the check. It is undisputed that the company intended to pay the true Mr. Lefkowitz.

The New Jersey Appellate Division, in an opinion affirmed by the supreme court per curiam, has held that simple conversion of checks by a dishonest employee through theft and subsequent forging of indorsements is not within the meaning of paragraph (1)(c). Snug Harbor Realty Co. v. First National Bank, 105 N.J. Super. 572, 253 A.2d 581 (App. Div.), aff'd, 54 N.J. 95, 253 A.2d 545 (1969). The court noted that the payees were bona fide creditors of the company. 105 N.J. Super. 572, 574, 253 A.2d at 582. The Third Circuit Court of Appeals, applying Pennsylvania's UCC 3-405, has also held that paragraph (1)(c) is inapplicable where a true debt is owed the payee. New Amsterdam Casualty Co. v. First Pennsylvania Bank & Trust Co., 451 F.2d 892, 898 (3d Cir. 1971). See also Official Comment 4.

UCC 3-405 does not apply here and provides no defense against summary judgment for Girard.

E. UCC 4-406(5) Defense

Finally, Mount Holly contends Girard is precluded from asserting breach of warranty by UCC 4-406(5).

4-406. *Customer's Duty to Discover and Report Unauthorized Signature or Alteration*

(1) When a bank sends to its customer a statement of account accompanied by items paid in good faith in support of the debit entries or holds the statement and items pursuant to a request or instructions of its customer or otherwise in a reasonable manner makes the statement and items available to the customer, the customer must exercise reasonable care and promptness to examine the statement and items to discover his unauthorized signature or any alteration on an item and must notify the bank promptly after discovery thereof.

(2) If the bank establishes that the customer failed with respect to an item to comply with the duties imposed on the customer by subsection (1) the customer is precluded from asserting against the bank

(a) his unauthorized signature or any alteration on the item if the bank also establishes that it suffered a loss by reason of such failure; and

(b) an unauthorized signature or alteration by the same wrongdoer on any other item paid in good faith by the bank after the first item and statement was available to the customer for a reasonable period not exceeding fourteen calendar days and before the bank receives notification from the customer of any such unauthorized signature or alteration.

(3) The preclusion under subsection (2) does not apply if the customer establishes lack of ordinary care on the part of the bank in paying the item(s).

(4) Without regard to care or lack of care of either the customer or the bank a customer who does not within one year from the time the statement and items are made available to the customer (subsection (1)) discover and report his unauthorized signature or any alteration on the face or back of the item or does not within 3 years from that time discover and report any unauthorized indorsement is precluded from asserting against the bank such unauthorized signatures or indorsement or such alteration.

(5) If under this section a payor bank has a valid defense against a claim of a customer upon or resulting from payment of an item and waives or fails upon request to assert the defense the bank may not assert against any collecting bank or other prior party presenting or transferring the item a claim based upon the unauthorized signature or alteration giving rise to the customer's claim.

Girard asserts two reasons why subsection (5) is unavailable to Mount Holly.

1. Applicability to Forged Indorsements

First, Girard argues that the phrase "the unauthorized signature or alteration" in this subsection does not refer to forged indorsements, and therefore the subsection cannot be used by Mount Holly here. However, the court concludes that "unauthorized signature" includes both forged drawer's signatures and forged indorsements. The text of subsection (2) of this section implicitly supports this construction. While paragraph (b) refers to "an unauthorized signature," paragraph (a) reads, referring to the drawer/customer, "*his* unauthorized signature." The "his" in paragraph (a) would be unnecessary if unauthorized signature included only the drawer's name. . . . The court also notes that UCC 3-406 uses the same phrase, and its accompanying Comment 7 specifically refers to forged indorsement situations. The New Jersey Appellate Division has held that the phrase in UCC 3-406 applies to forged indorsements. Gast v. American Casualty Co., 99 N.J. Super. 538, 542, 240 A.2d 682, 685 (App. Div. 1968).

While UCC 1-201(43) contains the language " '[u]nauthorized' signature or indorsement means . . ." and UCC 4-406(4) also uses both terms, this cannot be taken to indicate that an indorsement is not a signature, particularly given the language of UCC 3-414(2) which uses the terms interchangeably.

One commentator has written that paragraph (5) "appears not to cover the case of unauthorized indorsements." E. Peters, A Negotiable Instruments Primer 83 (2d ed. 1974). But Professor Peters still advocates incorporation of forged indorsements "either by legerdemain or by analogy." Id. Finally, other courts have applied this provision to forged indorsement situations without comment. . . .

2. UCC 4-406 Drawee's Defenses

Girard contends that even if subsection (5) applies to forged indorsement cases, the provision can be used to preclude its warranty claim only if it has failed to assert a valid defense "under this section," that is, one of the defenses stated in the other subsections of UCC 4-406. Girard further argues that each of these subsections is inapplicable as a matter of law.

Subsection (4) refers to failure of the drawer to report a forged indorsement within three years of receipt of the item, so is clearly not relevant to the instant case. Subsection (3) deals with the contributory negligence of the drawee bank and is also inapplicable. However, Mount Holly maintains that Penn Mutual failed to exercise reasonable care in reporting the item, as required by subsection (1), and therefore created a defense for Girard under subsection (2).

But subsection (1) applies only to failure to report a forged drawer's signature or an alteration. Mount Holly argues that alteration includes a forged indorsement. While the definition of material alteration in UCC 3-407 does not address this question, New Jersey Study Comment 1 to UCC 4-406 indicates that subsection (1) does not require scrutiny of indorsements. Furthermore, the language in paragraph (2)(b) would be redundant if the term "an unauthorized signature" included forged indorsements (as concluded above) and the term "alteration" also included such a forgery.[5] Subsection (4) would also be redundant as it names both indorsements and alterations. . . .

3. Drawee's UCC 3-406 Defense

Mount Holly contends that even if it cannot preclude Girard's claim on the basis of Girard's failure to assert a defense under UCC 4-406, it may still, under UCC 4-406(5), require that Girard assert a defense against its customer Penn Mutual based on UCC 3-406. Girard disagrees, stressing the UCC 4-406(5) language "If *under this section* a payor bank has a valid defense. . . ." [The court quotes UCC 3-406.]

According to Mount Holly, Penn Mutual was negligent in supervising the issuance of its checks, and this negligence substantially contributed to this unauthorized indorsement. Therefore, Mount Holly argues, Penn Mutual is

---

5. Inclusion of indorsements in paragraph (2)(b) is not inconsistent with their exclusion in subsection (1). Subsection (1) declares that a drawer must exercise care to discover a forged drawer's signature and must promptly report any such forgery; paragraph (2)(b) refers to later items with indorsements forged by the same wrongdoer who earlier forged the drawer's signature on an item that was not promptly reported.

precluded by UCC 3-406 from asserting the forgery against the drawee Girard, and the latter's failure to raise UCC 3-406 against Penn Mutual prevents Girard from recovering against Mount Holly under UCC 4-406(5).

Mount Holly's position warrants careful consideration. The court notes that UCC 3-405, where appropriate, may always be raised by the depository bank against the drawee. Under UCC 4-406(5) the depository bank may require the drawee bank to raise subsection (1) and (4) negligence against the drawer before the drawee passes liability back to prior parties. And UCC 3-406 allows the drawee to raise other forms of negligence against the drawer and relieve prior parties of liability.

But under Girard's interpretation of UCC 4-406(5), as long as the drawee chooses to credit its customer's account and not assert UCC 3-406, and instead sue the prior collecting or depository bank, UCC 3-406 drawer negligence will be ignored. This gap in the Code provisions can be very wide in certain situations. For instance where a drawer regularly leaves prepared checks where strangers can easily steal them, this gross negligence—cognizable under UCC 3-406 but not UCC 3-405 or 4-406(1) or (4)—will go unremedied if the drawer's bank chooses to credit its account and shift the liability back to the collecting bank. It is in fact likely that a drawee bank will be more willing to ignore its own customer's negligence when a remedy against another bank is available.

A depository bank often has the opportunity to prevent forgeries, but a clever wrongdoer can sometimes make it virtually impossible for a depository bank to detect a forged indorsement, even where the depository bank pays only after the check has cleared. . . . It is particularly difficult for the bank to detect the forgery where the check is deposited by an innocent party which took from the wrongdoer, and the bank may not always be able to later recover the full amount of the check from the innocent transferor.

Where the depository bank was diligent, and the drawer's negligence substantially contributed to the forgery, it seems arbitrary to allow the drawee bank to determine whether the negligent drawer or the innocent depository bank will bear the liability. As one commentator has stated, citing the posited situation as an example: "Gearing loss allocation to negligence is blatantly thwarted where one party, by waiving a defense, can immunize a negligent person from attack of others who must then bear the loss." Comment, 62 Yale L.J. 417, 450 & n.160 (1953). Since the drawee will often turn only to the depository bank for recovery, the policy of deterring negligent drawers, which is behind UCC 3-405, 3-406 and 4-406, is undermined. It should also be noted that it is just as easy for a large issuer of checks, such as Penn Mutual, to insure against forgery losses as it is for a depository bank to insure. See id. at 435-438.

Another commentator has written that incorporation of UCC 3-406 into the UCC 4-406 preclusion is the solution to this problem: "If the payor bank could ignore the drawer's negligence and pass the loss to the collecting bank, what cause of action would the latter have against the drawer? . . . To avoid this lack-of-remedy dilemma, section 4-406(5) should be read as requiring the payor bank to raise the section 3-406 negligence in the manner of that section, as a defense, but the collecting banks should bear the expense of the litigation win or lose since they are in the breach of their section 4-207(1)(a) warranty of good title either way." Whaley, Negligence and Negotiable Instruments, 53 N.C.L. Rev. 1, 21 (1974).

A few courts have stated or implied in dictum that this is a proper construction. Stone & Webster Engineering Corp. v. First National Bank & Trust Co., 345 Mass. 1, 184 N.E.2d 358 (1962) [see p. 885 infra]. . . .

However, the one court squarely addressing the issue ruled that UCC 3-406 cannot be incorporated into the UCC 4-406(5) preclusion. Mellon National Bank & Trust Co. v. Merchants Bank, 15 UCC Rep. 691 (S.D.N.Y. 1972) [the *Mellon* court concludes UCC 4-406(5) "clearly indicates that it refers to the waiver of the defenses created by UCC 4-406 and not of the defense based on a customer's negligent drawing of a check created by UCC 3-406."—EDS.] . . .

Despite the policy problems noted above, this court must concur with the *Mellon Bank* court. Not only is the language of subsection (5) clear, but Comment 7 to that section states: "Although the principle of subsection (5) might well be applied to other types of claims of customers against banks and defenses to these claims, the rule of the subsection is limited to defenses of a payor bank under this section. No present need is known to give the rule wider effect."

This court is further guided by the history of the Code, as was the *Mellon Bank* court, which stated: "In an early official draft of the Code, a similar provision [to UCC 4-406(5)] was included under UCC 4-207, the warranty section, and was thus applicable to a waiver of defenses based both on delay in reporting alterations and negligence in preparing checks. Supplement No. 1 [1955] to the 1952 Official Draft of Text and Comments of the Uniform Commercial Code, p. 31. However, in the adopted version of the Code, the provision was moved to UCC 4-406 and the phrase limiting it to that section was added. No comparable provision was included in UCC 3-406." 15 UCC Rep. 691, 693-694 & n.2.

These clear indications of the intent of the Code drafters compel a conclusion that Penn Mutual's alleged negligence under UCC 3-406 does not allow Mount Holly to use UCC 4-406(5) to preclude Girard's warranty claim. The policy and fairness considerations discussed above cannot override the definite mandate of the statute.[8]

___

8. The court finds distinguishable a case from this district which was not cited by Mount Holly but does indicate how the UCC 4-406(5) limitation might be circumvented. In Tormo v. Yormark, 14 UCC Rep. 962 (D.N.J.), *appeal dismissed,* No. 74-1961 (3d Cir. Oct. 23, 1974), Judge Coolahan held that a party which was both drawer and drawee of a draft could not sue the depository bank on a UCC 3-417(2) warranty because of the former's bad acts. The drawer-drawee had issued checks to an attorney who represented the intended beneficiary of the funds, although the drawee knew that the attorney, who later forged the indorsement of the beneficiary and absconded with the funds, had been convicted of certain crimes. The drawee's knowledge, the court held, created unclean hands and precluded the drawee's standing as a holder in good faith

F. Conclusion

The evidence in the record demonstrates that Mount Holly breached its UCC 4-207(1)(a) presentment warranty to Girard. Mount Holly, which has had ample opportunity for discovery, has raised no facts or law presenting a genuine issue for trial. Fed. R. Civ. P. 56(e). Summary judgment will be granted for plaintiff Girard in the amount of the Lefkowitz check, $28,269.54.

III. DEPOSITORY BANK'S DIRECT ACTION AGAINST DRAWER

Anticipating an adverse ruling on the warranty claim, Mount Holly has sued its transferor, Ms. Payung, and the drawer, Penn Mutual. By the claim against Penn Mutual, Mount Holly again seeks to assert Penn Mutual's purported negligence in order to shift the liability for the forged check.

The claim against Ms. Payung is not at issue here; presumably it will be based on her warranty of good title under UCC 3-417. That claim may allow Penn Mutual [Mount Holly?] to shift its liability back in the collection chain to Ms. Payung, who may be able to shift the loss to any other prior party. But the court cannot assume that Mount Holly's own warranty claim will be successful; even if held liable, Ms. Payung may not be able to satisfy a judgment. As is noted above, other forged indorsement situations could present facts making it impossible for the depository bank to recover from a prior party, particularly the wrongdoer. Therefore the court must consider this claim against Penn Mutual as possibly Mount Holly's only way of avoiding liability.

A. Choice of Law

While Mount Holly contends that New Jersey law should also apply to this claim, Penn Mutual asks the court to apply the law of its home state, Pennsylvania. The court assumes *arguendo* that Pennsylvania would *not* allow a depository bank-drawer action. As it is held below that New Jersey *would allow* such a claim, there is a conflict.

To resolve this choice of law problem, the court again turns to UCC 4-102(2) for guidance. ["(2) The liability of a bank for action or non-action with respect to any item handled by it for purposes of presentment, payment or collection is governed by the law of the place where the bank is located. In the case of action or non-action by or at a branch or separate office of a bank, its liability is governed by the law of the place where the branch or separate office is located."] Read literally, the provision requires application of the law of the

---

under the language of UCC 3-417. Assuming *arguendo* that this interpretation of the Code is valid and could be applied to the good faith term in UCC 4-207, this case is distinguishable from the present one since there can be no allegation here that Girard acted in bad faith. Even if Girard knew of Penn Mutual's problems with theft of its checks, such knowledge on the part of the drawee does not constitute the type of bad faith presented in *Tormo*.

state where the depository bank is located as it is the only "bank" in its action against the drawer. . . . Under this reading the term "liability" means the actual loss accruing to the bank if the claim is unsuccessful rather than the legal liability of the defendant in the action. This is somewhat contrary to the construction used above for the drawee-depository bank claim where it is held that "liability" means the depository bank's legal liability as defendant. Nevertheless, the court sees this as the only possible reading of the statute in the depository bank-drawer claim, and feels the result is a prudent one because it insures that all forged indorsement claims involving the depository bank will be governed by the law of its state. Where there is a forged indorsement the depository bank is essentially the central party since it is the one held presumptively liable under the Code scheme.

The court also believes that while a depository bank-drawer action must be based on common law, as is discussed infra, UCC 4-102(2) of the Code should cover the situation, given its broad language.[12]

But even if common law choice of law rules [for tort actions] are used the result is the same. . . .

B. Existence of a Cause of Action

1.   Under UCC 3-406

Mount Holly first contends that UCC 3-406 implicitly creates a cause of action against the drawer. Reliance on this section is misplaced. Mount Holly is not a drawee, payor or holder in due course. . . . Furthermore, Comment 5 to UCC 3-406 states: "This section does not make the negligent party liable in tort for damages resulting from the alteration." In the *Mellon Bank* case, cited above, the depository bank also attempted to bring a third-party claim based on UCC 3-406 against the allegedly negligent drawer, but the court dismissed the claim for the same reasons stated here. . . .

2.   Under Common Law

While it is clear that no provision of the Code provides a cause of action by the depository bank against the drawer for its negligence, this omission cannot be read as an intent by the legislature to preclude such an action based on common law principles. [The court quotes UCC 1-103.] . . .

Here a cause of action would further the Code policy favoring deterrence of the actor best able to prevent the fraud. Courts should be hesitant to improvise new remedies outside the already intricate scheme of Articles 3 and 4.

---

12. The only other choice of law provision in the Code that could conceivably apply is the general provision, UCC 1-105, which governs if UCC 4-102 does not. See UCC 1-105(2). UCC 1-105(1) states in pertinent part that the Code "applies to transactions bearing an appropriate relation to this state." This section appears to govern only liability created by other Code sections. Furthermore, the appropriate relation reference gives almost no guidance, and would in this case simply direct the court to common law rules. See Official Comment 3.

However, this new cause of action would not interfere with that scheme but extend its principles to a situation not specifically foreseen by the drafters. The Code cannot be read to preclude a common law action.

Plaintiff asserts that such an action should be based on ordinary negligence principles, as it alleges Penn Mutual's unreasonable failure to supervise its employees and check processing procedures has now resulted in an injury to Mount Holly. The New Jersey courts have never published an opinion discussing this type of claim, so the case must be approached as one of first impression.

The one recent case in another jurisdiction deciding whether there is a common law cause of action by a depository bank against a drawer is the *Mellon Bank* decision. There the depository bank also asserted a claim against the drawer based on common law, but the court held that such a claim would not be recognized.

A closely analogous situation is where a drawer attempts to sue a depository bank, another claim not specifically provided for in the Code. The courts have disagreed on this issue. Courts finding there can be no common law-based action have also relied on pre-Code decisions barring such claims. . . . These courts have also indicated that such a claim would circumvent the UCC 3-406 and 4-406 defenses by the drawee against the drawer. . . .

Unlike in these cases and in the *Mellon Bank* case, here no New Jersey pre-Code case covers the situation. Also, allowance of a cause of action would not circumvent any Code defenses; rather it would allow a defense based on UCC 3-406 which could not otherwise be raised because of the actions of the drawee.

A recent decision by the New York Court of Appeals allowing a drawer-depository bank suit stressed the need to shift liability to the negligent party. The court stated: "It is basic to the law of commercial paper that as between innocent parties any loss should ultimately be placed on the party which could most easily have prevented that loss." Underpinning & Foundation Constructors, Inc. v. Chase Manhattan Bank, 46 N.Y.2d 459, 386 N.E.2d 1319, 1323, 414 N.Y.S.2d 298, 302 (1979).

Here, too, a negligence action could allow the loss to be shifted to the party which was in the best position to have prevented the forgery. Such a policy is implicit in UCC 3-405, 3-406 and 4-406. While this situation is not encompassed by UCC 3-405 and subsections (1) and (4) of UCC 4-406, it is within the ambit of UCC 3-406. However, because of the rigid limitation written into UCC 4-406(5), the policy behind UCC 3-406 can be thwarted when the drawee decides not to sue its negligent customer.

Creation of a cause of action by the depository bank against the drawer would bridge this gap in the Code provisions, and allow relevant deterrence and compensatory policies, indorsed by the legislature through enactment of the Code, to reach this situation. The court therefore concludes that if the New Jersey Supreme Court were faced with the issue, it would . . . look to the "essential purpose and design," of the Code and create an interstitial cause of action for negligence by the depository bank against the drawer. Accordingly, the court holds that the law of New Jersey recognizes Mount Holly's claim against Penn Mutual.

C.   Parameters of the Cause of Action

As this action, though based on common law negligence, is a creature of the policies implicit in the Code, its shape should also derive from those policies. Since this action is designed to bridge a gap in the Code provisions, it should not extend to situations which the Code directly addresses. In accordance with these two principles, the holding here is limited in the following ways.

First, the depository bank may not sue the drawer directly for the types of negligence that are covered by subsections (1) and (4) of UCC 4-406; those types of negligence may only be addressed by the depository bank asserting an estoppel against the drawee bank under subsection (5).[13] The only types of negligence that are cognizable under the new action are those otherwise covered by UCC 3-406 where the drawer sues the drawee. The negligence must substantially contribute to the forgery. . . . Certainly this would cover the alleged failure of Penn Mutual to adequately supervise those employees having access to prepared checks. Whether it would also cover any delay by Penn Mutual in reporting the forgery where such a delay allowed a wrongdoer to withdraw funds need not be reached here since it is not clear if Mount Holly has charged that Penn Mutual was so negligent. Neither does the court rule on whether this cause of action extends to situations involving forged drawer's signatures or material alterations.

This cause of action would not be appropriate until the depository bank is adjudged or has admitted liability on a presentment warranty. Of course, such a judgment has been entered here. The court also believes a second prerequisite is appropriate to the special facts of this case. Since Mount Holly's prior transferor, Ms. Payung, has been sued by Mount Holly and has appeared in this court, and since she is charged with forging the Lefkowitz indorsement, the court believes that the claim against her should be tried before the claim against Penn Mutual. The first priority of the law should be to shift liability to the forger where that is possible. Therefore Mount Holly's claim against Penn Mutual is stayed pending a final disposition of its claim against Ms. Payung. If, after a good faith attempt to litigate the claim and collect a judgment, recovery is insufficient, then the stay of the claim against Penn

13. Where the drawer's negligent conduct under UCC 3-405 is involved the drawer will be liable regardless of the claims between parties since the section renders the indorsement effective precluding the drawer's claim against the drawee and the drawee's warranty claim against the depository bank. Since the depository bank cannot be held liable in this case, the bank would never need to raise UCC 3-405 conduct in a common law negligence action.

Mutual will be lifted and the action will proceed to trial. If full recovery is had from Ms. Payung, the claim against Penn Mutual will be barred.[14]

Finally, if the claim against the drawer is allowed to proceed, the drawer may raise the depository bank's own negligence in accepting the check as a defense barring the bank's recovery. Use of contributory negligence here parallels the requirement in UCC 3-406 that a drawee must act in accordance with reasonable commercial standards, and the restriction in UCC 3-419(3) that the depository bank which acts in accordance with such standards cannot be sued for conversion. . . . This also parallels UCC 4-406(3), which bars a drawee from raising the drawer's subsection (1) negligence where the drawee failed to use ordinary care in paying the item.[15]

The court finds support for inclusion of a contributory negligence defense from the fact that the outcome of litigation is similar under Code provisions governing the drawer-drawee suit. In that type of claim, the drawer will win where both drawer and drawee are negligent—just as a contributory negligence defense will absolve the negligent drawer in the cause of action here by the depository bank.

Another parallel is to the New Jersey Appellate Division's recent use of the "last clear chance" doctrine to dismiss a common law negligence claim by a drawer against a depository bank where the drawee bank had the opportunity to prevent an erroneous overpayment on a check. Western Union Telegraph Co. v. Peoples National Bank, 169 N.J. Super. 272, 276-278, 404 A.2d 1178, 1180-1181 (App. Div. 1979). In the instant case it might be found that Mount Holly had the last opportunity to prevent the forgery by not accepting or crediting the check.

However, the parallel to other situations is not perfect. Where both the depository bank and the drawer are negligent, but the drawee is not, the outcome will still depend on whether the drawee raises the drawer's negligence and fails to credit its customer. If the drawee successfully does this, it will not need to sue the depository bank and that bank's negligence will not create liability. But, as was noted above, the drawee will often fail to dispute its customer's claim, preferring to sue the depository or collecting bank where

---

14. If Ms. Payung took the check from the forger, as she alleges, then she can attempt to sue that party if she is found liable. She might also attempt to pursue a common law negligence claim against the drawer, although the court does not now reach the question of whether such a transferor may sue the drawer.

15. Some of the cases allowing a drawer to sue a depository bank have indicated that UCC 3-406 and 4-406 could be used as defenses by the bank to the drawer's claim, which has been held to be based on absolute liability doctrines of direct warranty, third-party beneficiary of a warranty and money had and received. . . . The cause of action created here uses UCC 3-406 as the basis of the bank's negligence claim against the drawer; where the law also permits the drawer to sue the bank and further allows the bank to raise UCC 3-406 drawer negligence as a defense against the drawer's absolute liability claim, then the outcome should be the same regardless of which party is plaintiff. However, no court has yet spoken on how the reasonable commercial standards and ordinary care provisions of UCC 3-406 and 4-406(3) would affect an action by the drawer. . . .

there is no UCC 4-406(5) estoppel. The new cause of action created here is, of course, designed to alleviate this gap in the Code. However, if a contributory negligence defense can be asserted against a direct negligence claim, then the depository bank's own negligence will put the loss on the bank, and its liability will still have been caused by the drawee's failure to raise its customer's negligence.

Yet another factor should be noted in connection with the instance where both drawer and depository bank are negligent. Where the drawee successfully asserts the drawer's negligence, the liability may still be shifted to the depository bank if the jurisdiction allows the drawer to then sue the depository bank directly but does not allow the depository bank to raise a UCC 3-406 drawer negligence defense to the claim. In that jurisdiction it would thus not matter whether the drawee chose to assert drawer negligence since the liability would eventually fall on the depository bank regardless, and the outcome would also not differ where the depository bank is barred from its own claim because of its own negligence. In addition, even where the depository bank has a UCC 3-406 defense to the drawer's claim, where both parties are negligent the bank would still be liable as a result of a drawer's action if the drawer can preclude the bank's UCC 3-406 defense by asserting the bank's failure to adhere to reasonable commercial standards. See footnote 15, supra.

All this would place the liability on the depository bank where both it and the drawer are negligent, as allowance of a contributory negligence defense in the cause of action in the instant case will do. The court approves this outcome since it believes deterrence of the parties taking from forgers is a higher priority than deterrence of negligent drawers. A better solution might be a comparative negligence system, but this court will leave such a radical step to the New Jersey legislature or supreme court.[16] This limited negligence cause of action may alter the result in only a few situations, but the court feels the sound principles behind various Code provisions will be served by allowing such a claim by the depository bank against the drawer.

D.   Conclusion

Third-party defendant Penn Mutual has supported its summary judgment motion solely with the legal argument that there can be no claim by third-party plaintiff Mount Holly against it. Since the court holds that Mount Holly may base an action on common law negligence, Penn Mutual's summary judgment motion is denied. For the reason indicated, this claim is stayed pending disposition of Mount Holly's claim against Darlene Payung.

---

16. The California Supreme Court has indicated in a brief dictum that comparative negligence may be used for UCC 4-406 defenses in actions by the drawer against the depository bank. Sun 'n Sand, Inc. v. United Cal. Bank, 21 Cal. 3d 671, 148 Cal. Rptr. 329, 582 P.2d 920, 939 (1978). See also 582 P.2d 920, 945 n.4 (Clark, J., concurring and dissenting).

NOTES & QUESTIONS

Drawer versus Depositary Bank. Should a drawer be able to sue a depositary bank for conversion or breach of warranty? If an action is recognized will the depositary bank be able to raise the defenses provided by the UCC to drawees and other payors? This issue is discussed in the following case.

STONE & WEBSTER ENGINEERING CORP. v. FIRST NATIONAL BANK & TRUST CO., 345 Mass. 1, 184 N.E.2d 358, 1 UCC Rep. 198 (1962): Stone & Webster drew three checks on its checking account with its Boston bank payable to Westinghouse in payment for goods and services furnished by Westinghouse. A Stone & Webster employee forged Westinghouse's indorsement, cashed the checks at Bank & Trust Co., and disappeared. The Boston bank paid the checks when presented for payment through the bank collection system. When the Boston bank refused to recredit its account Stone & Webster brought an action against Bank & Trust Co. The Massachusetts court held that the drawer did not have a cause of action against the depositary bank for conversion or money had and received. The court concluded that the drawer did not have valuable rights in the check where the check had not been delivered to a payee. It was argued that allowing a direct action would avoid circuity of litigation because under its holding the drawer first would have to proceed against the drawee for wrongful payment and drawee would then proceed against the collecting banks for breach of the warranty of title. The court pointed out, however, that a direct action against the depositary bank would deprive that bank of defenses, such as those set out in UCC 3-406 and 4-406, that the drawee could set up against the drawer but that were not available to a collecting bank.

Problem 17-16. On November 9 Contractor drew a check for $112,000 on its account with First National Bank payable to two subcontractors, Paving and Trimount, for work they had performed. Although the parties had agreed that Contractor would send the check to Trimount, Contractor inadvertently sent it to Paving, who without authority typed the indorsements of both Trimount and Paving and deposited the check for credit to its account with State Bank. First National paid the check when presented, and payment was reflected on the November bank statement received by Contractor on December 10. Earlier in December, however, an officer at First National had informed Contractor that the November 9 check had not been paid, and, without noting the information contained in the November bank statement, Contractor filed a stop payment order on December 12 and issued a new check to Trimount on December 14. In early January Contractor discovered the discrepancy and promptly filed with First National an affidavit of forgery signed by Trimount. First National promptly credited Contractor's account and two weeks later

sent a letter to State Bank requesting reimbursement on the theory that State
Bank had breached its UCC 4-207 warranty.

State Bank answers with the following arguments:

(1) First National waived defenses it had against Contractor under UCC
4-406 and First National is therefore estopped in its action against State Bank
by virtue of UCC 4-406(5).

(2) Both Contractor and First National were negligent, which precludes
judgment for First National by virtue of UCC 3-406 and 4-406.

(3) First National is barred from recovery because, under UCC 4-207(4),
it had delayed unreasonably in claiming a breach of warranty.

Advise First National on whether it should proceed against State Bank.

E.   ALTERATION

Allocation of losses due to alteration or unauthorized completion of a negotiable instrument follows the same pattern as the allocation of losses caused by
forged signatures, and, indeed, many of the same legal devices, such as warranties, are used. Assume, for example, that A draws a check to B for $15 and
B alters the amount to $1,500 before depositing the check in his bank. A's
bank pays the $1,500 when B's bank presents the check for payment. B closes
his bank account soon after and then disappears. A's bank did not follow his
order, which was to pay only $15, but the bank nevertheless may charge A's
account for $15, the original tenor of the check. UCC 4-401(2); cf. UCC 3-
413(2). A's bank may recover the remaining $1485 from B's bank for breach of
its warranty against material alteration. UCC 4-207(1)(c). Transfer warranties
may also be used to place the loss on the last person to deal with B, the
wrongdoer. UCC 4-207(2)(c), 3-417(2)(c). This normal allocation, however, is
subject to the same exceptions as in the case of forged signatures: A, the
drawer, may ultimately be responsible because of his negligence. UCC 3-406,
4-406.

In the case of alterations the Code does add one twist to the loss allocation
scheme: in some cases the drawer and other parties to an instrument may be
discharged because of a material and fraudulent alteration. UCC 3-407 provides:

(1) Any alteration of an instrument is material which changes the contract
of any party thereto in any respect, including any such change in
(a)   the number or relations of the parties; or
(b)   an incomplete instrument, by completing it otherwise than as authorized;
or

(c)   the writing as signed, by adding to it or by removing any part of it.

(2) As against any person other than a subsequent holder in due course

(a)   alteration by the holder which is both fraudulent and material discharges any party whose contract is thereby changed unless that party assents or is precluded from asserting the defense;

(b)   no other alteration discharges any party and the instrument may be enforced according to its original tenor, or as to incomplete instruments according to the authority given.

(3) A subsequent holder in due course may in all cases enforce the instrument according to its original tenor, and when an incomplete instrument has been completed he may enforce it as completed.

When considering the application of this provision remember that if a party is discharged on the instrument he will also be discharged on the underlying obligation. UCC 3-802.

Problem 17-17. Jones has his driveway paved by City Asphalt and pays for the work with a check for $4,000 drawn on First Bank and made payable to the order of City Asphalt. Foreman skillfully alters the amount of the check to $40,000 and gives it to Oil Company in payment of City Asphalt's past due trade account. Oil Company deposits the check in its account at State Bank, which forwards it to National Bank. When National Bank presents the check First Bank pays $40,000.

(a) Jones demands that First Bank recredit his account. Must First Bank do so? See UCC 4-401.

(b) If First Bank recredits Jones' account can it recover from National Bank? Will successive recoveries be obtainable against State Bank and Oil Company? See UCC 4-207(1), 4-207(2), 3-417(2).

(c) Suppose Jones is tipped off and stops payment on the check. It is returned to City Asphalt. Can City Asphalt enforce the check and, if so, for what amount? See UCC 3-407.

Problem 17-18. On Monday Customer orders merchandise and tells Seller that he will pay by having his employer obtain a certified check drawn payable to the order of Seller. Depositor, an accomplice of Customer, writes a check for $16 on his account at Bank and has an officer of Bank certify the check. Contrary to local banking custom the certification stamp does not indicate the amount of the check certified but the stamp does add the phrase "payable as originally drawn." Customer skillfully alters the amount of the check to $1,600 and on Tuesday delivers the check to Seller. When Seller presents the check for payment Bank dishonors the check because of the alteration. Seller asks you whether it should bring an action against Bank. Evaluate Seller's case. See UCC 3-406, 3-407, 3-413, 3-417.

CHAPTER 18

Documentary Transactions and Letters of Credit

Most sales transactions of any substantial size involve shipment of goods, frequently over long distances and across national borders. Sellers' legal remedies as to rejected goods have been examined in the sales materials, p. 585 supra. However, the practical utility of these remedies should be viewed in the context of a seller attempting to control disposition of goods in a distant or unfamiliar market. An unpaid seller of accepted goods usually has the status of an unsecured creditor for the amount of the agreed purchase price. Again, however, whether the seller's remedy is recovery in damages or for the price, collection against a recalcitrant buyer may involve litigation in an inconvenient forum.

Notwithstanding these risks, the underlying stability of modern commerce allows the bulk of commercial shipments to be treated on an "open account" basis. In certain situations, however, sellers will require greater security, such as when shipping to distant or unfamiliar markets; or to customers with no prior business relationship and no, or bad, credit history; or to customers, even those long-established, who are known to be financially distressed. In these contexts, among others, two devices have developed that significantly reduce the seller's risks: the documentary transaction and the letter of credit. In this chapter we will explore these devices, used not only to reduce payment risks but also as highly flexible mechanisms to assist the parties in financing the transaction.

A. DOCUMENTARY TRANSACTIONS

1. Basic Concepts

In Chapter 10 we first considered the legal and practical significance of documents of title, such as bills of lading and warehouse receipts. Students should

889

review those materials to re-acquaint themselves with the manner in which rights in the goods themselves are able to be transferred by transfer of the documents of title covering the goods. See text at p. 526 supra.

In Chapter 15 the use of the draft to effect payment in sales transactions was explained. See pp. 732 to 735 supra. UCC 4-104(1)(f) defines *documentary draft* broadly as "any negotiable or non-negotiable draft with accompanying documents, securities or other papers to be delivered against honor of the draft; . . ." Memphis Aero Corp. v. First American National Bank, p. 892 infra, is an illustration of the variant types of documents that may be involved. In this chapter, however, we will be principally concerned with drafts used in conjunction with bills of lading. The documentary transaction combines use of the draft and bill of lading in such a way as to significantly reduce the seller's risk that the buyer will reject the goods or refuse payment. In essence, the transaction becomes one in which tender of *documents*, rather than tender of *goods*, entitles the seller to payment. The niceties of this concept will be examined in the remainder of this section. The basic structure of the transaction, however, may be easily diagrammed. See Figure 18-1.

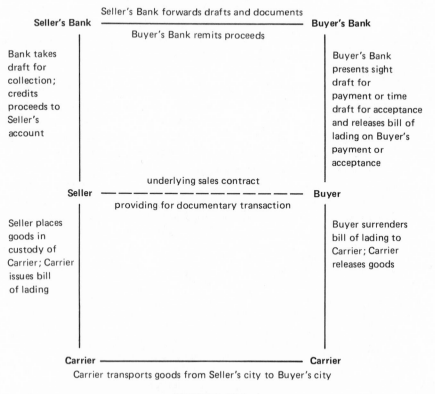

FIGURE 18-1
Basic Documentary Transaction

Let us examine the transaction illustrated in Figure 18-1, focusing on the sequence of events and the principal instruments, documents, and players involved.

Step 1. Seller places the contract goods in the custody of Carrier, who ships them to Buyer. At Seller's request, Carrier issues to Buyer a negotiable bill of lading drawn to Seller's order. See Form 10-2, supra. This bill of lading has three distinct characteristics: (1) it evidences receipt of the goods from Seller by Carrier; (2) it contains the terms of the contract for carriage of the goods; and (3) most important, as a negotiable bill of lading it confers upon its holder title to the underlying goods.

Step 2. Seller prepares a draft in the amount of the purchase price, drawn on the Buyer. See Form 15-2, Figure 15-2, supra, and text at pp. 732 to 735 supra.

Step 3. Seller attaches the draft to the bill of lading, and transfers both to Seller's Bank.

Step 4. Seller's Bank forwards the documentary draft through the bank collection system to a bank in Buyer's city. At the same time that the documents are being forwarded for collection, the goods may now be en route to Buyer in the custody of Carrier.

Step 5. Upon receipt of the documents Buyer's Bank presents them to Buyer for payment. A refusal to pay may constitute dishonor of the draft and breach of the sales contract. These issues will be explored more fully infra. In most cases, Buyer pays the draft, and the bill of lading, duly indorsed, is released to Buyer by the presenting bank.

Step 6. As a holder of a negotiable document by negotiation in due course, Buyer now has title to the goods, and the right to delivery of the goods by the carrier upon arrival. When the goods arrive Buyer surrenders the negotiable bill of lading to Carrier for cancellation, and Carrier will release the goods to Buyer.

In broad outline, most documentary transactions follow this simple pattern. Before proceeding further, ask yourself: what advantages does this form of transaction appear to have over shipment on open account? We turn below to a more detailed inquiry into that basic question.

A lawyer may be called on in varying capacities in connection with documentary transactions. In large transactions parties may call upon counsel to assist in documenting a specific sale, but lawyers may more frequently be engaged in review of the client's standard forms and procedures. Unfortunately, perhaps the most frequent role played will be in response to an urgent call when a dispute has already arisen in a transaction. In whatever capacity, a lawyer should be alert to several basic issues:

(1) how does a documentary transaction alter the rights and obligations of Seller and Buyer?

(2) what are the duties of banks engaged in the collection process?

(3) when is a transaction a documentary transaction?

When these basic issues have been clarified, we will turn to the additional use of documentary drafts to facilitate financing.

Problem 18-1. Seller sells Buyer 20 cartons of widgets, "F.O.B. Seller's plant, Houston." No provision is made in the contract for credit. When is payment due by Buyer? Do any of the following represent a breach of the sales contract by Seller?

(a) Seller ships the goods under a nonnegotiable bill of lading, naming Buyer as consignee.

(b) Seller ships the goods under a nonnegotiable bill of lading, naming Seller as consignee.

(c) Seller ships the goods under a negotiable bill of lading drawn to its own order. See UCC 2-319, 2-504, 2-505, 2-310, 2-513, 2-512.

(d) Is Seller obligated to pay the freight? May Seller ship "Freight Prepaid"? "Freight Collect"? C.O.D.? What is the effect if Seller ships C.O.D.? See UCC 2-310, 2-513.

Problem 18-2. Seller in Houston sells 20 cartons of widgets, "C.I.F. San Francisco." Seller ships the goods under a negotiable bill of lading drawn to Seller's order. Seller indorses the bill in blank and attaches it to a draft drawn on Buyer to Seller's order, also indorsed in blank. Seller takes the draft and bill to its bank, which forwards them to its correspondent bank in San Francisco. The San Francisco bank promptly notifies Buyer. However, the goods have not yet arrived, and Buyer refuses to pay the draft until the goods are available for inspection. What are the respective rights and liabilities of Seller, Buyer, and San Francisco Bank? See, in addition to the sections cited above, UCC 2-320, 4-501, 4-503, 4-504. See also the principal case that follows.

Problem 18-3. Suppose that under the facts of Problem 18-2 the underlying contract term was "F.O.B. San Francisco." How would this change your response? Suppose additionally that Seller instructs its bank to forward its sight draft, with instructions to make presentment "on arrival." How does this change your response? See UCC 2-319, 4-502, and authorities previously cited.

MEMPHIS AERO CORP. v. FIRST AMERICAN NATIONAL BANK
647 S.W.2d 219, 35 UCC Rep. 910 (Tenn. 1983)

HARBISON, J. This case arises under the Uniform Commercial Code. It involves a claim against a commercial bank for late return of a documentary draft which it had received by mail. The Chancellor and the Court of Appeals held that the bank was liable for the amount of the draft. We reverse and dismiss. . . .

Appellant, First American National Bank in Nashville (American), received from Trust Company of Georgia on November 14, 1974 the following instrument which is the subject of this suit.

The documents referred to as "Enclosures" accompanied the draft. Stamped on the back of the instrument was [an imprint].

Also accompanying the document was a "collection letter" or "advice":

Mr. Tim Comin, an officer of American, received the draft and the other documents. He immediately notified an official of Mid-South Aviation with whom he had dealt on numerous occasions for more than a year. This official had previously advised Mr. Comin that he had authorized the draft. When the instrument arrived, however, Mid-South Aviation did not have sufficient funds to pay it. Although repeated promises were made to Mr. Comin that funds would be made available, this was never done.

The underlying commercial transaction involved the purchase of a Piper aircraft by Mid-South, a local retailer, from a regional Piper dealer, Memphis Aero Corporation. The latter had acquired it from the manufacturer, whose subsidiary, Piper Finance Corporation, retained a security interest. When the local dealer, Mid-South, sold the plane it advised Memphis Aero to draw a draft on First American. Memphis Aero actually had this done by Piper Finance. It and Piper supplied the necessary accompanying title documents to be delivered by American to Mid-South upon payment of the draft. Piper sent the draft and other papers through its own bank, Trust Company of Georgia. The record does not show whether or not that bank gave provisional credit therefor to Piper.

Mid-South, a relatively new but high-volume Piper retail dealer in Nashville, was a customer of First American. It maintained a checking account at that bank through which it passed large sums in connection with the purchase and sale of aircraft. The account was not under the control of any officer or official of American, was never frozen for any purpose, nor did American have authority to pay documentary drafts therefrom without approval from the depositor. American had made commercial loans to Mid-South from time to time, some collateralized and some not. It never at any time attempted to set off the customer's checking account against those loans. Only officials of Mid-South had authority to draw checks against the account. American had made no previous agreements with Mid-South or with Piper and Memphis Aero to finance the purchase of the aircraft in question by Mid-South or to carry overdrafts of the latter. It had on some prior occasions made loans to enable Mid-South to purchase planes, but the latter dealt with numerous other banks and also obtained financing from Memphis Aero.

Mr. Comin, the bank officer who handled the documentary draft upon its receipt, had little experience with such instruments. However he immediately notified Mid-South of its arrival and was advised that the latter would acquire sufficient funds to cover the draft but that such funds were not available on the day of presentment. Although he was in communication with both Piper and Memphis Aero by telephone no later than November 26 and advised them of the situation, Mr. Comin did not notify their agent Trust Company of Georgia of the dishonor of the draft, nor did he return it and the title documents until about December 20.

There were several questions presented in the courts below, but as the case comes here the only issue is whether appellant, a "payor bank" under the Code [UCC 4-105(b)], is strictly liable for the amount of the draft under UCC

4-302(b)[3] or whether its liability is limited to damages proximately caused by its negligence under the general provisions of UCC 4-103(5). If the latter measure is applied, no recovery is warranted because the bank customer, which owed the debt out of which the transaction arose, never had sufficient assets to pay the draft, and the item was essentially worthless at all relevant times. The Court of Appeals correctly held that "there is no evidence that, if First American had given timely notice of dishonor and made timely return of the draft and documents, Memphis Aero could have collected the amount due from Mid-South. That is, there is no evidence that Memphis Aero lost any amount as a proximate result of the action or inaction of First American."

On the other hand, the strict liability imposed under UCC 4-302(b) is applicable only if the documentary draft was a "properly payable" item as contemplated in the Code, including the requirement stated in UCC 4-104(1)(i) of "availability of funds for payment at the time of decision to pay or dishonor."

Both the trial court and the Court of Appeals held that appellant, as a payor bank, was strictly liable under UCC 4-302(b), but the Court of Appeals did not address the issue of whether the draft was "properly payable." The Chancellor resolved this issue by holding that the payor bank was also a "joint drawee" of the documentary draft with its customer. The bank was, in fact, solvent and, therefore, had sufficient funds of its own to pay the draft. This was deemed to render it strictly liable under UCC 4-302(b) as a *payor bank*— although, as we understand it, liability under that section is not liability *on the document itself* but is liability for the mishandling (delay in giving notice or return) of the item. Making no distinction between liability of a drawee *on the instrument* and liability for mishandling by a *"payor bank,"* the Chancellor, following the insistence of appellee, virtually eliminated from the Code the requirement that before a payor bank can be held strictly liable for mishandling, a documentary draft must be "properly payable."

Appellee insists that the Code provision that "properly payable includes the availability of funds for payment at the time of decision to pay or dishonor" (UCC 4-104(1)(i)) means sufficient funds of the *payor bank* as well as sufficient funds of the *debtor* in the commercial transaction. Very little authority exists for this proposition. Some of the cases most relied upon by appellee and by the courts below arose and were decided under the equivalent of UCC 4-302(a)—strict liability for not handling demand items by the banking "midnight deadline." Liability is imposed under that provision of the Code, however, for mishandling items *"other than a documentary draft"* and *"whether properly payable or not."* There is a distinct difference between liability under subsection (a) and that under (b) of this Code section.

In other cases cited by appellee where liability has been imposed upon a

---

3. With some exceptions not material here, a "payor bank" is liable for the amount of certain items not involved in this case and "(b) any other properly payable item unless within the time allowed for acceptance or payment of that item the bank either accepts or pays the item or returns it and accompanying documents."

payor bank under subsection (b), there was no question that the debtor had on deposit with or made available to the payor bank sufficient funds to pay the draft. In still others, the issue was never discussed. One federal case, cited by appellee as a "leading case," merely stated that a payor bank is liable under subsection (b) if it does not pay or return an "item" within a reasonable time and made no reference to the "properly payable" requirement of that statute.[6] This decision was followed by another from the same circuit, holding that the payor bank was obligated to pay late-returned drafts even though there were insufficient funds made available by the debtor and even though the payment would have created an overdraft.[7]

In the present case the debtor at no time had or made available to the payor bank, appellant here, sufficient funds for payment of the draft, which was timely presented. In our opinion the draft was not a "properly payable" item under UCC 4-302(b) so as to render the payor bank strictly liable for its late return. Liability, therefore, is governed by UCC 4-103(5), and the action fails for insufficient proof for damages.

The Court of Appeals at several points drew an analogy between the liability of the drawee of a check and that of a payor bank respecting a documentary draft. There is a significant difference. Checks are usually referred to as "cash" or "demand" items, and the drawee must handle these under its midnight deadline, "whether properly payable or not." UCC 4-302(a). Sight drafts, unaccompanied by title documents, may also fall within that provision. . . . Both the Chancellor and the Court of Appeals correctly held in the present case, however, despite the contention of appellee to the contrary, that the instrument involved here was a "documentary draft" as defined in the UCC.[9] It was described by some witnesses as an "envelope draft." As shown on its face, it was accompanied by a bill of sale to an airplane, a release of lien on the same, and an application for registration of title in the name of the vendee (the debtor in the transaction). The accompanying "advice" or "collection letter" from the transmitting bank called it a "Draft on Mid-South Aviation, Inc., N573 38" [the serial number of the plane], and instructed the appellant to *"Deliver documents only on payment."* Clearly it was contemplated that the title papers were to be "delivered against honor of the draft," UCC 4-104(1)(f), and the draft was a "documentary draft," not a

6. Wiley, Tate & Irby v. Peoples Bank & Trust Co., 11 UCC Rep. 154, 161 (N.D. Miss. 1971), *aff'd*, 462 F.2d 179 (5th Cir. 1972). Earlier the same court had held the items not to be documentary drafts at all and had imposed liability under the subsection dealing with the "midnight deadline." This holding was reversed, the appellate court pointing out that documentary drafts are specifically excluded from that deadline. See Wiley, Tate & Irby v. Peoples Bank & Trust Co., 438 F.2d 513 (5th Cir. 1971). Upon remand the trial court imposed liability under UCC 4-302(b), holding that if the debtor had insufficient funds on deposit with or available to the payor bank, then the latter was strictly liable if it did not return the item or give notice of nonpayment.

7. Union Bank of Benton, Arkansas v. First Natl. Bank in Mt. Pleasant, Texas, 621 F.2d 790 (5th Cir. 1980). UCC 4-401 authorizes, *but does not require,* a bank to charge the account of a customer if it pays an *"otherwise* properly payable" item. See UCC 4-401 (emphasis added).

9. " 'Documentary draft' means any negotiable or nonnegotiable draft with accompanying documents, securities or other papers to be delivered against honor of the draft." [UCC 4-104(1)(f).]

check or a simple sight draft which had to be processed under UCC 4-302(a) "whether properly payable or not."

Further, there is no contention in this case that appellant had agreed that it would pay the draft out of its own funds, that it would lend funds to the purchaser of the airplane or "floor plan" the craft, or that it had obligated itself to the sellers (the drawer and payee) so as to render it liable *on the instrument* for not immediately accepting or paying the draft. It was instructed to present the draft to the purchaser of the plane and to deliver the title papers to the latter only upon payment. It did timely present the draft. It did not timely return the documents to the transferor bank or notify the latter that the purchaser had insufficient funds to meet its obligation. Therein it was negligent. Had this negligence caused loss to the creditor, liability would follow, but there is no evidence that this occurred. Eight business days elapsed between receipt of the draft by appellant and telephone communication between it and the creditor that the draft had been dishonored upon presentment. There is conflicting evidence as to whether this was or was not a reasonable time, but we accept the findings of the courts below that the appellant was negligent in this respect and in not notifying the transmitting bank, agent of the creditors. In that regard, however, we note that the creditors (Memphis Aero and its financing company Piper Finance) by-passed their own agent, Trust Company of Georgia, the transmitting bank, and dealt directly with appellant, the payor bank. While appellant held the draft for a total of thirty-six days, the fact that it was holding the dishonored draft was known to the creditors upon the eighth business day (the twelfth calendar day), at the latest. They thereafter tried to deal directly with the debtor, Mid-South Aviation, to repossess the aircraft and to arrange new financing for the debtor. Only after these efforts failed did they demand that appellant return the draft. It did so immediately.

It will be recalled that under UCC 4-302(b) a payor bank becomes liable for a properly payable item "unless within the time allowed for acceptance or payment" of that item the bank either accepts, pays or returns it.

No specific time is provided under this section of the UCC for the acceptance or payment of a documentary draft. Under special provisions of the Code dealing with the collection of documentary drafts, a collecting bank must "reasonably" notify "its customer" of dishonor. UCC 4-501. Unless otherwise instructed, a bank presenting a documentary draft must deliver the documents "to the drawee" on acceptance of the draft if payable more than three days after presentment or, otherwise, only on payment. UCC 4-503(a). Upon dishonor the presenting bank

> . . . must use diligence and good faith to ascertain the reason for dishonor, must notify its transferor of the dishonor and of the results of its effort to ascertain the reasons therefor and must request instructions. [UCC 4-503(b).]

A non-payor bank, that is one which is merely a collecting or presenting bank, is liable for damages proximately caused by its negligence in failing to carry out these duties. UCC 4-103(5), 4-105(d), 4-105(e). A "payor bank" becomes liable for the amount of the instrument if it fails to carry out its duties and if it is a "properly payable item." UCC 4-302(b).

It is clear that the "midnight deadline" applicable to the handling of checks and other demand items is not applicable to the handling of documentary drafts. Banking institutions are permitted a reasonable or "seasonable" time within which to present, remit or return. Wiley, Tate & Irby v. Peoples Bank & Trust Co., 438 F.2d 513 (5th Cir. 1971).

As noted by the Supreme Court of Virginia, and as abundantly illustrated by the testimony in the present record, "The custom followed by banks in handling documentary drafts is not uniform. And the time permitted for their payment or return varies. What is seasonable time, and what is due diligence and good faith, must necessarily depend upon the facts and circumstances of each case. The cashier of Citizens and Marine testified that while the policy of his bank was ten days without specific instructions, under certain circumstances, depending on the customer, an unpaid draft would be retained for a month before being returned." Suttle Motor Corp. v. Citizens Bank of Poquoson, 221 S.E.2d 784, 786 (Va. 1976).

A number of expert witnesses testified in the present case, representing banking institutions from different parts of this state. Others having knowledge of the subject testified to practices of banking institutions in New York, Atlanta and other parts of the United States. The time for holding a documentary draft, according to these witnesses, varies from two days to as much as ten days or longer. Witnesses from American testified that they customarily hold such drafts for about ten days.

We have already stated that we concur in the findings of the courts below that the holding period in the present case was unreasonable under all of the circumstances, although, in view of the direct communication between the creditors and the payor bank, it was not nearly so long or nearly so unreasonable as indicated by the courts below.

If, during the period while American was holding the draft, it had become "properly payable" and the bank had failed to pay or return, an entirely different case would be presented. That was the situation in Suttle Motor Corp., supra. There, while the bank was holding the drafts, funds came into its hands which should have been applied directly to the payment of those specific drafts. The title documents attached to the drafts should have been detached, delivered to customers who had made loans from the bank to purchase their automobiles, and the drafts paid out of the proceeds. Instead the bank applied those proceeds to other debts owed to it by the drawer of the drafts. It served its own interests, proximately and directly damaging the payee of the drafts who had caused them to be sent to the bank for collection. In one instance a bank customer named Harrell borrowed funds from the bank to finance the purchase of a car, and those loan proceeds were credited directly to the drawer of a draft which the bank was holding. The title papers attached to the draft were not delivered to the borrower, and the Supreme Court of

Virginia said: "Clearly the proceeds from the loan to Harrell should have been applied in payment of the Suttle draft, thereby enabling Harrell to obtain good title to her automobile." 221 S.E.2d at 787.

The court further said: "We do not have here a mere delay in the return of a draft. There was delay and inaction at a critical time when Poquoson was making a tremendous effort in its own behalf to reduce the losses which it obviously faced on the Batts and Hockaday account." 221 S.E.2d at 788.

These facts differ drastically from those presented in the present case. While the debtor, Mid-South Aviation, was indebted to American, the latter did not at any time divert funds or assets of Mid-South to the payment of its own claims when these should have been used to pay the draft which the bank was holding. This, indeed, is a case involving nothing more than "a mere delay in the return of a draft," and there is no evidence of any dereliction of duty or neglect other than failure of the bank official to give notice to the transferor bank or to give more prompt notice than he did to the creditors who undertook to deal directly with him.

No question was made in the Suttle Motor Corp. case, supra, but that liability was fixed under UCC 4-302(b). The drafts in that case clearly were or became "properly payable" while the bank was holding them, because sufficient funds of the debtor did come into the possession of the bank to pay the drafts—a situation entirely different from that involved here.

We concur in the conclusions of the courts below that American was a "payor bank" and that it was negligent, but since we do not find that the item was "properly payable," in our opinion liability should not have been imposed under UCC 4-302(b).

The judgments of the courts below are reversed and the suit is dismissed at the cost of appellee. . . .

NOTES & QUESTIONS

1. *Payor bank.* Examine the face of the draft reproduced in the text of the *Memphis Aero* case and read UCC 4-105(b). Do you agree with the court that American was a payor bank? If American was a payor bank, was it also a drawee? What was its liability as drawee?

2. *Liability on the instrument versus liability for late return.* The court states (correctly) that UCC 4-302(b) does not impose liability on the instrument. It also concludes that the item was not "properly payable." Do you agree with this second conclusion? Why does UCC 4-302 distinguish between "demand item[s] other than documentary drafts whether properly payable or not" (subsection (a)) and "any other properly payable item" (subsection (b))?

3. *The time for acting on documentary drafts.* If one assumes the item *were* properly payable, the bank would be liable if it did not either pay or return the item "within the time allowed." UCC 4-302(b). The court states that the

midnight deadline of 4-302(a) has no application to documentary drafts. How much time is allowed for a drawee/payor bank of documentary drafts payable at sight to determine to pay or return? The court also cites considerable testimony and case law for the proposition that a "reasonable" time is allowed. Does it matter, in this respect, whether American was acting as a payor bank or a presenting bank?

4. *Payor banks, collecting banks, and presenting banks.* Is the court's description of American as a payor bank consistent with its reference to UCC 4-501 to determine the timeliness of notice, and UCC 4-503 and 4-103(5) as to scope of liability? See UCC 4-105(d), UCC 4-105(e).

2.   Acceptance Financing

In the preceding materials, the documentary transaction has been viewed principally as a means of retaining the seller's control over the goods and lessening risks of nonpayment. By the use of *time* drafts, rather than *sight* drafts, the documentary transaction may also be viewed as a financing device. This is referred to as *acceptance financing*.

When a time draft is drawn upon and accepted by a merchant, it is referred to as a *trade acceptance*. When a time draft is drawn upon and accepted by a bank, it is referred to as a *bank acceptance*.[1] In either case, when the acceptance is returned to the Seller, it will have an item carrying both the acceptor's and the drawer's obligation to make payment at maturity. A discount market exists both for trade acceptances and bank acceptances—thus the Seller is able to realize most of the price of the goods sold, while the Buyer is not out of pocket until the draft matures.

Problem 18-4. Seller desires to sell goods to Buyer, but Buyer does not have the financial strength to pay for the goods immediately. Buyer requests

---

1. Certain bank acceptances are eligible for discount by Federal Reserve banks (and are hence referred to as eligible acceptances). Banks will readily discount eligible acceptances, since the Federal Reserve banks provide a dependable secondary market for rediscount. The term *eligible acceptance* is unfortunate, however, to the extent that a negative inference is drawn that other bank acceptances are somehow questionable. This is not so: they simply do not enjoy the benefit of possible rediscount with the Federal Reserve banks.

Eligibility is determined not by the nature of the instrument but by the nature of the transaction that gives rise to it. For this reason it is customary to stamp on the instrument a legend known as an eligibility certificate. This legend identifies the nature of the underlying transaction. Eligible acceptances do not otherwise vary in form from bank acceptances generally.

For our purposes, it is important to know that eligible acceptances include drafts of 180-days'-or-less tenor ". . . which grow out of transactions involving the importation or exportation of goods; or which grow out of transactions involving the domestic shipment of goods provided shipping documents conveying or securing title *are attached at the time of acceptance;* or which are secured *at the time of acceptance* by a warehouse receipt, or other such document conveying or securing title." [Emphasis added.] 12 U.S.C. §372 (1982). The classic treatise on acceptance financing is H. Harfield, Bank Credits and Acceptances (5th ed. 1974). See also J. Dolan, The Law of Letters of Credit: Commercial and Standby Credits (1984).

90 days' credit, allowing time to resell a portion of the purchased goods to finance the purchase price. Seller wishes to clinch the sale and suspects some competitors might afford Buyer the requested credit term. Seller is reluctant to tie up its own working capital to such an extent. Seller therefore makes a counter-proposal: Seller will ship the goods under a negotiable bill of lading and will draw a draft payable 90 days after sight. The parties agree on this transaction. Seller makes the shipment and forwards the documentary draft through its bank for presentment by a bank in Buyer's city. Under what conditions should presenting bank release the bill of lading to Buyer? After a proper release, what rights does Seller have against the goods? What rights on the draft, and against whom? If the presenting bank improperly releases the bill of lading, what rights will Seller have, and against whom? If Buyer dishonors the draft, what are the presenting bank's privileges and duties and what are the Seller's remedies? See UCC 3-802, 3-401, 3-413, 4-503, 4-504.

B.   LETTERS OF CREDIT

1.   *Basic Concepts: Commercial Credits*

Documentary transactions, explored in the preceding materials, reduce considerably the risks involved in carrying on business over long distances and in differing markets. Substantial risks remain, however. For instance, suppose that Seller forwards a documentary draft for collection through a bank in the buyer's locale. When the local bank presents the documents to the Buyer, Buyer wrongfully refuses to pay the draft and take up the documents. Since the bank is acting as Seller's agent, Seller retains control of the documents and the ability to control disposition of the goods. But if a New York manufacturer is selling special order goods to a Persian Gulf buyer, these legal rights may be of limited practical value. Commercial letters of credit originally developed in response to this and other risks present even in documentary transactions, particularly when carried on in overseas trade. In recent years, however, this highly flexible financing device has been extended into many novel situations.

A letter of credit is basically a means of assuring payment. It substitutes the credit of a highly creditworthy institution, such as a major commercial bank, for the credit of the payor in the underlying transaction (in a sale of goods, the buyer). Its use may be dictated by a payee's reservations concerning payor's ability to pay, willingness to pay, or both. In its simplest form, a letter of credit transaction involves three parties and three distinct sets of legal obligations. These may be illustrated as in Figure 18-2.

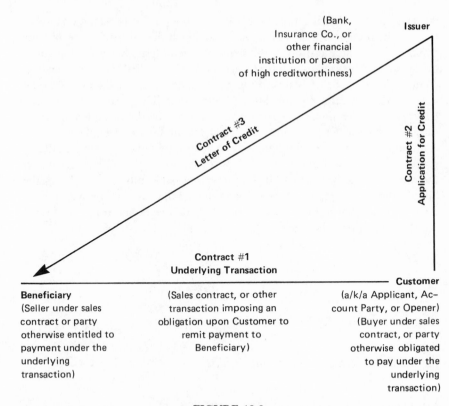

FIGURE 18-2
Basic Letter-of-Credit Relationship

In the transaction we have just considered, the sales contract between the New York seller and the Persian Gulf buyer constitutes the underlying transaction. In negotiating this contract, Seller may insist on a letter of credit. The parties may (and should) specify the financial institution that issues the credit, and the terms of the credit should also be specified. For instance, what documents must the seller (*beneficiary* under the credit) present to the *issuer*? Is the credit available by Seller's sight drafts? What is the total amount of the credit? How long will the credit remain available (i.e., what is its expiration date)? By what date should the buyer (*customer*) have established the letter of credit? You should clearly understand that the terms so established, although they define the nature of the credit that is to be issued, are simply terms of the sales contract. By agreeing to these terms, the buyer has specified the payment obligation under the contract in the same manner in which the parties might provide for cash payment or for buyer's acceptance of 30-day time drafts. If Buyer does not cause a conforming letter of credit to be issued he will breach the sales contract and seller may suspend performance or take other appropriate remedial action. But the terms of the contemplated letter of credit, as set forth in the sales contract, do not create any rights in the seller as against the issuer, and are immaterial to the seller's right as against the issuer to obtain payment under any credit that is subsequently issued.

In order to fulfill the obligation it has assumed under the sales contract, the buyer will now approach the bank designated. If the parties have failed to designate a bank the Code would define the buyer's obligation under UCC 2-325. However, since the seller's purpose in negotiating for a letter of credit is to assure payment, a well-counseled seller will insist that the issuing bank be satisfactory to it. An application for a commercial letter of credit will be filled out, usually on a standard form supplied by the bank. See Form 18-1 at p. 930 supra. This application constitutes the second contract in Figure 18-2.

The application establishes the terms of the credit between the issuer and the customer (also known as the account party in banking parlance). It is the buyer/customer's responsibility to make sure that the terms are identical to those set forth in the sales contract. If they are not, the buyer invites a breach of the sales contract or potential dispute at a later stage in the transaction. Should there be a discrepancy, the issuer is bound to the buyer only by the terms of the application, and a credit issued in accordance with the application will nonetheless not comply with the underlying sales contract.

An example, in the form of a simple problem, may clarify these principles.

Problem 18-5. Seller and Buyer sign an export log contract, allowing shipment during August and September. The contract calls for the Buyer to procure a letter of credit, with an expiration date of October 15, and requires as one condition of payment bills of lading evidencing loading of the logs on board during July and August. Due to an internal clerical error, Buyer completes an application for a credit that allows received-for-shipment bills of lading dated July or August and for a credit that expires October 1. Issuer issues a credit in conformity with the terms of the application. Has Buyer fulfilled its duty under the sales contract? Does Buyer have a contractual basis for requiring Issuer to issue a credit that conforms to the terms specified in the sales contract? Suppose Seller submits to Issuer documents conforming to the terms of the letter of credit but not to the terms of the sales contract itself?

The best course of action for a buyer receiving a nonconforming letter of credit is to seek an immediate amendment to conform the credit to the terms called for by the sales contract. Whether a buyer will in fact be able to obtain an amended credit will depend on a number of factors. These factors and other means of curing discrepancies are discussed in the text at p. 928 infra.

A second function of the application is to establish the bank's rights to reimbursement by its customer for amounts paid under the credit. If the credit is issued by a bank in a Code jurisdiction, UCC 5-115 provides a statutory basis for such reimbursement. However, a bank will almost certainly want additional rights, such as the right to establish an interest rate applicable to any amounts due, and will also wish to specify when it will be paid by its customer. In some instances the bank may be willing to allow its customer a credit period before reimbursement is due.

At the other end of the spectrum, the bank may require that its customer pay the bank the day before the bank's own payment under the credit. In some foreign countries it is the practice to require the customer to maintain with the issuer a blocked account in the amount of the credit or some percentage thereof before the bank will issue the credit at all. Although such a practice would be unusual in the United States, it is quite common for banks in this country to pursue similar objectives by incorporating a security agreement as part of the application. From a bank's perspective, when it engages its own credit on behalf of its customer, its risk is similar to any other extension of credit. If the credit finances a transaction in goods, the bank will normally have a security interest in the goods and in any documents of title covering them. However, the integrity of the seller may be completely unknown to the bank, which must therefore place its reliance principally on its own customer. Whether it will engage its credit on the basis of the customer's unsecured promise of reimbursement or whether it will require security obviously depends on the bank's prior experience with the customer, and on the customer's financial strength.

The third legal relationship involved in a letter of credit transaction is that between Issuer and Beneficiary. Again, this is an independent relationship, and the obligations that Issuer assumes under the letter of credit in favor of Beneficiary must be determined solely by reference to the letter of credit itself. The bank's obligation is unaffected by either the terms or the actual performance of the underlying sales contract. See UCC 5-109(1)(a). Nor may Beneficiary avail itself of the terms of credit application contract between Issuer and Customer. Uniform Customs and Practice for Documentary Credits (UCP), Art. 6 (1983 revision).[2]

When a seller has negotiated in the underlying transaction for issuance of a letter of credit, it is imperative that the purported credit be examined carefully by the seller/beneficiary as soon as it is established. In a practical sense,

2. The Uniform Customs and Practice for Documentary Credits (UCP) is the work product of the International Chamber of Commerce. It represents a formal compilation of banking usage with respect to many important issues of letter-of-credit practice. Virtually all United States banks issue commercial credits subject to the UCP, so its provisions are incorporated by reference into the terms of the credit. It is also adhered to by the banks of most, but not all, other nations. The UCP has been the subject of frequent revision, principally to keep pace with rapid changes in modes of transportation and transport documentation, and with the telecommunications revolution and its effect on bank operations. The UCP is often referred to by the ICC publication number of the respective edition: e.g., ICC 400 (1983 revision, effective October 1, 1984); ICC 290 (1974 revision); ICC 222 (1962 revision). Citations throughout the text will indicate whether they are to the 1974 or 1983 revision as follows: 1974 UCP Art.—; 1983 UCP Art.—.

the seller's ability to obtain payment is conditioned on compliance with the terms of the credit, whether or not those conditions reflect the language of the underlying contract. If ambiguities or discrepancies exist in the credit, or between the credit and the sales contract, they should be addressed immediately. Curative action may then be possible, as opposed to the prospect of costly litigation at a later point.

TOYOTA INDUSTRIAL TRUCKS U.S.A., INC. v. CITIZENS NATIONAL BANK v. PROMAT CORP.
611 F.2d 465, 28 UCC Rep. 484 (3d Cir. 1979)

ROSENN, Circuit Judge. . . . [Toyota Industrial, or Toyota,] was incorporated in September 1974 as a division of Toyota Motors Distributors, Inc. (Toyota Motors), a California corporation. In the spring of 1973, Toyota Motors was interested in retaining a distributor in the Pittsburgh, Pennsylvania area for its forklift trucks. Promat Corporation was selected by Toyota Motors to be its dealer, but before the dealership could be formalized, Toyota Motors required a line of credit to secure payment for its shipment of trucks to Promat. Toyota Motors subsequently entered into negotiations with CNB [Citizens National Bank] to establish such a line of credit. Vice-president and branch manager of CNB, Richard Shelton, wrote to Toyota Motors' authorized representative, Ray Tanner, on April 18, 1973, offering to extend a line of credit to Promat in the amount of $50,000. Toyota Motors, however, objected to the form of the agreement and wrote to CNB on May 1, 1973, asking CNB to issue a letter in conformity with Toyota Motors' standard bank revolving credit agreement with other distributors of its trucks. CNB cooperated and executed a letter on May 7, 1973, conforming to Toyota Motors' suggested terms. It is this letter which is the subject of the present controversy.

The letter of May 7, 1973, established a "line of credit" on behalf of Promat as a dealer in Toyota forklift trucks and required CNB to honor drafts covering shipments not "in excess of $50,000 on any one business day." Further, the letter required Toyota to attach to the drafts invoices and bills of sale evidencing title to the vehicles. CNB reserved the right to cancel the agreement by written notice at any time.

Toyota Motors sold its forklift truck product line to Toyota Industrial on December 31, 1974. As a part of this sale, Toyota Motors assigned all its rights arising under the credit arrangement with CNB dated May 7, 1973. Notice was sent to CNB evidencing such an assignment. From 1973 to 1976 CNB subsequently honored nineteen drafts submitted pursuant to the May 7, 1973 letter. CNB honored all of these drafts within thirty days of their presentment. From the first quarter of 1974 through 1975, CNB, without Toyota's knowledge, only paid the drafts *after* Promat had deposited sufficient funds with CNB to cover them. CNB also without Toyota's knowledge unilaterally altered the credit line available to Promat by reducing its maximum available credit from $50,000 to $25,000. CNB apparently altered both the procedure for honoring the drafts and the amount of available credit because of Promat's worsening financial position.

In August of 1975, Shelton was replaced by William T. Elliot as vice-president and branch manager of the CNB office with which Promat did business. In January of 1976, Promat's outstanding indebtedness to CNB was in excess of $32,000. Toyota presented a draft on January 7, 1976, in the amount of $24,425.52 with invoices for three forklift trucks that had been shipped to Promat. CNB did not honor this draft. Over a month passed without payment and on February 17, 1976, Toyota presented another draft in the amount of $24,330.75 with invoices representing shipment of three more fork-lift trucks to Promat. Up to this time, CNB had given Toyota no notice that it intended to dishonor any submitted drafts. The January 7 draft was apparently not paid because Promat failed to deposit sufficient funds to cover it. Similarly, Promat failed to deposit sufficient funds to cover the February 17 draft and Elliot, apparently without knowledge of the May 7, 1973 letter agreement with Toyota, dishonored both drafts and returned them unpaid to Toyota. Toyota objected to the dishonor of the two drafts and brought the letter agreement of May 7, 1973, to Elliot's attention at a meeting on March 8, 1976. CNB subsequently exercised its right to cancel the May 7, 1973 letter on March 17, 1976. . . .

Toyota brought a diversity action in the district court seeking to hold CNB for the wrongful dishonor of the two unpaid drafts. Asserting that the letter of May 7, 1973, was a letter of credit . . . Toyota demanded judgment in the amounts covered by the above dishonored drafts plus interest. . . .

Letters of credit have been commonly used in commercial transactions for centuries. A letter of credit is essentially a promise by the "issuer," (commonly a bank) to the "beneficiary," (usually a seller of goods) to extend credit on behalf of the beneficiary's customer, (usually a buyer of goods). A credit arrangement between a bank and a seller need not state that it is a letter of credit before the agreement is covered by Article Five of the Uniform Commercial Code. The UCC provides that Article Five applies "(a) to a credit issued by a bank if the credit requires a documentary draft or a documentary demand for payment. . . ." UCC 5-102(1)(a). Thus a letter of credit may arise when a bank agrees to extend credit on behalf of the seller's customer by honoring drafts substantiated by documentation of the transaction. There are, however, certain formal requirements that must be met before an Article Five letter of credit is established. The letter must be forwarded to the beneficiary, UCC 5-106(1)(b), and the letter must be signed, UCC 5-104(1). Although letters of credit require no consideration, UCC 5-105, they are nonetheless binding obligations.

The key issue in this case is whether the letter agreement between Toyota and CNB of May 7, 1973, constituted an Article Five letter of credit. CNB argues that the parties intended only a "revolving line of credit" by which CNB would extend an aggregate amount of credit on behalf of Promat not to exceed $50,000 on any one business day. Under CNB's interpretation of the letter, it would have been obligated to extend only that amount of credit, which when added to Promat's existing liability to the bank, equaled no more than $50,000. Thus, if Promat owed CNB $30,000 on a given day, CNB would be only required to honor drafts submitted by Toyota up to $20,000. The district court disagreed and found that the letter of May 7, 1973, was a valid letter of credit creating a $50,000 daily credit directly available to Toyota and that CNB's unilateral reduction of Promat's available credit had no effect on the May 7, 1973 letter. The district court concluded that CNB wrongfully dishonored the two drafts submitted by Toyota in January and February 1976. We agree.

The letter of May 7, 1973 meets the Article Five tests for a letter of credit. It specified that CNB will honor document[ary] drafts submitted by Toyota not to exceed $50,000 "for shipments or deliveries on any one business day." The letter was signed and sent to Toyota. Nothing more was required to establish the instrument as a letter of credit. Further, the letter specified that the credit arrangement was to be continuous until revoked by CNB upon written notice to Toyota. No conditions apart from documentation were included in the agreement. CNB's actions without notice to Toyota requiring Promat to first deposit sufficient funds to cover the drafts and reducing Promat's available credit could not relieve the bank of its obligation under the May 7, 1973 letter. The UCC provides:

> Unless otherwise agreed once an irrevocable credit is established as regards . . . the beneficiary it can be modified or revoked only with his consent. [UCC 5-106(2)]

The question then is whether CNB's dishonor of the two drafts submitted in 1976 was "wrongful."

Under Article Five "an issuer must honor a draft or demand for payment which complies with the terms of the relevant credit . . . ." UCC 5-114(1). Judge Teitelbaum appropriately found that "[t]he drafts were otherwise in compliance with the terms of the letter and were, therefore, improperly dishonored." Toyota complied with the terms of the letter by supplying the necessary documentation with the submitted drafts. No other action was required on its part.

Much of CNB's argument on appeal is that the term calling for CNB to honor drafts not in excess of $50,000 for shipments or deliveries on any one business day is ambiguous and that the district [court] failed to consider the prior dealings of the parties. Such dealings, CNB asserts, would establish the agreement as only establishing an aggregate maximum credit for Promat. Thus, it would not have been wrongful for CNB to dishonor the two 1976 drafts because when added to Promat's existing indebtedness, both would have exceeded the $50,000 maximum credit available.

The problem with CNB's position on appeal is that its argument in the district court concerning the prior dealings of the parties was directed at establishing the letter as a revolving credit line and not as a letter of credit. Upon careful examination of the record, we are unable to discover that CNB ever argued that even if it had issued a letter of credit, it did not wrongfully dishonor the drafts because if it had paid them it would have exceeded an aggregate $50,000 available to Promat. The issues of law set forth in the pre-trial stipulation executed by the parties do not raise this argument. Hence, we decline to consider this argument now raised for the first time on appeal. . . .

[The court's lengthy discussion of appellants' contention that Toyota failed to mitigate damages has been omitted.—Eds.]

In sum, we hold that the letter agreement of May 7, 1973, constituted a valid Article Five letter of credit and that Toyota was under no obligation to mitigate its damages because CNB was in an equal if not superior position to avoid the loss. Accordingly the judgment of the district court will be affirmed. Costs taxed against the appellant.

NOTES & QUESTIONS

1. *Formal requisites.* As the principal case indicates, the formal requisites for a valid letter of credit are minimal. The most direct statement appears in UCC 5-104, stating that it requires only a "writing" and a "signature by the issuer." Both these terms are given generous definitions in UCC 1-201. In practice, three general formats for letters of credit are in common use. One is the traditional format, which is simply written in the form of a letter addressed to the beneficiary, and states the terms of the credit. This format, responsible for the nomenclature "letter of credit," promotes by its very flexibility the risk of ambiguities as to the nature of the bank's obligation. The second is the form that commercial banks and some other issuers have developed having a stylized "fill-in-the-blanks" format, in part to minimize characterization issues. See Form 18-2 at p. 930 supra. The third form, used particularly in international trade, commonly telexes the terms of the credit. See Form 18-3. The use of telex credits finds specific support in UCC 5-104(2).

FORM 18-3

FORM OF TELEX CREDIT

SEABANK

FM CHINABANK HONGKONG TO SEABANK
DD 12-5-82

238/1770

ISSUED IRREVOCABLE DOCUMENTARY CREDIT 369/135802

FOR USD 2,494,000.—ON BEHALF OF THE SOUTH SEA TRADERS BANK LTD.

A/C WONG DAO TRADING (HK) CO FAVOURING EVERGREEN TRADING CO. INC., P.O. BOX NO. 902 HOQUIAM, WASHINGTON 98520   USA COVERING SHIPMENT OF:

DOUGLAS FIR LOGS 4,300,000 BMF AT USD 580.—PER 100 BMF CANDF QUINGDAO FROM USA TO QUINGDAO CHINA LATEST 31ST MAY 1982.   EXPIRES 10TH JUNE, 1982 IN USA TRANSHIPMENT AND PARTSHIPMENTS BOTH PROHIBITED (STOP)

DOCUMENTS REQUIRED:

BENEFICIARY'S DRAFTS DRAWN IN DUPLICATE ON THE SOUTH SEA TRADERS   BANK LTD A/C WONG DAO TRADING (HK) CO AT SIGHT (STOP)   SIGNED INVOICES IN TRIPLICATE (STOP)   FULL SET OF CLEAN ON BOARD OCEAN BILLS OF LADING IN TRIPLICATE MADE OUT TO ORDER AND BLANK ENDORSED MARKED FREIGHT PREPAID AND NOTIFYING CHINA NATIONAL FOREIGN TRADE TRANSPORTATION CORP QINGDAO CHINA (STOP)   BENEFICIARY'S LETTER ATTESTING THAT THE NATIONALITY OF THE CARRYING VESSEL HAS BEEN APPROVED BY THE OPENERS (STOP)   2 COPIES OF DETAILED LOG LIST INDICATING GROSS AND NET VOLUMES OF EACH LOG (STOP)   2 COPIES OF CERTIFICATE OF QUANTITY AND QUALITY AND VOLUME ISSUED BY THE SCALING BUREAU EVIDENCING SHIPMENT OF DOUGLAS FIR LOGS (STOP)   CERTIFIED COPY OF CABLE DISPATCHED TO OPENERS WITHIN 16 HOURS AFTER SHIPMENT ADVISING NAME OF VESSEL DATE QUANTITY WEIGHT AND VALUE OF SHIPMENT (STOP)

OTHER TERMS AND CONDITIONS:

5 PERCENT MORE OR LESS DRAWING AGAINST PROPORTIONATE QUANTITY OF GOODS SHIPPED ALLOWED (STOP)   ALL BANKING CHARGES OUTSIDE HONG KONG ARE FOR ACCOUNT OF BENEFICIARY (STOP)   CHARTER BILLS OF LADING ACCEPTABLE (STOP)   BILLS OF LADING MARKED ON DECK CARGO ACCEPTABLE (STOP)   INSURANCE TO BE COVERED BY ULTIMATE BUYER (STOP)   DOCUMENTS MUST

BE PRESENTED NOT LATER THAN 10 DAYS AFTER THE DATE
OF ISSUANCE OF THE SHIPPING DOCUMENTS (STOP)   DRAFTS
DRAWN UNDER THIS CREDIT ARE NEGOTIABLE BY SEABANK
ONLY (STOP)   THIS NEGOTIATING BANK MAY DEBIT THE
CHINA BANK HONG KONG UNITED STATES DOLLAR
ACCOUNT WITH SEABANK SEATTLE OFFICE (STOP)   DRAFTS
TOGETHER WITH THE RELATIVE DOCUMENTS TO BE
DISPATCHED TO THE CHINA BANK HONG KONG IN ONE
EXPRESS AIRMAIL (STOP)   THIS CREDIT IS SUBJECT TO ICC
(290) (STOP)   THIS CABLE IS THE OPERATIVE INSTRUMENT
AND NO CONFIRMATION WILL FOLLOW NEGOTIATION MAY
BE EFFECTED UNDER THIS CABLE ADVICE (STOP)   PLEASE
FORWARD THIS CABLE TO THE BENEFICIARY WITHOUT
ADDING YOUR CONFIRMATION (STOP)

CREDIT NO 369/135802

ENDCK

Practitioners should be aware that under the UCP, the telex is presumptively
the operative instrument, even if a letter in confirmation of terms follows. 1972
UCP Article 4. The 1983 UCP continues the ambiguity, however, by providing that the statement, ". . . full details to follow ["details to follow" in the
1974 revision.—Eds.] (or words of similar effect) . . ." signifies intent that
the mail confirmation be the operative credit. 1983 UCP Article 12(a), (6).
The 1983 UCP also strongly recommends that if the telex is intended as the
operative credit it should clearly indicate that the credit is issued "subject to
Uniform Customs and Practice for Documentary Credits, 1983 revision, ICC
Publication No. 400." 1983 UCP Art. 12(c).

   2. *Ambiguous documents.* As noted, the flexibility of Article 5 may serve as a
trap for the unwary, particularly when banks issue credits in the traditional
letter form, rather than utilizing a standard form of unambiguous character.
Consider the following letter, printed here with fictitious names, issued by the
branch manager of a small Oregon bank on the bank's letterhead at the
request of the bank's customer:

> Please consider this letter as an Irrevocable Letter of Credit in the amount
> of $14,655.00 by Seaside Bank, Tillamook County Branch, Nehalem, Oregon,
> for Virgil Scobie's DBA Nehalem River Dredging on the Quinault Tribe's
> dredging job that he has contracted to do for the U.S. Army Corps of Engineers,
> Seattle, Washington.
> We understand this letter of credit is in lieu of a Surety Bond (Revised
> Statutes 5.06.2) which Mr. Scobie will eventually obtain for you. When you
> receive this Bond and have accepted it, the Bank will expect you to release the

irrevocable letter of credit and return it to the Bank. If you have any questions, please call me at (503) XXX-XXXX.

> Very truly yours,
>
> /s/
>
> R. J. Stevens, Branch Mgr.

Is this a letter of credit? See UCC 5-102, 5-103. If you believe that it is, what are its terms? For instance, how does the beneficiary draw on it? What, if any, conditions must the beneficiary satisfy? What, if any, documents or instruments must be presented to the bank? If you do not believe that it is a letter of credit, what if any legal effect does the letter have?

3. *Definition of scope.* Note that in *Toyota* the court focuses initially on UCC 5-102. This section states the *scope* of Article 5, but by doing so it also provides a backhanded definition of *letter of credit.* All three subsections of UCC 5-102 refer to transactions within the scope of Article 5, when they involve "credits" with specified characteristics. However, *credit* is itself a defined term, UCC 5-103, that refers to engagements "of a kind within the scope of this Article (Section 5-102)." Thus there is a considerable degree of circularity in the definitional structure. Courts unavoidably play a major role in defining what types of engagements will be denominated letters of credit and subjected to the Article 5 regime. It is evident that this open-ended approach was quite intentional on the part of the draftsman, the late Dean Soia Mentschikoff. See UCC 5-102, comment 2.

4. *Consideration.* No consideration is required to establish a credit, nor is consideration required to support a subsequent modification of its terms. UCC 5-105. It is obvious that commercial institutions rarely issue credits except as part of a financial transaction. What then would be the difficulties if consideration were a requirement? Consider particularly in this regard traditional contract doctrines as to pre-existing duties.

5. *Revocable and irrevocable credit.* Letters of credit may be either revocable or irrevocable. The irrevocable letter of credit is considered the norm in American use, but this is not necessarily the practice in other countries. Furthermore, as noted, it is also the practice in the United States to issue credits "subject to" the UCP, which states that a credit silent on its face is to be interpreted as revocable.[3] Contrast this presumption with UCC 2-325. Article 5 itself is silent on this point. In *Toyota,* the court quotes UCC 5-106, which states that once an irrevocable credit has been established as against the beneficiary it can be modified or revoked only with the beneficiary's consent. The court makes no reference to UCC 5-106(3), which states: "Unless otherwise agreed after a revocable credit is established it may be modified or revoked by the issuer without notice to or consent from the customer or beneficiary." Was the credit in *Toyota* revocable or irrevocable?

---

3. 1983 UCP Art. 7(c). American banking associations attempted but failed to reverse this presumption during the 1983 revision of the UCP.

6. *Mitigation.* A lengthy discussion by the court concerning mitigation of damages has been omitted. In brief, the facts indicate that Toyota made a second shipment of trucks, for which it presented a draft on February 17. At that time, a draft presented January 7 had still not been paid. The court commented that the bank had never before failed to pay a draft, although there were prior instances of as much as 30 days' delay in effecting payment. It therefore regarded Toyota, which had received no formal notice of dishonor, as acting in good faith. Apparently by early March Toyota was fully aware of the precarious financial situation of the bank's customer (Toyota's buyer). Toyota had a contractual repurchase option, as well as the statutory rights of an unpaid seller. On the other hand, the bank itself held a perfected security interest in its customer's inventory. The court concluded that Toyota was under no duty to mitigate, since the bank was equally well situated to protect itself. Do you agree with the court's analysis of the above issues? Suppose that in early April, still having no formal cancellation of the letter of credit, Toyota had made four successive shipments of $50,000 each. Would Toyota be equally entitled to payment by the bank for those shipments, upon presentation of drafts and proper invoices? The bank, in urging Toyota's duty to mitigate, cited UCC 5-115. How does that section bear upon mitigation of damages in the event of dishonor?

2. *Development of the Standby Letter of Credit*

For many years, letters of credit were utilized almost exclusively in sales transactions, principally in the financing of imports and exports. The years since World War II, especially the last decade, have seen an enormous growth in the use of letters of credit in other commercial settings. By far the most important development has been the widespread use of so-called standby or guaranty letters of credit.

The standby credit shares the conceptual underpinning of the traditional commercial credit. The principle of the independent character of the issuer's obligation is equally applicable to standby credits, as is the principle of strict documentary compliance. With standby credits as with commercial credits, an issuing bank will examine the conformity of presented documents to the terms of the credit, not to the terms of the underlying transaction or to the facts that may lie behind those documents. If documents conform, the basic rule is that the beneficiary is entitled to honor of the credit. The bank's customer is relegated to disputing issues arising out of the underlying transaction with the beneficiary, the other party to the underlying transaction. In the interim, the bank will look to its customer for reimbursement for payments effected pursuant to the credit. However, the standby credit also is different from the traditional commercial credit in a very fundamental sense: none of the parties to the transaction ever expects it to be drawn upon. Like a guaranty, it is there, in the parties' contemplation, simply as a back up. Hence the names *guaranty* or *standby* credit. Consider the following examples of transactions in which standby credits have frequently been employed:

1. Before commencing construction of an office complex, developer secures construction financing from Lender #1. At the same time, a loan commitment is arranged with Insurance Company (Lender #2), which is to provide long-term take-out financing. Lender #2's commitment expires on June 30, 1984. Lender #2 requests a cash deposit of $180,000 to serve as liquidated damages in the event the loan is not taken down. Developer offers instead to provide a letter of credit issued by National Bank, naming Lender #2 as beneficiary, and providing that National Bank undertakes to honor Lender #2's sight draft in the amount of $180,000, if accompanied by Lender #2's certificate that the sum in question is due and owing to Lender #2 as liquidated damages for Developer's failure to take down the loan by the date specified in the loan commitment agreement.

2. Attorney wishes to appeal a judgment entered against his client, but the client balks at the substantial cash deposit required by Bonding Co. before it will issue a supersedeas bond. After further negotiation, it is agreed that client will arrange for a letter of credit in favor of Bonding Co. Client's bank takes from the client a note secured by real estate and for a charge of one point issues its letter of credit to Bonding Co. calling for payment of Bonding Co.'s sight draft up to the amount of the bond, if presented together with Bonding Co.'s certificate that such sum is due and owing Bonding Co. as a consequence of its payment under the bond. Client ties up no cash and pays no interest; the Bank will not be out funds unless and until a draw is made under the credit.

3. Manufacturer enters into a contract to manufacture specifically designed goods for Buyer. Manufacturer will incur substantial costs in the course of manufacture, and the goods will have no, or only a very limited, market if Buyer defaults on the contract. Manufacturer successfully negotiates inclusion in the sales contract of a term obligating Buyer to procure, prior to commencement of manufacture, a letter of credit in favor of Manufacturer in the amount of the purchase price, which may be drawn upon by Manufacturer's written demand, accompanied by Manufacturer's certificate that it has completed the manufacture of the specified goods.

4. In a mild variant of #3, contractor negotiates for inclusion of a similar clause in a construction contract.

5. Sizeable Company requires additional working capital. Rates in the commercial paper market are lower than commercial bank lending rates, so an issuance of notes would be a favorable alternative. Based on its own credit, Company's commercial paper would be rated A-3, so Company arranges to have its paper backed by a Bank letter of credit, available to the holder of the paper in the event of the Company's default. Bank's creditworthiness will raise the rating of the paper to A-1, and Company will save more by paying a lower interest rate on the paper than Bank will charge for issuing its credit.

What advantages to the account party (customer) can you identify in using a letter of credit in each of the above instances? Is there any advantage to the beneficiary? What alternative means of structuring the transactions in question have been rejected in favor of the use of a standby credit? How have the risks to which beneficiary is subject been affected by use of a standby credit? Is the issuer in such transactions subject to any different risks than in the case of commercial credits?

NEW JERSEY BANK v. PALLADINO
77 N.J. 33, 389 A.2d 454, 24 UCC Rep. 729 (1978)

SCHREIBER, J. This case involves the effect of a written assurance given by defendant First State Bank of Hudson County to plaintiff New Jersey Bank to induce it to loan Joseph P. Palladino $50,000. The document stated that if Palladino did not repay the $50,000 debt, which was evidenced by a note, defendant bank would honor that commitment. The crucial question is whether that paper was an illegal guaranty or a valid letter of credit.

The facts are essentially undisputed. In July 1972, Joseph P. Palladino sought a $100,000 loan from plaintiff New Jersey Bank. Plaintiff's Senior Vice-President and Senior Lending Officer, Everett B. Muh, after reviewing Palladino's financial statement indicated a willingness to advance the money for 90 days but wanted "some sort of collateral or support for the note." In response Palladino obtained a letter from defendant bank signed by its President, Edward Dooley, which read as follows:

> Dear Mr. Muh:
>   This letter will serve as a commitment to you that the First State Bank of Hudson County will assume the obligation arising from a note signed by Mr. Joseph P. Palladino on July 6, 1972, in the amount of $100,000. We will honor this commitment, 90 days after the date of the note, upon notice to us that the loan has not been paid by Mr. Joseph P. Palladino.

Thereupon, Palladino executed a 90-day note and plaintiff bank advanced $100,000.

Palladino deposited the $100,000 proceeds together with an additional $25,000 in his checking account with defendant bank. Of these funds, $5,790 were used to satisfy an overdraft on the account and $28,000 were applied to a reduction of Palladino's personal loan of $60,000 from defendant bank. At the time, Palladino was an officer or party in interest of Surf Realty Company, which was also indebted to defendant bank. The sum of $23,850 was transferred from Palladino's account to that of Surf Realty Company.

When Palladino did not repay the $100,000 loan, Mr. Muh in a letter dated October 6, 1972, called upon defendant bank to pay the $100,000 loan plus accrued interest of $2,020.80. President Dooley of defendant bank telephoned Mr. Muh and asked if plaintiff would accept a $50,000 reduction in the indebtedness and renew the note for the $50,000 balance. Mr. Muh accepted "with an understanding that Mr. Dooley would send me another letter covering the $50,000, and he agreed to do this." Defendant delivered a letter to plaintiff reading:

> This letter will serve as a commitment to you that the First State Bank of Hudson County will assume the obligations arising from a note signed by Mr. Joseph P. Palladino on October 12, 1972 in the amount of $50,000. We will honor this commitment six (6) months after the date of the note upon notice to us that the loan has not been paid by Mr. Joseph P. Palladino.

Relying upon the letter and the $50,000 reduction in the principal indebtedness, plaintiff renewed the loan upon Palladino's executing a new note for $50,000.

[Palladino defaulted on his note, and Muh successfully obtained a judgment against the bank on the basis of its assurance. On appeal, the Appellate Division reversed.]

The Appellate Division's reversal was grounded on the finding that the letter was a guaranty and was therefore illegal under N.J.S.A. 17:9A-213.1, which prohibits banks from guaranteeing obligations of others. . . . The Appellate Division also held that the defendant bank's letters were not letters of credit within the contemplation of the Uniform Commercial Code, Article 5, or of the Banking Act, N.J.S.A. 17:9A-25(3). . . .

Although state banks generally do not have the power to guarantee the obligations of others, the prohibition is not an absolute one. Section 213.1 of the Banking Act of 1948 reads:

> *Except as in this act or otherwise by law provided,* no bank or savings bank shall have power to guarantee the obligations of others. . . . [N.J.S.A. 17:9A-213.1 (emphasis supplied)]

An exception is found in that provision of the Banking Act which expressly endows banks with the power, whether or not specifically set forth in their certificates of incorporation,

> to issue letters of credit authorizing holders thereof to draw drafts upon it or upon its correspondents at sight or on time not exceeding one year; to guarantee, for a period not exceeding one year from the date of such guarantee, the payment by its customers of amounts due or to become due upon the purchase by such customers of real or personal property. [N.J.S.A. 17:9A-25(3)]

. . . Historically, the letter of credit was developed to facilitate the sale of goods between distant and unfamiliar buyers and sellers. It was an arrangement under which a bank, whose credit was acceptable to a seller, would at the instance of the buyer agree to pay drafts drawn on it by the seller, provided that certain documents, such as a bill of lading, accompanied the draft. See, e.g., Comment, Recent Extensions in the Use of Commercial Letters of Credit, 66 Yale L.J. 902, 903 (1957).

Expansion in the use of the letter of credit was a natural development in commercial banking. Elasticity in its use was made possible by the broad concept expressed in Article 5 of the Uniform Commercial Code, so that the letter was readily adaptable to embrace a new commercial banking practice which utilizes what is known as a standby letter of credit.[3] . . . This usage of a letter of credit is akin to a guaranty, for the bank's sole function is to act as surety for its customer's failure to pay. See Verkuil, Bank Solvency and Guaranty Letters of Credit, 25 Stan. L. Rev. 716, 725 (1973); Arnold and Bransilver, The Standby Letter of Credit—The Controversy Continues, 10 UCC L.J. 272, 278 (1978).

The standby letter of credit remains a primary obligation triggered by presentation of documentation as a precondition to payment. The bank which has issued the letter needs only to determine whether the document presented appears on its face to be in accordance with the terms and conditions of the credit. UCC 5-114. Its responsibility to honor the credit exists independently of the underlying obligation, even though the responsibility may be conditioned on notice of a breach of that underlying obligation. Chase Manhattan Bank v. Equibank, 550 F.2d 882 (3d Cir. 1977). See Barclays Bank D.C.O. v. Mercantile Natl. Bank, 481 F.2d 1224 (5th Cir. 1973), *cert. denied,* 414 U.S. 1139 (1974) (letter of credit to assure a lender of repayment of applicant's indebtedness); Prudential Ins. Co. v. Marquette Natl. Bank, 419 F. Supp. 734 (D. Minn. 1976) (letter of credit to assure lender of a commitment standby fee). . . . It is now well established that the issuance of a "standby letter of credit is a legitimate use by a bank of its credit, and not an unauthorized excursion by banks into the business of suretyship." Arnold and Bransilver, supra, 10 UCC L.J. at 282.

The Department of Banking has formally acknowledged the propriety of standby letters of credit in its regulations.[4] N.J.A.C. 3:11-9.1 defines a standby letter of credit as follows:

(a) A standby letter of credit is any letter of credit, or similar arrangement however named or described, which represents an obligation to the beneficiary on the part of the issuer:

---

3. H. Harfield has written that Article 5 "would stimulate the domestic use of the letter of credit and, like other potent fertilizers, bring it to instant luxuriance and fruition." Harfield, The Increasing Domestic Use of the Letter of Credit, 4 UCC L.J. 251 (1972).

4. Regulation H of the Federal Reserve System defines a standby letter of credit as "an obligation to the beneficiary on the part of the issuer (i) to repay money borrowed by or advanced to or for the account of the account party or (ii) to make payment on account of any evidence of indebtedness undertaken by the account party, or (iii) to make payment on account of any default by the account party in the performance of an obligation" (footnote omitted). 12 C.F.R. §208.8(d)(1) (1977) (footnote omitted). The Comptroller of the Currency and the F.D.I.C. have similar definitions. See 12 C.F.R. §7.1160(a) (1977) and 12 C.F.R. §337.2(a) (1977), respectively.

1. To repay money borrowed by or advanced to or for the account of the account party; or
2. To make payment on account of any indebtedness undertaken by the account party; or
3. To make payment on account of any default by the account party in the performance of an obligation.

(b) As defined in subsection (a) of this section, the term "standby letter of credit" does not include a commercial or traveler's letter of credit issued pursuant to section 25(3) of the Banking Act of 1948, such as:

1. Letter of credit used to facilitate the purchase and sale of goods;
2. Where the issuing bank has obtained, or will obtain, documents of title covering the goods; or
3. Where the credit is reasonably related to the actual value of the goods at the time of purchase and sale.

Substantial authority exists for holding that commitments constituting standby letters of credit are valid under the Uniform Commercial Code. . . .

These authorities recognize that the letter of credit is a highly useful device for insuring performance of an obligation to pay money and that its validity should not "depend upon the nature of the transaction in which it is used." Harfield, Code, Customs and Conscience in Letter-of-Credit Law, 4 UCC L.J. 7, 9 (1971). Harfield, a leading commentator in the field, also observed that "[a] commitment to honor a draft accompanied by a bill of lading reciting receipt on board of cases said to contain hog bristles is of no more legal stature than a commitment to honor a draft accompanied by a promissory note said to be in default as to payment of principal or interest. Its traditional sale-of-goods setting certainly does not imbue a letter of credit issued to finance the importation of cigarette tobacco with any greater social or economic utility than a letter of credit issued to ensure the faithful performance of a contract to construct a cancer clinic. The expanded and expanding use of letters of credit is both logical and useful." [Id.]

The Banking Act of 1948 and Article 5 of the Uniform Commercial Code, Letters of Credit, should be read in harmony with each other. The Appellate Division quite properly addressed itself to an interpretation of that section of the Banking Act of 1948 which entrusted banks with the authority "to issue letters of credit authorizing holders thereof to draw drafts upon it or upon its correspondents at sight or on time not exceeding one year . . . ." [N.J.S.A. 17:9A-25(3).] The one-year limitation, however, does not restrict the duration of a letter of credit, but is addressed to the time period during which a draft may be drawn on the letter. It only qualifies "drafts" rather than the more remote "letters of credit." If the Legislature had intended otherwise, it would have inserted a comma after the word "time." . . . That letters of credit are not subject to the one-year limitation is confirmed by the action of the Commissioner of Banking, whose regulations on standby letters of credit do not contain a one-year limitation period. N.J.A.C. 3:11-9.3. When considering the same issue in National Surety Corp. v. Midland Bank, 551 F.2d 21 (3d Cir. 1977),

Judge Garth in a careful analysis of the statute also concluded that our statute "has not restricted the duration of letters of credit issued by [state] banks to a one-year period." Id. at 35. We agree.

The October 11, 1972 letter of defendant First State Bank of Hudson County fulfilled all the requirements of a standby letter of credit. It advised plaintiff of a commitment to assume the obligation arising from a note signed by Joseph Palladino on October 12, 1972 in the amount of $50,000. It agreed to honor that commitment six months after the date of the note upon notice that the loan had not been paid. Here, then, defendant bank agreed to honor a demand for payment upon notice of nonpayment of the Palladino note.

Although the letter did not expressly direct that the notice must be written, the statute, UCC 5-103, requires a notice of default to be on paper. Undoubtedly, both parties to this commercial transaction, who were sophisticated businessmen and bankers, knew that a default notice must be written. It is common knowledge in the banking field that written records are made on all aspects of the banking operation. See N.J.S.A. 17:9A-247. Terms will be implied in a contract where the parties must have intended them because they are necessary to give business efficacy to the contract as written. . . . There is the strongest reason for interpreting a business agreement in the sense which will give it legal support. . . . With these principles in mind we find that the parties must have intended that the notice be in writing. Such a construction accords also with the proposition that when the terms of an agreement have more than one possible interpretation, by one of which the agreement would be valid and by the other void or illegal, the former will be preferred. . . . Furthermore, we note in passing that defendant bank has never contended that the letter of credit was invalid because it did not expressly require that the notice of default be in writing.

Defendant bank further contends that its contingent liability of $50,000 on the standby letter of credit would result in a violation of N.J.S.A. 17:9A-62A, which provides that the "total liabilities" of any person shall not exceed 10% of the capital funds of the bank. It was undisputed that in October 1972, the bank's capital funds were $1,776,540 and, therefore, its loans to Palladino could not exceed $177,654. Palladino was personally indebted to defendant for $32,000. The bank also claims that in computing Palladino's liabilities those of corporations in which he held a controlling interest must be included. N.J.S.A. 17:9A-60(7). It seeks to add a $125,000 indebtedness of Surf Realty Company and a $130,162 debt of Palbro Reality Co. However, the record does not support the conclusion that he held a controlling interest in either corporation at that time. But even if he did, contingent liabilities which might arise out of a letter of credit were not includable as a liability in the computation.[5]

This treatment accorded with the established practice that letters of credit

---

5. The New Jersey Department of Banking has recently adopted a regulation which requires that the contingent liability of a standby letter of credit be included in the computation of the lending limit. N.J.A.C. 3:11-9.2 (adopted July 20, 1977).

were considered contingent liabilities which were not reflected in a bank's balance sheet. Verkuil, supra, 25 Stan. L. Rev. at 727.[6]

It is important to recognize that defendant bank's obligation to pay plaintiff arose out of its independent contractual undertaking with plaintiff and that this obligation did not mature until presentation of a written notice that Palladino had not paid the note. . . .

Defendant First State Bank of Hudson County intentionally induced plaintiff to make the loan to Palladino by inviting reliance on the defendant's assurance. For defendant now to refuse to honor its commitment is disingenuous. Enforcement of that obligation in accordance with the terms of the standby letter of credit is fully warranted. The judgments of the Appellate Division are modified and those of the trial court reinstated.

CONFORD, P.J.A.D. (temporarily assigned), dissenting. As argued to the Court, this case apparently projected the question whether the long-standing general statutory policy against banks entering into agreements of guaranty or indemnification, N.J.S.A. 17:9A-213.1, should be breached without express legislative authorization under the aegis of so-called "standby letters of credit"—a device increasingly coming into general banking practice. . . . The controversy referred to is that between those who are concerned about the threat to solvency of banks in the expanded practice of standby letters of credit and those who believe such credit arrangements are a salutary development in banking practice. . . .

Whether or not the letter in litigation here is as a matter of form classifiable as a standby letter of credit, its substantial identity with a guarantee as commonly understood is so obvious that one would desire more explicit legislative approval of its validity as a bank obligation than was evident in 1972 when the instant transaction took place. I do not favor erosion of an apparently salutary statutory policy against bank guaranties through judicial ratification of a contrary commercial practice. It may well be that a new emerging policy of commercial convenience should swing the law in a new direction. But I should hope for a clear legislative signal to that effect.

The difference between conventional letters of credit and the standby variety in terms of threat to bank solvency is clear. In the former, typically used to finance sales of goods, the issuing bank's obligation arises only on the delivery of shipping documents evidencing title to the goods. The bank is therefore secure. In the standby letter of credit situation, by the time the bank is called upon to meet the demand of the beneficiary there has typically been a default of the bank customer to the beneficiary and there is no practicable

---

6. Interpretative Ruling No. 7.1160 of the U.S. Comptroller of the Currency in effect in 1972 provided: "An agreement to lend to a customer or to pay others for its account, under irrevocable sight letters of credit or otherwise, does not result in an obligation subject to the lending limit until the bank is required to make the advance or payment." This ruling was modified in August 1974 to state that a standby letter of credit is includable in computing the lending limit to a customer. 12 C.F.R. §7.1160 (1977).

recourse by the bank because of the insolvency of the customer. See Verkuil, 25 Stan. L. Rev. at 727-728. . . . Coupled with the fact that letters of credit are contingent liabilities not appearing on the bank's balance sheet, Verkuil, 25 Stan. L. Rev. at 727 . . . , the potential for danger to the public interest of an uncontrolled practice of dealing in standby letters of credit is manifest. The insolvency of the defendant bank before us may have some significance in this regard.

Prior to the adoption of the Uniform Commercial Code in this State in 1961 the only statutory reference to powers of banks to issue letters of credit was N.J.S.A. 17:9A-25(3) (L.1948, c.67), empowering banks "to issue letters of credit authorizing holders thereof to draw drafts upon it . . . ." This language is typically adapted to the traditional commercial letter of credit. The "standby" variety was in 1948 neither known nor within statutory contemplation. That a letter of credit was not then conceived as a potential exception to the general prohibition, by the same 1948 statute, of guaranties or indemnities by banks, see section 213.1 thereof (N.J.S.A. 17:9A-213.1), is evidenced by the remainder of N.J.S.A. 17:9A-25(3), mentioned above. In addition to authorizing issuance of letters of credit, that section permits a bank "to guarantee, for a period not exceeding one year from the date of such guarantee, the payment by its customers of amounts due or to become due upon the purchase by such customers of real or personal property." Thus the 1948 Legislature made clear the very limited extent to which it was willing to allow banks to make guaranties, while couching its authorization of letters of credit in terms of the conventional commercial financing device then well known.

The foregoing observations gain added pertinence from the very limited use of letters of credit in New Jersey, particularly prior to the adoption of the Uniform Commercial Code. The Introductory Comment to Chapter 5 ("Letters of Credit") by the chairman of the New Jersey Commission which studied the Code prior to its adoption states: "Before the Uniform Commercial Code there was no statutory regulation of Letters of Credit. This chapter has no prior legislative history. *Such letters are used primarily to finance international trade.* Only about 100 United States banks write Letters of Credit and 25 banks write 75% of them. *Very few are written by New Jersey banks.* Letters of credit should gain wide acceptance in domestic use and the clarification of the law respecting their issuance and the rights of all parties taking them should do much to advance their wider use by New Jersey banks." (emphasis added.)

In the light of this background it is difficult to perceive any actual intent by the New Jersey Legislature, in adopting the Code, to wipe out the strong preexisting statutory policy against guaranties and indemnities by banks. The standard letter of credit, as theretofore known in this State, and a guarantee by a bank are seen to be poles apart in nature and function.

It must be conceded, however, that UCC 5-102 and 5-103, read literally, would seem to validate what is technically within the definition of a standby letter of credit. A documentary demand, within the requirement of UCC 5-102(1)(a), can consist of a notice of default. UCC 5-103(1)(b). Thus a simple letter from a bank to a lender of money to the bank customer that within a stated period the bank will advance a stated sum to the lender upon receipt of a written notice of a default in the loan would seem, facially, to constitute a letter of credit within the Code. I am, however, relieved of the necessity of deciding whether such an engagement would be enforcible against an issuing bank, as against the statutory prohibition of guaranties by banks, by the circumstance that the letter in suit here does not meet the hypothetical case stated nor the intent of the statute even if conceived as authorizing standby letters of credit.

First, and most obvious, the letter in question does not call for the presentation of a document. It requires notice of default, but not a written notice, and it could hardly be denied that if the question of compliance with the Code or the prohibition of bank guaranties were not issues here the letter would be enforcible as between the parties on oral as well as written notice of default. The majority's attempt to bootstrap the validity of the document by resort to the maxim that the law will imply an intent by the parties that the writing be construed in a manner such as to lend validity to it must fail as otherwise the *essence* of the letter of credit—an undertaking by an issuer to pay upon the presentation of specified *documents*—is subverted. This is not a mere technism. It goes to the heart of the nature of a letter of credit. See Comment to UCC 5-102.

Second, the letter is not limited to an unequivocal undertaking to pay up to a specified sum on presentation of specified documents, but rather injects the bank squarely into the underlying relationship between the bank customer, Palladino, and the beneficiary plaintiff. It does this in the first paragraph of the letter, stating that the defendant "will assume the obligations arising from" the underlying $50,000 note given plaintiff by Palladino. While that assumption is made subject to the condition subsequent of receiving notice of default, it is nevertheless otherwise the acceptance by the bank of the status of accommodation co-debtor to the plaintiff for the $50,000 plus interest. Under such an assumption of liability the defendant would be creditable with any payment on account made by the debtor. . . . The unqualified absolutism of an undertaking to pay a specified sum of money on a stated proffer of documents, as requisite in a letter of credit, does not exist. Under the letter in question the bank's liability is subject to diminution or discharge depending upon later transactions between the bank customer and the beneficiary, and also to any uncertainty consequent upon disputes between the two as to the amount of the "obligation assumed" owing at any given time.

All of the authorities on letters of credit agree that a situation such as the foregoing defeats the basic intent of a letter of credit. As instructively stated in a recent article: "A fundamental legal principle with respect to letters of credit, embodied in . . . the UCC . . . is that the letter of credit is a contract separate from the underlying agreement, and consequently the rights of the issuer and the beneficiary under the letter of credit are determined only by the terms of the letter of credit itself (i.e., the presentation of the requisite documents), and are not affected by the performance or nonperformance by the applicant, issuer, or the beneficiary of their respective obligations under the underlying agreement and the application." Arnold and Bransilver, supra, 10 UCC L.J. at 274. . . .

The present circumstances, moreover, fix the character of the letter here involved as a true guarantee rather than a standby letter of credit. As explained by the same writers: "It is important to note, that despite their similarities, the standby letter of credit is not a guarantee. Recovery under a guarantee is predicated upon the primary obligor's nonperformance *in fact* of its guaranteed obligations. The guarantor is therefore only *secondarily* liable with respect to the *same* obligation of the primary obligor. Recovery under a standby letter of credit, on the other hand, requires only the presentation of the requisite documents (*whether or not* the applicant has in fact performed or even may legally perform, its obligations under the underlying agreement), and the issuer is *primarily* liable with respect to its obligations under the letter of credit (which obligations, needless to say, are different from those of the applicant under the underlying agreement)." (Emphasis in original.) Arnold and Bransilver, supra, 10 UCC L.J. at 279-280.

Under the analysis above of the letter-instrument before us, it is clear that the defendant bank's obligation *is* predicated on Palladino's nonperformance of his obligation to plaintiff since in the event of performance there would no longer exist the "obligation" which defendant "assume[d]" under the letter. Thus the letter is truly a guarantee, not a letter of credit, even of the standby variety.

For the reasons stated, I am in agreement with the Appellate Division that the letter in question is an illegal guarantee and cannot be enforced in this action because *ultra vires*.[7]

In reference to the alternative holding of the Appellate Division that the letter, if considered a letter of credit, exceeded the one-year limitation of N.J.S.A. 17:9A-25(3). . . . I agree with the majority that the Circuit Court of Appeals correctly decided that the one-year limitation in the section cited qualifies only time drafts drawn on a letter of credit and not letters of credit themselves. This conclusion is impelled not only by the most natural grammatical construction of the verbiage but by the circumstance that in the very next clause of the same provision a time limitation of one year for certain kinds of guaranties is phrased in terminology which is explicit and which could have been used in the provision as to letters of credit had it been the intent that the time limitation was to be applicable to letters of credit themselves rather than to time drafts.

---

7. The department regulations defining a standby letter of credit quoted in the majority opinion . . . are not here pertinent as they were adopted in 1976, long after the transaction in question. Moreover I doubt the authority of the Commissioner to promulgate them, as they do not require submission to the issuing bank of a document, as required by the Uniform Commercial Code.

And capping the case for the indicated result is the fact that in the same 1948 statute (c.67) which was the precursor of N.J.S.A. 17:9A-25(3) the Legislature also fixed a one-year period as the measure of staleness of a check. . . . Although the subsequent enactment of the Uniform Commercial Code changed the staleness period to six months, UCC 4-404, and see New Jersey Study Comment thereto, p. 523, the co-enactment in 1948 of the one-year limitation periods mentioned strongly indicates the time limitation in the letters-of-credit provision applied to drafts, not to letters of credit *per se.*

Despite my views as to the one-year limitation I would affirm the judgment of the Appellate Division for the reasons already stated. In view thereof I do not reach the question whether the letter of credit was illegal because resulting in total liabilities of the bank to one person exceeding 10% of the capital funds of the bank.

NOTES & QUESTIONS

Relation of UCC to state regulatory law. What is the relationship between §25(3) of New Jersey's Banking Act of 1948 and letters of credit within the scope of Article 5? Does the majority in *Palladino* conclude that the bank's assurance was a letter of credit within the meaning of Article 5? If so, do you concur? Does the UCC, by defining the legal effect of certain types of credits, alter state law regulating the authority of state banks to engage in certain types of activity? If the credit in *Palladino* is a standby credit within Article 5, and that law provides both the authority for and legal effect of such assurances in New Jersey, of what relevance is §25(3), including its time limitation? Is the court's reading of this time limitation convincing? What do you believe is its purpose? The court notes that the New Jersey Department of Banking has specifically acknowledged the propriety of standby credits by its regulations. Why does the definition of standby credit specifically exclude credits issued pursuant to §25(3)? The majority itself suggests that the basis for validity of standby credits issued by state-chartered New Jersey banks would be found in section 25(3) or in the Code. Is the Code the basis for the Department of Banking's regulation? Does the definition contained in the Department's regulation accord with the Code's definition of credits "within the scope of Article 5."

Note: Article 5, Standby Credits, and Bank Regulation

The rapid spread in the use of standby letters of credit promoted a spirited debate and has engendered substantial litigation as well. To understand fully the issues involved in this debate, some appreciation of the historical background is necessary. As *Palladino* indicates, it traditionally was held that a bank's guaranteeing the obligations of its customers or engaging itself as a surety were *ultra vires* acts. This doctrine is not generally shared by other countries, and its exact origins in this country are not altogether clear. However, it should be noted that early cases asserting the rule date from the mid-nineteenth century, when the compensated surety had not yet developed as a commercial phenomenon. Corporate law itself was still in a nascent state, and a similar rule prohibiting corporate guaranties then generally prevailed as to general business corporations. In either case, the bank or the business corporation was likely to be acting for the accommodation of an important customer of the bank, or an officer, director, or shareholder of the corporation. Again, in either case, the engagement was invariably gratuitous. See generally Lord, The No-Guaranty Rule and the Standby Letter of Credit Controversy, 96 Banking L.J. 46 (1979). Although the rule as to general business corporations was in time reversed by statute, the no-guaranty rule achieved a vitality of its own with respect to banking corporations, which were increasingly subject to separate statutory and regulatory regimes. However, little if any similarity exists between the circumstances under which the rule became established and modern situations in which banks might wish to engage in suretyship on a compensated basis, in competition with surety companies.

In any event, the rule did become established as the rule in most states for state-chartered commercial banks. Federally-chartered commercial banks have long been subjected to the same strictures by virtue of interpretation of 12 U.S.C. §24, which confers on national banks "all such incidental powers as shall be necessary to carry on the business of banking. . . ." Acting as a guarantor or surety has been held not to be such an "incidental" power.

Added complexity is provided by the highly-regulated environment of banking. Separate legislation affects state or national commercial banks, state or federal thrift institutions (such as savings banks or savings and loan associations), and other financial institutions such as insurance companies and investment bankers. Additionally, even a single type of institution, such as a commercial bank, may be either state or federally chartered. Accordingly, it will be subject to regulation, in the first instance, by either state banking authorities under local legislation or by the comptroller of the currency under the National Bank Act. Whether it is state or federally chartered, such a bank may also be subject to regulations of the Federal Reserve Board or the Federal Deposit Insurance Corporation (FDIC). The result is a crazy quilt of regulation and seemingly artificial distinctions, which has come under increasing attack as different segments of the financial services industry have sought to enter the "turf" of others. Particular segments of the industry have been hampered in their efforts to respond to such competition and to rapid economic change by the existing regulatory structure, which has in turn come under stress. The standby credit debate is best viewed within the broad contexts of history and of the range of structural issues currently facing the financial services industry.

In considering some of the issues raised in the preceding notes and questions, and in the majority and dissenting opinions in *Palladino,* some historical perspective may again be useful. Although prohibited from engaging their credit as a guarantor or surety, banks have long been held to possess the power to issue commercial letters of credit. The issuance of credits to facilitate trade was recognized under federal law as incidental to the business of banking, and state law was generally in accord. Insofar as the question involved in the standby credit debate related to the authority of banks to issue such credits, a correct answer would seem to turn on whether a standby credit more closely resembles (and therefore should be characterized as) a traditional letter of credit or as a guaranty. How well does either the majority or the dissent deal with this problem in *Palladino?* Verkuil, Bank Solvency and Guaranty Letters of Credit, 25 Stan. L. Rev. 716 (1973), contains by far the most incisive treatment of the issues originally posed. In the years since Dean Verkuil's article was published, bank regulators have moved to ameliorate some of the glaring deficiencies that then existed. See *Palladino,* nn.5 and 6.

Regulatory awareness of the problems posed by the widespread growth of the standby credit now exists. But it is less clear that the parties, including some banks and other financial institutions, themselves appreciate fully the nature of the respective risks in such transactions. Standby credit cases continue to generate an inordinate volume of litigation, some of which displays on its face the misconceptions of one or more parties to the transactions.

WICHITA EAGLE & BEACON PUBLISHING CO., INC. v. PACIFIC NATIONAL BANK, 343 F. Supp. 332, 11 UCC Rep. 167 (N.D. Cal. 1971), *rev'd,* 493 F.2d 1285, 14 UCC Rep. 156 (9th Cir. 1974): The bank issued the following instrument:

PACIFIC NATIONAL BANK OF SAN FRANCISCO

International Department
May 9, 1962

Marcellus M. Murdock; Victor
Delano; Katherine M. Henderson;
Marsh Murdock and Victoria Neff,
as the Trustees of the Pearl Jane
Murdock Trust; Wichita Eagle, Inc.;
and the Prairie Improvement
Company, Inc.

Gentlemen:

We hereby establish our Letter of Credit No. 17084 in your favor on the terms and conditions herein set forth for the account of Circular Ramp Garages, Inc. for the total sum of $250,000.00, available by drafts drawn at sight on the Pacific National Bank providing that all of the following conditions exist at the time said draft is received by the undersigned:

1. That Circular Ramp Garages, Inc. has failed to perform the terms and conditions of paragraph IV(a) of the lease dated February 28, 1962, as amended to April 28, 1962, between all of you as Lessor and Circular Ramp Garages, Inc. as Lessee, a copy of which lease is attached hereto.

2. That you have sent by registered United States mail, return receipt requested, with all postage and registration fees prepaid, a written notice to Circular Ramp Garages, Inc. at 343 Sansome Street, San Francisco 4, California, and to The Pacific Company specifying how Circular Ramp Garages, Inc. has failed to perform the terms and conditions of said paragraph IV(a) of said lease and further that you have delivered to the undersigned an affidavit signed by Marcellus M. Murdock stating that he sent said written notice in such manner to the above Circular Ramp Garages, Inc. and The Pacific Company Engineers and Builders, to which affidavit shall be attached the return receipt from said registered mail delivery, which affidavit and any attached return receipt shall show that said notice was delivered to said Circular Ramp Garages, Inc. and The Pacific Company Engineers and Builders more than thirty days prior to the date the draft is drawn by you against this Letter of Credit.

3. That either Circular Ramp Garages, Inc. or The Pacific Company Engineers and Builders has failed during said thirty days following the delivery of said notice to them to cure any actual default existing under the terms of said paragraph IV(a) of said lease as so specified in said written notice.

The credit extended under this lease shall terminate at the time and upon the happening of any of the following:

a. At the time that the City of Wichita, Kansas, refuses to issue a permit to construct a circular ramp parking garage building in accordance with plans and specifications submitted by Circular Ramp Garages, Inc. or its engineer or architect, on the property subject to said lease and fails to issue said permit to either Circular Ramp Garages, Inc. or the contractor hired to construct said building, provided, however, that said refusal is accepted as a final refusal by Circular Ramp Garages, Inc. or by said contractor. However, if Circular Ramp Garages, Inc. or said contractor has been unable to obtain such a permit by October 28, 1962 and either of them wishes to continue trying to obtain said permit, this Letter of Credit shall be automatically reduced at said date to a principal sum of $50,000.00 until terminated by any of the following conditions or events.

b. At the time that the contractor who is to construct said building obtains a performance bond from a surety company licensed to conduct a bonding business in Kansas insuring that said building will be completed in accordance with the plans and specifications therefor within three years after Circular Ramp Garages, Inc. is obligated to take possession of said premises or April 28, 1965, whichever date shall first occur.

c. At the time after such permit from the City of Wichita, Kansas, is obtained that no construction loan or takeout loan to finance the construction of said building is obtainable, if the reason that said loan is not obtainable is due to some provision in said lease between you and Circular Ramp Garages, Inc. which you refuse to amend pursuant to the requirements of said Lease. For the purposes of this paragraph it will be deemed that no such construction loan or takeout loan is obtainable if such has not been obtained after application to three lending companies which have theretofore made loans in Kansas for the purpose of constructing buildings or amortizing the cost thereof, if Circular Ramp Garages, Inc. then elects not to apply to any other lending company.

d. At the time that Circular Ramp Garages, Inc. has performed or caused to be performed the terms of said paragraph IV(a) of said lease.

e. At the end of three years from the date of this letter. Upon termination of the credit established under this letter you are to return the letter to the Pacific National Bank.

This Letter of Credit shall be irrevocable from its date providing that you accept the same within ten days from said date. Your acceptance is to be shown by the receipt by the undersigned of a copy of this letter with your acceptance shown by signing below.

Pacific National Bank of San Francisco

/s/   *A.G. Cinelli*

A.G. Cinelli Vice President

/s/   *D. Bannatyne*

D. Bannatyne for Cashier

The terms of the above Letter of Credit are accepted.
Dated May 17, 1962

/s/   *Marcellus M. Murdock*

Marcellus M. Murdock

This instrument was held to be a letter of credit by the district court, which further found that the beneficiary was entitled to recover the face amount of the credit ($250,000), less $87,000, a sum representing the enhanced value of a lease with Macy's that was entered into following default by the original lessee. 343 F. Supp. 332 (N.D. Cal. 1971). On appeal, the ninth circuit disagreed with the district court's characterization, stating in part:

"The instrument involved here strays too far from the basic purpose of letters of credit, namely, providing a means of assuring payment cheaply by eliminating the need for the issuer to police the underlying contract. Harfield, The Increasing Use of Domestic Letters of Credit, 4 UCC L.J. 251, 257 (1972); Ward & Harfield, Bank Credits and Acceptances 46, 136-138 (1958). The instrument neither evidences an intent that payment be made merely on presentation of a draft nor specifies the documents required for termination or payment. To the contrary, it requires the actual existence in fact of most of the conditions specified: for termination or reduction, that the city have refused a building permit; for payment, that the lessee have failed to perform the terms of the lease and have failed to correct that default, in addition to an affidavit of notice.

"True, in the text of the instrument itself the instrument is referred to as a 'letter of credit,' and we should, as the district court notes, 'give effect wherever possible to the intent of the contracting parties.' 343 F. Supp. at 338, 11

UCC Rep. at 174. But the relevant intent is manifested by the terms of the agreement, not by its label. . . . And where, as here, the substantive provisions require the issuer to deal not simply in documents alone, but in facts relating to the performance of a separate contract (the lease, in this case), all distinction between a letter of credit and an ordinary guaranty contract would be obliterated by regarding the instrument as a letter of credit." 493 F.2d at 1287.

Surprisingly, the ninth circuit's per curiam opinion contained no discussion of the *ultra vires* issue; it held the underlying provision of the Circular Ramps lease to be a valid liquidated damages clause under California law and modified judgment to allow recovery of the full $250,000, plus interest. For a discussion of whether a bank is estopped from refusing to honor an *ultra vires* guaranty, see Verkuil, Bank Solvency and Guaranty Letters of Credit, 25 Stan. L. Rev. 716, 724-727 (1973), and Comment, Recent Extensions in the Use of Commercial Letters of Credit, 66 Yale L.J. 902 (1957), cases cited at 915, n.50.

3.   *The Principles of Independence of the Credit and Strict Documentary Compliance*

COURTAULDS NORTH AMERICA, INC. v. NORTH CAROLINA NATIONAL BANK
528 F.2d 802, 18 UCC Rep. 467 (4th Cir. 1975)

Bryan, Senior Circuit Judge. A letter of credit with the date of March 21, 1973 was issued by the North Carolina National Bank at the request of and for the account of its customer, Adastra Knitting Mills, Inc. It made available upon the drafts of Courtaulds North America, Inc. "up to" $135,000.00 (later increased by $135,000.00) at "60 days date" to cover Adastra's purchases of acrylic yarn from Courtaulds. The life of the credit was extended in June to allow the drafts to be "drawn and negotiated on or before August 15, 1973."

Bank refused to honor a draft for $67,346.77 dated August 13, 1973 for yarn sold and delivered to Adastra. Courtaulds brought this action to recover this sum from Bank.

The defendant denied liability chiefly on the assertion that the draft did not agree with the letter's conditions, viz., that the draft be accompanied by a "Commercial invoice in triplicate stating inter alia that it covers . . . 100% acrylic yarn;" instead, the accompanying invoices stated that the goods were "Imported Acrylic Yarn."

Upon cross motions for summary judgment on affidavits and a stipulation of facts, the District Court held defendant Bank liable to Courtaulds for the amount of the draft, interest and costs. It concluded that the draft complied with the letter of credit when each invoice is read together with the packing lists stapled to it, for the lists stated on their faces: "Cartons marked:—100% Acrylic." After considering the insistent rigidity of the law and usage of bank credits and acceptances, we must differ with the District Judge and uphold Bank's position.

The letter of credit prescribed the terms of the drafts as follows:

> Drafts to be dated same as Bills of Lading. Draft(s) to be accompanied by:
>
> 1. Commercial invoice in triplicate stating that it covers 100,000 lbs. 100% Acrylic Yarn, Package Dyed at $1.35 per lb., FOB Buyers Plant, Greensboro, North Carolina Land Duty Paid.
> 2. Certificate stating goods will be delivered to buyers plant land duty paid.
> 3. Inland Bill of Lading consigned to Adastra Knitting Mills, Inc. evidencing shipment from East Coast Port to Adastra Knitting Mills, Inc., Greensboro, North Carolina.

The shipment (the last) with which this case is concerned was made on or about August 8, 1973. On direction of Courtaulds, bills of lading of that date were prepared for the consignment to Adastra from a bonded warehouse by motor carrier. The yarn was packaged in cartons and a packing list referring to its bill of lading accompanied each carton. After the yarn was delivered to the carrier, each bill of lading with the packing list was sent to Courtaulds. There invoices for the sales were made out, and the invoices and packing lists stapled together. At the same time, Courtaulds wrote up the certificate, credit memorandum and draft called for in the letter of credit. The draft was dated August 13, 1973 and drawn on Bank by Courtaulds payable to itself.

All of these documents—the draft, the invoices and the packing lists—were sent by Courtaulds to its correspondent in Mobile for presentation to Bank and collection of the draft which for the purpose had been endorsed to the correspondent.

This was the procedure pursued on each of the prior drafts and always the draft had been honored by Bank save in the present instance. Here the draft, endorsed to Bank, and the other papers were sent to Bank on August 14. Bank received them on Thursday, August 16. Upon processing, Bank found these discrepancies between the drafts with accompanying documents and the letter of credit: (1) that the invoice did not state "100% Acrylic Yarn" but described it as "Imported Acrylic Yarn," and (2) "Draft not drawn as per terms of [letter of credit], Date [August 13] not same as Bill of Lading [August 8] and not drawn 60 days after date" [but 60 days from Bill of Lading date 8/8/73]. Finding of Fact 24. Since decision of this controversy is put on the first discrepancy we do not discuss the others.

On Monday, August 20, Bank called Adastra and asked if it would waive the discrepancies and thus allow Bank to honor the draft. In response, the president of Adastra informed Bank that it could not waive any discrepancies because a trustee in bankruptcy had been appointed for Adastra and Adastra could not do so alone. Upon word of these circumstances, Courtaulds on August 27 sent amended invoices to Bank which were received by Bank on August 27. They referred to the consignment as "100% Acrylic Yarn," and thus would have conformed to the letter of credit had it not expired. On

August 29 Bank wired Courtaulds that the draft remained unaccepted because of the expiration of the letter of credit on August 15. Consequently the draft with all the original documents was returned by Bank.

During the life of the letter of credit some drafts had not been of even dates with the bills of lading, and among the large number of invoices transmitted during this period, several did not describe the goods as "100% Acrylic Yarn." As to all of these deficiencies Bank called Adastra for and received approval before paying the drafts. Every draft save the one in suit was accepted. . . .

The factual outline related is not in dispute, and the issue becomes one of the law. It is well phrased by the District Judge in his "Discussion" in this way: "The only issue presented by the facts of this case is whether the documents tendered by the beneficiary to the issuer were in conformity with the terms of the letter of credit."

The letter of credit provided: "Except as otherwise expressly stated herein, this credit is subject to the 'Uniform Customs and Practice for Documentary Credits (1962 revision), the International Chamber of Commerce Brochure No. 222.'" Finding of Fact 6.

Of particular pertinence, with accents added, are these injunctions of the Uniform Customs:

> *Article 7.*   Banks must examine all documents with reasonable care to ascertain that they *appear on their face* to be in accordance with the terms and conditions of the credit.
>
> *Article 8.*   In documentary credit operations all parties concerned deal in documents and not in goods. . . . If, upon receipt of the documents, the issuing bank considers that they *appear on their face* not to be in accordance with the terms and conditions of the credit, that bank must determine, on the basis of the documents alone, whether to claim that payment, acceptance or negotiation was not effected in accordance with the terms and conditions of the credit.
>
> *Article 9.*   Banks . . . do [not] assume any liability or responsibility *for the description* . . . quality . . . of the goods represented thereby. . . . The description of the goods in the commercial *invoice* must correspond with the description in the credit. *In the remaining documents the goods may be described in general terms.* . . .

[The court then quotes the following paragraphs of UCC 5-109:

> *§5-109.   Issuer's Obligation to Its Customer*
>
> (1) An issuer's obligation to its customer includes good faith and observance of any general banking usage but unless otherwise agreed does not include liability or responsibility
>
> > (a)   for performance of the underlying contract for sale or other transaction between the customer and the beneficiary; or . . .
> >
> > (c)   based on knowledge or lack of knowledge of any usage of any particular trade.

(2) An issuer must examine documents with care so as to ascertain that on their face they appear to comply with the terms of the credit but unless otherwise agreed assumes no liability or responsibility for the genuineness, falsification or effect of any document which appears on such examination to be regular on its face.]

In utilizing the rules of construction embodied in the letter of credit—the Uniform Customs and State statutes—one must constantly recall that the drawee bank is not to be embroiled in disputes between the buyer and the seller, the beneficiary of the credit. The drawee is involved only with documents, not with merchandise. Its involvement is altogether separate and apart from the transaction between the buyer and seller; its duties and liability are governed exclusively by the terms of the letter, not the terms of the parties' contract with each other. Moreover, as the predominant authorities unequivocally declare, the beneficiary must meet the terms of the credit—and precisely if it is to exact performance of the issuer. Failing such compliance there can be no recovery from the drawee. That is the specific failure of Courtaulds here.

Free of ineptness in wording the letter of credit dictated that each invoice express on its face that it covered 100% acrylic yarn. Nothing less is shown to be tolerated in the trade. No substitution and no equivalent, through interpretation or logic, will serve. Harfield, Bank Credits and Acceptances 73 (5th ed. 1974) commends and quotes aptly from an English case: "There is no room for documents which are almost the same, or which will do just as well." Equitable Trust Co. of N.Y. v. Dawson Partners, Ltd., 27 Lloyds' List Law Rpts. 49, 52 (1926). Although no pertinent North Carolina decision has been laid before us, in many cases elsewhere, especially in New York, we find the tenet of Harfield to be unshaken.

At trial Courtaulds prevailed on the contention that the invoices in actuality met the specifications of the letter of credit in that the packing lists attached to the invoices disclosed on their faces that the packages contained "cartons marked:—100% acrylic." On this premise it was urged that the lists were a part of the invoice since they were appended to it, and the invoices should be read as one with the lists, allowing the lists to detail the invoices. But this argument cannot be accepted. In this connection it is well to revert to the distinction made in *Uniform Customs,* supra, between the "invoice" and the "remaining documents," emphasizing that in the latter the description may be in general terms while in the invoice the goods must be described in conformity with the credit letter.

The District Judge's pat statement adeptly puts an end to this contention of Courtaulds: "In dealing with letters of credit, it is a custom and practice of the banking trade for a bank to only treat a document as an invoice which clearly is marked on its face an 'invoice.' " Findings of Fact 46.

This is not a pharisaical or doctrinaire persistence in the principle, but is altogether realistic in the environs of this case; it is plainly the fair and equitable measure. (The defect in description was not superficial but occurred in the statement of the *quality* of the yarn, not a frivolous concern.) The obligation of the drawee bank was graven in the credit. Indeed, there could be no departure from its words. Bank was not expected to scrutinize the collateral papers, such as the packing lists. Nor was it permitted to read into the instrument the contemplation or intention of the seller and buyer. Adherence to this rule was not only legally commanded, but it was factually ordered also, as will immediately appear.

Had Bank deviated from the stipulation of the letter and honored the draft, then at once it might have been confronted with the not improbable risk of the bankruptcy trustee's charge of liability for unwarrantably paying the draft moneys to the seller, Courtaulds, and refusal to reimburse Bank for the outlay. Contrarily, it might face a Courtaulds claim that since it had depended upon Bank's assurance of credit in shipping yarn to Adastra, Bank was responsible for the loss. In this situation Bank cannot be condemned for sticking to the letter of the letter.

Nor is this conclusion affected by the amended or substituted invoices which Courtaulds sent to Bank after the refusal of the draft. No precedent is cited to justify retroactive amendment of the invoices or extension of the credit beyond the August 15 expiry of the letter.

Finally, the trial court found that although in its prior practices Bank had pursued a strict-constructionist attitude, it had nevertheless on occasion honored drafts not within the verbatim terms of the credit letter. But it also found that in each of these instances Bank had first procured the authorization of Adastra to overlook the deficiencies. This truth is verified by the District Court in its Findings of Fact:

"42. It is a standard practice and procedure of the banking industry and trade for a bank to attempt to obtain a waiver of discrepancies from its customer in a letter of credit transaction. This custom and practice was followed by NCNB in connection with the draft and documents received from Courtaulds.

"43. Following this practice, NCNB had checked all previous discrepancies it discovered in Courtaulds' documents with its customer Adastra to see if Adastra would waive those discrepancies noted by NCNB. Except for the transaction in question, Adastra waived all discrepancies noted by NCNB.

"44. It is not normal or customary for NCNB, nor is it the custom and practice in the banking trade, for a bank to notify a beneficiary or the presenter of the documents that there were any deficiencies in the draft or documents if they are waived by the customer."

This endeavor had been fruitless on the last draft because of the inability of Adastra to give its consent. Obviously, the previous acceptances of truant invoices cannot be construed as a waiver in the present incident.

For these reasons, we must vacate the decision of the trial court, despite the evident close reasoning and research of the District Judge, [387 F. Supp.

92 (M.D.N.C. 1975)]. Entry of judgment in favor of the appellant Bank on its summary motion is necessary. . . .

NOTES & QUESTIONS

1. *Uniform customs and practice. Courtaulds* illustrates the importance of the UCP. Two revisions of the UCP have been effected since *Courtaulds,* which applied the 1962 revision. However, the same result would obtain under the present revision. See 1983 UCP Articles 3, 4, 41(c).

2. *Strict compliance.* Some initial doubt existed as to whether the strict compliance required under commercial credit practice should be imposed with equal vigor in standby credit transactions. At present, a decisive weight of authority supports the view that it should. Chase Manhattan Bank v. Equibank, 550 F.2d 882, 21 UCC Rep. 247 (3d Cir. 1977), is often cited as a leading case, although many cases are to the same effect. A limited body of contrary authority exists, principally in the first circuit. The court in Flagship Cruises, Ltd. v. New England Merchants National Bank, 569 F.2d 699, 24 UCC Rep. 745 (1st Cir. 1978), stated that minor discrepancies in documents were immaterial and provided no basis for dishonor, where there was "*no* possibility that the documents could mislead the paying bank to its detriment" (emphasis added). 569 F.2d at 705. Do you believe that there was a possibility of NCNB being misled to its detriment in *Courtaulds?*

3. *Waiver.* As *Courtaulds* indicates, a frequent response to minor documentary discrepancies is for the issuer to obtain waiver of the discrepancies by its account party. Why was that not done in the instance that led to the dispute? Note that NCNB had previously paid against similarly nonconforming documents. In each case NCNB had obtained waiver by its customer of the nonconformity, but apparently had in no case advised the beneficiary of the nonconformities of the tendered documents. In *Courtaulds* the original discrepancy was minor and was within the control of the beneficiary, yet the beneficiary was frustrated in its attempt to cure.

4. *Reasons for dishonor.* On August 27, the beneficiary sent amended invoices that conformed to the credit's terms, and the bank thereafter wired Courtaulds that the draft remained unaccepted because the credit had expired August 15. When did the bank receive the original documents? Is it clear to you what action the beneficiary must have taken prior to August 15? How long did NCNB have to act upon the documents following receipt? What is the effect of an issuer's failure to act within prescribed time limits? If an issuer dishonors, must it state the basis for its action? Does a failure to note particular nonconformities preclude the bank from later reliance upon them as grounds for dishonor? See UCC 5-112; 1983 UCP Art. 16(b), 16(d), 16(e). Cf. UCC 2-605.

5. *Discrepancies on issuance.* The principal case well illustrates the care that must be taken in preparing documents for presentment under a credit. As a corollary proposition, great care must also be taken in examining the terms of the credit when it is first established. If discrepancies between the credit and the underlying contract are only discovered at the time of presentment, time constraints or other difficulties may frustrate attempts to cure, obtain waiver, or provide indemnity to induce honor. Early discovery improves the likelihood that an amendment to the credit may be obtained. Who must consent to an amendment of an irrevocable credit? Banks normally impose a modest fee for amending a credit. But is an issuing bank under any obligation to amend a credit, even if both the beneficiary and the bank's customer desire the amendment? See AMF Head Sports Wear, Inc. v. Ray Scott's All-American Sports Club, 448 F. Supp. 222, 23 UCC Rep. 990 (D. Ariz. 1978). Why might the issuing bank refuse to amend its credit, when both its customer and the beneficiary desire the amendment?

4. *Variations on the Basic Letter-of-Credit Transaction*

In the principal cases discussed thus far, the transaction involved has corresponded to the simple three-party paradigm diagrammed in Figure 18-2, supra. In *Toyota* and *Palladino* the beneficiary made direct presentment to the issuing bank, and the credit called for immediate payment. *Courtaulds* added one additional factor, by calling for 60-day drafts rather than sight drafts. While the above patterns are very common, the use of time drafts rather than sight drafts is only one example of the many refinements or variations that may be made of the basic letter-of-credit transaction. A sophisticated use of these variations allows clients, working with their bankers and counsel, to create new devices tailored to the exact needs and desired risk allocations of a particular industry or transaction. In this section we will consider three specific issues: 1) the roles that may be played where banks other than the issuer are involved; 2) variation of the credit terms to provide for settlement by means other than payment of sight drafts; and 3) transfer of credits and assignment of proceeds of the credits to aid in financing transactions.

Throughout this section, the student should remain sensitive to one point: law in this area has not been made principally by the legislature or even the courts; instead, it has developed largely as the result of the creative response of the business, banking, and legal communities to rapidly changing practical demands. The role of the courts has been largely reactive rather than innovative. Dean Mentschikoff and the other draftsmen of the UCC were aware of the developing trends in letter-of-credit law, and consciously attempted to promote them, thus allowing the courts a free hand to validate further changes. See UCC 5-102(3) and Comment 1 thereto. However, while the Code successfully avoids imposing a straitjacket on further development, as a corollary it often provides minimal guidance in dealing with modern trends. The

UCP, which was revised in 1983 and represents a distillation of much of the private lawmaking of the last decade, most closely approximates a "restatement" of the law. To a large extent, the materials that follow will raise a practical problem, illustrate a currently utilized solution, and then invite the student to appraise the strengths and weaknesses of the solution and discover the extent to which explicit authority is found in either the Code or the UCP.

a. Additional Roles Typically Played by Banks in Letter-of-Credit Transactions

The simplest form of letter-of-credit transaction is illustrated in Figure 18-2, supra. Review that diagram. Below, a second diagram appears, which includes some of the additional roles that may be played by banks in such transactions. Refer to this diagram as you consider the problems that follow.

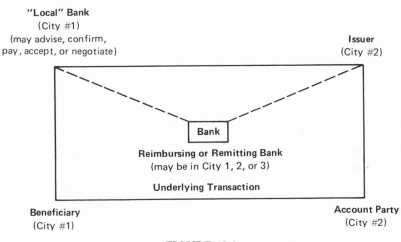

FIGURE 18-3
Bank Roles in Letter-of-Credit Transactions

Problem 18-6. Acme Distributing Company receives a document from St. Helens National Bank. The document states in part:

We wish to advise you that the enclosed credit has been opened in your favor by the Thai Military Bank, available in accordance with its terms by your draft upon us. This letter is solely an advice of the opening of the aforesaid credit.

Enclosed with the document was an irrevocable credit issued by the Thai Military Bank, stating the conditions of payment and that the credit would be available by Acme Distributing Company's drafts on St. Helens National Bank. A draft and documents drawn in conformity with the Thai Military Bank's credit are duly presented to St. Helens National Bank. However, subsequent to the issuance date and prior to the expiration date, the Thai government is toppled, and all remittances of Western currencies are prohibited. St. Helens National Bank accordingly refuses to accept the drafts drawn on it. What roles are being played by St. Helens National Bank in this transaction? What is the liability of St. Helens National Bank to Acme Distributing Company under this document for its failure to accept the conforming drafts and documents?

Problem 18-7. Assume on the same facts that St. Helens National Bank accepts the drafts, but later is informed of the coup in Thailand. It therefore refuses to pay the drafts at maturity. Is St. Helens National Bank liable to Acme Distributing Company? If so, for what amount and on what basis? Does the Thai Military Bank have any liability to St. Helens National Bank? On what basis? Might St. Helens National Bank have any liability to Thai Military Bank? On what basis?

Problem 18-8. Assume that Acme Distributing Company receives the same documents specified in Problem 18-6, except that the following sentence is omitted: "This letter is solely an advice of the aforesaid credit." In its place the letter states:

The above-named issuer of the credit engages with you that each draft drawn under and in compliance with the terms of the credit will be duly honored on delivery of documents as specified.

We confirm the credit and thereby undertake to honor each draft drawn and presented as above specified.

Answer the questions posed in the preceding two problems.

Problem 18-9. China Tu Shu is engaged in the importation of timber into the People's Republic of China. In its transactions with West Coast log exporters, a letter of credit usually is issued by the Bank of China. In the credits the Bank of China undertakes to honor drafts, accompanied by specified documents, drawn on the Bank of East Asia, for negotiation at the counters of the Hong Kong & Shanghai Bank, Ltd. The Bank of China usually forwards these credits through the log exporters' local bank, e.g., First Interstate Bank, Rainier National Bank, United States Bank of Oregon. Refer to Figure 18-3, supra. What are the roles being played by the various banks? As you understand this transaction, to whom shall an exporter make presentment of the drafts drawn under this credit? Who is liable to an exporter for wrongful dishonor of the credit? What rights to reimbursement do First Interstate, Hong Kong & Shanghai Bank, Ltd., or the Bank of East Asia have for funds remitted to the exporter on negotiation or presentment of conforming drafts? See UCC 5-107; 1983 UCP Art. 8, 9, 10, 11, 12, 16, 21.

b.   Variations in the Process of Settlement

All credits may be classified as payment credits, acceptance credits, or negotiation credits, according to the means by which the issuer is to settle the credit. In the simple case of the payment credit, the issuing bank settles simply by paying: *Toyota* and *Palladino* are examples of this type. Payment credits are frequently used in trade transactions, where the credit usually calls for payment of sight drafts accompanied by specified documents. The issuer may either pay directly (in which case the beneficiary must make presentment to the issuer) or may nominate a paying bank in the beneficiary's locale. Payment credits are also in common use as standby credits.

In either case, the seller bears the burden of financing performance up to the point that documents are tendered. On honor by the issuer the financing burden will shift to the buyer. Two interesting variations of the normal payment credit exist: the "red clause" credit, and the "deferred payment" credit. Both are designed to aid the parties in shifting the financing burden.

The red-clause credit allows its beneficiary to draw on the credit on a bare promise to present documents at a later date. The account party finances the beneficiary in the interim period between the draw on the credit and presentment of documents. Although use of such credits is not widespread, in certain trades they are well established. An example is the fish trade between Japan and the West Coast.

Problem 18-10. Nippon Trading Company makes large purchases of fish on the West Coast. These purchases are effected by Fishmonger. Nippon opens a red-clause credit with the Bank of Hokkaido, advised through Second National Bank of Nome, which is also nominated as paying bank.

Fishmonger draws against the credit, pays cash over the rail for catches, and subsequently presents invoices covering the purchased fish. What risks does this transaction present? What factors would mitigate these risks? What alternative means of financing Fishmonger's performance can you devise? As noted, red-clause credits have generally been restricted in use to a few particular trades. Another example of a use that is no longer prevalent is the export timber trade from the West Coast to Japan. What do these export trades have in common that may help account for the historical patterns that developed? Does it surprise you that the use of red-clause credits in the West Coast export trade has fallen off since World War II?

The deferred payment credit operates in a manner exactly converse to the red-clause credit. In this instance the beneficiary presents documents. Rather than making a contemporaneous presentment of a sight draft, however, the credit calls for the beneficiary to defer sight draft presentment for a specified number of days after presentment of the documents. The issuer engages to honor the sight drafts at that time, without further presentment of documents. Obviously the deferred payment credit amounts to the seller financing the buyer for the period of deferment.

As we shall see in the materials that immediately follow, this may also be accomplished if the credit calls for immediate acceptance of 90-day time drafts rather than by providing for deferred presentment of a sight draft 90 days after documents. In considering the materials regarding acceptance drafts, analyze the comparative advantages of the two devices from the perspective of the beneficiary, the issuer, and the account party.

Acceptance credits are simply credits whereby the issuing bank agrees to accept time drafts, rather than to pay sight drafts. Students should review the materials at pp. 732 to 735 supra, to clarify any questions they may have concerning the distinctions between sight and time drafts. *Courtaulds,* it will be recalled, involved the use of an acceptance credit and 60-day drafts. Again, the student should consult the material at p. 900 supra, for a consideration of the important financing role played by acceptances. Acceptance credits are similar to payment credits in the following respect: they may call for drafts to be drawn on the issuing bank itself, or they may nominate another bank (usually in the beneficiary's locale) as the accepting bank and authorize that bank to accept time drafts drawn on it.

Problem 18-11. Sumitomo Bank issues an irrevocable credit for the account of Mitsubishi Heavy Industries. The credit is in favor of Lake Charles Drillers and is available upon presentation of 120-day drafts (with appropriate documents) drawn on Southern National Bank. Southern National Bank advises the credit and is authorized by Sumitomo Bank to accept the drafts. Lake Charles presents a conforming draft and documents, which Southern refuses to accept. What recourse does Lake Charles have against Southern, Sumitomo, and Mitsubishi? See UCC 5-107; 1983 UCP Arts. 3, 4, 6, 10, 11, 16.

Problem 18-12. On the same basic facts, Southern accepts the draft, but refuses to pay it at maturity. What recourse does Lake Charles have against Southern, Sumitomo, and Mitsubishi? See UCC 3-413 and authorities previously cited.

Problem 18-13. On the same basic facts, Southern accepts the drafts and forwards the documents to Sumitomo, which rejects them and returns them to Southern. Assuming Southern pays the draft at maturity, what recourse does Southern have against Sumitomo and Lake Charles: (a) on the assumption the documents conform on their face to the terms of credit; and (b) on the assumption that discrepancies in the documents render them nonconforming? See UCC 5-111 and authorities previously cited.

A final means by which credits may be settled is by negotiation. In this instance, the issuing bank undertakes that drafts duly drawn under the credit will be negotiated by a designated bank. If the designated bank (negotiating bank) fails to negotiate duly drawn and presented drafts, the issuer will be obliged to pay the amount of the drafts. If the negotiating bank negotiates drafts, it will be entitled to reimbursement by the issuer. A bank may be nominated as negotiating bank in two ways: a straight credit will contain a specific nomination; a negotiation credit allows negotiation by any bank.[4] A bank that negotiates drafts without having been nominated does so at its own risk; a knowledgeable bank will normally take a documentary draft only for collection in such circumstances.

Two points, applicable to payment, acceptance, and negotiation credits alike, should be reiterated: (1) the mere nomination of a bank as a paying, accepting, or negotiating bank imposes no obligation to pay, accept, or negotiate—in favor of either the beneficiary or of the issuer. To the extent that the nominated bank is otherwise obligated in favor of the issuer (for instance, pursuant to terms of an agreement creating a correspondent relationship between the banks), the beneficiary may not avail itself of such agreements; (2) a nominated bank is *authorized* to act in accordance with the capacity in which it is nominated; to the extent that it pays, accepts, or nominates against apparently conforming documents, the issuer is bound to reimburse the nominated bank.

Problem 18-14. Banco di Roma (Banco) issues a negotiation credit in favor of Gulf Coast Traders, by which Banco engages with "drawers and/or

---

4. A "negotiation credit" in this sense, i.e., one authorizing any bank to negotiate drafts drawn under it, will customarily contain language such as:

> We hereby engage with *drawers and/or bona fide holders* that drafts drawn and negotiated in strict conformity with the terms of this credit will be duly honored on presentation and that drafts accepted within the terms of this credit will be honored at maturity. [Emphasis added.]

This contrasts with the engagement language of a so-called straight credit, which normally reads simply: "We hereby engage with *you* . . . [i.e., the beneficiary.]"

Negotiation is a word used with great imprecision in letter-of-credit practice. A "negotiation credit" in the strict sense (and in common bankers' parlance) has just been described. In this narrow sense, a negotiation credit contrasts with straight credits, which run only in favor of the beneficiary. More broadly, all credits calling for settlement by negotiation must be distinguished from payment and acceptance credits.

Confusion is increased by the fact that bankers, lawyers, and businessmen all frequently refer to the "negotiation" of the credit as a shorthand reference to the settlement process. For example, a lawyer might inquire of the issuer of a payment credit whether the credit had been negotiated yet; in this context, the lawyer technically may be inquiring whether a nominated paying bank has yet made payment.

bona fide holders" to honor drafts drawn in strict conformity with its letter of credit, up to an aggregate amount of $1,000,000. The credit is advised through Mississippi National Bank, which forwards the credit to Gulf Coast Traders and offers to serve as negotiating bank. Gulf Coast Traders prepares two forged sets of documents, each of which appears on its face to conform with the terms of the credit. One set, together with a duly drawn draft for $1,000,000, is taken to Mississippi National Bank, which negotiates the draft and forwards the documents to Banco. On the same afternoon, Gulf Coast Traders takes the second set of documents and a second draft for $1,000,000 to the Bank of Metairie. The Bank of Metairie requires Gulf Coast Traders to produce the original of the letter of credit. It then makes a notation on the credit identifying the draft, pays the draft, and sends the documents, draft, and letter of credit to Banco. These papers reach Banco the day after Banco has reimbursed Mississippi National Bank. What are the rights and liabilities of the parties? See UCC 5-108; 1983 UCP Arts. 11, 16.

Problem 18-15. In 1983, knowledgeable bankers in the Pacific Northwest estimated that roughly 90 percent of the commercial credits with which they dealt were negotiation credits. The remainder were straight credits. In the case of standby credits, however, the same bankers estimated that well over half the credits were straight credits. How would you account for the difference in these figures? You may wish to return to this question after studying section 5, infra.

c.   Financing the Beneficiary's Performance

In order to render the performance that will earn the beneficiary its right to draw on the credit, it may be necessary to obtain financing. For instance, before a log exporter is able to tender the bills of lading that may be called for under a credit, it is necessary for the exporter to acquire the timber and transport and place it in custody of the carrier. These needs are no different from the working capital needs of any other enterprise. If the exporter is cash rich, the needs may be met internally, or the exporter may obtain a garden-variety working capital loan from its bank. However, where the exporter knows that its ultimate buyer will provide a letter of credit in the export transaction, it may utilize this credit in solving its own financing needs.

Problem 18-16. Wing, in San Francisco, has the prospect of a $4 million dollar sale of powdered elk horns to Tai Pai Traders (TPT). TPT is willing to provide an irrevocable credit calling for payment of sight drafts up to an aggregate of $4 million, at a rate of $50/lb., when accompanied by invoices for powdered elk horns, inspection certificate, and received-for-shipment bills of lading issued by Nationalist Ocean lines. Wing can obtain 80,000 pounds of powdered elk horn from Horn Buyer at $40/lb. But he lacks $3.2 million, and Horn Buyer will not sell on credit. Horn Buyer has proposed the following:

that Horn Buyer submit documents, including invoices, at $40/lb. under Wing's letter of credit, together with a draft for $3.2 million; thereafter, that Wing submit his "substitute" invoices at $50/lb., together with a draft for $800,000, the balance available under the credit. Horn Buyer points out that the net result is that TPT will have a set of fully conforming documents and have paid $4 million for 80,000 pounds of powdered elk horn. Wing asks you to evaluate the feasibility of Horn Buyer's plan. See UCC 5-116; 1983 UCP Arts. 44, 54, 55.

Problem 18-17. Assume that for either legal or business reasons Wing rejects Horn Buyer's proposed structure for the transaction and instead proposes that Horn Buyer sell on credit and take a security interest in the goods sold and the proceeds of the letter of credit. As Horn Buyer's counsel, you are asked whether it is possible to structure the transaction in the suggested manner, what steps and documents are necessary to do so, and what if any dangers to Horn Buyer you see. Advise. See authorities previously cited.

Two additional alternatives exist: the back-to-back credit and the counter credit. Assume that TPT's credit, issued by the Bank of Taiwan, was advised through the Bank of America (B of A). Wing's own bank is the Hong Kong & Shanghai Bank, Ltd. A back-to-back credit may be obtained if Wing approaches the advising bank, B of A, and asks that it issue a second credit in favor of Horn Buyer. This credit calls for the same documents that Horn Buyer was to provide under Problem 18-16, supra, and requires performance within time limits allowing performance of the first credit. Wing offers the Bank of Taiwan credit as security. When Horn Buyer presents documents under the second (B of A) credit, B of A makes payment, substitutes Wing's invoices for Horn Buyer's, and makes presentment under the first (Bank of Taiwan) credit. From the proceeds, B of A reimburses itself and remits the excess to Wing.

The counter credit differs only slightly: Wing approaches his own bank, Hong Kong & Shanghai Bank, Ltd. Again a second credit is issued, with Horn Buyer as beneficiary. In this instance, as in the first, the counter credit must be carefully worded so that its performance effectively guarantees that Wing will be able to make a conforming tender of documents under the Bank of Taiwan credit.

The essential difference between the counter credit and the back-to-back credit lies only in the motivation for the second bank to issue its credit. A counter credit assumes a prior banking relationship, so that application for the credit will be treated on the same basis as other loan applications by the particular customer. The back-to-back credit relies on the fact that the advising bank is likely nominated as the paying, accepting, or negotiating bank under the first credit, and may structure the flow of documents to minimize risk of loss to itself. In neither instance is the bank under any obligation to issue the requested credit, and particularly in the back-to-back credit, where there is no prior relationship, many banks will refuse to do so. On the other hand, in both instances the second credit is quite independent of the first: if the second issuing bank performs, it will seek reimbursement from its customer (Wing) regardless of whether Wing successfully obtains payment under the first credit.

5.   *Remedies Prior to Payment Under the Credit*

Courts and commentators regularly recite the most basic principle of letter-of-credit law: the independence of the issuer's obligation from the performance (or nonperformance) of the obligation owed to the issuer's customer by the beneficiary. See Figure 18-2 and review section 3, supra. It is the independent character of the issuer's obligation that makes the letter of credit such a versatile device. At the same time, this independence subjects the customer/account party to grave risks at the hands of an unscrupulous beneficiary.

Consider the simple case of a seller who sells imperfect goods in a sale under a commercial credit. Assuming that the required documents are conforming, the bank will honor its credit and look to its customer for reimbursement. It is no matter to the bank that the goods are nonconforming: "In credit operations all parties concerned deal in documents, and not in goods, services and/or other performances to which the documents relate." 1983 UCP Art. 4. See also UCC 5-109. The buyer is not without remedy. If the goods are in fact nonconforming, appropriate remedies will lie for breach of the underlying sales transaction. Buyer may be forced to litigate this issue while out of pocket the contract price, but this is exactly the risk allocation the parties are assumed to have agreed to when they structured the transaction as a letter of credit transaction.

Suppose, however, that the buyer reasonably believes that the seller has simply forged documents and the entire transaction is a sham? Buyer will assert vigorously that it certainly did not bargain for that risk. Yet, if the bank pays under the credit, it will with equal certainty turn to the buyer for reimbursement.

If the buyer can discover and prove the above facts *before* the credit has been drawn upon, it will seem unreasonable to some that the bank should still be able to effect payment and throw the loss on the buyer. Yet the core of a credit's utility stems from the fact that it will be honored notwithstanding dispute as to the underlying transaction. Balancing these factors has proved a difficult task. The UCP provides little meaningful guidance in this area. The Code, in UCC 5-114, attempts to codify American case law as it existed at the time of adoption.

Although its language is convoluted, UCC 5-114 embodies only a few principles. The Code first reaffirms the independence of the issuer's obligations. UCC 5-114(1). But in certain circumstances, the UCC recognizes that it may be appropriate to give an issuer discretion. The UCC enumerates these instances in UCC 5-114(2):

> (2) Unless otherwise agreed when documents appear on their face to comply with the terms of a credit but a required document does not in fact conform to the warranties made on negotiation or transfer of a document of title (Section 7-507) or of a certificated security (Section 8-306) or is forged or fraudulent or there is fraud in the transaction:
>
> (a) the issuer must honor the draft or demand for payment if honor is demanded by a negotiating bank or other holder of the draft or demand which has taken the draft or demand under the credit and under circumstances which would make it a holder in due course (Section 3-302) and in an appropriate case would make it a person to whom a document of title has been duly negotiated (Section 7-502) or a bona fide purchaser of a certificated security (Section 8-302); and
>
> (b) in all other cases as against its customer, an issuer acting in good faith may honor the draft or demand for payment despite notification from the customer of fraud, forgery or other defect not apparent on the face of the documents but a court of appropriate jurisdiction may enjoy such honor.

In reality, this subsection sets up three rules:

(1) Paraphrasing UCC 5-114(2)(a): even in egregious circumstances, the issuer must honor, if the result of dishonor would be to throw the loss on an innocent party who has parted with value; but

(2) otherwise, the issuer may choose as it pleases, and knowingly place an eventual loss on the customer rather than risk its own liability for a possible wrongful dishonor; unless

(3) the customer/account party obtains an injunction.

Test your grasp of these principles by considering the following problems, in each case identifying the exact language in UCC 5-114 that seems to provide an answer.

Problem 18-18. Under a negotiation credit, Beneficiary obtains a fraudulently dated bill of lading, which shows shipment within the terms of the credit. Beneficiary has presented this document, which is regular on its face, and discounted conforming drafts with Negotiating Bank. Negotiating Bank demands payment from Issuing Bank. Should Issuing Bank pay? See also 1983 UCP Art. 16.

Problem 18-19. On facts similar to Problem 18-18, the credit has been advised through a bank in Beneficiary's locale. Presentment has been made directly to Issuing Bank. Issuing Bank has been tipped off that the documents are likely to be fraudulent and does not want to invite a dispute with its account party, a valued customer. On the other hand, it does not want to be held liable in a suit by Beneficiary if its information is incorrect. Advise.

Problem 18-20. On each set of facts in Problems 18-18 and 18-19, may the account party successfully enjoin honor of drafts presented under the credit?

Courts have been most troubled by the proper delineation of the "fraud in the transaction" concept in UCC 5-114. The cases and materials that follow deal with that issue.

UNITED BANK LTD. v. CAMBRIDGE SPORTING GOODS CORP.

41 N.Y.2d 254, 360 N.E.2d 943, 392 N.Y.S.2d 265, 20 UCC Rep. 980 (1976)

GABRIELLI, J. On this appeal, we must decide whether fraud on the part of a seller-beneficiary of an irrevocable letter of credit may be successfully asserted as a defense against holders of drafts drawn by the seller pursuant to the credit. If we conclude that this defense may be interposed by the buyer who procured the letter of credit, we must also determine whether the courts below improperly imposed upon appellant buyer the burden of proving that respondent banks to whom the drafts were made payable by the seller-beneficiary of the letter of credit, were not holders in due course. The issues presented raise important questions concerning the application of the law of letters of credit and the rules governing proof of holder in due course status set forth in article 3 of the Uniform Commercial Code. . . .

In April, 1971 appellant Cambridge Sporting Goods Corporation (Cambridge) entered into a contract for the manufacture and sale of boxing gloves with Duke Sports (Duke), a Pakistani corporation. Duke committed itself to the manufacture of 27,936 pairs of boxing gloves at a sale price of $42,576.80; and arranged with its Pakistani bankers, United Bank Limited (United) and The Muslim Commercial Bank (Muslim) for the financing of the sale. Cambridge was requested by these banks to cover payment of the purchase price by opening an irrevocable letter of credit with its bank in New York, Manufacturers Hanover Trust Company (Manufacturers). Manufacturers issued an irrevocable letter of credit obligating it, upon the receipt of certain documents indicating shipment of the merchandise pursuant to the contract, to accept and pay, 90 days after acceptance, drafts drawn upon Manufacturers for the purchase price of the gloves.

Following confirmation of the opening of the letter of credit, Duke informed Cambridge that it would be impossible to manufacture and deliver the merchandise within the time period required by the contract, and sought an extension of time for performance until September 15, 1971 and a continuation of the letter of credit, which was due to expire on August 11. Cambridge replied on June 18 that it would not agree to a postponement of the manufacture and delivery of the gloves because of its resale commitments and, hence, it promptly advised Duke that the contract was canceled and the letter of credit should be returned. Cambridge simultaneously notified United of the contract cancellation.

Despite the cancellation of the contract, Cambridge was informed on July 17, 1971 that documents had been received at Manufacturers from United purporting to evidence a shipment of the boxing gloves under the terms of the canceled contract. The documents were accompanied by a draft, dated July 16, 1971, drawn by Duke upon Manufacturers and made payable to United, for the amount of $21,288.40, one-half of the contract price of the boxing gloves. A second set of documents was received by Manufacturers from Muslim, also accompanied by a draft, dated August 20, and drawn upon Manufacturers by Duke for the remaining amount of the contract price.

An inspection of the shipments upon their arrival revealed that Duke had shipped old, unpadded, ripped and mildewed gloves rather than the new gloves to be manufactured as agreed upon. Cambridge then commenced an action against Duke in Supreme Court, New York County, joining Manufacturers as a party, and obtained a preliminary injunction prohibiting the latter from paying drafts drawn under the letter of credit; subsequently, in November, 1971 Cambridge levied on the funds subject to the letter of credit and the draft, which were delivered by Manufacturers to the Sheriff in compliance therewith. Duke ultimately defaulted in the action and judgment against it was entered in the amount of the drafts, in March, 1972.

The present proceeding was instituted by the Pakistani banks to vacate the levy made by Cambridge and to obtain payment of the drafts on the letter of credit. The banks asserted that they were holders in due course of the drafts which had been made payable to them by Duke and, thus, were entitled to the proceeds thereof irrespective of any defenses which Cambridge had established againt their transferor, Duke, in the prior action which had terminated in a default judgment. The banks' motion for summary judgment on this claim was denied and the request by Cambridge for a jury trial was granted. Cambridge sought to depose the petitioning banks, but its request was denied and, as an alternative, written interrogatories were served on the Pakistani banks to learn the circumstances surrounding the transfer of the drafts to them. At trial, the banks introduced no evidence other than answers to several of the written interrogatories which were received over objection by Cambridge to the effect that the answers were conclusory, self-serving and otherwise inadmissible. Cambridge presented evidence of its dealings with Duke including the cancellation of the contract and uncontested proof of the subsequent shipment of essentially worthless merchandise.

The trial court concluded that the burden of proving that the banks were not holders in due course lay with Cambridge, and directed a verdict in favor of the banks on the ground that Cambridge had not met that burden; the court stated that Cambridge failed to demonstrate that the banks themselves had participated in the seller's acts of fraud, proof of which was concededly present in the record. The Appellate Division affirmed. . . .

We reverse and hold that it was improper to direct a verdict in favor of the petitioning Pakistani banks. We conclude that the defense of fraud in the transaction was established and in that circumstance the burden shifted to petitioners to prove that they were holders in due course and took the drafts for value, in good faith and without notice of any fraud on the part of Duke (UCC 3-302). Additionally, we think it was improper for the trial court to permit petitioners to introduce into evidence answers to Cambridge's interrogatories to demonstrate their holder in due course status.

This case does not come before us in the typical posture of a lawsuit between the bank issuing the letter of credit and presenters of drafters drawn under the credit seeking payment (see generally White & Summers, Uniform Commercial Code §18-6, at 619-628). Because Cambridge obtained an injunction against payment of the drafts and has levied against the proceeds of the drafts, it stands in the same position as the issuer, and, thus, the law of letters of credit governs the liability of Cambridge to the Pakistani banks.[1] Article 5 of the Uniform Commercial Code, dealing with letters of credit, and the Uniform Customs and Practice for Documentary Credits promulgated by the International Chamber of Commerce set forth the duties and obligations of the issuer of a letter of credit.[2] A letter of credit is a commitment on the part of the issuing bank that it will pay a draft presented to it under the terms of the credit, and if it is a documentary draft, upon presentation of the required documents of title (see UCC 5-103). Banks issuing letters of credit deal in documents and not in goods and are not responsible for any breach of war-

1. Cambridge has no direct liability on the drafts because it is not a party to the *drafts* which were drawn on Manufacturers by Duke as drawer; its liability derives from the letter of credit which authorizes the drafts to be drawn on the issuing banks. Since Manufacturers has paid the proceeds of the drafts to the Sheriff pursuant to the levy obtained in the prior proceeding, it has discharged its obligation under the credit and is not involved in this proceeding.

2. It should be noted that the Uniform Customs and Practice controls, in lieu of article 5 of the code, where, unless otherwise agreed by the parties, a letter of credit is made subject to the provisions of the Uniform Customs and Practice by its terms or by agreement, course of dealing or usage of trade (UCC 5-102(4)). [UCC 5-102(4) was added to the New York text of the Code as a nonuniform provision. It provides: "(4) Unless otherwise agreed, this Article 5 does not apply to a letter of credit or a credit if by its terms or by agreement, course of dealing or usage of trade such letter of credit or credit is subject in whole or in part to the Uniform Customs and Practice for Commercial Documentary Credits fixed by the Thirteenth or by any subsequent Congress of the International Chamber of Commerce." The practical effect of the amendment has been minimal; the remainder of the court's footnote helps to explain why.—EDS.] No proof was offered that there was an agreement that the Uniform Customs and Practice should apply, nor does the credit so state (cf. Oriental Pacific [U.S.A.] v. Toronto Dominion Bank, 78 Misc. 2d 819, 357 N.Y.S.2d 957). Neither do the parties otherwise contend that their rights should be resolved under the Uniform Customs and Practice. However, even if the Uniform Customs and Practice were deemed applicable to this case, it would not, in the absence of a conflict, abrogate the precode case law (now codified in UCC 5-114) and that authority continues to govern even where article 5 is not controlling (see White and Summers, supra, at 613-614, 624-625). Moreover, the Uniform Customs and Practice provisions are not in conflict nor do they treat with the subject matter of UCC 5-114 which is dispositive of the issues presented on this appeal (see Banco Tornquist, S.A. v. American Bank & Trust Co., 71 Misc. 2d 874, 875, 337 N.Y.S.2d 489; Intraworld Indus. v. Girard Trust Bank, 461 Pa. 343, 336 A.2d 316, 322; Harfield, Practice Commentary, McKinney's Cons. Laws of N.Y., Book 62-1/2, UCC 5-114, p. 686). Thus, we are of the opinion that the Uniform Customs and Practice, where applicable, does not bar the relief provided for in UCC 5-114.

ranty or nonconformity of the goods involved in the underlying sales contract (see UCC 5-114(1); UCP, General Provisions and Definitions (c) and Art. 9; . . .). UCC 5-114(2), however, indicates certain limited circumstances in which an issuer *may* properly refuse to honor a draft drawn under a letter of credit or a customer may enjoin an issuer from honoring such a draft. Thus, where "fraud in the transaction" has been shown and the holder has not taken the draft in circumstances that would make it a holder in due course, the customer may apply to enjoin the issuer from paying drafts drawn under the letter of credit (see 3 N.Y. Law Rev. Comm. Report 1654-1659 (1955)). This rule represents a codification of pre-Code case law most eminently articulated in the landmark case of Sztejn v. J. Henry Schroder Banking Corp., 177 Misc. 719, 31 N.Y.S.2d 631, Shientag, J., where it was held that the shipment of cowhair in place of bristles amounted to more than mere breach of warranty but fraud sufficient to constitute grounds for enjoining payment of drafts to one not a holder in due course. . . . Even prior to the *Sztejn* case, forged or fraudulently procured documents were proper grounds for avoidance of payment of drafts drawn under a letter of credit (Finkelstein, Legal Aspects of Commercial Letters of Credit 231, 236, 247 (1930)); and cases decided after the enactment of the Code have cited *Sztejn* with approval. . . .

The history of the dispute between the various parties involved in this case reveals that Cambridge had in a prior, separate proceeding successfully enjoined Manufacturers from paying the drafts and has attached the proceeds of the drafts. It should be noted that the question of the availability and the propriety of this relief is not before us on this appeal. The petitioning banks do not dispute the validity of the prior injunction nor do they dispute the delivery of worthless merchandise. Rather, on this appeal they contend that as holders in due course they are entitled to the proceeds of the drafts irrespective of any fraud on the part of Duke (see UCC 5-114(2)(b)). Although precisely speaking there was no specific finding of fraud in the transaction by either of the courts below, their determinations were based on that assumption. The evidentiary facts are not disputed and we hold upon the facts as established, that the shipment of old, unpadded, ripped and mildewed gloves rather than the new boxing gloves as ordered by Cambridge, constituted fraud in the transaction within the meaning of UCC 5-114(2). It should be noted that the drafters of UCC 5-114, in their attempt to codify the *Sztejn* case and in utilizing the term "fraud in the transaction," have eschewed a dogmatic approach and adopted a flexible standard to be applied as the circumstances of a particular situation mandate.[5] It can be difficult to draw a precise line between cases involving breach of warranty (or a difference of opinion as to the quality of goods) and outright fraudulent practice on the part of the seller. To the extent, however, that Cambridge established that Duke was guilty of *fraud* in shipping, not merely nonconforming merchandise, but worthless fragments of boxing gloves, this case is similar to *Sztejn*.

5. In its original version UCC 5-114 contained the language "fraud in a required document" (see 3 1955 NY Law Rev. Comm. Report, pp. 1655-1658).

If the petitioning banks are holders in due course they are entitled to recover the proceeds of the drafts but if such status cannot be demonstrated their petition must fail. The parties are in agreement that UCC 3-307 governs the pleading and proof of holder in due course status. . . . Even though UCC 3-307 is contained in article 3 of the code dealing with negotiable instruments rather than letters of credit, we agree that its provisions should control in the instant case. UCC 5-114(2)(a) utilizes the holder in due course criteria of UCC 3-302 to determine whether a presenter may recover on drafts despite fraud in the sale of goods transaction. It is logical, therefore, to apply the pleading and practice rules of UCC 3-307 in the situation where a presenter of drafts under a letter of credit claims to be a holder in due course. In the context of UCC 5-114 and the law of letters of credit, however, the "defense" referred to in UCC 3-307 should be deemed to include only those defenses available under UCC 5-114(2); i.e., noncompliance of required documents, forged or fraudulent documents or fraud in the transaction. In the context of a letter of credit transaction and, specifically UCC 5-114(2), it is these defenses which operate to shift the burden of proof of holder in due course status upon one asserting such status. . . . Thus, a presenter of drafts drawn under a letter of credit must prove that it took the drafts for value, in good faith and without notice of the underlying fraud in the transaction (UCC 3-302). . . .

The courts below erroneously concluded that Cambridge was required to show that the banks had participated in or were themselves guilty of the seller's fraud in order to establish a defense to payment. But, it was not necessary that Cambridge prove that United and Muslim actually participated in the fraud, since merely notice of the fraud would have deprived the Pakistani banks of holder in due course status. . . .

Since the defense of fraud in the transaction was shown, the burden shifted to the banks by operation of UCC 3-307(3) to prove that they are holders in due course and took the drafts without notice of Duke's alleged fraud. . . . It was error for the trial court to direct a verdict in favor of the Pakistani banks because this determination rested upon a misallocation of the burden of proof; and we conclude that the banks have not satisfied the burden of proving that they qualified in all respects as holders in due course, by any affirmative proof. . . . The failure of the banks to meet their burden is fatal to their claim for recovery of the proceeds of the drafts and their petition must therefore be dismissed. . . .

[Order reversed, with costs, and the petition dismissed.]

NOTES & QUESTIONS

1. *Fraud in commercial credits.* The principal case is one of a small number of cases decided under UCC 5-114 that involve commercial credits. In contrast, the rapid spread in the use of standby credits, often by parties who do

not appear to have fully appreciated the risk allocations involved, has spawned a great deal of litigation over alleged fraud in the transaction. In such cases, should fraud in the inducement to enter into the underlying transaction be considered fraud in *the* transaction, or should the concept be considered more narrowly to only encompass fraudulent presentment of documents (for instance, documents lacking *any* basis in fact)? This issue is considered further in the next principal case. See also Note, Letters of Credit: Injunction as a Remedy for Fraud in UCC Section 5-114, 63 Minn. L. Rev. 487 (1979).

2. *Fraud in the transaction.* See n.5 of the principal case. Was there ". . . a required document . . . [that is] fraudulent . . . ?" Was it necessary to consider whether there was fraud in the transaction?

3. *Enjoining honor versus enjoining presentment.* In the typical injunction case the account party seeks to enjoin the issuer from honoring drafts: UCC 5-114 speaks to this situation. Is there any distinction if instead the account party seeks to enjoin the beneficiary or other holders from drawing or presenting drafts? Note that the principal case arises in a different context procedurally than either of the above situations (see n.1 of the case), although the court treats UCC 5-114 as dispositive of the substantive issue.

AMERICAN BELL INTERNATIONAL INC. v. ISLAMIC REPUBLIC OF IRAN
474 F. Supp. 420, 27 UCC Rep. 223 (S.D.N.Y. 1979)

MacMahon, District Judge. Plaintiff American Bell International Inc. ("Bell") moves for a preliminary injunction pursuant to Rule 65(a), Fed. R. Civ. P., and the All Writs Act, 28 U.S.C. §1651, enjoining defendant Manufacturers Hanover Trust Company ("Manufacturers") from making any payment under its Letter of Credit No. SC 170027 to defendants the Islamic Republic of Iran or Bank Iranshahr or their agents, instrumentalities, successors, employees and assigns. . . .

The action arises from the recent revolution in Iran and its impact upon contracts made with the ousted Imperial Government of Iran and upon banking arrangements incident to such contracts. Bell, a wholly-owned subsidiary of American Telephone & Telegraph Co. ("AT&T"), made a contract on July 23, 1978 (the "Contract") with the Imperial Government of Iran—Ministry of War ("Imperial Government") to provide consulting services and equipment to the Imperial Government as part of a program to improve Iran's international communications system.

The Contract provides a complex mechanism for payment to Bell totalling approximately $280,000,000, including a down payment of $38,800,000. The Imperial Government had the right to demand return of the down payment at any time. The amount so callable, however, was to be reduced by 20% of the amounts invoiced by Bell to which the Imperial Government did not object. Bell's liability for return of the down payment was reduced by application of this mechanism as the Contract was performed, with the result that approximately $30,200,000 of the down payment now remains callable.

In order to secure the return of the down payment on demand, Bell was required to establish an unconditional and irrevocable Letter of Guaranty, to be issued by Bank Iranshahr in the amount of $38,800,000 in favor of the Imperial Government. The Contract provides that it is to be governed by the laws of Iran and that all disputes arising under it are to be resolved by the Iranian courts.

Bell obtained a Letter of Guaranty from Bank Iranshahr. In turn, as required by Bank Iranshahr, Bell obtained a standby Letter of Credit, No. SC 170027, issued by Manufacturers in favor of Bank Iranshahr in the amount of $38,800,000 to secure reimbursement to Bank Iranshahr should it be required to pay the Imperial Government under its Letter of Guaranty.

The standby Letter of Credit provided for payment by Manufacturers to Bank Iranshahr upon receipt of:

> Your [Bank Iranshahr's] dated statement purportedly signed by an officer indicating name and title or your Tested Telex Reading: (A) "Referring Manufacturers Hanover Trust Co. Credit No. SC170027, the amount of our claim $_____ represents funds due us as we have received a written request from the Imperial Government of Iran Ministry of War to pay them the sum of _____ under our Guarantee No. _____ issued for the account of American Bell International Inc. covering advance payment under Contract No. 138 dated July 23, 1978 and such payment has been made by us."...

In the application for the Letter of Credit, Bell agreed—guaranteed by AT&T—immediately to reimburse Manufacturers for all amounts paid by Manufacturers to Bank Iranshahr pursuant to the Letter of Credit.

Bell commenced performance of its Contract with the Imperial Government. It provided certain services and equipment to update Iran's communications system and submitted a number of invoices, some of which were paid.

In late 1978 and early 1979, Iran was [torn by] revolutionary turmoil culminating in the overthrow of the Iranian government and its replacement by the Islamic Republic. In the wake of this upheaval, Bell was left with substantial unpaid invoices and claims under the Contract and ceased its performance in January 1979. Bell claims that the Contract was breached by the Imperial Government, as well as repudiated by the Islamic Republic, in that it is owed substantial sums for services rendered under the Contract and its termination provisions.

On February 16, 1979, before a demand had been made by Bank Iranshahr for payment under the Letter of Credit, Bell and AT&T brought an action against Manufacturers in the Supreme Court, New York County, seeking a preliminary injunction prohibiting Manufacturers from honoring any demand for payment under the Letter of Credit. The motion for a preliminary injunction was denied in a thorough opinion by Justice Dontzin on March 26, 1979, and the denial was unanimously affirmed on appeal by the Appellate Division, First Department.

On July 25 and 29, 1979, Manufacturers received demands by Tested Telex from Bank Iranshahr for payment of $30,220,724 under the Letter of Credit, the remaining balance of the down payment. Asserting that the demand did not conform with the Letter of Credit, Manufacturers declined payment and so informed Bank Iranshahr. Informed of this, Bell responded by filing this action and an application by way of order to show cause for a temporary restraining order bringing on this motion for a preliminary injunction. Following argument, we granted a temporary restraining order on July 29 enjoining Manufacturers from making any payment to Bank Iranshahr until forty-eight hours after Manufacturers notified Bell of the receipt of a conforming demand, and this order has been extended pending decision of this motion.

On August 1, 1979, Manufacturers notified Bell that it had received a conforming demand from Bank Iranshahr. At the request of the parties, the court held an evidentiary hearing on August 3 on this motion for a preliminary injunction. . . .

The current criteria in this circuit for determining whether to grant the extraordinary remedy of a preliminary injunction are set forth in Caulfield v. Board of Education, 583 F.2d 605, 610 (2d Cir. 1978): "There must be a showing of possible irreparable injury *and* either (1) probable success on the merits *or* (2) sufficiently serious questions going to the merits to make them a fair ground for litigation *and* a balance of hardships tipping decidedly toward the party requesting the preliminary relief." We are not persuaded that the plaintiff has met the criteria and therefore deny the motion. . . .

Plaintiff has failed to show that irreparable injury may possibly ensue if a preliminary injunction is denied. . . .

Although Bell has made no effort to invoke the aid of the Iranian courts, we think the current situation in Iran, as shown by the evidence, warrants the conclusion that an attempt by Bell to resort to those courts would be futile. . . . However, Bell has not demonstrated that it is without adequate remedy in this court against the Iranian defendants under the Sovereign Immunity Act which it invokes in this very case. 28 U.S.C. §§1605(a)(2), 1610(b)(2) (Supp. 1979). . . .

Even assuming that plaintiff has shown possible irreparable injury, it has failed to show probable success on the merits. . . .

In order to succeed on the merits, Bell must prove, by a preponderance of the evidence, that either (1) a demand for payment of the Manufacturers Letter of Credit conforming to the terms of that Letter has not yet been made . . . or (2) a demand, even though in conformity, should not be honored because of fraud in the transaction, see, e.g., UCC 5-114(2); United Bank Ltd. v. Cambridge Sporting Goods Corp., [p. 944 supra]. . . . It is not probable, in the sense of a greater than 50% likelihood, that Bell will be able to prove either nonconformity or fraud.

As to nonconformity, the August 1 demand by Bank Iranshahr is identical to the terms of the Manufacturers Letter of Credit in every respect except one: it names as payee the "Government of Iran Ministry of Defense, Successor to the Imperial Government of Iran Ministry of War" rather than the "Imperial Government of Iran Ministry of War." . . . It is, of course, a bedrock principle of letter of credit law that a demand must strictly comply with the letter in order to justify payment. . . . Nevertheless we deem it less than probable that a court, upon a full trial, would find nonconformity in the instant case.

At the outset, we notice, and the parties agree, that the United States now recognizes the present Government of Iran as the legal successor to the Imperial Government of Iran. That recognition is binding on American courts. . . . Though we may decide for ourselves the consequences of such recognition upon the litigants in this case . . ., we point out that American courts have traditionally viewed contract rights as vesting not in any particular government but in the state of which that government is an agent. . . .

Accordingly, the Government of Iran is the successor to the Imperial Government under the Letter of Guaranty. As legal successor, the Government of Iran may properly demand payment even though the terms of the Letter of Guaranty only provide for payment to the Government of Iran's predecessor . . .; and a demand for payment under the Letter of Credit reciting that payment has been made by Bank Iranshahr to the new government is sufficient. . . .

Finally, an opposite answer to the narrow question of conformity would not only elevate form over substance, but would render financial arrangements and undertakings worldwide wholly subject to the vicissitudes of political power. A nonviolent, unanimous transformation of the form of government, or, as this case shows, the mere change of the name of a government agency, would be enough to warrant an issuer's refusal to honor a demand. We cannot suppose such uncertainty and opportunity for chicanery to be the purpose of the requirement of strict conformity.

If conformity is established, as here, the issuer of an irrevocable, unconditional letter of credit, such as Manufacturers, normally has an absolute duty to transfer the requisite funds. This duty is wholly independent of the underlying contractual relationship that gives rise to the letter of credit. . . . Nevertheless, both the Uniform Commercial Code of New York, which the parties concede governs here, and the courts state that payment is enjoinable where a germane document is forged or fraudulent or there is "fraud in the transaction." UCC 5-114(2); United Bank Ltd. v. Cambridge Sporting Goods Corp., supra. Bell does not contend that any documents are fraudulent by virtue of misstatements or omissions. Instead, it argues there is "fraud in the transaction."

The parties disagree over the scope to be given as a matter of law to the term "transaction." Manufacturers, citing voluminous authorities, argues that the term refers only to the Letter of Credit transaction, not to the underlying commercial transaction or to the totality of dealings among the banks, the Iranian government and Bell. On this view of the law, Bell must fail to establish a probability of success, for it does not claim that the Imperial Government or Bank Iranshahr induced Manufacturers to extend the Letter by lies or half-truths, that the Letter contained any false representations by the Imperial Government or Bank Iranshahr, or that they intended misdeeds with it. Nor does Bell claim that the demand contains any misstatements.

Bell argues, citing equally voluminous authorities, that the term "transaction" refers to the totality of circumstances. On this view, Bell has some chance of success on the merits, for a court can consider Bell's allegations that the Government of Iran's behavior in connection with the consulting contract suffices to make its demand on the Letter of Guaranty fraudulent and that the ensuing demand on the Letter of Credit by Bank Iranshahr is tainted with the fraud.

There is some question whether these divergent understandings of the law are wholly incompatible since it would seem impossible to keep the Letter of Credit transaction conceptually distinct. A demand which facially conforms to the Letter of Credit and which contains no misstatements may, nevertheless, be considered fraudulent if made with the goal of mulcting the party who caused the Letter of Credit to be issued. Be that as it may, we need not decide this thorny issue of law. For, even on the construction most favorable to Bell, we find that success on the merits is not probable. Many of the facts alleged, even if proven, would not constitute fraud. As to others, the proof is insufficient to indicate a probability of success on the merits.

Bell, while never delineating with precision the contours of the purported fraud, sets forth five contentions which, in its view, support the issuance of an injunction. Bell asserts that (1) both the old and new Governments failed to approve invoices for services fully performed; (2) both failed to fund contracted-for independent Letters of Credit in Bell's favor; (3) the new Government has taken steps to renounce altogether its obligations under the Contract; (4) the new Government has made it impossible to assert contract rights in Iranian courts; and (5) the new Government has caused Bank Iranshahr to demand payment on the Manufacturers Letter of Credit, thus asserting rights in a transaction it has otherwise repudiated. . . .

As to contention (4), it is not immediately apparent how denial of Bell's opportunity to assert rights under the Contract makes a demand on an independent letter of credit fraudulent. Contentions (1), (2), (3) and the latter part of (5) all state essentially the same proposition—that the Government of Iran is currently repudiating all its contractual obligations with American companies, including those with Bell. Again, the evidence on this point is uncompelling.

Bell points to (1) an intragovernmental order of July 2, 1979 ordering the termination of Iran's contract with Bell, and (2) hearsay discussions between Bell's president and Iranian officials to the effect that Iran would not pay on the Contract until it had determined whether the services under it had bene-fited the country. . . . Manufacturers, for its part, points to a public statement in the Wall Street Journal of July 16, 1979, under the name of the present Iranian Government, to the effect that Iran intends to honor all legitimate contracts. . . . Taken together, this evidence does not suggest that Iran has finally and irrevocably decided to repudiate the Bell contract. It suggests equally that Iran is still considering the question whether to perform that contract.

Even if we accept the proposition that the evidence does show repudi-ation, plaintiff is still far from demonstrating the kind of evil intent necessary to support a claim of fraud. Surely, plaintiff cannot contend that every party who breaches or repudiates his contract is for that reason culpable of fraud. The law of contract damages is adequate to repay the economic harm caused by repudiation, and the law presumes that one who repudiates has done so because of a calculation that such damages are cheaper than performance. Absent any showing that Iran would refuse to pay damages upon a contract action here or in Iran, much less a showing that Bell has even attempted to obtain such a remedy, the evidence is ambivalent as to whether the purported repudiation results from nonfraudulent economic calculation or from fraudu-lent intent to mulct Bell.

Plaintiff contends that the alleged repudiation, viewed in connection with its demand for payment on the Letter of Credit, supplies the basis from which only one inference—fraud—can be drawn. Again, we remain unpersuaded.

Plaintiff's argument requires us to presume bad faith on the part of the Iranian government. It requires us further to hold that that government may not rely on the plain terms of the consulting contract and the Letter of Credit arrangements with Bank Iranshahr and Manufacturers providing for immedi-ate repayment of the down payment upon demand, without regard to cause. On the evidence before us, fraud is no more inferable than an economically rational decision by the government to recoup its down payment, as it is entitled to do under the consulting contract and still dispute its liabilities under that Contract.

While fraud in the transaction is doubtless a possibility, plaintiff has not shown it to be a probability and thus fails to satisfy this branch of the *Caulfield* test. . . .

If plaintiff fails to demonstrate probable success, he may still obtain relief by showing, in addition to the possibility of irreparable injury, both (1) suffi-ciently serious questions going to the merits to make them a fair ground for litigation, and (2) a balance of hardships tipping decidedly toward plaintiff. . . . Both Bell and Manufacturers appear to concede the existence of serious questions, and the complexity and novelty of this matter lead us to find they exist. Nevertheless, we hold that plaintiff is not entitled to relief under this branch of the *Caulfield* test because the balance of hardships does not tip *decid-edly* toward Bell, if indeed it tips that way at all.

To be sure, Bell faces substantial hardships upon denial of its motion.

Should Manufacturers pay the demand, Bell will immediately become liable to Manufacturers for $30.2 million, with no assurance of recouping those funds from Iran for the services performed. While counsel represented in graphic detail the other losses Bell faces at the hands of the current Iranian government, these would flow regardless of whether we ordered the relief sought. The hardship imposed from a denial of relief is limited to the admittedly substantial sum of $30.2 million.

But Manufacturers would face at least as great a loss, and perhaps a greater one, were we to grant relief. Upon Manufacturers' failure to pay, Bank Iranshahr could initiate a suit on the Letter of Credit and attach $30.2 million of Manufacturers' assets in Iran. In addition, it could seek to hold Manufacturers liable for consequential damages beyond that sum resulting from the failure to make timely payment. Finally, there is no guarantee that Bank Iranshahr or the government, in retaliation for Manufacturers' recalcitrance, will not nationalize additional Manufacturers' assets in Iran in amounts which counsel, at oral argument, represented to be far in excess of the amount in controversy here.

Apart from a greater monetary exposure flowing from an adverse decision, Manufacturers faces a loss of credibility in the international banking community that could result from its failure to make good on a letter of credit. . . .

Finally, apart from questions of relative hardship and the specific criteria of the *Caulfield* test, general considerations of equity counsel us to deny the motion for injunctive relief. Bell, a sophisticated multinational enterprise well advised by competent counsel, entered into these arrangements with its corporate eyes open. It knowingly and voluntarily signed a contract allowing the Iranian government to recoup its down payment on demand, without regard to cause. It caused Manufacturers to enter into an arrangement whereby Manufacturers became obligated to pay Bank Iranshahr the unamortized down payment balance upon receipt of conforming documents, again without regard to cause.

Both of these arrangements redounded tangibly to the benefit of Bell. The Contract with Iran, with its prospect of designing and installing from scratch a nationwide and international communications system, was certain to bring to Bell both monetary profit and prestige and good will in the global communications industry. The agreement to indemnify Manufacturers on its Letter of Credit provided the means by which these benefits could be achieved.

One who reaps the rewards of commercial arrangements must also accept their burdens. One such burden in this case, voluntarily accepted by Bell, was the risk that demand might be made without cause on the funds constituting the down payment. To be sure, the sequence of events that led up to that demand may well have been unforeseeable when the contracts were signed. To this extent, both Bell and Manufacturers have been made the unwitting and innocent victims of tumultuous events beyond their control. But, as between the innocents, the party who undertakes by contract the risk of political uncertainty and governmental caprice must bear the consequences when the risk comes home to roost. . . .

Accordingly, plaintiff's motion for a preliminary injunction, pursuant to Rule 65(a), Fed. R. Civ. P., is denied. However, Manufacturers Hanover Trust Company, its officers and agents are hereby enjoined from making any payments to Bank Iranshahr or the Islamic Republic of Iran, pursuant to the Letter of Credit, until August 6, 1979, at 3:00 P.M., to permit plaintiff to apply to the Court of Appeals for a stay pending appeal, if it is so advised.

So ordered.

NOTE

Injunctions in bankruptcy proceedings. Recent years have seen a growth of letter-of-credit litigation in bankruptcy proceedings, including actions seeking to enjoin payment. See Chaitman & Sovern, Enjoining Payment on a Letter of Credit in Bankruptcy, 38 Bus. Law. 21 (1982); McLaughlin, Letters of Credit as Preferential Transfers in Bankruptcy, 50 Ford. L. Rev. 1033 (1982); Baird, Standby Letters of Credit in Bankruptcy, 49 U. Chi. L. Rev. 130 (1982); Twist Cap, Inc. v. Southeast Bank, 1 B.R. 284 (Bankr. D. Fla. 1979); Westinghouse Credit Corp. v. Page, 18 B.R. 713 (Bankr. D.D.C. 1982).

Problem 18-21. Snakeyes carries on a high-rolling life of consumption and investment. In late 1980, he invests $250,000 in a tax-shelter gas drilling limited partnership program. His contribution is callable over a period of years, and he is required to obtain a standby letter of credit in favor of the limited partnership to back this commitment. In July, 1981, the issuer asks Snakeyes to execute a second deed of trust on his residence to secure his obligation to reimburse the bank if the credit is drawn on. In mid-September Snakeyes, faced with a series of reversals, files a petition in bankruptcy. The trustee now sues the bank to enjoin any payment under the credit, claiming: (1) the drilling program was fraudulently misrepresented to Snakeyes, and there is "fraud in the transaction" making equitable relief appropriate; (2) the letter of credit represents property of the estate and it would violate the automatic stay to draw on it; and (3) any payment under the credit would constitute a preferential transfer. Advise the bank. See UCC 5-109, 5-114; BC 542, 547.

The Iranian revolution produced many cases similar to *Bell.* Prior to the revolution, the Shah's government had entered into extensive contracts with Western companies. In common practice, these contracts called for partial prepayment by the Iranian agency to the contractor. This prepayment could be "called" by the agency under certain conditions, if the contract was cancelled or otherwise not properly performed. The amount subject to call often was reduced over a certain period of time or performance. For its part, the contractor would be required to furnish bank guarantees by an Iranian bank. Two separate guarantees might be involved, a guarantee of the repayment obligation and a guarantee of contract performance. Unlike United States banks, Iranian banks were not precluded from issuing guarantees. However, to secure repayment in the event its guarantee was called, an Iranian bank would require an American contractor to obtain a standby credit issued by a major United States bank in favor of the Iranian bank and in like amount to the guarantee. This credit would typically be available to the Iranian bank upon presentment of a demand certificate similar to that reproduced in *Bell*.

Bell is typical of early Iranian letter-of-credit litigation, where the account party sought an injunction against payment. Plaintiffs regularly failed to obtain the requested relief. Often this result involved simply an application of general principles regarding issuance of preliminary injunctions, rather than an elaborate interpretation of UCC 5-114. See, e.g., United Technologies Corp. v. Citibank, 469 F. Supp. 473, 27 UCC Rep. 212 (S.D.N.Y. 1979); KMW International v. Chase Manhattan Bank, 606 F.2d 10, 27 UCC Rep. 203 (2d Cir. 1979). While denying an unconditional injunction, however, the courts were more open to requiring that the issuer provide notice to the account party prior to honoring any demand under the credit. The opportunity was thus preserved for the account party to renew its request for relief on a less speculative basis.

As the Iranian crisis deepened, particularly following the taking of American hostages, courts seem to have softened their attitude towards plaintiffs and now more readily infer the likelihood of fraud. See, e.g., Itek Corp. v. First National Bank of Boston, 511 F. Supp. 1341 (D. Mass. 1981), *rev'd on other grounds,* 704 F.2d 1 (1st Cir. 1983); Touche Ross & Co. v. Manufacturers Hanover Trust Co., 107 Misc. 2d 438, 434 N.Y.S.2d 575 (Sup. Ct. 1980); Harris Corp. v. National Iranian Radio & Television, 691 F.2d 1344, 35 UCC Rep. 222 (11th Cir. 1982) (all enjoining payment).

For further commentary on the Iranian cases, see Note, "Fraud in the Transaction": Enjoining Letters of Credit During the Iranian Revolution, 93 Harv. L. Rev. 992 (1980); Weisz & Blackman, Standby Letters of Credit After Iran: Remedies of the Account Party, 1982 U. Ill. L. Rev. 355; Kimball & Sanders, Preventing Wrongful Payment of Guaranty Letters of Credit—Lessons from Iran, 39 Bus. Law. 417 (1984).

6. Remedies Following Presentment and Honor or Dishonor

Most letter-of-credit transactions proceed smoothly. When breakdowns occur, in recent years the most frequently litigated issue has been the ability of the account party to enjoin payment, which was discussed in the preceding section. However, disputes may arise following presentment and honor or dishonor. The types of breakdown may be usefully inventoried according to the perspective of the specific party: the beneficiary, customer, or issuer. Analysis in this area is not difficult, provided that the student keeps in mind the basic principles of letter-of-credit law: strict documentary compliance as the performance standard under the letter of credit itself, and the independence of the three sets of obligations involved in letter of credit transactions. (Review Figure 18-2, supra.) It is also helpful to bear in mind that the UCC and the UCP have both been heavily influenced by a vocal and well organized banking community. On the whole this community has done an excellent job of minimizing the exposure of issuers. Throughout the materials that follow, the student should remain alert to actions that the parties might have taken when structuring the transaction to avoid the problem that has arisen.

a.   The Beneficiary's Perspective

A Beneficiary may suffer loss in a variety of ways in a letter-of-credit transaction: failure to present conforming documents, insolvency of the issuer, or the issuer's wrongful refusal to honor conforming documents. Here we confine our attention to the issuer's wrongful refusal to honor.

Problem 18-22. Zephyr Runningwear (Zephyr) of Korea contracts to sell 50,000 pairs of quality running shoes to Sportshop, Inc., of Eugene, Oregon. The contract calls for an irrevocable credit to be issued by First Western Bank (FWB) in favor of Zephyr in the amount of the contract price, $250,000. FWB issues the credit. Prior to performance, however, medical research is publicized showing the harmful effects on the body of jogging. This results in a precipitous drop in the popularity of jogging and in the market for running shoes. FWB fears the imminent insolvency of Sportshop. On the advice of its house counsel, FWB rejects Zephyr's tender of conforming documents. It returns the documents to Zephyr and refuses payment. FWB's best estimate is that the goods can presently be sold for perhaps $100,000. Assuming Zephyr brings an action in Oregon and the UCC applies, to what damages is Zephyr entitled? Would it make any difference if FWB repudiates well prior to Zephyr's performance? See UCC 5-115 and also consider the following case.

BANCO DI ROMA v. FIDELITY UNION TRUST CO.
464 F. Supp. 817, 27 UCC Rep. 515 (D.N.J. 1979)

[Banco di Roma issued an irrevocable credit at the request of its customer, United Tractor Co. (United), Beirut, Lebanon. The credit's beneficiary was Consolidated Machinery Export Ltd. (Consolidated), Newark, N.J., and the credit was advised through Fidelity Union Trust Company (Fidelity). Fidelity advised two credits: one in favor of a certain Foley (the Foley credit) and one in favor of Consolidated (the Consolidated credit). One term of the Foley credit provided:

"1) Goods to be rendered FOB East New York or Newark *Destination Beirut Zone Franch In Transit Kuwait* (emphasis added)."

The term "Zone Franch" means Free Zone, that is, outside Lebanon's customs frontier. By telex, Banco di Roma instructed Fidelity that the Consolidated credit was to be similar to the Foley credit, except for the provision:

"2) Goods to be rendered FOB Newark stop"

Fidelity interpreted this term as a complete substitution for paragraph (1) of the Foley credit, and omitted any reference to the Free Zone destination in the Consolidated credit.

Consolidated presented a bill of lading and certificate of origin (both required under the letter of credit) which stated the destination as "Beirut," not "Beirut Free Zone In Transit Kuwait." Fidelity paid against these documents, and was reimbursed through Chemical Bank.—EDS.]

On May 7, 1975 Banco di Roma received the shipping documents from Fidelity. By telex dated May 9, 1975 Banco di Roma informed Fidelity that United had rejected the documents because of the incorrect destination term. Banco di Roma requested Fidelity to recredit its account at Chemical Bank and stated that it was holding the shipping documents at Fidelity's "disposition" awaiting "instructions."[3]

During the next month Fidelity managed to get the tractors designated Free Zone.[4] This was done with some difficulty because Banco di Roma was in possession of the title documents and refused Fidelity's requests for assistance. Banco di Roma several times renewed its request for reimbursement from Fidelity, reiterating that the documents were being held at Fidelity's "disposition" while Banco di Roma was awaiting "instructions."

Subsequently, attempts were made to resolve the matter by selling the tractors to a third party. Before such a sale was consummated, the tractors were destroyed during the civil disorder in Lebanon.

[In omitted portions of the opinion the court rejected arguments that Banco di Roma's instructions were ambiguous and that in any event no damage was caused because the tractors arrived in Beirut in timely fashion.—EDS.]

The foregoing analysis reveals that Banco di Roma's rejection of the documents submitted by Fidelity was proper. Consequently, on May 9, 1975 Banco di Roma had a valid claim against Fidelity for reimbursement.[15] Antici-

---

3. This telex, *on its face,* satisfied Banco di Roma's duty to Fidelity upon rejection of the documents. See UCC 5-112(2); UCP Article 8. [Citation is to the 1974 UCP. See 1983 UCP Art. 16—EDS.] As will be seen infra, the documents *in fact* were not held at Fidelity's "disposition."

4. The tractors were not physically moved. Whether or not something is in the Free Zone is a status designation.

15. By the time of the dishonor Fidelity had already obtained $298,816.15 from Banco di Roma through Chemical Bank.

pating this result, Fidelity asserts two additional defenses. First, Fidelity contends that Banco di Roma is estopped from recovery because it refused to assist in correcting the documents in order to designate the tractors Free Zone, which Fidelity alleges would have avoided all damages. Second, Fidelity asserts that Banco di Roma is barred from recovery because it refused to assist Fidelity in the sale of the tractors. To properly consider these defenses we must first look more carefully at the occurrences subsequent to May 9, 1975. Because this is a motion for summary judgment, we view these facts in a light most favorable to Fidelity.

After receiving Banco di Roma's May 9 telex rejecting the documents submitted under the letter of credit, Fidelity sought to have the status of the tractors changed to the Free Zone designation. An original Bill of Lading, which was in the possession of Banco di Roma, was required in order to effect this change swiftly. Fidelity therefore requested Banco di Roma's assistance in changing the designation of the tractors. Banco di Roma failed to provide any assistance. Consequently the move to the Free Zone was delayed. Banco di Roma now contends that since the period of validity of the letter of credit had expired, Banco di Roma had no duty to assist in having the tractors designated Free Zone because that could not retroactively cure the documentary defect. By telex dated June 20, 1975, Fidelity informed Banco di Roma that the tractors had been moved to the Free Zone and asserted that "it is our position that we have no further responsibility in this matter. We suggest that you immediately take whatever steps are necessary to secure the machinery."

For the next few months each party maintained that the other party was responsible for any loss involved. Fidelity, apparently proceeding in good faith, attempted to resolve the matter by finding a buyer for the two tractors. Since Banco di Roma possessed the documents of title to the tractors, Banco di Roma's cooperation was essential before any sale could take place. Banco di Roma, however, refused to cooperate with Fidelity on any possible sale until Fidelity first reimbursed Banco di Roma the $298,816.15.

Fidelity now alleges that it produced three separate buyers, each of whom would have "absolutely" bought the tractors but for Banco di Roma's refusal to make the title documents available. There is some documentary support for this claim. Any one of these sales, Fidelity asserts, would have generated enough money to cover all claims by Banco di Roma. We turn now to the legal effect of these allegations on Fidelity's liability.

UCC 5-112(2) provides that "[u]pon dishonor the bank may unless otherwise instructed fulfill its duty to return the draft or demand and the documents by holding them *at the disposal* of the presenter and sending him an advice to that effect" (emphasis added).[21] Having rejected the documents submitted by Fidelity, Banco di Roma informed Fidelity that it was holding the documents at Fidelity's "disposition." In fact, however, Banco di Roma's will-

---

21. A similar provision is found in UCP Article 8. [1983 UCP Art. 16.—Eds.]

ingness to hold the documents at Fidelity's disposition was conditioned upon prior reimbursement of the letter of credit amount.

We must therefore determine whether Banco di Roma acted properly in requiring reimbursement prior to holding the documents at Fidelity's disposition.

At the outset we note that neither UCC 5-112 nor UCP Article 8 requires prior reimbursement as a condition to holding documents at the presenter's disposition. Moreover, allowing a bank to demand prior reimbursement before holding dishonored documents at the presenter's disposition is contrary to one of the express purposes of UCC 5-112. Comment 2 to this section states: "Many letters of credit involve transactions in international trade and include as required documents the documents of title controlling the possession of goods on their way to the place of issuance of the credit. The ordinary rule requiring physical return of dishonored documentary drafts (Section 4-302) would therefore frequently work commercial hardship on the mercantile parties to the transaction; resale of the goods might be more difficult if the controlling documents of title were not available at the place of arrival of the goods. Subsection (2) therefore expressly permits the issuer to retain the documents as bailee for the presenter if it advises the presenter of its retention for that purpose." This Comment indicates that one of the purposes of UCC 5-112 is to facilitate mitigation of damages through resale of the goods underlying the letter of credit agreement. The facts of the instant case illustrate only too well how a requirement of prior reimbursement can impede the mitigation of damages. While we now, with the benefit of hindsight, determine that Banco di Roma properly rejected the documents submitted by Fidelity, our review of the many telexes sent by the parties convinces us that Fidelity in good faith disputed the correctness of Banco di Roma's dishonor. Fidelity's posture subsequent to the dishonor of the documents was that "no matter who is at fault" any damages resulting from United's rejection of the tractors should be minimized through transfer of the tractors to the Free Zone and through sale of the tractors. Banco di Roma, on the other hand, was steadfast in refusing Fidelity any cooperation until Fidelity first reimbursed Banco di Roma. We think that accepting Banco di Roma's position would be a bad rule, placing Fidelity between Scylla and Charybdis—either pay a contested claim before being allowed to mitigate damages or risk a much larger amount of damages should a court subsequently determine that Banco di Roma's dishonor was proper. Fidelity should not be compelled to make such an election. Banco di Roma should have held the documents at Fidelity's disposition, without precondition, and not impeded Fidelity's efforts to mitigate damages.

Our conclusion is bolstered by analogy to the law of contracts. Prior tender of benefits received under a contract is not a precondition to the duty to mitigate damages. Even a party injured by a breach of contract is under a duty to mitigate damages. . . . Thus, in an ordinary contract a party injured by a breach may be required to take affirmative steps in mitigation of damages without first receiving any restitution from the breaching party. Since in the instant case Banco di Roma was merely required to hold the documents at Fidelity's disposition,[25] as mandated by UCP 5-112 and UCC Article 8, we can find no justification for its position that Fidelity was first required to reimburse Banco di Roma. Therefore, we must now determine the consequences of Banco di Roma's improper behavior.

Neither the UCC nor the UCP expressly provide for the situation where the issuing bank fails to hold the documents at the disposition of the presenter.[26] That no provision of the UCC directly governs the rights and liabilities of parties in this case does not, however, end our inquiry into the Code. Section 5-102(3) of the UCC provides:

> [T]his Article deals with some but not all of the rules and concepts of letters of credit as such rules or concepts have developed prior to this act or may hereafter develop. The fact that this Article states a rule does not by itself require, imply or negate application of the same or a converse rule to a situation not provided for or to a person not specified by this Article.

Official Comment 2 to this section states, in part: "Subsection (3) recognizes that in the present state of the law and variety of practices as to letters of credit, no statute can effectively or wisely codify all the possible law of letters of credit without stultifying further development of this useful financing device. [T]herefore subsection (3) makes explicit the court's power to apply a particular rule by analogy to cases not within its terms, or to refrain from doing so."

The process of developing a rule to govern a letter of credit case not within the literal language of any provision in the UCC has been used by the Fifth Circuit. . . . We will develop a rule to govern the instant case by drawing upon the established law of contracts. Because Banco di Roma's dishonor on May 9, 1975 was proper, Fidelity is in a position analogous to that of a party who has breached a contract. Banco di Roma's unwillingness to hold the documents at Fidelity's disposition is analogous to breach of the duty to mitigate damages. The burden of proving that losses could have been avoided is always upon the party who has broken the contract. See A. Corbin, 5 Corbin on Contracts §1039 (1964). Accordingly, we find that Fidelity may reduce its

25. We need not decide whether a general duty of mitigation might be derived in an appropriate case through application of UCC 1-201(1), 5-102(3) by treating the Code as a source of commercial law and not merely as a statement of individual rules. See S. Nickles, Problems of Sources of Law Relationship Under the Uniform Commercial Code, 31 Ark. L. Rev. 1 (1977); cf. H. Harfield, Code Treatment of Letters of Credit, 48 Cornell L.Q. 92, 97 (1962).

26. Because the parties agreed that this transaction would be governed by the 1962 revision of the UCP, we decline to apply the rule prescribed in §8(f) of the 1974 revision of the UCP, which provides "[i]f the issuing bank fails to hold the documents at the disposal of the remitting bank, or fails to return the documents to such bank, the issuing bank shall be precluded from claiming that the relative payment, acceptance or negotiation was not effected in accordance with the terms and conditions of the credit." [See 1983 UCP Art. 16(e).—EDS.]

liability by any amounts that it establishes could have been avoided had Banco di Roma held the documents at Fidelity's disposition. We now proceed to apply this rule to facts of this case.

Fidelity contends that Banco di Roma's unwillingness to assist in designating the tractors Free Zone should bar it from any recovery. We disagree. The period of validity of the letter of credit had already expired by the time Fidelity attempted to designate the tractors Free Zone. The error committed by Fidelity in the statement of the destination in the documents submitted under the letter of credit could not be corrected nunc pro tunc. . . . [The court cites for this proposition *Courtaulds*, at p. 928 supra, where the beneficiary also attempted to represent conforming documents after the expiration of the credit.—Eds.] Once the tractors were designated Free Zone, Banco di Roma could not have required United to accept them. Banco di Roma is thus not precluded from recovery for failure to assist in redesignating the tractors Free Zone. Banco di Roma's recovery will be reduced, however, by the additional customs duties which accrued as a result of the delay in designating the tractors Free Zone caused by Banco di Roma's failure to hold the documents at Fidelity's disposition.

Finally, if Fidelity is successful in proving its assertion that the tractors would have been sold but for Banco di Roma's failure to hold the documents at Fidelity's disposition, then Fidelity's liability to Banco di Roma will be reduced by the amount of the obstructed sale.

NOTES & QUESTIONS

1. *Issuer's duty to mitigate.* The principal case litigates the issuer's duty to mitigate in the context of a defense to a claim for reimbursement made by a *rightfully* dishonoring issuer against the local bank acting on its behalf. Consider its applicability to a claim for damages by a beneficiary against a *wrongfully* dishonoring bank.

2. *Other defenses.* As noted, Fidelity also defended unsuccessfully on the grounds that no damage resulted because the tractors themselves arrived in Beirut on time, and that any loss was caused by Banco di Roma's own ambiguous instructions. Do you agree with the court's disposition of those issues? Cf. UCC 2-504; see 1983 UCP Arts. 5, 14.

b. The Customer's Perspective

Customers face substantial risks in letter-of-credit transactions. A deficient performance of the underlying contract may not prevent performance of the credit and the attendant liability of the customer to reimburse the issuer. As we have seen, it may be difficult or impossible for the customer to enjoin the issuer from honoring even forged or fraudulent documents.

Problem 18-23. Customer and Beneficiary enter into a C.I.F. sales contract. Customer completes an application for credit calling for appropriate documentation. Issuer issues a credit that fails to call for an insurance certificate. Assume that Beneficiary fails to procure insurance but tenders documents that comply with the credit as issued. If Issuer pays under the credit, is it entitled to reimbursement? Does UCC 5-114(3) address this case? See also UCC 5-109; cf. 5-107. If Issuer pays, may it recover against Beneficiary? Cf. UCC 5-111 and the principal case in the following subsection.

c.   The Issuer's Perspective

Issuer's risks may be classified broadly into two categories: risks of its customer's insolvency and risks of wrongful honor depriving the issuer of the right to seek reimbursement from its customer. Intermingled with these may be instances where there is also forgery of documents that are regular on their face, fraudulent documents, or fraud in the transaction.

Consider UCC 5-111 and the following case.

BANK OF EAST ASIA, LTD. v. PANG
140 Wash. 603, 249 P. 1060 (1926)

MAIN, J. The complaint in this action is based upon two drafts for the sums of twelve thousand five hundred dollars and seven thousand five hundred dollars respectively. To the amended complaint, which will be referred to as the complaint, a demurrer was interposed and sustained. The plaintiff declined to plead further and elected to stand upon the complaint, with the result that judgment was entered dismissing the action, from which it appeals.

The facts, as stated in the complaint, essential to present the law question to be determined, may be summarized as follows: The appellant, the Bank of East Asia, Ltd., was located at Shanghai, China, and will be referred to as the bank. The Sang Lee Company was engaged in business at the same place. The respondents Herbert Archie Pang and Law Wing Woo did business under the name of Union Trading Company at Seattle, Washington. The Sang Lee Company purchased steel products from the Union Trading Company and to facilitate the matter of payment the bank issued two letters of credit, the first of which was for twelve thousand five hundred dollars and was in words and figures as follows:

AMERICAN EXPRESS COMPANY, SEATTLE, WASHINGTON.

Mr. Grimmig, Building.
Mr. Eberle, For. Traff. Dept.
August 9, 1923

Irrevocable Export Credit No. 17196
Mention this Credit Number on all communications.

Union Trading Company,
Seattle, Washington

Dear Sir:

For account of our correspondent, named below, as ordered by cablegram we herewith open an irrevocable credit in your favor as follows: Amount $12,500 (Twelve thousand five hundred dollars). Expires Sept. 30th. Draft must be presented on or before that date. For account of Sang Lee Company. Covering shipment of steel products. Destination, Shanghai direct. Insurance—marine to be effected by shippers, available by draft on us at Sang Lee Co., Shanghai at 90 d/a (in dup.) accompanied by following shipping documents (in form satisfactory to us): Complete set of steamer B/L to order Bank of East Asia, Ltd. Marine and war risk insurance certificates in duplicate. Notify consignee. Invoice in triplicate.

P.S. Draft should bear the clause reading: "Payable with interest added at 7% from date of draft until approximate date of arrival of cover in New York."

Above credit opened by Bank of East Asia, Ltd.,
Shanghai, China

Yours truly,
Assistant Treasurer

This letter of credit by its terms is made irrevocable and was for the purpose of covering a shipment of steel products to the Sang Lee Company. The American Express Company was the agent of the bank for the purpose of making payment. On September 5, 1923, the Union Trading Company made a shipment of steel products and drew a draft in accordance with the letter of credit, as follows:

Seattle, September 5th, 1923.

Exchange for $12,500.00

At ninety days sight of this first of exchange (second unpaid) pay to the order of Bank of East Asia, Ltd., Shanghai, China, twelve thousand five hundred dollars only, value received, and charge the same to account of—

Drawn under your irrevocable export credit No. 17196. "Documents against payment." "Payable with interest added at 9% from date of draft until approximate date of arrival of cover in New York, U.S.A."

Union Trading Co.,
By *Archie Pang*, Manager.

To Messrs. Sang Lee Company,
Shanghai, China.

This draft with the documents attached was presented to the American Express Company and paid. The draft calls for acceptance at sight and payment in ninety days. It, together with the bill of lading and invoice, was transmitted to the bank and was by it presented to the Sang Lee Company and accepted. On the due date, the latter company was unable to take up the draft and it was duly protested and demand made upon the Union Trading Company to reimburse the bank. This demand was refused and the present action followed. The second draft and the proceedings thereunder was the same as that upon the first.

The bank claims, and so alleges in the complaint, that the steel products were not of the kind and quality which had been contracted for by the Sang Lee Company and that therefore it has a right, having paid the draft through its agent, to maintain an action directly against the Union Trading Company. The question is, whether the bank, having issued the letter of credit providing that payment would be made when certain documents were presented, can now rely upon the claimed fact that the steel products were of an inferior quality. The contract for these products was between Sang Lee Company and the Union Trading Company. The letter of credit was a contract between the bank and the Union Trading Company. There is no claim that the documents presented when the payment was made by the express company did not conform to the requirements of the letter of credit. The bank was dealing in documents and not merchandise. In National City Bank v. Seattle National Bank, 121 Wash. 476, 209 Pac. 705, 31 A.L.R. 347, the question was whether the documents presented conformed to the requirements of the letter of credit and arose between the agent of the bank issuing the letter and a bank presenting the draft and documents. In the course of the opinion in that case, the court made use of this language:

"We are not here concerned with the original contract between Sexton & Company and the importer, and need not inquire as to whether the terms of that contract were met, so as to fix the liability of the buyer. Bankers are not dealers in sugar in such a case as this, but are dealers in documents only, and whatever contract was made by the banks must be determined from the letter of credit itself. Here, as is the custom in such cases, the banker was presented with documents passed over his counter, and asked to pay a large sum of money in exchange for them. His duty was not to go out and determine by personal examination of the shipment, or by the employment of experts, whether the goods actually conformed to the contract between the buyer and seller, nor even to determine, either from his own knowledge or by expert advice, whether the documents called for goods which the buyer would be bound to accept. The banker knows only the letter of credit, which is his only authority to act, and the documents which are presented under it. If these documents conform to the terms of the letter of credit he is bound to pay. If not, he is equally bound not to pay."

In Laudisi v. American Exchange National Bank, 239 N.Y. 234, 146 N.E. 347, the plaintiff purchased a quantity of grapes which were to be shipped from California. As a method of paying for them, he made a contract with the defendant bank to issue to the vendor of the grapes a letter of credit under which the latter's draft for the purchase price was to be paid by the bank on presentation when accompanied by certain documents. The grapes were shipped to the plaintiff and the draft for the purchase price thereof was paid by the bank on account of the plaintiff on the presentation therewith of the documents. The plaintiff claimed, among other things, that the grapes shipped were much inferior to those which he had contracted to buy and had notified the bank that the grapes were not of the quality contracted for and requested it not pay the draft. The bank paid the draft and the action was brought against it by its customer on whose behalf the letter of credit was issued. It was there held that the contract between the customer and the bank under which the bank issued the irrevocable letter of credit was entirely distinct and apart from the contract between the customer and his vendor under which the goods were shipped. It was there said:

"The whole process of authorizing banks to issue letters of credit, under which the purchase price of goods is often paid for account of the vendee before he has had a chance to examine them, is largely based on confidence in the honesty of the vendor. If the vendee is suspicious of dishonesty he can guard against it by appropriate clauses in his contract. But, certainly, the courts ought to exercise no power of embarrassing or confusing widespread processes of commercial life by inserting in such contracts as this one clauses which it may deem in a particular case might have been quite properly placed there, but which as a matter of fact the parties were content to disregard and omit. The customer can impose and it will be the duty of the courts fairly to enforce all the restrictions and safeguards he desires. But they should not by strained interpretation impose those which he has omitted.

"There remains one feature to be briefly considered. Before the defendant paid the draft it was notified by the plaintiff that the grapes did not comply with the requirements of the contract but were much inferior thereto, and it was notified or requested not to pay the draft. We do not think that it is very earnestly urged by the plaintiff that this fact changed the relations and rights of the parties. It did not. The contract between the customer and the bank, under which the latter issues an irrevocable letter of credit, is entirely distinct and apart from the contract between such customer and, as in this case, his vendor under which goods are to be shipped. The question between the customer and the vendor is the one whether the goods comply with the contract, and if they do not the former has his appropriate right of actions. The question between the customer and the bank which issues the letter of credit is whether the documents presented with the draft fulfill the specific requirements, and if they do, speaking of such facts as exist in this case, the bank has the right to pay the draft no matter what may be the defects in the goods which have been shipped. The bank is not obliged to assume the burdens of a controversy between the vendor and vendee and incur the responsibility of establishing as an excuse for not paying a draft that the vendee's version is the correct one."

In neither of those cases is the exact question here presented decided, but the question is decided in Maurice O'Meara v. National Park Bank, 239 N.Y. 386, 146 N.E. 636. There the action was brought by the assignor of the vendor of a large quantity of newsprint paper against the bank which had issued a letter of credit. The bank when the drafts and documents called for in the letter of credit were presented refused to pay on the ground that the paper was not of the kind and quality which the vendee contracted for. It was held that the bank should pay and that it was not concerned whether the paper was as specified in the contract between the seller and purchaser. It was there said:

"The bank issued to plaintiff's assignor an irrevocable letter of credit, a contract solely between the bank and plaintiff's assignor, in and by which the bank agreed to pay sight drafts to a certain amount on presentation to it of the documents specified in the letter of credit. This contract was in no way involved in or connected with, other than the presentation of the documents, the contract for the purchase and sale of the paper mentioned. That was a contract between buyer and seller, which in no way concerned the bank. The bank's obligation was to pay sight drafts when presented if accompanied by genuine documents specified in the letter of credit. If the paper when delivered did not correspond to what had been purchased, either in weight, kind or quality, then the purchaser had his remedy against the seller for damages. Whether the paper was what the purchaser contracted to purchase did not concern the bank and in no way affected its liability. It was under no obligation to ascertain, either by personal examination or otherwise, whether the paper conformed to the contract between the buyer and seller. The bank was concerned only in the drafts and the documents accompanying them. This was the extent of its interest. If the drafts, when presented, were accompanied by the proper documents, then it was absolutely bound to make the payment under the letter of credit, irrespective of whether it knew, or had reason to believe, that the paper was not of the tensile strength contracted for. This view, I think, is the one generally entertained with reference to a bank's liability under an irrevocable letter of credit of the character of the one here under consideration. . . .

"The defendant had no right to insist that a test of the tensile strength of the paper be made before paying the drafts; nor did it even have a right to inspect the paper before payment, to determine whether it in fact corresponded to the description contained in the documents. The letter of credit did not so provide. All that the letter of credit provided was that documents be presented which described the paper shipped as of a certain size, weight, and tensile strength. To hold otherwise is to read into the letter of credit something which is not there, and this the court ought not to do, since it would impose upon a bank a duty which in many cases would defeat the primary purpose of such letters of credit. This primary purpose is an assurance to the seller of merchandise of prompt payment against documents.

"It has never been held, so far as I am able to discover, that a bank has the right or is under an obligation to see that the description of the merchandise contained in the documents presented is correct. A provision giving it such right, or imposing such obligation, might, of course, be provided for in the letter of credit. The letter under consideration contains no such provision. If the bank had the right to determine whether the paper was of the tensile strength stated, then it might be pertinent to inquire how much of the paper must it subject to the test. If it had to make a test as to tensile strength, then it was equally obligated to measure and weigh the paper. No such thing was intended by the parties and there was no such obligation upon the bank."

The only difference between that case and the one now before us is that there the bank refused to pay and the action was brought by the assignee of the seller of the merchandise. Here, the bank paid and now seeks to recover back from the Union Trading Company, the seller of the wire products. The principle controlling the two cases is the same. It is true, that in that case there was a dissenting opinion, supported not only by the writer thereof but by one other member of the court, in which the view was expressed that, when the question arose between the bank issuing the letter of credit and the vendor of the product, the bank had the right to allege and prove that the goods shipped were not of the kind and quality contracted for by the vendee. After mature consideration, we are of the view that the rule of the majority opinion is the better one. A bank, when it issues a letter of credit, has the right to write into it such requirements and conditions as it sees fit. If it does not do so and, as in this case, simply issues the letter of credit obligating itself to pay when certain documents are presented, then the terms of the contract are satisfied when documents conforming to the requirements of the letter of credit are presented.

It is alleged in the complaint in the present case that there was failure of consideration and fraud, but these allegations are based upon the fact that the products shipped were not of the kind and quality contracted for by the Sang Lee Company. As already pointed out, this is a question which cannot be inquired into when the action is by the bank against the seller of the product or by the seller of the product against the bank. . . .

Our attention is called to [Unif. Neg. Instr. L. §62], which provides that the drawer of a negotiable instrument, if dishonored, is required to pay the amount thereof to the holder or any subsequent endorser who may be compelled to pay it, but that the drawer may insert in the instrument any express stipulation negativing or limiting his liability. The general provision of that statute which permits the holder or any subsequent endorser of a negotiable instrument dishonored to maintain an action thereon against the drawer is not applicable in the present case, because the drafts here involved specifically state that they are drawn under the irrevocable letter of credit and by that the bank was required to pay when a draft and other documents specified were presented.

The judgment will be affirmed.

Appendix

REFERENCE MATERIALS

A useful summary of commercial law research materials is set out in Kavass, Uniform Commercial Code Research: A Brief Guide to the Sources, 88 Com. L.J. 547 (1983). For an attempt to classify and to characterize recent commercial law literature, see Winship, Contemporary Commercial Law Literature in the United States, 43 Ohio St. L.J. 643 (1982).

The official text of the Uniform Commercial Code is published by West Publishing Company. The latest edition, the ninth, was published in 1978. A useful concordance appears in 1 W. Hawkland, Uniform Commercial Code Series (1982).

For case law developments you should consult the Uniform Commercial Code Reporting Service (Callaghan). Case law digests and annotations are contained in the following publications:

Uniform Commercial Code Case Digest (Callaghan)

Bender's Uniform Commercial Code Service, Reporter-Digest, Vols. 6-6G

T. Quinn, Uniform Commercial Code Commentary and Law Digest (1978; supplemented semi-annually)

Uniform Laws Annotated, Uniform Commercial Code, Vols. 1-3. You may trace subsequent citations to Code cases in Shepard's Uniform Commercial Code Citations.

Secondary literature commenting on the Code and case law has proliferated. For a guide to this literature the major bibliography is M. Ezer, Uniform Commercial Code Bibliography (1972; Supp. M. Ezer 1973; Supp. A. Squillante 1978). Current bibliographies are published in the Business Lawyer (quarterly; highly selective); the Commercial Law Journal (semi-annual; comprehensive); the Uniform Commercial Code Law Journal (quarterly; selective summary of law review articles); the Uniform Commercial Code Law Letter (monthly; selective); and the American Law Institute, Annual Report (annual; comprehensive).

There are several useful general introductions to the Code. R. Braucher & R. Riegert, Introduction to Commercial Transactions (1977); J. White & R. Summers, Handbook of the Law under the Uniform Commercial Code (2d ed. 1980). See also B. Stone, Uniform Commercial Code in a Nutshell (2d ed. 1984). General treatises designed primarily for use by practitioners include R.

Alderman, A Transactional Guide to the Uniform Commercial Code (2d ed. 1983, 1st ed. by W. Hawkland 1964); R. Anderson, Uniform Commercial Code (3d ed. 1981); the multi-volume Bender's Uniform Commercial Code Service (looseleaf); and W. Hawkland, Uniform Commercial Code Series (1982; looseleaf).

Several journals specialize in commercial law matters. The most important include:

American Business Law Journal

Banking Law Journal

Boston College Law Review (formerly Boston College Industrial & Commercial Law Review)

Business Lawyer

Commercial Law Journal

Journal of Law and Commerce

Uniform Commercial Code Law Journal.

The April issue of the Business Lawyer includes a useful annual survey of commercial case law developments.

Numerous formbooks for practitioners have been published, usually with annotations. The most useful general formbooks include:

Bender's Uniform Commercial Code Service: Forms and Procedures under the Uniform Commercial Code, Vols. 5-5D

Uniform Laws Annotated, Uniform Commercial Code Forms and Materials (R. Henson & W. Davenport eds. 1968).

Useful brief manuals on documentation can be found in W. Hillman, Commercial Law Documentation (1982), and L. Mandell, The Preparation of Commercial Agreements (1978).

Professional responsibility problems of the commercial lawyer are set out with relevant although sometimes dated discussion materials in V. Countryman, Problems of Professional Responsibility under the UCC (1969).

Part I.   Introduction to Commercial Paper

Commercial Paper

The major treatises and handbooks for commercial paper are F. Hart & W. Willier, Commercial Paper Under the Uniform Commercial Code (1972; looseleaf); J. Brady, The Law of Bank Checks (H. Bailey 5th ed. 1979); W. Britton, Handbook of the Law of Bills & Notes (2d ed. 1961); W. Hawkland, Commercial Paper (2d ed. 1979); E. Peters, A Negotiable Instruments Primer (2d ed. 1974); J. Reitman & H. Weisblatt, Checks, Drafts and Notes (1984); C. Weber & R. Speidel, Commercial Paper in a Nutshell (3d ed. 1982); and Beutel's Brannan Negotiable Instruments Law (F. Beutel 7th ed. 1948).

For the Anglo-American history of negotiable instruments law, see Beutel's Brannan, supra, at 1-109; J. Holden, History of Negotiable Instruments in English Law (1955); Gilmore, Formalism and the Law of Negotiable Instruments, 13 Creighton L. Rev. 441 (1979).

Suretyship

Reference materials for the law of suretyship are somewhat dated. The Restatement of Security (1941) provides a useful commentary on both the principles of suretyship and the case law in this field. Scattered sections of the Restatement (Second) of Contracts (1981) place the suretyship contract in the general context of contract law. Detailed discussion may be found in L. Simpson, Handbook on the Law of Suretyship (1950); A. Stearns, The Law of Suretyship (J. Elder 5th ed. 1951); and 10 S. Williston, A Treatise on the Law of Contracts §§1211-1284A (W. Jaeger 3d ed. 1967). The principal study relating the law of suretyship to the Uniform Commercial Code is Peters, Suretyship Under Article 3 of the Uniform Commercial Code, 77 Yale L.J. 833 (1968).

Part II. Personal Property Secured Transactions

Secured Transactions

The major treatise, designed primarily for practitioners, is P. Coogan, W. Hogan, D. Vagts & J. McDonnell, Secured Transactions under the Uniform Commercial Code (1963; looseleaf). Shorter works include D. Baker, A Lawyer's Basic Guide to Secured Transactions (1983); B. Clark, The Law of Secured Transactions under the Uniform Commercial Code (1980); W. Davenport & D. Murray, Secured Transactions (1978); and E. Reiley, Guidebook to Security Interests in Personal Property (1981). Student hornbooks in this area include R. Henson, Handbook on Secured Transactions under the Uniform Commercial Code (2d ed. 1979) and H. Bailey III, Secured Transactions in a Nutshell (2d ed. 1981).

In a class by itself is G. Gilmore, Security Interests in Personal Property (1965).

A number of law journals specialize in problems of commercial finance law. Among the more important are:

Banking Law Journal

Commercial Finance Journal (Natl. Comm. Fin. Conf., Inc.)

Consumer Finance Law Bulletin (Natl. Consumer Fin. Assn., Law Forum)

Lending Law Forum

Personal Finance Law Quarterly Report (Conf. on Personal Fin. Law)

Specialized looseleaf reporters include Installment Credit Guide: Secured
Transactions Guide (CCH) and Consumer Credit Guide (CCH).

For the history of secured transactions, see G. Gilmore, supra, 1-286.

Bankruptcy

Following enactment of the Bankruptcy Reform Act in 1978 commentaries on bankruptcy law have proliferated. Collier on Bankruptcy (L. King 15th ed. 1979; looseleaf) remains the authoritative treatise. Among the numerous shorter works designed primarily for practitioners see A. Cohen, Bankruptcy, Secured Transactions and Other Debtor-Creditor Matters (1981); P. Murphy, Creditors' Rights in Bankruptcy (1981; looseleaf); B. Weintraub & A. Resnick, Bankruptcy Law Manual (1980); Bankruptcy Law and Practice (W. Norton ed. 1981; looseleaf); and Collier Bankruptcy Manual (L. King 3d ed. 1979; looseleaf). For pre-1978 law the major treatise is the 14th edition of Collier on Bankruptcy.

For the student D. Epstein, Debtor-Creditor Law in a Nutshell (2d ed. 1980) is a useful introduction to the law governing both federal bankruptcy and state law creditor remedies.

The American Bankruptcy Law Journal (formerly Ref. J.) is published quarterly by the National Conference of Bankruptcy Judges.

A growing number of reporting services publish bankruptcy court decisions. The most important are Bankruptcy Law Reporter (CCH); Bankruptcy Reporter (West); Collier's Bankruptcy Cases (1st series for pre-1978 law; 2d series for decisions under the 1978 Bankruptcy Code); and Bankruptcy Court Decisions. In addition, the UCC Reporting Service includes bankruptcy court decisions when they touch on the interpretation of the UCC.

For the history of bankruptcy and insolvency law in the United States, see P. Coleman, Debtors and Creditors in America: Insolvency, Imprisonment for Debt, and Bankruptcy, 1607-1900 (1974); C. Warren, Bankruptcy in United States History (1935); V. Countryman, A History of American Bankruptcy Law, 81 Com. L.J. 226 (1976); Riesenfeld, The Evolution of Modern Bankruptcy Law, 31 Minn. L. Rev. 401 (1947).

Part III.   Sales Transactions

Sales

The principal treatises on the law of sales are R. Duesenberg & L. King, Sales and Bulk Transfers under the Uniform Commercial Code (1966; looseleaf); G. Wallach, The Law of Sales Under the Uniform Commercial

Code (1981); and Williston on Sales (A. Squillante & J. Fonseca 4th ed. 1974).

Shorter works include W. Hawkland, Sales and Bulk Sales (3d ed. 1976); R. Nordstrom, Handbook on the Law of Sales (1970); M. Rigg & R. Alpert, Sale of Goods and Services (1982); J. Stockton, Sales in a Nutshell (2d ed. 1981); and L. Vold, Handbook on the Law of Sales (2d ed. 1959).

For a historical perspective see the following remarkable law review articles by Karl Llewellyn: Through Title to Contract and A Bit Beyond, 15 N.Y.U. L.Q. Rev. 159 (1938); Across Sales on Horseback, 52 Harv. L. Rev. 725; The First Struggle to Unhorse Sales, 52 Harv. L. Rev. 873 (1979). A broader historical perspective is provided by L. Trakman, The Law Merchant: The Evolution of Commercial Law (1983).

Documents of Title

The principal works analyzing the law of documents of title are R. Henson, Documents of Title Under the Uniform Commercial Code (1983) and R. Riegert & R. Braucher, Documents of Title (3d ed. 1978).

Warranties

For short treatises on the law of personal property warranties see B. Clark & C. Smith, The Law of Product Warranties (1984) and D. Whaley, Warranties and the Practitioner (1981).

Part IV.   Payment Systems

Payment Systems

On checks and bank collection see J. Brady, The Law of Bank Checks (H. Bailey 5th ed. 1979); B. Clark, The Law of Bank Deposits, Collections and Credit Cards (rev. ed. 1981); J. Clarke, H. Bailey & R. Young, Bank Deposits and Collections (4th ed. 1972); C. Smith, Negotiable Instruments and the Payments Mechanism (1983).

The impact of technological developments on the law of commercial paper is set out in N. Penney & D. Baker, The Law of Electronic Fund Transfer Systems (1980). See also W. Baxter, P. Cootner & K. Scott, Retail Banking in the Electronic Age: The Law & Economics of Electronic Fund Transfers (1977); Baxter, Bank Interchange of Transactional Paper: Legal and Economic Perspectives, 26 J. of L. & Econ. 541 (1983).

For a study of the history of bank collection legislation, see Scott, The Risk Fixers, 91 Harv. L. Rev. 737 (1978).

Letters of Credit

The principal secondary materials on letters of credit are J. Dolan, The Law of Letters of Credit: Commercial and Standby Credits (1984); H. Harfield, Letters of Credit (1979); W. Ward, Bank Credits and Acceptances (H. Harfield 5th ed. 1974).

Table of Cases

977

Table of Statutes

Index